Spain

THE ROUGH GUIDE

There are more than one hundred and fifty Rough Guide titles
covering destinations from Amsterdam to Zimbabwe

Forthcoming titles include
Beijing • Cape Town • Croatia • Ecuador • Switzerland

Rough Guide Reference Series
Classical Music • Drum 'n' Bass • English Football • European Football
House • The Internet • Jazz • Music USA • Opera • Reggae
Rock Music • Techno • World Music

Rough Guide Phrasebooks
Czech • Dutch • Egyptian Arabic • European Languages • French
German • Greek • Hindi & Urdu • Hungarian • Indonesian
Italian • Japanese • Mandarin Chinese • Mexican Spanish • Polish
Portuguese • Russian • Spanish • Swahili • Thai • Turkish • Vietnamese

Rough Guides on the Internet
www.roughguides.com

ROUGH GUIDE CREDITS

Text editor: Claire Saunders
Series editor: Mark Ellingham
Editorial: Martin Dunford, Jonathan Buckley, Jo
Mead, Kate Berens, Ann-Marie Shaw, Paul Gray,
Chris Schüler, Helena Smith, Judith Bamber,
Kieran Falconer, Orla Duane, Olivia Eccleshall,
Ruth Blackmore, Sophie Martin, Jennifer
Dempsey, Geoff Howard, Anna Sutton, Gavin
Thomas, Alexander Mark Rogers (UK); Andrew
Rosenberg, Andrew Taber (US)
Production: Susanne Hillen, Andy Hilliard, Link
Hall, Helen Ostick, James Morris, Julia Bovis,
Michelle Draycott, Cathy McElhinney

Cartography: Melissa Flack, Maxine Burke,
Nichola Goodliffe, Ed Wright
Picture research: Eleanor Hill, Louise Boulton
Online editors: Alan Spicer, Kate Hands (UK);
Geronimo Madrid (US)
Finance: John Fisher, Neeta Mistry, Katy
Miesiaczek
Marketing & Publicity: Richard Trillo, Simon
Carloss, Niki Smith, David Wearn (UK); Jean-
Marie Kelly, SoRelle Braun (US)
Administration: Tania Hummel, Charlotte
Marriott

ACKNOWLEDGEMENTS

On our eighth edition, **thanks** go to Hugh
  Broughton for architectural suggestion, and to
  Dr David Nash. Simon Baskett would like to
  thank Trinidad López for all her hard work and
  help with research for chapters One and Two.
  Phil Lee thanks Emma Reas and Martha
  Crean. Thanks from James McConnachie to
  Padre Jorge and the Brothers in Valdedios,
  and to Julia and Pablo in Santiago. Charles
  Young thanks Simon, Cristina and Ramon.
  Thanks from Ian Patterson to Toby Mundy,

Charis Evans, James Allmand-Smith, and
  especially Eva Mingarro Castillo.

At Rough Guides, thanks go to Claire Saunders
  and Paul Gray; Cameron Wilson and Nick
  Thompson for extra Basics research; Cathy
  McElhinney and Neil Cooper for typesetting;
  Maxine Burke and Stratigraphics for
  cartography; for mapping; Gillian Armstrong for
  proofreading; and James McConnachie for
  indexing.

PUBLISHING INFORMATION

This eighth edition published June 1999 by
  Rough Guides Ltd, 62–70 Shorts Gardens,
  London, WC2H 9AB. Reprinted, February 2000.
Distributed by the Penguin Group:
Penguin Books Ltd, 27 Wrights Lane, London W8 5TZ
Penguin Books USA Inc., 375 Hudson Street, New York
  10014, USA
Penguin Books Australia Ltd, 487 Maroondah Highway,
  PO Box 257, Ringwood, Victoria 3134, Australia
Penguin Books Canada Ltd, 10 Alcorn Avenue, Toronto,
  Ontario, Canada M4V 1E4
Penguin Books (NZ) Ltd, 182–190 Wairau Road,
  Auckland 10, New Zealand
Typeset in Linotron Univers and Century Old Style to an
  original design by Andrew Oliver.
Printed in England by Clays Ltd, St Ives PLC
Illustrations in Part One and Part Three by Edward Briant.

Illustrations on p.1 by Simon Fell & p.831 by David Lofus
© Mark Ellingham & John Fisher 1999
No part of this book may be reproduced in any form
  without permission from the publisher except for the
  quotation of brief passages in reviews.
944pp – Includes index
A catalogue record for this book is available from the
  British Library
ISBN 1-85828-419-8

Spain

THE ROUGH GUIDE

written and researched by

Mark Ellingham and John Fisher

with

Graham Kenyon and Jules Brown

revised and updated by

Simon Baskett, Melanie Cooke, Geoff Garvey, Phil Lee, James McConnachie, Ian Patterson, Alexandra Pratt and Charles Young

additional accounts by

Guy Barefoot, Manuel Domínguez, Jan Fairley, Teresa Farino and Gordon McLachlan

THE ROUGH GUIDES

CONTENTS

Introduction xi

● CHAPTER 4: ANDALUCÍA 203–323

● CHAPTER 5: OLD CASTILE AND LEÓN 324–385

● CHAPTER 6: EUSKADI: THE BASQUE PROVINCES AND NAVARRA 386–433

● CHAPTER 7: CANTABRIA AND ASTURIAS 434–476

• CHAPTER 12: VALENCIA AND MURCIA 733–778

• CHAPTER 13: THE BALEARICS 779–829

PART THREE — CONTEXTS — 831

LIST OF MAPS

MAP SYMBOLS

Motorway	Ruin
Major road	Spa
Minor road	Viewpoint
Steps	Lighthouse
Track	Caves
Path	Mountain range
Railway	Mountain peak
Ferry route	Hotel
Waterway	Parking
Chapter division boundary	Tourist office
National border	Post office
Airport	Telephone
Metro station	Building
Campsite	Park
Mountain refuge	Wood/forest
Monastery	Sand

INTRODUCTION

The first edition of this guide was published in 1983: just sixteen years ago but, looking back, almost another world. Spain then was emerging spectacularly and traumatically from the Franco era. Shots had been fired in parliament, in an unsuccessful coup attempt, while in Madrid and Barcelona, the *movida* – the belated "happening" and liberation – was in full swing. Rural and provincial Spain, meanwhile, appeared stuck in a timewarp, little changed since the 1950s or, occasionally, so it seemed, from the last century.

All that has changed. As the millennium approaches, Spain is firmly in western Europe, and one of the eleven EU nations to launch the single currency in 1999. Almost fifteen years of socialist government, followed by the election of a centre-right coalition, have utterly transformed the nation. There have been boom years, which reverberated down to building and development in even the smallest villages. In 1992, there was the famous triple whammy – the Olympics in Barcelona, Madrid as "European City of Culture", and the World Expo in Sevilla – alongside official celebration (and some critical analysis) of the five-hundredth anniversary of Columbus's expedition to the Americas. These days, Spain's economy, after years among the fastest-growing in Europe, has something of a hangover and unemployment has risen drastically to around twenty percent of the workforce.

Such realities, however, are almost a measure of how much Spain has moved from its isolation under Franco into the European mainstream. They also tell a very partial truth. Spaniards tend not to speak of *La España* – Spain – but *Las Españas*; come to that, they even talk of the capital in the plural – *Las Madriles*, the Madrids. Regionalism is almost an obsession and perhaps the most significant change in the post-Franco era has been the creation of a dozen *autonomías* – autonomous regions – with their own governments, budgets and cultural ministries. The old days of a unified nation, governed with a firm hand from Madrid, seem to have gone forever, as the separate kingdoms which made up the original Spanish state reassert themselves.

If you are coming to Spain for the first time, this regional diversity – of language, culture and artistic traditions, of landscapes, as well as politics – is likely to be the biggest surprise. The monuments, too, span an extraordinary range, from a history which takes in Romans, Moors and the "Golden Age" of Renaissance imperialism, as well as the regions' very different twentieth-century developments. Touring Castile and León, you confront the classic Spanish images of vast cathedrals and *reconquista* castles – literally hundreds of the latter; in the northern mountains of Asturias and the Pyrenees, tiny, almost organic Romanesque churches dot the hillsides and villages; Andalucía has the great Moorish palaces and mosques of Granada, Sevilla and Córdoba; in Barcelona there are the amazing *modernista* (Art Nouveau) creations of Antoni Gaudí.

Not that Spain is just about monuments. For most visitors, the landscape holds just as much fascination – and variety. The evergreen *rías* or estuaries of Galicia could hardly be more different from the high, arid plains of Castile, or the gulch-like desert landscapes of Almería. Spain is also one of the most mountainous countries in Europe, and there is superb walking and wildlife in a dozen or more sierras – and above all in the Picos de Europa and Pyrenees.

Then, of course, there are the Spaniards and their infectious enthusiasm for life. In the cities there is always something happening – in bars and clubs, on the streets – while the music and arts scenes are more vibrant than they have been for many years, with a resurgent "new flamenco", a film industry brought to international attention by the anarchic Pedro Almodóvar, and a superb array of modern galleries, including

Bilbao's spectacular new Guggenheim, and a trio devoted to the century's greatest Spanish artists, Picasso, Miró and Dalí. Even in out of the way places there's a surprising range of nightlife and entertainment, not to mention the daily pleasures of a round of *tapas*, moving from bar to bar, having a beer, a glass of wine or a *fino* (dry sherry) and a bite of the house speciality.

Another, almost limitless source of diversion are the traditional fiestas. They include established events like the great April *feria* in Sevilla, the pyrotechnic extravaganzas of *Las Fallas* in Valencia, and the running of the bulls in Pamplona, as well as thousands of local events, celebrating a town or village saint's day. As often as not, you'll happen on these quite unawares, to be carried away on a tide of exuberant street partying, concerts, and any number of bizarre activities, from parades of devils to full-blown tomato-throwing battles.

Where to go: some highlights

The identity and appeal of each of the regions is explored in the chapter introductions, and, if you're travelling around, there's a lot to be said for concentrating on one or two provinces, getting a feel for their individuality and character. If you want a broader sweep, though, definite **highlights** of Spanish travel include:

Barcelona. The Catalan capital is a must for the fantasy architecture of Antoni Gaudí; the great promenading street of the Ramblas; the Picasso museum; designer clubs and nightlife, par excellence; and, not least, FC Barcelona – the football team.

Madrid is not as pretty as Barcelona, by a long way, but has an irrepressible style and fantastic bars, both traditional and modern, plus three of Spain's top art galleries – the Prado, the Museo Thyssen-Bornemisza, and the Centro Reina Sofía.

Sevilla. Home of flamenco and all the clichés of the Spanish south; beautiful city quarters and major Christian and Moorish monuments; extraordinary festivals in Easter week, and, afterwards, at the April *feria*.

Toledo. Capital of medieval Spain and stunningly preserved, with synagogues, former mosques and an amazing cathedral; also houses a number of works by El Greco.

Salamanca. Spain's oldest university city remains a small, largely academic place, untouched by suburbs, and packed with Gothic and Renaissance buildings.

Moorish monuments. The best are in the Andalucían cities: the Alhambra palace in Granada, perhaps the most sensual building in Europe; the Mezquita, a former mosque, in Córdoba; and the Alcázar and Giralda tower in Sevilla.

Cathedrals, churches and monasteries. A tour of the top five Gothic cathedrals will take you through the Castilian cities of Toledo, León, Burgos, Salamanca and Segovia. Gorgeous Romanesque churches are to be found along the pilgrim route to Santiago, particularly in the Pyrenees, whilst Oviedo and the province of Asturias are home to the unique pre-Romanesque style. The façade of the great Santiago de Compostela is the highpoint of Spanish Baroque, Aragón has superb Mudéjar (Moorish-crafted) churches and towers, and the palace-monastery of El Escorial is the greatest expression of the late Renaissance in Spain.

Beaches. There is a lot more to Spanish beaches than the over-developed *costas*. Excellent and much less frequented strands are to be found around Cádiz and Almería in the south, and along the Asturian and Galician coasts in the north. If you want action and nightlife, it's hard to beat the island of Ibiza, one of the clubbing capitals of the world.

Medieval towns. Small-scale towns, once grand, now hardly significant, are often Spain at its best. Rewarding itineraries could include: Ciudad Rodrigo (Old Castile), Baeza and Úbeda (Andalucía), Trujillo and Cáceres (Extremadura), Albarracín (Aragón) and Santillana (Cantabria).

Roman sites. Mérida has the most significant sites and a superb museum; Segovia's aqueduct is stunning; other rewarding Roman ruins and sites include Italica (near Sevilla), Carmona, Tarragona and Empúries.

AIRLINES, AGENTS AND OPERATORS

British Airways 156 Regent St, London W1R
5TA (☎0345/222111; *www.british-airways.com*).
*From Heathrow or Gatwick to Madrid, Sevilla,
Jerez, Bilbao, Palma, Murcia, Barcelona, Malaga
and Gibraltar.*

Debonair 146 Prospect Way, London Luton
Airport, Luton, Bedfordshire LU2 9BA
(☎0541/500300; *www.debonair-airways.com*).
From Luton to Madrid and Barcelona.

EasyJet (☎01582/702900; *www.easyjet.com*).
From Luton to Madrid, Barcelona and Palma.

Iberia 29 Glasshouse St, London W1R
(☎0990/341341; *www.iberia.com*). *From Heathrow,
Gatwick and Manchester direct to Madrid,
Barcelona, Bilbao, Santiago, Sevilla, Malaga,
Alicante, Valencia, La Coruna and Oviedo with inter-
nal connections to most other airports in Spain.*

Virgin Express (☎0171/744 0004;
www.virgin-express.com). *From Heathrow to
Madrid and Barcelona.*

AGENTS AND OPERATORS

APA Travel 138 Eversholt St, London NW1
(☎0171/387 5337). *Spanish flight specialists.*

AVRO plc Vantage House, 1 Weir Road,
Wimbledon, London SW19 8UX (☎0181/715
0000). *Specialists in charter and scheduled
flights.*

B&B Abroad 5 World's End Lane, Green Street
Green, Orpington, Kent BR6 6AA
(☎01689/857838). *Specialist operator with a
wide range of bed-and-breakfast accommodation
from rustic farmhouses to luxurious country
manors. Also has hotel accommodation.*

Cox & Kings 4th Floor, Gordon House, 10
Greencoat Place, London SW1P 1PH (☎0171/ 873
5000). *Nature tours of the Aragonese Pyrenees
and Andalucía, staying in farmhouses.*

Exodus Expeditions 9 Weir Rd, London SW12
0LT (☎0181/675 5550). *Walking and cycling in
Andalucía, Mallorca and the Pyrenees.*

Explore Worldwide Ltd 1 Frederick St,
Aldershot, Hants GU11 1LQ (☎01252/760333).
*Walking in Andalucía, Sierra Nevada and the
Picos de Europa.*

Gourmet Birds Windrush, Coles Lane, Brasted,
Westerham, Kent TN16 1NN (☎01959/56327).
*One-week horse riding and bird watching in the
countryside around Ronda.*

Individual Travellers Bignor, Pulborough, West
Sussex RH20 1QD (☎01798/869461). *Farmhouses,
cottages and village houses all over Spain.*

Keytel International 402 Edgware Rd, London
W2 1ED (☎0171/402 8182). *Official UK agents for
the paradores.*

Owners Abroad First Choice House, Bettsway,
London Rd, Crawley, West Sussex RH10 2GX
(☎01293/554444). *Charter flights.*

Pilgrim Adventure 120 Bromley Heath Rd,
Downsend, Bristol BS16 6JJ (☎0117/657 3997).
Religious tours.

Portland Holidays Deansgate, Brazenose
House, Manchester M60 3PL (☎0990/002200).
Costa Brava and other Mediterranean packages.

Ramblers Holidays Box 43 Welwyn Garden City,
AL8 6PQ (☎01707/331133). *Walking and hiking
holidays throughout Spain.*

Rustic Blue Barrio de Ermita, 18412 Bubión,
Granada, Spain (☎958 763381, fax 958 763134;
rusticblue@cl.caja-grenada.es). *Spain-based
company specializing in rural holidays, from
traditional villages to furnished cave-dwellings in
the "real" Granada.*

Sherpa Expeditions 131a Heston Rd, Hounslow,
Middlesex TW5 0RD (☎0181/577 2717). *Trekking
in the Sierra Nevada, the Alpujarras, the
Pyrenees, the Picos de Europa and Mallorca.*

STA Travel 86 Old Brompton Rd, London SW7
(☎0171 361 6161); 117 Euston Rd, London NW1
(☎0171/361 6161); 25 Queen's Rd, Bristol BS8
1QE (☎0117/929 4399); 38 Sidney St, Cambridge
CB2 3HX (☎01223/366966); 36 George St, Oxford
OX1 2OJ (☎01865/792 8000); 75 Deansgate,
Manchester M3 2BW (☎0161/834 0668);
*www.statravel.co.uk. Independent travel special-
ists; discounted flights.*

Time Off 1 Elmfield Park, Bromley, Kent BR1 1LU
(☎0345/336622). *City breaks.*

Travellers Way The Barns, Hewell Lane,
Tardebigge, Bromsgrove, Worcs B60 1LP
(☎01527/836791). *Tailor-made holidays and city
breaks all over Spain, especially Andalucía.*

continued opposite

AGENTS AND OPERATORS cont

Usit CAMPUS 52 Grosvenor Gardens, London SW1 (☎0171/730 3402); 541 Bristol Rd, Selly Oak, Birmingham (☎021/414 1848); 37–39 Queen's Rd, Clifton, Bristol (☎0117/929 2494); 5 Emmanuel St, Cambridge (☎01223/324 283); 53 Forest Rd, Edinburgh (☎0131/225 6111); 166 Deansgate, Manchester (☎0161/833 2046); 13 High St, Oxford (☎01865/242067); www.usitcampus.com. *Also in YHA shops and on university campuses through-out Britain. Youth/student specialist.*

Waymark Holidays 44 Windsor Rd, Slough SL1 2EJ (☎01753/516477). *Walking holidays in Andalucía, the Pyrenees, the Picos de Europa and along the Camino de Santiago.*

Winetrails Greenways, Vann Lake, Ockley, Dorking EH5 5NT (☎01306/712111). *Ten-day wine tours through Navarra, Andalucía and La Rioja.*

At the time of writing, major carriers were offering the following scheduled flight return fares from London in low/high season: to Madrid £170/270; to Barcelona £180/250; to Málaga £210/280; to Bilbao £205/250. Fares from Manchester are generally £20–80 more expensive.

For a more flexible ticket, such as BA's Excursion fare, which is valid for six months, can be upgraded and is fully refundable, you're looking at around £485 from London to Madrid (£470 from Manchester) and £430 from London or Manchester to Barcelona. This has recently been bested by Air Europa's Economy fare from Gatwick to Madrid which costs only £280 return, allows for any type of change and is valid for a year. Note that it's usually cheaper to book scheduled flights through a travel agent than direct from the airline especially if you want youth or student discounts.

However, if you're looking for the least expensive option, the emerging cut-price airlines, such as EasyJet and Debonair, are ideal, offering mostly single fares, sold direct, on **no-frills flights**. These are great if you aren't sure of your itinerary and prices start from as little as £49 single from London to Barcelona. It is advisable to book as far ahead as possible as these airlines have limited cheap seats on each flight and regular seats are twice as expensive.

PACKAGES AND CITY BREAKS

Package holiday deals can be worth looking at, especially if you book early, late or out of season. While the cheaper, mass-market packages may seem to restrict you to some of the worst parts of the coast, remember that there's no compulsion to stick around your hotel. Get a good enough deal and it can be worth it simply for the flight – with transfer to a reasonably comfortable

hotel laid on for a night or two at each end. Bargains can be found at virtually any high street travel agent.

City breaks are often available at excellent package rates and destinations on offer include Barcelona, Madrid, Sevilla and Granada, flying from London or Manchester. Prices from London vary between around £240 (Madrid) and £310 (Sevilla) for three days (two nights); adding extra nights or upgrading your hotel is possible, too, usually at a fairly reasonable cost. The prices usually include return flights, airport transfer and bed and breakfast in a centrally located one-, two- or three-star hotel. Again, ask your travel agent for the best deal – especially for those under 26 – and check the addresses in the box opposite.

Fly-drive deals are well worth considering, too, as a combined air ticket and car rental arrangement can be excellent value. There are also some very good (and very attractive) deals available in **villas and apartments**, especially from companies who specialize in off-the-beaten-track farmhouses and the like. Several companies have started offering a range of *casas rurales*, on a similar basis to French *gîtes*. Other specialist companies offer an enticing range of **trekking holidays**, or, moving upmarket, tours based around the country's historic **paradores**.

BY TRAIN

With the **Channel Tunnel**, you've got the choice between making the crossing by boat or taking the Eurostar as far as Paris. Both options involve changing trains in **Paris** (and stations, from Nord to Austerlitz via Metro line 5), and again at the **Spanish border**. The standard rail and boat journey is around 27 to 29 hours, from London to Barcelona or Madrid; with the Eurostar, it's

start at around CAN$835 in the low season or CAN$1125 in the high season from Toronto or Montréal, and CAN$1215/ 1675 from Vancouver.

Travel CUTS is the most reliable student/youth agency, with some deals for non-students, too; alternatively, check the travel ads in your local newspaper and consult a good travel agent.

PACKAGE TOURS

Package tours may not sound like your kind of travel, but don't dismiss the idea out of hand. In addition to the fully escorted variety, many agents can put together very flexible deals, sometimes amounting to no more than a flight plus car or rail pass and accommodation; if you're planning to travel in moderate or luxury style, and especially if your trip is geared around special interests,

such packages can work out cheaper than the same arrangements made on arrival. A package can also be great for your peace of mind, if only to ensure a worry-free first week while you're finding your feet on a longer tour (of course, you can jump off the itinerary any time you like). Most companies will expect you to book through a local travel agent, and since it costs the same you might as well.

Plenty of tour companies offer whirlwind itineraries around Spain. Most of these also offer independent **city breaks** or more structured **escorted tours**. Other options include **trekking** (backpacking) in the Basque Pyrenees or basking on the **beaches** of the Costa del Sol. Typical prices for a week's independent winter break in Madrid, with round-trip airfare from New York

TOUR OPERATORS

Adventure Center
1311 63rd St, Suite #200, Emeryville, CA 94608
☎1-800/227-8747; 510/654-1879;
www.adventure-center.com
Active vacations in the Picos, Andalucía and the Sierra Nevada.

Abercrombie and Kent
1520 Kensington Rd, Oak Brook, IL 60521
☎1-800/323-7308; 630/954-2944;
www.abercrombiekent.com
Upmarket independent and fully escorted tours.

Central Holidays
120 Sullivan Ave, Englewood Cliffs, NJ 07632
☎1-800/227-5858; www.centralh.com
Agents for Iberia's tour department, Discover Spain Vacations. Group and independent tours.

Delta Vacations
PO Box 1525, Fort Lauderdale, FL 33312
☎1-800/872-7786; www.deltavacations.com
City breaks with optional car rental and city tours.

Easy Rider Tours
PO Box 228, Newburyport, MA 01950
1-800/488-8332; 978/463-6955;
www.easyridertours.com
Cycling/hiking tours.

EC Tours
12500 Riverside Dr, Suite #210, Valley Village, CA 91607-3423 ☎1-800/388-0877; www.ectours.com
Pilgrimages, historic city tours, wine and gourmet tours.

Escapade Tours
c/o Isram World of Travel
630 3rd Ave, New York, NY 10017

☎1-800/356-2405; www.isram.com
City breaks and multi-city packages.

M.I. Travel Inc
450 7th Ave, Suite 1805, New York, NY 10123
☎1-800/848-2314; 212/967-6565;
www.mitravel-melia.com
City packages and motorcoach tours.

Mountain Travel/Sobek
6420 Fairmount Ave, El Cerrito, CA 94530
☎1-888/MTSOBEK; www.mtsobek.com
Hiking in the Picos de Europa and Basque Pyrenees.

Petrabax Tours
9745 Queens Blvd, Rego Park, NY 11374
☎1-800/634-1188; www.petrabax.com
Motorcoach tours, parador bookings, plus a variety of set packages.

Saga Holidays
222 Berkely Street, Boston, MA 02116
☎1-800/343-0273.
Group travel for seniors.

Travel Go Round, Inc
90-05 Jericho Turnpike, Mineola, NY 11501
☎1-800/293-0076; www.travelgoround.com
City breaks, motorcoach tours, fly/drives, beach vacations and parador bookings.

Wilderness Travel
1102 9th St, Berkeley, CA 94710-1211
☎1-800/368-2794; 510/558-2488;
www.wildernesstravel.com
Hiking in the Pyrenees or Basque country.

DISCOUNT AGENTS, CONSOLIDATORS AND TRAVEL CLUBS

Airtech 588 Broadway, Suite 204, New York, NY 10017 (☎1-800/575-8324; 212/219-7000; *www.airtech.com*). *Standby seat broker; also deals in consolidator fares and courier flights.*

Air Courier Association 191 University Blvd, Suite 300, Denver, CO 80206 (☎1-800/282-1202; 303/215-0900; *www.aircourier.org*). *Courier flight broker.*

Council Travel Head Office, 205 E 42nd St, New York, NY 10017 (☎1-800/226-8624; 1-888/COUN-CIL; 212/822-2700); other offices include: 530 Bush St, Suite 700, San Francisco, CA 94108 (☎415/421-3473); 10904 Lindbrook Drive, Los Angeles 90024 (☎310/208-3551); 3300 M St NW, 2nd Floor, Washington, DC 20007 (☎202/337-6464); 1153 N Dearborn St, Chicago, IL 60610 (☎312/951-0585); 273 Newbury St, Boston, MA 02116 (☎617/266-1926). *Nationwide specialists in student travel.*

High Adventure Travel 353 Sacramento St, Suite 600, San Francisco, CA 94111 (☎1-800/350-0612; 415/912-5600; *www.highadv.com*). *Round the World tickets. Web site features interactive database that lets you build and price your own RTW itinerary.*

International Association of Air Travel Couriers 8 South J St, PO Box 1349, Lake Worth, FL 33460 (☎ 561/582-8320; *www.courier.org*). *Courier flight broker.*

Moment's Notice 7301 New Utrecht Ave, Brooklyn, NY 11204 (☎718/234-6295). *Discount travel club.*

New Frontiers/Nouvelles Frontières 12 E 33rd St, New York, NY 10016 (☎1-800/366-6387; 212/779-0600); 1001 Sherbrook East, Suite 720, Montréal, PQ H2L 1L3 (☎514/526-8444). *French*

discount travel firm, mostly to Europe. Other branches in LA, San Francisco and Quebec City.

STA Travel 10 Downing St, New York, NY 10014 (☎1-800/777-0112; 212/627-3111); 7202 Melrose Ave, Los Angeles, CA 90046 (☎213/934-8722); 51 Grant Ave, San Francisco, CA 94108 (☎415/391-8407); 297 Newbury St, Boston, MA 02115 (☎617/266-6014); 429 S Dearborn St, Chicago, IL 60605 (☎312/786-9050); 3730 Walnut St, Philadelphia, PA 19104 (☎215/382-2928); 317 14th Ave SE, Minneapolis, MN 55414 (☎612/615-1800). *Worldwide specialists in independent travel.*

TFI Tours International 34 W 32nd St, New York, NY 10001 (☎1-800/745-8000; 212/736-1140). *Consolidator.*

Travac 989 6th Ave, New York NY 10018 (☎1-800/872-8800). *Consolidator and charter broker mostly to Europe; has another office in Orlando.*

Travel Avenue 10 S Riverside, Suite 1404, Chicago, IL 60606 (☎1-800/333-3335). *Discount travel company.*

Travel CUTS 187 College St, Toronto, ON M5T 1P7 (☎1-800/667-2887; 416/979-2406). 180 MacEwan Student Centre, University of Calgary, Calgary, AB T2N 1N4 (☎403/282-7687); 12304 Jasper Av, Edmonton, AB T5N 3K5 (☎403/488-8487); 1613 Rue St Denis, Montréal, PQ H2X 3K3 (☎514/843-8511); 555 W 8th Ave, Vancouver, BC V5Z 1C6 (☎1-888/FLY CUTS; 604/822-6890); University Centre, University of Manitoba, Winnipeg MB R3T 2N2 (☎204/269-9530). *Canadian student travel organization.*

Unitravel 11737 Administration Drive, St Louis, MO 63146 (☎1-800/325-2222; 314/569-0900). *Consolidator.*

---

included, are $720 per person. If you're planning to stay in Spain's historic **paradores**, then expect to pay around $65–$95 per night for accommodation alone.

TRAVEL PASSES

If you're planning to do much **train** travel in Europe, then consider buying a **Eurail pass**, which comes in various forms, all of which must be bought before you leave home. Although not likely to pay for themselves if you're planning to stick to Spain, the passes allow unlimited free train travel in sixteen other countries.

The **Eurail Youthpass** (for under-26s) costs US$376 for fifteen consecutive days, $605 for one month or $857 for two months; if you're 26 or over you'll have to buy the **"first-class pass"**, available in 15-day ($538), 21-day ($698), one-month ($864), two-month ($1224) and three-month ($1512) increments. You stand a better chance of getting your money's worth out of a **Eurail Flexipass**, which is good for a certain number of travel days in a two-month period. This, too, comes in under-26/26 and over versions: ten days, $444/$634; and fifteen days, $585/$836. If you're travelling in a group of two or more, you might also want to consider the **Eurail Saverpass**, a single pass for multiple travellers. This costs $458 for fifteen consecutive days; $594 for 21; $734 for a month; $1040 for two months or $1286 for three. For groups of two or more there's also a **Flexi Saverpass**, which, like the Eurail Flexipass, is valid for a fixed number of days within a two-month period: $540 for ten days or $710 for fifteen days.

North Americans can also purchase passes exclusively for travel in Spain, including the **Spain Flexipass** and the **Spain Rail 'n' Drive** (see "Getting Around", p.27).

All these passes can be reserved through Rail Europe, 226 Westchester Ave, White Plains, NY 10604 (☎1-800/438-7245; *www.raileurope.com*) or travel agents.

North Americans considering travelling through Europe by **bus**, should check out the **Eurobus Pass**, which allows unlimited travel on special buses that ply fixed circuits of European cities. Spain is expected to join the itinerary by summer 1999. Check with Eurobus (☎1-800/387-6287) for rates and conditions. Note that only over-16s are eligible.

GETTING THERE FROM AUSTRALIA & NEW ZEALAND

There are no direct flights to Spain from Australia or New Zealand, but by combining services some airlines now offer travel to Madrid (and sometimes Barcelona) in conjunction with a stopover in Europe. KLM (via Amsterdam), Singapore Airlines (via Singapore) and British Airways (via London) provide the most direct services.

For extended trips, **Round the World** (RTW) tickets, valid for a year, are a good option, especially from New Zealand, where airlines offer fewer bonuses to fly with them. There are lots of different routes and airline combinations, but you generally get six stops – including Madrid or Barcelona – for A$2100–2800/NZ$2400–3100.

For details of Eurail and other useful **rail passes** contact: CIT – World Travel Group in Sydney ☎02/9267 1255; or Thomas Cook Rail Direct, ☎1300/361 941 for enquiries in Australia, ☎09/263 7260 for enquiries in New Zealand.

FARES

Fares change according to the time of year you travel. December and January are **high season**; February, and October through to mid-November, the low season; and the rest of the year the shoulder season. The current lowest standard return fares to Madrid (low/high season) are around A$1600/1900 from eastern Australia, A$1700/2100 from Perth and NZ$2100/2500 from Auckland.

Discount agents can usually provide far better prices than these, from A$1400/NZ$1900 for a low-season fare, though they charge heavily for cancellations or alterations. Students and anyone under 26 or over 60 may be eligible for further discounts, although this varies according to the season and the individual airline; check with STA Travel (see box, p.15).

AIRLINES

Air France 64 York St, Sydney (☎02/9244 2100); 310 King St, Melbourne (☎03/9920 3860); *www.airfrance-aust.com. Daily from Sydney and Melbourne, in combination with Qantas, to Madrid or Barcelona. Stopovers in Singapore, Hong Kong or Bangkok.*

Alitalia 9/118 Alfred St, Milson's Point, Sydney (☎02/9922 1555); 455 Bourke St, Melbourne (☎03/9600 0511); for reservations ☎1-300/653 747; 6th Floor, 229 Queen Street, Auckland (☎09/379 4455); *www.alitalia.it. Three Spanish connections a week from Sydney and Melbourne via Milan.*

British Airways Level 19, 259 George St, Sydney (☎02/8904 8800); 7th Floor, 114 William St, Melbourne (☎ 03/9603 1133); cnr Queen & Customs streets, Auckland (☎09/356 8690); *www.britishairways.com. Daily to seven cities in Spain via Bangkok/London or Kuala Lumpur/London from Sydney, Melbourne, Perth & Auckland. Daily from Brisbane via Singapore.*

Japan Airlines Darling Park, 14th Floor, 201 Sussex St, Sydney (☎02/9272 1111); 250 Collins St, Melbourne (☎03/9654 2733); 12/120 Albert Street, Auckland (☎09/379 9906). *Daily from Sydney to Madrid via Tokyo and Amsterdam (linking with KLM).*

KLM 5 Elizabeth St, Sydney (☎02/9231 6333); Nauru House, 80 Collins St, Melbourne (☎03/9654 5222); for reservations ☎1 800/505 747; *www.klm.com.au. Three times a week from Sydney (travellers from Melbourne, Adelaide and most regional areas fly Ansett to Sydney as part of the ticket) to Madrid or Barcelona via Amsterdam.*

Lauda Air 11th Floor, 143 Macquarie St, Sydney (☎02/9251 6155); 7th Floor, 84 William St, Melbourne (☎03/9600 4000); for reservations ☎1-800/642 438; *www.laudaair.com. Three a week from Sydney and Melbourne to Barcelona via Vienna where there is a one-night stopover.*

Qantas 70 Hunter St, Sydney (☎02/9951 4294); 50 Franklin St, Melbourne (☎03/9285 3000); Qantas House, 154 Queen St, Auckland (☎09/357 8900 or 0800/808 767); *www.qantas.com.au. Daily from Melbourne, Sydney and Perth (via Singapore or Bangkok) to London, connecting with British Airways for flights to Spain. Daily from Auckland via Sydney/Melbourne to London, and on to Spain.*

Singapore Airlines 17–19 Bridge St, Sydney (☎02/9350 0100); 414 Collins St, Melbourne (☎03/9254 0300); for reservations ☎13 1011; West Plaza Building, Lower Ground Floor, cnr Customs & Albert streets, Auckland (☎09/379 3209 or 0800/808 909); *www.singaporeair.com.au. Twice a week from Melbourne and Sydney to Madrid via Singapore. Daily from Auckland to Singapore (where there is a one-night stopover), then on to Madrid the next day.*

Thai International Airways 75–77 Pitt St, Sydney (☎02/9251 1922); 250 Collins St, Melbourne (☎03/9650 7522); reservations ☎1300/651 960; Kensington Swan Building, 22 Fanshawe St, Auckland (☎09/377 3886); *www.thaiair.com. Daily Spanish connections from Sydney via Bangkok. Twice weekly connections from Melbourne via Bangkok and three weekly from Auckland also via Bangkok.*

DISCOUNT AGENTS

AUSTRALIA

Accent on Travel 545 Queen St, Brisbane (☎07/3832 1777).

Anywhere Travel 345 Anzac Parade, Kingsford, Sydney (☎02/9663 0411).

Flight Centres 82 Elizabeth St, Sydney (☎02/9229 6611); 19 Bourke St, Melbourne (☎03/9650 2899); plus branches nationwide (nearest branch ☎13 1600); *www.flightcentre.com.*

I.B. Tours International Level 1, 47 New Canterbury Rd, Petersham, Sydney (☎02/9560 6722).

Ibertours 84 William St, Melbourne (☎03/9670 8388).

Northern Gateway 22 Cavenagh St, Darwin (☎08/8941 1394).

Passport Travel 401 St Kilda Rd, Melbourne (☎03/9867 3888).

Spanish Tourism Promotions 1st Floor, 178 Collins St, Melbourne (☎03/9650 7377).

STA Travel 855 George St, Sydney (☎02/9212 1255); 256 Flinders St, Melbourne (☎03/9654 7266); plus branches nationwide (nearest branch ☎13 1776); *www.statravel.com.au.*

continued overleaf

DISCOUNT AGENTS (cont)

AUSTRALIA

Thomas Cook 175 Pitt St, Sydney (☎02/9229 6611); 257 Collins St, Melbourne (☎03/9282 0333); branches in other state capitals (nearest branch ☎13 1771).

Topdeck Travel 65 Grenfell St, Adelaide (☎08/8232 7222).

Tymtro Travel 428 George St, Sydney (☎02/9223 2211).

NEW ZEALAND

Budget Travel 16 Fort St, Auckland (☎09/366 0061; ☎0-800/808 040 for nearest branch); *www.budgettravel.co.nz.*

Destinations Unlimited 3 Milford Rd, Milford, Auckland (☎09/373 4033).

Flight Centres National Bank Towers, 205–225 Queen St, Auckland (☎09/309 6171); plus branches nationwide (nearest branch ☎0-800/FLIGHTS); *www.flightcentre.com.*

STA Travel Travellers' Centre, 10 High St, Auckland (☎09/309 0458); 132 Cuba St, Wellington (☎04/385 0561); 90 Cashel St, Christchurch (☎03/379 9098); other offices in Hamilton, Palmerston North, Dunedin and major universities; *www.statravel.co.nz.*

Thomas Cook 159 Queen St, Auckland (☎09/379 3924; nearest branch ☎0-800/500 600).

RED TAPE AND VISAS

Citizens of most EU countries (and of Norway and Iceland) need only a valid national identity card to enter Spain for up to ninety days. Since Britain has no identity card system, however, British citizens have to take a passport. US, Canadian and New Zealand citizens do not need a visa for stays of up to ninety days. Australians do not need a visa for stays of up to thirty days, but for a longer visit (up to ninety days), will need to obtain one before arrival. Visa requirements do change and it is always advisable to check the current situation before leaving home.

To **stay longer**, EU nationals (and citizens of Norway and Iceland) can apply for a *permiso de residencia* (EU residence permit) once in Spain. A temporary residency permit is valid for up to a year, and you'll need a permanent one after that. Applications need to be made at the police station nearest to where you'll be taking up residency or at the relevant provincial police station. You'll either need to produce proof that you have sufficient funds (officially 5000ptas a day) to be able to support yourself without working – easiest done by keeping bank exchange forms every time you change money – or you'll need to have a contract of employment (*contrato de trabajo*) or become self-employed (for example as a teacher), which involves registering at the tax office. Other nationalities will either need to get a special visa from a Spanish consulate before departure (see opposte for addresses), or can apply – usually at any police station – for one ninety-day extension, showing proof of funds.

SPANISH EMBASSIES AND CONSULATES

Australia 15 Arkana St, Yarralumla, ACT 2600 (☎02/6273 3555); 4th Floor, 540 Elizabeth St, Melbourne, VIC 3000 (☎03/9347 1966); 24th Floor, St Martin Tower, 31 Market St, Sydney, NSW 2000 (☎02/9261 2433).

Britain 20 Draycott Place, London SW3 2RZ (☎0171/581 5921); Suite 1a, Brook House, 70 Spring Gardens, Manchester M22 2BQ (☎0161/236 1233).

Canada 74 Stanley Ave, Ottawa, Ontario K1M 1P4 (☎613/747-2252); 1 Westmount Sq #1456, Montréal, Quebec H3Z 2P9 (☎514/935-5235); Simcoe Place, 200 Front St, #2401, PO Box 15, Toronto, Ontario M5V 3K2 (416/977-1661).

Ireland 17a Merlyn Park, Ballsbridge, Dublin 4 (☎01/269 1640).

New Zealand No Spanish representation.

USA 2375 Pennsylvania Ave NW, Washington DC 20009 (☎202/728-2330); 150 E 58th St, New York, NY 10155 (☎212/355-4090); 545 Boylston St #803, Boston, MA 02116 (☎617/536-2506); 180 N Michigan Ave #1500, Chicago, IL 60601 (☎312/782-4588); 1800 Berins Drive #660, Houston, TX 77057 (☎713/783-6200); 5055 Wilshire Blvd #960, Los Angeles, CA 90036 (☎213/938-0158); 2655 Lejeune Rd #203, Coral Gables, Miami, FL 33134 (☎305/446-5511); 2102 World Trade Center, 2 Canal St, New Orleans, LA 70130 (☎504/525-4951); 1405 Sutter St, San Francisco, CA 94109 (☎415/922-2995).

HEALTH AND INSURANCE

As an EU country, Spain has free reciprocal health agreements with other member states (you should carry form E111, available from main post offices). Even so, some form of travel insurance is still all but essential. Note that bank and credit cards (particularly American Express) often provide certain levels of medical or other insurance, and travel insurance may also be included if you use a major credit or charge card to pay for your trip. With insurance you should be able to claim back the cost of any drugs prescribed by pharmacies, and European policies generally cover your baggage/tickets in case of theft, so long as you get a report from the local police. North American policies – see below – are more restrictive.

No **inoculations** are required for Spain, though if you plan on continuing to North Africa, typhoid and polio boosters are highly recommended. The worst that's likely to happen to you is that you might fall victim to an upset stomach. To be safe, wash fruit and avoid *tapas* dishes that look as if they were cooked last week.

For minor complaints go to a **farmacia** – they're listed in the phone book in major towns and you'll find one in virtually every village. Pharmacists are highly trained, willing to give advice (often in English), and able to dispense many drugs which would be available only on prescription in most other countries. They keep usual shop hours (9am–1pm & 4–7pm), but some open late and at weekends while a rota system keeps at least one open 24 hours. The rota is displayed in the window of every pharmacy, or you can check in one of the local newspapers under *Farmacias de guardia*.

In more serious cases you can get the address of an English-speaking doctor from the nearest relevant consulate, or with luck from a *farmacia*, the local police or Turismo. If you have special medical or dietary requirements, it is advisable to carry a letter from your doctor, translated into Spanish, indicating the nature of your condition and necessary treatments. In **emergencies** dial ☎091 for the *Servicios de Urgencia*, or look up the *Cruz Roja Española* (Red Cross) which runs a national ambulance service. Treatment at hospitals for EU citizens in possession of **form E111** is free; otherwise you'll be charged at private hospital rates, which can be as much as 14,000ptas per visit. Accordingly, it's essential to have comprehensive travel insurance.

BRITISH AND IRISH INSURANCE COVER

In **Britain**, travel insurance schemes (from around £25–30 a month) are sold by almost every travel agent and bank, or consider a specialist insurance firm. In **Ireland**, it's best to obtain your insurance through a travel specialist such as Usit (see p.9).

If you're going skiing in the Pyrenees, or engaging in any other high-risk outdoor activity, you'll probably have to pay an extra premium; ask your insurers for advice.

NORTH AMERICAN INSURANCE COVER

Before buying an insurance policy, check that you're not already covered. **Canadian provincial health plans** typically provide some overseas medical coverage, although they are unlikely to pick up the full tab in the event of a mishap. Holders of official **student/teacher**

/youth cards are entitled to accident coverage and hospital in-patient benefits – the annual membership is far less than the cost of comparable insurance. **Students** may also find that their student health coverage extends during the vacations and for one term beyond the date of last enrolment. **Homeowners' or renters'** insurance often covers theft or loss of documents, money and valuables while overseas.

After exhausting the possibilities above, you might want to contact a specialist travel insurance company; your travel agent can usually recommend one, or see the box below.

Travel insurance **policies** vary: some are comprehensive while others cover only certain risks (accidents, illnesses, delayed or lost luggage, cancelled flights, etc). In particular, ask whether the policy pays medical costs up front or reimburses you later, and whether it provides for medical evacuation to your home country. For policies that include lost or stolen luggage, check exactly what is and isn't covered, and make sure the per-article limit will cover your most valuable possession.

The best **premiums** are usually to be had through student/youth travel agencies – STA policies, for example, cost (with or without medical coverage respectively) $45/$35 (for up to 7 days), $60/$45 (8–15 days), $110/$85 (1 month), or $165/$135 (2 months). If you're planning to do any "dangerous sports" (skiing, mountaineering, etc), be sure to ask whether these activities are covered: some companies levy a surcharge.

TRAVEL INSURANCE COMPANIES

BRITAIN

Columbus Travel Insurance 17 Devonshire Square, London EC2 (☎0171/375 0011).

Endsleigh Insurance 97–107 Southampton Row, London WC1 (☎0171/436 4451).

NORTH AMERICA

Access America ☎1-800/284-8300.
Carefree Travel Insurance ☎1-800/323-3149.
Desjardins Travel Insurance Canada only, ☎1-800/463-7830.

STA Travel ☎1-800/777-0112.
Travel Guard ☎1-800/826-1300.
Travel Insurance Services ☎1-800/937-1387.

AUSTRALASIA

AFTA (Australian Federation of Travel Agents) 144 Pacific Hwy, North Sydney (☎02/9956 4800).

Cover-More Level 9, 32 Walker St, North Sydney (☎02/9202 8000 or 1-800/251 881); 57 Simon St, Auckland (☎09/377 5958).

Ready Plan 141–147 Walker St, Dandenong, Victoria (☎1-300/555 017), or through STA Travel; 10/63 Albert St, Auckland (☎09/379 3208).

UTAG (United Travel Agents Group) 122 Walker St, North Sydney (☎02/9956 8399 or 1-800/809 462).

AUSTRALIAN AND NEW ZEALAND INSURANCE COVER

In **Australia and New Zealand**, travel insurance schemes are available from most travel agents or direct from insurance companies. A typical policy will cost A$110/NZ$130 for two weeks, A$180/NZ$200 for one month or A$280/NZ$300 for two months. Most policies are similar in premium and coverage, but if you plan to indulge in high-risk activities, check the policy carefully to make sure you'll be covered.

TRAVELLERS WITH DISABILITIES

Spain is not exactly at the forefront of providing facilities for travellers with disabilities. That said, there are accessible hotels in the major cities and resorts and, by law, all new public buildings are required to be fully accessible; the staging of the 1992 Paralympic Games in Barcelona has done much to help attitudes and facilities there. There are also a number of active and forceful groups of disabled people: ONCE, the Spanish organization for the blind, is particularly active, its huge lottery bringing with it considerable power.

Transport is still the main problem, since buses are virtually impossible for wheelchairs and trains only slightly better (though there are wheelchairs at major stations and wheelchair spaces in some carriages – especially on the more modern trains such as the AVE between Madrid and Sevilla). Hertz has cars with hand controls available in Madrid and Barcelona (with advance notice), and taxi drivers are usually helpful. The Brittany Ferries crossing from Plymouth to Santander offers good facilities if you're **driving to Spain** (as do most cross-Channel ferries).

CONTACTS FOR TRAVELLERS WITH DISABILITIES

SPAIN

Spanish National Tourist Office (see p.21 for addresses). *Publishes a fact sheet, listing a variety of useful addresses and some accessible accommodation.*

ECOM (Federation of Spanish private organizations for the disabled) Gran Vía de las Corts Catalanas 562 principal, 2ª, 08011 Barcelona

(☎93 451 6904). *Produces an Access city guide for Barcelona.*

Organización Nacional de Ciegos de España (ONCE) Paseo de la Castellana 95, Planta 28, Madrid (☎91 597 4727); c/Calabria 66–76, Barcelona 08015 (☎93 325 92 00). *Sells Braille maps and can arrange trips for blind people; write for details.*

BRITAIN

Holiday Care Service 2nd Floor, Imperial Building, Victoria Rd, Horley, Surrey RH6 9HW (☎01293/774535). *Information on all aspects of travel.*

Mobility International Rue de Manchester 25, Brussels B1070 (☎00322/201 5711, fax 201 5763)

Information, access guides, tours and exchange programmes for British disabled travellers.

RADAR 12 City Forum, 250 City Rd, London EC1V 8AF (☎0171/250 3222). *A good source of advice on holidays and travel abroad.*

IRELAND

Disability Action Group 2 Annadale Ave, Belfast BT7 3JH (☎01232/491011). *Information on access for disabled travellers abroad.*

Irish Wheelchair Association Blackheath Drive, Clontarf, Dublin 3 (☎01/833 8241). *As above.* *continued overleaf*

MAP OUTLETS

IN BRITAIN

Glasgow John Smith and Sons, 57–61 St Vincent St, G2 5TB (☎0141/221 7472).

London National Map Centre, 22–24 Caxton St, SW1H (☎0171/222 2466); Stanfords, 12–14 Long Acre, WC2 (☎0171/836 1321);

The Travel Bookshop, 13–15 Blenheim Crescent, W11 (☎0171/229 5260).

Note: maps by **mail or phone order** are available from Stanfords (☎0171/836 1321).

IN IRELAND

Dublin Easons Bookshop, 40 O'Connell St (☎01/873 3811); Fred Hanna's Bookshop, 27–29 Nassau St (☎01/677 1255); Hodges Figgis Bookshop, 56–58 Dawson St

(☎01/677 4754); Waterstone's, 7 Dawson St (☎01/679 1415).

Belfast Waterstone's, Queens Bldg, 8 Royal Ave (☎01232/247 355).

IN NORTH AMERICA

Chicago Rand McNally, 444 N Michigan Ave, Chicago, IL 60611 (☎312/321-1751).

Montréal Ulysses Travel Bookshop, 4176 St-Denis, Montreal H2W 2M5 (☎514/843-9447).

New York The Complete Traveler Bookstore, 199 Madison Ave, New York, NY 10016 (☎212/685-9007); Traveler's Bookstore, 22 W 52nd St, New York, NY 10019 (☎212/664-0995).

San Francisco The Complete Traveler Bookstore, 3207 Fillmore St, San Francisco, CA 92123 (☎415/923-1511).

Seattle Elliot Bay Book Company, 101 S Main St, Seattle, WA 98104 (☎206/624-6600).

Toronto Open Air Books and Maps, 25 Toronto St, Toronto, M5R 2C1 (☎416/363-0719).

Vancouver International Travel Maps and Books, 552 Seymour St, Vancouver V6B 3J6 (☎604/687-3320).

Washington The Map Store Inc., 1636 1st St NW, Washington, DC 20006 (☎202/628-2608); Travel Books & Language Center, 4437 Wisconsin Ave, Washington, DC 20016 (☎1-800/220-2665).

Note: Rand McNally now has more than twenty stores across the US; call ☎1-800/234-0679 for the address of your nearest store, or for direct mail maps.

IN AUSTRALIA AND NEW ZEALAND

Adelaide The Map Shop, 16a Peel St, Adelaide, SA 5000 (☎08/8231 2033).

Auckland Specialty Maps, 58 Albert St, Auckland (☎09/307 2217).

Brisbane Worldwise Maps and Guides, 187 George St, Brisbane, QLD 4000 (☎07/3221 4330).

Melbourne Mapland, 372 Little Bourke St, Melbourne, VIC 3000 (☎03/9670 4383).

Perth Perth Map Centre, 884 Hay St, Perth, WA 6000 (☎08/9322 5733).

Sydney Travel Bookshop, 3/175 Liverpool St, Sydney, NSW 2000 (☎02/9261 8200).

A Catalunya-based company, Editorial Alpina, produces useful 1:40,000 or 1:25,000 **map-booklets** for most of the Spanish mountain and foothill areas of interest, and these are also on sale in many bookshops; the relevant editions are noted in the text where appropriate.

SPAIN ON THE INTERNET

Spain is represented pretty strongly on the Internet, with Web sites in both English and

Spanish offering information on most conceivable subjects. The Web sites detailed below are useful starting points and most contain numerous links on to more detailed areas. The *soc.culture.spain* Newsgroup is also highly recommended if you want to ask questions on any cultural matters.

City.Net: Spain

www.city.net/countries/spain/
City.Net's Web indexes are a superb resource, arranged in clear categories including travel and

sightseeing, news media and food and drink, and with a constant weather update as soon as you log in. All major Spanish cities are featured in some detail, and you can use the links to explore well beyond their boundaries.

Dónde
http://donde.uji.es/
Search engine for Spanish-language Web sites.

El País Digital
www.elpais.es/
Impressive digital version of Spain's major newspaper.

Fútbol de España
http://ibgwww.colorado.edu/~gayan/futbol/indice.html
Masses of stats, plus links to Web sites posted for most Spanish premier league teams.

Gournet Spain
www.winwork.es/gournet-spain/
Searchable restaurant database that – at present –promises rather more than it delivers.

Grupos Españoles en la Teleraña
www.get.es/
Collective site for a number of Spanish rock bands. Also details rock festivals.

Interbook
www.disbumad.es/
Major Spanish online bookstore, offering over a million titles.

Peseta Daily Exchange Rate
http://153.1.6.18/~ktmatu/rate-esp.html

Rough Guide to Europe (Spain)
www.hotwired.com/rough/europe/spain/
Full text of the Spanish section of our Europe book – with forums for readers' comments.

Si Spain
www.DocuWeb.ca/SiSpain/
Posted by the Spanish embassy in Ottawa, this is the largest – and best – Spain-oriented English-language site on the Web, bringing together reams of information on all aspects of Spanish culture, politics, history, and tourist information, as well as directing you to a host of specialist sites. A particularly neat feature is the searchable Fiesta Directory.

Spain Newsgroup
www.landfield.com/faqs/by-newsgroup/soc/soc.culture.spain.html
This is the main Newsgroup discussion forum for all matters Spanish.

Spatour
www.spatour.com
This site lists hotels, restaurants, campings, events and other tourist information for the whole of Spain. Excellent site, but unfortunately only available in Spanish at present.

Yahoo!: Spain
www.yahoo.com/Regional_Information/Countries/Spain/
The Spain section from this excellent Web directory.

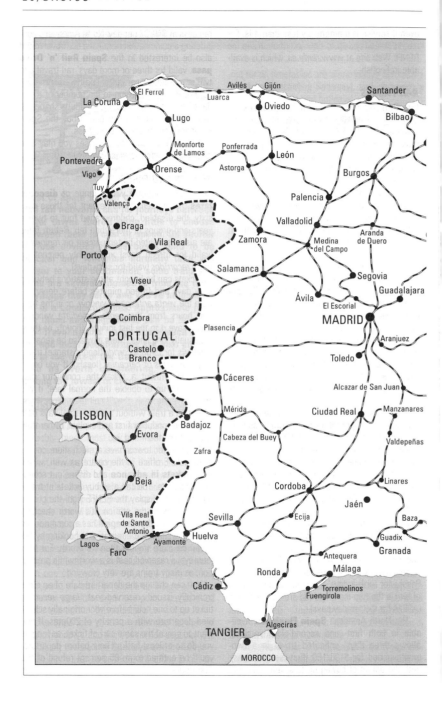

△ Paris

FRANCE

Toulouse

San Sebastián

Bayonne

Pau

Tarbes

Perpignan

Vitoria

Pamplona

Canfranc

ANDORRA

Cerbère

Logrono

Jaca

Figueres

Port Bou

Alfaro

Tudela

Huesca

Vic

Girona

Soria

Zaragoza

Lleida

Almazán

Calatayúd

Montblanc

Sitges

Barcelona

Medinaceli

Tarragona

Tortosa

Teruel

Menorca

Cuenca

Castellón de la Plane

Sóller

Inca

Palma

Mallorca

Sagunto

Valencia

Ibiza

Albacete

Formentera

Alicante

Murcia

Lorca

N

Almería

0 Kilometres 100

SPAIN: TRAINS

ACCOMMODATION

It's often worth **bargaining** over room prices, since the regulated prices don't necessarily mean much. In high season you're unlikely to have much luck (although many hotels do have rooms at different prices, and tend to offer the more expensive ones first) but at quiet times you may get quite a discount, even at fancier places. If there are more than two of you, most places have rooms with three or four beds at not a great deal more than the double-room price – a bargain, especially if you have children.

Hotel vouchers (*bonos*), available from local travel agents, often give substantial discounts at medium to upmarket hotels; simply present the voucher at the hotel instead of payment.

FONDAS, PENSIONES, HOSTALES AND HOTELES

Simple, reasonably priced rooms are still very widely available in Spain, and in almost any town you'll be able to get a double for around 2500–3500ptas, a single for 1500–2500ptas. Only in major resorts and a handful of "tourist cities" (such as Toledo or Sevilla) need you pay more.

We've detailed where to find places to stay in most of the destinations listed in the Guide, and given a price range for each (see below), from the most basic rooms to luxury hotels. As a general rule, all you have to do is head for the cathedral or main square of any town, invariably surrounded by an old quarter full of accommodation possibilities. In Spain, unlike most countries, you don't always have to pay more for a central location (this goes for bars and cafés, too), though you do tend to get a comparatively bad deal if you're travelling on your own as there are relatively few single rooms. Much of the time you'll have to negotiate a reduction on the price of a double.

The one thing all travellers need to master is the elaborate variety of types and places to stay. Least expensive of all are **fondas** (identifiable by a square blue sign with a white **F** on it, and often positioned above a bar), closely followed by **casas de huéspedes (CH** on a similar sign), **pensiones (P)** and, less commonly, **hospedajes**. Distinctions between all of these are rather blurred, but in general you'll find food served at both *fondas* and *pensiones* (some of which may offer rooms only on a meals-inclusive basis). *Casas de huéspedes* (literally "guest houses") were traditionally for longer stays; and to some extent, particularly in the older family seaside resorts, they still are.

ACCOMMODATION PRICES

All the establishments listed in this book have been price-graded according to the following scale. The prices quoted are for the **cheapest available double room in high season**; effectively this means that anything in the ① and most places in the ② range will be without private bath, though there's usually a washbasin in the room. In the ③ category and above you will probably be getting private facilities. Remember, though, that many of the budget places will also have more expensive rooms including en-suite facilities. Youth hostels are graded under ① as the price per person is less than half of the category's upper limit.

Note that in the more upmarket *hostales* and *pensiones*, and in anything calling itself a hotel, you'll pay a **tax** (IVA) of eight percent on top of the room price.

① Under 2000ptas	③ 3000–4500ptas	⑤ 6000–8000ptas	⑦ 12,000–17,500ptas
② 2000–3000ptas	④ 4500–6000ptas	⑥ 8000–12,000ptas	⑨ Over 17,500ptas

Slightly more expensive but far more common are **hostales** (marked **Hs**) and **hostal-residencias** (**HsR**). These are categorized from one star to three stars, but even so prices vary enormously according to location – in general the more remote, the less expensive. Most *hostales* offer good functional rooms, usually with private shower, and, for doubles at least, they can be excellent value. The *residencia* designation means that no meals other than perhaps breakfast are served.

Moving up the scale you finally reach fully-fledged **hoteles** (**H**), again star-graded by the authorities (from one to five). One-star hotels cost no more than three-star *hostales* – sometimes they're actually less expensive – but at three stars you pay a lot more, at four or five you're in the luxury class with prices to match. Near the top end of this scale there are also state-run **paradores**: beautiful places, often converted from castles, monasteries and other minor Spanish monuments. If you can afford them these are almost all wonderful. Even if you can't afford to stay, the buildings are often worth a look in their own right, and usually have pleasantly classy bars.

Outside all of these categories you will sometimes see **camas** (beds) and **habitaciones** (rooms) advertised in private houses or above bars, often with the phrase *camas y comidas* ("beds and meals"). If you're travelling on a very tight budget these can be worth looking out for – particularly if you're offered one at a bus station and the owner is prepared to bargain with you.

There are also **casas rurales** (rural houses), a scheme established along the lines of French *gîtes*. Accommodation at these can vary from bed and breakfast at a farmhouse to a rental cottage. Local Turismos have details.

Note if you have any **problems** with Spanish rooms – overcharging, most obviously – you can usually produce an immediate resolution by asking for the *libro de reclamaciones* (complaints book). By law all establishments must keep one and bring it out for regular inspection by the police. Nothing is ever written in it.

YOUTH HOSTELS, MOUNTAIN REFUGES, AND MONASTERIES

Albergues Juveniles (youth hostels) are rarely very practical, except in northern Spain (especially the Pyrenees) where it can be difficult for solo, short-term travellers to find any other bed in summer. Only about twenty Spanish *albergues* stay open all year – the rest operate just for the summer (or spring and summer) in temporary premises – and in cities they tend to be inconveniently located. The most useful are detailed in the Guide, or you can get a complete list (with opening times and phone numbers) from the YHA. Be warned that they tend to have curfews, are often block-reserved by school groups and demand production of a YHA card (though this is generally available on the spot if you haven't already bought one from your national organization). At around 1000ptas a person, too, you can quite easily pay more than for sharing a cheap double room in a *fonda* or *casa de huéspedes*.

In isolated mountain areas the Federación Madrilaña de Montañismo, Apodaca 16, Madrid 28004 (☎91 448 50 56), and two Catalunya-based clubs, the Federació d'Entitats Excursionistes de Catalunya (Rambla 41 Pral., 08002 Barcelona; ☎93 412 07 77; *www.feec.es*), and the Unió Excursionista de Catalunya de Gràcia (Santa Agata 30, 08012 Barcelona; ☎93 217 56 50; *www.gencat.es/entitats/unexcag.htm*), run a number of **refugios**: simple, cheap dormitory-huts for climbers and trekkers, generally equipped only with bunks and a very basic kitchen, and costing around 500ptas per person. Again off the beaten track, it is sometimes possible to stay at Spanish **monasterios** or **conventos**. Often severely underpopulated, these may let empty cells for a small charge. You can just turn up and ask – many will take visitors regardless of sex – but if you want to be sure of a reception it's best to approach the local Turismo first, and phone ahead. There are some particularly wonderful monastic locations in Galicia, Catalunya and Mallorca.

Those following the **Camino de Santiago** can also take advantage of monastic accommodation specifically reserved for pilgrims along the route; some of the best places are detailed in the text.

CAMPING

There are some 350 authorized **campsites** in Spain, predominantly on the coast. They usually work out at about 400–500ptas per person plus the same again for a tent (once again, discriminating against solo travellers) and a similar amount for each car or caravan, perhaps twice as much for a van. Only a few of the best located or most popular sites are significantly more expensive. Again, we've detailed the most useful in the text, but if you plan to camp extensively then pick up the free *Mapa de Campings* from the National Tourist Board, which marks and names virtually all of them. A complete *Guía de Campings*, listing full prices, facilities and exact locations, is available at most Spanish bookshops.

Camping outside campsites is legal – but with certain restrictions. There must be fewer than ten people in your group, and you're not allowed to camp "in urban areas, areas prohibited for military or touristic reasons, or within 1km of an official campsite". What this means in practice is that you can't camp on tourist beaches (though you can, discreetly, nearby) but with a little sensitivity you can set up a tent for a short period almost anywhere in the countryside. Whenever possible ask locally first.

If you're planning to do a lot of camping, an **international camping carnet** may be a good investment, available from home motoring organizations, or from one of the following: in Britain, the Camping and Caravan Club, Greenfield House, Westwood Way, Coventry CV4 8JH (☎01203/694995); and in the US and Canada, the Family Campers and RVers, 4804 Transit Rd, Building 2, Depew, NY 14043 (☎1-800/245-9755). The carnet serves as useful identification and covers you for third party insurance when camping.

EATING AND DRINKING

There are two ways to eat in Spain: you can go to a *restaurante* or *comedor* (dining room) and have a full meal, or you can have a succession of *tapas* (small snacks) or *raciones* (larger ones) at one or more bars.

At the bottom line a *comedor* – where you'll get a basic, filling, three-course meal with a drink, the **menú del día** – is the cheapest option, but they're often tricky to find, and drab places when you do. Bars tend to work out pricier but a lot more interesting, allowing you to do the rounds and sample local or house specialities.

BREAKFAST, SNACKS AND SANDWICHES

For **breakfast** you're best off in a bar or café, though some *hostales* and *fondas* will serve the "Continental" basics. The traditional Spanish breakfast is *chocolate con churros* – long tubular doughnuts (not for the weak of stomach) with thick drinking chocolate. But most places also serve *tostadas* (toast) with oil (*con aceite*) or butter (*con mantequilla*) – and jam (*y mermelada*), or more substantial egg dishes such as *huevos fritos* (fried eggs). *Tortilla* (potato omelette) also makes an excellent breakfast.

Coffee and pastries (*pasteles*) or doughnuts are available at most cafés, too, though for a wider selection of cakes you should head for one of the many excellent *pastelerías* or *confiterías*. In larger towns, especially in Catalunya, there will often be a *panadería* or *croissantería* serving quite an array of appetizing (and healthier) baked goods besides the obvious bread, croissants and pizza. For ordering coffee see p.42.

Some bars specialize in **sandwiches** (*bocadillos*), and, as they're usually outsize affairs in French bread, they'll do for breakfast or lunch. In a bar with *tapas* (see below), you can have most of what's on offer put in a sandwich, and you can often get them prepared (or buy the materials to do so) at grocery shops. Incidentally, a *sandwich* is a toasted cheese and ham sandwich, usually on sad processed bread.

TAPAS AND RACIONES

One of the advantages of eating in **bars** is that you are able to experiment. Many places have food laid out on the counter, so you can see what's available and order by pointing without necessarily knowing the names; others have blackboards (see box, p.38). **Tapas** are small portions, three or four small chunks of fish or meat, or a dollop of salad, which traditionally used to be served up free with a drink. These days you have to pay for anything more than a few olives (where you do get free food now, it will often be called a *pincho*), but a single helping rarely costs more than 200–400ptas unless you're somewhere very flashy. **Raciones** are simply bigger plates of the same, and can be enough in themselves for a light meal; *pinchos morunos* (small kebabs) are often also available. The more people you're with, of course, the better; half a dozen *tapas* or *pinchos* and three *raciones* can make a varied and quite filling meal for three or four people.

Tascas, **bodegas**, **cervecerías** and **tabernas** are all types of bar where you'll find *tapas* and *raciones*. Most of them have different sets of prices depending on whether you stand at the bar to eat (the basic charge) or sit at tables (up to fifty percent more expensive – and even more if you sit out on a terrace).

Wherever you have *tapas*, it is important to find out what the local **special** is and order it. Spaniards will commonly move from bar to bar, having just the one dish that they consider each bar does well. A bar's "non-standard" dishes, these days, can all too often be microwaved – which is not a good way to cook fried squid.

MEALS AND RESTAURANTS

Once again, there's a multitude of distinctions. You can sit down and have a full meal in a *comedor*, a

UNDERSTANDING SPANISH MENUS

As with *tapas* and *raciones*, restaurant dishes vary enormously from region to region. The list below is no more than a selection, with the main Spanish dishes and a handful of local specialities. Wherever possible you'll do best by going for the latter; some are mentioned in the regional chapters that follow, others you'll simply see people eating. *Quisiera uno asi* (I'd like one like that) can be an amazingly useful phrase.

BASICS

Aceite	Oil	Miel	Honey
Ajo	Garlic	Pan	Bread
Arroz	Rice	Pimienta	Pepper
Azúcar	Sugar	Sal	Salt
Huevos	Eggs	Vinagre	Vinegar
Mantequilla	Butter		

MEALS

Almuerzo	Lunch	La quenta	The bill
Botella	Bottle	Desayuno	Breakfast
Carta	Menu	Menú del día/cubierto	Fixed-price set meal
Cena	Dinner	Mesa	Table
Comedor	Dining room	Platos combinados	Mixed plate
Cuchara	Spoon	Tenedor	Fork
Cuchillo	Knife	Vaso	Glass

SOUPS (*SOPAS*) AND STARTERS

Caldillo	Clear fish soup	Sopa d'ajo	Garlic soup
Caldo	Broth	Sopa de cocido	Meat soup
Caldo verde or gallego	Thick cabbage-based	Sopa de gallina	Chicken soup
	broth	Sopa de mariscos	Seafood soup
Ensalada (mixta/verde)	(Mixed/green) salad	Sopa de pescado	Fish soup
Gazpacho	Cold tomato and	Sopa de pasta (fideos)	Noodle soup
	cucumber soup	Verduras con patatas	Boiled potatoes with
Pimientos rellenos	Stuffed peppers		greens

FISH (*PESCADOS*)

Anchoas	Anchovies (fresh)	Mero	Perch
Anguila/Angulas	Eel/Elvers	Pez espada	Swordfish
Atún	Tuna	Rape	Monkfish
Bacalao	Cod (often salt)	Raya	Ray, skate
Bonito	Tuna	Rodaballo	Turbot
Boquerones	Small, sardine-like fish	Salmonete	Mullet
Chanquetes	Whitebait	Sardinas	Sardines
Lenguado	Sole	Trucha	Trout
Merluza	Hake		

SEAFOOD (*MARISCOS*)

Almejas	Clams	Nécora	Sea-crab
Arroz con mariscos	Rice with seafood	Ostras	Oysters
Calamares (en su tinta)	Squid (in ink)	Paella	Classic Valencian dish
Centollo	Spider-crab		with saffron rice,
Cigalas	King prawns		chicken, seafood, etc
Conchas finas	Large scallops	Percebes	Goose-barnacles
Gambas	Prawns/shrimps	Pulpo	Octopus
Langosta	Lobster	Sepia	Cuttlefish
Langostinos	King prawns	Vieiras	Scallops
Mejillones	Mussels	Zarzuela de mariscos	Seafood casserole

SOME COMMON TERMS

al ajillo	in garlic	*alioli*	with mayonnaise
asado	roast	*cazuela, cocido*	stew
a la Navarra	stuffed with ham	*en salsa*	in (usually tomato) sauce
a la parilla/plancha	grilled	*frito*	fried
a la Romana	fried in batter	*guisado*	casserole
al horno	baked	*rehogado*	baked

MEAT (*CARNE*) AND POULTRY (*AVES*)

Callos	Tripe	*Hamburguesa*	Hamburger
Carne de buey	Beef	*Hígado*	Liver
Cerdo	Pork	*Lacón con grelos*	Trotter with turnips
Chuletas	Chops	*Lengua*	Tongue
Cochinillo	Suckling pig	*Lomo*	Loin (of pork)
Codorniz	Quail	*Pato*	Duck
Conejo	Rabbit	*Pavo*	Turkey
Cordero	Lamb	*Perdiz*	Partridge
Escalopa	Escalope	*Pollo*	Chicken
Fabada	Hot pot with butter	*Riñones*	Kidneys
asturiana/Fabes a la	beans, black pud-	*Ternera*	Veal
catalana	ding, etc		

VEGETABLES (*LEGUMBRES*)

Acelga	Chard	*Judías verdes, rojas,*	Green, red, black
Alcachofas	Artichokes	*negras*	beans
Arroz a la cubana	Rice with fried egg and	*Lechuga*	Lettuce
	tomato sauce	*Lentejas*	Lentils
Berenjenas	Aubergine/eggplant	*Menestra/Panache de*	Mixed vegetables
Cebollas	Onions	*verduras*	
Champiñones/Setas	Mushrooms	*Nabos/Grelos*	Turnips
Coliflor	Cauliflower	*Patatas (fritas)*	Potatoes (fries)
Esparragos	Asparagus	*Pepino*	Cucumber
Espinacas	Spinach	*Pimientos*	Peppers/capsicums
Garbanzos	Chickpeas	*Pisto manchego*	Ratatouille
Habas	Broad/fava beans	*Puerros*	Leeks
Judías blancas	Haricot beans	*Repollo*	Cabbage
		Tomate	Tomato
		Zanahoria	Carrot

FRUIT (*FRUTAS*)

Albaricoques	Apricots	*Melocotónes*	Peaches
Cerezas	Cherries	*Melón*	Melon
Chirimoyas	Custard apples	*Naranjas*	Oranges
Ciruelas	Plums, prunes	*Nectarinas*	Nectarines
Dátiles	Dates	*Peras*	Pears
Fresas	Strawberries	*Piña*	Pineapple
Granada	Pomegranate	*Plátanos*	Bananas
Higos	Figs	*Sandía*	Watermelon
Limón	Lemon	*Toronja/Pomelo*	Grapefruit
Manzanas	Apples	*Uvas*	Grapes

UNDERSTANDING SPANISH TERMS (cont.)

DESSERTS (*POSTRES*)

Arroz con leche	Rice pudding	*Helados*	Ice cream
Crema catalana	Catalan crème	*Melocotón en almíbar*	Peaches in syrup
	caramel	*Membrillo*	Quince paste
Cuajada	Cream-based dessert	*Nata*	Whipped cream
	served with honey	*Natillas*	Custard
Flan	Crème caramel	*Yogur*	Yogurt

CHEESE

Cheeses (*quesos*) are on the whole local, though you'll get the hard, salty *queso manchego* everywhere. Mild sheep's cheese (*queso de oveja*) from the León province is widely distributed and worth asking for.

---

usually get a whole bottle for two people, a *media botella* (a third to a half of a litre) for one.

The classic Andalucían wine is **sherry** – *vino de Jerez*. This is served chilled or at *bodega* temperature – a perfect drink to wash down *tapas* – and, like everything Spanish, it comes in a perplexing variety of forms. The main distinctions are between *fino* or *jerez seco* (dry sherry), *amontillado* (medium), and *oloroso* or *jerez dulce* (sweet), and these are the terms you should use to order. Similar – though not identical – are *montilla* and *manzanilla*, dry sherry-like wines from the provinces of Córdoba and Huelva. These, too, are excellent and widely available.

Cerveza, lager-type beer, is generally pretty good, though more expensive than wine. It comes in 300-ml bottles (*botellines*) or, for about the same price, on tap – a *caña* of draught beer is a small glass, a *caña doble* larger. Many bartenders will assume you want a *doble*, so if you don't, say so. Local brands, such as Cruz Campo around Sevilla or Alhambra in Granada, are often better than the national ones.

Equally refreshing, though often deceptively strong, is **sangría**, a wine-and-fruit punch which you'll come across at fiestas and in tourist bars; *tinto de verano* is basically the same red wine and soda or lemonade combination.

In mid-afternoon – or even at breakfast – many Spaniards take a *copa* of **liqueur** with their coffee. The best are *anís* (like Pernod) or *coñac*, excellent local brandy with a distinct vanilla flavour (try Magno, Soberano, or 103 to get an idea of the variety).

Most **spirits** are ordered by brand name, since there are generally less expensive Spanish equivalents for standard imports. Larios gin from Málaga, for instance, is about half the price of

Gordon's. Specify *nacional* to avoid getting an expensive foreign brand. Spirits can be very expensive at the trendier bars; however, wherever they are served, they tend to be staggeringly generous – the bar staff pouring from the bottle until you suggest they stop.

Mixed drinks are universally known as *Cuba libre* or *Cubata*, though strictly speaking this is rum and Coke. Juice is *zumo*; orange, *naranja*; lemon, *limón*; and tonic *tónica*.

SOFT DRINKS AND HOT DRINKS

Soft drinks are much the same as anywhere in the world, but try in particular *granizado* (slush) or *horchata* (a milky drink made from tiger nuts or almonds) from one of the street stalls that spring up everywhere in summer. You can also get these drinks from *horchaterías* and from *heladerías* (ice cream – *helados* – parlours), or in Catalunya from the wonderful milk bars known as *granjas*. Although you can drink the **water** almost everywhere it usually tastes better out of the bottle – inexpensive *agua mineral* comes either sparkling (*con gas*) or still (*sin gas*).

Café (coffee) – served in cafés, *heladerías* and bars – is invariably espresso, slightly bitter and, unless you specify otherwise, served black (*café solo*). If you want it white ask for *café cortado* (small cup with a drop of milk) or *café con leche* (made with lots of hot milk). For a large cup ask for a *doble* or *grande*. Coffee is also frequently mixed with brandy, cognac or whisky, all such concoctions being called *carajillo*. Iced coffee is *café hielo*. **Té** (tea) is also available at most bars, although bear in mind that Spaniards usually drink it black. If you want milk it's safest to ask for it afterwards, since ordering *té con leche* might well get you a glass of milk with a tea bag floating on top.

DRINKS AND BEVERAGES

Alcohol		Hot drinks		Soft drinks	
Beer	*Cerveza*	Coffee	*Café*	Water	*Agua*
Champagne	*Champán*	Espresso coffee	*Café solo*	Mineral water	*Agua mineral*
Wine	*Vino*	White coffee	*Café con leche*	. . . (sparkling)	. . .*(con gas)*
		Decaff	*Descafeinado*	. . . (still)	. . .*(sin gas)*
		Tea	*Té*	Milk	*Leche*
		Drinking	*Chocolate*	Juice	*Zumo*
		chocolate		Tiger nut drink	*Horchata*

Chocolate (hot chocolate) is incredibly thick and sweet, and is a popular early-morning drink after a long night on the town. For English-style (thin) hot chocolate, you may have to ask for a brand name, such as Cola Cao.

OPENING HOURS AND PUBLIC HOLIDAYS

Almost everything in Spain – shops, museums, churches, tourist offices – closes for a siesta of at least two hours in the hottest part of the day. There's a lot of variation (and the siesta tends to be longer in the south) but basic summer working hours are 9.30am–1.30pm and 4.30–8pm. Certain shops do now stay open all day, and there is a move towards "normal" working hours. Nevertheless, you'll get far less aggravated if you accept that the early afternoon is best spent asleep, or in a bar, or both.

Museums, with very few exceptions, follow the rule above, with a break between 1 and 4pm; watch out for Sundays (most open mornings only) and Mondays (most close all day). Admission charges vary, but there's usually a big reduction or free entrance if you show an ISIC or FIYTO card. Anywhere run by the Patrimonio Nacional, the national organization which preserves monuments, is free to EU citizens on Wednesday – you'll need your passport to prove your nationality. This includes some of the most important buildings in Spain, such as El Escorial and the Royal Palace in Madrid.

Note that the official beginning of **summer opening hours** for Patrimonio Nacional monuments – and some privately owned ones – vary from year to year, and are generally not announced until April/May. Where this is the case, we have given opening hours for "summer" and "winter"; contact the local Turismo for more up-to-date information.

Getting into **churches** can present more of a problem. The really important ones, including most cathedrals, operate in much the same way as museums and almost always have some entry charge to see their most valued treasures and paintings, or their cloisters. Other churches, though, are usually kept locked, opening only for worship in the early morning and/or the evening (between around 6–9pm), so you'll either have to try at these times, or find someone with a key. This is time-consuming but rarely difficult, since a sacristan or custodian almost always lives nearby

SPANISH NATIONAL HOLIDAYS

January 1, *Año Nuevo*, New Year's Day
January 6, *Epifanía*, Epiphany
Good Friday, *Viernes Santo*
Easter Sunday, *Domingo de la Resureccion*
Easter Monday, *Lunes de Pascua*
May 1, *Fiesta de Trabajo*, May Day/Labour Day
August 15, *La Asunción*, Assumption of the Virgin
October 12, *Día de la Hispanidad*, National Day
November 1, *Todos Santos*, All Saints
December 6, *Día de la Constitución*, Constitution Day
December 8, *Fiesta de la Hispanidad*
Christmas Day, *Navidad*

and most people will know where to direct you. You're expected to give a small tip, or donation. For all churches "decorous" dress is required, ie no shorts, bare shoulders, etc.

PUBLIC HOLIDAYS

Public holidays can (and will) disrupt your plans at some stage. Alongside the national holidays (see p.43) there are scores of local festivals (different in every town and village, usually marking the local saint's day); any of them will mean that everything except bars (and *hostales*, etc) locks its doors.

In addition, **August** is Spain's own holiday month, when the big cities – especially Madrid – are semi-deserted, and many of the shops and restaurants, even museums, close. In contrast, it can prove nearly impossible to find a room in the more popular coastal and mountain resorts at these times; similarly, seats on planes, trains and buses at this time should if possible be booked in advance.

FIESTAS, THE BULLFIGHT, FOOTBALL AND MUSIC

It's hard to beat the experience of arriving in some small Spanish village, expecting no more than a bed for the night, to discover the streets decked out with flags and streamers, a band playing in the plaza and the entire population out celebrating the local fiesta. Everywhere in the country, from the tiniest hamlet to the great cities, will take at least one day off a year to devote to partying. Usually it's the local saint's day, but there are celebrations, too, of harvests, of deliverance from the Moors, of safe return from the sea – any excuse will do.

Each festival is different. In the Basque country there will often be bulls running through the streets, or displays of the ancient Basque sports which resemble nothing so much as the Scottish Highland games; in Andalucía horses, flamenco and the guitar are an essential part of any celebration; in Valencia you'll see stylized battles between Christians and Moors, huge bonfires and stunning fireworks. But there is always music, dancing, traditional costume and an immense spirit of enjoyment. The main event of most fiestas is a parade, either behind a revered holy image, or a more celebratory affair with fancy costumes and *gigantones*, grotesque giant carnival figures which run down the streets terrorizing children.

Although these take place throughout the year – and it is often the obscure and unexpected event which proves to be most fun – there are certain occasions which stand out. **Semana Santa** (Easter week) and **Corpus Christi** (in early June) are celebrated all over the country with magnificent religious processions. Easter, particularly, is worth trying to coincide with – head for Sevilla, Málaga, Granada or Córdoba, where huge *pasos*, floats of wildly theatrical religious scenes, are carried down the streets, accompanied by weirdly hooded penitents atoning for the year's misdeeds.

Among the biggest and best-known of the other **popular festivals** are: the Cádiz *carnavales* (first to third week of February); the *Fallas de San José* in Valencia (March 15–19); Sevilla's enormous April *Feria* (a week at the end of the month); Jerez's Horse Fair (early May); the *Romería del Rocío*, an extraordinary pilgrimage to El Rocío near Huelva (arriving there on Whit Sunday); Pamplona's riotous *Fiesta de San Fermín*, most famous of the bull-runnings (July 6–14); the Feast of St James at Santiago de Compostela (July 25); and the mock battles between Christians and Moors in Elche (August 10–15), ending with a centuries-old mystery play.

The list is potentially endless, and although you'll find the major events detailed at the beginning of each chapter we can't pretend that this is an exhaustive list. Local tourist offices should have more information about what's going on in their area at any given time. Outsiders are always welcome at Spanish festivals, the one problem being that during any of the most popular you'll find it difficult and expensive to find a bed. If you're planning to coincide with a festival, try and book your accommodation well in advance.

> **Note** that saint's day festivals – indeed all Spanish celebrations – can **vary in date**, often being observed over the weekend closest to the dates given in our "Fiestas" listings at the beginning of each chapter.

BULLFIGHTS

Bullfights are an integral part of many Spanish festivals. In the south, especially, any village that can afford it will put on a **corrida** for an afternoon, while in big cities like Madrid or Sevilla, the main festival times are accompanied by a week-long (or more) season of prestige fights.

Los Toros, as Spaniards refer to bullfighting, is big business. Each year an estimated 24,000 bulls are killed before a live audience of over thirty million, and many more on televison. It is said that 150,000 people are involved, in some way, in the industry, and the top performers, the **matadores**, are major earners, on a par with the country's biggest pop stars. There is some opposition to the activity from animal welfare groups but it is not widespread: if Spaniards tell you that bullfighting is controversial, they are likely to be referring to practices in the trade. In recent years, bullfighting critics (who you will find on the arts pages of the newspapers) have been expressing their perennial outrage at the widespread but illegal shaving of bulls' horns prior to the *corrida*. Bulls' horns are as sensitive as fingernails, a few millimetres in, and deter the animal from charging; they affect the creature's balance, too, reducing the danger for the *matador* still further.

Notwithstanding such abuse (and there is plenty more), *Los Toros* maintain their **aficionados** throughout the country. Indeed, they are on the rise, with the elaborate language of the *corrida*

quite a cult among the young, as the days of Franco's patronage of bullfighting are forgotten, and TV stations pay big money for major events. To aficionados (a word that implies more knowledge and appreciation than "fan"), the bulls are a culture and a ritual – one in which the emphasis is on the way man and bull "perform" together – in which the art is at issue rather than the cruelty. If pressed on the issue of the slaughter of an animal, they generally fail to understand. Fighting bulls are, they will tell you, bred for the industry; they live a reasonable life before they are killed, and, if the bullfight went, so too would the bulls.

Whether you attend a *corrida*, obviously, is down to your own feelings and ethics. If you spend any time at all in Spain during the season (which runs from March through October), you will encounter *Los Toros*, at least on a bar TV, and that will as likely as not make up your mind. If you decide to go, try to see the biggest and most prestigious that is on, in a major city, where star performers are likely to despatch the bulls with "art" and a successful, "clean" kill. There are few sights worse than a *matador* making a prolonged and messy kill, while the audience whistles. Established and popular **matadores** include Enrique Ponce, César Rincón, Victor Mendes, Joselito, Litri, Paco Ojeda, Ortega Cano, José María Manzanares and Finito de Córdoba. Two newer stars in the headlines are El Cordobés – a young pretender of spectacular technique who claims to be his legendary namesake's illegitimate son – and Cristina Sánchez, the first woman to make it into the top flight for many decades. If you have the chance to see one, the most exciting and skilfull performances of all are by **mounted matadores**, or *rejoneadores*; this is the oldest form of *corrida*, developed in Andalucía in the seventeenth century.

THE CORRIDA

The *corrida* begins with a **procession**, to the accompaniment of a *paso doble* by the band. Leading the procession are two *algauziles* or "constables", on horseback and in traditional costume, followed by the three *matadores*, who will each fight two bulls, and their *cuadrillas*, their personal "team", each comprising two mounted *picadores* and three *banderilleros*. At the back are the mule teams who will drag off the dead bulls.

Once the ring is empty, the *algauzil* opens the *toril* (the bulls' enclosure) and the first bull appears – a moment of great physical beauty – to be "tested" by the *matador* or his *banderilleros* using pink and gold capes. These preliminaries conducted (and they can be short, if the bull is ferocious), the **suerte de picar** ensues, in which the *picadores* ride out and take up position at opposite sides of the ring, while the bull is distracted by other *toreros*. Once they are in place, the bull is made to charge one of the horses; the *picador* drives his short-pointed lance into the bull's neck, while it tries to toss his padded, blindfolded horse, thus tiring the bull's powerful neck and back muscles. This is repeated up to three times, until the horn sounds for the *picadores* to leave. For most neutral spectators, it is the least acceptable and most squalid stage of the *corrida*, and it is clearly not a pleasant experience for the horses, who have their vocal cords cut out.

The next stage, the **suerte de banderillas**, involves the placing of three sets of *banderillas* (coloured sticks with barbed ends) into the bull's shoulders. Each of the three *banderilleros* delivers these in turn, attracting the bull's attention with the movement of his own body rather than a cape, and placing the *banderillas* whilst both he and the bull are running towards each other. He then runs to safety out of the bull's vision, sometimes with the assistance of his colleagues.

Once the *banderillas* have been placed, the **suerte de matar** begins, and the *matador* enters the ring alone, having exhanged his pink and gold cape for the red one. He (or she) salutes the president and then dedicates the bull either to an individual, to whom he gives his hat, or to the audience by placing his hat in the centre of the ring. It is in this part of the *corrida* that judgements are made and the performance is focused, as the *matador* displays his skills on the (by now exhausted) bull. He uses the movements of the cape to attract the bull, while his body remains still. If he does well, the band will start to play, while the crowd *olé* each pass. This stage lasts around ten minutes and ends with the kill. The *matador* attempts to get the bull into a position where he can drive a sword between its shoulders and through to the heart for a *coup de grâce*. In practice, they rarely succeed in this, instead taking a second sword, crossed at the end, to cut the bull's spinal cord; this causes instant death.

If the audience are impressed by the *matador's* performance, they will wave their handkerchiefs and shout for an award to be made by the president. He can award one or both ears, and a tail – the better the display, the more pieces he

gets – while if the *matador* has excelled himself, he will be carried out of the ring by the crowd, through the *puerta grande*, the main door, which is normally kept locked. The bull, too, may be applauded for its performance, as it is dragged out by the mule team.

Tickets for *corridas* are 2000ptas and up – much more for the prime seats and prestigious fights. The cheapest seats are *gradas*, the highest rows at the back, from where you can see everything that happens without too much of the detail; the front rows are known as the *barreras*. Seats are also divided into *sol* (sun), *sombra* (shade), and *sol y sombra* (shaded after a while), though these distinctions have become less relevant as more and more bullfights start later in the day, at 6 or 7pm, rather than the traditional 5pm. The *sombra* seats are more expensive not so much for the spectators' personal comfort as the fact that most of the action takes place in the shade.

On the way in, you can rent **cushions** – two hours sitting on concrete is not much fun. Beer and soft drinks are sold inside.

ANTI-BULLFIGHT GROUPS

If you want to know more about the international **opposition to bullfighting**, contact the World Society for the Protection of Animals, 2 Langley Lane, London SW8 1TJ (☎0171/793 0540); PO Box 190, Boston, MA 02130 (☎617/522-7000); 44 Victoria Street, Suite 1310, Toronto, ON MGC 1Y2 (☎416/369-0044); 46 Nicholson St, St Leonards, Australia (☎02/9901 5277). Spain's main opposition to bullfighting is organized by ADDA (*Association para la Defensar de los Derechos de Animal*), c/Bailén 164, Local 2, Interior E08037, Barcelona (*www.intercom.es/adda/*). They co-ordinate the International Bullfight Campaign and also produce a bi-annual newsletter in Spanish and English.

FOOTBALL

To foreigners, the bullfight is easily the most celebrated of Spain's spectacles. In terms of popular support in modern Spain, however, it ranks far below **fútbol** (soccer). If you want the excitement of a genuinely Spanish afternoon out, a football stadium will usually have more passion than anything you'll find in the Plaza de Toros.

For many years, the country's two dominant teams have been **Real Madrid** and **F.C. Barcelona**, and these have shared the League and Cup honours more often than is healthy.

Recently, however, both teams have faced a bit more opposition than usual from clubs like **Atlético Bilbao**, **Sporting Gijón**, **Atlético Madrid**, **Real Sociedad** (a Basque team from San Sebastián), **Real Zaragoza**, and **Deportivo La Coruña** (from Galicia). **Sevilla**, where Maradona finished his European career, are the main team in Andalucía, though currently in the doldrums.

With the exception of a few big games – the Madrid derbies between Real and Atlético, and games between these teams and Barcelona – **tickets** are pretty easy to get; they start at around 1200ptas for First Division games. Trouble is very rare: English fans, in particular, will be amazed at the easy-going family atmosphere and mixed-sex crowds.

If you don't go to a game, the atmosphere can be pretty good **watching on TV** in a local bar, especially in a city whose team is playing away. Many bars advertise the matches they screen, which can include Sunday afternoon **English league and cup games**, if they have satellite.

MUSIC

An account of Spain's diverse music appears in the Contexts section of this guide. Enough to say, here, that you should catch all that is going on. You will see and hear plenty of regional specialities at any of the country's fiestas.

Traditional **flamenco** – the country's most famous sound – is best witnessed in its native Andalucía, and particularly at one of the major fiestas. There are also some specifically flamenco festivals in the summer, most notably at Cartagena and around Granada. Clubs and bars which feature flamenco performers tend on the whole to be expensive and tourist-oriented, while the *peñas* (clubs) are often members-only affairs. However, it is possible to find accessible places which cater for aficionados, and in Andalucía itself almost any flamenco guitarist you come across is likely to be extremely good. Just watch the cost of the drinks. In recent years, there has

been an exciting development in the shape of new flamenco bands, some of whom have attempted introducing jazz, rock and African elements into their music. Some of the best artists in this field are to be seen in Madrid.

If you're anywhere in Spain between about December 18 and January 3, watch for performances in local churches of **villancicos**. These are Christmas carols in local style – they can be flamenco, waltz or polyphonic – and are sung by fairly large *coral/rondalla* groups of instrumentalists and vocalists of both sexes. When they're good they're extremely beautiful, and it's obviously a non-boozy, family-oriented spectacle.

Rock music in Spain may tend to follow British and American trends, but the scene is livelier – and less slavishly derivative – than in almost any other west European country, at its best drawing from a broad range of influences in which traditional Spanish and Latin American rhythms play a major part. There are some excellent home-grown bands and regular gigs in most of the big cities, especially in the north. Both Madrid and Barcelona attract major **international concerts** from time to time, usually staged in their giant football stadiums. Wherever you are, keep an eye out for posters or check the entertainments sections in the local press – you'll find local bands airing their talents at just about any fiesta.

Because of relatively large expatriate populations, Madrid and Barcelona are also good places to hear **Latin American and African** music – again, keep your eye out for posters and check the club and dance-hall listings in the local papers.

There are several excellent **jazz festivals** in the summer: notably in San Sebastián in the middle of July, and in Barcelona, Santander and Sitges.

Worth checking out, too, is the International Festival of Guitar in Córdoba (early July), where most of the great **classical guitarists** put in an appearance along with exponents of Latin American and flamenco styles.

TROUBLE, THE POLICE AND SEXUAL HARASSMENT

While you're unlikely to encounter any trouble during the course of a normal visit, it's worth remembering that the Spanish police, polite enough in the usual course of events, can be extremely unpleasant if you get on the wrong side of them. There are three basic types: the *Guardia Civil*, the *Policía Municipal*, and the *Policía Nacional*, all of them armed.

AVOIDING TROUBLE

Almost all the problems tourists encounter are to do with **petty crime** – pickpocketing and bag-snatching – rather than more serious physical confrontations, so it's as well to be on your guard and know where your possessions are at all times. Sensible **precautions** include: carrying bags slung across your neck, not over your shoulder; not carrying anything in zipped pockets facing the street; having photocopies of your passport, and leaving passport and tickets in the hotel safe; and noting down travellers' cheque and credit card numbers. There are also several ploys to be aware of and situations to avoid as you do the rounds of the city.

• Thieves often work in pairs, so watch out for people standing unusually close if you're studying postcards or papers at stalls; keep an eye on your wallet if it appears you're being distracted. **Ploys** (by some very sophisticated operators) include: the "helpful" person pointing out birdshit (shaving cream or something similar) on your jacket while someone relieves you of your money; the card or paper you're invited to read on the street to distract your attention; the move by someone in a café for your drink with one hand (the other hand's in your bag as you react to save your drink).

• If you have a **car** don't leave anything in view when you park it; take the radio with you. Vehicles are rarely stolen, but luggage and valuables left in cars do make a tempting target and rental cars are easy to spot.

• **Looking for hotel rooms**, don't leave any bags unattended anywhere. This applies especially to blocks where the hotel or *hostal* is on the higher floors and you're tempted to leave baggage in the hallway or ground-floor lobby.

• The American Embassy in Madrid says it frequently receives reports of **roadside thieves** posing as "good Samaritans" to persons experiencing car and tyre problems. The thieves typically attempt to divert the driver's attention by pointing out a mechanical problem and then steal items from the vehicle while the driver is looking elsewhere. The problem is particularly acute with vehicles rented at Madrid's Barajas airport. Be cautious about accepting help from anyone other than a uniformed Spanish police officer, and, if you do break down, keep your valuables in sight or lock them in the vehicle.

WHAT TO DO IF YOU'RE ROBBED

If you're robbed, you need to **go to the police** to report it, not least because your insurance company will require a police report. Don't expect a great deal of concern if your loss is relatively small – and expect the process of completing forms and formalities to take ages. In the unlikely event that you're **mugged**, or otherwise threatened, never resist; hand over what's wanted and go straight to the police, who on these occasions will be more sympathetic.

If you have your passport stolen or lose all your money, you can contact your **consulate** (see "Listings" in the Guide for individual cities), which is required to assist you to some degree.

THE POLICE

There are three main types of **police**: the *Guardia Civil*, the *Policía Municipal* and the *Policía Nacional*.

The **Guardia Civil**, in green uniforms, are the most officious and the ones to avoid. Though their role has been cut back since they operated as Franco's right hand, they remain a reactionary force (it was a *Guardia Civil* colonel, Tejero, who held the Cortes hostage in the February 1981 failed coup).

If you do need the police – and above all if you're reporting a serious crime such as rape – you should always go to the more sympathetic **Policía Municipal**, who wear blue-and-white uniforms with red trim. In the countryside there may be only the *Guardia Civil*; though they're usually helpful, they are inclined to resent the suggestion that any crime exists on their turf and you may end up feeling as if you are the one who stands accused.

The brown-uniformed **Policía Nacional** are mainly seen in cities, armed with submachine guns and guarding key installations such as embassies, stations, post offices and their own barracks. They are also the force used to control crowds and demonstrations.

OFFENCES

There are a few **offences** you might commit unwittingly that it's as well to be aware of.

• In theory you're supposed to carry some kind of **identification** at all times, and the police can stop you in the streets and demand it. In practice they're rarely bothered if you're clearly a foreigner.

• **Nude bathing** or **unauthorized camping** are activities more likely to bring you into contact with officialdom, though a warning to cover up or move on is more likely than any real confrontation. **Topless** tanning is commonplace at all the trendier resorts, but in country areas, where attitudes are still very traditional, you should take care not to upset local sensibilities.

• Spanish **drug laws** are in a somewhat bizarre state at present. After the socialists came to power in 1983, cannabis use (possession of up to 8gm of what the Spanish call *chocolate*) was decriminalized. Subsequent pressures, and an influx of harder drugs, have changed that policy and – in theory at least – any drug use is now forbidden. You'll see signs in some bars saying *no porros* ("no joints"), which you should heed. However, the police are in practice little worried about personal use. Larger quantities (and any other drugs) are a very different matter.

Should you be **arrested** on any charge, you have the right to contact your **consulate**, although they're notoriously reluctant to get involved. If you've been detained for a drugs offence, don't expect any sympathy or help from your consulate.

SEXUAL HARASSMENT

Spain's macho image has faded dramatically and these days there are relatively few parts of the country where foreign women, travelling alone, are likely to feel threatened, intimidated, or attract unwanted attention.

Inevitably, the **big cities** – like any others in Europe – have their no-go areas, where street crime and especially drug-related hassles are on the rise, but there is little of the pestering and propositions that you have to contend with in, say, the larger French or Italian cities. The outdoor culture of terrazas (terrace bars) and the tendency of Spaniards to move around in large, mixed crowds, filling central bars, clubs and streets late into the night, help to make you feel less exposed. If you are in any doubt, there are always **taxis** – plentiful, reasonably priced, and certainly the safest way to travel late at night. Make full use of them, particularly in Madrid and Barcelona.

The major **resorts** of the *costas* have their own artificial holiday culture. The Spaniards who hang around in discos here or at fiesta fairgrounds pose no greater or lesser threat than similar operators at home. The language barrier simply makes it harder to know who to trust. *Déjame en paz* ("leave me in peace") is a fairly standard rebuff.

Predictably, it is in **more isolated regions**, separated by less than a generation from desperate poverty (or still starkly poor), that most serious problems can occur, and we have had a couple of reports of women being followed and attacked in remote parts of Andalucía. You do need to know a bit about the land you're travelling around.

In some areas you can walk for hours without coming across an inhabited farm or house, and you still come upon shepherds working for nothing but the wine they take to their pastures. It's rare that this poses a threat – help and hospitality are much more the norm – but you are certainly more vulnerable. That said, **trekking** is becoming more popular in Spain as a whole and many women happily tramp the footpaths, from Galicia to the Sierra Nevada. In the south, especially, though, it is worth finding rooms in the larger villlages, or, if you camp out, asking permission to do so on private land, rather than striking out alone.

WORK

Unless you have a particular skill and have applied for a job advertised in your home country, such as au pair work, the only real chance of long-term work in Spain is in language schools. If you intend to stay in Spain longer than three months, you'll need a *permiso de residencia* – see "Red Tape and Visas" (p.16). A word of warning: police are cracking down on people without these and may ask for passport/residence papers on the spot, especially out of the tourist season.

European Union citizens may find the EU's Web site for those planning to live or work abroad within the EU a useful resource; it can be found at *http://citizens.EU.int/*.

TEACHING AND OFFICE WORK

Finding a teaching job is mainly a question of pacing the streets, stopping in at every language school around and asking about vacancies. For the addresses of schools look in the *Yellow Pages*

under *Idiomas* or *Escuelas Idiomas*. However, there is much less work about than in the boom years of the early 1980s – schools are beginning to close down rather than open – and you'll need to persevere if you're to come up with a rewarding position. You'll need a TEFL (Teaching English as a Foreign Language) or ESL (English as a Second Language) certificate to give yourself any kind of chance.

Other options are to try advertising **private lessons** (better paid at 1500–2500ptas an hour, but harder to make a living at) on the *Philología* noticeboards of university faculties.

Another possibility, so long as you speak good Spanish, is **translation work**, most of which will be business correspondence – look in the *Yellow Pages* under *Traductores*. If you intend doing agency work, you'll usually need access to a fax and a PC.

TEMPORARY WORK

If you're looking for **temporary work** the best chances are in the **bars and restaurants** of the big Mediterranean resorts. This may help you have a good time but it's unlikely to bring in much money; pay (often from British bar owners) will reflect your lack of official status or work permit. If you turn up in spring and are willing to stay through the season you might get a better deal – also true if you're offering some special skill such as windsurfing (there are schools sprouting up all along the coast). Quite often there are jobs at **yacht marinas**, too, scrubbing down and repainting the boats of the rich; just turn up and ask around, especially from March until June. As a foreigner you've no hope at all of work on harvests – France is much more viable.

DIRECTORY

ADDRESSES are written as: c/Picasso 2, 4° izda. – which means Picasso street (*calle*) no. 2, fourth floor, left- (*izquierda*) hand flat or office; dcha. (*derecha*) is right; cto. (*centro*) centre. Other confusions in Spanish addresses result from the different spellings, and sometimes words, used in Catalan, Basque and Galician – all of which are to some extent replacing their Castilian counterparts – and from the gradual removal of Franco and other fascist heroes from the main avenidas and plazas. On this latter front, Avenidas del Generalísimo are on the way out all over the country (often changing to "Libertad" or "España"); so, too, are José Antonios, General Molas, Falanges, and Caudillos. Note that a lot of maps – including the official ones – haven't yet caught up; nor have a handful of right-wing-controlled towns. In some towns dual numbering systems are also in effect, and looking at the plates it's difficult to tell which is the old and which the new scheme.

AIRPORT TAX You can happily spend your last pesetas – there's no departure tax.

CONSULATES Practically every nation has an embassy in Madrid; there are also British consulates in Barcelona, Alicante, Bilbao, Ibiza, Málaga, Palma de Mallorca, Sevilla and Tarragona; US representation outside the capital is confined to Barcelona, Sevilla and Valencia.

ELECTRICITY Current in most of Spain is 220 or 225 volts AC (just occasionally it's still 110 or 125V); most European appliances should work as long as you have an adaptor for European-style two-pin plugs. North Americans will need this plus a transformer.

FEMINISM The Spanish women's movement, despite having to deal with incredibly basic issues (such as trying to get contraception available on social security), is radical, vibrant and growing fast. Few groups, however, have permanent offices, and if you want to make contact it's best to do so through the network of feminist bookshops in the major cities. Some of the more established are: Madrid – Librería de Mujeres, c/San Cristóbal 17, near Plaza Mayor (☎91 521 70 43); Valencia – Ideas, c/Gravador Esteve 33 (☎963 348318); Sevilla – Librería Fulmen, c/Zaragoza 36. In Barcelona, the most useful contact address is Ca la Dona, c/Caspe 38 (☎93 412 71 61), a women's centre used for meetings of over twenty feminist and lesbian organizations.

FILM Movie-going remains a remarkably cheap and popular entertainment, with crowded cinemas in every town. The majority of what's screened is the usual Hollywood fare poorly dubbed into Spanish, but in the cities you will find some films in their original language with subtitles. Look for *voz* or *versión original (subtitulada)*, abbreviated "v.o.", in the listings; "v.e." means *versión español*. An account of Spanish cinema is to be found in the Contexts section of this book.

FISHING Fortnightly permits are easily and cheaply obtained from any ICONA office – there's one in every big town (addresses from the local Turismo).

GAY LIFE Ibiza is now a major European gay resort and attitudes there, and in the major cities and resorts, are fairly relaxed. Madrid, Barcelona, Sitges and Cádiz in particular have large gay communities and a thriving scene. The age of consent is 18.

KIDS/BABIES don't pose great travel problems. *Hostales*, *pensiones* and *restaurantes* generally welcome them and offer rooms with three or four beds; RENFE allows children under four to travel free on trains, with 40 percent discount for those between four and twelve years; and some cities and resorts – Barcelona is particularly good – have long lists or special pamphlets on kids' attractions. As far as babies go, food seems to work out quite well (*hostales* often prepare food specially, or will let you use the kitchen to do so) though you might want to bring powdered milk – babies, like most Spaniards, are pretty contemptuous of the UHT (ultra-heat-treated) stuff generally available. If you're travelling in the north, or out of season, however, bear in mind that most *hostales* (as opposed to more expensive hotels) don't have any heating systems – and it can get cold. Disposable nappies and other standard needs are very widely available. Many *hostales* will be prepared to baby-sit, or at least to listen out for trouble. This is obviously more likely if you're staying in an old-fashioned family-run place than in the fancier hotels.

LANGUAGE COURSES are offered at most Spanish universities, and in a growing number of special language schools for foreigners. For details overseas and a complete list write to a branch of the Instituto Cervantes: the London one is at 102 Eaton Square, London SW1W (☎0171/235 0353; *www.cervantes.es/*) – other addresses from the nearest tourist office. Many American universities have their own courses based in Spain – or try the Education Office of Spain, 150 Fifth Avenue #600, Suite 918, New York, NY 10011 (☎212/741-5144).

LAUNDRIES You'll find a few self-service launderettes (*lavanderías automáticas*) in the major cities, but they're rare – you normally have to leave your clothes for the full (and somewhat expensive) works. Note that you're not allowed by law to leave laundry hanging out of windows over a street. A dry cleaner is a *tintorería*.

LEFT LUGGAGE After a long period of absence following terrorist actions in the late 1970s, self-service *consignas* are back at most important Spanish train stations. You'll find lockers large enough to hold most backpacks, plus a smaller bag, which cost about 400–600ptas a day; put the coins in to free the key. These are not a viable alternative for long-term storage, however, as they're periodically emptied out by station staff. Bus terminals have manned *consignas* where you present a claim stub to get your gear back; cost is about the same.

SKIING There are resorts in the Pyrenees, Sierra Nevada, and outside Madrid and Santander, all detailed in the relevant chapters. The SNTO's *Skiing in Spain* pamphlet is also useful. If you want to arrange a weekend or more while you're in Spain, Viajes Ecuador (the biggest travel firm in the country, with branches in most cities) is good for arranging cheap all-inclusive trips.

SWIMMING POOLS Even quite small Spanish towns have a public swimming pool, or *piscina municipal* – a lifesaver in the summer and yet another reason not to keep exclusively to the coast.

TIME Spain is one hour ahead of the UK, six hours ahead of Eastern Standard Time, nine hours ahead of Pacific Standard Time, except for brief periods during the changeovers to and from daylight saving. In Spain the clocks go back in the last week in March and forward again in the last week in September.

TOILETS Public ones are averagely clean but very rarely have any paper (best to carry your own). They're often squat-style. They are most commonly referred to and labelled *Los Servicios*, though signs may point you to *baños*, *aseos*, *retretes* or *sanitarios*. *Damas* (Ladies) and *Caballeros* (Gentlemen) are the usual distinguishing signs for sex, though you may also see the confusing *Señoras* (Women) and *Señores* (Men).

PART TWO

GUIDE

much clue as to what was here before Madrid became the **Habsburg** capital (in 1561), but the narrow alleys around the Plaza Mayor are still among the city's liveliest and most atmospheric. Later growth owed much to the French tastes of the **Bourbon** dynasty in the eighteenth century, when for the first time Madrid began to develop a style and flavour of its own.

The early **nineteenth century** brought invasion and turmoil to Spain as Napoleon established his brother Joseph on the throne. Madrid, however, continued to flourish, gaining some very attractive buildings and squares. With the onset of the twentieth century, the capital became the hotbed of the political and intellectual discussions which divided the country; *tertulias* (political/philosophical discussion circles) sprang up in cafés across the city (some of them are still going) as the country entered the turbulent years of the end of the monarchy and the foundation of the Second Republic.

The **Civil War**, of course, caused untold damage, and led to forty years of isolation, which you can still sense in Madrid's idiosyncratic style. The city can no longer be accused of provincialism, however, for it has changed immeasurably in the two decades since Franco died, guided by a poet-mayor, the late and much lamented Tierno Galván. His efforts – the creation of parks and renovation of public spaces and public life – have left an enduring legacy, and were a vital ingredient in the *movida madrileña*, the "happening Madrid", with which the city broke through in the 1980s. Madrid has now made the transition from provincial backwater to major European capital, at the same time preserving its own stylish and quirky identity.

Orientation, arrival and information

The city's layout is pretty straightforward. At the heart of Madrid – indeed at the very heart of Spain since all distances in the country are measured from here – is the **Puerta del Sol** (often referred to as just "Sol"). Around it lie the oldest parts of Madrid, neatly bordered to the west by the **Río Manzanares**, to the east by the park of **El Retiro**, and to the north by the city's great thoroughfare, the **Gran Vía**.

Within this very compact area, you're likely to spend most of your time. The city's three big museums – the **Prado**, **Thyssen-Bornemisza** and **Reina Sofía** – lie in a "magic triangle" just west of El Retiro, while over towards the river are the oldest, Habsburg parts of town, centred around the beautiful arcaded **Plaza Mayor**. After Gran Vía, the most important streets (*calles* – abbreviated as c/) are **c/de Alcalá** and its continuation, **c/Mayor**, which cut right through the centre from the main post office at **Plaza de Cibeles** to the Bourbon **Palacio Real**.

Arrival

If Madrid is your first stop in Spain, by **air, train or bus**, you are likely to arrive a little way from the centre. Transport into the centre, however, is relatively easy and efficient.

By air

The **Aeropuerto de Barajas** is 16km east of the city, at the end of Avenida de América (the NII road). It is in the process of being extended and modernized and now has three interconnecting terminals: T1 for nearly all international flights (*vuelos internacionales*); T2 for domestic flights (*nacionales*) plus some of Iberia's flights from continental Europe; T3 for the Puente Aéreo (the air shuttle from Barcelona). The journey to central Madrid is highly variable, depending on rush-hour traffic and can take anything from twenty minutes to an hour.

Outside the terminal, there is a **shuttle bus** every ten to fifteen minutes (5.17am–1.51am; 380ptas) to an underground terminal in the central Plaza Colón, with pedestrian entrance from the c/de Goya or Metro Serrano. If your plane arrives outside these times, there should be additional special connecting bus services. **Taxis** are always available outside, too, and cost around 2000ptas to the centre, unless you get stuck in traffic.

Half a dozen or so **car rental** companies have stands at the airport and can generally supply clients with maps and directions (see p.114 for addresses and phone numbers of car rental offices in the city). Other airport facilities include 24-hour currency exchange, a post office, a RENFE office for booking train tickets (daily 8am–9pm), a tourist office and hotel reservations desk.

By train

Trains **from France** and **north/northeast Spain** arrive at the **Estación de Chamartín**, a modern terminal isolated in the north of the city; it has all the usual big station facilities, including currency exchange. A metro line connects Chamartín with the centre, and there are also regular connections by the commuter *trenes de cercanías* with the much more central Estación de Atocha; just take any *cercanía* headed in that direction.

The **Estación de Atocha**, recently expanded and imaginatively remodelled, has two separate terminals: one for **Toledo** and other local services, the other for all points in **south and eastern Spain**, including the high speed AVE trains.

If you're coming from local towns around Madrid, you may arrive at **Príncipe Pío** (aka Estación del Norte), fairly close to the centre near the Royal Palace.

By bus

Bus terminals are scattered throughout the city, but the largest – used by all of the international bus services – is the **Estación Sur de Autobuses**, recently relocated on c/Méndez Alvaro on the corner of c/Retama, one and a half kilometres south of the Atocha train station (Metro Méndez Alvaro). For details of others, see the "Travel details" section at the end of this chapter (p.116).

By car

All the main roads into Madrid bring you right into the city centre, although eccentric signposting and even more eccentric driving can be very unnerving. The inner ring road, the M30, and the Paseo de la Castellana are all notorious bottlenecks, although virtually the whole city centre can be close to gridlock during the peak rush-hour periods (Mon–Fri 7.30–9.30am & 6–8.30pm). Be prepared for a long trawl around the streets to find parking, or – a lot safer – put your car in one of the many signposted *parkings*. Your own transport is really only of use for out-of-town excursions, so it's advisable to find a hotel with a car park and keep your car there during your stay in the city. If you are staying more than a couple of weeks, you can get long-term parking rates at neighbourhood garages.

Information and maps

There are year-round **Turismo** offices at the following locations: Aeropuerto de Barajas (Mon–Fri 8am–8pm, Sat 9am–1pm; ☎91 305 86 56); Estación de Chamartín (Mon–Fri 8am–8pm, Sat 9am–1pm; ☎91 315 99 76); Plaza Mayor 3 (Mon–Fri 10am–8pm, Sat 10am–2pm; ☎91 588 16 36); Mercado Puerta de Toledo, Ronda de Toledo 1 (Mon–Fri 9am–7pm, Sat 9.30am–1.30pm; ☎91 364 18 76); c/Duque de Medinaceli 2 (Mon–Fri 9am–7pm, Sat 9am–1pm; ☎91 429 49 51; Metro Banco de España). Atocha station also has an information kiosk with a hotel reservations service. You can **phone for information** on 901 300 600 (English spoken).

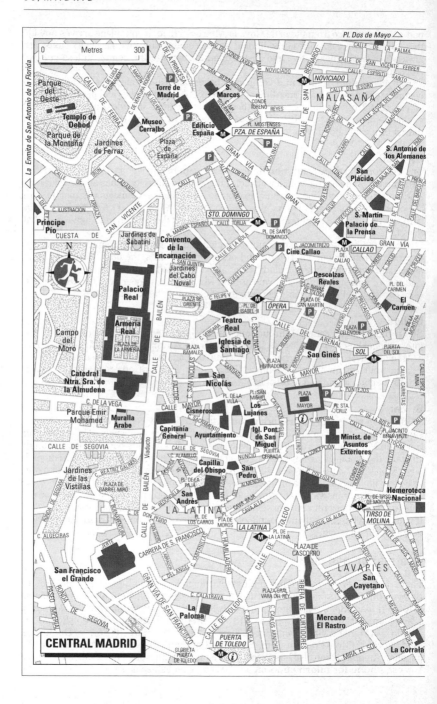

CENTRAL MADRID

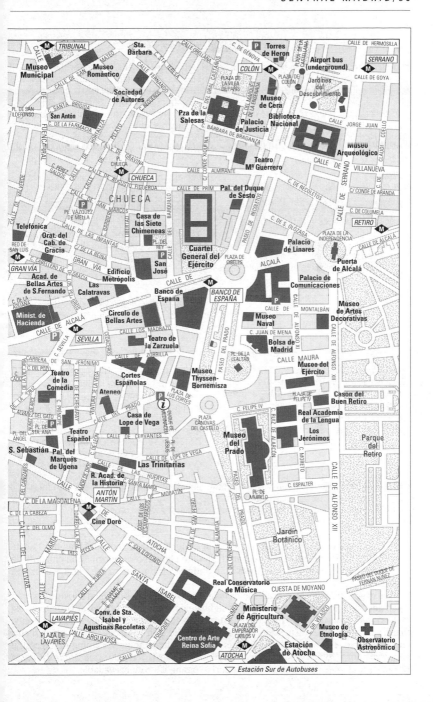

MADRID'S FIESTA

Look out for **fiestas** whenever you're in Madrid: there are dozens, some of which involve the whole city, others just an individual *barrio*. The more important dates are listed below.

Also well worth checking out are cultural festivals organized by the city council, in particular the **Veranos de la Villa** (July–Sept) and **Festival de Otoño** (Sept–Nov) concerts (classical, rock, flamenco), theatre and cinema. Many events are free and, in the summer, often open-air, taking place in the city's parks and squares. One of the nicest venues is the courtyard of the Antiguo Cuartel del Conde Duque (Metro Ventura Rodríguez), where weekly flamenco recitals are held. Full programmes are published in the monthly *En Madrid* tourist hand-out.

January
5 *Cabalgata de los Reyes* (Cavalcade of the Three Kings); an evening procession through the city centre in which children are showered with sweets.

February
Carnaval – the week before Lent – is the excuse for a lot of partying and fancy-dress parades.

March/April
Easter Week *Semana Santa* is celebrated in Madrid, but with less spirit and processional activity than in Toledo.

May
2 *Fiesta del Dos de Mayo* in Malasaña and elsewhere in Madrid. Bands and partying around the Plaza Dos de Mayo – a bit low-key in recent years, having been the funkiest festival in the city during the 1980s.

15 The *Fiestas de San Isidro* – Madrid's patron saint – spread for a week either side of this date, and are among the country's biggest festivals. A non-stop round of carnival events: bands, parades and loads of free entertainment. There's a band each night in the Jardines de las Vistillas (south of the Palacio Real), and the evenings there start

out with *chotis* (a dance typical of Madrid) music and dancing. The fiestas also herald the start of the bullfighting season.

June
13 *Fiesta de la Ermita de San Antonio de la Florida*; events around the church.

17–24 *Fiestas de San Juan*; bonfires and fireworks in El Retiro.

July
9–16 *La Virgen del Carmen*; local fiesta in Chamberí *barrio*, north of the city centre.

August
6–15 *Castizo fiestas*. Traditional *fiestas* of *San Cayetano, San Lorenzo* and *La Virgen de la Paloma* in La Latina and Lavapiés *barrios*. Much of the activity takes place around the Plaza de la Paja and the Jardines de las Vistillas.

December
31 New Year's Eve (*nochevieja*) is celebrated at bars, restaurants and parties all over the city, and there are bands in some of the squares. Puerta del Sol is the traditional place to gather, waiting for the strokes of the clock – it is traditional to swallow a grape on each strike.

In the **summer**, Turismo posts operate at popular tourist spots such as the Puerta del Sol and the Prado, and there are staff (in blue and yellow uniforms) on call outside the Palacio Real, *Ayuntamiento* (town hall) and the Prado, and in the Plaza Mayor and Puerta del Sol.

Free **maps** of Madrid are available from any of the Turismos detailed above. However, if you intend to do more than just a day's sightseeing, you would be well advised to invest in the Almax *Madrid Centro* map (350ptas), available from just about any kiosk in the city; this is very clear, 1:10,000 in scale, fully street-indexed, and has a colour plan of the metro on the reverse. The area covered on this represents just about everything of interest; if you want more, Almax also produces a rather less clear, 1:12,000-scale *Madrid Ciudad* (750ptas) that goes right out into the suburbs. Again, it's widely available.

Safety and crime

As far as safety goes, there's little cause for concern. Central Madrid is so populated – and so busy at just about every hour of the day and night – that it never seems to carry any "big city" threat. Which is not to say that **crime** is not a problem, nor that there aren't sleazy pockets to be avoided. Madrid has a big drug problem, all too evident around the Plaza de España and some of the streets just north of Gran Vía. Drugs, it is reckoned, account for ninety percent of crimes in Madrid, and if you are unlucky enough to be threatened for money, it's unwise to resist.

Tourists in Madrid, as everywhere, are prime targets for pickpockets and petty thieves. The main shopping areas, parks, the metro and anywhere with crowds, are their favourite haunts; burger bars and the Rastro market seem especially popular. Be aware that they often work in groups, and associates will try to distract your attention while your pocket is being picked. Unless you have rented expensive garage space, drivers may well find their cars broken into and the radio stolen. The **police** are sympathetic and will give you a report form for insurance claims. In an emergency, dial ☎112; English is usually spoken on this number.

City transport

Madrid is a pretty easy city to get around. The central areas are walkable, the metro is modern and efficient, buses serve out-of-the-way districts, and taxis are always available.

If you're using public transport extensively and staying long-term, **passes** (*abonos*) covering the metro, train and bus, and available for each calendar month, are worthwhile. If you have an InterRail or Eurail pass, you can use the RENFE urban and suburban trains (*cercanías*) free of charge – they're an alternative to the metro for some longer city journeys.

The metro

The **metro** is by far the quickest way of getting around Madrid, serving most places you're likely to want to get to. It runs from 6am until 1.30am; the flat fare is 130ptas for any journey, or 670ptas for a ten-trip ticket (*bono de diez viajes*), which can be used on buses too. Lines are colour-coded, and the direction of travel is indicated by the name of the terminus station. Extension of the existing network is at present underway, so some alterations to routes and station closures may occur up to the end of 1999. You can get a free colour map of the system (*plano del metro*) at any station.

Buses

The urban **bus network** is comprehensive but fairly complicated: in the text, where there's no metro stop, we've indicated which bus to take. There are information booths in the Plaza de Cibeles and Puerta del Sol, which dispense a huge route map (*plano de los transportes de Madrid*), and – along with other outlets – sell bus passes. Fares are the same as for the metro, at 130ptas a journey, or 670ptas for a ten-trip (*bono de diez viajes*) ticket which can be used on both forms of transport. When you get on a bus, you punch your ticket in a machine by the driver.

Buses run from 6am to midnight. In addition, there are several **all-night** lines around the central area: departures are half-hourly 12.30am–2am, hourly 2–6am, from Plaza de Cibeles and Puerta del Sol.

Taxis

One of the best things about Madrid is that there are thousands of **taxis** – white cars with a diagonal red stripe on the side – which are reasonably cheap; 700ptas will get you most places within the centre and, although it's common to round up the fare,

MADRID: METRO

PITIS
Arroyo del Fresno
Lacoma
Avda. Illustración
HERRERA ORIA
FUENCARRAL
PARQUE DE SANTA MARIA
Peñagrande
Barrio del Pilar
Begoña
Antonio Machado
Ventilla
Chamartin
San Lorenzo
Campo de las Naciones
BARAJAS
Valdeacederas
Duque de Pastrana
Mar de Cristal
Aeropuerto
Tetuán
PLAZA DE CASTILLA
Pío XII
Canillas
Valdezarza
Estrecho
Cuzco
Esperanza
Francos Rodriguez
Alvarado
Santiago Bernabéu
Colombia
Arturo Soria
CANILLEJAS
Metropolitano
CUATRO CAMINOS
Nuevos Ministerios
Republic Argentina
Concha Espina
Avda. de la Paz
Guzmán el Bueno
Cruz del Rayo
Alfonso XIII
Torre Arias
Ciudad Universitaria
Islas Filipinas
Canal
Rios Rosas
Gregorio Marañón
Prosperidad
Parque de las Avenidas
Barrio de la Concepción
Suanzes
MONCLOA
Quevedo
Alonso Cano
Iglesia
AVDA. DE AMÉRICA
Cartagena
Ciudad Lineal
LAS MUSAS
San Bernardo
Rubén Dario
Diego de León
VENTAS
Pueblo Nuevo
Ascao
ARGÜELLES
Ventura Rodriguez
Bilbao
Núñez de Balboa
Manuel Becerra
El Carmen
Quintana
Garcia Noblejas
Simancas
San Blas
Plaza de España
Noviciado
Lista
PRÍNCIPE PÍO
Santo Domingo
Tribunal
MARTINEZ
Colón
Serrano
Velázquez
Goya
Gran Via
Chueca
Principe de Vergara
O'Donnell
Lago
Callao
Sevilla
Banco de España
Retiro
Ibiza
Puerta del Angel
Sol
La Latina
Tirso de Molina
Sáinz de Baranda
OPERA
Batán
Alto de Extremadura
Puerta de Toledo
Antón Martin
Atocha
Estrella
Vinateros
Lucero
Lavapiés
Atocha Renfe
Artilleros
Campamento
Laguna
Acacias
Embajadores
Menéndez Pelayo
Conde de Casal
Pavones
Marqués de Vadillo
Pirámides
Palos de la Frontera
Valdebernardo
Empalme
Carpetana
Urgel
Pacífico
Vicálvaro
ALUCHE
Oporto
Plaza Elíptica
Delicias
Puente de Vallecas
San Cipriano
Nueva Numancla
Carabanchel
Vista Alegre
Opañel
Usera
LEGAZPI
Méndez Alvaro
Portazgo
Alto del Arenal
Puerta de Arganda
Abrantes
Buenos Aires
Miguel Hernández
Rivas Urbanizaciones
PAN BENDITO
Sierra de Guadalupe
Rivas Vaciamadrid
Villa de Vallecas
La Poveda
CONGOSTO
ARGANDA DEL REY

▪▪▪▪▪ Line 1	━━━ Line 5	▪▪▪▪ Line 9
◄◄◄ Line 2	◦◦◦◦ Line 6	━━━ Line 10
━▪━ Line 3	▪▪▪▪ Line 7	══ Line 11
◄◄◄◄ Line 4	━ ━ Line 8	

Station Due to open in 1999

you're not expected to tip. They charge supplements on the metered fair for baggage, for going outside the city limits (which includes going to the airport) and for night trips (11pm–6am). In any area in the centre, day and night, you should be able to wave down a taxi (available ones have a green light on top of the cab) in a couple of minutes. To phone for a taxi, call ☎91 547 82 00, ☎91 405 12 13 or ☎91 445 90 08.

Accommodation

Madrid has lots of accommodation, and – business hotels apart – most of it is pretty central. It is, on the whole, pretty functional, too. Few places, at any price range, have great character, and you're basically paying for location and facilities. At the lower end of the range, there are bargains to be had, with double rooms as low as 3000ptas a night – and less if you are looking for an extended stay. Move up a few notches and you can find plenty of places at around 5000–6000ptas a night, offering a comfortable room with a private bath or (more often) shower. Few places, however, justify paying prices much higher than that and, assuming money is limited and Madrid is not your only destination in Spain, you'd be better off splashing out for luxury elsewhere.

If you prefer to have others find you a room, there are accommodation services at the airport, the Estación Sur de Autobuses, Chamartín train station and elsewhere. Brújula is particularly helpful, with offices at Atocha station, Colón bus terminal and in the centre on the sixth floor of the Torre de Madrid, c/de la Princessa (Plaza de España; ☎91 559 97 05). The service covers the whole of Spain and is free apart from long-distance phonecalls.

Pensiones, hostales and hotels

The main factor to consider in choosing a hotel is location. If you want to be at the heart of the old town, you'll probably choose the areas around **Plaza de Santa Ana** or **Plaza Mayor**; if you're into nightlife, **Malasaña** or **Chueca** may appeal; if you want a bit of class, there are the **Paseo del Prado**, **Recoletos** or **Salamanca** areas. You'll notice that buildings in the more popular hotel/*hostal* areas often house two or three separate establishments, each on separate **floors**; these are generally independent of each other. Floors (*pisos*) are written as 1º (first floor in British parlance, second in American), 2º and so on, and often specify *izquierda* (*izq* or *izda*) or *derecha* (*dcha*), meaning to the left or to the right of the staircase. A problem with some of the *hostales* in larger buildings – on Gran Vía, for example – is that they are often inaccessible at night, unless you've been given a front-door key, as there's not always an entryphone or doorbell at street level. If you book a room and intend to arrive after, say, 9pm, check that you will be able to get in.

Around Estación de Atocha

Much of the cheapest accommodation in Madrid is to be found in the area immediately around the Estación de Atocha. However, the *pensiones* closest to the station are

---

ACCOMMODATION PRICE CODES

The codes used in our hotel listings denote the following price ranges:

① Under 2000ptas	④ 4500–6000ptas	⑦ 12,000–17,500ptas
② 2000–3000ptas	⑤ 6000–8000ptas	⑧ Over 17,500ptas
③ 3000–4500ptas	⑥ 8000–12,000ptas	

See p.34 for more details.

often grim, catering for migrants from the south looking for work, and the area can be a little threatening after dark. The three places below, however, are good, safe choices.

Hotel Mediodía, Plaza del Emperador Carlos V 8 (☎91 527 30 60, fax 91 530 70 08; Metro Atocha). Huge 165-roomed hotel right next to the Reina Sofía and the Estación de Atocha. The simple but comfortable rooms are excellent value. ⑤.

Hotel Mercator, c/Atocha 123 (☎91 429 05 00, fax 91 369 12 52; Metro Atocha). Smart hotel popular with tour groups. Good value and near the station. ⑦.

Pensión Mollo, c/Atocha 104, 4º (☎91 528 71 76; Metro Atocha/Antón Martín). Closest reasonable *hostal* to the station, although it is up a steep hill, so inconvenient if you're heavily laden. ③.

Around Plaza de Santa Ana

Plaza de Santa Ana is at the heart of Madrid nightlife, with cafés open until very late at night. The recommendations following are all within a block or two of the square. The metro stations Antón Martín, Sevilla and Sol are all close by.

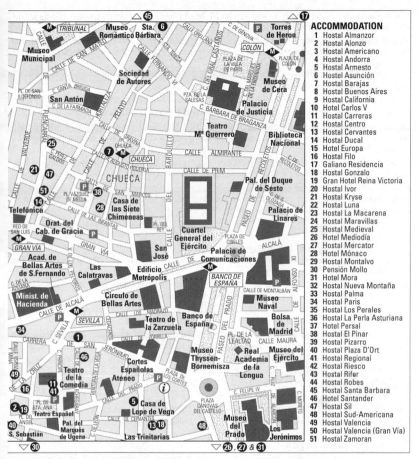

ACCOMMODATION

1 Hostal Almanzor
2 Hostal Alonzo
3 Hostal Americano
4 Hostal Andorra
5 Hostal Armesto
6 Hostel Asunción
7 Hostal Barajas
8 Hostal Buenos Aires
9 Hostal California
10 Hotel Carlos V
11 Hostal Carreras
12 Hostal Centro
13 Hostal Cervantes
14 Hostal Ducal
15 Hotel Europa
16 Hostal Filo
17 Galiano Residencia
18 Hostal Gonzalo
19 Gran Hotel Reina Victoria
20 Hostal Ivor
21 Hostal Kryse
22 Hostal Luna
23 Hostal La Macarena
24 Hostal Maravillas
25 Hostal Medieval
26 Hostal Mediodía
27 Hostal Mercator
28 Hotel Mónaco
29 Hostal Montalvo
30 Pensión Mollo
31 Hotel Mora
32 Hostal Nueva Montaña
33 Hostal Palma
34 Hostal Paris
35 Hostal Los Perales
36 Hostal La Perla Asturiana
37 Hotel Persal
38 Hostal El Pinar
39 Hostal Pizarro
40 Hostal Plaza D'Ort
41 Hostal Regional
42 Hostal Riesco
43 Hostal Rifer
44 Hostal Robes
45 Hostal Santa Barbara
46 Hotel Santander
47 Hostal Sil
48 Hostal Sud-Americana
49 Hostal Valencia
50 Hostal Valencia (Gran Vía)
51 Hostal Zamoran

Hostal Alonso, c/Espoz y Mina 17 (☎91 531 56 79; Metro Sol). Basic but good-value and friendly *hostal* popular for its location. Book ahead if you can. ②.

Hostal Carreras, c/Príncipe 18, 3º (☎91 522 00 36; Metro Sevilla). Large light rooms in this very pleasant *hostal*. ③.

Hostal Filo, Plaza de Santa Ana 15, 2ºizq. (☎91 522 40 56; Metro Sol). One of a few hotels above the beautiful Villa Rosa (which appeared in Almodóvar's *High Heels*). Pleasant rooms look out on to the square. ④.

Gran Hotel Reina Victoria, Plaza de Santa Ana 14 (☎91 531 45 00, fax 91 522 03 07; Metro Sol). Lovely old hotel in a historic building, where the bullfighters stay when they're in town. Rooms are a hefty 25,000ptas a night, but this is the pick of Madrid's class hotels in this price range. ⑧.

Hotel Persal, Plaza del Ángel 12 (☎91 369 46 43 or 91 368 37 26, fax 91 369 19 52; Metro Sol). Friendly and excellent-value 100-room hotel. All rooms have air conditioning, bathroom and TV. ⑤.

Hostal Plaza D'Ort, Plaza del Ángel 13 (☎91 429 90 41, fax 91 420 12 97; Metro Sol). Next door to the *Hotel Persal;* all rooms in this very clean *hostal* have a shower or bath, TV and telephone. There are also several self-catering apartments, making it a good family or group option. ④.

Hostal Regional, c/del Príncipe 18, 4º (☎91 522 33 73; Metro Sol). Small, basic rooms in an elegant old building off Plaza de Santa Ana. ③.

Hotel Santander, c/Echegaray 1 (☎91 429 95 51; Metro Sevilla). Spacious, spotless rooms in this pleasant, friendly two-star hotel. ⑤.

Hostal Valencia, c/ Espoz y Mina 7, 4º (☎91 521 18 45; Metro Sol). The very friendly multi-lingual owner of this six-room *hostal* will do everything he can to make your stay as comfortable as possible. Large rooms, all with bathroom and TV. ③.

Sol, Opera and Plaza Mayor

This really is the heart of Madrid and prices, not surprisingly, are a bit higher, though you can still find bargains in the slightly battered streets towards the Plaza Mayor.

Hostal Americano, Puerta del Sol 11, 3º and 4º (☎91 522 28 22, fax 91 522 11 92; Metro Sol). Nicely furnished *hostal*, with a pleasant communal living-room, but you're paying extra for the location. ④.

Hotel Carlos V, c/Maestro Vitoria 5 (☎91 531 41 00, fax 91 531 37 61; Metro Sol). Large, plush rooms at this turn-of-the-century hotel, in a pedestrianized part of town, just off c/Preciados behind the Descalzas Reales monastery. ⑦.

Hotel Europa, c/Carmen 4 (☎91 521 29 00, fax 91 521 46 96; Metro Sol). Well-established, family-run hotel with recently refurbished rooms. ⑥.

Hostal Ivor, c/Arenal 24, 2º (☎91 547 10 54; Metro Opera). Good standard hostal with comfortable en-suite rooms, all with TV. ④.

Hostal La Macarena, Cava de San Miguel 8, 2º (☎91 365 92 21, fax 91 364 27 57; Metro Sol). Fine, refurbished, family-run *hostal* (though the rooms are a little small) in a characterful alley just off the Plaza Mayor. ⑤.

Hostal Montalvo, c/Zaragoza 6 (☎91 365 59 10). Between Plaza Santa Cruz and Plaza Mayor; small, simple rooms (some with good views) with and without bath. ④.

Hotel Paris, c/Alcalá 2 (☎91 521 64 96, fax 91 531 01 88; Metro Sol). Smart, old-fashioned hotel right on the Puerta del Sol. Very good value for so central a position. ⑥.

Hostal La Perla Asturiana, Plaza de Santa Cruz 3 (☎91 366 46 00, fax 91 366 46 08; Metro Sol). Small rooms in this nicely located *hostal*, overlooking a pleasant square. ④.

Hostal Riesco, c/Correo 2–3 (☎91 522 26 92, fax 91 532 90 88; Metro Sol). Old-style, characterful place in a street just off Sol. All rooms are en suite. ④.

Hostal Rifer, c/Mayor 5, 4º (☎91 532 31 97; Metro Sol). Clean, bright rooms in the highest – and therefore quietest – of three options in this block. ③.

Hostal Rober, c/Arenal 26, 5º (☎91 541 91 75; Metro Opera). One of several reasonable *hostales* at the Opera end of Arenal. The thirteen rooms all have a bathroom and TV. ④.

Around Paseo del Prado

This is a quieter area, though still very central, which hosts some of the city's most expensive hotels – as well as some more modest options.

Hostal Almanzor, c/San Jerónimo 11, 2º (☎91 429 38 01; Metro Sol). Clean and welcoming, with a French-speaking *dueño*. ④.

Hostal Armesto, c/San Agustín 6, 1º (☎91 429 9031; Metro Antón Martín). Another clean and friendly option, in a quiet street near the tourist office. The best rooms overlook the pleasant little garden in the Casa de Lope de Vega next door. ④.

Hostal Cervantes, c/Cervantes 34, 2º (☎91 429 83 65 or 91 429 2745, fax 91 429 83 65; Metro Antón Martín). If you can't get in to the *Gonzalo* on the floor above, this is an equally friendly *hostal*, although slightly more expensive. All rooms have their own bathroom, TV and ventilator and are pleasantly furnished.④.

Hostal Gonzalo, c/Cervantes 34, 3º (☎91 429 27 14, fax 91 420 20 07; Metro Antón Martín). Don't let the ancient lift put you off – this recently refurbished hotel has bright, en-suite rooms and a charming owner. Highly recommended. ④.

Hotel Mora, Paseo del Prado 32 (☎91 420 15 69, fax 91 420 05 64; Metro Atocha). Friendly, recently refurbished, 62-room hotel. All rooms have air conditioning and some have pleasant views along the Paseo del Prado. Perfectly positioned for all the galleries on the Paseo del Arte. ⑤.

Hostal Sud-Americana, Paseo del Prado 12, 6º (☎91 429 25 64; Metro Antón Martín). Large, clean rooms with leafy views in this good-value *hostal* (though facilities are shared). Closed Aug. ④.

Along Gran Vía

The huge old buildings along the Gran Vía – which stretches all the way from Plaza de España to c/de Alcalá – hide a vast array of hotels and *hostales* at every price, often with a delightfully decayed elegance, though also noisy from outside traffic. After dark, the area can feel somewhat seedy.

Hostal Andorra, Gran Vía 33, 7º (☎91 531 66 03, fax 91 521 79 31; Metro Callao). Smart, clean and quiet, with bathrooms in all the rooms. ⑤.

Hostal Buenos Aires, Gran Vía 61, 2º (☎91 542 22 50, fax 91 542 28 69; Metro Plaza de España). Well-appointed *hostal*, at the Plaza de España end of this street. ⑤.

Hostal California, Gran Vía 38 (☎91 522 47 03, fax 91 531 61 01; Metro Callao). Well-placed, but somewhat pricey *hostal*. Bright, new and relatively quiet rooms. ⑥.

Hostal Valencia, Gran Vía 44, 5º (☎91 522 11 15, fax 91 522 11 13; Metro Callao). Best of a whole block of *hostales*, though rooms at the front can be noisy. ④.

North of Gran Vía

North of Gran Vía, there are further wedges of *hostales* on and around c/Fuencarral and c/Hortaleza, near Metro Gran Vía, and c/Luna, behind Metro Callao. Fuencarral itself can be almost as noisy as Gran Vía, however, so ask for a room facing away from the street; the streets around its southern end form a red-light district, so take care after dark. The higher the street numbers, the farther these streets are from Gran Vía – and the nearer to Malasaña (see below).

Hostal Ducal, c/Hortaleza 3, 2º (☎91 521 10 45, fax 91 521 50 64; Metro Gran Vía). Pleasant *hostal* with flower-laden verandas overlooking the city. All rooms are en suite. ④.

Hostal Kryse, c/Fuencarral 25, 1º (☎91 531 15 12, fax 91 522 81 53; Metro Gran Vía). One of a trio of clean, friendly places run by the same management. ④.

Hostal Luna, c/de Luna 6 (☎91 532 45 85; Metro Callao). Decent-value *hostal* (with shared facilities), overlooking drab square in an area with a strong Chinese character. ③.

Hostal Medieval, c/Fuencarral 46, 2º (☎91 522 25 49; Metro Chueca). Well-run, friendly place with a range of rooms, in an old building overlooking a square. ③–④.

Hotel Mónaco, c/Barbieri 5 (☎91 522 46 30, fax 91 521 16 01; Metro Gran Vía/Chueca). Wonderfully characterful hotel in a former bordello; the ornate bedrooms have elaborately curtained or partitioned bath areas. Highly recommended. ⑥.

Hostal Nueva Montaña, c/de la Luna 30 (☎91 521 60 85; Metro Plaza de España). Respectable, inexpensive option, reassuringly opposite a police station in a characterful old street, with shared bath. ②.

Hostal Pizarro, c/Pizarro 14, 1º (☎91 531 91 58; Metro Plaza de España). Comfortable, fairly upmarket *hostal* on a street just off c/de la Luna. ④.

Hostal Sil, c/Fuencarral 95, 3º (☎91 448 89 72; Metro Tribunal). Quiet *hostal* with air conditioning; very handy for Malasaña. ④.

Hostal Zamoran, c/Fuencarral 18 (☎91 532 20 60; Metro Gran Vía). Good-value *hostal*, with large, clean, en-suite rooms (all with TV). ④.

Malasaña

Malasaña, west of c/de Fuencarral and centred around Plaza Dos de Mayo, is an old working-class district, and one of the main nightlife areas of Madrid. The *hostales* here tend towards the basic, but if you stay you'll get a feel for what the city is really like – and you'll still be in walking distance of the sights.

Hostal Barajas, c/Augusto Figueroa 17 (☎91 532 40 78, fax 91 531 02 09; Metro Tribunal/Chueca). Unusually fancy *hostal* for this area, offering en-suite rooms, all with TV. ④.

Hostal Centro, c/de la Palma 11, 1º (☎91 447 00 47; Metro Tribunal). Reasonable and friendly budget choice, in an old family home, with shared facilities. ②.

Hostal Maravillas, c/Manuela Malasaña 23, 1º (☎91 448 40 00; Metro Noviciado). Lively location for this bland but low-priced *hostal*. ③.

Hostal Palma, c/de la Palma 17, 1º (☎91 447 54 88; Metro Tribunal). Basic but clean rooms (some with balcony), behind the metro station. ②.

Hostal Los Perales, c/de la Palma 61, 1º (☎91 522 71 91; Metro Noviciado). Best budget option in a building with several *hostales*. ②.

Chueca and Santa Bárbara

Chueca, east of c/de Fuencarral, is another nightlife centre, more so, these days, than Malasaña, with lots of music bars; it's also the city's *zona gay*. Plaza Chueca, however, is a hangout for junkies and dealers. The northern reaches of Chueca, around Plaza Santa Bárbara (Metro Alonso Martínez), are unintimidating and still full of nightlife.

Hostal Asunción, Plaza Santa Bárbara 8 (☎91 308 23 48, fax 91 310 04 78; Metro Alonso Martínez). Small but well-furnished rooms with bath, TV and mini-bar. Pretty position overlooking the square. ④–⑤.

Hostal El Pinar, c/San Bartolomé 2, 4º (☎91 531 01 34; Metro Chueca). Decent *hostal* that charges some of the lowest rates in the city – perhaps because the building looks as though it's about to collapse. ②.

Hostal Santa Bárbara, Plaza Santa Bárbara 4 (☎91 445 73 34, fax 91 446 23 45; Metro Alonso Martínez). Nice, newly refurbished *hostal* in a good location, with English-speaking Italian *dueño*. ⑤.

Recoletos and Salamanca

This is Madrid at its most chi-chi: the Bond Street/Rue de Rivoli region of smart shops and equally well-heeled apartment blocks. It's a safe, pleasant area, just north of the Parque del Retiro, but the pavements are notorious for dog shit – poodles being almost as ubiquitous here as fur coats.

Residencia Don Diego, c/Velázquez 45, 5º (☎91 435 07 60, fax 91 431 42 63; Metro Velázquez). This is a comfortable little hotel – and quite reasonably priced for the area. ⑥.

Galiano Residencia, c/de Alcalá Galiano 6 (☎91 319 20 00, fax 91 319 99 14; Metro Colón). Hidden away in a quiet street off the Paseo de la Castellana, this small hotel has a sophisticated feel and friendly service. Car parking facilities. ⑥.

Hotel Serrano, c/Marqués de Villamejor 8 (☎91 435 52 00, fax 91 435 48 49; Metro Rubén Darío). Small, modern hotel, handily sited between c/Velázquez and Paseo de la Castellana. Rooms look out on to a back courtyard so are fairly quiet. ⑦.

Youth hostels and campsites

Madrid has two youth hostels and, following the closure of *Camping Madrid* (still listed in some camping guides), just one "local" campsite.

Hostel Richard Schirmann, in the Casa de Campo (☎91 463 56 99, fax 91 464 46 85; Metro Lago or bus #33). Not very convenient (about 45min walk from Sol) but friendly, comfortable and clean with plenty of fresh air and an enjoyably noisy bar. You can call and they'll pick you up at Lago metro station, roughly 1km away; you certainly shouldn't walk there alone after dark as the area is frequented by prostitutes and their clients. ①.

Hostel Santa Cruz de Marcenado, c/Santa Cruz de Marcenado 28 (☎91 547 45 32; Metro Argüelles). This is twenty minutes' walk (or an easy metro ride) northwest of the centre, east of c/de la Princesa. It's a modern, reasonably pleasant building, with good local bars. Reception is open 9am–10pm, and doors stay open to 1.30am. Try to book ahead if at all possible. ①.

Camping Osuna, Avda. de Logroño, out near the airport, just north of the NII road to Barcelona (☎91 741 05 10; Metro Canillejas, then bus #105). Friendly, with good facilities, reasonable prices and plenty of shade, but the ground is rock-hard and, with planes landing and taking off overhead, it's extremely noisy. ①.

The City

Madrid's main sights occupy a compact area between the **Palacio Real** (Royal Palace) and the gardens of **El Retiro**. The great trio of museums – the **Prado**, **Thyssen-Bornemisza** and **Reina Sofía** – are ranged along the Paseo del Prado, over towards the Retiro. The oldest part of the city, an area known as **Madrid de los Austrias** after the Habsburg monarchs who built it, is centred on the gorgeous, arcaded **Plaza Mayor**, just to the east of the Palacio Real.

If you have very limited time, you might well do no more sightseeing than this. However, monuments are not really what Madrid is about, and to get a feel for the city you need to branch out a little, and experience the contrasting character and life of the various *barrios*. The most central and rewarding of these are the areas **around Plaza de Santa Ana and c/de las Huertas**, east of Puerta del Sol; **La Latina and Lavapiés**, south of Plaza Mayor, where the Sunday market, **El Rastro**, takes place; and **Malasaña and Chueca**, north of Gran Vía. By happy circumstance, these *barrios* have some of Madrid's finest concentrations of *tapas* bars and restaurants (see p.91).

Sol, Plaza Mayor and Opera: Madrid of the Austrias

Madrid de los Austrias – Habsburg Madrid – was a mix of formal planning, at its most impressive in the expansive and theatrical Plaza Mayor, and areas of shanty-town development, knocked up as the new capital gained an urban population. The central area of old Madrid still reflects both characteristics, with its twisting grid of streets, alleyways and steps, and its Flemish-inspired architecture of red brick and grey stone, slate-tiled towers, and Renaissance doorways.

Puerta del Sol

The obvious starting point for exploring Habsburg Madrid (and most other areas of the centre) is the **Puerta del Sol** (Metro Sol). This square marks the epicentre of the city – and, indeed, of Spain. It is from this point that all distances are measured, and here that six of Spain's *Rutas Nacionales* (the roads known as the NI, to Burgos, the NII, to Zaragoza, and so on) officially begin. On the pavement outside the clock-tower building on the south side of the square, a stone slab shows Kilometre Zero.

The square is a popular meeting place, especially by the fountain, or at the corner of c/del Carmen, with its statue of a bear pawing a bush – the city's emblem. These apart, there's little of note, though the square fulfils something of a public role when there's a demonstration or celebration. At the New Year, for example, it is packed with people

---

SUMMER IN MADRID

Madrid virtually shuts down **in the summer**; from around July 20 you'll suddenly find that half the bars, restaurants and offices are closed, and their inhabitants gone to the coast and countryside. Only in September does the city open properly for business again.

Luckily for visitors, and those *madrileños* who choose to remain, most sights and museums stay open, and a summer nightlife takes on a momentum of its own in outdoor terrace bars, or terrazas. In addition, the city council has in recent years initiated a major programme of summer entertainment, *Los Veranos de la Villa*. It's not a bad time to be in town at all, so long as you're not trying to get anything done.

Note that, throughout the year, most museums (and many bars and restaurants) **close on Monday**. Major attractions that stay open on Mondays include the Reina Sofía and the Palacio Real.

waiting for the clock to chime midnight. The square's main business, however, is shopping, with giant branches of the **department stores** El Corte Inglés and the French chain FNAC in c/de Preciados, at the top end of the square.

Plaza Mayor

Follow c/Mayor (the "Main Street" of the medieval city) west from the Puerta del Sol and you could easily walk right past Madrid's most important landmark: **Plaza Mayor**. This is set back from the street and, entered by stepped passageways, appears all the more grand in its continuous sweep of arcaded buildings. It was planned by Felipe II – the monarch who made Madrid the capital – as the public meeting place of the city, and was finished thirty years later in 1619 during the reign of Felipe III, who sits astride the stallion in the central statue. The architect was Juan Gómez de Mora, who was responsible for many of the civic and royal buildings in this quarter.

The square, with its hundreds of balconies, was designed as a theatre for public events, and it has served this function throughout its history. It was the scene of the Inquisition's *autos-de-fe* (trials of faith) and the executions which followed; kings were crowned here; festivals and demonstrations passed through; plays by Lope de Vega and others received their first performances; bulls were fought; and gossip was spread. The more important of the events would be watched by royalty from their apartments in the central **Casa Panadería**, a palace (now municipal offices) named after the bakery which it replaced. It was rebuilt after a fire in 1692 and decorated with a delightful – and to modern eyes, highly kitsch – array of allegorical figures, recently restored to their full glory.

Nowadays, Plaza Mayor is primarily a tourist haunt, full of expensive outdoor cafés and restaurants (best stick to a drink). However, an air of grandeur clings to the plaza, which still performs public functions. In the summer months it becomes an outdoor **theatre** and **music stage**; in the autumn there's a **book fair**; and in the winter, just before Christmas, it becomes a **bazaar** for festive decorations and religious regalia. Every Sunday, too, stamp sellers and collectors convene to talk philately together while their numismatic counterparts rummage through boxes of rare coins in an open-air market.

In the alleys just below the square, such as c/Cuchilleros and c/Cava de San Miguel, are some of the city's oldest *mesones*, or **taverns**. Have a drink in these in the early evening and you are likely to be serenaded by passing *tunas* – musicians and singers dressed in traditional costume of knickerbockers and waistcoats who wander around town playing and passing the hat. These men-only troupes are attached to various faculties of the university and are used by students to supplement their grants.

Plaza de la Villa, San Miguel and San Ginés

Farther west along c/Mayor, towards the Royal Palace, is **Plaza de la Villa**, a perfect example of three centuries of Spanish architectural development. Its oldest surviving building is the fifteenth-century **Torre de los Lujanes**, a fine Mudéjar (Moors working under Christian rule) tower, where Francis I of France is said to have been imprisoned in 1525 after his capture at the Battle of Pavia in Italy. Opposite is the old town hall, the **Ayuntamiento**, begun in the seventeenth century, but remodelled in a Baroque mode (tours at 5pm every Monday). Finally, fronting the square is the **Casa de Cisneros**, built by a nephew of Cardinal Cisneros in the sixteenth-century Plateresque ("silversmith") style.

Baroque is taken even further around the corner in c/San Justo, where the parish church of **San Miguel** shows the unbridled imagination of the eighteenth-century Italian architects who designed it.

Another fine – but much more ancient – church is **San Ginés**, north of Plaza Mayor on c/del Arenal. This is of Mozarabic origin (built by Christians under Moorish rule) and has an El Greco canvas of the money changers being chased from the temple. It is open only during services. Alongside the church, in somewhat uneasy juxtaposition, stands a cult temple of the twentieth century, the *Joy Eslava* disco, and, behind it, the **Chocolatería San Ginés**, a Madrid institution, which at one time catered for the early-rising worker but now churns out *churros* and hot chocolate for the late nightclub crowd (see p.106).

Descalzas Reales and Encarnación convents

A couple of blocks north of San Ginés is one of the hidden treasures of Madrid, the **Monasterio de las Descalzas Reales** at Plaza de las Descalzas Reales 3 (Metro Sol/Callao). This was founded by Juana de Austria, daughter of the Emperor Carlos V, sister of Felipe II, and, at age nineteen, already the widow of Prince Don Juan of Portugal. In her wake came a succession of titled ladies (*Descalzas Reales* means "Barefoot Royals"), who brought fame and, above all, fortune. The place is unbelievably rich, though beautiful and tranquil, too, and still in use as a convent, with shoeless nuns tending patches of vegetable garden.

Whistle-stop guided **tours** (Tues–Thurs & Sat 10.30am–12.45pm & 4–5.45pm, Fri 10.30am–12.45pm, Sun & holidays 11am–1.30pm; 650ptas, free on Wed for EU citizens) conduct visitors (usually in Spanish only) through the cloisters and up an incredibly fancy stairway to a series of chambers packed with art and treasures of every kind. The dormitories are perhaps the most outstanding feature, decorated with a series of Flemish tapestries based on designs by Rubens and a striking portrait of Saint Francis by Zurbarán. These were the sleeping quarters for all the nuns – who included, for a time, Saint Teresa of Ávila – except for the Empress María of Germany, who endowed the convent with her own luxurious private chambers. The other highlight of the tour is the *Joyería* (Treasury), piled high with jewels and relics of uncertain provenance. The nuns kept no records of their gifts, so no one is quite sure what many of the things are – there is a bizarre cross-sectional model of Christ – nor which bones came from which saint. Whatever the case, it's an exceptional hoard.

MADRID'S FREEBIES

Free entrance can be gained to many of Madrid's premier attractions. Sites classed as *Patrimonio Nacional* such as the Palacio Real, the Convento de la Encarnación, El Pardo (see p.90) and the Monasterio de las Descalzas are free to EU citizens on Wednesdays (bring your passport). Most museums are free for under 18s and the retired, and give substantial discounts to students (bring ID in all cases). In addition many museums and sights that normally charge entry set aside certain times when entrance is free. These include the following:

Centro de Arte Reina Sofía: Sat after 2.30pm & Sun 10am–2.30pm.
Ermita de San Antonio de la Florida: Wed 10am–2pm & 4–8pm & Sun 10am–2pm.
Museo de América: Sat 2–3pm & Sun 10am–2.30pm.
Museo Arqueológico: Sat 2.30–8.30pm & Sun 9.30am–2.30pm.
Museo de Artes Decorativas: Sun 10am–2pm.
Museo Cerralbo: Sun 10am–2pm & Wed 9.30am–2.30pm.
Museo del Ejército: Sat 10am–2pm.
Museo Lázaro Galdiano: Sat 10am–2pm.
Museo Municipal: Sun 10am–2pm & Wed 9.30am–8pm.
Museo del Prado: Sat after 2.30pm & Sun 9am–2pm.
Museo Romántico: Sun 10am–2pm.
Real Academia de Bellas Artes: Sat & Sun 9am–2.30pm.

Over towards the Palacio Real in Plaza de la Encarnación is the **Convento de la Encarnación** (Metro Opera; Wed & Sat 10.30am–12.45pm & 4–5.45pm, Sun 11am–1.45pm; 450 ptas, free on Wed for EU citizens). This was founded a few years after Juana's convent, by Margarita, wife of Felipe III, though it was substantially rebuilt towards the end of the eighteenth century. It houses an extensive but disappointing collection of seventeenth-century Spanish art, and a library-like reliquary which is reputed to be one of the most important in the Catholic world.

Opera: Plaza de Oriente and the cathedral

West of Sol, c/del Arenal leads to the **Teatro Real** or Opera (Metro Opera), which gives this area its name. Built in the mid-nineteenth century, it almost sunk a few decades later as a result of subsidence caused by underground canals; it has recently reopened after a ten-year refurbishment that should have lasted just four and which ended up costing a mind-boggling 25 billion pesetas.

Around the back, the opera house is separated from the Palacio Real by the **Plaza de Oriente**, a pleasant square that is surprisingly under-used, perhaps a hangover from the bad old days when Franco used to address crowds here; neo-Fascists still gather here on the anniversary of his death in November. However it, too, has undergone extensive renovation recently which may change things; the completion of a major pedestrianization project, diverting the busy c/Bailén beneath the square, has turned the plaza into one of the most agreeable open spaces in Madrid. One of the square's main attractions – and the focus of its life – is the elegant *Café del Oriente*, whose summer terraza is one of the stations of Madrid nightlife. The café (which is also a prestigious restaurant) looks as traditional as any in the city but was in fact opened in the 1980s, by a priest, Padre Lezama, who ploughs his profits into various charitable schemes.

The café apart, the dominant features of Plaza de Oriente are statues: forty-four of them, depicting Spanish kings and queens, which were designed originally to go on the palace facade but found to be too heavy (some say too ugly) for the roof to support. The **statue of Felipe IV** on horseback, in the centre of the square, clearly belongs on a different plane; it was based on designs by Velázquez, and Galileo is said to have helped with the calculations to make it balance.

Facing the Palacio Real to the south, across the shadeless Plaza de la Armería, is Madrid's cathedral, **Nuestra Señora de la Almudena** (Metro Opera; Mon–Sat 10am–1.30pm & 6–8.30pm, Sun 10am–2.30pm & 6–8.30pm). This was planned centuries ago, bombed out in the Civil War, worked upon at intervals since, plagued by lack of funds and eventually opened for business in 1993 by Pope John Paul II. Its Neoclassical bulk is as undistinguished inside as out, though the boutique-like Capilla Opus Dei has, at least, novelty value amid an array of largely unfilled chapel alcoves.

South again from here, c/Bailén crosses c/Segovia on a high **viaduct** which was constructed as a royal route from the palace to the church of San Francisco el Grande, avoiding the rabble and river which both flowed below. Close by is a patch of **Moorish wall** from the medieval fortress here, which the original royal palace replaced. Across the aqueduct, the **gardens** of Las Vistillas ("the views") beckon, with their summer terrazas looking out across the river.

El Palacio Real

The **Palacio Real** or Royal Palace (April–Sept Mon–Sat 9am–6pm, Sun & holidays 9am–3pm; Oct–March Mon–Sat 9.30am–5pm, Sun & holidays 9am–2pm; closed occasionally for state visits; free on Wed for EU citizens) scores high on statistics. It claims more rooms than any other European palace; a library with one of the biggest collections

N

Private apartments

Capilla

9 10 11

8

8 8

Antesala

8

Patio

8

8

Comedor de Gala

CALLE BAILÉN

12

13

19
20

Comedor
de diario

21

22

14

7
6

Salón de Tapices

5

Salón de
Columnas

Salón de
Guardias

1

15

4

18

16

3

2

Salón de
Gasparini

Salón del
Trono

Saleta
Oficial

17

Entrada (Ground floor)

PLAZA DE LA ARMERÍA

Cámara
Oficial

Farmácia

Toilets

Ticket
Office

1	Escalera Principal	**12**	Antecámara de la Reina Cristina
2	Antecámara de Gasparini	**13**	Saleta Reina Cristina
3	Salón de Gasparini	**14**	Salón de Espejos
4	Tranvía	**15**	Salón de Armas
5	Salón de Carlos III	**16**	Tranvía
6	Sala de Porcelana	**17**	Antecámara Oficial
7	Sala Amarilla	**18**	Salón de Grandes
8	Salas de Exposición	**19**	Salón de Billar
9	Cámara Fuerte	**20**	Salón Chino-Japonés
10	Relicario	**21**	Saleta de Estucos
11	Anterrelicario	**22**	Maderas Finas

PALACIO REAL

of books, manuscripts, maps and musical scores in the world; and an armoury with an unrivalled collection of weapons dating back to the fifteenth century. If you are around on the first Wednesday of every month at noon–1pm, look out for the changing of the guard outside the palace, a tradition which has recently been revived.

Optional **guided tours** in various languages (950ptas, usually with a wait for a group to form) have been abbreviated in recent years, now taking in around 25 (rather than 90) rooms and apartments, including the Royal Armoury Museum (when it's open) and Royal Pharmacy. Nevertheless, they're still a pretty hard slog, rarely allowing much time to contemplate the extraordinary opulence: acres of Flemish and Spanish tapestries, endless Rococo decoration, bejewelled clocks and pompous portraits of the monarchs, as well as a permanent display of Goya's cartoons and tapestries. You're probably better off going **without a guide** (850ptas), as each room is clearly signed and described in English anyway, the main disadvantage being trying to fight your way past the guided groups.

The palace and outhouses

The Habsburgs' original palace burned down on Christmas Day 1734. Its replacement, the current building, was based on drawings made by Bernini for the Louvre. It was constructed in the mid-eighteenth century and was the principal royal residence from then until Alfonso XIII went into exile in 1931; both Joseph Bonaparte and the Duke of Wellington also lived here briefly. The present royal family inhabits a considerably more modest residence in the western outskirts of the city, using the Palacio Real on state occasions only.

The **Salón del Trono** (Throne Room) is the highlight for most visitors, containing the new thrones installed for Juan Carlos and Sofía, the current monarchs, as well as the splendid ceiling by Tiepolo, a giant fresco representing the glory of Spain – an extraordinary achievement for an artist by then in his seventies.

The palace outbuildings and annexes include the **Armería Real** (Royal Armoury, currently closed for restoration), a huge room full of guns, swords and armour, with such curiosities as El Cid's sword and the suit of armour worn by Carlos V in his equestrian portrait by Titian in the Prado. Especially fascinating are the complete sets of armour, with all the original spare parts and gadgets for making adjustments. The **Biblioteca Real** (Royal Library, currently closed for restoration) is equally staggering, including a first edition of *Don Quixote* among its countless volumes. There is also an eighteenth-century **Farmacia**, a curious mixture of alchemist's den and laboratory, whose walls are lined with jars labelled for various remedies.

The gardens and the coach museum

Immediately north of the palace, the disappointing **Jardines Sabatini**, are also open to the public, while to the rear is the larger, and far more beautiful, park of the **Campo del Moro** (access only from the far west side off the Paseo de la Virgen del Puerto).

Within the park is the **Museo de Carruajes** (April–Sept Tues–Sat 10am–8pm, Sun 9am–3.30pm; Oct–March Tues–Sat 10am–6pm, Sun 9am–3.30pm; currently closed for restoration), which houses a collection of state coaches and the like from the sixteenth century to the present; your ticket to the Royal Palace entitles you to entry.

South of Plaza Mayor: La Latina, Lavapiés and El Rastro

The areas south of Plaza Mayor have traditionally been tough, working-class districts, with tenement buildings thrown up to accommodate the huge expansion of the population in the eighteenth and nineteenth centuries. In many places these old houses survive, huddled together in narrow streets, but the character of **La Latina** and **Lavapiés** is beginning to change as their inhabitants, and the districts themselves, become younger and more fashionable. The streets of Cava Baja and Cava Alta, for example, in La Latina, include some of the city's most fashionable bars and restaurants. These are attractive *barrios* to explore, particularly during the Sunday morning flea market, **El Rastro**, which takes place along and around the Ribera de Curtidores (Metro La Latina or Tirso de Molina).

Around La Latina

La Latina is a short walk from Plaza de la Villa (see p.70) and, if you're exploring Madrid de los Austrias, it's a natural continuation, as some of the squares, streets and

THE RASTRO

Madrid's flea market, **El Rastro**, is as much part of the city's weekend ritual as a Mass or a *paseo*. This gargantuan, thriving, thieving shambles of a street market sprawls south from Metro Latina to the Ronda de Toledo, especially along Ribera de Curtidores. Through it, crowds flood between 10am and 3pm every Sunday and increasingly on Fridays, Saturdays and public holidays too. On offer are secondhand clothes, military surplus items, budgies and canaries, sunshades, razor blades, fine antiques and Taiwanese transistors, cutlery and coke spoons – in fact just about anything you might (or more likely, might not) need.

Some of the goods – broken telephone dials, plastic shampoo bottles half-full of something which may or may not be the original contents – are so far gone that you can't imagine any of them ever selling. Other items may be quite valuable, but on the whole it's the stuff of markets around the world you'll find here: pseudo-designer clothes, bags and T-shirts. Don't expect to find fabulous bargains, or the hidden Old Masters of popular myth; the serious antique trade has mostly moved off the streets and into the shops along the street, while the real junk is now found only on the fringes. Nonetheless, the atmosphere of the Rastro is always enjoyable and the bars around these streets are as good as any in the city.

One warning: keep a close eye on your bags, pockets, cameras (best left at the hotel), and jewellery. The Rastro rings up a fair percentage of Madrid's tourist thefts.

churches here date back to the early Habsburg period. One of the most attractive pockets is around the recently renovated **Plaza de la Paja**, an acacia-shaded square, behind the large church of San Andrés. In summer, there is usually a terraza here, tucked well away from the traffic. If it is open, you might look into the Gothic **Capilla del Obispo**, which backs on to San Andrés; long under restoration, this has an elaborate Renaissance interior, endowed by one of Ferdinand and Isabella's counsellors.

Over to the west of here is one of Madrid's grandest, richest and most elaborate churches, **San Francisco el Grande** (Metro Puerta de Toledo/La Latina). Built towards the end of the eighteenth century as part of Carlos III's renovations of the city, it has a dome even larger than that of Saint Paul's in London. Inside (Tues–Sat: June–Sept 11am–1pm & 5–8pm; Oct–May 11am–1pm & 4–7pm; 50ptas with guided tour) are paintings by, among others, Goya and Zurbarán, and frescoes by Bayeu. They're not all that easy to see, however, as scaffolding is in place for a painfully slow restoration. Work is scheduled to be completed in 2012.

The Ribera de Curtidores, heart of the Rastro, begins just behind another vast church, **San Isidro**. Isidro is the patron saint of Madrid – his remains are entombed within – and his church acted as the city's cathedral prior to the completion of the Almudena by the Palacio Real. Relics apart, its chief attribute is size – it's as bleak as it is big. Next door is the **Instituto Real**, a school which has been in existence considerably longer than the church and counts among its former pupils such literary notables as Calderón de la Barca, Lope de Vega, Quevedo and Jacinto Benavente.

If you continue to the end of Ribera de Curtidores, whose antique shops (some, these days, extremely upmarket) stay open all week, you'll see a large arch, the **Puerta de Toledo**, at one end of the Ronda de Toledo. The only surviving relation to the Puerta de Alcalá in the Plaza de la Independencia, this was built originally as a triumphal arch to honour the conquering Napoleon. After his defeat in the Peninsular Wars, it became a symbol of the city's freedom. Just in front of the arch, the **Mercado Puerta de Toledo**, once the city's fish market, has pretensions to be a stylish arts and crafts centre, but in reality stands practically empty, apart from the under-used tourist office that lies within.

Lavapiés and the Cine Doré

A good point to start exploring Lavapiés is the Plaza Tirso de Molina (Metro Tirso de Molina). From here, you can follow c/Mesón de Paredes, stopping for a drink at *Taberna Antonio Sánchez*, at no. 13, down to **La Corrala**, on the corner of c/Sombrerete. This is one of many traditional *corrales* – tenement blocks – in the quarter, built with balconied apartments opening on to a central patio. Plays – especially farces and *zarzuelas* (a kind of operetta) – used to be performed regularly in Spanish *corrales*, and the open space here usually hosts a few performances in the summer. It has been well renovated and declared a national monument.

From Lavapiés, you are not far from the Centro de Arte Reina Sofía (see p.82), while to the north of the quarter, near Metro Antón Martín, is the **Cine Doré**, the oldest cinema in Madrid, dating from 1922, with a late *modernista*/Art Nouveau facade. It has been converted to house the Filmoteca Nacional, an art-film centre (see p.110) and it has a pleasant and inexpensive café/restaurant.

East of Sol: Plaza de Santa Ana and Huertas

The **Plaza de Santa Ana/Huertas** area forms a triangle, bordered to the east by the Paseo del Prado, to the north by c/Alcalá, and along the south by c/Atocha, with the Puerta del Sol at the western tip. The city reached this district after extending beyond the Royal Palace and the Plaza Mayor, so the buildings date predominantly from the nineteenth century. Many of them have literary associations: there are streets named after Cervantes and Lope de Vega (where one lived and the other died), and the *barrio* is host to the Atheneum club (literary guild), Círculo de Bellas Artes (Fine Arts Institute), Teatro Español, and the Cortes (parliament). Just to the north, there is also an important museum, the **Real Academia de Bellas Artes de San Fernando**.

For most visitors, though, the major attraction is that in this district are some of the best and most beautiful bars and *tascas* in the city. They are concentrated particularly around Plaza de Santa Ana, which – following a rather seedy period – has been smartened up by the council and is now one of the finest squares of the city.

Santa Ana and around

The bars around **Plaza de Santa Ana** (Metro Sol/Sevilla) really are sights in themselves. On the square itself, the dark panelled **Cervecería Alemana** was a firm favourite of Hemingway and has hardly changed since the turn of the century. It's a place to drink beer and go easy on *tapas* (the *empanadillas* are good), if you don't want to run up a significant bill. **Viva Madrid**, on the northeast corner at c/Manuel Fernández y González 7, should be another port of call, if only to admire the fabulous tilework, original zinc bar and a ceiling supported by wooden caryatids. Another notable place is the *Bar Torero* of the **Gran Hotel Reina Victoria**, the smart hotel flanking Plaza de Santa Ana; this is where bullfighters stay when in town, and the bar is packed with taurine memorabilia.

One block east from here is c/**Echegaray**, where one of the highlights is **Los Gabrieles** at no. 17. This is a bar with museum-piece *azulejos* (tiles), endowed by sherry companies in the late nineteenth century and fabulously inventive: there are skeletons climbing over barrels, Goya-esque idylls with sherry and bulls, and a superb co-opting of Velázquez's *Los Borrachos*.

Huertas, the Cortes and the Círculo de Bellas Artes

The area around c/de las Huertas itself is workaday enough – and again packed with bars. North of the street, and parallel, are two streets named after the greatest figures of Spain's seventeenth-century literary golden age, Cervantes and Lope de Vega. Bitter rivals in life, both are probably spinning in their graves now, since Cervantes is interred in the Convento de las Trinitarias on the street named after Lope de Vega, while the latter's house, the **Casa de Lope de Vega** (Tues–Fri 9.30am–2pm, Sat 10am–1.30pm; closed mid-July to mid-Aug; 200ptas), finds itself at c/de Cervantes 11 (Metro Antón Martín). The latter is well worth visiting for its reconstruction of life in seventeenth-century Madrid; ring the bell and someone will take you on a short tour (usually English is spoken).

A block to the north is **Las Cortes Españolas** (Metro Sevilla), an unprepossessing nineteenth-century building where the congress (the lower house) meets. Sessions can be visited by appointment only, though anyone can turn up (with a passport) for a tour on Saturday mornings (10.30am–1pm; closed Aug). You're shown, amongst other things, the bullet holes left by mad Colonel Tejero and his Guardia Civil associates in the abortive coup attempt of 1981.

Cut across to c/de Alcalá from the Plaza de las Cortes and you will emerge close to the **Círculo de Bellas Artes**, at Marqués de Casa Riera 2 (Metro Sevilla), a strange-looking 1920s building crowned by a statue of Pallas Athene. This is Madrid's best arts centre, and includes a theatre, music hall, cinema, exhibition galleries and a very pleasant bar – all marble and leather decor, with a nude statue reclining in the middle of the floor. It attracts Madrid's arts and media crowd but is not in the least exclusive, nor expensive, and there's an adjoining terraza, too. The Círculo is theoretically a members-only club, but it issues 100ptas day membership on the door, for which you get access to all areas.

Calle Alcalá to Cibeles

At the Círculo, you are on the corner of Gran Vía (see p.86), and, only a hundred metres to the east, c/de Alcalá meets the Paseo del Prado at the **Plaza de la Cibeles**. The wedding-cake building on the far side of this square is Madrid's main post office, the aptly entitled **Palacio de Comunicaciones**. Constructed from 1904 to 1917, it is vastly more imposing than the parliament and runs the Palacio Real pretty close. It's a fabulous place, flanked by polished brass postboxes for each province and preserving a totally Byzantine system within, where scores of counters each offer just one specific service, from telegrams to string, and, until quite recently, scribes.

Awash in a sea of traffic in the centre of the square is a **fountain** and statue of the goddess Cibeles, which survived the bombardments of the Civil War by being swaddled from helmet to hoof in sandbags. It was designed, as were the two other fountains gushing magnificently along the Paseo del Prado, by Ventura Rodríguez, who is honoured in modern Madrid by having a metro station and a street named after him. The fountain is the scene of celebrations for victorious Real Madrid fans (Atlético fans bathe in the fountain of Neptune just down the road).

Madrid's three principal art museums, the Prado (see p.78), Thyssen-Bornemisza (see p.81) and Centro de Arte Reina Sofía (see p.82), all lie to the south of here, along the Paseo del Prado. To the north, on Paseo de Recoletos, are a couple of the city's most lavish **traditional cafés**, the *Café Gijón* at no. 21 and *Café del Espejo* at no. 31 (see box, p.97).

Real Academia de Bellas Artes de San Fernando

Art buffs who have some appetite left after the Prado, Thyssen-Bornemisza and Reina Sofía, will find the **Real Academia de Bellas Artes de San Fernando**, at c/Alcalá 13 (Metro Sevilla; Tues–Fri 9am–7pm, Mon, Sat, Sun & holidays 9am–2.30pm; 300ptas, free Sat & Sun), next on their list. Admittedly, you have to plough through a fair number of dull academic canvases, but there are hidden gems, particularly in the second and third rooms. These include a group of small panels by **Goya**, in particular *The Burial of the Sardine*; portraits of the monks of the Merced order by Zurbarán and others; and a curious *Family of El Greco*, which may be by the great man or his son. Two other rooms are devoted to foreign artists, especially Rubens. Upstairs, there is a series of engravings by Picasso, and, scattered throughout the museum, is a dismembered *Massacre of the Innocents* by sculptor José Ginés.

Museo del Prado

The **Museo del Prado** (Metro Banco de España/Atocha; Tues–Sat 9am–7pm; Sun & holidays usually 9am–2pm, but closed on selected holidays; 500ptas, free on Sat after 2.30pm & Sun) is Madrid's premier tourist attraction, and one of the oldest and greatest collections of art in the world. Built as a natural science museum in 1775, the Prado opened to the public in 1819, and houses the finest works collected by Spanish royalty – for the most part avid, discerning, and wealthy buyers – as well as Spanish paintings gathered from other sources over the past two centuries. There are 7000 paintings in all, of which around 1500 (still a pretty daunting tally) are on permanent display. A plan to modernize and extend the museum (adding three nearby buildings) will enable the Prado to double the amount of works currently on show.

The museum's highlights are its Flemish collection – including almost all of **Bosch's** best work – and of course its incomparable display of Spanish art, in particular that of **Velázquez** (including *Las Meninas*), **Goya** (including the *Majas* and the *Black Paintings*), and **El Greco**. There's also a huge section of Italian painters (**Titian**, notably) collected by Carlos V and Felipe II, both great patrons of the Renaissance, and an excellent, recently inaugurated collection of seventeenth-century Flemish and Dutch pictures gathered by Felipe IV. Even in a full day you couldn't hope to do justice to everything here, and it's perhaps best to make a couple of more focused visits. If you are tempted to take advantage of the long opening hours, however, there's a decent cafeteria and restaurant in the basement.

Organization, catalogues and entrances
Major reorganization – for the installation of air-conditioning and a much-needed remodelling of the roof to provide more natural light – has been going on for years now, and although some of the national schools look to have found a permanent home (the main Spanish collection and the seventeenth-century Flemish and Dutch collection are almost sure to remain on the first floor) it's still uncertain where the others will eventually end up. Your best bet is to pick up one of the **free maps** on your way in – these are reprinted each time the collections are moved.

What follows is, by necessity, only a brief guide to the museum contents. Illustrated **guides and catalogues** (1100–2200ptas) describing and explaining the paintings are on sale in the museum shop and there are useful **colour booklets** (100ptas) on Velázquez, Goya, El Greco, Titian and Bosch available in their respective galleries.

There are two main **entrances** to the museum: the **Puerta de Goya**, which has an upper and a lower entrance opposite the Hotel Ritz on c/Felipe IV, and the **Puerta de Murillo** on Plaza de Murillo, opposite the botanical gardens. The Puerta de Goya upper entrance takes you up to the first floor (US second floor), with the seventeenth-century Flemish and Dutch art, giving way to the main Spanish collections; its ground-floor entrance currently steers you past Goya's *Black Paintings* (probably best seen after you've visited the rest of his work on the floor above) towards the early Flemish galleries and finally along to the classical sculpture at the Puerta de Murillo.

Spanish painting
The Prado's collections of Spanish painting begin with the cycles of twelfth-century **Romanesque frescoes**, reconstructed from a pair of churches from the Mozarabic (Muslim rule) era in Soria and Segovia. **Early panel paintings** – exclusively religious

fourteenth- and fifteenth-century works – include a huge *retablo* (altarpiece) by Nicolás Francés; the anonymous *Virgin of the Catholic Monarchs*; Bermejo's *Santo Domingo de Silos*; and Pedro Berruguete's *Auto-de-Fe*.

THE GOLDEN AGE: VELÁZQUEZ AND EL GRECO

Collections from Spain's Golden Age – the late sixteenth and seventeenth centuries under Habsburg rule – are prefigured by a collection of paintings by **El Greco** (1540–1614), the Cretan-born artist who worked in Toledo from the 1570s. You really have to go to Toledo to appreciate fully his extraordinary genius, but the portraits and religious works here, ranging from the Italianate *Trinity* to the visionary late *Adoration of the Shepherds*, are a good introduction.

Here you also confront the greatest painter of Habsburg Spain, **Diego Velázquez** (1599–1660). Born in Portugal, Velázquez became court painter to Felipe IV, whose family is represented in many of the works: "I have found my Titian," Felipe is said to have remarked of his appointment. Velázquez's masterpiece, *Las Meninas*, is displayed alongside studies for the painting: Manet remarked of it, "After this I don't know why the rest of us paint," and the French poet Théophile Gautier asked "But where is the picture?" when he saw it, because it seemed to him a continuation of the room. *Las Hilanderas*, showing the royal tapestry factory at work, *Christ Crucified*, *Los Borrachos* (The Drunkards) and *The Surrender of Breda* (note the compositional device of the lances) are further magnificent works. In fact, almost all of the fifty works on display (around half of the artist's surviving output) warrant close attention. Don't overlook the two small panels of the *Villa Medici*, painted in Rome in 1650, in virtually impressionist style.

In the adjacent rooms are examples of just about every significant Spanish painter of the seventeenth century, including many of the best works of **Francisco Zurbarán** (1598–1664), **Bartolomé Esteban Murillo** (1618–82), **Alonso Cano** (1601–67), **Juan de Valdes Leal** (1622–60), and **Juan Carreño** (1641–85). Note, in particular, Carreño's portrait of the last Habsburg monarch, the drastically inbred and mentally retarded Carlos II, rendered with terrible realism. There's also a fine selection of works by **José Ribera** (1591–1625), who worked mainly in Naples, and was influenced there by Caravaggio. His masterpieces are considered *The Martyrdom of St Bartholomew* and the dark, realist portrait of *Archimedes*.

GOYA

The final suite of Spanish rooms provides an awesome and fabulously complete overview of the works of **Francisco de Goya** (1746–1828), the largest and most valuable collection of his works in the world with some 140 paintings and 500 drawings and engravings. Goya was the greatest painter of Bourbon Spain, a chronicler of Spain in his time and an artist whom many see as the inspiration and forerunner of Impressionism and modern art. He was an enormously versatile artist: contrast the voluptuous *Maja Vestida* and *Maja Desnuda* (The Clothed and Naked Belles) with the horrors depicted in *Dos de Mayo* and *Tres de Mayo* (on-the-spot portrayals of the rebellion against Napoleon in the streets of Madrid and the subsequent reprisals). Then there are the series of pastoral cartoons – designs for tapestries – and, downstairs, the extraordinary *Black Paintings*, a series of murals painted on the walls of his home by the deaf and embittered painter in his old age. His many portraits of his patron, Carlos IV, are remarkable for their lack of any attempt at flattery while those of Queen María Luisa, whom he despised, are downright ugly.

Italian painting

The Prado's early Italian galleries are distinguished principally by **Fra Angelico**'s *Annunciation* (c. 1445) and by a trio of panels by **Botticelli** (1445–1510). The latter illustrate a deeply unpleasant story from the *Decameron* about a woman hunted by hounds; the fourth panel (in a private collection in the US) gives a happier conclusion.

With the sixteenth-century Renaissance, and especially its Venetian exponents, the collection really comes into its own. The Prado is said to have the most complete collection of Titian and painters from the Venice school in any single museum. There are major works by **Raphael** (1483–1520), including a fabulous *Portrait of a Cardinal*, and masterpieces from the Venetians, **Tintoretto** (1518–94), including *The Lavatorio*, bought by Felipe IV when Charles I of England was beheaded and his art collection was auctioned off, and **Veronese** (1528–88), as well as **Caravaggio** (1573–1610). The most important group of works, however, are by **Titian**. These include portraits of the Spanish emperors, *Carlos V* and *Felipe II* (Charles's suit of armour is preserved in the Palacio Real), and a famous, much-reproduced piece of erotica, *Venus, Cupid and the Organist* (two versions are displayed here), a painting originally owned by a bishop.

Flemish, Dutch and German painting

The biggest name in the **early Flemish collections** is **Hieronymus Bosch** (1450–1516), known in Spain as "El Bosco". The Prado has several of his greatest triptychs: the early-period *Hay Wain*, the middle-period *Garden of Earthly Delights* and the late *Adoration of the Magi* – all familiar from countless reproductions but infinitely more chilling in the original. Bosch's hallucinatory genius for the macabre is at its most extreme in these triptychs, but is reflected here in many more of his works, including three versions of *The Temptations of Saint Anthony* (though only the smallest of these is definitely an original). Don't miss, either, the amazing table-top of *The Seven Deadly Sins*.

Bosch's visions find an echo in the works of **Pieter Brueghel the Elder** (1525–69), whose *Triumph of Death* must be one of the most frightening canvases ever painted. Another elusive painter, **Joachim Patinir**, is represented by four of his finest works. From an earlier generation, **Rogier van der Weyden**'s *Deposition* is outstanding; its monumental forms make a fascinating contrast with his miniature-like *Pietà*. There are also important works by Memling, Bouts, Gerard David and Massys.

The collection of over 160 works of **later Flemish and Dutch** art has been imaginatively rehoused in a new suite of twelve rooms on the first floor. Grouped by themes, such as religion, daily life, mythology, and landscape, the rooms have been tastefully decorated, while many of the paintings have been given a new lease of life by their restoration to their startling original colours. There are enough works here to make an excellent comparison between the flamboyant Counter-Reformation propaganda of Flanders and the more austere bourgeois tastes of Holland.

Rubens (1577–1640) is extensively represented with the beautifully restored *Three Graces, The Judgement of Paris* and by a series of eighteen mythological subjects designed for Felipe IV's hunting lodge in El Pardo (though he supervised rather than executed these). There are, too, a fine collection of works by his contemporaries, including **Van Dyck**'s dramatic *Piedad* and his magnificent portrait of himself and Sir Endymion Porter. **Jan Brueghel**'s representations of the five senses and **David Teniers**' scenes of peasant lowlife also merit a closer look. For political reasons, Spanish monarchs collected few works painted in seventeenth-century Protestant Holland; an early **Rembrandt**, *Artemisia*, in which the artist's pregnant wife served as the model is, however, an important exception.

The **German rooms** are dominated by **Dürer** (1471–1528) and **Lucas Cranach the Elder** (1472–1553). Dürer's magnificent *Adam and Eve* was saved from destruction at the hands of the prudish Carlos III only by the intervention of his court painter, Mengs. The most interesting of Cranach's works are a pair of paintings depicting Carlos V hunting with Ferdinand I of Austria.

Casón del Buen Retiro

Just east of the Prado is the **Casón del Buen Retiro** (currently undergoing restoration) which used to be a dance hall for the palace of Felipe IV, but is now devoted to nineteenth-century Spanish art. It is included in the entrance ticket to the main museum but, considering the riches which have gone before, is not of compelling interest.

Museo Thyssen-Bornemisza

The **Museo Thyssen-Bornemisza** (Metro Banco de España; Tues–Sun 10am–7pm; 700ptas) occupies the old Palacio de Villahermosa, diagonally opposite the Prado, at the end of the Carrera de San Jerónimo. This prestigious site played a large part in Spain's acquisition – for a knock-down $350 million in June 1993 – of what many argue was the world's greatest private art trove after that of the British royals: 700-odd paintings accumulated by father-and-son German-Hungarian industrial magnates. Another trumpcard was Baron Thyssen's current (fifth) wife, "Tita" Cervera, a former Miss Spain once married to Tarzan actor Lex Barker, who steered the works to Spain against the efforts of Britain's Prince Charles, the Swiss and German governments, the Getty foundation, and other suitors.

A portrait of Tita – a kitsch (and dangerously anorexic) stunner – hangs in the great hall of the museum, alongside those of her husband and King Juan Carlos and Queen Sofía. Pass beyond, however, and you are into seriously premier-league art: **medieval to eighteenth-century** on the top floor, **seventeenth-century Dutch** and **Rococo and Neoclassicism to Fauves and Expressionists** on the first floor, and **surrealists**, **pop art** and the **avant-garde** on ground level. Highlights are legion in a collection that displays an almost stamp-collecting mentality in its examples of nearly every major artist and movement: how the Thyssens got hold of classic works by everyone from Duccio and Holbein, through El Greco and Caravaggio, to Schiele and Rothko, takes your breath away.

The museum, which has had no expense spared on its design, with stucco walls (Tita insisted on salmon pink) and marble floors, has a handy cafeteria and restaurant in the basement and allows re-entry, so long as you get your hand stamped at the exit desk. The basement is also home to a temporary exhibition space which has staged a number of interesting and highly successful shows (separate entry fee of 500ptas). There is also a shop, where you can buy the first instalments of the fifteen-volume catalogue of the baron's collection as well as the more modest, but informative, illustrated **guide** to the museum (1800ptas). Around half of the collection is now on show, either here, or at the Monestir de Pedralbes in Barcelona, which houses around eighty works of sacred art (see p.604).

European old masters: the second floor

Take a lift to the second floor and you will find yourself at the chronological start of the museum's collections: European painting (and some sculpture) from the fourteenth to eighteenth century. The core of these collections was accumulated in the 1920s and 1930s by the present baron's father, Heinrich, who was a friend of the art critics Bernard Berenson and Max Friedländer.

He was clearly well advised. The early paintings include incredibly good (and rare) devotional panels by the Sienese painter **Duccio di Buoninsegna**, and the Flemish artists, **Jan van Eyck** and **Rogier van der Weyden**. You then move into a fabulous array of Renaissance portraits, which include three of the very greatest of the period: **Ghirlandaio**'s *Portrait of Giovanna Tornabuoni*, **Hans Holbein**'s *Portrait of Henry VIII* (the only one of many variants in existence which is definitely genuine), and **Raphael**'s *Portrait of a Young Man*. A *Spanish Infanta* by **Juan de Flandes** may represent the first of Henry VIII's wives, Catherine of Aragón, while the *Young Knight* by **Carpaccio** is one of the earliest known full-length portraits. Beyond these is a collection of **Dürers** and **Cranachs** to rival that in the Prado, and as you progress through this extraordinary panoply, display cases along the corridor contain scarcely less spectacular works of sculpture, ceramics and gold- and silverwork.

Next in line are **Titian** and **Tintoretto**, and three paintings by **El Greco**, one early, two late, which make an interesting comparison with each other and with those in the Prado. **Caravaggio**'s monumental *St Catherine of Alexandria* is the centrepiece of an important display of works by followers of this innovator of chiaroscuro. And finally, as you reach the eighteenth century, there is a room containing three flawless **Canaletto** views of Venice.

Americans, impressionists and expressionists: the first floor

The present baron, Hans Heinrich Thyssen, began collecting, according to his own account, to fill the gaps in his late father's collection, after it was split among his siblings. He, too, started with old masters – his father thought nineteenth- and twentieth-century art was worthless – but in the 1960s started on German Expressionists, closely followed by Cubists, Futurists, Vorticists and De Stijl, and also American art of the nineteenth century. The first floor, then, is largely down to him.

After a comprehensive round of seventeenth-century Dutch painting of various genres, Rococo and Neoclassicism, you reach the **American painting** in Rooms 29 and 30. The collection, one of the best outside the US, concentrates on landscapes and includes James Goodwyn Clonney's wonderful *Fishing Party on Long Island Sound*, and works by James Whistler, Winslow Homer and John Singer Sargent. It is followed by a group of European **Romantics and Realists**, including Constable's *The Lock*, bought not so long ago for £10.8 million, forming one of a group of British representatives at the museum, along with a Henry Moore (Room 45) and a Sisley (Room 32).

Impressionism and post-**Impressionism** is another strong point of the collection – with works by Manet, Monet and Renoir from the former and Gauguin, Degas, Lautrec and Cézanne from the latter (Room 33) – and is especially strong in the choice of paintings by Vincent van Gogh, which include one of his last and most gorgeous works, *Les Vessenots*. **Expressionist** representatives, meanwhile, include an unusually pastoral Edvard Munch, *Evening* (Room 35), Egon Schiele's Mondrian-like *Houses on the River*, and some stunning work by Ernst Ludwig Kirchner, Wassily Kandinsky and Max Beckmann.

Avant-gardes: the ground floor

Works on the ground floor run from the beginning of the twentieth century through to around 1970. The good baron doesn't, apparently, like contemporary art: "If they can throw colours, I can be free to duck," he explained, following the gallery's opening.

The most interesting work in his "experimental avant-garde" sections is from the **Cubists**. There is an inspired, side-by-side hanging of parallel studies by Picasso (*Man with a Clarinet*), Braque and Mondrian (Room 41). Later choices – a scattering of Joan Miró, Jackson Pollock, Magritte and Dalí, Rauschenberg and Liechtenstein – do less justice to their artists and movements, though there is a great work by Edward Hopper, *Hotel Room*, and a fascinating **Lucian Freud**, *Portrait of Baron Thyssen*, posed in front of the Watteau *Pierrot* hanging upstairs.

Centro de Arte Reina Sofía

It is fortunate that the **Centro de Arte Reina Sofía** (Metro Atocha; Mon & Wed–Sat 10am–9pm, Sun 10am–2.30pm; 500ptas, free on Sat after 2.30pm and Sun), facing Atocha station at the end of Paseo del Prado, keeps slightly different opening hours and days to its neighbours. For this leading exhibition space and permanent gallery of modern Spanish art – its centrepiece is Picasso's greatest picture, *Guernica* – is another essential stop on the Madrid art circuit, and one that really mustn't be seen after a Prado-Thyssen overdose. There are audio-guide headphones in English for those who need a good introduction to Spanish art, by the second-floor entrance.

The museum, a vast former hospital, is a kind of Madrid response to the Pompidou centre in Paris. Transparent lifts shuttle visitors up the outside of the building, whose levels feature a cinema, excellent art book and design shops, a print, music and photographic library, a restaurant, bar and café in the basement and a peaceful inner courtyard garden, as well as the exhibition halls and the permanent collection of twentieth-century art (second and fourth floors).

The permanent collection

It is for **Picasso's Guernica** that most visitors come to the Reina Sofía, and rightly so. Superbly displayed, this icon of twentieth-century Spanish art and politics carries a shock that defies all familiarity. Picasso painted it in response to the bombing of the Basque town of Guernika by the German Luftwaffe, acting in concert with Franco, in the Spanish Civil War. In the preliminary studies, displayed around the room, you can see how he developed its symbols – the dying horse, the woman mourning her dead, the bull, the sun, the flower, the light bulb – and then return to the painting to marvel at how he made it all work.

The work was first exhibited in Paris in 1937, as part of a Spanish Republican Pavilion in the Expo there, and was then loaned to the Museum of Modern Art in New York, until, as Picasso put it, Spain had rid itself of fascist rule. The artist never lived to see that time but in 1981, following the restoration of democracy, the painting was, amid much controversy, moved to Madrid to hang (as Picasso had stipulated) in the Prado. Its recent transfer to the Reina Sofía in 1992, again prompted much soul-searching and protest, though for anyone who saw it in the old Prado annexe, it looks truly liberated in its present setting.

Guernica hangs midway around the permanent collection on the second floor, although Picasso himself is actually a starting point: symbolically, no painter represented here was born before Picasso (in 1881). It is preceded by strong sections on **Cubism** and the **Paris School**, in the first of which Picasso is again well represented, alongside an intriguing straight Cubist work by Salvador Dalí. There are also good collections of other avant-garde Spaniards of the 1920s and 1930s, including Juan Gris.

In the post-*Guernica* halls, **Dalí's** more familiar surrealism seems trite and **Miró** less engaging than usual. The final rooms are stimulating: entitled **"Proposals"**, they comprise an evolving display of contemporary art, both Spanish and foreign.

The Spanish realists, such as **Antonio López**, are on the fourth floor, where you will find a **Francis Bacon** and a **Henry Moore**, along with interesting works by **Tapiès** and **Chillida**.

Parque del Retiro and around

When you get tired of sightseeing, Madrid's many parks are great places to escape for a few hours. The most central and most popular of them is **El Retiro**, a delightful mix of formal gardens and wider open spaces. Around it, in addition to the Prado, Thyssen-Bornemisza and Reina Sofía galleries, are a number of the city's **smaller museums**, plus the startlingly peaceful **Jardines Botánicos**.

Parque del Retiro

Originally the grounds of a royal retreat (*retiro*) and designed in the French style, the **Parque del Retiro** (Metro Retiro) has been public property for more than a hundred

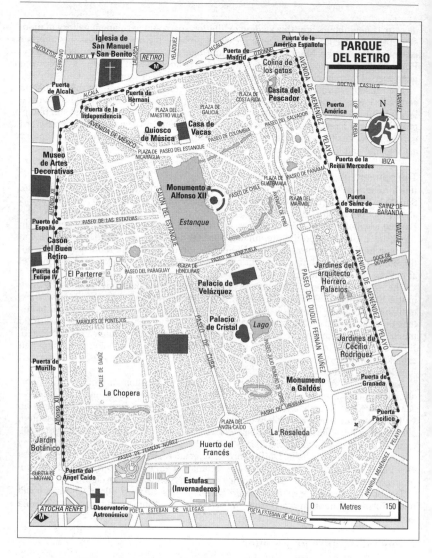

years. In its 330 acres you can jog (there is a council-sponsored track), row in the lake of **El Estanque** (you can rent boats by the Monumento a Alfonso XII), picnic (though not on the grass), have your fortune told, and – above all – promenade. The busiest day is Sunday, when half of Madrid, spouses, in-laws and kids, turn out for the *paseo*. Dressed for show, the families stroll around among the various activities, nodding at neighbours and building up an appetite for a long Sunday lunch.

Strolling aside, there's almost always something going on in the park, including a good programme of **concerts** and **ferias** organized by the city council. Concerts tend to be held in the Quiosco de Música in the north of the park. The most popular of the fairs is the *Feria del Libro* (Book Fair), held in early June, when every publisher and half the country's bookshops set up stalls and offer a 25 percent discount on their wares. At weekends there are **puppet shows** by the Puerta de Alcalá entrance (1pm, 7pm & 8pm) and on Sundays, you can often watch groups of Peruvian musicians or Catalans performing their counting-dance, the **sardana**.

Travelling art exhibitions are frequently housed in the beautiful **Palacio de Velázquez** (June–Sept Mon & Wed–Sat 11am–8pm, Sun 11am–6pm; Oct–May Mon & Wed–Sat 10am–6pm, Sun 10am–4pm; free) and the nearby **Palacio de Cristal** (due to open soon after restoration; free) and **Casa de Vacas** (daily 10.30am–2.30pm & 4–8pm; closed Aug; free). Look out, too, for **El Ángel Caído** (Fallen Angel), the world's only public statue to Lucifer, in the south of the park. A number of **stalls and cafés** along the Salón del Estanque sell drinks, *bocadillos* and *pipas* (sunflower seeds), and there are terrazas, too, for *horchata* and *granizados*. The park has a safe reputation, at least by day; in the late evening it's best not to wander alone. Note also that the area east of La Chopera is known as a cruising ground for gay prostitutes.

Puerta de Alcalá to San Jerónimo: some minor museums

Leaving the park at the northwest corner takes you to the Plaza de la Independencia, in the centre of which is one of the two remaining gates from the old city walls. Built in the late eighteenth century, the **Puerta de Alcalá** was the biggest in Europe at that time and, like the bear and bush, has become one of the city's monumental emblems.

South from here, you pass the **Museo de Artes Decorativas** (Metro Banco de España/Retiro; Tues–Fri 9.30am–3pm, Sat & Sun 10am–2pm; 400ptas, free on Sun), which has its entrance on c/Montalbán 12. The furniture and decorations here are not very thrilling but there are some superb *azulejos* and other decorative ceramics.

A couple of blocks west, in a corner of the Naval Ministry, at c/Montalbán 2, is a **Museo Naval** (Metro Banco de España; Tues–Sun 10.30am–1.30pm; free), strong, as you might expect, on models, charts and navigational aids from or relating to the Spanish voyages of discovery. The army has its museum, the **Museo del Ejército**, just to the south of here at c/Méndez Núñez 1 (Metro Retiro; Tues–Sun 10am–2pm; 100ptas, free on Sat). It is a traditional display, packed with arms and armour (including a sword of El Cid and *conquistador* breastplates), and models and memorabilia of various battles, from earliest times to the Civil War – in which Franco, here, remains the good guy.

South again, past the Prado's Casón del Buen Retiro annexe (part of the original Retiro palace, see p.81), is **San Jerónimo el Real**, Madrid's society church, where in 1975 Juan Carlos (like his predecessors) was crowned. Opposite is the **Real Academia Española de la Lengua** (Royal Language Academy), whose job it is to make sure that the Spanish language is not corrupted by foreign or otherwise unsuitable words; the results are entrusted to their official dictionary – a work that bears virtually no relation to the Spanish you'll hear spoken on the streets.

The botanical gardens and Atocha

Immediately south of the Prado are the delightful, shaded **Jardines Botánicos** (daily 10am–dusk; 200ptas). Opened in 1781 by Carlos III (known as *El Alcalde* – "the mayor" – for his urban improvement programmes), they once contained over 30,000 plants. The numbers are down these days, though the gardens were well renovated in the 1980s, after years of neglect, and the worldwide collection of flora is fascinating for any amateur botanist; don't miss the hothouse with its tropical collection and amazing cacti. Under an edict issued when the gardens were opened, *madrileños* are still theoretically entitled to help themselves to cuttings of any plant or medicinal herb.

On the other side of the botanical gardens is the sloping Cuesta de Moyano, lined with **bookstalls**. You can buy anything here, new or old, from secondhand copies of

Captain Marvel to Cervantes or Jackie Collins. There's always something of interest, often quite a selection of dog-eared paperbacks in English, and usually one or two surprises. You'd be lucky to find anything valuable, but prices are low and it's a pleasant stroll. Though it's at its busiest on Sundays, some of the stalls are open every day.

Across the way – and worth a look even if you're not travelling out of Madrid – is the **Estación de Atocha**. It's actually two stations, old and new: the former, a glorious 1880s glasshouse, was recently revamped as a kind of tropical garden. It's a wonderful sight from the walkways above, and train buffs will want to take a look at the high-speed AVE trains (Sevilla in two and a half hours) on the stations beyond.

Also in this area, the **Real Fábrica de Tapices** at c/Fuenterrabia 2 (Metro Menéndez Pelayo; Mon–Fri 9am–12.30pm; closed Aug; 250ptas) still turns out handmade tapestries, many of them based on the Goya cartoons in the Prado. They are fabulously expensive, but the entrance fee is a bargain if you ask for a tour of the fascinating manufacturing process.

Lastly, to the south of this area is Parque Enrique Tierno Galván (Metro Méndez Alvaro), which houses the **Planetarium** (shows at Tues–Fri 5.30pm & 6.45pm, Sat & Sun at 11.30am, 12.45pm, 5.30pm & 6.45pm; 450ptas) – an impressive 170-metre dome containing sophisticated projectors to explain the stars – and the futuristic Imax cinema (see p.110).

The Gran Vía, Chueca and Malasaña

The **Gran Vía**, Madrid's great thoroughfare, runs from Plaza de Cibeles to Plaza de España, effectively dividing the old city to the south from the newer parts northwards. Permanently jammed with traffic and crowded with shoppers and sightseers, it's the commercial heart of the city, and – if you spare the time to look up – quite a monument in its own right, with its turn-of-the-century, palace-like banks and offices, and the huge hand-painted posters of the cinemas. Look out, too, for the Moorish-style **Telefónica** building, which was the chief observation post for the Republican artillery during the Civil War, when the Nationalist front line stretched across the Casa de Campo to the west. And don't miss a cocktail at the Art Deco **Museo Chicote** at Gran Vía 12 (see p.103).

North of the Telefónica, c/de Fuencarral heads north to the Glorieta de Bilbao. To either side of this street are two of Madrid's most characterful *barrios*: **Chueca**, to the east, and **Malasaña**, to the west. Their chief appeal lies in an amazing concentration of bars, restaurants and, especially, nightlife. However, there are a few reasons – bars included – to look around here by day.

Chueca

Plaza de Chueca (Metro Chueca) has teetered on the verge of infamy, due to its popularity with drug dealers and prostitutes. But if this sounds like a place to avoid at all costs, then you're not in key with Madrid: most of the addicts have been moved on and there is now a strong neighbourhood feel, with kids and grannies giving a semblance of innocence by day, and a lively gay scene springing into action at night. It is also fronted by one of the best old-style *vermut* bars in the city, *Bodega Ángel Sierra*, on c/Gravina at the northwest corner.

From Plaza de Chueca east to **Paseo Recoletos** (the beginning of the long Paseo de la Castellana) are some of the city's most enticing streets. Offbeat restaurants, small private art galleries, and odd corner shops are to be found here in abundance and the **c/Almirante** has some of the city's most fashionable clothes shops too. On the parallel c/de Prim, **ONCE**, the national association for the blind, has its headquarters. ONCE is financed by a lottery, for which the blind work as ticket-sellers, and many come here to collect their allocation of tickets. The lottery has become such a major money-spinner that the organization is now one of the wealthiest businesses in Spain; oddly, perhaps, it is also the sponsor of one of the world's top cycling teams.

To the south, the Ministry of Culture fronts the **Plaza del Rey**, which is also worth a look for the other odd buildings surrounding it, especially the **Casa de las Siete Chimeneas** (House of Seven Chimneys), which is supposedly haunted by a mistress of Felipe II who disappeared in mysterious circumstances.

To the north, on the edge of the Santa Bárbara *barrio*, on c/Fernando VI, is the **Sociedad de Autores** (Society of Authors), housed in the only significant *modernista* building in Madrid, designed by José Grasés Riera, part of the Gaudí school. Nearby, the **Museo Romántico**, at c/San Mateo 13 (Metro Tribunal; Tues–Sat 9am–3pm, Sun 10am–2pm; 400ptas, free on Sun), has its admirers for its late-Romantic era furnishings, though casual visitors are unlikely to be impressed. The **Museo Municipal** at c/Fuencarral 78 (Metro Tribunal; Tues–Fri 9.30am–8pm, Sat & Sun 10am–2pm; 300ptas, free on Wed & Sun) is more interesting for its models and maps of old Madrid, which show the incredible expansion of the city in this century. A good selection of reasonably priced prints, posters and books is available in the museum shop. The building itself has a superb Churrigueresque facade.

Malasaña

The heart, in all senses, of Malasaña is the **Plaza Dos de Mayo**, named after the insurrection against Napoleonic forces on May 2, 1808; the rebellion and its aftermath are depicted in a series of Goyas at the Prado. The surrounding district bears the name of one of the martyrs of the uprising, fifteen-year-old Manuela Malasaña, who is also commemorated in a street (as are several other heroes of the time). On the night of May 1 all of Madrid shuts down to honour its heroes, and the plaza is the scene of festivities lasting well into the night.

More recently, the quarter was the focus of the *movida madrileña*, the "happening scene" of the late 1970s and early 1980s. As the country relaxed after the death of Franco and the city developed into a thoroughly modern capital under the leadership of the late lamented mayor, Galván, Malasaña became the mecca of the young. Bars appeared behind every doorway, drugs were sold openly in the streets, and there was an extraordinary atmosphere of new-found freedom. Times have changed – and *chocolate* (dope) sellers are less tolerated by residents and police alike. A good deal of renovation has been going on in recent years, but the *barrio* retains a somewhat alternative feel, with its bar custom spilling on to the streets, and an ever-lively scene in the Plaza Dos de Mayo terrazas.

There are no regular sights in this quarter but the streets have an interest of their own and some fine traditional bars – *Casa Camacho* at c/San Andrés 2 is a great place for *vermut*. There are also some wonderful old shop signs and architectural details, best of all the **old pharmacy** on the corner of c/San Andrés and c/San Vicente Ferrer, with its irresistible 1920s *azulejo* scenes depicting cures for diarrhoea, headaches and suchlike.

Plaza de España, Parque del Oeste and Casa de Campo

The **Plaza de España** (Metro Plaza de España), at the west end of Gran Vía, was home, until the recent flurry of corporate building in the north of Madrid, to two of the city's tallest buildings – the **Torre de Madrid**, which has a top-storey bar, and the **Edificio de España**. These rather stylish 1950s buildings look over an elaborate monument to Cervantes in the middle of the square, which in turn overlooks the bewildered-looking bronze figures of Don Quixote and Sancho Panza.

The plaza itself is a rather seedy place, and something of a junky hangout. However, to its north, **c/Martín de los Heros** is a lively place, day and night, with three of the city's best cinemas, and behind them the **Centro Princesa**, with shops, clubs, bars and a 24-hour branch of the ubiquitous VIPS – just the place to have your film developed at 4am, or a bite to eat before heading on to a small-hours club.

A block to the west is the **Museo Cerralbo**, c/Ventura Rodríguez 17 (Metro Ventura Rodríguez; Tues–Sat 9.30am–2.30pm, July closes 2pm; Sun 10am–2pm; closed Aug; 400ptas, free on Wed & Sun), an elegant mansion endowed with its collections by the Marqués de Cerralbo. The rooms, stuffed with paintings, furniture, armour and artefacts, provide insights into the lifestyle of the nineteenth-century aristocracy, though there is little of individual note.

Parque del Oeste – and Goya's Ermita frescoes

The **Parque del Oeste** stretches northwest from the Plaza de España, following the railway tracks of Príncipe Pío up to the suburbs of Moncloa and Ciudad Universitaria (see below). On its south side, five minutes' walk from the square, is the **Templo de Debod**, a fourth-century BC Egyptian temple given to Spain in recognition of the work done by Spanish engineers on the Aswan High Dam (which inundated its original site). Reconstructed here stone by stone, it seems comically incongruous but provides a good concert venue nonetheless. In summer, there are numerous terrazas in the park, while, year-round, a **teleférico** (Metro Argüelles/Ventura Rodríguez; April–Sept daily 11am–2.30pm & 4.30pm–dusk; Oct–March Sat, Sun & holidays noon–2.30pm & 4.30pm–dusk; 360ptas single, 515ptas return) shuttles its passengers high over the river from Paseo del Pintor Rosales to the middle of the Casa de Campo (see below). It was built to rival Barcelona's but doesn't quite have the topography to match.

Rail lines from commuter towns to the north of Madrid terminate at the **Príncipe Pío** (Estación del Norte), a quietly spectacular construction of white enamel, steel and glass which enjoyed a starring role in Warren Beatty's film *Reds*. About 300m from the station along the Paseo de la Florida is the *Casa Mingo* restaurant (see "Restaurants"), an institution for chicken and cider take-outs for the Casa de Campo and, almost alongside it, at Glorieta de la Florida 5, the **Ermita de San Antonio de la Florida** (Metro Príncipe Pío; Tues–Fri 10am–2pm & 4–8pm, closed afternoons in July & Aug; Sat & Sun 10am–2pm; 300ptas, free on Wed & Sun). If you can, go on Saturdays, when there are guided tours in English three times a day. This little church on a Greek cross plan was built by an Italian, Felipe Fontana, between 1792 and 1798, and decorated by **Goya**, whose frescoes are the only reason to visit. In the dome is a depiction of a miracle performed by St Anthony of Padua. Around it, heavenly bodies of angels and cherubs hold back curtains to reveal the main scene: the saint resurrecting a dead man to give evidence in favour of a prisoner falsely accused of murder (the saint's father). Beyond this central group, Goya created a gallery of highly realist characters – their models were court and society figures – while for a lesser fresco of the angels adoring the Trinity in the apse, he took prostitutes as his models. The *ermita* also houses the artist's mausoleum.

Moncloa

The wealthy suburb of **Moncloa** contains the Spanish prime ministerial home and is worth a visit even if you are not using the bus terminal for El Pardo and El Escorial (see p.90). The metro will bring you out opposite the imposing Ministry of Defence building and the impressive Arco de la Victoria, marking Napoleon's exit from the capital. Beyond this lies the leafy expanses of the Parque del Oeste and the campuses of the **Ciudad Universitaria**. During term time, the end of each day sees the area become one big student party, with huddles of picnickers and singing groups under the trees. Take the Plaza de Moncloa metro exit and the path on your right through the trees will lead you to the **Mirador del Faro** (Tues–Sun 10.30am–1.45pm & 4.30–7.15pm; 200ptas), a futuristic 92-metre-high tower with stunning views over the city and to the mountains beyond. Just past this, with its main entrance on Avenida Reyes Católicos 6, the **Museo de América** (Tues–Sat 10am–3pm, Sun 10am–2.30pm; 400ptas, free on Sat after 2pm and Sun) contains a fine collection of ceramics, gold and silverware from Spain's former colonies in Latin America, and a feather shawl dating back to 2000 BC.

Casa de Campo

If you want to jog, play tennis, swim, picnic, go to the fairground, or see pandas, then the **Casa de Campo** is the place to head. This enormous expanse of heath and scrub is in parts surprisingly wild for a place so easily accessible from the city; other sections have been tamed for more conventional pastimes. Far larger and more natural than the city parks, the Casa de Campo can be reached by metro (Batán or Lago), various buses (#33 is the easiest), or the aforementioned cable car. The walk from the Príncipe Pío station via the Puente del Rey isn't too strenuous either.

Throughout the park there are picnic tables and café-bars, a **jogging track** with exercise posts, a municipal open-air **swimming pool** (daily June–Sept 10.30am–8pm; 500ptas) close to Metro Lago, tennis courts, and rowing boats to hire on the **lake** (again near Metro Lago).

Sightseeing attractions include a **Zoo** (daily 10am–dusk; 1560ptas), which is perennially popular and has an impressive aquarium. Adjoining it is a large and recently modernized amusement park, the **Parque de Atracciones** (July & Aug daily noon–midnight, Fri & Sat till 2am; Sept–June daily noon–11pm, Sat till 1am; access only 575ptas, 2200ptas for a day ticket which includes most rides), with its assorted restaurants and cafés; during the summer, a variety of **concerts** are held in the auditorium within. Both are easiest reached by bus (#33 from Príncipe Pío), which will take you right to the gates; the Batán metro station is a ten-minute walk through scrubland. Be warned that many of the **main access roads** through the park have been taken over by prostitutes (banished from the city streets by the council), and can become crowded with kerb-crawlers, both day and night.

Salamanca and the Paseo de la Castellana

Salamanca, the area north of the Parque del Retiro, is a smart address for apartments and, even more so, for shops. The *barrio* is the haunt of *pijos* – universally denigrated rich kids – and the grid of streets between c/de Goya and c/José Ortega y Gasset contain most of the city's designer emporiums. The buildings are largely modern and undistinguished, though there is a scattering of museums and galleries that might tempt you up here, in particular the Lázaro Galdiano, the pick of Madrid's smaller museums.

Taking the area from south to north, the first point of interest is **Plaza de Colón** (Metro Colón), endowed at street level with a statue of Columbus (Cristóbal Colón) and some huge stone blocks arranged as a megalithic monument to the discovery of the Americas. Below it is the 1970s **Centro Cultural Villa de Madrid**, which is still a good place for film and theatre and occasional exhibitions. Across the square, if your taste runs to tableaux of matadors being gored, or vain attempts to recognize Juan Carlos, there is diversion at Paseo de Recoletos 41 in the **Museo de Cera** (Metro Colón; daily 10.30am–2pm & 4–8.30pm; 900ptas), a pretty lamentable wax museum.

Off the square, too, with its entrance at c/Serrano 13, is the **Museo Arqueológico Nacional** (Metro Serrano; Tues–Sat 9.30am–8.30pm, Sun 9.30am–2.30pm; 500ptas, free Sat 2.30–8.30pm & Sun). As the national collection, this has some impressive pieces, among them the celebrated Celto-Iberian busts known as *La Dama de Elche* and *La Dama de Baza*, and a wonderfully rich hoard of Visigothic treasures found at Toledo. The exhibition, however, is very old-fashioned and rooms are often closed for somnolent rearrangement, sometimes at very short notice. In the gardens, downstairs to the left of the main entrance, is a reconstruction of the Altamira Caves, with their prehistoric wall paintings.

The **Museo Lázaro Galdiano** (Metro Nuñez de Balboa/Rubén Darío; Tues–Sun 10am–2pm; closed Aug; 400ptas, free Sat) is some way north at c/Serrano 122. This former private collection was given to the state by José Galdiano in 1948 and spreads over the four floors and 37 rooms of his former home. It is a vast jumble of art works, with some very dodgy attributions, but includes some really exquisite and valuable pieces. Among painters represented are Bosch (two works: one, *St John the Evangelist on Patmos*, is important, the other may not be genuine), Gerard David, Dürer (perhaps) and Rembrandt, as well as a host of Spanish artists, including Berruguete, Murillo, Zurbarán and Velázquez. El Greco – whose *Adoration of the Magi* was painted long before he arrived in Spain – and Goya are also particularly well represented. *The Saviour*, hidden away in a room of Renaissance sculpture on the ground floor, is a beautiful little picture once claimed by the museum to be a Leonardo da Vinci. Other exhibits include a collection of clocks and watches, many of them once owned by Carlos V.

Not far to the west of here, across the Paseo de la Castellana, is another enjoyable gallery, the **Museo Sorolla**, c/General Martínez Campos 37 (Metro Rubén Darío/Iglesia; Tues–Sat 10am–3pm, July & Aug closes 2.30pm; Sun 10am–2pm; 400ptas, free Sun). This is a large collection of work by the painter Joaquín Sorolla (1863–1923), displayed in his old home and studio. The best paintings are striking, impressionistic plays on light and texture, others just obsessively preoccupied with beaches, naked bodies, and their reflections and refractions in the water.

Farther north along the Paseo de la Castellana, you reach the **Zona Azca** (Metro Nuevos Ministerios/Santiago Bernabéu), Madrid's newest business quarter, with its tallest skyscraper – the 43-storey Torre Picasso (designed by Minori Yamasaki, who also designed New York's Manhattan Twin Towers) – and corporate headquarters. Just beyond it, and easily the most famous sight up here, is the magnificent **Santiago Bernabéu** football stadium, home of Real Madrid.

El Pardo

Franco had his principal residence at **EL PARDO**, a former royal hunting ground, 9km northwest of central Madrid. A garrison still remains at the town – where most of the Generalísimo's staff were based – but the stigma of the place has lessened over the years, and it is now a popular excursion for *madrileños*, who come here for long lunches in the terraza restaurants, or to play tennis or swim at one of the nearby sports centres.

The tourist focus is the **Palacio del Pardo** (April–Sept Mon–Sat 10.30am–6pm, Sun 9.30am–1.30pm; Oct–March Mon–Sat 10.30am–5pm, Sun 9.30–1.30pm, closed occasionally for official visits; guided tours 650ptas, free Wed for EU citizens), rebuilt by the Bourbons on the site of a hunting lodge of Carlos V. The interior is pleasant enough, with its chapel and theatre, a portrait of Isabel la Católica by her court painter Juan de Flandes, and an excellent collection of tapestries, many after the Goya cartoons in the Prado. Guides detail the uses Franco made of the *palacio*, but pass over some of his stranger habits. He kept by his bed, for instance, the mummified hand of Santa Teresa of Ávila. Tickets to the palace are also valid for the **Casita del Príncipe**, though this cannot be entered from the gardens and you will need to return to the main road. Like the *casitas* (pavilions) at El Escorial, this was built by Juan de Villanueva, and is highly ornate.

You can reach El Pardo by local **bus** (every fifteen minutes until midnight from the bus terminal at Metro Moncloa), or by any city **taxi**.

Restaurants and tapas bars

The sections below review Madrid's best places for **eating and drinking**, essentially in conjunction with each other. They don't include out-and-out bars, where *madrileños* go later in the evening to drink, dance, listen to music, and, of course, to be seen; those follow in the next section, on nightlife.

Entries here include bars, *cafés*, *cervecerías* (beer halls), *marisquerías* (seafood bars) and *restaurantes* but have been divided simply between **"tapas bars"** and **"restaurants"**, depending on whether they concentrate more on bar food or sit-down meals. Sometimes this division is arbitrary, as many places have a bar area, where you can get *tapas*, together with a more formal *comedor* (canteen) or restaurant out the back or upstairs. At almost any of our recommendations you could happily eat your fill – money permitting – though at bars *madrileños* usually eat just a *tapa* or share a *ración* of the house speciality, then move on to repeat the procedure down the road.

Hours

The hours for having **cañas y copas** (drinks and *tapas*) are from around noon to 2pm, and 7pm to 10pm, though most bars will do you a snack at any hour of the day, and they generally stay open till midnight or beyond. Summer hours are generally later than winter, and Sundays are early to bed.

Restaurant meals (*comidas*) are taken very late: few *madrileños* will start lunch before 2pm or dinner much before 10pm, and if you turn up much earlier you may find yourself alone, or the restaurant (in the evening) not yet open. On the other hand, most people do arrive for dinner by 10.30pm; Madrid being Madrid, though, there are quite a number of late-night options and the listings magazines all have sections for restaurants open past midnight (*después de media noche/de madrugada*). Many restaurants close on Sundays and/or Mondays and for all or part of July and August.

Cuisines

Madrid's restaurants and bars offer every regional style of **Spanish cooking**: Castilian for roasts (*horno de asar* is a wood-burning oven) and stews (such as the meat and chickpea *cocido*), *gallego* for seafood, *andaluz* for fried fish, Levantine (Valencia/Alicante) for paella and other rice (*arroz*) based dishes, Asturian for winter stews like *fabada* and Basque for the ultimate gastronomy (and correspondingly high prices).

Over the last few years, dozens of **foreign cuisines** have appeared. There are some good Peruvian, Argentinian and Italian places and a scattering of enjoyable Indonesian and Japanese restaurants. With a few honourable exceptions, though, Indian and Chinese restaurants are fairly dire, as too, alas, are most of the Mexican and Brazilian ones.

RESTAURANT PRICES IN MADRID

We have graded **restaurants** as inexpensive (under 2000ptas a head for a meal and wine), moderate (2000–3500ptas) and expensive (over 3500ptas). You can of course pay very different amounts at any restaurant (or indeed *tapas* bar), depending on what you order and when: fish and seafood generally boost the bill, while a set lunchtime *menú del día* is often amazingly cheap (from as little as 800ptas for three courses).

Most – but by no means all – of the restaurants listed as "moderate" or "expensive" will accept **credit/charge cards** (*tarjetas*). If in doubt, phone ahead to check.

Sol, Plaza Mayor and Opera

The central area is the most varied in Madrid in terms of price and choice of food. Indeed, there can be few places in the world which rival the streets around Puerta del **Sol** for sheer number of places to eat and drink. Around the smarter **Opera** district, you need to be more selective, while on **Plaza Mayor** itself, stick to drinks. Unless we indicate otherwise, all these places are easily reached from **Metro Sol**.

Tapas bars

Las Bravas, c/Espoz y Mina 13. As the name suggests, *patatas bravas* (spicy potatoes) are the *tapa* to try at this bar, just south of Puerta del Sol; the *tortilla* is tasty, too. On the outside of the bar are novelty mirrors, a hangover from the days when this was a barber's and the subject of a story by Valle Inclán. You'll find other branches nearby at c/Alvarez Gato 3 and Pasaje Mathéu 5. Inexpensive for food and beer.

Casa del Abuelo, c/de la Victoria 12. Tiny, highly atmospheric bar serving just their sweet, rich red house wine and cooked prawns – try them *al ajilo* (in garlic) or *a la plancha* (fried).

Casa del Labra, c/de Tetuán 12 – opposite El Corte Inglés. Order a drink at the bar and a *ración* of cod fried in batter (*bacalao*) at the counter to the right of the door (see also "Restaurants", below).

La Gaditana, c/Cádiz 10. A sign outside claims this is the world's largest bar, as you "enter in Cádiz and leave in Barcelona": true enough, as it's at the corner of the two streets. The speciality is fried fish, Andaluz style.

Lhardy, Carrera de San Jerónimo 8 (☎91 521 33 85). *Lhardy* is one of Madrid's most famous and expensive restaurants. Once the haunt of royalty, it's a beautiful place but greatly overpriced. Downstairs, however, there's a wonderful bar, where you can snack on canapés, *fino* (dry sherry) and *consommé*, without breaking the bank.

Mejillonera El Pasaje, Pasaje Matheu. Mussels (*mejillones*) served in every way conceivable at one of many bars on this pedestrian-only alleyway between c/Espoz y Mina and c/de la Victoria, south of Puerta del Sol.

Mesón del Champiñones and **Mesón de la Tortilla**, Cava de San Miguel 17 & 15. These are two of the oldest *tabernas* in Madrid, just down the steps at the southwest corner of Plaza Mayor. They specialize, as you'd imagine, in mushrooms and *tortilla*, respectively. At weekends, both places come alive as people gather to sample the excellent wines and *sangría*.

Mesón Real c/Vergara 12 – just south of the Teatro Real (Metro Opera). Old-fashioned *taberna* with reasonably priced *tapas*.

Museo del Jamón, Carrera de San Jerónimo 6. The largest branch of this Madrid chain, from whose ceilings are suspended hundreds of *jamones* (hams). The best – and they are not cheap – are the *jabugos* from the Sierra Morena, though a ham croissant will set you back under 200ptas.

La Oreja de Oro, c/de la Victoria. Standing room only in this bar just opposite *La Casa del Abuelo*. Try the excellent *pulpo a la Gallega* (sliced octopus served on a bed of potatoes fried in olive oil and seasoned with cayenne pepper) washed down with Ribeiro wine served in terracotta bowls. Plenty of other seafood tapas on offer too. Closed Aug.

El Oso y El Madroño, c/de la Bolsa 4. A tiny *castizo* (traditional *madrileño*) bar where you can have a drink to the accompaniment of the *madrileño chotis* and chat to the barmen who seem to have been there forever. Specialities are *cocido*, snails, *sangría* and *jerez* (sherry).

Restaurants

El Abuelo, c/Núñez de Arce 3. There's a *comedor* at the back of this spit-and-sawdust bar, where you can order a selection of delicious and inexpensive *raciones* and a jug of house wine. Inexpensive.

El Botín, c/Cuchilleros 17 (☎91 366 42 17; Metro Sol/Tirso de Molina). One of the city's oldest restaurants, established in 1725, highly picturesque, and favoured by Hemingway. Inevitably, it's a tourist haunt but not such a bad one, with creditable if not tremendously inspired roasts – especially suckling pig (*cochinillo*) and lamb (*lechal*). The *menú* is 4000ptas but you could eat for less. Expensive.

Casa Ciriaco, c/Mayor 84 (☎91 548 50 66; Metro Opera). Attractive, old-style *taberna*, long reputed for traditional Castilian dishes – trout, chicken and so on, served up in old-style portions. The *menú* is 2100ptas; main *carta* dishes a bit less. Closed Wed & Aug. Moderate.

Casa Gallega, c/Bordadores 11 (☎91 541 90 55; Metro Opera/Sol). An airy and welcoming *marisquería* that has been importing seafood on overnight trains from Galicia since it opened in 1915. Costs vary greatly according to the rarity of the fish or shellfish that you order. *Gallego* staples such as *pulpo* (octopus) and *pimientos de Padrón* (tiny, randomly piquant peppers) are brilliantly done and inexpensive but the more exotic seasonal delights will raise a bill for two well into five figures. Another branch at Plaza San Miguel (☎91 547 30 55). Expensive.

Casa del Labra, c/de Tetuán 12 (☎91 531 00 81). A great, traditional place where the Spanish Socialist Party was founded, which retains much of its original 1869 interior. The restaurant is through the bar on the right: an old panelled room, with classic *madrileña* food. Moderate to expensive.

Casa Santa Cruz, c/de la Bolsa 12 (☎91 521 86 23). Formerly a hermitage and later the Stock Exchange, this beautiful place is not remotely cheap but the food has the same top quality as the decor. Expensive.

Pozo Real, c/del Pozo 6 (☎91 521 79 51). A bit of a businessman's haunt, but good for bargain *menú del día*, in a lovely old building. Moderate to expensive.

Taberna del Alabardero, c/Felipe V 6 (☎91 547 25 77; Metro Opera). A fine *taberna* in one of the nicest streets in this area, just behind the Plaza de Oriente. The cooking is Basque and, considering this, prices are relatively low, with a *menú del día* at 1100ptas. Inexpensive to moderate.

Around Santa Ana and Huertas

You should spend at least an evening eating and drinking at the historic, tiled bars in this central area. Restaurants are good, too, and frequented as much by locals as tourists.

Tapas bars

La Costa de Vejer, corner of c/Núñez de Arce & c/Alvarez del Gato (Metro Sol). The speciality here are prawns (*gambas*), grilled with garlic, which are an absolute must.

España Cañi, Plaza del Ángel 14 (Metro Sol). An attractive tiled exterior fronts this very relaxing bar with a fine selection of *tapas*; a great place to soak up flamenco sounds and the house *sangría*.

El Lacón, c/Manuel Fernández y González 8 (Metro Sol). Large Galician bar-restaurant with plenty of seats upstairs. Great *pulpo, caldo gallego* (meat and vegetable broth) and *empanadas* (pastry slices filled with tuna and vegetables). Closed Aug.

La Moderna, Plaza de Santa Ana 12 (Metro Sol). More popular with Spaniards than tourists, so better value than the *cervecerías* next door and always humming with activity at night.

La Taberna de Dolores, Plaza de Jesús 4 (Metro Antón Martín). Splendid canapés at this popular and friendly tiled bar at the bottom of Huertas. The beer is really good, and the food specialities include roquefort and anchovy, and smoked-salmon canapés. Get here early if you want a space at the bar.

La Trucha, c/Manuel Fernández y González 3 (Metro Antón Martín). If you're not going to end up at the restaurant here (see below), at least call in for a *tapa* at the bar. Smoked fish and *pimientos de Padrón* are specialities. Usually very crowded. Closed Sun.

Viña P, Plaza de Santa Ana 3 (Metro Sol). Very friendly staff serving a great range of *tapas* in a bar decked out with bullfighting mementos and posters. Try the asparagus, stuffed mussels and the mouthwatering *almejas a la marinera* (clams in a garlic and white wine sauce).

Restaurants

Asturias, c/Álvarez del Gato 5 (☎91 532 07 84; Metro Sol). With hams behind the bar and animal heads on the wall, you would expect the good meat dishes, but the fish is excellent too, as is the *tapas*. Inexpensive to moderate.

Casa Alberto, c/Huertas 18 (☎91 429 93 56; Metro Antón Martín). Traditional *taberna* with a zinc bar and a small dining room at the back. Closed Sun night & Mon. Moderate to expensive.

MADRID'S VEGETARIAN RESTAURANTS

Madrid can be an intimidating city for veggies, given the mass of ham, fish and seafood on display in bar and restaurant windows and on counters. However, you can order vegetables separately at just about any restaurant in the city – Argentine steakhouses, perhaps, excepted – and there is good pizza and pasta to be had at a number of Italian places. You can even find the odd vegetarian paella.

More crucially, the capital now has half a dozen decent and inexpensive **vegetarian restaurants**, scattered about the centre. These include:

Artemisa, c/Ventura de la Vega 4 (☎91 429 50 92; Metro Sevilla). A popular place (you may have to wait for a table), best for its veggie pizzas and an imaginative range of salads. No smoking – even more of a novelty than veggie food in Madrid. Closed Sun night. Moderate.

El Estragón, Plaza de La Paja 10 (☎91 365 89 82; Metro La Latina). Good vegetarian *tapas*, leek pie and chocolate cake. Economical *menú del día* at 1000ptas and a fine setting on the edge of this ancient plaza. Inexpensive to moderate.

El Granero de Lavapiés, c/Argumosa 10 (☎91 467 76 11; Metro Lavapiés). Excellent macrobiotic and vegetarian fare in a very

pleasant Latina street. Open Mon–Fri 1–4pm only. Closed Aug. Inexpensive.

La Granja, c/de San Andrés 11 (☎91 532 87 93; Metro Bilbao/Tribunal). Good-value set menu that changes every day, offering a choice of soup, salad, a main dish of vegetables, rice and fruits topped with sauce, dessert and drinks. Open Mon–Wed 1.30–4.30pm & 9pm–midnight, Thurs–Sun 1.30–4.30pm. Inexpensive.

Vegetariano, c/Marqués de Santa Ana 34 (☎91 532 09 27; Metro Tribunal). Excellent salads and Mediterranean vegetables. No smoking. Closed Sun night & Mon. Inexpensive.

Domine Cabra, c/Huertas 54 (☎91 429 43 65; Metro Antón Martín). Interesting mix of traditional and modern, with *madrileña* standards given the *nueva cocina* treatment. Closed Sun night. Moderate.

Donzoko, c/Echegaray 3 (☎91 429 57 20; Metro Sevilla). Very reasonable value Japanese restaurant with decent *sushi* and delicious *tempura*. Closed Sun. Moderate.

La Farfalla, c/Santa María 17 (☎91 369 46 91; Metro Antón Martín). The place to go for late-night food and a lively party atmosphere in the Huertas area. Good range of tasty pizzas and Argentinian-style meat. Open till 4am at weekends. Inexpensive.

El Inti de Oro, c/Ventura de la Vega 12 (☎91 429 67 03; Metro Sevilla). An ideal introduction to Peruvian cuisine. Try the *cebiche de merluza* (a refreshing raw fish salad) and the *aji de gallina* (chicken in walnut sauce); the local liqueurs are worth sampling too. Moderate.

Lerranz, c/Echegaray 26 (☎91 429 12 06; Metro Sevilla). Designerish touches to the decor and the food in this small bar/restaurant; the set menu is around 1000ptas. Moderate.

La Sanabresa, c/Amor de Diós 12 (☎91 429 03 38; Metro Antón Martín). A real local with a TV in one corner and an endless supply of customers who come for its excellent and reasonably priced dishes. Don't miss the grilled aubergines. Closed Sun. Inexpensive.

La Trucha, c/Manuel Fernández y González 3 – off c/Echegaray (☎91 429 58 33; Metro Antón Martín). This is a treat: call in to reserve a table while you have drinks at nearby *Los Gabrieles* and *La Venencia*, then fight your way through the bar to a half dozen tables at the back (or in the basement). Highlights include the *plato de verbena* (salmon and caviar canapés) and *fritura variada* (a huge platter of fried fish); decline the house wine and order a bottle instead. Moderate.

Gran Vía and Plaza de España

On the **Gran Vía**, burger bars fill most of the gaps between shops and cinemas. However, head a few blocks in and there's plenty on offer, including a good cluster of ethnic restaurants on c/San Bernardino (north of the Plaza de España).

Tapas bars

Bar La Mina, c/Martín de los Heros 27 (Metro Plaza de España). Pleasant bar with a range of *tapas* and *bocadillos*.

Stop Madrid, c/Hortaleza 11 (Metro Gran Vía). An old-time spit-and-sawdust bar, revitalized, with Belgian beers as well as *vermut* on tap; *tapas* are largely *jamón* and *chorizo*.

Restaurants

Adrish, c/San Bernardino 1 (☎91 542 94 98; Metro Plaza de España). One of the city's better Indian restaurants, nicely decorated and with a vast selection of dishes. The cooking is mild, so if you like your curries hot, let the waiter know. Closed Sun. Moderate.

Bali, c/San Bernardino 6 (☎91 541 91 22; Metro Plaza de España). Indonesian food; the speciality is the all-encompassing *rijsttafel*. Closed Sun night. Moderate.

El Buey, Plaza de la Marina Española 1 (☎91 541 30 41; Metro Santo Domingo). A meat-eaters' paradise specializing in steak which you fry up yourself on a hotplate. Very good side dishes, including a great leek and seafood pie and excellent homemade desserts. Moderate.

Las Dos Castillas, c/Caballero de Gracia 10 (☎91 522 18 15; Metro Gran Vía). Informal restaurant and bar with tasty Castilian classics. Inexpensive.

Nova Galicia, c/de Conde Duque 3 (☎91 559 42 60; Metro Plaza de España) Excellent-value Galician restaurant specializing in seafood *tapas* and *arroz con bogavante* (rice with lobster). Pass through the ordinary-looking front bar and into the dining room hidden behind. Closed second half of Aug. Moderate.

Paellería Valenciana, c/Caballero de Gracia 12 (☎91 531 17 85; Metro Gran Vía). Serves large Valencian-style paella, open lunchtimes only. Moderate.

La Latina and Lavapiés: the Rastro area

South from Sol and Huertas are the quarters of **La Latina** and **Lavapiés** whose tiny streets retain an appealing neighbourhood feel, and have a great selection of bars and restaurants.

Tapas bars

Almacén de Vinos, c/Calatrava 21 (Metro La Latina). A neighbourhood *tapas* bar in the best tradition. Well worth a call.

El Almendro, c/del Almendro 27 (Metro La Latina). On the corner of the Plaza de San Andrés, this is just the place for highly original seated *tapas*. Imaginatively presented and very tasty.

Almendro 13, c/del Almendro 13 (Metro La Latina). Fashionable wooden-panelled bar that serves great *fino* from chilled black bottles. Tuck into the original *tapas* of *huevos rotos* (fried eggs on a bed of crisps) and *roscas rellenas* (rings of bread stuffed with various meats).

Barranco, San Isidro Labrador 14 (Metro La Latina). Come here for *gambas* after a trek around the Rastro. Very popular.

Los Caracoles, Plaza Cascorro 18 (Metro La Latina). A favourite since the 1940s, this does a good range of *tapas* as well as its namesake *caracoles* (snails).

Cervecería el Doblete, Costanilla de San Andrés 10, just alongside Plaza de la Paja (Metro La Latina). Trendy bar, open late night, with nice canapés.

Taberna de Antonio Sánchez, c/Mesón de Paredes 13 (☎91 539 78 26; Metro Tirso de Molina). Seventeenth-century bar – said to be the oldest *taberna* in Madrid – decorated with a wooden interior and a stuffed bull's head (one of which killed Antonio Sánchez, the son of the founder). Lots of *finos* on offer, plus *jamón* and *queso tapas* or *tortilla de San Isidro* (with salted cod). Closed Sun night.

Restaurants

La Cacharrería, c/Morería 9 (☎91 365 39 30; Metro La Latina). Argentine restaurant – which means vast steaks and huge plates of chops, all expertly grilled. Order a salad to start as veggies aren't exactly abundant. Closed Sun & Aug. Moderate.

El Economico, c/Argumosa (Metro Lavapiés). Traditional workmen's *comedor* with an unbeatable 800ptas lunchtime *menú*. Inexpensive.

El Frontón, c/Tirso de Molina 7, 1º – entrance just off the square (Metro Tirso de Molina). Old, charming neighbourhood restaurant, where publishers and the like settle down for a long afternoon's lunch. Wide range of classic Castilian dishes – all delicious. Moderate.

El Juglar, c/Lavapíes 37 (Metro Lavapíes). An understandable favourite for locals who tuck in to hearty Spanish staples. Inexpensive.

Casa Lucio, c/Cava Baja 35 (☎91 365 32 52; Metro La Latina). *Madrileños* come here for the expected: classic Castilian dishes such as *cocido*, *callos* (tripe) and roasts, cooked to perfection. Prices have gone up a bit since the king visited but you can still eat well for under 4000ptas, if you're careful. Booking is essential. Closed Sat lunch & Aug. Expensive.

Posada de la Villa, c/Cava Baja 9 (☎91 366 18 60; Metro La Latina). The most attractive-looking restaurant in Latina, spread over three floors of a seventeenth-century mansion. Cooking is typically *madrileña*, including superb roast lamb. Reckon on a good 7000ptas per person for the works – though you could get away with less. Closed Sun night & Aug. Expensive.

El Schotis, c/Cava Baja 11 (☎91 365 32 30; Metro La Latina). Long-established *tasca* with an old-style bar up front. As at other places on this street, cooking is typically Castilian, with lots of red meat and roasts, but there's also fish and seafood. Closed Sun night & Aug. Moderate to expensive.

Viuda de Vacas, c/Cava Alta 23 (☎91 366 58 47; Metro La Latina). Highly traditional restaurant with quality Castilian fare. Closed Tues. Inexpensive to moderate.

Chueca and Santa Bárbara

Chueca – and **Santa Bárbara** to its north – have some superb traditional old bars and bright new restaurants, and a vast amount of nightlife. The southern part of Chueca, however, around the metro station, and south to Gran Vía, is also quite a big drug area, which can leave you feeling a little uneasy after dark.

Tapas bars

Cervecería Santa Bárbara, Plaza Santa Bárbara 8 (Metro Alonso Martínez). Popular meeting place in this part of town, with *cañas* and prawns to keep you going.

Santander, c/de Augusto Figueroa 25 (Metro Chueca). It's worth a visit to this bar in the heart of Chueca for the good range of *tapas*, including *empanadas*, *tortillas* and quiche lorraine, as well as a huge variety of fresh homemade canapés at reasonable prices. Closed Aug.

Taberna Ángel Sierra, c/Gravina 11, on Plaza Chueca (Metro Chueca). One of the great bars of Madrid, with a traditional zinc counter, constantly washed down. Everyone drinks *vermut*, which is on tap and delicious, and free *tapas* of the most exquisite *boquerones en vinagre* are despatched (*raciones*, too, for the greedy – though they are expensive).

Restaurants

Al Hoceima, c/Farmacia 8 (☎91 531 94 11; Metro Tribunal). Elegant little Moroccan restaurant, with decent *couscous* and *tajines* (casseroles). Closed Mon. Moderate.

Annapurna, c/Zurbano 5 (☎91 319 87 16; Metro Colón). To say this is the best Indian restaurant in Madrid is faint praise – however, *Annapurna* could hold its own in London, especially if you go for the *tandoori* dishes or *thali*. Closed Sat night & Sun & hols. Moderate.

Carmencita, c/Libertad 16 (☎91 531 66 12; Metro Chueca). Beautiful old restaurant, dating back to 1830, with panelling, brass, marble tables – and a new Basque-influenced chef. Lunch *menú* is a bargain 1200ptas. Closed Sat night & Sun & hols. Inexpensive to moderate.

La Carreta, c/Barbieri 10 (☎91 532 70 42; Metro Chueca/Banco de España). Argentinian restaurant, heavy on steaks and red meat. From Wed to Sun there's a trio playing tango; on Tues you can learn to dance. Open daily to 5am. Moderate to expensive.

Casa Gades, c/Conde de Xiquena 4 (☎91 532 30 51; Metro Chueca/Banco de España). Very attractive restaurant in a fashionable area on the edge of Chueca, owned by the flamenco dancer Antonio Gades. Food is a mix of Spanish and Italian. Closed Sun night & Mon. Moderate.

El Comunista (Tienda de Vinos), c/Augusto Figueroa 35 – between Libertad and Barbieri (Metro Chueca). Long-established *comedor*; its unofficial (but always used) name dates back to its time as a student haunt under Franco. The garlic soup is recommended. Inexpensive.

Hard Rock Café, Paseo de la Castellana 2 (☎91 435 02 00; Metro Colón). Predictable American fast-food and loud music, but with a pleasant terrace which overlooks Plaza de Colón. Open daily until 1.30am. Inexpensive.

El 26 de Libertad, c/de la Libertad 26 (☎91 522 25 22; Metro Chueca). Imaginative cuisine served up in an attentive, but unfussy manner in this brightly decorated restaurant popular with the Chueca locals. Closed Sun evening in July & Aug. Moderate.

Momo, c/Augusto Figueroa 41 (☎91 532 71 62; Metro Chueca). Kitsch decor and creative cuisine at very reasonable prices – 1200ptas for the *menu del día* – in this restaurant in the heart of Chueca.

CAFÉ LIFE

Madrid has a number of cafés that are institutions. They serve food but are much more places to drink coffee, have a *copa* or *caña*, or read the papers. They're also a meeting place for the semi-formal *tertulia* – a kind of discussion/drinking group, popular among Madrid intellectuals of the past and revived in the 1980s. Many cafés also have summer – or all-year – terrazas (outside terraces), though be aware that sitting outside puts up the prices. Other cafés and *pastelerias* are simpler affairs, good places to grab a breakfast croissant or a teatime snack. Good choices include:

Café los Austrias, Plaza de Ramales (Metro Opera). Relaxing café with marble table-tops and dark wood interior; a good stop after a visit to the Palacio Real.

Café Barbieri, c/de Ave María 45 (Metro Lavapiés). Well-known café with a vaguely intellectual reputation. It's a relaxed place with unobtrusive music, lots of wooden tables, old-style decor, newspapers, and a wide selection of coffees.

Café El Botánico, c/Espalter/Plaza Murillo (Metro Atocha). A quiet place to sit with a drink, opposite the south entrance of the Prado.

Café Central, Plaza del Ángel 10 (Metro Sol). A jazz club by night but a regular café by day, again with newspapers supplied.

Café Comercial, Glorieta de Bilbao (Metro Bilbao). One of the city's most popular meeting points – a lovely traditional café, well poised for the Chueca/Santa Bárbara area.

Café del Espejo, Paseo de Recoletos 31 (Metro Colón). Opened in 1991 but you wouldn't guess it – mirrors, gilt, and a wonderful glass pavilion, plus a leafy outside terraza.

Café Gijón, Paseo de Recoletos 21 (Metro Banco de España). Famous literary café – and a centre of the intellectual/arty *movida* in the 1980s – decked out in Cuban mahogany and mirrors. Has a summer terraza.

Café Manuela Malasaña, c/San Vicente Ferrer 29 (Metro Tribunal). Wonderful mirrors and fittings and a very civilized atmosphere, with live piano music and *tertulias*, in different languages, most nights.

Café de Oriente, Plaza de Oriente 2 (Metro Opera). Elegant, traditional-style café founded a decade or so ago by a priest, as part of a charity rehab programme for ex-convicts. Has a popular terraza.

Círculo de Bellas Artes, c/de Alcalá 42 (Metro Banco de España). Day membership to the Círculo is 100ptas, which gives you access to exhibitions, and to a most luxurious bar, where you can loll on sofas and have drinks at normal prices. Outside is a year-round terraza.

Croissantería, c/Corredera Alta de San Pablo – just off Plaza San Ildefonso (Metro Tribunal). Some of the best stuffed croissants in the city, plus ice cream and coffee.

La Mallorquina, Puerta del Sol 2 (Metro Sol). Good for breakfast or snacks – try one of their *napolitanas* (cream slices) in the sunny upstairs salon.

Yenes, c/Mayor 1 (Metro Sol). Wedge yourself on to a bar stool and enjoy a fine array of cakes and croissants; less bustling than *La Mallorquina* opposite.

Nabucco, c/Hortaleza 108 (☎91 310 06 11; Metro Alonso Martínez). Pleasant little Italian restaurant that serves pukka pizzas and a few pasta dishes. Open daily till 1am at weekends. Inexpensive.

La Tasca Suprema, c/Argensola 7 (☎91 308 03 47; Metro Alonso Martínez). Very popular neighbourhood local, worth booking ahead. Castilian home cooking to a T, including *cocido* on Mon & Thurs. Closed Sun & Aug. Inexpensive.

Malasaña and north to Bilbao

Malasaña is another characterful area, with a big nightlife scene and dozens of bars. Farther north, the area around Plaza de Olavide – a real neighbourhood square – offers some good-value places, well off any tourist trails.

Tapas bars

Casa Camacho, c/San Andrés 2 – just off Plaza Dos de Mayo (Metro Tribunal). Irresistible old *bodega*, with a traditional bar counter, *vermut* on tap, and basic *tapas*. An ideal place to start the evening. Packed out at weekends.

La Camocha, c/de Fuencarral 15 (Metro Bilbao). Asturian cider bar serving splendid *pulpo* and *almejas a la sidra*. You can use the special cider-pouring instruments stuck to the wall to make sure it is properly aerated.

Taberna La Nueva, c/Arapiles 7 (Metro Quevedo). Attractive, century-old *taberna* with an extensive range of *tapas*.

Restaurants

Balear, c/Sagunto 18 (☎91 447 91 15; Metro Iglesia). This Levantine restaurant serves only rice-based dishes, but they're superb. There's an inexpensive house *cava*, and you can turn up any time before midnight. What more could you want? Closed Sun & Mon night. Moderate.

Bar Maragato, c/San Andrés 14 (Metro Bilbao). A basic place to be among the locals; your best bet is egg and chips washed down with the local wine. Inexpensive.

La Gata Flora, Plaza Dos de Mayo 1 (☎91 521 20 20; Metro Tribunal). Argentine-Italian cooking of a pretty high quality, considering the low prices. Serves until midnight on weekdays, 1am on Fridays and Saturdays. Inexpensive.

La Giralda, c/Hartzenbush 12 (☎91 445 77 79; Metro Bilbao). An *andaluz* fish and seafood restaurant of very high quality: perfectly cooked *chipirones*, *calamares*, and all the standards, plus wonderful *mero* (grouper). A second branch, across the road at no. 15, does a similarly accomplished job on *pescados fritos*. Closed Sun & holidays. Moderate to expensive.

La Glorieta, c/Manuel Malasaña 37 (☎91 448 40 16; Metro Bilbao). Modern Spanish cooking – imaginative and tasty. Closed Sun night & Mon. Moderate.

Ma Bretagne, c/San Vicente Ferrer 9 (☎91 581 77 74; Metro Tribunal). Tiny place with good *crêpes*, open until after midnight. Closed Mon. Inexpensive.

Mesón Do Anxó, c/Cardenal Cisneros 6 (Metro Bilbao). A *gallego* café-restaurant with Formica tables – as unpretentious as they come – but serving superb *pulpo*, *pimientos de Padrón*, and other staples of the region. Closed Sun. Moderate.

Taberna Griega, c/Tesoro 6 (☎91 532 18 92; Metro Tribunal). Enjoyable Greek restaurant, with live bouzouki music most nights. Open until well after midnight. Inexpensive.

La Zamorana, c/Galileo 21 (☎91 447 11 69; Metro San Bernardo). Attractive, tiled restaurant, with good-value Basque cooking – including lots of dishes based on *bacalao* (dried cod). Closed Sat lunch & Sun. Moderate (just).

Paseo del Prado, Recoletos and Retiro

This is a fancier area with few bars of note but some extremely good restaurants, well worth considering, even if you're not staying in the *Ritz*.

Tapas bars

Mesón la Pilarica, Paseo del Prado 39 (Metro Atocha). One of the nearest decent places to the Prado on this road, this is a good place to sample *serrano* ham.

Restaurants

Al Mounia, c/Recoletos 5 (☎91 435 08 28; Metro Banco de España). Moroccan cooking at its best – indeed, it is equalled only by a couple of restaurants in Paris and Marrakesh. Be sure to try the *bastilla* (pigeon pie). Closed Sun, Mon & Aug. Expensive.

La Ancha, c/de Zorrilla 7 (☎91 429 81 86; Metro Sevilla/Banco de España). Highly regarded restaurant in a rather gloomy street behind the Cortes – hence popular with politicians. Mahogany-panelled décor, and imaginative variations on traditional Castilian dishes. Good-value lunchtime *menú*. Closed Sun & holidays. Moderate to expensive.

Dorna, c/Atocha 118 (☎91 527 52 99; Metro Atocha). Bustling place with somewhat brusque waiters, but a decent stop before (or after) a visit to the Reina Sofía. Inexpensive to moderate.

Paradis Madrid, c/Marqués de Cubas 14 (☎91 429 73 03; Metro Banco de España). There are paradises in Barcelona and New York – the chain is run by a Catalan duo – and the American influence is apparent in designerish details like a *carta* for olive oils. Nonetheless, the cooking is light, Mediterranean and tasty; try the wonderful *arroz negro* with seafood. Stays open till 1.30am if it's busy. Closed Sat lunch, Sun & Aug. Moderate.

Viridiana, c/Juan de Mena 14 (☎91 523 44 78; Metro Retiro). Bizarre temple of Madrid *nueva cocina*, offering mouthwatering creations like *solomillo* (sirloin) with black truffles, and herrings with avocado and mango, while also conducting pyrotechnic experiments (dishes often arrive decorated with small incendiary devices). You'll need to go to the bank first, as main courses are around 2500ptas and no cards are accepted. Closed Sun & Aug. Expensive.

Salamanca

Salamanca is Madrid's equivalent of Bond Street or Fifth Avenue, full of designer shops and expensive-looking natives. Recommendations below are correspondingly pricey but high quality.

Tapas bars

Alkalde, Jorge Juan 10 (☎91 567 33 59; Metro Serrano). This serves up Basque *tapas*, a treat which you could turn into a tasty meal.

Hevia, c/de Serrano 118 (Metro Núñez de Balboa). Plush venue and clientele for pricey, but excellent *tapas* and canapés – the hot Camembert is a must.

José Luís, c/Serrano 89 (☎91 563 09 58; Metro Serrano). A very chi-chi bar with dainty and delicious sandwiches laid out along the bar. You take what you fancy, in the safe knowledge that the barman will have notched up another few hundred pesetas to expand his chain of bars in the Americas.

Restaurants

El Amparo, Callejón Puigcerdá 8 (☎91 431 64 56; Metro Serrano). Most critics rate this designer restaurant among the top five in Madrid – and you'll need to book a couple of weeks ahead to get a table. If you strike lucky, the rewards are faultless Basque cooking from a woman chef, Carmen Guasp – "Guaspi" to the Spanish media. Main dishes are around the 3000ptas mark so expect a bill of at least 6000ptas a head. Closed Sat lunch & Sun. Expensive.

Casa Portal, c/Dr Castelo 26 (☎91 574 20 26; Metro Retiro). Superlative Asturian cooking – go for the *fabada* (beans and sausage stew) or *besugo* (bream). Closed Sun & Mon night & holidays & Aug. Moderate.

El Pescador, c/José Ortega y Gasset 75 (☎91 402 12 90; Metro Lista). One of the city's top seafood restaurants, run by *Gallegos* and with specials flown in from the Atlantic each morning. The clientèle can be a bit intimidating – it is reputedly one of Felipe González's favourites – but you'll rarely experience better seafood cooking. Closed Sun & Aug. Expensive.

TERRAZAS AND CHIRINGUITOS

Madrid is a different city during summer, as temperatures soar into the hundreds, and life moves outside, becoming even more late night. In July and August, those *madrileños* who haven't headed for the coast meet up with each other, from 10pm onwards, at one or other of the city's immensely popular **terrazas**. These can range from a few tables set up outside a café or alongside a **chiringuito** – a makeshift bar – in one of the squares, to extremely trendy (and very expensive) designer bars, which form the summer annexe of one or other of the major clubs or *discotecas*. Most places offer cocktails, in addition to regular drinks, and the better or more traditional ones also serve *horchata* (an almond-ish milk shake) and *granizado* (crushed-ice lemon). A few of the terrazas operate year-round.

Terrazas run by the **clubs** – such as *Stella* and *Zanzibar* – vary their sites year by year, often locating way out from the centre, necessitating long and expensive taxi rides. Still, if you do want to run into Pedro Almodóvar, Alaska and their chums, you'll have to track down *Stella*, wherever it currently happens to be.

Paseo de Recoletos and Paseo de la Castellana
The biggest concentration of terrazas is to be found up and down the grass strip in the middle of the Paseo de Recoletos and its continuation, Paseo de la Castellana. On the nearer reaches of Paseo de Recoletos are terrazas of the **old-style cafés** *Gran* (no. 8), *Gijón* (no. 21) and *Espejo* (no. 31), which are popular meeting points for *madrileños* of all kinds.

Past Plaza de Colón, the **trendier terrazas** begin, most pumping out music, and some offering entertainment – especially midweek, when they need to attract custom. They are extremely posey places, with clubbers dressing up for a night's cruise along the length – an expensive operation, with cocktails at 1000ptas a shot, and even a *caña* costing 600ptas. If you want to take in a good selection, walk up from Plaza de Colón for around 500m. Alternatively, take a taxi or the metro up to Plaza de Lima, where you'll find *Castellana 99* – a fashionable terraza and bar that's open year-round. For some reason, most of the Castellana terrazas are known only by their (approximate) street number.

Ribeira do Minho, c/Doctor Fleming 52 (☎91 359 7917; Metro Cuzco). A good place to sample top-quality traditional Galician food and wine. Expensive.

Suntory, Paseo de la Castellana 36 (☎91 577 37 33; Metro Rubén Darío). Authentic and upmarket Japanese restaurant, where a mixed sushi will set you back around 4000ptas. Closed Sun & holidays. Expensive.

Teatriz, c/Hermosilla 15 (☎91 577 53 79; Metro Serrano). As the name suggests, this was once a theatre, and the layout has been maintained by designers Philipe Stark and Mariscal – as trendy a European combination as could be conceived. Although primarily a nightspot (see p.105), there's a fine restaurant in the old "circle", with light, *nouvelle cuisine*-influenced dishes. (Surprisingly) moderate.

The west

Picnicking in the Casa de Campo aside, the west doesn't hold much in the way of culinary interest. However, one excellent restaurant deserves a mention.

Restaurants

Casa Mingo, Paseo de la Florida 2 – next to the chapel of San Antonio de la Florida (☎91 547 79 18; Metro Príncipe Pío). Famous Asturian café-restaurant where you eat roast chicken – which is basically all they serve – washed down with *sidra* (cider), and followed up by *yemas* (candied egg yolk) or aged Roquefort-like cheese (*cabrales*). Good value and great fun. You can also buy a take-out (chicken and cider) for a picnic in the Casa de Campo, if you prefer. Moderate.

Elsewhere in Madrid
Antiguo Cuartel del Conde Duque (Metro Ventura Rodríguez). This is a beautiful patio, inside an old military barracks. The council puts on weekly flamenco recitals and concerts in July & Aug, with a small admission charge, but most nights there's free entry.

Jardines de Conde Duque, at the corner of c/de Conde Duque 11 and c/Santa Cruz del Marcenado (Metro Ventura Rodríguez). The summer base of *Zanzibar* in recent years.

Jardines Las Vistillas, c/de Bailén – on the south side of the viaduct (Metro La Latina – though it's not very close). This area, due south of the royal palace, has a number of terrazas and *chiringuitos*. It's named for the "little vistas" to be enjoyed in the direction of the Guadarrama mountains to the northwest.

Paseo del Pintor Rosales (Metro Argüelles). There is a clutch of late-night terrazas around the base of the *teleférico*, with views across the river to the Casa de Campo.

Plaza de Comendadoras (Metro Ventura Rodríguez). One of the city's nicest squares, this has a couple of terrazas – attached to the *Café Moderno* and to a not very good Mexican restaurant.

Plaza Dos de Mayo (Metro Tribunal). The *chiringuito* on Malasaña's main square is always diverting, though the square has something of a reputation for drug addicts.

Plaza de Olavide (Metro Quevedo). An attractive neighbourhood square, with more or less year-round terrazas belonging to four or five cafés and *tapas* bars.

Plaza de Oriente (Metro Opera). The *Café de Oriente* terraza is a station of Madrid nightlife.

Plaza de Santa Ana (Metro Sol). Several of the *cervecerías* here have seats outside and there's a *chiringuito* in the middle of the square from June to September.

La Vieja Estación, Glorieta de Carlos V (Metro Atocha). Above the main entrance to Atocha station, this attracts a glamorous clientele ranging from football stars to TV personalities. If you don't fancy people-watching, there are concerts, talent contests and exhibitions laid on for good measure. Open 9pm–2am.

Nightlife

Madrid **nightlife** is a pretty serious phenomenon. This is the only city in Europe where you can get caught in traffic jams at 4am, when the clubbers are either going home or moving on to the dance-past-dawn discos.

As with everything *madrileño*, there is a bewildering variety of nightlife venue – all of which are covered, to some degree, in the area-reviews following. Most common are the **discobares** – bars of all musical and sexual persuasion, whose unifying feature is background (occasionally live) rock, dance or salsa music. These get going from around 11pm and will stay open routinely to 2am or 3am, as will the few quieter **cocktail bars** and **pubs**.

Discotecas – which we've separated in the listings – are rarely worth investigating until around 1am (the *madrugada* – early morning). Most of them pick their clientele through a dress code exclusivity and you may at times need to ingratiate yourself with the doorman. Being foreign, oddly enough, seems to make it easier to get in. **Entry charges** are quite common and quite hefty (600–3000ptas) at *discotecas* (and some of the more disco-like *discobares*) but tend to cover you for a first drink. Free entries can sometimes be picked up in tourist offices or bars. Be aware that many *discotecas* in Spain are fairly ephemeral institutions and frequently only last a season before opening

GAY AND LESBIAN MADRID

Much of Madrid's nightlife has a big gay input and gays will feel at home in most of the listings in our clubs/*discotecas* section. However, around Plaza Chueca, graffiti-plastered walls proclaim the existence of a *zona gay*, and the surrounding streets, especially c/de Pelayo, harbour at least a dozen exclusively gay bars and clubs, as well as a café that's traditionally gay – the *Café Figueroa* at c/Augusto Figueroa 17. Wandering about, be aware that Chueca is also something of a drug centre, so taxis are best late at night. The lesbian scene, such as it is, has a current focus in Lavapiés.

Gay Bars and Discotecas

Café Acuarela, c/Gravina 10 (Metro Chueca). Very comfortable café, stylish decor and the perfect place for a quiet drink. Popular with mixed crowd.

Bar LL, c/de Pelayo 11 (Metro Chueca). There's a bar at the front and a more intimate room at the back, where people sit around and talk or watch porn. Slightly older crowd, mainly singles. The bar offers free entry to an all-night sauna, Cristal, at c/Augusto Figueroa 17.

Cruising, c/Pérez Galdós 5 (Metro Chueca). This *discobar* is strictly for leather boys, with a dark room and bar upstairs and a small, intimate disco below. It has a slightly tense atmosphere and you

have to order your drinks at the door before you come in.

New Leather Bar, c/de Pelayo 42 (Metro Chueca). The name implies a leather scene but this bar has a mixed gay crowd.

Ricks, c/de las Infantas 26 (Metro Banco de España). Mixed straight/gay *discobar* which gets wild at weekends when every available space is used for dancing. Open and light, with a friendly atmosphere – plus table football at the back. Pricey drinks.

Shangay Tea Dance, at the *Flamingo Club*, c/Mesonero Romanos 13 (Metro Callao). A compulsory Sunday night stop, featuring live shows and 70s disco hits. 1000ptas entry including first drink. Sun 9pm–2am.

Lesbian Bars and Discotecas

Ambient, San Mateo 21 (Metro Alonso Martínez). Thriving bar with pool, table football, exhibitions, occasional live acts and a market on Sunday.

Frágil, c/Lavapiés 11 (Metro Lavapiés). A lively lesbian discobar.

Medea, c/de la Cabeza 33 (Metro Lavapiés/Antón Martín). The city's premier lesbian disco, although men are admitted if accompanied. Entrance charge (900ptas)

includes a cabaret on Thursday & Sunday. Smart decor, great music, pool table.

La Rosa, c/Tetuán 27 (Metro Sol). Lesbian disco run by a women's collective; again, accompanied men are admitted. Good selection of music and friendly atmosphere.

Truco, c/Gravina 10 (Metro Chueca). This gets busy but has a relaxed atmosphere.

up somewhere else under a different name, so it's a good idea to consult *La Guía del Ocio* or *Metropóli* (see p.107) for the very latest information.

Places with regular live music – rock, jazz, flamenco, salsa and classical – are covered in the "Performance" section, following on p.107.

Bars

Madrid's bar scene has, if anything, got more frenetic over the last few years, largely due to the appearance of *bakalao*, a Spanish (originally Ibizan) version of house music. In both *discobares* and *discotecas*, it's horribly popular, and *madrileños* have taken to the idea of all-night raving with unmitigated enthusiasm.

Perhaps in reaction to *bakalao*, the more traditional bar scene has revived and expanded, too. In the listings below, you'll find a fair number of *bares de copas* (drinking bars) where the music is restrained – and even a couple with chamber orchestras.

Sol, Opera and Plaza de Santa Ana

Cervecer'a Alemana, Plaza de Santa Ana (Metro Sol). Stylish old beer house frequented by Hemingway and, these days, seemingly every other American tourist. Order a *caña* and go easy on the *tapas*, as the bill can mount up fast.

Cervecería Santa Ana, Plaza de Santa Ana (Metro Sol). Cheaper than the *Alemana*, with tables outside, friendly service, and a good selection of *tapas*.

La Comedia, c/Príncipe 16 (Metro Sol). Modern, relaxing bar for a quiet drink by day, which gets livelier as the night progresses; from Thursday to Saturday it's open until 9am and is a favourite haunt for staff from earlier-closing bars.

La Fidula, c/Huertas 57 (Metro Antón Martín). A fine bar where you can sip *fino* to the accompaniment of classical tunes, performed from the tiny stage.

Los Gabrieles, c/Echegaray 17 (Metro Sol). This tiled bar is a Madrid monument and it's worth going earlier than is cool to appreciate the fabulous tableaux, created by sherry companies in the 1880s. Drinks are reasonable, considering the venue; *tapas* don't go much beyond olives and crisps. Very crowded after 10pm, especially at weekends.

Kasbah, c/Santa Maria 17 (Metro Antón Martín). With surreal ceiling ornaments and the latest sounds, this really swings at weekends, and so will you if you try one of their lethal slammers.

Naturbier, Plaza de Santa Ana 9 (Metro Sol). Next door to the *cervecerías Alemana* and *Santa Ana*, the *Naturbier* brews its own tasty, cloudy beer and serves a variety of German sausages to accompany it.

No se lo digas a nadie, c/Ventura de la Vega 7 (Metro Sol). This was founded (and is still run) by a women's co-op, though it has mellowed a bit in recent years (the toilets no longer proclaim *nosotros* and *ellos* – "us" and "them"). Nonetheless, it retains a political edge, hosting benefit events from time to time, and has a different atmosphere from other bars in this area. There is no door policy or dress code and the drinks are reasonably priced. Upstairs there's a pool table and plenty of places to sit; downstairs is a disco playing mainly dance music.

Salón del Prado, c/Prado 4 (Metro Sol). Elegant café-bar which hosts classical concerts on Thursday nights at 11pm. Turn up early if you want a table.

La Venencia, c/Echegaray (Metro Sol). For a real taste of old Madrid, this is a must: a long, narrow bar, serving just sherry – try the extra dry *fino* – cheese, and delicious cured tuna and olives. Decoration is unchanged for decades, with ancient barrels and posters.

Viva Madrid, c/Manuel Fernández y González 7 (Metro Antón Martín). Another fabulous tiled bar – both outside and in – with wines and sherry, plus basic *tapas*. Open to 2.30am and always crowded.

Gran Vía

Carpe Diem, Plaza Conde de Toreno 2 (Metro Plaza de España/Noviciado). Part of the takings of this single-roomed bar goes towards overseas projects and it often stages markets in aid of developing countries. Happy hour goes on until midnight, with a variety of Spanish pop and salsa played.

El Cock, c/de la Reina 16 – just behind Museo Chicote (Metro Gran Vía). A smart wooden-panelled bar, styled like a gentlemen's club, and very *de moda*. The music is good, although there's no dancing. *Cañas* or wine cost around 600ptas.

El Morocco, c/Marqués de Leganes 7 (Metro Santo Domingo). Latest venture by rock singer Alaska, long-time mover of the *movida*, and mate of Pedro Almodóvar. The crowds here could well be from an Almodóvar movie (it's likely that some, at least, have acted in one), and they get a club in their own image, including a cabaret show at 2am, the odd (and odd is the word) band, and a dance floor open till 9am. There's an occasional entrance charge and you'll need to look the part to get past the doorman.

Museo Chicote, Gran Vía 12 (☎91 532 67 37; Metro Gran Vía). *Chicote* is a piece of design history, virtually unaltered since it opened in 1931, full of Art Deco lines and booths and once a haunt of

IRISH PUBS

Although a pint of the "black stuff" has long been available in Madrid, specialist **Irish pubs** have sprung up all over the city in the last few years. Theme pubs based on village shops, Dublin streets, country cottages and breweries have all appeared, while the Celtic music scene has taken off in a big way with a number of bands now firmly established on the pub circuit. If you want to be assured of a great St Patrick's night or just feel a little homesick you could try some of the following:

Finbars, c/Marqués de Urquijo 10 (Metro Argüelles). Good range of live music on most nights in this self-styled pub/music shop.

Finnegans, Plaza de las Salesas 9 (Metro Colón). Large bar with several rooms, complete with bar fittings and wooden floors brought over from Ireland. English-speaking staff and TV sports.

La Fontana de Oro, c/de la Victoria 1 (Metro Sol). Although it's a heresy to have turned this ancient bar (dating back over two hundred years and featuring in Benito Pérez Galdós's book of the same name) into an Irish pub, it's an attractive and lively venue with some swinging Celtic sounds.

The Harp, c/Jesús del Valle (Metro Tribunal). Riotous bar which is packed at weekends. Occasional live music.

The Irish Rover, Avda. Brasil 7 (Metro Lima). On an Irish street behind the concrete jungle of the Azca centre, off the Paseo de la Castellana. Popular with young *madrileños* and packed at weekends.

The Quiet Man, c/Valverde 44 (Metro Tribunal). One of the first on the scene, designed in the style of a turn-of-the-century Dublin pub and full of authentic fittings.

Taberna del León de Oro, c/del León 10 (Metro Antón Martín). Popular bar, serving both Guinness and Newcastle Brown Ale to homesick foreign residents.

Buñuel and Hemingway. They will mix you any (expensive) cocktail, alcoholic or not. Busiest after midnight. Mon–Sat 5pm–1.30am.

Soma, c/Leganitas 25 (Metro Plaza de España). Popular "alternative" hangout in a series of labyrinthine darkened rooms.

La Latina and Lavapiés

Aloque, c/Torrecilla del Real 20 (Metro Antón Martín). Relaxed wine bar where you can try top-quality wine by the glass; the *tapas* are excellent too.

Avapiés, c/Lavapiés 5 (Metro Lavapiés/Tirso de Molina). Excellent music and nightly cabaret at around 10pm. Closes at 3.30am.

Maravillita, c/Zurita 39 (Metro Lavapiés). Loud music, and even louder clientele. Open till late.

El Tempranillo, Cava Baja 38 (Metro La Latina). Excellent little bar serving a vast range of Spanish wines by the glass – a great place to discover your favourite variety.

Chueca and Santa Bárbara

La Cervecería Internacional, c/Regueros 8 (Metro Alonso Martínez). Large beer hall masquerading as a beer festival, situated in the heart of the teenage disco belt around Plaza Santa Bárbara. Plenty of different draught beers, music videos and good *tapas*.

Cliché, c/del Barquillo (Metro Chueca). Best of many bars along this street – a relaxed yet funky place, with clientele as eclectic as the decor, and all ages from fifteen to fifty. Open till 3am.

La Fábrica de Pan, c/Regueros (Metro Chueca). Deep in the heart of Chueca, this has a relaxed atmosphere and good music. On any day of the week you'll find people drinking till 4am, or playing board games in the room at the back. Perhaps best enjoyed during the week, as it's a small place and gets packed at weekends. *Cañas* are a modest 350ptas.

Impacto, c/Campoamor 3 (Metro Alonso Martínez). Inside is a mini-labyrinth of little rooms and bars around every corner. A fairly trendy, slightly older crowd. Reasonably priced drinks and a good variety of music, despite the lack of dance floor. Door policy of sorts.

Kingston's, c/del Barquillo 29 (Metro Chueca). Relaxed multicultural *discobar*. Music ranges from soul and funk to reggae and rap. At the weekend professional dancers get things going.

Malasaña and north

Al Lab'Oratorio, c/de Colón 14 (Metro Tribunal). Famous 1980s bar with very loud rock music on the sound system, and often live on a little stage downstairs. No entry charge but the drinks are expensive.

Bar Plaza Dos de Mayo, Plaza Dos de Mayo (Metro Tribunal). Old-style wood and tiles bar, which gets packed at weekends. Good music, regular prices, and it opens up in the summer so you can watch the goings on in the square.

Café del Foro, c/San Andrés 38 (Metro Tribunal). Expensive but enjoyable bar with live music or some form of entertainment most nights. Attracts a slightly older, fairly smart crowd. The decor is designed by Costus, who was Almodóvar's side-kick. Open from 7pm till 3am or 4am.

Casa Quemeda, c/Cardenal Cisneros 56 (Metro Quevedo). Unusual for this bar-packed area in that it's old – all-wood decor – and very peaceful. There's a car stuck in the window – one of the first assembly-line models produced in the country. *Sangría* is a modest 900ptas a jug.

Hotel California, c/San Vicente Ferrer 28 (Metro Tribunal). Film-set interior with lots of intimate booths. Rock music, but not deafening, and a varied crowd. Fairly expensive drinks.

Las Noches del Cuplé, c/de la Palma 51 (Metro Tribunal). 6500ptas entry entitles you to food and live music, good value as long as you're into traditional music-hall Spanish, French songs and tangos.

Pepe Botella, c/San Andrés 12 – on Plaza Dos de Mayo (Metro Tribunal). Formerly a restaurant, now a relaxed wine bar, with friendly staff, decent music and no fruit machine.

Tupperware, c/Corredera Alta de San Pablo 26 (Metro Tribunal). *The* place to go for the latest on the indie scene, with a mixture of grunge, Brit pop and old classics from the punk era.

La Vaca Austera, c/de la Palma 20 (Metro Tribunal). American-style rock bar playing punk/indie classics, with pool tables, mixed clientele and friendly atmosphere.

Vía Lactea, c/Velarde 18 (Metro Tribunal). Call in here to see where the *movida* began. *Vía Lactea* was a key meeting place for Spain's designers, directors, pop stars and painters in the 1980s, and it retains its original decor from the time, billiard tables included. Stage downstairs. Young studenty clientele.

Warhol's Club, c/Luchana 20 (Metro Bilbao). Very popular *discobar* open until 10am – and until noon on Sundays. It is spread over two floors, with lots of chrome, glass, video screens, and ultraviolet lighting. Attracts an early-twenties crowd. No door policy.

Salamanca

Avión Club, c/Hermosilla 99 (Metro Goya). This was one of the most popular clubs in the gloomy post-Civil War years, when it was adopted by the remains of the left. It hasn't changed an iota in the last sixty years and even the pianist, at ninety-odd, is virtually original. Daily 7pm–3am.

El Cabaret de Madrid, c/Jorge Juan 20 (Metro Colón). Relaxing and characterful bar with downstairs cabaret acts that get going after 1am.

Teatriz, c/Hermosilla 15 (Metro Serrano). This former theatre, redesigned by the Catalan, Mariscal, together with Philipe Stark, is as elegant a club/bar as any in Europe. There are bars on the main theatre levels, watched over by a restaurant in the circle. Down in the basement there's a library-like area and small disco. Drinks are fairly pricey (1500ptas for spirits) but there's no entrance charge. Bar 9pm–3am; restaurant 1.30–4.30pm & 9pm–1am; closed Sat lunch, Sun & Aug.

Discotecas

Discotecas – or clubs – aren't always that different from *discobares*, though they tend to be bigger and flashier, with a lot of attention to the lights, sound system and decor, and stay open very late – most until 4am, some till 6am, and a couple till noon. In summer, many of the trendier clubs suspend operations and set up outdoor terrazas (see p.100).

CHOCOLATE BEFORE BED

If you stay up through a Madrid night, then you must try one of the city's great institutions – the **Chocolatería San Ginés** on Pasadizo de San Ginés, off c/del Arenal between the Puerta del Sol and Teatro Real. Established in 1894, this serves *chocolate con churros* to perfection – just the thing after a night's excess. There's an almost mythical *madrileño* custom of winding up at San Ginés after the clubs close (not that they do any longer), before heading home for a shower and then off to work. And why not?

San Ginés is open Tues–Sun 1am–7.30am plus Fri–Sun 7–10pm – the latter for weekend shoppers, when the *chocolate* is half price.

Sol, Opera and Plaza de Santa Ana

Joy Eslava, c/Arenal 11 (Metro Sol). This big-name disco is frequented by musicians, models and media folk, for whom the 2000ptas entry and rigorous door policy hold no fear. If you can't get in – and 3–5am is the hippest time here – console yourself with the *Chocolatería San Ginés* (see box, above), on the street behind.

Kapital, c/Atocha 125 (Metro Atocha). Seven floors to cater for most tastes, with two dance floors, a cinema and a top-floor terrace. Open Wed–Sat midnight–6am.

Palacio de Gaviria, c/Arenal 9 (Metro Opera/Sol). Aristocratic, nineteenth-century palace where you can wander through a sequence of extravagant salons, listen to a chamber concert in the ballroom, watch a live show or simply dance the night away. Entrance is 2000ptas which includes a first drink. After this, expect to pay 1500ptas a drink.

Stella, c/Arlabán 7 (Metro Sevilla). This has been one of Madrid's trendiest after-hours discos right from its launch by Alaska (see *El Morocco* under "Bars"). It attracts a gay/straight mix and gets going from about 5.30am; music is (or was) an inspired blend of salsa and tacky 1970s disco, and if it all palls, there's a bowling alley downstairs. You'll need to dress up.

Gran Vía

Arena, c/de la Princesa 1 (Metro Plaza de España). Big, modern and very popular former cinema, hosted at weekends by the minor Italian royal, Conde Lecquio, a man famous for being famous. Reggae and funk progresses to house music during the night.

El Calentito, c/Jacometezo 15 (Metro Callao). This is a fine place to experience wild, abandoned Madrid. It is tiny and cramped with strictly South American sounds: be prepared to dance with anyone! Drinks are modest. Open from 10pm but doesn't really get going till 4am. The entrance is easily missed – look out for the painted window.

Davai, c/Flor Baja 1, cnr Gran Via 59 (Metro Santo Domingo/Plaza de España). A multi-club operating under several different names during the week. The undoubted highlight at the moment is Thursday night when the Seventies are revived under the name Starsky and Hutch – the perfect opportunity to dust off your flares and platforms and wallow in great disco and funk classics.

Chueca and Santa Bárbara

Boccaccio, c/del Marqués de la Ensenada 16 (Metro Colón). This is an all-nighter, kicking off about midnight with a business-type crowd, with a younger, trendier crew taking over from 2am till noon. Plush interior with a bar upstairs and a disco down, playing mainly *bakalao*. Entrance is 1000ptas for men, free for women.

Pachá, c/de Barceló 11 (Metro Tribunal). An eternal survivor on the Madrid disco scene. Once a theatre and still very theatrical, it is exceptionally cool during the week, less so at the weekend when the out-of-towners take over. Good if you like techno.

Speakeasy, c/de Fernando VI 6 (Metro Alonso Martínez). Good-value, friendly disco that holds "International Parties" for foreigners new to the city. Good resident DJ.

Out of the centre

Cats, c/Julia Romeo 4 (Metro Guzmán El Bueno). Moncloa is a popular student area, towards the end of c/de la Princesa, and it has a good range of bars and discos. *Cats* is one of the best: a large

bar surrounded by various dance floors, podiums and chill-out areas. Young crowd and an emphasis firmly on dancing, to house and *bakalao*. Daily 9pm–5.30am.

Galileo Galilei, c/Galileo 100 (Metro Rios Rosas). Bar, concert venue and disco all rolled into one.
Check the *Guía del Ocio* to find out whether it's the night for cabaret, salsa or a singer-songwriter.

Space of Sound, Estación de Chamartín (Metro Chamartín). If you've still got energy left, this
after-hours club on top of the Chamartín train station will allow you to strut your stuff all morning;
if you can take the constant bombardment of *bakalao*, that is. Sat, Sun & holidays 6.30am–noon.

Performance: music, film and theatre

Most nights in Madrid, you can take in performances of **flamenco**, **salsa**, **rock** (local
and imported), **jazz**, **classical music** and **opera** at one or other of the city's venues.
Often, it's the smaller, offbeat clubs that are the more enjoyable, though there are plenty of big auditoria – including the football stadiums and bullring – for big-name
concerts. In summer, events are supplemented by the council's **Veranos de la Villa**
cultural programme and in autumn by the **Festival de Otoño**. These also encompass
theatre and **film**, both of which have fairly healthy year-round scenes.

Flamenco

Flamenco has undergone something of a revival in Madrid in the 1990s, in large part
due to the "new flamenco" artists, like Ketama and Joaquín Cortes, who are unafraid to
mix it with a bit of blues, jazz, even rock. The club listings below span the range
between purist flamenco and crossover experiments and most artists – even major stars
– appear in them. Paco de Lucía is a rare exception – when he plays with his band in
Madrid, it's usually in the bullring, Las Ventas. Clubs and cafés include:

Café de Chinitas, c/Torija 7 (☎91 559 51 35; Metro Santo Domingo). One of the oldest flamenco
clubs in Madrid, with a dinner-dance spectacular. It's expensive but the music is authentic and the
audience is predominantly Spanish. Reservations are essential, though you may get in late when

---

MADRID LISTINGS AND THE *MADRUGADA*

Listings information is in plentiful supply in Madrid. The newspapers *El País* and *El
Mundo* have excellent daily listings, and on Fridays both publish sections devoted to
events, bars and restaurants in the capital. Of the two, *El Mundo*'s **Metrópoli** is the better – a separate colour magazine, full of previews and details of the week's exhibitions,
films, theatre and concerts, and with extensive listings of clubs, bars and restaurants
(including opening hours and average prices – usually on the high side of what you'll
spend).

If your time in Madrid doesn't coincide with the Friday *Metrópoli* supplement, or you
want maximum info, pick up the weekly listings magazine **Guía del Ocio** (125ptas) at
any kiosk. It's not quite as clear or discriminating as *Metrópoli*, but it's functional enough.
The *Ayuntamiento* also publishes a monthly "What's On" pamphlet, **En Madrid**, which
is free from any of the tourist offices and lists forthcoming events in the city.
Alternatively, try calling the telephone listings service, which is in English, on ☎91 481
12 48. *In Madrid*, meanwhile, is a free monthly magazine – available in many bars – which
bills itself as "Madrid's English monthly for the Hip, Cool and Transient" and features
useful reviews of clubs and bars.

One word that might perplex first-timers in Madrid – and which crops up in all the listings magazines – is **madrugada**. This refers to the hours between midnight and dawn
and, in this supremely late-night/early-morning city, is a necessary adjunct to announcements of important events. *Tres de la madrugada* means an event is due to start at 3am.

people start to leave (at this time you don't have to eat and the entrance fee of around 4000ptas includes your first drink). Mon–Sat 9pm–2am.

Candela, c/del Olmo 2 (☎91 467 33 82; Metro Antón Martín). A legendary bar frequented by musicians with occasional shows too; the late, great Camarón de la Isla is reputed to have sung here until 11am on one occasion.

Caracol, c/Bernardino Obregón 18 (☎91 530 80 55; Metro Embajadores). The top names tend to appear here in a place popular with the young crowd, so it's worth making a reservation as early as possible. Flamenco is often mixed with jazz and blues; for pure flamenco, come on Thursday night.

Casa Patas, c/Cañizares 10 (☎91 369 04 96; Metro Antón Martín). Small club that gets its share of big names. The best nights are Thursday and Friday. Entrance 1500–200ptas. Closed Sun.

Corral de la Morería, c/de la Morería 17 (☎ 91 365 84 46; Metro La Latina). This is a good venue for some serious acts off the tourist circuit, but again expensive at about 4000ptas for the show plus a drink.

Peña Chaquetón, c/Canarias 39 (☎91 671 27 77; Metro Palos de la Frontera). Friday nights only, but worth the effort; turn up early if there's a big name or you won't get in. Don't worry about the "members only" sign on the outside.

La Soleá, Cava Baja 34 (☎91 365 33 08; Metro La Latina). This brilliant, long-established flamenco bar is the genuine article. People sit around in the salon, pick up a guitar or start to sing and gradually the atmosphere builds up until everyone else is clapping or dancing. Has to be seen to be believed. Mon–Sat 8.30pm–3am.

Rock and blues

Madrid is very much on the international rock tour circuit and you can catch big (and small) American and British acts in front of enthusiastic audiences. One of the more endearing Spanish habits is to translate all foreign names – including rock bands: thus, just as Prince Charles is always known as Príncipe Carlos, U2 are, of course, U–Dos. **Tickets** for most big rock concerts are sold by Madrid Rock, Gran Vía 25 (Metro Callao), FNAC, c/Preciados 28 (Metro Callao) and El Corte Inglés, c/ Preciados 1–4 (Metro Sol).

In the smaller clubs, you have a chance of seeing a very wide range of local bands. Madrid has long been the heart of the Spanish rock scene (see "Music" in Contexts).

Clubs

La Coquette, c/Arenal 22, entrance at c/de la Hileras 14 (Metro Opera). Small, smoky blues bar, where people sit around in the near dark watching the band perform on a tiny stage. Live music most nights.

Maravillas, c/San Vicente Ferrer 33 (☎91 523 30 71; Metro Tribunal). Small but usually uncrowded indie venue where bands play anything from jazz to funk to reggae, often till around 4am.

Siroco, c/San Dimás 3 (☎91 593 30 70; Metro San Bernardo). Live bands most nights at this popular little soul club, not far north of Gran Vía. Closed Sun.

Ya'sta La Trup, c/Valverde 10 (Metro Gran Vía). A weird and wonderful place for terminal insomniacs. Most nights there's a jam session from local rock musicians, then a disco plays rock and funk until about 8am. The door policy gets strict from 4am, so best turn up early.

Major concert venues

Auditorio Parque de Atracciones, Casa de Campo (Metro El Lago). Open-air summer venue.

Canciller 2, Pobladura del Valle 21 (Metro San Blas). Primarily a heavy rock venue, but also hosts blues and Celtic music gigs.

La Katedral, c/Fundadores 7 (Metro Manuel Becerra/O'Donnell). New venue, which has taken over from the now defunct *Revólver*, kicking off with recent concerts by indie bands including Echobelly and Supergrass.

Palacio de Deportes, Avda. Felipe II (Metro Goya). Large indoor sports arena usually used by Madrid's basketball teams and increasingly by the big-name artists on the Spanish leg of their

European tours. Fifteen thousand capacity, but the acoustics leave a lot to be desired. Oasis and the Spice Girls have appeared here.

Plaza de Toros de las Ventas, Las Ventas (☎91 356 22 00/91 726 48 00; Metro Ventas). The bull-ring is a pretty good concert venue, put to use in the summer festival. Tickets are usually one price, though you can pay more for a (good) reserved seat (*asiento reservado*).

La Riviera, Paseo Bajo Virgen del Puerto s/n, Puente de Segovia (Metro Puerta del Angel). Fun disco and concert venue right next to the river that has hosted some of the big names in recent years, from the trendy Lenny Kravitz to the not-so-trendy Lynyrd Skynyrd.

Sala Caracol, c/Bernardino Obregón 18 (Metro Embajadores). Originally a leading flamenco night spot, but now one of the most popular venues for touring groups including, of late, Eagle Eye Cherry and the Manic Street Preachers. Good acoustics and visibility.

Latin music

Madrid attracts big-name Latin artists and if you happen to coincide with the summer festival you'll stand a good chance of catching someone of the stature of salsa legend Joe Arroyo, or – a huge star in Spain – Juan Luís Guerra from the Dominican Republic. Gigs by the likes of these tend to take place at the venues listed above. The local scene is a good deal more low-key but there's enjoyable salsa, nonetheless, in a handful of clubs.

Café del Mercado, Ronda de Toledo 1, in the Centro Artesano Puerta de Toledo (☎91 365 37 86; Metro Puerta de Toledo). Live music every day in a spacious, comfortable club and a *Gran Baile de Salsa* every Friday and Saturday at 2am.

Massai, c/de la Victoria 6 (Metro Sol). Nightly salsa with some big-name bands.

Oba-Oba, c/Jacometrezo 4 (Metro Callao). Samba and lambada with lethal Brazilian *caiprinhas* from the bar.

Pasadena, c/de Fuencarral 29 (Metro Gran Vía). Large, popular venue with salsa a speciality.

Salsipuedes, c/Puebla 6 (☎91 522 84 17; Metro Callao/Gran Vía). Serious salsa dancing to a live orchestra most weekdays in a "tropical" setting. Strict door policy. Open from 11pm to 6am.

Jazz

Madrid doesn't rank with London, Paris or New York on the jazz front but the clubs are friendly, unpretentious places. Look out for the annual jazz festival staged at a variety of venues in November.

Bar Clamores, c/Albuquerque 14 (☎91 445 7938; Metro Bilbao). Large, low-key and enjoyable jazz bar with accomplished (if not very famous) artists, not too exorbitant drinks and a nice range of snacks. Last set finishes around 1.30am, though the bar stays open to 4am.

Café Central, Plaza del Ángel 10 (☎91 369 41 43; Metro Sol). This was voted no. 6 in a recent "Best Jazz Clubs of the World" poll in *Wire* magazine. It's certainly an attractive venue – small and relaxed – and it gets the odd big name, plus strong local talent. The Art Deco café is worth a visit in its own right.

Café Jazz Populart, c/de las Huertas 22 (☎91 429 84 07; Metro Antón Martín). Nightly sets from jazz and blues bands. It's open from 6pm, gets cooking around 11pm and stays open till 2am or so.

Segundo Jazz, c/Comandante Zorita 8 (☎91 554 94 37; Metro Nuevos Ministerios). Typical atmos-pheric basement club with live music during the week only. Last set at 2.15am.

Triskel Tavern, c/de San Vicente Ferrer 3 (☎91 523 27 83; Metro Tribunal). This Irish bar has a jazz night on Tuesday and it's worth popping in to see what's on.

Classical music and opera

The **Teatro Real** is the city's prestigious opera house and, along with the **Auditorio Nacional de Musica**, is home to the Orquesta Nacional de España. Equally enjoyable are the salons and small auditoriums for chamber orchestras and groups.

Auditorio Nacional de Música, c/Príncipe de Vergara 146 (☎91 337 01 00; Metro Cruz del Rayo). This is the home of the Spanish orchestra and host to most international visiting orchestras.

Centro de Arte Reina Sofía, c/Santa Isabel (Metro Atocha). This arts centre often has programmes of contemporary music.

La Corrala, c/Mesón de Paredes (☎91 530 96 00; Metro Lavapiés). A surviving tenement block, once typical of working class Madrid, which stages *zarzuelas* during the *Veranos de la Villa* summer season.

La Fídula, c/da las Huertas (Metro Antón Martín). A chamber orchestra plays most nights at 11.30pm in this café.

Fundación Juan March, c/Castelló 77 (☎91 435 42 40; Metro Núñez de Balboa). Small auditorium used for recitals two or three times a week.

Salón del Prado, c/Prado 4 (Metro Sol). Another café venue which hosts classical musicians on Thursday nights at 11pm.

Teatro Calderón, c/Atocha 18 (☎91 632 01 14; Metro Sol). Venue for a very popular annual opera season – a lot easier to get tickets here than at the Teatro Real.

Teatro Monumental, c/de Atocha 65 (☎91 429 81 19; Metro Atocha). A large theatre, offering orchestral concerts, opera, *zarzuela* and flamenco recitals. Tickets are sold for stalls (*butaca de patio*) or a series of dizzying circles (*entresuelo*).

Teatro Real, Plaza Isabel II (☎91 516 06 60; Metro Opera). Madrid's opera house.

La Zarzuela, c/Jovellanos 4 (☎91 524 54 00; Metro Sevilla). The main venue for Spanish operetta.

Film

Cines – cinemas or movie houses – can be found all over the central area. Major releases (which often make it here well before London) are dubbed into Spanish, though a number of cinemas have regular **original language** screenings, with subtitles; these are listed in a separate *versión original/subtitulada* (*v.o.*) section in the newspapers. **Tickets** for films cost around 750ptas but most cinemas have a *día del espectador* (usually Mon or Wed) with 400ptas admission. Be warned that on Sunday night half of Madrid goes to a movie and queues can be long.

Alphaville, **Renoir** and **Lumière**, c/Martín de los Heros – just north of the Plaza de España (Metro Plaza de España). This trio of multi-screen cinemas, within 200m of each other, show regular *v.o.* films.

Filmoteca/Cine Doré, c/Santa Isabel 3 (Metro Antón Martín). Beautiful old cinema, now home to an art-film centre, with imaginative programmes of classic and contemporary films, all shown in *v.o.* at an admission price of just 225ptas. In summer, there are open-air screenings on a little terraza – they're very popular, so buy tickets in advance.

Cines Ideal, c/Doctor Cortezo 6 (Metro Sol/Tirso de Molina). Six-screen complex which shows most films in *v.o.*

Imax Madrid, Parque Tierno Galván, Meneses (Metro Méndez Alvaro). Three different types of screen at this futuristic cinema – a giant flat one, a dome-shaped one for all-round viewing and one for 3D projections. Continuous shows: Mon–Fri 11.20am–1pm & 3.45pm–1am, Sat & Sun 11.20am–2.15pm & 3.45pm–1am; 850–1000ptas.

Theatre and cabaret

Madrid is enjoying a renaissance in theatre; you can catch anything from Lope de Vega to contemporary and experimental productions, and there's also a new wave of cabaret and comedy acts.

Círculo de Bellas Artes, c/de Alcalá 42 (☎91 531 77 00; Metro Sevilla). The Círculo includes a beautiful old theatre which puts on adventurous productions.

Centro Cultural de la Villa, Plaza de Colón (☎91 575 60 80; Metro Colón). Arts centre where you're likely to see some of the more experimental companies on tour as well as popular works and *zarzuela* performances.

Teatro Alfil, c/Pez 10 (☎91 521 58 27; Metro Noviciado). Alternative theatre and comedy.

Teatro Español, c/Príncipe 25 (☎91 429 62 97; Metro Sol/Sevilla). Classic Spanish theatre.

Teatro María Guerrero, c/Tamayo y Baus 4 (☎91 319 47 69; Metro Colón). This is the headquarters of the Centro Dramático Nacional which stages high-quality Spanish and international productions in a beautiful neo-Mudéjar interior.

Teatro Muñoz Seca, Plaza del Carmen 1 (☎91 521 37 90; Metro Sol). This theatre hosts regular performances of *Sainetes*, traditional Spanish plays.

Teatro Nuevo Apolo, Plaza Tirso de Molina 1 (☎91 429 52 38; Metro Tirso de Molina). Madrid's principal venue for major musicals.

Shopping

Shopping districts in Madrid are pretty defined. The biggest range of stores are along Gran Vía and around Puerta del Sol, which is where the **department stores** – such as El Corte Inglés – have their main branches. For **fashion** (*moda*), the smartest addresses are c/de Serrano, c/de Goya and c/de Velázquez, north of the Retiro, while more alternative designers are to be found in Malasaña and Chueca (c/Almirante, especially). The **antiques** trade is centred down towards the Rastro, on and around c/Ribera de Curtidores, or in the Puerta de Toledo shopping centre (Metro Puerta de Toledo), while for **general weirdness**, it's hard to beat the shops just off Plaza Mayor, where luminous saints rub shoulders with surgical supports and fascist memorabilia. The cheapest, trashiest **souvenirs** can be collected at the Todo a Cien Pesetas ("Everything 100ptas") shops scattered all over the city. If you want international or speciality shops, head for Madrid 2, a huge hypermarket next to Metro Barrio de Pilar or the upmarket ABC Serrano at c/Serrano 61 and Paseo de la Castellana 34 (Metro Nuñez de Balboa).

Most areas of the city have their own *mercados del barrio* – indoor **markets**, devoted mainly to food. Among the best and most central are those in Plaza San Miguel (just west of Plaza Mayor); La Cebada in Plaza de la Cebada (Metro La Latina); Antón Martín in c/de Santa Isabel (Metro Antón Martín); behind the Gran Vía in Plaza de Mostenses (Metro Plaza de España); on c/Gravina in Chueca (Metro Chueca); on c/Barceló in Malasaña (Metro Tribunal); and Maravillas in c/Bravo Murillo 122 (Metro Cuatro Caminos). The city's biggest market is, of course, **El Rastro** – the flea market – which takes place on Sundays in Latina, south of Plaza Mayor. For details of this great Madrid institution, see box, p.75. Other specialized markets include a secondhand **book market** on the Cuesta de Moyano, at the southwest corner of El Retiro.

OPENING HOURS AND LATE NIGHT SHOPPING

Usual **opening hours** are Monday–Friday 9.30am–2pm & 5–8pm, Saturday 10am–2pm. Nearly all shops are closed on Sunday, but the larger stores do open on the first Sunday of each month (not in Aug). There are however two chains of late-night shops – Vip's and 7 Eleven – that stay open into the small hours and on Sundays. Each branch sells newspapers, cigarettes, groceries, books, CDs – all the things you need to pop in for at 3am. Larger branches also have café-restaurants, one-hour photo developing and other services.

Central branches include:

Vip's (daily 9am–3am): Glorieta de Quevedo (Metro Quevedo); Gran Vía 43 (Metro Gran Vía); c/Fuencarral 101 (Metro Bilbao); c/Miguel Ángel 11 (Metro Rubén Darío); c/Serrano 41 (Metro Serrano); c/Velázquez 84 & 136 (Metro Velázquez).

7 Eleven (daily 24hr): c/de Arenal 28 (Metro Sol/Opera); c/Toledo 80 (La Latina); Agustín de Foxá 25 (Metro Plaza de Castilla); Avda. de América 18 (Metro Avda. de América); Capitán Haya 17–19 (Metro Lima); San Bernardo 33 (Metro Noviciados).

Crafts and miscellaneous

Alvarez Gómez, c/Serrano 14 (Metro Serrano). Gómez has been making the same perfumes in the same bottles for the past century. The scents – carnations, rose, violets – are as simple and straight as they come. Mon–Sat 9.30am–2pm & 4.45–8.15pm.

El Arco de los Cuchilleros, Plaza Mayor 9 – by the steps (Metro Sol). The location of this shop may be at the heart of tourist Madrid but the goods are a far cry from the swords, lace and castanets that fill most shops in the region. El Arco handles thirty or so workshops and artesans, who reflect Spanish *artesanía* at its most innovative and contemporary. They encompass ceramics (six of Madrid's top potters), leather (from Oviedo), wood (including some fine games), jewellery and textiles. Mon–Sat 11am–8pm, Sun 11am–2.30pm.

Conde Hermanos, c/Felipe II 2 (Metro Opera). Mon–Fri 9.30am–1.30pm & 4.30–8pm. **José Ramírez**, c/Concepción Jerónima (Metro Sol/Tirso de Molina). Mon–Fri 9.30am–2pm & 5–8pm, Sat 10am–2pm. Two of the most renowned guitar workshops in Spain; the latter even has a museum of antique instruments. Prices start at around 15,000ptas and head skywards for the quality models and fancy woods.

El Flamenco Vive, c/de la Unión 4 (Metro Opera). Specializes in all things Andalucian; flamenco music, guitars, percussion, dance accessories, books etc. Mon–Sat 10.30am–2pm & 5–9pm.

Fútbol Total, c/de Cardenal Cisneros 80 (Metro Quevedo). Just the place to get your Real, Atlético or even Rayo shirt. In fact the strip of practically every Spanish team is available, for around 7000ptas. Mon–Sat: July–Sept 10.30am–2pm & 5.30–8.30pm; Oct–June 10.30am–2pm & 5–9pm.

Casa Jiménez, c/Preciados 42 (Metro Callao). If you want to buy a fan that's a work of art, this is the place to come. Mon–Sat 10am–1.30pm & 5–8pm, closed Sat pm in July and all day Sat in Aug.

Palomeque, c/Hileras 12 (Metro Opera). A religious department store stocking everything from rosary beads and habits to your very own plastic baby Jesus. If you want to complete your postcard collection of Spanish saints and virgins, this is the place for you. Mon–Fri 10am–2pm & 5–8pm, Sat 10am–2pm.

Puck, c/Duque de Sesto 30 (Metro Goya). This is the best – indeed, about the only decent – toy shop in central Madrid. Mon–Sat 10am–1.30pm & 4.30–8pm.

Puerta de Toledo shopping centre, Metro Puerta de Toledo. This centre has over seventy shops specializing in antiques, jewellery and crafts. Closed Mon.

Seseña, c/de la Cruz 23 (Metro Sol). Tailor specializing in traditional *madrileño* capes for royalty and celebrities. Clients have included Luis Buñuel and Gary Cooper. Mon–Sat 10am–1.30pm & 4.30–8pm.

Casa Yustas, Plaza Mayor 30 (Metro Sol). Madrid's oldest hat shop, established in 1894. Pick from traditional designs for men's and women's hats (*sombreros*), caps (*gorras*) and berets (*boinas*). No cards. Mon–Fri 9.45am–1.30pm & 4.30–8pm, Sat 9.45am–1.30pm.

Books, comics and maps

Booksellers, c/José Abascal 48 (Metro Ríos Rosas). Specializes in English-language books; also stocks videos and has a decent childrens' section. Mon–Fri 9.30am–2pm & 5–8pm, Sat 10am–2pm.

Casa del Libro, Gran Vía 29 & Maestro Victoria 3 (Metro Callao). The city's biggest bookstore, with three floors covering just about everything, including a wide range of fiction in English. Mon–Sat 9.30am–9.30pm.

FNAC, c/Preciados 28 (Metro Callao). The book department of this huge store is a good place to sit and peruse English-language fiction.

Librería Antonio Machado, c/Fernando VI 17 (Metro Alonso Martínez). The city's best literary bookshop. All cards. Mon–Sat 10am–2pm & 5–8pm.

Servicio de Publicaciones del Instituto Geográfico Nacional, c/General Ibañez de Ibero (Metro Guzmán el Bueno). This is the place to get decent-scale walking maps of Spain.

La Tienda Verde, c/Maudes 23 & 38 (Metro Cuatro Caminos). Trekking and mountain books, guides and survey (*topográfico*) maps. Mon–Sat 9.30am–2pm & 4.30–8pm.

Fashion: clothes and shoes

Adolfo Domínguez, c/José Ortega y Gasset 4 & c/Serrano 96 (Metro Serrano). The classic modern Spanish look – subdued colours, free lines. Domínguez's designs are quite pricey but he has a cheaper *Basico* range. Both branches have men's clothes; women's are only available at the Ortega y Gasset branch. Mon–Sat 10am–2pm & 5–8.30pm (Serrano branch open for lunch).

Ararat, c/Conde Xiquena 13 (Metro Chueca) & c/Almirante 10 & 11 (Metro Cheuca). A trio of shops with clubby Spanish and foreign designs at reasonably modest prices. Men's clothes in Conde Xiquena, women's in c/Almirante. Mon–Sat 11am–2pm & 5–8.30pm.

Berlín, c/Almirante 10 (Metro Chueca). Women's clothes from vanguard European designers. Mon–Sat 11am–2pm & 5–8.30pm.

Blackmarket, c/Colón 3 (Metro Chueca). Adventurous clothes for women. Mon–Sat 10.30am–2pm & 5–8.30pm.

Camper, c/Gran Vía 54 (Metro Callao). Spain's best shoe-shop chain, with covetable designs at modest prices. There are lots of other branches around the city. Men and women. Mon–Sat 10am–2pm & 5–8.30pm.

Caracol Cuadrado, c/Justiniano 6 (Metro Serrano). Bargain store selling last season's designs from big names, including Sybilla – Spain's trendiest designer. Men and women. Mon–Sat 10.30am–2.30pm & 5–8.30pm.

Ekseptión, c/Velázquez 28 (Metro Velázquez). A dramatic walkway gives on to some of the most *moderno* clothes in Madrid, from Sybilla and Antoni Miró, among others. Expensive. Men and women. Mon–Sat 10.30am–2.30pm & 5–8.30pm.

Excrupulus Net, c/Almirante 7 (Metro Chueca). Groovy shoes from Spanish designers, Muxart and Looky. Men and women. Mon–Sat 11am–2pm & 5–8.30pm.

Glam, c/de Fuencarral 35 (Metro Gran Vía/Chueca) & c/Hortaleza 62 (Metro Chueca). The clientele and the clothes wouldn't look out of place in an Almodóvar film. Mon–Sat 10am–2pm & 5–9pm.

Hernanz, c/Toledo 30 (Metro Tirso de Molina). This shoe shop stocks *alpargatas* – espadrilles – in just about every imaginable colour. No cards. Mon–Fri 9.30am–1.30pm & 5–8.30pm, Sat 9.30am–1.30pm.

Josep Font-Luz D'az, c/Serrano 58 – patio (Metro Serrano). Beautiful, minimalist shop, selling original and expensive women's designs by this young and *muy de moda* Catalan duo. Women only. Mon–Sat 10am–2pm & 5–8.30pm.

Manuel Herrero, c/Preciados 7 (Metro Sol). Traditional shop specializing in leather; particularly good for coats and jackets.

Sybilla, c/Jorge Juan 12 (Metro Retiro). Sybilla was Spain's top designer of the 1980s – a Vivienne Westwood of Madrid, if you will. She remains at the forefront of the scene, and her prices show it. Women only. All cards. Mon–Sat 10am–2pm & 4.30–8.30pm.

Food and drink

Baco – La Boutique del Vino, c/San Bernardo 117 (Metro Quevedo). Good-value range of quality Spanish wines, *cavas*, brandies and even Asturian cider. No cards. Mon–Fri 11am–2pm & 5–8pm, Sat 10am–2pm.

Casa Mira, Carrera de San Jerónimo 30 (Metro Sol). Old, established *pasteleria*, selling delicious *turrón*, *mazapán*, *frutas glaseadas*, and the like. Daily 10am–2pm & 5–9pm.

Lafuente, c/Luchana 28 (Metro Bilbao). Wines from Spain and abroad, including lots from Rioja, Ribera del Duero and Galicia, plus *cavas*. Mon–Sat 10am–2pm & 5–8.30pm.

Lhardy, Carrera de San Jerónimo 8 (Metro Sol). This bar and deli is attached to one of Madrid's top restaurants – and is a lot more affordable. You can put together wonderful and elaborate picnics (the *croquetas* and *empanadillas* are legendary), assuming you can resist consuming them on the spot. Mon–Sat 9.30am–3pm & 5–9pm, Sun 9am–2pm.

Mallorca, c/Serrano 6 (Metro Serrano). The main branch of Madrid's best deli chain – like *Lhardy*, a pricey but fabulous treasure trove for picnics, or cakes or chocs for presents. All branches have small bars for drinks and canapés. Daily 9.30am–9pm.

Mariano Aguado, c/Echegaray 19 (Metro Sevilla). Fine selection of Spanish wines and, especially, sherries (*vinos de Jerez*). Mon–Sat 9.30am–2pm & 5.30–8.30pm.

Mariano Madrueño, c/Postigo San Martín 3 (Metro Callao). The place to get wines and liqueurs such as *Pacharán* sloe gin. Mon–Fri 9.30am–2pm & 5–8pm, Sat 9.30am–2pm.

Tienda Olivarero, c/Mejia Lequerica 1 (Metro Alonso Martinez). Outlet for olive growers' cooperative, with information sheets to guide you towards purchasing the best olive oils. Mon–Sat 9.30am–2pm & 5.30–7.30pm.

Records and CDs

FNAC, c/Preciados 28 (Metro Callao). Large French store with a huge collection of cassettes and CDs.

Madrid Rock, Gran Vía 25 – underground (Metro Gran Vía). A big, slightly chaotic store, good for rock CDs and concert tickets. Daily 10am–10pm.

Toni Martín, c/Martín de los Heros 18 (Metro Plaza de España). Rock CDs and discs, new and secondhand. Mon–Sat 10.30am–2pm & 5.30–8.15pm.

Listings

Airlines Most airlines have their offices along the Gran Vía or on c/de la Princesa, its continuation beyond the Plaza de España. Addresses include: Avianca, Gran Vía 88 (☎91 205 43 20; Metro Plaza de España); British Airways, c/Serrano 60 5° (☎91 305 42 12 or 91 205 43 17; Metro Serrano); Iberia, c/de Goya 29 (☎91 587 8156; Metro Serrano); KLM, Gran Vía 59 (☎91 247 81 00; Metro Santo Domingo); and TWA, Plaza de Colón 2 (☎91 310 3094; Metro Colón). The Iberojet counter at the airport sells discounted seats on all scheduled flights if you're prepared to queue up and take the risk of not getting on. Tickets for the Puente Aéreo to Barcelona are available in terminal two.

Airport information ☎91 305 83 43, fax 91 393 6200. See p.56 for details of transport to the airport.

American Express Plaza de las Cortes 2 – entrance on Marqués de Cubas (☎91 572 03 03; Metro Sevilla; Mon–Fri 9am–5.30pm & Sat 9am–noon for mail and transactions).

Banks and exchange The main Spanish banks are concentrated on c/Alcalá and Gran Vía. Opening hours are normally Mon–Fri 9am–2pm, but they're also often open on Sat 9am–1pm from October to May. International banks include: Bank of America, c/Capitán Haya 1 (☎91 555 50 00; Metro Santiago Bernabéu); Barclays, Plaza de Colón 1 (☎91 410 28 00; Metro Colón); Citibank, c/José Ortega y Gasset 29 (☎91 435 51 90; Metro Núñez de Balboa); and Lloyds, c/Serrano 90 (☎91 576 70 00; Metro Núñez de Balboa). In addition to the banks, branches of El Corte Inglés department store all have exchange offices with long hours and highly competitive rates; the most central is on Puerta del Sol. Aeropuerto de Barajas has a 24-hr currency exchange office.

Bicycle hire/repairs Try Bicicletas Chapinal, c/Alcalá 242 (☎91 404 18 53; Metro El Carmen; Mon–Fri 10am–1.30pm & 4.30–8pm, Sat 10am–2pm); Calmera, c/Atocha 98 (☎91 527 75 74; Metro Antón Martín; Mon–Sat 9.30am–1.30pm & 4.30–8pm); and Karacol, c/Montera 32 (☎91 532 90 73; Metro Gran Vía/Sol; Mon–Fri 10.30am–2pm & 5.30–8pm, Sat 10.30am–2pm).

Bullfights Madrid's main Plaza de Toros, the monumental Las Ventas (c/Alcalá 237; Metro Ventas), hosts some of the year's most prestigious events, especially during the May San Isidro festivities, though the main season runs from March to October. Tickets are available at the box office at Ventas (☎91 726 48 00/91 356 22 00; March–Oct Thurs–Sun 10am–2pm & 5–8pm) or at Localidades de Galicia (see "Ticket agencies" below); at the latter you pay around fifty percent more than the printed prices, which are for season tickets sold en bloc. There is a second bullring in the suburb of Carabanchel (Avda. Matilde Hernández; Metro Vista Alegre), about 4km to the southwest of the centre.

Car rental Major operators have branches at Aeropuerto de Barajas and around Madrid. Central offices include: Atesa, c/Infanta Mercedes 90 (☎91 571 19 31; Metro Estrecho); Avis, Gran Vía 60 (☎91 547 20 48; Metro Plaza de España); Europcar, c/San Leonardo 8 (☎91 721 12 22; Metro Plaza de España) – also an office in Atocha station; and Hertz, Atocha station (☎91 468 13 18; Metro Atocha). Rent Me, Plaza de Herradores 6, just off Plaza Mayor (☎91 559 08 22; Metro Sol), is a good-value local company.

Disability Madrid is not particularly well geared up for the disabled (*minusválidos*), although the situation is gradually improving. The Organización Nacional de Ciegos de España (ONCE) at c/de Prado 24 (☎91 589 46 00 or 91 577 37 56) provides the best specialist advice. Wheelchair-adapted taxis can be ordered from Radio Taxi (☎91 547 82 00).

Doctors English-speaking doctors are available at the Anglo-American Medical Unit, c/Conde de Aranda 1 (☎91 435 18 23; Metro Retiro; Mon–Fri 9am–8pm, Sat 10am–3pm).

Embassies include: Australia, Paseo de la Castellana 143 (☎91 579 04 28; Metro Cuzco); Britain, c/Fernando el Santo 16 (☎91 319 02 00; Metro Alonso Martínez); Canada, c/Núñez de Balboa 35 (☎91 431 43 00; Metro Núñez de Balboa); Ireland, Paseo de la Castellana 46 (☎91 577 89 31; Metro Rubén Darío); New Zealand, Plaza Lealtad 2 (☎91 523 02 26; Metro Sevilla); USA, c/Serrano 75 (☎91 577 40 00; Metro Rubén Darío).

Emergency For an **ambulance** dial ☎112 or 91 588 45 00 or 91 522 22 22 – or get a taxi, which will be quicker if no paramedics are necessary; ☎112 is also the number for the **police**.

First aid stations are scattered throughout the city and open 24hr a day: one of the most central is at c/Navas de Tolosa (☎91 521 00 25; Metro Callao).

Fitness/gyms If you want to work out, try the Holiday Gyms at Plaza República Dominicana 8 (☎91 457 80 00; Metro Colombia) and Serrano Jover 3 (☎91 547 40 33; Metro Argüelles). There are council-sponsored exercise tracks in El Retiro, the Casa de Campo and at the Complutense University campus.

Football The big teams are Real Madrid, recent champions of Europe, and their city rivals, Atlético Madrid. Tickets can be bought in advance (and usually on the day) at the stadium for most matches, though derbies between Real and Atlético, or visits to either by Barcelona, are always sell-outs. **Real Madrid**: Estadio Santiago Bernabéu, c/Concha Espina s/n (☎ 91 344 00 52; Metro Santiago Bernabéu). Ticket office Mon–Fri 6–9pm; match days 11am–1.30pm. Tickets from 2000ptas go on sale three days before each match. **Atlético Madrid**: Estadio Vicente Calderón, Paseo de la Virgen del Puerto 67 (☎91 366 47 07; Metro Pirámides). Ticket office Mon–Fri 5–8pm; two days before each match also open 11am–2pm. Tickets from 3000ptas. If you fancy a Sunday afternoon game, the English **Five-a-side League** (EFL) sometimes need players if teams are short, with games usually in Retiro (☎91 844 45 25).

Hospitals The most central are: El Clínico, Plaza de Cristo Rey (☎91 330 37 47; Metro Moncloa); Hospital Gregorio Marañon, c/Dr Esquerdo 46 (☎91 586 80 00; Metro O'Donnell); and Ciudad Sanitaria La Paz, Paseo de la Castellana 261 (☎91 358 28 31; Metro Diego de León).

Language courses Madrid has numerous language schools, offering intensive courses in Spanish language (and culture). One of the most established is International House, c/Zurbano 8 (☎91 310 13 14; Metro Alonso Martínez).

Laundry Central *lavanderías* include: c/del Barco 26 (Metro Gran Vía); c/de Cervantes 1–3 (Metro Sol); c/Donoso Cortés 17 (Metro Quevedo); c/de Hermosilla 121 (Metro Goya); and c/de la Palma 2 (Metro Tribunal).

Left luggage If you want to leave your bags there are *consignas* at the Estación Sur, Auto-Res and Continental Auto bus stations; and lockers at Atocha and Chamartín train stations.

Pharmacies *Farmácias* are distinguished by a green cross; each district has a rota with one staying open through the night – for details ☎098 or check the notice on the door of your nearest pharmacy or the listings magazines. Madrid also has quite a number of traditional **herbalists**, best known of which is Maurice Mességue, c/de Goya 64 (Metro Goya; Mon–Fri 10am–2pm & 5–8pm, Sat 10am–2pm).

Post office The main one is the Palacio de Comunicaciones in the Plaza de las Cibeles (Mon–Sat 8am–midnight, Sun 8am–10pm for stamps and telegrams; Mon–Fri 9am–8pm, Sat 9am–2pm for *Lista de Correos* – poste restante). Branch offices, for example on c/Cruz Verde on the edge of Malasaña, are open Mon–Sat 9am–2pm, but the easiest places to buy stamps are the *estancos*, recognizable by their brown and yellow signs bearing the word *Tabacos*.

Scooter hire If you want to chance the traffic, scooters are delivered to and collected from your hotel by Alquiler de Scooter (☎902 10 20 20) at a charge of 2000ptas a day. Also worth trying is Motoalquiler at c/Conde Duque 13 (☎91 542 06 57; Metro Noviciado).

Swimming pools and aquaparks The Piscina Canal Isabel II, Avda. de Filipinas 54 (daily 10am–8.30pm; Metro Ríos Rosas), is a large and well-maintained outdoor swimming pool, and the best central option. Alternatively, try the open-air *piscina* in the Casa de Campo (daily 10am–8.30pm; Metro El Lago); this is an older pool and best (or at least, cleanest) earlier in the day. Both these pools have café-bars attached. Also worth trying are the pools at Barrio del Pilar, Avda. Monforte de Lemos (Metro Barrio del Pilar/Begoña), and La Elipa, Parque de la Elipa, c/ O'Donnell s/n (Metro Estrella). There are also a number of aquaparks around Madrid. The closest is Aquamadrid 16 km out on the N2 Barcelona road (Bus Continental Auto #281, #282, #282, or #385 from Avda. de América). Note that the "swimming season" is from May to September, so outside these months, most outdoor pools are closed.

Telephones International calls can be made from any phone box or from any *telefónica*. The main *telefónica* at Gran Vía 30 (Metro Gran Vía) is open until midnight. Phone cards cost 1000ptas or 2000ptas and can be bought at post offices or *estancos*.

Thefts If you've had something stolen call ☎900 100 333 (English spoken).

Ticket agencies For theatre and concert tickets try Tele-Entradas, a telephone booking service run by Caja de Cataluña (☎91 538 33 33), Caja de Madrid (☎902 488488) and Servi-Caixa (☎91 902 33 22 11). None of these charge commission. Localidades Galicia, Plaza del Carmen 1 (☎531 27 32/☎531 91 31; Metro Sol), sells tickets for football games, bullfights, theatres and concerts.

Train tours The Tren de la Fresa (Strawberry train) is a steam train which runs each Saturday and Sunday (April–Oct) from Atocha to Aranjuez. Tours include free strawberries which are given out by women in period costume. Bookings from travel agents or the RENFE offices (see "Travel Details" below) or call ☎902 228822. Tours depart at 10am, return at 7.30pm and cost 2900ptas.

Travel agencies Viajes Zeppelin, Plaza Santo Domingo 2 (☎91 547 79 04; Metro Santo Domingo), are English-speaking, very efficient and offer some excellent deals on flights and holidays. Nuevas Fronteras, c/Luisa Fernanda 2 (☎91 542 39 90; Metro Ventura Rodríguez), and in the Torre de Madrid, Plaza de España (☎91 247 42 00) can be good for flights, or try Top Tours, c/Capitán Haja 20 (☎91 555 06 04; Metro Cuzco). For student and youth travel try TIVE, c/Fernando el Católico 88 (☎91 543 02 08; Metro Moncloa). Many other travel agents are concentrated on and around the Gran Vía and c/de la Princesa.

Walks Madrid's tourist offices can supply details of guided walks around the city, for around 500ptas a walk.

Women's groups The best places to make contact are at the Centro de La Mujer, c/del Barquillo 44, 10 (☎91 319 36 89; Metro Chueca), and at Madrid's feminist bookshop, the Librería de Mujeres, c/San Cristóbal 17, just east of Plaza Mayor (☎91 521 70 43; Metro Sol).

travel details

TRAINS

For train **information** and **reservations** call ☎91 328 90 20. **Tickets** can be bought at the individual stations, at Aeropuerto de Barajas arrivals and at the city centre RENFE office, c/de Alcalá 44 (☎91 562 33 33; Metro Banco de España; Mon–Fri 8am–8pm). All Madrid trains run through one or more of the two stations below. **Chamartín**, in the north, has the most services and includes through-trains to **Atocha**. If you arrive at (or are leaving from) Chamartín, you can use a *cercanía* train to/from Atocha, or catch the metro. Some through-trains also stop at the Recoletos and Nuevos Ministerios stations. Note that the new **high-speed AVE trains** to Córdoba and Sevilla run from Atocha. These must be booked in advance, either in person at Atocha, at the RENFE office in c/Alcalá 44, or by phone (☎91 328 90 20).

Atocha Station (Metro Atocha): Algeciras (1 daily; 11hr); Almería (1–2 daily; 6hr 45min); Aranjuez (every 15/30min; 40min); Badajoz (3 daily; 5hr 40min–7hr); Cáceres (5 daily; 4hr–4hr 30min); Cádiz (2 daily; 5hr); Córdoba (15 daily; 2hr; 1hr 40min AVE); Cuenca (4 daily; 2hr 30min); Granada (4 daily; 6hr); Huelva (1 daily; 4hr 30min); Jaén (3 daily; 4hr 15min); Jerez (3 daily; 4hr 10min); Málaga (11 daily; 4hr 30min–6hr 50min); Mérida (6 daily; 4–7hr); Segovia (7 daily; 2hr); Sevilla (19 daily; 3hr 15min; 2hr 30min AVE); Torremolinos (3 daily; 4–5hr); Valencia (6 daily; 3hr 45min). Plus most destinations in the south and west.

Chamartín (Metro Chamartín): Albacete (22 daily; 2hr); Alicante (7 daily; 4hr); Astorga (1 daily; 5hr); Ávila (17 daily; 2hr); Barcelona (9 daily; 7hr); Bilbao (2 daily; 5hr 30min–8hr 45min); Burgos (7 daily; 3hr 45min); Cáceres (7 daily; 4–5hr); Cartagena (4 daily; 5hr); El Ferrol (1 daily; 11hr); Guadalajara (every 30 min; 1hr); La Coruña (2 daily; 8hr 30min–11hr); León (8 daily; 4hr–4hr 30min); Lisbon (1 daily; 10hr); Lugo (1 daily; 9hr 30min); Oviedo (3 daily; 6hr); Pamplona (2 daily;

5hr); Paris (1 daily; 13hr 30min); Pontevedra (2 daily; 8hr 30min–10hr 30min); Salamanca (3 daily; 3hr 15min); San Sebastián (3 daily; 6hr 30min); Santander (3 daily; 5hr 30min); Santiago (2 daily; 7hr 15min–9hr 30min); Vigo (2 daily; 7hr 45min–8hr 30min); Zamora (2 daily; 3hr–3hr 30min); Zaragoza (13 daily; 3hr). Plus most other destinations in the east, northeast and northwest.

BUSES

A bewildering number of companies operate buses from Madrid, each from their own garage or terminus. Many of the services, however, run through the **Estación Sur de Autobuses** (☎91 468 42 00), to the south of Atocha on the circular #6 metro line.

Note that companies and services change with great frequency and it's always worth checking schedules with the Turismo or the **Information line** (☎91 435 22 66).

Estación Sur de Autobuses, c/Méndez Alvaro s/n (Metro Méndez Alvaro): Albacete (11 daily; 3hr); Alicante (8 daily; 5hr); Almería (3 daily; 6hr 30 min); Barcelona (15 daily; 7hr 30 min–8hr); Ciudad Real (2–4 daily; 3hr); Córdoba (7 daily; 4hr 30min); Gijón (12 daily; 5hr); Granada (13 daily; 5hr); Jaén (2–6 daily; 5hr); León (11 daily; 4hr 15min); Málaga (9 daily; 6hr); Palencia (5 daily; 3hr); Santiago (4 daily; 9hr); Sevilla (11 daily; 5hr 30min); Toledo (every 15min; 1hr); Zaragoza (17 daily; 4hr); and international services to France and Portugal.

Auto-Res, Fernández Shaw 1 (☎91 551 72 00; Metro Conde Casal): Badajoz (10 daily; 4hr 30min–5hr 15min); Cáceres (10 daily; 3hr 30min–4hr 15min); Cuenca (10 daily; 2hr–2hr 30min); Mérida (10 daily; 4–5hr); Salamanca (24 daily; 2hr 30min–3hr); Trujillo (10 daily; 4–5hr); Zamora (9 daily; 2hr 45min–3hr 15min).

Continental Auto, c/Alenza 20 (☎91 533 04 00; Metro Ríos Rosas): Aranda (4 daily; 2hr); Bilbao (11 daily; 4hr 30min); Burgos (11 daily; 2hr 45min); El Burgo de Osma (2 daily; 4hr); Guadalajara (13 daily; 45min); Logroño (5 daily; 4hr 30min–5hr 30min); Pamplona (4 daily; 5–6hr); San Sebastián (9 daily; 6–8hr); Santander (8 daily; 5hr 45min); Soria (6 daily; 2hr 30min–3hr).

La Sepulvedana, Paseo de la Florida 11 (☎91 530 48 00; Metro Príncipe Pío): Ávila (4 daily; 1hr 30min); Segovia (22 daily; 1hr 30min); and other points in Old Castile.

Herranz, Intercambiador de Autobuses de Moncloa, an underground terminal just above Metro Moncloa: El Escorial (approx. every 30min). Onward connections to El Valle de los Caídos.

CHAPTER TWO

AROUND MADRID

The lack of historic monuments in Madrid is more than compensated for by the region around the capital. Within a radius of 100km – and within an hour's travel by bus or train – are some of the greatest cities of Spain. Above all, there is Toledo, which preceded Madrid as the Spanish capital. Immortalized by El Greco, who lived and worked there for most of his later career, the city is a living museum to the many cultures – Visigothic, Moorish, Jewish and Christian – which have shaped the destiny of Spain. If you have time for just one trip from Madrid, there is really no other choice.

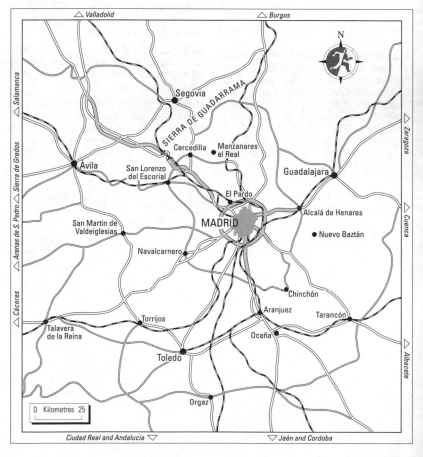

FIESTAS

February
Second weekend *Santa Agueda* women's festival in Segovia, when women take over city administration and parade and celebrate in traditional costume. Occurs to an extent throughout the province, especially in Zamarramala just outside the city.

Week before Lent *Carnaval* is the excuse for lively fiestas all over the place.

March/April
Holy Week *Semana Santa* is celebrated everywhere, but with great formality and processions in Toledo and a passion play on Saturday in Chinchón.

Mid-April *Fiesta del Anís y del Vino* in Chinchón.

May
Corpus Christi (variable – the Thursday after Trinity, which sometimes falls in June) sees a very solemn, costumed religious procession in Toledo.

June
24 *San Juan y San Pablo*. A lively procession with floats and music in Segovia.
30 In Hita (north of Guadalajara) the fiesta has a medieval theme, with performances of old theatre, feasts, dances, and sporting events including falconry and bull-lancing.

July
There's a big festival in Ávila in **mid-July**; a rowdy affair with bullfights, music and dances. In Segovia the festival runs over throughout **July and August**, with music, folk and dance festivities.

August
15 Celebrations for the *Virgen de la Asunción* in Chinchón include an *encierro*, with bulls running through the street.

25 Good fiestas in La Granja (near Segovia) and Orgaz (near Toledo).

The **third week of the month** marks the August fiestas in Toledo, in honour of the *Virgen del Sagrario*; amazing fireworks on the final weekend.

28 Bull running in Cuéllar (north of Segovia).

In the **last week in the month** there are some spectacular parades of giant puppets, and plenty of theatre, music and dance in Alcalá de Henares.

September
Aranjuez holds a fiesta over the **first weekend of the month**, and a re-enactment of the *Motín de Aranjuez* (Mutiny of Aranjuez).

October
Second week Ávila goes wild for the *Feria de Santa Teresa*. There are organ recitals in the churches too.

That said, **Segovia**, with its stunning Roman aqueduct and irresistible, Disney-prototype castle, puts up strong competition, while Felipe II's vast palace-mausoleum of **El Escorial** is a monument to out-monument all others. And there are smaller places, too, less known to foreign tourists: **Aranjuez**, an oasis in the parched Castilian plain, famed for its asparagus, strawberries and lavish Baroque palace; the beautiful walled city of **Ávila**, birthplace of Saint Teresa; and Cervantes's home town, **Alcalá de Henares**, with its sixteenth-century university. For walkers, too, trails amid the sierras of **Gredos** and **Guadarrama** provide enticing escapes from the midsummer heat.

All of the towns in this chapter can be visited as an easy day trip from Madrid, but they also offer interesting jumping-off points into Castile and beyond; details of onward travel follow each main entry. Wherever you're going, it's a good idea to pick up leaflets in advance from one of the tourist offices in Madrid.

Toledo

Despite its reputation as one of Spain's greatest cities, **TOLEDO** can prove to be a bit of a disappointment. Certainly, it's a city redolent of past glories, and is packed with

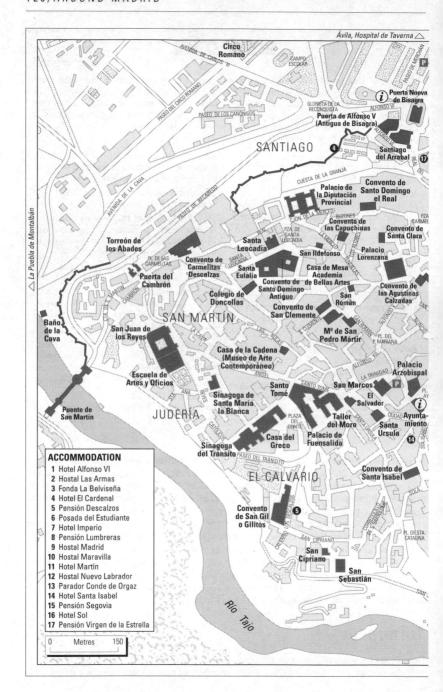

Ávila, Hospital de Taverna △

Circo Romano

CAMPO ESCOLAR

AVENIDA DE CARLOS III

PASEO DEL CIRCO ROMANO

PASEO DE LOS CANÓNIGOS

GLORIETA DE LA RECONQUISTA

Puerta Nueva de Bisagra

Puerta de Alfonso V (Antigua de Bisagra)

ALFONSO VI

SANTIAGO

Santiago del Arrabal

CUESTA DE LA GRANJA

Palacio de la Diputación Provincial

Convento de Santo Domingo el Real

BUZONES

Convento de las Capuchinas

Convento de Santa Clara

PZA CARMEL

Torreón de los Abades

Santa Leocadia

San Ildefonso

Palacio Lorenzana

Convento de Carmelitas Descalzas

Puerta del Cambrón

Santa Eulalia

Casa de Mesa Academia

Convento de Santo Domingo Antiguo

Convento de de Bellas Artes

San Román

Convento de las Agustinas Calzadas

Colegio de Doncellas

SAN MARTÍN

Convento de San Clemente

Baño de la Cava

San Juan de los Reyes

Mª de San Pedro Mártir

PL. DEL P. MARIANA

Casa de la Cadena (Museo de Arte Contemporáneo)

Escuela de Artes y Oficios

Palacio Arzobispal

Puente de San Martín

Santo Tomé

San Marcos

El Salvador

Sinagoga de Santa María la Blanca

JUDERÍA

Taller del Moro

Santa Úrsula

Ayuntamiento

Casa del Greco

Palacio de Fuensalida

Sinagoga del Tránsito

PASEO DEL TRÁNSITO

EL CALVARIO

Convento de Santa Isabel

ACCOMMODATION

1 Hotel Alfonso VI
2 Hostal Las Armas
3 Fonda La Belviseña
4 Hotel El Cardenal
5 Pensión Descalzos
6 Posada del Estudiante
7 Hotel Imperio
8 Pensión Lumbreras
9 Hostal Madrid
10 Hostal Maravilla
11 Hotel Martín
12 Hostal Nuevo Labrador
13 Parador Conde de Orgaz
14 Hotel Santa Isabel
15 Pensión Segovia
16 Hotel Sol
17 Pensión Virgen de la Estrella

Convento de San Gil o Gilitos

San Cipriano

San Sebastián

Río Tajo

0   Metres   150

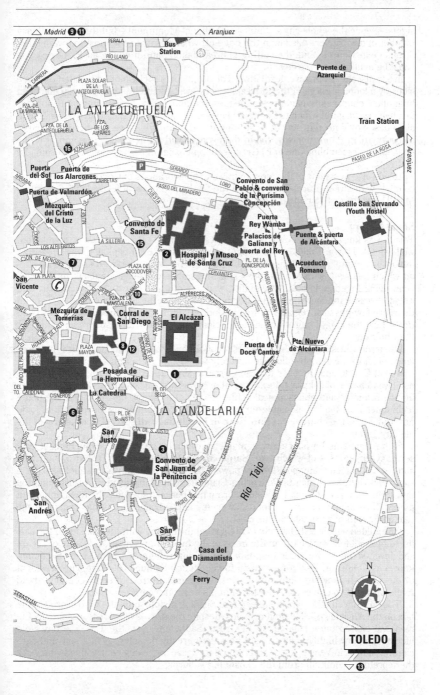

sights – hence the whole city's status as a National Monument – but the extraordinary number of day trippers has taken the edge off what was once the most extravagant of Spanish experiences. Still, the setting is breathtaking, and if you're an **El Greco** fan, you'd be mad to miss this city.

In a landscape of abrasive desolation, Toledo sits on a rocky mound isolated on three sides by a looping gorge of the Río Tajo. Every available inch of this outcrop has been built upon: churches, synagogues, mosques and houses are heaped upon one another in a haphazard spiral which the cobbled lanes infiltrate as best they can. To see Toledo at its best, you'll need to stay at least a night: a day trip will leave you hard pressed to see everything. More importantly, in the evening with the crowds gone and lit up by floodlights – resembling one of El Greco's moonlit paintings – Toledo is a different city entirely.

Toledo also hosts one of the most extravagant celebrations of **Corpus Christi** in the country, with street processions and all the works. Other local festivals take place on May 25 and August 15 and 20.

Some history

Toledo was known to the Romans, who captured it in 193 BC, as *Toletum*, a small but well-defended town. Taken by the Visigoths, who made it their capital, it was already an important cultural and trading centre by the time the **Moors** arrived in 712. The period which followed, with Moors, Jews and Mozárabes (Christians subject to Moorish rule) living together in relative equality, was one of rapid growth and prosperity and Toledo became the most important northern outpost of the Muslim emirates. Though there are few physical remains of this period, except the miniature mosque of **Cristo de la Luz**, the long domination has left a clear mark on the atmosphere and shape of the whole city.

When the Christian king Alfonso VI "reconquered" the town in 1085, with the assistance of El Cid, Moorish influence scarcely weakened. Although Toledo became the capital of Castile and the base for campaigns against the Moors in the south, the city itself was a haven of cultural tolerance. Not only was there a school of translators revealing the scientific and philosophical achievements of the East, but Arab craftsmen and techniques remained responsible for many of the finest buildings of the period: look, for example, at the churches of **San Román** or **Santiago del Arrabal** or at any of the old **city gates**.

At the same time Jewish culture remained powerful. There were, at one time, at least seven **synagogues** – of which two, **Santa María la Blanca** and **Tránsito**, survive – and Jews occupied many positions of power. The most famous was Samuel Levi, treasurer and right-hand man of Pedro the Cruel until the king lived up to his name by murdering him and stealing his wealth. From this period, too, dates the most important purely Christian monument, Toledo's awesome **cathedral** (the city has remained the seat of the Catholic primate to this day).

This golden age ended abruptly in the sixteenth century with the transfer of the capital to Madrid, following hard on the heels of the Inquisition's mass expulsion of Moors and Jews; some of the latter responded by taking refuge in Catholicism, becoming known as *Conversos*. Few Jews remain today, though Samuel Toledano, late president of the Spanish Israelite Community, was descended from a fifteenth-century grand rabbi, his family name considered proof of his descent from *Conversos*.

The city played little part in subsequent Spanish history until the Civil War (see the box on the **Alcázar**, p.130) and it remains, despite the droves of tourists, essentially the medieval city so often painted by El Greco. Sadly, however, the Tajo, the city's old lifeblood, is now highly polluted, and its waters greatly depleted by industry and agriculture. And, as in Venice, fewer and fewer people live in the city centre; most who work there prefer to commute from the expanding suburbs.

Toledo has been a byword for fine **steel** for a thousand years or more and the glint of knives in souvenir shops is one of the first things you'll notice on arrival. Some have traced the craft back to the Romans and it was certainly a growth industry when the Moors were here. By the seventeenth century, Samuel Butler was complaining that "the trenchant blade, Toledo trusty, for want of fighting was growing rusty". Today it's surprising that, except for a modern display in the Alcázar, there's little to see outside the shops; in these you can still admire attractive damascene steel swords and knives, with handles inlaid with decorative gold and silver filigree.

Arrival and information

Orientation is pretty straightforward in Toledo, with the compact old city looped by the Tajo, and the new quarters across the bridges. **Getting to the city**, too, is easy, with nine trains per day (fewer on Sat & Sun) from Madrid Atocha (7am–8.30pm; 1hr 15min), plus buses every thirty minutes from the Estación Sur (6.30am–10pm; 1hr 15min).

Toledo's **train station**, a marvellous 1919 mock-Mudéjar creation, is some way out on the Paseo de la Rosa, a beautiful twenty-minute walk – take the right-hand fork off the dual carriageway and cross the Puente de Alcántara – or a bus ride (#5 or #6) to the heart of town. The **bus station** is on Avenida de Castilla la Mancha in the modern, lower part of the city; buses run frequently to Plaza de Zocódover, though if you take short cuts through the *barrio* at the bottom of the hill just inside the walls, it's a mere ten minutes to the Puerta Nueva de Bisagra.

If you're **driving** – and from Madrid there's little point if you're not going on elsewhere – be aware that parking in Toledo is a problem: the only 24-hour car park is on Paseo del Miradero, below the Plaza de Zocódover, and it's expensive (1650ptas per day). If your hotel hasn't got its own parking facilities (and with creeping pedestrianization, this is increasingly likely), leave your car outside the city walls at, say, Paseo de Merchán; remember that the city tow truck is very active.

Information
Toledo's main **Turismo** (July & Aug Mon–Sat 9am–7pm, Sun 9am–3pm; Sept–June Mon–Fri 9am–6pm; ☎925 220843) is outside the city walls opposite the Puerta Nueva de Bisagra and next to a convenient taxi rank; it has full lists of places to stay, maps showing the monuments, admission times and charges.

There's also a smaller but more central Turismo run by the local *Ayuntamiento* in the plaza opposite the cathedral (Mon–Fri 9am–2pm & 4–6pm).

Accommodation

Booking a **room** in advance is important, especially at weekends, or during the summer. If you're on a limited budget, hotel choice is complemented by private rooms, but you'll need to arrive early in the day. At slow times of the year "agents" hover in the

ACCOMMODATION PRICE CODES

The codes used in our hotel listings denote the following price ranges:

① Under 2000ptas	④ 4500–6000ptas	⑦ 12,000–17,500ptas
② 2000–3000ptas	⑤ 6000–8000ptas	⑧ Over 17,500ptas
③ 3000–4500ptas	⑥ 8000–12,000ptas	

See p.34 for more details.

Plaza de Zocódover, pouncing on those arriving by bus and offering to find a room for a small fee. Since places are scattered all over town, and the guides will know which have space, this can save time and trouble.

Budget options

Hostal Las Armas, c/Armas 7 (☎925 221668). Small rooms in a pleasant old house, conveniently located next to Plaza de Zocódover; can be noisy at night. Open April–Oct. ③.

Fonda La Belviseña, Cuesta del Can 7 (☎925 220067). South of the Alcázar; cheap, good-value *fonda* and hence popular; the dozen rooms fill up quickly. ②.

Castillo San Servando (☎925 224554). Toledo's youth hostel and student residence is on the outskirts of town in a wing of the fourteenth-century Castillo San Servando; a fifteen-minute walk (signposted) from the train station. It's a good option, with a fine view of the city, and booking is advised. Closed mid-Aug to mid-Sept. ①.

Posada del Estudiante, Callejón de San Pedro 2 (☎925 214734). Hidden down a side street near the cathedral, this former student residence offers bargain accommodation. ②.

Pensión Lumbreras, c/Juan Labrador 9 (☎925 221571). Simple rooms around a courtyard; those on top floor have fine rooftop views. Rooms with bath available. ②.

Pensión Segovia, c/Recoletos 2 (☎925 211124). On a narrow street off c/Armas. Well-maintained and cheap; the rooms have washbasins – you pay extra for showers. ②.

Pensión Virgen de la Estrella, c/Real del Arrabal 18 (☎925 253134). Small, with shared facilities, but decent enough, on the main road up to the old town, near Puerta de Bisagra – ask at the bar of the same name across the road. ②.

Moderate and expensive options

Hotel Alfonso VI, c/General Moscardó 2 (☎925 222600, fax 925 214458). Pleasant hotel facing the Alcázar; some rooms with balconies have views of the Río Tajo. ⑦.

Hotel El Cardenal, Paseo de Recaredo 24 (☎925 224900, fax 925 222991). Splendid old palace with famous restaurant, located outside the city wall, near Puerta Nueva de Bisagra. ⑥.

Pensión Descalzos, c/Descalzos 30 (☎ & fax 925 222888). Centrally located *pensión*, handy for the main sights. Modern and a bit pricey, though some rooms without facilities are cheaper. ④.

Hotel Imperio, c/Cadenas 5 (☎925 227650, fax 925 253183). Modern and decently furnished with an in-house coffee shop and reasonable restaurant next door. Handy for Plaza de Zocódover. ⑤.

Hostal Madrid, c/Marqués de Mendigorría 7 (☎925 221114). Comfortable but a bit of a way from the old town. ④.

Hostal Maravilla, c/Barrio Rey 5 & 7 (☎925 223304, fax 925 228155). A prime location just off Plaza de Zocódover, and it's air-conditioned. ⑤.

Hotel Martín, c/Covachuelas 12 (☎ & fax 925 221733). Relatively new and good value for money, in a residential area close to the bus station. ⑤.

Hostal Nuevo Labrador, c/Juan Labrador 10 (☎925 222620, fax 925 229399). Conveniently placed *hostal*, with more rooms than most. ④.

Parador Conde de Orgaz, Cerro del Emperador (☎925 221850, fax 925 225166). Superb views of the city from the terrace of Toledo's top hotel, but a good walk from the centre. ⑦.

Hotel Santa Isabel, c/Santa Isabel 24 (☎925 253120, fax 925 253136). Best of the mid-range hotels, right in the centre, with safe parking. ④.

Hotel Sol, c/Azacanes 15 (☎925 213650, fax 925 216159). Good value, on a quiet side street just off the main road up to the Plaza de Zocódover before the Puerta del Sol. The owners also run the cheaper *hostal* across the street – ask at reception. ④.

Camping

Camping El Greco (☎925 220090). Much the best campsite in the area and a thirty-minute walk from the Puerta de Bisagra: cross the Puente de la Cava towards Puebla de Montalbán, then follow the signs. There are great views of the city from here – and a bar to enjoy them from – plus a swimming pool to cool off in after a hard day's sight-seeing. Open all year.

Camping Circo Romano, Avda. Carlos III 19 (☎925 220442). Nearer town, but a rundown site, worth considering only if the *El Greco* is full. Open all year.
Camping Toledo, Autovia Madrid–Toledo, km 63 (☎925 353013). 9km northeast of Toledo, off the Madrid road by the village of Olias del Rey. This is a handy site if you have your own vehicle. Open April–Sept.

The City

The street layout and labelling in Toledo can be confusing, but the old core is so small that you'll soon find your way round; part of the city's charm is that it's a place to wander and absorb, so don't overdose on "sights" if you can avoid it. You shouldn't leave without seeing at least the El Grecos, the cathedral, the synagogues and Alcázar, but give it all time and you may stumble upon things not listed in this or any other guidebook. Enter any inviting doorway and you may find stunning patios, rooms and ceilings, often of Mudéjar workmanship.

The cathedral

In a country so overflowing with massive religious institutions, the metropolitan **Catedral** has to be something special – and it is. A robust Gothic construction which took over 250 years (1227–1493) to complete, it has a richness of internal decoration in almost every conceivable style, with masterpieces of the Gothic, Renaissance and Baroque periods. The exterior is best appreciated from outside the city, where the 100-metre spire and the weighty buttressing can be seen to greatest advantage. From the street it's less impressive, so hemmed in by surrounding houses that you can't really sense the scale or grandeur of the whole.

There are eight doorways, but the main entrance is at present through the **Puerta Llana** on the southern side of the main body of the cathedral. Tickets (500ptas) for the various chapels, chapter houses and treasuries which require them are sold in the cathedral shop opposite. The main body of the cathedral is closed from 1 to 3.30pm; the parts which need tickets can be visited daily from 10.30am to 1pm and from 3.30 to 6.30pm (in September through to April, from 3.30 to 6pm). The *coro* is closed on Sunday morning, and the New Museums on Monday.

THE CORO AND CAPILLA MAYOR

Inside the cathedral, the central nave is divided from four aisles by a series of clustered pillars supporting the vaults, 88 in all, the aisles continuing around behind the main altar to form an apse. There is magnificent **stained glass** throughout, mostly dating from the fifteenth and sixteenth centuries, particularly beautiful in two rose windows above the north and south doors. Beside the south door (Puerto de los Leones) is a huge, ancient **fresco of Saint Christopher**.

At the physical heart of the church, blocking the nave, is the **Coro** (Choir), itself a panoply of sculpture. The carved wooden stalls are in two tiers. The lower level, by Rodrigo Alemán, depicts the conquest of Granada, with each seat showing a different village being taken by the Christians. The portraits of Old Testament characters on the stalls above were executed in the following century, on the north side by Philippe Vigarni and on the south by Alonso Berruguete, whose superior technique is evident. He also carved the large **Transfiguration** here from a single block of alabaster. The *reja* (grille) which encloses the *coro* is said to be plated with gold, but it was covered in iron to disguise its value from Napoleon's troops and has since proved impossible to renovate.

The **Capilla Mayor** stands directly opposite. Its gargantuan altarpiece, stretching clear to the roof, is one of the triumphs of Gothic art, overflowing with intricate detail and fanciful embellishments. It contains a synopsis of the entire New Testament, culminating in a calvary at the summit. On either side are the tombs of the mighty, including (on the left)

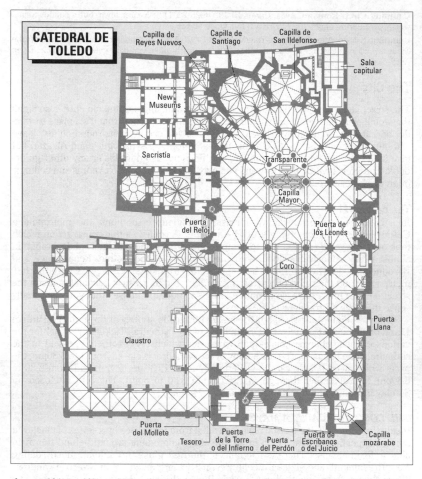

CATEDRAL DE TOLEDO

Capilla de Reyes Nuevos
Capilla de Santiago
Capilla de San Ildefonso
Sala capitular
New Museums
Sacristía
Transparente
Capilla Mayor
Puerta del Reloj
Puerta de los Leones
Coro
Puerta Llana
Claustro
Puerta del Mollete
Tesoro
Puerta de la Torre o del Infierno
Puerta del Perdón
Puerta de Escribanos o del Juicio
Capilla mozárabe

those of kings Alfonso VII and Sancho III and the powerful Cardinal Mendoza and (on the right) that of Sancho II.

Directly behind the main altar is an extraordinary piece of fantasy – the Baroque **Transparente**. Wonderfully and wildly extravagant, with its marble cherubs sitting on fluffy marble clouds, it's especially magnificent when the sun reaches through the hole punched in the roof for just that purpose. You'll notice a cardinal's hat hanging from the vaulting just in front of this. Spanish primates are buried where they choose, with the epitaph they choose, and with their hat hanging above them, where it stays until it rots. One of them chose to be buried here, and there are other pieces of headgear dotted around the cathedral.

CHAPELS AND TREASURES

There are well over twenty **chapels** around the walls, all of which are of some interest. Many of them house fine tombs, particularly the **Capilla de Santiago**, the octagonal **Capilla de San Ildelfonso** and the gilded **Capilla de Reyes Nuevos**.

In the **Capilla Mozárabe** Mass is still celebrated daily according to the ancient Visigothic rites. When the church tried to ban the old ritual in 1086 the people of Toledo were outraged. The dispute was put to a combat, which the Mozárabe champion won, but the church demanded further proof: trial by fire. The Roman prayer book was blown to safety, while the Mozárabe version remained, unburned, in the flames. Both sides claimed victory, and in the end the two rituals were allowed to coexist. If you want to attend mass, be there at 9.30am and look out for the priest – you may well be the only celebrant.

The Capilla de San Juan houses the riches of the cathedral **Tesoro** (Treasury), most notably a solid silver *custodia* (repository for eucharist wafers) ten-foot high and weighing over two hundred kilos. It was made by German-born silversmith Enrique de Arfe in the sixteenth century, and gilded seventy years later. An even more impressive accumulation of wealth is displayed in the **Sacristía** (Sacristy), where paintings include a *Disrobing of Christ* and portraits of the Apostles by El Greco, Velázquez's portrait of Cardinal Borja and Goya's *Christ Taken by the Soldiers*.

In the adjoining rooms, the so-called **New Museums** house works of art that were previously locked away or poorly displayed. Among them are paintings by Caravaggio, Gerard David and Morales, and El Greco's most important piece of sculpture (only a few pieces survive), a polychromed wooden group of San Ildefonso and the Virgin. The **Sala Capitular** (Chapter House) has a magnificent sixteenth-century *artesonado* ceiling and portraits of all Spain's archbishops to the present day.

Santo Tomé and the Casa del Greco

The outstanding attraction of Toledo, outshining even its cathedral, is El Greco's masterpiece, *The Burial of the Count of Orgaz*. It's housed, alone, in a small annexe to the church of **Santo Tomé** (daily 10am–6.45pm, winter 5.45pm; 150ptas) and depicts the count's funeral, at which Saint Stephen and Saint Augustine appeared to lower him into the tomb. It combines El Greco's genius for the mystic, exemplified in the upper half of the picture where the count's soul is being received into heaven, with his great powers as a portrait painter and master of colour. The identity of the sombre-faced figures watching the burial has been a source of endless speculation. On two identities, however, there is universal agreement; El Greco painted himself sixth from the right and his son in the foreground. Less certain are the identities of the rest of the mourners; Cervantes and Lope de Vega are unlikely to have been included as neither had achieved fame by 1586, but the odds are on for Felipe II's presence among the heavenly onlookers, even though he was still alive when it was painted. Perhaps of greater interest than "spot-the-celebrity" is the window which this painting provides on to sixteenth-century Spanish society. Jan Morris wrote that "it epitomises the alliance between God and the Spanish ruling classes (who) expect miracles as a matter of policy, and are watching the saints at work rather as they might watch . . . any foreign expert sent to do a job".

From Santo Tomé the c/de los Amarillos leads down to the old **Judería** (Jewish quarter) and to the **Casa del Greco** (Tues–Sat 10am–2pm & 4–6pm, Sun 10am–2pm; 400ptas, free Sat 4–6pm & Sun), which despite its name wasn't the artist's actual home – the building in fact dates from the beginning of this century – although the evidence suggests that he lived nearby. The living quarters, furnished in sixteenth-century style, are closed for restoration, but the museum part of the house displays many classic El Grecos, among them his famous *View and Map of Toledo* and another complete series of the Twelve Apostles, completed later than the set in the cathedral and subtly different.

The Taller del Moro, two synagogues and San Juan de los Reyes

Between Santo Tomé and the Casa del Greco you pass the entrance to the **Palacio de Fuensalida** (Palace of the Counts of Fuensalida), a beautiful fifteenth-century mansion

EL GRECO – AND A VIEW OF TOLEDO

Even if you've never seen Toledo – and even if you've no idea what to expect – there's an uncanny familiarity about your first view of it, with the Alcázar and the cathedral spire towering above the tawny mass of the town. This is due to **El Greco**, whose constant depiction of the city (as background, even, for the Crucifixion) seems to have stuck, albeit unwittingly, somewhere in everyone's consciousness. Domenico Theotocopoulos, "the Greek", was born in Crete in 1541 and settled in Toledo in about 1577 after failing to get work on the decoration of the Escorial. His paintings – the most individual, most intensely spiritual visions of all Spanish art – are extraordinary; however often he repeats the same subject, they always offer some surprise or insight.

For thrilling, uncluttered **views** of Toledo, walk along the Carretera de Circunvalación which runs along the south bank of the Tajo – the opposite bank from the city – from one of the medieval fortified bridges to the other. This takes about an hour, and will show to advantage the skyline so familiar from various El Grecos (though several other bridges have disappeared in the intervening centuries). For the panorama most resembling *Storm Over Toledo* (now in New York's Metropolitan Museum of Art), you have to climb the hill above the westerly bridge of San Martín.

Midway between the bridges, there is access to a little landing stage, by an old chain ferry, where for most of the year a **boatman** shuttles passengers across the river. This is an informal service and the boatman responds to waves or shouts from one or other bank; you tip whatever you feel is appropriate.

where Carlos V's Portuguese wife Isabel died. You used to be able to visit her treasures but the palace is now closed to the public. A garden separates it from the **Taller del Moro** (Tues–Sat 10am–2pm & 4–6.30pm, Sun 10am–2pm; 100ptas; combined ticket with the Museo de Arte Contemporaneo and the Museo de Arte Visigótico 150ptas), three fourteenth-century rooms of a Mudéjar palace which were later used by masons working on the cathedral, with magnificent Mudéjar decoration and doorways intact. It is approached through its own entrance in the c/Taller del Moro.

Almost next door to the Casa del Greco, on c/Reyes Católicos, is the **Synagoga del Tránsito**, built along Moorish lines by Samuel Levi in 1366. It became a church after the expulsion of the Jews, but is currently being restored to its original form. The interior is a simple galleried hall, brilliantly decorated with polychromed stucco-work and superb filigree windows. Hebrew inscriptions praising God, King Pedro and Samuel Levi adorn the walls. Nowadays it houses a small **Sephardic Museum** (Tues–Sat 10am–2pm & 4–6pm, Sun 10am–2pm; 400ptas), tracing the distinct traditions and development of Jewish culture in Spain. During restoration, however, the museum may be closed temporarily.

The only other surviving synagogue – **Santa María la Blanca** (daily 10am–2pm & 3.30–7pm, winter 6pm; 150ptas) – is a short way down the same street. Like El Tránsito, which it predates by over a century, it has been both church and synagogue, though it looks more like a mosque. Four rows of octagonal pillars each support seven horseshoe arches, all of them with elaborate and individual designs moulded in plaster, while a fine sixteenth-century *retablo* has been preserved from its time as a church. The whole effect is quite stunning, accentuated by a deep red floor tiled with decorative *azulejos*.

Continuing down c/Reyes Católicos, you come to the superb church of **San Juan de los Reyes** (daily 10am–1.45pm & 3.30–6.45pm, winter 5.45pm; 150ptas), its exterior bizarrely festooned with the chains worn by the Christian prisoners from Granada released on the reconquest of their city. It was originally a Franciscan convent founded by the "Catholic Kings", Fernando and Isabella, to celebrate their victory at the Battle of Toro, and in which, until the fall of Granada, they had planned to be buried. Designed by Juan Guas in the decorative late-Gothic style known as Isabelline (after the queen), its double-storeyed cloister is quite outstanding: the upper floor has an elaborate Mudéjar ceiling, and the crests of Castile and Aragón – seven arrows and a yoke – are carved everywhere in assertion of the new unity brought by the royal marriage. This theme is continued in the airy church where imperious eagles support the royal shields.

From the Puerta del Cambrón to Santo Cristo de la Luz

If you leave the city by the **Puerta del Cambrón** you can follow the Paseo de Recaredo, which runs alongside a stretch of Moorish walls, to the **Hospital de Tavera** (daily 10.30am–1.30pm & 3.30–6pm; 500ptas). This, a Renaissance palace with beautiful twin patios, houses the private collection of the Duchess of Lerma. The gloomy interior is a reconstruction of a sixteenth-century mansion scattered with fine paintings, including a *Day of Judgement* by Bassano; the portrait of Carlos V by Titian is a copy of the original in the Prado. The hospital's archives are kept here, too: thousands of densely hand-written pages chronicling the illnesses treated. The museum contains several works by El Greco and Ribera's gruesome portrait of a freak "bearded woman". Also here is the death mask of Cardinal Tavera, the hospital's founder, and in the church of the hospital is his ornate marble tomb – the last work of Alonso Berruguete.

Toledo's main gate, the **Puerta Nueva de Bisagra**, is marooned in a constant swirl of traffic, but it still seems a formidable obstacle for any would-be invader to overcome. Its patterned tile roofs bear the coat of arms of Carlos V. Alongside is the gateway that it replaced, the ninth-century Moorish portal through which Alfonso VI and El Cid led their triumphant armies in 1085. The main road bears to the left, but on foot you can climb towards the centre of town – after a glance at the intriguing exterior of the Mudéjar church of **Santiago del Arrabal** – by a series of stepped alleyways.

The Cuesta del Cristo de la Luz leads up here past the tiny mosque of **Mezquita del Cristo de la Luz**. Although this is one of the oldest Moorish monuments in Spain (it was built by Musa Ibn Ali in the tenth century on the foundations of a Visigothic church), only the nave, with its nine different cupolas, is the original Arab construction. The apse was added when the building was converted into a church, and is claimed to be the first product of the Mudéjar style. The head of a Visigoth peering out from one of the capitals is proof, if any were needed, of Moorish tolerance. According to legend, as King Alfonso rode into the town in triumph, his horse stopped and knelt before the mosque. Excavations revealed a figure of Christ, still illuminated by a lamp which had burned throughout three and a half centuries of Muslim rule – hence the name *Cristo de la Luz*.

The mosque itself, set in a small park and open on all sides to the elements, is so small that it seems more like a miniature summer pavilion, but it has an elegant simplicity of design that few of the great monuments can match. It has recently been fenced in and cannot normally be visited, but the caretaker lives across the street, at c/Cristo de la Luz 11, and will sometimes let visitors in; he might also show you through the garden where you can climb to the battlements of the **Puerta del Sol**, a great fourteenth-century Mudéjar gateway. Occasionally you'll see the mosque used for prayer by visiting Muslims.

The Alcázar

At the heart of modern Toledo is the **Plaza de Zocódover** (its name derives from the Arabic word *souk*), where everyone converges for an afternoon *copa*. Dominating this square, indeed all Toledo, is the bluff, imposing **Alcázar** (Tues–Sun 9.30am–2.30pm; 200ptas), entrance off Cuesta del Alcázar. There has probably always been a fortress at this commanding location, but the present building was originated by Carlos V, though it has been burned and bombarded so often that almost nothing remaining is original.

THE SIEGE OF THE ALCÁZAR

At the outset of the Spanish Civil War, on July 20, 1936, Colonel José Moscardó – a leading Nationalist rebel – and the cadets of the military academy under his command were driven into the Alcázar. They barricaded themselves in with a large group that included six hundred women and children, and up to a hundred left-wing hostages (who were never seen again).

After many phone calls from Madrid to persuade them to surrender, a Toledo attorney phoned Moscardó with an ultimatum: within ten minutes the Republicans would shoot his son, captured that morning. Moscardó declared that he would never surrender and told his son, "If it be true, commend your soul to God, shout *Viva España*, and die like a hero." (His son was actually shot with others a month later in reprisal for an air raid.) Inside, though not short of ammunition, the defenders had so little food they had to eat their horses.

The number of Republican attackers varied from 1000 to 5000, with people coming from Madrid to take pot shots from below. Two of the three mines they planted under the towers exploded but nothing could disturb the solid rock foundations. The besiegers tried spraying petrol all over the walls and setting fire to it, but with no effect. Finally, General Franco decided to relieve Moscardó and diverted an army that was heading for Madrid. On September 27, General José Varela commanded the successful attack on the town, which was followed by the usual bloodbath – not one prisoner being taken.

As the historian Raymond Carr put it "in civil war, symbols count". The day after Franco entered Toledo to consolidate his victory, he was declared head of state and spoke to the nation – according to Radio Castillo, he was "the authentic voice of Spain in the plenitude of its power".

The most recent destruction was in 1936 during one of the most symbolic and extraordinary episodes of the Civil War, involving a two-month siege of the Nationalist-occupied Alcázar by the Republican town (see box, above).

After the war, Franco's regime completely rebuilt the fortress as a monument to the glorification of its defenders – the fascist newspaper *El Alcázar* also commemorates the siege – and their propaganda models and photos are still displayed. Objectionable exercise though this is, it's a fascinating story, and the Alcázar also offers the best views of the town, its upper windows level with the top of the cathedral spire (though in recent years access has been restricted – part of the building is still occupied by the military). Across the river, next to a modern military academy, stands the ancient **Castillo de San Servando**, one wing of which is now a youth hostel.

Other museums

The **Hospital y Museo de Santa Cruz** (Mon 10am–2pm & 4–6.30pm; Tues–Sat 10am–6.30pm, Sun 10am–2pm; 200ptas), a superlative Renaissance building in itself, houses some of the greatest El Grecos in Toledo, including *The Assumption*, a daringly unorthodox work of feverish spiritual intensity, and a *Crucifixion* with the town as a backdrop. As well as outstanding works by Goya and Ribera, the museum also contains a huge collection of ancient carpets and faded tapestries (including a magnificent fifteenth-century Flemish tapestry called *The Astrolabe*), a military display (note the flags borne by Don Juan of Austria at the Battle of Lepanto), sculpture and a small archeological collection. Don't miss the patio with its ornate staircase – the entrance is beside the ticket office.

The **Museo de Arte Visigótico** (Tues–Sat 10am–2pm & 4–6.30pm, Sun 10am–2pm; 100ptas; combined ticket with the Museo de Arte Contemporaneo and the Museo de Arte Visigótico 150ptas) can be found in a very different, though equally impressive building, the church of **San Román**. Moorish and Christian elements – horseshoe arches, early murals and a splendid Renaissance dome – combine to make it the most interesting church in Toledo. Its twelfth-century Mudéjar tower originally stood apart from the main body of the church, in the manner of Muslim minarets. Visigothic jewellery, documents and archeological fragments make up the bulk of the collection.

A few new museums have opened in Toledo recently. Not far from the Visigothic museum, in the **Convento de Santo Domingo Antiguo**, the nuns display their art treasures in the old choir (Mon–Sat 11am–1pm & 4–7pm, Sun 4–7pm; winter open Sat, Sun & holidays only; 150ptas). More interesting is the high altarpiece of the church, El Greco's first major commission in Toledo. Unfortunately, most of the canvases have gone to museums and are here replaced by copies, leaving only two *St Johns* and a *Resurrection* in situ. The **Posada de la Hermandad**, near the market square at the back of the cathedral, is a recently restored Gothic building, now used for temporary exhibitions. Other exhibitions are staged at the **Museo de Arte Contemporáneo** (Tues–Sat 10am–2pm & 4–6.30pm, Sun 10am–2pm; 100ptas; combined ticket with the Museo de Arte Contemporaneo and the Museo de Arte Visigótico 150ptas) in the Casa de la Cadena, a refurbished sixteenth-century house near Santo Tomé. In the **Mezquita de las Tornerías** on c/de las Tornerías, the **Centro de Promoción de la Artesanía** (Tues–Sat 10am–2pm & 5–8pm, Sun 10am–2pm; free), houses good displays of beautiful local crafts, mainly pottery. The renovated eleventh-century mosque, deconsecrated by the Reyes Católicos around 1500, is worth a visit in itself.

Eating, drinking and nightlife

Toledo is a major tourist centre and inevitably many of its cafés, bars and restaurants are geared to passing trade. However, the city is as popular with Spanish as foreign visitors, so decent, authentic places do exist – and there's a bit of nightlife, too, for the local population.

Most **restaurants** in town do a good-value lunchtime *menú*, with game such as partridge (*perdiz*), pheasant (*faisán*) or quail (*cordoniz*) appearing in the more upmarket places, and everyone offering a tasty local speciality, *carcamusa* – a meat-stew in a spicy tomato sauce. In the evenings, on a budget, you need to be selective: this can be an expensive town. As a rule, the nearer you get to the centre, the more you'll pay.

Inexpensive restaurants

Alex, Plaza de Amador de los Ríos, at the top end of c/Nuncio Viejo. Reasonable-value restaurant with a much cheaper café at the side. Nice location and shady summer terrace.

Bar Alcázar aka *Champi*, c/Sierpe 5. Good range of *tapas* and *raciones*.

Bar Ludeña, Plaza Magdalena 10. One of many places around this square, offering a cheap *menú* and the best *carcamusa* in town.

Bar El Tropezón, Travesía de Santa Isabel 2. A stone's throw from the cathedral, this outdoor bar offers generous meals for under 1000ptas. The fish is particularly good.

Cafetería Nano, c/Santo Tomé 10. Good-value chain, where you can eat well for 1500ptas. You'll find it under the trees, near the church entrance.

La Catedral, c/Nuncio Viejo 1. Wide range of *tapas* and wines at this modern bar in the heart of the city.

La Cepa Andaluza, Avda. Méjico 11. Bar with dependable Andalucian cooking – fried fish and the like.

Pastucci Pizzeria, c/Sinagoga 10. Very reasonable pizzeria with a pleasant atmosphere.

Posada del Estudiante, Callejón de San Pedro 2. Secluded workers' café near the cathedral open only for very cheap lunchtime *menú* – well worth hunting out.

Restaurante Bisagra, c/Real del Arrabal 14. Reasonably priced *menú* in elegantly refurbished surroundings.

Restaurante Palacios, c/Alfonso X El Sabio 3. Friendly and popular local restaurant, with two *menús* – the cheaper one costing 900ptas.

Moderate and expensive restaurants

Casón de Los Lopez de Toledo, c/Silleria 3. Upmarket restaurant in a quiet street close to Plaza Zocódover with a tasty *menú* at 3000ptas.

La Lumbre, c/Real de Arrabal 3. Well-regarded restaurant, just above the Puerta de Bisagra, specializing in meat dishes and local cuisine.

Plácido, c/Santo Tomé 6. Good standard Toledan cuisine with a cool terrace and patio for the summer.

Restaurante Adolfo, c/Granada 6. One of the best restaurants in town, tucked behind a marzipan café, in an old Jewish town house (ask to see the painted ceiling downstairs), and serving very imaginative food. Allow 5000ptas a head. Closed Sun evening.

Restaurante Los Cuatro Tiempos, c/Sixto Ramón Parro 5 at southeast corner of the cathedral. Excellent mid-price restaurant with local specialities and good *tapas*.

Restaurante Maravilla, c/Barrio Rey 7. In the *hostal* of the same name, and offering an excellent *menú*, which includes traditionally prepared *perdiz*.

Venta de Aires, c/Circo Romano 35. Popular restaurant housed in a famous old inn, a little way out of the centre, with outdoor eating in the summer. Allow 4000ptas a head.

Late bars and entertainment

By Spanish standards, Toledo's **nightlife** is rather tame. You'll find most late-night bars running along c/de la Sillería and its extension c/de los Alfileritos, west of Plaza de Zocódover. *La Abadía*, c/Nuñez de Arce 3, is a fashionable but civilized bar and attracts an older crowd than most along here; it serves a large range of foreign beer.

Two alternative places are *Broadway Jazz Club*, on Plaza Marrón near the Taller del Moro, and *La Boîte de Garcilaso*, a similar place very nearby at the corner of c/Alfonso XII and c/Rojas; both have occasional live jazz.

Out of the tourist season (Sept–March), **classical concerts** are held in the cathedral and other churches; details can be obtained from the Turismo.

On from Toledo

The train line comes to a halt at Toledo but there are **bus** connections south to **Ciudad Real** (see p.170), west to **La Puebla de Montalbán** (see p.173) and **Talavera de la Reina** (see p.174) on the way to Extremadura, and east to **Cuenca** (see p.164). If you have transport of your own, or fancy slow progress by bus and on foot, the **Montes de Toledo** (see p.173), southwest of the city, are an interesting rural backwater.

More local excursions, by bus, to the south of Toledo, could include **Guadamur** (14km from Toledo), whose outstanding castle stands on a nearby hill top, and **Orgaz**, once home to the count of El Greco's masterpiece *The Burial of the Count of Orgaz*, now a quiet village with a beautiful plaza and small fifteenth-century castle overlooking the main road to Ciudad Real.

Aranjuez and Chinchón

The frequent Madrid–Toledo trains run via **Aranjuez**, a little oasis in the beginnings of New Castile, where the eighteenth-century Bourbon rulers set up a spring and autumn retreat. Their palaces and luxuriant gardens, and the summer strawberries (served with cream – *fresas con nata* – at roadside stalls) make an enjoyable stop. In summer (Sat & Sun mid-April–July & Sept–mid-Oct), an old wooden **steam train**, *Tren de la Fresa*, makes runs between Madrid and Aranjuez; it leaves Atocha station at 10am and returns from Aranjuez at 6.30pm, arriving back at Atocha at 7.30pm. Train enthusiasts won't begrudge the extra cost (3100ptas), which includes a guided bus tour in Aranjuez, entry to the monuments and *fresas con nata* on the train.

Nearby, too, connected by sporadic buses from Aranjuez at c/Almíbar 138 (Mon–Fri 4 daily; Sat 2 daily) and hourly services from Madrid, is **Chinchón**, a picturesque village that is home to Spain's best-known *anís* – a mainstay of breakfast drinkers across Spain.

Aranjuez

The beauty of **ARANJUEZ** is its greenery – it's easy to forget just how dry and dusty most of central Spain is until you come upon this town, with its lush palaces and luxuriant gardens. In summer, Aranjuez functions principally as a weekend escape from Madrid and most people come out for the day, or stop en route to or from Toledo. If you wanted to break your journey, you'd need to camp or book a room, as there's very little accommodation available.

The eighteenth-century **Palacio Real** (Tues–Sun: April–Sept 10am–6.15pm; Oct–March 10am–5.15pm; 650ptas, Wed free for EU citizens) and its **gardens** (daily: April–Sept 8am–8.30pm; Oct–March 8am–6.30pm) were an attempt by the Spanish Bourbon monarchs to create a Versailles in Spain; Aranjuez clearly isn't in the same league but it's a pleasant place to while away a few hours.

The palace is more remarkable for the ornamental fantasies inside than for any virtues of architecture. There seem to be hundreds of rooms, all exotically furnished, most amazingly so the **Porcelain Room**, entirely covered in decorative ware from the factory which used to stand in Madrid's Retiro park. The **Smoking Room** is a copy of one of the finest halls of the Alhambra in Granada, though executed with less subtlety. Most of the palace dates from the reign of the "nymphomaniac" Queen Isabella II, and many of the scandals and intrigues which led to her eventual abdication were played out here.

Outside, on a small island, are the fountains of the **Jardín de la Isla**. The **Jardín del Príncipe**, on the other side of the main road, is more attractive, with shaded walks along the river and plenty of spots for a siesta. At its far end is the **Casa del Labrador** (Tues–Sun: April–Sept 10am–6.15pm; Oct–March 10am–5.15pm; visits by appointment only – ☎91 891 0305; 500ptas, Wed free for EU citizens), which is anything but what its name (Peasant's House) implies. Richard Ford described it well over a century ago as "another plaything of that silly Charles IV, a foolish toy for the spoiled children of fortune, in which great expense and little taste are combined to produce a thing which is perfectly useless". Great expense is right, for the house contains more silk, marble, crystal and gold than would seem possible in so small a place, as well as a huge collection of fancy clocks. The guided tour goes into great detail about the weight and value of every item.

Also in the gardens, by the river, is the small **Casa de los Marinos** (Sailors' House) or **Museo de Faluas** (Tues–Sun: April–Sept 10am–6.15pm; Oct–March 10am–5.15pm; 325ptas, Wed free for EU citizens), a museum containing the brightly coloured launches in which royalty would take to the river.

A bus service occasionally connects the various sites, but all are within easy walking distance of each other, and the town's a very pleasant place to stroll around.

Practicalities

The best **hostal** choices are the *Rusiñol*, c/San Antonio 76 (☎ & fax 91 891 01 55; ②), in the centre of town, and *Hostal Castilla*, Carretera de Andalucia (☎91 891 26 27, fax 91 891 61 33; ④). The **campsite**, *Soto del Castillo*, Soto del Rebollo (☎91 891 13 95, fax 91 891 41 97), is on a far bend of the Río Tajo; it's equipped with a swimming pool, and hires out bicycles and rowing boats. You'll find a helpful **Turismo** in the Casa de Infantes, facing the Plaza de San Antonio (Tues–Sun 10am–2pm & 4–6pm; ☎91 891 04 27).

With plenty of fresh produce around (including the famous strawberries and asparagus in season), the splendid nineteenth-century Mercado de Abastos on c/Stuart is a good place to buy your own food for a picnic. If you're after a memorable restaurant meal, *Casa José*, c/Abastos 32, offers good nouvelle cuisine, while *Casa Pablo*, c/Almíbar 42, is more traditional, with walls covered with pictures of local dignitaries and bullfighters (but beware the seafood "soap" on the English menu!); its nearby offshoot, *Casa Pablete*, c/Stuart, is good for *tapas* (both are closed in August). Probably the best known restaurant is the pleasant riverside *El Rana Verde*, c/Reina 1, which dates back to the late nineteenth century and serves a wide ranging *menú* at 1600ptas.

Chinchón

CHINCHÓN, 45km southeast of Madrid, is an elegant little town, with a fifteenth-century castle and a fine Plaza Mayor, next to which stands the **Iglesia de la Asunción**, with a panel by Goya of *The Assumption of the Virgin*. It is as the home of *anís*, however, that the town is best known, and most visitors come to visit the three **distilleries** – a couple of which are housed in the castle. To follow a few tastings with a meal try the *Mesón del Comendador*, one of a cluster of good restaurants on the Plaza Mayor, or the *Mesón del Duende*; both are modestly priced. More expensive is the *Méson Cuevas del Vino*, once an olive oil mill and today with its own *bodega* (wine cellar). Accommodation in the town is expensive, but for the price of a coffee, you could visit the *parador* in a sixteenth-century convent.

If you're visiting over Easter, you'll be treated to the townsfolk's own enactment of the *Passion of Christ*, when participants and audience move around the town. In April 1995, the town launched its *Fiesta del Anís y del Vino*, an orgy of *anís* and wine tasting; understandably it was an immediate success and is now held every mid-April. An older annual tradition takes place on July 25, when the feast of St James (*Santiago* in Spanish) is celebrated with a bullfight in the Plaza Mayor.

El Escorial, El Valle de los Caídos and the Sierra de Guadarrama

Northwest of Madrid, in the foothills of the Sierra de Guadarrama, is one of Spain's best-known and most visited sights – Felipe II's vast monastery-palace of **El Escorial**. Travel writers tend to go into frenzies about the symbolism of this building – "a stone image of the mind of its founder" was how the nineteenth-century writer Augustus Hare described it – and it is indeed a key historic sight. The town around the monastery, **San Lorenzo del Escorial**, is an easy day trip from Madrid, or if you plan to travel on, rail and road routes continue to Ávila (see p.139) and Segovia (see p.146). The heart of the **Sierra de Guadarrama**, too, lies just to the north, offering Madrid's easiest mountain escape.

Tours from Madrid to El Escorial often take in **El Valle de los Caídos** (The Valley of the Fallen), 9km north. This is an equally megalomaniac yet far more chilling monument: an underground basilica hewn under Franco's orders, allegedly as a monument to the Civil War dead of both sides, though in reality as a memorial to the Generalísimo and his regime.

El Escorial

The monastery of **EL ESCORIAL** was the largest Spanish building of the Renaissance: rectangular, overbearing and severe, from the outside it more resembles a prison than a palace. Built between 1563 and 1584, it was originally the creation of Juan Bautista de Toledo, though his one-time assistant, **Juan de Herrera**, took over and is normally given credit for the design. **Felipe II** planned the complex as both monastery and mausoleum, where he would live the life of a monk and "rule the world with two inches of paper". Later monarchs had less ascetic lifestyles, enlarging and richly decorating the palace quarters, but Felipe's simple rooms, with the chair that supported his gouty leg and the deathbed from which he could look across into the church where Mass was constantly celebrated, remain the most fascinating.

There's more to see than you can fit into a single day without total exhaustion, and you're liable to end up agreeing with Augustus Hare that while the Escorial "is so profoundly curious that it must of necessity be visited, it is so utterly dreary and so hopelessly fatiguing a sight that it requires the utmost patience to endure it".

Arrival, information and accommodation

From **Madrid** there are up to 27 **trains** a day (5.45am–11.30pm from Atocha, calling at Chamartín, and up to twelve every weekday going on to Ávila), with **buses** running every thirty minutes on weekdays and hourly on weekends. If you arrive by train get straight on the local bus which shuttles you up to the centre of town – they leave promptly and it's a long uphill walk. If you're travelling by bus, stay on it and it will take you right up to the monastery. The **Turismo** (summer: Mon–Sat 11am–6pm & Sun 10am–3pm; winter: Mon–Fri 10am–2pm & 3–5pm, Sat & Sun 10am–3pm; ☎91 890 15 54) is at c/Floridablanca 10, just to the north of the visitors' entrance to the monastery.

If you want to stay in the town, San Lorenzo del Escorial, there's a range of **accommodation**, but none of it is particularly cheap and in summer it's essential to book in advance. At the lower end of the scale is *Hotel Tres Arcos*, c/Juan de Toledo 42 (☎91 890 68 97, fax 91 890 79 97; ④). A little more expensive are *Hostal Cristina*, c/Juan de Toledo 6 (☎91 890 19 61, fax 91 890 12 04; ④–⑤), and *Hotel Parilla Príncipe*, c/Floridablanca 6, near the Turismo (☎91 890 16 11, fax 91 890 76 01; ⑤). If you've got the cash to splash out, there's the *Hotel Florida* next to the Turismo (☎91 890 17 21, fax 890 17 15; ⑥), and the newly opened, and very plush, *Hotel Botánico*, c/Timoteo Padrós 16 (☎ 91 890 78 79, fax 91 890 81 58; ⑦), set in the verdant grounds of a former palace.

You'll also find a well-equipped **campsite** 6km out on the road to Ávila, *Caravaning El Escorial* (☎91 890 24 12, fax 91 896 10 62), and two **youth hostels**: *El Escorial*, c/Residencia 14 (☎91 890 59 24, fax 91 890 59 25; ②) and *Santa María del Buen Aire*, Finca la Herrería (☎91 890 36 40; members only; ②), which has a pool and camping space, but is usually packed with school groups. You're best off arriving in El Escorial early, spending the day here, and then continuing in the evening to Ávila or heading back to Madrid. Moving on to Segovia by train is a bit trickier as it involves backtracking to Villalba (15min) and hooking up with a Madrid–Segovia train from there.

The monastery

Visits to the **Real Monasterio del Escorial** (Tues–Sun: April–Sept 10am–6pm; Oct–March 10am–5pm; 850ptas, Wed free for EU citizens) used to be deeply regulated, with guided tours to each section. Recently, they've become more relaxed and you can use your ticket (purchased in the **visitors' entrance**) to enter, in whatever sequence you like, the basilica, sacristy, chapter houses, library and royal apartments. The outlying **Casita del Príncipe** (aka **de Abajo**) and **Casita del Infante** (aka **de Arriba**)

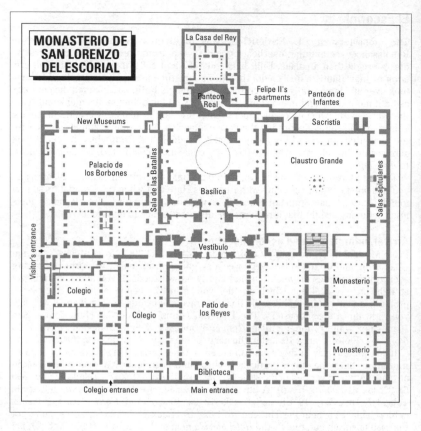

MONASTERIO DE SAN LORENZO DEL ESCORIAL

La Casa del Rey

Felipe II's apartments

Panteón Real

Panteón de Infantes

New Museums

Sacristía

Palacio de los Borbones

Sala de las Batallas

Claustro Grande

Salas capitulares

Basílica

Visitor's entrance

Vestíbulo

Colegio

Monasterio

Colegio

Patio de los Reyes

Monasterio

Biblioteca

Colegio entrance

Main entrance

charge separate admission. To avoid the worst of the crowds avoid Wednesdays and try visiting just before lunch, or pick that time for the royal apartments, which are the focus of all the bus tours. At present the Sala de Batallas – a long gallery lined with paintings of important imperial battles – and the Casita del Príncipe are closed as part of the programme of on-going restoration.

For sustenance or relief, you'll find a **cafetería** and **toilets** near the ticket office; drinks are OK but meals a bit of a rip-off.

THE BIBLIOTECA, PATIO DE LOS REYES, BASILICA AND COURTYARDS

A good starting point is to head for the west gateway, facing the mountains, and go through the traditional **main entrance**. Above it is a gargantuan statue of San Lorenzo holding a gridiron, the emblem of his martyrdom. Within is the **Biblioteca**, a splendid hall, with shelves designed by Herrera to harmonize with the architecture, and frescoes by Tibaldi and his assistants, showing the seven Liberal Arts. Its collections include the tenth-century *Codex Albeldensis*, Saint Teresa's personal diary, some gorgeously executed Arabic manuscripts, and a Florentine planetarium of 1572 demonstrating the movement of the planets according to the Ptolemaic and Copernican systems.

Beyond is the **Patio de los Reyes,** named after the six statues of the kings of Israel on the facade of the basilica straight ahead. Off to the left is a school, to the right the monastery, both of them still in use.

In the **Basilica,** notice the flat vault of the *coro* above your head as you enter, which is apparently entirely without support, and the white marble Christ carved by Benvenuto Cellini, and carried here from Barcelona on workmen's shoulders. This is one of the few things permanently illuminated in the cold, dark interior, but put some money in the slot to light up the main altarpiece and the whole aspect of the church is brightened. The east end is decorated by Italian artists: the sculptures are by the father-and-son team of Leone and Pompeo Leoni, who also carved the two facing groups of Carlos V with his family and Felipe II with three of his wives; Mary Tudor is excluded.

You can also wander at will in some of the Escorial's courtyards; most notable is the **Claustro Grande,** with frescoes of the life of the Virgin by Tibaldi, and the **Jardín de los Frailes** on the south side.

THE TREASURIES, MAUSOLEUM AND ROYAL APARTMENTS
The **Sacristía** and **Salas Capitulares** (Chapter Houses) contain many of the monastery's religious treasures, including paintings by Titian, Velázquez and José Ribera. Beside the sacristy a staircase leads down to the **Panteón Real,** the final resting place of all Spanish monarchs since Carlos V, with the exception of Felipe V and Fernando VI. Alfonso XIII, who died in exile in Rome, was recently brought to join his ancestors.

The deceased monarchs lie in gilded marble tombs: kings (and Isabella II) on one side, their spouses on the other. Just above the entry is the *Pudrería,* a separate room in which the bodies rot for twenty years or so before the cleaned-up skeletons are moved here. The royal children are laid in the **Panteón de los Infantes;** the tomb of Don Juan, Felipe II's bastard half-brother, is grander than any of the kings', while the wedding-cake babies' tomb with room for sixty infants is more than half full.

What remains of the Escorial's art collection – works by Bosch, Gerard David, Dürer, Titian, Zurbarán and many others, which escaped transfer to the Prado – is kept in the elegant suite of rooms known as the **New Museums.** Finally, there are the treasure-crammed **Royal Apartments.** On no account miss the spartan **quarters of Felipe II** and the adjacent **Maderas Finas** rooms with their magnificent inlaid wood.

OUTLYING LODGES
The **Casita del Príncipe** (Tues–Sun: April–Sept 10am–6.45pm; Oct–March 10am–5.45pm, at present closed for restoration; 325ptas, Wed free for EU citizens) and the **Casita del Infante** (Easter & 16 July–15 Sept Tues–Sun 10am–7pm; 325ptas, Wed free for EU citizens) are two eighteenth-century royal lodges, both full of decorative riches, and built by Juan de Villanueva, Spain's most accomplished Neoclassical architect – so worth seeing in themselves as well as for their formal gardens.

The Casita del Infante, which served as present King Juan Carlos's student digs, is a short way up into the hills and affords a good view of the Escorial complex; follow the road to the left from the main entrance and then stick to the contours of the mountain around to the right – it's well signposted. The Casita del Príncipe, in the Jardines del Príncipe below the monastery, is larger and more worthwhile, with an important collection of Giordano paintings and four pictures made from rice paste.

The Silla de Felipe
Around 7km out of town, is the **Silla de Felipe** – "Felipe's Seat" – a chair carved into a rocky outcrop with a view out towards the palace. His Majesty is supposed to have sat here to watch the construction going on. If you have a car, it still offers a great view; take the Ávila road and turn off after 3km.

Eating and entertainment

For **meals** and the like you'll need to head away from the monastery, up c/Reina Victoria into town. The *Hotel Parilla Príncipe* has a good restaurant, while *La Cueva*, c/San Antón 4, is elegant but expensive. Also at the top end of the scale, *Charolés*, c/Floridablanca 24, is renowned for its fish and stews. More reasonable is *La Fonda Genara*, Plaza de Las Animas 2, near the *coliseo*, which is filled with theatrical mementoes. The *Cervecería Los Pescaítos*, c/Joaquín Costa 8, is a friendly bar serving fish dishes. Alternatively, grab a *bocadillo* from a drinks stand on c/Floridablanca and save your appetite for later. For purely liquid refreshment *Bar Erriuga*, on c/Ventura Rodríguez 7, is one of the best bets.

If by design or default you end up staying the night in El Escorial, there are no fewer than eight **cinemas**, along with the eighteenth-century **Coliseo** where you'll find jazz and classical **concerts** and theatrical productions year-round. Details of shows can be picked up from the Turismo, or check out the free weekly *La Semana del Escorial*.

El Valle de los Caídos

The entrance to the **Valle de los Caídos** (Valley of the Fallen) lies 9km north of El Escorial: from here a road (along which you are not allowed to stop) runs 6km into the underground basilica. Above it is a vast cross, reputedly the largest in the world, and visible for miles along the road to Segovia. To visit El Valle de los Caídos from El Escorial, there is a local bus run by Herranz, which sells tickets at the *Bar Manises*, opposite the post office. The bus runs from El Escorial at 3.15pm, returning at 5.30pm (Tues–Sun).

The **basilica complex** (Tues–Sun: April–Sept 9.30am–7pm; Oct–Mar 10am–6pm; 650ptas, Wed free for EU citizens) denies its claims of memorial "to the Civil War dead of both sides" almost at a glance. The debased and grandiose architectural forms employed, the grim martial statuary, the constant inscriptions "Fallen for God and for Spain", and the proximity to El Escorial clue you in to its true function: the glorification of General Franco and his regime. The dictator himself lies buried behind the high altar, while the only other named tomb, marked simply "José Antonio", is that of his guru, the Falangist leader José Antonio Primo de Rivera, who was shot dead by Republicans at the beginning of the war. The "other side" is present only in the fact that the complex was built by the Republican army's survivors – political prisoners on quarrying duty.

From the entrance, a shaky funicular (Tues–Sun: April–Sept 11am–1.30pm & 4–6.30pm; Oct–Mar 11am–1.30pm & 3–5.30pm; 350ptas) ascends to the base of the **cross**, offering, as you can imagine, a superlative view over the Sierra de Guadarrama and a closer look at the giant, grotesque figures propping up the base of the cross.

The Sierra de Guadarrama

The routes from Madrid and El Escorial to Segovia strike through the heart of the **Sierra de Guadarrama** – a beautiful journey, worth taking for its own sake. The road is occasionally marred by suburban development, especially around **Navacerrada**, Madrid's main ski station, but from the train it's almost entirely unspoiled. There are plenty of opportunities for walking, but make sure you buy the appropriate maps in Madrid.

If you want to base yourself in the mountains for a while you'd do best to head for **Cercedilla**, 75 minutes by train on the Madrid–Segovia line – and a little way off the main road. Alternatively, over to the east, there is **Manzanares el Real**, with an odd medieval castle and a reservoir-side setting.

Cercedilla and the Puerto de Navacerrada

CERCEDILLA is an Alpine-looking village and an excellent base for summer walking; it is much frequented by *madrileños* at weekends. **Accommodation** is limited to the *Hostal El Aribel*, near the station (☎91 852 15 11, fax 91 852 15 61; ④), and two **youth hostels** up on the Dehesas road: *Villa Castora* (☎91 852 03 34, fax 91 852 24 11; ②) and, 2km up the road, *Las Dehesas* (☎91 852 01 35, fax 91 852 18 36; ②). Farther up still, you'll find a helpful information booth (☎91 852 22 13). There are several **eating** places in town; the station has a restaurant on the first floor or you could try the restaurant at *Hostal El Aribel*.

From Cercedilla, you can embark on a wonderful little train ride to the **Puerto de Navacerrada**, the most important pass in the mountains and the heart of the old area. The train runs hourly over weekends and holidays and passes through the **Parque Natural de Peñalara**, an extension of the upper Manzanares basin: watch out for roe deer and wild boar. Cercedilla station is also the base for the **Tren de la Naturaleza** (Sept–July Wed–Sun; 1150–1300ptas adults, 770–860ptas children) which sets off at 10.25am for a full day's nature education programme in the *parque*, returning at 4.45pm. For the more energetic there is a very pleasant five-hour round-trip **walk** along the pine-fringed *Calzada Romana* (old Roman road) up to the Puerto de la Fuenfría (1796m) with its striking views down into Segovia province.

From **Madrid** to Cercedilla, there are over twenty **trains** a day (6am–11pm from Atocha, calling at Chamartín, and 9 daily going on to Segovia) and **buses** leaving every half hour from the Intercambiador de Autobuses de Moncloa.

Manzanares el Real

Some 50km north of Madrid, on the shores of the Santillana *embalse* (reservoir), lies **MANZANARES EL REAL**, a town which in former times was disputed between the capital and Segovia. Nowadays it's a somewhat tatty resort, geared to Madrid weekenders, whose villas dot the landscape for miles around. Nearby however, the ruggedly beautiful **La Pedriza**, a spur of the Sierra de Guadarrama, has been declared a regional park, and has some enjoyable walks, as well as some much-revered technical climbs, notably the ascent to the jagged Peña del Diezmo. It is also home to a very large colony of griffon vultures.

In Manzanares itself, the one attraction is the **castle** (daily 10am–1pm & 3–5.30pm; free), which despite its eccentric appearance is a perfectly genuine fifteenth-century construction, built around an earlier chapel. It was soon modified into a palace by the architect Juan Guas, who built an elegant gallery on the south side, false machicolations on the other, and studded the tower with stones resembling cannon balls. The interior has been heavily restored.

As befits Manzanares, **accommodation** is expensive and limited to *Hostal Tranco* (☎91 853 00 63; ④), and *Hotel Parque Real* (☎91 853 99 12, fax 91 853 99 60; ⑤). However, there is usually space at one of the two **campsites**, *El Ortigal* (☎91 853 01 20) at the foot of La Pedriza or the well-equipped *La Fresneda* (☎ & fax 91 847 65 23) on the Carretera M608 towards Soto del Real. **Buses** from Madrid run hourly (7.30am–9.30pm) from c/Mateo Inurria 11 (Metro Plaza de Castilla).

Ávila

Two things distinguish ÁVILA: its eleventh-century **walls**, two perfectly preserved kilometres of which surround the old town, and the mystic writer **Santa Teresa**, who was born here and whose shrines are a major focus of religious pilgrimage. Set on a high plain, with the peaks of the Sierra de Gredos behind, the town is quite a sight, especially if you time it right and approach with the evening sun highlighting the golden tone of the walls and the details of the eighty-eight towers.

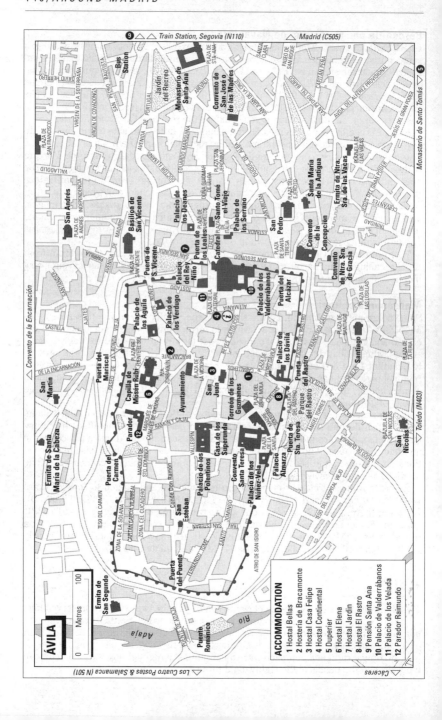

ÁVILA

Metres
0 — 100

△ Train Station, Segovia (N110)   △ Madrid (C505)

Monasterio de Santo Tomás ▽

▽ Cáceres

▽ Toledo (N403)

◁ Convento de la Encarnación

Ermita de San Segundo

Puente Románico

Río
Adaja

ACCOMMODATION

1 Hostal Bellas
2 Hostería de Bracamonte
3 Hostal Casa Felipe
4 Hostal Continental
5 Duperier
6 Hostal Elena
7 Hostal Jardín
8 Hostal El Rastro
9 Pensión Santa Ana
10 Palacio de Valderrábanos
11 Palacio de los Velada
12 Parador Raimundo

San Andrés
Basílica de San Vicente
Monasterio de Santa Ana
Convento de San José o de las Madres
Santa María de la Antigua
Ermita de Ntra. Sra. de las Vacas
Palacio de los Deanes
Catedral
Puerta de los Leales
Santo Tomé el Viejo
Palacio de los Serrano
San Pedro
Convento de la Concepción
Palacio del Rey Niño
Puerta de S. Vicente
Puerta de San Vicente
Palacio de los Verdugo
Palacio de los Águila
Puerta del Mariscal
Capilla de Mosén Rubí
Palacio de los Valderrábanos
Puerta del Alcázar
Convento de Ntra. Sra. de Gracia
Santiago
Ayuntamiento
San Juan
Torreón de los Guzmanes
Palacio de los Dávila
Puerta del Rastro
Parque del Rastro
Parador
Casa de los Superunda
Convento Santa Teresa
Palacio Almarza
Puerta de Sta. Teresa
Palacio de los Polentinos
Palacio de los Núñez-Vela
San Esteban
Puerta del Carmen
Puerta del Puente
San Nicolás
Ermita de Santa María de la Cabeza
San Martín

The walls were ordered by Alfonso VI, after his capture of the city from the Moors in 1090; they took his Muslim prisoners nine years to construct. At closer quarters, they prove a bit of a facade, as the old city within is sparsely populated and a little dishevelled, most of modern life having moved into the new developments outside the fortifications. However, the fine **Romanesque churches** dotted in and about the old city, plus good walks around the walls, make the town an excellent night's stopover, either combined with El Escorial, or en route to Salamanca.

Arrival and information

From **Madrid** there are up to seventeen **trains** a day to Ávila; **buses** are less frequent (seven on weekdays, three on weekends). The train station is a fifteen-minute walk to the east of the old town, or a local bus into Plaza de la Victoria. On foot, follow the broad Avenida José Antonio to its end, by the large church of Santa Ana, and bear left up c/del Duque de Alba to reach Plaza Santa Teresa. Buses use a terminal on the Avenida de Madrid, a little closer in: walking from here, cross the small park opposite, then turn right up c/Duque de Alba, or take a local bus to Plaza de la Victoria near the cathedral. **Driving**, follow signs for the walls (*murallas*) or the *parador* and you should be able to park just outside the old town.

Ávila's walls make orientation straightforward, with the **cathedral** and most other sights contained within. Just outside the southeast corner of the walls is the city's main square, **Plaza Santa Teresa**, and the most imposing of the old gates, the **Puerta del Alcázar**. Within the walls, the old market square, **Plaza de la Victoria**, fronts the *Ayuntamiento* at the heart of the old city.

The main **Turismo** (daily: July–Sept 9am–2pm & 5–7pm; Oct–June 10am–2pm & 4–7pm; ☎920 211387) is in the Plaza de la Catedral, and there's another, smaller office next to the Basílica de San Vicente (open July–Sept only; same hours).

Accommodation

There are numerous cheap *hostales* around the train station and along Avenida José Antonio, but you should be able to find something nearer the walled centre of town. You'll find a well-maintained **campsite**, *Camping Sonsoles* (☎920 256336; open June–Sept) 2km out on the Toledo road, near a football stadium.

Budget options

Hostal Continental, Plaza de la Catedral 4 (☎920 211502, fax 920 251691). An attractive old hotel, opposite the cathedral; its charms are fading fast, but the rooms are large and en suite and some have great views on to the square. ③.

Duperier, Avda. de Juventud (☎ & fax 920 221716). Small youth hostel (with 11pm curfew) out past the monastery, near the local swimming pool. Rooms with bath and meals available. Open July–mid Aug. ②.

Hostal Elena, c/Marqués de Canales y Chozas 1 (☎920 252496). Small *hostal* near the *parador*, with some en-suite rooms. ③.

Pensión Santa Ana, c/Alfonso de Montalvo 2 (☎920 220063). Fail-safe option between the train station and city centre. ③.

Moderate and expensive options

Hostal Bellas, c/Caballeros 19 (☎ & fax 920 212910). Friendly and fairly central, most rooms have showers and there are discounts out of season. ④.

Hostería de Bracamonte, c/Bracamonte 6 (☎920 251280). Atmospheric and elegant hotel, between the city walls and the Plaza de la Victoria, created from a number of converted Renaissance mansions. ⑥.

Hostal Casa Felipe, Plaza de la Victoria 12 (☎920 213924). Reasonable and centrally located; some rooms have showers and overlook the square. ④.

Hostal Jardín, c/San Segundo 38 (☎920 211074). Large *hostal* near Puerta de los Leales, which often has rooms when others are full. ④.

Palacio de Valderrábanos, Plaza de la Catedral 9 (☎920 211023, fax 920 251691). This former bishop's palace beats the *parador* for ambience. ⑦.

Palacio de los Velada, Plaza de la Catedral 10 (☎920 255100, fax 920 254900). Beautifully converted sixteenth-century palace and the priciest hotel in town; it's part of the Melia chain and bears their usual stamp of gracious living. ⑧.

Parador Raimundo de Borgoña, c/Marqués de Canales y Chozas 2 (☎920 211340, fax 920 226166). A converted fifteenth-century mansion – not the most exciting *parador* in Spain, but pleasant enough, with the usual comforts. It's the cheapest of Ávila's top hotels. ⑦.

Hostal El Rastro, Plaza del Rastro 1 (☎920 211218, fax 920 251626). A good mid-range option, this characterful old inn is set right against the walls, with a pleasant garden and popular restaurant. ④.

The Town

The focus of Ávila's sights is, inevitably, **Santa Teresa**, with whom most of the numerous convents and churches claim some connection. On the secular front, a circuit outside the **walls** makes a fine walk, and from the Puerta del Alcázar you can climb up and stroll around a section.

Santa Teresa in Ávila

The obvious place to start a tour of Teresa's Ávila is the **Convento de Santa Teresa** (daily 8.30am–1.30pm & 3.30–7.30pm; free), built over the saint's birthplace just inside the south gate of the old town – entered off the Paseo del Rastro. Most of the convent remains *de clausura* but you can see the very spot where she was born, now an elaborate chapel in the Baroque church, which is decorated with scenes of the saint demonstrating her powers of levitation to various august bodies. In a small reliquary (daily: 9.30am–1.30pm & 3.30–7.30pm; summer 10am–1pm & 4–7.30pm; free), beside the gift shop, are memorials of Teresa's life, including not only her rosary beads, but also one of the fingers she used to count them with.

Heading through the old town, and leaving by the Puerta del Carmen, you can follow a lane, c/de la Encarnación, to the **Convento de la Encarnación** (daily: 9.30am–1pm

---

SANTA TERESA DE ÁVILA

Santa Teresa (1515–82) was born to a noble family in Ávila and from childhood began to experience visions and religious raptures. At the age of seven she attempted to run away with her brother to be martyred by the Moors: the spot where they were recaptured and brought back, **Los Cuatro Postes**, is a fine vantage point from which to admire the walls of the town.

Teresa's religious career began at the Carmelite convent of La Encarnación, where she was a nun for twenty-seven years. From this base, she went on to reform the movement and found convents throughout Spain. She was an ascetic, but her appeal – and her importance to the Counter-Reformation – lay in the mystic sensuality of her experience of Christ, as revealed in her autobiography, for centuries a bestseller in Spain. As joint patron saint of Spain (together with Santiago – or St James), she remains a central pillar in Spanish Catholicism and schoolgirls are brought into Ávila by the bus load to experience first-hand the life of the woman they are supposed to emulate.

On a more bizarre note, one of Santa Teresa's mummified hands has now been returned to Ávila after spending the Franco years by the bedside of the great dictator.

& 4–7pm; winter 3.30–6pm; 150ptas). Each of the rooms here is labelled with the act Teresa performed, while everything she might have touched or looked at is on display. A small museum section also provides a reasonable introduction to the saint's life, with maps showing the convents, and a selection of her sayings – the pithiest, perhaps, "Life is a night in a bad hotel".

A third Teresan sight lies a couple of blocks east of the Plaza de Santa Teresa. This is the **Convento de San José** (daily 10am–1.30pm & 4–7pm; 150ptas), also known as San José, the first monastery that the saint founded, in 1562. Its museum contains relics and memorabilia, including the coffin in which Teresa once slept, and assorted personal possessions. The tomb of her brother Lorenzo is in the larger of the two churches.

Lastly, you might want to make your way up to **Los Cuatro Postes**, a little four-posted shrine, 1500m along the Salamanca road west of town. It was here, aged seven, that the infant Teresa was recaptured by her uncle, running away with her brother to seek Christian martyrdom from the Moors.

The cathedral and other sights

The three most beautiful churches in Ávila – the cathedral, San Vicente, and the Monasterio de Santo Tomás – are less directly associated with its most famous resident. Around the cathedral and Santo Tomé el Viejo (just outside the northeast corner of the walls), there is also a scattering of impressive **Renaissance mansions** – none of them are open to visitors but they give a glimpse of old Castilian wealth in their coats of arms and decorative facades.

Ávila's **Catedral** (daily: April–Oct 10am–7pm; Nov–March 10am–1.30pm & 3.30–5.30pm; closed 1–6 Jan, 15 Oct & 25 Dec; 250ptas) was started in the twelfth century but has never been finished, as evidenced by the missing tower above the main entrance. The earliest Romanesque parts were as much fortress as church, and the apse actually forms an integral part of the city walls. Their defensive function was real, with the twelfth-century Bishop Sancho providing sanctuary here for the young Alfonso IX, prior to his accession.

Inside, the succeeding changes of style are immediately apparent; the **Romanesque** parts are made of a strange red-and-white mottled stone, then there's an abrupt break and the rest of the main structure is pure white stone and **Gothic** forms. Although the proportions are exactly the same, this newer half of the cathedral seems infinitely more spacious. The *coro*, whose elaborate carved back you see as you come in, and two chapels in the left aisle, are **Renaissance** additions. Here you can admire the carved stalls in the *coro* (the work of a Dutch sculptor, Cornelius) and the elaborate marble tomb of a fifteenth-century bishop known as *El Tostado* (the "toasted" or "swarthy"). The thirteenth-century *sacristia* with its star-shaped cupola and gold inlay decor, and the treasury-museum with its monstrous silver *custodia* and ancient religious images are also worth a visit.

The basilica of **San Vicente** (daily 10am–1.30pm & 4–6.30pm; 200ptas), like the cathedral, is a mixture of architectural styles. Its twelfth-century doorways and the portico which protects them are magnificent examples of Romanesque art, while the church itself shows the influence of later trends. San Vicente was martyred on this site, and his tomb depicts a series of particularly gruesome deaths; in the crypt you can see the slab on which he and his sisters were executed by the Romans. This church shares with **San Pedro**, on Plaza de Santa Teresa, a warm pink glow from the sandstone of its construction – a characteristic aspect of Ávila but seen most clearly here.

The **Monasterio de Santo Tomás** (daily 11am–1pm & 4–7pm; *coro* and cloisters 150ptas) is a Dominican monastery founded in 1482, but greatly expanded over the following decade by Fernando and Isabella, whose summer palace it became. Inside are three exceptional cloisters, the largest of which contains an **oriental collection**, a strangely incongruous display built up by the monks over centuries of missionary work in the Orient. On every available surface is carved the yoke-and-arrows motif of the Reyes Católicos, surrounded by pomegranates, symbol of the newly conquered kingdom of Granada (*granada* means "pomegranate" in Spanish). In the **church** is the elaborate tomb of Prince Juan, Fernando and Isabella's only son, whose early death opened the way for Carlos V's succession and caused his parents so much grief that they abandoned their newly completed home here. It was subsequently damaged by Napoleon's troops, who stabled their horses in the church. Notice also the tomb of the prince's tutors, almost as elaborate as his own, and the thrones occupied by the king and queen during services. The notorious inquisitor Torquemada is buried in the sacristy. Santo Tomás is quite a walk downhill from the south part of town – you can get back up by the #1 bus, whose circular route takes in much of the old city.

The small **Museo Provincial** is housed in the sixteenth-century Palacio de los Deanes (Tues–Sat 10.30am–2pm & 4.30–7.30pm, Sun 10am–2pm; 200ptas, free Sat & Sun) which once housed the cathedral's deans. Today, its eclectic exhibits include collections of archeological remains, ceramics, agricultural implements, traditional costumes and furnishings from around the Ávila province, as well as some fine Romanesque statues and a wonderful fifteenth-century triptych depicting the life of Christ. The ticket also allows you entry to the museum store room in the church of Santo Tomé El Viejo just opposite.

It's possible to walk along the **city walls** from Puerta del Alcázar to Puerta del Rastro (Tues–Sun 10am–8pm; 200ptas); the view of the town is stunning. Tickets are available from the green kiosk by the Puerta del Alcázar.

Eating and drinking

Ávila has a decent if unexceptional array of **bars** and **restaurants**, some of them sited just outside the walls. Within the walls, a stroll from Plaza de la Victoria along c/de Vallespin will allow you to compare *menús* and prices. **Local specialities** include the Castilian standby *cordero asado* (roast lamb), *judias del barco con chorizo* (haricot beans with sausage), and *yemas de Santa Teresa* (candied egg-yolk) – the last of these sold in confectioners all over town. One to avoid is *mollejas* – cow's stomach. For **nightlife** head outside the city walls to c/Capitán Peña where the strip of four *discobares* next to each other keeps the walking to a minimum.

Bar El Rincón, Plaza Zurraquín 4. To the north of Plaza de la Victoria, this bar serves a generous three-course *menú* for 1500ptas.

Los Cancelas, c/Cruz Vieja 6. Next to the cathedral and in the hotel of the same name, this friendly restaurant is popular with locals; the *menú* is 1750ptas.

Casa Patas, c/San Millán 4. Pleasant bar, with good *tapas*, and a little *comedor* (evenings only), near the church of San Pedro. Closed Wed & Sept.

La Casona, Plaza de Pedro Dávila 6. Popular restaurant specializing in lamb with *menús* starting at 1600ptas.

Mesón del Rastro, Plaza del Rastro 1. Excellent bar, attached to the *hostal* of the same name, with a range of *tapas*. Behind it is a modest-priced restaurant, an old-fashioned place with solid, traditional food.

El Molino de la Losa, c/Bajada de la Losa 12 (☎920 211101). Converted fifteenth-century mill out by Los Cuatro Postes, with a deserved reputation and handy if you're with kids (there's a play area in the garden). The *menú* is 3000ptas. Closed Mon & mid-Oct to mid-March.

La Posada de la Fruta, Plaza de Pedro Dávila 8. Attractive, sunny, covered courtyard, this is a nice place for a drink.

On from Ávila

Ávila is quite a nexus with road and rail routes to Salamanca and Valladolid, from where you can get to just about anywhere in northern Spain, while to the east Segovia (see p.146) is less than two hours away by bus. Within striking distance, too, to the south, is the beautiful Sierra de Gredos (see below).

On the **Salamanca route**, both road and rail routes pass through **Peñaranda de Bracamonte**, a crumbling old town with a couple of large plazas and ancient churches. From here, if you have your own vehicle, you can continue to Salamanca on a slightly longer route through **Alba de Tormes**. Santa Teresa died here, and the Carmelite convent which contains the remains of her body (not much of it to judge by the number of relics scattered around Spain) is another major target of pilgrimage. There are the remains of a castle here too, and several other interesting churches.

Heading north **towards Valladolid**, road and rail both pass through **Medina del Campo** with its beautiful castle (see p.343).

The Sierra de Gredos

The **Sierra de Gredos** continues the line of the Sierra de Guadarrama, enclosing Madrid to the north and west. A major mountain range, with peaks in excess of 2500m, Gredos offers the best trekking in central Spain, including high-level routes across the passes as well as more casual walks around the villages.

By bus, the easiest access is from Madrid to **Arenas de San Pedro**, from where you can explore the range, and then move on west into the valley of La Vera in Extremadura (see p.175). If you have your own transport, you could head into the range south from Ávila along the C502, and you might prefer to base yourself in one of the villages on the north side of the range, along the **Tormes valley**, and do circular walks from there.

Arenas de San Pedro and Mombeltrán

ARENAS DE SAN PEDRO is a sizable town with a somewhat prettified **castle** and a good range of **accommodation**: pleasant options include the *Hostería Los Galayos* (☎ & fax 920 371379; ⑤), which also has a reliable restaurant, and *Hostal Castillo* (☎920 370091; ③). If you haven't already obtained **maps** of Gredos, you can pick up a functional pamphlet from the Turismo (open July–Sept only), or buy more detailed sheets from the bookshop Librería Nava.

MOMBELTRÁN, 12km north (an enjoyable, mainly downhill, walk from Arenas), is an attractive alternative stop, with its fifteenth-century **castle** of the Dukes of Albuquerque set against a stunning mountain backdrop. The village has two **hostales**, the *Albuquerque* (☎920 386032; ④) and *Marji* (☎920 386031; ④), and a summer-only **campsite**, *Prados Abiertos* (☎920 386061), 4km out of the centre.

El Arenal and El Hornillo

The main reason to stop in Arenas de San Pedro is to make your way up to the villages of El Hornillo and El Arenal, respectively 6km and 9km to the north, the trailheads for some excellent **mountain walks**. There are no buses but it's a pleasant walk up from Arenas to El Arenal on a track running between the road and the river – start out past the sports centre and swimming pool in Arenas.

EL ARENAL has the accommodation, including the *Hostal Isabel* (☎920 375148; ③), whose owner is knowledgeable about routes through the range. You can walk over the top of Gredos from El Arenal – the path via the pass at Puerto de la Cabrilla has been somewhat improved recently – and strike out along the ridge in either direction, to the main road at Puerto del Pico or back to El Arenal. **EL HORNILLO**, however, is the more common trailhead, and the beginning of the Circo de Gredos, one of the main recognized trekking routes over the Gredos watershed.

An alternative trek is to head due south from El Arenal, along a well-defined path over a broad pass to Candeleda (see below); this is a long day's walk but it's more or less all downhill.

The Circo de Gredos

The walk from El Hornillo over the **Gredos watershed** takes most of a day to accomplish, exchanging the pine and granite of the steep south slopes for the *matorral* (scrub thickets), cow pastures and wide horizons on the northern side. Over the top, you'll emerge on a twelve-kilometre stretch of paved road linking Hoyos del Espino, a village in the Tormes valley, and the so-called **Plataforma**, jumping-off point to the highest peaks of the Gredos. It's best to call it a day just above the Plataforma, where there's lots of camping space in the high Pozas meadows. From here, you can proceed up to the Circo de Laguna Grande, two hours' walk beyond Pozas on a well-defined path.

Circo de Laguna Grande and Circo de las Cinco Lagunas

The **Circo de Laguna Grande** is the centrepiece of the Gredos range, with its highest peak, **Almanzor** (2593m), looming above, surrounded by pinnacles sculpted into utterly improbable shapes. The valley with its huge lake is popular with day-trippers and weekenders, as you can drive up here from Hoyos del Espino, and its **refugio** (mountain hut) is often full, especially on weekends; camping out, however, is an accepted alternative.

The valley path, actually Alfonso XIII's old hunting route, continues west for a couple of hours before ending abruptly at the edge of a sharp, scree-laden descent into the **Circo de las Cinco Lagunas**. The drop is amply rewarded by virtual solitude, even in midsummer, and sightings of *Capra pyrenaica gloriae*, the graceful (and almost tame) Gredos mountain goat. Protected by law since the 1920s, they now number several thousand and frequent the north slopes of Gredos in the warmer months.

The Tormes valley: Navarredonda

On the north side of Gredos is the Tormes valley, trailed by the C500 to the main N110 at El Barco de Ávila. There is accommodation at **NAVARREDONDA**, including a **youth hostel** (☎920 348005; ②), a **campsite**, *Camping Navagredos* (☎920 207476; May–Sept) and Spain's first ever **parador** (☎920 348048, fax 920 348205; ⑦) at km43 on the C500.

Candeleda and Madrigal de la Vera

The village of **CANDELEDA**, on the Arenas–Jarandilla road, is nothing special but it's amazingly popular with Spanish summer holidaymakers, who book its *hostales* weeks in advance. If you're planning ahead, the best value is *Hostal La Pastora* (☎920 382127; ④) and the fanciest the *Hostal Pedrós* (☎920 380951; ③). Campers sometimes set up their tents alongside the river, west of town.

At **MADRIGAL DE LA VERA**, a more attractive village 12km to the west of Candeleda, there's an official campsite, *Alardos* (☎927 565066; March–Sept), and yet another route across the Gredos, this time leading to **Bohoyo**, a hamlet 4km southwest of El Barco de Ávila.

Segovia and around

After Toledo, **SEGOVIA** is the outstanding trip from Madrid. A relatively small city, strategically sited on a rocky ridge, it is deeply and haughtily Castilian, with a panoply of squares and mansions from its days of Golden Age grandeur, when it was a royal resort and a base for the Cortes (parliament). It was in Segovia – in the unremarkable church of San Miguel, off the Plaza Mayor – that Isabel la Católica was proclaimed queen.

For a city of its size, there is a stunning number of outstanding architectural monuments. Most celebrated are the **Roman aqueduct**, the **cathedral** and the fairy-tale **Alcázar**, but the less obvious attractions – the cluster of ancient churches and the many mansions found in the lanes of the old town, all in a warm, honey-coloured stone – are what really make it worth a visit. Just a few kilometres outside the city and reasonably accessible from Segovia are two Bourbon palaces, **La Granja** and **Riofrío**.

Arrival and information

Well-connected by road and rail, Segovia is an easy trip from Madrid with nine trains daily from Atocha, as well as up to 27 buses (operated by La Sepulvedana, Paseo de la Florida 11; Metro Príncipe Pío). The city's own **train station** is some distance out of town – take bus #3 to the central Plaza Mayor; the **bus station** is on the same route.

The **Turismo** (Mon–Fri 10am–2pm & 5–8pm, Sat 10am–2pm; summer Mon–Sat 10am–2pm & 5–8pm & Sun 10am–2pm; ☎921 460334), in the **Plaza Mayor**, offers a list of local accommodation plus a *Guía Semanal* with transport timetables and current events; most significant facts are displayed in the window if it's closed. You'll find a second tourist office in the busy **Plaza de Azoguejo** (daily 10am–8pm).

Accommodation

Most of the **accommodation** is to be found in the streets around the Plaza Mayor and Plaza de Azoguejo, but rooms can be hard to come by even out of season, so it's worth booking ahead if you're considering more than a day trip. Be warned that in winter, at over 1000m, the nights can be very cold and sometimes snowy, and the more basic rooms aren't generally heated.

Budget options

Pensión Aragón (☎921 460914) and **Pensión Cubo** (☎921 460917), both at Plaza Mayor 4. Rotten rooms but an ideal position and as cheap as they come. ②.

Emperador Teodosio, Paseo Conde de Sepúlveda 4 (☎921 441111). Pleasant, spacious youth hostel with no curfew, located between the train and bus stations. ②.

Pensión Ferri, c/Escuderos 10 (☎921 460957). On a street off Plaza Mayor, quiet, clean and with a small garden. ②.

Hostal Juan Bravo, c/Juan Bravo 12 (☎921 463413). Lots of big, comfortable rooms and plant-festooned bathrooms. ③.

Moderate and expensive options

Hotel Acueducto, c/Padre Claret 10 (☎921 424800, fax 921 428446). Pleasant hotel outside the city walls, near the aqueduct. The restaurant gets busy with bus parties during the day, but is quiet most evenings. ⑥.

Hostal Don Jaime, c/Ochoa Ondategui 8 (☎921 444787). Excellent *hostal* near Plaza de Azoguejo. All doubles have their own bathroom. ④.

Hostal Hidalgo, c/José Canalejas 3 (☎921 463529, fax 921 463531). Small, beautiful old building overlooking the church of San Martín, with a good restaurant. A recently opened sister *hostal, El Hidalgo 2*, at nearby c/Juan Bravo 21 (☎921 463529) is also worth a try. Both ④.

Hotel Infanta Isabel, c/Isabel la Católica 1 (☎921 461300, fax 921 462217). Comfortable new hotel – better value than the *parador* – ideally positioned on Plaza Mayor. ⑦.

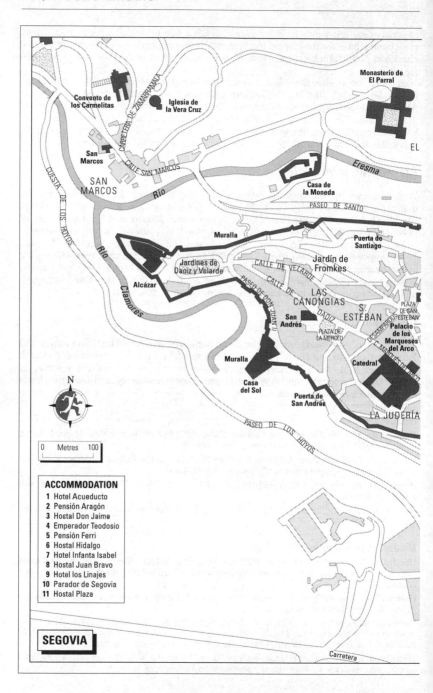

ACCOMMODATION

1 Hotel Acueducto
2 Pensión Aragón
3 Hostal Don Jaime
4 Emperador Teodosio
5 Pensión Ferri
6 Hostal Hidalgo
7 Hotel Infanta Isabel
8 Hostal Juan Bravo
9 Hotel los Linajes
10 Parador de Segovia
11 Hostal Plaza

SEGOVIA

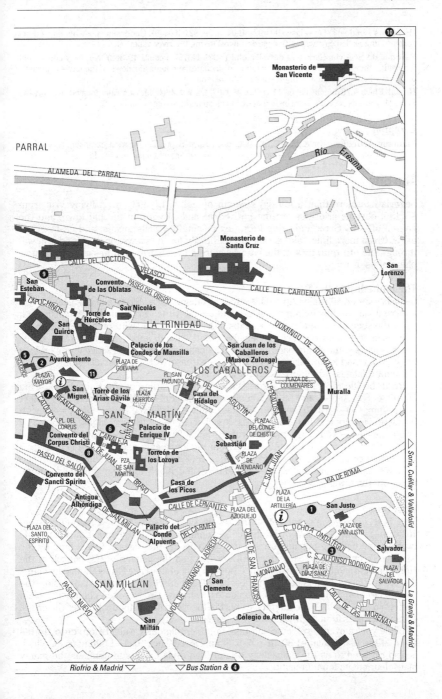

Monasterio de
San Vicente

PARRAL

Río Eresma

ALAMEDA DEL PARRAL

Monasterio de
Santa Cruz

San
Lorenzo

CALLE DEL DOCTOR
VELASCO

PASEO DEL OBISPO

CALLE DEL CARDENAL ZÚÑIGA

9
San
Esteban

Convento
de las Oblatas

DOMINGO DE GUZMÁN

CAPUCHINOS

San Nicolás

Torre de
Hércules

LA TRINIDAD

San
Quirce

5
2 Ayuntamiento

Palacio de los
Condes de Mansilla

San Juan de los
Caballeros
(Museo Zuloaga)

PLAZA DE
GUEVARA

LOS CABALLEROS

Muralla

PLAZA DE
COLMENARES

C. PEÑALOSA

PLAZA
MAYOR

i

PL. SAN
FACUNDO

CALLE DEL

11

7
San
Miguel

INFANTA ISABEL

Torre de los
Arias Dávila

PLAZA
HUERTOS

Casa del
Hidalgo

C. AGUSTÍN

PLAZA
DEL CONDE
DE CHESTE

CATÓLICA

PL. DEL
CORPUS

SAN

MARTÍN

6

Palacio de
Enrique IV

San
Sebastián

C. A. DÁVILA

8

Convento del
Corpus Christi

C. CANALEJA

C. DE JUAN

Torreón de
los Lozoya

PLAZA
DE
AVENDAÑO

C. SAN JUAN

VÍA DE ROMA

PASEO DEL SALÓN

BRAVO

PZA.
DE SAN
MARTÍN

Casa de
los Picos

Convento del
Sancti Spíritu

PLAZA
DE LA
ARTILLERÍA

1
San Justo

Antigua
Alhóndiga

DE SAN MILLÁN

CALLE DE CERVANTES

PLAZA DEL
AZOGUEJO

i

C. OCHOA ONDÁTEGUI

PLAZA DEL
SANTO
ESPÍRITU

Palacio del
Conde
Alpuente

DEL CARMEN

PLAZA
DE SAN
JUSTO

3

C. S. ALFONSO RODRÍGUEZ

El
Salvador

AVDA. DE FERNÁNDEZ LADREDA

CALLE DE SAN FRANCISCO

C.P.
MONTALVO

PLAZA DE
DÍAZ SANZ

PLAZA
DEL
SALVADOR

SAN MILLÁN

San
Clemente

PASEO NUEVO

San
Millán

Colegio de Artillería

CALLE DE LAS MORENAS

△ *Soria, Cuéllar & Valladolid*

△ *La Granja & Madrid*

Hotel Los Linajes, c/Dr Velasco 9 (☎921 460475, fax 921 460479). Good-value cosy hotel in a quiet corner of the walled city, with a fine garden overlooking the river valley. ⑤.

Parador de Segovia, Carretera de Valladolid (☎921 443737, fax 921 437362). Not very convenient for visiting the sights (you'll need a car), but for facilities and fantastic views of the city – especially beautiful when illuminated at night – it can't be beaten. ⑧.

Hostal Plaza, c/Cronista Lecea 11 (☎921 460303, fax 921 460305). Centrally located, just off the Plaza Mayor, this recently refurbished *hostal* is clean and also has a garage. ④.

Camping

Camping Acueducto (☎ & fax 921 425000; open April–Sept). The nearest campsite, a couple of kilometres out on the road to La Granja; take a #6 *Nueva Segovia* bus from the Plaza Mayor.

The City

Segovia has more than a full day's worth of sights. If you're on a flying visit from Madrid, obvious priorities are the **cathedral** and **Alcázar** in the old town, and the church of **Vera Cruz** and **aqueduct**, just outside the walls to west and east respectively. Given more time, take a walk out of the city for the **views**, or just wander at will through the **old quarters** of the city, away from the centre; each has a village atmosphere of its own.

The cathedral to the Alcázar

Segovia's **Catedral** (daily: April–Oct 9.15am–6.45pm; Nov–March 9.30am–5.45pm) was the last major Gothic building in Spain, and arguably the last in Europe. Accordingly it takes the style to its logical – or perhaps illogical – extreme, with pinnacles and flying buttresses tacked on at every conceivable point. Though impressive for its size alone, the interior is surprisingly bare so floral a construction and its space cramped by a great green marble *coro* at its very centre. The treasures are almost all confined to the museum (250ptas) which opens off the cloisters.

Down beside the cathedral, c/de Daoiz leads past a line of souvenir shops to the church of San Andrés and on to a small park in front of the **Alcázar** (daily: May–Sept 10am–7pm; Oct–April 10am–6pm; 375ptas). An extraordinary fantasy of a castle, with its narrow towers and flurry of turrets, it will seem eerily familiar to just about every visitor, having served as the model for the original Disneyland castle in California. It is itself a bit of a sham. Although it dates from the fourteenth and fifteenth centuries, it was almost completely destroyed by a fire in 1862 and rebuilt as a deliberately hyperbolic version of the original. Still, it should be visited, if only for the magnificent panoramas from the tower.

Vera Cruz

The best of Segovia's ancient churches is undoubtedly **Vera Cruz** (Tues–Sun 10.30am–1.30pm & 3.30–7pm, winter closes 6pm; closed Nov; 200ptas), a remarkable twelve-sided building outside town in the valley facing the Alcázar. It was built by the Knights Templar in the early thirteenth century on the pattern of the church of the Holy Sepulchre in Jerusalem, and once housed part of the True Cross (hence its name; the sliver of wood itself is now in the nearby village church at Zamarramala). Inside, the nave is circular, and its heart is occupied by a strange two-storeyed chamber – again twelve-sided – in which the knights, as part of their initiation, stood vigil over the cross. Climb the tower for a highly photogenic vista of the city.

While you're over here you could take in the prodigiously walled **Convento de las Carmelitas** (daily 10am–1.30pm & 4–8.30pm, closed Tues 10am–1.30pm; free), which is also referred to as the monastery of San Juan de la Cruz, and contains the gaudy mausoleum of its founder-saint.

The synagogue and a tour of the churches

One of the lesser-known sights of Segovia is the **Synagogue**, which now serves as the convent church of **Corpus Cristi**, in a little courtyard at the end of c/Juan Bravo near the east end of the cathedral. You can see part of its exterior from the Paseo del Salón, near which are the streets of the old *Judería*. It's very similar in style to Santa María la Blanca in Toledo, though less refined. During the last century it was badly damaged by fire, so what you see now is a reconstruction, but historic synagogues are so rare in Spain that this is still of interest. Opening times are unpredictable.

Just east of the synagogue is the **Plaza de San Martín**, one of the city's grandest squares, whose ensemble of buildings include the Torreón de Lozoya (open for exhibitions Mon–Sat 7–9pm & Sun noon–2pm & 7–9pm), and the twelfth-century church of **San Martín**, which demonstrates all the local stylistic peculiarities, though the best of none of them. It has the characteristic covered portico, a fine arched tower, and a typically Romanesque aspect; also, like most of Segovia's churches, it can be visited only when it's open for business, during early morning or evening services. In the middle of the plaza is a **statue of Juan Bravo**, a local folk hero who led the *comuneros* rebellion against Carlos V's attempts to take away their traditional rights. Around the square, notice the facades of the buildings, many of which display the local taste for plaster decoration (*esgrafado*) which is as common on new structures as it is on old. A good example is the **Teatro Juan Bravo** on the northern side of the plaza, opened in 1918.

North of here, the church of **La Trinidad** (daily 10am–2pm & 4.30–7.30pm) preserves the purest Romanesque style in Segovia: each span of its double-arched apse has intricately carved capitals, every one of them unique. Nearby – and making a good loop to or from the Alcázar – is the **Plaza San Esteban**, recently restored and worth seeing for its superb, five-storeyed, twelfth-century tower.

The aqueduct and more churches

The **aqueduct**, over 800m long and at its highest point towering some 30m above the Plaza de Azoguejo, stands up without a drop of mortar or cement. No one knows exactly when it was built, but probably around the end of the first century AD under either Emperor Domitian or Trajan. It no longer carries water from the Río Frío to the city and in recent years traffic vibration and pollution have been threatening to undermine the entire structure. If you climb the stairs beside the aqueduct you can get a view looking down over it from a surviving fragment of the city walls.

Another fine Romanesque church in the typical Segovian style, with tower and open porticoes, is **San Millán** (daily 10am–2pm & 4.30–7.30pm), which lies between the aqueduct and the bus station. Its interior has been restored to its original form. Also, beyond the aqueduct, you'll find **San Justo** (Tues–Sat: summer noon–2pm & 5–7pm; winter noon–2pm & 4–6pm) which has a wonderful Romanesque wall painting in the apse.

Museums

The **Museo de Segovia** (Tues–Sat 10am–2pm & 5–7pm, Sun 10am–2pm; 100ptas), which was recently reopened in the Casa del Sol, the former town abattoir perched on the walls between the Puerta de San Andrés and the Alcázar, has closed once more for further refurbishment. Its enlarged collection of fine arts, sculpture and ceramics, and ethnological and archeological exhibits should soon be open to the public once more. The **Casa-Museo de Antonio Machado**, c/Desamparados 5 (Tues–Sun 10am–2pm & 4.30–7.30pm, winter 4–6pm only), displays the spartan accommodation and furnishings of one of Spain's greatest poets of the early twentieth century; he is generally more associated with Soria but spent the last years of his life teaching here.

WALKS AROUND SEGOVIA AND THE MONASTERIO DEL PARRAL

Segovia is an excellent city for **walks**. Follow the signposted bypass road outside the city on the south side, and you'll get ever-changing views of the cathedral and the Alcázar from across the valley. The road then doubles back along the other side of the Alcázar, passing near the Convento de los Carmelitas and Vera Cruz.

From there you could continue to the **Monasterio del Parral** (Mon–Sat 10am–12.30pm & 4–6pm, Sun 10–11.30am; free); or better still, follow the track which circles behind Vera Cruz to the monastery. El Parral is a sizeable and partly ruined complex occupied by Hieronymites, an order found only in Spain. Ring the bell for admission and you will be shown the cloister and church; the latter is a late Gothic building with rich sculpture at the east end.

For the **best view** of all of Segovia, however, take the main road north for 2km or so towards Cuéllar. A panorama of the whole city, including the aqueduct, gradually unfolds.

Eating and drinking

Segovia takes its cooking seriously, with restaurants of Madrid quality – and prices. **Culinary specialities** include roast suckling pig (*cochinillo asado*), displayed in the raw in the windows of many restaurants, and the rather healthier *judiones*, large white beans from La Granja. There is a concentration of cheaper **bar-restaurants** on c/de la Infanta Isabella, off the Plaza Mayor, and late-night bars on c/Escuderos and c/Judería Vieja, and along Avenida Fernández Ladreda.

Inexpensive restaurants and bars

Bar José María, c/Cronista Lecea 11, just off Plaza Mayor. Bar-annex to one of Segovia's best restaurants (see below), serving delicious and modest-priced *tapas*.

Bar-Mesón Cuevas de San Esteban, c/Valdelaguila 15, off the top end of Plaza San Esteban. A cavern-restaurant and bar (serving draught beer), popular with locals and excellent value.

Cafetería-Restaurante Castilla, c/Juan Bravo 58. Generous helpings and friendly service – and you can eat out on a terrace.

La Codorniz, c/Escultor Marinas 3, opposite San Millán church. Inexpensive *menús* and lots of *combinados* involving *cordoniz* (quail).

El Cordero, c/del Carmen 4 & 6. Plenty of variety here, with no less than seven different *menús* to choose from, ranging in price from 1250 to 2500ptas.

La Escuela, c/San Millán 5. Youthful bar with occasional live bands.

Mesón El Campesino, c/Infanta Isabella 14. One of the best budget restaurants in town, serving decent-value *menús* and *combinados* to a young crowd. Closed Aug.

Restaurante La Almuzara, c/Marqués del Arco 3. Just behind the cathedral, this is a good-value, genuine vegetarian restaurant, with some non-veggie dishes on offer too. Closed Aug.

Tasca La Posada, c/Judería Vieja 19. A fine *bar-mesón* for *tapas*, *raciones*, or a *menú*.

La Vinatería de José Luis, c/Herreria 3. Imaginative *tapas* and good selection of wines in this friendly bar off c/Juan Bravo.

Moderate and expensive restaurants

Casa Amado, Avda. Fernández Ladreda 9 (☎921 432077). Popular local restaurant serving traditional dishes, near the Plaza Mayor. Allow 4000ptas per head. Closed Wed & Nov.

La Cocina de San Millán, c/San Millán 3 (☎921 436226). Nestling below the steps which lead up to the old town this cosy restaurant serves up imaginative cooking at reasonable prices. Closed Sun night & Jan 7–31.

Mesón de Cándido, Plaza Azoguejo 5 (☎921 428103). The city's most famous restaurant, reopened in 1992 by the founder's son and still the place for *cochinillo* and the like. The *menú* is 3000ptas, although with the *cochinillo* you are more likely to top 4000ptas.

Mesón del Duque, c/Cervantes 12 (☎921 430537). Rival to the nearby *Cándido*, and also specializing in Castilian roasts.

Mesón José María, c/Cronista Lecea 11, just off Plaza Mayor (☎921 461111). Currently reckoned to be the city's best and most imaginative restaurant, with modern variations on Castilian classics. The *menú* is a hefty 4000ptas but there are combinations costing around 2000ptas.

Narizotas, Plaza Medina Campo 1 (☎921 462679). Bar-restaurant with a bright, relaxed atmosphere, good service and innovative *menús*.

Santa Bárbara, c/Ezequiel González 32 (☎921 434806). Extensive menu and excellent seafood.

Out of town

La Posada de Javier, in the village of Torrecaballeros, 8km northeast on the N110 (☎921 401136). Serious *madrileño* – and *segoviano* – gourmands eat out in the neighbouring villages, and this lovely old farmhouse is one of the most popular choices. It is, however, pricey with a *menú* costing at least 4000ptas. Booking is essential at weekends. Closed Sun night, Mon & July.

La Granja and Riofrío

Segovia has a major outlying attraction in the Bourbon summer palace and gardens of **La Granja**, 10km southeast of the town on the N601 Madrid road, and connected by regular bus services. True Bourbon aficionados, with time and transport, might also want to visit a second palace and hunting museum 12km west of La Granja at **Riofrío**.

La Granja

LA GRANJA (or San Ildefonso de la Granja, to give it its full title) was built by the reluctant first Bourbon king of Spain, Felipe V, no doubt homesick for the luxuries of Versailles. Its glories are the mountain setting and the extravagant wooded grounds and gardens, but it's also worth casting an eye over the **palace** (April–May Tues–Sat 10am–1.30pm & 3–5pm, Sun 10am–2pm; June–Sept Tues–Sun 10am–6pm; Oct–March Tues–Sat 10am–1.30pm & 3–5pm, Sun 10–6pm; compulsory guided tour 650ptas, Wed free for EU citizens). Though destroyed in parts and damaged throughout by a fire in 1918, much has been well restored. The most striking thing about the long series of rooms is their perfect symmetry – you get the uncanny feeling, as you stand looking through the open doorways, of gazing into a mirror endlessly reflecting the same room. Everything is furnished in plush French imperial style but it's almost all of Spanish origin; the majority of the huge chandeliers, for example, were made in the **crystal factory** still operating in the village of San Ildefonso (April–Sept Tues–Sun 11am–8pm; Oct–March Tues–Sun 11am–7pm; 400ptas). The palace is also home to a superlative collection of sixteenth-century tapestries, one of the most valuable in the world.

The highlight of the **gardens** (daily 10am–7pm; 325ptas, Wed free for EU citizens) is its series of fountains, which culminate in the fifty-foot high jet of La Fama. They're really fantastic and on no account to be missed, which means timing your visit from 5.30pm on Wednesdays or weekends, when some are switched on. Only on a very few days of the year – normally 30 May, 25 July & 25 August – are all of the fountains set to work, with accompanying crowds to watch.

The **village** of San Ildefonso de la Granja is a lively place, with several **bars** and **restaurants** where you can while away any spare time: try the *Bar La Villa* off the main square for *tapas*, *Bar Zaca*, also off the square, for lunch, or *Bar Madrid*, near the palace. There's a range of **accommodation**, too, if you prefer to stay here than Segovia: try the *Hotel Roma* (☎921 470752; ⑤), right outside the palace gates, or the cheaper *Pensión Pozo de la Nieve*, c/Baños 4 (☎921 470598; ③).

Riofrío

The palace at **RIOFRÍO** (June–Sept Tues–Sun 10am–6pm; Oct–May Tues–Sat 10am–1.30pm & 3–5pm, Sun 10am–2pm; 650ptas) was built by Isabel, the widow of Felipe V, who feared she would be banished from La Granja itself by her stepson Fernando VI. He died however, leaving the throne for Isabel's own son, Carlos III, and Riofrío was not occupied until the nineteenth century when Alfonso XII moved in to mourn the death of his young queen Mercedes. He, too, died pretty soon after, which is perhaps why the palace has a spartan and slightly tatty feel.

The complex, painted in dusty pink with green shutters, is surrounded not by manicured gardens but by a **deer park**, which you can drive through but not wander into. Inside the palace, you have to join a guided tour, which winds through an endless sequence of rooms, none stunningly furnished. About half the tour is devoted to a **museum of hunting**; the most interesting items here are reconstructions of cave paintings, including the famous Altamira drawings.

North from Segovia

Heading **north from Segovia**, you're faced with quite a variety of routes. The train line heads northwest towards Valladolid and León, past the castles of **Coca** and **Medina del Campo** – two of the very finest in Spain. If you have transport of your own, or time for convoluted local bus routes, you can take in further impressive castles in Segovia province at **Pedraza**, **Turégano** and **Cuéllar**, and still more by striking north again to **Peñafiel** and the chain of castles along the River Duero. If you are looking for a night's stop in a small town, Pedraza and Turégano, around 40km from Segovia, would fit the bill nicely.

For details on this area, see the "Old Castile and Léon" chapter.

East of Madrid: Alcalá de Henares, Nuevo Baztán, Guadalajara and the Alcarria

East of the capital there's considerably less to detain you. The only tempting day trips are to the old university town of **Alcalá de Henares**, Cervantes's birthplace, and, for Baroque enthusiasts, to **Nuevo Baztán**, an eighteenth-century new town planned by José de Churriguera. Further afield, the largely modern city of **Guadalajara** has little to recommend it, although the region southwest of here, the **Alcarria**, has its charms, especially if you want to follow the footsteps of Spain's Nobel prizewinner, Camilo José Cela, who described his wanderings here in the 1940s in his book, *Viaje a la Alcarria*.

Alcalá de Henares

ALCALÁ DE HENARES, a little over 30km from Madrid, is one of Europe's most ancient university towns, and renowned as the birthplace of Miguel de **Cervantes**. In the sixteenth century the university was a rival to Salamanca's, but in 1836 the faculties moved to Madrid and the town went into decline. Almost all the artistic heritage was lost in the Civil War and nowadays it's virtually a suburb of Madrid. It is not somewhere you'd want to stay longer than it takes to see the sights, but that's no problem with regular trains (Chamartín or Atocha; every 15–30min) and buses (every 15min, operated by Continental Auto) from Madrid throughout the day.

The **Universidad Antigua** (guided tours: Mon–Fri 11.30am, 12.30pm, 1.30pm, 5pm & 6pm; Sat, Sun & holidays 11am–2pm & 5–8pm; 300ptas) stands at the heart of the old town in Plaza de San Diego. It was endowed by Cardinal Cisneros (also known as Cardinal Jiménez) at the beginning of the sixteenth century and features a fabulous Plateresque facade and a Great Hall, the **Paraninfo** (entered through the *Hostería del Estudiante*, an expensive restaurant at the back), with a gloriously decorated Mudéjar *artesonado* ceiling. Next door, the **Capilla de San Ildefonso** has another superb ceiling, intricately stuccoed walls, and the Italian marble tomb of Cardinal Cisneros.

Two buildings lay claim to Cervantes's birthplace. The **Museo Casa Natal de Cervantes** at c/Imagen 2 (Tues–Sun 10.15am–1.45pm & 4–6.45pm; free) is the more worthwhile: though the house itself is hardly thirty years old, it's authentic in style, furnished with genuine sixteenth-century objects, and contains a small museum with a few early editions of *Don Quixote* and other curiosities related to the author.

To the west of the university, the **Monasterio de San Bernardo**, Via Complutense (guided tours Mon–Fri 6pm; Sat 12.30pm, 1.30pm, 5pm, 6pm, 7pm; Sun 5pm, 6pm, 7pm; 350ptas), was founded by the Cistercians in 1617 and has recently opened its doors as a museum of religious art, recreating the atmosphere of a monastery of that era, complete with cells and kitchen.

Just off the central Plaza Cervantes is the **Cervantes Theatre**, whose eighteen-year restoration is nearing completion. Discovered beneath a crumbling old cinema by two drama students in 1980, the theatre, like Shakespeare's Globe, was a hub of rowdy heckling and lively dramatics throughout the first half of the seventeenth century. However, it now looks set to become the subject of a drama of its own, as a dispute over its future use develops between those who discovered it, and subsequently dedicated their lives to the project, and local bureaucrats from the regional authority.

The local **Turismo** (daily 10am–2pm & 5–7.30pm; closed Mon in July & Sept; ☎91 889 26 94), just off the central Plaza de Cervantes, has maps and further information, and from here nothing of interest is more than a short walk away. You'll find no shortage of places to eat centrally and, if you want to **stay**, there are several *pensiones* on the Plaza de Cervantes itself as well as the *Hostal Jacinto* (☎91 889 14 32; ③–④), conveniently located by the train station.

Nuevo Baztán

Twenty kilometres southeast of Alcalá, or 45km from Madrid, **NUEVO BAZTÁN** should appeal to anyone interested in architecture, planning or merely the unusual. It was designed and built in 1709–13 by José de Churriguera in response to a commission from the royal treasurer, who aimed to develop a local decorative arts industry. Today it's semi-deserted, though brash modern villas are being built nearby for well-heeled commuters to the capital. As a focus, Churriguera built a **palace** and **church** as a single architectural unit; the latter has a massive twin-towered facade and a central dome and *retablos* by the architect within. Behind the palace, now fenced off, is the **Plaza de Fiestas**, complete with balconies for watching celebrations. The houses of the workers comprise the rest of the settlement.

The best day to visit Nuevo Baztán is Sunday. Empresa Izquierdo, c/Goya 80 (Metro Goya), runs two buses daily from Madrid but only on Sunday do these allow you any time here, and this is also the only day the church is sure to be open.

Guadalajara

GUADALAJARA, north from Alcalá de Henares, is not terribly exciting despite its famous name. Severely battered during the Civil War, it's now a small industrial city, provincial and scruffy. There are, however, a few worthwhile buildings which survived bombardment, notably the **Palacio del Infantado** (Tues–Sat 10.15am–2pm & 4.30–7pm, Sun 10.15am–2pm; 200ptas) and an assortment of medieval churches. The *palacio*, the former home of the Duke of Mendoza, boasts a wonderful decorative facade and cloister-like patio, and now houses a fairly average local art museum. It is to be found a few blocks to the northwest of the town's large, park-like central square, Plaza Capitán Beixareu Rivera.

There's a friendly **Turismo** opposite the Palacio del Infantado (Mon–Fri 9am–3pm & 4–6pm, Sat 10am–6pm, Sun 10am–3pm; ☎949 220698). If you needed, or wanted, **to stay**, *Hotel España*, c/Teniente Figueroa 3 (☎949 211303, fax 949 211303; ④) is a decent budget option; even cheaper is *Pensión Galicia*, c/San Roque 16 (☎949 220059; ③). **Bars** and **restaurants** are plentiful, too. *Can Vic* on Plaza Fernando Beládiez is a good, low-priced place, or for a seafood and fish blow-out there's *Casa Victor* at c/Bardales 6. **Late-night** and **music bars** are mostly to be found along c/Sigüenza.

Moving on

The main road and rail lines from Madrid to Zaragoza and Barcelona both pass through Alcalá and Guadalajara, and continue more or less parallel throughout their journeys. Sigüenza (see p.162) and Medinaceli (see p.353) each make excellent resting points on your way. From Guadalajara you can also cut down to Cuenca, and from there continue towards Valencia and the coast. This is a very beautiful drive, past the great dams of the Embalse de Entrepeñas and Embalse de Buendía, and takes you through the heart of the Alcarria region.

The Alcarria

The **Alcarria** has few particular monuments but the wild scenery and sporadic settlements are eerily impressive, especially coming upon them so close to Madrid. Many of the high sierra villages, north of the N320, were deserted during the Nationalist advance on Madrid in the Civil War and today have only a handful of permanent inhabitants, plus a few *madrileño* weekenders who are restoring the old cottages.

The largest town of the region, **PASTRANA**, 15km south of the N320, merits a diversion. The museum of its vast **Colegiata** church (daily 10.30am–1.30pm & 4.30–6.30pm; 300ptas) contains some wonderful fifteenth-century tapestries depicting the conquest of Tangier and Asilah by Alfonso V of Portugal, as well as richly decorated ebony and bronze altarpieces from the Philippines. These were brought to Pastrana by the Princess of Eboli, duchess of the town, who after a court scandal was imprisoned in the palace overlooking the central square and allowed to sit out on the balcony overlooking the square (now known as Plaza de la Hora), for one hour a day. Also of interest is the **Convento del Carmen**, a ten-minute walk out of town. This Carmelite convent was founded by Saint Teresa and within you'll find a small museum of assorted religious art and yet more relics of the saint (daily 9.30am–1pm & 3.30–7pm; 300ptas). Part of this convent has recently become a **hotel**, the *Hospedería Real de Pastrana* (☎949 371060; ⑤). The only other place to stay is back in town at *Hostal Moratín*, c/Moratín 3 (☎949 370116; ③), a clean and comfortable place on the main road. Meanwhile, Pastrana's twisting streets, including its former **Jewish and Arab quarters**, offer endless rambling, and there's modest **Turismo** (☎949 370672) on the edge of town, but there's little diversion to be had in the evening.

travel details

BUSES

From Madrid

Estación Sur de Autobuses, c/Méndez Álvaro s/n (Metro Méndez Álvaro) to: Aranjuez (17 daily; 1hr); Toledo (every 30min; 1hr 15min); Arenas de San Pedro (5 daily; 2hr 15min).

La Veloz, Avda. del Mediterráneo 49 (Metro Conde de Casal) to: Chinchón (15 daily; 1hr).

Argabus, Avda. de Mediterráneo 49 (Metro Conde de Casal) to: Nuevo Baztan (2–3 daily; 1hr 15min).

Herranz, Intercambiador de Autobuses, Moncloa (Metro Moncloa) to: El Escorial (every 30min; 1hr).

La Sepulvedana, Intercambiador de Autobuses, Moncloa (Metro Moncloa) to: Cercedilla (every 30min; 45min).

La Sepulvedana, Paseo de la Florida 11 (Metro Príncipe Pío) to: Ávila (3–7 daily; 1hr 45min); Segovia (27 daily; 1hr 30min).

Continental Auto, Avda. de América (Metro Avda. de América) to: Alcalá (every 15min; 40min); Guadalajara (every 30min; 45min).

Intercambiador de Autobuses, Plaza de Castilla (Metro Plaza de Castilla) to: Manzanares del Real (hourly; 40min).

Ávila to: Arenas de San Pedro (1 daily Mon–Fri; 1hr 30min); Madrid (7 daily; 1hr 45min); Salamanca (4 daily; 1hr 30min); Segovia (2–3 daily; 1hr).

El Escorial to: Guadarrama (8 daily; 20min); Madrid (every 30min; 1hr); Valle de los Caídos (1 daily; 15min).

Segovia to: Ávila (2–3 daily; 1hr); La Granja (12 daily; 20min); Madrid (every 30min; 1hr 30min); Salamanca (1–3 daily; 2–3hr); Valladolid (5–9 daily; 2hr 30min).

Toledo to: Ciudad Real, for the south (1 daily; 2hr); Cuenca (1 daily Mon–Fri, 2hr 30min); Guadamur (3–6 daily; 20min); Madrid (every 30min; 1hr 15min); Orgaz (3–11 daily; 40min); La Puebla de Montelban (6 daily Mon–Fri, 1 daily Sat; 30min); Talavera de la Reina, for Extremadura (10 daily; 1hr 30min).

TRAINS

From Madrid

Atocha station (Metro Atocha) to: Alcalá via Chamartín (every 15–30min; 30min); El Escorial via Chamartín (27 daily; 1hr); Guadalajara via Chamartín (44 daily; 50min); Segovia via Chamartín (9 daily; 2hr); Toledo via Aranjuez (9 daily; 1hr 15min).

Chamartín (Metro Chamartín) to: Ávila (17 daily; 2hr); Cercedilla (23 daily; 1hr 25min).

Aranjuez to: Cuenca (5 daily; 2hr); Madrid (8 daily; 45min); Toledo (9 daily; 30min).

Ávila to: Madrid (35 daily; 1hr 30min–2hr); El Escorial (7 daily; 1hr 10min); Medina del Campo (14 daily; 40min); Salamanca (3 daily; 2hr); Valladolid (14 daily; 1hr).

Cercedilla to: Madrid (23 daily; 1hr 25min); Puerto de Navacerrada (12 daily; 30min); Segovia (9 daily; 1hr).

El Escorial to: Ávila (7 daily; 1hr 10min); Madrid (27 daily; 1 hr).

Segovia to: Cercedilla (9 daily; 1hr); Madrid (9 daily; 2hr).

Toledo to: Aranjuez (9 daily; 30min); Madrid (9 daily; 1hr 15min).

CHAPTER THREE

NEW CASTILE AND EXTREMADURA

The vast area covered by this chapter is some of the most travelled, yet least visited, country in Spain. Once south of Toledo (which is covered in the previous chapter, "Around Madrid"), most tourists thunder non-stop across the plains of New Castile to Valencia and Andalucía, or follow the great rivers through Extremadura into Portugal. At first sight this is understandable. **New Castile** in particular is Spain at its least welcoming: a vast, bare plain, burning hot in summer, chillingly exposed in winter. But the first impression is not an entirely fair one – away from the main highways the villages of the plain are as welcoming as any in the country, and in the northeast, where the mountains start, are the extraordinary cliff-hanging city of **Cuenca** and the historic cathedral town of **Sigüenza**. New Castile is also the agricultural and wine-growing heartland of Spain and the country through which Don Quixote cut his despairing swathe.

It is in **Extremadura**, though, that there is most to be missed. This harsh environment was the cradle of the *conquistadores*, men who opened up a new world for the Spanish empire. Remote before and forgotten since, Extremadura enjoyed a brief golden age when the heroes returned with their gold to live in a flourish of splendour. **Trujillo**, the birthplace of Pizarro, and **Cáceres** both preserve entire towns built with *conquistador* wealth, the streets crowded with the ornate mansions of returning empire builders. Then there is **Mérida**, the most completely preserved Roman city in Spain, and the monasteries of **Guadalupe** and **Yuste**, the one fabulously wealthy, the other rich in imperial memories. Finally, for little-visited wild scenery and superb fauna, northern Extremadura has the **Parque Natural de Monfragüe**, where even the most casual bird-watcher can look up to see eagles and vultures circling the cliffs.

NEW CASTILE

The region that was for so long called **New Castile** – and that until the 1980s held Madrid in its domain – is now officially known as **Castilla-La Mancha**. Although the heavily cultivated plains that cover much of the terrain are less bleak than they once were – the name La Mancha comes from the Arab *manxa*, meaning steppe – the main points of interest are widely spaced on an arc drawn from Madrid, with little between that rewards exploration. If you are travelling east on **trains and buses** towards Aragón, there's little to justify a stop other than Sigüenza (en route to Zaragoza) or Cuenca (en route to Teruel). To the south, Toledo has bus links within its own province

FIESTAS

February

First weekend *La Endiablada* at Almonacid Marquesado (near Cuenca), a very old festival which sees all the boys dressing up as devils and parading through the streets.

Week before Lent *Carnival* everywhere.

March/April

Holy Week (*Semana Santa*) celebrated with magnificent ritual (floats, penitents, etc) in Cuenca.

Pascua (Passion of the Resurrection). Major Easter fiesta in Trujillo.

April 23 *San Jorge*. Celebrations characterized by tremendous enthusiasm continue for several days in Cáceres.

May

First weekend at Cáceres. WOMAD Festival (see p.187)

Late May fair at Cáceres. Also – again with no fixed date – *Cabalata*, muleteer races, at Atienza (30km northeast of Sigüenza).

June

23–27 *San Juan*. Particularly manic festival in the picturesque town of Coria (50km west of Plasencia) with a bull let loose for a few hours a day, everyone dancing and drinking in the streets, and running for their lives when it appears.

July

Drama Festival in Mérida throughout July and into August, when the plays move onto Alcántara.

Spanish Classical Drama Festival at Almagro (25km southwest of Ciudad Real) throughout July – from the first Thursday until the last Sunday of the month.

14 July Fiestas start in La Puebla de Montalbán, in the Montes de Toledo. Bulls are let loose in the streets.

August

First Tuesday *Fiesta de Martes Mayor*, Plasencia.

24–25 *San Bartolomé*. Fiestas at any town or church named after the saint, particularly at Jerez de los Caballeros.

September

First week *Vendimia* – grape harvest – celebrations at Valdepeñas; major fair at Trujillo also early in the month.

7–17 *Virgin of Los Llanos*, Plasencia.

Week leading up to third Sunday Festivals in Jarandilla and Madrigal de la Vera with bulls running in front of cows – which are served up on the final day's feast.

October

1 *San Miguel*. Fiestas at any town or church named after the saint, particularly at Badajoz.

---

but heading for Andalucía or Extremadura you'd do better returning to Madrid and starting out again; the Toledo rail line stops at the town.

If you do have **transport**, and are **heading south**, the Toledo–Ciudad Real road, the Montes de Toledo, and the marshy Parque Nacional de las Tablas de Daimiel, all provide good alternatives to the sweltering NIV *autovía*. **Heading east**, through Cuenca to Teruel, the best route is to follow the Río Jucar out of the province, by way of weird rock formations in the Ciudad Encantada and the source of the Río Tajo. **Heading west**, into Extremadura, the NV is one of the dullest and hottest roads in Spain, and can be avoided by following the C501 through the Sierra de Gredos (see previous chapter, "Around Madrid") or cutting on to it from Talavera de la Reina; this would bring you to the Monastery of Yuste by way of the lush valley of La Vera.

The sections following cover the main sights and routes of New Castile in a clockwise direction, from northeast to southwest of Madrid.

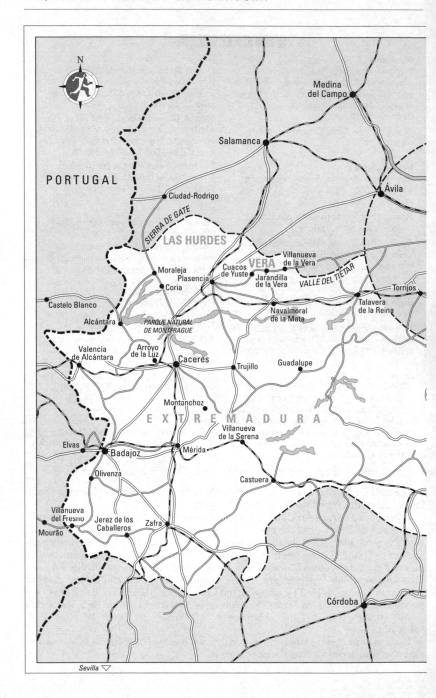

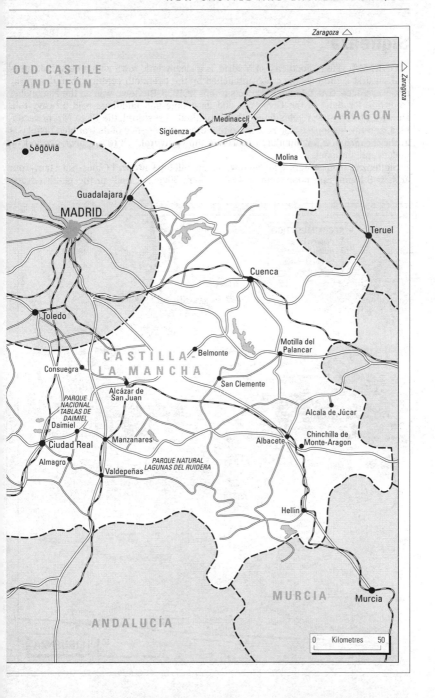

Sigüenza

SIGÜENZA, 120km northeast of Madrid, is a sleepy little town with a beautiful cathedral. At first sight it seems quite untouched by the twentieth century, though appearances are deceptive: taken by Franco's troops in 1936, the town was on the Nationalist front line for most of the Civil War, and its people and buildings paid a heavy toll. However, the post-war years have seen the cathedral restored, the Plaza Mayor recobbled, and the bishop's castle rebuilt, so that the only evidence of its troubled history is in the facades of a few buildings, including the cathedral bell tower, pock-marked by bullets and shrapnel.

Sigüenza's main streets lead you towards the hill-top **Catedral** (Tues–Sat 11am–1pm & 4.30–6.15pm, Sun noon–1pm & 4.30–5.30pm; 300ptas), built in the pinkish stone

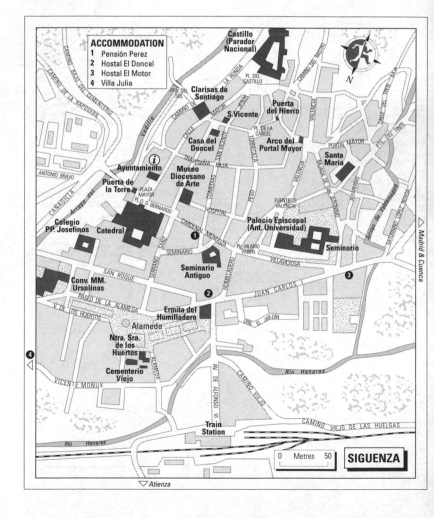

which characterizes the town. Begun in 1150 by the town's first bishop, Bernardo of Toledo, it is essentially Gothic, with three rose windows, though it has been much altered over the years. Facing the main entrance is a huge marble *coro* with an altar to a thirteenth-century figure of the Virgin. The cathedral's principal treasure is the alabaster tomb of Martín Vásquez de Arce, known as *El Doncel* (the page boy); a favourite of Isabella la Católica, he was killed fighting the Moors in Granada. On the other side of the building is an extraordinary doorway: Plateresque at the bottom, Mudéjar in the middle and Gothic at the top – an amazing amalgam, built by a confused sixteenth-century architect. Take a look, too, at the sacristy, whose superb Renaissance ceiling has 304 heads carved by Covarrubias. In a chapel opening off this (with an unusual cupola, best seen in the mirror provided) is an El Greco *Annunciation*.

More treasures are displayed in the **cloister**, while further art works from local churches and convents, including a saccharine Zurbarán of *Mary as a Child*, are displayed in the **Museu Diocesano del Arte** (closed for refurbishment at time of writing), just off the square.

From the **Plaza Mayor**, overseen by the cathedral's pencil-thin bell tower and last used for bull fighting in 1985, you can walk up to the castle, passing en route the church of **San Vicente**. This is much the same age as the cathedral and is interesting mainly as a chance to see just how many layers of remodelling had to be peeled off by the restorers; an ancient figure of Christ above the altar is the only thing to detain you inside.

The **castle** started life as a Roman fortress, was adapted by the Visigoths and further improved by the Moors as their *Alcazaba*. Reconquered in 1124, it became the official residence of the warlike Bishop Bernardo and his successors. The Civil War virtually reduced the castle to rubble, but it was almost completely rebuilt in the 1960s and converted to a *parador*.

Practicalities

There's a rather lacklustre **Turismo** in the town hall, at the top end of the Plaza Mayor (Tues–Fri 9am–2pm, Sat 9am–3pm & 4–7pm, Sun 9am–3pm; ☎949 393251). **Accommodation** is not usually a problem. Central places include the *Pensión Perez*, c/García Atance 9 (☎949 391263; ①), *Hostal El Doncel*, Paseo de la Alameda 3 (☎949 391090, fax 949 390080; ⑤), and the slightly more upmarket *El Motor*, Avda. Juan Carlos I 2 (☎949 390827, fax 949 390007; ⑤). The *Villa Julia*, Paseo de las Cruces 27 (☎949 393339; ⑤), is a pricey but extremely comfortable *casa rural* (private house) with just five double en-suite rooms, while the *Parador de Sigüenza* (☎949 390100, fax 949 391364; ⑦) is a bit soulless but has fine views from the upper floors. For **meals**, try the hotel restaurants at *El Motor* and *El Doncel*, or settle for excellent *tapas* at the *Cafetería Atrio* on the Plaza Mayor.

Heading north from Sigüenza, **Medinaceli** is just over the border in Old Castile, a couple of stops on the Zaragoza line (only slow trains call at Sigüenza and Medinaceli). Heading south, a good route for drivers leads **towards Cuenca**, past great reservoirs watered by the Tajo and Guadiela rivers, and skirting around the **Alcarria** region.

Cuenca and around

The mountainous, craggy countryside around **CUENCA** is as dramatic as any in Spain, and all the more so in the context of New Castile. The city itself, too, the capital of a sparsely populated province, is an extraordinary-looking place, enclosed on three sides by the deep gorges of the Huécar and Júcar rivers, with balconied houses hanging over the cliff top – the finest of them converted to a Museum of Abstract Art. No surprise, then, that this is a popular weekend outing from Madrid; to get the most from a visit, try to come on a weekday, and take the time to stay a night and absorb the atmosphere.

Arrival and information

The old town of Cuenca – the **Ciudad Antigua** – stands on a high ridge, looped to the south by the Río Huécar and the **modern town** and its suburbs. If you're driving in, follow signs for the *Catedral* and try one of the car parks up in the old town. Arriving by **train** or **bus** you'll find yourself at the southern edge of the modern part of town: the bus station is just beyond the train station. Calle Ramón y Cajal leads from either to the Puerta de Valencia, from where it's a steep climb up to the old town; bus #1 or #2 will save you the walk. You can **rent a car** at the train station from Arexi-Rent-A-Car (☎969 234148).

Cuenca's very helpful **Turismo** is at Plaza Mayor (daily 9.30am–2pm & 4–6pm; ☎969 232119, fax 969 235356), and can provide information and maps on the whole province.

Accommodation

You'll find most **places to stay** in the new town, with a concentration of *hostales* along c/Ramón y Cajal, but there are several reasonably priced options in the old town.

Budget options

Pensión Central, c/Alonso Chirino 9 (☎969 211511). Good-value *pensión* offering large rooms with separate bath. ②.

Pensión Cuenca, Avda. República Argentina 8 (☎969 212574). Modern *pensión* located near the train and bus stations offering some rooms with showers. ②–③.

Pensión Marín, c/Ramón y Cajal 53 (☎969 221978). Basic, but clean and central. ②.

Pension Real, c/Larga 39 (☎969 229977). The last building in the old town, with commanding views of Cuenca. Nineteen rooms with shared bathroom/shower. ③.

Pension Tabanqueta, c/Trabuco 13 (☎969 211290). The best *pensión* in town with wonderful views and a lively bar which serves good food at affordable prices. Shared bathrooms. ③.

Moderate and expensive options

Hotel Alfonso VIII, Parque de San Julián 3 (☎969 212512, fax 969 214325). Nicely located – but pricey – hotel in the new town, facing the park. ⑥.

Hotel Arévalo, c/Ramón y Cajal 29 (☎969 223812). Centrally located hotel with secure parking. ④.

Hostal Avenida, Avda. Carretería 25 (☎969 214343, fax 969 212335). Near the park, and well located for the old town, this *hostal* is functional but comfortable. All rooms have TV and bath. ④.

Hotel Figón de Pedro, c/Cervantes 17 (☎969 224511). Well-run hotel at the heart of the modern town, with an excellent restaurant. ④.

Hotel Leonor de Aquitania, c/San Pedro 58–60 (☎969 231000). Cuenca's prime hotel, beautifully situated in the old town, with superb views and prices to match. ⑥.

Parador de Cuenca, Convento de San Pablo (☎969 232320, fax 969 232534). Expensive and nothing special; head for *Leonor de Aquitania* for better value and views. ⑦.

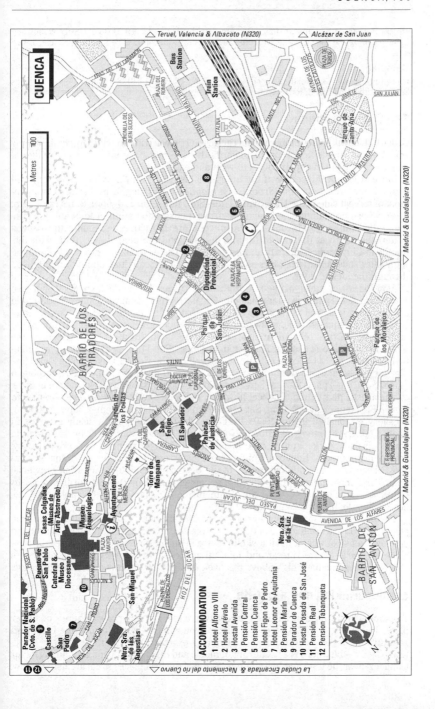

CUENCA

Teruel, Valencia & Albacete (N320) — Alcázar de San Juan

Madrid & Guadalajara (N320)

Madrid & Guadalajara (N320)

La Ciudad Encantada & Nacimiento del río Cuervo

0 Metres 100

Bus Station
Train Station

Diputación Provincial

Parque de San Julián

Palacio de Justicia
El Salvador
San Felipe

Torre de Mangana

Ayuntamiento

Museo Arqueológico

Casas Colgadas (Museo de Arte Abstracto)

Catedral & Museo Diocesano

Puente de San Pablo

Parador Nacional (Cvto. de S. Pablo)

Castillo

San Pedro

Ntra. Sra. de las Angustias

San Miguel

Ntra. Sra. de la Luz

BARRIO DE LOS TIRADORES

BARRIO DE SAN ANTON

HOZ DEL JÚCAR

PASEO DEL JÚCAR

AVENIDA DE LOS ALFARES

ACCOMMODATION

1 Hotel Alfonso VIII
2 Hotel Arévalo
3 Hostal Avenida
4 Pensión Central
5 Pensión Cuenca
6 Hotel Figón de Pedro
7 Hotel Leonor de Aquitania
8 Pensión Marín
9 Parador de Cuenca
10 Hostal Posada de San José
11 Pensión Real
12 Pensión Tabanqueta

Hostal Posada de San José, c/Julián Romero 4 (☎969 211300, fax 969 230365). Lovely old building in the old town near the cathedral, with only 30 rooms (21 with bath), so be sure to book ahead. ⑥.

Camping

Camping Cuenca, 6km north of the city on the CU921 (☎969 231656). Surrounded by shady pines and open from mid-March to December.

The Ciudad Antigua

Cross one of the many bridges over the River Huécar and you start to climb steeply (most of the streets are stepped) towards the **Ciudad Antigua**, a narrow wedge of lanes, petering out in superb views to west and east.

More or less at the centre of the quarter is the Plaza Mayor, a fine space, entered through the arches of the Baroque *Ayuntamiento* and ringed by cafés. Occupying most of its east side is the **Catedral** (Tues–Sat 11am–2pm & 4–6pm, Sun 11am–2pm; free), whose ugly, unfinished facade betrays a misguided attempt to beautify a simple Gothic building. The interior is much more attractive, especially the carved Plateresque arch at the end of the north aisle, and the chapel next to it, with distinctly un-Christian carvings round its entrance. The east chapel, directly behind the high altar, has a superb *artesonado* ceiling, which can just about be glimpsed through the locked door.

Alongside is a small **Museo Catedralicio** (Tues–Fri 11am–2pm & 4–6pm, Sat 11am–2pm & 4–8pm, Sun 11am–2.30pm; 200ptas) which contains some beautiful gold and silver work as well as doors by Alonso Berruguete. The ceiling here, now a sea of Baroque icing-sugar shades, was originally a beautiful Mudéjar work like the one in the east chapel. Further religious treasures are to be found down c/Obispo Valero in the **Museo Diocesano** (Tues–Sat 11am–2pm & 4–6pm, Sun 11am–2pm; 200ptas), including two canvasses by El Greco, a magnificent *Crucifixion* by Gerard David, and a Byzantine diptych unique in Spain. Right opposite is a new and excellent **Museo Arqueológico** (Tues–Sat 10am–2pm & 4–7pm, Sun 10am–2pm; 300ptas), showcasing local Roman finds.

The artistic highlight of Cuenca, however, has to be the **Museo de Arte Abstracto** (Tues–Fri 11am–2pm & 4–6pm, Sat 11am–2pm & 4–8pm, Sun 11am–2.30pm; 500ptas), a gallery established in the 1960s by Fernando Zóbel, one of the leading artists in Spain's "abstract generation". It is now run by the prestigious Fundación Juan March, which displays works from a core collection of abstract painting and sculpture by, among many others, Eduardo Chillida, José Guerrero, Lucio Muñoz, Antonio Saura and Fernando Zóbel, and hosts some of the best exhibitions to be found in provincial Spain. The museum itself is a stunning conversion from the extraordinary *Casas Colgadas* ("hanging houses"), a pair of fifteenth-century houses, with cantilevered balconies, literally hanging from the cliff face.

There are other monuments signposted in Cuenca, but the greatest attraction is the place itself. Have a drink in one of the bars opposite the cathedral in the Plaza Mayor and you get a sense of what it must feel like to live in one of the suspended houses, or walk along the gorge of the Huécar and look up at the *Casas Colgadas* and the other less secure-looking buildings high above the river. At night the effect is even more dramatic.

Eating, drinking and nightlife

The tourist heart of Cuenca is the Plaza Mayor, and for evening *copas*, there's no better place. You can have meals here, too, though you will eat better down at the **bars and restaurants** of the modern town. Cuenca isn't exactly full of **nightlife** – this is small-town Castile – but there is a scattering of music and disco-bars in and around c/Doctor Galíndez, near the train and bus stations. Some of the best places to eat are listed below.

Figón de Pedro, c/Cervantes 15 (☎969 226821). Renowned restaurant, serving classic Castilian roasts, and a superb *mero* dish. Closed Sun evening & Mon. Moderate to expensive.

Mesón Casas Colgada, c/Canónigos 3 (☎969 223509). A good restaurant up in the old town, housed in a fine hanging house. Features suckling pig and other Castilian specialities. Closed Thurs evening. Expensive.

La Ponderosa, c/San Francisco 20. The best *tapas* selection in a street full of worthwhile *mesónes*. Closed Sun.

Posada San Julián, c/de las Torres 1. A nice local with decent, inexpensive *menús*.

Restaurante Plaza Mayor. Local specialities and liquor (*resolí*) served in this restaurant on the main plaza. Allow 2000–3000ptas per head.

Taverna Tintes, c/Tintes 7. Recently refurbished, this popular and atmospheric local serves up a wide range of moderately priced dishes. Closed Mon.

Togar, Avda. República Argentina 3. Popular restaurant with cellar serving local dishes and regional specialities. Allow 3000ptas per head.

La Ciudad Encantada – and on towards Albarracín

The classic excursion from Cuenca is to the **Ciudad Encantada**, a 20-square-kilometre "park" of limestone outcrops, sculpted by erosion into a bizarre series of abstract, natural and animal-like forms. A few of the names – "fight between an elephant and a crocodile", for example – stretch the imagination a little, but the rocks are certainly amazing, and many of the creations really do look knocked into shape by human hands.

The most interesting area of sculptures is enclosed (admission daily 9am–dusk; 200ptas), and the extensive car park and restaurants outside testify to its popularity with weekending *madrileños*. However, off season, or during the week, you can have the place almost to yourself. You will need transport to get to the park, which is around 20km northeast of Cuenca, on signed backroads towards Albarracín. If you get stuck, there is a **hostal**, the *Ciudad Encantada* (☎969 288194; ⑤) opposite the entrance gate.

To the source of the Tajo

If you have transport, the route west from the Ciudad Encantada, towards Albarracín (see the "Aragón" chapter) is a delight, edging through the verdant **Júcar Gorge** and across the wild, scarcely populated Serranía de Cuenca. En route, still in Cuenca Province, you might stop at **UÑA**, a village sited between a lagoon and barrage, where the *Hotel Agua Riscas* (☎969 281332; ⑤) has decent rooms, a panoramic restaurant and a garden bar.

Just over the provincial border, in Teruel Province, the road between Uña and Frías de Albarracín runs past a point known as García, where a signpost directs you to the **source of the Río Tajo**. Below a hideous 1960s sculpture, a trickle of muddy water seeps out, setting the course of one of Iberia's great rivers on its way to the Atlantic Ocean at Lisbon.

Belmonte, El Toboso and Alarcón

Travelling south from Cuenca – or west from Toledo – Cuenca Province has a couple more places where you might consider breaking your journey if you have your own transport: the castle villages of **Belmonte** (on the N420) and **Alarcón** (just off the NIII to Valencia).

Belmonte and El Toboso

The village of **BELMONTE** is partly encircled by a vast curtain wall, at the corner of which is a magnificent fourteenth-century **castle** (daily 10am–2pm & 4–7pm; 200ptas).

Partially rebuilt in the last century, it is really little more than a shell, although belated restoration is revealing what must once have been stunning Mudéjar *artesonado* ceilings. The village, too, has seen better days, though it has a fine collegiate church, and a pleasant little **hotel**, *La Muralla* (☎967 171045; ②).

Continuing west from Belmonte, Cervantes enthusiasts might consider a detour to the attractive village of **EL TOBOSO**, on a minor road south of the N301. This was the home of Don Quixote's mistress, Dulcinea, whose "house" has of course been identified and turned into a small museum (Tues–Sat 10am–2pm & 4–6.30pm, Sun 10–2pm; 100ptas), with an adjoining *hostal* and restaurant. West again from here, you could cut across country – and past the NIV – to **Consuegra** (see opposite), with its dozen windmills.

Alarcón

ALARCÓN occupies an impressive defensive site sculpted by the burrowings of the Río Júcar. Almost completely encircled and walled, the village is accessible by a spit of land just wide enough to take a road which passes through a succession of **fortified gateways**. Unlike Belmonte, Alarcón has a bit of life about it, at least at weekends, as many of the old escutcheoned houses have been restored as retreats by *madrileños*.

At the top of the village is an exquisite **castle**, eighth-century in origin and captured from the Moors in 1184 after a nine-month siege. This has been converted to house an expensive **parador**, the *Parador Marqués de Villena* (☎969 331350, fax 969 330303; ⑧), one of the country's smallest and most characterful. More affordable accommodation is provided by the *Pensión El Infante*, c/Dr Tortosa 6 (☎969 331360; ④). Either option should be booked ahead in summer or at weekends.

Albacete Province

Travelling between Madrid or Cuenca and Alicante or Murcia, you'll pass through **Albacete Province**, one of Spain's more forgettable corners. Hot, arid plains, for the most part, this is very much the Spain of Castilla-La Mancha, with a dull provincial capital, **Albacete**, to match. Scenically, the only relief is in the hyperactive **Río Júcar**, which, in the north of the province, sinks almost without warning into the plain.

The Río Júcar: Alcalá del Júcar

If you are driving, it is worth a detour off the main roads east to cross the Río Júcar, cutting between **Casas-Ibáñez** (on the N322) and **Ayora** (on the N330) by way of the village of **ALCALÁ DEL JÚCAR**. Almost encircled by the river, this is an amazing sight, with its houses built one on top of the other and burrowed into the white cliff face. Several of these **cuevas** (caves) have been converted into bars and restaurants and they are well worth a stop, with rooms carved up to 170m through the cliff and windows overlooking the river on each side of the loop. They're open daily in summer but otherwise only at weekends. Alcalá also boasts a **castle**, adapted at intervals over the past 1500 years, though today just a shell – with views. If you want to stay, there are two **hostales** on the main road at the bottom of the village.

Albacete

ALBACETE was named *Al-Basit* – the plain – by the Moors, but save for a few old backstreets, it is basically a modern city. The underworked Turismo lists only two places of interest on its map. You could dispense with one of these, the **Catedral**, which is noted only for the presence of Ionic columns astride its nave instead of normal pillars. The **Museo de Albacete** (Tues–Sat 10am–2pm & 4.30–7pm, Sun 9am–2pm; 200ptas), however, has a more than respectable archeological and ethnographical collection, whose prize exhibits are five small Roman dolls, perfectly sculpted and jointed, and an array of local Roman mosaics. For Spaniards, Albacete is synonymous with high-quality knives, a speciality which, as with Toledo, can be traced back to the Moors: if you're after some top cutlery, now's your chance.

Albacete has plenty of **accommodation**, but there's no real reason to stay. Don't be tempted, either, by signs to Albacete's *parador*, a modern creation southeast of the town, right on the flight path of a military airfield.

Chinchilla de Monte Aragón

Thirteen kilometres southeast of Albacete, **CHINCHILLA DE MONTE ARAGÓN** is a breezy hill-top village worth a look if you're passing by, though most of its grand mansions and churches are either decayed or locked up for restoration. The hill-top **fortress**, so impressive from the road below, is a windy ruin not really worth the climb, but the **Convento de Santo Domingo**, in the lower part of the village, has interesting fourteenth-century Mudéjar work. There is also a small but nationally represented **Museo de Cerámica** at c/de la Penuela, open on Saturday afternoons and Sundays.

Ciudad Real and the heartland of La Mancha

There is a huge gap in the middle of the tourist map of Spain between Toledo and the borders of Andalucía, and from Extremadura almost to the east coast. This, the province of **Ciudad Real**, comprises the heartland of **La Mancha**. The tourist authorities try hard to push their *Ruta de Don Quixote* across the plains, highlighting the windmills and other Quixotic sights. The signposted route, which starts at Belmonte and finishes at Consuegra, can be done in a day, but much of it is fanciful, and, unless you're enamoured of the book, it's of only passing interest.

Nonetheless, there are a few places which merit a visit if you've got time to spare, most notably **Consuegra**, for the best windmills, **Almagro**, for its arcaded square and medieval theatre, and **Calatrava**, for the castle ruins of its order of knights.

Consuegra

CONSUEGRA lies just to the west of the NIV *autovía*, roughly midway from Madrid to Andalucía, and has the most picturesque and typical of Manchegan settings, below a ridge of twelve restored (and highly photogenic) windmills. The first of these is occupied by the town's **Turismo**, with uncertain opening hours (indeed, truly Quixotic), but good for information on the *Ruta de Don Quixote*, while others house shops and workshops. They share their plateau with a ruined **castle**, once the headquarters of the order of St John in the twelfth century, which offers splendid views of the plain from its windswept ridge. The town below, in spite of having perhaps the most potholed roads in Spain, is also attractive, with a lively Plaza Mayor and many Mudéjar churches.

Places to stay are limited to the friendly *Hostal-Restaurant San Paul* (☎925 481315; ④) in the centre, and the busy and comfortable *Hotel Las Provincias* (☎925 482000; ④), within walking distance on the main road north of town.

DON QUIXOTE

The romantic adventures of **Don Quixote**, set against the backdrop of La Mancha, with its castles, windmills, cornfields and vineyards, have captivated readers ever since *Don Quixote de La Mancha* was first published in 1604.

Not a novel in the modern sense, **Miguel Cervantes'** book is a sequence of episodes following the adventures of a country gentleman in his fifties, whose mind has been addled by romantic tales of chivalry. In a noble gesture, he changes his name to Don Quixote de la Mancha, and sets out on horseback, in rusty armour, to right the wrongs of the world. At his side throughout is **Sancho Panza**, a shrewd, pot-bellied rustic given to quoting proverbs at every opportunity. During the course of the book, Quixote, an instantly sympathetic hero, charges at windmills and sheep (mistaking them for giants and armies), makes ill-judged attempts to help others, and is mocked by all for his efforts. Broken-hearted but wiser, he returns home, and, on his deathbed, pronounces: "Let everyone learn from my example... look at the world with common sense and learn to see what is really there."

Cervantes' life was almost as colourful as his hero's. The son of a poor doctor, he fought as a soldier in the sea battle of **Lepanto**, where he permanently maimed his left hand and was captured by pirates and put to work as a slave in Algiers. Ransomed and sent back to Spain, he spent the rest of his days writing novels and plays in relative poverty, dying ten years after the publication of *Don Quixote*, "old, a soldier, a gentleman and poor".

Spanish academics have spent as much time dissecting the work of Cervantes as their English counterparts have Shakespeare's. Most see the story as a satire on the popular romances of the day, with the central characters representing two forces in Spain; Quixote the dreaming, impractical nobililty, and Sancho the wise and down-to-earth peasantry. There are also those who read in it an ironic tale of a visionary or martyr frustrated in a materialistic world, while yet others see it as an attack on the church and establishment. Debates aside, this highly entertaining adventure story, rich in characters, and with an eminently lovable hero, is said to have been reprinted so often that, worldwide, it is second only to the Bible in the printing stakes.

Out of the wealth of artistic interpretations inspired by Cervantes's holy fool (including a bizarre and original short story by Jorge Luís Borges), perhaps the most enduring are Jules **Massenet's** folksy opera and **Strauss's** symphonic poem, in which the hero is portrayed by a lofty cello.

Ciudad Real

CIUDAD REAL, capital of the province at the heart of this flat country, makes a good base for excursions and has connections by bus with most villages in the area. It has a few sights of its own, too, including a Mudéjar gateway, the **Puerta de Toledo**, which fronts the only surviving fragment of its medieval walls, at the northern edge of the city on the Toledo road. Farther in, take a look at fourteenth-century **San Pedro**, an airy, Gothic edifice, housing the alabaster tomb of its founder and a good Baroque *retablo*, and the **Museo Provincial** (Tues–Sat 10am–2pm & 5–7pm, Sun 5–7pm; free), a modern building, opposite the cathedral, with two floors of local archeology and a third devoted to artists of the region.

The local **Turismo** (Mon–Fri 9am–2pm; ☎926 212003) is at c/Alarcos 21 in the centre of town, and the **bus station** on c/Inmaculada Concepción. Ciudad Real's new **train station**, with high-speed AVE connections to Madrid, lies out of town on the Daimiel road; bus #5 connects with the central Plaza de Pilar.

Accommodation is not always easy to find, particularly at the lower end of the scale, so it's worth booking ahead. Decent options include *Pensión Esteban*, c/Reyes 15 (☎926 224578; ③), *Pensión Angelo*, c/Galicia 49 (☎926 228592; ③), *Pensión Escudero*, c/Galicia 48 (☎926 252309; ④) and *Hotel Santa Cecilia*, c/Tinte 3 (☎926

228545, fax 926 228618; ⑦). An impressive range of **tapas bars** includes *Casa Lucio*, c/Gato 5 and *Gran Mesón*, Ronda Ciruela 34, which also has a swankier restaurant, *Miami Park*, down the road at no. 48.

Almagro

Twenty kilometres east of Ciudad Real is **ALMAGRO**, an elegant little town, which for a period in the fifteenth and sixteenth centuries was quite a metropolis in southern Castile. Today, its main claim to fame is the **Corral de las Comedias**, a perfectly pre-oorvod ointoonth contury opou-air theatre, unique in Spain. Plays from its sixteenth- and seventeenth-century heyday – the golden age of Spanish theatre – are performed regularly in the tiny auditorium and in July it hosts a fully-fledged theatre festival. By day, the theatre in the Plaza Mayor is open to visitors (summer Tues–Fri 10am–2pm & 5–8pm, Sat 10am–2pm & 5–7pm, Sun 11am–2pm; winter Tues–Fri 10am–2pm & 4–7pm, Sat 10am–2pm & 4–6pm, Sun 11am–2pm; 400ptas). Across the square on Callejon de Villar the **Museo del Teatro** (same hours as theatre), houses photos, posters, model theatres and other paraphernalia, but is probably only of passing interest to anyone other than theatre buffs.

The **Plaza Mayor** itself is magnificent: more of a wide street than a square, it is arcaded along its length, and lined with rows of green-framed windows – a north European influence brought by the Fugger family, Carlos V's bankers, who settled here. Also resident in Almagro for a while were the Knights of Calatrava (see below), though their power was on the wane by the time the **Convento de la Asunción de Calatrava** was built in the early sixteenth century. Further traces of Almagro's former importance are dotted throughout the town in the grandeur of numerous **Renaissance mansions**. Back in the Plaza Mayor, you can have an open-air snack or browse among the shops in the arcades, where **lace-makers** at work with bobbins and needles are the main attraction. On Wednesday mornings there's a lively **market** in c/Ejido de San Juan.

WET LA MANCHA AND TWO PARKS

A respite from the arid monotony of the Castilian landscape, and a treat for bird-watchers, is provided by the oasis of **La Mancha Húmeda** ("Wet La Mancha"). This is an area of lagoons and marshes, both brackish and fresh, along the high-level basin of the **Río Cigüela** and **Río Guadiana**. Although drainage for agriculture has severely reduced the amount of water, so that lakes almost dry up in the summer, there is still a good variety of interesting plant and bird life to be found here. You're best off visiting from April to July when the water birds are breeding, or from September to mid-winter when birds are passing through on migration.

Major parks between Ciudad Real and Albacete include the **Parque Nacional de las Tablas**, 11km north of **Daimiel**, which is renowned for its bird life. There's an **information centre** (daily 8am–9pm; ☎926 693118) alongside the marshes, but the park is accessible only by car or taxi, and Daimiel has little **accommodation** on offer; you can try the upmarket *Hotel Las Tablas* (☎926 852107, fax 926 852189; ⑤).

More traveller-friendly is the **Parque Natural de las Lagunas de Ruidera**, which lies northeast of Valdepeñas (with frequent buses from Albacete). You'll find an **information centre** (daily 10am–2pm & 5.30–9pm; ☎926 528116) on the roadside, and several nature trails inside the park, as well as swimming and boating opportunites. You can also stay overnight; **accommodation** ranges from a campsite, *Los Molinos* (☎926 528089; July to mid-Sept), to *Pensión La Noria* (☎926 528032; ③) and the comfortable *Hotel Albamanjón* (☎926 699048, fax 926 699120; ⑥).

Practicalities

There's a small **Turismo** just south of Plaza Mayor on c/Mayor de Carnicerías 5 (Tues–Sun 11am–2pm & 6–8pm; ☎926 860717). Almagro invites a stay more than anywhere in this region, and there is a fair range of **accommodation**. Cheapest options are the *Fonda Peña*, c/Emilio Piñuela 10 (☎926 860317; ②), near the church of San Bartolomé, and, next to the convent, the *Hospedería Municipal*, Ejido de Calatrava (☎926 882087, fax 926 882122; ④). The *Hotel Don Diego*, on the Ronda de Calatrava (☎926 861287, fax 926 860574; ⑤), due east of the plaza, is a good mid-range hotel, and there is also a very good *parador* (☎926 860100, fax 926 860150; ⑧) in a former Franciscan convent.

A number of **bars**, good for *tapas*, are to be found around the Plaza Mayor, and the *bodega* at the *parador* is worth a stop for a drink, too. The best **restaurant** in town is the *Mesón El Corregidor* at Jerónimo Ceballos 2 (closed Mon & first week in Aug); it's moderately expensive at 3250–4100ptas per head. A cheaper option is *La Cuerda*, in front of the train station at Plaza del General Jorreto 6, which has a good *menú* specializing in fish and *arroz* for 1200ptas (closed Mon evening and first fortnight in Sept).

Moving on, Almagro has one direct **train** a day to Madrid, and five trains and six **buses** daily to Ciudad Real; buses stop near the *Hotel Don Diego* on the Ronda de Calatrava.

Calatrava La Nueva

The area known as the **Campo de Calatrava**, south of Almagro and Ciudad Real, was the domain of the **Knights of Calatrava**, a Cistercian order of soldier-monks at the forefront of the reconquest of Spain from the Moors. So influential were they in these parts that Alfonso X created Ciudad Real as a royal check on their power. Even today, dozens of villages for miles around are suffixed with their name.

In the opening decades of the thirteenth century, the knights pushed their headquarters south, as land was won back, from Calatrava La Vieja, near Daimiel, to a commanding hill top 25km south of Almagro, protecting an important pass – the Puerto de Calatrava – into Andalucía. Here, in 1216, they founded **Calatrava La Nueva**, a settlement that was part monastery and part castle, and whose main glory was a great Cistercian church. The site (Tues–Sat: summer 10am–2pm & 5–8pm; winter 10am–2pm & 4–6pm; 400ptas) is reached by turning west off the main road (C410) and following the signposts uphill. Once there, you will get a good idea of what must have been an enormously rich and well-protected fortress. The church itself is now completely bare but preserves the outline of a striking rose window and has an amazing stone vaulted entrance hall.

On the hill opposite is a further castle ruin, known as **Salvatierra**, which the knights took over from the Moors.

Valdepeñas and beyond

The road from Ciudad Real through Almagro continues to **VALDEPEÑAS**, centre of the most prolific wine region in Spain and handily situated just off the main Madrid–Andalucía motorway. You pass many of the largest **bodegas** on the slip road into town, coming from the north and Madrid; most of them offer free tastings – ask at the **Turismo** on the Plaza Mayor (Tues–Sun 9am–2pm & 4–8pm; ☎926 312552). Wine aside, the only "sight" is a **windmill**, again on the Madrid road, which is supposedly the biggest in Spain; it houses a museum of the works of local artist Gregorio Prieto. Behind it is the public swimming pool.

South from Valdepeñas

Heading south beyond Valdepeñas you enter Andalucía through the narrow mountain **Gorge of Despeñaperros** (literally, "throwing over of the dogs"), once a notorious spot for bandits and still a dramatic natural gateway which signals a change in both climate and vegetation, or as Richard Ford put it (travelling south to north), "exchanges an Eden for a desert".

The first towns of interest across the regional border, and more tempting places to break your journey than anywhere in this part of La Mancha, are **Úbeda** and **Baeza**. Both towns are connected by bus with the train station of **Linares-Baeza**, which is also where you'll change trains if you're heading for Córdoba. The provincial capital of **Jaén**, the first city on the main bus and train routes, is comparatively dull.

The Montes de Toledo and west into Extremadura

The **Montes de Toledo** cut a swathe through the upper reaches of La Mancha, between Toledo, Ciudad Real and Guadalupe. If you're heading into Extremadura, and have time and transport, the deserted little roads across these hills (they rise to just over 1400m) provide an interesting alternative to the main routes. This is an amazingly remote region to find so close to the centre of Spain: its people are so unused to visitors that in the smaller villages they may imagine you're an itinerant vendor. Covered below, too, is the **main route west** from Toledo into Extremadura, which runs just north of the hills.

Toledo to Navalmoral

The C502, west of Toledo, provides a direct approach into **Extremadura**, linking with the NV from Madrid to Trujillo, and with roads north into the valley of **La Vera** (see sections following). It follows the course of the Río Tajo virtually all the way to **Talavera de la Reina**, beyond which an attractive minor road, from **Oropesa**, with its castle *parador*, runs to **El Puente del Arzobispo** and south of the river to the Roman site of **Los Vascos**.

La Puebla de Montalbán – and Montalbán Castle

LA PUEBLA DE MONTALBÁN, the first town west of Toledo, offers one of the best approaches into the Montes de Toledo. In itself, it is an unexceptional little place but it has a claim to fame as the birthplace of **Fernando de Rojas**, a precursor of the Golden Age dramatists, whose play *La Celestina* was first published in 1500 and is still performed in Spain. He is remembered by a plaque in the Plaza Mayor on the *Ayuntamiento*, a building, like those surrounding it, endowed with an attractive facade of pillars and balconies. Across the square, the sixteenth-century **Palacio de los Condes de Montalbán** is an impressive, rambling affair, brooding behind small, barred windows.

There's a **hostal** on the Toledo side of town, the *Legázpiz* (☎925 750032; ①), though little reason to stay unless you happen to coincide with the July fiestas, which include bull-running through the streets.

South of La Puebla de Montalbán, the C403 leads into the foothills of the Montes de Toledo. At kilometre-stone 31 (15km south of La Puebla), a track leads 2km west to the **Castillo de Montalbán**. This is clearly visible from the road – a low, golden-brown edifice with central turrets – though close up you discover that only the walls actually survive. The interior is open for visits on Saturday mornings.

Talavera de la Reina, Oropesa and Navalmoral de la Mata

Continuing west from La Puebla de Montalbán you reach TALAVERA DE LA REINA, an unremarkable town at the junction of major road and rail routes. The town has long been one of the most important centres of ceramic manufacture in Spain, and there are thirty functioning porcelain factories still here. If you decide to stop, take a look round the many shops down the main street displaying the local products: much is the usual mass-produced tourist trash, but there are still a few genuine craftsmen working here. The most attractive part of town is the park on the banks of the Río Tajo, where you'll find a friendly **Turismo**, a *hostal* and a few places to eat.

Far more promising for a night's stop is **OROPESA**, which lies 33km farther west, overlooking the busy NV. The *Parador Virrey de Toledo* (☎925 430000, fax 925 430777; ⑦) is installed in part of the village **castle**, a warm, stone building on a Roman site, rebuilt from Moorish foundations in the fifteenth century by Don García Álvarez de Toledo. Below it, stretches of the old town walls survive, along with a few noble mansions and a pair of Renaissance churches.

West again, **NAVALMORAL DE LA MATA** has nothing to offer other than its road, rail and bus connections to more engrossing places such as the **Monastery of Yuste** across the rich tobacco-growing area to the north, **Plasencia** to the west, and **Trujillo** and **Guadalupe** to the south.

El Puente del Arzobispo and Los Vascos

EL PUENTE DEL ARZOBISPO, 14km south of Oropesa, is like Talavera, famed for the production of pottery and decorated tiles. It stands astride the Río Tajo and, approaching from the south, you drive in across the ancient **bridge** over the river which gives the place its name. According to legend this was built after the villagers appealed to a fourteenth-century archbishop to build them a bridge across the river. At first he refused, and when pressed pulled a ring from his finger and flung it into the Tajo, saying that he would build the bridge when the ring came back to him. Three days later he cut open his dinner of fish from the river, only to find the ring inside.

Today the ceramics industry dominates, with small factories and shops selling their products everywhere. The wares are not terribly exciting but the tiles do brighten up the Plaza Mayor, with its tile-covered benches, and the exuberantly ornate archbishop's house. The other local attraction is the ruined **Roman city of Los Vascos**, in beautiful country some 10km southeast of town, near the village of Navalmoralejo. There's little to see beyond a few walls, but it's an enjoyable excursion.

Into the hills

The most accessible route into the Montes de Toledo is the C410 south of La Puebla de Montalbán and its castle, which runs through the backwater village of **Las Ventas Con Peña Aguilera**. Rock-studded hills, including a curious outcrop shaped like three fat fingers, overlook the village – the name Peña Aguilera means "Crag of Eagles" – and to the south you reach the main pass over the Montes de Toledo, the **Puerto del Milagro**, with great views of the hills dipping down on either side to meet the plain.

Southwest of Las Ventas, a tiny road leads to **San Pablo de los Montes**, a delightful village of fine stone houses nestling against the mountains. Beyond here, you can walk over the hills to the spa of **Baños del Robledillo**, a spectacular five -to six- hour trek (get directions locally).

Keeping to the C403, past the Puerto del Milagro, you can drive through lovely scenery towards Ciudad Real, or turn right at the El Molinillo junction to follow a road through the hills via Retuerta del Bullaque to **Navas de Estena**. Here the road curves round to the north again, passing a large crag with caves 5km beyond Navas, allowing you to loop round to Navahermosa and on to the C401 to Guadalupe.

The western villages

If isolated villages and obscure roads appeal, you could strike south from the C401, or west from the C403 (past the Puerto del Milagro), into the most remote part of the Montes de Toledo. The latter approach would take you some 54km, without a village, before you reached **Valdeazores**, itself scarcely inhabited with a population of just 35. You could bypass this, if you wanted, following a road past the Cijara reservoir, and on to the N502 at Puerto Rey, passing nothing save the odd *finca* (farmhouse).

Coming from the C401, the first place you reach is **Roblado del Buey**, where there's a single bar. From here, a pine forest extends south to Los Alares. To the west, and the only place in these parts that gets any visitors, is Piedraescrita, a well-kept village with an incredibly spruce bar, and a miraculous image of the Virgin that pulls in the odd Spanish pilgrim. West again is the area's main administrative centre, **Robledo del Mazo**, with a doctor, chemist and bar.

EXTREMADURA

Extremadura is slowly getting on the tourist trail – and deservedly so. The grand old *conquistador* towns of **Trujillo** and **Cáceres** are excellent staging posts en route south from Madrid or from Salamanca to Andalucía; **Mérida** has numerous Roman remains and an exemplary museum of local finds; and there is superb bird life in the **Parque Natural de Monfragüe**. Almost inaccessible by public transport, but well worth visiting, is the great **Monastery of Guadalupe**, whose revered icon of the Virgin has attracted pilgrims for the past five hundred years.

This section of the chapter is arranged north to south, starting with the lush hills and valley of **La Vera**, the first real patch of green you'll come to if you've driven along the NV west from Madrid.

La Vera and the Monasterio de Yuste

La Vera lies just south of the Sierra de Gredos (see p.145), a range of hills tucked above the **Río Tiétar** valley. It is characterized by the streams or *gargantas* which descend from the mountains and in spring and summer attract increasing bands of weekenders from Madrid. At the heart of the region is the **Monasterio de Yuste**, the retreat chosen by Carlos V to cast off the cares of empire.

Jarandilla and around

La Vera really comes into its element between Candeleda and Jarandilla de la Vera, along the C501, as the *gargantas* flow down from the hills. They are flanked in summer by some superb seasonal **campsites**: *Minchones* (☎927 565403; Easter & June to mid-Sept) is just outside **Villanueva de la Vera**, a village which gained British media notoriety in the 1980s with its *Pero Palo* fiesta, in which donkeys are horribly mistreated. It seems strange to imagine any cruelty, given the rural idyll hereabouts and the incredibly house-proud appearance of the villages, especially **Losar**, which has an almost surreal display of topiary.

The main village in these parts is **JARANDILLA DE LA VERA**, a good target if you want a roof over your head, with a choice of three **hostales**, the *Marbella* (☎927 560218; ④), *Jaranda* (☎927 560206; ⑤) and *Posada de Pizarro* (☎927 560727; ⑤), plus a fifteenth-century **castle-parador**, the *Parador Carlos V* (☎927 560117, fax 927 560088; ⑦), in the castle where the emperor stayed during the construction of Yuste.

If you've got a tent to pitch, head for the attractive *Camping Jaranda* (☎927 560454; April–Dec). In the village there is a scattering of bars and a Roman bridge. Buses run through here, en route between Madrid and Plasencia; the stop is outside *Bar Charly* on the main road.

There is good walking around Jarandilla. A track into the hills leads to the village of **El Guijo de Santa Barbara** (4.5km) and then ends, leaving the ascent of the rocky valley beyond to walkers. An hour's trek away is a pool known as *El Trabuquete* and a high meadow with shepherds' huts known as *Pimesaíllo*. On the other side of the valley – a serious trek needing a night's camping and good area maps – is the *Garganta de Infierno* (Stream of Hell) and natural swimming pools known as *Los Pilones*.

The Monasterio de Yuste

There is nothing especially dramatic about the **Monasterio de Yuste** (daily: summer 9am–12.30pm & 3–6.30pm; winter 9am–12.30pm & 3–6pm; 100ptas, Thurs morning free), the retreat created by Carlos V after renouncing his empire: just a simple beauty and the rather gloomy accoutrements of the emperor's last years. The monastery had existed here for over a century before Carlos's retirement and he had earmarked the site for some years, planning his modest additions – which included a pleasure garden – while still ruling his empire from Flanders. He retired here with a retinue that included an Italian clockmaker, Juanuelo Turriano, whose inventions were his last passion.

The imperial apartments are draped throughout in black, and exhibits include the little sedan chair in which he was brought here, and another designed to support the old man's gouty legs. If you believe the guide, the bed and even the sheets are the very ones in which Carlos died, though since the place was sacked during the Peninsular War and deserted for years after the suppression of the monasteries, this seems unlikely. A door by the emperor's bed opens out over the church and altar so that even in his final illness he never missed a service.

Outside, there's a snack bar and picnic spots, and you'll find a track signposted through the woods to Garganta La Olla (see below).

Cuacos

The monastery is 2km into the wooded hills from **CUACOS**, an attractive village with a couple of squares, including the tiny Plaza de Don Juan de Austria, named after the house (its upper floor reconstructed) where Carlos's illegitimate son Don Juan lived when visiting his father. The surrounding houses, their overhanging upper floors supported on gnarled wooden pillars, are sixteenth-century originals, and from the beams underneath the overhang tobacco is hung out to dry after the harvest. There are several **bars**, a good family-run **hotel**, *La Vera* (☎927 172178; ⑤), and a shady **campsite**, *Carlos I* (☎927 172092; April to mid-Sept).

Jaraíz de la Vera and Garganta La Olla

West towards Plasencia, one last place you might be tempted to stop is **JARAÍZ DE LA VERA**. This has pleasant walking and a couple of reasonable **places to stay**: *Hostal Dacosta* (☎927 460219; ③), and the comfortable *Hotel Jefi* (☎927 461363; ④), which has a good restaurant.

Just outside Jaraíz, a left turning leads to **GARGANTA LA OLLA**, a beautiful, ramshackle mountain village set among cherry orchards. There are several things to look out for: the **Casa de Putas** (a brothel for the soldiers of Carlos V's army, now a butcher's but still painted the traditional blue) and the **Casa de la Piedra** (House of Stone), a house whose balcony is secured by a three-pronged wooden support resting on a rock. The latter is hard to find; begin by taking the left-hand street up from the square and then ask.

From Garganta, there is a short-cut track to the Monasterio de Yuste (see above).

El Valle de Jerte

Immediately north of La Vera, the main Plasencia–Avila road follows the valley of the **Río Jerte** to the pass of Puerto de Tornavacas, the boundary with Ávila Province. The villages here are more developed than those of La Vera but the valley itself is renowned for its cherry trees, which for a ten-day period in spring cover the slopes with white blossom. If you're anywhere in the area at this time, it's a beautiful spectacle.

If you have transport, you can follow a minor road across the sierra to the north of the valley from **Cabezuela del Valle** to **Hervás**, where there's a fascinating former Jewish quarter. This is the highest road in Extremadura, rising to 1430m.

On the **southern side** of the valley, the main point of interest is the **Puerto del Piornal** pass, just behind the village of the same name. The best approach is via the villages of **Casas del Castañar** and **Cabrero**. Once at the pass you can continue over to Garganta La Olla in La Vera.

Plasencia

Set in the shadow of the Sierra de Gredos, and surrounded on three sides by the Río Jerte (from the Greek *Xerte*, meaning "joyful"), **PLASENCIA** looks more impressive from afar than it actually is. Once you get up into the old city the walls are hard to find – for the most part they're propping up the back of houses – and the cathedral is barely half-built. However, Plasencia has some lively bars and a fine, arcaded **Plaza Mayor**, flanked by cafés and every Tuesday morning the scene of a farmers' **market**, held here since the twelfth century.

Arrival and information

Plasencia's **Turismo** is on c/del Rey 8, off the Plaza Mayor (summer Tues–Fri 9am–2pm & 5–7.30pm, Sat & Sun 9am–2pm; winter Tues–Fri 9am–2pm & 4–6.30pm, Sat & Sun 9am–2pm; closed on alternate weekends; ☎927 422159). If you arrive by **bus**, you'll be about fifteen minutes' walk from the centre: the **train** station is much farther out – take a taxi. If you're driving, be warned that navigation in and around town is notoriously difficult. There are up to five trains a day to and from Madrid and many more buses.

Accommodation

Good **places to stay** include two reasonably priced places near the Plaza Mayor: the *Hostal La Muralla*, c/Berrozana 6 (☎927 413874; ③), and *Hotel Rincón Extremeño*, c/Vidrieras 6 (☎927 411150, fax 927 420627; ④), which has twelve en-suite rooms with TV and air conditioning. For more comfort, there's *Hotel Los Alamos* on the Cáceres road facing the tobacco factory (☎927 411550, fax 927 411558; ④), and *Hotel Alfonso VIII*, c/Alfonso VIII 32 (☎927 410250, fax 927 418042; ⑦), on the main road near the post office; both of these have good, but pricey **restaurants**. There's a **campsite** with a swimming pool 5km out on the Ávila road, *La Chopera* (☎927 416660; March–Sept).

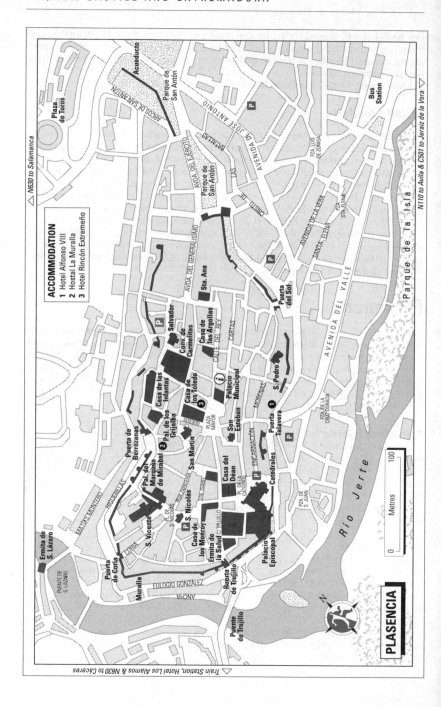

△ N630 to Salamanca

▷ N110 to Avila & C501 to Jeraiz de la Vera

▽ Train Station, Hotel Los Alamos & N630 to Cáceres

ACCOMMODATION
1 Hotel Alfonso VIII
2 Hostal La Muralla
3 Hotel Rincón Extremeño

PLASENCIA

Parque de la Isla

Río Jerte

0   Metres   100

Acueducto
Plaza de Toros
ARCOS DE SAN ANTÓN
Parque de San Antón
Bus Station
PZA. LUIS DE ZÚÑIGA
AVENIDA DE JOSÉ ANTONIO
LAS
AVDA. DEL EJÉRCITO
Parque de San Antón
BATALLAS
AVENIDA DE LA VERA
PZA. STA. ELENA
SANTA. ELENA
CRISTO DE LAS
AVDA. DEL GENERALISIMO
Sta. Ana
Puerta del Sol
AVENIDA DEL VALLE
Salvador
Conv. de Carmelitas
Casa de las Argollas
CALLE DEL REY
CARTAS
Casa de las Infantas
Casa de los Toledo
Palacio Municipal
S. Pedro
MORENAS
PZA. DE LA CRUZ DORADA
Pal. de los Grijalba
SOSTRO
PLAZA MAYOR
San Esteban
Puerta Talavera
Puerta de Berrozanas
Pal. del Marqués de Mirabal
San Martín
P. ENCARNACIÓN
Catedrales
HIGUERILLAS
MATÍAS MONTERO
Casa del Déan
PLAZA DE STA. ISABEL
PLAZA DE S. NICOLÁS
P. DE LA CATEDRAL
PZA. DE S. JUAN
Ermita de S. Lázaro
PUENTE DE S. LÁZARO
S. Vicente
CORIA
C/DE S/NICOLÁS
S. Nicolás
Casa de los Montero
Ermita de la Salud
C/ TRUJILLO
Palacio Episcopal
Puerta de Coria
Muralla
EULOGIO GONZÁLEZ
ANCHA
Puerta de Trujillo
Puente de Trujillo

N

The Town

Plasencia's **Catedral** (summer Mon–Sat 9am–1pm & 5–7pm, Sun 9am–1pm; winter Mon–Sat 9am–12.30pm & 4–6pm, Sun 9am–12.30pm) is in fact two churches – old and new – built back-to-back. Work began on the second at the beginning of the sixteenth century and continued under two architects for almost forty years, but when neither managed to finish it, the open end was simply bricked up. The fact that the completed building would have been a particularly lofty Gothic construction only adds to the foreshortened feel of the interior. It does have some redeeming features, most notably the Renaissance choir stalls intricately carved by Rodrigo Alemán and described with some justice by the National Tourist Board as "the most Rabelaisian in Christendom". The older, Romanesque part of the cathedral now houses the obligatory **museum,** and the 150ptas entrance fee includes access to the similarly aged **cloisters.** Free tours of the cathedral (in Spanish) can be booked at the nearby tourist office.

Opposite the cathedral is the **Casa del Deán** (Dean's House), with an interesting balcony like the prow of a ship. Continuing away from the cathedral along c/Blanca you come out at the **Plaza de San Nicolás**, where, according to local tradition, the church was built to prevent two local families from shooting arrows at each other from adjacent houses. On c/Trujillo, near the hospital, the **Museo Etnográfico Textil Provincial** (Wed–Sat 11am–2pm & 5–8pm, Sun 11am–2pm; free) is worth a look for its colourful costumes and local crafts, excellently displayed in a fourteenth-century hospital. Many of the exhibits are still much in evidence in the more remote villages in the north of Plasencia province.

Eating and drinking

Bars are thick on the ground, with over fifty in the old town alone. This is the land of the *pincho*, a little sample of food provided free with your beer or wine – among which is the local *pitarra* wine. A high tally of promising bars is to be found in c/Maldonado (also known as c/Patalón; go down c/Talavera from the main square and it's the second turning on the left); *La Herradura* is good for *pinchos* and *pitarra*, and the *Asador el Refugio* for fish, squid and octopus *pinchos*. In the next street down, *Bar Media Luna* is famous for its ham – it's expensive, but if you're lucky you'll get a taste as a *pincho*, and the place is very atmospheric.

Finding good **restaurants** is less easy, but try the area between the cathedral and the Plaza Mayor. Easily the best budget option is that attached to the *Hostal La Muralla*. Another good, and rather fancier, place is *El Acueducto*, c/Valentina Mirón 17, near the monument from which it takes its name.

Las Hurdes and the Sierra de Gata

Las Hurdes, the abrupt rocky lands north of Plasencia, have always been set apart and are a rich source of mysterious tales. According to legend, the region was unknown to the outside world until the time of Columbus, when two lovers fleeing from the Court of the Duke of Alba chanced upon it. The people who welcomed them were supposedly unaware of the existence of other people or other lands. Shields and other remnants belonging to the Goth Rodrigo and his court of seven centuries earlier were discovered by the couple, giving rise to the saying that the Hurdanos are descendants of kings.

Fifty years ago, the inhabitants of the remoter areas were still so unused to outsiders that they hid in their houses if anyone appeared. **Luis Buñuel** filmed an unflatteringly grotesque documentary, *Las Hurdes: Tierra Sin Pan* ("Land Without Bread"), here in 1932, in which it was hard to discern any royal descent in his subjects. Modernity has crept up on the villages these days, though they can still feel very remote. To explore the region, you really need transport of some kind and certainly a detailed local **map** – regular Spanish road maps tend to be pretty sketchy.

Las Hurdes villages

You could approach Las Hurdes from Plasencia, Salamanca or Ciudad Rodrigo (the region borders the Sierra Peña de Francia – see p.338). From Plasencia or Salamanca, the approach is along the C512. Turn off along this road at Vegas de Coria and you will reach **NUÑOMORAL**, a good base for excursions, with an excellent and inexpensive **hostal**, *El Hurdano* (☎927 433012; ①); this does big dinners, and there is a bank alongside – not a common sight in these parts. For hire of mules, donkeys and horses at reasonable prices, ask for Amable in *Bar Emiliano* at the top of the town opposite the medical centre. Nuñomoral is also the village best connected to the outside world, with early-morning buses to both Ciudad Rodrigo and Plasencia.

In this rocky area, tiny terraces have been constructed on the river bed as the only way of getting the stubborn land to produce anything. To the north of Nuñomoral, the tiny village of **La Huetre** is worth a visit; take a left fork just before the village of Casares de las Hurdes. The typical slate-roofed houses are in better than usual condition and have an impressive setting, surrounded by steep rocky hills. The villages of **Avellanar, Horcajo, Fragosa** and **Erias** all have traditional houses. Walkers might also head for the remote and disarmingly primitive settlement of **El Gasco**, over to the west of Fragosa, where there is a huge waterfall beneath the Miacera Gorge.

The Sierra de Gata

The **Sierra de Gata** creates a westerly border to Las Hurdes, in a series of wooded hills and odd outcrops of higher ground. It is almost equally isolated – in some of the villages the old people still speak *maniego*, a mix of Castilian Spanish and Portuguese – and its wooded valleys are in parts stunningly beautiful. Unfortunately, much has been damaged in recent summers by forest fires, which, like similar fires in Las Hurdes, are said to have been deliberately started to claim insurance money.

For a trip into the heart of the region, follow the C513 to the west of **Villanueva de la Sierra**. A couple of kilometres past the Río Arrago, a very minor road veers north towards **Robledillo de Gata**, a village of old houses, packed tightly together. A shorter, easier detour, south of the C513, around 5km on, is provided by the hill-top village of **Santibáñez el Alto**, whose oldest houses are built entirely of stone, without windows. At the top of town, look out for a tiny bullring, castle remains and the old cemetery – there's a wonderful view over the Borbollón reservoir from here. Another 3km along the C513, a turn-off to the north takes you on a winding road up to **GATA**, a pretty village with rooms at the *Pensión Avenida* (☎927 441079; ②).

On to the west, keeping to the C513, is **HOYOS**, the largest village of the region, with some impressive mansions. There's only one hostal in the village, *Fonda Navarro*, c/La Paz 23 (☎927 514018; ②), but there's pleasant **camping** 3km below the village by a natural swimming pool, created by the damming of the river. Lastly, further along the C513, another turning leads north to **SAN MARTÍN DE TREVEJO**, one of the nicest of the many lonely villages around; if you're here at mealtime there's good, cheap village fare in great abundance at the *Bar Avenida del 82* (also referred to as the *Casa de Julia*).

South to Cáceres: Coria and Palancar

Heading south from the Sierra de Gata towards Cáceres along the C526, **CORIA** makes an interesting stop. It looks nothing much from the main road, but a visit reveals a cool and quiet old town with lots of stately whitewashed houses, enclosed within third- and fourth-century **Roman walls**.

For the most part the walls are built into and around the houses, but a good stretch is visible between the deserted tower of the fifteenth-century **Castillo**, built by the Dukes of Alba, and the **Catedral** (daily 10am–1pm & 3–6.30pm), which has beautifully carved west and north portals in the Plateresque style of Salamanca. Inside, the choir stalls and *retablo* are worth seeing. The building overlooks a striking medieval bridge across the fields, the river having changed course three hundred years ago.

There's plenty of **accommodation** in Coria. The *Pensión Casa Piro*, Plaza del Rollo 6 (☎927 500027; ②), is cheap and well-placed, facing a gate in the walls; *Hotel Los Kekes*, Avda. Sierra de Gata 49 (☎927 500901, fax 927 500900; ④), has more comforts and a decent restaurant.

Convento del Palancar

A detour off the C526, south of Coria, will take you to the **Convento del Palancar**, a monastery founded by San Pedro de Alcántara in the sixteenth century and said to be the smallest in the world at only seventy square metres. It's hard to imagine how a community of ten monks could have lived in these cubbyholes, though San Pedro himself set the example, sleeping upright in his cubicle. A small monastic community today occupies a more modern monastery alongside; ring the bell (daily except Wed 9.30am–1pm & 4–7.30pm) and a monk will come and show you around.

To reach Palancar, turn left off the C526 just after Torrejoncillo and follow the road to **Pedroso de Acim**; a left turn just before the village leads to the monastery.

The Parque Natural de Monfragüe

South of Plasencia a pair of dams, built in the 1960s, have turned the **Río Tajo** into a sequence of vast reservoirs. It's an impressive sight, driving across one of the half dozen bridges, and it's a tremendous area for wildlife. Almost at random here, you can look up to see storks, vultures and even eagles, circling the skies.

The best area for concerted wildlife viewing – and some very enjoyable walks – is the **PARQUE NATURAL DE MONFRAGÜE**, Extremadura's only protected area, which extends to either side of the Plasencia–Trujillo road, with its park headquarters at **Villareal de San Carlos**. The landscape is a wonderful diversity of rivers, woods, scrubland and pasture, and attracts an incredible range of flora and fauna. It has been spared the blights of much of the region hereabouts, which, after the completion of the dams, saw the widescale destruction of wildlife habitats and the indiscriminate planting of inflammable eucalyptus by the rapidly expanding paper industry, despite the fire risk involved.

There are over two hundred **species of animals** in the park, including the ultra-rare Spanish lynx (which you are most unlikely to see). Most important is the **bird population**, especially the black stork – this is the only breeding population in western Europe – and birds of prey such as the black vulture (not averse to eating tortoises), the griffon vulture (partial to carrion intestine), the Egyptian vulture (not above eating human excrement), the rare Spanish imperial eagle (identifiable by its very obvious white shoulder patches), the golden eagle and the eagle owl (the largest owl in Europe).

Ornithologists should visit Monfragüe in May and June, botanists in March and April, and everybody should avoid July to September, when the heat is stifling.

Park practicalities

The easiest **approach to the park** is along the C524 from Plasencia to Trujillo, which runs past the park headquarters at Villareal de San Carlos. Transport of your own is an advantage unless you are prepared to do some walking. There is just one **bus** along the road, which runs daily between Plasencia and Torrejón El Rubio, 16km south of Villareal de San Carlos, and on Mondays and Fridays covers the whole distance to Trujillo. It's not a promising hitching route, though at weekends you should get a lift with Spanish bird-watchers.

VILLAREAL DE SAN CARLOS has a couple of bars and a restaurant, plus an **information centre** (daily 9am–2.30pm & 4–6pm; ☎927 199134), where you can pick up a colourful leaflet, with a map detailing three colour-coded walks from the village. There is also a seasonal shop, selling wildlife T-shirts and the like, and a useful guide to the park (in Spanish) by José Luís Rodríguez.

There's no **accommodation** in Villareal, and camping is prohibited in the park, but there are two friendly pensions in **TORREJÓN EL RUBIO**: the *Monfragüe* (☎927 455026; ②) and the *Avenida* (☎927 455050; ③); more expensive, but good value for money, is the *Hotel Carvajal*, Plaza de Pizarro 54 (☎927 455254; ④). The nearest **campsite** is *Camping Monfragüe* (☎927 459220), a well-equipped, year-round site with a swimming pool and restaurant, 12km north of Villareal, on the Plasencia road. It is near the turning to the train station of Palazuelo-Empalme (a stop for slow trains on the Madrid–Cáceres line) and it also has **bikes for rent** (for 1500ptas a day) to get to Monfragüe.

Into the park

Walking in Monfragüe, it is best to stick to the colour-coded **paths** leading from Villareal de San Carlos. Each of them is well paint-blobbed and leads to rewarding bird-watching locations. Elsewhere, it is not easy to tell where you are permitted to wander, and all too easy to find yourself out of the park area in a private hunting reserve.

The **Green Route**, to the Cerro Gimio, is especially good, looping through woods and across streams, in a landscape unimaginable from Villareal, to a dramatic cliff-top viewing station. The longer **Purple Route** heads south of Villareal, over a bridge across the Río Tajo, and past a fountain known as the *Fuente del Francés* after a young Frenchman who died there trying to save an eagle. Two kilometres farther is a great crag known as the *Peñafalcón*, which houses a large colony of griffon vultures, and the Castillo de Monfragüe, a castle ruin high up on a rock, with a chapel next to it; there is an observation post nearby. All these places are accessible from the C524 and if you're coming in on the bus, you could ask to get off here.

On the south side of the park, towards Trujillo, you pass through the **dehesas**, strange Africa-like plains which are among the oldest woodlands in Europe. The economy of the *dehesas* is based on grazing, and the casualties among these domestic animals provide the vultures of Monfragüe with their daily bread.

Trujillo

TRUJILLO is the most attractive town in Extremadura: a classic *conquistador* stage-set of escutcheoned mansions, stork-topped towers and castle walls. Much of it looks virtually untouched since the sixteenth century, and is redolent above all of the exploits of the conquerors of the Americas; Francisco Pizarro, the conqueror of Peru, was born here, as were many of the tiny band who with such extraordinary cruelty aided him in defeating the Incas.

Arrival and information

Trujillo could be visited easily enough as a day trip from Cáceres, but if you can book, it is worth staying the night. There is no train station, but the town is well served by buses, with up to eight a day to and from Madrid. Coming in by **bus**, you'll arrive in the

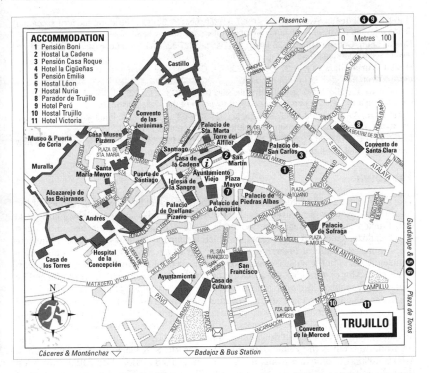

ACCOMMODATION
1 Pensión Boni
2 Hostal La Cadena
3 Pensión Casa Roque
4 Hotel la Cigüeñas
5 Pensión Emilia
6 Hostal Léon
7 Hostal Nuria
8 Parador de Trujillo
9 Hotel Perú
10 Hostal Trujillo
11 Hotel Victoria

lower town, just five minutes' walk from the Plaza Mayor/Plaza de la Constitución, where there is a **Turismo** (Tues–Sun: summer 9am–2pm & 5–7pm; winter 9am–2pm & 4–6pm; ☎927 322677). If you're driving, follow the signs to the Plaza Mayor, where, with luck, you'll be able to park.

Accommodation

Places to stay are in high demand – so book ahead if you can. The Turismo can provide accommodation lists. The nicest rooms are around the Plaza Mayor, or, if money is no object, at the *parador*.

Budget options

Pensión Boni, c/Domingo de Ramos 7 (☎927 321604). Cheap and meticulously run, just off the northeast corner of the Plaza Mayor. ③.

Pensión Casa Roque, c/Domingo de Ramos 30 (☎927 322313). Excellent and well-located *pensión*. The owner runs the *Margarita* gift shop on the Plaza Mayor. ③.

Pensión Emilia, c/General Mola 28 (☎927 320083). Clean but slightly shabby *pensión*. ③.

Hostal Trujillo, c/Francisco Pizarro 4 (☎927 322274). A pleasant *pensión* between the Plaza Mayor and the bus station. ③.

Moderate and expensive options

Hostal La Cadena, Plaza Mayor 8 (☎927 321463). Attractive hotel, with rooms overlooking all the action and a decent restaurant. ④.

Hotel Las Cigüeñas, Avda. Madrid (☎927 321250, fax 927 321300). Pleasant, modern accommodation down on the main road, but a bit inconvenient for the major sites. ⑥.

Hostal Léon, General Mola 23–25 (☎927 321792, fax 927 322137). Decent *pensión* with the advantage of secure parking. ⑤.

Hostal Nuria, Plaza Mayor 27 (☎927 320907). Comfortable *hostal* with good views over the Plaza Mayor. ④.

Parador de Trujillo, Plaza Santa Beatriz de Silva (☎927 321350, fax 927 321366). Luxurious accommodation in a sixteenth-century former *convento* north of the Plaza Mayor. ⑦.

Hotel Perú, Avda. Madrid (☎927 320745, fax 927 320749). A large, drab hotel above a bar, whose one virtue is that it may have rooms long after everywhere else is full. ④.

Hotel Victoria, Plaza de Campillo 22 (☎927 321819, fax 927 323084). Recently opened, friendly hotel, with a pool, good restaurant and comfortable en-suite rooms with TV. ⑥.

The Town

Trujillo is a very small place, still little larger than its extent in *conquistador* times. At the centre of a dense web of streets is the **Plaza Mayor** (also known as the Plaza de la Constitución), a grand square overlooked by a trio of palaces and churches, and ringed by a half-dozen cafés and restaurants, in which life for most visitors revolves. In the centre is a bronze statue of Pizarro – oddly, the gift of an American sculptor, one Carlos Rumsey, in 1929. In the square's southwest corner is the **Palacio de la Conquista** (currently closed for restoration), the grandest of Trujillo's mansions with its roof adorned by statues representing the twelve months. Just one of many built by the Pizarro clan, it was originally inhabited by Pizarro's half-brother and son-in-law Hernando, who returned from the conquests to live here with his half-Inca bride (Pizarro's daughter). Diagonally opposite, and with a skyline of storks, is the bulky church of **San Martín**. Its tombs include, among others, that of the family of Francisco de Orellana, the first explorer of the Amazon. Adjacent is the **Palacio de los Duques de San Carlos** (daily 9am–1pm & 4–6pm; 100ptas), home to a group of nuns who moved out of their dilapidated convent up the hill and restored this palace in return for the lodgings. The chimneys on the roof boast aggressively of cultures conquered by Catholicism in the New World – they are shaped like the pyramids of Aztecs, Incas and others subjected to Spanish rule.

From the plaza, c/de Ballesteros leads up to the walled upper town, past the domed **Torre del Alfiler** with its coats of arms and storks' nests, and through the gateway known as the Arco de Santiago. Here, to the left, is **Santa María Mayor** (daily: summer 10.30am–2pm & 5–7.30pm; winter 10.30am–2pm & 4.30–6.30pm; 50ptas), the most interesting of the town's many churches. The building is basically Gothic but contains a beautiful raised Renaissance *coro* noted for the technical mastery of its almost flat vaults. There is a fine Hispano-Flemish reredos by Fernando Gallego, and tombs including those of the Pizarros – Francisco was baptized here – and Diego García de Paredes, a man known as the "Sansón Extremeño" (Extremaduran Samson). Among other exploits, this giant of a man, armed only with his gargantuan sword, is said to have defended a bridge against an entire French army and to have picked up the font, now underneath the *coro*, to carry holy water to his mother.

Farther up the hill, in the Pizarros' former residence, the **Casa Museo Pizarro** (daily: summer 11am–2pm & 4–8pm; winter 11am–2pm & 4–6.30pm; 150ptas), is a small, dull and overpriced affair, with little beyond period furniture and a few panels on the conquest of Peru. More detailed exhibits on the conquest are to be found in the nearby **Museo de la Coria** (Sat & Sun 11.30am–2pm; free), which is housed in an old Franciscan convent.

The **castle** is now virtually in open countryside; for the last hundred metres of the climb you see nothing but the occasional broken-down remnant of a wall clambered over by sheep and dogs. The **fortress** itself, Moorish in origin but much reinforced by later defenders, has recently been restored, and its main attraction is the panoramic view of the town and its environs from the battlements. Looking out over the barren heath which rings Trujillo, the extent to which the old quarter has fallen into disrepair is abundantly evident, as is the castle's superb defensive position.

Of the many other town mansions, or *solares*, the most interesting is the **Palacio de Orellana-Pizarro**, just west of the main square (daily 9.30am–2pm & 4–7pm; free). Go in through the superb Renaissance arched doorway to admire the courtyard: an elegant patio decorated with the alternating coats of arms of the Pizarros – two bears with a pine tree – and the Orellanas.

Eating and drinking

There are plenty of **bar-restaurants** right in the Plaza Mayor. Perhaps the best of them is *Mesón La Troya*, which offers huge *menús* for between 1900 and 2500ptas –you'll probably find a giant salad and omelette on your plate before they've even asked what you want to order, and thereafter helpings are automatically replenished, should you somehow have room for them. The *Pizarro*, also on the plaza, is a rather more fancy restaurant (around 3000ptas a head), or there are excellent *raciones* and *tapas* at the *Bar Las Cigüeñas* (in the hotel of the same name). If you're driving, you could try out *La Majada*, 4km south of town on the road to Mérida for good fish, local sausages and partridge.

Guadalupe

The small town of **GUADALUPE** is dominated in every way by the great **Monasterio de Nuestra Señora de Guadalupe**, which for five centuries has brought fame and pilgrims to the area. It was established in 1340, on the spot where an ancient image of the Virgin, said to have been carved by Saint Luke, was discovered by a shepherd fifty or so years earlier. The delay was simply a question of waiting for the Reconquest to arrive in this remote sierra, with its lush countryside of forests and streams.

Arrival, information and accommodation

Guadalupe's generally helpful **Turismo** is in the Plaza Mayor (Tues–Sun 9am–2pm & 5–7pm; ☎927 154128). **Banks** and a **post office** are to be found close by this central square, near the steps of the monastery church. **Buses** leave from either side of Avenida de Barcelona uphill from the *Ayuntamiento*, 200m from the Plaza Mayor: Mirat operates services to Trujillo and Cáceres, Doalde runs buses to Madrid.

Accommodation

There are plenty of **places to stay** in Guadalupe and the only times you're likely to have difficulty finding a room are during Easter Week or around September 8, the Virgin's festival day. The **campsite**, *Las Villuercas* (☎927 367139; open all year), is 2km out of town towards Trujillo, close to the main road.

Hostal Alfonso XI, c/Alfonso Onceno 21 (☎ & fax 927 154184). Comfortable, nicely furnished *hostal*. ④.

Hostal Isabel, Plaza Santa María 13 (☎927 367126). Modern *hostal* offering rooms with bath, and a bar downstairs. ③.

Hostal Lujuan, c/Gregorio López 19 (☎927 367170). Decent, mid-priced rooms, reasonably central and with a reliable restaurant (the *menú* costs 1100ptas). ③.

Parador de Guadalupe, c/Marqués de la Romana 12 (☎927 367075, fax 927 367076). Beautiful *parador*, housed in a fifteenth-century hospital, with a swimming pool and immaculate patio gardens. ⑦.

Hospedaría del Real Monasterio, Plaza Juan Carlos 1 (☎927 367000, fax 927 367177). Housed in a wing of the monastery and popular with Spanish pilgrims; it's expensive, but is better value than the *parador*. ⑥.

Hostal Taruta, c/Alfonso Onceno 16 (☎927 154144). This *hostal* can arrange rooms in private houses if its own are fully booked, and offers discounts for full-board, with meals in a nearby restaurant. ③.

The Town

In the fifteenth and sixteenth centuries, Guadalupe was among the most important pilgrimage centres in Spain: Columbus named the Caribbean island in honour of the Virgin here, and a local version was adopted as the patron saint of Mexico. Much of the monastic wealth, in fact, came from returning *conquistadores*, whose successive endowments led to a fascinating mix of styles. The **monastery** was abandoned in the nineteenth-century dissolution, but early this century was reoccupied by Franciscans, who continue to maintain it.

The town itself is a fitting complement to the monastery and countryside, a net of narrow cobbled streets and overhanging houses around an arcaded plaza, the whole overshadowed by the monastery's bluff ramparts. There's a timeless feel, only slightly diminished by modern development on the outskirts, and a brisk trade in plastic copies of religious treasures.

The church and monastery

The **monastery church** (daily 9am–8.30pm; free) opens on to the Plaza Mayor (aka Plaza de Santa María). Its gloomy Gothic interior is, like the rest of the monastery, packed with treasures from generations of wealthy patrons. Note especially the incredibly ornate *rejas* (grilles).

The entrance to the **monastery** proper (daily 9.30am–1pm & 3.30–6.30pm; 300ptas) is to the left of the church. The (compulsory) guided tour begins with a Mudéjar **cloister** – two brick storeys of horseshoe arches with a strange pavilion or tabernacle in the middle – and moves on to the **museum**, with an apparently endless collection of rich vestments, early illuminated manuscripts and religious paraphernalia, along with some fine art works including a triptych by Isenbrandt and a small Goya. The **Sacristía**, beyond, is the finest room in the monastery. Unaltered since it was built in the seventeenth century, it contains eight paintings by Zurbarán, which, uniquely, can be seen in their original context – the frames match the window frames and the pictures themselves are a planned part of the decoration of the room.

Climbing higher into the heart of the monastery, you pass through various rooms filled with jewels and relics before the final ascent to the Holy of Holies. From a tiny room high above the main altar you can look down over the church while a panel is spun away to reveal the climax of the tour – the **image of the Virgin** herself, bejewelled, richly dressed, and blackened by centuries of candle smoke (replicas of this image are sold in the town's many souvenir shops).

On the way out, drop in at the **Hospedaría del Real Monasterio**, around to the right. The bar in its Gothic cloister, with lovely gardens outside, is one of the world's more unusual places to enjoy a *Cuba libre*.

Eating and drinking

You can **eat** at most *hostales* and *pensiones*. The *Hostal Lujuan* has a particularly good-value *menú* for 1100ptas, while the *Hospedaria del Real Monasterio* has a courtyard setting. Perhaps the best restaurant in town is the *Mesón del Cordero* at c/Alfonso Onceno 27, a reasonably priced place with home cooking and grand views from the dining room. More modern and with a younger clientele is the *Restaurante Castillo*, c/Huerta del Hospital 6; specialities include the Extremaduran trout and pork chop.

The Sierra de Guadalupe: routes to Trujillo

A truly superb view of the town set in its sierra can also be enjoyed from the road (C713) north to Navalmoral. Five kilometres beyond, the **Ermita del Humilladero** marks the spot where pilgrims to the shrine traditionally caught their first glimpse of the monastery.

The surrounding **Sierra de Guadalupe** is a wild and beautiful region, with steep, rocky crags abutting the valley sides. If you have your own transport, a good route is to strike northwest of the C401 at **Cañamero**, up to the village of **Cabañas del Castillo**, a handful of houses, most of them empty as only twelve inhabitants remain, nestling against a massive crag and ruined castle. Beyond here, you can reach the main **Navalmoral–Trujillo road** close to the **Puerto de Miravete**, a fabulous viewpoint, with vistas of Trujillo in the far distance. Another great drivers' route, again leaving the C401 at Cañamero, is to follow the narrow road **through Berzocana** to Trujillo.

Cáceres

CÁCERES is in many ways remarkably like Trujillo. At its centre is an almost perfectly preserved walled town, the *Ciudad Monumental*, packed with *solares* built on the proceeds of American exploration, while even more than in Trujillo every available tower and spire is crowned by a clutch of storks' nests. As a provincial capital, however, Cáceres is a much larger and livelier place, especially in term-time, when the students of the University of Extremadura are in residence. With its Roman, Moorish and *conquistador* sights, and a lively bar and restaurant scene, it is an absorbing and highly enjoyable city. It also provides a dramatic backdrop for an annual **WOMAD** festival, held over the first weekend in May and attracting up to 20,000 spectators.

The walled **old town** stands at the heart of Cáceres, with a picturesque **Plaza Mayor** just outside its walls. Almost everything of interest is contained within – or a short walk from – this area, and you would do well to base yourself as close to it as possible.

Arrival and information

If you arrive by **train or bus**, you'll find yourself around 3km out from the old town, at the far end of the Avenida de Alemania. It's not an enjoyable walk, so take bus #1, which runs down the *avenida* to Plaza de San Juan, a square adjoining the Plaza Mayor; an irregular shuttle bus from the train station (free if you show a rail ticket) also runs into town, to the Plaza de América, a major traffic junction west of the old town. If you're driving, be warned that increasing pedestrianization is making access to some streets impossible by car; your best bet is to try and park in the Plaza Mayor.

Cáceres has a helpful **Turismo** (Mon–Fri 9am–2pm & 4–7.30pm, winter closes 6.30pm; Sat & Sun 9am–2pm; ☎927 246347) in the Plaza Mayor; the main **post office** is at c/Miguel Primo Rivera 2, near the Plaza de América; and numerous **banks** dot the central grid.

Accommodation

There is usually plenty of **accommodation** to go round (much of it overpriced), but it's a good idea to book ahead if you're visiting during Easter.

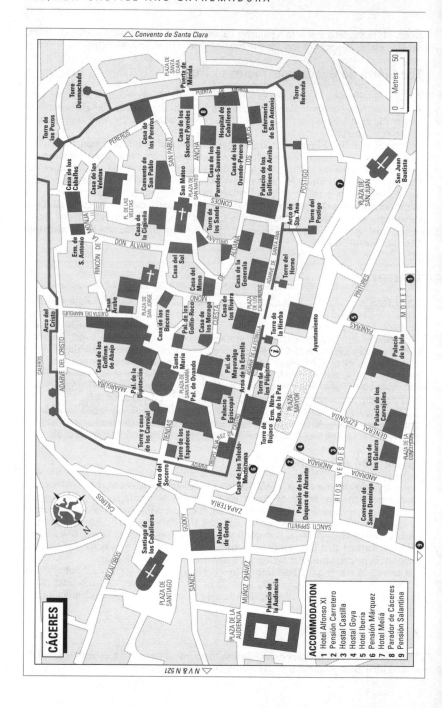

△ Convento de Santa Clara

△ N V & N 521

CÁCERES

0 Metres 50

ACCOMMODATION
1 Hotel Alfonso XI
2 Pensión Carretero
3 Hostal Castilla
4 Hostal Goya
5 Hotel Iberia
6 Pensión Márquez
7 Hotel Meliá
8 Parador de Cáceres
9 Pensión Salantina

Budget options

Pensión Carretero, Plaza Mayor 23 (☎927 247882). Best value in town – large rooms, spotless bathrooms and a TV lounge. ②.

Pensión Castilla, c/Ríos Verdes 3 (☎927 244404). Just off the Plaza Mayor, with small, clean rooms, and separate bath. ③.

Pensión Márquez, c/Gabriel y Galán 2 (☎927 244960). Decent, low-budget option just off the Plaza Mayor; it's popular, so check in early. ②.

Pensión Salmantina, c/General Margallo 36-A (☎927 244218). This centrally located *pensión* is the cheapest place in town, with shared bathroom and small, extremely basic rooms. ①.

Moderate and expensive options

Hotel Alfonso IX, c/Moret 20 (☎927 246400, fax 927 247811). Nicely located on a pedestrianized street off c/Pintores, this slightly aged hotel offers en-suite rooms with air conditioning and satellite TV. ⑤.

Hostal Goya, Plaza Mayor 11 (☎927 249950, fax 927 213758). Upmarket (and good-value) *hostal* on the Plaza Mayor, with en-suite rooms. ⑤.

Hotel Iberia, c/Pintores 2 (☎927 247634, fax 927 248200). Tastefully restored building in a corner of the Plaza Mayor. ④.

Hotel Meliá, Plaza de San Juan 11 (☎927 215800, fax 927 214070). Part of the growing Meliá chain, this hotel is in a sixteenth-century palace, just outside the walls of the old town, and is in many ways a nicer place than the *parador*. ⑧.

Parador de Cáceres, c/Ancha 6 (☎927 211759, fax 927 211729). The *parador* occupies a *conquistador* mansion in the *Ciudad Monumental* – the only hotel within the walls. ⑧.

The Town

The **walls** of the *Ciudad Monumental* are basically Moorish in construction, though parts date back to the Romans – notably the **Arco del Cristo** – and they have been added to, refortified and built against pretty much throughout the centuries. The most intact section, with several original adobe Moorish towers, runs in a clockwise direction, facing the walls from the Plaza Mayor.

Around the old town

Entering the old town – the **Parte Vieja**, as it's also known – from the Plaza Mayor, you pass through the low **Arco de la Estrella**, an entrance built by Manuel Churriguera in the eighteenth century. To your left, at the corner of the walls, is one of the most imposing *conquistador solares*, the **Casa de Toledo-Montezuma** with its domed tower. It was to this house that a follower of Cortés brought back one of the New World's more exotic prizes, a daughter of the Aztec emperor, as his bride. The building has recently been restored – it was in imminent danger of collapse – to house the provincial historical archives, and it also stages occasional exhibitions.

Walking straight ahead through the Arco de la Estrella, brings you into the **Plaza de Santa María**, flanked by another major *solar*, the Casa de los Golfines de Abajo, the Palacio Episcopal, and the Gothic church of Santa María – Cáceres's finest. Inside, you can illuminate a fine sixteenth-century carved wood *retablo*, while in the surrounding gloom are the tombs of many of the town's great families.

A couple of blocks away, at the town's highest point, is the Plaza de San Mateo, flanked by the church of **San Mateo**, another Gothic structure with fine chapels, and the **Casa de la Cigüeña** (House of the Stork), whose narrow tower was the only one allowed to preserve its original battlements when the rest were shorn by royal decree. It is now a military installation and, although the tower features on half the postcards in Cáceres, soldiers discourage the taking of further snapshots.

In the Plaza de las Veletas is the **Casa de las Veletas**, which houses the archeology and ethnology sections of the **Museo Provincial** (Tues–Sat 9.30am–2.30pm, Sun

10.15am–2.30pm; 300ptas, free to EU citizens). The collections here take second place to the building itself. Typical of the local style, its beautifully proportioned rooms are arrayed around a small patio and preserve the *aljibe* (cistern) of the original Moorish Alcázar with its horseshoe arches. It also has an extraordinary balustrade, created from Talavera ceramic jugs.

From here, a footbridge leads to the museum's contemporary art section in the **Casa de los Caballos** (House of Horses). Two floors of modern art and sculpture include works by Miró, Picasso and Eduardo Arroyo, alongside up-and-coming contemporary artists.

Something could be said about almost every other building within the old walls, but notice above all the **family crests** – in particular on the **Casa del Sol** – and the magnificent facade of the **Casa de los Golfines de Abajo**. It was in this latter *conquistador* mansion that Franco had himself proclaimed *Generalísimo* and head of state in October 1936. Near the Casa del Sol is another *solar*, the **Casa del Mono** (House of the Monkey), which is now a public library; the facade is adorned with grotesque gargoyles and a stone monkey is chained to the staircase in the courtyard.

Outside the walls

Outside the walls, wander up to the sixteenth-century church of **Santiago de los Caballeros**, which fronts the plaza of the same name, opposite a more or less contemporary mansion, **Palacio de Godoy**, with its corner balcony. The church, open only for Masses, has a fine *retablo* by Alonso Berruguete.

You might take time, too, for a visit to the **Casa Árabe** (daily 10.30am–2pm & 6–8pm; 100ptas), off Plaza San Jorge at Cuesta del Marqués 4. The owner of this Moorish house has had the bright idea of decorating it more or less as it would have been when occupied by its original owner. The Alhambra it's not, and the red lights in the "harem" are a dubious touch, but it at least provides a context for all the horseshoe arches and curving brick ceilings.

If you want to enjoy a good **view** of the old town, go through the Arco del Cristo down to the main road and turn right on to c/de Fuente Concejo, following the signs for about five minutes or so, and you have the whole town set out below you.

Eating and drinking

There is a good range of **bars, restaurants and bodegas** in and around the Plaza Mayor, while the old town offers a bit more style at not too inflated a price.

Restaurants

El Asador, c/Moret 34. Reasonably priced restaurant, off c/Pintores, serving local dishes and fronted by a popular *tapas* bar.

Atrio, Avda. de España 30. Good, upmarket restaurant, southwest of Plaza Mayor, with extensive menu. Closed Sun evening. Allow 4500–5500ptas per head.

El Corral de las Cigüeñas, Cuesta de Aldana 6. A beautiful spot to enjoy a meal in the old town, with tables in a large, palm-shaded courtyard; reasonably priced *platos combinados*.

El Figón de Eustaquio, Plaza de San Juan 12. This features an extensive list of regional dishes, cooked with care and flair. It's not cheap; allow 3000–5000ptas a head.

El Palacio del Vino, c/Ancha 4. Pleasant, traditional *mesón* near the *parador* in the old town; allow around 2500ptas a head.

El Pato, Plaza Mayor 24. Popular restaurant fronting the square – slightly more expensive than its neighbours but probably worth the extra.

El Puchero, Plaza Mayor 10. The cheapest restaurant on the plaza, with an ever-popular *terraza*.

Rialto, Plaza de la Concepción 29. No frills but good-value restaurant popular with young locals.

Bars

Bar del Jamón, Plaza de San Juan 10. Small place to enjoy *pitarra* and a *pincho*.

El Extremeño, Plaza del Duque 10 – off the Plaza Mayor. A student favourite with Guinness on tap and beer sold by the metre.

La Machacona, c/Andrada 8 – down an alley under the arcades off the Plaza Mayor. Good place to hear Latin sounds and occasional live music.

El Torre de Babel, c/Pizarro 8. Laid-back café with occasional live music, plus clothes and jewellery stalls downstairs.

Northwest of Cáceres: Arroyo and Alcántara

Northwest of Cáceres is the vast **Embalse de Alcántara**, one of a series of reservoirs harnessing the power of the Río Tajo in the last few kilometres before it enters Portugal. The scheme swallowed up large tracts of land and you can see the old road and railway to Palencia disappearing into the depths of the reservoir (their replacements cross the many inlets on double-decker bridges), along with the tower of a castle.

The C523 loops away to the south of the reservoir, through **Arroyo de la Luz** and **Brozas**, each with fine churches, before reaching **Alcántara**, with its superb Roman bridge across the Tajo. The Portuguese border – and the road to Costelo Branco and Coimbra – is just a dozen kilometres beyond.

Arroyo de la Luz and Brozas

ARROYO DE LA LUZ (Stream of Light), despite its romantic name, is one of the least memorable Extremaduran towns. However, it does have one sight of note: the gaunt, late Gothic church of **La Asunción**, which houses a huge *retablo* of twenty panels by Luís Morales. This Extremaduran artist (1509–86) is known to the Spanish as "El Divino", though his heart-on-sleeve style has never found much favour with art historians. His work is certainly a lot more impressive seen here, in situ, than in a museum. To view it, ask for the keys from the local police at the side door of the *Ayuntamiento*, which faces the south side of the church, and bring a couple of 100-ptas coins for the meter.

Arroyo has a single **hostal**, inevitably called the *Divino Morales* (☎927 270257; ④), at the edge of town where the buses stop, and a couple of basic restaurants. A more pleasant place to eat, drink, or stay, however, is the old *Hostal La Posada* (☎927 395019; ④) at **BROZAS**, 35km on towards Alcántara. Brozas itself is an old *conquistador* town, centred on a seventeenth-century castle. Its Gothic church of Santa María La Mayor has a spectacular Baroque *retablo*. More impressive still are the fantastic views over the plain and the low hills to the south.

Alcántara

The name **ALCÁNTARA** comes from the Arabic for "bridge" – in this case a beautiful six-arched **Puente Romano** spanning a gorge of the Río Tajo. Completed in 105 AD, and held together without mortar, it was reputed to be the loftiest bridge ever built in the Roman empire, although it's far from certain which bits, if any, remain genuinely Roman.

The bridge is quite a distance from the town itself, which is built high above the river; if you're on foot, don't follow the signs via the road – instead, head to the far side of the town and down a steep cobbled path.

Further Roman remains include a **triumphal arch** dedicated to Trajan and a tiny **classical temple**. The dominating landmark, however, is the recently restored **Convento San Benito**, erstwhile headquarters of the Knights of Alcántara, one of the

JAMÓN SERRANO: A GASTRONOMIC NOTE

Extremadura, to many Spaniards, means **ham**. Together with the Sierra Morena in Andalucía, the Extremaduran sierra is the only place in the country which supports the pure-bred Iberian pig, source of the best *jamón serrano*. For its ham to be as highly flavoured as possible, the pig, a subspecies of the European wild boar exclusive to the Iberian peninsula, is allowed to roam wild and eat acorns for several months of the year. The undisputed kings of hams in this area, praised at length by Richard Ford in his *Handbook for Travellers*, are those that come from **Montánchez**, in the south of the region. The village is midway between **Cáceres** and **Mérida**, so if you're in the area try some in a bar, washed down with local red wine – but be warned that the authentic product is extremely expensive, a few thinly cut slices often costing as much as an entire meal. The local wine known as *pitarra* is an ideal accompaniment..

great orders of the reconquest. For all its enormous bulk, the convent and its church are only a fragment; the nave of the church was never built. Outside, the main feature is the double-arcaded Renaissance gallery at the back; it serves as the backdrop for a season of classical plays which moves here from Mérida in August. Entry to the convent (Mon–Fri 10am–1.45pm & 5–7pm, Sat 10.45am–1.45pm; free) is through the adjacent *Fundación de San Benito*, who have been making attempts to restore the cloister and the Plateresque east end with its elaborate wall tombs.

Alcántara also contains the scanty remains of a **castle**, numerous **mansions** and street after street of humbler whitewashed houses. The place is marvellous for scenic walks, whether in the town, along the banks of the Tajo, or – best of all – in the hills on the opposite bank.

Practicalities

The **Turismo**, Avenida de Merida 21 (May–Sept Tues–Fri 10am–2pm & 4–6pm, Sat & Sun 10.30am–12.30pm; Oct–April Tues–Fri 10am–2pm & 4.30–6.30pm, Sat & Sun 10.30am–12.30pm; ☎927 390863), is very helpful and can provide a town map.

The town has one official **hostal**, the *Kantara Al Saif*, Avenida de Mérida (☎927 390246, fax 927 390833; ③), with an adjoining restaurant and café. Alternatively try the *Hostal Puente Romano* in Avenida de Merida (☎927 390246; ③), which has clean and comfortable en-suite rooms. **Buses**, which run twice a day to and from Cáceres, stop at a little square ringed by cafés at the entrance to the historic part of the town. Here you can **eat** cheaply at *Restaurante El Gorrón*, and at *Restaurante Antonio*, near the Turismo building.

Mérida

The former capital of the Roman province of Lusitania, **MÉRIDA** (the name is a corruption of *Augusta Emerita*) contains more **Roman remains** than any other city in Spain. Even for the most casually interested, the extent and variety of the remains here are compelling, with everything from engineering works to domestic villas, by way of cemeteries and places of worship, entertainment and culture. With a little imagination, and a trip to the modern museum, the Roman city is not difficult to evoke – which is just as well, for the modern city, in which the sites are scattered, is no great shakes.

Each July and August, the Roman theatre in Mérida hosts a **theatre festival**, including performances of classical Greek plays and Shakespeare's Roman tragedies.

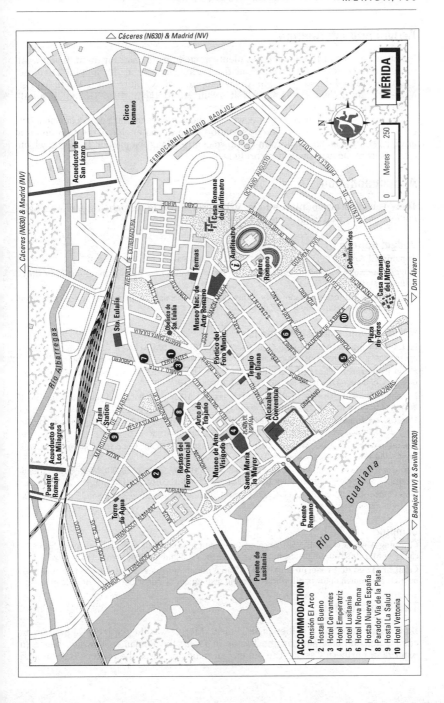

△ Cáceres (N630) & Madrid (NV)

MÉRIDA

N

0   Metres   250

Cáceres (N630) & Madrid (NV)

▽ Don Álvaro

▽ Badajoz (NV) & Sevilla (N630)

FERROCARRIL MADRID BADAJOZ

Circo
Romano

Acueducto de
San Lázaro

Río Albarregas

Acueducto de
Los Milagros

Puente
Romano

Torre
de Agua

Train
Station

Sta. Eulalia

Obelisco de
Sta. Eulalia

Museo Nac. de
Arte Romano

Termas

Casa Romana
del Anfiteatro

Anfiteatro

Teatro
Romano

Casa Romana
del Mitreo

Columbarios

Plaza
de Toros

Pórtico del
Foro Munic.

Templo
de Diana

Alcazaba y
Conventual

Arco de
Trajano

Restos del
Foro Provincial

Museo de Arte
Visigodo

Santa María
la Mayor

Puente
Romano

Río Guadiana

Puente de
Lusitania

Río

ACCOMMODATION
1 Pensión El Arco
2 Hostal Bueno
3 Hotel Cervantes
4 Hotel Emperatriz
5 Hotel Lusitania
6 Hotel Nova Roma
7 Hostal Nueva España
8 Parador Vía de la Plata
9 Hostal La Salud
10 Hotel Vettonia

Arrival and information

Mérida sees a lot of visitors and has plenty of facilities to cater for them. If you want maps, guidebooks or information on the region, look in at the helpful **Turismo** (summer Mon–Fri 9am–1.45pm & 5–6.45pm, Sat & Sun 9am–1.45pm; winter Mon–Fri 9am–1.45pm & 4–5.45pm, Sat & Sun 9am–1.45pm; ☎924 315353), just outside the gates to the theatre and amphitheatre site.

The **train station** is pretty central, with the theatre site and Plaza de España no more than ten minutes' walk away. The **bus station** is on the other side of the river and is a grittier twenty minutes' walk from the town centre, along Avenida de Libertad, which extends from the new single-arch bridge.

Accommodation

There is no shortage of **places to stay**, but prices tend to be high; if you're on a tight budget, be prepared to do some searching.

Budget options

Pensión El Arco, c/Cervantes 16 (☎924 318321). Cheap and friendly *pensión*. ②.

Hostal Bueno, c/Calvario 9 (☎924 311013). Basic but clean *hostal* – all the rooms have (tiny) bathrooms. ③.

Hostal La Salud, c/Vespasiano 41 (☎ & fax 924 312259). Small, simple rooms in this good-value *hostal* near the Acueducto de los Milagros. ③.

Moderate and expensive options

Hotel Cervantes, c/Camilo José Cela 8 (☎924 314961, fax 924 311342). Comfortable hotel, off c/Cervantes, with secure parking. Ask to see the rooms, as some are on the small side. ⑤.

Hotel Emperatriz, Plaza de España 19 (☎924 313111, fax 924 313305). Attractive old hotel in a former palace, bang on the main square, and with a patio garden. ⑥.

Hotel Lusitania, c/Oviedo 12 (☎924 316112, fax 924 316109). Reliable but unremarkable hotel, best kept in reserve if everywhere else is full. ⑤.

Hotel Nova Roma, c/Suavez Somontes 42 (☎924 311261, fax 924 300160). Large, modern hotel in central location. Book ahead if you're coming during the theatre festival. ⑥.

Hostal Nueva España, Avda. de Extremadura 6 (☎924 313356). Good-value *hostal* with large rooms, out towards the train station. ④.

Parador Vía de la Plata, Plaza Constitución 3 (☎924 313800, fax 924 319208). Well-run and friendly *parador* in an eighteenth-century Baroque convent, near the Arco de Trajano. ⑦.

Hotel Vettonia, c/Calderón de la Barca 26 (☎924 311462). Comfortable, small hotel with easy parking right outside. ④.

Camping

Camping Mérida (☎924 303453). Located 4km out of town on the Trujillo road (N430), this is the closer of Mérida's two campsites, but is very near the road and has little shade. Open all year.

Camping Lago de Proserpina (☎924 313236). A much more pleasant site, by the reservoir (see below), 5km north of town, offering swimming, fishing and windsurfing. Open April to mid-Sept.

The Roman sites

Built on the site of a Celto-Iberian settlement, Mérida was the tenth city of the Roman empire and the final stop on the *Vía de la Plata*, the Roman road which began in Astorga in northern Castile. The old city stretched as far as the modern bullring and

Roman circus, covering only marginally less than the triangular area occupied by the modern town. Visiting the sites, a single 750ptas **ticket** covers the ancient theatre, amphitheatre, Roman villas and the Alcazaba.

The bridge, Alcazaba and around the centre

The obvious point to begin your tour is the magnificent **Puente Romano**, the bridge across the islet-strewn Río Guadiana. It is sixty arches long (the seven in the middle are fifteenth-century replacements) and was still in use until the early 1990s, when the new **Puente de Lusitania** – itself a structure to admire – was constructed.

Defence of the old bridge was provided by a vast **Alcazaba** (Tues–Sat 10am–2pm & 4–6pm, Sun 10am–2pm; combined ticket 750ptas), built by the Moors to replace a Roman construction. The interior is a rather barren archeological site, although in the middle there's an *aljibe* to which you can descend by either of a pair of staircases.

North of the Alcazaba, past the sixteenth-century Plaza de España, the heart of the modern town, is the so-called **Templo de Diana**, adapted into a Renaissance mansion, and farther along are remains of the **Foro**, the heart of the Roman city. To the west of the plaza, a convent houses the **Museo de Arte Visigodo** (Tues–Sun: summer 10am–2pm & 5–7pm; winter 10am–2pm & 4–6pm; 400ptas), with an unexciting collection of about a hundred lapidary items. Just behind here is the great **Arco Trajano**, once wrongly believed to be a triumphal arch; it was, in fact, a monumental gate to the forum.

The theatre and amphitheatre

A ten-minute walk northeast of the Plaza de España will take you to Mérida's main archeological site (daily: summer 9am–1.45pm & 5–7.15pm; winter 9am–1.45pm & 4–6.15pm; combined ticket 750ptas), containing the theatre and amphitheatre. Immediately adjacent are a Roman Villa and the museum of Roman art.

The elaborate and beautiful **Teatro Romano** is one of the best preserved anywhere in the Roman empire. Constructed around 15 BC, it was a present to the city from Agrippa, as indicated by the large inscription above the passageway to the left of the stage. The stage itself, a two-tier colonnaded affair, is in a particularly good state of repair, while many of the seats have been entirely rebuilt to offer more comfort to the audiences of the annual July and August season of classical plays.

Adjoining the theatre is the **Anfiteatro**, a slightly later and very much plainer construction. As many as 15,000 people – almost half the current population of Mérida – could be seated to watch gladiatorial combats and fights with wild animals.

The **Casa Romana del Anfiteatro** (daily: summer 9am–1.45pm & 5–7.15pm; winter 9am–1.45pm & 4–6.15pm; combined ticket 750ptas) lies immediately below the museum, and offers an approach to it from the site. It has wonderful mosaics, including a vigorous depiction of grape-treading.

The Museo Nacional de Arte Romano

The **Museo Nacional de Arte Romano** (May–Sept Tues–Sun 10am–2pm & 5–7pm, Oct–April Tues–Sun 10am–2pm & 4–6pm; 400ptas), constructed in 1986 above the Roman walls, is a wonderfully light, accessible building, using a free interpretation of classical forms to present the mosaics and sculpture as if emerging from the ruins. Rafael Moneo, its architect, and currently quite a star in Spain, achieved perfectly his aim here, to allow visitors "to see the entire collection almost in a glance".

The exhibits, displayed on three levels of the basilica-like hall, live up to their showcase. They include statues from the theatre, the Roman villa of **Mithraeus** (see below) and the vanished forum, and a number of mosaics – the largest being hung on the walls so that they can be examined at each level. There are frescoes, too, including a complete room, reconstructed. Individually, the finest exhibits are probably the three statues, displayed together, depicting Augustus, the first Roman emperor; his son Tiberius, the second emperor; and Drusus, Augustus's heir apparent until (it is alleged) he was murdered by Livia, Tiberius's mother.

Farther out: the hippodrome, aqueducts and Mitreo villa

The remaining monuments are farther out from the centre, on the other side of the railway tracks. From the museum, it's a ten-minute walk out along the Avenida de Extremadura to the **Circo Romano**, essentially an outline, where horses and chariots once raced. Across the road from here, a stretch of the **Acueducto de San Lázaro** leads off towards the Río Albarregas.

The more impressive aqueduct, however, is the **Acueducto de los Milagros**, of which a satisfying portion survives in the midst of vegetable gardens, west of the train station. Its tall arches of granite, with brick courses, brought water to the city in its earliest days from the reservoir at Proserpina, 5km away (see below). The best view of the aqueduct is from a low and inconspicuous **Puente Romano** across the Río Albarregas; it was over this span that the *Vía de la Plata* entered the city.

Two further sights are the church of **Santa Eulalia**, by the train station, which has a porch made from fragments of a former Temple of Mars, and a second Roman villa, the **Mitreo**, in the shadow of the Plaza de Toros, south of the museum and theatres. The villa has a magnificent but damaged mosaic depicting river gods. A short walk away is a Roman burial ground with two family sepulchres.

Proserpina and Cornalvo reservoirs

You can swim in the **Embalse de Proserpina**, a Roman-constructed reservoir 5km north of town, and a popular summer escape, with a line of holiday homes. Alternatively, if you have transport, head to the **Embalse de Cornalvo**, 18km east of Mérida (turn left after the village of Trujillanos). There's a Roman dyke here, and a small national park has recently been created in the area.

Eating and drinking

The whole area between the train station and the Plaza de España is full of **bars and cheap restaurants** – fliers for many of which will be stuffed into your hands outside the theatre site entrance. Alternatively, search out one of the following:

Bar-Restaurante Briz, c/Félix Valverde Lillo 5, just off Plaza de España. Reliable restaurant (with lively *tapas* bar attached) offering local specialities and a 1350ptas *menú*. Closed Sun evening.

Casa Benito, c/San Francisco 3. Bullfighters' ephemera line the walls of this bar, which serves the local speciality *tapas* and *pitarra* wine – you can eat here for 1300ptas. Closed Sun.

Mesón Restaurante Casa Nano, c/Casterlar 3. Nice restaurant with a *menú* at around 3000ptas.

Restaurante Nicolás, c/ Félix Valverde Lillo 13. Good range of Extremaduran dishes and *menú* at 3500ptas. Closed Sun evenings and mid-Sept.

Restaurante Rufino, Plaza de Santa Clara 2 (☎924 312001). Traditional dishes in pleasant surroundings at this centrally located restaurant. Allow 3500ptas a head.

Badajoz

The valley of the Río Guadiana, followed by road and rail, waters rich farmland between Mérida and **BADAJOZ**. The main reason for visiting this provincial capital, traditional gateway to Portugal and the scene of innumerable sieges, is still to get across the border – it's not somewhere you'd want to stay long. Crude modern development has largely overrun what must once have been an attractive old centre, and few of the monuments have

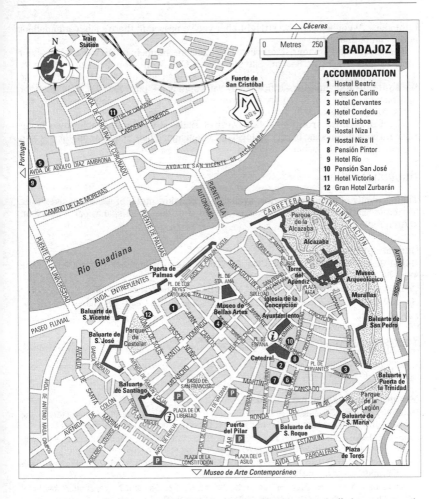

△ *Cáceres*

BADAJOZ

| | Metres | | 250 |

ACCOMMODATION

1 Hostal Beatriz
2 Pensión Carillo
3 Hotel Cervantes
4 Hotel Condedu
5 Hotel Lisboa
6 Hostal Niza I
7 Hostal Niza II
8 Pensión Pintor
9 Hotel Río
10 Pensión San José
11 Hotel Victoria
12 Gran Hotel Zurbarán

▽ *Museo de Arte Contemporáneo*

survived. The troubled history of Badajoz, springing from its strategically important position on the Río Guadiana, is in many ways more interesting than its present day. Founded by the Moors in 1009, the city was taken by the Christian armies of Alfonso IX in 1230, used as a base by Felipe II against the Portuguese in 1580, stormed by British forces under the Duke of Wellington in 1812, and taken by Franco's Nationalist troops in 1936.

Arrival and information

If you're arriving by **bus**, you'll have a fifteen-minute-plus walk to the centre, as the station is awkwardly located in wasteland beyond the ring road at the southern edge of the city. Your best bet is to hop on city bus #3 or #4. The **train station** is still farther from the action, on the far side of the river, up the road which crosses the Puente de Palmas. Any bus crossing the bridge will take you there, or it's a cheap taxi ride. If you're looking for **parking**, follow the signs to the Turismo from the Puerta de Palmas and turn right along Avenida de Huelva straight after you've passed it; there's a big attended lot at the end of this street.

The town has two tourist offices. The efficient municipal **Turismo** (May–Sept Mon–Fri 10am–2pm & 6–8pm, Sat 9am–1pm; Oct–April Mon–Fri 9am–1.30pm & 4–6pm, Sat 9am–1pm; ☎924 224981), is in c/de San Juan, just off Plaza de España, while the **Junta de Extremadura** office (daily 9am–2pm & 5–7pm; ☎924 222763), good for information on the whole region, is down the hill on Plaza de la Libertad – follow the signs from any approach to the town.

The **Portuguese frontier** is 4km west of Badajoz (the first sizable town being Elvas). You can cross the border by local or long-distance bus, and by train; there's also an overnight train to Lisbon, via Elvas.

Accommodation

There's plenty of **accommodation** available in Badajoz, much of it inexpensive, if not terribly desirable. The best location is around the Plaza de España, particularly on c/Arco Agüero.

Budget options

Hostal Beatriz, c/Abril 20 (☎924 233556). Small but adequate rooms in this budget *hostal*; some with bath, some with washbasins only. ③.

Pensión Carillo, c/Arco Agüero 39 (☎924 223881). Good-value *pensión*, near the cathedral. ③.

Hostal Niza I, c/Arco Agüero 34 (924 223881). Cheap but decent *hostal*, with shared facilities. ②.

Pensión Pintor, c/Arco Agüero 26 (924 224228). Cheap but charming *pensión* on the first floor of this building, offering good value for money. ②.

Pensión San José, c/Arco Agüera 39 (☎924 220568). Beautiful old house with big rooms, but shared facilities. ②.

Hotel Victoria, c/Luís de Camões 3 (☎924 271662). Good-value hotel near the train station, but a fair distance from the centre. Double rooms have bath and TV. ③.

Moderate and expensive options

Hotel Cervantes, c/Trinidad 2 (☎924 223710, fax 924 222935). On the Plaza Cervantes, by the cathedral, this hotel has impressive common areas but rather ordinary rooms. ④.

Hotel Condedu, c/Muñoz Torrero 27 (☎924 224641, fax 924 220003). Comfortable and well-located hotel (also known as *Hotel Conde Duque*), handy for the museum and cathedral. ⑤.

Gran Hotel Zurbarán, Paseo Castelar (☎924 223741, fax 924 220142). Priciest hotel in town, with swimming pool and renowned restaurant. ⑧.

Hotel Lisboa, Avda. Díaz Ambrona 13 (☎924 223741, fax 924 220142). Large, comfortable hotel with en-suite rooms and a very reasonably priced restaurant. ⑤.

Hostal Niza II, c/Arco Agücro 45 (☎924 223173). Comfortable, en-suite rooms in this small *hostal* (check in early as it fills up quickly). ④.

Hotel Río, Avda. Adolfo Díaz Ambrona 13 (☎924 272600, fax 924 273874). At the far end of Puente de la Universidad, with swimming pool, parking and a good restaurant (closed weekends & Aug). ⑦.

The Town

At the heart of old Badajoz is the **Plaza de España** and the squat thirteenth-century **Catedral** (Tues–Sat 11am–1pm; free), a fortress-like building, prettified a little during the Renaissance by the addition of a portal and embellishment of the tower.

Northeast of the square, c/de San Juan leads to **Plaza Alta**, once an elegant arcaded concourse, now seedy, and what remains of the town's fortress, the **Alcazaba**. This is largely in ruins but preserves Moorish entrance gates and fragments of a Renaissance palace inside. Part of it houses a **Museo Arqueológico** (Tues–Sun 10am–5pm; free), with local Roman and Visigothic finds. Defending the townward side is the octagonal Moorish **Torre del Aprendiz**, or *Torre Espantaperros* ("dog-scarer" – the dogs in question being Christians).

The Río Guadiana is the city's only other distinguished feature, and in particular the graceful **Puente de Palmas**, or Puente Viejo, spanning its course. The bridge was designed by Herrera (architect of the Escorial) as a fitting first impression of Spain, and leads into the city through the **Puerta de Palmas**, once a gate in the walls, now standing alone as a sort of triumphal arch.

From the plaza behind this arch, c/Santa Lucía leads to the **Museo de Bellas Artes** (Mon–Sat 9am–2pm; free), which includes works by local boy Luís Morales, and a couple of good panels by Zurbarán. Near Plaza de la Constitución and off Avenida Calzadillas Maestre, is the **Museo de Arte Contemporáneo** (Tues–Sat 10.30am–1pm & 5–8pm, Sun 10.30am–1pm; free). This striking building houses a wealth of modern paintings, installations and sculpture, by artists from Spain, Portugal and Latin America.

Eating and drinking

The area around c/Conde Duque, a couple of blocks below the Plaza de España, is the most promising site for reasonably priced food and lively bars.

Bar-Restaurante El Tronco, c/Muñoz Torrero 16. Perhaps the best reason to stay in town – this has a vast range of superb-value bar snacks and excellent, fiery regional food in the restaurant.

Los Gabrieles, c/Vicente Barrantes 21 (☎924 220001). Classic local cuisine, served in huge portions and at very reasonable cost. Closed Sun & mid-June (check beforehand).

El Sótano, c/Virgen de la Soledad 6. Extremaduran dishes, on a pedestrianized street near the cathedral. Allow 3500ptas per head.

La Toja, Avda. Elvas 22 – the Portugal road. This is the class restaurant in Badajoz, run by a *gallego*, so serving food from Extremadura and Galicia. Moderately pricey. Closed Sun evenings & mid-Aug.

Southern Extremadura

The routes **south from Mérida or Badajoz** cross territory that is mostly harsh and unrewarding, fit only for sheep and the odd cork or olive tree, until you come upon the foothills of the Sierra Morena, on the borders of Andalucía. En route, **Olivenza**, a town that has spent more time in Portugal than Spain, is perhaps the most attractive stop, and offers a road approach to Évora, the most interesting city of southern Portugal.

Olivenza

Twenty-five kilometres southwest of Badajoz, whitewashed **OLIVENZA** seems to have landed in the wrong country; long disputed between Spain and Portugal, it has been Spanish since 1801. Yet not only are the buildings and the town's character clearly Portuguese, the oldest inhabitants still cling to this language – you may overhear them chatting as they relax in the main square where the buses stop. There's a local saying here: "the women from Olivenza are not like the rest, for they are the daughters of Spain and the granddaughters of Portugal".

There's a **Turismo** kiosk on the main square (Tues–Fri 9am–2pm & 5–7pm, Sat & Sun 9.15am–2pm, but closed alternate weekends when the castle museum will provide information; ☎924 490125). The town has long been strongly fortified, and traces of the **walls and gates** can still be seen, even though houses have been built up against them.

They extend up to the **castle**, which has three surviving towers, and an ethnographic **museum** (summer Sat 7–9pm & Sun 11am–2pm; winter Sat 4.30–6pm & Sun 11am–2pm) within.

Right beside the castle is the seventeenth-century church of **Santa María del Castillo**, and around the corner, **Santa María Magdalena**, built a century later (both open mornings only). The latter is in the distinctive Portuguese Manueline style, with arcades of twisted columns; the former is a more sober Renaissance affair with three aisles of equal height and a notable work of art in the huge "Tree of Jesse" *retablo*. Both have sturdy bell towers and light, airy interiors adorned with *azulejo* and ornate Baroque altars.

Just across the street from Santa María Magdalena is a former **palace**, now the public library, with a spectacular Manueline doorway. Continuing down this street, then taking the first turning on the left on to c/Coridad, you come to the early sixteenth-century **Hospital**, which still serves its original purpose. Its chapel (staff will open it up for you on request) is covered with early eighteenth-century *azulejos*.

Should you want to stay in Olivenza, there's a **hotel** on the fringes of town, at the exit to Badajoz, the *Heredero* (☎924 490835, fax 924 491261; ⑤), which has a restaurant. Those on a budget should head for *Los Amigos* (☎924 490725; ②), back in town on Avenida del Perú, or the *Pensión Centro* in c/Paseo Filarmonica (☎924 490198; ②). You'll find a public **swimming pool** by the football ground, on Avenida Portugal, near the Badajoz exit.

Towards Portugal

Twelve kilometres northwest of Olivenza, a road heading towards Portugal stops abruptly at the ruined bridge of **Puente Ayuda**, where the Río Guadiana forms the border between the two countries. There's no way on other than to swim but it's a picturesque picnic spot; the river runs across many exposed rock beds giving good fishing and it's also an ideal spot for some discreet camping. To **enter Portugal**, you need to follow the C436 south from Olivenza for 39km to the Spanish border at **Villanueva del Fresno**. From here it's 16km to **Mourao**, the first Portuguese town on this approach, which is on the main road (and bus route) to Évora.

South to Jerez de los Caballeros

The road from **Badajoz to Jerez de los Caballeros** is typical of southern Extremadura, striking across a parched landscape whose hamlets – low huts and a whitewashed church strung out along the road – look as if they have been dumped from some low-budget Western set of a Mexican frontier town. It's a cruel country which bred cruel people, if we are to believe the names of places like Valle de Matamoros (Valley of the Moorslayers), and one can easily understand the attraction which the New World and the promise of the lush Indies must have held for its inhabitants.

It is hardly surprising, then, that **JEREZ DE LOS CABALLEROS** produced a whole crop of *conquistadores*. The two most celebrated are Vasco Núñez de Balboa, discoverer of the Pacific, and Hernando de Soto (also known as the Conqueror of Florida), who in exploring the Mississippi became one of the first Europeans to set foot in North America. You're not allowed to forget it either – the bus station is in the Plaza de Vasco Núñez de Balboa, complete with a statue of Vasco in the very act of discovery, and from it the Calle Hernando de Soto leads up into the middle of town.

It's a quiet, friendly place, where many tourists pass through but few stay. Grass grows up through many of the cobbled streets and there's no hurry about anything. From a distance it is the church towers that dominate the walled old town: a passion for building spires gripped the place in the eighteenth century, when three churches erected new ones. The silhouette of each is clearly based on that of the Giralda at Sevilla, but they are all distinctively decorated: the first is **San Miguel**, in the central Plaza de España, made of carved brick; the second is the unmistakable red-, blue-, and ochre-glazed tower of **San Bartolomé**, on the hill above it, with a striking tiled facade; and the third, rather dilapidated, belongs to **Santa Catalina**, outside the walls.

Above the Plaza de España the streets climb up to the restored remains of a **castle** of the Knights Templar (this was once an embattled frontier town), mostly late thirteenth-century but with obvious Moorish influences. Adjoining the castle, and predating it by over a century (as do the town walls), is the church of **Santa María**. Built on a Visigothic site, it's more interesting seen from the battlements above than it is from the inside. In the small park below the castle walls, a café commands fine views of the surrounding countryside, including the magnificent sunsets.

Places to stay are few. By far the cheapest is the *Pensión El Gordito*, Avda. de Portugal 104 (☎924 731452; ①), which is good for the price. The more upmarket alternatives are the *Hotel Oasis*, c/El Campo 18 (☎ & fax 924 731453; ④) and *Hostal Las Torres*, on the road out to Oliva de la Frontera (☎924 731168; ②). The *Oasis* has the only real **restaurant** in town; for *tapas* and *pitarra* wine, try *La Ermita*, an old chapel on c/Dr Benitez. There's a small **Turismo** in the *Ayuntamiento* (daily 8.30am–3pm & 5.30–7.30pm; ☎924 730384).

Zafra

If you plan to stick to the main routes or are heading south from Mérida, **ZAFRA** is rather less of a detour, though it's also much more frequented by tourists. It's famed mainly for its **castle** – now converted into a *parador* – which is remarkable for the white marble Renaissance patio designed by Juan de Herrera. Two beautiful arcaded plazas, the Plaza Grande and the Plaza Chica, adjoin each other in the town centre.

The most attractive of several interesting churches is **Nuestra Señora de la Candelaria** (daily 7–7.30pm only), with nine panels by Zurbarán in the *retablo* and a chapel by Churriguera; the entrance is on c/José through a small gateway, around the side of the church. The tombs of the Figueroa family (the original inhabitants of the castle) in the **Convento de Santa Clara** (daily 5–6.30pm), just off the main shopping street, c/Sevilla, are worth a look; ring the bell to get in. This region is famous for its wines, and you can visit the **Bodega Medina**, c/Cestria (Mon–Fri 2–8pm); call in at the **Turismo** in the Plaza de España (Mon–Fri 9.30am–4.30pm, Sat & Sun 10.30am–2.30pm; ☎924 551036) to make an appointment. **Accommodation** options include the *parador* (☎924 554540, fax 924 551018; ⑦), *Hotel El Ancla*, Plaza de España 8 (☎924 554382; ⑥), *Hotel Las Palmeras*, Plaza Grande 14 (☎924 552208; ④), and *Hostal Carmen*, Avda. Estación 9 (☎924 551439; ④), which also boasts an excellent medium-priced restaurant. The cheapest and best-value place in town is the friendly *Hostal Arias* (☎924 554855, fax 924 554888; ③), 200m out of town on the Carretera Badajoz–Granada, which has en-suite rooms and a good restaurant with a 1200ptas *menú*.

South of Zafra: the Sierra Morena

Beyond Zafra the main road and the railway head straight down through the **Sierra Morena** towards **Sevilla**. By **road** it's more interesting – though bus services are less frequent – to go through **Fregenal de La Sierra** (where the road from Jerez de los Caballeros joins up) into the heart of the sierra around Aracena. On the **train** you can reach another interesting region by getting off at the station of Cazalla-Constantina; while if you're heading for **Córdoba** and eastern Andalucía, you should change at Los Rosales before reaching Sevilla.

travel details

BUSES

Albacete to: Alicante (6 daily; 2hr 30min); Cuenca (2 daily; 3hr); Madrid (8 daily; 3hr); Murcia (6 daily; 2hr 15min); Parque Natural de las Lagunes de Ruidera (Mon–Sat 1 daily; 2hr); Valencia (9 daily; 3hr).

Badajoz to: Cáceres (4 daily; 2hr); Caya (Portuguese frontier – 4 daily; 30min); Córdoba (3 daily; 5hr); Lisbon (4 daily; 7hr); Madrid (7 daily; 4hr 30min–5hr); Mérida (10 daily; 45min); Olivenza (12 daily; 30min); Sevilla (4 daily; 4hr 30min); Zafra (8 daily; 1hr 30min).

Cáceres to: Alcántara (2 daily; 1hr 30min); Arroyo de la Luz (Mon–Sat 11 daily; 30min); Badajoz (4 daily; 1hr 45min); Coria (4 daily; 1hr 30min); Guadalupe (2 daily; 4hr); Madrid (7 daily; 4hr); Mérida (3 daily; 1hr); Plasencia (4–5 daily; 1hr 30min); Salamanca (5 daily; 3hr 30min); Sevilla (5–7 daily; 4hr); Trujillo (9 daily; 45min).

Ciudad Real to: Almagro (8 daily; 1hr); Córdoba (1 daily; 4hr 30min); Jaén (2 daily; 4hr); Madrid (4 daily; 4hr); Toledo (1 daily; 3hr), Valdepeñas (3 daily; 2hr).

Cuenca to: Albacete (2 daily; 3hr); Barcelona (2 daily; 9 hr); Madrid (7 daily; 2hr 30min); Teruel (2 daily; 3hr); Valencia (2 daily; 4hr).

Guadalupe to: Cáceres (2 daily; 4hr); Madrid (2 daily; 4hr); Trujillo (2 daily; 2hr–2hr 30min).

Madrid to Albacete (7 daily; 3hr 45min); Badajoz (7 daily; 4hr 20min); Cáceres (4 daily; 4hr); Cuenca (7 daily; 2hr 30min); Jarandilla (1 daily; 3hr 30min); Mérida (7 daily; 4hr); Plasencia (1–2 daily; 4hr); Talavera de la Reina (6 daily; 1hr 30min); Trujillo (8 daily; 3hr 30min).

Mérida to: Badajoz (10 daily; 45min); Cáceres (2–4 daily; 1hr); Guadalupe (4 daily; 2 hr); Jerez de los Caballeros (1 daily; 2hr); Madrid (6–7 daily; 5hr); Sevilla (12 daily; 3hr 30min, some stopping in Zafra); Trujillo (4 daily; 1hr); Zafra (5 daily; 1hr).

Navalmoral to: Jarandilla (2 daily; 3hr); Plasencia (2 daily; 2–4hr); Trujillo (6 daily; 1hr).

Plasencia to: Cáceres (4–5 daily; 1hr 30min); Jarandilla (2 daily; 2hr); Madrid (2 daily; 4hr); Salamanca (5 daily; 2hr).

Talavera de la Reina to: Guadalupe (2 daily; 2hr 30min); Madrid (15 daily; 1hr 30min); Toledo (10 daily; 1hr 30min).

Trujillo to: Cáceres (7 daily; 1hr 30min); Guadalupe (2 daily; 2hr 30min); Madrid (9–11 daily; 3hr); Mérida (4 daily; 2hr).

TRAINS

Albacete to: Alicante (6–7 daily; 1hr 30min); Madrid (6–8 daily; 2hr 30min); Valencia (4 daily; 1hr 55min).

Badajoz to: Cáceres (4 daily; 2hr); Lisbon via Elvas (2 daily; 5hr); Madrid (4 daily; 5–7hr); Mérida (7 daily; 1hr); Plasencia (3 daily; 3hr 20min); Sevilla (1 daily; 5hr via Mérida).

Cáceres to: Badajoz (4 daily; 2 hr); Lisbon (1 overnight; 5hr); Madrid (5 daily; 3hr 30min–5hr); Mérida (5 daily; 1hr); Plasencia (4 daily; 1hr 30min); Sevilla (1 daily; 5hr 30min); Zafra (2 daily; 2hr 10min).

Ciudad Real to: Almagro (5 daily; 1hr 15min); Madrid (18 daily; 1–3hr).

Cuenca to: Madrid (4 daily; 2hr 30min); Valencia (3 daily; 3hr 15min).

Madrid to: Albacete (15 daily; 2hr 10min); Almagro (1 daily; 2hr 30min); Badajoz (3 daily; 5hr 30min–7hr 30min); Cáceres (5 daily; 3hr 30min–4hr 30min); Ciudad Real (7 daily AVE high-speed service; 55min & 2 daily ordinary; 3hr); Cuenca (4–6 daily; 2hr 30min); Mérida (6 daily; 6hr); Navalmoral (5 daily; 2hr 30min); Plasencia (5 daily; 3hr 30min); Sigüenza (10 daily; 1hr 30min–2hr); Talavera de la Reina (5–7 daily; 2hr).

Mérida to: Badajoz (7 daily; 1hr); Cáceres (1–2 daily; 1hr); Madrid (3 daily; 4–6hr); Plasencia (2 daily; 2hr 30min); Sevilla (1 daily; 4hr 30min).

Plasencia to: Badajoz (3 daily; 3hr 20min); Cáceres (4 daily; 1hr 30min); Madrid (4 daily; 3hr 30min); Mérida (2 daily; 2hr 30min).

Sigüenza to: Barcelona (1 daily; at least 6hr 30min), via Zaragoza (3–4hr); Madrid (9 daily; 1 hr 30min–2hr 15min); Medinaceli (1 daily; 15min).

CHAPTER FOUR

ANDALUCÍA

Above all else – and there is plenty – it's the great **Moorish monuments** that compete for your attention in **Andalucía**. The Moors, a mixed race of Berbers and Arabs who crossed into Spain from Morocco and North Africa, occupied *al-Andalus* for over seven centuries. Their first forces landed at Tarifa in 710 AD and within four years they had conquered virtually the entire country; their last kingdom, Granada, fell to the Christian Reconquest in 1492. Between these dates they developed the most sophisticated civilization of the Middle Ages, centred in turn on the three major cities of **Córdoba**, **Sevilla** and **Granada**. Each one preserves extraordinarily brilliant and beautiful monuments, of which the most perfect is Granada's **Alhambra palace**, arguably the most sensual building in all of Europe. **Sevilla**, not to be outdone, has a fabulously ornamented Alcázar, the greatest of all Gothic cathedrals. Today, Andalucía's capital and seat of the region's autonomous parliament is a vibrant contemporary metropolis that's impossible to resist. Córdoba's exquisite **Mezquita**, the grandest and most beautiful mosque constructed by the Moors, is a landmark building in world architecture and also not to be missed.

These three cities have, of course, become major tourist destinations, but the smaller **inland towns** of Andalucía are often totally unspoiled. These offer amazing potential; Renaissance towns such as **Úbeda**, **Baeza** and **Osuna**, **Guadix** with its cave suburb, Moorish **Carmona** and the stark white hill towns around **Ronda**, are all easily accessible by local buses. Travelling for some time here you'll also get a feel for the landscape of Andalucía: occasionally spectacularly beautiful but more often impressive on a huge, unyielding scale, distinguished by a patchwork of colours and the interaction of land and buildings, or the gradual appearance of villages grouped beneath a castle and church.

The province also takes in mountains – including the **Sierra Nevada**, Spain's highest range. You can ski here in February, and then drive down to the coast to swim the same day. Perhaps more compelling, though, are the opportunities for walking in the lower slopes, **Las Alpujarras**. Alternatively, there's good trekking amongst the gentler (and much less-known) hills of the **Sierra Morena**, north of Sevilla.

On the **coast** it's easy to despair. Extending to either side of **Málaga** is the **Costa del Sol**, Europe's most heavily developed resort area, with its beaches hidden behind a remorseless density of concrete hotels and apartment complexes. However, the province takes in two alternatives, much less developed and with some of the best beaches in all Spain. These are the villages **between Tarifa and Cádiz** on the Atlantic, and those **around Almería** on the southeast corner of the Mediterranean. The Almerian beaches allow warm swimming through all but the winter months; those near Cádiz, more easily accessible, are fine from about June to September. Near Cádiz, too, is the **Coto Doñana**, Spain's largest and most important nature reserve.

The realities of life in **contemporary Andalucía** can be stark. **Unemployment** in the province is the highest in Spain – over thirty percent – and an even larger proportion of the population is still engaged in agriculture. Rural life is bleak; you soon begin to notice the appalling economic structure, at its most extreme in this

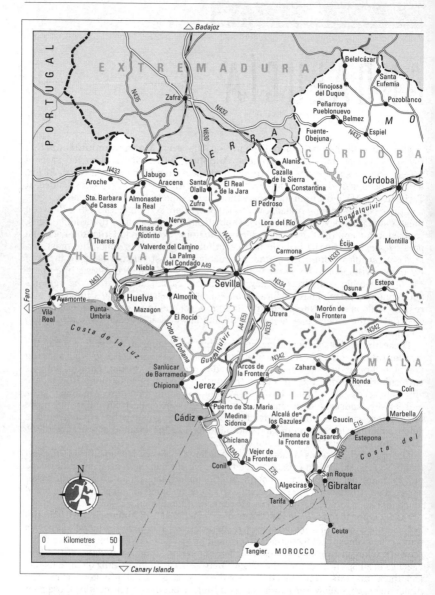

part of Spain, of vast absentee-landlord estates and landless peasants. The *andaluz* villages, bastions of anarchist and socialist groups before and during the Civil War, saw little economic aid or change during the Franco years – or indeed since, even though the PSOE Socialist party has its principal power base in Andalucía and, since 1980, the province has been an autonomous region with a substantial degree of self-government.

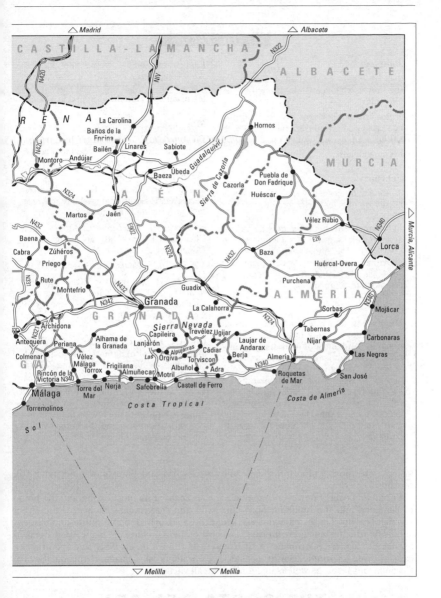

The day labourers, *jornaleros*, earn a precarious living from seasonal work, and as recently as 1986 the regional government instituted land reform in an effort to head off a peasants' revolt. Numerous instances of land occupation have resulted in violent clashes between labourers and the Civil Guard. Throughout the 1990s, tourism, and ventures such as Expo '92 in Sevilla, have brought some changes – above all radical improvements in infrastructure, with new road and rail projects aimed at providing

FIESTAS

January

1–2 *La Toma* – celebration of the entry of the Reyes Católicos into the city – at Granada.

6 *Romería de la Virgen del Mar* pilgrimage procession from Almería.

17 *Romería del Ermita del Santo*. Similar event at Guadix.

February

1 *San Cecilio* fiesta in Granada's traditionally gypsy quarter of Sacromonte.

February/March *Carnaval* is an extravagant week-long event (leading up to Lent) in all the Andalucian cities. Cádiz, above all, celebrates, with uproarious street parades, fancy dress, flamenco and camp-comic competitions.

April

Holy Week (*Semana Santa*), too, has its most elaborate and dramatic celebrations in Andalucía. You'll find memorable processions of floats and penitents at Sevilla, Málaga, Granada and Córdoba and to a lesser extent in smaller towns such as Jerez, Arcos, Baeza and Úbeda. All culminate with dramatic candlelight processions on the dawn of Good Friday, with Easter Day itself more of a family occasion.

Last week (or 1–2 weeks after Easter) Week-long *Feria de Abril* at Sevilla: the largest fair in Spain. A small April fair – featuring bull running – is held in Vejer.

May

First week *Cruces de Mayo* in Córdoba celebrates the Holy Cross and includes a "prettiest patio" competition in a town full of prize examples.

Early May (usually the week after Sevilla's fair) Somewhat aristocratic *Horse Fair* at Jerez de la Frontera.

3 *Moros y Cristianos* ("Moors and Christians") carnival at Pampaneira (Alpujarras).

17 *San Isidro Romería* at Setenil (Cádiz).

Pentecost (7 weeks after Easter) *Romería del Rocío*, when horse-drawn carriages and processions converge from all over the south on El Rocío (Huelva).

Corpus Christi (variable – Thursday after Trinity). Bullfights and festivities at Granada, Sevilla, Ronda, Vejer and Zahara de la Sierra.

Last week *Feria de la Manzanilla*, Sanlúcar de Barrameda. Prolonged binge to celebrate the town's major product with flamenco and sporting events on the river beach.

faster connections within the region and with Madrid and Barcelona – but much still remains to be done.

For all its poverty however, Andalucía is also Spain at its most exuberant: the home of flamenco and the bullfight, and those wild and extravagant clichés of the Great Spanish Dream. These really do exist and can be absorbed at one of the hundreds of annual **fiestas**, **ferias** and **romerías**. The best of them include the giant **April Feria** in Sevilla, the ageless pilgrimage to **El Rocío** near Huelva in late May, and the dramatically moving **Semana Santa** (Easter) celebrations at Málaga, Granada, Sevilla, Córdoba and Jerez, as well as in countless small villages.

THE COSTA DEL SOL

The outstanding feature of the **Costa del Sol** is its ease of access. Hundreds of charter flights arrive here every week, and it's often possible to get an absurdly cheap ticket from other cities in Europe, particularly London. **Málaga airport** is positioned

June

Second week *Feria de San Bernabé* at Marbella, often spectacular since this is the richest town in Andalucía.

13 *San Antonio* Fiesta at Trevélez (Alpujarras) with mock battles between Moors and Christians.

Third week The Algeciras fair and fiesta, another major event of the south.

23–24 *Candelas de San Juan* – bonfires and effigies at Vejer and elsewhere.

30 Conil *feria*.

End June/early July *International Festival of Music and Dance*: major dance/flamenco groups and chamber orchestras perform in Granada's Alhambra palace, Generalife and Carlos V palace.

July

Early July The *International Guitar Festival* at Córdoba brings together top international acts from classical, flamenco and Latin American music.

End of month *Virgen del Mar* – Almería's major annual shindig, with parades, horse-riding events, concerts and lots of drinking.

August

5 Trevélez observes a midnight *romería* to Mulhacén.

13–21 *Fería de Málaga* – one of Andalucía's most enjoyable fiestas for visitors, who are heartily welcomed by the ebullient *malagueños*.

15 *Ascension of the Virgin Fair* with *casetas* (dance tents) at Vejer and elsewhere. Riotous *Noche del Vino* wine festival at Competa (Málaga).

Third week The first cycle of horse races along Sanlúcar de Barrameda's beach, with heavy official and unofficial betting; the second tournament takes place a week later.

23–25 *Guadalquivir festival* at Sanlúcar de Barrameda with bullfights and an important flamenco competition.

September

First two weeks Ronda's annual *feria* with flamenco contests and *Corrida Goyesca* – bullfights in eighteenth-century dress.

1–3 Celebration of the *Virgen de la Luz* in Tarifa: processions and horseback riding.

First/second week *Vendimia* (celebration of the vintage) at Jerez.

29–Oct 2 *Feria* in Órjiva (Alpujarras).

October

1 *San Miguel* fiesta in Granada's Albaicín quarter and elsewhere, even at Torremolinos.

15–23 *Feria de San Lucas* – Jaén's major fiesta, dating back to the fifteenth century.

midway between Málaga, the main city on the coast, and **Torremolinos**, its most grotesque resort. You can easily reach either town by taking the electric train which runs every thirty minutes (daily 6.30am–11.30pm) along the coast between Málaga and **Fuengirola**. Granada, Córdoba and Sevilla are all within easy reach of Málaga; so too, and covered in this section, are **Ronda** and the "White Towns" to the west, and a handful of relatively restrained coastal resorts to the east. **Beaches** along this stretch are generally grit-grey rather than golden, but the sea is reliably clean, after a lot of work on the sewerage system.

Economically, the coastal hinterland is undergoing a gradual resurgence, in contrast to the general decline in the rest of Andalucía. In recent years the cultivation of subtropical fruits such as mangos, papayas, guavas, lychees and avocados has replaced the traditional orange, lemon and almond trees. Most farm labourers, however, can't afford coastal land; those who buy are often former migrants to France and Germany who have been forced to return because of the unemployment situation there.

THE CARRETERA NACIONAL N340

A special note of warning has to be made about the Costa del Sol's **main highway**, which is one of the most dangerous roads in Europe. Nominally a national highway, it's really a 100-kilometre-long city street, passing through the middle of towns and *urbanizaciones*. Drivers treat it like a motorway, yet pedestrians have to get across, and cars are constantly turning off or into the road – hence the terrifying number of accidents, with over a hundred fatalities a year on average. A large number of these involve inebriated British package tourists who are further handicapped by lack of familiarity with left-hand-drive vehicles and traffic patterns. The first few kilometres, between the airport with its various car hire offices and Torremolinos, are among the most treacherous of the entire N340. The worst stretch is heading west from Marbella: around thirty accidents a year occur on each kilometre between Marbella and San Pedro.

Construction has now begun on a four-lane toll **motorway** to replace it – the Autostrada del Sol – stretching from Nerja (east of Málaga) to Estepona in the west. The first sections linking Málaga with Fuengirola and Nerja are already open, and the full length is due to be completed in 2000, although this date may well be overshot due to the numerous towns and villages along the route attempting to divert this monster away from their communities. In the meantime, don't make dangerous (and illegal) left turns from the fast lane, and be particularly careful after heavy rain, when the hot, oily road surface sends you easily into a skid. Pedestrians should cross at traffic lights, a bridge or an underpass where possible.

Málaga

MÁLAGA seems at first an uninviting place. It's the second city of the south (after Sevilla), with a population of half a million, and it's also one of the poorest: official unemployment figures for the area estimate the jobless at one in four of the workforce. Yet though many people get no farther than the train or bus stations, and though the clusters of highrises look pretty grim as you approach, it has its attractions. The central zone has a number of interesting churches and museums, not to mention the **birthplace of Picasso** and the new **Picasso Museum**, housing an important collection of works by Málaga's most famous son. Around the old fishing villages of **El Palo** and **Pedregalejo**, now absorbed into the suburbs, are a series of small beaches and a *paseo* lined with some of the best **fish and seafood cafés** in the province. And overlooking the town and port are the Moorish citadels of the **Alcazaba** and **Gibralfaro** – excellent introductions to the architecture before pressing on to the main sites at Córdoba and Granada.

Arrival and information

From the **airport**, the **electric train** provides the easiest approach to Málaga (every 30min; 135ptas). From the Arrivals hall, go up one floor to the *Salidas* or Departures hall, take any exit and then turn right to reach a pedestrian overpass at the end of the airport building. Follow the *Ferrocarril* signs and cross the overpass to the unmanned station; the sweet kiosk, if open, sells tickets or you can buy one on the train. Make sure that you're on the Málaga platform (the farthest away from you) and stay on the train right to the end of the line: the **Guadalmedina** stop (about a 12min ride). The stop before this is RENFE, the main **train station**, a slightly longer walk into the heart of town (bus #3 runs from here to the centre every 10min or so).

The **bus station** is just behind the RENFE station, a bit to the right as you face the RENFE logo from the esplanade. All buses (run by a number of different companies) operate from this terminal. In midsummer it's best to arrive an hour or so early for the bus to Granada, since tickets can sell out.

Arriving in Málaga by **car** you'll face the serious problem of parking; one good-value guarded car park (about 200ptas per day) is located along the east bank of the Río Guadalmedina (Avda. Comandante Benitez), below the Alameda. As **theft from cars** is rampant in Málaga you should strip your vehicle of all valuables before leaving it on the street overnight, or else use a hotel with a garage. You should also remove any visible stickers bearing a car rental company's name or logo as these are a magnet for thieves.

Málaga also has the remnants of a **passenger ferry port**, though these days there's a service only to the Spanish enclave of Melilla in Morocco. If you're heading for Fès and eastern Morocco, this is a useful connection – particularly so for taking a car over – though most people go for the quicker services at Algeciras and Tarifa to the west. Sailings are daily except Sunday, currently leaving at 1pm; the crossing takes seven and a half hours. Tickets are available from Transmediterranea at c/Juan Díaz 4 (☎95 222 43 91).

The **Turismo**, Pasaje de Chinitas 4 (Mon–Fri 9.30am–1.30pm, Sat 9.30am–1pm; ☎95 221 34 45), can provide full accommodation lists and a large, detailed map of the city. There's also a helpful branch at the bus station.

Accommodation

Málaga boasts dozens of **fondas** and **hostales**, so budget rooms are rarely hard to come by, and there are some real bargains available in winter. You may well get offers at the train (or possibly the bus) station, and so long as the rooms are fairly central these will probably be as good as any. Further upmarket, the town has a large number of central **hotels** of all categories, with some of the more luxurious sited to the east of the bullring, close to the sea. Numerous budget accommodation possibilities are to be found in the area just south of the Alameda Principal, and in the streets east and west of c/Marques de Larios which cuts between the Alameda and Málaga's main square, the Plaza de la Constitucion; these are probably the best places to start looking. Málaga's **campsite** has closed; the nearest sites along the coast is at Torremolinos heading west (see p.219).

Budget options

Albergue Juvenil Málaga, Plaza de Pio XII (☎95 230 85 00, fax 95 230 85 04). Modern youth hostel on the eastern outskirts of town, with double and single rooms, disabled facilities and its own sun terrace. The #18 bus from the Alameda will drop you nearby. ①.

Hostal Avenida, Alameda Principal 5 (☎95 221 77 29). Right on the Alameda but not too noisy; some rooms with bath. ③.

Casa Huéspedes Bolivia, c/Casas de Campos 24 (☎95 221 88 26). Clean and simple with a friendly proprietor. ③.

Hostal Córdoba, c/Bolsa 9–11 (☎95 221 44 69). Inexpensive, simple rooms in a family-run establishment near the cathedral. ②.

ACCOMMODATION PRICE CODES

The codes used in our hotel listings denote the following price ranges:

① Under 2000ptas	④ 4500–6000ptas	⑦ 12,000–17,500ptas
② 2000–3000ptas	⑤ 6000–8000ptas	⑧ Over 17,500ptas
③ 3000–4500ptas	⑥ 8000–12,000ptas	

See p.34 for more details.

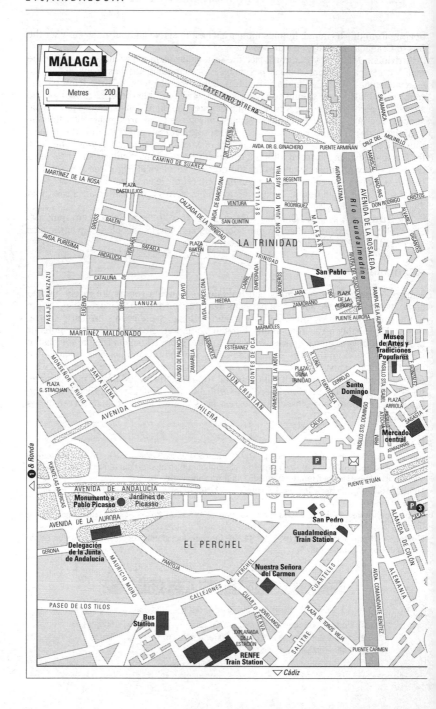

MÁLAGA

0   Metres   200

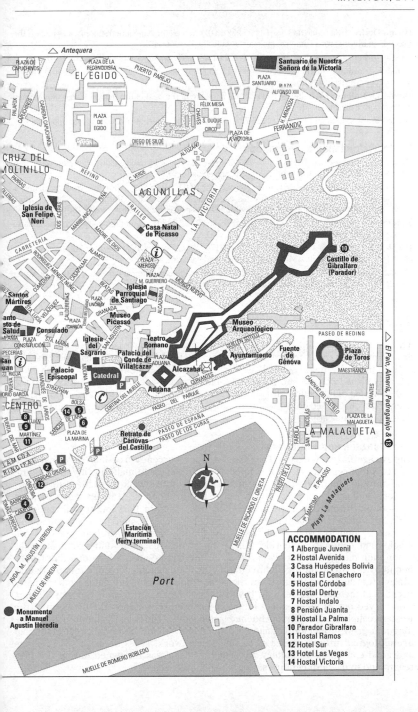

△ Antequera

Santuario de Nuestra
Señora de la Victoria

PLAZA DE
CAPUCHINOS

PLAZA DE LA
RECONQUISTA

PUERTO PAREJO

EL EGIDO

PLAZA
SANTUARIO

PLAZA
ALFONSO XIII

FÉLIX MESA
CHAVES

S. DUQUE

PLAZA
DE
EGIDO

CIRCO

PLAZA DE
LA VICTORIA

H. MENDOZA

DIEGO DE SILOÉ

FERRÁNDIZ

CRUZ DEL
MOLINILLO

REFINO

C. VERDE

LAGUNILLAS

LA VICTORIA

Iglesia de
San Felipe
Neri

FRAILES

Casa Natal
de Picasso

DIOS ACERAS

MANIBLANCA

MADRE DE DIOS

i

PLAZA
MERCED

CARRETERIA

ALAMOS

PLAZA
M. GUERRERO

MUNDO NUEVO

Santos
Mártires

Iglesia
Parroquial
de Santiago

ALCAZABILLA

anto
sto de
Salud

Museo
Picasso

Castillo de
Gibralfaro
(Parador)

Consulado

Museo
Arqueológico

PASEO DE REDING

Iglesia
del
Sagrario

Teatro
Romano

GUILLEN SOTELO

Fuente
de
Génova

Plaza
de Toros

Palacio
Episcopal

Palacio del
Conde de
Villalcázar

Ayuntamiento

MAESTRANZA

Catedral

Alcazaba

CÁNOVAS DEL CASTILLO

CERVANTES

Aduana

AVDA. CERVANTES

CENTRO

PASEO DEL PARQUE

PLAZA DE LA
MALAGUETA

8

JUAN

14

DE LARIOS

5

DE LARA

6

LA MALAGUETA

MARTÍNEZ

9

11

PLAZA DE
LA MARINA

PASEO DE ESPAÑA

PASEO DE LOS CURAS

Retrato de
Cánovas
del Castillo

2

12

N

4

Estación
Marítima
(ferry terminal)

7

MUELLE DE RICARDO G. ORUETA

Playa La Malagueta

Port

Monumento
a Manuel
Agustín Heredia

MUELLE DE ROMERO ROBLEDO

ACCOMMODATION
1 Albergue Juvenil
2 Hostal Avenida
3 Casa Huéspedes Bolivia
4 Hostal El Cenachero
5 Hostal Córdoba
6 Hostal Derby
7 Hostal Indalo
8 Pensión Juanita
9 Hostal La Palma
10 Parador Gibralfaro
11 Hostal Ramos
12 Hotel Sur
13 Hotel Las Vegas
14 Hostal Victoria

Hostal Derby, c/San Juan de Dios 1 (☎95 222 13 01). Excellent value fourth-floor *hostal*, just off the Plaza de la Marina, with some rooms overlooking the harbour. ③.

Hostal Indalo, c/Casas de Campos 5 (☎95 221 19 74). Clean, airy rooms without bath. ③.

Pensión Juanita, c/Alarcón Luján 8 (☎95 221 35 86). Basic, but clean and central *pensión* on the fourth floor (with a lift). ③.

Hostal La Palma, c/Martínez 7 (☎95 222 67 72). One of the best of the budget places; sometimes willing to give discounts. ③.

Hostal Ramos, c/Martínez 8 (☎95 222 72 68). Clean, basic alternative to *La Palma*, opposite. ②.

Moderate and expensive options

Hostal El Cenachero, c/Barroso 5 (☎95 222 40 88). Clean, quiet and reasonably priced *hostal*; left off the seafront end of c/Córdoba. All rooms are en suite. ④.

Parador Gibralfaro, Monte de Gibralfaro (☎95 222 19 02, fax 95 222 19 04). You won't get a better panoramic view of the coast than from this eagle's nest on top of the Gibralfaro hill; but it's quite small as *paradors* go, and the service sometimes lacks grace. Has its own garage. ⑦.

Hotel Sur, c/Trinidad Grund 13 (☎95 222 48 03, fax 95 221 24 16). Quiet, efficient and central hotel with secure garage; all rooms have bath and TV. ④.

Hotel Las Vegas, Paseo de Sancha 22 (☎95 221 77 12, fax 95 222 48 89). Smart hotel, reasonably close to the beach, with its own swimming pool and car park. ⑥.

Hostal Victoria, c/Sancha de Lara 3 (☎952 224223). Pleasant, upmarket *hostal* with good-value double and single rooms, just north of the Alameda. ⑤.

The City

The city's position well east of the airport, and the ring road that carries traffic around it, means that most visitors to the Costa del Sol rarely visit the heart of Málaga itself. All this may be about to change, as the city embarks on a costly face-lift, with plans to create enormous hotel-lined promenades along the beaches to the east and west of the centre already well advanced. Away from the seafront glitz, how-ever, it's to be hoped that the city's unique and vibrant character will survive the development unscathed.

The Alcazaba and Gibralfaro

The **Alcazaba** (daily except Tues 9.30am–8pm; currently free but there may be a charge when restoration work is finished) is the place to make for if you're killing time between connections. It lies just fifteen minutes' walk from the train or bus stations, and can be clearly seen from most central points. At its entrance stands a lost-looking **Roman theatre**, accidentally unearthed in 1951 and now a venue for various outdoor entertainments. The citadel, too, is Roman in origin and inter-spersed among the Moorish brick of the double- and triple-arched gateways are blocks and columns of marble. The main structures (now undergoing a major restoration during which only parts of the site will be open at any one time) were begun by the Moors in the eighth century, probably soon after their conquest since Málaga was an important port, but the palace higher up the hill dates from the early decades of the eleventh century. It was the residence of the Arab emirs of Málaga, who carved out an independent kingdom for themselves upon the break-up of the western caliphate. Their independence lasted a mere thirty years, but for a while the kingdom grew to include Granada, Carmona and Jaén. The palace, restored as an **archeological museum**, has some fine stucco work, 1920s Moorish-style ceilings and good collections of pottery, for which Málaga was renowned during the thir-teenth and fourteenth centuries.

Above the Alcazaba, and connected to it by a long double wall, is the **Gibralfaro cas-tle** (daily 9.30am–8pm; free). Take the road to the right of the Alcazaba, then a path up through gardens, a ramble of towers, bougainvillea-draped ramparts and sentry-box-shaped Moorish wells (you can also approach from the town side, as the tourist coach-es do, but this is a very unattractive walk and not one to be done alone after sundown). Last used in 1936 during the Civil War, the castle affords terrific views over the city. The nearby *parador* has a pleasant terrace café and restaurant.

The cathedral and fine art museum

Most conspicuous from the heights is Málaga's peculiar, unfinished **Catedral** (Mon–Sat: April–Sept 10am–6.45pm; Oct–March 10am–12.45pm & 4–6.45pm; 200ptas). Constructed between the sixteenth and eighteenth centuries, it is still lacking a tower on the west front as a radical *malagueño* bishop donated the earmarked money to the American War of Independence against the British. Unfortunately – and despite its huge scale – it also lacks any real inspiration and is distinguished only by an intricate-ly carved and ultrarealistic seventeenth-century *sillería* (choir stall) by noted sculptor Pedro de Mena.

The **Museo de Bellas Artes**, just around the corner from the cathedral on c/San Agustín, is about to be reborn as the new **Museo Picasso**, housing a major collection of the artist's work from his childhood and early years, as well as 140 important works from the Picasso family's Paris collection. At the time of writing the opening date has been put back to the year 2000, but the Turismo will have the latest details. The Bellas Artes collection – which includes works by Zurbarán, Murillo and Pedro de Mena – is to be moved to the **Antiguo Convento de la Trinidad** across the Guadalmedina river, but again you'll need to confirm opening dates and times with the Turismo. Picasso was born a hundred metres away from his museum in the Plaza de la Merced, where the **Casa Natal de Picasso** (Mon–Sat 10am–2pm & 6–8pm, Sun 10am–2pm; free) is home to the Fundación Picasso, a centre for scholars researching the painter's life and work. There's a photo display of Picasso's life here, as well as occasional exhibitions, but despite welcoming staff there's currently not an awful lot more to see. It was in the bars surrounding the square that the infant Pablo saw the first solid shape that he wanted to commit to paper: *churros*, those oil-steeped fritters that *malagueños* love to dip into their breakfast chocolate.

The Jardín Botánicos La Concepción and El Retiro

There are a couple of pleasant trips out of town if you want to escape the fumes and concrete. The recently opened **Jardín Botánico La Concepción** (guided visits daily except Mon: June–Sept 10am–7.30pm; Oct–May 10am–5.30pm; 435ptas) is a spectacular tropical garden, with many of its botanical specimens planted in the nineteenth century. To get there, bus #2 from the north side of the Alameda will drop you at the gates on Saturday and Sunday, and on weekdays at its terminus 700m short, leaving a ten-minute walk to the entrance; alternatively, you can take a taxi from town for about 750ptas one-way. The garden has no restaurant or bar but makes an ideal location for a discreet picnic.

The **El Retiro Jardín Botánico** (April–Sept 9am–8pm; Oct–March 9am–6pm; 1250ptas) lies just west of the airport in Churriana and makes an excellent place to kill a couple of hours while waiting for a flight. Founded by an eighteenth-century bishop of Málaga, the tranquil gardens are studded with fountains, lakes and sculptures and contain more than eight hundred species of plants and trees. The gardens also hold Andalucía's largest **aviary**, where more than a thousand exotic birds from all over the world can be viewed in depressingly cramped cages. El Retiro has a restaurant and bar but is not well served by public transport; to get there with your own vehicle, take the

N340 out of Málaga towards the airport, leaving the road at the Coín–Churriana exit, just beyond the airport turnoff. The garden is signposted on the right, a little beyond Churriana village some 4km from the *autovía*.

Eating and drinking

Málaga has no shortage of places to **eat** and **drink**, and, though it's hardly a gourmet paradise, the city has a justified reputation for its seafood.

Málaga's greatest claim to fame is undoubtedly its **fried fish**, acknowledged as the best in Spain. You'll find many fish restaurants grouped around the Alameda, although for the very best you need to head out to the suburbs of Pedregalejo and El Palo, served by bus #11 (from the Paseo del Parque). On the seafront *paseo* at **Pedregalejo**, almost any of the cafés and restaurants will serve you up terrific fish. Farther on, after the *paseo* disappears, you find yourself amid fishing shacks and smaller, sometimes quite ramshackle, cafés. This is **El Palo**, an earthier sort of area for the most part, with a beach and fishing huts, and in summer or at weekends an even better place to eat.

Inexpensive restaurants

Bar Los Pueblos, c/Ataranzas, almost opposite the market. Serves satisfying, inexpensive food all day – bean soups and *estofados* are its specialities; *gazpacho* is served in half-pint glasses.

Bar El Puerto, c/Comisario. A good *marisquería* in a narrow alley on the northern side of the Alameda.

La Cancela, c/Denis Belgrano 3, off c/Granada. A *malagueño* institution with an economical *ménu* and outdoor tables in a pleasant, pedestrianized street.

Er Compá, c/Compás de la Victoria 24, opposite the church of Nuestra Señora de la Victoria. Pleasant small *mesón* offering a good value *menú* for under 1000ptas.

Maite, c/Esparteros 5. In an alley that's a bit difficult to find, just west of c/Larios, and offering a rock-bottom priced *ménu*.

Mesón de Jamón, Plaza María Guerrero 5, just off the Plaza Merced. Good-value *menú* and a selection of *jamón* and cheese *tapas*.

Restaurante Arcos, Alameda 31. Efficient central place serving all-day *platos combinados* and late-night meals – for breakfast they also serve *pan tostada* with wholemeal bread, *pan integral*.

La Tarantela, c/Granada 67. Tasty pizzas and salads.

El Tintero II, El Palo. Right at the far east end of the seafront, just before the *Club Náutico* (stay on bus #11 and ask for "Tintero Dos"), this is a huge beach restaurant where the waiters charge round with plates of fish (all costing the same for a plate) and you shout for, or grab, anything you like. The fish to go for are, above all, *mero* (a kind of gastronomically evolved cod) and *rosada* (equally indefinable), along with Andalucian regulars such as *boquerones* (fresh anchovies), *gambas* (prawns), *calamares*, *chopos*, *jibia* (different kinds of squid) and *sepia* (cuttlefish).

La Traya, c/Circo 1, at the end of c/Victoria. Good fish bar that's inexpensive and very popular. Ask for directions at Plaza Victoria as it's not easy to find. Closed Thurs.

Moderate to expensive restaurants

Al-Yamal, c/Blasco de Garay 3, near *Hostal El Cenachero*. Good Arab restaurant serving up meat in spicy sauces, couscous and other typical Arab food.

Antonio Martín, Paseo Maritimo. One of Málaga's renowned fish restaurants and the traditional (and expensive) haunt of *matadores* celebrating their successes in the nearby bullring.

Parador Gibralfaro, Monte Gibralfaro (bus #35). Superior dining on the terrace with spectacular views over the coast and town. The *menú* is excellent value at around 3000ptas.

Bars

A number of **traditional bars** serve the sweet **Málaga wine** (Falstaff's "sack"), made from muscatel grapes and dispensed from huge barrels; try it with shellfish at *Antigua*

Casa Guardia, a great old nineteenth-century bar at the corner of c/Pastora, on the Alameda's north side. The new season wine, Pedriot, is incredibly sweet; much more palatable is Seco Añejo, which has matured for a year.

Málaga has plenty of good **tapas bars**: *Gorki*, in c/Strachan near the Turismo is a popular place at *aperitivo* time, whilst the diminutive size of *Orellana* at c/Moreno Monroy 5, slightly north, is in inverse proportion to its reputation as one of the best *tapas* bars in town. Cheaper and earthier options include *La Manchega*, off the west side of c/Larios, and the *Antigua Reja* on Plaza de Uncibay off c/de Méndez Núñez.

Nightlife

You'll find most of Málaga's **nightlife** northeast of the cathedral along and around c/Granada, c/Beatas, c/Comedias and the streets circling Plaza de Uncibay, as well as in Malagueta, south of the bullring. At weekends and holidays dozens of youthful disco-bars fill the crowded streets in these areas with a cacophony of sound, and over the summer – though it's dead out of season – the scene spreads out along the seafront to the suburb of Pedregalejo. Here, the streets just behind the beach host most of the action, and dozens of discos and smaller bars lie along and off the main street, Juan Sebastián Elcano.

Anden, Plaza de Uncibay. Disco-bar with a wild crowd and open till very late.

Chotis, Paseo de Reding, near the bullring. Lively music bar with plenty of atmosphere, and open 11.30pm until dawn. Next door, the disco-bar *Pries 18* is also good and keeps similar hours.

La Chancla, on the beach in Pedregalejo. One of a recent rash of bars on the beach, this one bursts forth at midnight and continues until 3am or later.

El Pimpi, c/Granada 62. Cavernous night spot with flashing TV screens and a wide selection of sounds.

Salsa, at the top of c/Denis Belgrano, off c/Granada. Salsa, karaoke, samba and mambo on weekday nights. Dance tuition is also on offer for those who want to polish their moves.

Sancha 21, c/Salvador Rueda, near the junction with Paseo Sancha in Malagueta. Late-night haunt (opens 11pm till dawn), which often attracts a lively crowd dancing to Spanish and international music.

Siempre Asi, c/Convalecientes, north of Plaza Uncibay. Another late bar opening 11pm–3.30am and specializing in Spanish rock and techno.

Vankuver, Pasaje Mitjana, just off Plaza Uncibay. Wide range of international sounds and open until dawn. The adjacent *La Botellita* offers a change of scene, does Spanish music and has a wide range of drinks at non-club prices.

El Chorro Gorge and Antequera

North of Málaga are two impressive sights, the magnificent limestone **gorge** near **El Chorro** and the prehistoric **dolmen caves** at **Antequera**. They lie close to the junction of roads inland to Sevilla, Córdoba and Granada and on direct train lines, and both are possible as day trips from Málaga. Approaching Antequera along the old road from Málaga via Almogía and Villenueva de la Concepción, you also pass the entrance to the popular national park, **El Torcal**.

El Chorro Gorge

Fifty kilometres north of Málaga, Garganta del Chorro is an amazing place – an immense cleft in a vast limestone massif – but its most stunning feature is a concrete catwalk, *El Camino del Rey*, which threads the length of the gorge, hanging precipitously halfway up its side. Built in the 1920s as part of a burgeoning hydroelectric scheme, it used to figure in all the guidebooks as one of the wonders of Spain; today it's largely fallen into disrepair, though a deal has recently been struck between the Madrid and Málaga governments to fund renovation works, due to begin in 1999. At present, despite a few wobbly – and decidedly dangerous – sections (one tourist fell to her death in 1998), with random holes in the concrete through which you can see the gorge hundreds of feet below, it's still possible to walk much of its length. You will, however, need a very good head for heights, and at least a full day starting from Málaga. If you've neither, it's possible to get a glimpse of both gorge and *camino* from any of the trains going north from Málaga – the line, slipping in and out of tunnels, follows the river for a considerable distance along the gorge, before plunging into a last long tunnel just before its head.

If you want to explore the gorge, and walk the *camino*, head for **EL CHORRO**, served by direct trains from Málaga. In the village there's an excellent **campsite** (☎95 211 26 96) with pool, reached by heading downhill to your right for 400m after getting off the train. Near the station, *Bar-Restaurante Garganta del Chorro* (☎95 249 72 19; ③) has pleasant rooms inside a converted mill. Signs from the station will also direct you 2km to the *Finca La Campana* (☎ & fax 95 211 20 19), with an economical bunkhouse (①) and a couple of apartments (③), which also offers courses in rock climbing, caving and paragliding, rents out mountain bikes and can arrange horse-riding and hiking excursions.

Into the gorge

From El Chorro it's a beautiful 12km to the start of the path and the gorge. From the train station, take the road signposted *Pantano de Guadalhorce*, which crosses over the dam, turns to the right and leads towards the hydroelectric plant. After 10km you'll come upon the bar-restaurant *El Mirador*, poised above the various lakes and reservoirs of the Guadalhorce scheme. From the bar a dirt track on the right (just manageable by car) covers the 2km to an abandoned power plant at the mouth of the gorge. The footpath to the left of this will take you into the chasm and to the beginning of **El Camino**.

Although it is marked "No Entry", you'll probably come upon a number of young Spaniards exploring the catwalk. The first section, at least, seems reasonably safe – despite places where it is only a metre wide and where parts of the handrail are missing – and this is in fact the most dramatic part of the canyon. Towards the end, where the passageway gets really dangerous, the gorge widens and it's possible to climb down and follow the riverbank or have a swim.

Antequera and around

ANTEQUERA, on the main rail line to Granada, is an ordinary, modern town but it does have peripheral attractions in a Baroque church, **El Carmen** (Tues–Fri & Sun 10am–2pm, Sat 10am–2pm & 4–7pm; 200ptas), which houses one of the finest *retablos* in Andalucía, and a group of three prehistoric **dolmen caves**. The most impressive and famous of these is the **Cueva de Menga** (Tues–Fri 10am–2pm & 3–5.30pm, Sat & Sun 10am–2pm; free), its roof formed by an immense 180-ton monolith. To reach this, and the nearby **Cueva de Viera** (same hours), take the Granada road out of town – the turning, rather insignificantly signposted, is after about 1km on the left. A third cave, **El Romeral**, (same hours) is rather different (and later) in its structure, with a domed ceiling of flat stones; it is again to the left of the Granada road, 2km further on, behind a sugar factory with a chimney.

If you want to stay in Antequera there's a good **pensión**, *Madrona*, c/Calzada 25 (☎95 284 00 14; ③), near the market, which serves excellent food. Antequera also has a rather unattractive modern *parador* and several *hostales* on the roads in and out of town.

El Torcal, 13km south of Antequera, is the most geologically arresting of Spain's national parks. A massive high plateau of glaciated limestone tempered by a lush growth of hawthorn, ivy and wild rose, it's painlessly explored using the **walking routes** that radiate from the centre of the park – trails are outlined in a leaflet available from the **Centro de Recepción** (Tues–Sun 10.30–2pm & 4–6pm; ☎95 222 58 00). The only **waymarked route** (in green) is also the shortest (1.5km) and most popular, and in summer you may find yourself competing with gangs of school kids who arrive en masse for vaguely educational trips. A longer five-kilometre trail is more peaceful, great for strolling and taking in the looming limestone formations, eroded into vast, surreal sculptures. Camping is no longer allowed inside the park but there is a **campsite**, *Camping Torcal* (April–Sept), just off the A3310 6km south of Antequera. Five daily buses (Mon–Fri) run from Málaga (one on Sun).

East from Málaga: the coast to Almería

The eastern stretch of the **Costa del Sol**, from Málaga to Almería, is uninspiring. Though far less developed than the wall-to-wall concrete from Torremolinos to Marbella in the west, it's not exactly unspoiled. If you're looking for a village and a beach and not much else, then you'll probably want to keep going at least to Almería.

Nerja and around

There's certainly little to tempt anyone before **NERJA**. This was a village before it was a resort, so it has some character, and development (more villas, fewer tower blocks) has been shaped around it. The beaches are reasonably attractive, too, with a series of coves within walking distance if you want to escape the main mass of crowds. Bici Nerja at Pasaje Canterero 1, near the bus station, and Mountain Bike Holidays, c/Cristo 10, **rent bikes** if you want a little more freedom about where you go off to swim. There are plenty of great **walks** around Nerja, well-documented in a locally available guide, *Twelve Walks Around Nerja* by Elma and Denis Thompson. Elma also leads guided walks from November to May (☎95 252 13 41).

Nerja's chief tourist attraction, the **Cuevas de Nerja** (daily 10.30am–2pm & 4–8pm; 650ptas), 3km from the town, are a heavily commercialized series of caverns, impressive in size – and home to the world's longest known **stalactite** at 63m – though otherwise not tremendously interesting. They also contain a number of prehistoric paintings, but these are not presently on public view.

Practicalities

Nerja's main drawback, and a thorny problem through most of the summer, is scarce **accommodation**. There are a dozen or so *hostales*, most reserved well in advance, although some have arrangements with *casas particulares* who mop up the overflow. Budget choices include *Hostal Montesol*, c/Pintada 130, just off Plaza Cantarero near the bus station (☎95 252 00 14; ③) or, close to the Turismo, *Hostal Atenbeni*, c/Diputación 12 (☎95 252 13 41; ③). The excellent *Hotel Cala-Bella*, c/Puerta del Mar 10 (☎95 252 07 00; ④), has superb sea views and its own restaurant. Overlooking one of Nerja's most popular beaches, Playa de Burriana, is the *Parador Nacional*, c/Almuñécar 8 (☎95 252 00 50, fax 95 252 19 97; ⑦), with a lift down the cliff, and sharing the same views is the *Hotel Paraíso del Mar*, c/Carabeo 22 (☎95 252 16 21; ⑤). The **campsite**, *Nerja Camping* (☎95 252 97 14; open all year), with pool, bar and restaurant, is 4km east of town. Full accommodation lists are available from the helpful Turismo, Puerta del Mar 2 (April–Sept 10am–2pm & 5–9pm; ☎95 252 15 31). The **bus station** is on Avenida de Pescia, close to Plaza Cantarero, and there are hourly buses from here to the *cuevas*.

Almuñécar

Beyond Nerja the road climbs inland, running high above the coast until it surfaces at
LA HERRADURA, a fishing village-resort suburb of Almuñécar, and a good place to
stop off and swim; there's also a summer campsite, *La Herradura* (☎958 640056).
ALMUÑÉCAR itself is marred by a number of towering holiday apartments, though
if you've been unable to find a room in Nerja you might want to stay here for a night.
The rocky beaches are rather cramped and have grey sand, but the esplanade behind
them, with palm-roofed bars (many offer free *tapas*) and restaurants, is fun, and the old
town attractive.

Half a dozen good-value **fondas** and **hostales** ring the central Plaza de la Rosa in the old
part of town; the cosy *Hostal Plaza Damasco*, c/Cerrajos 8 (☎958 630165; ③), and *Hostal
Victoria*, Plaza de la Victoria (☎958 630022; ③), are two of the best. If you want to be right
by the beach, try *Hostal Tropical*, Avenida de Europa (☎958 633458; ③), comfortable and
good value considering its position. The **campsite** here, *El Paraiso* (☎958 632370; open all
year), at the eastern end of the seafront, can become an overcrowded hell-hole in summer;
an alternative is *Camping Don Cactus* (☎958 623109; open all year) on the beachfront at
Motril, 12km further on.

You can pick up a town map at the **Turismo** (Mon–Sat 10am–2pm & 4–9pm; ☎958
631125), which is located in an imposing neo-Moorish mansion on Avenida de Europa,
and you'll find the **bus station**, with frequent connections to Málaga and Granada, at
the junction of Avenida Juan Carlos I and Avenida Fenicia, northeast of the centre.

Salobreña and beyond

SALOBREÑA, 10km farther east on the coast road, is infinitely preferable to Almuñécar.
A white hill-top town gathered beneath the shell of a Moorish castle and surrounded by
sugar-cane fields, it's set back 2km from the sea and is thus comparatively little developed.
Its beach – a black sandy strip, only partially flanked by hotels and seafront *chiringuitos* –
is a far more relaxed affair than that at Almuñecar. Along and off c/de Hortensia, the main
avenue that winds down from the town to the beach, are a few **pensiones** and **hostales**;
Pensión Arnedo, c/Nueva 15 (☎958 610227; ②), has the least expensive rooms. *Pensión
Mari Carmen* (☎958 610906; ②), over the road, is equally good, with fans in the rooms.
Buses arrive and leave from Plaza de Goya, close to the **Turismo** (Tues–Sun
9.30am–1.30pm & 5–8pm; ☎958 610314).

Just before **Motril**, the N323 heads north to Granada, a great route, skirting the
Sierra Nevada. The coast road continues towards Almería through an unremarkable
sprawl of resorts of which the most worthwhile is **CASTELL DE FERRO**. It's quite
sheltered, still preserving remnants of its former existence as a small fishing village,
with good, wide beaches to the east and west. Avoid the small town beach which is dirty
and uninspiring. If you want to stay, head for the seafront where there are numerous
possibilities: *Hostal Bahía*, Plaza de España 12 (☎958 656060; ③) is worth trying. The
closest **campsite** to town is *El Sotillo* (☎958 656078; June–Sept), near the beach. For
the coast further east, see p.319.

The Costa del Sol resorts

West of Málaga – or more correctly, west of Málaga airport – the real **Costa del Sol** gets
going, and if you've never seen this level of touristic development it's quite a shock. These
are certainly not the kind of resorts you could envisage in Greece or even Portugal, with
their 1960s and 1970s hotel and apartment tower blocks. In recent years, there has been

a second wave of property development, this time villa homes and leisure complexes, funded by massive international investment. It's estimated that 300,000 foreigners now live on the Costa del Sol, the majority of them British and other northern Europeans, though custom marina developments like Puerto Banús have also attracted Arab money.

Approached in the right kind of spirit it is possible to have fun in **Torremolinos** and, at a price, in **Marbella**. But if you've come to Spain to be in Spain, or even just to forget what inner-city housing looks like, put on the shades and keep going at least until you reach Estepona.

Torremolinos

The approach to Torremolinos – easily done on the electric train from Málaga – is a rather depressing business. There are half a dozen beaches and stops, but it's a drab, soulless landscape of kitchenette apartments and half-finished developments.

TORREMOLINOS, to its enduring credit, is certainly different: a vast, grotesque parody of a seaside resort which in its own kitschy way is fascinating. This bizarre place, lined with sweeping (but crowded) beaches and infinite shopping arcades, crammed with (genuine) Irish pubs and (probably less genuine) real estate agents, has a large permanent expatriate population of British, Germans and Scandinavians. It's a weird mix, which, in addition to thousands of retired people, has attracted – due to a previous lack of extradition arrangements between Britain and Spain – an extraordinary concentration of British crooks. Torremolinos's social scene is strange, too, including, among the middle-of-the-road family discos, a thriving, pram-pushing, gay transvestite scene. All in all it's an intriguing blend of the smart and the squalid, bargains and rip-offs.

Practicalities

If any of these possibilities attracts you – or you're simply curious about the awfulness of the place – it's easy enough to **stay**. There are plenty of cheap *hostales* sandwiched between the highrise horrors: *Pensión Beatriz*, c/Peligros 4 (☎95 238 51 10; ③), and *Hostal Micaela*, c/Bajondillo 4 (☎95 238 33 10; ③), are both near the beach and fairly cheap. The resort's **campsite** (☎95 238 26 02) lies 3km east of the centre on the main Málaga–Cádiz highway, 500m from the sea; get there by taking the *cercanía* train to the Los Alamos stop or on bus *Línea B* from outside the *Irish Corner* bar in the central Plaza Costa del Sol. The **Turismo** in Plaza Picasso (daily 8am–3pm; ☎95 237 11 59) can provide more information on what accommodation's available.

The sheer competition between Torremolinos's **restaurants**, **clubs** and **bars** is so intense that if you're prepared to walk round and check a few prices you can have a pretty good night out on remarkably little. The more elegant part of the resort lies to the east at **La Carihuela**, where there's a decent beach, good seafood restaurants along the seafront and a pleasant *hostal*, *Prudencio*, Paseo Carmen 41 (☎95 238 14 52; ③).

Fuengirola

FUENGIROLA, half an hour along the train line from Torremolinos, is very slightly less developed and infinitely more staid. It's not so conspicuously ugly, but it is distinctly middle-aged and family-oriented. The huge, long beach has been divided up into restaurant-beach strips, each renting out lounge chairs and pedal-boats. At the far end is a windsurfing school.

Rooms are difficult to find in August, but at other times you could try the basic *Hostal Coca*, c/de Cruz 3 (☎95 247 41 89; ③), or *Hostal Italia* (☎95 247 41 93; ③), next door, which has rooms with bath, balcony and room-safe for not much more. Fuengirola's nearest **campsite**, *La Rosaleda* (☎95 246 01 91; open all year), lies just east of the town, reached by a turnoff near the junction of the N340 and the road to Mijas. For excellent **seafood**, try the mid-priced *Bar La Paz Garrido* on the Avenida de Mijas just north of the Plaza de la Constitución; alternatively, quantity is the gimmick at two "as much as you can eat for 750ptas" places on the seafront, *Versalles*, Paseo Maritimo 3, and *Las Palmeras* nearby.

Marbella and around

MARBELLA stands in considerable contrast, after another sequence of apartment-villa *urbanizaciones*, to most of what's come before. It is undisputedly the "quality resort" of the Costa del Sol, where restaurants and bars are more stylish and everything costs considerably more. It has the highest per capita income in Europe and more Rolls Royces than any European city apart from London (although many of the classy cars here are rumoured to have been stolen elsewhere and re-registered in Spain). In an ironic twist of history, there's been a massive return of Arabs to the area, especially since King Fahd of Saudi Arabia built a White House lookalike, complete with adjacent mosque, on the town's outskirts.

To be fair, it's all decidedly tasteful and the town has been spared the worst excesses of concrete architecture inflicted upon Torremolinos. Marbella also retains the greater part of its **old town** – set back a little from the sea and the new development. Centred on the Plaza de los Naranjos and still partially walled, the old town is hidden from the main road and easy to miss; to get there, turn left out of the bus station, walk straight for about 500m and then turn left again. Slowly, this original quarter is being bought up and turned into "quaint" clothes boutiques and restaurants, but this process isn't that far advanced. You can still sit in an ordinary bar in a small old square and look up beyond the whitewashed alleyways to the mountains of Ronda.

The truly rich don't stay in Marbella itself. They secrete themselves away in villas in the surrounding hills or lie around on phenomenally large and luxurious yachts at the marina and casino complex of **Puerto Banús**, 6km out of town towards San Pedro. If you're impoverished, this fact is worth noting as it's sometimes possible to find work scrubbing and repairing said yachts – and the pay can be very reasonable. As you'd expect, Puerto Banús has more than its complement of cocktail bars and seafood restaurants, most of them very good and very pricey.

Practicalities

You'll find Marbella's only budget **pensiones** in the old town – of which the lowest priced are *Hostal Juan*, c/Luna 18 (☎95 2779475; ③), and *Hostal Isabel*, c/Luna 24 (☎95 2771978; ②), both good and near the main road on the way in to town. At c/Trapiche 2 to the north of the old town, the *Albergue-Campamento Youth Hostel* (①) has even cheaper beds in double and four-person en-suite rooms and a **campsite** too, but is not quite so central. There are plenty of more expensive places, too: *Hostal Enriqueta*, c/los Caballeros 18 (☎95 2827552; ④), is comfortable and quiet, as is the charming *Hostal La Pilarica*, c/San Cristóbal 31 (☎95 2774252; ③), in a street lined with potted plants – the work of the enthusiastic residents. The best seaside **campsite** for the town is *Marbella Playa* (☎95 283 39 98), located, confusingly, 12km east of the centre with a good beach.

If you need help in finding a room it is probably worth calling in at the **Turismo** in Plaza de los Naranjos (Mon–Sat 9am–9pm; ☎95 282 35 50), if only for their town plan and list of addresses.

Estepona and beyond

The coast continues to be upmarket (or "money-raddled" as Laurie Lee put it) until you reach **ESTEPONA**, about 30km west, which is a more or less Spanish resort – inasmuch as that's possible round here. It lacks the enclosed hills that give Marbella character, but the hotel and apartment blocks which sprawl along the front are restrained in size, and there's space to breathe. The fine sand beach has been enlivened a little by a promenade studded with flowers and palms, and, away from the seafront, the old town is very pretty, with cobbled alleyways and two delightful plazas.

The **fish market** is definitely worth seeing: Estepona has the biggest fishing fleet west of Málaga, and the daily dawn ritual in the port, where the returning fleets auction off the fish they've just caught, is worth getting up early for – be there at 6am, since by 7am it's all over.

From May onward, Estepona's **bullfighting** season gets underway in a modern bullring reminiscent of a Henry Moore sculpture. At the beginning of July, the *Fiesta y Feria* week transforms the place, bringing out whole families in flamenco-style garb.

Beyond Estepona, 8km along the coast, there's a minor road leading into the hills to **CASARES**, one of the classic Andaluz "White Towns" (see p.230). In keeping with the genre, it clings tenaciously to a steep hillside below a castle, and has attracted its fair share of arty types and expatriates. But it remains comparatively little known; bus connections are just about feasible for a day-trip.

Further west, 3km inland from the village of Manilva, are some remarkably well-preserved **Roman sulphur baths**. If you want to partake of these health-giving waters you'll have to be prepared to dive into a subterranean cavern, and to put up with the overpowering stench of sulphur, which clings to your swimwear for weeks.

The beaches beyond Estepona have greyish sands (a trademark of the Costa del Sol that always seems surprising – you have to round the corner at Tarifa before you meet yellow sand) and there are more greyish developments, before the road turns inland towards San Roque and Gibraltar.

Estepona practicalities

Estepona's **bus station** is on Avda. de Espana, to the west of the centre behind the seafront. The efficient and centrally located **Turismo** (Mon–Fri 9.30am–9pm, Sat & Sun 9.30am–1.30pm; ☎95 280 09 13) is at Avda. San Lorenzo 1, near the seafront. For **rooms**, *Hostal El Pilar* (☎95 280 00 18; ③), on the pretty Plaza Las Flores, and the friendly *Pensión San Miguel*, c/Terraza 16 (☎95 280 26 16; ②), a little to the west, with its own bar, are both good bets. Estepona's nearest **campsite** is *La Chullera III* (☎95 289 01 96; open all year), 8km south of town, just beyond the village of San Luís de Sabanillas. The town is well-provided with **places to eat**, among them a bunch of excellent *freidurías* and *marisquerías* along c/Terraza, the main street which cuts through the centre. There's an excellent *churrería* towards the southern end of c/Mayor (one block back from, and parallel to, the promenade) – get there before 11am as they sell out early. Another good place for buying food is the covered **market** in the mornings. If you're sufficiently motivated, you could also head out of town **to eat**. South along the coast past the new Puerto de la Duquesa marina, is the tiny fishing village of **La Duquesa El Castillo**, which has two excellent restaurants, *Restaurante Antonio* being the better of the two, with an excellent-value *tapas* bar attached.

San Roque and La Línea

Situated 35km beyond Estapona in Cádiz province, **SAN ROQUE** was founded by the people of Gibraltar fleeing the British, who had captured the Rock and looted their homes and churches in 1704. They expected to return within months, since the troops had taken the garrison in the name of the Archduke Carlos of Austria, whose rights Britain had been promoting in the War of the Spanish Succession. But it was the British flag that was raised on the conquered territory – and so it has remained.

The **"Spanish-British frontier"** is 8km away at LA LÍNEA, obscured by San Roque's huge oil refinery. After sixteen years of (Spanish-imposed) isolation, the gates were finally reopened in February 1985, and crossing is now a routine affair of passport stamping. Be warned that if you're planning a stay in Gibraltar, accommodation there is very expensive and in summer the few budget places available are in tremendous demand; La Línea is more realistic, although even here prices have risen and it's now more expensive than neighbouring towns. There are no sights as such; it's just a fishing village which has exploded in size due to the jobs in Gibraltar and Algeciras.

Practicalities

At the heart of La Línea is the large, modern Plaza de la Constitución, where you'll find the *Correos*. The **Turismo** (Mon–Fri 8am–3pm, Sat 9am–1pm; ☎956 769950) and **bus station** are both on Avda. 20 Abril, just off the plaza; the Turismo's town map labelling *hostales* is useful. Off the east side of the square an archway leads to the smaller, pedestrianized Plaza Cruz de Herrera, with lots of reasonably priced **bars** and **restaurants**, among which *La Nueva Mesón Jerezana* does good *fino* and *jamón*. Slightly north lies c/Real, the main pedestrianized shopping street and another area with plenty of bars and cafés: just off the north side is *La Venta*, c/Dr Villar 19, which does a good-value *menú* and an excellent paella, while to the south of c/Real at Avda. de España 22 is an excellent *marisquería*, *Bar Aquarium*. C/Clavel, signposted from the main plaza to the Plaza de Toros, has more options: *Bar Alhambra* halfway down is basic and excellent value. The **market**, north of c/Real, is also worth a visit for food.

The same areas have most of the budget **hostales**. The friendly *La Campana*, c/Carboneras 3, just off Plaza de la Constitutión (☎956 173059; ③) is clean, and has rooms with bath and TV; if this is full, *Hotel-Restaurante Carlos* (☎956 762135; ③) is almost opposite with the same facilities. Slightly further north, *Hostal Florida*, c/Sol 37 (☎956 171300; ③), is another possibility, with a good-value restaurant downstairs. In the Plaza de Iglesia, at the end of c/Real, the basic *La Giralda* (②) has a friendly owner, free hot showers and a hotplate in the kitchen for preparing simple meals.

Local **buses** from La Línea to Algeciras take thirty minutes, with departures every hour. The closest main-line **train station** is San Roque-La Línea, 12km away, from where you can pick up a train to Ronda and beyond. Buses link La Línea with Sevilla (daily; 4hr), and as far as Ayamonte on the Portuguese border (7hr).

Gibraltar

GIBRALTAR's interest is essentially its novelty: the genuine appeal of the strange, looming physical presence of its rock, and the dubious one of its preservation as one of Britain's last remaining colonies. For most of its history it has existed in a limbo between two worlds without being fully part of either, which makes it a curious place to visit, not least to witness the bizarre process of its opening to mass tourism from the Costa del Sol. Ironically, this threatens both to destroy Gibraltar's highly individual hybrid society and at the same time to make it much more British, after the fashion of the expatriate communities and huge resorts of the Costa. In recent years the economic boom Gibraltar enjoyed throughout the 1980s, following the re-opening of

PHONING GIBRALTAR

From Spain: dial ☎9567 + number.
From other countries: dial international access code, then ☎350 (country code for Gibraltar) + number.

the border with Spain, has started to wane, and the likely future of the colony – whether its population agrees to it or not – is almost certain to involve closer ties with Spain.

Arrival, information and orientation

The town and rock have a necessarily simple layout. **Main Street** (La Calle Real) runs for most of the town's length, a couple of blocks back from the port; from the frontier it's a short bus ride or about a ten-minute walk. If you have a **car**, don't attempt to bring it to Gibraltar – the queues at the border are always atrocious, and parking is a nightmare. Use the underground car parks in La Línea, 3km away, instead (it's worth paying for the extra security) and either catch the **bus** (20min past or 10min to the hour) from the border, or walk. If you do join the queue to drive in, ignore anyone who tries to sell you a "visa" – it's usually an old bus ticket.

In and around Main Street are most of the shops, together with most of the British-style pubs and hotels. For information, the main **tourist office** (Mon–Fri 10am–6pm, Sat 10am–2pm; ☎74805) is in Cathedral Square, and there are also offices at the airport, the Gibraltar Museum, Market Place and the Waterport coach park. The John Mackintosh Hall at the south end of Main Street is a useful resource – it's the cultural centre, with exhibitions and a library. The local paper is the *Gibraltar Chronicle*, a stultifyingly parochial daily with little of interest to visitors. Much of Gibraltar – with the exception of the cut-price booze shops – closes down on Saturday afternoon, but the tourist sites remain open, and this can be a quiet time to visit.

The **currency** used here is the **Gibraltar pound** (the same value as the British pound, but different notes and coins); if you pay in pesetas while in Gibraltar, you generally fork out about five percent more. It's best to change your money once you arrive in Gibraltar, since the exchange rate is slightly higher than in Spain and there's no commission charged. Gibraltar pounds can be hard to change in Spain.

Accommodation

Shortage of space on the rock means that **places to stay** are at a premium, and you're much better off visiting on day trips from Algeciras (buses on the hour and half-hour; 30min) or La Línea. The only remotely budget beds are at the *Toc H Hostel* on

WORKING IN GIBRALTAR

If you're staying around a while, Gibraltar is not a bad place to **look for work**, although competition abounds, so be persistent, and if you're working officially, taxes are high. Gibraltar Radio broadcasts vacancies on Tuesday at about noon, but door-to-door (or site-to-site) footslogging is vital. Another possibility is crewing work on a yacht – look at the noticeboard in the chandler's store on Marina Bay, or put an ad there yourself; at the end of summer the yacht marina fills up with boats heading for the **Canaries**, **Madeira** and the **West Indies** and many take on crew to work in exchange for passage.

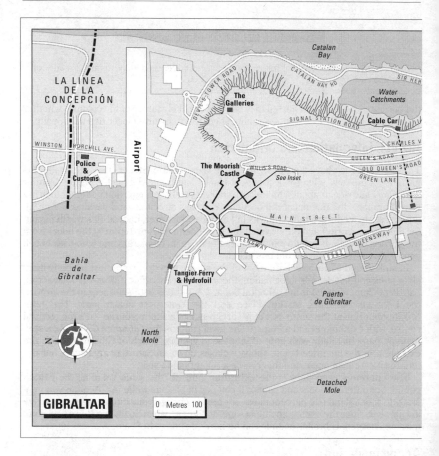

Line Wall Rd (☎73431; about £5 a person) – and these are none too comfortable and almost always occupied by long-term residents – or the tiny *Seruya's Guest House* at 92 Irish Town (☎73220; about £15 a double), which is also invariably full. There are also dorm beds at the basic **youth hostel** at the Montagu Bastion, Line Wall Rd (☎51106; about £10). Otherwise, you're going to have to pay normal British hotel prices: the next step up includes the *Queen's Hotel* on Boyd St (☎74000, fax 40030), the *Bristol* in Cathedral Square (☎76800, fax 77613), or the *Cannon Hotel* on Cannon Lane (☎ & fax 51711), all charging around £30–60 for a double room.

If this tempts you to find a bit of sand to bed down on, forget it: no camping is allowed and if you're caught sleeping rough or inhabiting abandoned bunkers, you are more than likely to be arrested and fined. This law is enforced by Gibraltar and Ministry of Defence police, and raids of the beaches are regular.

Around the Rock

From near the end of Main Street you can hop on a **cable car** (Mon–Sat 9.30am–6pm, last trip down 5.45pm; £4.90 return) which will carry you up to the summit – **The Top**

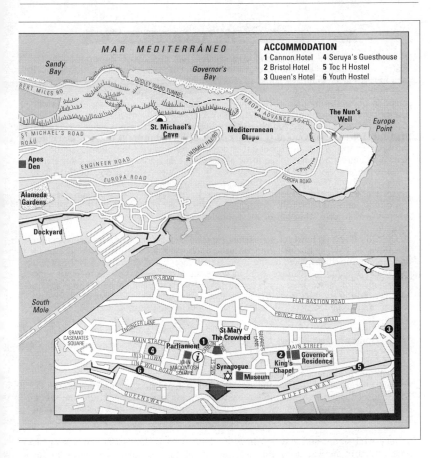

of the Rock as it's logically known – via **Apes' Den** halfway up, a fairly reliable viewing point to see the tailless monkeys and hear the guides explain their legend. From The Top you can look over to the Atlas Mountains and down to the town, its elaborate water catchment system cut into the side of the rock, and ponder whether it's worth heading for one of the beaches. From the Apes' Den it's an easy walk south along Queens Road to **Saint Michael's Cave** (free entry with cable car ticket), an immense natural cavern which led ancient people to believe the rock was hollow and gave rise to its old name of *Mons Calpe* (Hollow Mountain). The cave was used during the last war as a bomb-proof military hospital and nowadays hosts occasional concerts. If you're adventurous you can arrange at the tourist office for a guided visit to Lower Saint Michael's Cave, a series of chambers going deeper down and ending in an underground lake.

Although you can take the cable car both ways, it's an interesting walk up via Willis's Road to visit the **Tower of Homage**. Dating from the fourteenth century, this is the most visible surviving remnant of the old **Moorish Castle**. Further up you'll find the **Upper Galleries**, blasted out of the rock during the Great Siege of 1779–82, in order to point guns down at the Spanish lines. To walk down, take the **Mediterranean Steps** – they're

BRITISH SOVEREIGNTY IN GIBRALTAR

Sovereignty of the Rock (a land area smaller than the city of Algeciras across the water) will doubtless eventually return to Spain, but at present neither side is in much of a hurry. For Britain it's a question of precedent – Gibraltar is in too similar a situation to the Falklands/Malvinas, which conflict pushed the Spanish into postponing an initial frontier-opening date in 1982. For Spain, too, there are unsettling parallels with the *presidios* (Spanish enclaves) on the Moroccan coast at Ceuta and Melilla – both at present part of Andalucía. Nonetheless, the British presence is in practice waning and the British foreign office clearly wants to steer Gibraltar towards a new, harmonious relationship with Spain. To this end they are running down the significance of the military base, and now only a token force of less than a hundred British troops remain – most of these working in a top-secret hi-tech bunker buried deep inside the Rock from where the Royal Navy monitors the sea traffic through the straits (accounting for a quarter of the world movement of all shipping). The Royal Naval Dockyard has now been replaced with Gibrepair, a commercial ship repair yard which, in the long term, should lead to diversification of the Gibraltar economy and reduce dependence on Britain.

The Gibraltarians, however, are firmly opposed to a return to **Spanish control** of the Rock. In 1967, just before Franco closed the border in the hope of forcing a quick agreement, the colony voted on the issue – rejecting it by 12,138 votes to 44. Most people would probably sympathize with that vote – against a Spain that was then still a dictatorship – but more than thirty years have gone by, Spanish democracy is now secure, and the arguments are becoming increasingly tenuous. Despite its impressive claims to law and order, Gibraltar is no model society either; its dirty jobs, for instance, are nearly all done by Moroccans, who were recruited en masse to replace Spanish workers after the border between Gibraltar and Spain was closed by Franco in 1969, and who have always been treated as second-class citizens. This was underlined recently by tough new immigration laws stripping them of residence, pension and health care rights, which were upheld by the colony's supreme court, despite appeals against "ethnic cleansing".

May 1996 saw a change in the trend of internal **politics**, with the defeat of Joe Bossano's Labour government (following two previous landslide victories). Voters, concerned that Bossano's pugnacious anti-Spanish stance jeopardized a viable economic

not very well signposted and you have to climb over O'Hara's Battery, a very steep descent most of the way down the east side, turning the southern corner of the Rock. You'll pass through the Jews' Gate and into Engineer Road. From here, return to town through the Alameda Gardens and the **Trafalgar Cemetery**, overgrown and evocative, with a good line in imperial epitaphs. The grand tour of the Rock takes a half to a full day, and all sites on it are open from 10am to 7pm in summer, 10am to 5.30pm in winter; if you visit all the attractions, buy a reduced-price ticket which includes the cave as well.

Back **in town**, incorporated into the **Gibraltar Museum** (Mon–Fri 10am–6pm, Sat 10am–2pm; £2), two well-preserved and beautiful fourteenth-century **Moorish Baths**. This, along with the **casino**, and the **miniature golf**, is about the extent of it. Gibraltar has plans to reclaim an area equivalent to that of the present town from the sea, and is currently doing feasibility surveys on pumping up sand from the seabed. But at present there is just the one tiny fishing village at **Catalan Bay**, which is where you'll find the **beach** with most character. The inhabitants of the village like to think of themselves as very distinct from the townies on the other side of the Rock. About 48km of recent tunnels, or **galleries**, have been bored through the Rock for military purposes – these are now being adapted to help solve the territory's traffic-flow crisis brought on by the extraordinary surplus of cars.

future in which Spain must realistically play a role, elected a new Social Democratic administration led by Peter Caruana. However, whilst Caruana talked of opening up a more **constructive dialogue with Spain** during the election campaign, once in control he soon began to voice the traditional Gibraltarian paranoia. His stance has caused some dismay in Madrid and London, who were both behind Spain's offer in 1997 to give the colony the status of a Spanish autonomous region (similar to that of the Basques and Catalans) inside the Spanish state. The proposal was rejected out of hand by Caruana. Caruana has also been urged by Britain (under pressure from Spain) to crack down on the smuggling of contraband cigarettes over the Spanish border and to curb the activities of the Rock's 24,000 "offshore" financial institutions – many of which Spain claims are guilty of drugs and money-laundering.

What most outsiders don't realize about the political situation is that the Gibraltarians feel very vulnerable, caught between the interests of two big states; they are well aware that both governments' concerns are primarily strategic and political rather than with the wishes of the people of Gibraltar. Until very recently people were sent over from Britain to fill all the top civil service and Ministry of Defence jobs, a practice which, to a lesser degree, still continues – the present Governor is Richard Luce, a former British cabinet minister. Large parts of the Rock are no-go areas for "natives"; the South District in particular being taken up by military facilities. Local people also protest about the Royal Navy nuclear-powered submarines which dock regularly at the naval base, and secrecy surrounds the issue of whether nuclear warheads and/or chemical and biological weapons are stored in the arsenal, probably deep inside the Rock itself.

Yet Gibraltarians still cling to British status – perhaps simply because they have known nothing other than British rule since the former population was displaced – and all their institutions are modelled on English lines. Contrary to popular belief, they are of neither mainly Spanish nor British blood, but an ethnic mix descended from Genoese, Portuguese, Spanish, Minorcan, Jewish, Maltese and British ancestors. English is the **official language**, but more commonly spoken is what sounds to an outsider like perfect Andalucian Spanish. It is in fact **llanito**, an Andalucían dialect with borrowed words which reflect its diverse origins; ironically – in view of most of the colony's antipathy to their Iberian neighbour – only a Spaniard from the south can tell a Gibraltarian from an Andalucían.

Eating and drinking

Restaurants are far more plentiful than places to stay, though by Spanish standards they are still relatively expensive: pub snacks or fish and chips are reliable standbys. Main Street is crowded with touristy places, among which *Smiths Fish and Chip Shop*, at no. 295 near the Convent, is worth a try – but avoid the curries. Other good choices are the *Penny Farthing* on King Street, always busy for home-cooked food at reasonable prices (take-away too); and *La Cantina*, a slightly more expensive Mexican place. Decent pasta in all its varieties is served up at *Buddies Pasta Casa*, on Cannon Lane. The *Market Café* in the public market and *Splendid Bar* in George's Lane both serve inexpensive meals and *tapas*. *Sacarrello's Coffee House* in Irish Town is more upmarket, but you can just have a drink here and look at their collection of old postcards upstairs showing the development of Gibraltar.

Pubs all tend to mimic traditional English styles (and prices), the difference being that they are open all day and often into the wee hours. For pub food, the *Royal Calpe*, Main Street, *Calpe Hounds*, Cornwalls Lane, and *Clipper*, Irish Town, are among the best. Of the obvious pubs grouped together on Main Street, the *Royal Calpe* has a beer garden, and *The Horseshoe* and the *Gibraltar Arms* have tables outside; places on Main

Street, however, tend to be rowdy – full of squaddies and visiting sailors at night. For a quieter alternative, try the *Captain's Cabin* in John Mackintosh Square or the *Cannon Bar* in Cannon Lane. The *Star Bar*, 12 Parliament Lane, off the west side of Main Street near the Post Office, is reputedly Gibraltar's oldest and a favourite hang-out of Lord Nelson when it traded under its original name, *La Estrella*.

Onward travel

One decidedly functional attraction of Gibraltar is its role as a **port for Morocco**. The timetable is erratically subject to weather conditions even at the best of times (the trip is invariably very rough), and the faster hydrofoil and catamaran sailings no longer run. The only service currently operating is a ferry to Tangier on Monday and Wednesday at 7.30am and Friday at 6.30pm, with the return on Sunday and Tuesday at 3pm and Friday at 9am; the trip takes about three hours. Tickets cost around £18 one-way or £30 return, but things tend to change frequently and you should confirm timetables and ticket prices with the operator, Tourafrica, in the International Commercial Centre, Casemates Square (☎77666, fax 76754). By plane, GB Airways has services to and from Casablanca (a 1hr flight) running on Monday, Thursday and Friday; in winter there's a reduced service. Up-to-date information and plane tickets can be had from Bland Travel (☎77012, fax 76189) in Irish Town, who also sell **RENFE** tickets for travelling on through Spain.

Algeciras

ALGECIRAS occupies the far side of the bay to Gibraltar, spewing out smoke and pollution in the direction of the Rock. The last town of the Spanish Mediterranean, it must once have been an elegant resort; today it's unabashedly a port and industrial centre, its suburbs extending on all sides, and almost all construction is of modern vintage. When Franco closed the border with Gibraltar at La Línea it was Algeciras that he decided to develop to absorb the Spanish workers formerly employed in the British naval dockyards, thus breaking the area's dependence on the Rock.

Most travellers are scathing about the city's ugliness, and unless you're waiting for a bus or train, or heading for Morocco, there's admittedly little reason to stop. Yet some touch of colour is added by the groups of Moroccans in transit, dressed in flowing jellabas and yellow slippers, and lugging unbelievable amounts of possessions (see box). Algeciras has a real port atmosphere, and even passing through it's hard to resist the urge to get on a boat south, if only for a couple of days in Tangier. Once you start to explore, you'll also discover that the old town has some very attractive corners which seem barely to have changed in fifty years, especially around the Plaza Alta. The number of people passing through also guarantees endless possibilities for food and drink.

Practicalities

If you're waiting for a morning ferry, or want to stay awhile, Algeciras has plenty of budget **hostales** and **pensiones** in the grid of streets between the port and the train station. There are several in c/Duque de Almodóvar, c/José Santacana and c/Rafael de Muro. Try *Levante*, c/Duque de Almodóvar 21 (☎956 651505; ③), *Vizcaíno*, c/José Santacana 9 (☎956 655756; ②), or the more comfortable *González*, c/José Santacana 7

MOROCCANS IN ALGECIRAS

It's easy to take a romantic view of the exotic hustle and bustle in the port area, but there's a miserable story behind some of it. Algeciras is the main port for **Moroccan migrant workers**, who drive home every year during their holidays from the factories, farms and mines of France, Germany and the Low Countries. Half a million cross Spain in the six weeks from the end of June to the beginning of August, often becoming victims of all levels of racial discrimination (they are still referred to as *los Moros*), from being ripped off to being violently attacked and robbed.

(☎956 652843; ③). The romantic *Hotel Anglo-Hispano*, Avda. Villanueva 7 (☎956 572590; ④), near the port, has a marble-tiled lobby dripping with faded grandeur. Algeciras's luxurious new **youth hostel**, Ctra. Nacional 340 (☎956 679060; ①), has pool, tennis courts and double rooms with bath, but lies 8km west of town on the Tarifa road; buses heading for Tarifa will drop you there if you ask. Should you have trouble finding space, pick up a town plan and check out the list in the **Turismo**, c/Juan de la Cierva (Mon–Fri 9.30am–1.30pm & 5–8pm, Sat 9.30am–1.30pm; ☎956 572636 English spoken), towards the river and train line from the port. Prices tend to go up dramatically in midseason, but lots of simple *casas de huéspedes* cluster round the market.

The port area also has plenty of **places to eat**. Across the train line from the Turismo and invariably crowded is the good value *Casa Gil* at c/Sigismundo Moret 2. Fifty metres further along the same street, *Casa Sánchez*, at the corner of c/Río, is another good place with a *menú*, and they also have **rooms** (②). The **markets** are useful places to buy food, as well as fascinating places to visit; the main one is held on Plaza Palma, down by the port. In the centre, especially around the Plaza Baja, are plenty of excellent *tapas* bars. Plaza Alta is noticeably more expensive.

Onward travel

If you are tempted to pop over to Morocco, it's easily enough done: in the summer, there are eight **crossings to Tangier** each day (2hr 30min, or 1hr 30min with a fast ferry), and six to the Spanish *presidio* of **Ceuta** (1hr 30min), little more than a Spanish Gibraltar with a brisk business in duty-free goods, but a relatively painless way to enter Morocco. Scheduled catamaran and hydrofoil services, including all-inclusive day-trips to Tangiers, are suspended at the time of writing, and the latest information on these and other crossings can be obtained from Viájes Transafric (see below), Transmediterranea (☎956 663850), Comarit (☎956 633997) or the Turismo (see above). Tickets (about 3200ptas one-way to Tangiers) are available at scores of travel agents all along the waterside and on most approach roads, and include the reliable Viájes Transafric, Avda. Marina 4 (☎956 654311).

Wait till Tangier – or if you're going via Ceuta, Tetouan – before buying any Moroccan currency; rates in the embarkation building kiosks are very poor. Make sure that your ticket is for the next ferry, and beware the ticket sellers who congregate near the dock entrance wearing official Ceuta/Tangier badges: they add a whopping "commission" to the normal price of a ticket. InterRail/Eurail card holders are entitled to a twenty percent discount on the standard ferry price; if you have trouble getting this, go to the official sales desk in the embarkation building.

At Algeciras the **train line** begins again, heading north to Ronda, Córdoba and Madrid. The route to Ronda – one of the best journeys in Andalucía – is detailed below; there are six departures a day. For Madrid (and Paris) there's a night express, currently leaving at 11pm, and also Linebus/Iberbus coaches to Paris and London. For Málaga, hourly **buses** leave from a bar on the main seafront avenue, just back from the port; from here too, there are less frequent, direct connections to Granada. Buses to Barcelona leave from outside the harbour offices, but the journey is appallingly slow at 21 hours, with a change in Málaga. For Tarifa, Cádiz, Sevilla and most other destinations you'll need the **main bus station**, in c/San Bernardo, behind the port, next to *Hotel Octavio* and just short of the **train station**: to get there follow the train tracks. The bus to La Línea also goes every half-hour from here.

Ronda and the White Towns

Andalucía is dotted with small, brilliantly whitewashed settlements – the **Pueblos Blancos** or "White Towns" – most often straggling up hillsides towards a castle or towered church. Places like **Mijas**, up behind Fuengirola, are solidly on the tourist trail, but even here the natural beauty is undeniable. All of them look great from a distance, though many are rather less interesting on arrival. Perhaps the best lie in a roughly triangular area between Málaga, Algeciras and Sevilla; at its centre, in a region of wild mountainous beauty, is the spectacular town of **Ronda**.

To Ronda from the coast

Of several possible approaches to Ronda from the coast, the stunningly scenic route up from Algeciras is the most rewarding – and worth going out of your way to experience. From Málaga, most of the buses to Ronda follow the coastal highway to San Pedro before turning into the mountains: dramatic enough, but rather a bleak route, with no villages and only limited views of the sombre rock face of the Serranía (an alternative route, via Álora and Ardales, is far more attractive). The train ride up from Málaga is better, with three connecting services daily, including a convenient 6pm departure after the last bus leaves.

The **Algeciras route** – via Gaucín – is possible by either bus or train, or, if you've time and energy, can be walked in four or five days. En route, you're always within reach of a river and there's a series of hill towns, each one visible from the next, to provide targets for the day. Casares is almost on the route, but more easily reached from Estepona (see p.221).

Castellar de la Frontera

The first "White Town" on the route proper is **CASTELLAR DE LA FRONTERA**, a bizarre village within a castle, whose population, in accord with some grandiose scheme, was moved downriver in 1971 to the "new" town of La Almoraima. The relocation was subsequently dropped and a few villagers moved back to their old houses, but most of them were taken over by retired hippies (mainly German, mainly affluent). The result didn't entirely work, with suspicion from the locals and hostile exclusivity from some of the new arrivals fuelling tensions which remain today. Plans to rebuild the town into a tourist centre, complete with *parador*, appear to have ground to a halt. There are a couple of German-run bars, but the village has a brooding, claustrophobic atmosphere, and you may want to move on after a brief look around. The only accommodation, *Hostal El Pinar*, c/León Esquirel 4 (☎956 693022; ②), is in the new town.

Jimena de la Frontera and Gaucín

JIMENA DE LA FRONTERA is a far larger and more open hill town, rising to a grand Moorish castle with a triple-gateway entrance. There are several bars, a beautiful old **fonda** (which has no sign – ask for the *Casa María*, c/Sevilla 36; ①), and the more expensive *Hostal El Anon* (④) on c/Consuelo, as well as another *hostal* at the train station, a little way out of town. The best place for **food** is *Restaurante-Bar Cuenca*, Avenida de los Deportes, on the way into town, which does wonderful *tapas* and meals.

Beyond Jimena it's a sixteen-kilometre climb through woods and olive groves to reach **GAUCÍN**, though there are bars halfway at the hamlet of San Pablo. Gaucín, almost a mountain village, commands tremendous views (to Gibraltar and the Moroccan coast on a very clear day) and makes a great place to stop over. Its charming *fonda*, the *Nacional* (c/San Juan de Dios 8), closed its doors a couple of years back after 125 years, but is steeped in history and still serves **meals**. **Rooms** and food are also to be had at *Hostal Moncada*, c/Luís Armiñian (☎95 2151156; ②), next to the *gasolinera* as you enter the village from Jimena (get a room at the back for a view). You can reach the village by bus, but far more rewarding is the thirteen-kilometre, mostly uphill, walk from its **train station**. Though it's now known as Gaucín, this station is actually at El Colmenar, on the fringes of the Cortés nature reserve: if you need to rest up before the trek (getting on for 3hr) there's a *hostal, Bar-Restaurante Flores* (☎95 215 30 26; ②) and several bars here. Should you chicken out, the *hostal* can arrange a taxi ride (about 2000ptas one way).

The train line between Gaucín and Ronda passes through a handful of tiny villages. En route, you can stop off at the station of Benaoján-Montejaque: from here it's an hour's trek to the prehistoric **Cueva de la Pileta** (see p.234). From Benaoján, Ronda is just three stops (and thirty minutes) down the line.

Ronda

Rising amid a ring of dark, angular mountains, the full natural drama of **RONDA** is best appreciated as you enter the town. Built on an isolated ridge of the sierra, it's split in half by a gaping river gorge, **El Tajo**, which drops sheer for 130m on three sides. Still more spectacular, the gorge is spanned by a stupendous eighteenth-century arched bridge, the **Puente Nuevo**, while tall whitewashed houses lean from its precipitous edges.

Much of the attraction of Ronda lies in this extraordinary view, or in walking down by the Río Guadalévin, following one of the donkey tracks through the rich green valley. Bird-watchers should look out for the lesser kestrels, rare in northern Europe, nesting in and launching themselves from the cliffs beneath the Alameda park. Lower down you can spot crag martins. The town itself is also of interest and, surprisingly, has sacrificed little of its character to the flow of day-trippers from the Costa del Sol.

Arrival, information and accommodation

Ronda's **train** and **bus stations** are both in the Mercadillo quarter to the northeast of the bullring. Trains arrive on Avenida Andalucía, a ten-minute walk or easy bus ride from the centre, and all the bus companies use the terminal close by on Plaza Redondo. The **Turismo** (Mon–Fri 10am–2pm; ☎95 287 12 72) is at the northern end of Plaza de España, and can help with accommodation.

All the **places to stay** are also in the Mercadillo quarter, within easy walking distance of the central Plaza de España.

Pensión La Española, c/José Aparicio 3 (☎95 287 10 52). Cosy refurbished rooms with bath in the alley behind the Turismo, some with amazing views, plus a terrace restaurant. ⑤.

Parador de Ronda, Plaza de España (☎95 287 75 00, fax 95 287 81 88). Ronda's spanking new *parador* has spectacular views overlooking El Tajo, plus a pool, terrace bar and restaurant, and all the facilities you'd expect from a hotel in this category. ⑦.

Hotel Polo, Mariano Soubirón 8 (☎95 287 24 47, fax 95 287 24 49). Luxurious option if you're feeling extravagant. ⑥.

Pensión La Purísima, c/Sevilla 10 (☎95 287 10 50). Friendly, good-value *pensión*. ②.

Ronda Sol, c/Cristo 11 (☎95 287 44 97). Decent, low-priced option, near the intersection with c/Sevilla. ②.

Hotel Royal, c/Virgen de la Paz 42 (☎95 287 11 41, fax 95 287 81 32). Comfortable accommodation opposite the Alameda. ④.

Hostal San Francisco, c/Cabrera-Prim 18 (☎95 287 32 99). At the end of c/Sevilla and just off Plaza Carmen Abela, this *hostal* is excellent value, and all rooms come with bath. ②.

Hostal Virgen del Rocío, c/Nueva 18 (☎95 287 74 25). Pleasant small *hostal* offering rooms with bath, just off the east side of the Plaza de España. ③.

The Town

Ronda divides into three parts: on the near (northwest) side of the gorge, where you'll arrive, is the largely modern **Mercadillo** quarter. Across the bridge is the old Moorish town, the **Ciudad**, and its **San Francisco** suburb.

The **Ciudad** retains intact its Moorish plan and a great many of its houses, interspersed with a number of fine Renaissance mansions. It is so intricate a maze that you can do little else but wander at random. However, at some stage, make your way across the bridge and along the c/Santo Domingo, also known as c/Marqués de Parada, which winds round to the left. At no. 17 is the somewhat arbitrarily named **Casa del Rey Moro**, an early eighteenth-century mansion built on Moorish foundations. The house has recently been opened to the public with a stiff entrance fee (daily 10am–7pm; 500ptas), and from its garden a remarkable underground stairway, the *Mina*, descends to the river; these 365 steps (which can be slippery after rain), guaranteeing a water supply in times of siege, were cut by Christian slaves in the fourteenth century.

Farther down the same street is the **Palacio del Marqués de Salvatierra**, a splendid Renaissance mansion with an oddly primitive, half-grotesque frieze of Adam and Eve on its portal; the house is still used by the family but can usually be visited (Mon–Wed, Fri & Sat 11am–2pm & 5–7pm, Sun 11am–2pm; mildly interesting guided tour for 300ptas). Just down the hill you reach the two old town bridges – the **Puente Viejo** of 1616 and the single-span Moorish **Puente de San Miguel** – and nearby, on the southeast bank of the river, are the distinctive hump-shaped cupolas and bizarre glass roof-windows of the old **Baños Árabes** (Tues–Sat 9.30am–1.30pm & 4–7pm, Sun 10.30am–1pm; free). Dating from the thirteenth century, and wonderfully preserved, the barrel-vaulted ceiling and brickwork octagonal pillars, supporting horseshoe arches, underline the sophistication of the period.

At the centre of the Ciudad quarter stands the cathedral church of **Santa María Mayor** (daily 10am–8pm; 200ptas), originally the Arab town's Friday mosque. Externally it's a graceful combination of Moorish, Gothic and Renaissance styles with the belfry built on top of the old minaret. The interior is decidedly less interesting, but you can see an arch covered with Arabic calligraphy, and just in front of the current street door, a part of the old Arab *mihrab*, or prayer niche, has been exposed. Across the square – perhaps the finest in Ronda – is the **Casa de Mondragón**, probably the real palace of the Moorish kings (Mon–Fri 10am–7pm, Sat & Sun 10am–3pm; 200ptas). Inside, three of the patios preserve original stucco work and there's a magnificent carved ceiling, as well as a museum covering local archeology and aspects of Moorish Ronda.

Near the end of the Ciudad are the ruins of the **Alcázar**, destroyed by the French in 1809 ("from sheer love of destruction", according to Richard Ford), and now partially occupied by a school. Once it was virtually impregnable – as indeed was this whole fortress capital, which ruled an independent and isolated Moorish kingdom until 1485, just seven years before the fall of Granada – now it's full of litter and stray sheep.

The principal gate of the town, through which passed the Christian conquerors (led personally by Fernando), stands to the southeast of the Alcázar at the entrance to the suburb of San Francisco.

The **Mercadillo** quarter, which grew up in the wake of the Christian conquest, is of comparatively little interest, with just a couple of buildings worth a quick look. The first is a remarkably preserved inn where Miguel Cervantes once slept, the sixteenth-century **Posada de las Ánimas** (also known as the Hogar del Pensionista) in c/Cecilia, the oldest building in the quarter. The other is the **bullring** (10am–8pm; 300ptas), close by the Plaza de España and the beautiful cliff-top *paseo* from which you get good views of the old and new bridges. Ronda played a leading part in the development of bullfighting and was the birthplace of the modern *corridas* (tournaments). The ring, built in 1781, is one of the earliest in Spain; at its September *feria*, *corridas* take place in eighteenth-century costume, and the fight season here is one of the country's most important. You can visit the bullring to wander around the arena, and there's a museum inside.

The Puento Nuevo bridge's bar (now closed) was originally the town prison and last saw use during the Civil War, when Ronda was the site of some of the south's most vicious massacres. Hemingway, in *For Whom the Bell Tolls*, recorded how prisoners were thrown alive into the gorge. These days, Ronda remains a major military garrison post and houses much of the Spanish Africa Legion, Franco's old crack regiment, who can be seen wandering around town in their tropical green coats and tasselled fezes. They have a mean reputation.

Eating and drinking

Most of the bargain **restaurants** are grouped round the far end of the Plaza del Socorro, though there are also some to be found near the Plaza de España.

Bar-Restaurant Royal, c/Virgen de la Paz 42. Above the bullring and opposite the Alameda, serving up *platos combinados* and a *ménu*. They also do *tapas* and have a terrace.

Bodega La Giralda, c/Nueva 19. Traditional *tapas* in a great setting.

Café Alba, c/Espinel 44. Piping hot *churros* and delicious breakfast coffee.

Doña Pepa, Plaza del Socorro. Family-run establishment with a separate cafeteria-bar serving *bocadillos* and freshly-squeezed orange juice.

Don Miguel, Plaza de España. Good restaurant with *rondeño* specialities, a *menú* and a terrace offering a marvellous view of the Tajo.

Hotel Polo, Mariano Soubirón 8 (☎95 287 24 47). Pricey but excellent restaurant.

Marisquería Paco, Plaza del Socorro 8. Fresh seafood and good *tapas*, washed down with a beer at tables on the square.

Peking, c/Los Remedios 1. Reasonably priced Chinese food, near the Plaza de España.

La Rosalejo, c/Borrego 7. Off the northeast corner of the Plaza del Socorro, this is another good bar with a wide range of *tapas*.

Around Ronda

Ronda makes an excellent base for exploring the superb countryside in the immediate vicinity or for visiting more of the "White Towns"; 15km away, **Setenil**, dug into the cliffs and with cave dwellings, is one of the most unusual.

Walks around Ronda

Good walking routes from Ronda are pretty limitless. One of the best, and a good way to get a sense of the town as a rural market centre set among farmland, is to take the path down to the gorge from the Mondragón palace terrace. In the fields below there's a network of paths and some stupendous views. A couple of hours' walk will bring you to the main road to the northwest where you can hitch or walk back the 4–5km into the Mercadillo. Another excursion is to an old, unused **aqueduct** set in rocky pasture – from the market square just outside the Ciudad in the San Francisco area, take the straight residential street which leads up and out of town. After about an hour this ends in olive groves, by a stream and a large water trough. A path through the groves leads to the aqueduct.

Farther afield, if you're mobile or energetic, are the ruins of a **Roman theatre** at a site known as **Ronda La Vieja**, 12km from the town and reached by turning right 6km down the main road to Arcos/Sevilla. At the site (Tues–Fri 10am–6pm, Sat & Sun noon–6.30pm; free) a friendly farmer, who is also the guardian, will present you with a plan (Spanish only) and record your nationality for statistical purposes.

Based on Neolithic foundations – note the recently discovered prehistoric stone huts beside the entrance – it was as a Roman town in the first century AD that Acinipo (the town's Roman name), reached its zenith. Immediately west of the theatre, the ground falls away in a startlingly steep escarpment, and from here there are fine views all around, taking in the hill village of Olvera to the north. From here a track leads off towards the strange "cave village" of Setenil (see below).

The Cueva de la Pileta

West from Ronda is the prehistoric **Cueva de la Pileta** (daily 9am–1pm & 4–6pm; 800ptas), a fabulous series of caverns with some remarkable paintings of animals (mainly bison), fish and what are apparently magic symbols. These etchings and the occupation of the cave date from about 25,000 BC – hence predating the more famous caves at Altamira – to the end of the Bronze Age. The tour lasts one hour on average, but can be longer, and is in Spanish – though the guide does speak a little English. There are hundreds of bats in the cave, and no artificial lighting, so visitors carry lanterns with them; you may also want to take a jumper, as the caves can be extremely chilly. Be aware if you leave a car in the car park that thieves are active here.

To reach the caves take an Algeciras-bound local train (4 daily; 35min) to the Estación Benaoján-Montejaque, or a bus, which drops you a little closer, in Benaoján. There's a bar at the train station if you want to stock up on drink before the hour-long walk (6km) to the caves. Follow the farm track from the right bank of the river until you reach the farmhouse (approximately 30min). From here, a track goes straight uphill to the main road just before the signposted turning for the caves. If you're driving, follow the road to Benaoján, and take the turn-off, from where it is about 4km.

Setenil, Olvera and Teba

North of Ronda, and feasible as a day trip from the town, are Setenil and Olvera. **SETE-NIL**, on a very minor road to Olvera, is the strangest of all the white towns, its cave-like streets formed from the overhanging ledge of a gorge. Many of the houses – sometimes two or three storeys high – have natural roofs in the rock. There are a couple of bars, and a reasonably priced **hotel**, *El Almendral* (☎956 134029, fax 956 134444; ③), on the road just outside town. Four buses a day run from Ronda, or it's a possible walk from Ronda La Vieja. The train station is a good 8km from the village itself.

OLVERA, 15km beyond, is dominated by a fine Moorish castle. There's just one bus a day from Ronda, but there are a couple of **pensiones** if you want to stay and explore the region: *Maqueda*, c/Calvario 35 (☎956 130733; ②), and *Olid*, c/Llana 13 (☎956 130102; ②), which is beautifully situated on the river, with olive groves and the stark backdrop of the Sierra de Lijar.

TEBA is a small community situated in the mountains five or six kilometres south of the N342 between Campillos and Olvera, or straight up on the C341 from Ronda. It's easily seen from the N342 and is approached by way of a single, clearly marked road which winds its way up to the town. The lower square, Plaza de la Constitución, has all the **accommodation**: three clean, friendly and relatively inexpensive places, of which the best is *Hostal Sevillano*, c/San Francisco 26 (☎95 274 80 11; ②), just off the plaza. Sights around the village include the enormous Baroque church of **Santa Cruz** (daily 5–6pm), which is stuffed full of treasures, and the Plaza de España where there's a monument in Scottish granite to Robert Bruce. Bruce's recently rediscovered heart played a part in the battle against the Moors here in 1331; one of his knights carried it as a talisman and threw it into the Moorish ranks to encourage his timid soldiers to charge. On the hill above the town are the remains of a **Moorish castle**, constructed on Roman ruins, which has a superb keep. The views from here over the surrounding countryside are spectacular and the whole village has a calm and prosperous air.

Towards Cádiz and Sevilla

Ronda has good transport connections in most directions (see "Travel details" at the end of this chapter). Almost any route to the north or west is rewarding, taking you past a whole series of White Towns, many of them fortified since the days of the Reconquest from the Moors – hence the mass of "de la Frontera" suffixes.

Grazalema, Ubrique and Medina Sidonia

Perhaps the best of all the routes, though a roundabout one, and tricky without your own transport, is to **Cádiz** via Grazalema, Ubrique, and Medina Sidonia. This skirts the nature reserve of **Cortes de la Frontera** (which you can drive through by following the road beyond Benaoján) and, towards Alcalá de los Gazules, runs through forests of cork oaks.

Twenty-three kilometres from Ronda, **GRAZALEMA** is a striking place, now the centre of the Sierra de Grazalema Natural Park, with the **Puerto de las Palomas** (Pass of the Doves, at 1350m the second highest pass in Andalucía), rearing up behind. Cross this, and you descend to Zahara and the main road west (see below).

UBRIQUE, 20km southwest, is a natural mountain fortress which was one of the last Republican strongholds in the Civil War. According to Nicholas Luard's book, *Andalucía*:

> It proved so difficult for the besieging nationalists to take they eventually called up a plane from Sevilla to fly over the town and drop leaflets carrying the message: "Ubrique, if in five minutes from now all your arms are not piled in front of the Guardia Civil post and the roofs and terraces of your houses are not covered in white sheets, the town will be devastated by the bombs in this plane". The threat was effective, although not quite in the way the nationalists had intended. Without spreading a single white sheet or leaving a gun behind them Ubrique's citizens promptly abandoned the town and took to the hills behind.

This is a Civil War story typical of these parts. More unusual, however, is that the town today is relatively prosperous, surviving very largely on its medieval guild craft of leather-making.

MEDINA SIDONIA, farther west on the minor roads, is the old ducal seat of the Guzmáns, one of Spain's most famous families. Depopulated and now somewhat ramshackle, it nevertheless offers glimpses of sixteenth-century grandeur.

Zahara de la Sierra

Heading directly to Jerez or Sevilla from Ronda, a beautiful rural drive, you pass below **ZAHARA DE LA SIERRA** (or *de los Membrillos* – "of the Quinces"), perhaps the most perfect example of these fortified hill *pueblos*. Set in beautiful country, a landmark for miles around, its red-tiled houses huddle round a church and castle on a stark outcrop of rock. Once an important Moorish town, its capture by the Christians in 1483 opened the way for the conquest of Ronda – and ultimately Granada. Again there's a clutch of **places to stay** – a *casa de huéspedes* (c/San Juan 9, with no sign opposite the church; ②), a *pensión, Los Estribos* (c/Fuerte 3; ☎956 137445; ③) near the swimming pool, as well as the excellent *Hostal Marqués de Zahara* (c/San Juan 3; ☎956 137261; ④) with a good **restaurant**. Zahara's pleasant **campsite** (open April–Sept) lies 3km outside the village along the old Ronda road; here you can rent a tent complete with camp beds.

Arcos de la Frontera

Of more substantial interest, and serving as a better place to break the journey, is **ARCOS DE LA FRONTERA**. This was taken from the Moors in 1264, over two centuries before Zahara fell – an impressive feat, for it stands high above the Río Guadalete on a double crag and must have been a wretchedly impregnable fortress. This dramatic location, enhanced by low, white houses and fine sandstone churches, gives the town a similar feel and appearance to Ronda – only Arcos is poorer and, quite unjustifiably, far less visited. The streets of the town, despite particularly manic packs of local bikers, are if anything more interesting, with their mix of Moorish and Renaissance buildings. At the heart is the Plaza de España, easily reached by following the signs for the *parador*, which occupies one side of it. Flanking another two sides are the castle walls and the large Gothic-Mudéjar church of **Santa María de la Asunción**; the last side is left open, offering plunging views to the river valley.

PRACTICALITIES

Budget **accommodation** in the **old town** is confined to the *Pensión de Callejón de las Monjas* (☎956 702302; ③), immediately behind the church of Santa María, and the very friendly *Bar San Marcos*, c/Marquéz de Torresoto 6 (☎956 700721; ③), the better option, with its own restaurant. Otherwise you're restricted to the elegant *parador* (☎956 700500, fax 956 701116; ⑦), perched on a rock pedestal, or the *Hotel Marqués de Torresoto*, c/Marqués de Torresoto 4; (☎956 700517; ⑤), housed in a converted seventeenth-century mansion complete with colonnaded patio and Baroque chapel. In the **new town** you'll find a couple of places on either side of the main street, c/Corredera, including the excellent *Hotel Fonda Comercio* (☎956 700057; ③). Alternatively, try the more upmarket *Hostal Voy-Voy*, c/Ponce de León 9 (☎956 701320; ④), or *Hostal Andalucía*, Carretera Nacional 342 (☎956 702718; ③), close to each other on the western edge of town.

Eating and drinking tends to be expensive in the old quarter, where most of the hotels have their own restaurants. *El Convento* at c/Marques de Torresoto 7 is recommended for a splurge, while a more modest good-value option is *La Terraza* in the gardens of the Paseo de Andalucía, which serves a wide variety of *platos combinados* at outdoor tables.

Just out of town, towards Ronda, a road leads down to a couple of sandy **beaches** on the riverbank (buses every half-hour), a rather swanky two-star *hostal* and a **campsite**, *Arcos de la Frontera* (☎956 700514), close to the Bornos reservoir; if you swim here, or farther along toward the namesake village, take care – there are said to be whirlpools in some parts.

SEVILLA, THE WEST AND CÓRDOBA

With the major exception of **Sevilla** – and to a slightly lesser extent **Córdoba** – the west and centre of Andalucía are not greatly visited. The coast here, certainly the Atlantic **Costa de la Luz**, is a world apart from the Mediterranean resorts, with the entire stretch between Algeciras and Tarifa designated a "potential military zone". This probably sounds grim – and in parts, marked off by *Paso Prohibido* signs, it is – but the ruling has also had happier effects, preventing foreigners from buying up land and placing strict controls even on Spanish developments. So, for a hundred or more kilometres, there are scarcely any villa developments and only a modest number of hotels and campsites – small, easy-going and low-key even at the one growing resort of **Conil**. On the coast, too, there is the attraction of **Cádiz**, one of the oldest and, though it's now in decline, most elegant ports in Europe.

Inland rewards include the smaller towns between Sevilla and Córdoba, Moorish **Carmona** particularly. But the most beautiful, and neglected, parts of this region are the dark, ilex-covered hills and poor rural villages of the **Sierra Morena** north of Sevilla. Perfect walking country with its network of streams and reservoirs between modest peaks, this is also a botanist's dream, brilliant with a mass of spring flowers.

On a more organized level, though equally compelling if you're into bird-watching or wildlife, is the huge nature reserve of the **Coto Doñana**, spreading back from Huelva in vast expanses of *marismas* – sand dunes, salt flats and marshes. The most important of the Spanish reserves, Doñana is vital to scores of migratory birds and to endangered mammals like the Iberian lynx. It can be visited by Land Rover tour from the new beach resort complex of **Matalascañas/Torre de Higuera**, accessible from Huelva or Sevilla.

Sevilla

"Seville," wrote Byron, "is a pleasant city, famous for oranges and women." And for its heat, he might perhaps have added, since **SEVILLA**'s summers are intense and start early, in April. But the spirit, for all its nineteenth-century chauvinism, is about right. Sevilla has three important monuments and an illustrious history, but what it's essentially famous for is its own living self – the greatest city of the Spanish south, of Carmen, Don Juan and Figaro, and the archetype of Andalucian promise. This reputation for gaiety and brilliance, for theatricality and intensity of life, does seem deserved. It's expressed on a phenomenally grand scale at the city's two great festivals – **Semana Santa** (in the week before Easter) and the **April Feria** (which starts two weeks after Easter Sunday and lasts a week). Either is worth considerable effort to get to. Sevilla is also Spain's second most important centre for **bullfighting**, after Madrid.

Despite its considerable elegance and charm, the underlying conditions in the city have been bleak in recent years. Sevilla has definite modern wealth, having cornered the Spanish arms industry and its lucrative export trade to Latin America, but it also lies at the centre of a depressed agricultural area and has an unemployment rate of nearly forty percent – among the highest in Spain, along with Málaga and Jaén. The total refurbishment of the infrastructure, including impressive new roads and bridges, a high-speed rail link and a revamped airport may help – but the long-term effects will take a while to assess.

Meantime, **petty crime** is a big problem, and the motive for stealing is usually cash to feed drug addiction. Bag-snatching is common (often Italian-style, from passing *motos*), as is breaking into cars. There's even a special breed called *semaforazos* who break the windows of cars stopped at traffic lights and grab what they can. Western-style amateur bank

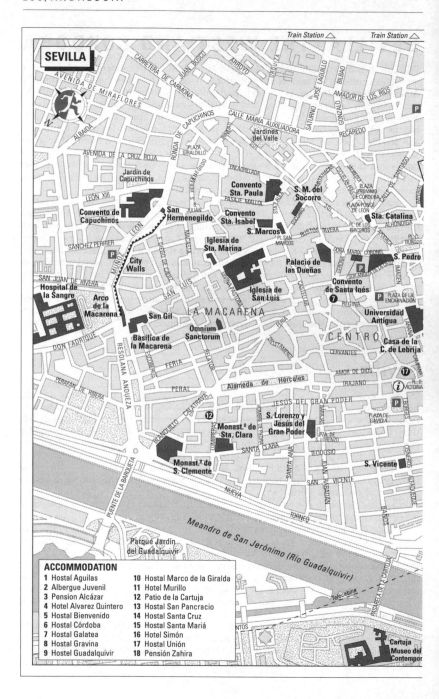

SEVILLA

Train Station △   Train Station △

CARRETERA DE CARMANA
JUAN BOSCH
ARROYO
AVENIDA DE MIRAFLORES
CALLE MARÍA AUXILIADORA
JOSÉ LAGUILLO
URQUITA
BILBAO
SATURNO
GONZALO
AMADOR DE LOS RÍOS
RECAREDO
ALBAIDA
RONDA DE CAPUCHINOS
PLAZA GIRALDILLO
Jardines del Valle
AVENIDA DE LA CRUZ ROJA
Jardín de Capuchinos
ENLADRILLADA
Convento Sta. Paula
S. M. del Socorro
PLAZA JERÓNIMO DE CÓRDOBA
PLAZA PONCE DE LEÓN
LEÓN XIII
San Hermenegildo
Convento de Capuchinos
Convento Sta. Isabel
Sta. Catalina
ALHÓNDIGA
S. Marcos
PL DE LOS TERCEROS
SÁNCHEZ PERRIER
Iglesia de Sta. Marina
PL SAN MARCOS
BUSTOS TAVERA
S. Pedro
City Walls
Palacio de las Dueñas
DOÑA MARÍA CORONEL
SAN JUAN DE RIVERA
Hospital de la Sangre
Arco de la Macarena
Iglesia de San Luis
Convento de Santa Inés ❼
PLAZA DE LA ENCARNACIÓN
DON FADRIQUE
San Gil
LA MACARENA
Universidad Antigua
CENTRO
Basílica de la Macarena
Omnium Sanctorum
Casa de la C. de Lebrija
PERAFÁN DE RIBERA
RESOLANA ANDUEZA
FERIA
RELATOR
CERVANTES
AMOR DE DIOS
TRAJANO
ⓘ
PERAL
Alameda de Hércules
JESÚS DEL GRAN PODER
PLAZA DE GAVIDIA
⓬
S. Lorenzo y Jesús del Gran Poder
Monast.ª de Sta. Clara
SANTA CLARA
PZA DE S. LORENZO
Monast.ª de S. Clemente
TEODOSIO
S. Vicente
PUENTE DE LA BARQUETA
NUEVA
SAN VICENTE
TORNEO
Meandro de San Jerónimo (Río Guadalquivir)
Parque Jardín del Guadalquivir
Telecabina
PASARELA DE LA CARTUJA
Cartuja Museo del Contempor

ACCOMMODATION

1 Hostal Aguilas	10 Hostal Marco de la Giralda
2 Albergue Juvenil	11 Hotel Murillo
3 Pensión Alcázar	12 Patio de la Cartuja
4 Hotel Alvarez Quintero	13 Hostal San Pancracio
5 Hostal Bienvenido	14 Hostal Santa Cruz
6 Hostal Córdoba	15 Hostal Santa Mariá
7 Hostal Galatea	16 Hotel Simón
8 Hostal Gravina	17 Hostal Unión
9 Hostel Guadalquivir	18 Pensión Zahira

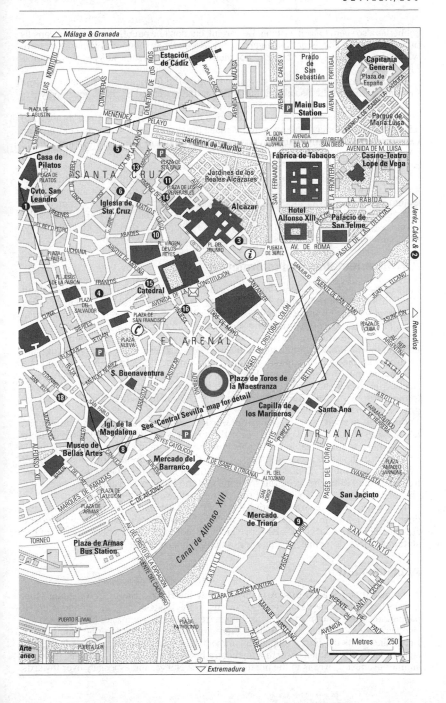

△ Málaga & Granada

Estación de Cádiz

Prado de San Sebastián

Capitania General

Plaza de España

PLAZA DE S. AGUSTIN

LUIS MONTOTO

CONTRERAS

DEMETRIO DE LOS RIOS

AVDA. DE CANT.

AVENIDA DE MÁLAGA

AVENIDA DE CARLOS V

AVENIDA DE PORTUGAL

AVENIDA DE ISABEL LA CATOLICA

Parque de María Luisa

MENÉNDEZ PELAYO

Jardines de Murillo

Main Bus Station

PL. DON JUAN DE AUSTRIA

AVENIDA DEL CID

GLORIETA SAN DIEGO

AVENIDA DE M. LUISA

Casa de Pilatos

Cvto. San Leandro ❶

PLAZA DE PILATOS

SANTA CRUZ

PLAZA DE STA. CRUZ ❺ ❸

❻

Iglesia de Sta. Cruz

PLAZA DE LOS VENERABLES ❶❶ ❶❹

Jardines de los Reales Alcázares

Alcázar

Fábrica de Tabacos

Casino-Teatro Lope de Vega

LA RÁBIDA

Hotel Alfonso XIII

Palacio de San Telme

VIRGENES

DEL REY D. PEDRO

ABADES

ARGOTE DE MOLINA

PL. VIRGEN DE LOS REYES

PL. DEL TRIUNFO ❸

PUERTA DE JEREZ

SAN FERNANDO

AV. DE ROMA

PASEO DE LAS DELICIAS

❶❼

❿

LUCHANA

PLAZA ALFALFA

PL. JESUS DE LA PASIÓN

❹

FRANCOS

PLAZA DEL SALVADOR

❶❺ Catedral

❶❻

AVENIDA DE LA CONSTITUCIÓN

SANTANDER

PASEO DE CRISTÓBAL COLÓN

PUENTE DE SAN TELMO

JUAN S. ELCANO

PLAZA DE CUBA

ASUNCIÓN

AV. REP. ARGENTINA

CUNA

CURTIDORES

PLAZA DE SAN FRANCISCO

LAS MAYAS

EL ARENAL

PLAZA NUEVA ℗

PLAZA DE SAN FRANCISCO

S. Buenaventura

❶❽

O'DONNELL

RIOJA

TETUAN

MÉNDEZ NÚÑEZ

SAN PABLO

ZARAGOZA

CASTELAR

ADRIANO

Plaza de Toros de la Maestranza

BETIS

SALADO

ARJONA

Igl. de la Magdalena ❽

Museo de Bellas Artes

REYES CATÓLICOS

See 'Central Sevilla' map for detail

Capilla de los Marineros

Santa Ana

TRIANA

PLAZA AMADEO JANNONE

FARMACÉUTICO MÚ. HERRERA

ARDILLA

ALFONSO XII

BAILÉN

P. DE ISABEL II (TRIANA)

Mercado del Barranco

PL. DEL ALTOZANO

SAN JORGE

PURFZA

BETIS

PAGES DEL CORRO

EVANGELISTA

San Jacinto

MARQUES DE PARADAS

PLAZA DE LA LEGIÓN

PLAZA DE ARMAS

Plaza de Armas Bus Station

AV. DE CRISTO DE LA EXPIRACIÓN

Canal de Alfonso XIII

CASTILLA

Mercado de Triana ❾

SAN JACINTO

SAN VICENTE DE PAUL

TORNEO

PUERTO FLUVIAL

PLAZA PATROCINIO

CLARA DE JESÚS MONTERO

MANUEL ARELLANO

TEJARES

AVENIDA DE SANTA CECILIA

0 Metres 250

Arte aneo

PUERTA SUR

▽ Extremadura

◁ Jeréz, Cádiz & ❷

◁ Remedios

robberies also seem to be in fashion. Be careful, but don't be put off. As one of the consuls in Sevilla put it: "This is not a dangerous city. No one gets mugged. I know of no town where the streets are safer at night." For violence against persons, at least, this is probably true.

Sevilla's most famous present-day native son is the former prime minister, **Felipe González**, who led the Socialist administration that governed Spain for fourteen years until 1996. Another, more bizarre Sevillano is one **Gregorio XVII**, who calls himself the true Pope; in defiance of his excommunication by the Vatican, "Pope Greg" is leader of a large ultra-reactionary order which has made the dead Franco a saint and has built an extensive new "Vatican" in the countryside to the south of the city. Gregorio himself conspicuously enjoys the good life and stalks the city's bars, dressed in full silken regalia, along with his "papal" entourage.

The connection with Felipe González may have had something to do with Sevilla sharing the world stage with Barcelona in 1992, to celebrate the 500th anniversary of Columbus's discovery of the New World. Vast investment and the participation of over one hundred countries went some way to justifying the billing of **Expo '92** as the "event of the century", although the hype surrounding it was later to be equalled by the colossal (and still unpaid) debts the mammoth enterprise left behind.

Arrival, orientation and information

Split in two by the Río Guadalquivir, Sevilla is fairly easy to find your way about (though hell if you're driving). The **old city** – where you'll want to spend most of your time – takes up the east bank. At its heart, side by side, stand the three great monuments: the **Giralda tower**, the **cathedral** and the **Alcázar**, with the cramped alleyways of the **Barrio Santa Cruz**, the medieval Jewish quarter and now the heart of tourist life, extending north of them. West of here is the main shopping and commercial district, its most obvious landmarks the **Plaza Nueva** and **La Campana**, and the smart pedestrianized **c/Sierpes** which runs between them. Across the river is the earthier, traditionally working-class district of **Triana**, flanked to the south by the **Los Remedios** *barrio*, the city's chic residential zone where the great April *feria* takes place .

Points of arrival, too, are straightforward, though the **train station**, Santa Justa, is a fair way out on Avenida Kansas City, the airport road. Bus #27 will take you from outside here to the Plaza de la Encarnación (roughly dead centre of our city map), from where all sights are within easy walking distance. The **airport** bus, operated by Amarillos (hourly; 750ptas), terminates in the centre at the Puerta de Jerez, at the top of Avenida Roma between the Turismo and the Fábrica de Tabacos. It works out cheaper to take a taxi (1000ptas) if there there are two people or more.

The **main bus station** is at the Prado de San Sebastián. Most companies and destinations go from here: exceptions include buses for Badajoz, Extremadura and Huelva, which are served by La Estrella and Empresa Damas, operating out of the station at Plaza de Armas by the Puente del Cachorro on the river.

Accommodation

The most attractive **area to stay** is undoubtedly the **Barrio Santa Cruz**, though this is reflected in the prices. In mid-season or during the big festivals you can find yourself paying ridiculous amounts for what is little more than a cell; rooms are relatively expensive everywhere, in fact. Nonetheless there are reasonable places to be found in the Barrio and on its periphery (especially immediately north, and south towards the bus station) and they're at least worth a try before heading elsewhere. Slightly farther out, another promising area is to the north of the Plaza Nueva, and especially over towards

SEMANA SANTA AND THE FERIA DE ABRIL

Sevilla boasts two of the largest festival celebrations in Spain. The first, **Semana Santa** (Holy Week), always spectacular in Andalucía, is here at its peak with extraordinary processions of masked penitents and carnival-style floats. The second, the **Feria de Abril**, is unique to the city: a one-time market festival, long converted to a week-long party of drink, food and flamenco. The *feria* follows hard on the heels of *Semana Santa*. If you have the energy, experience both.

SEMANA SANTA

Semana Santa may be a religious festival, but for most of the week solemnity isn't the keynote – there's lots of carousing and frivolity, and bars are full day and night. In essence, it involves the marching in procession of brotherhoods of the church (*cofradías*) and penitents, followed by *pasos*, elaborate platforms or floats on which sit seventeenth-century images of the Virgin or Christ. For weeks beforehand the *cofradías* painstakingly adorn the hundred or so *pasos*, spending vast amounts on costumes and precious stones. The bearers (*costaleros*) walk in time to stirring, traditional dirges and drumbeats from the bands, which are often punctuated by impromptu and moving street-corner *saetas* – short, fervent, flamenco-style hymns about the Passion and the Virgin's sorrows.

The last lap of the official **route** for every *paso*, goes from La Campana along c/Sierpes through the cathedral, and around the Giralda and the Bishop's Palace. Throughout the week *pasos* leave churches all over town from early afternoon onward, snaking through the city and back to their resting place many hours later. **Good Friday** morning is the climax, when the *pasos* leave the churches at midnight and move through the town for much of the night. The highlight is the arrival at the cathedral of the *paso* bearing *La Macarena*, an image of the patroness of bullfighters and, by extension, of Sevilla itself.

The pattern of events changes every day; a loose **timetable** is issued with local papers and is essential if you want to know which events are where – the ultra-Catholic *ABC* paper has the best listings. On Maundy Thursday women dress in black and it's considered respectful for tourists not to dress in shorts or T-shirts. Triana is a good location on this day, and there's always a crush of spectators outside the cathedral and on c/Sierpes, the most awe-inspiring venue. Plaza de la Virgen de los Reyes under the Giralda is a good viewing point, but the best way of all to see the processions is to pick them up near their starting and finishing points in the respective *barrios*; here you'll see the true *teatro de la calle* – theatre of the streets.

FERIA DE ABRIL

The *Feria de Abril* is staged a fortnight after Semana Santa ends and lasts non-stop for a week. For its duration a vast area on the far bank of the river, the *Real de la Feria*, is totally covered in rows of *casetas*, canvas pavilions or tents of varying sizes. Some of these belong to eminent *sevillano* families, some to groups of friends, others to clubs, trade associations or political parties. In each one – from around nine at night until perhaps six or seven the following morning – there is flamenco singing and dancing. Many of the men and virtually all the women wear traditional costume, the latter in an astonishing array of brilliantly coloured, flounced gypsy dresses.

The sheer size of this spectacle is extraordinary, and the dancing, with its intense and knowing sexuality, a revelation. But most infectious of all is the universal spontaneity of enjoyment; after wandering around staring with the crowds you wind up a part of it, drinking and dancing in one of the "open" *casetas* which have commercial bars. Among these you'll usually find lively *casetas* erected by the anarchist trade union CNT and various leftist groups.

Earlier in the day, from 1pm until 5pm, Sevillana society **parades** around the fairground in carriages or on horseback. An incredible extravaganza of display and voyeurism, this has subtle but distinct gradations of dress and style; catch it at least once. Each day, too, there are **bullfights** (at around 5.30pm; very expensive tickets in advance from the ring), generally reckoned to be the best of the season.

the river and the Plaza de Armas bus station. It's always worth trying to bargain the price down a little, though you may not always succeed.

At peak times you may face quite a walk. The list below is no more than a start, and it's worth checking at the places you'll pass between all these.

Budget options

Hostal Águilas, c/Águilas 15 (☎95 421 31 77). Small and quiet *hostal*, near the Casa de Pilatos. ③.

Albergue Juvenil Sevilla, c/Isaac Peral 2 (☎95 461 31 50). Crowded youth hostel some way out in the university district; take bus #34 from Puerta de Jerez or Plaza Nueva. ①.

Pensión Alcázar, c/Deán Miranda 12 (☎95 422 84 57, fax 95 442 16 59). Tiny *pensión* in a small street beside the Alcázar; good value if they have space. ③.

Hostal Bienvenido, c/Archeros 14 (☎95 441 36 55). East of c/Santa María la Blanca, this *hostal* offers simple small rooms but has a nice roof terrace. ③.

Hostal Gravina, c/Gravina 46 (☎95 421 64 14). Pleasant, family-run *hostal* close to the Museo de Bellas Artes. They also own nearby *Hostal Paco* (c/Pedro del Toro 7) which has slightly more expensive rooms with bath. Both ③.

Hostal Guadalquivir, c/Pagés del Corro 53 (☎95 433 21 00, fax 95 433 21 04). Barrio Triana's only *hostal* is atmospheric and friendly; some rooms en suite. ③.

Hostal San Pancracio, c/Cruces 9 (☎95 441 31 04). Decent range of room options here, some with bath – so check what's available. ③.

Hostal Santa Cruz, c/Lope de Rueda 12 (☎95 421 76 95). Tiny and charming *hostal* with delightful patio and some rooms with bath, close to the Plaza Santa Cruz. ③.

Hostal Santa María, c/Hernando Colón 19 (☎95 422 85 05). Small *hostal* on a noisy street, but in the Giralda's shadow and cheap. ③.

Hostal Unión, c/Tarifa 4 (☎95 421 17 90). Slightly east of the Plaza Duque de la Victoria and one of the best-value places in this area. Clean, economical rooms with bath. ③.

Moderate and expensive options

Hotel Álvarez Quintero, c/Álvarez Quintero 12 (☎95 422 12 98, fax 95 456 41 41). Near the cathedral, this converted former *bodega* has a delightful seventeenth-century patio and great views from some rooms, especially nos. 201–206. ⑦.

Hostal Córdoba, c/Farnesio 12 (☎95 422 74 98). Good standard *hostal*, offering some rooms with bath, close to the church of Santa Cruz. ④.

Hostal Galatea, Plaza San Juan de la Palma 4 (☎95 456 35 64, fax 95 456 35 17). Friendly *hostal* in a restored town house in the heart of the atmospheric Macarena quarter. ④.

Hostal Marco de la Giralda, c/Abades 30 (☎95 422 83 24). Good value for somewhere so close to the cathedral. ④.

Hotel Murillo, c/Lope de Rueda 7 (☎95 421 60 95, fax 95 421 96 16). Traditional hotel in restored mansion with all facilities plus amusingly kitsch features such as suits of armour and paint palette key rings. Close to the Plaza Santa Cruz. ⑤.

Patio de la Cartuja, c/Lumbreras 8, off west side of Alameda's northern end (☎95 490 02 00, fax 95 490 20 56). Stylish and excellent-value hotel created from an old *sevillano corral*; en-suite apartments with balconies, kitchen and lounge are set around a tiled patio. ⑤.

Hotel Simón, c/García de Vinuesa 19 (☎95 422 66 60, fax 456 22 41). Well-restored mansion in an excellent position across from the cathedral. Can be a bargain out of season. ⑤.

Pensión Zahira, c/San Eloy 43 (☎95 422 10 61, fax 95 421 30 48). Comfortable air-conditioned rooms with bath. ④.

Camping

Camping Sevilla (☎95 451 43 79). Right by the airport, so very noisy but otherwise not a bad site. The airport bus will get you there or take bus #70 from outside the main Prado de San Sebastián bus station and ask to be dropped at "Parque Alcosa".

Club de Campo (☎95 472 02 50). About 12km out in Dos Hermanas, with a pool. Better than *Villsom*, nearby on the main Cádiz road. Half-hourly Amarillos buses from the main bus station.

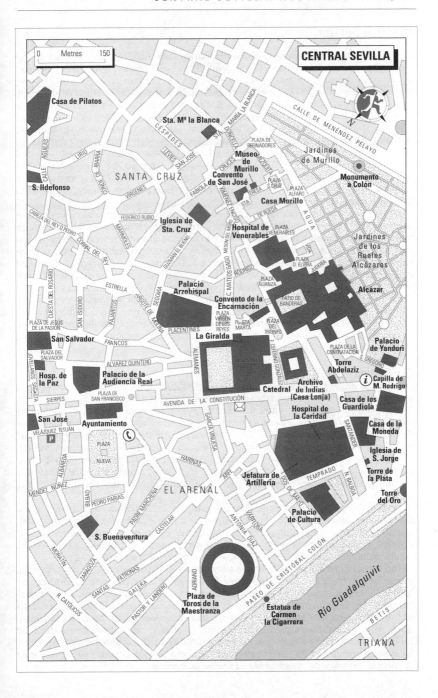

Moorish Sevilla

Sevilla was one of the earliest **Moorish conquests** (in 712) and, as part of the Caliphate of Córdoba, became the second city of *al-Andalus*. When the Caliphate broke up in the early eleventh century it was by far the most powerful of the independent states (or *taifas*) to emerge, extending its power over the Algarve and eventually over Jaén, Murcia and Córdoba itself. This period, under a series of three Arabic rulers from the Abbadid dynasty (1023–91), was something of a golden age. The city's court was unrivalled in wealth and luxury and was sophisticated too, developing a strong chivalric element and a flair for poetry – one of the most skilled exponents being the last ruler, al-Mu'tamid, the "poet-king". But with sophistication came decadence and in 1091 Abbadid rule was usurped by a new force, the **Almoravids**, a tribe of fanatical Berber Muslims from North Africa, to whom the Andalucians had appealed for help against the rising threat from the northern Christian kingdoms.

Despite initial military successes, the Almoravids failed to consolidate their gains in *al-Andalus* and attempted to rule through military governors from Marrakesh. In the middle of the twelfth century they were in turn supplanted by a new Berber incursion, the **Almohads**, who by about 1170 had recaptured virtually all the former territories. Sevilla had accepted Almohad rule in 1147 and became the capital of this last real empire of the Moors in Spain. Almohad power was sustained until their disastrous defeat in 1212 by the combined Christian armies of the north, at Las Navas de Tolosa. In this brief and precarious period Sevilla underwent a renaissance of public building, characterized by a new vigour and fluidity of style. The Almohads rebuilt the Alcázar, enlarged the principal **mosque** and erected a new and brilliant minaret, a tower over 100m tall, topped with four copper spheres that could be seen from miles round: the Giralda.

The Giralda

The Sevilla minaret was the culmination of Almohad architecture and served as a model for those at their imperial capitals of Rabat and Marrakesh. It was used by the Moors both for calling the faithful to prayer (the traditional function of a minaret) and as an observatory, and was so venerated that they wanted to destroy it before the Christian conquest of the city. This they were prevented from doing by the threat of Alfonso (later King Alfonso X) that "if they removed a single stone, they would all be put to the sword". Instead the **Giralda** (Mon–Sat 10.30am–5pm, Sun 2–6pm; 700ptas combined ticket with the cathedral, free Sun), named after the sixteenth-century *giraldillo* or weather vane on its summit, became the bell tower of the Christian cathedral.

Beyond doubt the most beautiful building in Sevilla, it continues to dominate the skyline. You can ascend to the bell chamber for a remarkable view of the city – and, equally remarkable, a glimpse of the Gothic details of the cathedral's buttresses and statuary. But most impressive of all is the tower's inner construction, a series of 35 gently inclined ramps wide enough to allow two mounted guards to pass.

The Moorish structure took twelve years to build (1184–96) and derives its firm, simple beauty from the shadows formed by blocks of brick trelliswork, different on each side, and relieved by a succession of arched niches and windows. The original harmony has been somewhat spoiled by the Renaissance-era addition of balconies and, to a still greater extent, by the four diminishing storeys of the belfry – added, along with the Italian-sculpted bronze figure of "Faith" which surmounts them, in 1560–68, following the demolition by an earthquake of the original copper spheres. Even so, it remains in its perfect synthesis of form and decoration one of the most important and beautiful monuments of the Islamic world.

Christian Sevilla

After the **Reconquest of Sevilla** by Fernando III in 1248, the Almohad mosque was consecrated to the Virgin Mary, as was the practice with all Spanish mosques taken from Islam, and it became the Christian cathedral. Thus it survived until 1402, when the cathedral chapter dreamt up plans for a new and unrivalled monument to Christian glory: "a building on so magnificent a scale that posterity will believe we were mad". To this end the mosque was demolished, while the canons, inspired by their vision of future repute, renounced all but a subsistence level of their incomes to further the building. From the old structure only the Giralda and the Moorish entrance court, the **Patio de los Naranjos**, were spared. The patio is entered to the north of the Giralda, from c/Alemanes, through the **Puerta del Perdón** – the original main gateway, sadly marred by Renaissance embellishments. In the centre of the patio remains a Moorish fountain, itself incorporating a sixth-century Visigothic font, used for the ritual ablutions before entering the mosque.

The cathedral

The **Catedral** (Mon–Sat 10.30am–5pm, Sun 2–6pm; 700ptas combined ticket with the Giralda, free Sun) was completed in just over a century (1402–1506), an extraordinary achievement for, in accord with the plans of the chapter, it is the largest Gothic church in the world. As Norman Lewis says, "It expresses conquest and domination in architectural terms of sheer mass." Though it is built upon the huge, rectangular base-plan of the old mosque, the Christian architects (probably under the direction of the French master architect of Rouen Cathedral) added the extra dimension of height. Its central nave rises to 42 metres, and even the side chapels seem tall enough to contain an ordinary church. The total area covers 11,520 square metres, and new calculations, based on cubic measurement, have now pushed it in front of Saint Paul's in London and Saint Peter's in Rome as the largest church in the world.

Sheer size and grandeur are, inevitably, the chief characteristics of the cathedral. But as you grow accustomed to the gloom, two other qualities stand out with equal force: the rhythmic balance and interplay between the parts, and an impressive overall simplicity and restraint in decoration. All successive ages have left monuments of their own wealth and style, but these have been limited to the two rows of side chapels. In the main body of the cathedral only the great box-like structure of the **coro** stands out, filling the central portion of the nave.

The *coro* extends and opens on to the **Capilla Mayor**, dominated by a **vast Gothic retablo** composed of 45 carved scenes from the life of Christ. The lifetime's work of a single craftsman, Pierre Dancart, this is the supreme masterpiece of the cathedral – the largest and richest altarpiece in the world and one of the finest examples of Gothic woodcarving. The guides provide staggering statistics on the amount of gold involved.

Behind the Capilla Mayor (and directly to your left on entering the cathedral) you pass the domed Renaissance **Capilla Real**, built on the site of the original royal burial chapel and containing the body of Fernando III (*El Santo*) in a suitably rich, silver shrine before the altar. The large tombs on either side of the chapel are those of Fernando's wife, Beatrice of Swabia, and his son, Alfonso the Wise. At the end of this first aisle are a series of rooms designed in the rich Plateresque style in 1530 by Diego de Riano, one of the foremost exponents of this predominantly decorative architecture of the late Spanish Renaissance. Through a small antechamber here you enter the curious oval-shaped **Sala Capitular** (Chapter House), whose elaborate domed ceiling is mirrored in the marble decoration of the floor. It contains a number of paintings by Murillo – the finest of which, a flowing *Conception*, occupies a place of honour high above the bishop's throne. Alongside this room is the grandiose **Sacristía Mayor** which houses the treasury. Amid a confused collection of silver reliquaries and monstrances – dull and prodigious wealth

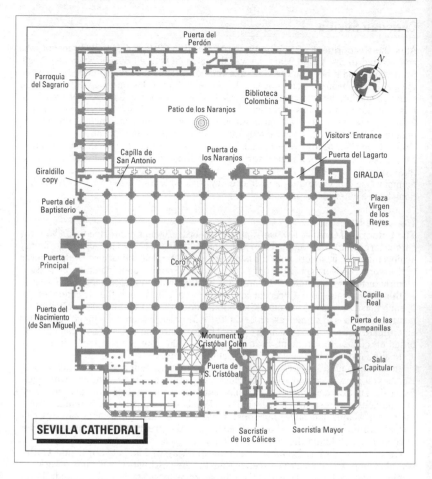

SEVILLA CATHEDRAL

Puerta del Perdón

Parroquia del Sagrario

Biblioteca Colombina

Patio de los Naranjos

Visitors' Entrance

Capílla de San Antonio

Puerta de los Naranjos

Puerta del Lagarto

Giraldillo copy

GIRALDA

Puerta del Baptisterio

Plaza Virgen de los Reyes

Puerta Principal

Coro

Capilla Real

Puerta del Nacimiento (de San Miguel)

Puerta de las Campanillas

Monument to Cristóbal Colón

Puerta de S. Cristóbal

Sala Capitular

Sacristía de los Cálices

Sacristía Mayor

– are displayed the keys presented to Fernando by the Jewish and Moorish communities on the surrender of the city; sculpted into the latter in stylized Arabic script are the words "May Allah render eternal the dominion of Islam in this city."

Just beyond the entrance to the sacristy is an enormous nineteenth-century **Monument to Christopher Columbus** (*Cristóbal Colón* in Spanish), erected originally in the cathedral of Havana. By a wry stroke of irony, however, Cuban independence was declared seven years later and it had to be shipped to Sevilla. The mariner's coffin is held aloft by four huge allegorical figures, representing the kingdoms of León, Castile, Aragón and Navarra; note how the lance of León is piercing a pomegranate, symbol of Granada, the last Moorish kingdom to be reconquered.

If the monument inspires you, or you have a fervent interest in Columbus's travels, visit the **Lonja**, the city's old stock exchange, opposite the cathedral. This now houses the remarkable **Archives of the Indies** (Mon–Fri 10am–1pm; free). Among the selection of documents on display are Columbus's log and a changing exhibition of ancient maps and curiosities.

SEVILLA'S PARISH CHURCHES

Sevilla's parish **churches** display a fascinating variety of architectural styles. Several are converted mosques with belfries built over their minarets, others range through Mudéjar and Gothic (sometimes in combination), Renaissance and Baroque. Most are kept locked except early in the morning, or in the evenings from about 7 until 10pm – a promising time for a church crawl, especially as they're regularly interspersed with bars.

For a good circuit make first towards Gothic **San Pedro**, where a marble tablet records Velázquez's baptism, and **San Marcos**, with a fine minaret tower. Nearby, in this old cobbled part of town, is the fifteenth-century **Convento de Santa Paula** (Tues–Sun 10.30am–12.30pm & 4.30–6.30pm; free), its church decorated with a vivid ceramic facade and superb *azulejos*, with an excellent museum containing fine artworks by Zurbarán and Ribera among others. Farther on you meet the last remaining stretch of Moorish **city walls** – remains of the Almoravid fortifications which once spanned 12 gates and 166 towers. Now there's only one gate, the **Puerta Macarena**; beside it a basilica houses the city's cult image and patroness of matadors, *La Esperanza Macarena*, a tearful Virgin seated in the midst of gaudy magnificence.

Looping down towards the river, you reach the **Monasterio de Santa Clara** (entered from c/Santa Clara no. 40) – once part of the palace of Don Fadrique, brother of Alfonso X, and with a Romanesque-Gothic tower dating from 1252. A couple of blocks away are the distinctive columns (two at the far end are Roman) of the **Alameda de Hércules**. This leads back towards the town centre, with two more churches worth a look on the way: the Renaissance chapel of the **Universidad Antigua** and Baroque **San Salvador**, the latter built on the site of Sevilla's first Friday mosque (part of whose minaret is incorporated in its tower).

The Alcázar

Rulers of Sevilla have occupied the site of the **Alcázar** (Tues–Sun 9.30am–7pm; 600ptas) from the time of the Romans. Here was built the great court of the Abbadids, which reached a peak of sophistication and exaggerated sensuality under the cruel and ruthless al-Mu'tadid – a ruler who enlarged the palace in order to house a harem of eight hundred women, and who decorated the terraces with flowers planted in the skulls of his decapitated enemies. Later, under the **Almohads**, the complex was turned into a citadel, forming the heart of the town's fortifications. Its extent was enormous, stretching to the Torre del Oro on the bank of the Guadalquivir.

Parts of the Almohad walls survive, but the present structure of the palace dates almost entirely from the Christian period. Sevilla was a favoured residence of the Spanish kings for some four centuries after the reconquest – most particularly of **Pedro the Cruel** (1350–69) who, with his mistress María de Padilla, lived in and ruled from the Alcázar. Pedro embarked upon a complete rebuilding of the palace, employing workmen from Granada and utilizing fragments of earlier Moorish buildings in Sevilla, Córdoba and Valencia. Pedro's works form the nucleus of the Alcázar as it is today and, despite numerous restorations necessitated by fires and earth tremors, it offers some of the best surviving examples of **Mudéjar architecture** – the style developed by Moors working under Christian rule. Later monarchs, however, have left all too many traces and additions. Isabella built a new wing in which to organize expeditions to the Americas and control the new territories; Carlos V married a Portuguese princess in the palace, adding huge apartments for the occasion; and under Felipe IV (c. 1624) extensive renovations were carried out to the existing rooms. On a more mundane level, kitchens were installed to provide for General Franco, who stayed in the royal apartments whenever he visited Sevilla.

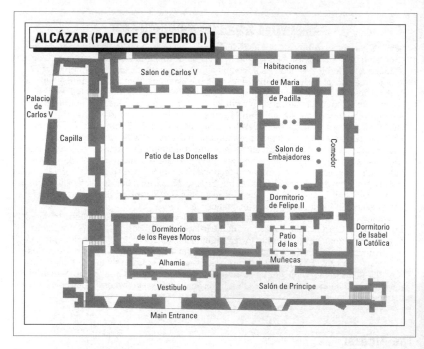

ALCÁZAR (PALACE OF PEDRO I)

Palacio de Carlos V

Capilla

Salon de Carlos V

Habitaciones de Maria de Padilla

Patio de Las Doncellas

Salon de Embajadores

Comedor

Dormitorio de Felipe II

Dormitorio de los Reyes Moros

Patio de las Muñecas

Dormitorio de Isabel la Católica

Alhamia

Vestibulo

Salón de Principe

Main Entrance

Entrance – the Casa del Océano

The Alcázar is entered from the Plaza del Triunfo, adjacent to the cathedral. The gateway, flanked by original Almohad walls, opens on to a courtyard where Pedro (who was known as "the Just" as well as "the Cruel", depending on one's fortunes) used to give judgement; to the left is his **Sala de Justicia**. The main facade of the palace stands at the end of an inner court, the **Patio de la Montería**; on either side are galleried buildings erected by Isabella. This principal facade is pure fourteenth-century Mudéjar and, with its delicate, marble-columned windows, stalactite frieze and overhanging roof, is one of the finest things in the whole Alcázar. But it's probably better to look round the **Casa del Océano** (or *de las Américas*), the sixteenth-century building on the right, before entering the main palace. Founded by Isabella in 1503, this gives you a standard against which to assess the Moorish forms. Here most of the rooms seem too heavy, their decoration ceasing to be an integral part of the design. The only notable exception is the chapel with its magnificent *artesonado* ceiling inlaid with golden stars; within is a fine altarpiece depicting Columbus (in gold) and Carlos V (in a red cloak) sheltering beneath the Virgin. In the rear, to the left, are portrayed the kneeling figures of the Indians to whom the dubious blessings of Christianity had been brought by the Spanish conquest.

The palace

As you enter the **Main Palace** the "domestic" nature of Moorish and Mudéjar architecture is immediately striking. This involves no loss of grandeur but simply a shift in scale: the apartments are remarkably small, shaped to human needs, and take their beauty from the exuberance of the decoration and the imaginative use of space and light. There is, too, a deliberate disorientation in the layout of the rooms which makes the palace seem infinitely larger and more open than it really is. From the entrance court a narrow passage leads straight into the central courtyard, the **Patio de las Doncellas** (Patio of the Maidens), its name recalling the Christians' tribute of one hundred virgins presented annually to the Moorish kings. The court's stucco work, *azulejos* and doors are all of the finest Granada craftsmanship. Interestingly, it's also the one room where Renaissance restorations are successfully fused – the double columns and upper storey were built by Carlos V, whose *Plus Ultra* ("yet still further") motto recurs in the decorations here and elsewhere.

Past the **Salón de Carlos V**, distinguished by a superb ceiling, are three rooms from the original fourteenth-century design built for María de Padilla (who was popularly thought to use magic in order to maintain her hold over Pedro – and perhaps over other gallants at court, too, who used to drink her bath water). These open on to the **Salón de Embajadores** (Salon of the Ambassadors), the most brilliant room of the Alcázar, with a stupendous *media naranja* (half-orange) wooden dome of red, green and gold cells, and horseshoe arcades inspired by the great palace of Medina Azahara outside Córdoba. Although restored, for the worse, by Carlos V – who added balconies and an incongruous frieze of royal portraits to commemorate his marriage to Isabella of Portugal here – the salon stands comparison with the great rooms of Granada's Alhambra. Adjoining are a long dining hall (*comedor*) and a small apartment installed in the late sixteenth century for Felipe II.

Beyond is the last great room of the palace – the **Patio de las Muñecas** (Patio of the Dolls), which takes its curious name from two tiny faces decorating the inner side of one of the smaller arches. It's thought to be the site of the harem in the original palace. In this room Pedro is reputed to have murdered his brother Don Fadrique in 1358; another of his royal guests, Abu Said of Granada, was murdered here for his jewels (one of which, an immense ruby which King Pedro later gave to Edward, the "Black Prince", now figures in the British crown jewels). The upper storey of the court is a much later, nineteenth-century restoration. On the other sides of the patio are the **bedrooms** of Isabella and of her son Don Juan, and the arbitrarily named Dormitorio del los Reyes Moros (Bedroom of the Moorish Kings).

Palacio de Carlos V and the gardens

To the left of the main palace loom the large and soulless apartments of the **Palacio de Carlos V** – something of an endurance test, with endless tapestries and pink-orange or yellow paintwork. Their classical style asserts a different and inferior mood. Best to hurry through to the beautiful and rambling **Alcázar gardens**, the confused but enticing product of several eras, where you can take a well-earned rest from your exertions. Here are the vaulted baths in which María de Padilla is supposed to have bathed (in reality, an auxiliary water supply for the palace), and the tank specially built for Felipe V in 1733, who whiled away two solitary years at the Alcázar fishing in this pool and preparing himself for death through religious flagellation. Also here is an unusual maze of myrtle bushes and the **pavilion of Carlos V**, the only survivor of several he built in the gardens.

The Plaza de España and María Luisa Park

Laid out in 1929 for an abortive "Fair of the Americas", the Plaza de España and adjoining María Luisa Park are among the most pleasant – and impressive – public spaces in Spain. They are an ideal place to spend the middle part of the day, just ten minutes' walk to the east of the cathedral.

En route you pass by the **Fábrica de Tabacos**, the city's old tobacco factory and the setting for Bizet's *Carmen*. Now part of the university, this massive structure was built in the 1750s and for a time was the largest building in Spain after El Escorial. At its peak in the following century it was also the country's largest single employer, with a workforce of some 4000 women *cigarreras* – "a class in themselves" according to Richard Ford, who were forced to undergo "an ingeniously minute search on leaving their work, for they sometimes carry off the filthy weed in a manner her most Catholic majesty never dreamt of."

The **Plaza de España**, beyond, was designed as the centrepiece of the Spanish Americas Fair, which was somewhat scuppered by the Wall Street crash. A vast semicircular complex, with its fountains, monumental stairways and mass of tile work, it would seem strange in most Spanish cities but here it looks entirely natural, carrying on the tradition of civic display. At the fair, the Plaza de España was used for the Spanish exhibit of industry and crafts, and around the crescent are *azulejo* scenes and maps of each of the provinces – an interesting record of the country at the tail end of a moneyed era.

Spaniards and tourists alike come out to the plaza – slightly shabby now – to potter about in the little boats hired out on its tiny strip of canal, or to hide from the sun and crowds amid the ornamental pools and walkways of the **Parque de María Luisa**. The park is designed like the plaza in a mix of 1920s Art Deco and mock-Mudéjar. Scattered about, and round its edge, are more buildings from the fair, some of them amazingly opulent, built in the last months before the Wall Street crash undercut the scheme's impetus – look out, in particular, for the stylish **Guatemala building**, off the Paseo de la Palmera.

Towards the end of the park, the grandest mansions from the fair have been adapted as **museums**. The farthest contains the city's **archeology collections** (Tues 3–8pm, Wed–Sat 9am–8pm, Sun 9am–2.30pm; 250ptas, free to EU citizens). The main exhibits are Roman mosaics and artefacts from nearby Italica, along with a unique Phoenician statuette of Astarte-Tanit, the virgin goddess once worshipped throughout the Mediterranean. Opposite, the fabulous-looking **Popular Arts Museum** (Tues 3–8pm, Wed–Sat 9am–8pm, Sun 9am–2.30pm; 250ptas, free to EU citizens), is often besieged by school kids but has interesting displays relating to traditional arts and crafts and the April *feria*.

Barrio Santa Cruz, the river and Triana

Santa Cruz is very much in character with the city's romantic image, its streets narrow and tortuous to keep out the sun, the houses brilliantly whitewashed and barricaded with *rejas* (iron grilles) behind which girls once kept chaste evening rendezvous with their *novios*. Almost all of the houses have patios, often surprisingly large, and in summer these become the principal family living room. One of the most beautiful is within the Baroque **Hospicio de los Venerables Sacerdotes** (daily 10am–2pm & 4–8pm; guided visits every 30min 600ptas), near the centre in a plaza of the same name – one of the few buildings in the Barrio worth actively seeking out.

Of numerous mansions, by far the finest is the so-called **Casa de Pilatos** (daily 9am–7pm; 1000ptas), built by the Marqués de Tarifa on his return from a pilgrimage to Jerusalem in 1519 and popularly thought to have been in imitation of the house of Pontius Pilate. In fact it's an interesting and harmonious mixture of Mudéjar, Gothic and Renaissance styles, featuring brilliant *azulejos*, a tremendous sixteenth-century stairway and the most elegant domestic patios in the city.

Down by the **Guadalquivir** are more pedal-boats for idling away the afternoons, and at night a surprising density of local couples. The main riverside landmark here is the twelve-sided **Torre del Oro**, built by the Almohads in 1220 as part of the Alcázar fortifications. It was connected to another small fort across the river by a chain which had to be broken by the Castilian fleet before their conquest of the city in 1248. The tower was later used as a repository for the gold brought back to Sevilla from the Americas – hence its name. It now houses a small **naval museum** (Tues–Fri 10am–2pm, Sat & Sun 11am–2pm; 100ptas).

One block away, with its entry on c/Temprado, is the **Hospital de la Caridad** (Mon–Sat 9am–1.30pm & 3.30–6.30pm; 400ptas), founded in 1676 by Don Miguel de Manara, the inspiration for Byron's Don Juan. According to the testimony of one of Don Miguel's friends, "there was no folly which he did not commit, no youthful indulgence into which he did not plunge . . . (until) what occurred to him in the street of the coffin." What occurred was that Don Miguel, returning from a reckless orgy, had a vision in which he was confronted by a funeral procession carrying his own corpse. He repented his past life, joined the Brotherhood of Charity (whose task was to bury the bodies of tramps and criminals), and later set up this hospital for the relief of the dying and destitute, for which purpose it is still used. Don Miguel commissioned a series of eleven paintings by Murillo for the chapel, six of which remain. Alongside them hang two *Triumph of Death* pictures by Valdés Leal. One, depicting a decomposing bishop being eaten by worms (beneath the scales of justice labelled *Ni más, Ni menos* – No More, No Less), is so powerfully repulsive that Murillo declared that "you have to hold your nose to look at it".

Farther along, past the Plaza de Armas station, lies the **Museo de Bellas Artes** (Tues 3–8pm, Wed–Sat 9am–8pm, Sun 9am–3pm; 250ptas, free to EU citizens). Housed in recently modernized galleries in a beautiful former convent, this is definitely worth a visit; highlights of an outstanding collection include the paintings by Zurbarán of Carthusian monks at supper, El Greco's portrait of his son, and works by Murillo, Ribera and Montañes.

The **Museo de Murillo**, c/Santa Teresa 8 (Tues–Fri 10am–2pm & 4–7pm, Sat 10am–2pm, Sun 10am–2pm & 4–7pm; free), at the far end of the Jardines de Murillo, is the artist's former home, and is furnished with contemporaneous artworks, craftsmanship and furniture – though no original artworks of his own.

Triana and La Cartuja

Over the river is the **Triana** *barrio*, scruffy, lively and well away from the tourist trails. This was once the heart of the city's gypsy community and, more specifically, home of the great flamenco dynasties of Sevilla who were kicked out by developers earlier this century and are now scattered throughout the city. The gypsies lived in extended families in tiny, immaculate communal houses called *corrales* around courtyards glutted with flowers; today only a handful remain intact. Triana is still, however, the starting point for the annual pilgrimage to El Rocío (at the end of May), when a myriad of painted wagons leave town, drawn by oxen. It houses, too, the city's oldest working ceramics factory, Santa Ana, where the tiles, many still in the traditional, geometric Arabic designs, are painted by hand.

At Triana's northern edge lies **La Cartuja** (Tues–Sun 11am–9pm; 300ptas, free Tues for EU citizens), a fourteenth-century former Carthusian monastery expensively restored as part of the Expo '92 world fair. Part of the complex is now given over to the **Museo del Arte Contemporáneo** (Tues–Sat 10am–9pm, Sun 10am–3pm; 300ptas, free Tues for EU citizens), which, in addition to work by *andaluz* artists, frequently stages important exhibitions by international artists.

The remnants of much the **Expo '92 site** itself have been incorporated into the **Isla Mágica** (March–Oct 11am–11pm; 3300ptas, half-day 2300ptas), an amusement park based on sixteenth-century Spain, with water and rollercoaster rides, shows and period street animations.

Outside the city: Roman Italica

The Roman ruins and remarkable mosaics of **ITALICA** (Tues–Sat 9am–8pm, Sun 9am–3pm; 250ptas, free to EU citizens) lie some 9km to the north of Sevilla, just outside the village of Santiponce. There's also a well-preserved **Roman theatre** in Santiponce itself, signposted from the main road.

Italica was the birthplace of three emperors (Trajan, Hadrian and perhaps Theodosius) and was one of the earliest Roman settlements in Spain, founded in 206 BC by Scipio Africanus as a home for his veterans. It rose to considerable military importance in the second and third centuries AD, was richly endowed during the reign of Hadrian (117–138), and declined as an urban centre only under the Visigoths, who preferred Sevilla, then known as *Hispalis*. Eventually the city was deserted by the Moors after the river changed its course, disrupting the surrounding terrain.

Throughout the Middle Ages the ruins were used as a source of stone for Sevilla, but somehow the shell of its enormous **amphitheatre** – the third largest in the Roman world – has survived. Today it's crumbling perilously, but you can clearly detect the rows of seats, the corridors and the dens for wild beasts. Beyond, within a rambling and unkempt grid of **streets** and **villas**, about twenty **mosaics** have been uncovered. Most are complete, including excellent coloured floors with birds, Neptune and the Seasons, and several fine black-and-white geometric patterns.

Getting to Italica, buses depart every half-hour from the Plaza de Armas station for the twenty-minute journey; you need the Empresa Casal service to Santiponce, which departs from Bay 33. Santiponce is not well-endowed with facilities but the *Venta Canario* almost opposite the Italica site entrance does reasonable *platos combinados* and is famous for its grilled steaks served on wooden slabs with *papas arrugadas* – small baked potatoes in *mojo* spicy sauce.

Eating and drinking

Sevilla is packed with lively and enjoyable bars and restaurants, and you'll find somewhere to eat and drink at just about any hour. With few exceptions, anywhere around the sights and the **Barrio Santa Cruz** will be expensive. The two most promising central areas are down **towards the bullring** and north of here towards the Plaza de Armas bus station. The **Plaza de Armas** area is slightly seedier but has the cheapest *comidas* this side of the river. Wander down c/Marqués de Paradas, and up c/Canalejas and c/San Eloy, and find out what's available. Across the river in **Triana**, c/Betis and c/Pureza are also good cheap hunting grounds.

Restaurants

La Albahaca, Plaza Santa Cruz 29. Charming, traditional and expensive restaurant with outdoor tables in the one of the city's prettiest squares. Closed Sun.

El Arenal, c/García de Vinuesa. Good *freiduría* (fried fish shop) in the rewarding area between the bullring and the cathedral.

Bar Modesto, c/Cano y Cueto. At the north end of Santa Cruz, this mid-priced bar-restaurant offers a tempting *menú* (2000ptas) and great *tapas*.

Bar-Pizzeria El Artesano, c/Mateos Gago 11. Very reasonably priced, in the Barrio Santa Cruz and popular with young locals.

Bodegón Pez Espada, c/Hernando Colón 8. Near the cathedral, and one of the few inexpensive places to eat in the Barrio Santa Cruz. Excellent seafood and *paella* with a buffet where you can refill your plate as many times as you like.

Café Rayuela, c/Miguel de Mañara 9. Pleasant lunch-time venue serving *raciones* and salads at outdoor tables in a pedestrianized street behind the Turismo.

Café-Bar Veracruz, opposite the Torre del Oro near the river. Simple roadside place offering a bargain 1000ptas *menú*; makes a good lunch stop.

Hotel Alfonso XIII, c/San Fernando 2 (☎95 422 28 50). Swankiest place in town – worth a look at this beautiful building and its stunning patio even if you don't sit down in the pricey restaurant.

Jalea Real, c/Sor Ángela de la Cruz 37, near the church of San Pedro. Excellent vegetarian restaurant run by a friendly and enthusiastic *sevillana*. Closed Mon.

Jerez en Sevilla, San Eloy s/n, near Plaza Duque de la Victoria. Bar serving tasty *churros* and *chocolate*.

Kiosko de las Flores. Just across the Puente de Triana (Isabel II bridge), tucked into the side of the bridge, this is one of Sevilla's best-loved fried fish emporia serving *tapas* in the bar and *raciones* at outdoor tables near the river – just the place on a summer night. Closed Mon.

La Mandragora, c/Albuera 11, just north of the Maestranza bullring, across c/Reyes Católicos. Sevilla's second vegetarian restaurant with a wide range of dishes and a *menú*.

Restaurante de los Gallegos, c/Capataz Franco. In a tiny alleyway off c/Martín Villa, near the Plaza del Duque de la Victoria, this restaurant is such good value that locals queue up at lunchtime to eat here.

Restaurante San Francisco, Plaza San Francisco. Stylish restaurant near the cathedral.

Río Grande, c/Betis 70. This Triana restaurant has the best view in town from its terrace on the river's west bank, and a medium-priced *menú*.

San Marco, c/Meson del Moro 6, Santa Cruz. Delicious and good-value Italian food served inside a remarkable twelfth-century Moorish bathhouse. Equally good are their other restaurants at c/Cuna 6, near Plaza del Salvador, and c/Betis 68, in Triana.

La Sopa Boba, c/Bailén 34, just off the Plaza del Museo on the Museo de Bellas Artes' doorstep. Tasty experimental home cooking, with a good-value *menú*.

Zucchero, c/Golfo, to the east of Plaza Alfalfa. Small and friendly Italian vegetarian restaurant.

Bars

For straight drinking and occasional *tapas* you can be much less selective. There are **bars** all over town – a high concentration of them with barrelled sherries from nearby Jerez and Sanlúcar (the locals drink the cold, dry *fino* with their *tapas*, especially shrimp); a *tinto de verano* is the local version of *sangría* – wine with lemonade, a great summer drink. Outside the centre, you'll find lively bars in the **Plaza Alfafa** area, and across the river in **Triana** – particularly in c/Castilla, c/Betis, and in and around c/Salado. A new zone that has emerged recently as a focus for artistic, student and gay barhoppers is the **Alameda** (de Hércules).

In summer much of the action emigrates to the bars along the **river's east bank** to the north of the Triana bridge as far as the spectacular Puente de la Barqueta, built for Expo '92. Many of these open for a season only, springing up the following year under a new name and ownership.

The **gay scene** has a cluster of bars on the city side of the Puente Isabel II, where *Isbiliyya*, *Tocame* and other bars get lively around midnight.

Anima, c/Miguel Cid 80, north of the Museo de Bellas Artes. Lovely old tiled bar which mounts periodic art and photo exhibitions.

La Barqueta, just south of the bridge of the same name. Stylish open-air bar which puts on music, concerts, theatre and shows throughout the summer.

Bar Eslava, c/Eslava 3–5, near the church of San Lorenzo. Excellent *tapas* bar with restaurant attached.

Bar Giralda, c/Mateus Gagos. Excellent bar in converted ancient Moorish bathhouse, with a wide selection of *tapas*.

Bar Modesto, c/Cano y Cueto, at the north end of Santa Cruz (ask for it by name, it's well known). Perhaps the best *tapas* bar in the city, with just about every imaginable snack.

Casa Morales, c/García de Vinuesa. Fine traditional bar with barrelled wine.

La Gitanilla, c/Ximénez de Enciso. One of the liveliest places in Santa Cruz, with inexpensive drinks, but pricey *tapas*.

La Otra Orilla, Paseo de Nuestra Señora de la "O" s/n, near the Puente de Triana. Riverside open-air bar owned by the proprietors of *La Barqueta* (above) with a similar ambience.

El Refugio, c/Huelva 5. Slightly west of Plaza del Salvador, this serves a wide variety of snacks, including vegetarian *tapas*.

El Rinconcillo, c/Gerona, by the church of Santa Catalina. Sevilla's oldest bar (founded in 1670) does a fair *tapas* selection as well as providing a hangout for the city's literati.

El Siete, c/Goles 44, near the Pasarela La Cartuja footbridge. Good little bar attached to this art gallery/performance space.

Las Teresas, Plaza Santa Teresa. Good beer and sherry served in this atmospheric bar with hanging cured hams and tiled walls lined with faded *corrida* photos. It's also worth stopping here for breakfast the morning after.

Nightlife

Sevilla is a wonderfully late-night city, and in summer and during fiestas, the streets around the central areas are often packed out at 2am.

Flamenco

Flamenco – or more accurately *sevillanas* – music and dance are offered at dozens of places in the city, some of them extremely tacky and expensive. Unless you've heard otherwise, avoid the fixed "shows" or *tablaos* (many of which are a travesty, even using recorded music). The spontaneous nature of flamenco makes it almost impossible to timetable into the two-shows-a-night cabaret demanded by impresarios. The nearest you'll get to the real thing is at *Los Gallos*, in the Plaza Santa Cruz, which has a professional cast. However, it is pricey (3000ptas including one drink), and you'd probably do just as well at *El Tamboril*, a renowned flamenco **bar** in the opposite corner of the same square. Singers and dancers aren't guaranteed to drop in (around midnight is best), but when they do, you're in for an unforgettable night.

Another excellent bar which often has spontaneous flamenco (try Mon or Thurs after 10pm) is *La Carbonería*, c/Levies 18, just to the northeast of the church of Santa Cruz. It used to be the coal merchant's building (hence the name) and is a large, simple and welcoming place. *Quita Pesares*, in the Plaza Jerónimo de Córdoba near the church of Santa Catalina, is run by a flamenco singer, and is a chaotic place where there's often impromptu music when things get lively around midnight.

Live music and clubs

For **rock music** the bars around Plaza Alfalfa and the Alameda de Hércules have most of the best action. Recommended music bars on the Alameda which often stage live gigs include *Bulebar* (no. 83), *La Habanilla* at the northern end, *El Baron Rampante* in c/Arias Montano about half way along and *Fun Club* on the Alameda proper. Over in Triana, *Druida*, c/Rodrigo de Triana, often has live music. **Live jazz** can be found at *Bluemoon*, c/J.A. Cavestany s/n, near the Santa Justa train station, or the newly opened and popular *Naima*, just off the Alameda at c/Trajano 47 (both closed Aug). The vibrant café-bar *La Imperdible*, Plaza San Antonio de Padua, between the Alameda de Hércules and the river, puts on live jazz on Tuesdays, with various other entertainment throughout the week. Major **concerts**, whether touring British and American bands or big Spanish acts like Paco de Lucía, Alejandro Sanz or Ketama, usually take place in the old Expo site across the river in Cartuja or in one or other of the football stadiums. Check *El Giraldillo* (the Turismo's free listings magazine), the local paper *El Correo* or street posters for possibilities. The official agents for many concerts are Viajes Meliá, Avda. de la Constitución 30.

A strong night-time **club and disco** scene in Triana livens up c/Betis, whilst across the river near the Puente Isabel II, the disco-pub *Poseidon*, c/Marqués de Paradas, has free entrance, moderately priced drinks, and is open till 3am.

Listings

Airport Mainly internal flights run by Iberia (c/Almirante Lobo; ☎95 422 89 01; 95 451 61 11 for flight information). Amarillos buses run between the airport and the Puerta de Jerez (see "Arrival, orientation and information", p.240).

Banks Numerous places on the Avda. de la Constitución and around Plaza Duque de la Victoria. American Express is represented by Viajes Alhambra (c/Coronel Segui 3, off Plaza Nueva; ☎95 421 29 23). El Corte Inglés stores offer good exchange rates, low commission and long hours.

Bike rental Motorcycles available from Alkimoto, c/Recaredo 28 (☎95 444 11 15), east of the Casa de Pilatos. Cycles (a great way to see the city) for hire at: Paco Mira on the Jardines de Murillo (opposite *Bar Modesto*); El Ciclismo, Paseo Catalina de Ribera 2 (☎95 441 19 59); Biki Rent Sevilla, Plaza de España (☎95 421 94 74).

Books/newspapers Reasonable selection of English books – mainly on Spain – at Librería Pascuallazaro, c/Sierpes 4, and in El Corte Inglés on Plaza Duque de la Victoria. There's a good newspaper stand at the Campana end of c/Sierpes, and British newspapers and the *International Herald Tribune* are also sold in the International bookshop on c/Reyes Católicos.

Bullfights Details and tickets from the Plaza de Toros or (with commission) from the kiosks in c/Sierpes.

Car rental Most agents are along the Avda. de la Constitución. One of the lowest-priced national operators, represented in the foyer of the *Hotel Alfonso XIII* (by the tobacco factory), is Atesa (☎95 441 97 12). You could also try a local operator, Triana Rent a Car, c/Almirante Lobo 7 (☎95 456 44 39), near the Torre del Oro.

Cinema Most movies showing are listed in *El Giraldillo*, the Turismo's listings magazine. "*V.O*" indicates a screening in the original language. A new "*V.O*" venue, Cine Avenida, c/Marqués de Paradas 15, has recently opened. Open-air "*cines de verano*" (July & Aug) are great places for a beer and a *tapa* while watching a movie, and can be found at the Prado de San Sebastián, c/Pagés del Corro 39 in Triana and the Buhaira in Avda. Eduardo Dato near Sevilla CF's football stadium.

Consulates Australia, c/Federico Rubio 14 (95 422 02 40); Canada, Avda. de la Constitución 30, 2° 4 (☎95 422 94 13); Ireland, Plaza Santa Cruz 6, 6° (☎95 421 63 61); UK, Plaza Nueva 87 (☎95 422 88 75); USA, Paseo de las Delicias 7 (☎95 423 18 83).

Feminism Best contact is the Librería Feminista at c/Zaragoza 36.

Flea market A *rastro* takes place on Thursday mornings along the c/Feria past the Plaza Encarnación, and a bigger one on Sunday at the Alameda de Hércules.

Football Sevilla has two major teams – Sevilla CF (who play at the Sánchez Pizjuan stadium) and Real Betis (currently the better one, who use Estadio Benito Villamarín). Match schedules are in the local or national press.

Hiking maps 1:50,000, 1:100,000 and 1:200,000 military maps from the Servicio Geográfico del Ejército (Plaza de España building, Sector Norte). Maps may also be purchased from CNIG, Edificio Sevillas, c/San Francisco Javier 9 (☎95 464 42 56).

Hospital English-speaking doctors available at the Hospital Universidad, Avda. Dr Fedriani (☎95 424 81 81). Dial ☎091 for emergency treatment.

Police Bag-snatching is big business. If you lose something, get the theft documented at the Plaza de la Gavidia station (☎95 428 93 00), near Plaza de la Victoria. Dial ☎091 in emergency.

Post office Avda. de la Constitución 32, by the cathedral; *Lista de Correos* (poste restante) open Mon–Fri 9am–8pm, Sat 9am–1pm.

Telephones c/Sierpes 11, down a passageway (Mon–Sat 9am–1pm & 5.30–9pm).

Train information For tickets/info go to the RENFE office, off the Plaza Nueva at c/Zaragoza 29 (☎95 442 26 93 for information and reservations).

The Sierra Morena

The longest of Spain's mountain ranges, the **Sierra Morena** extends almost the whole way across Andalucía – from Rosal on the Portuguese frontier to the dramatic pass of Despeñaperros, north of Linares. Its hill towns marked the northern boundary of the old Moorish Caliphate of Córdoba and in many ways the region still signals a break, with a shift from the climate and mentality of the south to the bleak plains and villages of Extremadura and New Castile. The range is not widely known – with its highest point a mere 1110m, it's not a dramatic sierra – and even Andalucíans can have trouble placing it.

Climate, flora and fauna

The Morena's climate is mild – sunny in spring, hot but fresh in summer – but it can be very cold in the evenings and mornings. Tracks are still more common than roads, and tourism, which the government of Andalucía is keen to encourage, has so far meant little more than a handful of new signs indicating areas of special interest.

A good **time to visit** is between March and June, when the flowers, perhaps the most varied in the country, are at their best. You may get caught in the odd thunderstorm but it's usually bright and hot enough to swim in the reservoirs or splash about in the clear springs and streams, all of which are good to drink. If your way takes you along a river, you'll be entertained by armies of frogs and turtles plopping into the water as you approach, by lizards, dragonflies, bees, hares and foxes peering discreetly from their holes – and, usually, no humans present for miles round.

The locals maintain that, while the last bears disappeared only a short time ago, there are still a few wolves in remoter parts. Of more concern to anyone trekking in the Sierra Morena, however, are the **toros bravos** (fighting bulls), since you are quite likely to come across them. They should always be in fenced-off pastures with explicit signs warning you to keep out (*toros peligros* are the words to look out for), but these often disappear or are not put up in the first place. Should you be unfortunate enough to have a close encounter it's worth knowing that the black bulls are the only dangerous ones; the red ones, although equipped with some daunting headgear, are said not to be aggressive. Apparently, too, a group of bulls is less to be feared than a single one, and a single one only if he directly bars your way and looks mean. The thing to do, according to expert advice, is to stay calm, and without attracting the bull's attention, go round. If you even get a whiff of a fighting bull, though, it might well be best to adopt the time-honoured technique – drop everything and run.

Getting around the sierra

East–west **transport** in the sierra is very limited. Most of the bus services are radial and north–south, with Sevilla as the hub, and this leads to ridiculous situations where, for instance, to travel from Santa Olalla to Cazalla, a distance of some 53km, you must take a bus to Sevilla, 70km away, and then another up to Cazalla – a full day's journey of nearly 150km just to get from one town to the next. The best solution if you want to spend any amount of time in Morena is to organize your routes round **treks**. A bicycle, too, could be useful, but your own car much less so – this is not Michelin car-window-view territory. If you have a **bike**, you'll need plenty of gears, especially for the road between El Real de la Jara and El Pintado (Santa Olalla–Cazalla), while the roads round Almonaster, and between Cazalla and Constantina, are very bad for cycling.

Buses from Sevilla to the sierra leave from the Plaza de Armas station. If you just want to make a quick foray into the hills, **Aracena** is probably the best target (and the most regularly served town). If you're planning on some walking it's also a good starting point: before you leave Sevilla, however, be sure to get yourself a good **map** from the military Servicio Geográfico in the Plaza de España – these are well-produced and cheap, and though crammed with misleading information they do point you in the right direction to get lost somewhere interesting.

Aracena – and its sierra

The highest town in the Sierra Morena – guarded to its south by a small offshoot of the range – **ARACENA** has sharp, clear air, all the more noticeable after Sevilla. Capital of the western end of the sierra with 10,000 inhabitants, it's a substantial but pretty town, rambling up the side of a hill topped by the **Iglesia del Castillo**, a Gothic-Mudéjar church built by the Knights Templar around the remains of a Moorish castle.

Although the church is certainly worth the climb, Aracena's principal attraction is the **Gruta de las Maravillas** (daily 10.30am–1.30pm & 3–6pm; 850ptas), the largest and arguably the most impressive cave in Spain. Supposedly discovered by a local boy in search of a lost pig, the cave is now illuminated and there are guided tours as soon as a dozen or so people have assembled. On Sunday there is a constant procession, but usually plenty of time to gaze and wonder. The cave is astonishingly beautiful, and funny too – the last chamber of the tour is known as the Sala de los Culos (Room of Buttocks), its walls and ceiling an outrageous, naturally sculpted exhibition, tinged in a pinkish orange light. Close by the cave's entrance are a couple of excellent restaurants, open lunchtime only. Aracena is at the heart of a prestigious *jamón*-producing area, so try to sample some, and, when they're available, the delicious wild asparagus and local snails – rooted out from the roadside and in the fields in spring and summer respectively.

Practicalities

Aracena has a **Turismo**, located at the Gruta (Mon–Sat 10am–2.30pm & 3.30–6.30pm; ☎959 128206). There are limited **places to stay** – the best of which, at the bottom end of the scale, is *Casa Manolo*, below the main square at c/Barberos 6 (☎959 128014; ②). Alternatively, the *Hotel Sierra de Aracena*, Gran Vía 21 (☎955 126175; ④), offers relative luxury. There's also a **campsite** (☎959 501005; open April–Sept) about 5km out on the Sevilla road, then left for 500m on the road towards Corteconcepción. For **meals**, the medium-priced *Restaurante José Vicente*, Avda. Andalucía 51, opposite the park, specializes in *jamón* and pork dishes, including a mouthwatering *solomillo* (pork loin). Decent *tapas* and *platos combinados* are on offer at the more basic *Café-Bar Manzano*, at the southern end of the main square. If you intend to do some **walking in the sierra**, ask the Turismo for a pamphlet entitled *Senderismo* (paths) which details waymarked trails between the local villages.

Villages around Aracena

Surrounding Aracena you'll find a scattering of attractive but economically depressed villages, most of them dependent on the **jamón industry** and its curing factory at Jabugo. *Jamón serrano* (mountain ham) is a *bocadillo* standard throughout Spain and some of the best, *jamón de bellotas* (acorn-fed ham), comes from the Morena, where herds of sleek grey pigs grazing beneath the trees are a constant feature. In October the acorns drop and the pigs, waiting patiently below, gorge themselves, become fat and are promptly whisked off to be slaughtered and then cured in the dry mountain air.

The **sierra villages** – Jabugo, Aguafría, Almonaster La Real – all make rewarding bases for walks, though all are equally ill-served by public transport. The most interesting is **ALMONASTER LA REAL**, whose castle encloses a tiny ninth-century mosque, **La Mezquita** (daily 10am–sunset), with what is said to be the oldest **mihrab** in Spain. Tacked on to the mosque is the village bullring which sees action once a year in August during the annual fiesta. The village also has a couple of **places to eat and stay**: the very hospitable *Pensión La Cruz* (☎955 143135; ③), in the centre with a good restaurant, and *Hostal Casa García* (☎955 143109; ③), which also has a fine restaurant, with great *jamón* and *ensaladilla*. There are some superb paint-splashed waymarked walks northwest of the village, off the Cartegana road; a leaflet detailing these and other walks in the area can be found at the *Ayuntamiento* on Plaza de la Constitución.

Zufre and east to Cazalla and Constantina

From Aracena a single daily **bus** – currently at 5.45pm, connecting with the bus from Sevilla – covers the 25km southeast to Zufre (for those going farther afield, there's also a direct bus to Lisbon). Ten kilometres out of Aracena you come upon the **Embalse de Aracena**, one of the huge reservoirs that supply Sevilla, and from here a lovely but circuitous route will take you down towards Zufre along the **Rivera de Huelva**. From Zufre east there are no buses directly linking the villages en route to Cazalla.

Zufre

ZUFRE must rank as one of the most spectacular villages in Spain, hanging like a miniature Ronda on a high palisade at the edge of a ridge. Below the crumbling Moorish walls, the cliff falls away hundreds of feet, terraced into deep green gardens of orange trees and vegetables. Within the town the **Ayuntamiento** and **church** are both interesting examples of Mudéjar style, the latter built in the sixteenth century on the foundations of a mosque. In the basement of the *Ayuntamiento*, too, are a gloomy line of stone seats, said to have been used by the Inquisition. The focus of town, however, is the **Paseo**, a little park with rose gardens, a balcony, a bar at one end and a casino (bar-club) at the other. Here the villagers gather for much of the day: there is little work either in Zufre or its surrounding countryside. Finding food and drink shouldn't be a problem, but there's no official **accommodation** in Zufre; ask around, however, and there's a fair chance of finding a private room.

Santa Olalla

SANTA OLALLA DEL CALA, the next village to the east, is a walkable 16km from Zufre – a flattish route through open country with pigs and fields of wheat and barley, and then a sudden view of the Moorish **castillo** above the town. There have been several half-hearted attempts to reconstruct the castle but they haven't been helped by its adaptation in the last century as the local cemetery – the holes for coffins in the walls rather spoil the effect. Below its walls is the fifteenth-century parish church, with a fine Renaissance interior.

Coming from Zufre it's a surprise to find **hostales** in Santa Olalla, but the town is actually on the main Sevilla–Badajoz road and sees a fair amount of traffic – and regular buses to both cities. These stop outside the *Bar Primitivo*, c/Marina 3 (☎955 190052; ②), an admirable place to sleep, eat or just drink, all for a very reasonable price; its name is that of the owner, and no judgement.

Real de la Jara

After 4km of winding through stone-walled olive groves, the road flattens out into a grassy little valley above the **Río Calla** – a spot where the villages of Real and Olalla hold their joint *romería* at the end of April. These country *romerías* are always good to stumble upon, and if you happen on one in the Sierra Morena you should be well looked after. Proceedings start with a formal parade to the local *ermita* but they're very soon given over to feasting and dancing, the young men wobbling about on donkeys and mules in a wonderful parody of the grand *hidalgo* doings of Jerez and Sevilla, children shrieking and splashing in the river, and everyone dancing *sevillanas* to scratchy cassettes.

REAL DE LA JARA is 8km further east of Santa Olalla and much in the same mould, with two Moorish *castillos* (both in ruins), an over-priced and eccentrically run *casa de huéspedes* at c/Real 66 (②), and a very welcome public swimming pool. Cazalla de la Sierra, the next village, is some 45km along a mountainous route which sees few cars.

Cazalla and the Central Sierra

Another regional sierra "capital", **CAZALLA DE LA SIERRA** seems quite a metropolis. Not only does it have four **fondas** (the best is in Plaza Iglesia, the rest are in the main street, c/Llana) but there's a hotel, *Posada del Moro* (☎954 884326, fax 954 161437 ⑤), numerous bars and even a pub – pronounced "pa" in *andaluz* – where the locals go to drink cocktails and listen to jazz and rock music. If this is all too much of a shock, a more traditional bar and restaurant, but still lively, is the *Boleras* in Plaza Manuel Nosea – right next to the Guardia Civil's headquarters in a beautiful former nunnery.

The place to make for, however, is **La Plazuela**, where you'll find the local casino. This is essentially a place to drink and relax – quieter and more comfortable than most of the bars – and serves as a kind of club, with locals paying a nominal monthly membership charge. Most towns of Cazalla's size have one, and tourists and visitors are always welcome to use the facilities free of charge – worth doing since the membership rule means everybody drinks at reduced prices.

The main sight is the church of **Nuestra Señora de la Consolación** at the southern end of town, an outstanding example of *andaluz* "mix and match" architecture – begun in the fourteenth century, continued with some nice Renaissance touches and finally completed in the eighteenth century.

There are also some fine spots within easy wandering distance of Cazalla: a walk of just 5km will take you east to the **Ermita del Monte**, a little eighteenth-century church on a wooded hill above the Rivera de Huesna.

Cazalla is well-served by public transport. **Buses** run to the Estación de Cazalla y Constantina, twenty minutes to the east, at 6.45am and 1pm. From here there are three or four **trains** a day northwest to Zafra and Extremadura, and a similar number follow the river down towards El Pedroso and ultimately Sevilla. If you're making for El Pedroso, though, you might consider walking from the station – a lovely route, with great river swimming and a fabulous variety of valley flora and fauna; it takes about five hours. Daily buses also connect Cazalla with Sevilla.

El Pedroso and Constantina

EL PEDROSO is a pretty little town with a notable Mudéjar church. Accommodation is limited and basic; the woman who runs the station *cantina* supplies **rooms**. Across the road is an excellent **tapas bar**, the *Serranía*, which serves up local specialities such as venison, hare, pheasant and partridge.

Eighteen kilometres further to the east – and perhaps as good a place as any to cut back to Sevilla if you're not counting on trekking the whole length of the range – lies **CONSTANTINA**, a lively and beautiful mountain town with a population of almost 15,000. High above the town is the impressive **Castillo de la Armada**, surrounded by shady gardens descending in terraces to the old quarters. At the base is the parish **church**, once again with a Mudéjar tower, Moorish influence having died hard in these parts.

There are two **fondas** in the main street, c/Mesones, and just off it, a decent *hostal*, *Pensión Angelita*, c/El Peso 28 (☎95 588 17 25; ②), which has some rooms with bath. There's also a summer **youth hostel**, c/Cuesta Blanca s/n (☎95 588 15 89, fax 95 588 16 19; ①), slightly out of town, with a restaurant and pool. Travelling to Sevilla, there are two buses a day at 6.45am and 3pm.

The Costa de la Luz

Stumbling on the villages along the **Costa de la Luz**, between Algeciras and Cádiz, is like entering a new land after the dreadfulness of the Costa del Sol. The journey west from Algeciras seems in itself a relief, the road climbing almost immediately into rolling green hills, offering fantastic views down to Gibraltar and across the straits to the just-discernible white houses and tapering mosques of Moroccan villages. Beyond, the Rif Mountains hover mysteriously in the background and on a clear day, as you approach Tarifa, you can distinguish Tangier on the edge of its crescent-shaped bay.

Tarifa

TARIFA, spreading out beyond its Moorish walls, was until the mid-1980s a quiet village, known in Spain, if at all, for its abnormally high suicide rate – a result of the unremitting winds that blow across the town and its environs. Today it's a prosperous, popular and at times very crowded resort, following its discovery as Europe's prime **windsurfing** spot. There are equipment rental shops along the length of the main street, and regular competitions held year-round. Development is fast as a result of this new-found popularity, but for the time being it remains a fairly attractive place.

If windsurfing is not your motive, there can still be an appeal in wandering the crumbling ramparts, gazing out to sea or down into the network of lanes that surround the fifteenth-century, Baroque-fronted church of **San Mateo**. The **castle** was the site of many a struggle for this strategic foothold into Spain. It is named after Guzmán el Bueno (the Good), Tarifa's infamous commander during the Moorish siege of 1292, who earned his tag for a superlative piece of tragic drama. Guzmán's nine-year-old son had been taken hostage by a Spanish traitor and surrender of the garrison was demanded as the price of the boy's life. Choosing "honour without a son, to a son with dishonour", Guzmán threw down his own dagger for the execution. The story – a famous piece of heroic resistance in Spain – had echoes in the Civil War siege of the Alcázar at Toledo, when the Nationalist commander refused similar threats, an echo much exploited for propaganda purposes.

A new attraction in Tarifa are the popular **whale and dolphin spotting** excursions to the Strait of Gibraltar which leave daily from the harbour. The trip is a fairly steep 4500ptas, but this includes another trip free of charge if there are no sightings. Places must be booked in advance at the FIRRM (Foundation for Information & Research on Marine Mammals; ☎ & fax 956 627008 or mobile ☎919 459441) at c/Pedro Cortés 3, slightly west of San Mateo, off c/El Bravo.

Practicalities

The **Turismo** (Mon–Fri 10am–2pm & 6–8pm; ☎956 680993) on the central Paseo la Alameda can help with maps and accommodation. Tarifa has plenty of **places to stay**, though finding a bed in summer can be a struggle, with crowds of windsurfers packing out every available *hostal*. The *Hostal-Restaurante Villanueva*, Avda. Andalucía 11 (☎956 684149; ②), is very clean and has a good restaurant. In the same area are more *hostales* and an attractive hotel with sea views, *La Mirada*, c/San Sebastián 43 (☎956 680626; ④). The excellent *Hostal La Calzada*, c/Justina Pertiñes 7 (☎956 680366; ③), by San Mateo church, and the charming *Pensión Correo*, c/Coronel Móscardo 8 (☎956 680206; ②), located in the old post office, just south of the cathedral entrance, are both good places. Finally, there are two reasonable *casas de huéspedes*: *Casa Concha*, c/Rosendo (②), around the corner from *La Calzada*, and *Facundo*, c/Callao (☎956 680624; ②), 200m out on the main road to Cádiz. Just off the highway on c/Amador de los Ríos, *Hostal las Fuserías* (③) is better than it looks, with a laundry area and a shady courtyard, and preferable to the overpriced *Hostería Tarifa* (☎956 684076, fax 956 681078; ④) on the same street.

You'll find the **bus station**, a supermarket, a laundry and many of the larger hotels on the main Cádiz–Algeciras road.

For **meals**, the *Chan, Villanueva* and *Agobio*, all within a few hundred metres of each other just outside the western wall, have cheap *menús*, and *Pizzería Transito Tropical*, c/Sancho IV El Bravo 32, a couple of streets east of the Alameda, is a good Italian place. Most pleasant for lunch is the *Bar Alameda* on the Alameda, which does reasonable *platos combinados*. Of the dozen other **bars**, the German-run *Bistro Point* is a windsurfers' hangout and a good place for finding long-term accommodation as well as secondhand windsurfing gear. In the centre and down the side of San Mateo's church, *Mesón El Cartijo*, c/General Copons, is a bit more upmarket with a good-value *menú*, whilst *Bar Morilla*, facing the church's main entrance, is a good *tapas* stop.

On to Morocco

Tarifa offers the tempting opportunity of a quick approach **to Morocco**, with Tangier feasible as a day trip by boat; tickets are available from the Tourafrica office on the quayside, who will also have the latest information on the faster hydrofoil crossings, suspended at the time of writing. The boat currently leaves at 9.30am, returning from Tangier at 4.30pm or 6pm. The crossing takes an hour, leaving you just enough time for a brief look around. An overnight stay probably makes more sense, especially as a return ticket costs around 6000ptas. It's wise to book a few days ahead, as tour companies often take over the whole boat. This crossing is a lot more expensive than going from Algeciras, but might be a better bet if the latter is chock-a-block in summer or when Moroccans are returning home for the two major Islamic festivals (which rotate between January, February and March). There's also a car ferry from Tarifa to Tangier which leaves daily at 9.30am, returning at 3.30pm.

Tarifa Beach

Heading northwest from Tarifa, you find the most spectacular **beaches** along the whole Costa de la Luz – wide stretches of yellow or silvery-white sand, washed by some magical rollers. The same winds that have created such perfect conditions for windsurfing can, however, be a problem for more casual enjoyment, sandblasting those attempting to relax on towels or mats and whipping the water into whitecaps.

The beaches lie immediately west of the town. They get better as you move past the tidal flats and the mosquito-ridden estuary – until the dunes start, and the first camper vans lurk among the bushes. At **TARIFA BEACH**, a little bay 9km from town, there are restaurants, a windsurfing school, campsites and a *hostal* (③) at the base of a tree-tufted bluff. For more seclusion head for one of the numerous **beach-campsites** on either side, signposted from the main road or accessible by walking along the coast. All of these – the main ones are *Río Jara* (☎956 680570), *Tarifa* (☎956 439040), *Torre de la Peña* (☎956 684903) and *Paloma* (☎956 684203) – are well-equipped, inexpensive and open all year.

The coast west of Tarifa

Around the coast from *Paloma* campsite are extensive ruins of the Roman town of **BOLONIA**, or *Baelo Claudia* as the Romans knew it, where you can make out the remains of three temples and a theatre, as well as numerous houses (Tues–Sun; guided tours only at 10am, 11am, noon, 1pm, 4pm, 5pm & 6.15pm; 100ptas, free to EU citizens). The site can be reached down a small side road which turns off the main Cádiz road 15km after Tarifa. There's also a fine beach here with bars and eating places. Alternatively it's a good walk along the coast from either Paloma or, from the west, Zahara de los Atunes (3–4hr).

TUNA FISHING

The catch of the **bluefin tuna** is a ritual which has gone on along the Costa de la Luz for a thousand years and, today, still employs many of the age-old methods. The bluefin is the largest of the tuna family, weighing in at around 200 kilos each, and the season lasts from April to June as the fish migrate south towards the Mediterranean, and from early July to mid-August when they return, to be herded and caught by huge nets. The biggest market is Japan, where tuna is eaten raw as sushi. Tuna numbers, however, are declining and the season shortening – probably the result of overfishing – much to the concern of the people of Conil de la Frontera and Zahara de los Atunes, for whom the catch represents an important source of income.

ZAHARA, a small fishing village beginning to show signs of development, has a fabulous eight-kilometre-long beach. There's a smallish plush hotel, *Hotel Antonio* (☎956 439141, fax 956 439135; ⑥) just back from it, and three *hostales*, all fairly expensive and usually full until at least the end of September. The friendly *Hostal Monte Mar* (☎956 430947; ③), however, on the beach, is a real bargain. Camping is also feasible, but don't forget the insect repellent.

Vejer de la Frontera

While you're on the Costa de la Luz, be sure to take time to visit **VEJER DE LA FRONTERA**, a classically white, Moorish-looking hill town set in a cleft between great protective hills that rear high above the road from Tarifa to Cádiz. If you arrive by bus, it's likely to drop you well below the town at two *hostal-restaurantes*; *La Barca de Vejer* (☎956 450369, fax 956 451083; ③) does superb *bocadillos de lomo*. The road winds up for another 4km, but just by one of the bus-stop cafés there's a donkey path that takes only about twenty minutes to reach the town. This is a perfect approach – for the drama of Vejer is in its isolation and its position, which gradually unfold before you. If you don't fancy the walk, though, taxis are usually available. The **Turismo**, at c/San Filmo 6 (Mon–Fri 10.30am–2pm & 6.30–8.30pm, Sat 10.30am–1.30pm; ☎956 450191), can provide a good town map and accommodation list.

Until the last decade, the women of Vejer wore long, dark cloaks that veiled their faces like nuns' habits; despite being adopted as the town's tourist icon, this custom seems now to be virtually extinct, but the place has a remoteness and Moorish feel as explicit as anywhere in Spain. There's a castle and a church of curiously mixed styles (mainly Gothic and Mudéjar) but the main fascination lies in exploring the brilliant white and labyrinthine alleyways, wandering past iron-grilled windows, balconies and patios, and slipping into a succession of **bars**. Try the *Bar Chirino* on La Plazuela, which contains a photographic history of the town.

Outside August, finding **accommodation** shouldn't be a problem. There's the slightly pricey but excellent *Hostal la Janda*, c/Cerro Clarisas s/n (☎956 450142; ③), or the delightful, upmarket *Hotel Convento San Francisco* (☎956 643570; ⑤) on La Plazuela, which also stocks maps if the Turismo is closed. Both are rather hidden away, so ask for directions. Cheaper rooms are available at a charming *casa particular* on the Plaza de España (no. 17), in the old town (☎956 450843; ②). Vejer's **campsite** (☎956 450098; June–Sept) lies below the town on the main N340 Málaga to Cádiz road.

Conil

Back on the coast, a dozen or so kilometres on, **CONIL** is an increasingly popular resort. Outside July and August, though, it's still a good place to relax, and in mid-season the only real drawback is trying to find a room. Conil town, once a poor fishing village, now seems entirely modern as you look back from the beach, though when you're actually in the streets you find many older buildings too. The majority of the tourists are Spanish (with a lesser number of Germans), so there's an enjoyable atmosphere, and if you are here in mid-season, a very lively nightlife.

The **beach**, Conil's *raison d'être*, is a wide bay of brilliant yellow stretching for miles to either side of town and lapped by an amazingly, not to say disarmingly, gentle Atlantic – you have to walk halfway to Panama before it reaches waist height. The area immediately in front of town is the family beach; up to the northwest you can walk to some more sheltered coves, while across the river to the southeast is a topless and nudist area. Walking along the coast in this direction the beach is virtually unbroken until it reaches the cape, the familiar-sounding **Trafalgar**, off which Lord Nelson achieved victory and met his death on October 21, 1805. If the winds are blowing, this is one of the most sheltered beaches in the area. It can be reached by road, save for the last 400 metres across the sands to the rock.

Practicalities

Most **buses** use the Transportes Comes station: walk towards the sea and you'll find yourself in the centre of town. There's a helpful **Turismo** (Mon–Fri 8.30am–2.30pm & 6–9pm, Sat 10am–2pm & 6–9pm, Sun 10am–1pm; ☎956 440501) at c/Carretera, north of Plaza de España. **Accommodation** needs are served by numerous hotels and *hostales*. The central *Pensión La Villa*, Plaza de España 6 (☎956 441053; ③), is one of the most reasonable. Conil also has private rooms for rent; the easiest way to find one of these is to go to the first "supermarket" on the right-hand side of the road to Playa Fontanilla (the road opposite the *Rinkon Way* open-air disco), where they have a complete list – there are good ones at c/Velásquez 1. Nearby **campsites** include *Fuente del Gallo* in the nearby *urbanización*, Fuente del Gallo (☎956 440137; March–Oct), a three-kilometre walk despite all signs to the contrary.

Conil has lots of good seafood **restaurants** along the front; try the *ortiguillas* – deep-fried sea anemones – which you see only in the Cádiz area. For a really excellent, modest-priced meal, search out the *Bar-Restaurante Peña Federata de Caza*, on the road uphill towards the nearby town of Barbate. During the summer, Conil's **nightlife** attraction is *Las Carpas* ("the tents"), a huge triple disco complex on the beach which caters for all ages and features techno, salsa, dance bands and flamenco shows. It's all provided by the town council and, best of all, it's free.

Cádiz

CÁDIZ is among the oldest settlements in Spain, founded about 1100 BC by the Phoenicians and one of the country's principal ports ever since. Its greatest period, however, and the era from which the central part of town takes most of its present appearance, was the eighteenth century. Then, with the silting up of the river to Sevilla, the port enjoyed a virtual monopoly on the Spanish-American trade in gold and silver, and on its proceeds were built the cathedral – itself golden-domed (in colour at least) and almost Oriental when seen from the sea – the public halls and offices, and the smaller churches.

Inner Cádiz, built on a peninsula-island, remains much as it must have looked in those days, with its grand open squares, sailors' alleyways and high, turreted houses. Literally crumbling from the effect of the sea air on its soft limestone, it has a tremendous atmosphere – slightly seedy, definitely in decline, but still full of mystique.

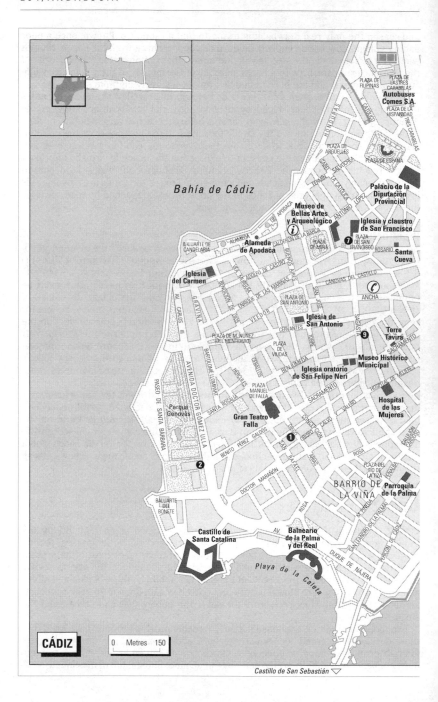

Bahía de Cádiz

PLAZA DE FILIPINAS

PLAZA DE LASTRES CARABELAS

Autobuses
Comes S.A.

PLAZA DE LA HISPANIDAD

PLAZA DE ARGUELLES

PLAZA DE ESPAÑA

Palácio de la
Diputación
Provincial

Museo de
Bellas Artes
y Arqueológico

Iglesia y claustro
de San Francisco

PLAZA DE SAN FRANCISCO

Santa
Cueva

BALUARTE DE CANDELARIA

ALAMEDA

Alameda
de Apodaca

PLAZA DE MINA

Iglesia
del Carmen

CANOVAS DEL CASTILLO

ANCHA

PLAZA DE SAN ANTONIO

Iglesia de
San Antonio

PLAZA DE M. NUÑEZ
(DEL MENTIDERO)

PLAZA DE VIUDAS

Torre
Tavira

Museo Histórico
Municipal

Iglesia oratorio
de San Felipe Neri

PLAZA MANUEL DE FALLA

Hospital
de las
Mujeres

Parque
Genovés

Gran Teatro
Falla

BALUARTE
DEL
BONETE

PLAZA DEL
TIO DE
LA TIZA

BARRIO DE
LA VIÑA

Parroquia
de la Palma

DOCTOR MARAÑON

Castillo de
Santa Catalina

Balneario
de la Palma
y del Real

Playa de la Caleta

PASEO DE SANTA BARBARA

AVENIDA DOCTOR GOMEZ ULLA

CÁDIZ

0   Metres   150

Castillo de San Sebastián ▽

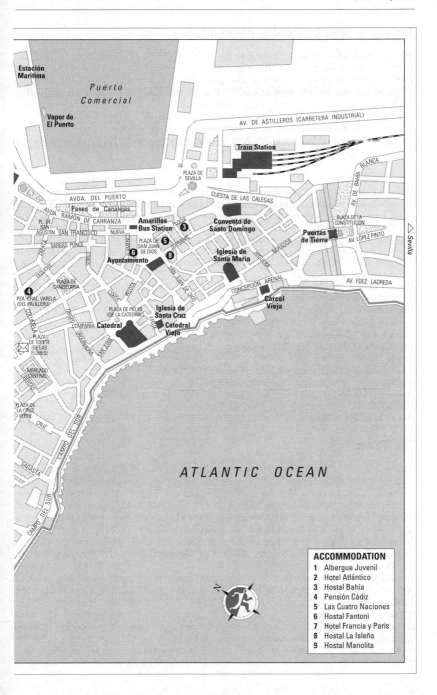

Arrival, information and accommodation

Arriving by **train** you'll find yourself on the periphery of the old town, close to the Plaza de San Juan de Dios, busiest of the many squares. By **bus** you'll be a few blocks farther north, along the water – either at the Los Amarillos terminal (which serves Rota, Chipiona and the resorts west of Cádiz) or just beyond in the Plaza de Hispanidad at the Estación de Comes (used by buses from Sevilla, Tarifa and most other destinations toward Algeciras). Los Amarillos also runs a twice-daily service through Arcos to Ubrique, with a connection there to Ronda – by far the best route. There's a **Turismo** on Plaza de Mina (Mon–Fri 9am–2pm & 5–8pm; ☎956 241001; a kiosk in the plaza opens Sat, Sun & holidays 10am–1pm).

Accommodation

Radiating around the Plaza de San Juan de Dios is a dense network of alleyways crammed with **hostales**, **fondas** and straightforward dosshouses or brothels. More salubrious places to stay are to be found a couple of blocks away, towards the cathedral or Plaza de Candelaria.

Albergue Juvenil, c/Diego Arias 1, close to Plaza Manuel de Falla (☎ & fax 956 221939). Excellent new hostel in restored mansion with dormitory, single and double rooms. Hires out bicycles to residents, as well as offering courses in flamenco and trips both around the city and to surrounding beauty spots. ①–③.

Hotel Atlántico, Parque Genovés 9 (☎956 226905, fax 956 214582). Modern *parador* with Atlantic views and an outdoor pool. ⑦.

Hostal Bahía, c/Plocias (☎956 259061). Excellent, friendly *hostal*, offering rooms with bath. ④.

Pensión Cadiz, c/Feduchy 20 (☎956 285801). Basic but clean *pensión*. ②.

Las Cuatro Naciones, c/Plocia 3 (☎956 255539). Clean, unpretentious place with low-priced rooms, close to Plaza San Juan de Dios. ②.

Hostal Fantoni, c/Flamenco 5 (☎956 282704). Good-value *hostal* with en-suite rooms. ②.

Hotel Francia y París, Plaza San Francisco 2 (☎956 222348, fax 956 222431). Comfortable accommodation in this quiet and central *Belle Époque* hotel. ⑤.

Hostal La Isleña, Plaza de San Juan de Dios (☎956 287064). Basic but clean *hostal* right on the square. ②.

Hostal Manolita, c/Benjumeda 2 (☎956 211577). Simple rooms in a friendly, family-run place. ③.

The Town

Unlike most other ports of its size, Cádiz seems immediately relaxed, easy-going, and not at all threatening, even at night. Perhaps this is due to its reassuring shape and compactness, the presence of the sea making it impossible to get lost for more than a few blocks. But it probably owes this tone as much to the town's tradition of liberalism and tolerance – one maintained all through the years of Franco's dictatorship even though this was one of the first towns to fall to his forces, and was the port through which the Nationalist armies launched their invasion. In particular, Cádiz has always accepted its substantial gay community, who are much in evidence at the city's brilliant *carnaval* celebrations.

Cádiz is more interesting in its general ambience – its blind alleys, cafés and backstreets – than for any particular buildings. As you wander, you'll find the **Museo de Bellas Artes**, at Plaza de Mina 5 (Tues 2–8pm, Wed–Sat 9am–8pm, Sun 9.30am–2.30pm; 250ptas; free to EU citizens), just across from the Turismo. This contains an impressive local archeological display and a quite exceptional series of saints painted by **Francisco Zurbarán**, brought here from the Carthusian monastery at Jerez and one of only three such sets in the country (the others are at Sevilla and

Guadalupe) preserved intact, or nearly so. With their sharply defined shadows and intense, introspective air, Zurbarán's saints are at once powerful and very Spanish – even the English figures such as Hugh of Lincoln, or the Carthusian John Houghton, martyred by Henry VIII when he refused to accept him as head of the English Church. Perhaps this is not surprising, for the artist spent much of his life travelling round the Carthusian monasteries of Spain and many of his saints are in fact portraits of the monks whom he met.

The **sea fortifications** and waterside **alamedas** are very striking and give direction to walks around the town. Even if you don't normally go for High Baroque it's hard to resist the attraction of the huge and seriously crumbling eighteenth-century **Catedral Nueva** (Mon–Sat 10.30am–1pm; museum open Tues–Sat 10.30am–12.30pm; 500ptas), decorated entirely in stone, with no gold or white in sight, and absolutely perfect proportions. In the crypt is buried Manuel de Falla, the great *gaditano* composer of such Andalucía-inspired works as *Nights in the Gardens of Spain* and *El Amor Brujo*.

Over on the seaward side of the mammoth complex, the "old" cathedral, **Santa Cruz**, is also worth a look, its interior liberally studded with coin-in-the-slot votive candles. A **Roman theatre** (Tues–Sun 11am–1pm; free) has recently been excavated behind. To the north of the cathedral along c/Sacramento the **Torre Tavira** (daily 10am–8pm; 400ptas) is an eighteenth-century mansion with the tallest tower in the city, from where there are great **views** over the city and sea beyond; it also houses an entertaining camera obscura. Lastly, there are two churches of note for the paintings they contain. Foremost of these is the chapel of the **Hospital de Mujeres** (daily 9am–6pm; free) – ask the porter for admission – which has a brilliant El Greco of *St Francis in Ecstasy*. The other, an oval, eighteenth-century chapel, **Santa Cueva** (Mon–Fri 10am–1pm; 50ptas), on c/San Rosario, has three frescoes on Eucharistic themes by Goya.

Eating and drinking

Take-away **fried fish** was invented in Cádiz (despite English claims to the contrary) and there are numerous *freidurías* (fried-fish shops) around the town – including the highly recommended *Freiduría Las Flores* on the square of the same name to the north-west of the cathedral – as well as stands around the beach in season. In the **bars**, *tortilla de camarones* (shrimp omelette) is a superb local speciality. The Plaza de San Juan de Dios, protruding across the neck of the peninsula from the port and the first long stretch of Cádiz's naval dockyards, has several cafés and inexpensive **restaurants**. *La Caleta*, whose interior is built like the bow of a ship, serves wonderful *champiñones al Jerez* (mushrooms in sherry), *chipirones en su tinta* (squid in ink) and other hearty *raciones*; it also has a *comedor* with excellent value *menús*. In the square's top right-hand corner, *El 9*, *Pasaje Andaluz* and *La Económica* are also good. Also try the tiny Plaza Tío de la Tiza, in the old quarter near the beach, which has dozens of good fish places, with outdoor tables in summer, or the more upmarket *El Faro*, c/San Félix 15, nearby, one of the best fish restaurants in Andalucía.

The Cádiz coast

Cádiz has two beaches – the **Playa de la Victoria**, to the left of the promontory approaching the town, and the none-too-clean **Playa de la Caleta** – but for clearer waters it's best to cross the bay to **Puerto de Santa María**. Farther along the coast towards Sanlúcar de Barrameda, beaches are more or less continuous, with two of the best flanking the resorts of **Rota** and **Chipiona**. These are both popular weekend retreats from Cádiz, and during July and August pretty much packed.

Puerto de Santa María

PUERTO DE SANTA MARÍA is the obvious choice, a traditional family resort for both *gaditanos* (as inhabitants of Cádiz are known) and *sevillanos* – many of whom have built villas and chalets along the fine **Playa Puntillo**. This strand is a little way out from the town (a ten- to fifteen-minute walk or a local bus), a pleasant place to while away an afternoon; there's a friendly beach bar where for ridiculously little you can nurse a litre of *sangría* (bring your own food). In the town itself the principal attraction is a series of **sherry bodegas** – long, whitewashed warehouses flanking the streets and the banks of the river. Until the train was extended to Cádiz, all shipments of sherry from Jerez came through Santa María, and its port is still used to some extent. Most of the firms offer free tours and tastings to visitors (Tues–Sat from around 10am–noon), though this is not a regular process and you need to phone in advance or organize a visit through the Turismo, either in Cádiz or Puerto de Santa María itself. Choose from *Osborne y Cía* (☎956 861600), *Luís Caballero* (☎956 861300) or, in a beautiful, converted, seventeenth-century convent, *Fernando A Terry* (☎956 862700).

The **ferry** from Cádiz is quicker and cheaper than the bus; the twenty-minute trip across the bay departs from the Estación Marítima at 8.30am (summer only), 10am, noon, 2pm, 6.30pm and 8.30pm (summer only), returning to Cádiz at 9am, 11am, 1pm, 3.30pm & 7.30pm (summer only), with extra sailings in season according to demand (especially in the evening). The **Turismo** is situated at c/Guadalete 1 (daily 10am–2pm & 5.30–7.15pm; ☎956 542413), near the Plaza de Galevas Reales where the ferry drops you, where you'll also find some excellent seafood **restaurants**. A bus from the Plaza de Galevas Reales goes to the **campsite** at Playa Las Dunas (☎956 870112; open all year), near the beach with plenty of shade.

Rota and Chipiona

ROTA, 16km along the coast, is marred by its proximity to one of the three major **US bases** in Spain – installed in the 1950s as part of a deal in which Franco exchanged strips of Spanish sovereign territory for economic aid and international "respectability". As a resort, it's no great shakes, but does boast two splendid beaches, and enough discos, bars and fish restaurants to satisfy your needs should you decide to stay.

CHIPIONA, at the edge of the next point, is simpler: a small, straightforward seaside resort crammed with family *pensiones*. Older tourists come here for the **spa waters**, channelled into a fountain at the church of Nuestra Señora de Regla, but for most it's the **beaches** that are the lure. South of the town and lighthouse is the long **Playa de Regla**, where, outside July and August, it's easy enough to leave the crowds behind; northeast, towards Sanlúcar, are sand bars and rocks. If you're planning on staying in the town, the **hostales** along the beach are the most attractive; in mid-season you'll need help getting a room from the women who meet new arrivals at the bus station. The **campsite**, *Pinar de Chipiona* (☎956 372321; open all year), is 3km out of town towards Rota.

Sanlúcar de Barrameda

Like Puerto Santa María, **SANLÚCAR DE BARRAMEDA** also has its sherry connections. Set at the mouth of the Guadalquivir, it's the main depot for **Manzanilla** wine, a pale, dry variety much in evidence in the bars, which you can also sample during visits (booked in advance by phone) to the town's **bodegas**: *Bodega Antonio Barbadillo*, c/Eguilaz 11 (☎956 365103; Thurs 12.30pm only; 300ptas), the town's major producer, and *Vinícola Hidalgo*, c/Banda Playa 24 (☎956 360516; Mon–Fri 12.30pm; free), which makes the famous La Gitana brand. Sanlúcar is also the setting for some exciting horse races along the beach in the last two weeks of August, the best time to be here.

There's not a great deal to see, although the attractive old quarter in the upper town or *barrio alto* is worth taking time to explore. The town's port was the scene of a number of important maritime exploits: Magellan set out from here to circumnavigate the globe, Pizarro embarked to conquer Peru and 4km upriver in Bonanza, Columbus sailed on his third voyage. The few buildings of interest – the **ducal palaces** of **Medina Sidonia** (Wed 10am–1pm; free), and **Montpensier** (Mon–Fri 10am–2pm; free), the latter known locally as the Palacio de Orleáns y Borbón and decorated in a wild neo-Mudejar style, the thirteenth-century church of **Nuestro Señora de la O** with its fine Gothic-Mudejar portal, and parts of a Moorish **Castillo de Santiago** – are all perched above the main part of town on the Cuesta de Belén.

The best thing about Sanlúcar is its shell-encrusted **river beach** and warm waters, a couple of kilometres' walk from the town centre and usually quite deserted. This is flanked, on the opposite shore, by the beginnings of the **Coto Doñana National Park** (see below), whose vast marshy expanses (strictly regulated access) signal the end of the coast road to the west. Visits to the park from Sanlúcar are now possible with a new boat cruise which, while it doesn't allow for serious exploration, is nevertheless a wonderful introduction to this remarkable area. The trip lasts approximately four hours and allows two short guided walks inside the park. The *Real Fernando* leaves daily from the Bajo de Guia quay (☎956 363813; April–Sept 8.30am & 4.30pm, Oct–March 10am; 2100ptas).

Accommodation isn't easy to find in summer, but try *Pensión Blanca Paloma*, Plaza San Roque 9 (☎956 363644; ③), with a magnificent position, or the friendly *Fonda Román*, c/Barrameda 17 (☎956 366001; July–Aug only; ②), slightly east of the centre. Otherwise seek assistance from the **Turismo**, Calzada del Ejército (Mon–Fri 10am–2pm, Sat & Sun 11am–2pm; ☎956 366110), on the avenue leading to the sea, who can also provide a good town map.

Jerez de la Frontera

JEREZ DE LA FRONTERA, inland towards Sevilla, is the home and heartland of sherry (itself an English corruption of the town's Moorish name – *Xerez*) and also, less known but equally important, of Spanish brandy. It seems a tempting place to stop, arrayed as it is round the scores of wine *bodegas*. But you're unlikely to want to make more than a quick visit (and tasting) between buses; the town itself, while pleasant, is hardly distinctive unless you happen to arrive during one of the two big **festivals** – the May Horse Fair (perhaps the most refined of the Andalucian *ferias*), or the celebration of the vintage towards the end of September. That said, Jerez has a long and distinguished **flamenco** tradition and if you're interested in finding out more about Andalucía's great folk art then a visit to the **Centro Andaluz de Flamenco**, Plaza de San Juan (Mon–Fri 9am–2pm; free), is a must, where you can see videos of past greats and get information on flamenco venues in the town.

The **tours of the sherry and brandy processes** can be interesting – almost as much as the sampling that follows – and, provided you don't arrive in August when much of the industry closes down, there are a great many firms and *bodegas* to choose from. The most central is **González Byass** (open all year; tours Mon–Fri 400ptas, Sat 500ptas; advance booking on ☎956 357000). Tours are given here, as with most other firms, between 9 or10am and 1pm, with an extra late-afternoon tour on weekdays, and are conducted in English – very much the second language in Jerez's sherry fraternities. **Pedro Domeque**, c/San Ildefonso 3 (open all year; tours Mon–Sat 500ptas, Sun 600ptas; advance booking on ☎956 151500) is the second of Jerez's "big two" and has similiar hours plus Sunday visits. Many of the firms were founded by British Catholic refugees, barred from careers at home by the sixteenth-century Supremacy Act, and even now they form a kind of Anglo-Andalucian tweed-wearing and polo-playing aristocracy (on display, most conspicuously, at the Horse Fair). The González cellars – the *soleras* – are perhaps the oldest in Jerez, and, though it's no longer used, preserve an old circular chamber designed by Eiffel (of the tower fame). If you feel you need comparisons, you can pick up a list of locations and opening times of the other *bodegas* from the Turismo (see below) or from any travel agent in the centre when this is closed.

The most attractive of the town's buildings – including an imposing Gothic-Renaissance **Catedral de San Salvador** (daily 5.30–8pm & for morning service), and an impressive eleventh-century Moorish **Alcázar** (Mon–Fri 10am–2pm & 4–6pm, Sat 10am–2pm; 200ptas) next to the González *bodega* – are within a couple of minutes' walk of the central Plaza del Arenal. The excellent new **Archeological Museum** (Tues–Fri 10am–2pm & 4–7pm, Sat & Sun 10am–2.30pm; 250ptas) lies five minutes north of the centre in the Plaza del Mercado on the edge of Jerez's ancient *gitano* (gypsy) quarter, the Barrio de Santiago; star exhibits include a seventh-century BC Greek military helmet, a Visigothic sarcophagus and a fine Caliphal bottle vase. Evidence of Jerez's great enthusiasm for horses can be seen at the **Royal Andalucian School of Equestrian Art**, Avda. Duque de Abrantes s/n, which offers the chance to watch them performing to music (weekly show Thurs noon; 2500ptas; reservations ☎956 307798); the better-value rehearsals (Mon, Tue, Wed & Fri 11am; 500ptas) have no music.

Practicalities

The **Turismo** (Mon–Fri 9am–2pm & 5–7pm, Sat 9am–2pm; ☎ & fax 956 331150) is at Alameda Cristina 7, to the north of the central Plaza del Arenal, and can provide a good town map. For **accommodation**, the best budget bedrooms are at *Pensión Los Amarillos*, c/Melina 39 (☎956 342296; ②), which you reach by turning left from the bus station and walking three blocks. The nearby *Hostal Las Palomas*, c/Higueras 17 (☎956 343773; ②) has clean and simple rooms, while a bit further out is the good-value **Albergue-Juvenil**, Avda. Carrero Blanco 30 (☎956 143901, fax 956 143263; ①), a ten-minute walk south from the centre, or easily reached with buses #1 or #13 from the Plaza del Arenal. Moving upmarket, there's the excellent *Hostal San Andrés*, c/Morenos 12 (☎956 340983, fax 956 343196; ③) which has rooms with bath, and the friendly *Hostal Torres*, c/Arcos 29 (☎956 323400; ④), north of the bus station, with similar facilities and two charming patios.

The **train** and **bus** stations are more or less next door to each other, eight blocks east of the González *bodega* and the central Plaza del Arenal.

Huelva Province

The **province of Huelva** stretches between Sevilla and Portugal, but aside from its scenic section of the Sierra Morena (see p.255) to the north and a chain of fine **beaches** to the west of the provincial capital it's a pretty dull part of Andalucía, laced with large areas of swamp – the *marismas* – and notorious for mosquitoes. This dismal habitat is, however, particularly suited to a great variety of wildlife, especially birds, and over 60,000 acres of the delta of the Río Guadalquivir (the largest roadless area in western Europe) have been fenced off to form the **national park of the Coto Doñana**. Here, amid sand dunes, pine woods, marshes and freshwater lagoons, live scores of flamingos, along with rare birds of prey, lynx, mongooses and a startling variety of migratory birds.

Coto Doñana National Park

The seasonal pattern of its delta waters, which flood in winter and then drop in the spring, leaving rich deposits of silt, raised sandbanks and islands, give **Coto Doñana** its special interest. Conditions are perfect in winter for ducks and geese, but spring is more exciting: the exposed mud draws hundreds of flocks of breeding birds. In the marshes and amid the cork oak forests behind you've a good chance of seeing squacco herons, black-winged stilt, whiskered tern, pratincole and sand grouse, as well as flamingos, egrets and vultures. There are, too, occasional sightings of the Spanish imperial eagle, now reduced to fourteen breeding pairs. In late summer and early autumn, the *marismas* dry out and support far less bird life. The park is also home to some 25 pairs of lynx.

The park, however, is under threat from development. Even at current levels the drain on the water supply is severe, and made worse by pollution of the Guadalquivir by farming pesticides, Sevilla's industry and Huelva's mines. The seemingly inevitable disaster finally occurred in 1998 when an upriver mining dam used for storing toxic waste burst, unleashing millions of litres of pollutants into the Guadiamar river which flows through the park. The noxious tide was stopped just 2km from the park's boundary, but catastrophic damage was done to surrounding farmland, with nesting birds decimated and fish poisoned, with as yet unforeseeable consequences.

Equally disturbing are the proposals for a huge new tourist centre to be known as the **Costa Doñana**, on the very fringes of the park. Campaigning by national and international environmental bodies resulted in this project being shelved, but the threat remains, much of the pressure stemming from local people who see much-needed jobs in the venture. Large demonstrations have been organized by both sides, and an uneasy truce endures with persistent and mysterious outbreaks of vandalism against park property.

Visiting the park

Visiting the Doñana involves a certain amount of frustration. At present it's open only to a boat cruise from Sanlúcar (see p.269) and to brief, organized **tours** (spring & summer daily 8.30am & 5pm; 2500ptas a seat) by Land Rover – four hours at a time along one of five charted, eighty-kilometre routes. The starting point for these, and the place to book them (essential and as far ahead as possible in high season), is at the Centro de Recepción del Acebuche (☎959 448711 or 959 448739; English spoken), 5km north of Matalascañas towards El Rocío and Almonte, or at the Cooperativa Marismas del Rocío, Plaza del Acebuchal 16, El Rocío (☎959 430432, fax 959 430451). The tours are quite tourist-oriented, and point out only spectacular species like flamingos, imperial eagles, deer and wild boar. If you're a serious ornithologist and are equally interested in variations on little brown birds, the tour isn't for you. Instead, enquire at the Centro about organizing a private group tour; there are birdwatching **hides** (daily 8am–8pm) at El Acebuche, La Rocina and El Acebron, as well as a 1500-metre footpath from El Acebuche, which creates a mini-trek through typical *cotos* or terrains to be found in the reserve. Although binoculars are on hire, they sometimes run out, and you'd be advised to bring your own. The natural history exhibition at the Centro is in itself worthy of a visit.

Matalascañas

Birds and other wildlife apart, the resort settlement of **MATALASCAÑAS** on the park's coastal edge is unlikely to excite; with its five large hotel complexes and a concrete shopping centre, it would be difficult to imagine a more complete lack of character. In summer, too, the few **hostal rooms** are generally booked solid and, unless you plan in advance (any Sevilla travel agent will try to reserve you a room), you'll probably end up camping – either unofficially at the resort itself, or at the vast *Camping Rocío Playa* (☎959 430238; open all year), down the road towards Huelva. This site is a little inconvenient without your own transport if you're planning to take regular trips into the Doñana, but if you just want a **beach**, it's not a bad option. Playa Doñana and its continuation Playa Mazagón (with another campsite, *Doñana Playa*; ☎959 536281; open all year) stretch the whole distance to Huelva, and with hardly another foreign tourist in sight. This route is covered by three daily buses in both directions.

El Rocío

The other and more usual approach to Matalascañas is via Almonte, a small, unmemorable town, and **EL ROCÍO**, a tiny village of white cottages and a church stockade where perhaps the most famous pilgrimage-fair of the south takes place annually at Pentecost. This, the **Romería del Rocío**, is an extraordinary spectacle, with whole village communities and local "brotherhoods" from Huelva, Sevilla and even Málaga converging on horseback and in lavishly decorated ox carts. Throughout the procession, which climaxes on the Saturday evening, there is dancing and partying, while by the time the carts arrive at El Rocío they've been joined by busloads of pilgrims. What they have all come for – apart from the fair itself – is the commemoration of the miracle of Nuestra Señora del Rocío (Our Lady of the Dew), a statue found, so it is said, on this spot and resistant to all attempts to move it elsewhere. The image, credited with all kinds of magic and fertility powers, is paraded before the faithful early on the Sunday morning.

El Rocío is a nice place to stay, with wide, sandy streets and a frontier-like feeling. There are two good **hostales**: the *Hostal Isidro*, Avda. los Ansares 59 (②), and *Hostal Cristina*, c/Real 32 (☎959 406513; ③). Moving upmarket, there's a choice between the inviting *Hotel Toruño*, Plaza Acebuchal 22 (☎959 442323, fax 959 442338; ⑤), and the even plusher *Puente del Rey*, Avda. Canaliega 1 (☎959 442575, fax 959 442070; ⑤). In the spring, as far as **bird-watching** goes, the town is probably the best base in the area. The *marismas* and pine woods adjacent to the town are teeming with birds, and following tracks east and southeast of El Rocío, along the edge of the reserve, you'll see many species (up to a hundred if you're lucky).

Huelva and the coast down to Portugal

Large, sprawling and industrialized, **HUELVA** is the least attractive and least interesting of Andalucía's provincial capitals. It has claims as a "flamenco capital", but unless you're really devoted it's unlikely you'll want to stop long enough to verify this. By day – and in the evening as well – the most enticing thing to do is to take the hourly ferry (summer only) across the bay to **Punta Umbría**, the local resort, also linked by a new road bridge spanning the marshlands of the Río Odiel estuary. This is hardly an inspiring place either, but it does at least have some life, a fair beach, numerous *hostales* and a campsite.

The Columbus Trail

Nearby, across the Río Tinto estuary, the monastery of La Rábida and the villages of Palos and Moguer are all places connected with the voyages of Columbus to the New World.

La Rábida (Tues–Sun hourly tours 10am–1pm & 4–6.15pm; free), 8km from Huelva and easily reached by bus, is a charming and tranquil fourteenth-century Franciscan monastery whose abbot was instrumental in securing funds for the voyage from Fernando and Isabella. The new **Harbour of the Caravels** (April–Sept Tues–Fri 10am–2pm & 5–9pm, Sat & Sun 11am–8pm; Oct–March Tues–Fri 10am–2pm, Sat & Sun 11am–8pm; 420ptas) has full-size replicas of the three caravels which made the epic voyage to the New World. At **Palos**, 4km to the north, is the church of **San Jorge** where Columbus and his crew heard Mass before setting sail from the now silted-up harbour. A further 8km north, at the whitewashed town of **MOGUER**, is the fourteenth-century **Convent of Santa Clara** in whose church Columbus spent a whole night in prayer as thanksgiving for his safe return. The small town is a beautiful place, the birthplace of the Nobel prize-winning poet Juan Ramón Jiménez, and boasts a scaled-down, whiter version of Sevilla's Giralda attached to the church of **Nuestra Señora de la Granada**. If you want to stay overnight, *Hostal Pedro Alonso Niño*, c/Pedro Alonso Niño 13 (☎959 372392; ②), is delightful and has excellent-value en-suite rooms.

Plaza Mayor, Madrid

Alcázar, Segovia

Monumento a Alfonso XII in Parque del Retiro, Madrid

NEIL SETCHFIELD

View of Toledo from Río Tajo

EDMUND NÄGELE

Sierra Nevada landscape, Andalucía

Sardines, Costa del Sol

Roman aqueduct, Segovia

Cuenca, New Castile

Bull fighting poster

Semana Santa, Córdoba

Alpujarras village, Andalucía

West to Portugal

From Huelva it's best either to press on inland to the Sierra Morena or straight **along the coast to Portugal**. There are a number of good beaches and some low-key resorts noted for their seafood, such as **Isla Cristina**, along the stretch of coastline between Huelva and the frontier town of **Ayamonte**, but not much more to detain you. A good bus service along this route and a new road suspension bridge across the Rio Guadiana estuary and border, linking Ayamonte and **Villa Real de Santo Antonio**, make for a relatively painless crossing into Portugal. From this approach, a good first night's target in Portugal is Tavira, on the Algarve train line.

Sevilla to Córdoba

The direct route from **Sevilla to Córdoba**, 135km along the valley of Guadalquivir, followed by the train and some of the buses, is a flat and rather unexciting journey. There's far more to see following the route just to the south of this, via **Carmona** and **Écija**, both interesting towns, and even more if you detour further south to take in **Osuna** as well. There are plenty of buses along these roads so there's no real need to stay – **Carmona** in particular is an easy day trip from Sevilla.

Carmona

Set on a low hill overlooking a fertile plain, **CARMONA** is a small, picturesque town with a fifteenth-century tower built in imitation of the Giralda. This is the first thing you catch sight of and it sets a tone for the place – an appropriate one, since the town shares a similar history to Sevilla, less than 30km distant. It was an important Roman city (from which era it preserves a fascinating subterranean necropolis) and under the Moors was often governed by a brother of the Sevillan ruler. Later, Pedro the Cruel built a palace within its castle, which he used as a "provincial" royal residence.

The buses stop right by the old Moorish **Puerto de Sevilla**, a grand and ruinous fortified gateway to the old town. Inside the walls, narrow streets wind up past Mudéjar churches and Renaissance mansions. There's a map of the town pinned up in the porch of **San Pedro** (the church with the Giralda-type tower): get your bearings and head uphill to the **Plaza San Fernando** (or Plaza Mayor), modest in size but dominated by splendid Moorish-style buildings. Behind it there's a bustling fruit and vegetable market most mornings.

Close by to the east is **Santa María**, a fine Gothic church built over the former main mosque, whose elegant patio it retains; like many of Carmona's churches it is capped by a Mudéjar tower, possibly utilizing part of the old minaret. Dominating the ridge of the town are the massive ruins of **Pedro's palace**, destroyed by an earthquake in 1504 and now taken over by a remarkably tasteful but very expensive *parador* (see below). To the left, beyond and below, the town comes to an abrupt and romantic halt at the Roman **Puerta de Córdoba**, from where the old Córdoba road (now a dirt track) drops down to a vast plain.

The extraordinary **Roman necropolis** (guided tours June–Sept Tues–Fri 9am–2pm, Sat & Sun 10am–2pm; Oct–May Tues–Fri 10am–2pm & 4–6pm, Sat & Sun 10am–2pm; 250ptas, free to EU citizens) lies on a low hill at the opposite end of Carmona; walking out of town from San Pedro take c/Enmedio, the middle street (parallel to the main Sevilla road) for about 450m. Here, amid the cypress trees, more than nine hundred family tombs dating from the second century BC to the fourth century AD can be found. Enclosed in subterranean chambers hewn from the rock, the tombs are often frescoed and contain a series of niches in which many of the funeral urns remain intact. Some of the larger tombs have vestibules with stone benches for funeral banquets, and several retain carved family emblems (one is of an elephant, perhaps symbolic of long life). Most spectacular is the Tumba de Servilia – a huge colonnaded temple with vaulted side chambers. Opposite is a partly excavated **amphitheatre**, though as yet it isn't included in the tour.

Practicalities

The **Turismo** (Mon–Fri 9am–2pm, Sat & Sun 10.30am–1.30pm; ☎95 441 90 95) is located in the Plaza de Fernando (aka Plaza de Arriba), in the centre of the old town, and can provide a map. Budget **accommodation** is limited: the best bet is *Pensión El Comercio* (☎95 414 00 18; ③), built into the town's gateway, or try the seedy, but clean, *El Potro*, c/Sevilla 78 (☎95 414 14 65; ②), 100m back along the Sevilla road. The *Parador Alcázar del Rey Don Pedro* (☎95 414 10 10, fax 95 414 17 12; ⑧), in the ruins of the palace, is Carmona's most atmospheric upmarket hotel, and even if you don't stay it's worth calling at the bar for a drink to enjoy the fabulous views from its terrace.

The old town is an expensive place for **food**; try the *tapas* bars on c/Fuente which descends to the right before **San Pedro**. Beyond the church, the *Gamero* restaurant serves reasonably priced *platos combinados* and has a *menú*. *El Potro* also has a decent and economical, if rather soulless, restaurant.

Écija

Sevilla and Córdoba are reputedly the hottest cities of Spain; **ÉCIJA** lies midway between them in a basin of low sandy hills. It's known, with no hint of exaggeration, as *la sartenilla de Andalucía* ("the frying pan of Andalucía"). In mid-August the only possible strategy is to slink from one tiny shaded plaza to another, or with a burst of energy to make for the riverbank.

The effort is worth it, since this is one of the most distinctive and individual towns of the south, with eleven superb, decaying church towers, each glistening with brilliantly coloured tiles. It has a unique domestic architecture, too – a flamboyant style of twisted and florid forms, best displayed in the **Calle de los Caballeros**, a whole street full of mansions and palaces, a block or two south of the Plaza Mayor (where the bus stops). Most interesting of the churches is **Santa Cruz**, the old mosque.

A couple of **hostales** are located near the centre: try *Pensión Santa Cruz*, c/Romero Gordillo 8 (☎95 483 02 22; ③), off the eastern end of the Plaza Mayor; others are to be found on the outskirts, off the Sevilla–Córdoba road. For a little more luxury, there's the air-conditioned *Hotel Platería*, c/Garci López (☎95 483 50 10; ⑤). The **Turismo** (Mon–Fri 9am–3pm; ☎95 590 02 40) is located in the *Ayuntamiento* on the Plaza Mayor and will provide a good town map.

Osuna

OSUNA (like Carmona and Écija) is one of those small Andalucian towns which are great to explore in the early evening: slow in pace and quietly enjoyable, with elegant streets of tiled, whitewashed houses interspersed by fine **Renaissance mansions**. The best of these are in c/Carrera, running down from the Plaza Mayor, and in c/San Pedro which intersects it (no. 16 has a superb geometric relief round a carving of the Giralda). The Plaza Mayor has a marvellous **casino** – with 1920s Mudéjar-style decor and a grandly bizarre ceiling – which is open to all visitors and makes an excellent place to drink.

Two huge stone buildings stand on the hill top: the old university (suppressed by reactionary Fernando VII in 1820), and the lavish sixteenth-century **Colegiata** (guided tours Tues–Fri 10.30am–1.30pm & 3.30–6.30pm, Sat & Sun 10.30am–1.30pm; 300ptas), which contains the gloomy but impressive **pantheon and chapel** of the dukes of Osuna, descendants of the kings of León and once "the lords of Andalucía", as well as a **museum** displaying some fine artworks, including canvases by Ribera. Opposite the entrance to the Colegiata, is the Baroque convent of **La Encarnación** (same hours as above; 250ptas), which has a fine plinth of ninth-century Sevillan *azulejos* round its cloister and gallery.

Osuna has a reasonable range of **accommodation**. Lowest priced is the friendly *Pensión Esmerelda*, c/Tesoro 7 (☎95 582 10 73; ②), through the double arch off the Plaza Mayor and straight ahead. There are also several bars that offer noisy rooms along c/Carrera. More upmarket alternatives are *Hostal Cinco Puertas*, c/Carrera 79 (☎95 481 12 43; ③), or, opposite, the *Hostal Caballo Blanco*, c/Granada 1 (☎95 481 01 84; ④), which has some better rooms with bath. Both of these also serve decent meals.

Córdoba

CÓRDOBA stands upstream from Sevilla beside a loop of the Guadalquivir, which was once navigable as far as here. It is today a minor provincial capital, prosperous in a modest sort of way. Once, however, it was the largest city of Roman Spain, and for three centuries it formed the heart of the western Islamic empire, the great medieval caliphate of the Moors.

It is from this era that the city's great sight dates: the **Mezquita**, the grandest and most beautiful mosque ever constructed by the Moors in Spain. It stands right in the centre of the city, surrounded by the old Jewish and Moorish quarters, and is a building of extraordinary mystical and aesthetic power. Make for it on arrival and keep returning as long as you stay; you'll find its beauty and power increase with each visit, as of course is proper, since the mosque was intended for daily and regular attendance.

The Mezquita apart, Córdoba itself is a place of considerable charm. It has few grand squares or mansions, tending instead to introverted architecture, calling your attention to the tremendous and often wildly extravagant **patios**. These have long been acclaimed, and they are actively encouraged and maintained by the local council, which runs a "Festival of the Patios" in May. Just 7km outside the town are the ruins of the extravagant palace complex of **Medina Azahara** which is undergoing fascinating reconstruction.

Arrival and information

Finding your way around Córdoba is no problem. From the **train station** on Avenida de America, the broad Avenida del Gran Capitán leads down to the old quarters and the Mezquita. Bus terminals are numerous and scattered around the city. The main company, Alsina Graells, is at Avda. de Medina Azahara 29 (the continuation of c/Gondomar), two or three blocks to the west of the Paseo de la Victoria gardens; it runs services to and from Sevilla, Granada and Málaga.

The **Turismo** (Mon–Fri 9.30am–8pm, Sat 10am–8pm, Sun 10am–2pm; Nov–March Mon–Sat closes 6pm; ☎957 471235) is at the Palacio de Congresos y Exposiciones in c/Torrijos alongside the Mezquita. There's also a small municipal office nearby in Plaza Judá Leví, west of the Mezquita (Mon–Sat 9am–2pm & 4.30–6.30pm, Sun 9am–2pm; ☎957 200522), which gives out an illustrated brochure on places to visit, with a town plan. For information on fringe theatre and music, the **Casa de Cultura** is at Plaza del Potro 10.

Accommodation

Places to stay can be found all over Córdoba, but the best are concentrated in the narrow maze of streets above the Mezquita. Less obvious are some recently refurbished *fondas* in the Plaza de la Corredera. This is a wonderful, ramshackle square, like a decayed version of Madrid's Plaza Mayor, and worth a look whether you stay or not; it hosts a small morning market.

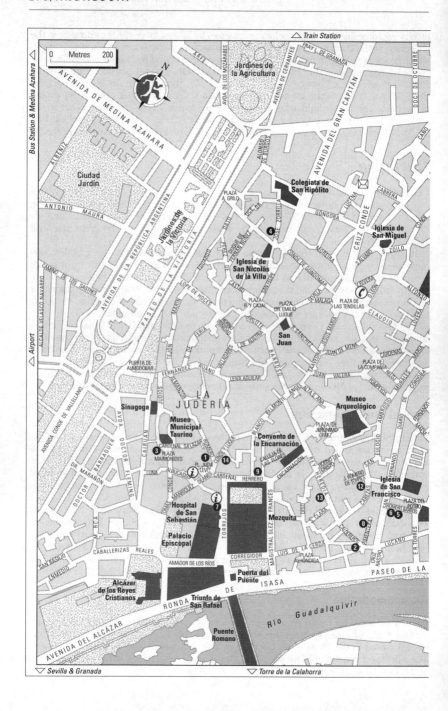

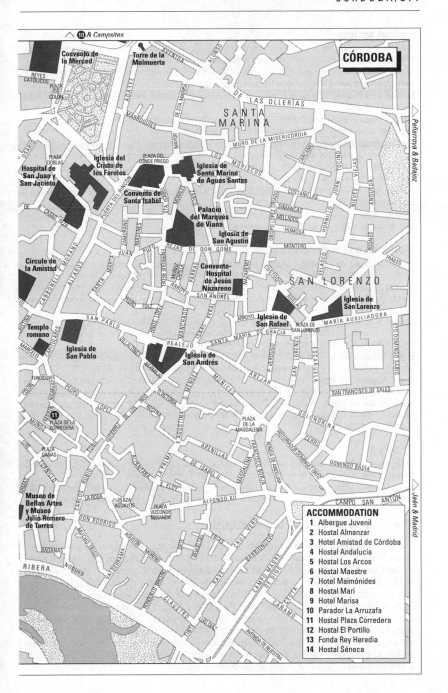

∧ **10** & *Campsites*

CÓRDOBA

Convento de la Merced
Torre de la Malmuerta
REYES CATÓLICOS
PLAZA DE COLÓN

DE LAS OLLERÍAS

SANTA MARINA

MURO DE LA MISERICORDIA

PLAZA DOBLAS
Hospital de San Juan y San Jacinto
Iglesia del Cristo de los Faroles
PLAZA DEL CONDE PRIEGO
Iglesia de Santa Marina de Aguas Santas

Convento de Santa Isabel
Palacio del Marqués de Viana

Iglesia de San Agustín

DE DON GOME

Círculo de la Amistad
Convento-Hospital de Jesús Nazareno

SAN LORENZO

Iglesia de San Lorenzo

Templo romano
SAN PABLO
Iglesia de San Rafael
PLAZA DE SAN LORENZO
MARÍA AUXILIADORA

Iglesia de San Pablo
REALEJO
SANTA MARTA DE GRACIA
Iglesia de San Andrés

SAN FRANCISCO DE SALES

MUNICES

PLAZA DE LA MAGDALENA

GOLONDRINA

CERRO

DOMINGO BADIA

11 PLAZA DE LA CORREDERA

PLAZA CAÑAS

ARENILLAS

C. DE ISABEL II

PLAZA AGUAYOS
PLAZA VIZCONDE MIRANDA

ALFONSO XII

CAMPO SAN ANTÓN

Museo de Bellas Artes y Museo Julio Romero de Torres

RIBERA

ACCOMMODATION

1 Albergue Juvenil
2 Hostal Almanzar
3 Hotel Amistad de Córdoba
4 Hostal Andalucía
5 Hostal Los Arcos
6 Hostal Maestre
7 Hotel Maimónides
8 Hostal Mari
9 Hotel Marisa
10 Parador La Arruzafa
11 Hostal Plaza Corredera
12 Hostal El Portillo
13 Fonda Rey Heredia
14 Hostal Séneca

△ *Peñarroya & Badajoz*

△ *Jaén & Madrid*

Budget options

Albergue Juvenil, Plaza Judá Leví (☎957 290166, fax 957 290500). Córdoba's excellent modern youth hostel (with twin en-suite rooms), which also serves meals. ①.

Hostal Almanzor, Corregidor Luís Cerda 10 (☎957 485400). East of the Mezquita, this small, but very charming *hostal* has rooms with or without bath. ②–③.

Hostal Los Arcos, c/Romero Barros 14 (☎957 485643, fax 957 486011). Delightful *hostal* with a pleasant patio. ③.

Hostal Mari, c/Pimentera 6 (☎957 479575), off c/Calderos to the east of the Mezquita. This clean and pleasant *hostal* is one of the lowest priced in town. ②.

Hostal Plaza Corredera, c/Rodríguez Marín 15 at the corner of Plaza Corredera (☎957 470581). Clean, friendly and recently refurbished, with great views over the plaza from some rooms. ②.

Hostal El Portillo, c/Cabezas 2 (☎957 472091, fax 957 472091). Beautiful old *hostal* offering both singles and doubles. ②.

Fonda Rey Heredia, c/Rey Heredia 26 (☎957 474182). One of three very reasonable *fondas* on this street. ③.

Hostal Séneca, c/Conde y Luque 7 (☎ & fax 957 473234), just north of the Mezquita. Breakfast also available at this attractive and good-value *hostal*. ③.

Moderate and expensive options

Hotel Amistad de Córdoba, Plaza de Maimónides 3 (☎957 420335, fax 957 420365). Wonderful hotel incorporating two eighteenth-century mansions, near the old wall in the Judería. ⑦.

Hostal Andalucía, c/José Zorilla 3, near the church of San Hipolito (☎957 476000, fax 957 478143). Handy hotel for drivers who want to avoid the Mezquita maze, offering pleasant rooms with bath, and easy parking. ④.

Hostal & Hotel Maestre, c/Romero Barros 4 & 16 (☎ & fax 957 475395). Excellent *hostal* between c/San Fernando and the Plaza del Potro; their neighbouring hotel has air-conditioned rooms with TV. If you're carrying a *Rough Guide*, they'll offer you free parking. ④.

Hotel Maimónides, c/Torrijos 4 (☎957 471500, fax 957 483803). This upmarket hotel has a particularly central and attractive location, near to the Turismo – it also has a garage. ⑦.

Hotel Marisa, c/Cardenal Herrero 6 (☎957 473142, fax 957 474144). Two-star hotel with a superb position immediately outside the Mezquita. ⑤.

Parador La Arruzafa, Avda. de la Arruzafa (☎957 275900, fax 957 280409). Córdoba's modern *parador* is located on the outskirts of the city 5km north, but it does have a pool and every other amenity to justify the price. ⑦.

Camping

Campamento Municipal (☎957 472000). Córdoba's local campsite (with pool) is 2km north on the road to Villaviciosa, and is served by bus #12 from the Puente Romano. Open all year.

Camping Los Villares (☎957 330145). If you have your own transport, this site (7km north of the city) is a better option, set in woodland with nature trails and with a restaurant. Open all year.

Moorish Córdoba and the Mezquita

Córdoba's **domination of Moorish Spain** began thirty years after its conquest – in 756, when the city was placed under the control of **Abd ar-Rahman I**, the sole survivor of the Umayyad dynasty which had been bloodily expelled from the eastern caliphate of Damascus. He proved a firm but moderate ruler, and a remarkable military campaigner, establishing control over all but the north of Spain and proclaiming himself Emir, a title meaning both "King" and "Son of the Caliph". It was Abd ar-Rahman who commenced the building of the Great Mosque (*La Mezquita*, in Spanish), purchasing from the Christians the site of the cathedral of St Vincent (which, divided by a partition wall, had previously served both communities). This original mosque was completed by his son **Hisham** in 796 and comprises about one-fifth of the present building, the first dozen aisles adjacent to the Patio de los Naranjos.

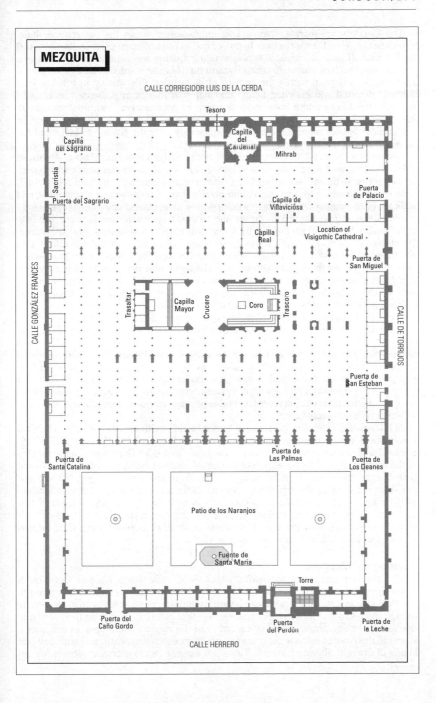

MEZQUITA

CALLE CORREGIDOR LUIS DE LA CERDA

Tesoro

Capilla del Sagrario

Capilla del Cardenal

Mihrab

Sacristia

Puerta del Sagrario

Puerta de Palacio

Capilla de Villaviciosa

Capilla Real

Location of Visigothic Cathedral

Puerta de San Miguel

CALLE GONZÁLEZ FRANCES

Trasaltar

Capilla Mayor

Crucero

Coro

Trascoro

Puerta de San Esteban

Puerta de Las Palmas

Puerta de Santa Catalina

Puerta de Los Deanes

Patio de los Naranjos

Fuente de Santa Maria

CALLE DE TORRIJOS

Torre

Puerta del Caño Gordo

Puerta del Perdón

Puerta de la Leche

CALLE HERRERO

The **Cordoban Emirate**, maintaining independence from the eastern caliphate, soon began to rival Damascus both in power and in the brilliance of its civilization. **Abd ar-Rahman II** (822–52) initiated sophisticated irrigation programmes, minted his own coinage and received embassies from Byzantium. He in turn substantially enlarged the mosque. A focal point within the culture of *al-Andalus*, this was by now being consciously directed and enriched as an alternative to Mecca; it possessed an original script of the Koran and a bone from the arm of Muhammad, and, for the Spanish Muslim who could not go to Mecca, it became the most sacred place of **pilgrimage**. In the broader Islamic world it ranked third in sanctity after the Kaaba of Mecca and the Al Aksa mosque of Jerusalem.

In the tenth century Córdoba reached its zenith under a new emir, **Abd ar-Rahman III** (912–61), one of the great rulers of Islamic history. He assumed power after a period of internal strife and, according to a contemporary historian, "subdued rebels, built palaces, gave impetus to agriculture, immortalized ancient deeds and monuments, and inflicted great damage on infidels to a point where no opponent or contender remained in *al-Andalus*. People obeyed en masse and wished to live with him in peace." In 929, with Muslim Spain and part of North Africa firmly under his control, Abd ar-Rahman III adopted the title of "Caliph". It was a supremely confident move and was reflected in the growing splendour of Córdoba, which had become the largest, most prosperous city of Europe, outshining Byzantium and Baghdad (the new capital of the eastern caliphate) in science, culture and scholarship. At the turn of the tenth century it had 27 schools, 50 hospitals (with the first separate clinics for the leprous and insane), 900 public baths, 60,300 noble mansions, 213,077 houses and 80,455 shops.

The **development of the Great Mosque** paralleled these new heights of confidence and splendour. Abd ar-Rahman III provided it with a new minaret (which has not survived), 80m high, topped by three pomegranate-shaped spheres, two of silver and one of gold and each weighing a ton. But it was his son **al-Hakam II** (961–76), to whom he passed on a peaceful and stable empire, who was responsible for the most brilliant expansion. He virtually doubled its extent, demolishing the south wall to add fourteen extra rows of columns, and employed Byzantine craftsmen to construct a new *mihrab* or prayer niche; this remains complete and is perhaps the most beautiful example of all Moorish religious architecture.

Al-Hakam had extended the mosque as far to the south as was possible. The final enlargement of the building, under the chamberlain-usurper **al-Mansur** (977–1002), involved adding seven rows of columns to the whole east side. This spoiled the symmetry of the mosque, depriving the *mihrab* of its central position, but Arab historians observed that it meant there were now "as many bays as there are days of the year". They also delighted in describing the rich interior, with its 1293 marble columns, 280 chandeliers and 1445 lamps. Hanging inverted among the lamps were the bells of the pilgrimage cathedral of Santiago de Compostela. Al-Mansur made his Christian captives carry them on their shoulders from Galicia – a process which was to be observed in reverse after Córdoba was captured by Fernando el Santo (the Saint) in 1236.

Entering the Mezquita

As in Moorish times the **Mezquita** (April–Sept daily 10am–7.30pm; Oct–March 10am–5pm; 750ptas, free entrance at side doors 8.30am–10am) is approached through the **Patio de los Naranjos**, a classic Islamic ablutions court which preserves both its orange trees and its fountains for ritual purification before prayer. Originally, when in use for the Friday prayer, all nineteen naves of the mosque were open to this court, allowing the rows of interior columns to appear an extension of the tree with brilliant shafts of sunlight filtering through. Today, all but one of the entrance gates is locked and sealed and the mood of the building has been distorted from the open and vigorous simplicity of the mosque, to the mysterious half-light of a cathedral.

Nonetheless, a first glimpse inside the Mezquita is immensely exciting. "So near the desert in its tentlike forest of supporting pillars," Jan Morris found it, "so faithful to Mahomet's tenets of cleanliness, abstinence and regularity". The mass of supporting pillars was, in fact, an early and sophisticated innovation to gain height. The original architect had at his disposal columns from the old Visigothic cathedral and from numerous Roman buildings; they could bear great weight but were not tall enough, even when arched, to reach the intended height of the ceiling. His solution (which may have been inspired by Roman aqueduct designs) was to place a second row of square columns on the apex of the lower ones, serving as a base for the semicircular arches that support the roof. For extra strength and stability (and perhaps also deliberately to echo the shape of a date palm, much revered by the early Spanish Arabs) the architect introduced another, horseshoe-shaped arch above the lower pillars. A second and purely aesthetic innovation was to alternate brick and stone in the arches, creating the red-and-white striped pattern which gives a unity and distinctive character to the whole design.

The Mihrab

This uniformity was broken only at the culminating point of the mosque – the domed cluster of pillars surrounding the sacred **Mihrab**, erected under al-Hakam II. The *mihrab* had two functions in Islamic worship: it indicated the direction of Mecca (and hence of prayer) and it amplified the words of the *imam*, or prayer leader. At Córdoba it was also of supreme beauty. As Titus Burckhardt wrote, in *Moorish Art in Spain*:

> *The design of the prayer niche in Córdoba was used as a model for countless prayer niches in Spain and North Africa. The niche is crowned by a horseshoe-shaped arch, enclosed by a rectangular frame. The arch derives a peculiar strength from the fact that its central point shifts up from below. The wedge-shaped arch stones or voussoirs fan outwards from a point at the foot of the arch and centres of the inner and outer circumferences of the arch lie one above the other. The entire arch seems to radiate, like the sun or the moon gradually rising over the edge of the horizon. It is not rigid; it breathes as if expanding with a surfeit of inner beatitude, while the rectangular frame enclosing it acts as a counterbalance. The radiating energy and the perfect stillness form an unsurpassable equilibrium. Herein lies the basic formula of Moorish architecture.*

The inner vestibule of the niche (which is roped off – forcing you to risk the wrath of the attendants in getting a glimpse; if you don't want to pay yourself, wait for it to be lit up for someone else) is quite simple in comparison, with a shell-shaped ceiling carved from a single block of marble. The chambers to either side – decorated with exquisite Byzantine mosaics of gold, rust-red, turquoise and green – constitute the *maksura*, where the caliph and his retinue would pray.

The cathedral and other additions

Originally the whole design of the mosque would have directed worshippers naturally towards the *mihrab*. Today, though, you almost stumble upon it, for in the centre of the mosque squats a Renaissance **cathedral coro**. This was built in 1523 – nearly three centuries of enlightened restraint after the Christian conquest – and in spite of fierce opposition from the town council. The erection of a *coro* and *capilla mayor*, however, had long been the "Christianizing" dream of the cathedral chapter and at last they had found a monarch – predictably Carlos V – who was willing to sanction the work. Carlos, to his credit, realized the mistake (though it did not stop him from destroying parts of the Alhambra and Sevilla's Alcázar); on seeing the work completed he told the chapter, "You have built what you or others might have built anywhere, but you have destroyed something that was unique in the world." To the left of the *coro* stands an earlier and happier Christian addition – the Mudéjar **Capilla de Villaviciosa**, built by Moorish craftsmen in 1371 (and now partly sealed up). Beside it are the dome and pillars of the **earlier mihrab**, constructed under Abd ar-Rahman II.

The **belfry**, at the corner of the Patio de los Naranjos, is contemporary with the cathedral addition. If it's open after restoration, the climb is a dizzying experience. Close by, the **Puerta del Perdón**, the main entrance to the patio, was rebuilt in Moorish style in 1377. Original "caliphal" decoration (in particular some superb lattice-work), however, can still be made out in the gates along the east and west sides of the mosque.

Rest of the town

After the Mezquita, Córdoba's other remnants of Moorish – and indeed Christian – rule are not individually very striking. The river, though, with its great **Arab waterwheels** and its **bridge** built on Roman foundations, is an attractive area in which to wander. The wheels, and the ruined mills on the riverbank, were in use for several centuries after the fall of the Muslim city, grinding flour and pumping water up to the fountains of the Alcázar, or Palace Fortress. This originally stood beside the Mezquita – on the site now occupied by the **Episcopal Palace** (Mon–Fri 10.30am–2pm & 4–6.30pm, Sat 9.30am–1.30pm; 150ptas, free with Mezquita ticket), now a museum of religious art with some fine examples of medieval wood sculpture – but after the Christian conquest it was rebuilt a little to the west by Fernando and Isabella, hence its name, **Alcázar de los Reyes**. The buildings (Tues–Sat 10am–2pm & 6–8pm, Sun 9.30am–3pm; 425ptas, free Fri) are a bit dreary, having served as the residence of the Inquisition from 1428 to 1821. However, they display some fine mosaics from Roman Córdoba, among which is one of the largest complete Roman mosaics in existence, and the **gardens** are attractive.

Judería
Between the Mezquita and the beginning of the Avenida del Gran Capitán lies the **Judería**, Córdoba's old Jewish quarter and a fascinating network of lanes – more atmospheric and less commercialized than Sevilla's, though souvenir shops are beginning to gain ground. Near the heart of the quarter, at c/Maimónides 18, is a **synagogue** (Tues–Sun 10am–2pm & 3.30–5.30pm; 50ptas, free to EU citizens), one of only three in Spain – the other two are in Toledo – that survived the Jewish expulsion of 1492. This one, built in 1316, is minute, particularly in comparison to the great Santa María in Toledo, but it has some fine stucco work elaborating on a Solomon's-seal motif and retains its women's gallery. Outside is a statue of Maimónides, the Jewish philosopher, physician and Talmudic jurist, born in Córdoba in 1135.

Nearby is a rather bogus **Zoco** – an Arab *souk* turned into a crafts arcade – and, adjoining this, a small **Museo Taurino** (Tues–Sat 10am–2pm & 6–8pm, Sun 9.30am–3pm; 425ptas, free Fri). The latter warrants a look, if only for the kitschy nature of its exhibits: row upon row of bulls' heads, two of them given this "honour" for having killed matadors. Beside a copy of the tomb of Manolete – most famous of the city's fighters – is exhibited the hide of his taurine nemesis, Islero. If bullfighting is your thing, it's also possible to go on a guided tour of the city's **bullring** (tours on the hour, 10am–1pm & 4–7pm); complete with distastefully reverential commentary, this includes even the high-tech emergency room. Ask at the Turismo for further details.

Other museums and mansions

More interesting, perhaps, and really more rewarding, is the **Museo Arqueológico** (Tues 3–8pm, Wed–Sat 9am–8pm, Sun 9am–3pm; 250ptas, free to EU citizens). During its original conversion, this small Renaissance mansion was revealed as the unlikely site of a genuine Roman patio. As a result it is one of the most imaginative and enjoyable small museums in the country, with good local collections from the Iberian, Roman and Moorish periods. Outstanding is an inlaid tenth-century bronze stag found at the Moorish palace of Medina Azahara (see below) where it was used as the spout of a fountain.

A couple of blocks below the Archeological Museum, back towards the river, you'll come upon the **Plaza del Potro**, a fine old square named after the colt (*potro*) which adorns its fountain. This, as local guides proudly point out, is mentioned in *Don Quixote*, and indeed Cervantes himself is reputed to have stayed at the inn opposite, the **Mesón del Potro**, which is now used for *artesanía* displays and art exhibitions. On the other side of the square is the **Museo de Bellas Artes** (Tues 3–8pm, Wed–Sat 9am–8pm, Sun 9am–3pm; 250ptas, free to EU citizens) with paintings by Ribera, Valdés Leal and Zurbarán. Across its courtyard is a small museum (Tues–Sat 10am–2pm & 6–8pm; 425ptas, free Fri) devoted to the Cordoban artist **Julio Romero de Torres** (1885–1930), painter of some sublimely dreadful canvases, most of which depict reclining female nudes with furtive male guitar players.

In the north of town, towards the train station, are numerous Renaissance churches – some converted from mosques, others showing obvious influence in their minarets – and a handful of convents and palaces. The best of these, still privately owned, is the **Palacio del Marqués de Viana** (guided tours daily except Wed: April–Sept 9am–2pm; Oct–March 10am–1pm & 4–6pm; 500ptas) whose main attraction for many visitors are its twelve flower-filled patios.

Eating and drinking

Bars and **restaurants** are on the whole reasonably priced – you need only to avoid the touristy places round the Mezquita. There are lots of good places to eat not too far away in the Judería and in the old quarters off to the east, above the Paseo de la Ribera.

Restaurants

Bar–Restaurante Federación de las Peñas, c/Conde y Luque 8. Moorish-style patio dining room which despite its name is open to non-members, and offers a variety of economical *menús*.

Bar-Restaurante Millán, Avda. Dr. Fleming 14, just northwest of the Alcázar. Tranquil, economical restaurant with a charming *azulejo*-lined room. The *rabo de toro* (Córdoba's traditional dish – a very superior oxtail stew) and *salmorejo* (a thick Cordoban version of *gazpacho* with hunks of ham and egg) are excellent here.

Casa Paco Acedo, beneath the ancient Torre de Malmuerta at the northen end of town. The house speciality is a memorable *rabo de toro*.

El Churrasco, c/Romero 16 (not c/Romero Barros). Expensive restaurant, with a long-standing reputation for its *churrasco* (a grilled pork dish, served with pepper sauces) and *salmorejo*.

Restaurante Cafetín Halal, c/Rey Heredia 28. Islamic cultural centre serving excellent, inexpensive food with vegetarian options. No alcohol.

Restaurante La-La-La, c/Cruz del Rastro. Situated on the river and serving inexpensive *menús*.

Taberna Salinas, c/Tundidores 3, just off the Plaza Corredera. Excellent place serving great *salmorejo*.

Taberna Santa Clara, c/Osio 2, corner of c/Rey Heredia. Very friendly, with good value *menús*, served in a delightful patio.

Bars

The local barrelled **wine** is predominantly Montilla-Moriles – brewed in the towns of the same name just to the south – which vaguely resembles mellow, dry sherry, and is magnificent here on its own turf. The *Bar Plateros* opposite the *Hostal Maestre* specializes in Montilla and also has great *tapas*; the same chain has another branch at c/Deanes 5, near the top left-hand corner of the Mezquita. Good *tapas* and *bocadillos* can be found at the tiny *Casa Elisa*, c/Almanzor near Puerto del Almodobar, northwest of the Mezquita. One bar not to be missed is the century-old *Taberna San Miguel*, behind the church of the same name to the north of Plaza Tendillas. It's an ancient old place, hung with guitars and faded *corrida* posters, where the *tapas*, especially *callos* (tripe) and *manitas* (trotters) in sauce, are excellent.

You'll find the best, and most authentic, **flamenco** in town at *Tablao Cardenal*, c/Torrijos 10 (next to the Turismo), though it doesn't come cheap at 3000ptas a ticket. Performances begin at 10.30pm and you can book a good table by phone (☎957 483320; closed Sun & Mon).

Medina Azahara

Seven kilometres to the northwest of Córdoba lie the vast and rambling ruins of **Medina Azahara**, a palace complex built on a dream scale by **Caliph Abd ar-Rahman III**. Naming it after a favourite, az-Zahra (the Radiant), he spent one-third of the annual state budget on its construction each year from 936 until his death in 961. Ten thousand workers and 1500 mules and camels were employed on the project and the site, almost 2000m long by 900m wide, stretched over three descending terraces. In addition to the palace buildings, it contained a zoo, an aviary, four fish ponds, 300 baths, 400 houses, weapons factories and two barracks for the royal guard. Visitors, so the chronicles record, were stunned by its wealth and brilliance: one conference room was provided with pure crystals, creating a rainbow when lit by the sun; another was built round a huge pool of mercury.

Medina Azahara was a perfect symbol of the western caliphate's extent and greatness, but it was to last for less than a century. **Al-Hakam II**, who succeeded Abd ar-Rahman, lived in the palace, continued to endow it, and enjoyed a stable reign. However, distanced from the city, he delegated more and more authority, particularly to his vizier Ibn Abi Amir, later known as **al-Mansur** (the Victor). In 976 al-Hakam was succeeded by his eleven-year-old son Hisham II and, after a series of sharp moves, al-Mansur assumed the full powers of government, keeping Hisham virtually imprisoned at Medina Azahara, to the extent of blocking up connecting passageways between the palace buildings.

Al-Mansur was equally skilful and manipulative in his wider dealings as a dictator, retaking large tracts of central Spain and raiding as far afield as Galicia and Catalunya; consequently Córdoba rose to new heights of prosperity. But with his death in 1002 came swift decline as his role and function were assumed in turn by his two sons. The first died in 1008; the second, Sanchol, showed open disrespect for the caliphate by forcing Hisham to appoint him as his successor. At this a popular revolt broke out and the caliphate disintegrated into civil war and a series of feudal kingdoms. Medina Azahara was looted by a mob at the outset and in 1010 was plundered and burned by retreating Berber mercenaries.

The site

For centuries **the site** (May–Oct Tues–Sat 10am–1.30pm & 6–8.30pm, Sun 10am–1.30pm; phone for Nov–April hours on ☎957 329130; 250ptas, free to EU citizens) continued to be looted for building materials; parts, for instance, were used in the Sevilla Alcázar. But in 1944 excavations unearthed the remains of a crucial part of the palace – the **Royal House**, where guests were received and meetings of ministers held.

This has been meticulously reconstructed, and, though still fragmentary, its main hall must rank among the greatest of all Moorish rooms. It has a different kind of stucco work from that at Granada or Sevilla – closer to natural and animal forms in its intricate Syrian *Hom* (Tree of Life) motifs. Unlike the later Spanish Arab dynasties, the Berber Almoravids and the Almohads of Sevilla, the caliphal Andalucians were little worried by Islamic strictures on the portrayal of nature, animals or even men – the beautiful hind in the Córdoba museum is a good example – and it may well have been this aspect of the palace that led to such zealous destruction during the civil war.

The reconstruction of the palace gives a scale and focus to the site. Elsewhere you have little more than foundations to fuel your imaginings, amid an awesome area of ruins, hidden beneath bougainvillea and rustling with cicadas. Perhaps the most obvious of the outbuildings yet excavated is the **mosque**, just beyond the Royal House, which sits at an angle to the rest of the buildings in order to face Mecca.

To reach Medina Azahara, follow the Avenida de Medina Azahara out of town, on to the road to Villarubia and Posadas. About 4km down this road, make a right turn, after which it's another two or three kilometres. Alternatively, take a bus from the Calle de la Bodega station and ask the driver to drop you off at the intersection ("Cruz de Medina Azahara") for the final three-kilometre walk. A taxi will cost you about 3000ptas one-way for up to five people.

EASTERN ANDALUCÍA

There is no more convincing proof of the diversity of Andalucía than its eastern provinces: **Jaén**, with its rolling, olive-covered hills; **Granada**, dominated by Spain's highest peaks, the Sierra Nevada; and **Almería**, waterless and in part semi-desert.

Jaén is slightly isolated from the main routes around Andalucía, but if you're coming down to Granada from Madrid you might want to consider stopping over in the small towns of **Úbeda** or **Baeza**, both crammed with Renaissance architectural jewels and served on the main train line by their shared station of Linares-Baeza. Úbeda also serves as the gateway to **Cazorla** and its neighbouring natural park.

Granada, a prime target of any Spanish travels, is easily reached from Sevilla, Córdoba, Ronda, Málaga or Madrid. When you've exhausted the city, there are dozens of nearby possibilities, perhaps most enticing being the walks in the **Sierra Nevada** and its lower southern slopes, **Las Alpujarras**. The **Almería beaches**, least developed of the Spanish Mediterranean, are also within striking distance of Granada and Málaga.

Jaén Province

There are said to be over 150 million olive trees in the **province of Jaén**. They dominate the landscape as infinite rows of green against the orange-red earth, occasionally interspersed with stark white farm buildings. It's beautiful on a grand, sweeping scale, though concealing a bitter and entrenched economic reality. The majority of the olive groves are owned by a mere handful of families, and for most residents this is a very poor area.

Jaén

JAÉN, the provincial capital and by far the largest town, is an uneventful sort of place with traces of its Moorish past in its ruined castle and in the largest surviving Moorish baths in Spain. The town is centred around the Plaza de la Constitución and its two arterial streets, Paseo de la Estación and Avenida de Madrid. The **Turismo**, c/Arquitecto

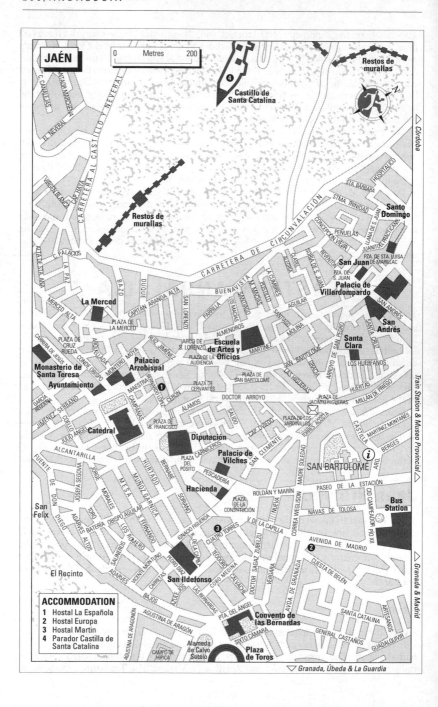

JAÉN

0 Metres 200

④ Castillo de
Santa Catalina

Restos de
murallas

△ *Córdoba*

Restos de
murallas

STA. BARBARA

STMA. TRINIDAD

**Santo
Domingo**

PEÑUELAS

JUANITO EL PRACTICANTE

PZA. DE STA. LUISA DE MARILLAC

San Juan

**Palacio de
Villardompardo**

SAN ANDRÉS

**San
Andrés**

BUENAVISTA

La Merced

PLAZA DE
LA MERCED

**Escuela
de Artes y
Oficios**

**Santa
Clara**

LOS HUÉRFANOS

PLAZA DE
CRUZ
RUEDA

**Palacio
Arzobispal**

PLAZA DE LA
AUDIENCIA

**Monasterio de
Santa Teresa**

Ayuntamiento

PLAZA DE
SAN BARTOLOMÉ

❶

PLAZA DE
CERVANTES

DOCTOR ARROYO

PLAZA DE
JACINTO HIGUERAS

PLAZA DE LOS
JARDINILLOS

Catedral

PLAZA DE
S. FRANCISCO

ÁLAMOS

Diputación

**Palacio de
Vilches**

SAN CLEMENTE

SAN BARTOLOMÉ

ℹ

ALCANTARILLA

PLAZA CARNICEROS

PLAZA
DEL
PÓSITO

PESCADERÍA

Hacienda

PASEO DE LA ESTACIÓN

Train Station & Museo Provincial ▷

ROLDÁN Y MARÍN

PLAZA
DE LA
CONSTITUCIÓN

**Bus
Station**

**San
Felix**

NAVAS DE TOLOSA

❸

❷

AVENIDA DE MADRID

△ *Granada & Madrid*

CUATRO TORRES

El Recinto

San Ildefonso

PTA. DEL ÁNGEL

**Convento de
las Bernardas**

SANTA CATALINA

AGUSTINA DE ARAGÓN

CAMPO DE
HÍPICA

Alameda
de Calvo
Sotelo

SIXTO CÁMARA

**Plaza
de Toros**

GENERAL CASTAÑOS

▽ *Granada, Úbeda & La Guardia*

ACCOMMODATION

1 Hostal La Española
2 Hostal Europa
3 Hostal Martín
4 Parador Castilla de
   Santa Catalina

Bergés 1 (Mon–Fri 8.30am–1pm, Sat 10am–12.30pm; ☎953 222737), with good town maps, is just off Paseo de la Estación, and the **train station** is farther north along the same street. Jaén's bus station is off Avenida de Madrid on Pio XII.

West of the main plaza is the imposing Renaissance **Catedral** (daily 8.30am–1pm & 5–8pm; free), and to the north, between the churches of San Andrés and Santo Domingo, you'll find the painstakingly restored Moorish **hammam** (Tues–Fri 9am–8pm & 5–8pm, Sat & Sun 9.30am–2.30pm; free). The baths were originally part of an eleventh-century Moorish palace, over which was constructed the Palacio de Villadompardo. Jaén's **Museo Provincial**, Paseo de la Estación 29 (Tues–Fri 10am–2pm & 4–7.30pm, Sat & Sun 10am–2pm; 250ptas; free to EU citizens), has a large archeological collection including some remarkable fifth-century BC Iberian sculptures.

Practicalities

If you want to **stay**, budget options include the basic *Hostal Martín*, c/Cuatro Torres 5 (☎953 220633; ②), near the Plaza de la Constitución, and *Hostal La Española*, c/Bernardo López 9 (☎953 230254; ③), by the cathedral. There are more expensive options on the Paseo de la Estación and Avda. de Madrid, including *Hostal Europa*, Plaza de Belén 1, just off Avda. de Madrid (☎953 222700, fax 953 222692; ⑤). Overlooking the town, built in the shell of a Moorish castle and with superb views, is the *Parador Castillo de Santa Catalina* (☎953 230000, fax 953 230930; ⑦), one of the best-value *paradores* in Spain.

Calle Nueva, immediately east of Plaza de la Constitución, has a whole crowd of **bars** and **places to eat** – *La Gamba de Oro* and *Bodegón de Pepe* are good.

Baeza and Úbeda

Less than an hour from Jaén are the rarely visited, elegant towns of **Baeza** and **Úbeda**. Each has an extraordinary density of exuberant Renaissance palaces and richly endowed churches, plus fine public squares. Both towns were captured from the Moors by Fernando el Santo and, repopulated with his knights, stood for two centuries at the frontiers of the reconquered lands facing the Moorish kingdom of Granada.

Baeza

BAEZA is tiny, compact and provincial, with a perpetual Sunday air about it. At its heart is a combined Plaza Mayor and *paseo*, flanked by cafés and very much the hub of the town's limited animation.

The **Plaza de Leones**, an appealing cobbled square enclosed by Renaissance buildings, stands slightly back at the far end. Here, on a rounded balcony, the first Mass of the Reconquest is reputed to have been celebrated; the mansion beneath it houses the **Turismo** (Mon–Fri 9am–2.30pm, Sat 10am–12.30pm; ☎953 740444), where you can pick up an English-language walking-tour brochure of the town.

Finest of Baeza's mansions is the **Palacio de Jabalquinto** (patio open daily 11am–1pm & 5–7pm; free), now a seminary, with an elaborate "Isabelline" front (showing marked Moorish influence in its stalactite decoration). Close by, the six-teenth-century **Catedral** (daily 10.30am–1pm & 5–7pm; free), like many of Baeza and Úbeda's churches, has brilliant painted *rejas* (iron screens) by Maestro Bartolomé, a local craftsman. In the cloister, part of the old mosque has been uncovered, but the cathedral's real novelty is a huge silver *custodia* – cunningly hidden behind a painting of Saint Peter which whirls aside for a 100ptas coin.

There are some good walks around town: wandering up through the Puerta de Jaén on the Plaza de los Leones and along the Paseo Murallas/Paseo de Don Antonio

Machado takes you round the edge of Baeza with good views over the surrounding plains. You can cut back to the Plaza Mayor via the network of narrow stone-walled alleys – with the occasional arch – that lie behind the cathedral.

Accommodation is scarce: try the *Hostal El Patio*, c/Conde Ramones 13, near the Plaza de Leones (☎953 740200; ②), an old Renaissance mansion set around an enclosed courtyard with a wood-beamed dining hall; or the *Hostal Comercio* (☎953 740100; ②) at c/San Pablo 21, a main road at the end of the central square. Best of the upmarket places is the central *Hotel Baeza*, c/Concepción 3, near the Plaza de España (☎953 748130, fax 953 742519; ⑥), partly set inside a restored Renaissance palace. Good bets for **food** and **drink** include the ancient *Cafetería Mercantil*, on the Plaza España, which offers decent *tapas* and *raciones* and, across the street, *La Gondola*, with an economical *menú* and decent pizzas. For a bit more style try the pleasant terrace of the *Restaurante Sali* around the corner at Cardenal Benavides 9.

The nearest **train station** is Linares-Baeza on the direct line from Madrid and 13km from Baeza (there is a connecting bus for most trains, except on Sun). Most bus connections are via Úbeda.

Úbeda

ÚBEDA, 9km east of Baeza, is a larger town with modern suburbs. Follow the signs to the *Zona Monumental* and you'll eventually reach the **Plaza de Vázquez de Molina**, a tremendous Renaissance square which overshadows anything in Baeza.

Most of the buildings round this square were the late sixteenth-century work of Andrés de Vandelvira, the architect of Baeza's cathedral and numerous churches in both towns. The *Ayuntamiento*, originally a palace for Felipe II's secretary, now houses the **Turismo** (Mon–Fri 10am–2pm; ☎953 750897), who can provide a map of the town. At the opposite end of the plaza is the church of **El Salvador**, erected by Vandelvira, though actually designed by Diego de Siloé (architect of the Málaga and Granada cathedrals). This is the finest church in Úbeda, its highlight a gilded, brilliantly animated *retablo* of the Transfiguration; to enter you have to go through the sacristy at the side – ring for the caretaker at the fine doorway in the white wall on c/Francisco de Cobos. Across town, the idiosyncratic church of **San Pablo**, Plaza del Generalísimo, has a thirteenth-century balcony (a popular feature in Úbeda) and various Renaissance additions.

Most of the budget **accommodation** options are grouped around the main **bus station** in Avenida de Ramón y Cajal, in the modern part of town. The *Hostal Castillo* at no. 16 (☎953 750430; ③), and the *Hostal Sevilla* at no. 9 (☎953 750612; ③), are both reasonable, and have better rooms with bath. For some of the least expensive rooms in town, try *Hostal San Miguel*, Avda. Libertad 69 (☎953 752049; ②), a fifteen-minute walk from the bus station. In the centre of town, the only option is the *Parador Condestable Dávalos*, Plaza de Vázquez de Molina 1 (☎953 750345, fax 953 751259; ⑦), in a fabulous sixteenth-century Renaissance mansion.

There are plenty of **places to eat** around Avenida Ramón y Cajal: *El Gallo Rojo*, c/Torrenueva 3, has outdoor tables in the evening; *El Olivo*, Avda. Ramón y Cajal 6, serves good *platos combinados*; and *Hostal Castillo* has its own excellent restaurant.

Cazorla and the Parque Natural

During the reconquest of Andalucía, **CAZORLA**, linked by bus to Úbeda, Jaén and Granada, acted as an outpost for Christian troops. The two castles which dominate the town testify to its turbulent past – both were originally Moorish but later altered and restored by their Christian conquerors. Today it's the main base for visits to the **Parque Natural de las Sierras de Segura y Cazorla**, a vast protected area of magnificent river gorges and forests. Cazorla also hosts the **fiesta de Cristo del**

Consuelo, with fairgrounds, fireworks and religious processions on September 16–21.

Cazorla itself is constructed around three main squares. Buses arrive in the busy, commercial Plaza de la Constitución, where there's a privately run **tourist information centre**, Quercus, offering Land Rover day-trips (5000ptas) into the park. The town's official **Turismo** (April–Sept Mon–Fri 10.30am–2pm; ☎953 710102) is at Paseo del Cristo 17, 100m north of Plaza de la Constitución, and can provide a useful town map. The main c/de Muñoz connects with the second square, the Plaza de la Corredera (or *del Huevo*, "of the Egg", because of its shape). The seat of the administration, the *Ayuntamiento*, is here, a fine Moorish-style palace at the far end of the plaza.

Beyond, a labyrinth of narrow, twisting streets leads to Cazorla's liveliest square, the **Plaza Santa María**. This takes its name from the old cathedral which, damaged by floods in the seventeenth century, was later torched by Napoleonic troops. Its ruins, now preserved, and the fine open square form a natural amphitheatre for concerts and local events as well as being a popular meeting place. The square is dominated by **La Yedra**, an austere, reconstructed castle tower, which houses the **Museo de Artes y Costumbres** (Mon–Sat 9.30am–2.30pm), an interesting folklore museum displaying domestic utensils and furniture.

Cazorla practicalities

There is a surprising range of **accommodation** in Cazorla. *Pensión Taxi*, Travesía de San Antón 7 (☎953 720525; ②), off Plaza de la Constitución, is at the bottom end; as a resident, you can also eat for very little in their *comedor*. Better rooms are available at the *Hostal Guadalquivir*, c/Nueva 6 (☎953 720268; ③), off Plaza de la Corredera – it's spotlessly clean and very friendly, though disconcertingly close to the municipal slaughterhouse for those with sensitive ears. In the square itself, the friendly *Hostal Betis* (☎953 720540; ②) has some rooms overlooking the plaza, or there's the *Andalucía*, c/Martínez Falero 42 (☎953 721268; ③). There is also a clutch of more upmarket places, of which the *Villa Turistica de Cazorla*, Ladera de San Isidro s/n (☎953 710100, fax 953 710152; ⑥), is the best; it's a five-minute walk from Plaza de Santa Maria along c/Fuente de la Peña. If you have a car there are some very attractive alternatives out in the sierra, including the *Sierra de Cazorla* (☎953 720015, fax 953 720017; ⑤), 2km outside the town, with a pool, and the *Parador el Adelantado* (☎953 727075, fax 953 727077; ⑦), a dull modern building also with pool in a wonderful setting 25km away in the park. Cazorla also has a **youth hostel**, at Mauricio Martínez 2 (☎953 710329; ①), open April to October, Christmas and Easter. Ask at the *Mesón la Cueva* (see below) if you want to **rent an apartment** for a longer stay.

Several spit-and-sawdust **bars** with good *tapas* cluster round the Plaza Santa María, along with the rustic *Mesón la Cueva*, which offers authentic local food cooked on a wood-fired range – though when they are overrun in high season things can tend to deteriorate. Other places where you can **eat** well are the two *mesones* on Plaza de la Corredera; the one next to the church is excellent value and the other prepares exquisite fish – both serve *tapas* and *raciones* rather than full meals. There are two discos (weekends only) and several "pubs" with loud music.

The Parque Natural

Even casual visitors to the park are likely to see a good variety of wildlife, including *Capra hispanica* (Spanish mountain goat), deer, wild pig, birds and butterflies. Ironically, though, much of the best viewing will be at the periphery, or even outside the park, since the wildlife is most successfully stalked on foot and walking opportunities within the park itself are surprisingly limited.

THE RÍO BOROSA WALK

The classic walk along the **Río Borosa** can currently be done as a day trek even if you are relying on public transport – though you should check the bus timetables before setting out. The early-morning bus to Coto Ríos can drop you at the visitors' centre at Torre de Vinagre where the route begins. Cross the road and take the path to the side of the Jardín Botanico. When you reach an electricity pylon turn left on to a downhill track. After passing a campsite and sportsfield to the left cross a footbridge over the river and turn right, aiming for a white building peeping above the trees. Soon you'll pass a small campsite (with an open-air bar in summer) and about a kilometre from the footbridge you'll come to a car park at a trout hatchery (*piscifactoría*).

From here follow the rough track along the northwest (right) bank of the Borosa, swift and cold even in summer. Within a few minutes a signposted footpath diverges to the right; this also marks the beginning of the **gorge**. Two or three wooden bridges now take the path back and forth across the river, which is increasingly confined by sheer rock walls. At the narrowest points the path is routed along planked catwalks secured to the limestone cliff. The walk from Torre de Vinagre to the end of the narrows takes about two hours.

There the footpath rejoins the track; after another half-hour's walk you'll see a turbine and a long metal pipe bringing water from **two lakes** – one natural, one a small dam – up the mountain. The road crosses one last bridge over the Borosa and stops at the turbine house. When you get to a gate, beyond which there's a steeply rising gully, count on another full hour up to the lakes. Cross a footbridge and start the steep climb up a narrow track over the rocks below the cliff (at one point the path passes close to the base of the palisade – beware falling stones). At the top of the path is a cavernous amphitheatre, with a waterfall in winter. The path ends about halfway up the cliff, where an artificial tunnel has been bored through rock; walk through it to get to the lake.

Allow three and a half hours' walking time from Torre del Vinagre, slightly less going down. It's a very full day's excursion but you should have plenty of time to catch the afternoon bus back, which currently passes the visitors' centre at 5.45pm.

INFORMATION

The official **information office** for the park is located in Cazorla at c/Martínez Falero 11, just off Plaza de la Constitución. It's worth getting a good map from here, either the 1:100,000 map, *Parque Natural de las Sierras de Cazorla y Segura*, or the 1:50,000 version, *Cazorla*.

TRANSPORT AND ACCOMMODATION

Public transport into the park is sparse. Two daily **buses** (except Sun) link Cazorla with **Coto Ríos** in the middle of the park: one at 5.45am, the other at 2.30pm; there's also a 6.30pm bus on Saturday. The return from Coto (not Sun) leaves at 5.30pm. Distances between points are enormous, so to explore the park well you'll need a car or be prepared for long treks. Such problems are complicated by the fact that most of the *camping libre* (free camping) areas shown on the 1:100,000 map have been closed recently; one still functioning is to be found beyond El Tranco on the dam. There is more accommodation at Coto Ríos, with three privately run **campsites** and a succession of *hostales*. Before setting out you should get the latest update on transport and accommodation from the Turismo in Cazorla.

WALKS

There are only three signposted **tracks** in the park, all pitifully short. One leads from the Empalme de Vadillo to the Puente de la Herrera via the Fuente del Oso (2km each way); another of about 1700m curls round the Cerrada (narrows) de Utrero near Vadillo-Castril village; and the best marked segment, through the lower Borosa gorge (see above), is also a mere 1700m long.

Granada

If you see only one town in Spain it should be **GRANADA**. For here, extraordinarily well preserved and in a tremendous natural setting, stands the **Alhambra** – the most exciting, sensual and romantic of all European monuments. It was the palace-fortress of the Nasrid Sultans, rulers of the last Spanish Moorish kingdom, and in its construction Moorish art reached a spectacular and serene climax. But the building seems to go further than this, revealing something of the whole brilliance and spirit of Moorish life and culture. There's a haunting passage in Jan Morris's book, *Spain*, which the palace embodies: "Life itself, which was seen elsewhere in Europe as a kind of probationary preparation for death, was interpreted [by the Moors] as something glorious in itself, to be ennobled by learning and enlivened by every kind of pleasure."

Arrival and information

Virtually everything of interest in Granada – including the hills of **Alhambra** (to the east) and **Sacromonte** (to the north) – is within easy walking distance of the centre.

The **train station** is a kilometre or so out on the Avda. de Andaluces, off Avda. de la Constitución (Avda. Calvo Sotelo); to get into town, bus #4 runs direct to Gran Vía, and bus #11 takes a circular route – inbound on the Gran Vía de Colón and back out via the Puerta Real and Camino de Ronda. The most central stop is by the cathedral on the Gran Vía.

MOORISH GRANADA

Granada's glory was always precarious. It was established as an **independent kingdom** in 1238 by **Ibn Ahmar**, a prince of the Arab Nasrid tribe which had been driven south from Zaragoza. He proved a just and capable ruler but all over Spain the Christian kingdoms were in the ascendant. The Moors of Granada survived only through paying tribute and allegiance to Fernando III of Castile – whom they were forced to assist in the conquest of Muslim Sevilla – and by the time of Ibn Ahmar's death in 1275 theirs was the only surviving Spanish Muslim kingdom. It had, however, consolidated its territory (stretching from just north of the city down to a coastal strip between Tarifa and Almería) and, stimulated by refugees, developed a flourishing commerce, industry and culture.

By a series of shrewd manoeuvres Granada maintained its autonomy for two and a half centuries, its rulers turning for protection, in turn as it suited them, to the Christian kingdoms of Aragón and Castile and to the Merinid Muslims of Morocco. The city-state enjoyed a particularly confident and prosperous period under **Yusuf I** (1334–54) and **Mohammed V** (1354–91), the sultans responsible for much of the existing Alhambra palace. But by the mid-fifteenth century a pattern of coups and internal strife became established and a rapid succession of rulers did little to stem Christian inroads. In 1479 the kingdoms of Aragón and Castile were united by the marriage of Fernando and Isabella and within ten years had conquered Ronda, Málaga and Almería. The city of Granada now stood completely alone, tragically preoccupied in a **civil war** between supporters of the sultan's two favourite wives. The Reyes Católicos made escalating and finally untenable demands upon it, and in 1490 war broke out. **Boabdil**, the last Moorish king, appealed in vain for help from his fellow Muslims in Morocco, Egypt and Ottoman Turkey, and in the following year **Fernando and Isabella** marched on Granada with an army said to total 150,000 troops. For seven months, through the winter of 1491, they laid siege to the city, and on January 2, 1492, Boabdil formally surrendered its keys. The Christian Reconquest of Spain was complete.

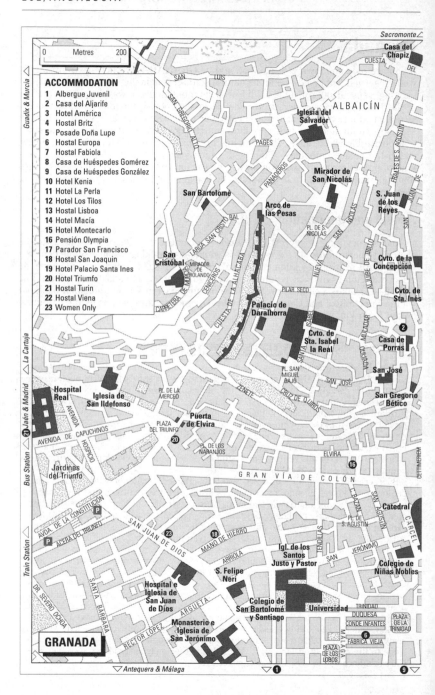

ACCOMMODATION

1 Albergue Juvenil
2 Casa del Aljarife
3 Hotel América
4 Hostal Britz
5 Posade Doña Lupe
6 Hostal Europa
7 Hostal Fabiola
8 Casa de Huéspedes Gomérez
9 Casa de Huéspedes González
10 Hotel Kenia
11 Hotel La Perla
12 Hotel Los Tilos
13 Hostal Lisboa
14 Hotel Macía
15 Hotel Montecarlo
16 Pensión Olympia
17 Parador San Francisco
18 Hostal San Joaquin
19 Hotel Palacio Santa Ines
20 Hotel Triumfo
21 Hostal Turin
22 Hostal Viena
23 Women Only

GRANADA

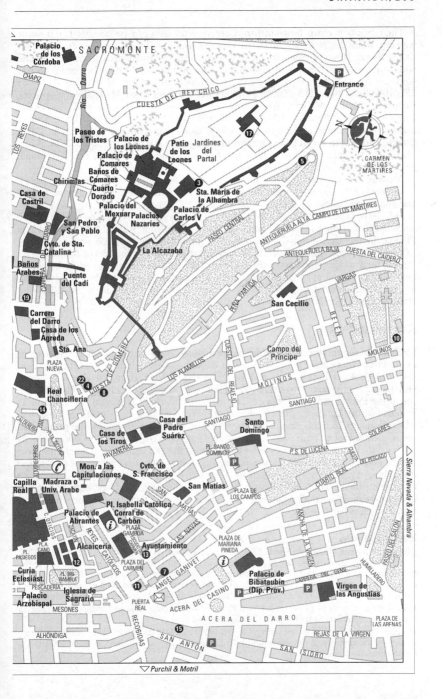

Palacio de los Córdoba

SACROMONTE

CHAPIZ

Río Darro

CUESTA DEL REY CHICO

P
Entrance

LOS REYES

Paseo de los Tristes

Palacio de los Leones

Patio de los Leones

Jardines del Partal

17

N

5

CARMEN DE LOS MÁRTIRES

Palacio de Comares
Baños de Comares
Cuarto Dorado
Palacio del Mexuar

Chirimías

Casa de Castril

San Pedro y San Pablo

Cvto. de Sta. Catalina

Baños Árabes

19

Puente del Cadí

Palacios Nazaries

3
Sta. María de la Alhambra

Palacio de Carlos V

La Alcazaba

PASEO CENTRAL

ANTEQUERUELA ALTA   CAMPO DE LOS MÁRTIRES

ANTEQUERUELA BAJA   CUESTA DEL CAIDERO

PEÑA PARTIDA

VARGAS

San Cecilio

BELÉN

MOLINOS

Carrera del Darro
Casa de los Agreda

Sta. Ana

PLAZA NUEVA

CUESTA DEL REALEJO

LOS ALAMILLOS

Campo del Príncipe

10

22 4
8

Real Chancillería

CUESTA DE GOMÉREZ

M O L I N O S

SANTIAGO

SOLARES

14

CALDERERÍA

PTA. SITENA

Casa del Padre Suárez

SANTIAGO

Santo Domingo

P. S. DE LUCENA

CUESTA DEL PESCADO

Casa de los Tiros

PAVANERAS

PL. SANTO DOMINGO

P

CUARTO REAL

ALHAMICEROS

Mon. a las Capitulaciones

Cvto. de S. Francisco

San Matías

PLAZA DE LOS CAMPOS

PASEO DEL SALÓN

Capilla Real

Madraza o Univ. Árabe

SAN MATÍAS

PLAZA DE MARIANA PINEDA

ANCHA DE LA VIRGEN

HUMILLADERO

REYES CATÓLICOS

Palacio de Abrantes

Pl. Isabella Católica
Corral de Carbón

i

PLAZA GAMBOA

LAS NAVAS

Alcaicería

13

Ayuntamiento

PLAZA DEL CARMEN

7

ANGEL GANIVET

i

Palacio de Bibataubín
(Dip. Prov.)

P

CARRERA DEL GENIL

Virgen de las Angustias

Curia Eclesiást.

PL. BIB-RAMBLA

11

Iglesia de Sagrario

PUERTA REAL

ACERA DEL CASINO

P

PLAZA DE LAS ARENAS

Palacio Arzobispal

MESONES

RECOGIDAS

A C E R A   D E L   D A R R O

REJAS DE LA VIRGEN

ALHÓNDIGA

15

SAN ANTÓN

P

SAN ISIDRO

△ Sierra Nevada & Alhambra

▽ *Purchil & Motril*

The city's new **main bus station**, Carretera de Jaén s/n (☎958 185011), is some way out of the centre in the northern suburbs, and handles all services except those to the Sierra Nevada, Valencia and Barcelona. The #3 bus leaves from outside and will drop you near the cathedral (a fifteen-minute journey). For information on bus services on departure check with the individual companies: Alsina Graells (☎958 185010) at the main bus station runs services to and from Madrid, Jaén, Úbeda, Córdoba, Sevilla, Málaga, Alpujarras, Motril, Guadix, Almería and the coast; Empresa Bonal (☎958 273100), Avda. Calvo Sotelo 19, has buses to the north side of Sierra Nevada; Empresa Autedia (☎958 563636), c/Rector Martín 10, off Avda. Calvo Sotelo, runs more services to Guadix; and Empresa Bacoma (☎958 284251), Avda. Andalucía 12, near the train station, has buses to Valencia/Alicante and Barcelona. All terminals are on the #11 bus route.

Arriving **by air**, there's a bus (5 daily except Sat; 30min) connecting the airport, 17km west of the city on the A92 *autovía*, with Plaza Isabel La Católica; alternatively, a taxi should cost about 2500ptas.

Full details and bus timetables – and much else besides – should be posted on the walls of the **Turismo** (Mon–Sat 9am–7pm, Sun 10am–2pm; ☎958 225990), c/Mariana Pineda, in the Corral del Carbón near the cathedral, just off the eastern side of c/Reyes Católicos. You can also buy **maps and guides** for the Sierra Nevada here, though for a wider selection try the Librería Dauro at c/Zacatín 3 (a pedestrian street between the cathedral and c/Reyes Católicos). There's also a helpful (and less frenetic) **municipal tourist office** (Mon–Fri 9.30am–7pm, Sat 10am–2pm; ☎958 226688) at Plaza Mariana Pineda 10.

Accommodation

Finding a **place to stay** in the centre of town, along the Gran Vía, c/Reyes Católicos or in the Plaza Nueva and Puerta Real is easy enough except at the very height of season (Semana Santa is impossible), and prices are no higher than elsewhere in Spain. Otherwise, try the streets to either side of the Gran Vía, at the back of the Plaza Nueva, round the Puerta Real and Plaza de Carmen (particularly c/de Navas), the Plaza de la Trinidad in the university area (and east of there), or along the Cuesta de Gomérez, which leads up from the Plaza Nueva towards the Alhambra. **Hostales** and **pensiones** are so plentiful round here – and turnaround of guests so regular – that individual places are hard to recommend. Those below are no more than an indication of some that have proved good; the main problem, almost anywhere, is **noise**. However, a new road to the Alhambra, diverting traffic away from the centre, has transformed the Cuesta de Gomérez, which is now a semi-pedestrianized street (taxis only). Don't bother trying to find "interesting" accommodation in the Albaicín area – there is only one upmarket *hostal* which is listed below

Budget options

Albergue Juvenil, Camino de Ronda 171, at the junction with Avda. Ramón y Cajal (☎958 284306, fax 958 285285). If you arrive late in the day, Granada's youth hostel is conveniently close to the train station: turn left on to Avda. de la Constitución and left again on to Camino de Ronda. From the bus station, take bus #11. Lots of facilities include a summer pool and good en-suite double and four-person rooms, but it's rather institutional and can be booked up for days ahead in summer. ①.

Hostal Britz, Cuesta de Gomérez 1 (☎958 223652). Very comfortable and well-placed *hostal*, en route to the Alhambra. Some rooms with bath. ③.

Posada Doña Lupe, Avda. del Generalife s/n (☎958 221473, fax 958 221474). A stone's throw from the new entrance to the Alhambra, with great-value rooms (with and without bath) and a rooftop pool. ②.

Hostal Europa, c/Fábrica Vieja 16, off Plaza Trinidad (☎958 278744). Friendly and small, with plenty of other *hostales* nearby. ③.

Hostal Fabiola, c/Ángel Gavinet 5 (☎958 223572). Close to the Puerta Real; on the third floor and relatively quiet. All rooms with bath and many with sun balcony. ③.

Casa de Huéspedes Gomérez, Cuesta de Gomérez 2 (☎958 226398). Simple but convenient for the Alhambra and centre. ②.

Casa de Huéspedes González, c/Buensuceso, between Plaza de Trinidad and Plaza de Gracia, east of the cathedral. Perfectly decent rooms in this good-value *casa*. ②.

Pensión Olimpia, c/Alvaro de Bazán 6, off Gran Vía de Colón opposite Banco de Jeréz. Friendly, central *pensión* offering good-value accommodation. ②.

Hotel La Perla, c/Reyes Católicos 2 (☎958 223415). Simple hotel right in the centre, near the cathedral, but this is a noisy street. ③.

Hostal San Joaquín, c/Mano de Hierro 14, close to the church of San Juan (☎958 282879). Great, rambling old *hostal*, with simple rooms and charming patios. ③.

Hostal Turin, Ancha de Capuchinos 16 (☎958 200311). Also near the train station, off the Jardines del Triunfo, this *hostal* is inexpensive and well run. ②.

Hostal Viena, c/Hospital de Santa Ana 2 (☎958 221859). In a quiet street (first left off Cuesta de Gomérez), this is a friendly, Austrian-run *hostal* offering some rooms with bath. ③.

Women Only, c/San Juan de Dios 14, press buzzer for 4th floor. Nameless private accommodation for women only in student area. Clean, friendly and helpful. ①.

Moderate and expensive options

Casa del Aljarife, Placeta de la Cruz Verde 2 (☎ & fax 958 222425). The Albaicín's solitary *hostal* occupies a restored seventeenth-century mansion and has charming en-suite air-conditioned rooms. ⑤.

Hotel América, Real de la Alhambra 53 (☎958 227471, fax 958 227470). Simple, one-star hotel, in the Alhambra grounds; you're paying for the location, but recent price hikes now question whether it's worth it. Booking essential. ⑥.

Hotel Kenia, c/Molinos 65 (☎958 227506). This well-converted old mansion is on a quiet position on slopes below Alhambra, south of the centre. ⑤.

Hostal Lisboa, Plaza del Carmen 27 (☎958 221413). Clean and comfortable central *hostal*, offering rooms with and without bath. ③–④.

Hotel Macía, Plaza Nueva 4 (☎958 227536, fax 958 227535). Centrally-located hotel, with comfortable rooms overlooking the atmospheric square. ⑤.

Hotel Montecarlo, c/Acera de Darro 44 (☎958 257900, fax 958 255596). Another central hotel, offering rooms with video and air-conditioning. ⑤.

Parador San Francisco, Real de la Alhambra (☎958 221440, fax 958 222264). Without question the best – and most expensive – place to stay in Granada; a converted monastery in the Alhambra grounds. Advance booking essential. ⑧.

Hotel Palacio Santa Inés, Cuesta de Santa Inés 9 (☎958 222362, fax 958 222465). Sumptuous six-room hotel in a restored sixteenth-century mansion on the edge of the Albaicín, with views of the Alhambra. ⑧.

Hotel Triunfo, Plaza del Triunfo 19 (☎958 207444, fax 958 207673). Well-appointed upmarket hotel on the edge of the Albaicín, flanked by an imposing Moorish arch, the Puerta de Elvira. ⑦.

Hotel Los Tilos, Plaza de Bib-Rambla 4 (☎958 266712, fax 958 266801). Plain, two-star hotel well located near the cathedral. ⑤.

Camping

Camping Sierra Nevada, Avda. de Madrid 107 (☎958 150062; March–Oct). Closest site to the centre (bus #3 from the centre or a 2-min walk from the bus station, turning right outside), and probably the best too.

El Último, Camino Huetor Vega 22 (☎958 123069). Not much farther out, via Avda. de Cervantes, and with a pool.

The Alhambra

There are three distinct groups of buildings on the Alhambra hill: the **Palacios Nazaríes** (Royal Palace, or Nasrid Palaces), the palace gardens of the **Generalife**, and the **Alcazaba**. This latter, the fortress of the eleventh-century Ziridian rulers, was all that existed when Ibn Ahmar made Granada his capital, but from its reddish walls the hill top had already taken its name: *Al Qal'a al-Hamra* in Arabic means literally "the red". Ibn Ahmar rebuilt the Alcazaba and added to it the huge circuit of walls and towers which forms one's first view of the castle. Within the walls he began a palace, which he supplied with running water by diverting the River Darro nearly 8km to the foot of the hill; water is an integral part of the Alhambra and this engineering feat was Ibn Ahmar's greatest contribution. The Palacios Nazaríes was essentially the product of his fourteenth-century successors, particularly Mohammed V, who built and redecorated many of its rooms in celebration of his accession to the throne (in 1354) and the taking of Algeciras (in 1369).

After their conquest of the city, **Fernando and Isabella** lived for a while in the Alhambra. They restored some rooms and converted the mosque but left the palace structure unaltered. As at Córdoba and Sevilla, it was **Emperor Carlos V**, their grandson, who wreaked the most insensitive destruction, demolishing a whole wing of rooms in order to build a Renaissance palace. This and the Alhambra itself were simply ignored by his successors and by the eighteenth century the Palacios Nazaríes was in use as a prison. In 1812 it was taken and occupied by **Napoleon's forces**, who looted and damaged whole sections of the palace, and on their retreat from the city tried to blow up the entire complex. Their attempt was thwarted only by the action of a crippled soldier who remained behind and removed the fuses.

Two decades later the Alhambra's "rediscovery" began, given impetus by the American writer **Washington Irving**, who set up his study in the empty palace rooms and began to write his marvellously romantic *Tales of the Alhambra* (on sale all over Granada – and good reading amid the gardens and courts). Shortly after its publication, the Spaniards made the Alhambra a **national monument** and set aside funds for its restoration. This continues to the present day and is now a highly sophisticated project, scientifically removing the accretions of later ages in order to expose and meticulously restore the Moorish creations.

Approaches to the Alhambra

The standard **approach** (on foot or by bus) to the Alhambra is along the Cuesta de Gomérez, the semi-pedestrianized road which climbs uphill from Granada's central Plaza Nueva. The only vehicles allowed to use this road in daytime are taxis and the **Alhambrabus**, a dedicated minibus service (daily 7am–10pm, every 10min; 100ptas) linking Plaza Nueva with the Alhambra palace. To get there **by car** you will need to use the route which is signed from the Puerta Real, to the south of the cathedral; the road leads you to the Alhambra's car park, close to the new entrance.

Should you decide to **walk** up the hill (a pleasant twenty-minute stroll from the Plaza Nueva), after a few hundred metres you reach the **Puerta de las Granadas**, a massive Renaissance gateway erected by Carlos V. Here two paths diverge to either side of the road: the one on the right climbs up towards a group of fortified towers, the **Torres Bermejas**, which may date from as early as the eighth century. The left-hand path leads through the woods past a huge terrace-fountain (again courtesy of Carlos V) to the main gateway – and former entrance – of the Alhambra. This is the **Puerta de la Justicia**, a magnificent tower which forced three changes of direction, making intruders hopelessly vulnerable. It was built by Yusuf I in 1340 and preserves above its outer arch the Koranic symbol of a key (for Allah the Opener) and an outstretched hand, whose five fingers represent the five Islamic precepts: prayer, fasting, alms-giving, pilgrimage to Mecca and the oneness of God. The **new entrance** to the Alhambra – at the eastern end, near to the Generalife gardens – lies a further five-minute walk uphill, reached by following the wall to your left.

Within the citadel stood a complete "government city" of mansions, smaller houses, baths, schools, mosques, barracks and gardens. Of this only the **Alcazaba fortress** and the **Palacios Nazaríes** remain; they face each other across a broad terrace (constructed in the sixteenth century over a dividing gully), flanked by the majestic though incongruous **Palace of Carlos V**.

Within the walls of the citadel, too, are the beautiful *Parador San Francisco* (a converted monastery, where Isabella was originally buried – bar open to anyone), and the *Hotel América*. There are a handful of drinks stalls around as well, including one, very welcome, in the Portal gardens (towards the Carlos V Palace after you leave the Palacios Nazaríes).

Admission

Tickets to the complex (April–Sept Mon–Sat 9am–8pm, Sun 9am–6pm; Oct–March daily 9am–6pm; 750ptas) can be purchased at the entrance but be prepared for queues of one to two hours in high season. Indeed, the overwhelming number of visitors to the Alhambra has now made it less than certain that visitors turning up on the day during high season will be guaranteed entry, and if your time in Granada is restricted you are strongly advised to book ahead using the methods described below, or turn up as early as possible in the morning (the ticket office opens thirty minutes before the gates).

One way **to avoid the queues** is to purchase tickets from the offices of the Caja General de Ahorros de Granada bank, Plaza Isabel la Católica 6, in the town centre. On the same square at no. 1 the Banco Bilbao Vizcaya also sells tickets and accepts advance bookings in person under the same conditions as the Alhambra's main office (see below). You should note that both banks only sell tickets during normal banking hours, charge 100ptas commission per ticket and are computer-linked to the Alhambra which means that when the daily allocation of 8,400 admissions has been reached, no further tickets will be sold. The Alhambra's **reservation system** (☎958 220912, fax 958 210584; they prefer faxes) allows you to book a time for your visit prior to arrival which must be at least a week and less than one year ahead.

The tickets have **sections** for each part of the complex – Alcazaba, Palacios Nazaríes, Generalife – and these must be used on the same day. In an attempt to cope with the drastic overcrowding of recent years, tickets are stamped with a half-hour time slot (usually up to an hour ahead) during which you *must* enter the Palacios Nazaríes section; once inside you can stay as long as you like.

The Alhambra is also open for **floodlit visits** (limited to only the central part of the complex; 750ptas) from 10pm until midnight on Tuesday, Thursday and Saturday nights from April to September (out of season Sat only, 8–10pm), and occasional concerts are held in its courts. The two **museums** in the Palace of Carlos V have separate admission fees and hours (see p.302).

Entry to the Alhambra

The **new entrance** to the Alhambra now brings you into the complex at the eastern end, near to the Generalife gardens. However, as you will have a time slot for entering the Royal Palace (usually up to an hour ahead), it makes sense chronologically and practically to start your visit with the Alcazaba at the Alhambra's opposite, or western, end. To get there from the entrance, walk up the short avenue lined with cypresses to a three-way fork, taking the signed path to the Alhambra. Cross the bridge over the moat following signs to the Alcazaba and Palacios Nazaríes, and you will eventually

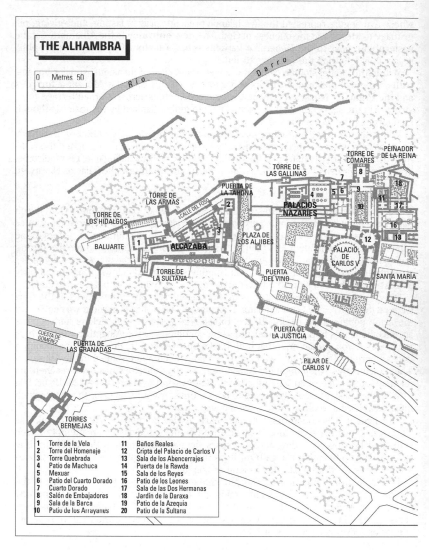

THE ALHAMBRA

0 Metres 50

1	Torre de la Vela	**11**	Baños Reales
2	Torre del Homenaje	**12**	Cripta del Palacio de Carlos V
3	Torre Quebrada	**13**	Sala de los Abencerrajes
4	Patio de Machuca	**14**	Puerta de la Rawda
5	Mexuar	**15**	Sala de los Reyes
6	Patio del Cuarto Dorado	**16**	Patio de los Leones
7	Cuarto Dorado	**17**	Sala de las Dos Hermanas
8	Salón de Embajadores	**18**	Jardín de la Daraxa
9	Sala de la Barca	**19**	Patio de la Azequia
10	Patio de los Arrayanes	**20**	Patio de la Sultana

pass the gates of the *Parador de San Francisco* (on your right), and the *Hotel America*, to enter the Calle Real. Continue alongside the Palace of Carlos V to pass through the **Puerto del Vino** – named from its use in the sixteenth century as a wine cellar – into the Alcazaba, the earliest, though most ruined part of the fortress.

The Alcazaba

The **Alcazaba** is the best place to start your visit and get a grip on the whole site. At its summit is the **Torre de la Vela**, named after a huge bell on its turret which until recent

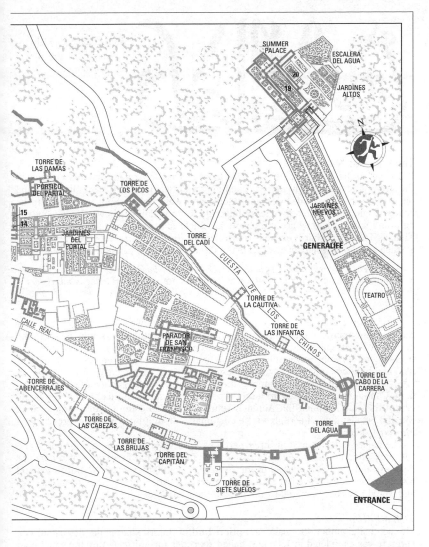

years was rung to mark the irrigation hours for workers on Granada's vast and fertile plain. It was here, at 3pm on January 2, 1492, that the Cross was first displayed above the city, alongside the royal standards of Aragón and Castile and the banner of Saint James. Boabdil, leaving Granada for exile in the Alpujarras, turned and wept at the sight, earning from his mother Aisha the famous rebuke: "Do not weep like a woman for what you could not defend like a man". The **Aljibe**, a cistern beneath the area between the Alcazaba and Casa Real, is open for viewing on Monday, Wednesday and Friday from 9.30am to 1.30pm.

Wa-la-ghaliba illa-Llah
stylized inscription from
the Alhambra

The Palacios Nazaríes

It is amazing that the **Palacios Nazaríes** has survived, for it stands in utter contrast to the strength of the Alcazaba and the encircling walls and towers. It was built lightly and often crudely from wood, brick and adobe, and was designed not to last but to be renewed and redecorated by succeeding rulers. Its buildings show a brilliant use of light and space but they are principally a vehicle for ornamental stucco decoration. This, as Titus Burckhardt explains in *Moorish Culture in Spain*, was both an intricate science and a philosophy of abstract art in direct contrast to pictorial representation:

> *With its rhythmic repetition, [it] does not seek to capture the eye to lead it into an imagined world, but, on the contrary, liberates it from all pre-occupations of the mind. It does not transmit any specific ideas, but a state of being, which is at once repose and inner rhythm.*

Burckhardt adds that the way in which patterns are woven from a single band, or radiate from many identical centres, served as a pure simile for Islamic belief in the oneness of God, manifested at the centre of every form and being. **Arabic inscriptions** feature prominently in the ornamentation. Some are poetic eulogies of the buildings and builders, others of various sultans (notably Mohammed V). Most, however, are taken from the Koran, and among them the phrase *Wa-la ghaliba illa-Llah* (There is no Conqueror but God) is tirelessly repeated. It is said that this became the battle cry of the Nasrids upon Ibn Ahmar's return from aiding the Castilian war against Muslim Sevilla; it was his reply to the customary, though bitterly ironic, greetings of *Mansur* (Victor).

The palace is structured in three parts, each arrayed round an interior court and with a specific function. The sultans used the **Mexuar**, the first series of rooms, for business and judicial purposes. In the **Serallo**, beyond, they received embassies and distinguished guests. The last section, the **Harem**, formed their private living quarters and would have been entered by no one but their family or servants.

THE MEXUAR

The council chamber, the main **reception hall** of the Mexuar, is the first room you enter. It was completed in 1365 and hailed (perhaps formulaically) by the court poet Ibn Zamrak as a "haven of counsel, mercy, and favour". Here the sultan heard the pleas and petitions of the people and held meetings with his ministers. At the room's far end is a small oratory, one of a number of prayer niches scattered round the palace and immediately identifiable by their distinctive alignment (to face Mecca). This "public" section of the palace, beyond which few would have penetrated, is completed by the Mudéjar **Cuarto Dorado** (Golden Room), decorated under Carlos V, whose *Plus Ultra* motif appears throughout the palace, and the **Patio del Cuarto Dorado**. This has perhaps the grandest facade of the whole palace, for it admits you to the formal splendour of the Serallo.

THE SERALLO

The Serallo was built largely to the design of Yusuf I, a romantic and enlightened sultan who was stabbed to death by a madman while worshipping in the Alhambra mosque. Its rooms open out from delicate marble-columned arcades at each end of the long **Patio de los Arrayanes** (Patio of the Myrtles).

At the court's north end, occupying two floors of a fortified tower, is the royal throne room, known as the **Salón de Embajadores** (Hall of the Ambassadors). As the sultan could be approached only indirectly, it stands at an angle to the entrance from the Mexuar. It is the largest room of the palace, perfectly square and completely covered in tile and stucco decoration. Among the web of inscriptions is one that states simply "I am the Heart of the Palace". Here Boabdil signed the terms of his city's surrender to the Catholic kings, whose motifs (the arms of Aragón and Castile) were later worked into the room's stunning wooden dome, a superb example of *lacería*, the rigidly geometric "carpentry of knots". Here too, so it is said, Fernando met with Columbus to discuss his plans for finding a new sea route to India – which led to the discovery of the Americas. The dome itself, in line with the mystical-mathematical pursuit of medieval Moorish architecture, has a complex symbolism representing the seven heavens. Carlos V tore down the rooms at the southern end of the court; from the arcade there is access to the gloomy **Chapel Crypt** of his palace which has a curious "whispering gallery" effect.

THE HAREM

The **Patio de los Leones** (Court of the Lions), which has become the archetypal image of Granada, constitutes the heart of the harem section of the palace. The stylized and archaic-looking lions beneath its fountain probably date, like the patio itself, from the reign of Mohammed V, Yusuf's successor; a poem inscribed on the bowl tells how much fiercer they would look if they weren't so restrained by respect for the sultan. The court was designed as an interior garden and planted with shrubs and aromatic herbs; it opens on to three of the palace's finest rooms, each of which looks on to the fountain.

The most sophisticated rooms in this part of the complex, apparently designed to give a sense of the rotary movement of the stars, are the two facing each other across the court. The largest of these, the **Sala de los Abencerrajes,** has the most startlingly beautiful ceiling in the Alhambra: sixteen-sided, supported by niches of stalactite vaulting, lit by windows in the dome and reflected in a fountain on the floor. This light and airy quality stands at odds with its name and history, for here Abu'l-Hasan (Boabdil's father) murdered sixteen princes of the Abencerraje family, whose chief had fallen in love with his favourite, Zoraya; the rust stains in the fountain are popularly supposed to be the indelible traces of their blood.

At the far end is the **Sala de los Reyes** (Hall of the Kings), whose dormitory alcoves preserve a series of unique paintings on leather. These, in defiance of Koranic law, represent human scenes; it's believed that they were painted by a Christian artist in the last decades of Moorish rule. The second of the two facing chambers on the court's north side, the **Sala de las Dos Hermanas** (Hall of the Two Sisters), is more mundanely named – from two huge slabs of marble in its floor – but just as spectacularly decorated, with a dome of over five thousand "honeycomb cells". It was the principal room of the sultan's favourite, opening on to an inner apartment and balcony, the **Mirador de Daraxa** (known in English as the "Eyes of the Sultana"); the romantic garden patio below was added after the Reconquest.

Beyond, you are directed along a circuitous route through **apartments** redecorated by Carlos V (as at Sevilla, the northern-reared emperor installed fireplaces) and later used by Washington Irving. Eventually you emerge at the **Peinador,** or Queen's Tower, a pavilion that served as an oratory for the sultanas and as a dressing room for the wife of Carlos V; perfumes were burned beneath its floor and wafted up through a marble slab in one corner.

From there, passing the **Patio de la Reja** (Patio of the Grille) added in the seventeenth century, you reach the **Baños Reales** (Royal Baths). These are tremendous, decorated in rich tile mosaics and lit by pierced stars and rosettes once covered by coloured glass. The central chamber was used for reclining and retains the balconies where singers and musicians – reputedly blind to keep the royal women from being seen – would entertain the bathers.

TOWERS AND THE PALACIO DE CARLOS V

Before leaving the palace compound, there are a number of the **towers** worth a look. Most are richly decorated – particularly the first, the **Torre de las Damas** (Ladies' Tower) – which stands in front of its own patio (restored to the original design).

The exit from the Palacios Nazaríes leads you to the entrance and courtyard of **Carlos V's palace**, where bullfights were once held. The palace itself (begun in 1526 but never finished) seems totally out of place here, but is in fact a distinguished piece of Renaissance design in its own right – the only surviving work of Pedro Machuca, a former pupil of Michelangelo. On its upper floors is a mildly interesting **Museo de Bellas Artes** (Tues 2.30–6pm, Wed–Sat 9am–6pm, Sun 9am–2.30pm; 250ptas, free for EU citizens) with some notable examples of *andaluz* wood sculpture. The lower floor holds the **Museo Hispano-Musulman** (Tues–Sat 10am–2pm; 250ptas, free for EU citizens), a small but fascinating collection of Hispano-Moorish art, displaying many items discovered during the Alhambra restoration; the star exhibit is a beautiful fifteenth-century **Alhambra vase**, made from local red clay enamelled in blue and gold. Note, however, that both museums frequently fail to open on their advertised days.

To reach the Generalife gardens, retrace your steps along the Calle Real to the three-way fork near the entrance.

The Generalife

Paradise is described in the Koran as a shaded, leafy garden refreshed by running water where the "fortunate ones" may take their rest. It is an image which perfectly describes the **Generalife**, the gardens and summer palace of the sultans. Its name means literally "garden of the architect" and the grounds consist of a luxuriantly imaginative series of patios, enclosed gardens and walkways.

By chance, an account of the gardens during Moorish times, written rather poetically by the fourteenth-century court vizier and historian Ibn Zamrak, survives. The descriptions that he gives aren't all entirely believable, but they are a wonderful basis for musing as you lie around by the patios and fountains. There were, he wrote, celebrations with horses darting about in the dusk at speeds that made the spectators rub their eyes (a form of festival still indulged in at Moroccan *fantasías*); rockets shot into the air to be attacked by the stars for their audacity; tightrope walkers flying through the air like birds; and men bowled along in a great wooden hoop, shaped like an astronomical sphere.

Today, devoid of such amusements, the gardens are still evocative – above all, perhaps, the **Patio de los Cipreses** (aka Patio de la Sultana), a dark and secretive walled garden of sculpted junipers where the Sultana Zoraya was suspected of meeting her lover Hamet, chief of the unfortunate Abencerrajes. Nearby, too, is the inspired flight of fantasy of the **Camino de las Cascadas**, a staircase with water flowing down its stone balustrades. This is just above the wonderful little **Summer Palace**, with its various decorated belvederes. From just below the entrance to the Generalife the **Cuesta del Rey Chino** – an alternative route back to the city – winds down towards the River Darro and the old Arab quarter of the Albaicín (see below).

The Albaicín and around the town

If you're spending just a couple of days in Granada it's hard to resist spending both of them in the Alhambra. There are, however, a handful of minor Moorish sites and, climbing up from the Darro, the run-down medieval streets of the **Albaicín**, the largest and most characteristic Moorish quarter that survives in Spain. In addition, it's worth the distinct readjustment and effort of will to appreciate the city's later Christian monuments.

The Albaicín and other Moorish remains

The Albaicín stretches across a fist-shaped area bordered by the river, the Sacromonte hill, the old town walls and the winding Calle de Elvira (parallel to the Gran Vía de Colón, the main avenue which bisects central Granada). The best approach is along the Carrera del Darro, beside the river. At no. 31 in this street are the remains of the **Baños Árabes** (Tues–Sat 10am–2pm; free), marvellous and very little-visited Moorish public baths. At no. 43 is the **Casa de Castril** (Tues 3–8pm, Wed–Sat 9am–8pm, Sun 9am–3pm; 250ptas, free to EU citizens), a Renaissance mansion which houses the town's **Archeological Museum**. Of particular note here are some remarkable finds from the Neolithic Cueva de los Murciliegos (Cave of the Bats) in the Alpujarras; there are also exhibits from Granada's Phoenician, Roman, Visigothic and Moorish periods. Beside the museum a road ascends to the church of San Juan (with an intact thirteenth-century minaret) and to **San Nicolás**, whose square offers a **view of the Alhambra** considered to be the best in town.

Outside the Albaicín are two of the most interesting Moorish mansions: the **Corral del Carbón**, a fourteenth-century *caravanserai* (an inn where merchants would lodge and, on the upper floors, store their goods), now home of the Turismo; and the nearby **Casa de los Tiros**, actually built just after the Reconquest, which has a curious facade adorned with Greek deities and a number of stone muskets projecting from the upper windows. Perhaps the most interesting Moorish building in the lower town, though, and oddly one of the least well known, is the so-called **Palacio Madraza**, a strangely painted building opposite the Capilla Real. Built in the early fourteenth century, this is a former Islamic college (*medressa* in Arabic) and retains part of its old prayer hall, including a magnificently decorated *mihrab*. It is open somewhat sporadically for exhibitions; you may have to knock for admission.

The Capilla Real, cathedral and churches

The **Capilla Real** (April–Sept Mon–Sat 10.30am–1pm & 4–7pm, Sun 11am–1pm; Oct–March Mon–Fri 10.30am–1pm, Sat & Sun 11am–1pm; 300ptas) itself is an impressive

---

SECURITY IN THE ALBAICÍN

Although you certainly shouldn't let it put you off visiting the atmospheric **Albaicín quarter**, it's worth bearing in mind that the area has recently seen an escalating number of **thefts** from tourists, typically carried out by drug addicts to fund their addiction. To ensure your visit is a happy one, take all the usual precautions: avoid carrying around large amounts of money or valuables, and keep what you have in safe pockets instead of shoulder bags. If you do get something snatched, don't offer resistance; crime in these streets rarely involves attacks to the person, but thieves will be firm in getting what they want. Finally, try not to look like an obvious tourist (map/guidebook in hand is a dead giveaway) and keep to the streets where there are other people about, particularly at night.

building, flamboyant late Gothic in style and built ad hoc in the first decades of Christian rule as a mausoleum for Los Reyes Católicos, the city's "liberators". The actual **tombs** are as simple as could be imagined: Fernando (marked with an "F") and Isabella, flanked by their daughter Joana ("the Mad") and her husband Felipe ("the Handsome"), resting in lead coffins placed in a plain crypt. But above them – the response of their grandson Carlos V to what he found "too small a room for so great a glory" – is a fabulously elaborate **monument** carved in Carrara marble by Florentine Domenico Fancelli in 1517, with sculpted Renaissance effigies of the two monarchs; the tomb of Joana and Felipe alongside is a much inferior work by Ordoñez. In front of the monument is an equally magnificent **reja**, the work of Maestro Bartolomé of Baeza, and a splendid **retablo** behind depicts Boabdil surrendering the keys of Granada.

Isabella, in accordance with her will, was originally buried on the Alhambra hill (in the church of San Francisco, now part of the *parador*) but her wealth and power proved no safeguard of her wishes; recently the candle that she asked should perpetually illuminate her tomb was replaced by an electric bulb. In the Capilla's **Sacristy** is displayed the sword of Fernando, the crown of Isabella and her outstanding personal collection of medieval Flemish paintings – including important works by Memling, Bouts and van der Weyden – and various Italian paintings, including works by Botticelli and Pedro Berruguete.

For all its stark Renaissance bulk, Granada's **Catedral**, adjoining the Capilla Real and entered from the door beside it (daily: April–Sept 10.30am–1.30pm & 4–7pm; Oct–March 10.30am–1.30pm; 300ptas), is a disappointment. It was begun in 1521, just as the chapel was finished, but was then left incomplete well into the eighteenth century. At least it's light and airy inside, though, and it's fun to go round putting coins in the slots to light up the chapels, where an El Greco *St Francis* and sculptures by Pedro de Mena and Montañes will be revealed.

Other churches have more to offer, and with sufficient interest you could easily fill a day of visits. North of the cathedral, ten minutes' walk along c/San Jerónimo, the Baroque **San Juan de Dios**, with a spectacular *retablo*, is attached to a majestically portalled hospital (still in use). Close by is the elegant Renaissance **Convento de San Jerónimo** (daily: April–Sept 10am–1.30pm & 4–7pm; Oct–March 10am–1.30pm; 300ptas), founded by the Catholic kings, though built after their death, with two imposing patios.

Lastly, on the northern outskirts of town, is the **Cartuja** (April–Sept Mon–Sat 10am–1.30pm & 4–7.30pm, Sun 10am–noon; Oct–March Mon–Sat 10am–1.30pm, Sun 10am–noon; 300ptas), perhaps the grandest and most outrageously decorated of all the country's lavish Carthusian monasteries. It was constructed at the height of Baroque extravagance – some say to rival the Alhambra – and has a chapel of staggering wealth, surmounted by an altar of twisted and coloured marble. It's a further ten- to fifteen-minute walk beyond San Juan de Dios (or take bus #8 from the centre going north along Gran Vía de Colón).

Fuente Vaqueros Lorca museum

To the west of the city, in the village of Fuente Vaqueros, the birthplace of Federico García Lorca, Andalucía's greatest poet and dramatist, has been transformed into a **museum** (guided visits on the hour Tues–Sun 10am–1pm & 6–8pm; 200ptas), and contains a highly evocative collection of Lorca memorabilia. Buses operated by Ureña (hourly from 8am; 20min) leave from Granada's Avenida de Andaluces, fronting the train station.

Eating and drinking

Granada certainly isn't one of the gastronomic centres of Spain; nevertheless, like so many Spanish cities, the centre has plenty of lively **bars** serving good, inexpensive food and staying open late. All along c/Calderería Nueva you'll find health-food stores, and numerous Moroccan tea-rooms. This street, and the Mercado Municipal at the southern end of c/Agustín, are useful for assembling **picnics** for Alhambra visits. Inexpensive **restaurants** can be found among the inevitable tourist traps all over Granada. The warren of streets between **Plaza Nueva** and **Gran Vía** has plenty of good-value places, particularly *tapas* bars, as does the area around **Plaza del Carmen** (near the *Ayuntamiento*) and along c/Navas leading away from it. Another good location is the **Campo del Principe**, a pleasant square below the south side of the Alhambra hill, with a line of open-air restaurants serving inexpensive *menús*.

City centre

Bar Gambino, Plaza Mariana Pineda. Bar with a *comedor* serving delicious roast chicken.

Bar-Restaurante Sevilla, c/Oficios, opposite the entrance to the Capilla Real. One of the few surviving pre-war restaurants, and a haunt of Lorca, with a good-value *menú*.

Café-Bar Sampedro, Plaza Mariana Pineda. Good *tapas* in this café-bar next door to the *Gambino*.

Cafetería-Restaurante La Riviera, c/Cettimeriem 5. Popular café with a good *menú económico*, including a vegetarian option.

Cepillo, c/Pescadería, off c/Príncipe behind the Alcaicería. Very popular with locals for its great-value *menús* – fish and squid are the specialities.

Cunini, c/Pescadería 9. One of Granada's established upmarket (and expensive) restaurants, serving mainly fish, with an outstanding (and cheaper) *tapas* bar attached.

Gargantua, Placeta Sillería 7, near c/Reyes Católicos. Excellent atmosphere and food.

El Mesón, Plaza Gamboa 2. Behind the *Ayuntamiento*, this medium-to-expensive restaurant serves classic Granada food, such as *habas y jamón*.

Mesón Gallego Noemi, c/Trinidad 8, off Plaza Trinidad. Good and cheap little Galician restaurant.

Mesón Yunque, Plaza San Miguel Bajo in Albaicín. Great atmosphere, tasty dishes served at indoor and outdoor tables and a mainly student clientele.

Naturi Albaicín, c/Caldererría Nueva 10. Imaginative vegetarian cooking, serving up fine salads, stuffed mushrooms, and the like.

Nueva Bodega, c/Cettimeriem 3. Traditional restaurant, with a crowd of locals at the bar where the prices are cheaper.

Patio Andaluz, Escudo del Carmen 10. Very lively with one of the lowest-priced *menús* in town.

Restaurante León, c/Pan 3. Good place to linger, with *menús* at all prices; *tapas* are served at the bar during the week.

Around town

El Amir, General Narváez 3, in the south of the city near the the Plaza de Gracia. Superb, and expensive, Arab restaurant with delicious hummus and falafel, wonderful dishes of rice and ground meat with pine nuts and cinnamon, and meatballs in a spicy sauce.

Café-bar Ochando, Avda. de los Andaluces. Situated right by the train station and open 24 hours, this café is handy for late or early travellers, and serves a good breakfast.

La Estancia, c/Pedro Antonio de Alarcón. Medium-priced French restaurant on the eastern edge of the university area.

Hindi, c/de la Cruz 2, near the Plaza de Gracia. Indian vegetarian restaurant – a rarity for Spain.

El Mesón, La Esquina, La Gotera and Sol, c/Pedro Antonio de Alarcón. A string of good *tapas* bars along this street.

Nightlife

Enjoyable central **bars** include *Bodegas Castañeda* on the corner of c/Elvira and c/Almireceros, near the top of the Gran Vía, a traditional, though modernized, *bodega*; *La Buhardilla*, unsigned, on nearby c/Sillería; and *Bar Sabanilla*, c/San Sebastián 14, off the southeast corner of Plaza Bib Rambla, which claims to be the oldest in Granada, and serves free *tapas* with every drink. All these stay open until around midnight.

If you want to go on **drinking through the early hours**, head out to the student areas round the university. Calle San Juan de Dios (and its continuations c/Gran Capitán and Plaza Gran Capitán), Carril del Picón and c/Pedro Antonio de Alarcón are all extremely lively: try *Los Girasoles*, San Juan de Dios 25. In term time, students also gather in **pubs** to the west of the centre along c/Pedro Antonio de Alarcón. and around the Campo del Príncipe (an area of growing popularity), a square on the eastern slopes of the Alhambra. Another popular district, with new bars opening by the month, is the zone around Plaza Nueva, c/Elvira and the Paseo de los Tristes.

Good **disco-bars** (in a city not inclined to raving) include *La Estrella*, Plaza Cuchilleros, off Plaza Nueva (good for mixed rock and flamenco); the long-established *Planta Baja*, Horno de Abad, off Carril de Picón; *Blus*, c/Montalbán, also off Carril de Picón (which specializes in blues and rock); and *Camborio*, a fashionable place in Sacromonte. *Granada 10*, c/Carcel Baja 10, near the cathedral, is a grand old cinema which re-opens as a disco when the films finish. Two good **women's bars** are *La Sal*, c/Marqués de Falces, and *Pie de la Vela*, Paseo Tristes just off Plaza Nueva, while *Rincon de San Pedro*, Carrera del Darro, is a mixed-music **gay bar**.

One of the most touristy and heavily promoted of the **flamenco** shows is *Los Jardines Neptuno*, c/Arabial (near the Parque García Lorca in the south of the city), which in summer you should avoid; in winter, however, it's better, with an intimate atmosphere and a log fire in the bar. *Echevaria*, c/Postigo Cuna (off Gran Vía), is a jazz/flamenco bar with a great atmosphere and live performances.

Sacromonte

Like many cities of Andalucía, Granada has an ancient and still considerable gypsy population, from whose clans many of Spain's best flamenco guitarists, dancers and singers have emerged. Traditionally the gypsies inhabit cave homes on the **Sacromonte hill**, and many still do, giving displays of *zambras* to the tourists. These can occasionally be good, though more often they're straight-faced and fabulously shameless rip-offs: you're hauled into a cave, leered at if you're female, and systematically extorted of all the money you've brought along (for the dance, the music, the castanets, the watered-down sherry . . .). The simple solution is to take only as much money as you want to part with. Turn up mid-evening; the lines of caves begin off the Camino de Sacromonte, just above the Casa del Chapiz. When the university is in session, several of the cave dwellings are turned into **discos**, packed with students at weekends.

The Sierra Nevada

The mountains of the **Sierra Nevada** (soon to be awarded the status of a National Park) rise to the south of Granada, a startling backdrop to the city, snowcapped for much of the year and offering good trekking and also skiing from late November until late May. The ski slopes are at **Solynieve**, an unimaginative, developed resort just 28km away. From here, you can make the two- to three-hour trek up to **Veleta** (3470m), the second highest peak of the range (and of Spain); this is a perfectly feasible day trip from Granada by bus. For more serious enthusiasts, the renowned trek across the sierra is the **Ruta de los Tres Mil**.

The best **map** of the Sierra Nevada and of the lower slopes of the Alpujarras (see p.308) is the one co-produced by the Instituto Geográfico Nacional and the Federación Española de Montañismo (1:50,000), which is generally available in Granada.

Flora and fauna

The Sierra Nevada is particularly rich in **wild flowers**, with fifty varieties unique to these mountains. **Wildlife** abounds away from the roads; one of the most exciting sights is the

Cabra hispanica, a wild horned goat which you'll see standing on pinnacles, silhouetted against the sky. Bird-watching is also superb, with the colourful hoopoe – a bird with a stark, haunting cry – a common sight.

The Veleta/Mulhacén ascent

The Sierra Nevada is easily accessible from Granada. Throughout the year, Autocares Bonal (☎958 273100) runs a bus to the Solynieve resort, southeast of the city and, just above this, to the *Parador de Sierra Nevada* (see below). The bus leaves from *Bar Ventorillo*, Paseo Violón, next to the Palacio de Congresos, southeast of the centre (#1 going east along Gran Vía, will drop you off very near) at 8am and 10am daily (with an extra 3pm service Sat & Sun), returning from the *parador* at 9am and 5.30pm daily (extra services at 1pm & 7.30pm Sat & Sun) passing the Solynieve ski resort ten minutes later. If there are passengers, the bus will continue the short distance beyond the *parador* to the *Albergue Universitario* (see below).

With your own transport, take the Acera del Darro east from the Puerta Real and follow the signs for the Sierra Nevada. At the 22km mark and signposted just off the road is the **Sierra Nevada Natural Park Information Centre** (daily 10am–2.30pm & 4.30–7pm; ☎958 340625), which sells guidebooks, maps and hats (sun protection is vital at this altitude), and has a permanent exhibition on the park's flora and fauna. There's also a pleasant **cafetería** with a stunning terrace view.

From the *parador*, the Capileira road (closed to vehicles) continues to climb and actually runs past the **peak of Veleta**; now asphalted, it is perfectly – and tediously – walkable, but most hikers follow the well-worn shortcuts between the snakes the road is forced to make. With your own transport it's possible to shave a couple of kilometres off the walk to the summit by ignoring the no-entry signs at the car park near to the *Albergue Universitario* and continuing on to a second car park further up the mountain from which point the road is then barred. Although the peak of the mountain looks deceptively close from here, you should allow two to three hours up to the summit and two hours down. The **views** beyond the depressing trappings of the ski resort are fabulous: the Sierra Subbética of Córdoba and the Sierra de Guadix to the north, the Mediterranean and Rif mountains of Morocco to the south, and nearby to the south-east, the towering mass of **Mulhacén** (3479m), Spain's highest peak.

With a great deal of energy you could conceivably walk the mountain route all the way to Capileira, though it's a good 25km. An hour beyond Veleta you pass just under Mulhacén, two hours of exposed and windy ridge-crawling from the road.

Solynieve

SOLYNIEVE is a hideous-looking ski resort and regarded by serious Alpine skiers as something of a joke. But with snow lingering so late in the year, it does have obvious attractions. The Turismo in Granada can advise on snow conditions and accommodation at the resort (many hotels open only during the ski season), or contact either the Federación Andaluz de Esquí, Paseo de Ronda 78 (☎958 250706), or the Sierra Nevada Club (☎958 249111). For budget **accommodation** try the modern and comfortable *Albergue Juvenil*, c/Peñones 22 (☎958 480305, fax 958 481377; open all year), on the edge of the ski resort, where you can get great-value double (②) and four-bed rooms (④), all en suite. They also rent out skis and equipment in season. Other places here are incredibly **expensive** in season, with even the cheapest doubles priced at the higher end of our ⑥ category.

Three kilometres away in isolated Peñones de San Francisco are a couple more options: the *Albergue Universitario* (☎958 481003, fax 958 480122; open all year; ③ half board), has bunk rooms, doubles, and a restaurant, while the bleakly modern

Parador Sierra Nevada (☎958 480661, fax 958 480212; ⑤), no longer part of the state *parador* chain, opens only in the ski season. The only **campsite** in this area is at the Ruta del Purche (☎958 340407; open all year), 15km out of Granada and half-way to Solynieve, with a supermarket and restaurant. The bus will drop you at the road leading to the site (a good kilometre walk).

Ruta Integral de los Tres Mil (High Peaks Traverse)

The classic **Ruta Integral de los Tres Mil**, a complete traverse of all the sierra's peaks over 3000m high, starts in Jeres del Marquesado on the north side of the Sierra Nevada (due south of Guadix) and finishes in Lanjarón, in the Alpujarras; an exhausting three-to four-day itinerary. A slower pace entails overnight stays near Puntal de Vacares, in the Siete Lagunas valley, at the Félix Méndez shelter and at the Cerro Caballo hut. Slightly shorter, and more practicable, variations involve a start from the Vadillo refuge in the Estrella valley (northwest of Vacares), or from Trevélez in the Alpujarras, and a first overnight at Siete Lagunas.

Whichever way you choose, be aware that the section between Veleta and Elorrieta calls for rope, an ice axe (and crampons before June) and good scrambling skills. There is another difficult section between Peñón Colorado and Cerro de Caballo. If you're not up to this, it is possible to **detour** round the Veleta–Elorrieta section, but you will end up on the ridge flanking the Lanjarón river valley on the east rather than on the west; here there is a single cement hut (the *Refugio Forestal*), well-placed for the final day's walk to Lanjarón.

For **any exploration of the Sierra Nevada**, do take a tent and ample food. If you cannot reach or find the huts (which are marked correctly on the 1:50,000 map), and the weather turns nasty, you will need to be able to fend for yourself.

An easier alternative

The full *Ruta* is probably more than most people – even hardy trekkers – would want to attempt. A modified version, starting in **Trevélez** and ending in **Lanjarón** (with the detour noted above), is more realistic, though still strenuous.

Ascending Mulhacén from Trevélez is a full six hours up, four hours down – assuming that you do not get lost or rest (both unlikely) and that there is no snowpack on Mulhacén's east face (equally unlikely until July). If you decide to try, be prepared for an overnight stop. Heading out of Trevélez, make sure that you begin on the higher track over the Crestón de Posteros, to link up with *acequias* (irrigation channels) coming down from the top of the Río Culo Perro (Dog's Arse River) valley; if you take the main, tempting trail which goes toward Jeres del Marquesado, and then turn into the mouth of the Río Culo Perro, you face unbelievable quagmires and thorn patches. The usual place to **camp** is in the Siete Lagunas valley below the peak, allowing an early-morning ascent to the summit before the mists come up.

Continuing the traverse, you can drop down the west side of Mulhacén (take care on this awkward descent) to the dirt road coming from Veleta. Follow this toward Veleta, and you can turn off the road to spend a second night at Félix Méndez hut (main area not open until after spring snow melt, meal service thereafter; the hut's annexe with four bunks should always be open). Moving on, to the west, plan on a third night spent at either Cerro Caballo or the *Refugio Forestal*, depending on your capabilities.

Las Alpujarras

Beyond the mountains, further south from Granada, lie the great **valleys of the Alpujarras**, first settled in the twelfth century by Berber refugees from Sevilla, and later the Moors' last stronghold in Spain.

The valleys are bounded to the north by the Sierra Nevada, and to the south by the lesser sierras of Lujar, La Contraviesa and Gador. The eternal snows of the high sierras keep the valleys and their seventy or so villages well watered all summer long. Rivers have cut deep gorges in the soft mica and shale of the upper mountains, and over the centuries have deposited silt and fertile soil on the lower hills and in the valleys; here the villages have grown, for the soil is rich and easily worked. The intricate terracing that today preserves these deposits was begun as long as 2000 years ago by Visigoths or Ibero-Celts, whose remains have been found at Capileira.

The **Moors** carried on the tradition, and modified the terracing and irrigation in their inimitable way. They transformed the Alpujarras into an earthly paradise, and here they retired to bewail the loss of their beloved lands in *al-Andalus*, resisting a series of royal edicts demanding their forced conversion to Christianity. In 1568 they rose up in a final, short-lived revolt, which led to the expulsion of all Spanish Moors. Even then, however, two Moorish families were required to stay in each village to show the new Christian peasants, who had been marched down from Galicia and Asturias to repopulate the valleys, how to operate the intricate irrigation systems.

Through the following centuries, the land fell into the hands of a few wealthy families, and the general population became impoverished labourers. The Civil War passed lightly over the Alpujarras: the occasional truckload of Nationalist youth trundled in from Granada, rounded up a few bewildered locals, and shot them for "crimes" of which they were wholly ignorant; Republican youths came up in their trucks from Almería and did the same thing. Under Franco the stranglehold of the landlords increased and there was real hardship and suffering. Today, the population has one of the lowest per capita incomes in Andalucía, with – as a recent report put it – "a level of literacy bordering on that of the Third World, alarming problems of desertification, poor communications and a high degree of under-employment".

Ironically, the land itself is still very fertile – oranges, chestnuts, bananas, apples and avocados grow here – while the recent influx of **tourism** is bringing limited wealth to the region. The so-called "High" Alpujarras have become popular with Spanish tourists; Pampaneira, Bubión and Capileira, all within half an hour's drive from Lanjarón, have been scrubbed and whitewashed. Though a little over-prettified, they're far from spoiled, and have acquired shops, lively bars, good unpretentious restaurants and small, family-run *pensiones*. Other villages, less picturesque, or less accessible, have little employment, and are sustained only by farming.

Approaches: Lanjarón and Órjiva

The road **south from Granada to Motril** climbs steeply after leaving the city, until at 860m above sea level it reaches the **Puerto del Suspiro del Moro** – the Pass of the Sigh of the Moor. Boabdil, last Moorish king of Granada, came this way, having just handed over the keys of his city to the Reyes Católicos (see "The Alhambra"). From the pass you catch your last glimpse of the city and the Alhambra. Just beyond Béznar, is the turning to Lanjarón and Órjiva, the market town of the region. There are several buses a day from both Granada and Motril to **Lanjarón** and **Órjiva**, and one a day from Almería in the east.

There's also a bus which goes to Ugíjar, in the "Low" Alpujarras, from Granada, via a less scenic route through Lanjarón, Órjiva, Torvizcón, Cadiar, Yegen and Valor; about four hours to the end of the line. A bus direct to the High Alpujarras leaves the main Granada bus station at 10.30am (terminating at Pitres), noon and 5.15pm daily. It goes via Trevélez as far as Bérchules; in the other direction it leaves Bérchules at 5am and 5pm, passing Trevélez half an hour later, arriving in Granada at 8.45am and 8.45pm respectively (with a service from Pitres to Granada at 3.30pm).

Lanjarón

LANJARÓN has been subject to tourism and the influence of the outside world for longer than anywhere else in the valley, good enough reason perhaps for passing straight through to the higher villages. Its attraction is the curative powers of its waters, sold in bottled form throughout Spain. Between June and October the spa baths are open, and the town fills with the aged and infirm. The place itself is little more than a ribbon of buildings, mostly modern, flanking the road through the village, the Avenida. Alpujarra, and its continuation, the Avenida. Andalucía. Below, marking Lanjarón's medieval status as the gateway to the Alpujarras, is a Moorish castle, now dilapidated and barely visible. A ten-minute stroll reveals its dramatic setting – follow the signs down the hill from the main street and out on to the terraces and meadows below the town.

The countryside and mountains within a day's walk of Lanjarón, however, are beyond compare. Walk up through the backstreets behind the town and you'll come across a track that takes you steeply up to the vast spaces of the **Reserva Nacional de la Sierra Nevada**. For a somewhat easier day's walk out of Lanjarón, go to the bridge over the river just east of town and take the sharply climbing, cobbled track which parallels the **river**. After two to two-and-a-half hours through small farms, with magnificent views and scenery, a downturn to a small stone bridge permits return to Lanjarón on the opposite bank. Allow a minimum of six hours.

Should you wish to try a cure at the **Balneario**, Avda. Alpujarra (open March–Dec), a basic soak will cost about 1500ptas, with add-ons for massage, mud baths and all kinds of other alarming-sounding *tracciónes* and *inyecciónes*. Opposite is Lanjarón's semi-official **information kiosk** (office hours; ☎958 770282).

There's no shortage of **hotels** and **pensiones** in the town. The grand-looking *Hotel España*, Avda. Alpujarra 42 (☎ & fax 958 770187; ③), next door to the *balneario*, is very friendly and has a pool. Further along the road, a signed turnoff leads downhill to the delightful *Apartamentos Castillo Alcadima*, c/General Rodrigo 3 (☎ & fax 958 770809; ④), which has excellent studio apartments with kitchenette and stunning balcony views over the castle below the town, as well as a pool and pleasant terrace restaurant. The proprietor also hires out mountain bikes and offers horse riding treks and rock climbing courses. Towards the east end of town, *Bar Galvez*, c/Real 95 (☎958 770702; ②), is inexpensive and has excellent meals, while 1km east of town, there are peaceful en-suite rooms and excellent *tapas* at the *Pensión El Mirador* (☎958 770350; ②).

Lanjarón has plenty of **restaurants** and *tapas* bars too. The *Manolete*, c/Queipo de Llano 107, is much esteemed by the locals for its *tapas*, while *Bar Los Briscos* in the square off Avenida. Andalucía is the place to go for seafood. *Bar Suizo* looks like a Swiss tearoom but the food here is excellent. More expensive, *El Club*, Avda. Andalucía 18, serves Alpujarran dishes and is reckoned to be the best restaurant in town.

There's even a nightclub, *Noche Azul*, on the corner of the main square, with two Italian ice-cream parlours opposite.

Órjiva

Eleven kilometres east of Lanjarón is **ÓRJIVA** (also spelled Órgiva), the "capital" of the western Alpujarras. It is closer to the heart of the valley but still really a starting point; if the bus goes on to Capileira, you may want to stay on it. If you're **driving** it's worth noting that petrol stations get scarcer from this point on.

Órjiva is a lively enough town, though, with a local produce market on Thursdays, and a number of good bars and hotels. On the main street is a sixteenth-century Moorish palace which today houses various shops. A yoga centre, Cortijo Romero, just 1km east of Órjiva, often has programmes of shiatsu and other activities besides yoga – a sign of the times hereabouts; Órjiva, and surrounding farms and villages, are attracting a growing band of expatriate "New Age" Europeans. The **mercado** building in town is now full of wholefood stalls and jugglers, and there's a **tepee village**, "El Beneficio" on the edge of town, where assorted Europeans and their offspring ensure freezing winters under canvas.

For budget **accommodation**, one of the nicest places is the pretty *Alma Alpujarreña* (☎958 784085; ③), a little beyond the traffic lights at the town's main (and solitary) intersection, with a leafy terrace restaurant. Cheaper rooms are to be had at *Bar El Semáforo* (②) set a little back from the traffic lights along Avenida. Gonzalez Robles, and on the way in there's another decent *hostal*, the recently refurbished *Hostal Mirasol* (☎958 785159; ②–③), which has rooms with and without bath. Órjiva's **campsite** (☎958 784307; open all year), with a pool, bar and restaurant, lies 2km south of town, reached by continuing along the road (C333) where the bus drops you. For **food** both the *Alma Alpujarreña* and the *Hostal Mirasol* do good *tapas* and reasonable *menús*. The best *tapas*, though, are at the *Bar El Semaforo*, particularly the *calamares*. For good meals at reasonable prices try the quiet, family-run *Mirasierra* at the bottom of town.

The mountains behind Órjiva form the **Sierra de Lujar**, running into the **Sierra la Contraviesa**. The whole range of hills on the south side of the valley was once densely forested, indeed many years ago the whole of the Alpujarras was well covered with trees. But in 1980 a great forest fire swept for miles along the hillsides, scorching the life from the trees but leaving the wood undamaged; tens of thousands of acres of forest were ruined overnight. It's alleged that a pulp paper company paid hoodlums to start the fire – the next day they were buying up the dead trees at a fraction of the real price.

The High (Western) Alpujarras

The best way to experience the **High Alpujarras** is to walk and there are a number of paths between Órjiva and Cadiar, at the farthest reaches of the western valleys (see box, p.312). Equip yourself with the Instituto Geográfico Nacional/Federación Española de Montañismo 1:50,000 map, which covers all the territory from Órjiva up to Berja, and a compass. Alternatively, a bus leaves daily from Lanjarón at 1pm and winds through all the upper Alpujarran villages; hitching, too, is generally good in these rural areas, though cars are few and far between.

Cañar, Soportújar and Carataunas

Heading on from Órjiva, the first settlements you reach, almost directly above the town are **CAÑAR** and **SOPORTÚJAR**, the latter a maze of sinuous white-walled

---

HOUSES IN THE ALPUJARRAS

Houses in the valleys are built of grey stone, flat-roofed and low; whitewashing them is a recent innovation. The coarse walls are about 750cm thick, for summer coolness and protection from winter storms. Stout beams of chestnut, or ash in the lower valleys, are laid from wall to wall; on top of these is a mat of canes or split chestnut; upon this flat stones are piled, and on the stones is spread a layer of *launa*, the crumbly grey mica found on the tops of the Sierra Nevada. It must, and this maxim is still observed today, be laid during the waning of the moon for the *launa* to settle properly and thus keep rain out. Gerald Brenan wrote in *South from Granada* of a particularly ferocious storm: "As I peered through the darkness of the stormy night, I could make out a dark figure on every roof in the village, dimly lit by an esparto torch, stamping clay into the holes in the roof."

TREKKING IN THE ALPUJARRAS

Half a century ago the **Camino Real** (Royal Way), a mule track that threaded through all the high villages, was the only access into the Alpujarras. Today the little that's left is quiet, used only by the occasional local mule or foreign walker. At their best, Alpujarran paths follow mountain streams, penetrate thick woods of oak, chestnut and poplar, or cross flower-spangled meadows; in their bad moments they deteriorate to incredibly dusty firebreaks, forestry roads or tractor tracks, or (worse) dead-end in impenetrable thickets of bramble and nettle. Progress is slow, grades are sharp and the heat (from mid-June to Sept) is taxing. A reasonable knowledge of Spanish is a big help.

For the determined, the most rewarding **sections of treks** include:

Pitres to Mecina Fondales: Twenty minutes' trek, and then a good hour-plus from neighbouring Ferreirola to Busquistar.

Busquistar toward Trevélez: One hour's trek, and then two-plus hours of road walking.

Pórtugos toward Trevélez: Two hours' trek, meeting the tarmac a little beyond the end of the Busquistar route.

Trevélez to Berchules: Four hours' trek, but the middle two hours is dirt track.

Trevélez to Juviles: Three hours' trek, including some sections of firebreak.

alleys. Like many of the High Alpujarran villages, they congregate on the neatly terraced mountainside, planted with poplars and laced with irrigation channels. Both have bars where you can get a **meal** and Soportújar can provide excellent-value ensuite **rooms** for the night; ask at *Bar Correillo* (☎958 787578; ②) on c/Real (behind the church). Both villages are perched precariously on the steep hillside with a rather sombre view of Órjiva in the valley below, and the mountains of Africa over the ranges to the south. Just below the two villages, the tiny hamlet of **CARATAUNAS** is particularly pretty, and offers a comfortable place to stay, *El Montañero* (☎958 787528; ④), which has a pool and offers a variety of activities, such as mountain biking, horse riding and mountain walks.

The Poqueira Gorge and up to Capileira

Shortly after Carataunas the road swings to the north, and you have your first view of the **Poqueira Gorge**, a huge sheer gash into the heights of the Sierra Nevada. Trickling deep in the bed of the cleft is the Río Poqueira, which has its source near the peak of Mulhacén. The steep walls of the gorge are terraced and wooded from top to bottom, and dotted with little stone farmhouses. Much of the surrounding country looks barren from a distance, but close up you'll find that it's rich with flowers, woods, springs and streams.

A trio of villages – three of the most spectacular and popular in the Alpujarras – teeters on the steep edge of the gorge among their terraces. The first is **PAMPANEIRA**, neat, prosperous and pretty. Around its leafy main square is Nevadensis, an **information centre** (Mon & Tues 10am–3pm, Wed–Sat 10am–2pm & 4–6pm, Sun 10am–3pm; ☎958 763127) for the Natural Park of the Sierra Nevada as well as a number of bars, restaurants and **pensiones**; try *Casa Diego* by the fountain (☎958 763015; ②), or the plusher *Hostal Ruta del Mulhacen* (☎958 763010, fax 958 763010; ③) on the main road for rooms with bath. A weaving workshop just down the hill specializes in traditional *alpujarreño* designs. On the very peak of the western flank of the Poqueira Gorge is the **Tibetan Buddhist Monastery of Al Atalaya**. The Spanish reincarnation of the head lama – one Yeshé – is currently undergoing training under the Dalai Lama in the Himalayas. Lectures on Buddhism are held regularly and facilities exist for those who want to visit the monastery for periods of retreat (enquire at Global Spirit, see below).

BUBIÓN is next up the hill: there's a fancy hotel, *Villa Turística del Poqueira* (☎958 763111, fax 958 763136; ⑦) and a comfortable *pensión*, *Las Terrazas* (☎958 763034, fax 958 763252; ③), which also has some excellent apartments (☎958 763217; ④) downhill at c/Parras, which come with terrace, kitchen and satellite TV. A decent **restaurant**, *La Artesa* at c/Carretera 2, turns out *alpujarreño* specialities and has an economical *menú*. There is also a ranch, *Dallas*, 2km above the village, which will arrange **horseback riding**; trips of from one to five days are offered in groups with a guide (☎958 763135, 958 763034 or 958 763038). The private **tourist office**, Global Spirit (☎958 763054) on the main road, can also book horse-riding tours and help with accommodation.

Capileira

CAPILEIRA is the highest of the three villages (the seasonal road across the heart of the Sierra Nevada, "Europe's highest road", ends here, although it is currently closed to cars but not to hikers), with many **bars, hostales and restaurants** – the *Casa Ibero* (aka the *Mesón Alpujarreón*) serves excellent food and has vegetarian options; the *Mesón-Hostal Poqueira* (☎ & fax 958 763048; ③) is good value for en-suite rooms, and also offers one of the best *menús* in the province. One of the quietest places in town, well away from the main road, is the *Fonda Restaurante El Tilo*, Plaza Calvario (☎958 763181; ②), which also does a *menú*. The **kiosco** at the centre of the village near where the bus drops you hands out a village map and acts as an information office; just downhill from here lies the village's **museum**, containing displays of regional dress and handicrafts, as well as various bits and pieces belonging to, or produced by, Pedro Alarcón, the nineteenth-century Spanish writer who made a trip through the Alpujarras and wrote a (not very good) book about it.

In addition to the direct daily afternoon **bus** from Granada, continuing to Murtas and Bérchules, anything going to Ugíjar and Berja will come very close to Capileira; the bus out to Granada passes by at 6.20am, 3.50pm and 6.20pm.

Capileira is a handy base for easy **day walks** in the Poqueira Gorge. For a not-too-strenuous example, take the northernmost of three paths below the village, each with bridges across the river. This sets off from alongside the *Pueblo Alpujarreño* villa complex. The path winds through the huts and terraced fields of the river valley above Capileira, ending after about an hour and a half at a dirt track within sight of a power plant at the head of the valley. You can either retrace your steps or cross the stream over a bridge to follow a dirt track back to the village. In May and June, the fields are tended – laboriously and by hand, as the steep slopes dictate. Reasonably clear paths or tracks also lead to **Pampaneira** (2–3hr, follow lower path to the bridge below Capileira), continuing to Carataunas (1hr, mostly road) and Órjiva (45min, easy path) from where you can get a bus back. In the other direction, taking the Sierra Nevada road and then the first major path to the right, by a ruined stone house, you can reach **Pitres** (2hr), Pórtugos (30min more) and Busquistar (45min). Going in the same direction but taking the second decent-sized path (by a sign encouraging you to "conserve and respect nature"), **Trevélez** is some five hours away – you can also get to Pórtugos this way.

Along the High Route to Trevélez

PITRES and PÓRTUGOS, the next two villages on the High Route, are perhaps more "authentic" and less polished. You're more likely to find **rooms** here during high season, while all around spreads some of the best Alpujarran walking country. For **accommodation** in Pitres try the *Fonda Sierra Nevada* (②), on the main square. On the village's eastern edge the *Refugio de los Albergues* (☎958 766004; ①), is an old Civil War hostel with very cheap dormitory beds and cooking facilities. Pitres's **campsite**, *Balcón de Pitres* (☎958 766111; March–Oct), with restaurant and pool, is located in a stunning position just out of town. Pórtugos has the *Hostal Mirador* (☎958 766014; ③), on the main square, and a *fonda* (②) at Los Castaños, 1km east.

Down below the main road are the three villages of Mecina Fondales, Ferreirola and Busquistar; along with Pitres, these formed a league of villages known as the *Taha* under the Moors. **FERREIROLA** and **BUSQUISTAR** are especially attractive, as is the path between the two, clinging to the north side of the valley of the Río Trevélez. You're out of tourist country here and the villages display their genuine characteristics to better effect; there's an **inn**, the recently refurbished *Hostal Mirador de la Alpujarra* (☎ & fax 958 857470; ④), just uphill from the church in Busquistar, which also has a restaurant. A walking circuit of the three from either Pitres or Pórtugos need take no more than three hours, though in practice you'll probably want to linger along the way.

TREVÉLEZ, at the end of an austere ravine carved by the Río Trevélez, is purportedly Spain's highest permanent settlement. In traditional Alpujarran style it has upper and lower *barrios*, overlooking a grassy, poplar-lined valley where the river starts its long descent. The village is also well provided with **hostales**, located in both the lower and upper squares, and with *camas* advertised over a few bars. Try *Pensión Regina*, Plaza Francisco Abellán (☎958 858564; ③), or *Hostal Fernando* (☎958 858565; ③), on the road into town. The *Hotel La Fragua*, c/Antonio 4 (☎958 858626, fax 958 858614; ④), in the upper *barrio*, is another possibility, and has an excellent restaurant. Other **restaurants** include the *Río Grande*, down near the bridge, which serves good, solid food and is often the only place open in the evening. *Jamón serrano* is a local speciality and obsession, and a good place to try it is *Mesón del Jamón* above the Plaza de la Iglesia.

Although Capileira is probably the more pleasant base, Trevélez is traditionally the jump-off point for the **high sierra peaks** (to which there is a bona fide path) and for treks across the range (on a lower, more conspicuous track). The latter is still used, and begins down by the bridge on the eastern side of the village. After skirting the bleak Horcajo de Trevélez (3182m), and negotiating the Puerto de Trevélez (2800m), the path drops gradually down along the north flank of the Sierra Nevada to Jeres del Marquesado (see the *Ruta de los Tres Mil*, p.308).

East from Trevélez

Heading east from Trevélez, you come to **JUVILES**, an attractive town straddling the road. At its centre is an unwhitewashed, peanut-brittle-finish church with a clock that's slightly slow (like most things round here). A single all-in-one *fonda-restaurante*-store, *Bar Fernandez* (☎958 769168; ②; meals on demand), is simple and very friendly, with great views from the second floor east over the valley to Cadiar. *Pensión Tino* (☎958 769174; ②), a little back along the main street, has rooms with bath and serves *raciones*.

BÉRCHULES, a high village of grassy streams and chestnut woods, lies only 4km beyond Juviles, but a greater contrast can hardly be imagined. It is a large, abruptly demarcated settlement, three streets wide, on a sharp slope overlooking yet another canyon. The *Fonda-Restaurante Carayol* (☎958 769092; ②) and *La Posada* (☎958 852541; ②) on the central Plaza Victoria both have decent **rooms**, and there's an excellent grocery – a godsend if you're planning on doing any walking out of here, since most village shops in the Alpujarras are primitive. For **food**, *Bar Vaqueras*, also on Plaza Victoria, does good *tapas*.

Just below Bérchules, **CADIAR**, the central town of the Alpujarras, is more attractive than it seems from a distance, and there are a handful of **hostales** and *camas* if you want to stay; the friendly *Hostal Montoro*, c/San Isidro 20 (☎958 768068; ②), near the central plaza, has heated rooms, and the very good *Bar-Restaurante La Pará de La Suerte*, near the gas station as you come in from Berchules, is owned by the same people. There's a colourful **produce market** on the 3rd and 18th of every month, sometimes including livestock, and from October 5th to the 9th a **Wine Fair** takes place, turning the waters of the fountain literally to wine.

Cadiar and Bérchules mark the end of the western Alpujarras, and a striking change in the landscape; the dramatic, severe, but relatively green terrain of the Guadalfeo and Cadiar valleys gives way to open rolling land that's much more arid, a prelude to the deserts of Almería that lie ahead.

Eastern Alpujarras

The villages of the eastern Alpujarras display many of the characteristics of those to the west but as a rule they are poorer and much less visited by tourists. There are vineyards on the hills in the south of this region and the good dry red wine available in most of the Alpujarran villages, west or east, is always worth asking for.

Yegen and Ugíjar

In **YEGEN**, some 7km northeast of Cadiar, there's a plaque on the house where **Gerald Brenan** lived during his ten or so years of Alpujarran residence. His autobiography of these times, *South from Granada*, is the best account of rural life in Spain between the wars, and describes the visits made here by Virginia Woolf, Bertrand Russell and the arch-complainer Lytton Strachey. Disillusioned with the strictures of middle-class life in England after World War I, Brenan rented a house in Yegen and shipped out a library of 2000 books, from which he was to spend the next eight years educating himself. He later moved to the hills behind Torremolinos, where he died in 1987, a writer better known and respected in Spain (he made an important study of Saint John of the Cross) than in his native England.

Brenan connections aside, Yegen is still one of the most characteristic Alpujarran villages, with its two distinct quarters, cobbled paths and cold-water springs. It has a **fonda**, *Bar La Fuente* (☎958 851067; ②), opposite the fountain in the square, or there are rooms with bath at *El Tinao* (☎958 851212; ③), on the main road. Heading east out of the village, more upmarket accommodation is available at *El Rincón de Yegen* (☎958 851270; ④), where heated rooms come with TV and there are apartments for longer stays, a restaurant offering an economical *menú* and a pool.

UGÍJAR, 12km on from Yegen, is the largest community of this eastern part, and an unassuming, quiet, market town. There are easy and enjoyable walks to the nearest villages (up the valley to Mecina-al-Fahar, for example), and plenty of **places to stay**: try the relatively luxurious *Pensión Pedro*, c/Fabrica, near the church (☎958 767149; ②), which has en-suite rooms and a restaurant, or *Vidaña* (☎958 767010, fax 958 854004; ②), on the main road, with a terrace restaurant. If you're on the tightest of budgets you could try the very cheap *camas* place opposite the bus stop in the central plaza. There is a **bus** service on to Almería (3hr).

The Southern Ranges

The tiny hamlets of the southern Alpujarras have an unrivalled view of the Mediterranean, the convexity of the hills obscuring the awful development that mars the coast. There are few villages of any size, but the hills host the principal **wine-growing district** of the Alpujarras. For a taste of the best of its wine, try the *venta* (wine shop) at Haza del Lino (Plain of Linen); the house brew is a full-bodied rosé.

Inland towards Almería: Guadix

An alternative **route from Granada to Almería** runs via **GUADIX**, a crumbling old Moorish town with a vast and extraordinary cave district. This, the **Barrio Santiago**, still houses some 10,000 people and it's well worth a stop.

The quarter extends over a square mile or so in area, just beyond the ruined **Alcazaba** (daily 9.30am–1.30pm & 3–6.30pm; 100ptas), which is signposted as you come into the old walled part of town and is entered from the adjoining theological school. The entrance to the Barrio is behind the whitewashed church of Santiago. The lower caves, on the outskirts, are really proper cottages with upper storeys, electricity, television and running water. But as you walk deeper into the suburb, the design quickly becomes simpler – just a whitewashed front, a door, a tiny window and a chimney. Penetrating right to the back you'll come upon a few caves which are no longer used: too squalid, too unhealthy, their long-unrepainted whitewash a dull brown. Yet right next door there may be a similar, occupied hovel, with a family sitting outside and other figures following dirt tracks still deeper into the hills. A new **Cueva Museo** opposite the church of San Miguel, in Plaza Padre (Mon–Fri 10am–2pm & 4–6pm, Sat 10am–2pm; 175ptas), provides insight into cave culture, with intriguing reconstructions of troglodytic life.

Guadix itself is a pleasant, modest old place with a grand Plaza Mayor and some good-looking mansions. If you want to **stay**, try the *Fonda García* (☎958 660596; ②), just inside the walls by a prominent Moorish gateway, the Puerta San Turcuato, or either of the *hostales* on the main Carretera Murcia at the edge of town: *Hostal Río Verde* (☎958 660729; ③) and *Pensión Mulhacén* (☎958 660750; ③). For **food**, the *Mesón Cato*, Pasajede la Purisima 6, just off the Plaza Mayor, has a *menú*, and the *Restaurante El Albergue*, Avda. Medina Olmos 48, next to the bus station, is also a reasonable place.

Buses run direct from Granada to Guadix (Empresa Autodia from c/Rector Marín). The bus station in Guadix is a five-minute walk outside the walls.

On from Guadix

En route towards Almería you pass through more of the strange, tufa-pocked landscape from which the Guadix caves are hewn. The main landmark is a magnificent sixteenth-century castle high above **La Calahorra** (keys from c/de los Claveles 2 if you find it closed). Guadix–Almería buses normally follow the train line, along the minor N324 over the last section. If you're driving, you might want to keep going straight on the main road, meeting the Almería–Sorbas road at what has become known as **Mini Hollywood** (see p.320), the preserved film set of *A Fistful of Dollars*.

Almería Province

The **province of Almería** is a strange corner of Spain. Inland it has an almost **lunar landscape** of desert, sandstone cones and dried-up riverbeds. On the coast it's still largely unspoiled; lack of water and roads frustrated development in the 1960s and 1970s and it is only now beginning to take off. A number of **good beaches** are accessible by bus, and in this hottest province of Spain they're worth considering during what would be the "off season" elsewhere, since Almería's summers start well before Easter and last into November. In midsummer it's incredibly hot (frequently touching 100°F/38°C in the shade), while all year round there's an intense, almost luminous, sunlight. This and the weird scenery have made Almería one of the most popular film locations in Europe – much of *Lawrence of Arabia* was shot here, along with scores of spaghetti westerns.

Almería

ALMERÍA is a pleasant, modern city, spread at the foot of a stark grey mountain. At the summit is a tremendous **Alcazaba** (daily 9am–1.30pm & 3.30–6.30pm; 250ptas, free for EU citizens), probably the best surviving example of Moorish military fortification, with three huge walled enclosures, in the second of which are the remains of a mosque, converted to a chapel by the Reyes Católicos. In the eleventh century, when Almería was an independent kingdom and the wealthiest, most commercially active city of Spain, this citadel contained immense gardens and palaces and some 20,000 people. Its grandeur was reputed to rival the court of Granada but comparisons are impossible since little beyond the walls and towers remains, the last remnants of stucco work having been sold off by the locals in the eighteenth century.

From the Alcazaba, however, you do get a good view of the coast, of Almería's **cave quarter** – the Barrio de la Chanca on a low hill to the left – and of the city's strange fortified **cathedral** (Mon–Fri 10am–5pm, Sat 10am–1pm, Sun service hours; 300ptas), built in the sixteenth century at a time when the southern Mediterranean was terrorized by the raids of Barbarossa and other Turkish and North African pirate forces; its corner towers once held cannons. There's little else to do in town, and your time is probably best devoted to sampling the cafés, *tapas* bars and *terrazas* in the streets circling the Puerta de Purchena, strolling along the main Paseo de Almería down towards the harbour, and taking day trips out to the beaches along the coast. The city's own **beach**, southeast of the centre beyond the train lines, is long but dismal.

THE LANDSCAPE OF ALMERÍA

The landscape of Almería, like much of southern Spain, is dominated by mountain chains composed of hard, ancient rocks, separated by lower-lying basins filled with younger, softer rocks. The highest mountains – the Sierra Nevada, Sierra de Gádor, Sierra de Baza and the Sierra de los Filabres, which reach altitudes of over 2000 metres – were created by the collision of the African and Eurasian tectonic plates which took place at around the same time as the Alps were being formed, ending some ten million years ago. The basins between the mountain ranges were once below sea level and rivers cut into them, leading to the creation of the stunning landscapes that we see today.

Almería is also one of the driest parts of Europe, with an average rainfall of only 250–300mm per year. When rainfall does occur, however, it can be of very high intensity: the storms which swept the region in the winter of 1993 deposited 247mm of rain in just four days, causing flash flooding and severe erosion of hill slopes – something the region is prone to with its semi-arid climate and relatively sparse vegetation cover.

The landscape which most vividly illustrates the interaction between tectonic uplift and erosion is the area of "badlands" to the west of **Tabernas**, which can be best viewed from the road behind Mini Hollywood leading up to the radio mast on the summit of the Sierra Alhamilla. The badlands have been caused by tributaries of the Tabernas and Gérgal rivers cutting into soft limestone and sandstone deposits between the Sierra Alhamilla and Sierra de los Filabres. As the basin was uplifted, so the rivers cut deeper into the landscape, creating the stunning setting used by numerous Almería-made Westerns.

There are also a number of excellent raised beaches near **Mojácar** and **La Garrucha**, which were once at sea level but have been uplifted by tectonic movements to heights of several metres above the present beach. You'll have to be quick to see them, however, as many of the better sites are being progressively bulldozed to make way for villa developments.

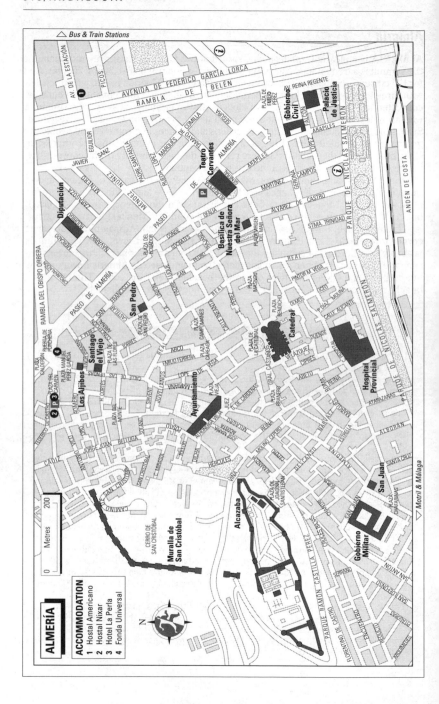

Practicalities

The **Turismo** (Mon–Fri 9am–7pm, Sat 10am–2pm; ☎950 27 43 55) is on c/Parque de Nicolás Salmerón facing the commercial harbour. They have a list of most buses out of Almería in all directions, as well as train and boat schedules. Almería's gleaming new international **airport** is 8km out of town with a connecting bus service (#14) every half-hour to the junction of the Rambla del Obispo Orbera and the Rambla de Bélen, east of the Puerta de Purchena. The city also has a **daily boat to Melilla** on the Moroccan coast throughout the summer, an eight-hour journey which can pay dividends in both time and money over Algeciras if you're driving – information from Ferrimaroc office on the harbour (☎950 274800).

Rooms are not normally difficult to come by at any time of the year, and a good place to start looking is around the Puerta de Purchena, the hub of the modern town. Just off this intersection, the recently refurbished *Hotel La Perla*, Plaza del Carmen 7 (☎950 238877, fax 950 275816; ⑤) is Almería's oldest hotel. Just behind is a cheaper option, *Hostal Nixar*, c/Antonio Vico 24 (☎950 237255, fax 950 237255; ④); ask for a high, airy room. On the square itself, the atmospheric *Fonda Universal*, Puerta de Purchena 3 (☎950 235597; ②), with a fabulous foyer staircase, is very basic but clean. Close to the bus station, *Hostal Americano*, Avda. de la Estación 6 (☎950 258011; ④), is handily placed if you're arriving on a late bus. The nearest **campsite**, *La Garrofa* (☎951 235770; open all year), is on the coast at La Garrofa, some 5km west, easily reached by the buses to Aguadulce and Roquetas de Mar (where there's another, giant site; ☎950 235770; open all year).

When it comes to **eating** and **drinking**, the Puerta de Purchena is a great place to head for, particularly at night. On the north side, in a small street, *Restaurante Alfareros*, c/Marcos 6, has an excellent-value *menú*. On the opposite side of the junction, there's a popular *marisquería*, *Bar El Alcázar*, Paseo de Almería 4, with plenty of *tapas* possibilities. Just in from here, you'll find an alley, c/Tenor Iribarne, filled with tables from many other *tapas* establishments, and close by, *Bodegas Las Botas*, c/Fructuoso Perez 3, is well worth seeking out. For **bars**, try the streets around Plaza Masnou off the southern end of the Alameda.

The beaches and inland

Almería's best **beaches** lie on its eastern coast; those to the west of the city, particularly Aguadulce and Roquetas de Mar, have already been exploited and although they're not quite as bad as many on the Costa del Sol, they're not a lot better either. Either place is an easy day trip, however, with hourly buses along the coast.

El Cabo de Gata and San José

Heading east, the closest resort with any appeal is the modest **EL CABO DE GATA**, where there is a lovely expanse of coarse sand. Five buses a day run between here and Almería, making an intermediate stop at Retamar, a retirement/holiday development. Arriving at El Cabo, you pass a lake, the **Laguna de Rosa**, protected by a conservation society and home to flamingos and other waders throughout the summer. Around the resort are plentiful bars, cafés and shops, plus a fish market. Accommodation is limited and in high season often impossible to find; the two *fondas* (③) above the bars (*Playa* and *Mediterraneo*) on the beach are both quite expensive. Nearby there's a **campsite**, *Cabo de Gata* (☎950 160443; open all year). The beach gets windy in the afternoons, and it's a deceptively long walk eastwards to **Las Salinas** (The Salt Pans – exactly that) for a bar and café.

Beyond lies **SAN JOSÉ**, also reached by bus from Almería. This is an established and popular resort, set back from a sandy beach in a small cove, with shallow water, and fine beaches within walking distance. **Accommodation**, however, can be hard to come by in summer. *Casa de Huéspedes Costa Rica* (③), on the main road a little way out, is one of the most inexpensive and also serves a reasonable *menú*. *Hostal Bahía* (☎950 380114; ⑤) is a comfortable modern hotel in the centre. A good **campsite** (☎950 380166; April–Oct) on the beach offers hope if everywhere seems full. There are again numerous excellent bars and cafés, and a well-stocked supermarket.

Next along the coast is **LOS ESCULLOS**, with a reasonable beach and a pleasant, if slightly overpriced, beachfront hotel-restaurant, *Casa Emilio* (☎950 389761; ④). **LA ISLETA** is another fishing town, with a sleepy atmosphere, a sandy beach and a **hostal** overlooking the harbour, *Hostal Isleta de Moro* (☎951 389713; ④); this reasonably priced place has a popular bar for *tapas*, but is often full (or choosy about its customers). At **LAS NEGRAS**, farther on, there's a cove with a pebbly beach and a few bars; there's a brand-new **hostal**, *Carmen Ortiz* (☎950 388081; ④) close to the village *estanco*; if it's full, you can enquire here about a room in a private house.

Inland: Mini Hollywood

Rather livelier than the eastern resorts is the strip of coast between Carboneras and La Garrucha, centred on the town of Mojácar. This is some way up the coast and to get there you'll have to travel through some of Almería's distinctive desert scenery (see box, p.317). There are two possible routes: via Níjar to Carboneras, or via Tabernas and Sorbas to Mojácar.

NÍJAR is a neat, white and typically Almerían town, with narrow streets designed to give maximum shade, and it makes a good base from which to explore the coast. There are two or three small **hostales**; try *Montes* (☎951 360157; ②), with a *comedor*, on the main road into town. There's also a pizzeria on this road, one of very few places to eat here. Níjar's **pottery** is attractive – traditional patterns and mineral dyes giving it an archaic quality. Blankets and rugs made in the local textile workshops are on sale too.

The most dramatic landscapes, however, lie farther north, between **TABERNAS** and **SORBAS**. Both towns look extraordinary, especially Sorbas, whose houses overhang an ashen gorge, but neither is really a place to linger – this is the middle of a desert. Just outside Tabernas, in a particularly gulch-riven landscape, is **Mini Hollywood** (daily: July–Sept 10am–9pm; Oct–June 10am–7pm; 1500ptas, 2200ptas including zoo), the set of the spaghetti western *A Fistful of Dollars* and various other movies. This has been preserved and opened up as a tourist attraction: you can wander into the saloon for a drink, and three times a day in season (noon, 5 & 8pm) the fantasy is carried a step further with an acted-out "show" including a mock bank raid. The complex has now also added a **zoo**, though its cages are depressingly small.

Mojácar

MOJÁCAR, Almería's main and growing resort, takes its name from the ancient hill village which lies a couple of kilometres back from the sea, a striking agglomeration of white cubist houses wrapped round a harsh outcrop of rock. In the 1960s, when the main Spanish *costas* were being developed, this was virtually a ghost town, its inhabitants having long since taken the only logical step, and emigrated. The town's fortunes suddenly revived, however, when the local mayor, using the popularity of other equally barren spots in Spain as an example, offered free land to anyone willing to build within a year. The bid was a modest success, attracting one of the decade's multifarious "artist colonies", and now, twenty years later, they are quickly being joined by package-holiday firms and second-home professionals. A plush new 280-room hotel has opened in the town, as well as a *parador* on the beach, and a burgeoning foreign jet-set now lives here for half the year and migrates in summer.

If you want to stay in the **upper village** there are a handful of small **hostales**; try *Casa Justa*, c/Morote 5 (☎950 478372; ③). For cheap eats up here, *Rincón de Embrujo*, on the plaza, does a good-value *menú*. Down at **the beach**, there's a good **campsite**, *El Cantal de Mojácar* (☎951 478204; open all year), lots of fine beach bars (currently a little over-whelmed by Spanish techno), rooms to let and several hostales. Among the *hostales*, try either the friendly *Puntazo* (☎951 478229, fax 951 478265; ④), to the south of the *centro comercial* on the seafront, or the nearby *Hostal Bahía* (☎951 478010; ③); the latter has a fine seafood restaurant. The modern *Parador Reyes Católicos* (☎951 478250, fax 951 478183; ⑥) is set in a palm-tree landscape right by the beach. For a decent no-frills meal, head for the *Cafetería Rosa*, facing the south side of the *centro comercial*. The beach itself is excellent and the waters (like all in Almería) are warm and brilliantly clear.

Bus services, incidentally, reflect Mojácar's popularity with Catalans; you can arrange a ticket to Barcelona, from the beach, at the Viajes Solar travel agent at the La Gaviota complex.

Carboneras and La Garrucha

South of Mojácar beach lie a succession of small, isolated coves, the most accessible of them reached down a rough coastal track that turns off towards the sea just under 4km down the road to Carboneras. The scenic Mojácar–Carboneras road itself winds perilously through the hills some way inland, and offers only occasional access to some tempting beaches. There's no bus on this stretch either, and you'd need to be very intent on escaping the crowds to want to drive this way.

CARBONERAS has an average beach and a couple of **hostales**: *La Marina*, c/General Mola 1 (☎951 454070; ②), is reasonable, slightly marred by the shadow of a massive cement factory around the bay. Beyond, a small road extends to the isolated fishing hamlet of **AGUA AMARGA**, an infinitely more attractive spot with a fine beach backed by a tasteful crop of villas and the solitary *Pensión Family* (☎ & fax 950 138014; ⑤), where you'll need to book well ahead in high season. Both Carboneras and Agua Amarga are served by bus from Almería.

North from Mojácar there's easier access, with occasional buses and reasonably easy hitching, to **LA GARRUCHA**, a lively, if unattractive, town and fishing harbour. This is in the process of development, with villas now thick on the ground and many more in the offing, but it does have a life of its own besides tourism. There are several expensive **hostales** and a summer-only **youth hostel**, but you're more likely to visit its reasonable beach as a good afternoon's break from Mojácar. There are also some fine seafront fish restaurants; try *Los Porrones* at the south end of the promenade.

travel details

TRAINS

Algeciras to: Córdoba (4 daily; 4hr 30min); Granada (4 daily; 4hr 45min–6hr); Madrid (3 daily; 12hr 30min–15hr; 6hr 40min with AVE from Córdoba). All Algeciras trains via Ronda and Bobadilla.

Almería to: Granada (3 daily; 2hr); Guadix (3 daily; 1hr 30min); Madrid (2 daily; 6hr 30min–10hr); Sevilla (4 daily; 5hr 30min).

Cádiz to: Madrid (AVE 2 daily; 5hr); Sevilla (11 daily; 1hr 45min).

Córdoba to: Algeciras (1 daily; 4hr 30min); Cádiz (2 daily; 3hr); Jáen (1daily; 1hr 40min); Madrid (5 daily; 4hr 30min–8hr, via Linares-Baeza 2hr 30min–3hr; AVE 2 daily; 2hr 10min); Málaga (2 daily; 2hr 30min); Sevilla (6 daily; 45min–1hr 20min).

Granada to: Algeciras (3 daily; 4hr 30min); Almería (3 daily; 2hr 45min); Antequera (3 daily; 1hr 50min); Córdoba (2 daily; 3hr); Guadix (3 daily; 1hr 15min); Linares-Baeza (1 daily; 2hr 30min); Madrid (2 daily; 6–8hr); Málaga (5 daily; 2hr);

Ronda (3 daily; 3hr); Valencia (3 daily; 8–12hr, 1 via Linares-Baeza).

Huelva to: Sevilla (3 daily; 1hr 30min); Madrid (AVE 1 daily; 4hr 15min); Zafra (2 daily; 4hr 30min).

Jaén to: Córdoba (1 daily; 1 hr 30min); Madrid (2 daily; 4–5hr); Sevilla (1 daily; 3hr 15min).

Málaga to: Algeciras (3 daily; 3hr); Córdoba (2 daily; 3hr 10min; AVE 6 daily; 2hr 10min); Fuengirola (every 30min; 50min); Granada (3 daily; 3hr 30min); Madrid (5 daily; 7–10hr; AVE 5 daily; 4hr 10min); Ronda (3 daily; 3hr); Sevilla (6 daily; 3–4hr); Torremolinos (every 30min; 30min).

Sevilla to: Badajoz (4 daily; 5–7hr); Cádiz (12 daily; 1hr 30min–2hr); Córdoba (16 daily; 45min–2hr); Huelva (2 daily; 1hr 30min); Madrid (12 daily; AVE 3hr 15min or 6–9hr); Mérida (4 daily; 3hr 30min).

BUSES

Algeciras to: Cádiz (9 daily; 3hr); La Línea (for Gibraltar: hourly; 30min); Madrid (1 daily; 10hr); Sevilla (6 daily; 3hr 30min); Tarifa (11 daily; 30min).

Almería to: Agua Amarga (2 weekly, Mon & Fri; 1hr 30min); Carboneras (2 daily; 1hr 30min); Alicante (2 daily; 7hr); Carboneras (2 daily; 1hr 45min); Córdoba (2 daily; 6–8hr); Granada (5 daily; 2hr 30min); Guadix (2 daily; 2hr 30min); Laujar de Andarax (3 daily; 1hr); Mojácar (4 daily; 2hr); Níjar (1 daily; 1hr); Cabo de Gata/San José (2 daily; 45min/1hr); Sevilla (3 daily; 5–6hr); Tabernas (6 daily; 45min); Ugíjar/Las Alpujarras (2 daily; 1hr 30min).

Cádiz to: Algeciras (8 daily; 2hr 45min); Arcos de la Frontera (5 daily; 2hr); Chipiona (9 daily; 1hr 30min); Conil (6 daily; 1hr); Granada (2 daily; 8hr); Jerez de la Frontera (8 daily; 45min); Málaga (3 daily; 5hr); El Puerto de Santa María (24 daily; 40min); Sanlúcar de Barrameda (8 daily; 1hr 15min); Sevilla (12 daily; 1hr 30min); Tarifa (1 daily; 2hr); Vejer de la Frontera (7 daily; 1hr 15min).

Córdoba to: Badajoz (1 daily; 6hr 30min); Écija (4 daily; 1hr 15min); Granada (8 daily; 2hr 30min); Jaén (5 daily; 2hr); Málaga (5 daily; 3hr); Madrid (6 daily; 4hr 30min); Sevilla (12 daily; 2hr 30min).

Granada to: Alicante (5 daily; 4hr 45min–6hr 45min); Almería (10 daily; 2hr 15min–4hr 15min); Cádiz (2 daily; 5hr); Cazorla (2 daily; 4hr 30min);

Córdoba (8 daily; 2hr 30min); Guadix (12 daily; 1hr); Málaga (15 daily; 2hr); Madrid (9 daily; 5–6hr); Motril (9 daily; 1hr 30min); Ronda (3 daily; 3hr); Sevilla (9 daily; 3hr 30min–4hr 30min); Sierra Nevada/Alpujarras (5 daily to Lanjarón and Órjiva in 1hr; 2 daily to most of the other villages along most of the routes); Solyieve (2 daily; 45min); Valencia (5 daily; 7hr 30min); Úbeda/Baeza (7 daily; 2hr 30min–3hr 30min).

Huelva to: Aracena (2 daily; 2hr–3hr via Jaén); Ayamonte/Portuguese frontier (8 daily; 1hr); Isla Cristina (3 daily; 1hr); Moguer/Palos (12 daily; 45min); Punta Umbria (hourly; 30min); Sevilla (14 daily, 6 direct; 1hr 45min); .

Jaén to: Almería (1 daily; 4hr); Baeza (10 daily; 1hr 15min); Cazorla (3 daily; 1hr 45min); Córdoba (8 daily; 2hr); Granada (12 daily; 2hr); Madrid (6 daily; 5hr 30min); Málaga (3 daily; 4hr); Sevilla (3 daily; 3hr 30min); Úbeda (10 daily; 1hr 30min).

Málaga to: Algeciras (11 daily; 3hr 30min); Almería (8 daily; 4hr 30min); Almunecar (11 daily; 1hr 45min); Cádiz (3 daily; 4hr 30min); Córdoba (5 daily; 4hr); Fuengirola (every 40min; 45min); Gibraltar (1 daily; 4hr 30min); Granada (16 daily; 2hr 30min); Huelva (1 daily; 5hr 30min); Jaén (3 daily; 4hr 30min); Jerez (1 daily; 4hr 30min); Madrid (6 daily; 6hr); Marbella (every 30min; 1hr 30min); Motril (10 daily; 2hr 30min); Nerja (11 daily; 1hr 30min); Ronda (11 daily; 2hr 30min); Salobrena (11 daily; 1hr 45min); Sevilla (10 daily; 3hr–4hr 30min); Torremolinos (every 15min; 30min); Úbeda-Baeza (1 daily; 5hr).

Ronda to: Arcos de la Frontera (3 daily; 1hr 45min); Cádiz (2 daily, 3hr 30min); Jerez (3 daily, 2hr 30min); Olvera (2 daily; 30min); San Pedro de Alcántara (6 daily; 2hr, continuing to Málaga); Setenil (2 daily; 15min); Sevilla (4 daily; 3hr 15min); Ubrique (2 daily; 45min).

Sevilla to: Aracena (2 daily; 2hr); Ayamonte (access to Portugal's Algarve – 3 daily; 2hr 15min); Badajoz (2 daily via Zafra, 2 daily via Jerez de los Caballeros; 5hr); Cádiz (11 daily; 1hr 30min–2hr 30min); Carmona (16 daily; 45min); Córdoba (12 daily; 1hr 45m–3hr 15min); Écija (3 daily; 2hr); El Rocío (5 daily; 2hr 30min); Granada (9 daily; 3–4hr); Huelva (13 daily; 1hr 30min); Jerez (9 daily; 1hr 15min–2hr); Madrid (9 daily; 6–10hr); Málaga (10 daily; 3hr); Matalascañas (5 daily; 2hr 30min); Mérida (6 daily; 3hr 30min); Ronda (5 daily; 2hr).

FERRIES

Algeciras to: Ceuta (6 boats daily; 1hr 30min); Tangier (8 ferryboats daily; 2hr 30min).

Almería to: Melilla seasonal boat (daily except Sun; 8hr).

Cádiz to: the Canary Islands of Tenerife (36hr) and Las Palmas (43hr) every two days in season, every five out; Fl Puerto de Santa María (4–6 daily; 20min).

Gibraltar to: Tangier thrice weekly ferry (Mon, Wed & Fri; 3hr).

Málaga to: Melilla (daily except Sun; 7hr 30min).

Tarifa to: Tangier (daily except Sun; 1hr).

CHAPTER FIVE

OLD CASTILE AND LEÓN

T
he foundations of modern Spain were laid in the kingdom of **Castile**. A land of frontier fortresses – the *castillos* from which it takes its name – it became the most powerful and centralizing force of the Reconquest, extending its domination through military gains and marriage alliances. By the eleventh century it had merged with and swallowed **León**; through Isabella's marriage to Fernando in 1469 it encompassed Aragón, Catalunya and eventually the entire peninsula. The monarchs of this triumphant and expansionist age were enthusiastic patrons of the arts, endowing their cities with superlative monuments, above which, quite literally, tower the great Gothic cathedrals of Salamanca, León and Burgos.

Salamanca and **León** are the two outstanding highlights, ranking in interest and beauty alongside the other great cities of Spain, Toledo, Sevilla and Santiago. Try to take in some of the lesser towns, too, such as **Ciudad Rodrigo**, **El Burgo de Osma**, **Zamora** or the village of **Covarrubias**. In all of them you'll be struck by a wealth of mansions and churches incongruous with present, or even imagined past, circumstances and status. In the people, too, you may notice something of the classic Castilian *hidalgo* archetype – a certain haughty solemnity of manner and a dignified assumption of past nobility, however straitened present circumstances.

Over the past decade, the historic cities have grown to dominate the region more than ever. Although the Castilian soil is fertile, the harsh extremes of land and climate don't encourage rural settlement, and the vast central plateau – the 700- to 1000-metre-high *meseta* – is given over almost entirely to grain. Huge areas stretch into the horizon without a single landmark, not even a tree. Surprisingly, however, the Duero River, which has the most extensive basin in Spain, runs right across the province and into Portugal. And despite being characterized by *meseta* landscape, there are enclaves of varied scenery – in particular, the **valley of Las Batuecas** and the lakeland of the **Sierra de Urbión**, where the Duero begins its course.

The sporadic and depopulated villages, bitterly cold in winter, burning hot in summer, are rarely of interest – travel consists of getting as quickly as you can from one grand town to the next. The problem with many of the smaller places, and even some of the larger ones, is that they have little appeal beyond their monuments: **Toro**, **Tordesillas** and **Valladolid**, for example, are important historically, but their "sights" lack a stimulating setting. The most impressive of the castles are at **Coca**, **Gormaz** and **Berlanga de Duero**. The other architectural feature of the region is the host of Romanesque churches, monasteries and hermitages, a legacy of the **Camino de Santiago** (pilgrim route) which cut across the top of the province.

FIESTAS

January
30 Processions in Burgos to honour
San Lesmes.

February
3 *Romería* to Ciudad Rodrigo.
Week before Lent *Carnaval* is also particularly lively in Ciudad Rodrigo.

March/April
Holy Week is if anything even more
fanatically observed than in most areas –
processions in all the big cities, particularly Valladolid, León, Salamanca and
Zamora. The one at Medina de Rioseco is
also worth aiming for. Good Friday in
Bercanos de Aliste (Zamora) is almost
chillingly solemn, participants dressed in
white gowns which will later become
their shrouds. The **week after Easter** is
marked by the *Fiesta del Ángel* in Aranda
de Duero and Peñafiel.

May
12 *Día de Santo Domingo* celebrated
with a traditional fiesta in Santo Domingo
de la Calzada.
Pentecost (variable) is marked by the
week-long *Feria Chica* in Palencia and
with more religious celebrations in
Miranda de Ebro.
Corpus Christi (variable) sees celebrations in Palencia and Valladolid; in
Benavente the *Toro Enmaromado* runs
through the streets in the evening,
endangering the lives of everyone. The
following day sees the festival of *El
Curpillos* in Burgos.

June
11 Logroño's *Fiestas Bernabeas* run
around this date.
12 *Día de San Juan de Sahagún* celebrated in Salamanca (of which he is patron)
and his birthplace, Sahagún.
24 *Día de San Juan* sees a secular fiesta
with bullfights and dance in León and
more religious observances in Palencia.
The following week sees a big fiesta in
Soria.

23–26 *Fiesta de San Juan* at San Pedro
de Manrique (northeast of Soria) – the
first night opens with the famous barefoot firewalking of the *Paseo del Fuego*,
described in Norman Lewis's *Voices of
the Old Sea.*
29 *Día de San Pedro.* In Burgos the start
of a two-week-long *feria;* lesser events in
León, and in Haro there's the drunken
Batalla del Vino celebrating local wine
production.

July
22 In Anguiano performance of the
famous stilt dance – *danza de los zancos.*

August
15 Colourful festivals for the Assumption
in La Alberca, Coca and Peñafiel.
16 *Día de San Roque* fiesta in El Burgo
de Osma.
Last week *Fiesta de San Agustín* in
Toro, with the "fountain of wine" and
encierros, and in Medinaceli, musical
evenings with medieval and
Renaissance music.

September
8 A big day everywhere – the first day of
Salamanca's major fiesta, beginning the
evening before and lasting two weeks, as
well as a famous bull running in
Tordesillas.
21 *Día de San Mateo.* Major *ferias* in
Valladolid and especially Logroño, where
the Rioja harvest is celebrated.

October
First Sun *Fiesta de las Cantaderas* in
León.
Valladolid's *International Film Week* also
falls in Oct.

November
13 The *Toro Júbilo* runs through the
streets of Medinaceli on the night of the
nearest Saturday.

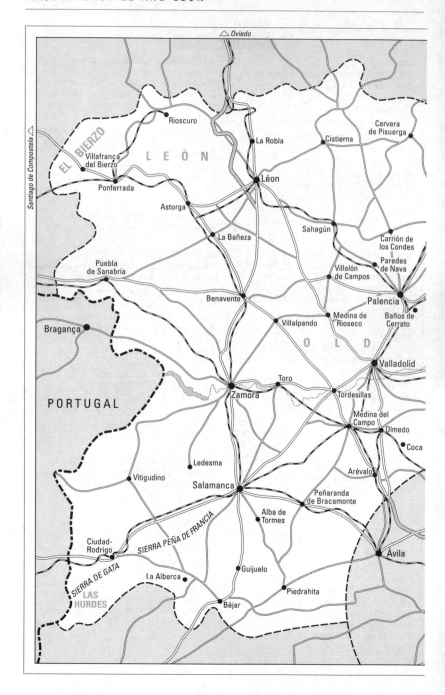

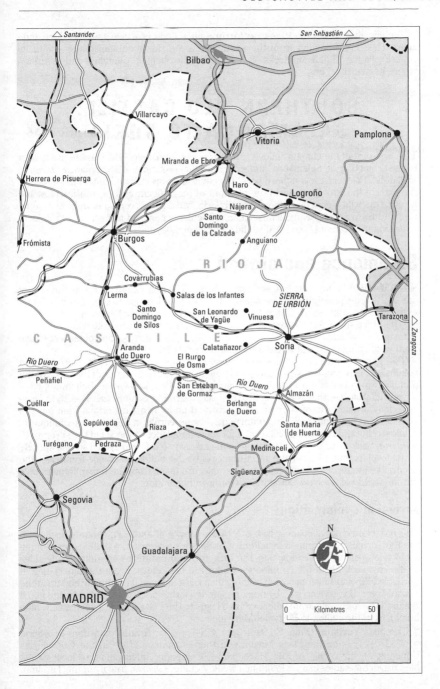

△ Santander   San Sebastián △

Bilbao

Villarcayo

Vitoria   Pamplona

Miranda de Ebro

Herrera de Pisuerga   Haro   Logroño

Nájera

Santo
Domingo
de la Calzada   Anguiano

Frómista   Burgos   R I O J A

Covarrubias

Lerma   Salas de los Infantes   SIERRA
DE URBIÓN

Santo
Domingo   San Leonardo
de Silos   de Yagüe   Vinuesa   Tarazona △

C A S T I L E   △ Zaragoza

Aranda   Calatañazor   Soria
Río Duero   do Duero   El Burgo
de Osma

Peñafiel   San Esteban   Río Duero
de Gormaz   Almazán

Cuéllar   Berlanga
de Duero

Sepúlveda   Riaza   Santa María
de Huerta

Turégano   Pedraza   Medinaceli

Sigüenza

Segovia

N

Guadalajara

MADRID   0   Kilometres   50

Technically, parts of the **Picos de Europa** lie in León province, and there are good approaches to the region from the south. However, this mountain range – with its superb villages, wildlife and treks – is covered in the chapter "Cantabria and Asturias", where its heartland lies.

SOUTHERN OLD CASTILE: SALAMANCA TO SORIA

This first part of the chapter follows a route across **Southern Old Castile**, from west to east, starting at Salamanca and covering the provinces of Salamanca, Zamora, Valladolid, Palencia, the northern part of Segovia and Soria. From Zamora on, it follows the path of the **Río Duero** with its plethora of magnificent castles, to the crags and lakes of the wild Sierra de Urbión beyond Soria. Most of this region is well covered by **bus** and **train** routes, with Salamanca, in particular, a nexus of transport, with links to Ávila/Madrid, Zamora/León, Valladolid/Burgos and beyond.

Salamanca and around

SALAMANCA is the most graceful city in Spain. For four centuries it was the seat of one of the most prestigious universities in the world and, despite losing this reputation in the seventeenth century, it has kept the unmistakable atmosphere of a seat of learning. It's still a small place, untouched by the piles of suburban concrete which blight so many of its contemporaries, and is given a gorgeous harmony by the golden sandstone from which almost the entire city seems to be constructed.

Two great architectural styles were developed, and see their finest expression, in Salamanca. **Churrigueresque** takes its name from José Churriguera (1665–1723), the dominant member of a prodigiously creative family. Best known for their huge, flamboyant altarpieces, they were particularly active around Salamanca. The style is an especially ornate form of Baroque, long frowned upon by art historians from a north European, Protestant tradition. **Plateresque** came earlier, a decorative technique of shallow relief and intricate detail named for its resemblance to the art of the silversmith (*platero*); Salamanca's native sandstone, soft and easy to carve, played a significant role in its development. Plateresque art cuts across Gothic and Renaissance frontiers – the decorative motifs of the university, for example, are taken from the Italian Renaissance but the facade of the New Cathedral is Gothic in inspiration.

Arrival and information

The **old centre** of Salamanca, with the **Plaza Mayor** at its heart, spreads back from the Río Tormes, still spanned by a Roman bridge. It's a compact, walkable area, bounded by a loop of avenues and *paseos*. The **bus and train stations** are on opposite sides of the city, each about fifteen minutes' walk from the centre. From the bus station at Avda. de Filiberto Villalobos 73–83 simply turn right and you'll eventually end up in the Plaza Mayor. If you've arrived by train, go left down the Paseo de la Estación and you'll reach Plaza de España, from where c/Toro leads to the Plaza Mayor; alternatively, take bus #1 from the station to Plaza del Mercado.

The main **Turismo** (Mon–Fri 9am–2pm & 5–7pm, Sat & Sun 10am–2pm & 5–8pm; ☎923 279124) is on the Plaza Mayor, and there's another office in the Casa de las Conchas, on the corner of Rúa Mayor and c/Compañía. Information on local events plus travel timetables can be found in a weekly guide, *Lugares*, free from the Turismo.

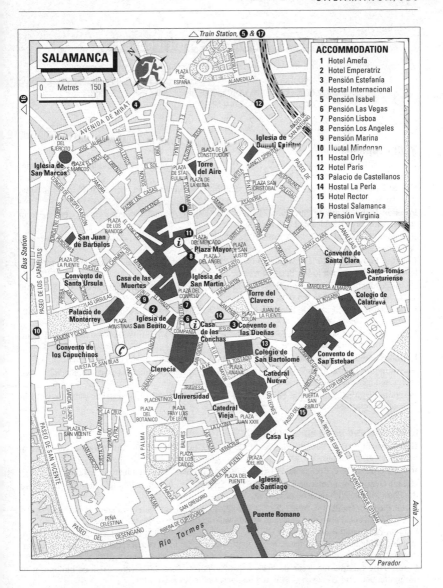

ACCOMMODATION

1 Hotel Amefa
2 Hotel Emperatriz
3 Pensión Estefanía
4 Hostal Internacional
5 Pensión Isabel
6 Pensión Las Vegas
7 Pensión Lisboa
8 Pensión Los Angeles
9 Pensión Marina
10 Hostal Mindonan
11 Hostal Orly
12 Hotel Paris
13 Palacio de Castellanos
14 Hostal La Perla
15 Hotel Rector
16 Hostal Salamanca
17 Pensión Virginia

Accommodation

Prices for **accommodation** in Salamanca are reasonable, but it can be hard to find a room in high season – especially at fiesta time in September. During the summer months you may well be approached at the train /station and offered *casas particulares* (private rooms). These are often the lowest-priced options available as many of the *pensiones* are more or less permanently occupied by students during the academic year.

Budget options

Pensión Estefanía, c/Jesús 3 (☎923 217372). No frills, but reliable, clean and tidy, and on a quiet street. Most rooms have small balconies. ②.

Hostal Internacional, Avda. de Mirat 15 (☎923 262799). A convenient place near Plaza de España; good value. ③.

Pensión Isabel, Plaza de Barcelona 24–25 (☎923 249254). A small, modern *pensión*, near the train station, with three doubles and two triples. ③.

Pensión Lisboa, c/Meléndez 1 (☎923 214333). The best *pensión* on the street, maybe even in Salamanca. ③.

Pensión Los Angeles, Plaza Mayor 10 (☎923 218166). Friendly service and spacious, airy rooms, four of them looking on to the Plaza Mayor. ②.

Pensión Marina, c/Doctrinos 4, 3° (☎923 216569). A very friendly and clean place, but it's small, so try to get there early in the day. ②.

Hostal Mindonao, Paseo de San Vicente 2 (☎923 263080, fax 923 263080). Pleasant *hostal* with good en-suite rooms. ③.

Hostal La Perla Salmantina, c/Sánchez Barbero 7 (☎923 217656). Well-placed *hostal*, with comfortable rooms and separate showers. ②.

Hostal Salamanca, c/Escoto 13–15 (☎923 269141). A new youth hostel in a good location. ①.

Pensión Las Vegas, c/Meléndez 13 (☎923 218749). A very popular low-price choice with large rooms and frilly bathrooms. ②.

Pensión Virginia, Paseo de la Estación 109–115, 2° (☎923 241016). A well-run *pensión*, right in front of the train station. ③.

Moderate and expensive options

Hotel Amefa, c/Pozo Amarillo 18–20 (☎923 218189, fax 923 260200). Understated, good-quality hotel in an excellent location. ⑥.

Hotel Emperatriz, c/Compañía 44 (☎923 219200). A central hotel in a historic building. ④.

Hostal Orly, c/Pozo Amarillo 3 (☎923 216215). Small but well-equipped hotel a stone's throw from the Plaza Mayor. With its own garage. ④.

Hotel París, c/Padilla 1–5 (☎923 262970, fax 923 260991). Great value with en-suite bathrooms and colour TV; just off Paseo de Canalejas, within walking distance of the city centre. ⑤.

Palacio de Castellanos, c/ San Pablo 58–64 (☎923 261818, fax 923 261819). An outstanding hotel in a fine old building, dating from the fifteenth century. Its most remarkable feature is its cloister, covered by a glass ceiling and converted into a huge drawing room. ⑥.

Parador de Salamanca, Toso de Feria 2 (☎923 268700, fax 923 215438). Modern building with swimming pool and great views, situated just across the Roman bridge. ⑦.

Hotel Rector, Paseo del Rector Esperabé 10 (☎923 218482, fax 923 214008). A superb hotel, small enough to feel personal (just fourteen rooms) and abounding in style and luxury. ⑦.

Camping

Camping Regio (☎923 138888, fax 923 138044). Salamanca's excellent campsite is open all year round, 4km along the Ávila road behind the *Hotel Regio*.

The City

The city's architectural sights seem endless: two **cathedrals**, one Gothic, the other Romanesque, vie for attention with Renaissance **palaces** and gems of Plateresque decoration. The **Plaza Mayor** is the finest in Spain; and the surviving university buildings are tremendous throughout – all of them distinguished by the same warm stone.

For a stunning panoramic view, go to the extreme south of the city and cross its oldest surviving monument, the much-restored **Puente Romano** (Roman Bridge), some 400m long and worth seeing in itself.

Around the Plaza Mayor

The grand **Plaza Mayor** is the hub of Salamantine life. You get the impression that everyone passes through its cafés and arcaded walks at least ten times a day. Its bare central expanse, in which bullfights were staged as late as 1863, is enclosed by one continuous four-storey building decorated with iron balconies and medallion portraits. It was the work of Andrea García Quiñones and Alberto Churriguera, younger brother of José, and nowhere is the Churrigueras' inspired variation of Baroque so refined as here.

From the south side of the plaza (facing the *Ayuntamiento*), Rúa Mayor leads to the vast Baroque church of **La Clerecía**, seat of the Pontifical University. At present you can visit only the patio (Mon–Fri 9am–1.30pm & 4.30–8.30pm, Sat 9am–1pm) as the church is opened just for Mass. Opposite stands the city's most distinctive (and reproduced) building, the early sixteenth-century mansion, **Casa de las Conchas** (House of Shells), so called because its facades are decorated with rows of carved scallop shells, symbol of the pilgrimage to Santiago.

The University

From the Casa de las Conchas, c/Libreros leads to the **Patio de las Escuelas** and the Renaissance entrance to the **University** (Mon–Fri 9.30am–1pm & 4–7pm, Sat & Sun 10am–1pm; 300ptas). The ultimate expression of Plateresque, this building symbolizes the tremendous reputation of Salamanca in the early sixteenth century.

The **facade** of the university is covered with medallions, heraldic emblems and a profusion of floral decorations, amid which lurks a hidden frog said to bring good luck and marriage within the year to anyone who spots it unaided. The centre is occupied by a portrait of Isabella and Fernando, surrounded by a Greek inscription commemorating their devotion to the university; above them is the coat of arms of Carlos V, grandson and successor of Isabella.

Inside, the old **lecture rooms**, surprisingly small for a seat of learning that once boasted over 7000 students, are arranged round a courtyard. The **Sala de Fray Luís de León** preserves the original benches and the pulpit where this celebrated professor lectured. In 1573, the Inquisition muscled its way into the room and arrested Fray Luís for alleged subversion of the faith; five years of torture and imprisonment followed, but upon his release he calmly resumed his lecture with the words *"Dicebamus hesterna die..."* ("As we were saying yesterday...").

The Patio de las Escuelas is surrounded by other university buildings including the **Escuelas Menores**, which served as a kind of preparatory school for the university proper (same hours and admission as university). It has a fine zodiacal ceiling, formerly in the chapel, moved here after two-thirds of it was destroyed by tremors from the 1755 Lisbon earthquake. Again lecture rooms open off a beautiful Renaissance cloister, whose walls are inscribed with records of academic successes (*vitores*).

THE UNIVERSITY AT SALAMANCA

Salamanca University was founded by Alfonso IX in the 1220s, and after the union of León and Castile swallowed up the University of Palencia to become the most important in Spain. Its rise to international stature was phenomenal and within thirty years Pope Alexander IV proclaimed it equal to the greatest universities of the day. As at Oxford, Paris and Bologna, theories formulated here were later accepted as fact throughout Europe. It made major contributions to the development of international law, and Columbus sought support for his voyages of discovery from the enlightened faculty of astronomy. The university continued to flourish under the Reyes Católicos, even employing a pioneering woman professor, Beatriz de Galindo, who tutored Queen Isabella in Latin. In the sixteenth century it was powerful enough to resist the orthodoxy of Felipe II's Inquisition but, eventually, freedom of thought was stifled by the extreme clericalism of the seventeenth and eighteenth centuries. Books were banned for being a threat to the Catholic faith, and mathematics and medicine disappeared from the curriculum. Decline was hastened during the Peninsular War when the French demolished 20 of the 25 colleges, and by the end of the nineteenth century there were no more than 300 students.

In recent decades, numbers have been replenished, though, like so many of Spain's universities, it still suffers an intellectual hangover from the appointments and backward operation of Franco's regime. Although socially prestigious, it ranks low academically, well behind Madrid, Barcelona and Sevilla. It does, however, run a highly successful language school – nowhere else in Spain will you see so many young Americans.

The cathedrals and Art Nouveau museum

The **Catedral Nueva** (daily: April–Sept 9am–2pm & 4–8pm; Oct–March 9am–1pm & 4–6pm; free) was begun in 1512 as a declaration of Salamanca's prestige, and in a glorious last-minute assertion of Gothic architecture. It was built within a few yards of the university and acted as a buttress for the Old Cathedral which was in danger of collapsing. The main Gothic-Plateresque facade is contemporary with that of the university and equally dazzling in its wealth of ornamental detail. For financial reasons, construction spanned two centuries and thus the building incorporates a range of styles, with some Renaissance and Baroque elements and a tower modelled on that of the cathedral at Toledo. Alberto Churriguera and his brother José both worked here – the former on the choir stalls, the latter on the dome.

The Romanesque **Catedral Vieja** (cloisters and museum daily, the rest daily except Sat: April–Sept 9.30am–1.30pm & 4–7.30pm; Oct–March 9am–1pm & 4–6pm; 300ptas) is dwarfed by its neighbour, which now also provides the only entrance to it. Its most striking feature is the massive fifteenth-century *retablo* by Nicolás Florentino. Fifty-three paintings of the lives of the Virgin and Christ are surmounted by a powerfully apocalyptic portrayal of the Last Judgement; a thirteenth-century fresco on the same theme is hidden away in the **Capilla de San Martín** at the back of the building. The cathedral's distinctive *media naranja* dome, shaped like the segments of an orange, derives from Byzantine models and is similar to those at Zamora and Toro. The exterior is known as the **Torre de Gallo** (Cock Tower) and can be seen from the Patio Chico next to the New University's south entrance.

The chapels opening off the cloisters were used as university lecture rooms until the sixteenth century. One, the **Capilla de Obispo Diego de Anaya**, contains the oldest organ in Europe (mid-fourteenth-century); the instrument shows Moorish influence and, in the words of Sacheverell Sitwell, "is one of the most romantic, poetical objects imaginable". In the Chapter House there's a small **museum** with a fine collection of works by Fernando Gallego, Salamanca's most famous painter. Active in the late fifteenth century, he was a brilliant and conscious imitator of early northern Renaissance artists such as Roger van der Weyden.

Right behind the Old Cathedral stands Salamanca's newest and quirkiest museum, the **Museo Art Nouveau y Art Deco** (April to mid-Oct Tues–Fri 11am–2pm & 5–9pm, Sat & Sun 10am–9pm; mid-Oct to March Tues–Fri 11am–2pm & 4–7pm, Sat & Sun 11am–8pm; 300ptas). The development of these two, closely linked, movements – Art Nouveau and Art Deco – from the belle époque years at the turn of the century through to the 1930s, is illustrated here by a miscellany of objects including paintings, bronze statues, porcelain figures, lamps, vases, jewellery and furniture. Among the most notable exhibits are the glass vases and lamps created by Emile Gallé (room 5), one of the most eminent Art Nouveau artists; the famous scent bottles René Lalique designed for Guerlain and Worth (room 4); and Hagenauer's highly stylized and instantly recognizable carved figures (room 13). The chief attraction, however, is the building itself, Casa Lys, which was built for an Art Nouveau enthusiast at the turn of the century and appears to be half-constructed from amazing, vibrantly painted glass. A spirit of playfulness permeates the museum and makes for a light-hearted, if somewhat incongruous, contrast to Salamanca's religious monuments.

San Esteban, Santa Clara and around

Churriguera's work is again evident in Salamanca's magnificent monastic buildings. The **Convento de San Esteban** (Mon–Fri 9am–1.30pm & 4–8pm, Sat & Sun 9.30am–1.30pm & 4–8pm; 200ptas), whose facade is another faultless example of Plateresque art, is a short walk down c/del Tostado from the large Plaza de Anaya at the side of the New Cathedral. Its facade is divided into three horizontal sections and covered in a tapestry of sculpture, the central panel of which depicts the stoning of its patron saint, St Stephen. The east end of the church is occupied by a huge Baroque *retablo* by José Churriguera, a lavish concoction of columns, statuary and floral decoration. The monastery's cloisters, through which you enter, are magnificent too.

The most beautiful cloisters in the city, however, stand across the road in the **Convento de las Dueñas** (daily 10.30am–1pm & 4.30–7pm; 200ptas). Built on an irregular pentagonal plan in the Renaissance-Plateresque style of the early sixteenth century, the imaginative upper-storey capitals are wildly carved with human heads and skulls. On the opposite side of San Esteban stands the monumental Churrigueresque **Colegio de Calatrava**.

Nearby, on Plaza San Román, is the newly restored **Convento de Santa Clara** (Mon–Fri 10am–1.40pm & 4–6.40pm, Sat & Sun 9am–2.40pm; 100ptas), a thirteenth-century building, outwardly plain but with beautiful interior features which encompass virtually every important feature of Spanish architecture and design. In 1976 the walls of the chapel, whitewashed during a long-forgotten cholera epidemic, were found to be covered with an important series of frescoes from the thirteenth to the eighteenth century, while further probing of the ceiling revealed medallions similar to those in the Plaza Mayor. Romanesque and Gothic columns, and a stunning sixteenth-century polychrome ceiling, were also uncovered in the cloister. But the most incredible discovery was made in the church, where the Baroque ceiling constructed by Churriguera was found to be false; rising above this, you can see the original fourteenth-century beams, decorated with heraldic motifs of the kingdoms of Castile and León. The prize-winning restoration is fascinating, and the icing on the cake is perhaps the city's best view of the bulk of the New Cathedral.

The final monument in this quarter worthy of special note is the **Torre del Clavero**, a fifteenth-century turreted octagon. It's at the far end of the Plaza de Colón, behind the convent of Las Dueñas.

West of the Plaza Mayor

Salamanca's remaining buildings of interest are situated in the **western part of the city**. If you follow c/de la Compañía from the Casa de las Conchas, you pass the Plaza

San Benito, which has some fine houses, and come to the Plaza Agustinas. In front is the large **Palacio de Monterrey**, a sixteenth-century construction with end towers, unfortunately not seen to best advantage in the narrow street. Across from it is the seventeenth-century Augustinian monastery usually called **La Purísima**, for which Ribera painted several fine altarpieces, including the main *Immaculate Conception*.

Behind the Palacio de Monterrey is another interesting convent, **Las Ursulas** (daily 11am–1pm & 4.30–6pm; 100ptas). In its church is the marble tomb of Archbishop Alonso Fonseca, a superb piece of Renaissance sculpture by Diego de Siloé. Facing the east wall of this church is the impressive facade of the **Casa de las Muertes** (House of the Dead).

Diagonally opposite the park from Las Ursulas, c/de Fonseca leads to the magnificent Plateresque palace still commonly known as the **Colegio de los Irlandeses**. For centuries this served as the Irish seminary, until in the 1950s it was decided to concentrate resources at home. It is a corporate work by many of the leading figures of Spanish architecture in the early sixteenth century, led by Juan de Álava. The Renaissance patio is a particular delight, with beautifully carved portrait medallions, each distinctly characterized. In the chapel there's a *retablo* with paintings and sculptures by Alonso Berruguete. Now a teacher-training college, the patio and chapel can in theory be visited from 10am to 2pm and from 4 to 7pm, although in practice whether you're allowed in or not seems to depend on the whim of the caretaker.

Eating, drinking and nightlife

Salamanca is a great place for hanging out in bars and cafés. Those in the Plaza Mayor are nearly twice the usual price but worth every peseta. Close at hand in the Plaza del Mercado (by the **market**, itself a good source of provisions), there's a row of lively **tapas bars**, while for simple drinking with a chance to sample some *pinchos* (a selection of *tapas*), head for the cluster of bars round the Cine Van Dyck. There is another good selection round Plaza de la Fuente, and the university area also offers loads of good-value **bars and restaurants** catering to student budgets. Also worth a mention is the stylish café *Music Arte*, Plaza Corillo, an oasis for tea drinkers in a land of coffee, and a good place for **breakfast**.

Restaurants and tapas bars

Bar Marín, c/del Prado 11. Good reputation for its summer speciality, frogs' legs fried in batter.

El Bardo, c/Compañía 8. Very good-value restaurant with a partly vegetarian *menú*, located next to the Casa de las Conchas.

Chez Victor, c/Espoz y Mina 26. Upmarket French-influenced restaurant specializing in game. Reckoned to be Salamanca's finest. Closed Sun night, Mon & Aug.

La Covachuela, Portales de San Antonio 24 (just off the Plaza Mayor). Worth a drink and *tapas* in this small bar to see the waiter and his coin-flipping exploits – a Salamantine tourist attraction in his own right.

Mesón Cervantes, Plaza Mayor 15. If you want to eat on the Plaza Mayor without blowing your budget, this place does cheap *platos combinados* (but don't expect anything special).

Restaurante Río de la Plata, Plaza Peso 1. Quality Castilian home cooking at reasonable prices, just off c/San Pablo, at the Plaza Mayor end. Closed Mon & July.

Restaurante Roma, c/Rúiz Aguilera 8. Inexpensive place to try *chanfaina* – a rice-based dish with meats cooked in spicy juices and the nearest Spanish cuisine gets to a curry.

Nightlife

Salamanca has many laid-back **cafés** where you can hear live music – try *El Corrillo* in Plaza San Benito for jazz, or *El Callejón*, Gran Vía 68, for folk. Also good for folk is the excellent *Country Bar* at c/Juan de Almeida 5 (round the corner from *El Gran Café*

Moderno – see below). There's no sign anywhere, just an unpromising black door, but downstairs you'll find a small, atmospheric tavern covered wall-to-wall in beautiful, swirling mosaics (the owner is a Gaudí fanatic).

There's a whole host of **clubs** and disco-bars, many along Gran Vía: *El Gran Café Moderno* at no. 75 has an excellent DJ and live sets; just around the corner, *De Laval Genovés*, popularly known as "Submarino" due to its nautical decor, plays good music, has three bars and stays open until 5am. *Camelot*, next to the Palacio de Monterrey on c/Bordadores, and *El Puerto de Chus*, Plaza de San Julian, are much frequented by foreign students.

Listings

American Express c/o Viajes Salamanca, Plaza Mayor 11 (☎923 211414).

Bookshops Salamanca's largest bookshop, Cervantes, Plaza de Santa Eulalia 13, stocks a range of English-language books; a smaller selection is available at Librería Portonaris at Rúa Mayor 35.

Bus information ☎923 236717.

Car rental Major operators include Avis, Paseo de Canalejas 49 (☎923 269753), Europcar, c/Maestro Ávila 3 (☎923 262334) and Hertz, Avda. de Portugal 131 (☎923 243134). For a local operator, try Goyacar, Paseo Dr Torres Villarroel 49 (☎923 233526).

Language courses Spanish language courses are big business in Salamanca. For a complete list of schools, contact the Turismo. The following is a small selection: Colegio de España, c/Compañía 65 (☎923 214788, fax 923 218791); Colegio de Estudios Hispanicos, c/Bordadores 1 (☎923 214837, fax 923 215607); Cursos Internacionales de la Universidad de Salamanca, Patio de Escuelas Menores (☎923 294408, fax 923 294504).

Laundry There are a couple of self-service *lavanderías* out by Plaza del Oueste (northwest of the ring road) but none in the centre.

Post office The main *Correos* is at Gran Vía 25.

Taxis There are two 24 hour companies: Radio Tele-Taxi (☎923 250000) and Radio Taxi (☎923 271111).

Train information ☎923 120202.

Around Salamanca

The countryside around Salamanca is an attractive swathe of New Castile, particularly along the Río Tormes, which flows into the Duero to the northwest.

Alba de Tormes

The small hillside town of **ALBA DE TORMES**, 20km southeast of the city, makes an interesting day's excursion. The main attraction here is the **Convento de Carmelitas** (daily 9am–1.30pm & 4–6.30pm, Oct–April closes 7.30pm), founded by Santa Teresa in 1571, with its ornate Renaissance facade and a rather dubious reconstruction of the cell in which Teresa died. Alba is a centre for making traditional Castilian **pottery**, and you can watch its manufacture at Bernardo Pérez Correas on c/Matadero near the river. If you want to **stay the night**, the lowest-priced rooms are at the *Hostal América*, across the bridge on c/La Guía (☎923 300071; ③). For spacious accommodation with bath try the *Hotel Alameda*, Avda. Juan Pablo II (☎923 300031, fax 923 370281; ④), which also has a good restaurant. The town is served by local buses from Salamanca.

North to Zamora: Ledesma

Heading northwest from Salamanca, a delightful minor road via Ledesma makes an excellent alternative route to **Zamora**. For most of the way this route trails the beautiful Río Tormes, where there's excellent fishing (for giant carp), herons and storks in the trees, enormous, delicious mushrooms (*setas*) in autumn and a variety of meadow flowers in spring. **LEDESMA** itself – little more than a large village these days – retains its ancient walls, the remains of a Roman bridge and baths, and a couple of attractive churches. If you're staying overnight, the *Fonda Mercado* (no phone; ②) is good. The greenery round here seems atypical of Castile – it's created in large part by the **Embalse de Almendra**, a dam almost at the Portuguese border, whose reservoir stretches all the way back to Ledesma.

Ciudad Rodrigo and the Sierra Peña de Francia

In the far southwest corner of Salamanca province, the unspoiled frontier town of **Ciudad Rodrigo** – astride the road and rail line to Portugal – is worth a detour even if you don't plan to cross the border. East of the town lies the **Sierra Peña de Francia**, with good walking and a stunning village, **La Alberca**, the whole of which has been declared a national monument.

Ciudad Rodrigo

CIUDAD RODRIGO is a quiet old place which, despite an orgy of destruction during the Peninsular War, preserves streets full of **Renaissance mansions**. If you follow the walls round – a pleasant walk and a good way to see the town – you'll pass an austere castle (now a *parador*), which overlooks a Roman bridge on the Río Águeda and commands an enticing view across into Portugal.

Focal point of the town is the **Catedral** (daily 10am–1pm & 4–6.30pm), built in a mixture of styles but originally Transitional Gothic: take a look at the highly unusual eight-part vaults, dome-like in shape. You'll need to find the sexton to see the building's other interesting features: the *coro*, with wonderfully grotesque stalls carved by Rodrigo Alemán, who also created those at Toledo and Plasencia; the narthex, with statues of Apostles; and the cloisters (guided tours 200ptas), half of which are fourteenth-century and half sixteenth-century with lurid carvings of biblical scenes.

A pagoda-like monument to **General Herrasti** and his men (see box) stands in the little square beside the cathedral. A plaque in the corner of the walls near this marks the site of the Great Breach through which the British entered Ciudad Rodrigo; from outside, the gaping hole is clearly visible. The British guns were on the two ridges opposite (the lower one with the block of flats, the other higher up beyond the rail

---

CIUDAD RODRIGO IN THE PENINSULAR WAR

Along with Badajoz, Ciudad Rodrigo was a crucial border-point in the Peninsular War. No army could cross safely between Spain and Portugal unless these two towns to its rear were secured. Ciudad Rodrigo fell to the French in 1810, despite valiant resistance from General Herrasti's Spanish garrison – in admiration for whose bravery, the French permitted them to march away from the devastated city.

Britain's Duke of Wellington re-took Ciudad Rodrigo with a devastatingly rapid siege in 1812. Aware that French reinforcements were approaching, Wellington had announced "Ciudad Rodrigo must be stormed this evening" – his soldiers duly did so, embarking on a triumphant rampage of looting and vandalism. When order was restored, the troops paraded out dressed in a ragbag of stolen French finery. A bemused Wellington muttered to his staff, "Who the devil *are* those fellows?"

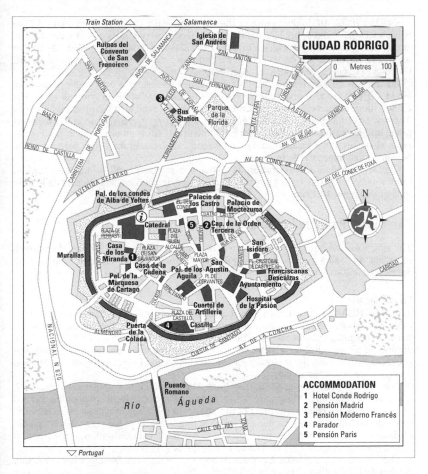

line). This side of the cathedral is thus covered with cannonball dents; half the railing is smashed from the top of the dome and the tympanum above the door is wrecked.

Ciudad Rodrigo's empty streets are ideal for wandering with no particular purpose, though if you're curious, the local tourist pamphlets provide great detail on the churches and palaces. Two of the most imposing are the **Palacio de los Castro** and **Palacio de Moctezuma**, both on Plaza Conde; the latter is now the town Casa de la Cultura, used as a library and exhibition centre.

Practicalities

Ciudad Rodrigo has a **Turismo** (Mon–Fri 9am–2pm & 5–7pm, Sat & Sun 10am–2pm & 5–8pm; ☎923 460561), facing the cathedral at the entrance to the town.

For reasonable budget **rooms** (including a quadruple with a fridge and sink), try *Pensión Madrid*, c/Madrid 20 (☎923 462467; ②). Other budget options include the impeccably clean *Pensión Moderno Francés*, c/Campo de Toledo 8 (☎923 461968; ②), conveniently located opposite the bus station, and the excellent *Pensión París*, c/Toro

10 (☎923 461372; ③), in the centre of the old town. *Hotel Conde Rodrigo*, Plaza de San Salvador (☎923 461408, fax 923 461408; ⑤), offers more comfort and is located in an attractive square, while *Parador Enrique II* (☎923 460150, fax 923 460404; ⑦) has an unrivalled location in the castle. There's a **campsite**, *La Pesquera*, by the river, just off the road to Cáceres (☎923 481348; April–Sept).

Among several **bars** on the Plaza Mayor, *El Arco* serves fairly good-value *platos combinados*. There are also several *tapas* bars in the roads radiating away on all sides. For dinner, there are several good **restaurants** along the c/de los Gigantes, including *El Rodeo* at no. 10. Outside the walls, *Mesón los Cazadores* at c/San Martín 3 does great *tapas*, and if you have transport, you'll find plenty of substantial *menús* in the restaurants along the main Salamanca–Portugal road. The restaurant at the *parador* is the best and most expensive in town.

Ciudad Rodrigo's **train station** is about ten minutes' walk along the road to Lumbreras: there's one train a day into Portugal leaving at 6am, and another daily train to Irún leaving at 12.45am.

The Sierra Peña de Francia

The village of La Alberca is a good place to head for, both in its own right, and as a starting point for walks in the **Sierra Peña de Francia**. There are daily buses from Salamanca, but only on Sunday does the timetable make a day trip possible.

La Alberca

LA ALBERCA has an extraordinary collection of houses, constructed from diverse materials: wood, pebbles, stone and rubble built in amongst the rocks. Due to its national monument status, plenty of tidying-up is going on, and "local craft" shops have sprung up all over, but the character of a rural community remains; horses still take precedence over cars, the restorers use donkeys instead of vans, and goats, sheep and poultry often block the streets.

The most elegant houses are in the **Plaza Mayor**, which is dominated by a calvary. Look into the church in the square behind for its elaborate polychromed pulpit, carved in a popular style. These days most of the houses in the Plaza Mayor seem to serve as cafés for the tourist trade, but there is an air of timelessness to the place. Many age-old traditions, including costume, have survived, and the local celebration of the Feast of Assumption on August 15 is considered to be the best in Spain.

There's a shortage of budget **accommodation**, the only reliable place being *Pensión Hernandez* off the Plaza Mayor (☎923 415039; ②). If money's no problem, the four-star *Hotel Doña Teresa* (☎923 415308, fax 923 415309; ⑤), on the road to Mogarraz, is very chic and well-equipped (with jacuzzi, gym, sauna and sunbeds), while the long-established *Hotel Las Batuecas* (☎923 415188, fax 923 415055; ⑤), on the road to Las Batuecas, has a more rustic feel and an excellent restaurant. There is a campsite (with a pool) on the Salamanca road (☎923 415195; April–Sept).

La Peña de Francia

A very circuitous road behind La Alberca climbs to the summit of the **Peña de Francia**. The road emerges from the trees halfway up to give fine panoramas not only of the mountain itself (disfigured by a television tower serving the whole province and beyond) and the plains below, but also out over the wild hills of Las Hurdes to the south and the Sierra de Gredos to the east. At the top you can have lunch or refreshments at the *hospedería* of the **Monasterio Peña de Francia**, which is occupied during the summer by Dominicans from San Esteban in Salamanca.

Valle de Las Batuecas

Another excellent trip from La Alberca is south to the **Valle de Las Batuecas**, a national reserve bordering Las Hurdes (see p.179). This makes an impressive day-long walk or a beautiful drive; you'll need to take a picnic, for although fresh water abounds, there isn't a bar, restaurant or even house in sight until you reach the village of Las Mestas, just over the Extremaduran border, some 19km away.

From La Alberca, take the minor road south out of the village. After 2km you'll come to the pass of **El Portillo**, surrounded by solemn, rugged hills. From here, the road dips and loops spectacularly, offering a different vista at every turn. You reach the valley floor at the 12km point, and a short road leads to the gate of the **Carmelito Monastery**, founded at the beginning of the seventeenth century for a community of hermits. One of the first tasks of the monastery was to exorcize the demons and evil spirits which supposedly inhabited the nearby valleys of Las Hurdes. In 1933, the great film-maker **Luis Buñuel** stayed in the monastery – then a hotel – while shooting his early masterpiece, *Land Without Bread*, about the extremely primitive lifestyle of the people of these valleys. Today, two superannuated monks pass their last years in this most beautiful of locations.

A footpath skirts the outside of the monastery's perimeter wall and follows the course of the river, which forms a gorge with splendid rock formations. There are **caves** with prehistoric rock paintings here, but unfortunately the most important ones have had to be closed in order to preserve them from deterioration and vandalism.

If you're walking back to La Alberca after exploring the valley, you're faced with a daunting climb; there is little traffic, although the chances of a lift from cars that do pass are good. By car, it makes a good round trip to keep going beyond **Las Mestas**, turning east at the T-junction and crossing back into Salamanca province via **Miranda del Castañar**, with its pretty views and romantic, crumbling castle.

Zamora to Valladolid

Zamora is the quietest of the great Castilian cities, with a population of just 65,000. Its province is pretty low-key, too, though with a cluster of historic names. The road east from Zamora follows the **Río Duero** into the heartland of Old Castile, taking in **Toro**, the site of the battle which established Fernando and Isabella on the Spanish throne in 1476, and **Tordesillas**, where the treaty which ratified the division of lands discovered in the New World was signed in 1494.

Zamora

In medieval romances, **ZAMORA** was known as *la bien cercada* (the closed one) on account of its strong fortifications; one siege here lasted seven months. Its old quarters, still walled and medieval in appearance, are spread out along the sloping banks of the Río Duero (known as the Douro once it crosses into Portugal). In and around the old centre are a dozen Romanesque churches whose unassumingly beautiful architecture is the city's greatest distinctive feature. Most of them date from the twelfth century and reflect Old Castile's sense of security following the victorious campaigns against the Moors by Alfonso VI and El Cid – notably the recapture of Toledo in 1085.

Arrival and information

The **train station** and the **bus terminal** are adjacent to each other, fifteen minutes' walk from the centre; to reach the Plaza Mayor, follow Avenida de las Tres Cruces to the Plaza de Alemania on the edge of the old town. The **Turismo** (Mon–Fri 9am–2pm & 5–7pm, Sat & Sun 10am–2pm & 5–8pm; ☎980 531845) is at c/Santa Clara 20 – take

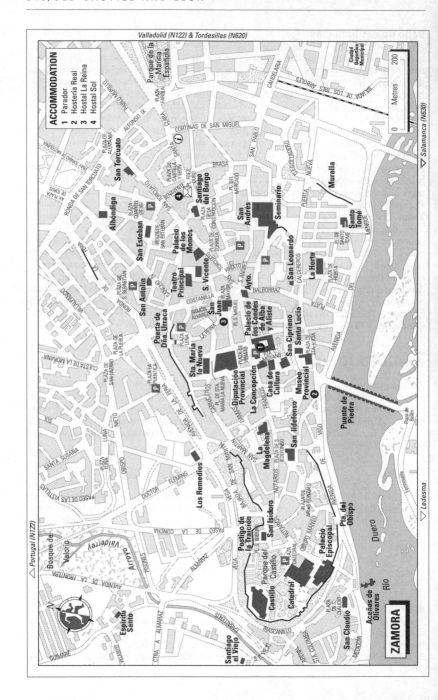

c/Pelayo, the second road to the left, from the Plaza de Alemania. Drivers should note that there's free and central parking on Plaza Claudio Moyano behind the Casa de Cultura. Leaving town, the rail line heads northwest to Orense and Santiago in Galicia. If you're heading east along the Duero, the minor road to Toro (along the south bank of the river) offers good opportunities for bird-watching or fishing.

Accommodation

Zamora has a reasonable spread of **accommodation**, most of it centred in the old quarter. Except during Easter week few places run out of space, but if you do get stuck the Turismo can help you out.

Parador Condes de Alba de Aliste, Plaza de Viriato 1 (☎980 514497, fax 980 530063). One of Spain's most beautiful *paradores*, situated in a fifteenth-century ducal palace and with a superb restaurant. ⑥.

Hostería Real de Zamora, Cuesta Pizarro 7 (☎980 534545, fax 980 534522). A former Palacio de Inquisidores, this 400-year-old building, with its beautiful Renaissance patio, is now a small and excellent hotel. ⑨.

Hostal La Reina, c/La Reina 1 (☎980 533939). Best budget accommodation in town, with good, clean rooms overlooking the Plaza Mayor and a very friendly *dueña*. ②.

Hostal Sol, c/Benavente 2, 3° (☎980 533152). Modern rooms, a little on the small side, but smart and well-equipped (all with bathroom, TV and phone). In the same block as two other, slightly more expensive, *hostales*: *Hostal Luz*, belonging to the same owners, and *Hostal Chiqui* (☎980 531480). ③.

The Town

The **Catedral**, enclosed within the ruined citadel at the far end of town, is a fitting climax to Zamora's series of churches. Begun in 1151, it is again Romanesque overall, though the grandiose north entrance is in the classical style of the High Renaissance. A Byzantine-inspired dome, looking quite out of place, is its most striking feature, showing the same turrets and "fish-scale" tiles as the Old Cathedral at Salamanca. The carved choir stalls, which depict lusty carryings-on between monks and nuns, were closed for a long time at the orders of a particularly sanctimonious bishop, but are now on view again. The cathedral museum (Tues–Sat: April–Sept 11am–2pm & 5–8pm; Oct–March 11am–2pm & 4–6pm; 300ptas), houses the city's celebrated and unsurpassed "Black Tapestries". The patrons who commissioned these fifteenth-century Flemish masterpieces clearly demanded their money's worth, since every inch is woven in stunning detail. Traditional Greek and Roman themes were chosen but often contemporary dress and weaponry intruded, illustrating how nobles in the Middle Ages liked to see themselves as heroes from the past.

Among the other Romanesque churches, **San Juan de Puerta Nueva** (Tues–Sun 11am–2pm & 5–8pm) and **Santiago del Burgo** (same hours) are the most rewarding, while attached to **Santa María la Nueva** is an unusual **Museo de la Semana Santa** (April–Sept Mon–Sat 10am–2pm & 4–8pm, Sun 10am–2pm; Oct–March Mon–Sat 10am–2pm & 4–6pm, Sun 10am–2pm; 300ptas). This contains the *pasos* – statues depicting the Passion of Christ – which are paraded through the streets at Easter.

Eating and drinking

You'll find most **restaurants and cafés** on or around the Plaza Mayor, and on the side streets off c/Santa Clara. For late-night drinking and music, head for the bars at the top of c/Balborraz.

Café Cariátide, c/Benavente 5. Pleasant and spacious café with a wide range of *tapas* and a restaurant attached.

Café Viriato, c/Viriato. Attracts a young crowd at night (open until 5am at weekends); by day this is a good place to enjoy a quiet drink outside on the terrace.

España, c/Ramón Álvarez. Long-established and very popular with locals, this cheap but basic restaurant is situated just off the Plaza Mayor.

Toro

TORO, 30km from Zamora, looks dramatic: "an ancient, eroded, red-walled town spread along the top of a huge flat boulder," as Laurie Lee described it when he arrived here with a group of travelling German musicians. Its raw, red, hillside site is best contemplated from the rail line several hundred feet below the town in the Duero valley. At closer quarters it turns out to be a pleasant, rather ordinary provincial town, though embellished with one outstanding Romanesque reminder of past glory.

Toro did, however, play a role of vital significance in both Spanish and Portuguese history. The **Battle of Toro** in 1476 effectively ended Portugal's interest in Spanish affairs and laid the basis for the unification of Spain. On the death of Enrique IV in 1474, the Castilian throne was disputed: almost certainly his daughter Juana la Beltraneja was the rightful heiress, but rumours of illegitimacy were stirred up and Enrique's sister Isabella seized the throne. Alfonso V of Portugal saw his opportunity and supported Juana. At Toro the armies clashed in 1476 and the Reyes Católicos – Isabella and her husband Fernando – defeated their rivals to embark upon one of the most glorious periods in Spanish history.

Toro had long been a major military stronghold enjoying considerable royal patronage, and the monument that hints most strongly at this former importance is the **Colegiata Santa María la Mayor** (daily: summer 10.30am–1.30pm & 5–7.30pm; winter 11.30am–1.30pm). The West Portal (c. 1240) is one of the best-preserved and most beautiful examples of Romanesque art, its seven recessed arches carved with royal and biblical themes. All such portals were originally painted in a variety of colours, and this one remains close to its pristine decorative state. If locked, enquire at the **Turismo** (Mon–Fri 9am–2pm & 5–7pm, Sat & Sun 10am–2pm & 5–8pm) in the *Ayuntamiento* on the plaza for the keys.

The Dominican **Monasterio Sancti Spiritus** on the western edge of town (10.30am–12.30pm & 5–7pm, closed last Sun in the month, Lent and Advent; 300ptas) is worth a visit, too. It's a rambling fourteenth-century building containing some genuine treasures in amongst the mass of exhibits; chiefly a series of sixteenth-century Flemish tapestries depicting the betrayal and crucifixion of Christ. In the church is the tomb of Beatriz of Portugal (wife of Juan I of Castile, died 1410), who lived here for various periods after she was widowed at the age of eighteen.

Toro's **train station** is a steep twenty-minute walk below the town and there's a **hostal**, *La Estación* (☎980 692936; ②) alongside. In the town itself there's a choice between *Hostal Doña Elvira* at c/Antonio Miguélez 47 (☎980 690062; ③), and the upmarket *Hotel Juan II*, Plaza del Espolón 1 (☎980 690300, fax 980 692376; ⑤).

Tordesillas

TORDESILLAS, like Toro, can boast an important place in Spain's history. It was here, under the eye of the Borgia Pope Alexander VI, that the **Treaty of Tordesillas** (1494) divided "All Lands Discovered, or Hereafter to be Discovered in the West, towards the Indies or the Ocean Seas" between Spain and Portugal, along a line 370 leagues west of the Cape Verde Islands. Brazil, allegedly discovered six years later, went to Portugal – though it was claimed that the Portuguese already knew of its existence but had kept silent to gain better terms. The rest of the New World, including Mexico and Peru, became Spanish.

Further fame was brought to Tordesillas by the unfortunate **Juana la Loca** (Joanna the Mad), who spent 46 years in a windowless cell here. She had ruled Castile jointly with her husband Felipe I (the Handsome) from 1504–6 but was devastated by his early death and for three years toured the monasteries of Spain, keeping the coffin

33 CASH-1   5266 0098 001

SPAIN: THE ROUGH G   QTY 1   12.99
TOTAL   12.99

CARD NUMBER   6759404787115050440
ISSUE NUMBER   1
EXPIRY DATE   0901
MERCHANT ID   5710333Z
AUTHORISATION CODE 0002648
SWITCH   SALE   12.99

19.09.00 19:29

perpetually by her side, stopping from time to time to inspect the corpse. In 1509 she reached the Convent of Santa Clara in Tordesillas, where first Fernando (her father) and later Carlos V (her son) declared her insane, imprisoning her for half a century and assuming the throne of Castile for themselves.

Juana's place of confinement could have been worse. The **Real Monasterio de Santa Clara** (April–Sept Tues–Sat 10am–1pm & 3.30–6.30pm, Sun 10.30am–1.30pm & 3.30–5.30pm; 425ptas, free Wed, 225ptas for Arab baths by appointment: ☎983 770071) overlooks the Duero and is known as "The Alhambra of Castile" for its delightful Mudéjar architecture. It was built as a royal palace by Alfonso el Sabio (the Wise) in 1340 and its prettiest features are the tiny "Arab Patio" with horseshoe arches and Moorish decoration and the superb *artesonado* ceiling of the main chapel, described by Sacheverell Sitwell as "a ceiling of indescribable splendour, as brilliant in effect as if it had panes or slats of mother-of-pearl in it".

Further places of interest in Tordesillas include the long medieval **bridge** over the Duero, the arcaded **Plaza Mayor** and the church of **San Antolín** (April–Sept daily 10am–2pm & 4–7pm; 200ptas), now a museum with an impressive collection of sculpture and excellent views from its tower. Next door, the Casa de Tratado houses the small but useful **Turismo** (daily 10am–2pm & 4–6pm; ☎983 770061).

Practicalities

If you intend **staying** in Tordesillas be warned that it stands on a major crossroads (of the Madrid–Galicia road and the direct Salamanca–Valladolid route) and *hostales* tend to be expensive. The lowest-priced is the *Lorenzo* (☎983 770228; ③). Upmarket options are the modern *parador* (☎983 770051, fax 983 771013; ⑦) and *El Montico* (☎983 795000, fax 983 795008; ⑥), complete with tennis courts, pools, and a gym. All these places are on the Salamanca road; for somewhere more central, *Los Toreros*, Avda. de Valladolid 26 (☎983 771900; ⑤), has immaculate rooms and a good restaurant. There's also a well-equipped campsite (☎983 770953; April–Sept) across the road from the *parador*. Inexpensive **places to eat**, including the busy *Viky*, can be found on the Plaza Mayor and along c/San Antolín. For a splurge, the restaurant at the *parador* is excellent.

Medina del Campo

MEDINA DEL CAMPO, 24km south of Tordesillas, and the major rail junction before Valladolid, stands below one of the region's great castles. The Moorish design of the brick-built **Castillo La Mota** (daily 11am–2pm & 4–6pm) is similar to that at Coca further east, but less exotic and more robust. It was intended as another stronghold for the same family, the Fonsecas, but they were thrown out by the townsfolk in 1473. Queen Isabella lived here for several years (and died, in 1504, in a room overlooking the town's Plaza Mayor), after which the castle was reincarnated as a prison, then as a girls' boarding school, and more recently as a Casa de la Cultura. You can go inside the castle walls, but there are no rooms to see, and it is the exterior which is impressive.

In the fifteenth and sixteenth centuries, Medina del Campo (Market of the Field) was one of the most important market towns in the whole of Europe, with merchants converging from as far afield as Italy and Germany to attend its fairs. The largest sheep market in Spain is still held here and the beautifully ramshackle **Plaza Mayor** is evocative of the days when its bankers determined the value of European currencies.

Budget **rooms** are offered by *Pensión Medina* (☎983 802603; ②) and the smarter *Mesón la Plaza* (☎983 811246; ③), both on the Plaza Mayor (also known as Plaza de la Hispanidad). You could also try *Hostal La Mota* (☎983 800450; ④) at c/Fernando el Católico 4, on the other side of the bridge from the centre. For **meals**, try *Restaurante Monaco* on the Plaza Mayor, a splendid place with a bargain *menú*.

Valladolid

VALLADOLID, at the centre of the *meseta*, ought to be exciting. Many of the greatest figures of Spain's Golden Age – Fernando and Isabella, Columbus, Cervantes, Felipe II – lived in the city at some point and for many years it vied with Madrid as the royal capital. In reality its old quarter is today an oppressive labyrinth of dingy streets, and those of its palaces that survive do so in a woeful state of decline. Many of the finest have been swept away on a tide of speculation and official incompetence – to be replaced by a dull sprawl of highrise concrete. Modern Valladolid may be an expanding industrial city of 400,000 inhabitants but it has lost much that was irreplaceable.The one time you might actively seek to be in Valladolid is **Semana Santa** – Easter week – when it is host to some of the most extravagant and solemn processions in Spain.

Arrival and information

Arrival points and information are centred around the Campo Grande, a large triangular park where Napoleon once reviewed his troops. The **train station** is on Paseo de Campo Grande; the **bus station** is a ten-minute walk west at c/Puente Lodgante 2. There are two **Turismos**, one in a corner of the Campo at Plaza de Zorilla 3 (Tues–Sat 10am–1.30pm & 5–7.30pm, Sun 10am–2pm), the other on the corner of c/Correos and c/Primo de Rivera (Mon–Sat 10am–2pm & 5–7pm, Sun 10am–2pm; ☎983 372085). A good **travel bookshop**, Beagle, at c/Cascajares 2 (opposite the cathedral), stocks a wide range of maps.

Accommodation

If you want to stay in Valladolid, there's a reasonable choice of **rooms**, but they're spread all over town. You'll find several budget possibilities near the train station and also in the seedy area around the cathedral.

Budget options

Pensión Dani, c/Perú 11, 1° (☎983 300249). Excellent-value, clean rooms with scrubbed wooden floors just off the road leading to Plaza de Zorilla. ②.
Pensión Dos Rosas, c/Perú 11, 2° (☎983 207439). The second of two superb-value *pensiónes* owned by sisters in the same building. ②.
Residencia Juvenil Río Esgueva, c/Cementerio 2 (☎983 251550 or 983 340044). Advance booking is essential at this youth hostel, which, like most in Spain, is usually full of school groups. ①.
Hostal Val II, Plaza del Val 6 (☎983 375752). Reasonable rooms in the market area, north of Plaza Mayor. ③.

Moderate and expensive options

Pensión La Cueva, c/Correos 4 (☎983 330072). Decent en-suite rooms in a great location. ④.
Hotel La Enara, Plaza de España 5 (☎983 300211, fax 983 300311). A good, central place with plenty of character. ④.
Hotel Imperial, c/del Paseo 4 (☎983 330300, fax 983 330813). Charming hotel in a beautiful, sixteenth-century building, near the Plaza Mayor. ⑤.
Hotel El Nogal, c/Conde Ansurez 10 (☎983 340333, fax 983 354965). Stylish and upmarket with comfortable rooms and its own restaurant. ⑤.
Hostal Residencia París, c/Especería 2 (☎983 370625, fax 983 358301). Centrally located with its own car park and good-quality rooms. ⑤.
Hotel Roma, c/Héroes del Alcázar de Toledo 8 (☎983 351833, fax 983 355461). Smart rooms in a great location, with a good restaurant attached. ⑥.

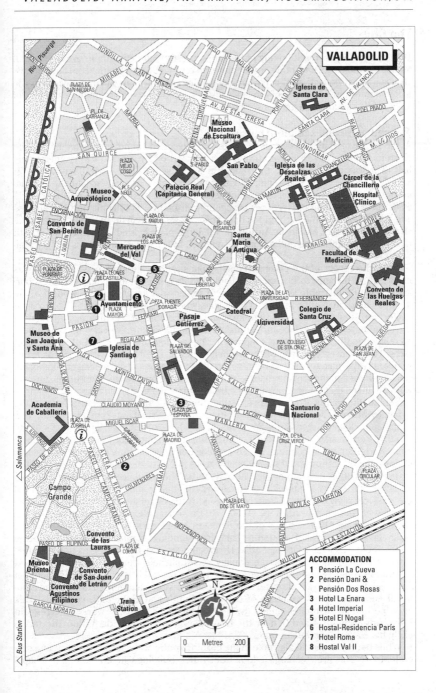

VALLADOLID

Río Pisuerga

RONDILLA DE SANTA TERESA

TIRSO DE MOLINA

PLAZA DE SAN NICOLAS

MIRABEL DE SANTA TERESA

AV. DE STA. TERESA

PORTILLO DE BALBOA

AV. DE PALENCIA

P. DEL PRADO

Iglesia de Santa Clara

SANTA CLARA

REAL DE BURGOS

M. V. de DIOS

PL. DE CARRANZA

IMPERIAL

CARDENAL TORQUEMADA

GONDOMAR

PADILLA

SAN QUIRCE

PLAZA VIEJO COSO

Museo Nacional de Escultura

PL. DE S. PABLO

San Pablo

ANGUSTIAS

Iglesia de las Descalzas Reales

TORRECILLA

CALLE CHANCILLERIA

SAN MARTIN

RAMON Y CAJAL

Cárcel de la Chancillería

Hospital Clínico

SAN V. Y FORES

Museo Arqueológico

PL. NELI

Palacio Real (Capitanía General)

FELIPE II

PL. DEL ROSARILLO

Santa María la Antigua

ESGUEVA

PARAISO

Facultad de Medicina

ENCARNACION

PLAZA DE S. MIGUEL

PLAZA DE LOS ARCES

Convento de San Benito

PASEO DE ISABEL LA CATOLICA

L. GUILLEN

Mercado del Val

L. CANO

ANGUSTIAS

COLON

Convento de las Huelgas Reales

PLAZA DE PONIENTE

ⓘ

PLAZA LEONES DE CASTILLA

⑤

⑧

CADENAS

PL. DE LIBERTAD

PLAZA DE LA UNIVERSIDAD

R. HERNANDEZ

HUELGAS

LORENZO

CORREOS

④

Ayuntamiento

⑥

①

PLAZA MAYOR

PZA. FUENTE DORADA

TINTE

Catedral

Colegio de Santa Cruz

MERCED

PLAZA DE SAN JUAN

Museo de San Joaquín y Santa Ana

PASION

ZUÑIGA

⑦

REGALADO

DUQUE DE LA VICTORIA

Pasaje Gutiérrez

FRAY LUIS DE LEON

Universidad

PZA. COLEGIO DE STA. CRUZ

CARDENAL MENDOZA

Iglesia de Santiago

SANTIAGO

MONTERO CALVO

PLAZA DEL SALVADOR

LOPEZ GOMEZ

SALVADOR

SANTA

DON SANCHO

MARIA DE MOLINA

DOCTRINOS

Academia de Caballería

CLAUDIO MOYANO

③

PLAZA DE ESPAÑA

JOSE M. LACORT

Santuario Nacional

S. ILDEFONSO

PLAZA DE ZORRILLA

MIGUEL ISCAR

GABRIELA CONSORCIO

MANTERIA

VEGA

PZA. DE LA CRUZ VERDE

ⓘ

PASEO DE ZORRILLA

PLAZA DE MADRID

②

CIPERO

PANADEROS

TUDELA

PLAZA CIRCULAR

△ Salamanca

Campo Grande

PASEO DEL CAMPO GRANDE

ACERA DE RECOLETOS

COLMENARES

GAMAZO

PLAZA DE DOS DE MAYO

NICOLAS

SALMERON

LABRADORES

DE LA ESTACION

PASEO DE FILIPINOS

Convento de las Lauras

PLAZA DE COLON

INDEPENDENCIA

NUEVA

Museo Oriental

Convento de San Juan de Letrán

ESTACION

Convento Agustinos Filipinos

GARCIA MORATO

Train Station

△ Bus Station

N

0   Metres   200

ACCOMMODATION

1 Pensión La Cueva
2 Pensión Dani &
   Pensión Dos Rosas
3 Hotel La Enara
4 Hotel Imperial
5 Hotel El Nogal
6 Hostal-Residencia París
7 Hotel Roma
8 Hostal Val II

The City

Despite the despoliation of many of the city's finest monuments, there are a couple of terrific examples of late Gothic architecture, an excellent Oriental museum and – above all – the finest collection of sculpture assembled anywhere in Spain. Aside from the national museum, almost all of the city's historic churches contain further examples of Valladolid's passionate religious sculpture.

The cathedral and sculpture museum

At the centre of things, as ever, is the **Catedral**, designed but not completed by Juan de Herrera (architect of El Escorial) and later worked on by Alberto Churriguera; only half of it was ever built, but the model in its museum (Tues–Fri 10am–1.30pm & 4.30–7pm, Sat & Sun 10am–2pm; 250ptas) shows how classically grand the original design was. What stands is a disappointment: the vast dimensions and sweeping arches do have something of Herrera's grandeur, but the overall effect is one of plainness and severity. Inside, the highlight is the *retablo mayor* by Juan de Juni, which was actually made for **Santa María la Antigua** in the large plaza behind: a Gothic church with modest flying buttresses and a Romanesque bell tower which culminates in a pyramidal roof.

From the corner of the plaza diagonally opposite the cathedral, c/de las Angustias leads a short distance to Plaza de San Pablo and its unmistakable church. The exuberant facade of **San Pablo** is a wild mixture of styles – the lower part is a product of the lavish form of late Gothic known as Isabelline, whereas the upper part is a Plateresque confection, similar to the New Cathedral and San Esteban at Salamanca. The building is treated purely as a surface for whimsical and highly decorative carvings which bear no relation to the structure that supports it. The facade of the adjacent **Colegio de San Gregorio**, a purer example of the Isabelline style, is adorned with coats of arms, sculpted twigs, naked children clambering in the branches of a tree and several comical, long-haired men carrying maces. It's a lot like icing on a cake – Jan Morris, for one, was convinced that the flamboyant facades must be edible.

Behind the gaudy front, there's serious business, for San Gregorio houses the dynamic **Museo Nacional de Escultura** (Tues–Sat 10am–2pm & 4–6pm, Sun 10am–2pm; 400ptas, free Sat 4–6pm and Sun), where the most brilliant works of the Spanish Renaissance are on display. Much the most important figures in this movement were Alonso Berruguete, Diego de Siloé and Juan de Juni: all three were active in the sixteenth century and spent several years in Florence where they perfected the realistic depiction of anatomy, fell heavily under the influence of Michelangelo and immersed themselves in the Italian Renaissance. Their genius lies in the adaptation of the classical revival to the religious intensity of the Spanish temperament. The masterpiece of **Alonso Berruguete** (1486–1561) is a massive, dismantled *retablo* which occupies the first three rooms of the museum – a remarkable demonstration of his skills in painting, relief sculpture and free-standing statuary. **Diego de Siloé** (1495–1565) was even more versatile. He created a classical building from the Gothic cathedral at Granada and was an equally accomplished sculptor – see his *Sagrada Familia* in room 12 and the carved choir stalls in room 11. Works of the Frenchman **Juan de Juni** (1507–77) show an almost theatrical streak and foreshadowed the emotional and naturalistic sculpture of the seventeenth and eighteenth centuries. This later period is best exemplified by the agonizingly realistic work of **Gregorio Fernández** (rooms 4 and 5, near the ticket desk) and **Alonso de Villabrille** (especially his *Head of San Pablo*, room 27).

While here, you should also take in the beautiful **patio** with lace-like tracery, and several Moorish-inspired ceilings taken from other buildings in the city. The chapel (entrance is immediately left of the main door, opposite the ticket booth) has many interesting exhibits, including another *retablo* by Alonso Berruguete, this time intact (hours are the same as for the museum).

The university and a miscellany of museums

Valladolid is also a famous academic centre. The **Universidad**, just beyond the cathedral, has a portal by Narciso Tomé, the man who built the *Transparente* in Toledo Cathedral – one of his very few surviving works. Farther on, part of the university administration is housed in the **Colegio de Santa Cruz**, a late fifteenth-century edifice which signals the introduction of Renaissance architecture to Spain. The beautiful three-storey patio and cloister are open to the public during office hours.

In a surprisingly different vein there's a delightful **Museo Oriental** (Mon–Sat 4–7pm, Sun 10am–2pm; 350ptas) on the Paseo de los Filipinos, just off the Campo Grande. This occupies a dozen rooms in the Colegio de Agustinos, which sent missionaries to China and the Philippines for four centuries until their expulsion in 1952. Countless exquisite gems of Chinese art are on show. Among the most striking are some beautiful paintings of nature on rice paper (mainly Sung dynasty; room 9), three gorgeous porcelain pieces entitled *The Three Happy Chinamen: Fu, Shou and Lou* (Qing epoch; room 2) and some stunning ivory carvings from the Philippines (room 14). On the way out you can look at the lavishly decorated interior of the church, a good example of the academic style of Ventura Rodríguez, fashionable in the late eighteenth century.

Other museums include the **Museo de Valladolid** (Tues–Fri 9.45am–2pm & 4–7.15pm, Sat & Sun 9.45am–2.15pm; 200ptas, free Sat & Sun), an archeological museum and art gallery, just up from Plaza San Miguel in a Renaissance mansion. The **Museo de San Joaquín y Santa Ana** (Mon 5–8pm, Tues–Sat 10am–1pm & 5–8pm, Sun 10am–1pm; 300ptas) is filled mostly with religious dust-collectors but has a few good statues, plus three Goya paintings in the chapel.

Eating, drinking and nightlife

The central area is the best place for **eating and drinking**. Near Santa María la Antigua, c/Marqués de Duero, c/Paraíso and c/Esgueva are full of good *tapas* bars, and the Plaza Mayor is also a popular place to linger. Valladolid's youth congregate at night in the modern **bars** of the Paco Suárez area, around Plaza Coca and c/San Lorenzo. For something a little different try the ancient *El Penicilino* on Plaza de la Libertad, with an atmosphere more like an apothecary than a bar; its speciality is a lurid pink concoction. There's also **live jazz** in the *Café España*.

Café León d'Or, Plaza Mayor. Relaxed central café; a good place to watch the world go by.

Casa de Galicia, opposite the Colegio de Santa Cruz. Excellent, inexpensive dishes.

Casa San Pedro Regalado, Plaza del Ochavo 1 (next to *Hostal París*). Traditional Castilian fare and a good atmosphere, close to the Plaza Mayor.

La Criolla, c/Correos. One of many restaurants in town serving the Valladolid speciality, *lechazo asado* (roast lamb).

Mesón Panero, c/Marina Escobar 1 (☎983 301673; closed Sun night). The city's gastronomic temple – pricey, but not horribly so.

La Mina, c/Correos. An enjoyable bar behind the plaza, near the post office.

La Pedriza, c/Colmenares 10. No menu – only roast lamb served here (and at its best); moderately priced.

Taberna Pan con Tomate, Plaza Mayor 18. Good *tapas* bar with a modest restaurant attached.

Taberna el Pozo, c/de Campañas 2 (off c/Correos). Moderately priced Castilian specialities, very popular with locals.

Palencia

PALENCIA is Castile's least known and least impressive province and its capital city is no exception. Despite a rich past, it has no great sights. There are numerous plazas, usually dominated by Romanesque churches built in a rather gaunt white stone, but while all are pleasant, none is outstanding.

The **Catedral** (daily 9.30am–1.30pm & 4–6.30pm, closed Sun pm), a fourteenth- to fifteenth-century Gothic building, is plain by Spanish standards, except for the two south portals. Inside, most of the decoration is contemporary with, or only slightly later than, the architecture, thanks to the patronage of Bishop Fonseca. Soon after it was completed, Palencia fell into decline – hence the almost complete absence of Baroque trappings. Buy a ticket in the sacristy to see the artistic treasures; one of the staff will take you to the crypt (part Visigothic, part Romanesque) and the museum in the cloisters, which includes a very early *San Sebastián* by El Greco and Flemish tapestries. In addition, lights are switched on so you can see the various altars, and the chapel doors opened – a facility not always available in Spain. The highlight is probably the *retablo mayor*, which contains twelve beautiful little panels, ten of them painted by Juan de Flandes, court painter to Isabella la Católica – it's the best collection of his work anywhere.

Not far from the cathedral is the Río Carrión, spanned by a picturesque old bridge known as **Puentecillas**, which contrasts well with the sturdier and later **Puente Mayor**. If you have time to kill, you could also search out one of Spain's more personal and idiosyncratic museums, the **Museo Historia del Calzado** (daily except Thurs & Sun noon–2pm & 7–9pm) above the shop of the master shoemaker, Julio Vibot Tristán, at c/Barrio y Mier 10, off c/Mayor. Señor Vibot is cobbler to the royal family and this is your chance to find out about Juan Carlos's taste in footwear: there's a well-marked display of beautifully crafted shoes, the fruits of sixty years in the trade, as well as shoes from different ages belonging to various historical figures.

Practicalities

Palencia's **bus and train stations** are both on the Plaza Calvo Sotelo; at its far corner, the long c/Mayor opens out, and the **Turismo** (daily 9am–2pm & 5–7pm; ☎979 740068) is near the end of it. Close by is the friendly and spotless *El Salón*, Avda. República Argentina 10 (☎979 726442; ③); *Hostal Ávila*, at c/Conde Vallellano 5 (☎979 711910, fax 979 711910; ④), is more luxurious but good value. For good *tapas* and *raciones* try *La Taberna Plaza Mayor* in the southeast corner of the plaza, or *Don Jamón* off its northeast corner. *Lorenzo*, Avda. Casado del Alisal 10 (closed Sept 10–Oct 10), is the top restaurant and quite modestly priced.

Around Palencia

South of Palencia, at the ugly, modern town of **Venta de Baños**, is an important train junction. If you are changing trains here, it's well worth following the signs to the village of **BAÑOS DE CERRATO** 2km out of town. This has the oldest church in the peninsula – *Monumento Nacional 1* in the catalogue: a seventh-century basilica (Tues–Sun 10am–1pm & 4–7pm) dedicated to **San Juan** by the Ostrogoth King Recesvinto. It has tiny lattice windows, horseshoe arches and incorporates materials from Roman buildings. The caretaker lives opposite. Across the road is a spring with delicious water.

PAREDES DE NAVA, on the train line to León, has another church of interest, **Santa Eulalia** (summer 11am–2pm & 4–7pm; winter closes 6pm). The great sculptor Alonso Berruguete was born here, as were many of his lesser-known relatives, and the parish church (with a beautifully tiled Romanesque tower) has been turned into a small museum full of their work. The collection is arranged in every available space, and includes pieces by many of the best-known of Berruguete's contemporaries, gathered from all the churches of this little town. Paredes also has three **fondas**, all with restaurants.

For those interested in pursuing the **pilgrimage route**, the town of Frómista (see p.372) on the Santander road, is within easy reach of Palencia. Otherwise, castle country to the south is an obvious destination.

Castles south of the Duero

It is said there were once ten thousand castles in Spain. Of those that are left, some five hundred are in a reasonable state of repair, and Castile has far more than its fair share of them. The area south of Valladolid, and towards Segovia, is especially rich – ringed with a series of fortresses, many of them built in the fifteenth century to protect the royal headquarters.

Coca

Sixty kilometres south of Valladolid and accessible by bus, **COCA** is the prettiest fortress imaginable. Less a piece of military architecture than a country house masquerading as one, it's constructed from narrow pinkish bricks, encircled by a deep moat and fantastically decorated with octagonal turrets, merlons and elaborate castellation – an extraordinary design strongly influenced by Moorish architecture. The building dates from about 1400, and was the base of the powerful **Fonseca family**. The interior (Mon–Thurs 8am–8.30pm & Fri 8.30am–3pm) is used by the Ministry of Agriculture so it's advisable to phone ahead to check opening hours (☎911 586062).

The village of Coca itself is pretty lifeless, but there are a few bars and if you ask in these you should be able to find a room for the night. While here, try to see the inside of the parish church of **Santa María**, where there are four tombs of the Fonseca family carved in white marble in the Italian Renaissance style. The power of the dynasty is indicated by the fact that they were able to hire Bartolomé Ordóñez, the sculptor of the tombs of the Reyes Católicos in Granada.

Cuéllar, Turégano, Pedraza and Sepúlveda

The route south by road from Valladolid passes another impressive ancient castle at **Cuéllar**. Even more stunning is the one at **Turégano**, 28km north of Segovia; it's essentially a fifteenth-century structure enclosing an early thirteenth-century church, and you have to track down the sexton of the parish church to get inside.

East of Turégano, just off the main Segovia–Soria road, there are rewarding diversions to be made to Pedraza and Sepúlveda, both extraordinarily pretty villages. **PEDRAZA** is almost perfectly preserved from the sixteenth century, a homogeneity enhanced by the uniformity of the rich brown stone in which it's constructed. The village is protected on three sides by a steep valley; the only entrance is the single original gateway (which used to be the town prison) from where the narrow lanes spiral gently up towards a large **Plaza Mayor**, still used for a **bullfighting festival** in the first week in September. Pedraza also has a **castle** (privately owned), where the eight-year-old Dauphin of France and his younger brother were imprisoned in 1526, given up by their father François I who swapped his freedom for theirs after he was captured at the battle of Pavia.

SEPÚLVEDA is less of a harmonious whole, but has a more dramatic setting, strung out high on a narrow spit of land between the Castilla and Duratón river valleys. Its physical and architectural high point is the distinctive Romanesque church of **El Salvador** (open third Sun in month), below which is a ruined castle out of which the town hall protrudes.

Both villages can be reached by bus from Valladolid, but are best avoided at weekends, when every young *madrileño* with a Mercedes seems to descend on them for the local speciality, roast lamb. Sepúlveda is the better bet for **accommodation** with three *hostales*: *Hernanz*, c/Conde de Sepúlveda 4 (✆921 540378, fax 921 540520; ④); *Postigo*, a few doors along (✆921 540172; ④); and *Villa de Sepúlveda* on the Ctra Boceguillas (✆921 500302; ④). Pedraza has two hotels, both expensive (and luxurious): *De la Villa*, c/Calzada (✆921 508651, fax 921 508652; ⑦), and *La Posada de Don Mariano*, c/Mayor 14 (✆ & fax 921 509886; ⑥).

The Pantano de Burgomillodo and Riaza

In addition to its castles, this area of Old Castile is rich in **wildlife**. The **Pantano de Burgomillodo**, a reservoir just to the west of Sepúlveda, is a particularly exciting spot for bird-watchers, surrounded by heaths of wild lavender which are the haunt of griffon vultures and other exotic species. From here you can head towards El Burgo de Osma on the road through **RIAZA**, skirting the foothills of the Sierra de Guadarrama. It's a lovely route, and Riaza itself is a pleasant place to stop with several good bars (try *El Museo*) and restaurants, and a couple of places offering rooms. There's also a station here on the main line from Madrid to Burgos.

Along the Duero: Valladolid to Soria

The **Duero**, east from Valladolid to Soria, is trailed by a further panoply of castles and old market towns; the river long marked the frontier between Christian and Arab territory. Road (and bus) routes follow the river, allowing leisurely and rewarding small-town stops.

Peñafiel

The reason for stopping at **PEÑAFIEL**, 60km east of Valladolid, is to see its fabulous elongated **castle** (Tues–Sun 11am–1.30pm & 4–8pm, winter closes 7pm; 200ptas), which bears an astonishing resemblance to a huge ship run aground: it is 210m long but only 23m across, with its central tower playing the role of the ship's bridge. Built in 1466 out of the region's distinctive white stone, the castle was designed around the narrow ridge upon which it stands, a location best appreciated from the top of the tower.

From the "prow" of the castle there's a tremendous view of Peñafiel, and good views too from the hill at the foot of the castle, particularly from the **Plaza del Cosa**. This large square is extraordinary in itself; its buildings are wooden, with several tiers of loggias, and it makes the most spectacular bullring in Spain when bullfights are held in August. It's also where you'll find the **Turismo** (April–Sept Tues–Sat 10am–2pm & 5.30–8pm, Sun 10am–2pm). Nearby is **San Pablo**, now a college, with a superb brick Gothic-Mudéjar apse, to which a Plateresque chapel was later added.

Practicalities

If you need a **place to stay**, the *Hostal Linares,* across the river from the old village at Mercado Viejo 11 (✆983 880942; ④), offers a few basic rooms, and several that are considerably more comfortable. In the old quarter, *Chicopa* is a beautifully located *tapas* bar next to the *Ayuntamiento*, which sometimes rents (tidy) rooms above the bar (✆983 880782; ③). For something more luxurious, Peñafiel offers one of the region's best hotels: the *Hotel Ribera de Duero*, Avda. Escalona 17 (✆983 873111, fax 983 881616; ⑥), is in a splendid old building (which until recently housed a suitcase factory) with very stylish rooms, most of them looking directly on to the castle. For **dinner**, the *Molino de Palacios* serves traditional Castilian dishes in a converted sixteenth-century watermill over the Duratón River, while *Bar Plata*, at c/Franco 22, does good *tapas* and is a bit of a nightspot. There are five daily **buses** (fewer on Sundays) to and from Valladolid (1hr) and Aranda de Duero (30min).

Aranda de Duero

Another 35km east, and at a junction with the Madrid-Burgos *autopista*, is **ARANDA DE DUERO**, a busy commercial town which has managed to retain the feel of a graceful and picturesque village, and is at its liveliest for the Saturday morning market. If you're passing through, take a look at the south facade of **Santa María**, an ornate Isabelline work in which even the doors are carved.

Restaurants vie with each other in Aranda to tempt you with the local treat of roast lamb (*cordero* or *lechazo asado*); particularly good is *Casa Florencio* at c/Isilla 4; for something cheaper, try *Arandos* at c/Pedrote 5. **Places to stay** include *Pensíon Sole*, c/Puerta Nueva 16 (☎947 500607; ③), and *Julia* at c/San Gregorio 2 (☎947 501200; ⑤). There is a very well-equipped **campsite**, with pool, *Costaján* (☎947 502070; open mid-June to mid-Sept), on the main N1 heading north of town. **Buses** from Valladolid to Peñafiel continue to Aranda, then eastwards on to El Burgo de Osma.

El Burgo de Osma and around

EL BURGO DE OSMA, the episcopal centre of Soria Province, is a wonderfully picturesque place, with crumbling town walls and ancient colonnaded streets overhung by houses supported on precarious wooden props. In the relaxed village atmosphere of the Plaza Mayor, its **Catedral** (daily 10am–1pm & 4–7pm), one of the richest in Spain, seems more than usually over the top. Basically Gothic in style, it has had many embellishments over the years, notably the superb Baroque tower decorated with pinnacles and gables which dominates the town. If you buy a visitor's ticket (350ptas), lights will be switched on for you to see the theatrical *retablo mayor* by Juan de Juni and his pupils, and a series of dark chapels, one of which contains a powerful Romanesque carving of the Crucifixion. You will also be escorted to the cloisters and the museum. Most impressive of all is the thirteenth-century painted stone tomb of San Pedro de Osma – a uniquely naturalist treatment for its age.

Practicalities

You can get some idea of Osma's former importance from the fact that it was once the seat of a university. The sixteenth-century building, now a school, is at the edge of town, near where the **buses** stop. Nearby are a couple of **places to stay**: the budget *Hostal Casa Agapito*, c/Universidad 1 (☎975 340212; ②), and the more upmarket *Hostal La Perdiz*, tucked behind the petrol station at c/Universidad 33 (☎975 360476; ④). There is an excellent new hotel, *El Mirador* (☎975 360408; ④), behind the Plaza Mayor on c/Marques de Vadillo, which has smart, modern rooms and a good choice of **tapas** in its bar. If money is no object, the town's best hotel is *Il Virrey* (☎975 341311, fax 975 340855; ⑤) on the Plaza Mayor. There's also a **campsite**, *La Pedriza* (☎975 340806; June–Sept); take the first left off c/Mayor and then turn right along c/Rodrigo Yusto.

There is now a very friendly and helpful **Turismo** (☎975 360116) at Plaza Mayor 1, which can provide information on the **bus** routes (including unscheduled stops) to Valladolid and Soria.

San Esteban de Gormaz and Gormaz

Thirteen kilometres to the west of El Burgo de Osma, **SAN ESTEBAN DE GORMAZ** has a ruined castle and a pair of Romanesque churches. There's also a pleasant **hostal**, *El Moreno*, Avda. del Generalísimo 1 (☎975 350217; ③), which could be useful if you find everything full in Osma.

GORMAZ, 15km south of El Burgo de Osma, is a particularly intriguing fortification since it was originally built in the caliphate style, and two Moorish doorways dating from the tenth century have survived. Later captured and modified by Christians, it was one of the largest fortified buildings in the West – there are 28 towers in all, ruined but impressive. The inside is a shell, but there are good panoramas from here, and the wonderful views as you approach make the long walk up less daunting. Gormaz itself is little more than a hamlet, without any accommodation.

Calatañazor

Just off the main El Burgo–Soria road lies **CALATAÑAZOR**, a severely depopulated medieval village with walls and the ruins of a castle, chiefly remarkable for its **houses**, with their distinctive conical chimneys, decorative coats of arms and wooden balconies. A village guide is based at the *mesón*, where good simple meals are served. The only available **accommodation** is the *Hostal Calatañazor*, c/Real 10 (☎975 340570; ④), an ancient house on the main village street, but the place makes a good half-day excursion from either El Burgo de Osma or Soria, 30km east.

Berlanga de Duero and around

BERLANGA DE DUERO, east again along the Duero, stands just off the main road between El Burgo de Osma and Almazán; it can also be reached from Soria by daily **bus** (departure 6.30pm, return 6.45am).

Once again, the main attraction is a **castle**, whose massive cylindrical towers and older double curtain wall, reminiscent of Ávila, loom above the town. The way up is through a doorway in a ruined Renaissance palace at the edge of town (watch out for the lethal uncovered hole dropping down to an underground cavern); entrance is free. The other dominant monument is the **Colegiata** (usually open), one of the last flowerings of the Gothic style. Its unusually uniform design is a consequence of rapid construction – it was built in just four years. Berlanga also has an old-world **Plaza Mayor** (where markets are held regularly), several fine mansions, arcaded streets, an impressive entrance gateway and the unique **La Picota** – a pillar of justice to which offenders were tied (it's on a wasteground outside the old town, where the buses stop).

The only **place to stay** in Berlanga is at the upmarket *Hotel Fray Tomás*, c/Real 16 (☎975 343033; ⑤), which also has a very good restaurant.

Ermita de San Baudelio de Berlanga

Eight kilometres south of Berlanga, the tiny **Ermita de San Baudelio de Berlanga** (Nov–March Wed–Sat 10.30am–2pm & 4–6pm, Sun 10.30am–2pm; April–June & Sept–Oct Wed–Sat 10.30am–2pm & 4–7pm, Sun 10.30am–2pm; July & Aug Wed–Sat 10.30am–2pm & 5–9pm, Sun 10.30am–2pm; 100ptas) is the best-preserved and (with San Miguel de Escalada, see p.373) most important example of Mozarabic style in Spain. It was even better before the 1920s: five years after being declared a national monument, its marvellous cycle of frescoes was acquired by an international art dealer and exported to the USA. After much fuss, the Spanish government got some of them back on indefinite loan, but they are now kept in the Prado.

In spite of this loss, the hermitage remains a beauty. Its eight-ribbed interior vault springs from a central pillar, while much of the space is taken up by the tribune gallery of horseshoe arches. Some original frescoes do remain, including two bulls from the great sequence of animals and hunting scenes of the nave. You can also see the entrance to the cave below, which the hermit, San Baudelio, made his home.

Almazán

Some 35km due south of Soria lies **ALMAZÁN**, which despite a lot of ugly modern development still possesses complete **medieval walls**, pierced by three gateways. On the Plaza Mayor stands the fine Renaissance **Palacio Hurtado de Mendoza**, with a Gothic loggia at the rear, visible from the road around the walls. The church of **San Miguel**, across from the palace, has a memorable interior, with Romanesque and early Gothic features, and a remarkable dome in the Cordoban style; the altar has a relief of the martyrdom of Saint Thomas à Becket. To gain access, try the parish offices in the adjacent Plaza Santa María, opposite the church of the same name.

Places to stay include *Hostal El Arco*, c/San Andrés 7 (☎975 310228; ③), and *Hostal Mateos*, c/San Lázaro (☎975 301400; ②), across the river. The latter is also one of the few places to eat in town, along with *Restaurante Toma*, c/Manuel Cartel 11. However, you are not likely to want to stay long, and there are regular **bus** and **train** connections to Soria.

Medinaceli

MEDINACELI, perched in an exhilarating, breezy position above the Río Jalón, is something of a ghost town – steeped in history and highly evocative of its former glory as a Roman and Moorish stronghold. It's 76km south of Almazán and positioned on the main Madrid–Barcelona rail line. If you arrive this way, it's a three-kilometre climb by road up from the station to the village, though you can take a short cut straight up the hill to a distinctive Roman arch. The **Roman arch** – a triple arch in fact – is worn but impressive, and unique in Spain. Its presence is something of a mystery as such monuments were usually built to commemorate military triumphs but the cause of celebration at Medinaceli is unknown. Nearby stands the dilapidated Moorish **castle**, now a mere facade sheltering a Christian cemetery.

The quiet streets are full of ancient mansions with proud coats of arms, the grandest of which is the **Palacio de los Duques de Medinaceli** on the dusty and desolate Plaza Mayor, a square that looks like a disused film set. The palace was the seat of the family regarded as rightful heirs to the Castilian throne until, in 1275, Fernando, eldest son of Alfonso el Sabio (the Wise), died before he could assume his inheritance. His two sons were dispossessed by Fernando's brother Sancho el Valiente (the Brave), and their descendants, the Dukes of Medinaceli, long continued to lay claim to the throne. Today Medinaceli is a declining village with no more than 900 inhabitants, though its *duquesa* remains the most betitled woman in Spain.

There are several **places to stay** by the train station; *Hostal Nicolás* (☎975 326004; ④) and *Hotel Duque de Medinaceli* (☎975 326111, fax 975 326472; ④) are both very pleasant. If you prefer to stay up in the old village there's *El Mirador* (☎975 326264; ④), or the *Hostal Medinaceli* (☎975 326102; ④), next to the Roman arch. *Las Llaves* (closed Sun evening & Mon), on the Plaza Mayor, is an attractive **restaurant**, stuffed with antiques.

Southwest of Medinaceli, Sigüenza (see p.162) is just 20km away across the border in New Castile, a couple of stops on any Madrid-bound train.

Santa María de Huerta

On the Aragonese border, 25km and just half an hour by train or bus from Medinaceli, lies **SANTA MARÍA DE HUERTA**. This tiny community is dominated by a Cistercian **monastery** (9am–1pm & 3–6.30pm), whose story of royal and noble patronage was brought to a sudden end by the First Carlist War in 1835. The buildings were repopulated in 1930, and the main church has recently been restored. The highlight of the complex is the French-Gothic refectory (1215–23), whose superb sexpartite vaulting and narrow pointed windows are worthy of the best church, let alone a dining room. Adjacent stands the kitchen with a mammoth chimney protruding above Plateresque upper cloisters. The village has a single **pensión**, *Santa María* (☎975 327218; ②), and on the Zaragoza road, a former *parador*, now privately run, the *Hotel Santa María de Huerta* (☎975 327011, fax 975 327011; ⑥).

Soria and around

SORIA is a modest little provincial capital – an attractive place, despite encroaching suburbs. It stands between a ridgeback of hills on the banks of the Duero, with a castle ruin above, a medieval centre dotted with mansions and Romanesque churches, and one of the country's greatest cloisters.

Arrival, information and accommodation

Soria's **train and bus stations** are both on the fringes of the city; the former, which has had its services ruthlessly pruned in the last few years, is at the extreme southwest corner. A new bus station has been built on Avda. de Valladolid in the modern northwest quarters; to walk from one to the other, you can follow the ring road without having to go into the centre. **Moving on** from Soria there's a rich choice of destinations: west to Burgos, east into Aragón or north to Logroño and the Basque country. If you're heading into the immediate countryside around Soria, Ociotur at c/Sagunto 4 (☎975 228923) organizes climbing, mountaineering, cross-country skiing and other **outdoor activities**. A helpful **Turismo** (daily 10am–2pm & 5–8pm; ☎975 212052) is in the Plaza Ramón y Cajal, opposite the entrance to the large Alameda de Cervantes, a spacious park which is one of Soria's most attractive features.

Accommodation

Soria's tourists are rarely in great numbers, so finding a **place to stay** shouldn't be a problem. There are plenty of centrally located budget options, and a reasonable choice of mid-range and upmarket hotels.

Hostal Alvi, c/Albera 2 (☎975 228112, fax 975 228240). Well-equipped, with electric shutters in every room and private parking. ④.

Pensión Carlos, Plaza del Olivio 2 (☎975 211555). Clean, adequate rooms in an excellent location. ②.

Pensión Ferial, Plaza del Salvador 6 (☎975 221244). Spacious, good-value rooms and a welcoming *dueña*. ②.

Parador Antonio Machado, Parque del Castillo (☎975 240800, fax 975 240803). A modern *parador* in a beautiful hill-top location, with great views. ⑦.

Hostal La Posada, Plaza San Clemente 6 (☎975 223603). Good rooms in this nicely located *hostal*, set in the corner of a lovely square. ④.

Pensión El Sol, c/Ferial 8 (☎975 227202). Don't be put off by the dingy exterior – the rooms inside are spotless. ②.

Hostal Viena, c/García Solier 1 (☎975 222109, fax 975 228140). Past its best but the rooms are spacious and comfortable, and the place has its own restaurant. ④.

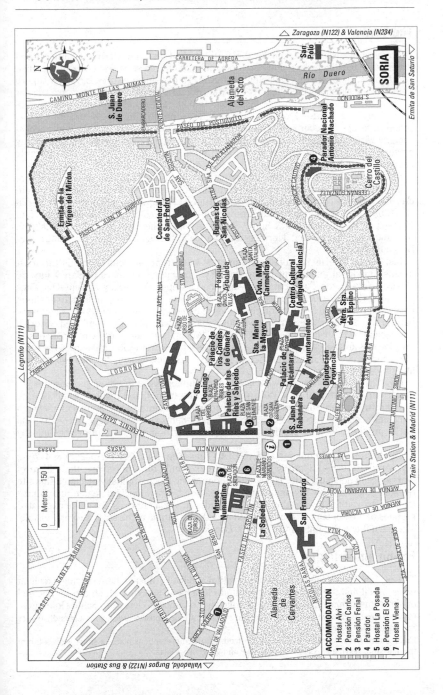

The Town

The centre of town is marked by the **Concatedral de San Pedro**, a rather stolid Plateresque building, whose interior (open only for church services) takes the Spanish penchant for darkness to a ridiculous extreme. To the side are three bays of a superb Romanesque cloister, which belonged to the cathedral's predecessor.

From the cathedral, follow the main road that skirts the old town to reach the convent church of **Santo Domingo**. A twelfth-century building, its beautiful rose-coloured facade is decorated symmetrically with sixteen "blind" arches and a wheel window with eight "spokes". The recessed arches of the main portal are excellently preserved and magnificently sculpted with scenes from the life of Christ, currently being renovated.

Also worth a look in the centre of town is **San Juan de Rabanera** (daily 11am–1pm & 3–5pm), another fine Romanesque church, the massive sixteenth-century **Palacio de los Condes de Gomara** and the **Museo Numantino** (May–Sept Tues–Sat 9am–2pm & 5–9pm, Sun 10am–2pm; Oct–April Tues–Sat 9.30am–7.30pm, Sun 10am–2pm; 200ptas, free Sat & Sun). This features excellent displays of the finds from Numancia (see below) and Tiermes, another Celto-Iberic and Roman city, south of El Burgo de Osma.

Just across the Duero, some ten minutes' walk from the centre, stands the most freakish medieval monument in the country. The ruined cloisters of **San Juan de Duero** (Nov–March Tues–Sat 10am–2pm & 3.30–6pm; April–May & Sept–Oct Tues –Sat 10am–2pm & 4–7pm; June–Aug Tues–Sat 10am–2pm & 5–9pm, Sun 10am–2pm; free) are remarkable for their original and imaginative synthesis of styles. They were built in the thirteenth century by Mudéjar masons who playfully combined Moorish interlaced and cusped arches with Christian Romanesque and early Gothic shapes. If the cloisters are closed, you can get a partial aerial view from a low hill across the road. The church, converted into a museum, is more orthodox in style, but has two unusual little freestanding temples inside.

From here, there's a good walk south along the banks of the river, passing the former Templar church of **San Polo** (now a private home), and coming, after 2km, to the **Ermita de San Saturio**, a two-tiered complex including an octagonal chapel with thirteenth-century frescoes (10am–2pm & 4.30–8pm). The landscape here is typical of the province, with its parched, livid, orange earth and the solemn river lined by poplars.

The barren site of Roman **NUMANCIA** (Tues–Sun: May–Oct 10am–2pm & 4–7pm; Nov–April 10.30am–1.30pm & 4.30–6pm; free) stands on a hill above the village of **Garray**, 8km north of Soria. The Celto-Iberian town which originally occupied this site resisted Scipio and his legions for over a year, and, when finally defeated, the inhabitants destroyed the town rather than surrender it. What survives are some excavated remains of the Roman city that replaced it, with the outline of the streets clearly visible. They're not exciting unless you're an archeologist.

Eating and drinking

The city's **bars and restaurants** are plentiful and lively, most of them serving excellent *tapas*. You'll find the best selection around Plaza San Clemente, which can be reached either from the main c/Collado, or by following c/Aduana Vieja from Santo Domingo.

Casa Augusto, Plaza Mayor 5. An excellent restaurant in a central location with a friendly owner and an affordable *menú*.

Casa Soria, Avda. Mariano Vicén 5 (open from 7am). Unpretentious place, a short walk south of the Turismo, serving excellent-value *menús* and good breakfasts.

Maroto, Paseo del Espolón 20. Conservative and quite pricey, this is where Soria's well-heeled come to dine. Good Castilian food, beautifully presented. Closed Thurs.
La Posada, Plaza San Clemente 6. As well as offering rooms, this bar serves some of the best *tapas* in town.
Santo Domingo II, Avda. Vieja 15. Fairly upmarket restaurant, just south of Santo Domingo, offering a wide range of fish and meat dishes.

Río Lobos Canyon and the Sierra de Urbión

Some of Castile's loveliest and least-visited countryside lies northwest of Soria, on either side of the N234 to Burgos. South of this road a **Parque Natural** has been created around the canyon of the Río Lobos. To the north rises the **Sierra de Urbión**, a lakeland region much loved by the Sorian-born poet, Antonio Machado. The Cañón Río Lobos can also be approached on minor roads from El Burgo de Osma, to the south.

Río Lobos Canyon

The whole area of the **Parque Natural del Cañón del Río Lobos** is impressive, with fantastically shaped rocks on both sides of the canyon. The most interesting part lies 1km from the park's car park, southeast of San Leonardo de Yagüe. Here, as well as some of the prettiest rock formations, there's a **Romanesque chapel** founded by the Templars (kept locked) and, behind this, a beautiful natural **cave**. From here, the path continues through the Lobos gorge; at times the river is a mere trickle – its tributaries have dried up completely, providing ready-made walking tracks. For this, or more adventurous treks into the high ground, you really need proper walking boots, but any shoes will do on the main paths. The park will appeal to bird-watchers; eagles and vultures are often seen, even though they are not protected here.

    SAN LEONARDO DE YAGÜE makes a convenient base, with a good **hostal**, the *Torres*, c/Magdalena 4 (☎975 376156; ④). Alternatively, you can **camp** in the officially designated areas around the entrance to the park (☎975 363565; mid-March to mid-Oct).

Vinuesa and the Sierra de Urbión

For the **Sierra de Urbión**, the most obvious base is **VINUESA**, situated just north of an enormous man-made reservoir, **Pantano de la Cuerda del Pozo**. On a slow country bus route between Soria and Burgos, it's a spaciously laid-out village with many fine old houses and plenty of **accommodation** to choose from down by the bridge: *Viscontium* (☎975 378354, fax 975 378362; ③) and *Santa Inés* (☎975 378126; ③) are two attractive *hostales*, owned by brothers; *Hostal Urbión* on Avda. Constitución (☎975 378494; ③) also has good rooms and in the middle of the village there's an excellent *pensión*, *Mesón Tito*, c/Reina Sofía (☎975 378031; ②). All these places except the last have their own restaurant. There's also a **campsite** 2km along the Montenegro road (☎975 378331; April to mid-Oct), which has bikes for hire.

    Nineteen kilometres north of Vinuesa lies the most famous of the lakes, the beautiful **Laguna Negra**. There's no public transport to it, but a good road leads through thickly wooded country before climbing steeply up the green mountainside. For the last couple of kilometres, by the side of a ravine, the road is much rougher; finally, a path leads to the lagoon. Ice Age in origin, set in an amphitheatre of mountains from which great boulders have fallen, it presents a primeval picture – Machado was inspired to write some of his most purple verse here. The area remains delightfully unspoiled, though, and the **bar** (June–Sept only) and **picnic area** are out of sight, 3km down the mountain.

Serious hikers can make a tortuous ascent from the Laguna Negra to the **Laguna de Urbión**, just over the border in Logroño Province – a route that takes in a couple of other tiny, glacially formed lakes. A less taxing version of the same excursion is to take the long way round, from the village of **Duruelo de La Sierra**, some 20km west of Vinuesa.

THE CAMINO DE SANTIAGO: FROM LOGROÑO TO LEÓN

This part of the chapter is laid out in an east–west direction, following, more or less, the **Camino de Santiago**, the great pilgrim route to the shrine of Saint James at Compostela (see p.490). The route had many variants but its most popular point of entry to Spain was – indeed is – at the pass of Roncesvalles in the Pyrenees. From there, the old paths strike south through Navarra to Logroño and then west across Castile through the great cathedral cities of **Burgos** and **León**. These are major architectural sights but each of the smaller towns along the *camino* has some treasure or reminder – a bridge, a Romanesque church, or a statue of the saint. For uncommitted pilgrims, the highlights of the route can be taken in by car, bus, or sometimes train.

Old Castile, in this section, is used in a loose, historical sense, for this region actually takes in two other provinces. In the east is **La Rioja**, Spain's premier wine-producing region, with its capital in **Logroño** and wine trade centre in nearby **Haro**. Over to the west is the old kingdom of **León**, whose northern reaches merge with Asturias in the Picos de Europa mountains (see p.456).

Logroño

LOGROÑO is a modern, prosperous city, lacking in great monuments, but pleasant enough with its broad, elegant streets and open squares. It has a lively old section, too, stretching down towards the Río Ebro from the twin-towered **Catedral de Santa María la Redonda**. Here the city becomes more than just an extended parade of shop-lined avenues and modern parks, and the narrow streets bustle with unexpected energy.

Whether you stay or not, you're likely to pass through Logroño at some point since it lies on the borders of Old Castile, the Basque provinces and Navarra, a position that has stimulated commerce and light industry. Most importantly, however, this is the very heart of the **Rioja wine region**.

The Town

Before the wine trade and industry brought prosperity to Logroño, it owed its importance for some six centuries to the **Camino de Santiago**. In almost every town on the route you can still find a church dedicated to the saint; in Logroño it stands close to the iron bridge over the Río Ebro – the lofty sixteenth-century Gothic structure of **Santiago el Real**. High on its north side, above the main entrance, is a magnificent eighteenth-century Baroque equestrian statue of the saint, mounted in full glory in his role of *Matamoros* (Moorslayer), on a stallion which Edwin Mullins, in his fascinating book *The Pilgrimage to Santiago*, describes as "equipped with the most heroic genitals in all Spain, a sight to make any surviving Moor feel inadequate and run for cover".

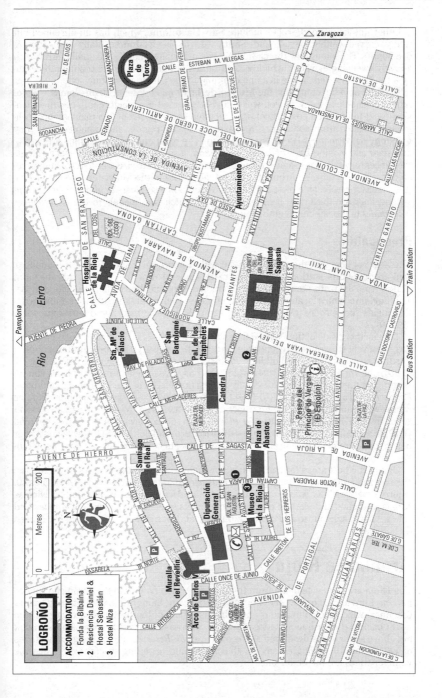

△ Zaragoza

△ Pamplona

Ebro

Rio

△ Train Station

▽ Bus Station

LOGROÑO

ACCOMMODATION

1 Fonda la Bilbaína
2 Residencia Daniel &
  Hostal Sebastián
3 Hostal Niza

Plaza de Toros

Ayuntamiento

Instituto Sagasta

Hospital de la Rioja

Sta. Mª de Palacio

San Bartolomé

Pal. de los Chapiteles

Catedral

Santiago el Real

Diputación General

Museo de la Rioja

Muralla del Revellín

Arco de Carlos V

Paseo del Príncipe de Vergara (El Espolón)

PUENTE DE PIEDRA

PUENTE DE HIERRO

PASARELA

Metres 0 200

Other fine Logroño churches include **San Bartolomé**, which has an unrefined but richly carved Gothic portal, and **Santa María la Redonda** (daily 8am–1pm & 6–8.30pm). The latter, now the cathedral, was originally a late Gothic hall church with a lovely sweeping elevation which was extended at both ends in the eighteenth century – the twin-towered facade is a fine example of the Churrigueresque style.

In addition to the churches, the **Museo de la Rioja** (Tues–Sat 10am–2pm & 4–9pm, Sun 11.30am–2pm; free), is well worth a visit. Located in an eighteenth-century mansion (next to the main post office), its collection is composed of two main groups: religious art taken from abandoned monasteries in the region, and nineteenth-century paintings on permanent loan from the Prado. The most impressive exhibits are on the first floor and include *Las Tablas de San Millán*, a series of beautifully preserved fourteenth-century paintings, and a roomful of remarkable, life-size wooden carvings created in 1597 by Pedro de Arbulo for the *retablo mayor* of the Monasterio de la Estrella. It's a pleasure to be able to see this kind of sculpture so close-up and well-lit. On the second floor are the Prado paintings, most of which won medals in the *Exposiciones Nacionales* in the late nineteenth century.

Practicalities

The heart of Logroño, the gardens of the wide **Paseo del Espolón**, is a few minutes' walk from the **bus station** (straight up c/del General Vara del Rey, crossing the Gran Vía) or from the **train station** (up the Avenida de España, then right at the bus station). The **Turismo** is now located in a new building set back from the c/del General Vara del Rey inside the gardens (Mon–Sat 10am–2pm & 4.30–7.30pm, Sun 10am–2pm; ☎941 291260).

The northern side of the Paseo del Espolón marks the start of the old quarter, which has the liveliest bars and restaurants and the lowest-priced **accommodation**. On a bustling street in the same building, *Residencia Daniel,* c/San Juan 21 (☎941 252948; ②–③), and *Hostal Sebastián* (☎941 242800; ③) are two excellent budget places run by sisters, but they can be noisy, especially during the festival of San Bernabé in mid-June. *Fonda La Bilbaína*, c/Gallarza 10 (☎941 254226; ②–③), is also recommended, and has rooms with and without baths. For more comfort, try *Hostal Niza*, c/Gallarza 13 (☎941 206044; ⑤). The local **campsite**, *La Playa*, Avda. de la Playa (☎941 252253; open all year), is a kilometre out of town across the Río Ebro, and lies beside its own sandy river beach; campers get free entrance to a nearby sports complex with an enormous outdoor pool.

One of the best areas for eating is c/San Juan, with good **tapas bars** including the *Beronés* and *La Cueva*. Perhaps the best **restaurant** in Logroño is *Leitos*, c/Portales 30, where a *menú del día* will cost around 1700ptas. *Meridiana*, Marqués de San Nicolás 136, is also good and slightly cheaper. For snacks – including superb *empanadas* and cakes – make a detour to *El Paraíso*, a **bakery** at c/San Agustín 27, next to the Museo de la Rioja.

Around La Rioja

The **Rioja** area takes its name from the Río Oja, which flows into the Tirón and thence into the Ebro to the northwest of Logroño. Effectively, though, it is the Ebro that waters the vines, which are cultivated on both banks. Many of the best vineyards are on the north bank in the Basque province of Alava – an area known as the *Rioja Alavesa*. Look out above all for wines described as *Reserva* or *Gran Reserva*, and for the great vintages of '68, '69 and '70 – though many say that with controls getting stricter every year, the younger wines are the better ones.

LA RIOJA'S WINE

Wine is at the very heart of La Rioja's identity, and few people will pass through Haro without wanting to buy a few bottles. It's a good idea to equip yourself with some **vocabulary** so you know what you're buying: *cosecha* (which literally means harvest), when used on its own refers to young wines in their first or second year, which tend to have a fresh and fruity flavour; *crianzas* are wines which are at least in their third year, having spent at least one year in an oak cask and several months in the bottle; *reservas* are vintages that have been aged for three years with at least one year in the oak; and *gran reservas* have spent at least two years in oak casks and three years in the bottle. Good years to look out for include '75,'78,'81,'82,'91,'94 and '95.

The most convenient **place to buy** your wine is at Mi Bodega, c/Santo Tomás 13 (just off the Plaza de la Paz), whose dark cellars stock a vast range of wines at *bodega* prices; a similar outlet is El Rincón de Quintín near the bus station. You can expect to buy decent *crianzas* from around 500ptas and *reservas* from around 800ptas. The *bodegas* themselves, most of which are down by the train station, are reluctant to open their doors unless you're with a group; your best bet is to try to get on a tour organized by the Turismo or ask at the campsite (see p.362) about getting one together. Failing this, try hanging around the gates looking interested but not too thirsty. Among the most famous *bodegas* are Bodegas Bilbaínas, CVNE (pronounced Cune), and Muga. If you want to find out more about how the wine's produced, the high-tech **Museo del Vino** (Tues–Sat 10am–2pm; 300ptas, free Wed), in the Estación Erológico on c/Breton de los Herreros, behind the bus station, has detailed and highly complicated displays of the processes involved, but no tastings.

Haro

The main centre of Rioja production is **HARO**, an attractive, working town, 40km northwest of Logroño. In addition to **wine tasting** possibilities, it has some lovely reminders of a grand past, notably the Renaissance church of **San Tomás**, an imposing sight on any approach to town, with its wedding-cake tower. The old quarter around it is attractive in a low-key, faded kind of way, its lower margins marked by the **Plaza de la Paz**, a glass-balconied square whose mansions overlook an archaic bandstand.

The best time to be in Haro is in the last week of June, during the fiestas of San Juan, San Felices and San Pedro. All the *bodegas* bring their wares to the main square for tastings and bargain buys; there are free outdoor concerts, and you'll see parades through the streets of elaborately costumed characters on giant stilts. The climax of these fiestas is the riotous *batalla del vino* on June 29, when thousands of people climb the Riscos de Bilibio (a small mountain near the town) to be drenched from head to foot in wine; if this annual ritual does not take place, the Riscos will by law be passed to the jurisdiction of Miranda de Ebro.

Practicalities

Haro's **train station** is some distance out of town; to get to the centre, walk down the hill to the main road, turn right and when you reach the bridge (campsite off to the right), cross it and head straight uphill. **Buses** stop in Plaza Castañares, a ten-minute walk from the centre (follow signs for *centro* straight up c/la Ventilla). The **Turismo** is on Plaza M. Florentino Rodríguez (Mon–Sat 10am–2pm & 4.30–7.30pm, Sun 10am–2pm; ☎941 303366).

There's plenty of budget **accommodation** in town: *Pensión la Peña*, Plaza de la Paz 17, 2° (☎941 310022; ③), has spotless rooms, most of them with a balcony overlooking the plaza, and you'll find more modern (though smaller) rooms attached to *Bar-Restaurante Vega*, Plaza Juan García Gatio 1 (☎941 312205; ③). *El Maño*, Avda. de la Rioja 27 (☎941

310229; ④), is very comfortable, but if it's luxury you're after, head for *Los Agostinos*, a superb hotel in a converted Augustinian monastery, c/San Agustín 2 (☎941 311308, fax 941 303148; ⑦). There's also an excellent **campsite** (☎941 312737; open all year), down by the river below town with a bar and swimming (in the river or pool) nearby.

Even the humblest *menú del día* in town is transformed by a bottle of Rioja, and you'll get more wine – and very cheaply – in the many good **bars** that lie between the *Ayuntamiento* and the church of San Tomás. Best of the **restaurants** are *Beethoven*, c/San Tomás 5 (☎941 311181; closed Mon night, Thurs, July 1–15 & Dec), and *Terete*, c/General Franco 26 (☎941 310023; closed Sun night & Mon); prices at both are mid-range and the cooking is serious.

The pilgrim route west from Logroño

From Logroño, the **Camino de Santiago** heads through Santo Domingo de la Calzada and out across northern Castile – a long, straight trek to Burgos, León and Astorga – before heading over the mountains into Galicia.

Nájera

The first town of note west of Logroño is **NÁJERA**, which is dramatically situated below a pink rock formation, and has an interesting Gothic monastery, **Santa María la Real** (daily 9.30am–12.30pm & 4–7.30pm; 100ptas). This contains a royal pantheon of ancient monarchs of Castile, León and Navarra – a host of sarcophagi and statues, some of which seem to have been made long after the death of the sitter. Best of all is the cloister of rose-coloured stone and elaborate tracery, closer to the Manueline style of Portugal than anything in Spain. There is nothing more to detain you, but the town caters for modern pilgrims with several cheap restaurants, a **hostal**, *San Fernando* (☎941 363700, fax 941 363399; ⑤), and a *fonda*.

Santo Domingo de la Calzada

SANTO DOMINGO DE LA CALZADA, 46km west of Logroño, owes its very existence to the pilgrimage. It takes its name from a saint who settled here in the eleventh century and devoted his life to assisting travellers by paving roads, tending the sick, and engineering bridges (hence *Calzada*, or causeway).

These days it's a dull, unattractive place for the most part, though the saint's **causeway** survives at the end of town, on the Burgos road. His tomb lies in the crypt of the **Catedral** (Mon–Sat 10am–6.30pm; 250ptas), whose detached Baroque tower looms above everything in the centre of town. Santo Domingo was once a fortified town (fragments of the walls can still be seen) and the cathedral's massive west porch used to serve as a fortress. The interior is strongly evocative of what a medieval cathedral must have looked like, with a *coro*, tombs, *rejas* – and a pair of caged chickens.

These are kept in celebration of the local version of a legend popular throughout Spain and Portugal. A young German pilgrim is said to have resisted the advances of an innkeeper's daughter who "wolde have had hym to medyll with her carnally". She retaliated by falsely accusing him of theft, for which offence he was summarily strung up on the gallows. There he was kept alive by the miraculous intervention of Santo Domingo, to the disbelief of the local judge who was busily munching on a roast. "He's as dead as those chickens," claimed the judge, whereupon the birds crowed their disagreement and flew off the table.

Beside the cathedral stands a **pilgrims' hospice**, now converted to a *parador* (see below), and a handful of fine Renaissance **mansions**.

Practicalities

There's a **Turismo** at the Casa de Cultura, c/Mayor 70 (July–Sept Mon–Sat 10am–2pm & 4.30–7.30pm, Sun 10am–2pm; ☎941 341230). By far the best budget **accommodation** is offered by *Bar Albert*, Plaza Harmosilla 6, behind the bus stop (☎941 340827; ②). Alternatives include *Hostal Río* at c/Etchegoyen 2 (☎941 340085; ③), the large and comfortable *Hostal Santa Teresita* at c/Pinar 2 (☎941 340700, fax 941 343304; ④), and the fabulous *parador* on Plaza del Santo, next to the cathedral (☎941 340300, fax 340325; ⑦). For **meals**, *Bar Albert*, and *El Vasco* at Avda. Rey Juan Carlos 17, offer good inexpensive *menús*. *Mumm*, at c/Madrid 5, is a pleasant *mesón* with a summer terraza; next door is the *Discoteca Royal* and opposite, *Liv*, the town's two main **nightspots**. **Buses** run to Burgos five times a day, or you can head north to the Basque provinces and the coast.

Burgos

BURGOS was for some five hundred years the capital of Old Castile and with its dark-stone old town and castle it remains redolent of these years of power and military strength. It has historic associations as the home of El Cid, in the eleventh century, and as the base two centuries later of Fernando el Santo (Fernando III), the reconqueror of Murcia, Córdoba and Sevilla. It was Fernando who began the city's famous Gothic **cathedral**, one of the greatest in all Spain, though it, too, seems to share in the solemnity and severity of the city's history.

To Spaniards, the city has more modern military connotations. A large military garrison has been stationed here virtually since the Civil War, when Franco temporarily installed his fascist government in the city. Burgos, in addition, owes much of its modern industry and expansion to Franco's "Industrial Development Plan", a strategy to shift the country's wealth away from Catalunya and the Basque country and into Castile. Even now, such connotations linger.

The most exciting times to be in Burgos are during **El Curpillos**, which takes place the day after the feast of Corpus Christi, and at the end of June for the two-week **Fiesta de San Pedro**, when *Gigantillos* parade in the streets, and bullfights and all-night parties take place.

Arrival, orientation and information

Orientation in Burgos could not be simpler, since wherever you are the cathedral makes its presence felt. The Río Arlanzón bisects the city and neatly delimits the old quarters. The main pedestrian bridge is the **Puente de Santa María**, nearest the cathedral and facing the gateway of the same name. On the "new side" of the river this bridge opens out into Plaza de Vega and c/de Madrid, which is the main area for bars, restaurants and *hostales*.

The **bus station** is right in the centre of the city at c/Miranda 4; the **train station** is a short walk away at the bottom of Avenida Conde Guadalhorre. The **Turismo** (Mon–Fri 9am–2pm & 5–7pm, Sat & Sun 10am–2pm & 5–8pm; ☎947 203125) is at Plaza de Alonso Martínez 7, around the side of the cathedral and up c/Laín Calvo; there's also a small regional office (Mon–Sat 10am–2pm & 5.30–8.30pm, Sun noon–2pm) on Asunción de Nuestra Senora, close to the cathedral.

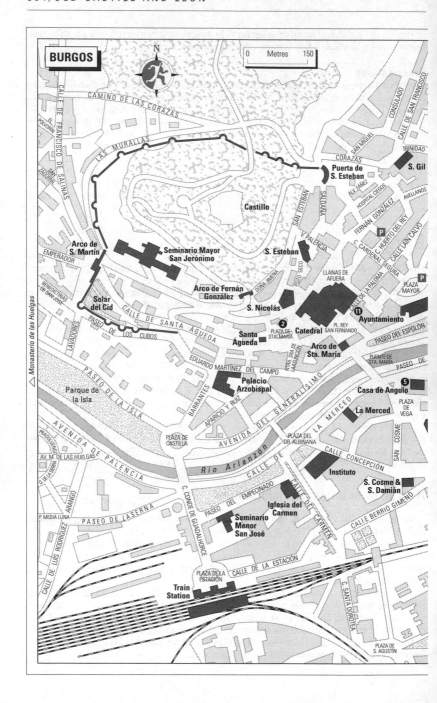

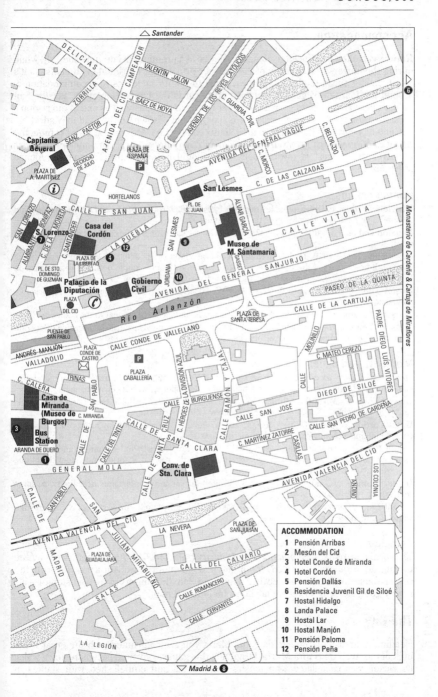

△ Santander

DELICIAS

ZORRILLA

VALENTIN JALÓN

J. SÁEZ DE HOYA

AVENIDA DEL CID CAMPEADOR

AVENIDA DE LOS REYES CATÓLICOS

C. GUARDIA CIVIL

SANZ PASTOR

Capitanía General

DIECIOCHO DE JULIO

PLAZA DE ESPAÑA
P

AVENIDA DEL GENERAL YAGÜE

C. MURPO

C. BELOR-IJO

PLAZA DE A. MARTÍNEZ
(i)

HORTELANOS

C. DE LAS CALZADAS

SAN LORENZO

ALMIRANTE BONIFAZ

C. DE LA MONEDA

C. DE SANTANDER

CALLE DE SAN JUAN

S. Lorenzo
(7)

Casa del Cordón
(12)

LA PUEBLA

PLAZA DE LA LIBERTAD
(4)

PL. DE S. JUAN

San Lesmes

SAN LESMES

ALVAR GARCÍA

CALLE VITORIA

(9)

Museo de M. Santamaría

GRASSET

PL. DE STO. DOMINGO DE GUZMÁN

Palacio de la Diputación

PLAZA DEL CID
(i)

Gobierno Civil

JORDANA

(10)

AVENIDA DEL GENERAL SANJURJO

PASEO DE LA QUINTA

Río Arlanzón

PLAZA DE SANTA TERESA

CALLE DE LA CARTUJA

PUENTE DE SAN PABLO

ANDRÉS MANJÓN

PLAZA CONDE DE CASTRO

CALLE CONDE DE VALLELLANO

MOLINILLO

PADRE DIEGO LUIS VITORES

VALLADOLID

TRINAS

P

PLAZA CABALLERÍA

C. MATEO CEREZO

C. CALERA

SAN PABLO

CALLE DE LA DIVISIÓN AZUL

C. HÉROES DE

CALLE RAMÓN Y CAJAL

DIEGO DE SILOÉ

Casa de Miranda (Museo de Burgos)

C. MIRANDA

CALLE DE SANTA CRUZ

BURGUENSE

CALLE SAN JOSÉ

CALLE SAN PEDRO DE CARDEÑA

(3)

Bus Station

ARANDA DE DUERO
(1)

CALLE DE

CALLE DEL TINTE

CALLE DE SANTA CLARA

C. MARTÍNEZ ZATORRE

CASILLAS

GENERAL MOLA

Conv. de Sta. Clara

AVENIDA VALENCIA DEL CID

LOS COLONIA

ANDINO

CALLE DE

SAN PABLO

SAN

JULIÁN MIRABUENO

AVENIDA VALENCIA DEL CID

LA NEVERA

PLAZA DE SAN JULIÁN

MADRID

PLAZA DE GUADALAJARA

CALLE DEL CALVARIO

SALAS

CALLE ROMANCERO

CALLE CERVANTES

LA LEGIÓN

ACCOMMODATION

1 Pensión Arribas
2 Mesón del Cid
3 Hotel Conde de Miranda
4 Hotel Cordón
5 Pensión Dallás
6 Residencia Juvenil Gil de Siloé
7 Hostal Hidalgo
8 Landa Palace
9 Hostal Lar
10 Hostal Manjón
11 Pensión Paloma
12 Pensión Peña

▷ Monasterio de Cardeña & Cartuja de Miraflores

▽ Madrid & (8)

Accommodation

Rooms can often be difficult to come by; they're at a premium in late June and July, while during the university year many of the cheaper *pensiones* are brimful of students, so it's worth calling ahead to check. The best place to try for inexpensive accommodation is around the Plaza de Vega, and any road off towards the bus station as far as c/de San Pablo. There are plenty of smart, upmarket hotels in town, as well as one of the region's most luxurious and memorable places to stay just out of town on the road to Madrid.

Genuine pilgrims who can prove their status can obtain free rooms at a new **refuge**, the *Albergue Municipal de Peregrino*, in the Colegio San Lorenzo on Paseo Fuentecillas near the river to the west of town. Ideally, you should report to the Turismo on Alonso Martínez first.

Budget options

Pensión Arribas, c/Defensores de Oviedo 6 (☎947 266292). One of the city's lowest-priced and most reliable *pensiones*, situated near the bus station. ②.

Pensión Dallás, Plaza de Vega 6 (☎947 205457). Good-value rooms in this *pensión* right on the river front. ③.

Residencia Juvenil Gil de Siloé, Avda. de General Vigón (☎947 220362). Meals are available at this youth hostel. To get there, walk east along Avda. del General Yagüe until you reach Plaza de Bilbao; turn left and the hostel is about 10m farther up. Open July–Sept. ①.

Hostal Hidalgo, c/Almirante Bonifaz 14 (☎947 203481). Large, airy rooms with very friendly atmosphere. ③.

Pensión Paloma, c/Paloma 39 (☎947 276574). Warm and clean, bang next to the cathedral. ③.

Pensión Peña, c/Puebla 18 (☎947 206323). This welcoming, newly refurbished *pensión* offers outstanding value in a quiet, but central location. ②.

Moderate and expensive options

Mesón del Cid, Plaza de Santa María 8 (☎947 208715, fax 947 269460). Facing the cathedral, this is the top hotel in the centre of town in a handsome old building, with its own parking. ⑦.

Hotel Conde de Miranda, c/Miranda 4 (☎947 265267, fax 947 291028). Smart and comfortable rooms (if rather pricey), located conveniently above the bus station. ⑤.

Hotel Cordón, c/Puebla 6 (☎947 265000, fax 947 200269). A smart hotel in a beautiful, glass-balconied building, recently refurbished throughout. ⑥.

Landa Palace, Carretera Madrid–Irún (☎947 206343, fax 947 264676). A stunning and fabulously expensive hotel in a medieval tower, just out of town on the road to Madrid, complete with antique furnishings and a renowned restaurant. ⑧.

Hostal Manjón, c/Conde Jornada 1 (☎947 208689). Clean and comfortable, near the river; some rooms have private bath. ③–④.

Hostal Lar, c/Cardenal Benlloch 1 (☎947 209655). Friendly, family-run *hostal*; all rooms en suite with TV and phone. ④.

Camping

The local **campsite**, *Camping Fuentes Blancas* (☎947 486016; April–Sept) is out by the Cartuja de Miraflores (see p.369 for directions), 45 minutes' walk or a bus ride from the centre (buses once an hour between 11am and 9pm, leaving from the Cid statue) – it's a very good site with excellent facilities, including a pool.

The City

Heading in across the Puente de Santa María you are confronted with the great white bulk of the **Arco de Santa María**. Originally this gateway formed part of the town walls; its facade was castellated with towers and turrets and embellished with statues in

1534–36 in order to appease the wrath of Carlos V after Burgos's involvement in a revolt by Spanish noblemen against their new Belgian-born king. Carlos's statue is glorified here in the context of the greatest Burgalese heroes: Diego Porcelos, founder of the city in the late ninth century; Nuño Rasura and Laín Calvo, two early magistrates; Fernán González, founder of the Countship of Castile in 932; and **El Cid Campeador**, who was surpassed only by Santiago *Matamoros* in his exploits against the Moors. El Cid was born Rodrigo Díaz in the village of Vivar, just north of Burgos, though his most significant military exploits actually took place around Valencia; *Cid*, incidentally, derives from the Arabic *sidi* (lord), and *Campeador* means "supreme in valour". There's a splendid **equestrian statue** of him – with flying cloak, flowing beard and raised sword – lording over the **Puente de San Pablo**, the main road-bridge to the old town. The statue, one of the city's principal landmarks, stands at the end of the **Paseo del Espolón**, a fashionable tree-lined promenade round which most of the evening life takes place.

The cathedral

The old quarters of Burgos are totally dominated by the **Catedral** (daily 9.30am–1pm & 4–7pm), whose "wild and slightly mad roof-line" does indeed (as Mullins observed) "seem to hang by invisible threads above the city". Its florid filigree of spires and pinnacles is among the most extraordinary achievements of Gothic art; however, the building is such a large complex of varied and opulent sections that it's difficult to appreciate it as a whole. It is the sheer accumulation of masterpieces – both inside and out – that impresses. Burgos has outstanding individual achievements in ironwork, wood carving and sculpture, and almost every entrance and chapel seems to be of interest. Oddly enough, the most ornate entrance of all, the **Puerta de la Pellejería** at the northeast corner, is in a Renaissance-Plateresque style, quite different from the bulk of the exterior. The cathedral is currently undergoing extensive renovation and, unfortunately, much of the facade is covered by scaffolding. The main entrance is on the southern side, facing the river.

THE CHAPELS

Inside the cathedral you're immediately struck by the size and number of side chapels, the greatest of which, the **Capilla del Condestable**, is almost a cathedral in itself. The most curious, though, is the **Capilla del Santo Cristo** (first right) which contains what must be one of the most bizarre and mystical icons in Christendom. This is the *Cristo de Burgos*, a cloyingly realistic image of Christ (c. 1300), endowed with real human hair and nails and covered with the withered hide of a water buffalo, still popularly believed to be human skin. Legend has it that the icon was modelled directly from the Crucifixion and that it requires a shave and a manicure every eighth day.

The adjacent **Capilla de la Consolación** has a distinctive, early sixteenth-century star-shaped vault – a form adapted from the Moorish "honeycomb" vaults of Granada. Similar influences can also be seen in the cathedral's central dome (1568), highlighted with gold and blue and supported on four thick piers which fan out into remarkably delicate buttresses – a worthy setting for the **tomb of El Cid**, marked by a simple slab in the floor below.

The sumptuous, octagonal **Capilla del Condestable**, behind the high altar, contains a third superb example of star-vaulting. Here the ceiling is designed to form two eight-pointed stars, one within the other. The chapel, with its profusion of stone tracery, was founded in 1482 by Fernández de Velasco, Constable of Castile, whose marble tomb lies before the altar; the architect was the German Simón de Colonia. Between 1442 and 1458 his father Hans (Hispanicized as Juan) had built the twin openwork spires of the west facade, possibly modelling them on the spires planned for the cathedral in his home city of Cologne. In the third generation, Francisco de Colonia built the central dome and the Puerta de la Pellejería. Another father-and-son combination of artists was that of Gil and Diego de Siloé, the former from Flanders but his son born and raised in Spain. Gil worked on the *retablo* in the Capilla de Santa Ana (second left), while Diego's masterpiece, one of the crowning achievements of the cathedral, is the glorious **Escalera Dorada**, a double stairway in the north transept. To get into some of these smaller chapels you'll have to buy a Treasury ticket (400ptas), which also admits you to the cloisters, the Diocesan museum inside them, and the **Coro** at the heart of the cathedral, which affords the best view into the dome.

San Nicolás and San Esteban

Overlooking the plaza in front of the cathedral stands the fifteenth-century church of **San Nicolás**. Unassuming from the outside, it has an altarpiece within by Francisco de Colonia, which is as rich as anything in the city. At the side of San Nicolás, c/Pozo Seco ascends to the early Gothic church of **San Esteban**, which is now a museum.

Monasterio de las Huelgas and the Cartuja de Miraflores

Inevitably the lesser churches of Burgos tend to be eclipsed by the cathedral, but on the outskirts are two monasteries which are by no means overshadowed. The closer, the Cistercian **Monasterio de las Huelgas** (April–Sept Tues–Sat 10.30am–1.15pm & 3.30–5.45pm, Sun 10.30am–2.15pm; Oct–March Tues–Sat 11am–1.15pm & 4–5.45pm, Sun 10.30am–2.15pm; 650ptas, free Wed), is remarkable for its wealth of Mudéjar craftsmanship. It lies on the "new side" of the river, a twenty-minute walk from the city centre: cross Puente de Santa María, turn right and follow the signs along the riverbank. Founded in 1187 as the future mausoleum of Alfonso VIII and Eleanor of Aquitaine, daughter of Henry II of England, it became one of the most highbrow and powerful convents in Spain. It was popularly observed that "if the Pope were to marry, only the Abbess of Las Huelgas would be eligible!" The main **church**, with its typically excessive Churrigueresque *retablo*, contains the tombs of no fewer than sixteen Castilian monarchs and nobles. That of the Infanta Blanca (died 1325), daughter of Afonso III of Portugal, is vigorously carved with heraldic insignia surrounded by Moorish borders. Priceless embroidery, jewellery and weaponry of a suitably regal splendour were discovered inside the tombs and are exhibited in a small museum.

The highlight of the convent is its Mudéjar-Gothic **cloister**. Here again are the familiar eight-pointed stars, along with rare peacock designs – a bird holy to the Moors. The **Capilla de Santiago**, an obvious reminder that Las Huelgas stood on the pilgrim route, also has a fine Mudéjar ceiling and pointed horseshoe archway. Its cult statue of Saint James has an articulated right arm, which enabled him to dub Knights of the Order of Santiago (motto: "The Sword is Red with the Blood of Islam") and on occasion even to crown kings. At the other end of the pilgrim scale the convent was responsible for the nearby Hospital del Rey where food and shelter were provided free for two nights. It is presently in a very bad state of neglect, although the portals merit a visit.

The **Cartuja de Miraflores** (Mon–Sat 10.15am–3pm & 4–6pm, Sun 11.20am–12.30pm, 1–3pm & 4–6pm; free) is famous for three dazzling masterpieces by Gil de Siloé. The buildings are still in use as a monastery and most are closed – you can, however, visit the **church**, built between 1454 and 1488 by Juan and Simón de Colonia. In accordance with Carthusian practice, it is divided into three sections for the public, the lay brothers and the monks. In front of the high altar lies the star-shaped joint tomb of Juan II and Isabella of Portugal, of such perfection in design and execution that it forced Felipe II and Juan de Herrera to admit "we did not achieve very much with our Escorial". Isabella la Católica, a great patron of the arts, commissioned it from Gil de

Siloé in 1489 as a memorial to her parents. The same sculptor carved the magnificent altarpiece, which was plated with the first gold shipped back from America. His third masterpiece is the tomb of the Infante Alfonso, through whose untimely death in 1468 Isabella had succeeded to the throne of Castile.

Miraflores lies in a secluded spot about 4km from the centre: turn left from the Puente de Santa María along c/de Valladolid, from where the *Cartuja* is well signposted. There's a good restaurant in the nearby park. A bus runs on Sunday but returns right after the well-attended Mass; there's also a bus to the nearby campsite (see p.366).

Eating, drinking and nightlife

You'll find plenty of **restaurants** in Burgos serving the traditional dishes, *cordero asado* (roast lamb) and *morcilla* (a kind of black pudding with rice), but there's also a wide choice of other food, and, due to the large student population, a lively **bar** scene.

Restaurants, cafés and tapas bars

Café-bar Luz, Plaza de Vega 3. Lovely café with a summer terraza where you can sample *chocolate con bizcochos* and other goodies while you watch the world go by.

Casa Ojeda, c/Vitoria 5. A good choice, however deep your pocket, with a smart restaurant upstairs, a less expensive *comedor* downstairs, or *tapas* at the bar.

Gaona, c/Virgen de la Paloma. A more formal and upmarket Spanish restaurant, very close to the cathedral.

Marisquería Bringas, c/Laín Calvo 50. Very good fish restaurant when you're fed up with *asados* and Castilian cuisine.

Mesón el Avellano, c/Avellanos. One of several excellent *tapas* bars along this lively street.

Prego, c/Huerto del Rey. Reasonably priced Italian eatery.

Nightlife

There's a lively atmosphere in the city's bars and cafés, particularly at weekends. Nightlife depends on the time of night – the action progresses from the **bars** on c/San Juan, c/Laín Calvo, c/Huerto del Rey and c/San Lorenzo in the early evening, to the pedestrianized area at the foot of the cathedral from around 10pm onwards. Here, try *El Oliver* or *Casco Viejo*, which also serves great *tapas*, in c/Llanas de Afuera; in c/Llanas de Adentro (a small courtyard reached via the passage next to *Casco Viejo*), there's *El Rincón*, *Espadería* and *La Nuit*. After 3am, head for the **clubs** in the new district of Bernardos round c/Las Calzadas and Avenida General Yagüe. Most places play loud rock and dated heavy metal but two places with a more relaxed atmosphere and soothing jazz music are *Café La Cabala*, c/Puebla 7, and – back towards the cathedral – *Café de España*, at c/Laín Calvo 12.

Listings

Bus information ☎947 265565.

Car rental Operators include Díaz Espartosa, Avda. General Vigón 52 (☎947 223803); Europcar, c/Santa Clara 32 (☎947 273745); and Hertz, c/General Mola 5 (☎947 201675).

Laundry Lavasec, Plaza Santiago 4, has self-service facilities.

Post office The main office is at Plaza de Conde de Castro, by the Puente San Pablo.

Taxis Autotaxi (☎947 277777) and Radio Taxi (☎947 481010) both offer a 24-hour service.

Train information ☎947 203560.

Southeast of Burgos

Southeast of Burgos, off the road to Soria, are a trio of sights: the town of **Covarrubias**, a medieval treasure on the Río Arlanza; the great monastery of **Santo Domingo de Silos**; and, at **Quintanilla de las Viñas**, a tiny Visigothic church and hermitage.These are easy excursions if you have transport. If you don't, you'll need commitment and time to get the daily (5pm) bus from Burgos to Silos, via Lerma. Pilgrims, of course, used to (and still do) walk to Silos as a detour from the *camino*.

Santo Domingo de Silos

The Benedictine abbey of **SANTO DOMINGO DE SILOS** is one of Spain's greatest Christian monuments. Its main feature is a great double-storey eleventh-century **Romanesque cloister** (Mon–Sat 10am–1pm & 4–7pm, Sun noon–1pm & 4–7pm; 250ptas) whose beautiful sculptural decoration is in many ways unique. The most remarkable features of the cloister are eight almost life-sized **reliefs** on the corner pillars. They include *Christ on the Road to Emmaus*, dressed as a pilgrim to Santiago (complete with scallop shell), a detail that shows that pilgrims made a detour from the route to see the tomb of Santo Domingo, the eleventh-century abbot after whom the monastery is named.

The same sculptor was responsible for about half of the **capitals**. Besides a famous bestiary, these include many Moorish motifs, giving rise to speculation that he may even have been a Moor. Whatever the case, it is an early example of the effective mix of Arab and Christian cultures, which was continued in the fourteenth century with the painted Mudéjar vault showing scenes of everyday pastimes. A quite different sculptor carved many of the remaining capitals, including the two that ingeniously tell the stories of the Nativity and the Passion in a very restricted space. A third master was responsible for the pillar with the Annunciation and Tree of Jesse, which is almost Gothic in spirit.

Visits to the monastery also include entry to the eighteenth-century **pharmacy**, which has been reconstructed in a room off the cloister, and the **museum**, which houses the tympanum from the destroyed Romanesque church.

The **church** itself is an anticlimax, a rather nondescript construction designed by the eighteenth-century academic architect Ventura Rodríguez. Its Romanesque predecessor was too dark for the taste of the times; fortunately, the cloister's size and spaciousness saved it from a similar fate. The monks are considered one of the two or three best choirs in the world, and it's particularly worth attending the morning Mass (9am) or even better, vespers, which currently start at 7pm.

Staying at Silos

Men can **stay** in the monastery itself (☎947 380768), if they contact the Guest Master (*Padre Hospedería*) in advance; he prefers people to stay a few days. This is a wonderful bargain, with comfortable single rooms and good food at a ridiculously low cost (2095ptas per night). There are also some excellent places to stay in the village: the recently upgraded *Hotel Arco de San Juan* in the Pradera de San Juan (☎947 390074, fax 947 390074; ⑤), very near the cloister entrance, which has a lovely garden; the new, clean and well-furnished *Hostal Cruces* in the Plaza Mayor (☎947 390064; ④), which has an informative, English-speaking manager and serves good-value evening meals; and the *Hotel Tres Coronas de Silos*, Plaza Mayor 6 (☎947 390047, fax 947 390065; ⑥), an imposing stone house which dominates the square.

THE GREGORIAN CHANTS OF SANTO DOMINGO

In 1994, the monks of Santo Domingo de Silos made rock and roll history when their album of **Gregorian chants**, *Canto Gregoriano*, became a huge Christmas hit, selling over six million copies. The Benedictine brothers had been making low-key recordings for years; it wasn't until EMI had them digitally remastered and glossily packaged that the monks achieved pop-star status. Almost overnight, the brothers found themselves at the centre of a media frenzy, with thousands of visitors and paparazzi swarming into the monastery to get a look at the singing monks. The success story had a sour edge: *Canto* was used in discos, and, more disturbingly, in porn movies; punters were urged to buy tacky, monk-style T-shirts (which were brown instead of Benedictine black); and the follow-up album, *Canto Noel*, intended by EMI as another yuletide hit, actually contained chants from the Easter liturgy. Nevertheless, the releases continue, tourists still flock in, and the Gregorian chant is now firmly established in the imagination of the record-buying public (in 1996 monks of Glenstal Abbey in Ireland topped the Irish charts). Whether Silos will be able to keep up with the new competition is another matter; recruits are low and the average age is steadily climbing. But while the brothers' vocal chords may rust, their numerous gold discs are destined to hang brightly in their sophisticated music room for many years to come.

The gorges of Yecla

The landscape around Silos is some of the most varied in Castile. A short walk up the hill gives a superb bird's-eye view of the village and the surrounding countryside and a couple of kilometres away are the impressive **gorges of Yecla**.

To reach these, take the road to Burgos, heading west of Silos, and turn left at the first road you come to, shortly after leaving the village. You cross two rivers in quick succession, the Mataviejas and the Yecla. A few hundred metres later, a path off to the left leads through an incredibly narrow rocky gorge – the **Desfiladero de la Yecla** – which was impassable until a series of wooden walkways and plank bridges was built in the 1930s. It makes a spectacular hike, with the birds of prey circling high in the thin strip of visible sky.

If you continue west from the gorge rather than heading straight back to Silos, you can climb to the picturesque hill-top village of **Hinojar de Cervera**, and descend on the far side, after a couple of kilometres, to the **Cueva de San García**. This is a small cave containing various faded and rudimentary specimens of prehistoric art.

Covarrubias

The superbly preserved small town of **COVARRUBIAS** is just under 20km north of Silos, on the C110 between Lerma and the Burgos–Soria road. The main sight is the town itself: many of its white houses are half-timbered, with shady arcades, and remnants of the fortifications are still standing, including a tenth-century tower. The **Colegiata** (Mon & Wed–Sun 10.30am–2pm & 4–7pm; 250ptas) looks plain from the outside, but a visit to the interior is a must. Inside you'll find a late Gothic hall church crammed with tombs, giving an idea of the grandeur of the town in earlier times. The organ is an amazing seventeenth-century instrument still in good working order; you'll probably have to be content with hearing a recording. There are several good paintings in the museum, but the chief attraction is a triptych whose central section, a polychromed carving of the *Adoration of the Magi*, is attributed to Gil de Siloé.

Public **transport** is limited: there's no bus service between Covarrubias and Silos, although it is just possible to see both towns in a day on foot – the alternative is to come direct on the single daily bus from Burgos. If you plan to stay in Covarrubias, bear in mind that apart from the expensive (but excellent) *Hotel Arlanza*, Plaza Mayor 11 (☎947 406441, fax 947 406359; ⑥), the only other place to stay is above the restaurant *Casa Galín* (☎947 406552; ③), which is also the best place to **eat** in the village.

Quintanilla

An equally important monument, this time a rare Visigothic survival, is to be found at **QUINTANILLA DE LAS VIÑAS**, which lies 4km north of Mazanriegos on the main Burgos–Soria road, about 40km southeast of Burgos. Signs labelled *Turismo* lead to a house where the caretaker of the **Ermita de Santa María** lives; if he isn't there, he'll probably be at the hermitage itself, 1km farther north. It's a simple building, of which only the transept and the chancel survive. Dating from about 700, it's remarkable for its unique series of sculptures: the outside bears delicately carved friezes, and inside there's a triumphal arch with capitals representing the sun and moon, and a block which is believed to be the earliest representation of Christ in Spanish art.

Burgos to León

The pilgrim route west from Burgos to León is one of the most rewarding sections in terms of art and architecture. The N120 between the two cities passes through **Carrión de los Condes** and **Sahagún**, and the other stops on the *camino* are only a short detour off the main road.

Frómista

FRÓMISTA was the next important pilgrimage stop after Burgos. The present-day town is much decayed, with a fraction of the population it once had. There's only one sight of any note – the extremely beautiful church of **San Martín**, which was originally part of an abbey which no longer exists, and is now deconsecrated (daily 10am–2pm & 4.30–8pm, winter 10am–2pm & 3–6.30pm; free). Carved representations of monsters, human figures and animals run right around the church, which was built in 1066 in a Romanesque style unusually pure for Spain, with no traces of later additions. In fact, what you can see now is a result of a turn-of-the-century restoration which was perhaps rather too thorough, although it is pleasing to the eye. Its beauty is enhanced by being completely devoid of furnishings; there's nothing to detract from the architecture, and the only colour is provided by twin wooden statues of San Martín and Santiago. The other church associated with the pilgrimage, **Santa María**, is near the train station, but it is also redundant and is kept locked.

If you want to **stay** there are two comfortable places, *Pensión Camino de Santiago* (☎988 810053; ③) on the square on the road north to Santander, and *Pensión Marisa* (☎988 810023; ③), behind San Martín. The latter does a discreet and very popular lunchtime *menú*. The *Hostería de Los Palmeros*, Plaza Mayor (☎988 810067), is a former medieval pilgrims' *hostal* now converted into an excellent restaurant. The **Turismo** (daily in summer 10am–2pm & 4.30–8pm; ☎979 810113) is at the crossroads in the centre of town where the **buses** stop. Frómista is connected with Burgos by a daily bus, although it's reached more easily from Palencia since it lies on the Palencia–Santander rail line.

Villalcázar de Sirga

Thirteen kilometres from Frómista lies **VILLALCÁZAR DE SIRGA**, notable for a **church** built by the Knights Templar: from a distance it seems to crush the little village by its sheer mass, and originally its fortified aspect was even more marked. The Gothic style here begins to assert itself over the Romanesque, as witnessed by the figure sculpture on the two portals and the elegant pointed arches inside. The **Capilla de Santiago** has three polychromed tombs, among the finest of their kind and contemporary with the building. If the church is closed, as it usually is, take the street to the left in front of it and turn left at the corner; the sexton's house is the first brick building on the right.

In the square itself are a few medieval houses, one of which has been converted into the excellent **restaurant**, *El Mesón de Villasirga*. There is no accommodation, however, and Villalcázar is probably best seen as a day's excursion from Carrión de los Condes, 5km away.

Carrión de los Condes

The dusty, quiet atmosphere of **CARRIÓN DE LOS CONDES** belies its sensational past. It's reputed to be the place where, before the Reconquest, Christians had to surrender one hundred virgins annually to the Moorish overlords – a scene depicted on the portal of **Santa María** (situated at the edge of town, where the buses stop). For fine sculpture, however, look at the doorway of **Santiago's** own church in the centre of town, overlooking the Plaza Mayor. Time has not treated this kindly – burned out during the last century, the church was rebuilt but now stands disused and neglected. The upper frieze reveals a debt to classical art, but the extraordinarily delicate covings above the door, which depict the trades and professions of the Middle Ages, are finer. The town's third main monument is the Plateresque cloister of the **Monasterio de San Zoilo**, located over the sixteenth-century bridge; a side room off the cloister contains the tombs of the counts of Carrión, from whom the town's name comes. The nuns of **Santa Clara** have opened a small **museum** (April–Sept Tues–Sun 10.30am–12.30pm & 5–7pm; Oct–March Tues–Sun 10.30am–12.30pm & 4–6pm, closed Oct 15–Nov 15) with a moderately interesting collection, including one of Spain's oldest organs. Their main work of art, however, the theatrical *Pietà* by Gregorio Fernández, is kept in the church, which is open only for the early-morning Mass.

For **accommodation**, *Hostal La Corte* at c/Santa María 34 (☎979 880138; ③) in Carrión is good value, and boasts an excellent cheap **restaurant**. Another restaurant, *El Resbalón*, c/Marqués de Santillana, also offers rooms (☎979 880433; ②), though they have seen better days. By far the most atmospheric place to stay is at the splendid *Hotel Real Monasterio San Zoilo* (☎979 880049, fax 979 881090; ⑤), recently converted from part of the monastery. There's plenty of room for unofficial **camping** down by the river, or in the shady and modern official campsite, *El Edén* (☎979 881152), also by the river and back from the main road. Carrión is linked by **bus** to both Burgos and Palencia.

Sahagún and San Miguel de Escalada

From Carrión the route west continues to **Sahagún**. No other town so clearly illustrates the effect of the decline from the heyday of the pilgrimage. Once the seat of the most powerful monastery in all Spain, it's now a largely modern town, above which the towers of the remaining old buildings rear up like dinosaurs in a zoo. The nearby monastery at **San Miguel de Escalada** has similarly slipped into insignificance.

Sahagún

SAHAGÚN is generally thought to be the birthplace of the brick churches built by the Moorish craftsmen who stayed on to work for the Christians after the Reconquest. Unfortunately, the great monastery these days is little more than a memory, and its main surviving sections – the gateway and belfry – date from a period of reconstruction in the seventeenth century. However, the twelfth-century parish churches of **San Tirso** and **San Lorenzo** remain, each with a noble tower. San Lorenzo has the most imposing exterior, but the inside has been completely transformed, and is open only for Mass at the weekend. The town's guide is based at San Tirso, where work has begun on the long-term project of removing the whitewash and returning the place to its original form (April–Sept Tues–Sat 10.30am–1.30pm & 5–8pm, Sun 10am–3pm; Oct–March Tues–Sat 10.30am–1.30pm & 4–7pm, Sun 10.30am–1.30pm). The guide will also show you **La Peregrina**, up the hill from San Tirso, a thirteenth-century monastery built by Mudéjars – it's in a shocking state of disrepair, but a beautiful little chapel with stucco work has been restored.

Finally, you should see the little **museum** in the **Monasterio Santa Cruz** (daily 10.30am–12.30pm & 4–6.30pm), through the archway from San Tirso; the nuns here have inherited the great *custodia* made by Enrique de Arfe, founder of a dynasty of silversmiths. Its big sister is the famous one at Toledo; like that one, the only airing it gets is during the Corpus Christi celebrations. The nuns prefer to open up to groups but try anyway if you're on your own – many pilgrims pass by here to get the official stamp for their *Camino de Santiago* card.

Sahagún has plentiful low-priced **accommodation**. Down by San Tirso there's the *Fonda Asturiana* (☎987 780073; ②), a building that would look more at home in Biarritz; up beyond the Plaza Mayor on Avenida de la Constitución, *Alfonso VI* (☎987 781144, fax 987 781258; ④) and, farther up, *La Cordoniz* (☎987 780276, fax 987 780186; ④) are modern and smart. Along here, *Hostal-Restaurante Don Pacho* (☎987 780775; ③) has good-value rooms and a nice **restaurant**.

Sahagún lies on the Palencia–León rail line. **Buses** leave from the Plaza Mayor but are very infrequent and many services have limited stops along this section of the pilgrim route. Buses from León to Carrión pass through Sahagún, but do not stop, nor issue tickets to here, so you will have to ask the driver specifically to drop you off.

San Miguel de Escalada

Although León is just a short distance farther on from Sahagún, the medieval pilgrim would probably first have made a slight detour to see the monastery of **SAN MIGUEL DE ESCALADA**, a precious Mozarabic survival from the tenth century. Founded by refugee monks from Córdoba, it's a touching little building, with a simple interior of horseshoe arches, and a later portico, again Moorish in style. Getting there by public transport, however, presents a problem; although there are two buses a day to and from León, one turns back thirty minutes after it arrives, while the other requires spending the night – and there's nowhere to stay.

León

Even if they stood alone, the stained glass in the cathedral of **LEÓN** and the Romanesque wall paintings in its Royal Pantheon would merit a very considerable journey, but there's much more to the city than this. For León is as attractive – and enjoyable – in its modern quarters as it is in those parts that remain from its heyday: a prosperous provincial capital and lively university town.

Arrival, orientation and information

León's modern sectors have been imaginatively laid out with wide, straight streets radiating like spokes from three focal plazas. The first of these is the **Glorieta de Guzmán el Bueno** near the river and the **train station**. Just south of here is the **bus station** on Paseo Ingeniero Miera.

From the Glorieta one can see straight down the Avenida de Ordoño II and across the **Plaza de Santo Domingo** to the towers of the cathedral. Just off the Plaza de Santo Domingo stands the **Casa de Botines**, an uncharacteristically restrained work by Antoni Gaudí. The third key square is the **Plaza de Calvo Sotelo**, connected to the Glorieta by the Avenida de Roma. Head straight up from Plaza de Santo Domingo to the cathedral and you'll arrive in the Plaza Regia; here, directly opposite the cathedral's great west facade, stands the main **Turismo** (Mon–Fri 9am–2pm & 5–7pm, Sat & Sun 10am–2pm & 5–8pm; ☎987 237082). León's old quarter lies to the south of the cathedral, occupying the streets around the Plaza Mayor and Plaza San Martin; it now seems a little shabby in the daytime, especially in comparison to the smart modern city centre.

Accommodation

Budget accommodation is scattered all over León; there's no particular concentration and you don't have to leave the main streets. Handiest for the train station (and for the free parking the length of Paseo de Papalaguinda) are the places along the Avenida de Roma. Rooms round the Plaza Mayor are less expensive but dingy and noisy, and often full of permanent residents – certainly not worth a long trail with heavy bags.

Budget options

Hostal Bayón, c/Alcázar de Toledo 6 (☎987 231446). Best budget accommodation in town: stripped pine floors, high ceilings, large windows, quiet rooms and firm beds throughout. ③.

Hostal Covadonga, Avda. de Palencia 2, 1° (☎987 222601). Adequate *hostal* in a lovely location, with parking opposite by the river. ③.

Hostal España, c/del Carmen 3 (☎987 236014). Good-value, clean *hostal*. ②.

Hostal Oviedo, Avda. de Roma 26 (☎987 222236). Good budget place near the train station. ②.

Pensión Puerta del Sol, c/Puerta del Sol 1 (☎987 211966). Reasonable rooms overlooking the attractive Plaza Mayor; about the only *pensión* here not permanently occupied by students. ②.

Fonda Roma, Avda. de Roma 4 (☎987 224663). Dark, old and inexpensive, run by a delightful old woman. ①.

Moderate and expensive options

Hostal Guzmán el Bueno, c/López Castrillón 6 (☎987 236412). Quiet rooms and handily placed near Palacio de los Guzmanes. ④.

Hostal Residencia Londres, Avda. de Roma 1 (☎987 222274). Spotless rooms (all with bathroom, TV and phone) with nice views; good value. ④.

Hostal Orejas, c/Villafranca 8 (☎987 252909). Comfortable rooms with bath and TV. ④.

Parador San Marcos, Plaza San Marcos 7 (☎987 237300, fax 987 233458). Has been described as the best hotel in the world, with antiques in the rooms. ⑧.

Hotel París, c/Generalísmo Franco 20 (☎987 238600, fax 987 271572). Modern rooms in a former palace close to the cathedral. ⑤.

The City

In 914, as the Reconquest edged its way south from Asturias, Ordoño II transferred the Christian capital from Oviedo to León. Despite being sacked by the dreaded al-Mansur

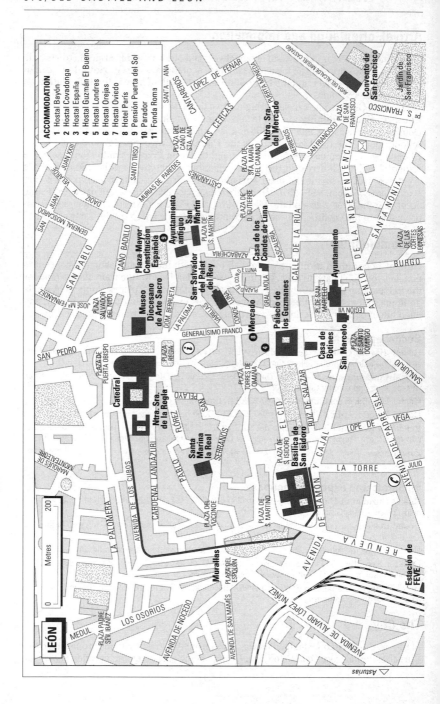

LEÓN

Metres
0   200

ACCOMMODATION
1 Hostal Bayón
2 Hostal Covadonga
3 Hostal España
4 Hostal Guzmán El Bueno
5 Hostal Londres
6 Hostal Orejas
7 Hostal Oviedo
8 Hotel París
9 Pensión Puerta del Sol
10 Parador
11 Fonda Roma

Convento de San Francisco

Jardín de San Francisco

Ntra. Sra. del Mercado

Ayuntamiento antiguo

San Martín

Plaza Mayor Constitución Española

Museo Diocesano de Arte Sacro

San Salvador del Palat del Rey

Casa de los Condes de Luna

Ayuntamiento

Mercado

Palacio de los Guzmanes

Casa de Botines

San Marcelo

Catedral

Ntra. Sra. de la Regla

Santa Marina la Real

Basílica de San Isidoro

Murallas

Estación de FEVE

△ *Asturias*

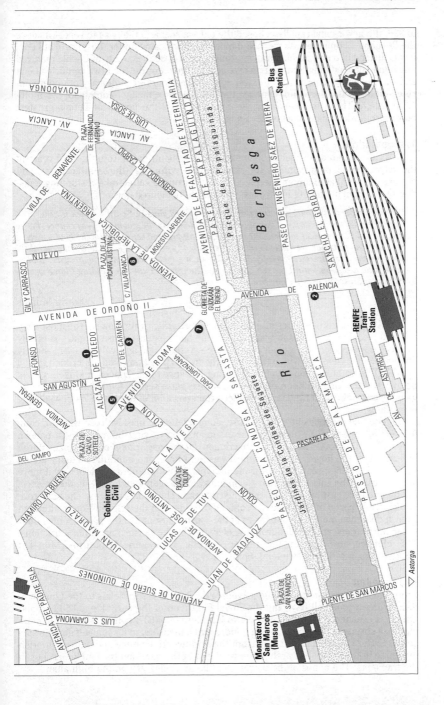

in 996, the new capital rapidly eclipsed the old – a scenario that was to repeat itself as the Reconquest unfolded. As more and more territory came under the control of León, it was divided into new administrative groupings: in 1035 the county of Castile matured into a fully fledged kingdom with its capital at Burgos. For the next two centuries León and Castile jointly spearheaded the war against the Moors – as often as not under joint rule – until, by the thirteenth century, Castile had come finally to dominate her mother kingdom. These two centuries were nevertheless the period of León's greatest power, from which date most of her finest monuments.

The cathedral

León's Gothic **Catedral** (daily 8.30am–2pm & 4–7.30pm) dates from the final years of the city's period of greatness. Its stained-glass **windows** (thirteenth-century and onwards) are equal to any masterpiece in any European cathedral – a stunning kaleidoscope of light streaming in through walls of multicoloured glass.

> *It is not simply that León Cathedral has the best stained glass in Spain – which it does: to enter the chill, twilit interior of this place and look round in the gloom until, by chance, the sun chooses that moment to come out is, I felt, to comprehend something of the hold which the Christian faith has been able to retain over so many people and for so long. In general, Spanish churches are exceptionally dark, and in my view exceptionally oppressive; and León is no exception – until the sun comes out. Then, more than any building I have ever set eyes on, it seems to burst into fire.*

> Edwin Mullins

As Edwin Mullins describes in *A Pilgrimage to Santiago*, this is one of the most magical and harmonious sights in Spain, and while such extensive use of glass is purely French in inspiration, the colours used here – reds, golds and yellows – are strictly Spanish. Other elements which take the cathedral farther away from its French model are the cloister (admission 300ptas, including entrance to the Diocesan Museum – see below) and the later addition of the *coro*, whose glass screen (added this century to give a clear view up to the altar) enhances the sensation of light with its bewildering refractions.

Outside, the magnificent **west facade**, dominated by a massive rose window, comprises two towers and a detached nave supported by flying buttresses – a pattern repeated at the south angle. The inscription *locus appelationis* on the main porch indicates that the Royal Court of Appeal was held here, and amid the statuary a king ponders his verdict, seated on a throne of lions. Above the **central doorway** a more sublime trial – the Last Judgement – is in full swing: angels weigh souls in the balance, the damned are cast into the fire and the righteous sing God's praises. The sculpture on this triple portal of the facade is some of the finest on the Pilgrim Route, although later in date than most. The doorways of the south transept and the polychromed door to the north transept (shielded from the elements by the cloister) are other attractions. The cloister now houses the rather eclectic **Diocesan Museum** (Mon–Sat 9.30am–1pm & 4–6.30pm, winter 4–6pm).

The Pantéon

From the Plaza de Santo Domingo, Avenida de Ramón y Cajal leads to the church of **San Isidoro** (open all day) and the Royal Pantheon of the early kings of León and Castile. Fernando I, who united the two kingdoms in 1037, commissioned the complex as a shrine for the bones of San Isidoro and a mausoleum for himself and his successors. The church dates mainly from the mid-twelfth century and shows Moorish influence in the horseshoe arch at the west end of the nave and the fanciful arches in the transepts. The bones of the patron saint lie in a reliquary on the high altar.

The **Pantéon** (July & Aug Mon–Sat 9am–2pm & 3–8pm, Sun 9am–2pm; Sept–June Tues–Sat 10am–1.30pm & 4–6.30pm, Sun 10am–1.30pm, closed Feb 1–15; 400ptas), comprising two surprisingly small crypt-like chambers, was constructed between 1054 and 1063 as a narthex or portico preceding the west facade of the church. It's one of the earliest Romanesque buildings in Spain, and the carvings on the portal which links the Pantéon and church herald the introduction of figure sculpture into the peninsula. In contrast, the capitals of the side piers and the two squat columns in the middle of the Pantéon are carved with thick foliage which is still rooted in Visigothic tradition. Towards the end of the twelfth century, the vaults were vividly covered in some of the most significant, imaginative and impressive paintings of Romanesque art. They are extraordinarily well preserved and their biblical and everyday themes are perfectly adapted to the architecture of the vaults. The central dome is occupied by Christ Pantocrator surrounded by the four Evangelists depicted with animal heads – allegorical portraits which stem from the apocalyptic visions in the Bible's Book of Revelation. One of the arches bordering the dome is decorated with quaint rustic scenes which represent the months of the year. Eleven kings and twelve queens were laid to rest here but the chapel was desecrated during the Peninsular War and the remaining tombs command little attention in such a marvellous setting.

You can also visit the treasury and library – the former contains magnificent reliquaries, caskets and chalices from the early Middle Ages, but only reproductions of the manuscripts are on view.

San Marcos

If the Pantéon is a perfect illustration of the way Romanesque art worked its way into Spain along the Pilgrim Route from France, the opulent **Monasterio de San Marcos** (reached from the Plaza de Calvo Sotelo via Avenida de José Antonio) stands as a more direct reminder that León was a station on this route. Here, on presentation of the relevant documents, pilgrims were allowed to regain their strength before the gruelling Bierzo mountains west of León. The original monastery was built in 1168 for the Knights of Santiago, one of several chivalric orders founded in the twelfth century to protect pilgrims and lead the Reconquest. Eventually these powerful, ambitious and semi-autonomous knights posed a political threat to the authority of the Spanish throne, until in 1493 Isabella la Católica subtly tackled the problem by "suggesting" that her husband Fernando be "elected" Grand Master. Thus the wealth and power of this order was assimilated to that of the throne.

In time, the order degenerated to little more than a men's club – Velázquez, for instance, depicts himself in its robes in *Las Meninas* – and in the sixteenth century the monastery was rebuilt as a kind of palatial headquarters. Its massive facade is lavishly embellished with Plateresque appliqué designs: over the main entrance Santiago is once again depicted in his battling role of *Matamoros*; more pertinently, protruding above the ornate balustrade of the roofline, are the arms of Carlos V, who inherited the grand mastership from Fernando in 1516. The monastery is now a *parador*, and is off-limits to non-residents beyond its foyer and (modern) bar and restaurant. You can, however, ask specifically to see the *coro alto* of the church (access only from the hotel), which has a fine set of stalls by Juan de Juni.

Adjacent to the main facade stands the **Iglesia San Marcos**, vigorously speckled with the scallop shell motif of the pilgrimage. Its sacristy houses a small **museum** (Tues–Sat 10am–2pm & 5–7.30pm, Sun 10am–2pm), whose most beautiful and priceless exhibits are grouped together in a room separated from the lobby of the hotel by an oddly symbolic thick pane of glass. Foremost among them are a thirteenth-century processional cross made of rock crystal and an eleventh-century ivory crucifix – a tiny piece of Romanesque sculpture, primitive and strangely proportioned, but with the peculiar mark of faith about it.

Eating, drinking and nightlife

The time of year to be in León is during Semana Santa, and for the **fiestas** of San Juan and San Pedro in the last week of June – the celebrations, concentrated around the Plaza Mayor, get pretty riotous, with an enjoyable blend of medieval pageantry and buffoonery. For the rest of the year, the liveliest **bars and restaurants** tend to be those in the small square of San Martín and the dark, narrow streets which surround it – an area known as **Barrio Húmedo** for the amount of liquid sloshing around all weekend. All the bars here will give you a *pincho* with every drink, so you can eat pretty well if you drink enough, especially hopping from bar to bar ordering *cortos* – small tumblers of beer for about 70ptas. The garlic-smothered potatoes dished up in *El Rincón del Gaucho* are particularly delicious.

Café Carmela, c/Caño Badillo 7. Lively café specializing in liqueur coffees, with magazines to browse through.

Casa Pozo, Plaza San Marcelo 15 (☎987 223039). Excellent *bodega* for traditional Leónese dishes, behind the new *Ayuntamiento*; *menús* from 1400ptas. Closed Sun & July 1–15.

Mesón Leones del Racimo de Oro, Caño Badillo 2 . An authentic and modest-priced *mesón*, with a good *menú*. Closed Sun night & Tues.

Nuevo Racimo de Oro, Plaza San Martín 8. Slightly formal and expensive, but worth it. Closed Sun in summer and Wed in winter.

Restaurante Fornos, c/Cid 8. Great food and atmosphere. Closed Sun night & Mon.

Listings

Bus information ☎987 211000.

Car rental Operators include Avis, c/Condesa Sagasta 34 (☎987 270075); Europcar, c/Juan de Badajoz 7 (☎987 271980); and Santa María, c/Alcalde M. Castaño 10 (☎987 207218).

Post office The main branch is at the southern end of Avda. de Independencia, by the Plaza de San Francisco.

Taxis Radio Taxi (☎987 242451); Taxi Trabajo del Camino (☎987 802035).

Train information RENFE ☎987 270202; FEVE ☎987 271210.

Astorga and beyond

For the fittest of the pilgrims it was one day's walk 29 miles southwest of León to the next major stop at Astorga. On the way – at **Puente de Orbigo** – you pass the most ancient of the bridges along the route (probably the oldest in all Spain), now bypassed by the new road and offering a delightful and popular spot for a riverside stroll or picnic. As you get closer to Galicia, the terrain becomes mountainous and offers spectacular views. Beyond the valley town of **Ponferrada**, weary pilgrims confronted the mountains of **El Bierzo**, a region linked historically with León though distinct in more than just geography; in remoter villages you'll hear *gallego* spoken and see rather hopeful graffiti demanding independence for the area.

Astorga

ASTORGA resembles many of the smaller cities along the way: sacked by the Moors in the eleventh century, it was rebuilt and endowed with the usual hospices and monasteries, but as the pilgrimage lost popularity in the late Middle Ages the place fell into decline. Many of its buildings were ravaged during the Peninsular War and today it seems to be crumbling gently into a peaceful old age.

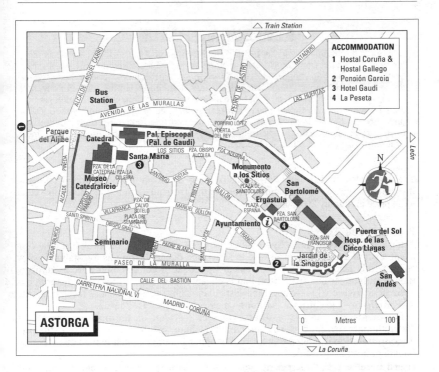

Not without the odd flurry, though, for the bizarre **Palacio Episcopal** – commissioned by a Catalan bishop from his countryman Antoni Gaudí – injects some real vitality. Its appearance will not surprise anyone who has seen Gaudí's work in Barcelona. Surrounded by a moat and built of light grey granite, it resembles some horror-movie Gothic castle from the mountains of Transylvania with an equally striking, remarkably spacious interior. For half a century it stood empty and was considered a scandalous and expensive white elephant, but nowadays it houses the unique and excellent **Museo de los Caminos** (June–Sept daily 10am–2pm & 4–8pm; Oct–May Mon–Sat 11am–2pm & 3.30–6.30pm; 250ptas or 400ptas joint ticket with Diocesan Museum). A host of knick-knacks throws interesting sidelights on the story of the pilgrimage: hanging on the wall are examples of the documents issued at Santiago to certify that pilgrims had "travelled, confessed and obtained absolution", and there are photographs of the myriad villages and buildings along the way, and charts to show the precise roads taken through the towns.

Nearby – though stylistically worlds apart – stands the **Catedral**. Built between 1471 and 1693, it combines numerous architectural styles, but without any notable success. The **Diocesan Museum** (daily 10am–2pm & 4–8pm; 400ptas joint ticket with Museo de los Caminos; entrance to the left of the main facade), is interesting, however, especially for its beautiful twelfth-century wooden tomb painted with scenes from the lives of Christ and the Apostles.

While you're here, you could also take in the **Museo del Chocolate**, c/José María Goy (Mon–Sat noon–2pm & 6–8pm, Sun noon–2pm; free) which charts the growth of Astorga's flourishing chocolate industry during the eighteenth and nineteenth centuries.

THE MARAGOTAS

Astorga is the traditional market town of the **Maragatos**, a mysterious race of people, possibly descended from the Berbers of North Africa, who crossed into Spain with the first Moorish incursions of the early eighth century. Marrying only among themselves, they maintained their traditions and individuality well into recent decades. For several centuries almost the entire carrying trade of Spain was in their hands, but muleteers no longer have a role. Nowadays you're unlikely to come across them unless you're plodding through the fields along the Pilgrim Route, and their only obvious legacy to the town is a pair of colourful clockwork figures dressed in Maragato costume who jerk into action to strike the hour on the town hall clock in Plaza de España.

There are also guided tours (in Spanish) along the **Ruta Romana** which take you through Astorga's Roman remains; enquire at the Turismo for times and departure point – the price is roughly 200–300ptas.

Practicalities

Astorga connects with León by train but the **train station** is a long way from the centre of town. It makes far more sense to arrive and depart by **bus** as the station is very conveniently placed opposite the Palacio Episcopal. If you're coming from Santiago, there's an Intercar bus at 10.30am that is cheaper than most of the trains. Astorga has a small **Turismo** (June–Sept Mon–Sat 10am–2pm; ☎987 616838), located in the *Ayuntamiento* – the entrance is through a side door on c/ La Bañeza.

For **meals**, try one of the several cafés or *comedors* on the main square by the Ayuntamiento or in the streets which radiate off it towards the cathedral. **Accommodation** is limited to a handful of options in or just outside the city centre, so booking ahead is advisable.

Hostal Coruña, Avda. Ponferrada 72 (☎987 615009). Decent *hostal*, outside the walls but convenient for the bus station. ③.

Hostal Gallego, Avda. de Ponferrada 78 (☎987 615450). Close to the *Coruña*, but smarter and more expensive. ④.

Pensión García, c/Bajjada Postigo 3 (☎987 616046). Just south of the *Ayuntamiento*, opposite the children's playground; basic but clean, with a good *comedor*. ③.

Hotel Gaudí, c/Eduardo de Castro 6 (☎987 615654, fax 987 615040). Astorga's top hotel, with classy rooms looking directly on to Gaudí's palace. The restaurant's *menú* changes daily – a good place for a splurge. ⑥.

La Peseta, Plaza de San Bartolomé (☎987 617275, fax 987 615300). Smart but overpriced *hostal* whose main raison d'être is its excellent restaurant, which has won many awards over the years. ⑤.

Ponferrada

At first sight the heavily industrialized, bowl-shaped valley, centred on the large town of **PONFERRADA**, seems to have little to offer, but the mountainous terrain around has scenery as picturesque as any in Spain. The town of Ponferrada itself sums up this dichotomy, dominated by a huge slag heap and spreading suburbs, yet with a quiet, unspoiled old quarter. The two are separated by a river blackened by coal mining and spanned by the iron bridge that has given Ponferrada its name. Above the sharp valley the fancy twelfth-century turrets and battlements of the **Castillo de los Templarios** (Tues–Sat 10.30am–1.30pm & 4–7pm, Sun 10.30am–1.30pm) may look like gingerbread, but they were built to protect pilgrims against the very real threat of the Moors, and the arcaded streets and overhanging houses of the old quarter grew up in their protective shadow. A quaint *Puerta del Reloj* (Clock Gateway) leads into the

Plaza Mayor, with a late seventeenth-century *Ayuntamiento*, similar in design to its contemporary counterpart at Astorga.

There are several churches in the town but the most important is a short walk away in the northeast outskirts: **Santo Tomás de las Ollas**, a small Mozarabic church dating from the tenth century with nine round Moorish horseshoe arches and Visigothic elements.

Practicalities

Bus and **train** stations, and most **accommodation**, are in the new part of town which can be quite difficult to find your way around – Avenida de la Puebla is the main road which leads to the river; after crossing the bridge head right up the hill to reach the centre of the old town. The **Turismo** is on the road next to the castle (Mon–Sat 10am–2pm & 5–7pm; ☎987 424236), and has a useful map of the town. The only rooms up here are at the adequate *Pensión Mondelo*, c/Flores Osorio 3 (☎987 416351; ②), just off c/del Reloj. In the new town, the best low-price places to try are *Hostal Santa Cruz*, c/Marcelo Macías 4 (☎987 428351; ③), and the more basic *Hostal Marán*, c/A. López Pelaez 29 (☎987 428379; ②). The *Hotel de Madrid*, Avda. de la Puebla 44 (☎987 411550, fax 987 411861; ③), also has a good **restaurant**, and, for real luxury, Ponferrada has its own palace hotel, *Del Temple*, Avenida de Portugal (☎987 410058, fax 987 423525; ⑥). The *Bar/Restaurante Gundín*, near the *Santa Cruz*, offers good-value *menús*.

Las Médulas

Twenty kilometres southwest of Ponferrada lies **LAS MÉDULAS**, the jagged remains of Roman stripmining for gold. Nine hundred thousand tonnes of the precious metal were ripped from the hillsides using carefully constructed canals, leaving an eerie scene reminiscent of Arizona, peppered with caves and needles of red rock. From **Carucedo**, a road leads for 4km up to the village of Las Médulas; from here you can walk right through the zone. It's a good idea to make for the ridge overlooking the whole desolation; the quarry visible in the background from here is a reminder of how nature can turn man's devastation into beauty given a few thousand years. Another road leads from this viewpoint back down to Carucedo; the round trip takes about four or five hours.

Villafranca del Bierzo

The last halt before the climb into Galicia, **VILLAFRANCA DEL BIERZO** was where pilgrims on their last legs could chicken out of the final trudge. Those who arrived at the Puerta del Perdón (Door of Forgiveness) at the church of **Santiago** could receive the same benefits as in Santiago de Compostela itself. The simple Romanesque church is of little interest, and the impressive castle opposite is in private hands and unvisitable, but the town is a pleasant enough spot to spend a few hours, with slate-roofed houses, cool mountain air and the clear Burbia River providing a setting reminiscent of the English Lake District. Of the other churches the most rewarding is **San Francisco** just off the Plaza Mayor; it has a beautiful Mudéjar ceiling, a *retablo* so warped that it makes you dizzy to contemplate it, and an unusual well. If either church is locked, the bookshop on the plaza has the keys.

Places to stay include the modern *Parador de Villafranca del Bierzo*, Avenida Calvo Sotelo (☎987 540175, fax 987 540010; ⑥), and the *Hostal Comercio*, Puente Nuevo 2 (☎987 540008; ②), a beautiful fifteenth-century house whose spacious rooms are a real bargain. *Don Nacho*, in a little alley off the Plaza Mayor, is a good place to **eat**, serving *tapas*, *menús* and fish specialities. Regular half-hourly **buses** from Ponferrada stop right outside the *parador*.

travel details

BUSES

Burgos to: Aranda (7 daily; 1hr 15min); Bilbao (8 daily; 2–3hr); Carrión de los Condes (1 daily; 1hr 30min); Ciudad Rodrigo (1 daily; 5hr); Covarrubias (1 daily; 1hr); Frómista (1 daily; 1hr); León (1 daily; 3 hours); Logroño (7 daily; 2hr); Madrid (12 daily; 3hr); Palencia (3 daily; 1hr); Pamplona (1 daily; 3hr 30min); Sahagún (1 daily; 2hr 30min); Salamanca (1 daily; 2hr 45min); San Sebastián (8 daily; 3hr); Santander (5 daily; 2hr 30min); Santo Domingo de la Calzada (5 daily; 1hr 30min); Santo Domingo de Silos (1 daily; 1hr 30min); Soria (3 daily; 3hr–3hr 30min); Valladolid (3 daily; 1hr 45min); Vinuesa (2 daily; 2hr 45min); Zamora (1 daily; 2hr 45min); Zaragoza (4 daily; 3hr 45min).

León to: Astorga (16 daily; 45min); Bilbao (1 daily; 3 hours); Burgos (2 daily; 3hr); Logroño (2 daily; 4hr); Lugo (1 daily; 4hr 30min); Madrid (8 daily; 4hr 30min); Oviedo (8 daily; 1hr 45min); Palencia (1 daily; 2 hours); Ponferrada (11 daily; 2hr); Potes (1 daily; 3hr); Salamanca (5 daily; 2hr 40min); Santander (1 daily; 3hr); Valladolid (8 daily; 1hr 30min); Villafranca del Bierzo (3 daily; 3hr); Zamora (3 daily; 2hr 30min); Zaragoza (2 daily; 8hr).

Logroño to: Barcelona (3 daily; 6hr); Bilbao (4 daily; 2hr 30min); Burgos (7 daily; 2hr); Haro (5 daily; 1hr); León (2 daily; 4hr); Pamplona (4 daily; 2hr); Santander (6 daily; 3hr 30min); Santo Domingo de la Calzada (9 daily; 45min); Soria (5 daily; 1hr 30min); Vitoria (8 daily; 1hr); Zamora (2 daily; 4hr 30min); Zaragoza (6 daily; 2–3hr).

Palencia to: Burgos (3 daily; 1hr); Carrión de los Condes (3 daily; 45min); La Coruña (3 daily; 6hr); León (1 daily; 2 hours); Lugo (5 daily; 5hr 30min); Madrid (6 daily; 3hr); Salamanca (3 daily; 2hr 30min); Valladolid (9 daily; 1hr); Zamora (2 daily; 2hr 30min); Zaragoza (2 daily; 5hr).

Salamanca to: Alba de Tormes (16 daily; 30min); Aranda de Duero (2 daily; 3hr); Ávila (4 daily; 1hr 30min); Badajoz (2 daily; 4hr 30min); Barcelona (2 daily; 11hr 30min); Burgos (1 daily; 2hr 45min); Cáceres (4 daily; 3hr 30min); Ciudad Rodrigo (10 daily; 1hr 30min); Madrid (14 daily; 2hr 30min); Palencia (3 daily; 2hr 30min); Peñafiel (2 daily; 2hr); Plasencia (4 daily; 2hr); San Esteban de Gormaz (2 daily; 3hr 45min); Santander (2 daily; 5hr 30min); Sevilla (4 daily; 7hr); Soria (2 daily; 4hr

30min); Valladolid (4 daily; 1hr 30min); Zamora (hourly; 50min).

Soria to: Barcelona (2 daily; 6hr); Berlanga de Duero (1 daily; 1hr 15min); Burgos (3 daily; 3hr–3hr 30min); El Burgo de Osma (2 daily; 1hr); Logroño (5 daily; 1hr 30min); Madrid (11 daily; 2hr 30min); Medinaceli (2 daily; 1hr 15min); Pamplona (5 daily; 2–3hr); Peñafiel (3 daily; 2hr 30min); Salamanca (2 daily; 4hr 30min); Valladolid (3 daily; 3hr); Vinuesa (2 daily; 45min); Zaragoza (5 daily; 2hr 15min).

Valladolid to: Burgos (3 daily; 1hr 30min); El Burgo de Osma (1 daily; 2hr 30min); León (8 daily; 2hr); Madrid (16 daily; 2hr 40min); Palencia (9 daily; 1hr); Peñafiel (5 daily; 1hr); Salamanca (4 daily; 1hr 30min); Zamora (9 daily, 3 on Sun; 1hr 15min); Zaragoza (3 daily; 7hr 30min).

Zamora to: Barcelona (2 daily; 12hr 30min); Burgos (1 daily; 2hr 45min); León (3 daily; 2hr 30min); Logroño (2 daily; 4hr 30min); Palencia (2 daily; 2hr 30min); Salamanca (hourly; 50min); Valladolid (9 daily, 3 on Sun; 1hr 15min); Zaragoza (2 daily; 6hr 15min).

TRAINS

Burgos to: Ávila (2–3 daily; 2hr 30min); Barcelona (4 daily; 8hr 30min); Bilbao (3–6 daily; 3hr 30min); Ciudad Rodrigo (1 daily; 4hr 15min); Haro (3 daily; 1hr 40min); Irún (7 daily; 3hr 30min); León (4 daily; 2hr); Logroño (4 daily; 2hr); Lugo (2–4 daily; 6hr 30min–7hr 30min); Madrid (5 daily; 3hr); Palencia (4 daily; 1hr); Valladolid (14 daily; 1hr 20min); Vitoria (9 daily; 1hr 30min–2hr); Zamora (1 Mon, Sat & Sun; 3hr 10min); Zaragoza (4 daily; 4hr).

León to: Ávila (2–4 daily; 2hr 30min–3hr); Barcelona (3 daily; 9hr 30min–11hr); Bilbao (1–2 daily; 5hr); Burgos (5 daily; 2hr); A Coruña (3–5 daily; 7hr); El Ferrol (1 daily Mon–Sat; 7hr); Logroño (2 daily; 3hr 45min); Lugo (3–5 daily; 5hr); Madrid (3–5 daily; 4hr–6hr 20min); Medina del Campo (11 daily; 2hr); Orense (4 daily; 3hr 50min–4hr 50min); Oviedo (5 daily; 2hr); Santiago de Compostela (1 daily; 5hr 40min); Valladolid (2–4 daily; 1hr 30min); Vigo (2–4 daily; 5hr 45min–6hr 45min); Vitoria (2–3 daily; 3hr 30min); Zaragoza (3 daily; 5hr 30min).

Logroño to: Barcelona (4 daily; 6hr 30min); Bilbao (2–3 daily; 2hr 30min); Burgos (3–4 daily; 2hr); León (2 daily; 3hr 45min); Madrid (1 daily except Sat; 4hr 45min); Valladolid (1–2 daily; 3hr); Vigo (1 daily; 11hr 20min); Zamora (1 Mon, Sat & Sun; 5hr 30min); Zaragoza (4–6 daily; 1hr 50min).

Medina del Campo to: Barcelona (1–3 daily; 11hr–12hr 30min); Bilbao (2–4 daily; 5hr); León (3–4 daily; 2hr); Lugo (1 daily except Sat; 7hr); Madrid (12 daily; 2hr 15min); Orense (3–4 daily; 3hr 40min); Oviedo (2–3 daily; 4hr); Vigo (3–4 daily; 5hr 45min–7hr 45min); Zamora (3–4 daily; 1hr); Zaragoza (2–3 daily; 6hr–7hr 30min).

Valladolid to: Ávila (5–9 daily; 1hr); Barcelona (1–2 daily; 10hr–12hr); Bilbao (2–4 daily; 4hr 30min); Burgos (14 daily; 1hr 20min); León (2–4 daily; 1hr 30min); Lisbon (1 daily; 9hr); Logroño (1–2 daily; 3hr 30min); Madrid (7–10 daily; 2hr 30min); Palencia (30min); Salamanca (4–5 daily; 1hr 30min); San Sebastián (4 daily; 4–5hr); Zamora (1 Mon, Sat, & Sun; 1hr 30min); Zaragoza (1–2 daily; 5hr 30min–6hr 30min).

Zamora to: Ávila (3 daily; 1hr); Barcelona (1 Thurs, Sat & Sun; 13hr 30min); A Coruña (2 daily; 5hr 20min); Madrid (3 daily; 3hr 10min); Medina del Campo (3–4 daily; 1hr); Santiago de Compostela (2 daily; 4hr 20min); Toro (1 Thurs, Sat & Sun; 30min); Valladolid (1 Thurs, Sat & Sun; 1hr 30min); Vigo (3 daily; 4hr); Zaragoza (1 Thurs, Sat & Sun; 8hr 30min).

CHAPTER SIX

EUSKADI: THE BASQUE PROVINCES & NAVARRA

Euskadi is the name the Basque people give to their own land, an area that covers the three Basque provinces – **Gipuzkoa**, **Bizkaia**, and **Araba**, known collectively as the País Vasco – together with much of **Navarra**, and part of southwestern France. It's an immensely beautiful region – mountainous, green and thickly forested. It rains often, and much of the time the countryside is shrouded in a fine mist. But the summers, if you don't mind the occasional shower, are a glorious escape from the unrelenting heat of the south.

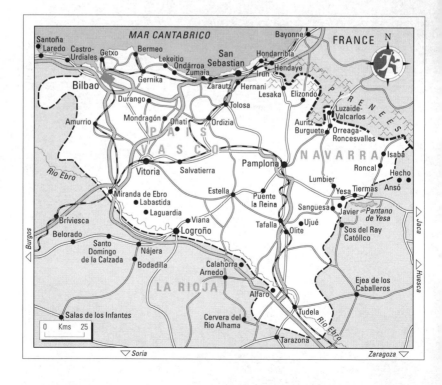

Despite the heaviest industrialization on the peninsula, Euskadi is remarkably unspoiled – neat and quiet inland, rugged and enclosed along the coast – and transport everywhere is easy and efficient. **San Sebastián** is the big draw on the coast, a major resort with superb but crowded beaches, but there are any number of lesser-known, equally attractive villages along the coast all the way to Bilbao, and beyond into Asturias and Galicia. **Bilbao** itself is home to the magnificent new **Guggenheim Museum**, while inland there's **Pamplona**, with its exuberant **Fiestas de San Fermín**, as well as many other destinations with charms of their own, from the drama of the **Pyrenees** to the quiet elegance of **Vitoria**.

The Basques

The origin of **the Basques** is something of a mystery. They are a distinct people, generally with a different build from the French and Spanish and a different blood group distribution from the rest of Europe. Certainly their language, the complex *Euskara*, is one of the most ancient spoken in Europe, predating the migrations from the east which brought the Indo-European languages some 3000 years ago. It is now considered to go back in time as far as the Basque race itself and to have evolved within the present territory rather than to have been introduced from elsewhere.

Establishing concrete data has been complicated by the fact that *Euskara* did not appear in written form until the sixteenth century (in the French Basque country). The language has largely been maintained and has even evolved through the oral traditions of *bertsolariak*, or popular poets specializing in improvised verse, a tradition still alive today. The vocabulary itself implies a way of thinking going well back beyond the Christian era, as evidenced by terms referring to ancient burial sites such as dolmens and cromlechs. Further evidence is suggested in the strong tradition of Basque mythology relating to *gentiles*, or legendary giants, supposedly responsible for building these sites, ancient ways and bridges.

Some think that the Basque people are the last surviving representatives of Europe's aboriginal population, a theory borne out by archeological finds earlier this century. Skull fragments of late Cro-Magnon man believed to date from the Paleolithic era, around 9000 BC, have been shown to be identical to present-day Basque cranial formation. Much anthropological work, above all by the revered Joxe Miguel Barandiaran (who died in December 1991, aged 101), lends itself to the view that the Basques have continuously inhabited the western Pyrenees, largely in isolation, for thousands of years. Indeed, over the centuries they have had very little contact with the peoples who originally migrated into Europe, partly due to being surrounded by impenetrable mountains and partly because they were considered barbarians by potential invaders.

Basque nationalism

For almost the entire history of Spain, the Basques jealously defended their *fueros* – the ancient rights under which they ruled themselves almost as an independent republic. Richard Ford wrote in the nineteenth century that "these highlanders, bred on metal-pregnant mountains, and nursed amid storms in a cradle indomitable as themselves, have always known how to forge their iron into arms, and to wield them in defence of their own independence". It was not until 1876 and the final defeat of the Carlists, whom the Basques supported as upholding their own traditionalist values, that the victorious liberals finally abolished the *fueros* altogether as an act of vengeance on the Basques.

Although the conservative **Basque National Party** (PNV) emerged towards the end of the nineteenth century, it is only in this century that **Basque nationalism** has become associated with the political left, mostly in reaction to the terrors of Franco's regime. Cut off from their Republican allies by Navarra, which sided with the

BASQUE NAMES

Almost everywhere in the province, street and road signs are in both Basque and Castilian, but the latter is often painted over. Recently, many town halls have officially chosen to use the Basque names and this is reflected on new tourist brochures and maps. We have, therefore, used the Basque name for towns, giving the Castilian in brackets. Some towns, however, including Pamplona and Bilbao, are still generally referred to by their Castilian names and in these cases we have supplied the Basque name in brackets.

It is worth noting a couple of key letter changes which may help to decipher initially confusing words on, for example, menus and signs: notably, the Castilian *ch* becomes *tx* (*txipirones* as opposed to *chipirones*), *v* becomes *b* and *y* becomes *i* (*Bizkaia* as opposed to *Vizcaya*). Above all, *Euskara* features a proliferation of *k*s, as this letter replaces the Castilian *c* (*Gipuzkoa* instead of *Guipúzcoa*) and is used to form the plural.

Castilian name	Basque name	Castilian name	Basque name
Fuenterrabía	Hondarribia	Motrico	Mutriku
Oñate	Oñati	Lequetio	Lekeitio
Zarauz	Zarautz	Guernica	Gernika
Guetaria	Getaria	Mundaca	Mundaka
Pasajes	Pasaia Donibane	Marquina	Markina
Zumaya	Zumaia	Pamplona	Iruña
Bilbao	Bilbo	San Sebastián	Donostia
Vitoria	Gasteiz		

Nationalists, the Basque provinces were conquered in a vicious campaign that included the infamous German bombing of **Gernika** in 1937. Franco's vengeful boot went in hard, and as many as 21,000 people died in his attempts to tame the Basques after the war. Public use of the language was forbidden, and central control was asserted with the gun. But state violence succeeded only in nurturing a new resistance, the **ETA** (*Euskadi ta Askatasuna* – "Freedom for the Basques"), whose most spectacular success was the assassination in Madrid of Franco's right-hand man and probable successor, Admiral Carrero Blanco. Even today the military and the Guardia Civil behave as an army of occupation, and the more radically minded Basques of the *Abertzale* (nationalist) movement continue to support ETA's aims, if not their methods.

Following the **return to democracy**, things changed. The Basque parliament has been granted a fair degree of devolution, with its own president, parliament and tax collection – there's even a regional police force, the *ertzaintza* (distinguished by its red berets) much in evidence in the streets, and the Basque **language** is taught in schools and universities. The Basque flag (the *Ikurriña*) flies everywhere – the exterior design of Euskadi's pavilion at Expo '92 in Sevilla was of a giant illuminated *Ikurriña*.

After Spain's general election in March 1996, the conservative popular party (PP) failed to secure enough seats to form a government, and was forced to make a pact with Basque and Catalan nationalists. Conciliatory measures included transferring 32 convicted ETA terrorists to jails close to the Basque country. **Herri Batasuna** (the political arm of the ETA) campaigned relentlessly against the previous government's policy of dispersing Basque prisoners around Spain. It was still not enough for the ETA, who continued their campaign of terror, with the **tourist industry** as their target. In July 1996 they planted a dozen bombs in resorts along the Cosa Dorada and the Costa del Sol, in areas particularly popular with British tourists, and on July 20, 35 British holidaymakers, including three children, were injured in an ETA explosion at Reus airport, near Barcelona.

Since then, however, the situation has improved. Influenced by the emerging peace settlement in Northern Ireland, in the summer of 1998 ETA declared an **indefinite ceasefire** and agreed to talks with the Spanish government. This is regarded as a major breakthrough and, it is hoped, will lead to a permanent ceasefire and a politically negotiated settlement.

Polls show that while wanting increased autonomy, many Basques oppose forming a breakaway state. The economic recession no doubt has much to do with this; the *País Vasco*'s former industrial glories are now reduced to rusty, outdated factories and closed-down steel foundries and shipyards; terrorism keeps away new investment and unemployment is extremely high. There's little doubt that a substantial portion of the Basque population now feels that more will be achieved through the new channels of compromise and conciliation, than by the old ETA methods.

Food

Basque cuisine is accepted as Spain's finest, and the people here are compulsive eaters: try *bacalao* (cod) *a la vizcaina*, *merluza* (hake) *a la vasca*, *chipirones en su tinta* (squid cooked in its ink) or *txangurro* (spider crab), which you'll find in very reasonably priced roadside *caseríos* (*baserri* in Basque), on the outskirts of towns throughout the region. You'll also come across traditional Basque food in the form of *tapas* (known in the Basque country as *pinchos*) in virtually every bar, freshly cooked and always excellent.

The tradition of **gastronomic societies**, unique to the Basque country, deserves special mention: first founded in the mid-nineteenth century, they came about originally as socializing places for different craftsmen. Controversy has surrounded them due to the traditional barring of women (although this is changing); all cooking is done by men who pay a token membership fee for the facilities. Members prepare elaborate dishes to perfection as a hobby and it can be said that true Basque cookery has largely retreated to these societies. The so-called *Nueva Cocina Vasca* (New Basque Cookery), heavily influenced by French cuisine, is becoming increasingly evident on menus.

Sport

The **Basque sport** of *jai alai*, or *pelota*, is played all over Spain, but in Euskadi even the smallest village has a *fronton* or pelota court, and betting on the sport is rife among Basques. Other unique Basque sports include *aizkolaritza* (log-chopping), *harri-jasotzea* (stone-lifting), *soka-tira* (tug-of-war) and *segalaritza* (grass-cutting). The finest exponents of the first two in particular are popular local heroes (the world champion stone-lifter Iñaki Perurena's visit to Japan resulted in the sport being introduced there – he remains the only lifter to surpass the legendary 315-kilo barrier). All Basque sports form an important part of the many local fiestas.

BASQUE: SOME COMMON WORDS			
Kaixo	Hello	*Aireportua*	Airport
Agur	Goodbye	*Hotela*	Hotel
Gabon	Goodnight	*Aparkalekua*	Car park
Egun on	Good morning	*Hondartza*	Beach
Mesedez	Please	*Jatetxea*	Restaurant
Bai	Yes	*Turismo Bulegoa*	Tourist Office
Ez	No	*Udaletxea*	Town Hall
Ongi etorri	Welcome	*Ertzantza*	Autonomous Police
Eguna	Day	*Udaltzaingoa*	Municipal Police

Accommodation

The main drawback to travelling in the region is that prices (apart from for food) are higher than in much of Spain, particularly for **accommodation**, although there is a considerable difference between prices on the Cantabrian coast and inland (with the exception of Pamplona). Accommodation in smaller towns had a substantial boost with the introduction of the Basque government's **agroturismo**, or homestay, programme, which offers the opportunity to stay in traditional Basque farmhouses and private homes, usually in areas of outstanding beauty, at very reasonable cost. They are identified by a red and green circular sign with the word *nekazalturismoa*. In Navarra these are known as **casas rurales**. Lists showing facilities and prices may be obtained from regional tourist offices (who also handle bookings); alternatively, you can reserve through the central booking offices for País Vasco (☎94 620 11 88) and Navarra (☎948

FIESTAS

January
19–20 *Festividad de San Sebastián*, 24 hours of festivities, including *tamborrada* (a march with pipes and drums).

February
15–20 *Carnaval* in Bilbao, San Sebastián and Tolosa.

March
4–12 A series of pilgrimages to the castle at Javier, birthplace of San Francisco Javier.

April
Extensive Easter celebrations in Vitoria.
28 *Fiesta de San Prudencio* is celebrated with *tamborradas*, and a re-enactment of the retreat is staged in Vitoria.

June
24 *Fiestas de San Juan* in Lekeitio, Laguardia-Biasteri and Tolosa.

July
First week sees the great fiesta at Zumaia with dancing, Basque sports and an *encierro* on the beach.
7–14 *Fiestas de San Fermín* in Pamplona, featuring running with the bulls.
16–20 International Jazz Festival in Vitoria.
22 *Fiesta de la Magdalena* in Bermeo, with torch-lit processions of fishing boats and the usual races and Basque sports.
25 *Santiago Apóstol*, International Paella Competition in Getxo.
Mid to late July Jazz Festival in San Sebastián.
Last week in July *Fiesta de San Pedro* in

Mundaka (2km south of Bermeo), with Basque dancing.
31 *Día de San Ignacio Loyola*, celebrated throughout, but above all in Loyola and Getxo where there are fireworks, jazz and a cycling competition.

August
First weekend Patron saint's celebration in Estella.
4–9 *Fiesta de la Virgen Blanca* in Vitoria with bullfights, fireworks and *gigantones*.
15 *Semana Grande* witnesses an explosion of celebration, notably in Bilbao, with Basque games and races; Zarautz with rowing regattas; Gernika and Tafalla with an *encierro* and San Sebastián where the highlight is an International Fireworks Competition.

September
First week *Euskal Jaiak* (Basque feasts) in San Sebastián.
4 *Fiesta de San Antolín* in Lekeitio, where the local youth attempt to knock the head off a goose.
9 *Euskal-Jaia* in Zarautz and *Día del Pescador* in Bermeo.
12 Sangüesa holds its own *encierros*.
14 Patron saint's day in Olite, with yet more bulls.
19–28 International Film Festival in San Sebastián.

December
Christmas Celebrations are particularly exuberant in Pamplona. At midnight on Christmas Eve there's an open-air Mass by firelight in Labastida (Alava).

229328). Except in the very small villages, there is usually a *fonda* or *hostal*; alternatively, entering any bar and asking for a room will generally produce results.

Irún and around

The Basque province of Gipuzkoa adjoins the French frontier, and its border town, **Irún**, is one of the major road and rail entry points into Spain. There are fast connections on to San Sebastián, although if you're travelling more slowly, the fishing ports of **Hondarribia** and **Pasaia Donibane** (Pasajes San Juan) are worth a stop. The main route to the south crosses into Navarra and leads via the beautiful Valle de Bidasoa to Pamplona (Iruña).

Irún

Like most border towns, **IRÚN**'s chief concern is how to make a quick buck from passing travellers, and the main point in its favour is the ease with which you can leave; there are trains to **Hendaia** (Hendaye) in France and to San Sebastián throughout the day, and regular long-distance and international connections. If arriving by train from Paris (or elsewhere in France) at Hendaia, note that it is far quicker to take the *topo* (mole train, so-called because of all the tunnels it goes through) from the separate platform on the right outside Hendaia's main station; it runs every thirty minutes to Irún station at Avda. de Colón 52 and to San Sebastián. Of the town's few attractions, the **Ermita de Santa Elena**, c/Ermita, a museum containing Roman remains discovered here in 1969, is worth a visit.

Practicalities

If you do need to spend the night, there are plenty of bars and places to **eat**, and prices are markedly lower than in France or San Sebastián (which is no place to arrive late at night with nowhere to stay). In the vicinity of Irún's main train station are several small, reasonably priced **hostales** and **restaurants** specializing in good local food. *Hostal Irún*, c/Zubiaurre 5 (☎943 611637; ③), and *Bar Pensión los Fronterizos*, c/Estación 7 (☎943 619205; ④), have some of the lowest-priced rooms; for more comfort try the nearby *Hotel Alcazár*, Avda. Iparralde 11 (☎943 620900, fax 943 622797; ⑤), *Lizaso*, c/Aduana 5–7 (☎943 611600; ④) or *Matxinbenta*, Paseo Colón 21 (☎943 621384; ④). There is also a **agroturismo**, *Mendiola*, Ventas, Landexte (☎943 629763; ④), a little way out of town on the A-8.

Hondarribia

The fishing port of **HONDARRIBIA** (Fuenterrabía), 6km north of Irún and overlooking Hendaia, is a far more attractive prospect, with its tamarisk-lined main street, Calle San Pedro, flanked with traditional, wood-beamed Basque houses interspersed with bars offering some of the best seafood and *pinchos* around. During the summer, the fine **beaches** just beyond the town are an escape from the ultra-crowded *La Concha* in San Sebastián.

Hondarribia has a picturesque, walled old town entered through the fifteenth-century **Puerta de Santa María**. Calle Mayor, leading up to the Plaza de Armas, has further fine examples of wood-beamed houses, some displaying the family coats of arms above doorways, and the square itself is dominated by the **Palacio de Carlos Quinto**, started originally in the tenth century by Sancho the Strong of Navarra and subsequently extended by Carlos V in the sixteenth. It is now a luxurious *parador* (see below), and it's worth at least having a drink at the bar inside.

Practicalities

There is a very helpful **Turismo** on Javier Ugarte 6 (☎943 645458, fax 943 645466; July–Aug Mon–Sat 9am–8pm, Sun 10am–2pm; Sept–June Mon–Fri 9am–1.30pm & 4–6.30pm, Sat 10am–2pm).

There are several good **hostales** in town; try *Hostal Álvarez Quintero*, c/Beñat Etxepare 2 (☎943 642299; ④), in the Edificio Miramar near the Turismo, or *Txoko-Goxua*, Murrna 22, Aptdo. 189 (☎943 644658; ③), in the old town. The **youth hostel**, *Juan Sebastián Elcano*, is on Carretera Faro (☎943 641550, fax 943 640028; ①); fork left beyond c/San Pedro on the way to the beaches. The three-star *Río Bidasoa*, c/Nafarroa Behera (☎943 645408, fax 943 645170; ⑦), has its own pool, while the *Parador Nacional El Emperador*, Plaza Armas (☎943 645500, fax 943 642153; ⑦), is stunningly located in the town's fortified *palacio*. Nearby in Plaza Obispo, the *Hotel Obispo* (☎943 645400, fax 943 642386; ⑦) also offers stylish accommodation. The closest **campsite**, *Camping Jaizkibel* (☎943 641679; open all year), is 2km out of town along Carretera Guadalupe towards Pasaia Donibane (Pasajes). Also outside town, just by the chapel of Nuestra Señora de Guadalupe, is a signposted turn-off to an **agroturismo**, *Artzu*, in Montaña (☎943 640530; ④), offering accommodation in an old restored farmhouse.

The bars along c/San Pedro are the best hunting ground for **food** and **drink**. In the old town, tucked away in a narrow, cobbled alley two streets behind c/Mayor, the *Mamutzar* restaurant serves a good-value *menú del día*, and next door *tapas* is available in the tiny but lively *Hamlet* bar.

Frequent **buses** leave from c/San Pedro to San Sebastián. The stretch of coastline from here as far as the port of Pasaia is particularly rugged and has long been a haven for smugglers.

Pasaia Donibane

The one place you might consider stopping for any length of time en route between Irún and San Sebastián is the port of Pasaia. While much of the town is highly industrialized, the old town, **PASAIA DONIBANE** (Pasajes San Juan), has retained its charm. The narrow cobbled c/San Juan (Victor Hugo once lived at no. 65, the house built over the tunnel) leads to the plaza with its colourful houses. Pasaia Donibane is famous for its waterside **fish restaurants**, many of which offer good-value *menús del día* and even choosing from the evening menus here works out considerably less expensive than those in San Sebastían's old quarter. A **launch** (*txalupa*) runs throughout the day and evening across the harbour to Pasajes San Pedro, from where frequent buses run to San Sebastián's Boulevard.

Towards Pamplona

If you're heading straight down to Pamplona, you'll pass through the **Bidasoa valley** with its string of beautifully preserved towns, the best of which are Bera-Vera de

Bidasoa, Lesaka and Etxalar. South from Etxalar, the road forks right and the N121 leads over the Velate Pass to Pamplona. The left fork takes you up to the Baztán valley (see p.430). Both valleys are on direct bus routes from San Sebastián/Irún and Pamplona.

Bera-Vera de Bidasoa

BERA-VERA DE BIDASOA offers some of the finest examples of old wood-beamed and traditional stone houses in the region; the brightly painted buildings along c/Altzarte and the main square are particularly attractive. About a hundred metres off the square, just past the old border crossing, is the former house (no. 24) of the Basque writer Pío Baroja; at the time of writing this is closed indefinitely, but you can check the latest situation with the Turismo in Pamplona (see p.420).

If you want to **stay,** there's the small *Fonda Chantre*, c/San Esteban 15 (☎948 630239; ③), or the more comfortable *Euskalduna*, c/Bidasoa 5 (☎948 630392; ④), with a good restaurant offering a *menú del día* and local specialities. Alternatively, head for the pleasant *casa rural* just outside town: *Casa Etxeberzea*, Barrio de Zalain (☎948 630272; ④).

Five kilometres east of Bera at the top of Luzuniaga Pass right on the French border, **Monte Larrun** is an easy climb: from the top you'll get spectacular views across the Pyrenees and the French Basque coast. There's a bar-restaurant at the top which serves tourists taking the funicular from the French side.

Lesaka

South of Bera along the Bidasoa valley, a right turn leads to **LESAKA**. Despite the eyesore of a large factory on the outskirts of town, it's a beautiful place dominated by the hill-top parish church in which the pews bear family names of the local farms and mansions. On the banks of the irrigation channel which flows through town is one of the best remaining examples of a *casa torre* (fortified private house) of a design peculiar to the Basque country, dating back to the days when north Navarra was in the hands of a few powerful and constantly feuding families.

Places to stay include the simple *Pensión Tolareta*, Plaza Berria 2 (☎948 637106; ②), above a clothes shop, just off the main square, and the more upmarket *Hotel Bereau* (☎948 627509, fax 948 627647; ⑤), near the main road. The *Ekaitza Café*, at Plaza Berria 13 (☎948 627547; ④), rents out an apartment in the summer – ask for the proprietor, Miguel Ángel.

Etxalar

ETXALAR is a tiny place, 4km off the main road, but is perhaps the best-preserved town of the valley, famous for the impressive array of Basque funerary steles in the churchyard. There's a lovely **casa rural** in the centre, *Casa Domekenea* (☎948 635031; ③), and another, *Casa Herri-Gain* (☎948 635208; ③), perched on a steep hill, with fantastic views of the surrounding area.

San Sebastián

The undisputed queen of the Basque resorts, **SAN SEBASTIÁN** (Donostia) is a picturesque – and expensive – seaside town with good beaches. Along with Santander, it has always been the most fashionable place to escape the heat of the southern summers, and in July and August it's packed. Though it tries hard to be chic, San Sebastián is too much of a family resort to compete in those terms with the South of France, which is all to its good. Set around the deep, still bay of La Concha and enclosed by rolling low hills, it's beautifully situated; the old town sits on the eastern promontory, its back to the wooded slopes of Monte Urgull, while newer development has spread along the banks of the Urumea, around the edge of the bay to the foot of Monte Igeldo and on the hills overlooking the bay.

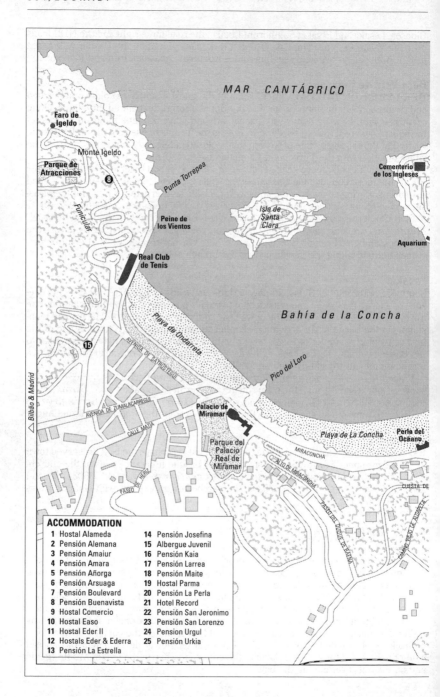

MAR CANTÁBRICO

Faro de Igeldo

Monte Igeldo

Parque de Atracciones

⑧

Funicular

Punta Torrepea

Peine de los Vientos

Real Club de Tenis

Isla de Santa Clara

Cementerio de los Ingleses

Aquarium

Bahía de la Concha

Playa de Ondarreta

⑮

AVENIDA DE SATROSTEGUI

AVENIDA DE ZUMALACARREGUI

CALLE MATIA

Pico del Loro

◁ Bilbáo & Madrid

PASEO DE HERIZ

Palacio de Miramar

Parque del Palacio Real de Miramar

Playa de La Concha

MIRACONCHA

ALTO DE MIRACONCHA

Perla del Océano

CUESTA DE

PASEO DEL DUQUE DE BAENA

CAMINO VIEJO DE AIGORETA

ACCOMMODATION

1 Hostal Alameda
2 Pensión Alemana
3 Pensión Amaiur
4 Pensión Amara
5 Pensión Añorga
6 Pensión Arsuaga
7 Pensión Boulevard
8 Pensión Buenavista
9 Hostal Comercio
10 Hostal Easo
11 Hostal Eder II
12 Hostals Eder & Ederra
13 Pensión La Estrella

14 Pensión Josefina
15 Albergue Juvenil
16 Pensión Kaia
17 Pensión Larrea
18 Pensión Maite
19 Hostal Parma
20 Pensión La Perla
21 Hotel Record
22 Pensión San Jeronimo
23 Pensión San Lorenzo
24 Pension Urgul
25 Pensión Urkia

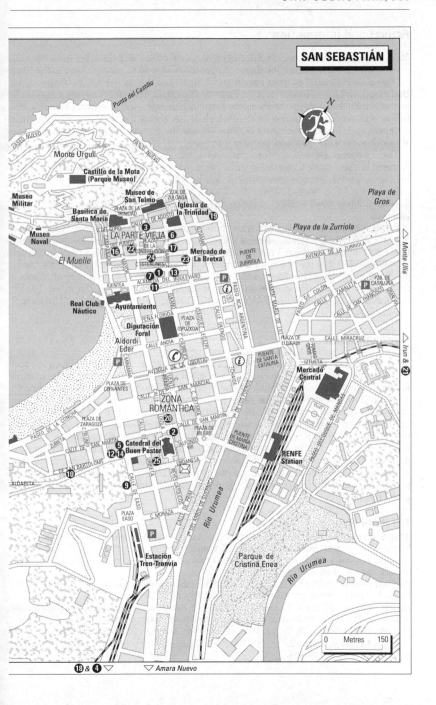

SAN SEBASTIÁN

Punta del Castillo

PASEO NUEVO

Monte Urgull

Castillo de la Mota
(Parque Museo)

Museo
Militar

Museo de
San Telmo

PZA DE
ZULOAGA

Playa de
Gros

Basilica de
Santa María

PLAZA DE LA
TRINIDAD

Iglesia de
la Trinidad

Playa de la Zurriola

CALLE 31 DE AGOSTO

Museo
Naval

LA PARTE VIEJA

AVENIDA DE LA ZURRIOLA

El Muelle

PLAZA
DE LA
CONSTITUCIÓN

Mercado de
La Bretxa

PUENTE DE
ZURRIOLA

Monte Ulia

ESTERLINES

PASEO
DE
COLON

P2A DE
CATALUÑA

IGENTEA

ALAMEDA DEL BOULEVARD

PASEO RCA. ARGENTINA

CALLE DE SAN FRANCISCO

Irun & 21

Real Club
Náutico

Ayuntamiento

PEÑA FLORIDA

PLAZA
DE
GIPUZKOA

PLAZA DE
EUSKADI

CALLE MIRACRUZ

Diputación
Foral

CALLE ANDIA

PUENTE
DE SANTA
CATALINA

IZTUETA

Aldordi
Eder

AVENIDA DE LA LIBERTAD

Mercado
Central

PLAZA DE
CERVANTES

ZONA
ROMÁNTICA

SAN MARCIAL

CALLE DE SAN MARTIN

PLAZA DE
ZARAGOZA

CALLE DE SAN MARTIN

PLAZA DE
BILBAO

PASEO DE LA CONCHA

ALFONSO
VIII

PUENTE
DE MARIA
CRISTINA

ZUBIETA

Catedral del
Buen Pastor

URDANETA

RENFE
Station

C. DE SAN BARTOLOMÉ

REYES CATÓLICOS

Río Urumea

ALDAPETA

C. MORAZA

CALLE DE PRIM

CALLE DE EASO

PLAZA
EASO

Parque de
Cristina Enea

Río Urumea

Estación
Tren-Tranvía

0   Metres   150

18 & 4

Amara Nuevo

Arrival and information

Most **buses** arrive at Plaza Pío XII, fifteen minutes' walk along the river from the centre of town (the ticket office for these companies is around the corner next to the river on Paseo de Bizkaia), but from Pasaia and Astigarraga they arrive on the Alameda del Boulevard, and from Hondarribia on Plaza de Gipuzkoa. The main-line **train station** is across the Río Urumea on the Paseo de Francia, although local lines from Hendaia and Bilbao via Zarautz and Zumaia (both of which do not accept InterRail passes) have their terminus on c/Easo. The **airport** is 22km outside the city centre, near Hondarribia; an airport bus runs every fifteen minutes into town.

The **Turismo** (Mon–Sat 8am–8pm, Sun 10am–1pm; ☎943 481166) is on c/Reina Regente in the Teatro Victoria Eugenia. For a greater selection of pamphlets there is the very useful Basque government tourist office (Mon–Fri 9.30am–1.30pm & 3.30–6.30pm, Sat 9am–1.30pm & 3.30–6.30pm; July & Aug also open Sun 9.30am–1.30pm; ☎943 426282) at Paseo de los Fueros 1, just off the main Avenida de la Libertad.

San Sebastián is something of a travel hub for the region. Viajes TIVE, c/Tomás Gros 3 (☎943 276934), is a youth/student **travel agency** that sells tickets for international buses and discount plane tickets. Another good travel agency is Viajes Aran, c/Elkano 1 (☎943 429009). For travel **books and maps** (both local and elsewhere), and for books on all things related to the Basque country, head for Graphos on the corner of Alameda del Boulevard and c/Mayor. Also recommended are Bilintx, c/Esterlines 10, Dr Camino, c/31 de Agosto 32–36, and the new library, Koldo Mitxelena, c/Urdaneta 9 (☎943 482750).

Accommodation

Places to stay, though plentiful, can be pricey and hard to come by in season – if you arrive in July or August, or during the film festival in September, you'll have to start looking early in the day, or book ahead if possible. There is no great difference in rates between the cheapest places in the *parte vieja* (old quarter) and elsewhere, although *hostales* along the Alameda del Boulevard do tend to be slightly pricier. There is often more chance of finding space in the cathedral (*centro*) area around c/Easo, c/San Martín, c/Fuenterrabía and the lively c/San Bartolomé, or on the other side of the river in **Gros**, behind the main train station in **Egia**, or in the new part of town, **Amara Nuevo**, on the way to the Anoeta sports complex. Asking in bars in any of the above-mentioned areas about unofficial private rooms can produce a result – although the Turismo strongly recommends sticking to licensed hotels and guest houses.

The Parte Vieja

Albergue Juvenil, Paseo de Igeldo (☎943 310268, fax 943 214090). San Sebastián's youth hostel, known as *La Sirena*, is just a few minutes' walk from the end of Ondarreta beach. ①.

Pensión Amaiur, c/31 de Agosto 44, 2° (☎943 429654). Pleasant, friendly *pensión* with carpeted doubles and a few triples. ④.

Pensión Arsuaga, c/Narrica 3, 3° (☎943 420681). Simple, spacious doubles; can be chilly in winter but has its own restaurant and offers good full-board deals. ③.

Hostal La Estrella, Plaza de Sarriegi 1 (☎943 420997). Attractive old *hostal*, offering rooms with or without shower, either overlooking the plaza or Alameda del Boulevard. ④.

Pensión Kaia, c/Puerto 12, 2° (☎943 431342). Pleasant, modern rooms with bath. ④.

Pensión Larrea, c/Narrica 21, 1° (☎943 422694). Clean, new rooms but on a busy street corner, and a bit cramped and noisy. ④.

Hostal Parma, c/General Jauregui 11 (☎943 428893). Nicely located between *parte vieja* and Pasco Nuevo, this *hostal* offers comfortable rooms with all amenities, the best ones overlooking the sea. ⑥.

Pensión San Jerónimo, c/San Jerónimo 25, 2° (☎943 420830). Adequate *pensión*, though the rooms are spartan and the hallway and stairs somewhat the worse for wear. ④.

Pensión San Lorenzo, c/San Lorenzo 2, 1° (☎943 425516). Guests can use the kitchen to prepare food in this small *ponsión*. ③.

Pensión Urgul, c/Esterlines 10, 3° (☎943 430047). Airy, spotless and tastefully furnished rooms –there are only five, so arrive early or book (no lift). ③.

Alameda del Boulevard

Hostal Alameda, Alameda del Boulevard 23 (☎943 421687). Old, characterful building showing its age. Some rooms are available en suite. ③–⑤.

Pensión Boulevard, Alameda del Boulevard 24, 1° (☎943 429405). Comfortable, modern rooms, but without washbasins and only one is en suite. ⑤.

Hostal Eder II, Alameda del Boulevard 16, 2° (☎943 426449). Elegant hallway with fine wood panelling leads to spacious rooms, some with bath. ⑤.

Centro

Pensión Alemana, c/San Martín 53, 1° (☎943 462544, fax 943 461771). Perfectly located on the street by the cathedral, and with en-suite rooms, this *pensión* is highly recommended. ⑥.

Pensión Añorga, c/Easo 12, 1° (☎943 467945). Large *pensión* on two floors; fairly plain, but the rooms are clean and some have bath. ③.

Hostal Comercio, c/Urdaneta 24 (☎943 464414). Simply furnished *hostal*, offering reasonable rooms with washbasin and fan heaters. ④.

Hostal Easo, c/San Bartolomé 24 (☎943 453912). Relatively low-priced rooms with washbasin or shower. ④.

Hostal Eder, and **Hostal Ederra**, c/San Bartolomé 33 and 25 (☎943 4649696 & 943 426449). Two smart *hostals* run by the same management as the *Eder II* in Alameda del Boulevard. Easter & July–Sept only. ⑤.

Pensión Josefina, c/Easo 12, 3° (☎943 461956). This *pensión* has a couple of large rooms facing the street, but otherwise offers only cramped singles and doubles with little or no natural light. ④.

Pensión La Perla, c/Loiola 10 (☎943 428123). Excellent-value *pensión*, near the cathedral and the food market, offering spotless rooms with bath. ④.

Pensión Urkia, c/Urbieta 12, 3° (☎943 424436). Run by the sister of *La Perla*'s owner, this *pensión* has equally good rooms with bath. ④.

Out of the centre

Pensión Amara, Isabel II 2, 1° (☎943 468472). Clean, comfortable acommodation in this highly recommended *pensión*. ④.

Hotel Buenavista, Barrio de Igeldo (☎943 210600). Typical Basque chalet on the main road to Monte Igeldo, featuring great sea views and a good restaurant. ④.

Pensión Maite, Avda. de Madrid 19, 1° B (☎943 470715). Good, clean rooms with bath and TV; handy for bus station, Astoria cinema and Anoeta football stadium. The owners also run the *Bar Maite* opposite. ④.

Hotel Record, Calzada Vieja de Ategorrieta (☎943 271255, fax 943 278521). At the far end of Gros and a pleasant alternative to the bustle of the *parte vieja* and *centro*; well-connected by bus or a fifteen-minute walk from the centre, with plenty of parking. All rooms with shower or bath; the larger have terraces. ⑥.

Camping

Igeldo, Barrio de Igeldo (☎943 214502). San Sebastián's campsite is excellent, although it's a long way from the centre on the landward side of Monte Igeldo, reached by bus #16 from the Alameda del Boulevard. Open all year.

The Town

The **parte vieja** (old quarter) is the town's highlight – cramped and lively streets where the crowds congregate in the evenings to wander among the many small bars and shops or sample the shellfish from the street traders down by the fishing harbour.

Here, too, are San Sebastián's chief sights: the elaborate Baroque facade of the eighteenth-century church of **Santa María**, and the more elegantly restrained sixteenth-century Gothic church of **San Vicente**. The centre of the old quarter is **La Plaza de la Constitución** (known by the locals simply as La Consti) – the numbers on the balconies of the apartments around the square refer to the days when it was used as a bullring. Situated just off c/31 de Agosto (the only street to survive the great fire of August 31, 1813), behind San Vicente, is the excellent **Museo de San Telmo** (Tues–Sat 10.30am–1.30pm & 4–8pm, Sun & fiestas 10.30am–2pm; free), whose displays – around the cloisters of a former convent – include a fine Basque ethnographic exhibition on the first floor and the largest collection of discoidal funerary steles in the Basque country. There are regular exhibitions of work by modern Basque painters and the convent chapel (daily 4–8pm) is decorated with a series of frescoes by José Sert, depicting scenes from Basque life. In the same square as the side entrance to the museum is the oldest surviving gastronomic society in the city, the **Artesana**.

Behind the plaza rises **Monte Urgull**, crisscrossed by winding paths. From the mammoth figure of Christ on its summit there are great views out to sea and back across the bay to the town. On the way down you can stop at the **Aquarium** (mid-May to mid-Sept daily 10am–1.30pm & 4–8pm; mid-Sept to mid-May Tues–Sun 10am–1.30pm & 4–7.30pm; 1100ptas) on the harbour; it contains the skeleton of a whale caught in the last century and an extensive history of Basque navigation, although not a great deal of fish. Close by, at Paseo de Muelle 24, is the **Museo Naval** (mid-June to mid-Sept Tues–Sat 10am–1.30pm & 5–8.30pm, Sun 11am–2pm; mid-Sept to mid-June Tues–Sat 10am–1.30pm & 4–7.30pm, Sun 11am–2pm), with video facilities and exhibits tracing the tradition and history of Basque fishing.

Fantastic views across the bay can be had from the top of **Monte Igeldo**: take the bus marked *Igeldo* from the Boulevard or walk round the bay to its base near the tennis club, from where a **funicular** (daily summer 10am–8pm, winter 11am–6pm; every 15min; 170ptas round-trip) will carry you to the summit.

Beaches

There are **three beaches** in San Sebastián: Playa de la Concha, Playa de Ondarreta and Playa de la Zurriola. **La Concha** is the most central and the most celebrated, a wide crescent of yellow sand stretching round the bay from the town. Despite the almost impenetrable mass of flesh here during most of the summer, this is the best of the beaches, enlivened by sellers of peeled prawns and cold Cokes and with great swimming out to the sand bars and boats moored in the bay. Out in La Concha bay is a small island, **Isla de Santa Clara**, which makes a good spot for picnics; a boat leaves from the port every half-hour in the summer (daily, 10am–8pm; 250ptas round-trip).

La Concha and **Ondarreta** are the best beaches for swimming – the latter is a continuation of the same strand beyond the rocky outcrop which supports the **Palacio de Miramar**, once a summer home of Spain's royal family. Set back from Ondarreta beach are large villas, some of the most expensive properties in Spain, and mostly owned by wealthy families from Madrid who vacation here – the area used to be known as La Diplomática for this reason and has a reputation for being rather more staid than the central area, although the lively district of **El Antiguo** with its many bars is only a few minutes' walk beyond.

Playa de la Zurriola has been rebuilt and is now very good for surfing and far less crowded. The elegant promenade, however, has been blighted by the construction of a huge concrete cube; this new centre, due to open in the summer of 1999, will contain restaurants, shops, an auditorium for concerts and an art gallery. One of the best views of the whole town and bay may be had by climbing up the steps to the cider house on the side of **Monte Ulia** from the far end of the beach. This walk can easily be extended for about 5km along the coast to the lighthouse overlooking the entrance to Pasaia harbour.

Eating, drinking and entertainment

If you're in the mood for a gastronomic treat, San Sebastián has some of the best **restaurants in Spain** (note that most are closed Sunday evening and Monday), as well as plenty of lively **bars**. You'll find most places around the *parte vieja*. Prices tend to reflect the popularity of the old quarter, especially in the waterside restaurants, but the lunchtime *menús del día* are generally good value, and the *pinchos* and *raciones* in the bars are a great way to eat cheaply in the evenings. For those on a budget, the **Mercado de la Bretxa** is conviently situated in the centre of the *parte vieja* on c/San Juan.

Restaurants and tapas bars

Akelarre, Paseo de Padre Orcolaga 56 (☎943 212052). In Barrio Igeldo, this is one of the city's top restaurants with wonderful sea views. Allow over 5000ptas a head.

Arzak, Alto de Miracruz 21, Monte Ulia (☎943 278465). A shrine of Basque cuisine, with three Michelin rosettes and a superb *menú* for around 8000ptas.

Domenico's, c/Zubieta 3. Upmarket Italian restaurant, very popular with the locals.

Bar Etxadi, c/Reyes Católicos 9. Lively bar-restaurant for *raciones* and inexpensive *menús*.

Gaztelu, c/31 de Agosto 22. Fine choice in the *parte vieja* where you can choose from a selection of reasonably priced *raciones*.

Mama Mia's, c/Triunfo 8. Good, inexpensive Italian restaurant serving vegetarian dishes.

Casa Maruxa, Paseo de Bizkaia 14, Amara. Specializes in food from Galicia and attracts the crowd on their way to the Astoria cinema complex just around the corner.

Morgan Jatetxea, c/Narrica 7. Specializes in the French-influenced new Basque school of cookery and also has dishes suitable for vegetarians – especially tasty first courses. It's quite normal to order two of these instead of the more meat- and fish-orientated main courses.

Casa Nicolasa, c/Aldamar 4 (☎943 421762). Classic – and expensive – Basque cookery.

Casa Senra, c/San Francisco. Good-value restaurant in Gros.

Oriental, c/Reyes Católicos 6. Best of the bunch of Chinese restaurants in terms of quality of food, price and extremely friendly atmosphere.

Cafetería Ubarrechenea, c/San Martín 42. Excellent and economical *menús*.

Warrechena, c/Mayor. Very popular with locals and visitors alike, this serves up standard Spanish fare and is one of the least expensive places to eat in the *parte vieja*.

Bars and clubs

In the evenings, you'll find no shortage of action, with **clubs** and **bars** everywhere. The two main areas are the **parte vieja**, where you'll find *Bar Uraitz*, *Bar Eibartarra* and *Bar Sariketa*, all on the lively c/Fermín Calbetón, and the area around **c/Reyes Católicos**, where a large number of the city's more expensive music pubs are located: try *Pokhara*, *Kalima*, *La Bodeguilla* or *El Nido*, which plays a wide selection of music. Calle San Bartolomé, a few streets back from the Concha promenade, attracts a very young crowd. For **jazz**, try *BeBop*, *Etxekalte* or *Altxerri*, all on the edge of the *parte vieja*. In Gros there are also a couple of excellent German-style pubs, *El Chofre* and *Bidea*, with a range of imported beers.

Once the pubs close, usually by about 3.30am, the night continues at the *Komplot* in c/Pedro Egaña, at *Bataplán* on the Concha promenade, and at *La Piscina* and *Tenis*, both at the far end of Ondarreta beach, where there is often live music (especially salsa) well into the small hours.

SIDRERÍAS

If you're in San Sebastián between late January and early May, a visit to one of the many **sidrerías** (*sagardotegiak* in Basque, or cider houses) in the area around **Astigarraga**, about 6km from town, is a must – take the red Hernani-bound bus from the Alameda del Boulevard or a taxi for about 1000ptas.

Cider production is one of the oldest traditions in the Basque country – until the Civil War and the subsequent move towards industrialization, practically every farmhouse in Gipuzkoa and to a lesser extent the other provinces produced cider, which was a valuable commodity used as barter. Barter remained the main form of exchange in rural communities here until comparatively recently, and the farms were practically open houses where local people socialized – the *bertsolariak* tradition of oral poetry originated in these places – and drank cider. Cider houses are again flourishing, and for 1500–2500ptas you can feast on enormous steaks, grilled fish and codfish omelette followed by local cheese and walnuts, drink unlimited quantities of cider and in general enjoy the raucous atmosphere. Of the fifty or so *sidrerías*, some of the most accessible include *Petritegi* and *Gartziategi*, just a few kilometres out of town, while many of the more rustic (ie authentic) ones, such as *Sarasola* and *Oiarbide*, are on the so-called *ruta de las sidrerías* (cider trail) beyond Astigarraga. Check in the Turismo for a full list with phone numbers.

Festivals

Throughout the summer there are constant **fiestas**, many involving Basque sports including the annual rowing (*trainera*) races between the villages along the coast. The **Jazz Festival**, at different locations throughout the town for five days in July, invariably attracts top performers as well as hordes of people on their way home from the fiesta in Pamplona. There is also the **Film Festival** in the second half of September and frequent theatrical and musical performances throughout the year at both the Victoria Eugenia and the Teatro Principal. The Turismo produces a monthly guide to what's on.

Listings

Banks Most banks have their main branches along Avda. de la Libertad, including Banco Central Hispano at no. 17 and Banco Bilbao Bizkaia on the corner with c/Hernani.

Bike rental You can rent mountain bikes from Comet, Avda. de la Libertad 6 (☎943 426637).

Car rental Atesa, Amezketa 7 (☎943 463013); Avis, c/Triunfo 2 (☎943 461527); Hertz, c/Zubieta 5 (☎943 461084); and Europcar, RENFE station, Paseo de Francia (☎943 322304).

Hiking information Contact Club de Montaña de Kresala, c/Euskalerría 9 (☎943 420905), or Noresta, c/María Lili (☎943 293520), a travel and map bookstore that also rents skis and trekking gear.

Post office The *Correos* is at c/Urdaneta, just south of the cathedral (Mon–Fri 8am–9pm, Sat 9am–2pm).

Swimming pool The sports centre in Anoeta, Polideportivo de Anoeta (☎943 458797), has an open-air pool, track, tennis courts and a gym. There's a pool, Termas La Perla, at Paseo de la Concha (☎943 458856), which also has a gym and sauna.

Telephones There is a *telefónica* on c/San Marcial 29, one block from Avda. de la Libertad (Mon–Sat 9.30am–11pm).

Inland from San Sebastián: a circuit through Gipuzkoa

Gipuzkoa is the smallest province in Spain and public transport is good, meaning that most places of interest can be visited comfortably as a day trip from San Sebastián.

Alternatively, try the circuit set out below which can also act as a stepping stone to Vitoria and places further south.

Tolosa and Ordizia

Twenty-four kilometres south of San Sebastián is **TOLOSA**, famous for its **carnival** in February, celebrated here with fervour and considered by Basques to be superior to San Sebastián's (it was the only one whose tradition was maintained throughout the Franco era). In October, the town hosts an international choir festival. Although fairly industrialized, Tolosa has an extensive old quarter with an impressive old town square and is a lively place for a weekend night out. Make sure you sample a plate of *alubias* (kidney beans) in one of the many eating places – they're considered the best in Euskadi. If you want to **stay**, try *Hostal Oyarbide*, Plaza Gorriti 1 (☎943 670017; ④), or the more upmarket *Hotel Oria*, c/de Oria 2 (☎ & fax 943 654688; ⑤).

A further 20km south, on the main railway line to Vitoria, is **ORDIZIA**, the fastest growing town in the Oria valley. If your visit coincides with a Wednesday, don't miss the weekly **market** of farm products when all the farmers in the region converge on the town to buy and sell livestock, cheese and the like.

Walks around Ordizia

Ordizia is backed by the impressive peak of **Txindoki**, rising above the town like a mini-Matterhorn. You can climb it in about three hours from Larraitz, the highest village, and the whole thing can be done as a day trip from San Sebastián or Tolosa.

The **Sierra de Aralar** stretching beyond Txindoki is a great place for a few days' walking – one possibility is to walk all the way from Larraitz to the **monastery of San Miguel** in Navarra (7–8 hours in all, largely on the flat over the plateau), where it's possible to stay and eat cheaply, and from where a road leads down the escarpment to **Huarte** on the main Vitoria–Pamplona rail line. In winter the range becomes a popular centre for cross-country skiing.

Segura and the monastery of Aranzazu

One of the most attractive inland villages in Gipuzkoa is **SEGURA**, southeast of Ordizia. An original seignorial village from where the powerful Guevara family once wielded power, there are various old mansions once belonging to the Guevaras and other families of note along its long, winding main street. Today, it's a sleepy backwater which comes alive during the **Easter processions** (not otherwise much celebrated in Euskadi) and which hosts one of the best village fiestas in Euskadi in mid-June.

Segura, and Zegama farther south, were important stops on the ancient **Pilgrim Route** to Santiago, which joined up with the main route in Santo Domingo de la Calzada (La Rioja). The old Roman way the pilgrims once followed is still partly in evidence and you can walk a section of it as an easy day trip, even without your own transport (although you should double check all transport details before setting out). Take an early Vitoria-bound train from San Sebastián to **OTZAURTE**, a small halt south of Zegama. From here it's an hour's walk to the refuge of **San Adrián** (open weekends throughout the year and daily in summer; meals available). The best-preserved section of Roman road on the mountain is just beyond the natural tunnel of San Adrián above the refuge, from where it's downhill (2hr) to **Araia**, the first town in Araba just off the Vitoria–Pamplona road; from here, a bus departs at 3.15pm for Vitoria and trains leave from the station 2km beyond town.

Alternatively, head west across the plateau or along the spectacular ridge of Aitzkorri to the refuge of **Urbia** (same hours as San Adrián) and the monastery of **Aranzazu**

(3–4hr), where there are several *hostales* and hotels, best value of which is *Hospedería de Aranzazu* (☎943 781313; ③), or the slightly more expensive *Sindica* next door (☎943 781303; ④). This is the prime place of pilgrimage for Basques – **Our Lady of Aranzazu** is the patron saint of Gipuzkoa – and is located in a particularly spectacular setting, clinging to the mountainside above a gorge. Although a monastery on this site dates back to the fifteenth century, the present futuristic-looking building was built in 1950 and features contemporary work by the sculptors Chillida (the doors) and Oteiza (part of the facade). It gets packed out on Sundays when worshippers come from all over the province and elsewhere.

Oñati

OÑATI, 8km below Aranzazu, is without doubt the most interesting inland town in Gipuzkoa, with some fine examples of Baroque architecture among its many historic buildings; indeed the Basque painter Zuloaga described it as the "Basque Toledo".

The old **university** dominates the town, built in 1548 and the only functioning university in Euskadi for hundreds of years. The facade with its four pilasters adorned with figures, and the serene courtyard, are particularly impressive. The Baroque town hall and parish church of **San Miguel** are at opposite ends of the arcaded Plaza de los Fueros. In the church crypt are buried all the Counts of Oñati from 988 to 1890; the cloister is unusual in that it is actually built over the river. Other fine buildings around the town include various *casas torres* of the type also found in north Navarra, private family mansions and the Plateresque-style monastery of **Bidaurreta**.

Practicalities

You'll find a very helpful **Turismo** at Foru Enparantza 11 (daily; ☎943 783453), which can arrange visits to the university and parish church, and provide a free map of the town, as well as plenty of leaflets detailing walking and motoring routes to places of interest nearby.

The *Bar-Restaurante Echeverria*, R.M. Zuazola 15 (☎943 780460; ③), is the only **hostal** in the town centre – the **restaurant** below also offers a reasonable *menú del día*. Enquire at the Turismo about an **agroturismo** – try *Enparantza*, Olabarrieta 25 (☎943 782152; ③), or *Arregi*, Garagaltza 21 (☎943 780824; ④) – or the possibility of a private room.

There is a daily **bus** from Oñati to Bilbao, and another to Vitoria, changing at Mondragón.

The Costa Vasca

Heading west from San Sebastián, both road and rail run inland, following the Río Oria, towards the coast at Zarautz. Along the way, the pretty fishing village of **Orio** on the estuary makes an enjoyable break in the journey. From **Zarautz** onwards, the coastline of the **Costa Vasca** is glorious – rocky and wild, with long stretches of road hugging the edge of the cliffs – all the way to Bilbao. There are buses that take the motorway along this route, but even if you're not planning to stop (and there are plenty of picturesque villages to tempt you to do so) it's worth taking the old road for the scenery. The farther you go, the less developed the resorts are.

Zarautz

ZARAUTZ itself is certainly not the most attractive spot along the coast. Developed as a fashionable overspill of San Sebastián, the old village has been swamped by a line of hotels and pricey cafés sandwiched between the busy road and the busier beach, a popular place for surfers. The town and surrounding area (and, to a lesser extent, towns farther along the coast towards Bizkaia) are famous for the production of *txakoli*, a strong, dry white wine – the vineyards cling to hillsides along the coast from here to Getaria.

Practicalities

The well-stocked **Turismo** is on c/Nafarroa (Mon–Sat 9am–1pm & 3.30–7pm, Sun 10am–2pm; ☎943 830990), the busy main road through town; staff here can advise on **accommodation**. One of the best places to stay is a large and well-situated *agroturismo*; *Agerre-Goikoa* (☎943 833248; ④), above the *Talai-Mendi* campsite. The **youth hostel**, *Monte Albertia*, San Inazio 25 (☎943 132910, fax 943 130006; ②), on the Meagas road out of town, is open all year. Zarautz has two **campsites**, *Gran Camping Zarauz* (☎943 831238; open all year) on the cliff tops overlooking the beach, reached from town on the old San Sebastián road, with a marked turning on the left up the hill, and the cheaper *Talai-Mendi* (☎943 830042), a short walk from the beach but open only from July to mid-September.

Getaria

Five kilometres on is **GETARIA**, a tiny fishing port sheltered by the hump-backed islet of **El Ratón** (The Mouse). It's a historic little place, one of the earliest towns on the coast, preserving the magnificent fourteenth-century church of San Salvador, whose altar is raised theatrically above the heads of the congregation. The first man to sail around the world, Juan Sebastián Elcano, was born here around 1487, and his ship was the only one of Magellan's fleet to make it back home. Every four years on August 6, during the village's **fiestas**, Elcano's landing is re-enacted on the beach; the next will be in 1999. The *Mayflower* bar overlooking the harbour is worth a visit for the round-the-wall nautical map of the entire Basque coast, and there's a small but interesting **art gallery** of oil reliefs by local painter Elorza, which is free of charge.

Practicalities

Getaria has a small, summer-only **Turismo** at Aldamar Parkea 2 (mid-July to mid-Sept Mon 3–9pm, Wed 11.15am–1.15pm & 3–9pm, Thurs–Sun 10.15am–2.15 & 3–9pm; ☎943 140957); when it's closed, use the Turismo in Zarautz.

Check the prices at the tempting fish **restaurants** before you eat; many are expensive. **Accommodation** options include *Pensión Getariano*, c/Errieta Kalea 3 (☎943 140567; ⑤) and three somewhat cheaper *agroturismos* a few kilometres up the hillside on the way to Meagas; check with the Turismo for details.

Zumaia, Azpeitia and around

The coast becomes still more rugged on the way to **ZUMAIA** – an industrial-looking place at first sight, but with an attractive centre and pleasant waterfront along the estuary of the Río Urola. Zumaia's local **fiesta** in the first days of July is one of the region's most exuberant, with Basque sports, dancing and bullocks let loose on the beach to test the mettle of the local youth.

Zumaia has two very different **beaches** – one of these, over the hill behind the town, is a large splash of grey sand enclosed by extraordinary sheer cliffs of layered slate-like rock which channel the waves in to produce some of the best surfing on the coast. There are spectacular walks along the cliff tops to the west. The other beach, across the river from the port, is yellow and flat, sheltered by a little pine forest. On the road behind this you'll find the **Villa Zuloaga** (June 6–Sept 15 Wed–Sun 4–8pm; 400ptas), former home of the Basque painter Ignacio Zuloaga, and now a small art museum displaying his work and that of other Basque artists, together with a rather bizarre exhibition of bull-fighting memorabilia.

There's a **Turismo** in the main square (July–Sept Mon 4–7.30pm, Tues–Sat 10am–1.30pm & 4–7.30pm; ☎943 143396), where you'll also find the only **accommodation** in town, *Bar Tomás* (☎943 861916; ③); if the rooms here are full, the owner should be able to organize a private room elsewhere without too much trouble.

Inland from Zumaia, 1km from the town of **AZPEITIA**, is the imposing eighteenth-century Baroque **Basilica of Loyola** (daily 8.30am–2pm & 3–9pm), built in honour of San Ignacio de Loyola, the founder of the Society of Jesus, with an impressive rotunda and marble decor – this is a major pilgrimage spot. Also nearby is the town of **ZESTOA**, which lies north of Azpeitia and has a rich supply of thermal and mineral waters. The luxurious (and pricey) *Gran Hotel Balneario Cestona* (☎943 147140, fax 943 147140; ⑦) lies just off the main road (Carretera Provincial) and offers a wide range of spa treatments including thermal showers.

Mutriku

Beyond **Deva** (Deba), itself an unprepossessing place, the main road veers inland and the coastal route becomes still wilder as it enters the province of Bizkaia. The road is narrow and slow, but there are a fair number of buses from San Sebastián and hitching is surprisingly easy. There's a **Turismo** near the port in Deva, at Puerto 1 (open July to Sept only; ☎943 602452).

MUTRIKU, despite some ugly recent construction above the town, has some attractive narrow streets leading down steeply to the fishing harbour. It's the centre of another *txakoli*-producing area. Admiral Churruca, the "Hero of Trafalgar" to locals, was born here; his imposing statue faces the incongruous church of Nuestra Señora de Asunción, built along the lines of a Greek temple. Mutriku boasts no fewer than five **campsites** around several small beaches, and there is also a choice of **agroturismos**, *Casa Matzuri* (☎943 603001; ③), just beyond town on the road to Ondarroa, and *Koostei* (☎943 583008; ③), perched high up in the hills several kilometres from the main road, which offers horse riding. Beyond Mutriku, the road temporarily turns inland and reaches the coast once more at the beach of **Saturrarán**, very popular and crowded in summer, when there's a **campsite** (☎943 603847; June–Sept).

Ondarroa

Around the headland from Saturrarán, **ONDARROA**, the first coastal town in Bizkaia, presents a very different aspect from the other small resorts farther east. Here, the usual town beach and attractive tree-lined *rambla* end at a no-nonsense **fishing port** filled with an eclectic set of trawlers. In the early morning, an endless succession of trucks files in from the coastal road to fill up with fish – the traffic is so great that a large bridge has been built across the bay to channel the fishing trucks directly to the port. On the quayside, burly fishermen haul up skips of quivering fish from the bowels of their vessels and hurl them into the back of the waiting trucks. You're unlikely to want to stay more than one night, but Ondarroa is an interesting place to stop over, particularly in August when the town hosts its **fiestas**.

Practicalities

If you want to **stay**, head for the *Hostal Vega*, c/Antiguako Ama 8 (☎94 683 00 02; April–Sept only; ④), right by the fishing port and overlooking the water; the rooms are spacious and clean, some with massive picture windows, and the terrace **restaurant** serves a good 1200ptas *menú*, incorporating whatever's been landed that day. The **bars** at the harbour stay open late (some 24hr) as deckhands come and go, and, stuffed with a tempting array of seafood *pinchos*, they're accommodating enough to keep the promenading locals and occasional stray tourist happy.

Lekeitio

LEKEITIO is another good bet along this stretch. Still an active fishing port, it has two fine **beaches** – one beside the harbour, the other, much better, across the river to the east of town. There's little choice in **accommodation**: try the *Hotel Beitia*, Avda. Pascual Abaroa 25 (☎94 684 01 11, fax 94 684 21 65; ⑤), and the *Hostal Piñupe*, Avda. Pascual Abaroa 10 (☎94 684 29 84, fax 94 684 07 72; ⑤), both of which are very popular in summer, when the town becomes a prime destination for the masses from Bilbao. Depending on how adventurous you feel, you could always sleep on the beach, where there are showers and, in season at least, a couple of restaurants. Lekeitio is literally teeming with **bars**, many offering food. An official **campsite**, *Endai* (☎94 684 24 69; Easter & mid-June to mid-Sept only) can be found on the main road to Ondarroa; alternatively, head for *Leagi* (☎94 684 23 52), which is open all year. There is a summer-only **agroturismo**, *Mendexakua* (☎94 624 31 08; ④), in the village of Mendexa, 3km inland. Horse-riding, mountain biking and kayaking are all available nearby.

Elantxobe

The road turns inland from Lekeitio, but the fishing village of **ELANTXOBE** (Elanchove), almost entirely in its original condition, is worth a detour back to the coast. Perched high above a small harbour, the village is connected to it by an incredibly steep cobbled street lined with attractive fishermen's houses. Calle Mayor continues up to the cemetery from where a signposted track leads to **Mount Ogoño** – the highest cliff on the Basque coast at 280m.

Elantxobe has a couple of small **restaurants** in c/Mayor but no accommodation – make it a day trip, or stay at either *Pensión Arboliz* (☎94 627 62 83; ④) or the **agroturismo**, *Etxetxu* (☎94 627 63 37; ③), both located in Arboliz, 1km from the crossroads in the direction of Gernika.

Direct **buses** run between Elantxobe and Gernika (twice daily) or, from Lekeitio, take the Gernika bus to the crossroads at Ibarrangelua and walk 1km down to the village.

Gernika and around

Immortalized by Picasso's nightmare picture (finally brought home to Spain after the fall of Franco, and now exhibited in the Centro de Arte Reina Sofía, Madrid), **GERNIKA**, inland and west of Lekeitio, is the traditional heart of Basque nationalism. It was here that the Basque parliament used to meet, and here, under the **Tree of Gernika** (the *Gernikako Arbola*), that their rights were reconfirmed by successive rulers. Sadly it was also Gernika's fate to be chosen for the first-ever saturation bombing raid on a civilian centre – an attempt to blast the soul out of Basque resistance in the Civil War. In only four hours on April 27, 1937 more than 1600 people were killed and the town centre destroyed.

The parliament building, the **Casa de las Juntas** (Mon–Sat 10am–2pm & 4–7pm, Sun 10am–1.30pm; free), is well worth a visit for the stained-glass window depicting the tree and important scenes and monuments from the region. The adjacent church of **Santa María la Antigua**, adorned with portraits of the various nobles of Bizkaia who pledged allegiance to the *fueros*, has traditionally served as a kind of church/ parliament, used for Assemblies. The parliament, church and tree remained miraculously unscathed by the bombing, but the rest of the town was rebuilt and is now nondescript. For a Basque, at least, a visit here is more pilgrimage than tourist trip. A walk through Europa Park with its ornamental gardens, fast-flowing stream and peace sculptures by Henry Moore and Eduardo Chillida captures something of the elegiac atmosphere.

Practicalities

There's a helpful **Turismo**, at c/Artekale 8 (Mon–Sat 10am–1pm & 4–7.30pm, Sun 10am–1pm; ☎94 625 58 92) in the arcaded main street, with one of the best selections of pamphlets in English on all areas of Euskadi and details of **places to stay**. Otherwise, head for *Hostal Iratxe*, Industri Kalea 4 (☎94 625 64 63; ③), or for more luxury, *Gernika*, Carlos Gangoiti 17 (☎94 625 49 49, fax 94 625 58 74; ⑥). If you have your own transport, the Turismo can make bookings at any one of four **agroturismos** within a ten-kilometre radius of town. There's a good, inexpensive **menú** at *Jatetxea Madariaga*, c/Juan Madariaga 10. Hourly **buses** run via Zornotza to Bilbao starting at 7.10am. There is also a regular service to Bermeo (12 daily).

The Cueva de Santimamiñe

Five kilometres from Gernika, on the Lekeitio road, lies the **Cueva de Santimamiñe** (guided tours Mon–Fri at 10am, 11.15am, 12.30pm, 4.30pm & 6pm; free). Inside are extraordinary rock formations and some Paleolithic cave paintings of bison. See them now, since the long-term plan for the cave may eventually result in permanent closure, due to deterioration brought about by rising temperatures.

Without your own transport, it may be worth coming on an organized tour (details from tourist offices in Gernika or Bilbao), as there is no public transport to the cave. The thrice daily Gernika–Lekeitio bus can, however, drop you at Kortezubi from where it's a two-kilometre walk. It's a steep climb up to the entrance and you may have to wait as numbers are limited to fifteen at one time – a good **bar-restaurant** in the car park helps pass the time. If you do have to wait, or wish to spend longer, the area is very scenic and walking trails from the cave are well signposted. Opposite the *Lekiza* restaurant (look out for *agroturismo* signs), a road leads to the farmhouse *Bizketxe* (☎94 625 49 06; ④) situated in a tiny unspoilt Basque village, tucked away in a beautiful green valley and highly recommended (you can book at the Gernika Turismo). An alternative is peaceful *Morgota* (☎94 625 27 72; ④), in nearby Kortezubi.

Mundaka and Bermeo

Continuing the route west, the Río Mundaka flows from Gernika into a narrow estuary fringed by hilly pine woods and dotted with islets. There's a succession of sandy coves to swim in, but the best spots are at Pedernales and especially **MUNDAKA**, where there's a **campsite**, *Portuondo* (☎94 687 63 68; open all year), high above the water with steps leading down to a rocky beach, and magnificent surfing. A passenger ferry plies across the bay (twice daily; June–Sept only) to an excellent stretch of white sand, **Playa de Laída**, on the far side of the estuary at the base of Monte Ogoño. There is a group of holiday villas here and another campsite, *Camping Arketa* (☎94 627 81 18); it's a small site, so book beforehand.

The local train line from Gernika gives good access to the estuary beaches and continues beyond Mundaka to **BERMEO**, whose fishing fleet is the largest remaining in these waters, a riot of red, green and blue boats in the harbour. The beach isn't the best, but try some of the fish in the restaurants around the port – the local standards, *merluza* (hake) and *bacalao* (cod), are particularly good. Also worth checking out while you're here is the **Museo del Pescador** (Tues–Sat 10am–1.30pm & 4–7.30pm, Sun 10am–1.30pm), a three-storey converted building near the harbour, full of local interest and more general maritime displays. Bermeo's **Turismo** (daily 10am–1pm & 5–8pm; ☎946 186543), just opposite the train station at Askatasun Bidea 2, has a good pamphlet detailing a walk through the narrow streets and can arrange **accommodation**. There are several *agroturismos* in the area, and in town the *Hostal Ainhoa*, Arostegi 25 (☎94 618 65 61; ③), is clean and comfortable.

Westwards, on the way to Baquio, the hermitage of **San Juan de Gaztelugatxe** stands on a rocky islet, connected by a long and winding flight of steps to the shore at one of the most rugged parts of the Bizkaian coast. If you're travelling by bus, ask the driver to let you off at the cliff-top crossroads and walk down. Near Baquio, the road passes **Lemóniz**, infamous for the government's attempt to build a nuclear power station and the Basques' fierce resistance to it. The half-finished project was shelved when two of its directors were assassinated by ETA, and the area is now privately owned.

Bilbao

Stretching for some 14km along the narrow valley of the heavily polluted Río Nervión, **BILBAO** (Bilbo) is a large city that rarely feels like one, its urban sprawl having gradually engulfed a series of once-separate communities. Even in the city centre you can always see the green slopes of the surrounding mountains beyond the highrise buildings. A prosperous, modern city, animated in its busy centre and surrounded by grim, graffiti-covered slums and smoke-belching factories, Bilbao is still struggling to come to terms with its industrial past. However, recent years have seen something of a cultural renaissance in the city, most impressively with the opening of the Guggenheim Museum in October 1997. The city also has incredibly friendly inhabitants, and some of the best places to eat and drink in the whole of Euskadi.

Arrival and information

Arriving in Bilbao can be confusing, since there's a welter of different **bus** and **train** stations, although there has been an effort recently to simplify this with the new **Termibús station** (☎94 439 52 05; Metro San Mamés), which fills an entire block between Luis Briñas and Gurtubay in the new part of town. Most long-distance and international bus companies use Termibús, including Alsa, Bilmanbús, Enatcar, Saia, La Unión and Pesa. The main exceptions are Ansa, c/Autonomiá 17 (☎94 444 31 00), which runs buses to Madrid, Barcelona, Burgos and León; La Unión, c/Henao 29 (☎94 424 08 36), for services to Vitoria; and Vascongados (☎94 454 05 44) which covers local routes to Gernika and Lekeito (buses depart from a tunnel next to Estación de Abando on Hurtado de Amézaga).

The main RENFE train station is the **Estación de Abando** on Plaza Circular, but local services to San Sebastián, Gernika and Durango use the **Estación Atxuri** (Achuri), on the other side of the river, to the south of the *casco viejo*. FEVE services, along the coast to Santander and beyond, stop at the highly decorative **Estación de Santander**, on the riverbank right below the Estación de Abando.

From Bilbao **airport**, buses run every forty minutes to a bus station on c/Sendeja alongside the river next to the Puente del Ayuntamiento; ask the driver if you want to get off at an earlier stop on the route through town. A one-way trip is 130ptas.

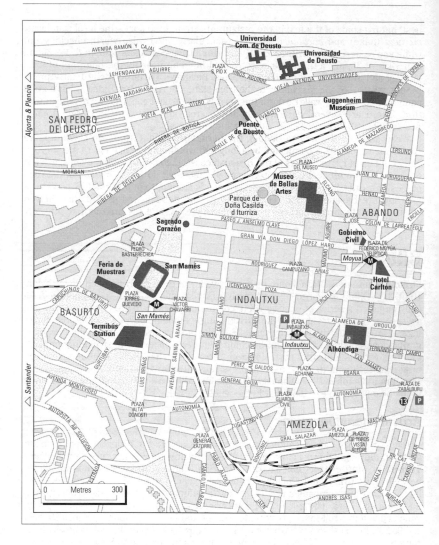

The **P&O ferry** from Portsmouth in the UK docks at **Santurtzi** across the river from Getxo (Algorta), to the north of the city centre. An unusual way to cross the Río Nervión is by the hundred-year-old *puente colgante* (hanging bridge); a regular bus runs from the docks to the centre of town.

Information and orientation

The **Turismo** (Mon–Fri 9am–2pm & 4–7.30pm, Sat 9am–2pm, Sun 10am–2pm; ☎94 479 57 60) is located inside the Teatro Arriga by the Puente del Arenal, while a very helpful Turismo on Getxo's seafront at Muelle de Areaga (☎94 469 38 00) is handy for those arriving off the ferry who don't wish to head straight into Bilbao.

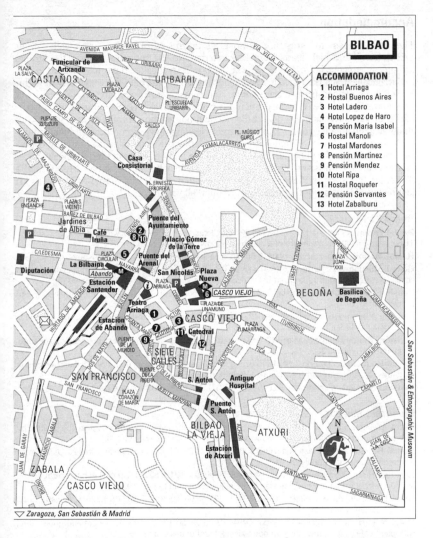

BILBAO

ACCOMMODATION
1 Hotel Arriaga
2 Hostal Buenos Aires
3 Hotel Ladero
4 Hotel Lopez de Haro
5 Pensión Maria Isabel
6 Hostal Manoli
7 Hostal Mardones
8 Pensión Martinez
9 Pensión Mendez
10 Hotel Ripa
11 Hostal Roquefer
12 Pensión Servantes
13 Hotel Zabalburu

▽ *Zaragoza, San Sebastián & Madrid*

▷ *San Sebastián & Ethnographic Museum*

Most facilities are along the city's main thoroughfare, the **Gran Vía**, where you'll find all the major **banks**, public buildings, expensive shops and El Corte Inglés. It leads through the heart of the modern city to the huge stadium of **San Mames**, the "cathedral of football" as the Basques would have it.

Transport around the city has recently been revolutionized by the completion of a **metro** system, free maps of which are available from the Turismo. An easy, efficient service runs every four minutes along the single line from Plentzia (to the north east of Getxo) to Bolueta, south of the city centre. The 27 stops are divided into three zones, but all journeys within the city centre (including the *casco viejo*) are within one zone and cost 135ptas.

Accommodation

The best **places to stay** are almost all in the *casco viejo* – especially along **c/Bidebarrieta**, which leads from Plaza Arriaga to the cathedral, and in the streets around it: c/Lotería, c/Santa María and c/Barrencalle Barrena, which is off c/Barrencalle. Calle Barrencalle itself is best avoided – the bars get very noisy at night. Rock-bottom options (rather grim *fondas* and *casas de huéspedes*) are on the east bank around the Estación de Abando, particularly round the back on c/San Francisco. The parallel c/de las Cortes is the red-light district, and not for the nervous; avoid it if you can. Another good area for rooms is in the streets leading down from Plaza Circular around c/Buenos Aires (Metro Abando). Staying in **Getxo** is a good alternative to city centre accommodation and can be particularly useful the night before catching the ferry.

The nearest **campsites** are to the east, on the beaches at Sopelana, *Sopelana* (☎94 676 21 20; bus towards Plentzia or Metro Sopelana), and Gorliz, *Gorliz* (☎94 677 19 11; just beyond Plentzia); both campsites are open all year.

Budget options

Hostal Ladero, c/Lotería 1, 4° (☎94 415 09 32). Clean, good-value rooms with modern furnishings. There is also a fifth-floor annexe reached by a narrow spiral staircase. ②.

Hostal Manoli, c/Libertad 2 (☎94 415 56 36). Spacious, clean rooms off Plaza Nueva. ②.

Hostal Mardones, c/Jardines 4 (☎94 415 31 05). Entrance at the side of a newspaper kiosk with smart, clean rooms with or without bath. Preferable to annexe on the second floor. ③.

Pensión Maria Isabel, c/Amistad 5, 4° (☎94 424 85 66). Basic, but clean and well-run, and useful for the station. ③.

Pensión Martínez, c/Villarías 8 (☎94 423 91 78). Located near *Hostal Buenos Aires*, this *pensión* is clean, small and friendly. ③.

Pensión Mendez, c/Santa María 13 (☎94 416 03 64). In the *casco viejo* near the Stock Exchange; clean and convenient. ②.

Hostal Roquefor, c/Lotería 2 (☎94 415 07 55). On the second and fourth floors of a dark and musty building. The best (and lightest) rooms overlook the cathedral square. ④.

Pensión Servantes, c/Somera 14 (☎94 415 15 57). This is the cheapest of the lot. ②.

Moderate and expensive options

Hotel Arriaga, c/Ribera 3 (☎94 479 00 01). Best of the medium-range hotels, near the Teatro, by the river; modern, comfortable rooms with bath and TV; garage available. ⑤.

Hostal Buenos Aires, Plaza Venezuela 1, 3° (☎94 424 07 65). Comfortable and well-run *hostal* with a pleasant lounge and small bar. ⑤.

Hotel Igeretxe, Playa Ereaga, Getxo (☎94 460 70 00, fax 94 460 85 99). Upmarket hotel right on the seafront with a bar where you can watch the ships coming in to port. ⑦.

Hotel López de Haro, Obispo Orueta 2 (☎94 423 55 00, fax 94 423 45 00). Luxury, five-star hotel near the Jardines de Albia. ⑥.

Hotel Neguri, Avda. Algorta 14, Getxo (☎94 491 05 09, fax 94 491 19 43). Decent and good value, with plenty of facilities, including an open-air pool and tennis courts. ⑥.

Hotel Ripa, c/Ripa 3 (☎94 423 96 77). Just over Puente del Arenal from the *casco viejo*, on the street by the waterfront; good-value rooms with bath and TV. ⑤.

Hotel Zabálburu, Pedro Martínez Artola 8 (☎94 443 71 00). Good, clean doubles and handy for some of the major bus terminals. ⑤.

The City

Although Bilbao suffered severely from flooding at the end of 1983, there has been little permanent damage and many of the older areas have been dazzlingly refurbished. The **casco viejo**, the old quarter on the east bank of the river, holds many of the city's sights: the beautiful **Teatro Arriaga**, the elegantly arcaded **Plaza Nueva** (or *de los Mártires*), the Gothic **Catedral de Santiago** and the **Museo Arqueológico, Ethnográfico e Histórico Vasco** at c/Cruz 4 (Tues–Sat 10am–1.30pm & 4–7pm, Sun 10.30am–1.30pm; free). The museum is housed in the former School of San Andrés with its beautiful cloister and large selection of coats of arms of the former Bizkaian nobility – a very pleasant retreat from the city bustle. It's in the old town too that the best bars and restaurants are situated, among the thronged narrow streets and anti-quated shops contained in the *siete calles* (seven streets) area bordered by c/de la Ronda and c/Pelota.

However, the biggest attraction in Bilbao is undoubtedly Frank O'Gehry's remark able titanium-covered **Guggenheim Museum** (Tues–Sun 11am–8pm; 700ptas), which dominates the quayside next to the Puente de Salve. The museum, now the largest gallery in the world, is the result of a major co-operative venture between the Basque government – who will be underwriting the construction and operational costs for the next twenty years – and the Guggenheim Foundation, who bring not only their exper-tise and prestige to the project, but, perhaps more importantly, also the loan of collec-tions from their other three museums, in particular the New York Guggenheim.

Described by architect Philip Johnson as "the greatest building of our time", the structure itself is as much of an attraction as the works of art it holds. Its controversial undulating curves of titanium and stone culminate in a forty-metre glass and steel rotunda, which creates an immense feeling of space and light inside, a direct contrast to the seeming chaos of the exterior.

Nineteen galleries radiate from the rotunda, while a further ten, including a spectac-ular 130-metre space under the La Salve bridge, are devoted to temporary exhibitions. The rotating **collection** holds over 250 works of modern art, and includes paintings and sculptures by such Spanish luminaries as Picasso, Miró, Chillida and Tàpies, as well as works from further afield by, amongst others, Kandinsky, Braque, Ernst, Pollock, Rothko and De Kooning, together with specially commissioned site-specific works. For up-to-date information on current exhibitions and programmes, visit the Guggenheim's Web site at *www.guggenheim/org/bilbao/*.

Over the river on the northern edge of the new town is the excellent **Museo de Bellas Artes**, Plaza del Museo 2 (Tues–Sat 10am–1.30pm & 4–7.30pm, Sun 10am–2pm; free), in the Parque de Doña Casilda de Iturriza. This is considered one of Spain's most important collections, and includes works by El Greco, Zurbarán and Goya, modern works by Gauguin and Bacon and paintings by Basque artists Zulorga and Echevarría.

Beaches

The city is well-served with **beaches** along the mouth of the estuary and around both headlands. For day trips you should go to **Sopelana** (Metro Sopelana) and the other beaches around **Plentzia** (Metro Plentzia) north of the city. The pretty old quarter of **Getxo** (Metro Algorta), with its white houses and green-painted doors, has an impressive waterfront promenade fringed with private mansions belonging to Bilbao's millionaire set.

Eating, drinking and nightlife

Bilbao is definitely one of those cities where the most enjoyable way to eat is to move from bar to bar, snacking on *tapas*. The city can be very lively at night – and totally wild during the August **fiesta**, with scores of open-air bars, live music and impromptu danc-ing everywhere, and a truly festive atmosphere. The *casco viejo* has all the most inter-esting places to **eat and drink**, with almost wall-to-wall places on c/Santa María and c/Barrencalle Barrena.

If you want to get together something of your own, the attractive **Mercado de la Ribera**, on c/de la Ribera towards the Estación Atxuri, offers a dazzling array of fresh produce.

Restaurants and tapas bars

Café Gargantua, c/Barrencalle Barrena. Simple café serving sandwiches, and a selection of different priced *menús* and *platos combinados*.

Café-Restaurante Kalean, c/Santa María. Very popular, offering excellent economical *nueva cocina vasca*. After midnight, there's a resident pianist and great atmosphere.

Garibolo, c/Fernandez del Campo 7 and Alameda de Urquijo 33 (both in the centre just north of the Gran Vía). Good vegetarian restaurant, with two sites and few surprises.

Herriko Taberna, c/de la Ronda 20. Excellent place for a straightforward, inexpensive meal; a strong Basque nationalist atmosphere and a great *menú*.

Kasko, c/Santa María. Trendy café, with a reasonable evening *menú* for 1300ptas.

Taberna Aitor, c/Barrencalle Barrena. Excellent *tapas* bar and one for football fans, with the bonus of a beautiful wooden interior.

Taberna Txiriboga, c/Santa María. Lively *tapas* bar in the heart of the *casco viejo*.

Taberna Txomin Barullo, c/Barrencalle. Great café-bar with nationalist murals, specializing in more experimental *nueva cocina vasca* (lunch *menú* only Thurs–Sun) at reasonable prices.

Bars and entertainment

Bars can be found all through the **casco viejo**, but they are particularly lively around c/Pelota, c/Barrencalle, c/Santa María, c/de la Ronda and c/Torre. *Lamiak* on c/Pelota is a café-bar full of students, with good music and a noticeboard worth checking for events, women's groups, work, flatshares and the like. *Txokolanda* is a **gay** bar, upstairs from *Solokuetxe*, reached via steps from c/de la Ronda, and, along with the *Lasaí* bar on c/de la Ronda itself, is one of the last places to close. For a relaxed drink in the early evening, head for the outdoor tables in the beautiful Plaza Nueva, not as pricey as you might expect. Bilbao's **historic cafés** include the *Boulevard* on c/Ribera near the Teatro Arriaga and the *Granja* in Plaza Circular.

In the **new town**, lively areas with a slightly smarter atmosphere are near the Plaza Circular, between the Alameda de Mazarredo and c/de Buenos Aires, especially on c/Ledesma, a street teeming with bars and especially popular during early evening. *Bar Iruña*, on Colón de Larreategui, parallel to c/Ledesma, is marvellously atmospheric.

Farther east, south of the Gran Vía, around the junction of c/de Licenciado Poza and Gregorio de Revilla, an area known as **Pozas** is highly popular before lunch and in the early evening; *Ziripot* is a bar worth trying here. For action well into the night, one of the in-places is the cluster of bars known as the **Ripa** on the modern city side of the riverbank between Puentes del Arenal and Ayuntamiento, with a mixed crowd ranging from Basque yuppies to rockabillies.

Finding **live music** can be tricky, as the posters which advertise bands seem to be covered by others within hours of going up. The local paper *El Correo* probably has the best listings, and also details movies, few of which are in English: one place you can regularly see films in their original language is the Filmoteca at the Museo de Bellas Artes – films generally start around 5pm.

Listings

Airport information ☎94 486 93 00.

American Express c/o Viajes Cafranga, Alameda de Recalde 68 (☎94 444 48 62).

Bookshops Libropolis, c/General Concha 10, is a large travel bookshop with the most complete range of maps and guides in the city; Borda, c/Cueva de Santimamiñe at Plaza Nueva, stocks a wide range of local guides as well as some English-language publications; Mendiko Etxea, c/Autonomía

9, specializes in local trekking and cycling guides. The best place to buy English and other foreign newspapers (one day late) is Librería Cámara on c/Euskalduna 10, four streets up on the right from Plaza de España along Hurtado de Amézaga.

Car rental Avis is at Alameda Dr Areilza 34 (☎94 427 57 60) and Europcar (☎94 442 28 49) is at c/Rodríguez Arias.

Consulates The British consulate is at Alameda Urquijo 2 (☎94 415 77 22), and the US at Avda. de Ejército 11 (☎94 475 83 00).

Hospital Hospital Bilbao, Avda. de Montevideo 18 (☎94 486 93 14). Call ambulances on ☎94 441 00 81.

Post office The main *Correos* is at Alameda Urquijo 19 (Mon–Fri 8am–9pm, Sat 9am–2pm).

Taxi Radio Taxi Bizkaia (☎94 426 90 26) or Radio Taxi Bilbao (☎94 444 88 88).

Telephones There is a *telefónica* at c/Baroeta Aldamar 7, close to the Plaza de España.

Travel agents Barcelo Viajes, Rodríguez Arias 8, and TIVE, Iparraguirre 3 (☎94 423 18 62), which specializes in student/youth travel and international buses.

Inland routes from Bilbao

Inland Bizkaia is well off the beaten track yet has much to offer, with spectacular walking and climbing country, particularly around Durango, and remarkable limestone caves, accessible as a day trip from Bilbao.

Around Durango

The otherwise uninspiring factory town of **DURANGO** (easily accessible by train from Atxuri station) is the gateway to the impressive **Duranguesado Massif.** To explore this area of rocky peaks, the best access point is the Urkiola Pass (on the Durango–Vitoria road and bus route) from where it's about three hours to the highest peak, **Amboto.** This summit is a favourite with Basque walkers and climbers – the final scramble to the top can be a bit vertigo-inducing. Alternatively, head for the beautiful Atxondo valley off the Durango–Elorrio road. If you don't have your own transport, take the hourly buses as far as the signposted crossroads and then walk 2.5km to the village of **Axpe-Marzana**, nestling at the base of Amboto – a good base for a couple of days' walking. There is an **agroturismo**, *Imitte-Etxebarria* (☎94 623 16 59; ④), 500m before the village.

Markina and Bolibar

Also east of Bilbao, on the bus route to Ondarroa, the attractive town of **MARKINA** is famous for producing many of the finest *pelota* players – the *frontón* here is known as *La Universidad de la Pelota*. If you want to stay, try *Hostal Vega* in the main square (☎94 686 60 15; ③). From Markina you can visit the tiny village of **BOLIBAR**, ancestral home of the South American liberator, where there is a small museum depicting the great man's feats (Tues–Fri 10am–1pm, Sat & Sun 12–2pm; July & Aug also daily 5–7pm). From the village a short, restored stretch of a coastal branch of the Camino de Santiago leads up to the **Colegiata de Zenarruza**, (daily 10.30am–1.30pm & 4–7pm; Mass 12pm), a former pilgrims' *hostal* and hospital containing a beautiful sixteenth-century cloister and Romanesque church. There's a gift shop here, which also sells local produce.

Orduña

Thirty-five kilometres south of Bilbao is **ORDUÑA**, a curious enclave of Bizkaia in Alava Province (served by several trains a day from Abando station). The Plaza de los Fueros boasts a collection of fine old buildings including the Neoclassical former customs house and a belfry where a pair of storks have taken up residence – apparently one of only three such nests in Euskadi. In the plaza is an old shop selling the local speciality, *Mantecadas de Badillo*, a kind of sweet spongecake, sold straight from the oven.

You can walk up to **Fraileburu** (monk's head), a peculiarly shaped rock at the top of the escarpment immediately south of the town which is regarded as one of the prime hang-gliding and paragliding spots in Spain.

West to the limestone caves

The little-known area of **ENCARTACIONES**, west of Bilbao, makes another rewarding day trip, with places to stay if you want to extend your visit. Head for the village of **Carranza** on the Bilbao–Ramales road (one hour by train on the Santander line out of Abando station; no public transport onwards to the caves). Four kilometres west of Carranza on the main road, just past a curious thermal spa resort run by German monks at **MOLINAR**, where you can stay and eat (☎94 680 60 02), a road heads up the mountain to the tiny village of **Ranero** and the **Cuevas de Pozalagua** (3km). Half the enjoyment is the trip up through the craggy limestone outcrops of the mountainside which take on an almost lunar appearance, but the **caves** themselves (Sat & Sun 11am–2pm & 4–7pm; 500ptas; groups must ring ahead – ☎94 680 60 12) are equally remarkable for their eccentric coral-like stalactites. Unfortunately, some of the formations have been damaged by previous dynamiting in local quarries, but there are many other opportunities for speleology in the area, including visits to the **Torca de Carlista**, further into the mountain, one of the world's largest cave chambers.

Vitoria and around

VITORIA (Gasteiz), the capital of Alava, crowns a slight rise in the heart of a fertile plain. Founded by Sancho el Sabio, King of Navarra, it was already a prosperous place by the time of its capture by the Castilian Alfonso VIII in 1200. Later, as the centre of a flourishing wool and iron trade, Vitoria became seriously rich, and the town still boasts an unusual concentration of Renaissance palaces and fine churches. It's off the tourist circuit but is by no means dull. The university here – or rather, its students – have made this one of northern Spain's "in" cities, and the old town is full of rowdy bars and *tabernas,* not to mention an abundance of excellent Basque restaurants, making it as pleasant a place to pass a few days away from the crowds as you'll find.

Arrival and information

The **bus station** is across town on c/Francia, a two-minute walk (straight up the cobbled Cantón de San Francisco Javier Colegio) from the old town. You'll find a useful **Turismo** (Mon–Sat 9am–1pm & 4–8pm, Sun 10am–2pm; ☎943 131321), on c/Ramón y Cajal (in the corner of the park), close to the **train station**, with lots of colourful brochures and a good free map. A second Turismo, a bit farther away from the centre, is on the corner of Avenida de Gasteiz and c/de Chile (Mon–Sat 10am–7pm, Sun 11am–2pm; ☎945 161598 or 945 161599).

The **post office**, c/de Postes, and most other services, including **banks**, are located in the central area around the Plaza de la Virgen Blanca.

Accommodation

The only time you might have trouble locating a room is during Vitoria's annual **jazz festival** in the third week of July, or during the town **fiesta** at the beginning of August. There are several budget **places to stay** near the train station, around the junction of c/de los Fueros and Ortiz de Zarate and near the bus station, but it's far nicer to stay in the old quarter near the action.

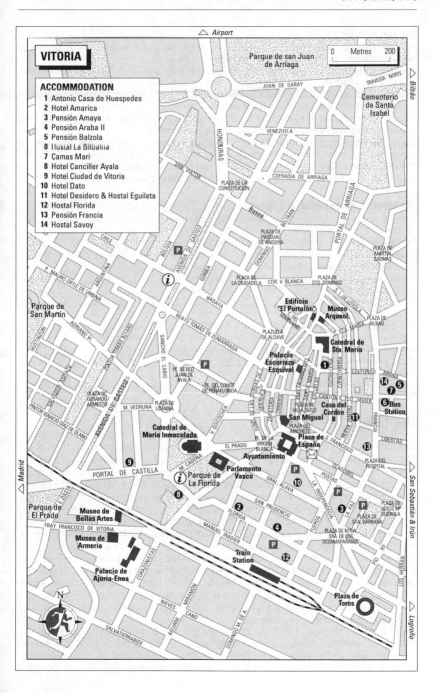

VITORIA

ACCOMMODATION
1 Antonio Casa de Huespedes
2 Hotel Amarica
3 Pensión Amaya
4 Pensión Araba II
5 Pensión Balzola
6 Hostal La Bilbaína
7 Camas Mari
8 Hotel Canciller Ayala
9 Hotel Ciudad de Vitoria
10 Hotel Dato
11 Hotel Desidero & Hostal Eguileta
12 Hostal Florida
13 Pensión Francia
14 Hostal Savoy

Budget options

Antonio Casa de Huéspedes, c/Cuchillería 66 (☎945 268795). A rambling old building with friendly management, but a long hike to the bathrooms. ②.

Pensión Araba 2, c/Florida 25 (☎945 232588). Centrally located *pensión*, offering four clean rooms with or without bath. ③.

Pensión Balzola, c/Prudencio María de Verástegui 6, 2° (☎945 256279). Simple but clean, with doubles and singles; ring bell beside CH sign. ②.

Hostal Eguileta, c/Nueva Fuera 32 (☎945 251700, fax 945 251722). Cheaper annexe of the *Hotel Desiderio* opposite, offering reasonable doubles with washbasin. ③.

Hostal Florida, c/Manuel Iradier 33 (☎945 260675). Comfortable, well-furnished rooms on the first street down from the station towards the bullring. Has more expensive rooms with bath. ③.

Pensión Francia, c/Francia 4 (☎945 287380). Decent doubles and singles with shared bath. ④.

Camas Mari, c/Prudencio María de Verástegui (☎945 277303). Clean rooms with shared bath. ③.

Moderate and expensive options

Hotel Amarica, c/Florida 11 (☎945 130506). Popular modern hotel, offering two singles and eight doubles with bath and satellite TV. ⑤.

Pensión Amaya, c/La Paz 15 (☎945 255497). No single rooms, but all have bath. ④.

Hostal La Bilbaina, c/Prudencio María de Verástegui 2 (☎945 254400, fax 945 279757). Comfortable rooms above a large *cafetería*, all with bath and cable TV. ④.

Hotel Canciller Ayala, c/Ramón y Cajal 5 (☎945 130000, fax 945 133505). One of Vitoria's top hotels, situated on the edge of the Parque de la Florida. ⑦.

Hotel Ciudad de Vitoria, Portal de Castilla 8 (☎945 141100, fax 945 143616). Comfortable, upmarket accommodation. ⑦.

Hotel Dato, c/Dato 28 (☎945 147230, fax 945 232320). Excellent-value hotel on main pedestrian mall down from the station. There's a different colour scheme in every room, and colourful batik bedspreads. All rooms with bath and some have enclosed balcony. ④.

Hotel Desiderio, Colegio San Prudencio 2 (☎945 251700, fax 945 521722). Spacious rooms with bath and TV. ⑤.

Hostal Savoy, c/Prudencio María de Verástegui 4 (☎945 250056). Decent *hostal*, which belongs to the *cafetería* of the same name. ④.

The Town

The streets of the Gothic old town spread out like a spider's web down the sides of the hill, surrounded on level ground by a neater grid of later development. You'll get the feel of Vitoria simply by wandering through this old quarter. Although parts of it can be rather shabby, it is on the whole a harmonious place, the graceful mansions and churches all built from the same greyish/gold stone. The porticoed **Plaza de España**, especially, is a gem, a popular location for early-evening strolling and drinking.

Take time to visit the church of **San Miguel**, just above the Plaza de España, which marks the southern end of the old town. Outside its door stands the fourteenth-century stone image of the Virgen Blanca, revered patron of the city. The streets below hold any number of interesting buildings, one of the finest being the **Escoriaza-Esquivel Palace** with its sixteenth-century Plateresque portal, on c/Fray Zacarías. A little further, the old Gothic cathedral of **Santa María**, c/Correría 116 (Tues–Fri 10am–2pm & 4–6.30pm, Sat 10am–2pm, Sun & fiestas 11am–2pm; free) has a superb west doorway, intricately and lovingly carved, whilst inside a delicate stone gallery runs around most of the higher sections of the naves.

Behind the cathedral, down the hill on the left, the **Portalón** is the most impressive of the surviving trading houses of Renaissance Vitoria, its dusty red brick and wooden beams and balconies in marked contrast to the golden stone of the rest of the town. Today it is an extremely good, but expensive restaurant (see below). Over the road you'll find the province's **Museo Arqueológico** (same opening times as Santa María; free). Southwest of the centre, on the attractive, pedestrianized, tree-lined Paseo de Fray Francisco, is the **Museo de Bellas Artes** (same opening times as Santa María; free), which has a substantial collection of works by Spanish and Basque contemporary artists. An annexe of this museum houses the unusual **Museo de Naipes** with over 6000 exhibits of playing cards from all corners of the globe. Nearby, the **Museo de Armería**, Paseo de Fray Francisco 3 (same opening times as Santa María; free), features imaginative displays of medieval weapons and suits of armour.

Eating and drinking

The streets of the **old town** – particularly c/Cuchillería, c/Pintorería, c/Hurrería and c/Zapatería – are lined with lively **bars**, **tabernas** and **bodegas**, differentiated only by music and perhaps decor. Each, however, manages to spill on to the narrow pavements at night. For a good selection of restaurants and *tapas* bars head for the **casco histórico** to sample a selection of Basque dishes. Farther down, on the pedestrianized section of c/Dato, you'll find a variety of bars and cafés with charming terraces which offer a quieter ambiance. Equally pleasant are the outdoor cafés of Plaza de España and those on the other pedestrian throughfares in the lower section of the new town.

Casa Felipe, c/Fueros 28 (☎945 134554). Reasonably priced restaurant specializing in local dishes.

Ikea, Portal de Castilla 27 (☎945 144747). Expensive, fashionable spot serving good Basque food. Closed Sun night & Mon.

Kirol, c/Cuchillería. This café-bar has an amazing selection of *raciones*.

Mesa, c/Chile 1 (☎945 228494). Basque specialities for around 3500ptas a head and a good-value *menú* for 1800ptas. Closed Wed.

El Portalón, c/Correría 15 (☎945 142755). Expensive restaurant specializing in traditional Basque cooking, set in beautiful 16th-century surroundings. Closed Sun.

Teide, Avda. de Gasteiz 61 (☎945 221023). Solid Basque cuisine at moderate prices.

Around Vitoria

Attractive though the town is, a significant part of Vitoria's charm is the beauty of the surrounding **countryside**. Almost every hamlet of mountainous Euskadi has something of interest: an old stone mansion proudly displaying the family coat of arms, a richly decorated church, or a farmhouse raised Swiss-style on stilts. In the immediate vicinity of Vitoria are many notable places, most at which are accessible by public transport.

The nearby **Pantanos de Zadorra** is a large scenic reservoir very popular with the locals; the waterside villages of Gamboa-Ullibarri and Landa (both served by bus three times daily) make a pleasant retreat on a hot summer's day. A few kilometres to the west of Vitoria, another popular day trip is to the village of **MENDOZA**, dominated by a fortified tower-house now established as the **Museo de Heraldica** (summer Tues–Fri 11am–2pm & 4–7.30pm, Sat & Sun 10am–2.30pm; winter Tues–Sun 11am–2.30pm; free), which contains a fascinating collection of coats of arms of the Basque nobility through the ages and an exhibition of the history of the principal clans and their often bloody feuds.

To the east, on the **Llanada Alavesa** (Plain of Alava) are some of the best-preserved villages of inland Euskadi. Take the side road off the main N1 *autovía* via **NARVAJA**, where there is an **agroturismo**, *Koipe-Enea* (☎945 300298; ③), to reach **ZALDUON-DO** and **ARAÍA** (served by a twice daily bus from Vitoria). From the latter two it's possible to walk on a branch of the Camino de Santiago to the San Adrián tunnel and its refuge (see p.401).

The main town on the plain, **SALVATIERRA,** makes a good base for exploration. The old walled quarter rises above the countryside offering splendid views, and the Gothic church of Santa María is visible for miles around. Situated on the main Vitoria–Pamplona/Irún rail line, the town has a couple of small *fondas*; one attached to the *Bar Merino* opposite the church of San Juan in Plaza Mayor (☎945 300052; ③), and the other at c/Mayor 53 (②).

South of Vitoria lies the wine-growing district of **Rioja Alavesa** and its town of **LAGUARDIA,** which is served by regular buses from Vitoria. There is a useful **Turismo,** c/Sancho Abarca (Mon–Fri 10am–2pm & 4–6.30pm, Sat 10am–2pm, Sun 10.45am–2pm; ☎941 100845), which has a free map of the town as well as information on the many *bodegas* in the area – visits usually require a phone call beforehand. Laguardia itself is an interesting old walled town of cobbled streets and historic buildings, entered through the Puerta de San Juan. The Turismo has keys to the church of Santa María de los Reyes with its ornately carved Gothic doorway. One of the best places to **stay** is *Larretxari*, c/Portal de Páganos (☎941 600763; ④), a small *agroturismo* in the old town. You can also rent out rooms at *Batzori*, c/Mayor 17 (☎941 600114; ③), or for more comfort, there are two *hostales* on the main road; *Pachico Martínez*, c/Sancho Abarca 20 (☎941 600009; ⑤), and *Marixa*, c/Sancho Abarca (☎941 600165; ⑤). If you're looking for a place to **eat**, *La Muralla*, Paganos 42, and *Los Rojillos*, c/Mayor 57, both serve a good *menú del día* for under 1000ptas.

Pamplona

PAMPLONA (Iruña) has been the capital of Navarra since the ninth century, and long before that was a powerful fortress town defending the northern approaches to Spain at the foothills of the Pyrenees. Even now it has something of the appearance of a garrison city, with its hefty walls and elaborate pentagonal citadel. With a long history as capital of an often semi-autonomous state, Pamplona has plenty to offer around its old centre, the *casco antiguo* – enticing churches, a beautiful park, the massive citadel – and it's an enjoyable place to be throughout the year. But for anyone who has been here during the thrilling week of the **Fiestas de San Fermín,** a visit at any other time can only be an anticlimax.

San Fermín

From midday on July 6 until midnight on July 14 the city gives itself up entirely to riotous non-stop celebration. The centre of the festivities is the **encierro,** or the running of the bulls, which draws tourists from all over the world, but this has become just one aspect of a massive fair along with bands, parades and dancing in the streets 24 hours a day. You could have a great time here for a week without ever seeing a bull, and even if you are violently opposed to bullfighting, the *encierro* – in which the animals decisively have the upper hand – is a spectacle not to miss.

Six bulls are released each morning at eight (traditionally it was an hour earlier, so that the festival started on the seventh hour of the seventh day of the seventh month) to run from their corral near the Plaza Santo Domingo to the bullring. In front, around, and occasionally under them run the hundreds of locals and tourists who are foolish or drunk enough to test their daring against the horns. It was Hemingway's *The Sun Also Rises* that really put "Los San Fermines" on the map and the area in front of the Plaza de Toros has been renamed Plaza Hemingway by a grateful council. His description of it as "a damned fine show" still attracts Americans by the thousands. No amount of outsiders, though, could outdo the locals in their determination to have a good time, and it's an indescribably exhilarating event in which to take part.

PAMPLONA

0   Metres   200

Train Station

RÍO ARGA

JOAQUIN

BELUNZA

ERROTAZAR

Arga

PUENTE DE ROCHAPEA

San Sebastián & Vitoria

AV. GUIPUZCOA

PUENTE PLAZAOLA

Río

Basílica de la Virgen de la O

Monumento a Gayarre

Ant. Casa Capellanes

Conv. de las Agustinas Recoletas

Fuente de la Beneficencia

Parque de la Taconera

Iglesia de las Carmelitas Descalzas

Palacio Teresiana

Iglesia de S. Lorenzo

Pál. de los Vasallo

NAVAS DE TOLOSA

BOSQUECILLO

TACONERA

DESCALZOS

MAYOR

JARAUTA

S. ANTON

S. GREGORIO

Museo de Navarra

Parque y Corralillos

Sto. Domingo

Palacio del Virrey

Portal de Francia

Conv. de las Carmelitas Descalzas

PL. DE S. JOSE

NAVARRERIA

Catedral

Parque de la Tejería

Ayuntamiento

San Cernín

Cámara de los Comptos Reales

PLAZA DE LOS BURGOS

PLAZA CONSISTORIAL

MERCADERES

CURIA

CAMPANA

DORMITALERÍA

Palacio Arzobispal

PLAZA DEL CASTILLO

Gobierno Foral y Archivo general de Navarra

PLAZA DE TOROS

PASEO DE HEMINGWAY

S. NICOLÁS

NUEVA

ZAPATERÍA

PLAZA DE S. FRANCISCO

S. Nicolás

Monumento a los Fueros

Basílica de San Ignacio

PASEO SARASATE

PLAZA DEL VINCULO

ESTELLA

Bus Station

PADRE MORET

GRAL. CHINCHILLA

Avenida del Ejército

SANCHO EL MAYOR

SAN IGNACIO

CORTES DE NAVARRA

RONCESVALLES

AVENIDA CARLOS III

EMILIO

ARRIETA

AMAYA

Leyre

PLAZA DE LAS MERINDADES

AVENIDA DE LA BAJA NAVARRA

LEYRE

Citadel

PLAZA DE LA PAZ

CONDE OLIVETO

PLAZA PRINCIPE DE VIANA

San Miguel

YANGUAS Y MIRANDA

TUDELA

VILLOSLADA

PL. DE LA CRUZ

SAN FRANCISCO

NAVARRO

SANGUESA

CALATAYUD

TAFALLA

BERGAMIN

N

PLAZA DE LOS FUEROS

AVENIDA DE ZARAGOZA

Casa de Misericordia

AVENIDA DE GALICIA

▽ Zaragoza & Madrid

ACCOMMODATION

1 Fonda La Aragoñesa	8 Hotel Europa
2 Hostal Artazcos	9 Fonda La Montañesa
3 Hostal Bearán	10 Pensión Oliveto
4 Camas	11 Hostal Otano
5 Casa Garcia	12 Hotel La Perla
6 Casa de Huespedes	13 Bar-Restaurante El Redin
7 Hotel Enslava	14 Hotel Yoldi

Arrival and information

Although Pamplona is a sizable city, the old centre is remarkably compact – nothing you're likely to want to see is more than five minutes from the main **Plaza del Castillo**. The **train station** is on Avda. San Jorge; bus #9 runs every ten minutes from here to the citadel end of the Paseo de Sarasate, a few minutes' walk from the Plaza del Castillo. There's a handy central RENFE ticket office at c/Estella 8 (Mon–Fri 9.30am–2pm &

SAN FERMÍN - THE FACTS

ACCOMMODATION AND SECURITY

Don't expect to find **accommodation** during the fiesta unless you have booked well in advance – the town is packed to the gills. However, the Turismo opposite the bullring fills with old women willing to let **rooms** for the night at exorbitant prices. If you have no luck, accept that you're going to sleep on the ramparts, in the park or plaza (along with hundreds of others), and deposit your valuables and luggage at the bus station on c/Conde Oliveto – it's inexpensive, and you can have daily access (this fills early in the week, too – hang around and be insistent). There are also showers here.

Probably the **best plan**, though, is not to stay here at all: find a room somewhere else (Vitoria or Estella for instance), get plenty of sleep, leave your luggage there, and arrive in Pamplona by bus, staying as long as you can survive on naps in the park before escaping for some rest and a clean-up. You can always come back again. The first few days are best – by the end the place is getting pretty filthy.

Alternatively, there's a **campsite**, *Ezcaba* (☎948 330315), 7km out of town on the road to France. You have to be there a couple of days before the fiesta to get a place. Facilities include good toilets and showers but they can't really handle the numbers during San Fermín – be prepared for long queues or for going "primitive", and bear in mind that the shop is only really well stocked in the drinks department. The main bonus is that security is tight – admission is by pass only and there's a guard who patrols all night. For the period of the fiesta there is a **free campsite**, by the river just below *Ezcaba*. Security is doubtful, however. The bus service, which goes to all the campsites, is poor (about five a day, first at 6am, last at 1am), but it's easy to hitch or, more expensively, get a lift on one of the tour buses that stay at the official campsite (they leave in time to see the *encierro*).

Wherever you sleep, keep an eye on everything you have with you – there's a very high rate of **petty crime** during the festival; cars and vans are broken into with alarming frequency and people are often robbed as they sleep, occasionally with violence. Several **banks** and a **post office** are open mornings during the festival, so changing travellers' cheques is no problem. Note that everything is closed over the weekend.

EL ENCIERRO

To watch the *encierro* it's essential to arrive early (about 6am) – crowds have already formed an hour before it starts. The best **vantage points** are near the starting point around the Plaza Santo Domingo or on the wall leading to the bullring. If possible, get a spot on the outer of the two barriers – don't worry when the one in front fills up and blocks your view, as all these people will be moved on by the police before the run. The event divides into two parts: firstly there's the actual running of the bulls, when the object is to run with the bull or whack it with a rolled-up newspaper. It can be difficult to see the bulls amid all the runners but you'll sense the sheer terror and excitement down on the ground; just occasionally this spreads to the watching crowd if a bull manages to breach the wooden safety barriers. Then there's a separate event after the bulls have been through the streets, when bullocks with padded horns are let loose on the crowd in the bullring. If you watch the actual running, you won't be able to get into the bullring (too many people), so go on two separate mornings to see both things. For the bullring you have to arrive at about 6am to get the free lower seats. If you want to pay

4.30–7.30pm, Sat 9.30am–1pm; ☎948 227282). The **bus station** is more central, on c/Conde Oliveto just in front of the citadel: schedules are confusing, given the number of companies operating from here – check the timetable posted at the station, or pick up one at the helpful **Turismo** (summer daily 10am–7pm; winter Mon–Fri 10am–2pm

for a seat higher up buy from the ticket office outside, not from the touts inside, who will rip you off. On Sunday you have to pay.

We advise against it, but if you do decide to **run**, remember that although it's probably less dangerous than it looks, at least one person gets seriously injured (sometimes killed) every year. Find someone who knows the ropes to guide you through the first time, and don't try any heroics; bulls are weighed in tons and have very sharp horns. Don't get trapped hiding in a doorway and don't get between a scared bull and the rest of the pack. Traditionally women don't take part, though more and more are doing so; if you do, it's probably best to avoid any officials, who may try to remove you. A glass of *Pacharán*, the powerful local liqueur, is ideal for a dose of courage.

The only official way in is at the starting point, Plaza Santo Domingo, entered via Plaza San Saturnino; shortly before the start the rest of the course is cleared, and then at a few minutes before eight you're allowed to make your way along the course to your own preferred starting point (you should walk the course beforehand to get familiar with it). To mark the start, two rockets are fired, one when the bulls are released, a second when they are all out (it's best if these are close together, since the bulls are far safer if they're running as a herd rather than getting scared individually). As soon as the first goes you can start to run, though if you do this you'll probably arrive in the ring well before the bulls and be booed for your trouble; if you wait a while you're more likely to get close to the bulls. Although there are plenty of escape points, these are only for use in emergency – if you try to get out prematurely you'll be shoved back.

OTHER EVENTS

There are plenty of other hazardous things to do in Pamplona, especially once the atmosphere has got the better of a few people's judgement. Many people (especially tourists) have fun hurling themselves from the fountain in the centre of town and from surrounding buildings (notably *La Mesillonera* – the mussel bar), hoping their friends will catch them below. Needless to say, several people each year are not caught by their drunken pals.

Other events include **music** from local bands nightly from midnight in the bars and at Plaza del Castillo, continuing until about 4am in the fairground on the Avda. de Bayona, which is where local political groupings and other organizations have their stands. There are **fireworks** every evening in the citadel (about 11pm), and a **funfair** on the open ground beside it. Competing **bands** stagger through the streets all day playing to anyone who'll listen. If things calm down a bit you can sunbathe, take a shower, catch up on sleep and even swim at the public **swimming pool** outside the walls below the Portal de Zumalacárregui.

Bullfights take place daily at 6.30pm, with the bulls that ran that morning. Tickets are expensive (about 2000–12,000ptas), and if you have no choice but to buy from the touts, wait until the bullfight has begun, when you can insist on paying less (the price drops with each successive killing). You can also buy tickets the day before from the ticket office in Plaza de Toros (opens 8am), but be prepared to queue. At the end of the week (midnight, July 14) there's a mournful candlelit procession, the **Pobre De**, at which the festivities are officially wound up for another year.

If you're hooked on danger, many **other Basque towns** have fiestas which involve some form of *encierro*. Among the best are Tudela (July 24–28), Estella (first weekend in August, and one of the few which has no official ban on women participants), Tafalla (mid-Aug) and Ampuero in Santander Province (Sept 7–8).

& 4–7pm, Sat 10am–2pm; ☎948 220741) on c/Duque de Ahumada 3, just off Plaza del Castillo. The staff will also arrange accomodation, including advance bookings if you intend to strike out into the Pyrenees. During San Fermín, a municipal information bus also operates (10am–2pm & 5–8pm).

Banks are scattered throughout the central area, with much restricted, morning-only hours during the fiesta – one that also opens in the afternoons (4–6pm) is the Caja de Ahorros de Navarra in c/Roncesvalles. There's a central **post office** (Mon–Fri 8am–9pm, Sat 9am–7pm) on c/Estella, next to the RENFE office. A **laundry** (in case your clothes have borne the brunt of the festivities) can be found at c/de Descalzos, a couple of minutes' walk from the Plaza de San Francisco.

Accommodation

Most of the budget **fondas** and **hostales** are in c/San Nicolás and c/San Gregorio, off the Plaza del Castillo. Even outside San Fermín, when prices can double or triple, rooms fill up quickly in summer, and it might be easier to accept that you'll have to pay a little more to avoid the hassle of trudging around. If you want to continue looking, the streets around the cathedral, across the Plaza del Castillo, yield other possibilities. Farther away from the Plaza del Castillo and the old town, there are several *hostales* in the more modern, yet not so interesting, central area.

Budget options

Fonda La Aragonesa, c/San Nicolás 32 (☎948 223428). Reasonable *fonda* offering doubles with washbasin. ②.

Hostal Artázcoz, c/Tudela 9, 2° (☎948 225164, fax 948 223426). Well-established *hostal* going back more than forty years; all rooms have en-suite facilities. ③.

Camas, c/Nueva 24, 1° (☎948 227825). Next to the upmarket *Hotel Maisonnave*; well-furnished doubles and singles. ③.

Casa García, c/San Gregorio 12 (☎948 223893). Double rooms without bath above a restaurant, with very reasonable full-board rate. ③.

Casa de Huéspedes Santa Cecilia, c/Navarrería 17, 1° (☎948 222230). Spacious rooms in a former palace right by the fountain much splashed in during San Fermín. The place looks foreboding with a massive heavy door and grey facade, but the owner is extremely welcoming. ③.

Fonda La Montañesa, c/San Gregorio 2 (☎948 224380). Doubles and singles; nothing very special. ②.

Moderate and expensive options

Hostal Bearán, c/San Nicolás 25 (☎ & fax 948 223428). Comfortable, clean *hostal* offering rooms with TV. ⑤.

Hotel Eslava, Plaza Virgen de la O 7 (☎948 222270, fax 948 225157). Cosy, comfortable hotel run by the Eslava family in a quiet corner of the old city – views from balconies overlooking the plaza. Singles and doubles, with a bar in the basement. ⑥.

Hotel Europa, c/Espoz y Mina 11 (☎948 221800, fax 948 229235). Just off Plaza del Castillo; a good three-star hotel with a fine restaurant. ⑦.

Pensión Oliveto, Avda. de Conde Oliveto 3 (☎948 249321), Just across the road from the bus station; nice rooms without bath but with satellite TV and plenty of hot water. ④.

Hostal Otano, c/San Nicolás 5 (☎948 225095, fax 948 212012). Well-run *hostal* above bar and restaurant which have been in the family since 1929. The restaurant serves a popular *menú del día* for 1300ptas. ④.

Hotel La Perla, Plaza del Castillo 1 (☎948 227706). Great character; a few rooms have balcony overlooking the street (prices triple during San Fermín). Ernest Hemingway stayed in Room 217. ⑥.

Bar-Restaurante El Redín, c/del Merced 5 (☎948 222182). Nicely located in the street by the market, within a stone's throw of the start of the *encierro*. Mostly double rooms with a bar-restaurant downstairs; full board available. ④.

Hotel Yoldi, Avda. de San Ignacio 11 (☎948 224800, fax 948 212045). This is where the bullfighters and VIPs from the *taurino* world stay during San Fermín. Garage parking. ⑦.

The Town

The **Plaza del Castillo**, a tree-lined square ringed with fashionable cafés, is the centre of the town and of much of its activity. The narrow streets of the former *Judería* fill the area to the south and west, towards the city walls by the cathedral; virtually the only trace of a large Jewish community that thrived here before the persecutions and expulsions of the Inquisition. From the opposite side of the square, c/San Nicolás runs down towards the citadel and the more modern area of the city to the east. It's in c/San Nicolás and its continuation, c/San Gregorio, that you'll find most of the *hostales* and *fondas*, a number of excellent small restaurants and loads of raucous little bars.

The **Catedral de Santa María** is basically Gothic, built over a period of 130 years from the late fourteenth to the early sixteenth century but with an unattractive facade added in the eighteenth. It doesn't look promising, but the interior, containing the tomb of Carlos III and Eleanor in the centre of the nave, and the ancient *Virgen de los Reyes* above the high altar, is fine, and the cloister is magnificent. The **Museo Diocesano** (Tues–Sat 9am–10.30am & 6–8pm, Sun 9–10.30am; free) is entered via the cloisters and is housed in two superb buildings, the refectory and the kitchen – both are worth seeing in their own right. Don't miss the many sculpted doorways in the cloister, particularly the *Puerta de la Preciosa* and the chapel with a lovely star vault, built by a fourteenth-century bishop to house his own tomb.

Behind the cathedral is one of the oldest parts of the city, an area known as **La Navarrería**. Here you'll find the best section of the remaining **city walls** with the Baluarte de Redín and Portal de Zumalacárregui (or de Francia) looking down over a loop of the Río Arga. If you head out through the gate, paths lead down to the river from where you get the full force of the impregnability of these defences. Follow the inside of the walls and you'll come to the **Museo de Navarra** (Tues–Sat 10am–2pm & 5–7pm, Sun 11am–2pm; 300ptas) in the magnificent old hospital building on c/Santo Domingo. Inside is displayed material on the archeology and history of the old kingdom of Navarra, along with some good mosaics and an art collection that includes a portrait of the Marqués de San Adrián by Goya. Heading back to the plaza via c/Santo Domingo and the Plaza Consistorial you'll pass the **market** and the fine Baroque **Ayuntamiento**.

There's much more to be seen along the streets of the old town, with ancient churches and elegant buildings on almost every street. In particular, though, take time to wander around the parks and gardens that surround and include the ruinous **Citadel**, Avenida Ejército, with its views over the new part of town and a gallery (Tues–Sat 11.30am–1.30pm & 6–8pm, Sun 11am–2pm; free). From here you can follow the line of the old walls through the **Parque de la Taconera** and down to the river by an alternative route.

Eating and drinking

For good, inexpensive **menús**, and a wide range of **tapas** and *bocadillos*, head for the streets around c/Major, in particular c/San Lorenzo. The elegant *Café Iruña*, on Plaza del Castillo, is the place to sit over a leisurely coffee and take in the action, or try the more modern yet equally enjoyable *Café Niza* opposite the Turismo on c/Duque de Ahumada. For **breakfast** in peaceful surroundings and a chance to read the paper, there's no better place than *Café Alt Wien*, known to the locals as *El Vienés*, in the Jardines de la Taconera – it can get crowded with families in the afternoon.

Restaurants

Alhambra, c/Bergamín 7. Good for local dishes, especially the stuffed lamb.

Campana, c/Campana 12. Serves one of the best *menús* in town, near the church of San Saturino.

Casa Otano, c/San Nicolás. Popular *menú del día* at this restaurant which excels in *cocina Navarra*. Closed Sun night.

La Cepa, c/San Lorenzo 2. Fine selection of *tapas* and *bocadillos*.

Deportivo, c/Tafalla 34. Reasonably priced, tasty home cooking. Closed Thurs.

Ibañeta, c/San Nicolás 15. Basic, but good-value dishes at this lively restaurant. Closed Sun night & Mon.

Josexto, Plaza Príncipe de Viana (☎948 222097). One of the best – and priciest – restaurants in town.

Méson del Caballo Blanco, c/Redín. Lots of character at this surprisingly inexpensive restaurant serving up *raciones* and traditional local cooking. Evenings only.

O'Connors, Paseo Sarasate 22. A recently opened pub serving a strange but excellent mixture of Irish and Spanish *tapas*. Very popular with locals.

Sarasate, c/San Nicolás 19. Very decent vegetarian restaurant.

Southern Navarra

South of Pamplona, the country changes rapidly; the mountains are left behind and the monotonous plain so characteristic of central Spain begins to open out. The people are different, too – more akin to their southern neighbours than to the Basques of the north. There are regular bus and train services south to **Tudela**, the second city of Navarra, passing through **Tafalla** and **Olite**, once known as the "Flowers of Navarra", though little remains of their former glory.

Tafalla

TAFALLA, 35km south of Pamplona, is a shabby provincial town apparently left behind by modern Spain. If you find yourself here, it's worth going to the parish church of **Santa María**, where there's a huge *retablo*, one of the finest in Spain. It was carved by Juan de Ancheta, among the most recognized of the Basque country's artists.

There are a couple of overpriced places to **stay**: *Pensión Arotza*, Plaza de Navarra 3 (☎948 700716; ⑤; reception in *Bar Tubal*), and *Hostal Tafalla* (☎948 700300, fax 948 703052; ⑤), on the main Pamplona–Zaragoza road, next to the service station.

Olite

OLITE is a more attractive proposition. Now hardly more than a village, it boasts a magnificent **castle** (summer Mon–Sat 10am–2pm & 4–8pm, Sun 10am–2pm; winter Mon–Sat 10am–2pm & 4–5pm, Sun 10am–2pm; 300ptas) which was once the residence of the kings of Navarra. An amazing ramshackle ramble of turrets, keeps and dungeons, it is slowly being restored, and part of the building already houses a *parador*. There are also two gorgeous old churches, Romanesque **San Pedro** and Gothic **Santa María**, the latter with a superb carved *retablo*.

You'll find a useful **Turismo** in Plaza Carlos III, in the medieval gallery (Mon–Fri 10am–2pm & 4–7pm, Sat & Sun 10am–2pm; ☎948 712434). **Accommodation** in Olite is expensive. Apart from the *Parador Príncipe de Viana*, Plaza de los Teobaldos 2 (☎948 740000, fax 948 740201; ⑦), there are a couple of other pricey hotels: *Casa Zanito*, Rúa Mayor 16 (☎948 740002, fax 948 712087; ⑥), among the old streets, is the more atmospheric, but is frequently full during the summer; *Hotel Carlos III el Noble*, Rúa de Medios 1 (☎948 740644; ⑤), is slightly less expensive and offers a popular and good-value *menú* for 1300ptas, but your best bet if you're on a budget is *Pensión Vidaurre*, in Plaza Carlos III (☎948 740597; ③). If you want to camp, head for *Camping Ciudad de Olite* on the Tafalla–Peralta Road (☎948 712443; open all year).

Ujué

East of Tafalla and Olite in the direction of Sangüesa, a winding road branches off to the right at San Martín de Unx (a good place to stock up on wine from the local *bodega*), to the hill-top village of **UJUÉ** – one of the real jewels of Navarra. It's a perfect medieval defensive village perched up on the terraced hillside above the harsh, arid landscape and dominated by the thirteenth-century Romanesque church of **Santa María** (daily 10am–8pm), where the heart of King Charles II of Navarra is supposedly preserved inside the altar. The church has Gothic additions dating from the fourteenth century and, from its balconied exterior, the view extends over the whole southern Navarra region of La Ribera. The main doorway contains some intricate sculptures depicting the Last Supper and the Three Kings.

From the main square, where you can eat *migas de pastor, almendras garrapiñadas*, and other dishes from the region, a couple of pedestrianized cobbled streets plunge down to another beautiful little square and a *casa rural, Casa Isolina Jurio* (☎948 739037; ③); a second smaller one in the village, *Casa El Chófer* (☎948 739011; ③), also has a couple of rooms. There are at least ten *casa rurales* in the area, which can be booked through the Turismo in Olite; ask here also about a guide and transport to the village from San Martín de Unx, as there is no public transport.

Tudela

The route south continues to **TUDELA** on the banks of the Ebro. On arrival, it seems as ugly a town as you could ever come across, but don't despair – a short walk down the main street takes you into the old town and an entirely different atmosphere. Around the richly decorated **Plaza de los Fueros** are a jumble of narrow lanes apparently little changed since the Moorish occupation of the city was ended by Alfonso I of Aragón in 1114. The twelfth-century **Colegiata de Santa Ana** is a fine, strong, Gothic construction. It has a rose window above the intricately carved alabaster west doorway which portrays a chilling vision of the Last Judgement. Inside there's an unusual *retablo* and some beautiful old tombs, while the Romanesque cloister has some deft primitive carvings, many badly damaged. The bizarre thirteenth-century **bridge** over the Ebro looks as if it could never have carried the weight of an ox cart, let alone seven centuries of traffic on the main road to Zaragoza.

There is a **Turismo** on Plaza Vieja 1 (☎948 821539), and a couple of pricey **hostales** in the main street through the new part of town: best value is *Hostal Remigio*, just off Plaza de los Fueros, at c/Gaztambide 4 (☎948 820850; ④), which also has more expensive rooms with bath; *Delta*, Avda. Zaragoza 29 (☎948 821400, fax 948 821400; ⑤), has rooms with TV and video; or try the *Casa de Huéspedes* at c/de Carniceras 13 (☎948 821039; ②), above the *Restaurante La Estrella* in the old town. You'll find many other places to **eat and drink** around the Plaza de los Fueros; *Bar Arbella* is good for fresh *calamares fritos*.

The Pilgrim Route

The ancient **Pilgrim Route** to Santiago passed through Aragón (see p.551) and into Navarra just before Leyre, travelling through the province via **Sangüesa, Puente la Reina** (where it met an alternative route crossing the Pyrenees at Roncesvalles) and **Estella**, before crossing into Old Castile at Logroño.

Yesa and the Monasterio de Leyre

The first stop for the pilgrims in Navarra is the **Monasterio de San Salvador de Leyre** (daily 10am–9pm), which stands amid mountainous country 4km from Yesa, on the main Pamplona–Jaca road, connected with both places by a daily **bus** in either

---

THE CAMINO DE SANTIAGO IN NAVARRA

Following the European Parliament's decision to designate the **camino** Europe's first "cultural itinerary", Navarra has invested considerably in improving facilities along the route. There are around a dozen pilgrims' *hostales* within Navarra which bona fide pilgrims can use – to qualify you must show a letter of introduction from your parish church or town hall at the place where you plan to start the route (in Spain this is usually Roncesvalles or Somport, or the church of San Cernino or the Archbishop's palace in Pamplona). You'll be given a "passport" as an accredited pilgrim which is then stamped at each *hostal* along the route. Most of the *hostales* have hot showers, some have kitchens and are either free or charge only a nominal 500ptas fee. A few of the *hostales* may be open only during the summer months, but regional Turismos in Navarra can provide up-to-date details.

The route itself is clearly marked as long-distance footpath GR65. Long stretches do run alongside the main Pamplona–Estrella–Logroño road, but wherever possible the official walking route avoids major highways.

---

direction. **YESA** has several **hostales**, the best being *El Jabalí* (☎948 884042; ④), on the main road, with a pool and restaurant.

From the village a good road leads up to Leyre, arriving at the east end of the monastery. Although the convent buildings are sixteenth- to eighteenth-century, the church is largely Romanesque; its tall, severe apses are particularly impressive. After languishing in ruins for over a century, it was restored and reoccupied by the Benedictines in the 1950s and now looks in immaculate condition. The leaflet available in English at the porter's lodge is useful to shed light on the complicated sculptured facade of the church. Inside, the crypt, with its sturdy little columns, can be illuminated by putting a coin in the slot. Try to catch a service if you can; the Benedictines here employ the Gregorian chant in their Masses and are well worth hearing.

The former pilgrims' guest house here is now run as a two-star **hotel**, the *Hospedería de Leyre* (☎948 884100, fax 948 884137; ⑤), which, although far more expensive than staying in Yesa, is still a remarkable bargain. Men can stay at the monastery itself for a nominal fee, but anyone wanting to do this should phone ahead (☎948 884011).

Javier

From Yesa it's only a few kilometres south to **JAVIER**, birthplace of San Francisco Xavier – one of the first Jesuits – and home to a fine **castle** (daily 10am–1pm & 4–7pm; free). Javier had nothing to do with the Pilgrim Route, but it is something of a place of pilgrimage in its own right, with a museum of the saint's life in the restored keep. Look out for the set of extraordinary demonic murals – recently discovered – depicting the Dance of Death.

It's a popular picnic spot and there's a **hotel** in the grounds, *Hotel Xavier* (☎948 884006, fax 948 884078; ⑥), which has a good restaurant. Alternatively, try the cheaper *El Mesón*, Plaza de Javier (☎948 884035, fax 948 884226; ⑤ with bath). Javier and Pamplona are connected by one daily **bus**.

Sangüesa

The Pilgrim Route proper stops next at **SANGÜESA**, a small, delightful town preserving many outstanding monuments, including several churches from the fourteenth century and earlier. See above all the south facade of the church of **Santa María Real** (at the far end of town beside the river), which has an incredibly richly carved doorway and sculpted buttresses: God, the Virgin and the Apostles are depicted amid a chaotic company of warriors, musicians, craftsmen, wrestlers and animals. The entrance is flanked by two groups of three statues, one of which is signed by the artist Leodagarius (c. 1200); the other sculptor known to have worked on the doorway was the Master of San Juan de la Peña.

Sangüesa is an enjoyable place simply to wander around. Many of its streets have changed little in centuries and aside from the churches – Romanesque Santiago is also lovely – there are some handsome mansions, the remains of a royal palace and a medieval hospital.

Practicalities

Sangüesa's helpful **Turismo** is at Alfonte el Batallador 20 (Mon–Fri 10am–2pm & 4–7pm, weekends & fiestas 10am–2pm; ☎948 860329). Unfortunately, there's not much in the way of **accommodation**: the *Pensión Las Navas*, c/Alfonso el Batallador 7 (☎948 870077; ③), opposite the main bus stop, is the only convenient place to stay, though there's also a fairly fancy hotel, *Yamaguchi* (☎948 870127, fax 948 870700; ⑤), on the road to Javier. Three **buses** daily run to and from Pamplona and one (leaving Sangüesa very early) goes to the Aragonese town of Sos del Rey Católico, 12km away.

Puente La Reina

Perhaps no town is more perfectly evocative of the days of the medieval pilgrimage than **PUENTE LA REINA**, 20km southwest of Pamplona. This is the meeting place of the two main Spanish routes: the Navarrese trail, via Roncesvalles and Pamplona, and the Aragonese one, via Jaca, Leyre and Sangüesa. From here onward, all the pilgrims followed the same path to Santiago.

At the eastern edge of town, the **Iglesia del Crucifijo** was originally a twelfth-century foundation of the Knights Templar, its porch decorated with scallop shells (the badge of the Santiago pilgrims). To one side is the former pilgrims' hospice, later in date, but still one of the oldest extant. In town, the tall buildings along c/Mayor display their original coats of arms, and there's another pilgrim church, Santiago, whose portal is sadly worn, but which has a notable statue of Saint James inside. The **bridge** at the end of the street gives the town its name. The finest medieval bridge in Spain, it was built at the end of the eleventh century by royal command and is still used by pedestrians and animals only – an ugly modern bridge has been constructed for vehicular traffic.

Practicalities

Accommodation in town is limited to *Hostal Puente*, Paseo de los Fueros (☎948 340146; ⑤), which is friendly, clean and serves good food, though it can be noisy. *Mesón del Peregrino* (☎948 340075, fax 948 341190; ⑧), an ancient building with a modern pool, just out of town on the main road towards Pamplona offers more luxury, or try next door at the *Hotel Jakue* (☎948 341017, fax 948 341120; ⑥) for rooms of a good standard. There's a good **campsite**, *El Molino* (☎948 340604, fax 948 340082; open all year) at **Mendigorria**, 5km south, with a large swimming pool. There are several places to **eat**, most near the main road which, thankfully, skirts the town. *La Conrada*, at Cerco Nuevo 77 (near Hostal Puente), has an excellent set menu for around 1500ptas, while *Sidrería Ilzarbe*, on c/Irundibea, offers delicious cider and *tapas*.

Estella

Twenty kilometres west lies **ESTELLA**, a beautiful town rich in monuments and high in interest. During the nineteenth century this was the headquarters of the Carlists in the Civil Wars, and each May there is still a pilgrimage up a nearby mountain to honour the dead. **Plaza de los Fueros** marks the centre of town, but most of the more interesting buildings are on the opposite side of the river in the Barrio San Pedro de la Rúa.

Next door is the twelfth-century **Palacio de los Reyes de Navarra**, a rare example of large-scale Romanesque civil architecture, part of which is now open as an art gallery (Tues–Sat 11am–1pm & 5–7pm; Sun & fiestas 11am–1pm; free) devoted to the painter Gustave de Maeztu.

Estella has a wealth of churches, including the fortified pilgrimage church of **San Pedro de la Rúa**, which is only open for half an hour before the daily 7pm Mass and the noon Mass on Sunday. The main doorway shows unmistakable Moorish influence. From the former *Ayuntamiento*, an elegant sixteenth-century building opposite the *palacio*, c/de la Rúa leads past many old merchants' mansions. Further along, past a stud farm, you reach the abandoned church of Santo Sepulcro with a carved fourteenth-century Gothic doorway. Cross the hump-backed bridge, take the first left, then right uphill, and you come to the church of **San Miguel**: not a terribly inspiring building in itself but with a north doorway that is one of the gems of the Pilgrim Route. Its delicate capitals are marvellous, as are the modelled reliefs of the *Three Marys at the Sepulchre* and *St Michael Fighting the Dragon*. The dingy interior is a letdown after this, and in any case may only be visited just before or just after Mass (Mon–Fri 7pm, Sun 8.30am, 11.30am & 1pm).

Practicalities

Immediately after crossing the bridge, you'll find Estella's well-stocked **Turismo**, at c/San Nicolás 1 (March–Dec Mon–Fri 10am–2pm & 4–7pm, Sat & Sun 10am–2pm; ☎948 554011), which can provide you with a free map of the town. If you want to **stay**, many of the budget places are located round the Plaza de los Fueros. *Fonda San Andrés*, Plaza de Santiago 58 (☎948 550448; ④), is a good choice, while in the streets nearby several cheaper options include *El Volante*, c/Merkatondoa 2 (☎948 553975; ③), and *Fonda Izarra*, c/Calderería (☎948 550678; ③), which has a comfortable bar. For more comfort, head for *Hostal Cristina*, Baja Navarra 1 (☎948 550772, fax 948 550750; ⑤). There's also a **casa rural**, *Casa Laguao* (☎948 520203; ③), 8km north in the village of Abarzuza, and a **campsite**, *Camping Lizarra* (☎948 551733).

Estella has plenty of **bars**, many serving good *platos combinados*; the **restaurants**, on the other hand (except those attached to the *fondas*), are expensive, although most offer a lunchtime *menú* for 800–1200ptas.

Buses operate to Pamplona (11 daily), Logroño (7 daily) and San Sebastián (4 daily).

Estella to Logroño

From Estella, the Pilgrim Route follows the main road to Logroño and there are a number of interesting stops. At **IRACHE**, near the village of Ayegui, there's a **Cistercian monastery** (Mon 10am–2pm & 5–7pm, Tues 10am–2pm, Wed–Fri 10am–2pm & 5–7pm, Sat & Sun 9am–2pm & 4–7pm), which boasts an ornate Plateresque cloister. Beside the adjacent Museo de Vino (principally a showroom for *Bodega Irache*), are two taps in the wall, ostensibly for use by pilgrims – out of one comes water and from the other, red wine. Seventeen kilometres farther on is **LOS ARCOS**, whose handsome church of **Santa María** (daily 9am–2pm) has a Gothic cloister. If you decide to **stay**, *Hostal Ezequiel* (☎948 640296, fax 948 640278; ④) is clean and comfortable, and has a special pilgrim rate; alternatively, *Hotel Monaco*, Plaza del Coso 22 (☎948 640000, fax 948 640025; ③ with bath) is a good bet.

Of more direct interest is **TORRES DEL RÍO**, 7km farther still. This unpretentious village is built round the church of the **Holy Sepulchre**, a little octagonal building whose function is uncertain – it may have been a Knights Templar foundation or a funeral chapel. The names of the local women who look after the monument are posted on the wall of the church, and any one of them may be found to show visitors around (access at any reasonable time), for a small charge. Inside it's a surprise to find that the dome is of Moorish inspiration.

VIANA, the last stop before the border and where Cesare Borgia died, is an attractive place with many beautiful Renaissance and Baroque palatial houses, in addition to the Gothic church of Santa María with its outstanding Renaissance carved porch. Logroño is only 10km away, but Viana's **pensión**, *La Granja*, c/Navarro Villoslada 19 (☎948 045078, ③), has comfortable rooms with bath. Viana also has a useful **Turismo** in Plaza de los Fueros (Mon–Fri 10am–2pm & 4.45–8pm, Sat 10.15am–2pm; ☎948 446302).

The Pyrenees

The mountains of Navarra may not be as high as their neighbours to the east, but they're every bit as dramatic and far less developed. And there's not – as yet – a single ski lift in the province. The historic **pass of Roncesvalles** is the major route through the mountains from Pamplona, and always has been; it is celebrated in the *Song of Roland* and, more recently, by Jan Morris who called it "one of the classic passes of Europe and a properly sombre gateway into Spain". It was the route taken by countless pilgrims throughout the Middle Ages; Charlemagne's retreating army was decimated here by Basque guerrillas avenging the sacking of Pamplona; Napoleon's defeated armies fought a running battle along the pass as they fled Spain; and thousands of refugees from the Civil War made their escape into France along this narrow way.

The beautiful Pyrenean valleys, particularly the **Valle de Baztán** north of Pamplona, and the **Valle de Salazar** to the southeast, are a perfect place to relax, and they offer inexpensive and plentiful accommodation with the largest number of **casas rurales** in the province.

Auritz-Burguete and Orreaga-Roncesvalles

Northeast of Pamplona, the N135 winds upwards until it reaches the neighbouring villages of **Auritz-Burguete** and **Orreaga-Roncesvalles**, about half an hour's walk apart. The surrounding country is superb for walking, or simply to sit back and admire. Beyond these villages, the road continues into France via the border town of Luzaide-Valcarlos.

Auritz-Burguete

AURITZ-BURGUETE has a pleasing, villagey atmosphere, and if you've come on the daily bus from Pamplona you've little choice but to **stay** here, as it doesn't arrive till 8pm. The best place is the wonderfully renovated *Hotel Restaurant Loizu* (☎948 760008, fax 948 790444; ⑥) on the main road. Others on the main road include the *Hostal Burguete* (☎948 760005; ④) and the *Juandeaburre* (☎948 760078; ③). Better still, try one of the *casas rurales* for a more family atmosphere; *Casa Loigorri* (☎948 760016; ③), *Lopirini* (☎948 760068; ③), next to the bank, or *Casa Vergara* (☎948 760044; ④), which has more expensive rooms with bath. There's also a **campsite**, *Urrobi* (☎948 760200), 3km south of the village at **Aurizberri-Espinal** on the Pamplona road.

Orreaga-Roncesvalles

The few buildings at **ORREAGA-RONCESVALLES** are clustered around the **Colegiata** with its beautiful Gothic cloister. A side chapel houses a prostrate statue of

Sancho VII el Fuerte (the Strong); measuring 2.25m long, it is supposedly life-size. Here also are the chains that Sancho broke in 1212 at the battle of Navas de Tolosa against the Moors – a symbol which found its way into the Navarrese coat of arms. A small **museum** (summer daily & weekends all year 11am–1.30pm & 4–6pm) next to the monastery has relics of centuries of pilgrimage and a great deal of (mainly bogus) exhibits relating to the ambush of Charlemagne. A beautiful half-hour walk from the back of the monastery (on the marked path) will take you up to the pass of the **Puerto de Ibañeta** – this is said to be the very route taken by Charlemagne.

Accommodation is fairly limited: there's the *Hostal Casa Sabina*, right next to the monastery (☎948 760012; ④), or the newer *La Posada* (☎948 760225; ⑤), run by the monastery. If you're a walker or cyclist following the Pilgrim Route, you might be able to stay in a dormitory at the monastery; ask for Father Javier Navarro. There is also a small **Turismo** on Antiguo Molino (☎948 760193).

Luzaide-Valcarlos

If you're continuing into France – a journey redolent with history – you'll come to the border village, **LUZAIDE VALCARLOS**, 18km on. There's no bus on this road but hitching is easy. Valcarlos is a typical border town full of souvenirs and booze – though the views are better than usual – with the *Hostal Maitena* (☎948 790210; ④) conveniently situated on the main road should you need to stay. On the Frenchward side of the village, the excellent *Casa Etxezuria* (☎948 790011; ③) has a couple of beautifully furnished rooms and offers luxury at a bargain price – this place has become a big success with pilgrims following the Camino de Santiago, so phone in advance if possible. There are also houses with rooms to let – ask in the bars.

Valle de Baztán

Due north of Pamplona, the N121 climbs over the Velate pass at **Mugaire** near the **Senori de Bértiz gardens**, a former private estate now designated as a Parque Natural and recreation area. At Oronoz, a left fork heads up the scenic Valle de Bidasoa with its interesting old towns (see p.393) to Irún and San Sebastián. Continuing along the right fork, you enter the **Valle de Baztán** with its string of tiny villages, beautiful countryside and cave formations.

Elizondo

The centre of this most typically Basque of Navarran valleys is **ELIZONDO**. The town is full of fine Basque Pyrenean architecture, especially alongside the river, but above all, it serves as a good base for exploring the beautiful villages and countryside in the area.

There are several places to **stay** in Elizondo. The best option is *Casa Jaén* (☎948 580487; ③), but it has only two rooms; *Pensión Eskisaroi*, c/Jaime Urrutia 40 (☎948 580013; ③), is a good second choice. There are also two considerably more expensive places: the three-star *Hotel Baztán* (☎948 580050, fax 948 452323; ⑥) on the Pamplona road south of town, complete with garden and pool; and in the town itself, *Hostal Saskaitz*, c/María Azpilikueta 10 (☎948 580488, fax 948 580615; ⑥). Four **buses** run daily from both Pamplona and San Sebastián, but there is no public transport to the smaller villages beyond.

Around Elizondo

In nearby **ARIZCUN** is the seventeenth-century Convent of Our Lady of the Angels with its striking Baroque facade and, just beyond the village, a typical example of a fortified house (very common in the valley) where Pedro de Ursua, the leader of the Marañones expedition up the Amazon in 1560 in search of El Dorado, was born. You can **stay** in Arizcun at the friendly and well-run *Pensión Etxeberría*, c/Txuputo 43 (☎948 453013; ③), which also serves good lunches and dinners.

Just before the spectacular, narrow **Izpegui Pass** is **ERRATZU**, another gem, with a few well-preserved *casas rurales*: one is a fourteenth-century palatial home, *Casa Etxebeltzea* (☎948 453157; ④), and another, *Casa Marimartinenea*, (☎948 453117; ③), still has livestock on the ground floor.

MAIA, a few kilometres to the north, where the last battle for the independence of Navarra took place, is another unspoilt village worth a stop. The gateway to its single street displays the village shield depicting a red bell – most houses still proudly show off the shield above their doorways.

The caves of Zugarramurdi

North of Elizondo, the main road climbs over the **Otxondo Pass** to the villages of Urdax and Zugarramurdi, a good stopover between Pamplona and the French Basque coastal towns of Biarritz and Bayonne. The only public transport on this stretch is the noon bus from Elizondo – check in town first.

ZUGARRAMURDI is famous for its **caves** whose centrepiece is the giant natural arch through which the *regata de infierno* (hell's stream) flows. It was a major centre for witchcraft in the Middle Ages and consequently the area bore the brunt of persecution at the time of the Inquisition. Underneath the arch, *akelarres* or witches' sabbaths allegedly took place and have passed into Basque legend. The village itself is very pretty and a good place to base yourself for excursions into the surrounding countryside – one possibility is to walk on the track beyond the caves into France to another set of caves at **Sare**.

Zugarramurdi is well-served with **casas rurales**, although they often get booked out at weekends; *Casa Sueldeguía* (☎948 599088; ③) and *Casa Teltxeguia* (☎948 599167; ③) are both in the centre of the village, or there is a **campsite**, *Camping Josenea* (☎948 599011; open all year), by the main road near Urdax.

Valle de Salazar

Southeast of Pamplona, 10km before Yesa, the road to Lumbier leads into the beautiful Salazar valley, the most spectacular part of which is the **Foz de Arbayún** – a deep gorge, visible from a viewing platform by the road, which may be descended by the intrepid. One kilometre from **LUMBIER** is the entrance to the Foz de Lumbier, a major nesting place for **eagles** which can usually be spotted high up in the walls of the gorge or circling overhead. There's a **campsite** at Lumbier, *Camping Iturbero* (☎948 880405; open Easter–Oct, rest of the year weekends only).

Forty kilometres farther on you reach the unspoilt Pyrenean town of **OCHAGAVÍA**, served by one bus daily from Pamplona, except Sunday. The most attractive parts of town are the tree-lined streets on both sides of the river, which is crossed by a series of low stone bridges. There are no fewer than twelve **casas rurales** (②) here offering accommodation in attractive traditional stone houses for which the town is famous; *Casa Navarro* (☎948 890355) and *Casa Osaba* (☎948 890011) are both good choices (consult the *Guía de alojamientos: turismo rural* for a full list – free from the Turismo in Pamplona). One of the best places in town to eat is the innovative, but reasonable, gourmet **restaurant** at the *Hostal Laspalas*, c/Urrutia 49 (☎948 890015; ④), with such goodies as carrot soup, salmon *en papillote* and decadent sweets.

The **forest of Irati** to the north is one of the most extensive pine and beech forests in Europe, and **Monte Ori**, the first 2000m peak in the Pyrenees rising from the Atlantic side, offers some excellent walking and climbing options with views every bit as spectacular as the highest peaks. For those using public transport, the forest is inaccessible, but there are some excellent walks in the hills surrounding Ochagavía. Ask for details at Ochagavia's **Turismo** (☎948 890004), on the opposite side of the river to the bus stop.

Valle de Roncal – the Parque Natural Pirenaico

If you're really serious about exploring the mountains, the **Valle de Roncal** farther east is considerably more rewarding, although very popular in July and August. The bus route from Pamplona passes north of Sangüesa, and briefly into Aragón by the huge reservoir, Embalse de Yesa, before heading north up the valley of the Esca and back into Navarra. It's a lovely route, crisscrossing the river all the way up through Burgui and Roncal to Isaba. There is a **Turismo** (☎948 475136) in **RONCAL**, as well as a *hostal*, the *Zaltua*, c/Castillo 23 (☎948 475008; ④), and also several *casas rurales*, best of which is *Casas Villa Pepita* (☎948 475133; ③), a large private mansion which also provides good meals at very reasonable cost. If you want to stay round here, though, you're much better off continuing to Isaba.

Isaba and around

ISABA has plenty of rooms available in private houses, the majority of which are now grouped as **casas rurales**, although expect to have to try several places at weekends as Isaba (along with Ochagavía) is a major touring centre for the western Pyrenees and gets invaded by the hordes from Pamplona, Bilbao and elsewhere. There's also the *Albergue Oxanea* (①), a sort of private **youth hostel** where you sleep in dormitories; the *Hostal Lola*, c/Mendigatxa 17 (☎948 893012, fax 948 893012; ④), and *Pensión Txabalkua*, c/Izargentea 16 (☎948 893083; ③), both offering good food; *Pensión Txiki* (☎948 893118; ④), above the bar-restaurant of the same name; as well as a fairly luxurious hotel, the *Isaba* (☎948 893000, fax 948 893030; ⑥). The **campsite**, *Asolaze* (☎948 893034; open all year), is at the edge of the Parque Natural, 6km up the road towards the border, or with discretion you can camp freelance along the banks of the river beyond the village.

Despite its convenience, there's too much new building in Isaba for it to be really attractive. For the best walking and magnificent views, continue up the valley of the Río Belagua to the *Refugio de Belagua*, a mountain refuge (popular in July and August) almost on the border, in the middle of the **Parque Natural**, high among the peaks in a landscape of extraordinary beauty. In summer the bus from Pamplona continues this far, or there's an 8am service up from Isaba. There's a **restaurant and bar**, *Venta de Juan Pito*, Puerto de Belagua (☎948 893080), and if you bring a sleeping bag you can hire a basic bed for the night – bring your own food if you plan to stay long. There are many **walks** you can undertake from here – some very ambitious – to make the most of which you need a proper **map** (Editorial Alpina 1:40,000 *Ansó-Hecho* covers the park) and a compass. There are also plenty of easy strolls; details in the *Refugio*.

travel details

TRAINS

Bilbao Estación de Abando to: Alicante (5 daily; 16hr); Barcelona (2 daily; 10–12hr); Logroño (6 daily; 2hr 30min); Madrid (1 daily; 8hr); Orduña (hourly; 1hr); Salamanca (1 daily; 9hr).

Estación Atxuri to: Durango (10–12 daily; 1 hr); Gernika (15 daily; 2hr).

Estación de Santander to: Karranza (4 daily; 1hr); Santander (5 daily; 2hr).

Estación Las Arenas (San Nicolás) to: Getxo (every 30min; 25 min); Leioa (every 30min; 35min); Plentzia (every 30min; 45min).

Irún to: Hendaia, France (every 30min 7am–10pm; 5min); Paris (2 daily; 8hr); San Sebastián (every 30min 5am–11pm; 30min).

Pamplona to: Madrid (1 daily; 6hr); San Sebastián (1 daily; 2hr 30min); Tudela (1 daily; 1hr 15min); Vitoria (1 daily; 1hr); Zaragoza (7 daily; 2hr 30min).

San Sebastián to: Bilbao (9 daily; 2hr 30min–3hr); Burgos (12 daily; 4hr); Irún (every 30min; 30min); Madrid (4 daily; 6hr 30min–8hr 30min); Ordizia (every 30min; 50min); Pamplona (6 daily; 2–3hr); Salamanca (2 daily; 9hr); Valencia (1 daily; 12hr); Vitoria (7 daily; 1hr 50min); Zaragoza (4 daily; 4–5hr).

Vitoria to: Miranda del Ebro (1 daily; 1hr 25min); Pamplona (1 daily; 1hr); San Sebastián (7 daily; 2hr 30min).

BUSES

Bilbao to: Burgos (4 daily; 2hr); Elantxobe (3 daily; 1hr 30min); Gernika (16 daily; 40min); Lekeitio (4 daily; 1hr 30min); Logroño (1 daily; 2hr 15min); Onati (2 daily; 2hr); Ondarroa via Markina (2 daily; 1hr 30min); Pamplona (3 daily; 4hr); San Sebastian (hourly, 1hr 10min); Santander (5 daily; 2hr 30min); Vitoria (8 daily; 1hr 30min); Zaragoza (3 daily; 5hr).

Irún to: Pamplona (3 daily; 2hr); San Sebastián (constantly; 30min).

Pamplona to: Bilbao (3 daily; 4hr); Burguete (1 daily; 1hr 30min); Elizondo (4 daily; 2hr); Estella (11 daily; 1hr); Irún (3 daily; 2hr); Isaba (1 daily; 2hr); Jaca (2 daily in summer, 1 in winter, except Sun; 2hr); Logroño (4 daily; 2hr); Madrid (2 daily; 6hr); Ochagavía (1 daily, except Sun; 2hr); Puenta la Reina (hourly; 30min); Roncal (1 daily; 1hr 45min); San Sebastián (6 daily; Autovista 1hr; others 3hr); Tafalla (6 daily; 1hr); Tudela (6 daily; 1hr 30min); Vitoria (9 daily, fewer Sun; 1hr 30min); Yesa (1 daily; 1hr); Zaragoza (2–3 daily; 4hr).

San Sebastián to: Bilbao (13 daily; 1hr 10min); Elizondo (3 daily; 2hr); Hondarribia (every 20min; 30min); Irún (constantly; 30min); Lekeitio (3–5 daily; 2hr); Lesaka (2 daily; 1hr 15min); Pamplona (6 daily; Autovista 1hr; others 3hr); Bera-Vera de Bidasoa (2 daily; 1hr); Vitoria (7 daily; 2hr 30min); Zarautz (hourly; 30–40min); Zumaia (4 daily; 1hr).

Vitoria to: Araía (via villages of Llanada Alavesa; 2 daily; 1hr); Bilbao (8 daily; 1hr 30min); Durango (4 daily; 1hr); Estella (4 daily; 1hr 15min); Laguardia (4 daily; 1hr 45 mins); Logroño (8 daily; 1hr); Pamplona (9 daily, fewer Sunday; 1hr 30min); Pantanos de Zadorra (3 daily; 30min); Santander via Castro Urdiales (3 daily; 2hr).

CHAPTER SEVEN

CANTABRIA AND ASTURIAS

The northern provinces of Cantabria and Asturias are popular holiday terrain for Spaniards and French, but hardly touched by the mass tourism of the Mediterranean coast, mostly because of the somewhat unreliable weather. But the sea is warm enough for swimming through the summer months, and the sun does shine, if not every day; it is the warm, moist climate too, which gives rise to the wealth of forests and rich vegetation which give the region its name, *Costa Verde*, or the Green Coast. The provinces also boast old and elegant seaside towns, and a landscape that becomes more dramatic the further west you travel, with tiny, isolated coves along the coast and, inland, the fabulous Picos de Europa, with peaks, sheer gorges, flora and fauna enough to satisfy walkers and trekkers of all levels.

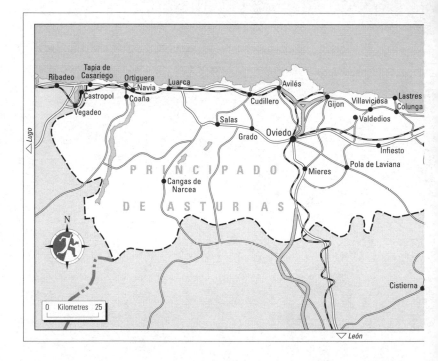

Cantabria, centred on the city of Santander, was formerly part of Old Castile, and was long a conservative bastion amid the separatist leanings of its coastal neighbours. **Santander**, the modern capital, is an elegant, if highly conventional, resort, with one of Spain's few remaining ferry links with Britain – to Plymouth. More attractive, low-key resorts lie to either side, crowded and expensive in the Spanish and French holiday season – August especially – but generally enjoyable; the best are **Castro Urdiales**, to the east, and **Comillas** and **San Vicente** to the west. Inland, there is a series of **prehistoric caves**, several of which can be seen at **Puente Viesgo**, near Santander, though the most famous, **Altamira**, can no longer be visited.

To the west is mountain-locked **Asturias**, an idiosyncratic, Celtic land that was the one part of Spain never to be conquered by the Moors. It is a little like Wales, both in its scenery – harsh mountains and rugged coves – and in its idiosyncratic traditions, which include status as a principality (the heir to the Spanish throne is known as the *Príncipe de Asturias*) and a culture that includes bagpipes and cider (*sidra* – served from above head height to add fizz). The Welsh comparisons extend, too, to Asturias's base of heavy industry, especially mining and steelworks, and a long-time radical and maverick workforce. Having conducted wildcat strikes during the early days of the Republic, Asturian miners were among the staunchest defenders of the Republic against Franco.

The coastline is a delight, so long as you steer clear of the steel mills of Avilés and the factories of Gijón, with wide, rolling meadows leading down to the sea. Tourism here is largely local, with a succession of old-fashioned and very enjoyable **seaside towns**: small places such as **Ribadesella**, **Llanes** and **Luarca**. Inland, everything is dominated by the **Picos de Europa**, though a quiet pleasure on the peripheries of the mountains, as in Cantabria, is the wealth of Romanesque, and even rare pre-Romanesque, churches

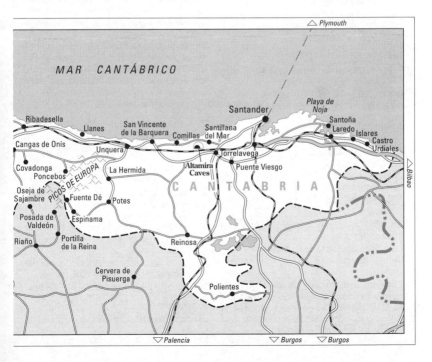

found in odd corners of the hills. These reflect the history of the old Asturian kingdom – the embryonic kingdom of Christian Spain – which had its first stronghold in the mountain fortress of **Covadonga**, and was slowly to spread south with the Reconquest. The churches are often at their best when you come upon them by accident, rounding a corner in the countryside, though **Santa María del Naranco**, just outside Oviedo, is worth a special effort to see; **Oviedo** itself, a delightful regional capital, is perhaps the only big city on this part of the coast meriting a longer stay.

The Picos de Europa, as noted earlier, take in parts of León, as well as Cantabria and Asturias, though for simplicity the whole region is covered in this chapter.

FIESTAS

January

22 Saint's day fiesta at San Vicente de la Barquera.

February/March
Start of Lent Week-long *carnaval* festivities in Avilés, Gijón, Oviedo, Mieres, Santoña – fireworks, fancy dress and live music.

April

Holy Week Celebrations include the *bollo* (cake) festival on Easter Sunday and Monday at Avilés.

First Sunday after Easter *La Folia*, torch-lit maritime procession at San Vicente de la Barquera.

June

28 *Coso Blanco* nocturnal parade at Castro Urdiales.

29 Cudillero enacts *La Amuravela* – an ironic review of the year – and then proceeds to obliterate memories.

July

10 Fiesta at Aliva.

15 Good solid festival at Comillas with greased-pole climbs, goose chases and other such events.

16, 17 & 18 Fiestas in Tapia de Casariego.

25 Festival of Saint James at Cangas de Onis.

Last Sunday *Fiesta de los Vaqueros* – cowboys – at La Brana de Aristebano near Luarca.

Through July Weekly fiestas in Llanes, with Asturian dancers balancing pine trees on their shoulders and swerving through the streets. Also, tightrope walking and live bands down at the harbour.

August

First or second weekend, Mass canoe races from Arriondas to Ribadesella down the Río Sella, with fairs and festivities in both towns.

First Sunday Asturias Day, celebrated above all at Gijón.

12 Fiesta at Llanes.

15 *El Rosario* at Luarca – the fishermen's fiesta when the Virgin is taken to the sea.

31 Battle of the Flowers at Laredo.

Last week Fairly riotous festivities for San Timoteo at Luarca: best on the final weekend of the month, with fireworks over the sea, people being thrown into the river, and a Sunday *romería*.

Through August Music and cultural festival at Santander. This being one of the wealthiest cities of the north, you can usually depend on the festival featuring some prestigious acts.

September

7–8 Running of the bulls at Ampuero (Santander).

14 Bull running by the sea at Carreñón (Oviedo).

16 Llanes folklore festival, strong on dancing.

19 Americas Day in Asturias, celebrating the thousands of local emigrants in Latin America; at Oviedo there are floats, bands and groups representing every Latin American country. The exact date for this can vary.

21 *Fiesta de San Mateo* at Oviedo, usually a continuation of the above festival.

29 San Miguel *romería* at Puente Viesgo.

November

30 Small regatta for San Andrés day at Castro Urdiales.

The FEVE railway

Communications in this region are generally slow, with the one main road following the coast through the foothills to the north of the Picos de Europa. If you're not in a hurry, you may want to make use of the **FEVE rail line**, which is unmarked on many maps and independent of the main RENFE system; note that rail passes are not valid on this service. The FEVE line begins at Bilbao in the Basque country and follows the length of the Cantabrian coast (with trains serving the triangle of Gijón, Avilés and Oviedo) to Ferrol in Galicia: a terrific route, skirting beaches, crossing *rías* and snaking through a succession of limestone gorges. An expensive "train hotel" runs at night, but it's not a practical way of getting about and it's certainly not the best way of seeing the scenery.

Santander

Long a favourite summer haunt of *madrileños*, **SANTANDER** is an elegant, refined resort – much in the same vein as Biarritz and San Sebastián – though away from the beaches, the modern city is rather unattractive. Some people find Santander a clean and restful base – indeed it's a popular centre for summer Spanish language courses – while others (especially younger Spaniards) will tell you it's dull and snobbish. On a brief visit, the balance is probably tipped in its favour by its variety of excellent beaches and the sheer style of its setting, despite the lack of sights in the town. The narrow Bahía de Santander is dramatic, with the city and port on one side in clear view of open countryside and high mountains on the other – a great first view of Spain if you're arriving on the ferry from Plymouth.

In the summer, the city holds an **international university**, augmented by a **music and cultural festival** throughout August. You'll need to book accommodation well ahead if you plan to stay at these times.

Information and orientation

The **centre** of Santander is a compact grid of streets, set between the city's two ports, the **Puerto Grande** (where the ferries arrive) and the **Puerto Chico** (which serves pleasure boats). The main square is **Plaza de Velarde**, where you'll find the **Turismo** for the Cantabrian region (daily 9am–1pm & 4–7pm). Nearby, on Paseo Pereda, is the informative municipal **Turismo** (summer daily 9am–2pm & 4–9pm; winter Mon–Fri 9.30am–1.30pm & 4–7pm, Sat 10am–1pm; ☎942 310708). Around the waterfront to the east, **La Magdalena**, a wooded headland, shelters **Playa Magdalena**, on its near side, and, beyond, the two-kilometre-long sands of **El Sardinero**, with its beachside suburb.

The **RENFE** and **FEVE** train stations are side by side on the Plaza Estaciones, just back from the waterside, under an escarpment which hides the main roads. A largely subterranean **bus station** faces them directly across the square. The **Aeropuerto de Santander** (☎942 202100) is 4km out of town at Parayas on the Bilbao road – an inexpensive taxi ride.

City buses #1, #3, #4, #7, and #E shuttle daily between the centre and El Sardinero.

Accommodation

July and August aside, Santander usually has enough **accommodation** to go round. There is a choice of locations between the **centre** or **El Sardinero**, though many of the *pensiones* and *hostales* at the latter don't open until July.

In the centre

Pensión Los Caracoles, Marina 1 (☎942 212697). Centrally located and good-value *pensión*. ③.

Hostal Residencia La Corza, c/Hernán Cortés 25 (☎942 212950). Clean, friendly and very central. ③.

Pensión Gómez, c/Vargas 57A (☎942 376622). Small, friendly base not far from the station, offering rooms with or without bath. ④.

Hostal La Mexicana, Juan de Herrera 3 (☎942 222350). Well-located and friendly *hostal*, offering clean rooms with bath. ④.

Pensión La Porticada, c/Méndez Núñez 6 (☎942 227817). Spotless, friendly and right next to the bus and train stations. ④.

Hotel Real, Paseo Pérez Galdós 28 (☎942 272550, fax 942 274573). Elegant, upmarket hotel, near the Playa de la Magdalena, with good sea views. ⑧.

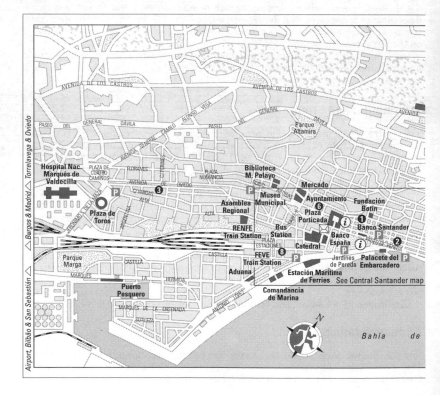

El Sardinero

Hostal Residencia Luisito, Avda. de los Castros 11 (☎942 271971). Pleasant *hostal* just back from the beach. Open July–Sept only. ③.

Hotel Hoyuela, Avda. de los Hoteles 7 (☎942 282628, fax 942 280040). Traditional, upmarket and expensive hotel, perfect for the beach. ⑧.

Hostal Paris, Avda. de los Hoteles 6 (☎942 272350, fax 942 271744). Upmarket *hostal* well placed just off Plaza Italia with some stylish balconied rooms. Open all year. ⑤–⑥.

Hotel Sardinero, Plaza de Italia 1 (☎942 271100, fax 942 278943). Smart beachside hotel with style and character. ⑦.

Hostal La Torre, Avda. de los Castros 53 (☎942 275071). A good ten-minute walk from the beach, but one of the few Sardinero *hostales* that stays open all year round. ④.

Camping

Camping Bellavista (☎942 391530; open all year) and **Camping Cabo Mayor** (☎942 391542; June 15–Sept 30). Two well-equipped sites, flanking the Sardinero beach, 2km north of the Casino, on a bluff known as Cabo Mayor. Take bus #9 to Cueto from opposite the Ayuntamiento.

The Town

Santander was severely damaged by fire in 1941, when it lost most of its former pretensions, along with its medieval buildings. What was left of the old city was reconstructed

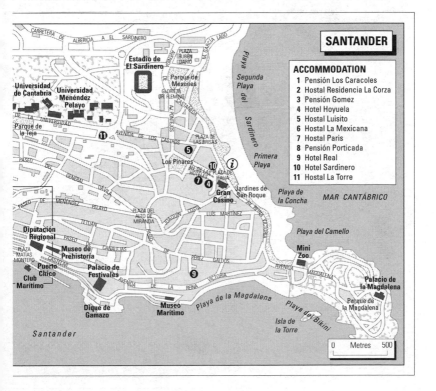

SANTANDER

ACCOMMODATION
1 Pensión Los Caracoles
2 Hostal Residencia La Corza
3 Pensión Gomez
4 Hotel Hoyuela
5 Hostal Luisito
6 Hostal La Mexicana
7 Hostal Paris
8 Pensión Porticada
9 Hotel Real
10 Hotel Sardinero
11 Hostal La Torre

on the grid around the cathedral, but, while the avenues are pleasant enough, and some of the shops have their appeal, there is little of interest beyond a couple of museums. The appeal of the town lies firmly in its beaches.

Santander's **Catedral** (Mon–Fri 10am–1pm & 4–7.30pm, weekends & fiestas 10am–1pm & 4.30–8.45pm) is a dull building, almost uniquely bereft of treasures, save for its Gothic-Romanesque **crypt** (separate entrance; daily 8am–1pm & 4–8pm). The **Museo Municipal** (June–Sept Mon–Fri 10.30am–1pm & 5.30–8pm, Sat 10.30am–1pm; Oct–May Mon–Fri 10am–1pm & 5–8pm, Sat 10am–1pm; free), nearby, is not much more promising, overburdened with nineteenth-century portraits. If you have time to fill, better to look in at the **Museo Marítimo** (summer Tues–Sat 11am–1pm & 4–7pm, Sun 11am–2pm; winter Tues–Sat 10am–1pm & 4–6pm, Sun 11am–2pm; free), near the port, whose exhibits range from pickled two-headed sardines to entire whale skeletons, plus a real-life aquarium.

Kids might also enjoy the little seaside **zoo** (9am–10pm; free), on the Peninsula de la Magdalena, with its lions and polar bears. This is housed in the gardens of the old **Palacio Real**, built at the end of the last century by Alfonso XIII, to whose residence Santander owed its initial fashionable success.

If you're planning to visit the caves at Puente Viesgo (see p.447), you might look in at the **Museo Provincial de Prehistoria**, c/Juan de la Costa 1 (Tues–Sat 10am–1pm & 4–7pm, Sun 11am–2pm; free). This is well arranged, displaying and reconstructing finds from the province's numerous prehistorically inhabited caves.

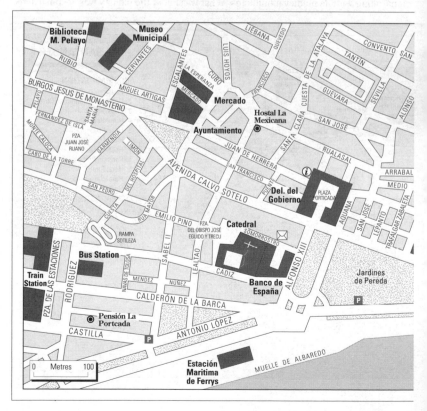

The beaches

The first of Santander's beaches, **Playa de la Magdalena**, begins on the near side of the headland. A beautiful yellow strand, sheltered by cliffs and flanked by a summer **windsurfing** school, it is deservedly popular. So, too, is **El Sardinero** itself: a further 2km of beach, beyond the headland, with its own flag announcing it one of the eight cleanest beaches in the world. If you find both beaches too crowded, there are long stretches of dunes and excellent views across the bay at **Somo** (which has windsurfers to rent and a summer **campsite**) and **Pedreña**; to get to them, jump on the taxi-ferry which leaves every fifteen minutes from the central Puerto Chico (350ptas return).

Eating, drinking and nightlife

There is a huge choice of **cafés**, **bars** and **restaurants** in the centre, around the **Puerto Pesquero** (the fishing port), and at **El Sardinero**, while if you want to picnic or cook for yourself, there's a good food market behind the *Ayuntamiento*.

Being a university town and a pretty flash resort, Santander also has plenty of **nightlife**, at its liveliest from Thursday to Saturday. **Calle Río de la Pila** is the heart of the scene – a whole street of bars, with people spilling out into the small hours; a slightly older crowd is to be found 300m uphill (and left out of c/Río de la Pila) in **Plaza Cañadio** and out towards the **Puerto Chico**. Bright young Santanderians also leave

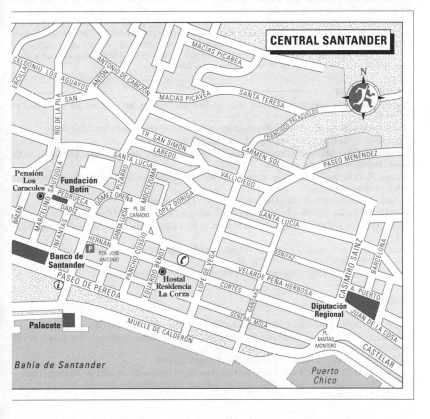

town for **Renedo** on Saturday nights and **Solares** on Sundays, both nearby small towns, connected by RENFE and FEVE trains respectively.

Tapas bars and restaurants

Bodega Bringas and **Bodega Mazon**, c/Hernán Cortés 47 and 57. These *bodegas* serve tasty local food, wine and *sidra*, amidst vast wine vats. *Bringas* is open evenings only and reputed for its *anchoas* and *pimientos*; *Mazon* is good for *chipirones* and *tortilla*.

Bodega del Riojano, c/Río de la Pila, 5. Traditonal *bodega* with stacks of casks and good *tapas*. Popular with thirty-something crowd.

Bar Cantabria, c/Río de la Pila 12. *Tapas* bar serving up wonderful *empanadas* and *pinchos*, with a little dining room at the back.

Bar Cigaleña, c/Daoiz y Velaverde. Atmospheric bar decorated with old bottles.

Bar El Solórzano, c/Peña Herbosa 17. Great neighbourhood bar with traditional music, *vermut* on tap, and the whole array of Cantabrian seafood.

La Cañía, c/Joaquín Costa 45, Sardinero. Unpretentious restaurant with excellent seafood and a good *menú*.

Cervecería Lisboa, Plaza Italia, Sardinero. Ever-popular restaurant in front of the casino, with a summer *terraza*, and a good choice of *platos combinados*.

La Conveniente, c/Gómez Oreña 19. Nineteenth-century *bodega* with live music, fried fish and other delicious, but pricey snacks.

La Gaviota, **Las Peñucas** and **Vivero**, c/Marqués de la Ensanada, Puerto Pesquero. Three popular and unpretentious seafood restaurants down by the fishing port. You can spend anything, from a few hundred pesetas for a *menú del dia* or plate of sardines, to a small fortune for fishy exotica.

Restaurante Cañadio and **Bar Cañadio**, Plaza Cañadio (☎942 314149). The *Cañadio* is the city's best restaurant, known far and wide for the sublime fish and regional cooking of its chef, Paco Quirós. If you can't spare 4000ptas and up, don't despair – just join the foodies snacking on a fabulous spread of canapés at the much more modest bar. Closed Sun.

Bars and clubs

Agua de Valencia, c/Perines. Popular place to start the evening, with a killer house cocktail at 800ptas a jug.

Blues, Plaza Cañadio. Blues and jazz music bar, with an expensive connecting restaurant.

Castelar–5, c/Castelar 5. Pleasant music bar with a summer *terraza*.

Cerveceria Cruz Blanca, c/Hernán Cortés 16. Another popular place to begin the evening, with a huge variety of international beers.

Escena, Plaza Rubén Darío, at the north end of Sardinero. Old-time dance club still frequented for *rumbas* and *sevillanas*.

El Grifo, Plaza Cañadio. Youthful bar with a choice of fifteen beers.

Maria's and **Indian's**, both on c/Casmiro Saiuz and open for dancing till dawn.

Pacha, c/General Mola 45. Biggest club in town with two floors (dance/latino) and a quieter bar area.

Rocambole, c/de Hernán Cortés 36. Late-night club attracting a young and trendy crowd from 3am; Motown music and expensive drinks.

Web-Site Story, c/Menéndez Pelayo 5. Funky café-pub with Internet access.

Listings

American Express c/o Viajes Altair, c/Calderón de la Barca 11 (☎942 311700).

Car rental Atesa, c/Marcelino Sanz de Santuola, 2 (☎942 222926); Budget, c/San Luis 8 (☎942 238485); Europcar, c/Rodríguez 9 (☎942 214706).

Consulates British Consulate, Paseo Pereda 27 (☎942 224100).

Ferry tickets Tickets for the Brittany Ferries crossing to Plymouth are sold by Modesto Piñeiro at their office at the ferry dock (☎942 214500). Advance reservations are essential in summer, both for cars and passengers.

Hospital Santander's General Hospital is on Avda. Valdecilla (☎942 335577).
Post office The city's main *Correos* is on Avda Alfonso XIII (Mon–Fri 8am–9pm, Sat 9am–2pm).
Telephones The *Telefónica* is at c/de Hernán Cortés 37; in Sardinero there is a *locutorio* beside the casino.
Trekking Federación Cantabria de Montaña, c/Rubio 2 (☎942 373378), provides information and organizes treks in the Picos de Europa.

East along the coast to Castro Urdiales

The coast east of Santander has been heavily developed, with villas and apartment complexes swamping most of the coves. **Noja**, until recently remarkable only for the strange-shaped rocks along its shore, now has seven campsites, while **Laredo** has become one of the north's major holiday resorts. Things improve as you move east, however, to the beach at **Islares**, or to the old town of **Castro Urdiales**.

Laredo and around

LAREDO pulls in a young, Spanish crowd with its summer profusion of pubs, clubs and discos. In parts, though, it's still an attractive place. For a spell in the last century it was Cantabria's provincial capital, and the village-like core of the old town, the **Puebla Vieja**, rambles back from the harbour, with occasional traces of its former walls and gates, climbing up towards a splendid thirteenth-century parish church, **Santa María de la Ascunción** (daily 10am–1pm & 4–7.30pm). Beyond the church you can climb quickly out of town to the cliffs and to grand open countryside, while below lies the best **beach** this side of San Sebastián, a gently shelving crescent of sand, 5km long and well protected from the wind.

Practicalities

All **buses** stop outside the small ticket office adjoining the *Cafetería Orio*, on c/Jose Antonio 10. There isn't much in the way of budget **accommodation** in Laredo. The cheapest place you'll find is *Habitaciones Cantabria* on c/Menéndez Pelayo 7 (☎942 605073; ③); otherwise, *Hotel Montecristo*, c/Calvo Sotelo 2 (☎942/605700; ⑤), and *Hotel El Cortijo*, c/González Gallego 3 (☎942 605600; ⑥; open July–Sept), are both handy for the beach, and *Pensón Esmeralda*, c/Fuente Fresnedo 4 (☎942 605219; ④), is close to the nightlife in town. If money is no object, *Hotel El Risco*, Blvd. Arenosa (☎942 605030, fax 942 605055; ⑦), perched on top of a hill with great views out to sea, is a fine bet; alternatively, head for the elegant *Hotel El Ancla*, c/Gonzáles Gallego 10 (☎942 605500, fax 942 611602; ⑦). There are two **campsites** (June–Sept) close to the beach: *Laredo* (☎942 605035) and *Costa Esmeralda* (☎942 603250).

You'll find bars and *cafeterías* on the beach, while in town Rúa de San Marcial has a good selection of **restaurants**. If you want the town's best, it is the *Mesón del Marinero* (☎942 606008) on c/Zamanillo, a creative, though pricey, shellfish specialist; *El Pescador*, on the seafront, is another good option – their catch of the day is always excellent.

Santona

Just across the bay from the west end of Playa de Laredo lies the resort of **SANTONA**. Ferries run across the water to the small beach, or it's thirty minutes from Laredo by hourly bus. Santona is, remarkably, still a working fishing port; you can watch the catch being unloaded and sample it in the tiny bars grouped around the streets leading up from the port, particularly c/General Salinas. There are grand views across the bay to Laredo from the hilltop castle of **Fuente de San Martín**.

Islares

If you're looking for somewhere more peaceful, the village of **ISLARES**, east from Laredo, beyond the headland, is pleasant and as yet little developed, although it is somewhat overshadowed by the coast road roaring past on the hillside above. There's a beach a short walk past the houses, well sheltered by cliffs, a very modest-sized **campsite** (☎942 863152) and just a handful of *hostales* and *pensiones*. *El Langostero* (☎942 862212; ④), just off the main highway and virtually on the beach is clean with nice views and its own restaurant. Closer to the main road, *Pensión Playamonte* (☎942 862696; ③) is a cheaper, but noisier option. *Hostal Areníllas*, (☎942 860900), Islares's original *hostal*, is still a good bet, though it can be very crowded in July and August.

Castro Urdiales

CASTRO URDIALES is a congenial and good-looking resort, less developed than Laredo, though rooms and space on the beaches are still at a premium in high season and at weekends, when everyone descends from Santander and Bilbao. At such times, the main "town beach", **Playa del Brazomar**, a small strip of sand, hemmed in by a cement esplanade used for sunbathing, and bordered by two large hotels, can be very busy. However, the crowds can be left behind by heading further east to more secluded coves, or west to **Playa Ostende**, with its rough, dark sand. From this latter beach, there's an unusual walk back to town along the cliffs, most of which seem to be hollow – you can hear the sea pounding beneath you. Along the route is a tiny bay where the sea comes in under a spectacular overhang.

As well as its tourist functions, the town retains a considerable fishing fleet, gathered around a beautiful natural harbour. Above this looms a massively buttressed Gothic church, **Santa María**, and a lighthouse, built within the shell of a Knights Templar castle. These are linked to the remains of an old hermitage by a dramatically reconstructed **Roman bridge**, under which the sea roars at high tide. The old quarter, the **Mediavilla**, is relatively unspoiled, with arcaded streets and tall, glass-balconied houses. The **Turismo** (summer Mon–Sat 10am–2pm & 5–8pm, winter hours vary) is found on the main jetty, alongside an open-air fish grill serving fresh sardines and tuna in summer.

Accommodation

The town's best budget **accommodation** is scattered throughout the narrow, pedestrianized streets of the old town. For modern and expensive hotels, head towards the beach and the newer part of town. There is a **campsite** in Barrio Campijo near the beach; *Castro*, Camino Allende Laguna (☎942 870300, fax 942 870306).

Hostal Alberto, Avda. República Argentina, 2 (☎942 862757). Comfortable rooms with or without bath. ③.

Pensíon Catamaran, c/Victorina Gainza (☎942 870066). Modern rooms in noisy position opposite the bus station; try for a room that doesn't face the road, as noise starts early. ④.

Hostal El Cordobes, c/Ardigales 15 (☎942 860089). Attractive, old-fashioned *hostal* with good choice of clean, spacious rooms with or without bath. ④–⑤.

Hostal La Mar, c/La Mar 27 (☎942 870524, fax 942 862828). Smart, refurbished *hostal* in the old town, well connected for bars and restaurants. ⑤.

Hotel Miramar, Avda. de la Playa 1 (☎942 860200, fax 942 870942). Modern hotel close to the beach with good panoramic views of the port. ⑥.

Hotel Las Rocas, Avda. de la Playa (☎942 860400, fax 942 861382). Expensive hotel close to the beach in a residential area. ⑦.

Hotel La Sota, c/La Correría 1 (☎942 871188, fax 942 871284). Just behind the *Ayuntamiento*, this hotel makes a good base for exploring the harbour and castle. ⑤.

Hostal El Viejo Baracaldo, c/Ardigales 4 (☎942 872404). Small, inexpensive *hostal* in the old town, offering rooms with or without bath. ③.

Eating and drinking

Castro Urdiales has no shortage of places to **eat**. If you're on a budget, head for the less expensive places around the *Ayuntamiento* at the castle end of the harbour, where there are some excellent fish/seafood bars around the square and on c/El Carrerias. The lively c/Ardigales is packed with *mesones* and *tabernas*, and is also the centre of the **nightlife** scene, with two discos, *Mambo* and *Safari*, and more fashionable disco-pubs and late night bars continuing on down the same street into c/La Rua.

Bar Agora, c/Ardigales. Very reasonable Basque-run establishment with outdoor tables.

Bar Rincón, c/La Mar. Typical Basque setting with sawdust floors and men in berets; expect good *pinchos* and great atmosphere.

El Marichu, c/Ardigales. An excellent selection of *pinchos* – the mushrooms in oil and garlic are especially good.

Mesón Marinero, c/Correría 23 (☎942 860005). Castro's renowned fish restaurant, in a huge building opposite the *Ayuntamiento*, can be pricey, but if you sit at the bar and choose from the wide selection of *raciones* you can eat very well and relatively cheaply.

Restaurante Baracaldo, c/Matilde de la Torre 11 (☎942 862012). Highly recommended restaurant with good seafood *menú*.

Moving on

The **bus stop**, shared by the companies Alsa-Turytrans and Encartaciones, is next to the *Cafetería Catamaran*, c/Victorina Gainza, four blocks from the front, where you'll also find a small ticket office. There are through services to towns between Irún and Gijón from here, while buses to **Bilbao** leave from the side road just next to the *Cafe-Bar Ronda* on the main N634.

Santillana and the prehistoric caves

If you see a postcard in Santander depicting gorgeous sandstone churches and mansions, it is **Santillana del Mar**, an outrageously picturesque village, 26km west of Santander, which has been prettified beyond belief for tourism. It remains beautiful, by the skin of its teeth, but in season it's a major tourist spot, and can be a nightmare to visit. The crowds would be even worse were the caves at **Altamira**, on the edge of the village, still open to visitors, for these contain Spain's most dramatic prehistoric drawings. Two other caves, less well known, but still preserving Altamira-epoch paintings, are accessible, and located at **Punte Viesgo**, 24km south of Santander on the N623 Burgos road.

Santillana

Jean-Paul Sartre (in *Nausea*) describes **SANTILLANA DEL MAR** as *"le plus joli village d'Espagne"* – an unlikely source, but none the less accurate for that. The village (once you reach it past the bus and car parks) is all ochre-coloured stone houses, mansions, and farms. Despite the name – *del Mar* – Santillana actually stands some three or four kilometres back from the sea and, while its fine houses flaunt their aristocratic origins, the village itself has long been completely rural. Its single pedestrianized street, with one loop and two plazas, saunters back from the access road towards a wonderful Romanesque collegiate church and then stops abruptly amidst farms and fields.

Santillana's fifteenth- to eighteenth-century **mansions**, vying with each other in the extravagance of their coats of arms, are as splendid as they are anomalous. One of the best is the **Casa de los Hombrones**, named after two moustachioed figures, flanking its grandly sculpted escutcheon. Another, the **Casa de Bustamentes**, established its credentials with a simple motto: "The Bustamentes marry their daughters to kings."

Although many of the mansions still belong to the original families, their noble owners rarely visited in this century or the last; indeed, up until the 1970s, villagers kept their cattle in some of the less-used mansions.

Just down from the Casa de los Hombrones is the **Museo de la Inquisición** (daily 10am–10pm; 600ptas), an excellent, if disturbing museum housing torture instruments, with historical notes in English. The village church, **La Colegiata** (daily 9am–1pm & 4–7pm) is dedicated to Santa Juliana, an early martyr whose tomb it contains; she is legendarily supposed to have captured the devil and is depicted with him in tow in various scenes around the building. Its most outstanding feature, however, is the twelfth-century **Romanesque cloister** (300ptas), one of the best preserved in the whole country, with its squat, paired columns and lively capitals carved with animals and hunting scenes.

Also worth a look is the seventeenth-century **Convento de Regina Coeli** (same hours and tickets as the Colegiata cloisters), on the main road just across from the entrance to the village. This houses an exceptional museum of painted wooden figures and other religious art: pieces brilliantly restored by the nuns and displayed with great imagination to show the stylistic development of certain images, particularly of San Roque, a healing saint always depicted with his companion, a dog who licks the wound in his thigh. There is a resident ghost, too, on the first floor.

Practicalities

There are several direct **buses** daily to Santillana from Santander run by Autobuses Cantabria from the main station (first bus July–Aug 7.30am); you are dropped outside the convent with the town straight ahead across the main road. Buses on to Comillas and San Vicente de la Barquera leave from the same place at 8am, 11.10am, 1.40pm and 6.45pm although the service is reduced at weekends. You can also get to the village by regular buses from Torrelavega, which is on the FEVE railway line. You'll find a **Turismo** (Mon–Sat 9.30am–1.30pm & 4–8pm, Sun 10am–1.30pm & 4–7.30pm; ☎942 818251) in the Plaza de Ramón Pelayo – the square opposite the *parador*.

Santillana is an attractive **overnight stop** if you are travelling out of season, and it has rooms to suit most budgets, although these can be booked out in summer. Least expensive are the *casas de huéspedes* (guest houses), just off Plaza de Ramón Pelayo, and the *habitaciones* advertised by many of the bars in high season. *Casa Angelica*, c/Los Hornos 3 (☎942 818238; ③), is a decent, low-budget option, while *Casa Fernando*, (☎942 818018; ②), a little out towards Altamira, and more modern, is also good value. For more comfort, head for *Casa La Solana*, at the top of c/Los Hornos (☎942 818106; ⑤), a beautifully restored country house, perched above the hustle and bustle of the village. The grand old *Hotel Altamira*, Cantón 1 (☎942 818025, fax 942 840136; ⑥), is a good choice if you can afford to splash out, but Santillana's choicest accommodation is the *Parador Gil Blas*, housed in one of the town's finest mansions in the heart of the village (☎942 818000, fax 942 818391; ⑦). There is also a **campsite**, *Camping Santillana* (☎942 818250), 1km out along the Altamira road, which is large and soulless, but has a pool and good facilities.

Restaurants in Santillana are abundant but largely unexceptional. *Mesón de Los Villa*, c/Santo Domingo 5, is pleasant, serving meals outside in a little orchard in summer; *La Viga* has a lovely courtyard restaurant and is also one of the few bars staying open late.

The prehistoric caves

The prehistoric **Caves of Altamira** lie 2km west of Santillana. Dating from around 12,000 BC, they consist of an extraordinary series of caverns, covered in paintings of bulls, bison, boars and other animals etched in red and black with a few confident and impressionistic strokes. When discovered in the 1870s they were in near-perfect condition, with striking and vigorous colours, but in the 1950s and 1960s the state of the murals seriously deteriorated, and they are now **closed** to prevent the build-up of surplus moisture (from breathing) in the cavern's atmosphere. Visitors with a serious academic interest can apply (at least one year in advance) to the Museo Altamira (39330 Santillana de Mar, Cantabria; ☎942 818005), but most tourists will have to make do with a couple of lesser grottoes at the site and the small **museum** (Tues–Sun 9.30am–2.30pm).

A more rewarding cave visit is to hand at **PUENTE VIESGO**, 27km out of Santander on the N623 road to Burgos (SA Continental bus from the main station in Santander). Around the village, set amid magnificent rolling green countryside, are four separate **prehistoric caves**, two of which, **Castillo** and **Las Monedas**, are open to tours (May–Oct Wed–Sun 9.30am–1pm & 3–7.30pm; Nov–April Wed–Sun 9.30am–2pm & 3–5pm; Castillo 225ptas; Monedas 125ptas). These are magnificent, with stalactites and stalagmites in the weirdest shapes, in addition to the remarkable paintings – clear precursors to the later developments at Altamira.

If you want to stay, the village has a luxurious four-star hotel on c/Manuel Pérez Mazo, the *Gran Hotel Balneario* (☎942 598061, fax 942 598261; ⑦), as well as a few budget places: *Hostal La Terraza* (☎942 598102; ③; open June–Aug), and *La Troncal* (☎942 598117; ②), set back a bit from the bus stop. A couple of other places open up for the summer season.

South of Santander: Reinosa and the Ebro

South of Santander lies a large area of quiet Cantabrian countryside, dominated by the extensive **Pantano del Ebro**. The N611 to Palencia brushes the shores of this reservoir and passes through **Reinosa**, a transport hub for the region and a pleasant old town if you want to break your journey. To the west, the high Sierra de Peña Labra has **skiing** opportunities, with a small resort at **Alto Campoo**, 24km from Reinosa. To the east, the **Río Ebro** trails a lovely valley, past a succession of unspoilt villages, Romanesque architecture and cave churches.

Reinosa

REINOSA is a pretty, characteristically Cantabrian town with lots of glass-fronted balconies and *casonas* – seventeenth-century townhouses – displaying the coat of arms of their original owners. The **Turismo** occupies one of these, midway down the main street, Avda. de la Puente, near the distinctive Baroque church of **San Sebastián**.

Two inexpensive **places to stay** are *Pensión San Cristóbal*, c/Julióbriga 1 (☎942 751486; ③), and the nearby *Hostal Residencia Sema* (☎942 750047; ③), at c/Julióbriga 14, which is near the station and has a good restaurant. For a bit more comfort, head for *Hotel Rubén*, c/Abrego 12 (☎942 754914; ④), or, across the bridge, *Hostal Tajahierro*, c/Pellila 8 (☎942 753524; ④). For a small town, Reinosa has a surprising range of traditional **bodegas** and **mesones**. On the main street, *Pepe de los Vinos* is a good place for a glass of wine and a snack, while the restaurants *Avenida* and *Los Ángeles* offer more substantial meals; the latter is open late. While you're here, don't miss the tasty *pantortillas* (sweet pastries), which can be bought from most bakeries.

If you are pressing on deeper into the countryside, two local **buses** daily go south to Polientes, leaving at 9.50am and 6pm, and another two travel east around the reservoir to **Cabanas** and **Arija**, departing at 10.45am and 6pm.

Skiing: Alto Campoo

Twenty-four kilometres to the west of Reinosa lies the ski resort of **ALTO CAMPOO**, served by regular buses in season. It's a tiny resort, with a ski school, 17km of pistes and a three-star **hotel**, *La Curza Blanca* (☎942 779250, fax 942 779250; ⑤).

Along the Ebro: Polientes

East of Reinosa, a network of tiny, winding roads trail the Ebro river, passing through villages of no more than a few houses. The largest of these is **POLIENTES**, a lovely place, totally rural, though with a couple of places to stay: a **pensión** (③), by the bus stop, and a *hostal* just down the road, *Sampatiel* (☎942 776053, fax 942 776136; ③) – in season, be sure to ring before you arrive, as the *hostal* has only six rooms. The café/bar in the main square serves good **food** (it's run by the mayor) and the *hostal* does a good value *menú*, too.

East of Polientes, you'll need your own transport to continue along the valley and on to the Santander–Burgos road. Twelve kilometres from Polientes is the village of **San Martín de Elines**, with a twelfth-century Romanesque **Colegiata** containing medieval sarcophagi, and a church set into rock. At nearby **Cadalso**, you'll find another smaller rock church.

The coast: Comillas to Gijón

The coastline **west of Santillana** and **into Asturias** is dotted with a succession of enticing resorts. Most of them are popular in a small-scale, local sort of way, and have been spared the highrise hotel and apartment treatment; amid the villages and river valleys there are coves which see only the occasional weekender from Santander. The coast is tracked, most of the way, by the **FEVE rail line**, and the countryside, with a massed backdrop of hills rolling into the Picos de Europa, is invariably magnificent.

Comillas

COMILLAS, the first resort west of Santillana del Mar, is a curious rural town with pretty cobbled streets and squares, and an inland feel, despite it being only just set back from the sea. It has a pair of superb beaches: the **Playa de Comillas**, the closest, with a little anchorage for pleasure boats and a few beach cafés, and the longer and less developed **Playa de Oyambre**, 2km west out of town towards the cape.

Oddly out of place in the otherwise provincial town is a trio of mansions, including a Gaudí-designed villa, **El Capricho**, a short (and signposted) walk from the centre. This is now a restaurant but its gardens are open to visitors, and it's certainly worth a look even if you're not staying in Comillas, with its playful miniaturizations, futuristic use of colour and whimsical tower.

Next door to El Capricho, is another nineteenth-century *modernista* flourish, the **Palácio de Marqués de Comillas**, designed by Gaudí's associate, Juan Martorell. It is closed to visitors but can be seen from the garden of El Capricho. The Marqués, an industrialist friend of Alfonso XII, also commissioned the huge **Seminario Pontífico**, on the hillside above, from Domenech y Montaner, another of the Barcelona *modernista* group.

Practicalities

Comillas is actually skirted by the FEVE line, though it has good **bus** connections with San Vicente de la Barquera to the west and Santillana and Santander to the east. Buses arrive at and leave from the Paseo de Solatorre, the main road at the bottom of the town overlooked by El Capricho. **Accommodation** is better priced than surrounding resorts, but in season you will need to book ahead, or arrange a private room through the **Turismo** (Mon–Sat 10am–1pm & 5–9pm, Sun & fiestas 11am–1pm & 5–8pm; ☎942 720768), centrally located at c/La Aldea 2.

You'll find good budget rooms at *Pensión Bolingas*, c/Guzo de la Torre (☎942 720841; ③), which is clean, friendly and just off the main square, and at *Pensión Casa Aldea*, c/La Aldea (☎942 720300; ③), which has a superb restaurant downstairs. *Pensión Villa*, Cuesta Carlos Diaz de la Campa 21 (☎942 720217; ③), has two buildings, one modern and comfortable above the main square and another more characterful house just off the Plaza de Ibañez. More upmarket choices include *Hotel Josein*, c/Santa Lucía 27 (☎942 720225; ⑤), with excellent coastal views, *Hostal Esmeralda*, c/Antonio López 7 (☎942 720097, fax 942 722258; ⑥), a beautifully furnished place at the top of the town, and the *Fuente Real*, c/Sobrellano 19 (☎942 720155; ④), right beside El Capricho. There are **campsites** at both beaches, with the *Comillas* (☎942 720074; July–Aug) significantly better than *El Rodero* at Oyambre (June–Oct).

Comillas has good **food** to offer. At the bottom end of the scale, *Picoteo*, just down from the *Esmeralda*, does generous meals at rock-bottom prices, while for good, cheap *tapas*, try the *Bar Filipinas* at the crossroads next to the bus stop. The main square is packed with outdoor tables and café-restaurants, most specializing in *barcas* (huge platters) of seafood. If you want to really splash out, credit cards can pay for Gaudí decor and Spanish nouvelle cuisine at *El Capricho* (☎942 720365).

Given its size, Comillas has a surprisingly lively nightlife, with a clutch of **disco-pubs** on c/Pérez de la Riva, above the sloping Plaza Generalísimo, including the excellent *Don Porfirio*, with gardens and a small dancefloor.

San Vicente de la Barquera

The approach to **SAN VICENTE DE LA BARQUERA** is dramatic, with the town, marooned on both sides by the sea, entered across a long causeway, while inland, hills rise towards the Picos de Europa. Looking down from the hill which looms over the centre of town are an impressive Renaissance **ducal palace** and Romanesque-Gothic church, **Santa María de los Ángeles**, the latter with restored, gilded altarpieces and a famous reclining statue of the Inquisitor Corro. The town itself, a thriving fishing port with a string of locally famed but expensive seafood restaurants, has had its old core encroached upon, and is split by the main coast road with its thundering lorries, but it still makes a good overnight stop. The seafront is more dedicated to work than tourism, but there's a good sweep of sand flanked by a small forest fifteen minutes across the causeway.

Practicalities

The local **Turismo** (daily 9.30am–2pm & 4.30–9pm; ☎942 710797) is on the main road, at Avda. Generalísimo 20. **Accommodation** is easy enough to find. The central *Pensión La Paz*, c/Mercado 2 (☎942 710180; ③), is clean and spacious; *Pensión Liebana* (☎942 710211; ③) is at the top of the stairs leading from the back of the main square. More expensive options include *Hotel Boga Boga*, Plaza José Antonio 9 (☎942 710135, fax 942 710151; ⑤), and on the main road, *Hotel Luzón*, Avda. Miramar (☎942 710050, fax 942 710050; ⑤). There is a pleasant **campsite** (☎942 711461) in the woods beside the beach. For **food**, *Bar Colón*, on the right as you head westwards out of town, does good *raciones*, while a good place to try seafood or *sorropoton*, the local speciality tuna stew, is *El Pescador*, further down the same road and just beyond the Turismo.

Using public transport, San Vicente is best left or approached by **bus** (Alsa serves the coast and Palomera or Cantabrica cover inland routes), as the FEVE station is about 4km south at **La Alcebasa**. Buses leave from the stop near the causeway; details of timetables and tickets are available at Fotos Noly, opposite the bus stop.

Into Asturias: Unquera to Ribadesella

Asturias begins 9km west of San Vicente, at **UNQUERA**. Here buses for the Picos turn south towards **Potes**, and here too the FEVE railway comes into its own after the inland stretch from Santander. Unquera itself is fairly dire, its only bright spots being the restaurants *Ríomar* and *Granja*; the latter also serves as the local bus stop and is just across from the FEVE station. You'll find a small **Turismo** in Plaza de Don Alfonso Gonzáles Egüen (Mon–Fri 10am–1.30pm & 4–7.30pm, Sat 10am–12.30pm).

If you're on the train or bus, you'll do much better staying on until **Llanes**, Asturias's easternmost resort – and one of its most attractive.

Llanes

LLANES is a delightful seaside town crammed between the foothills of the Picos and a particularly dramatic stretch of the coast. To the east and west stretch sheer cliffs, little-known beaches and a series of beautiful coves, yours for the walking. The three town beaches are small, but pleasant, while the excellent **Playa Ballota** is only 3km to the east, with its own supply of spring water down on the sand (and a nudist stretch). A long *rambla*, the **Paseo de San Pedro**, runs along the top of the dramatic cliffs above the western town beach, the Playa del Sablón.

In the centre, a tidal stream lined with cafés and seafood restaurants runs down into a small harbour. On the west bank, tall medieval walls shelter a number of older buildings in various stages of restoration or decay, including a medieval tower, the semi-ruined Renaissance palaces of the **Duques de Estrada** and the **Casa del Cercau** (both closed for restoration), and the **Basilica**, built in the plain Gothic style imported from southern France, although the sculpted east door is preserved from an earlier Romanesque building. Around town you'll also see numerous larger houses built by *indianos*, nineteenth-century emigrants returning from the Americas eager to show off their newly acquired wealth.

Llanes makes an excellent base (or rest-cure) for the Picos, with good transport connections via nearby Unquera. Those with their own transport could also visit a curious bronze age monolith 10km east along the coast road at **Peña Tu**.

PRACTICALITIES

There's a useful **Turismo** in the Torre Medieval (daily 10am–2pm & 4–6pm; ☎98 540 01 64), which can help with accommodation. Llanes's cheapest **rooms** are at the *Bar Colón* (☎98 540 08 83; ②), overlooking the river, while other good budget options include the old-fashioned and spacious *Hospedaje El Río*, Avda. de San Pedro 3 (☎98 540 11 91; ③), and *Don Paco* (☎98 540 01 50; ③), which is run along *parador* lines in a converted seventeenth-century convent. *Pensión Iberia*, c/Las Barqueras (☎98 540 08 91; ③), is a good budget fallback near the bus station. For more comfort, *Salton's Hotel* (☎98 540 19 87, fax 98 540 19 88; ⑤) overlooks the Playa del Sablón, while *Pensión La Guía*, Plaza Parres Sobrino 1 (☎98 540 25 77; ④), is smart and central. A wide selection of *casas rurales* in this area includes *La Torre* (☎98 541 72 07; ⑥), 5km away in Andrín. There is a large **campsite**, *Las Baracenas* (☎98 540 28 87; June–Sept), five minutes from town, although the smaller *Entre Playas* (☎98 540 08 88; June–Oct), on the headland between the two town beaches to the east, has the better situation.

For good **seafood** – and Asturian *sidra* – head for *La Marina*, a restaurant shaped like a boat at the end of the harbour, where you can sit outside and tuck into swordfish steaks and sardines, or for one of the simple open-air **café-restaurants** by the river just inland from the bridge, which serve up above-average seafood *raciones*. At the *El Campanu*, and others here, you'll pay between 600ptas and 2000ptas a dish; drink the *sidra* or the local white wine. *El Bodegón*, hidden in the tree-shaded Plaza de Siete Puertas, is good for *sidra* and Asturian *raciones*; for more formal meals and *menús*, try the restaurant behind *Bar Colón*, or one of the fairly similar places round the corner on c/Manuel Cué.

Villahormes and Nueva

Following the coast (and FEVE line), the next tempting stop to the west of Llanes is **VILLAHORMES**. This is an unprepossessing-looking place: no more than a train station, a handful of houses, a café-bar and a very shabby-looking *hostal*. Follow the rusty signpost to **Playa de la Huelga**, however, and, after 1500m of drivable track, you reach one of the best swimming coves imaginable, with a rock arch in the bay and an enclosed sea pool for kids to splash around in safety. It is flanked by a pleasant bar-restaurant. The **Playa de Gulpiyuri**, 1km to the north east, is an unusual beach set back from the shore line but fed by an underground channel of sea water.

A thirty-minute walk west of Villahormes, or five minutes more on the train, will get you to another hamlet, **NUEVA**, tucked into a fold of the hills, 3km inland from another gorgeous little cove. If you decide to **stay**, head for the *Ereba* (☎98 541 01 39; ④), a pleasant *casa rural*; there is also a **campsite**, *Calores* (☎98 541 03 36).

Ribadesella

RIBADESELLA, 18km west of Llanes, is an unaffected old port, split into two by the Sella River, and bridged by a long causeway. On the east side is the old town, with the bus and FEVE stations and dozens of great little bars and *comedores* on the streets parallel to the **fishing harbour**. Freshly caught fish is still unloaded after midnight at the *lonja* and, although the catch is increasingly small, it's fun to hang out until then in the bars. On the west side, the new town contains the more upmarket accommodation, the excellent town **beach**, and the **Cueva Tito Bustillo** (April to mid-Sept Wed–Sun 9.30am–12.30pm & 3–5pm; 300ptas), an Altamira-style cave more impressive for its stalactites than its paintings, though it has a museum of prehistoric finds from the area. Only 375 visitors are allowed into the caves each day, so in summer you'll need to arrive first thing in the morning to get in.

Practicalities

Arriving by train, you'll emerge at the **FEVE station**, at the top end of town, on Carretera Santander; the **bus station** is on the main road at the entrance to the old town. There is a **Turismo** (summer only daily 10am–10pm; ☎98 586 00 38) in an original *hórreo* (granary), just by the causeway in the new town.

Accommodation is a bit pricier than usual, although the impecunious may be able to find *camas*, and there's a **youth hostel** on c/Ricardo Cangas (☎98 586 13 80; ③) in an old house on the east side of the estuary, although it is often booked out by groups. Among the *hostales*, try the *Sueve*, La Bolera 13 (☎98 586 03 69; ④), and the *Covadonga* (☎98 586 02 22; ④), at the end of Gran Vía at c/Manuel Caso de la Villa 7. Ribadesella's top hotel, the old-fashioned *Gran Hotel del Sella* (☎98 586 01 50, fax 98 585 74 40; ⑦), fronts the beach and the newly built promenade. Also recommended is the *Hostal El Pilar* (☎98 586 04 46; ④), 2km south of the beach at Puente del Pilar, which has a restaurant serving traditional Asturian food. There is a *casa rural, La Llosona* (☎98 585 78 87; ④), 1km south of the new town in Granda-Ardines, with great views of the surrounding area, and there are also two **campsites**: *Los Sauces*, near the beach on Carretera San Pedro la Playa (☎98 586 13 12; June–Sept), and *Ribadesella* (☎98 585 82 93; April–Sept), just south of Puente del Pilar, at Sebreño.

For **meals**, the *Rompoelas* is a classic if slightly pricey *marisquería* in the old town, with piles of seafood lining its long wooden counter; alternatively, there's *Casa Basilio* on c/Manuel Caso de la Villa, which serves great *tapas*.

Lastres and Villaviciosa

Beyond Ribadesella the railway turns inland, as do most tourists, heading for Cangas de Onis and the western flanks of the Picos de Europa. The route into the mountains – the N634 and M625 – is a superb one, following the valley and gorge of the Río Sella. The coast itself deteriorates the closer you get to Gijón, Asturias's main industrial port, though there are a few last highlights, including the small resort of **La Isla** and the town of **Colunga**, both of which are noted for their seafood and cider, and the fishing villages of **Lastres** and **Villaviciosa**. Colunga has a useful **Turismo**, located in an original *hórreo* (traditional wooden grain store) in the town park (Tues–Sat 10am–2pm & 5–8pm, Sun 10am–3pm).

Lastres
LASTRES, a couple of kilometres north of Colunga off the Santander–Gijón highway, is a tiny fishing village built on a steep cliffside with a new harbour and a couple of good beaches on its outskirts. It has escaped much tourist attention so far and if you've just come from a few strenuous days' trekking in the Picos, this would be as good a spot as any to recuperate. **Buses** run from Ribadesella every two hours in summer.

Two neighbouring **restaurants** on the road down to the port, *Sidrería El Escanu* and *Bar Bitacora*, serve good seafood, with terrace views. There is only a handful of **hotels**, but *Casa Eutimio* (☎98 585 00 12; ⑤), near the port in Plaza San Antonio, and with its own seafood restaurant, is a good bet, and the nearby *Miramar*, Bajada al Puerto (☎98 585 01 20; ④) has some rooms with great sea views. The *Hostal Mary Paz* (☎98 585 02 61; ④), at the top of town, is a last resort, while if you've money to spare, there's also a luxury hotel, the *Palacio de los Vallados*, Pedro Villarta (☎98 585 04 44, fax 98 585 05 17; ⑥). There are two *casas rurales: Pipo* in the tiny village of Sales, 4km away (☎98 585 65 90; ④), and *Costa Verde* (☎98 585 63 73) in Pernús, the next village along. The excellent beach, Playa la Griega, 2km to the east, has a **campsite**, *Costa Verde* (☎98 585 63 73).

Villaviciosa and around
VILLAVICIOSA, 30km from Gijón, is set in beautiful Asturian countryside, on the shores of the Río Villaviciosa, and with green rolling hills behind. There's a market on Wednesday and an atmospheric old town where you'll find the thirteenth-century church of Santa María and the best restaurants. Visits to the cider factory, El Gaitero, reveal how Spain's most famous cider is manufactured (Mon–Fri 9am–12.30pm & 3–5.30pm, Sat 9am–12.30pm; free). There's a good **beach** for swimming nearby – Playa Rodiles, visible from the main road.

You'll find good-value **rooms** at the friendly *Pensión Sol*, c/Sol 27 (☎98 589 11 30; ③), and at the modern *Hostal El Congreso*, c/Generalísimo 25 (☎98 599 61 56; ④), with its own restaurant. More upmarket places include *Hotel Carlos I*, Plaza Carlos I (☎98 589 01 21, fax 98 589 00 51; ⑤), and the new *Hotel Casa España*, opposite (☎98 589 20 30, fax 98 589 26 82; ⑥). The **Turismo** (summer only Tues–Sat 10am–2pm & 5–8pm; ☎98 589 17 59) is in Parque Vallina.

Nine kilometres southwest of Villaviciosa, tucked away in the beautiful Puelles valley, lies the Cistercian monastery of **Valdedios** (daily: May–Oct 11am–1pm & 4.30–6.30pm; Nov–April 11am–1pm). Abandoned for many years, the buildings are now being restored and a small community of monks returned in 1992. It's worth a look around the grounds and impressive thirteenth-century monastery church, where you can attend one of the five offices sung daily, but the main sight is the wonderful **Iglesia de San Salvador**, built in the ninth century in the unique style known as Asturian, or pre-Romanesque; look out for the columns borrowed from a nearby Roman ruin and the beautiful geometric motifs in the stone windows. There are eight buses daily between Oviedo and Villaviciosa which stop at San Pedro de Ambas. From here, it's a one-kilometre walk downhill to the monastery, where it's sometimes possible to stay in the new **hospedería** (☎98 589 23 24).

Gijón and Avilés

Gijón and **Avilés** are Asturias's major industrial cities: daunting places, with their smoking factory chimneys, and best passed by if you are looking for a seaside holiday. However, each of the cities has something going for it: Gijón in its big-city "feel", nightlife and summer **film festival** (late June/early July); Avilés in its well-preserved old centre. In addition, both cities know how to party, especially during **Carnaval** (see box, p.455) and during **Semana Santa**, when Avilés hosts some of the country's most spectacular parades.

Gijón

GIJÓN, the largest city in Asturias, was completely rebuilt after its destruction in the Civil War. It was the scene of one of the most intensive bombardments of the war, when, in August 1936, miners armed with sticks of dynamite stormed the barracks of the Nationalist-declared army. The beleaguered colonel asked ships from his own side, anchored offshore, to bomb his men rather than let them be captured.

Arrival, orientation and information

The city **centre** is a fairly small area, just south of the old town and headland. Its three main squares, separated by a couple of blocks each, are, from south to north, Plaza del Humedal, Plaza del Carmen and Plaza del Marqués (flanked by the palace described below). Two of the **train stations** (FEVE and RENFE local services) and the **bus station** (a wonderful piece of Art Deco) are just off Plaza del Humedal. Long-distance RENFE services use a third train station on Avenida. de Juan Carlos I. The **Turismo** (☎98 534 60 46) is off the Plaza del Marqués.

Accommodation

Finding a **place to stay** is rarely a problem, with a broad range of places to cater for all budgets. Most of the accommodation is concentrated at the lower end of town, beyond the Playa San Lorenzo; good streets to head for include c/San Bernardo, c/Santa Lucía and c/Pedro Duro.

Hotel Asturias, Plaza Mayor 11 (☎98 535 98 15, fax 98 534 68 72). Friendly hotel on the atmospheric main square between the beach and port. ⑤.

Hostal Gijón, c/Tineo 5 (☎98 535 98 15). Cheap, basic bed for the night, not far from the bus station. ③.

Pensión Gonzalez, c/San Bernardo 30 (☎98 535 58 63). Highly recommended *pensión* with large, airy rooms in a well-furnished old mansion-house. **Pensión Argentina** (☎98 534 44 81) upstairs is also a good bet. Both ③.

Hostal Manjón, Plaza del Marqués 1 (☎98 535 23 78). Nicely located *hostal*; ask for a room overlooking the harbour. ⑤.

Hostal Narcea, c/San Juan de la Cruz 5 (☎98 539 32 87). One of the cheapest places to stay, slightly outside the centre. ③.

Parador Molino Viejo, Parque de Isabel la Católica (☎98 537 05 11, fax 98 537 02 33). Luxury accommodation, set in an attractive park at the east end of the beach. ⑦.

The City

Once past the industrial outskirts, Gijón has quite a breezy, open feel about it, with a grid of streets backing onto the sands of the **Playa de San Lorenzo**, a surprisingly unpolluted beach. In winter, you'll find the occasional hardy surfer out here, while in the summer the whole city seems to descend for the afternoons and weekends. The old part of town, **Cimadevilla**, occupies a headland northwest of the beach. Its chief monument is the eighteenth-century **Palacio de Revillagigedo**, built in a splendid mix of neo-Baroque and neo-Renaissance styles; it houses occasional exhibitions. Facing the palace, in the centre of the square, is a statue of Pelayo, the seventh-century king who began the Reconquest.

West again from Cimadevilla is the pretty **Puerto Deportivo**, the harbour area which is a focus for the city's evening and weekend *paseo*. This apart, there's little more in the way of sights – though Gijón offers serious shopping, if that's of interest – other than a few scattered museums. The most interesting of these is the bagpipe museum, the **Museo de Gaita**, Paseo Dr Fleming (summer Tues–Sat 11am–1.30pm & 5–9pm, Sun 11am–2pm; winter Tues–Sat 10am–1pm & 5–8pm; free), an amazing array of instruments from all over the Celtic world and beyond. Gijón is home to one of the Spain's premier **football** clubs, Sporting Gijón; they play at a stadium just east of the beach.

Eating and drinking

The streets around the seafront and immediately behind contain a mass of little **café-restaurants**, all reasonably priced and most with a *menú*. **Fish** is a speciality here.

La Botica, c/San Bernardo 2. Typical *sidrería* (cider house) on the Plaza Mayor.

Casa Justo, Avda. del Hermanos Felgueroso 50. Superb *sidrería* with a good restaurant behind it.

Casa Zabala, c/Viz Compgrade (☎98 53417 31). Good, traditional Asturian specialities, including *fabada*, a rich sausage and bean stew. Closed Sun & Feb.

La Marina, c/Trinidad 9. Fine *sidra* and *tapas*.

La Pondala, Avda. Dionisio Cifuentes, Somio (☎98 536 11 60). Upmarket restaurant, famous for its seafood and rice. Closed Thurs & Nov.

El Retiro, c/Begoña 26, La Ruta. Asturian cooking with an excellent value 1000ptas *menú*.

Torremar, c/Ezcurdía 120. Wonderful place for *sidra* and *parillas* (grills).

Nightlife

Gijón's **nightlife** scene centres around the area known as **La Ruta**, a grid enclosed by c/Santa Lucía, c/Buen Suceso and c/Santa Rosa, five minutes' walk from the harbour. There are scores of **disco-bars**, including the noisy and trendy *La Gruta de la Ruta*, and *El Viñedo*, which has a quieter, more old-fashioned feel. Later on, the **club and disco** scene is focused around **El Náutico** near the beach: *Amnesia*, c/Jacobo Olaneta, plays up-to-date dance; *Guananamera*, farther down the road, plays salsa and latino.

Avilés

AVILÉS, 20km from Gijón and inland, has most of the Asturian steel industry, and the unwelcome honour of being one of Europe's most polluted cities. As you approach, from any direction, it's not hard to see why: line upon line of grim factories ring the

CARNIVAL IN ASTURIAS

Carnaval, the *mardi gras* week of drinking, dancing and excess, takes place over late February and early March. In Spain, the celebrations are reckoned to be at their wildest in Tenerife, Cadiz and Asturias – and, in particular, **Avilés**.

Events begin in **Avilés** on the **Saturday** before Ash Wednesday, when virtually the entire city dons fancy dress and takes to the streets. Many costumes are bizarre works of art ranging from toothbrushes to mattresses and packets of sweets. By nightfall, anyone without a costume is likely to be drenched in some form of liquid, as gangs of nuns, Red Indians and pirates roam the streets. Calle Galiana is central to the action, and the local fire brigade traditionally hoses down the street, and any passing revellers, with foam. A parade of floats also makes its way down this street, amid the frenzy.

The festivities, which include live music, fireworks and fancy-dress competitions, last till dawn. It's virtually impossible to find accommodation but the celebrations continue throughout Asturias during the following week, so after a full night of revelling you can just head on to the next venue. The first buses leave town at 6.45am. Sunday is, in fact, a rest day before *Carnaval* continues in **Gijón** on the **Monday** night. Much the same ensues and fancy dress is again essential; La Ruta is the place to be for the start of the night, with people and events shifting between Plaza Mayor and the harbour area till dawn. On **Tuesday** night, the scene shifts to **Oviedo**: the crowds are smaller here and events are less frantic, but a fair part of the city again dons costume. There's a parade along Calle Uria, a midnight fireworks display in the Plaza Escandelera, and live bands in the Plaza Mayor.

Finally, on the Friday after Ash Wednesday, **Mieres**, a mining town, just south-east of Oviedo, plays host to *Carnaval*. Events take place in an area known as Calle del Vicio, which locals claim contains the highest concentration of bars in the province.

town, putting off even the hardiest of travellers. But press on to the tiny, arcaded old centre of town and you can forget they exist.

Arrival, information and accommodation

Avilés is a good transport junction and you may well find yourself here changing buses or trains. The **FEVE**, **RENFE** and **bus stations** are all sited in the same terminus on Avenida. Telares just down from Parque Muelle and the old town. The **airport**, Aeropuerto de Asturias, lies 13km away in Ranon, just off the N632 (☎ 98 512 75 00); Aviaco flies direct to Stansted in the UK three times a week. The Viaca travel agency, at Plaza de la Merced, 5 (☎98 556 18 44), can be useful for last-minute flights and train tickets.

The city's **Turismo** (Mon–Fri 9.30am–2pm; ☎98 554 43 25), is off Plaza de España, at c/Ruíz Gómez 21, and the main post office is on c/Doctor Graiño, in front of Parque Las Meanas.

Staying in Avilés is surprisingly tricky as **accommodation** is scarce, and the few reasonably priced *hostales* are invariably full of business-people. At the bottom end of the scale, head for *Pensión Serafín*, c/Santa Apolonia 60 (☎98 557 27 28; ③), just off Plaza de España, or *Pensión Villablanca*, c/El Acero 5 (☎98 554 51 70; ③). More expensive, is the *Hotel Luzana*, c/Fruta 9 (☎98 556 58 40, fax 98 556 49 12; ⑥), also just off Plaza de España and with a good restaurant, while the upmarket *Hotel San Félix*, Avda. Los Telanes 48 (☎98 556 51 46, fax 98 552 17 79; ⑤), is slightly out of town.

The City

The city's pleasant **old district**, strewn with fourteenth- and fifteenth-century churches and palaces, is about five minutes' walk from the bus and train terminus and not difficult to find. Most of the shops, bars and places to stay are here, too, and there's also a large and very pretty park, the Parque de Ferrera. Among several churches worth a closer look are the Romanesque church, **San Nicolás de Bari** on c/San Francisco, and the thirteenth-century **Santo Tomás**. La Iglesia de los Padres Franciscanos contains the tomb of the erstwhile governor of Florida, Don Pedro Menéndez de Avilés. There are also three superb palaces, notably the Baroque **Camposagrado**, built in 1663, in Plaza Camposagrado, the seventeenth-century **Palacio de Marqués de Ferrera** in Plaza de España and the **Palacio de Llano Ponte**, which is now a cinema.

Eating, drinking and nightlife
The streets around Plaza de España are full of promising **bars and restaurants**, in particular c/del Ferrería, c/Rivero and c/Galiana. *Casa Lin*, Avda. Telares 3, is a fine *sidrería* with excellent seafood, while *Casa Tataguyo*, Plaza Carbayedo 6, a beautiful 1870s *mesón* (the oldest in town), serves Asturian specialities; both are moderately priced. Late night, there are **music bars** on c/Galiana, an all-nighter at c/González Albarca 6, off Plaza de la Merced, and *Paradis*, a popular disco on c/Cátamara.

The Picos de Europa

The **PICOS DE EUROPA**, although not the highest mountains in Spain, are the favourite of many walkers, trekkers and climbers. The range is a miniature masterpiece: a mere forty kilometres across in either direction, shoehorned in between three great **river gorges**, and straddling the provinces of Asturias, León and Cantabria. The whole area has recently been created a National Park, although there remain problems in co-ordinating the activities of the three provinces. Asturians see the mountains as a symbol of their national identity, and celebrate a cave-church at **Covadonga**, in the west of the range, as the birthplace of Christian Spain.

Walks in the Picos de Europa are amazingly diverse, considering the size of the region, and they include trails for all levels of activity – from a casual morning's walk to two- and three-day treks. The most spectacular and popular walks are along the twelve-kilometre **Cares Gorge** – a route you can take in whole or part – and around the high peaks reached from a cable car (*teleférico*) at **Fuente Dé**. But there are dozens of other paths and trails, both along the river valleys and woodlands, and up in the mountains. Take care if you go off the marked trails: the slowly undulating plateaus you appreciate from a distance can too easily turn out to be a series of chasms and gorges that entail backtracking, winding around and scrambling up to points you never wished to be at.

In addition to the walking, the Picos **wildlife** is a major attraction. In the Cares Gorge you're likely to see griffon vultures, kestrels, black redstarts, rock thrushes, and, most exciting of all for the initiated, wallcreepers. Wild and domestic goats abound, with some unbelievably inaccessible high mountain pastures. Wolves are easy to imagine in the grey boulders of the passes, but bears, despite local gossip, and their picturesque appearances on the tourist board maps, are not a likely sight. An inbred population of about sixty specimens of *Ursus ibericus* remains in the eastern mountains, most of them tagged with radio transmitters.

The Picos have long been on the map for trekkers and, over the last few years, as road access has opened up the gorges and peaks, have been brought increasingly into the mainstream of tourism. The most popular areas can get very crowded in July and August, as can the narrow roads, and the *teleférico* at Fuente Dé. If you have the choice, and are content with lower-level walks, spring is best, when the valleys are gorgeous and the peaks still snowcapped, although the changing colours of the beech forests in autumn give some competition.

You can **approach** – and leave – the Picos along half a dozen roads: from León, to the south; Santander and the coast, to the northeast; Oviedo and Cangas de Onis, to the northwest.

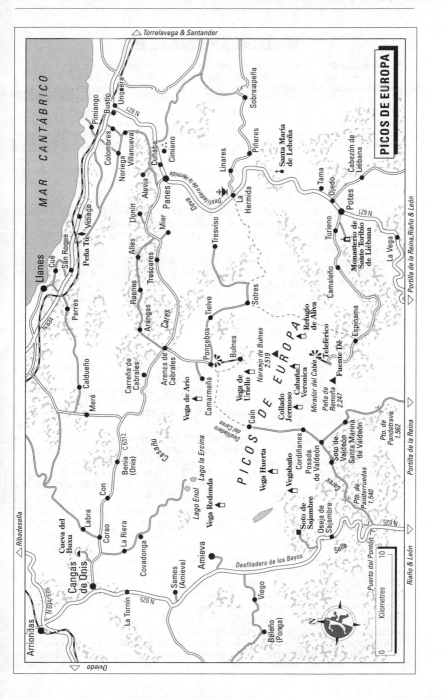

PICOS PRACTICALITIES

Accommodation *Albergues, pensiones* and *hostales* have proliferated in recent years in the more popular villages, but whenever you can it is worth phoning ahead to book a room – especially in summer or at weekends, when whole towns can be booked solid. Up in the mountains there are a number of alpine *refugios*, which range from organized hostels to free, unstaffed huts where you'll need to bring your own food and sleeping bag. Camping beside the *refugios* is accepted, and there are about half a dozen campsites, too, scattered around the villages. Camping outside these sites is officially prohibited anywhere below 1600m, and subject to on-the-spot fines, but unofficially you won't be disturbed once away from populated areas.

Banks are located on the periphery of the region: at Potes, Arenas de Cabrales, Riaño and Cangas de Onis.

Bikes Mountain bikes can be rented at various outlets in Potes.

Buses There are bus services along the main roads but they're limited to one or two a day and very sketchy out of season. You can complement these, however, with bike rental, and hitching – which is easy enough with fellow tourists, and can often be arranged at campsites.

Climate There are good days even in the depths of winter for walking below the snowline, though high altitudes dictate a spring–summer walking season, from late June to September, for mountain treks. At all times of year, be warned that clouds can build up very fast and Asturian rain is cold and heavy; alternatively, or in tandem, sudden mists can blot out visibility. Accordingly, rain gear and a compass are virtually mandatory. In summer lower-level cloud often obscures the tops, while higher up it is bright and clear. Reliable **water sources** are sporadic along the trails and you'll need to carry a bottle.

Equipment Walking in summer, or on low-level routes, you don't necessarily need any experience or special equipment, at least on the routes described in this guide; all of these treks are practicable as long as you're reasonably fit. If you wander off the marked routes or attempt any actual climbing, proper equipment and experience are essential – otherwise you may quickly find yourself in trouble. What with the abundance of sharp, loose stones, and stiff gradients, **walking boots** are a distinct plus, and **sunglasses** are useful to combat the glare.

Maps Best are the Adrados editions, in two 1:25,000 sheets, one covering the western, El Cornión massif, the other covering the central and eastern massifs. Adrados also publish good walking and climbing guides with routes graded by difficulty. Less directed at walkers, and hence not quite as useful, is the official Topografico Nacional de España series which covers the area in four 1:25,000 sheets. All these maps are available in Cangas de Onis, Potes, Sotres, Bulnes or Arenas de Cabrales.

Mountain federations You can get further information on trekking and climbing in the Picos from these organizations: Federacíon Asturiana de Montaña, c/Melquiades Álvarez 16, Oviedo (☎98 521 10 99; Mon–Fri 6.30–7.30pm) and Federacíon Cantabria, c/Rubio 2, Santander (☎942 373378).

National Park offices There are three offices, one in each province, providing information on routes, activities and wildlife within the park, although you may find each one short of information on the other two regions: Casa Dago, Cangas de Onis, Asturias (☎98 584 91 54); San Pelayo, Cantabria (☎942 733201); Posada de Valdeón, Castilla y León (☎987 740549). The National Park service also runs a number of free guided walks in summer.

Potholing federations For details on potholing in the area, contact Apt. de Correos 540, Oviedo (☎98 521 17 90; Fri 7–9pm), Apt. de Correos 51, Santander or at c/Alfonso X el Sabio 1, Burgos (☎947 222427). Permits are needed from the National Park offices.

From the coast to Potes

The N621 heads inland from the coast at **UNQUERA**, right on the Cantabria–Asturias border, between San Vicente de la Barquera and Llanes. From there, it follows the twisting course of the Río Deva, past **PANES**, where the C6312 forks west, along the upper reaches of the Río Cares to Arenas de Cabrales (see p.464) and Cangas de Onís. There are buses along this latter route (currently 7.45am and 5pm) from **Bustio**, just west of Unquera; you can also pick them up in Panes, around half an hour later, from the *Bar de la Cortina* across the bridge. There is also a very good **information office** (☎989 574656) in Panes, opposite the Caja de Asturias, where you can set up walks and horse riding.

Panes to Potes: the Deva Gorge

Continuing from Panes towards Potes, you enter the eerily impressive gorge of the Río Deva, the **Desfiladero de La Hermida**, whose sheer sides are so high that they deny the village of **LA HERMIDA** any sunlight from November to April. There are one or two **places to stay** here if you want to break your journey; the *Hostal Marisa* (☎ & fax 942 731030; ④), on the road out towards Potes, is clean and modern, and there's a *posada rural*, *Campo* (☎ & fax 942 744135; ⑤ with bath). The popular **bar-restaurant** *Pagnin*, beneath *Hostal Marisa*, serves up fine traditional cooking. From nearby **Urdón**, a rough road leads west to Sotres (see p.462); it's a pleasant walk, with mountains looming up around you.

Around 10km beyond La Hermida, the village of **LEBEÑA** lies just east of the main road. It is worth a detour to see the church of **Santa María**, built in the early tenth century by "Arabized" Christian craftsmen and considered the supreme example of Mozarabic architecture. It makes an interesting visit with its thoroughly Islamic geometric motifs and repetition of abstract forms, and is set in beautiful countryside – the Hermida gorge having by now opened out into sheltered vineyards and orchards.

Potes and around

POTES is the main base on the east side of the Picos, still not all that high above sea level at 500m but beautifully situated in the shadow of tall white peaks. It is a small town and market centre (there's an open-air **flea market** on Monday mornings), with winding alleys and plenty of small shops, and, although devoted largely to tourism, it retains some identity beyond it. Look out for the Torre del Infanto, which dates back to the thirteenth century and is now the site of the *Ayuntamiento*.

This is a useful town to change money in, with the last banks before the mountains, and, if you haven't already done so, to buy **trekking maps**. The latter are available from a number of shops, including Fotos Bustamante, in the main square, Plaza Jesús del Monasterio. You can rent **mountain bikes**, and arrange paragliding and canyoning at Picos Aventura next to the bridge.

Six kilometres south of Potes is the church of **Santa María Piasca**. This is pure Romanesque in style, beautifully proportioned, and with some terrific exterior sculpture. Like Santo Toribio de Liébana (see below) it was once a Cluniac monastery, and is flanked by the ruins of monastic and conventual buildings.

Practicalities

You'll find a useful **Turismo** (June–Sept Mon–Sat 9am–2pm & 4–7pm; ☎942 730820), under the clock tower just behind the *Ayuntamiento*, in Plaza Jesús del Monasterio.

Potes has a good range of **accommodation**. If you want to be in town, *Casa Cayo*, c/Cántabra 6 (☎942 730150, fax 942 730119; ④), is very pleasant, with a lively bar and decent restaurant downstairs; at the end of the same road, *Casa Cuba* (☎942 730064; ②) is much more basic. For a bit more comfort, head for the modern *Picos de Europa*, San Roque 6 (☎942 732061, fax 942 732060; ⑤), the first hotel on the left coming into town from Panes, or the *Rubio* (☎942 730015, fax 942 730405; ⑤) next door, which has its own garage.

If you're unsure just how to tackle the Picos and don't speak much Spanish, the English-owned *Casa Gustavo Guesthouse,* (☎942 732010; ③) is ideal, although 3km away in Aliezo. **Skiing** and **canoeing trips** for residents (and allcomers) are on offer here, and the guesthouse has an office in the UK (☎01629/813346), which takes bookings. Also good for activities is *Albergue El Portalón*, 6km south of Potes at Vega de Liébana (☎942 736048; ①). This is a hostel, with dormitory rooms, and an *"Escuela del aire libre"* (Outdoor Activity Centre) offering **paragliding**, mountain biking, climbing and trekking.

In summer there are three Palomera (☎942 880611) **buses** daily from Potes to Fuente Dé (8.15am, 1pm and 8pm; returning at 9am, 5pm and 8.45pm). Services also run to Unquera and on to Santander three times a day (7am, 9.45am and 5.45pm).

Potes to Espinama and Fuente Dé

The road from **Potes** to **Espinama** and **Fuente Dé** runs below a grand sierra of peaks – the Macizo Oriental – and past a handful of villages, built on the slopes. In summer, and at weekends, there is near constant traffic towards the *teleférico* at Fuente Dé, which has spoilt the villages on the road. However, all have attractive walking, with woodland and streams, and from Espinama you can cut across the range to Sotres.

Turieno and Liébana

TURIENO, 3km west of Potes along the road to Espinama, is a quiet village, in sight of some tall peaks and well placed for acclimatizing to the mountains, with lots of short walks along narrow mule tracks to villages where the locals don't see many tourists and may well open up the bar just for you. The walk to the hamlets of **Lon** and **Brez** is especially worthwhile, through a profusion of wild flowers and butterflies. Turieno has a good rural hotel, the *Casa de Labranza Javier* (☎942 732122; ④), 2km out of town in an idyllic setting, and an attractive **campsite**, *La Isla* (☎942 730896; open April–Oct), situated behind an orchard, with **pony-trekking** on offer and a swimming pool. If it's full, the *San Pelayo* campsite in Baró (☎942 733087; April–Oct), a little farther up the road towards Espinama, is just as good.

Close by Turieno, but off the main road from Potes, is the eighth-century **Monasterio de Santo Toribio de Liébana** (daily 10am–2pm & 4–8pm; free), one of the earliest and most influential of medieval Spain. Although much-reconstructed, it preserves fine Romanesque and Gothic details, the largest claimed piece of the True Cross, and some extraordinary Mozarabic paintings (now replaced by reproductions) of the Visions of the Apocalypse.

Cosgaya

COSGAYA, midway between Potes and Espinama, can be an attractive base. If you feel like a little luxury before or after trekking, the Alpine-looking *Hotel del Oso* (☎942 733018, fax 942 733036; ⑤) is the place, set in neat paddocks beside a tidy stream, and with a swimming pool in summer. The *Posada de la Casona* (☎942 733077; ④), a seventeenth-century farmhouse, hidden away in the woods off the side of the road, is equally relaxing. Inexpensive rooms are provided by the *Mesón de Cosgaya* (☎942 733047; ④), which also does excellent meals.

Espinama

Twenty kilometres from Potes, **ESPINAMA** is really into the mountains. Like Cosgaya, its position and one-time isolation is marred by the road running through, but there are plenty of walks in the nearby woods and meadows for those seeking rural tranquillity.

You'll find comfortable accommodation at any of the four **hostales**: the excellent *Hospedaje Sobrevilla* (☎942 736669; ④) off the main road, the *Remoña* (☎ & fax 942 736605; ④), the *Puente Deva* (☎942 736658; ④) and the *Nevandi* (☎942 736608; ④). All of these serve **meals**, with the *Vicente Campo* (*Puente Deva*'s restaurant) having the edge, if only for its feel of a wayfarers' inn, and a crackling fire in winter. The village also has a grocery store which provides for picnics and trekking snacks.

Fuente Dé and the *teleférico*

The road comes to a halt 4km past Espinama, in a steep-sided cul-de-sac of rock. This is the source of the Río Deva; debate as to whether its name should be Fuente de Deva or Fuente de Eva has left it called simply **FUENTE DÉ**. Here you can stay at the modern **parador**, *Río Deva*, next to the cable car (☎942 736651, fax 942 736654; ⑥; April–Oct only), or the attractive *Hotel Rebeco* (☎ & fax 942 756600; ⑤), nearby. There's also a **campsite**, *El Redondo* (☎942 736699), with a basic dormitory (①) and the *teleférico* (cable car) with a ticket office and café attached.

The **teleférico** lurches alarmingly up 900m of sheer cliff. It's an extremely popular excursion throughout the year, and in summer a wait to ascend of between two and three hours is by no means uncommon, especially in the middle of the day. A system of numbered tickets (1300ptas return, 800ptas one-way) means that you can wait in the shelter of the **café-bar** at the bottom, as long as your Spanish is up to interpreting the garbled announcements of the PA. Remember that you may well have to queue again for an hour or two before coming down, which is not nearly so congenial in the mountain chill.

At the top is an extraordinary mountainscape, in which Spanish day-trippers wander around in bathing suits. However, within a few minutes' walk there is hardly a soul. If you are on for a walk, you can follow a bulldozer track 4km to the **Refugio de Aliva** (☎942 563736; ⑤), which has hotel-like rooms and prices, a restaurant, and its own *fiesta* on July 2. From there, you can wind your way back down to Espinama on another rough track. It is also possible to arrange a lift in a **jeep** from the top of the *teleférico*, either to Aliva or to Sotres (see below).

Espinama to Sotres – and beyond

The **trek from Espinama to Sotres** is a superb route along a dirt track, practicable by jeep, or around five hours on foot. If you are walking, set out north from the *Peña Vieja* bar in Espinama, under an arching balcony, and on to the twisting track behind. This, climbing stiffly, winds past hand-cut hay fields and through groups of barns, until tall cliffs on either side rise to form a natural gateway. Through this you enter a different landscape of rocky summer pasture and small streams. As you near the highest point the track divides at a small barn. Ignore the left-hand path which leads up to the Refugio de Aliva and the top of the cable car, and take the track ahead past a chapel (visible from the junction) up to the ridge forming the pass.

Over the divide the scenery changes again, into a mass of crumbling limestone. In spring or winter, the downhill stretch of track here is slippery and treacherous to all but goats – and perhaps jeeps. The hamlet of **Vegas de Sotres**, at the bottom of the hill, has a seasonal bar selling drinks; from there you need to climb again slightly to reach Sotres, which, when it appears, has a grim, almost fortified feel, clinging to a cliff edge above a stark green valley.

Sotres

SOTRES is an established walkers' base – it is a trail head for some superb treks – and has three fairly basic **places to stay**. The best of these is the *Pensión Casa Cipriano* (☎98 594 50 24; ③), which also has a *comedor* with a 1200-ptas *menú* and a basic *albergue* (①). The better *albergue*, however, is the new *Peña Castil* (☎98 594 50 70; ①), and there is also another *pensión*, *La Perdiz* (④), a little further up the street.

The village **store** does good meals, and sells cured sheep's and cow's milk cheeses, as well as the five-month-fermented *cabrales*, a local speciality similar to Roquefort.

East to Tresviso and Urdón

Until the late 1980s, only a mule path led east from Sotres to **TRESVISO**. This is now a paved road, though still a beautiful route. If you prefer your walking a bit rougher, you can cut down a footpath from this road, 5km out of Sotres, which leads through the **Valle de Sobra** down to **La Hermida**; the final stretch is a spectacular switchback.

In Tresviso, the local bar has clean, modern rooms (☎942 744 444; ③) and a restaurant.

West to Bulnes

Most walkers head west from **Sotres to Bulnes**, heading up to the broad, windy pass of **Pandébano** using the dirt road. At present this is navigable by car, with care, although it is due to be closed to private traffic. At the top are high meadows still used for summer pasture by villagers from Bulnes, who live in simple stone dwellings there during the summer months. An old, steep cobbled path leads down to Bulnes.

BULNES is a delight, a remnant of the Picos before roads brought tourists and better living conditions. However a **funicular railway** from Poncebos is due to open in summer 1999, much to the relief of residents who have been agitating for a road for many years, and to the anger of environmental groups who say the mountain ecosystem will not be able to cope with the predicted thousands of visitors. For now at least, Bulnes remains a sleepy village, in two parts, Castillos and La Villa. All the facilities are in La Villa, including two decent bars with meals and dormitories, the *Bar/Albergue Bulnes* (☎98 584 59 34; ①) and the quieter *Bar Guillermina/Albergue Peña Main* (☎98 584 59 39; ①). Camping here is tolerated, too.

The Naranjo de Bulnes – and across the massif

From the pass at Pandébano and from Bulnes village there are well-used paths up to the **Vega de Urriello**, high pasture at the base of the **Naranjo de Bulnes**, a sugarloaf peak which is one of the "sights" of the Picos. The approach from Pandébano is easier, along a newly regraded track, taking between two and three hours. The direct path up from Bulnes is heavy-going, and can take up to six hours in bad conditions, with a slippery scree surface which can prove very difficult and dangerous when wet. Once up on the plateau you'll find a *refugio* (altitude 953m), and (a rarity in the Picos) a permanent spring, as well as large numbers of campers and rock-climbers, for whom the Naranjo is a popular target.

Seasoned trekkers equipped for an overnight stop can continue across the central massif to the top of the **Fuente Dé** funicular, through a roller-coaster landscape unforgiving of mistakes – go in a group and with proper gear. Alternatively, you can bypass Fuente Dé and instead make a slow lap around the highest peaks. This involves a night's camp at **Vega de Liordes** and a descent down the ravine of **Asotín**, ending at **Cordiñanes** at the top of the Cares Gorge.

The Cares Gorge

The classic walk in the Picos – and deservedly so – is the **Cares Gorge**, which separates the central massif from the western one of Cornión. The most enclosed section

between Caín and Poncebos – a massive cleft more than 1000m deep and some 12km long – bores through some awesome terrain along an amazing footpath hacked out of the cliff face. It's maintained in excellent condition by the water authorities (it was built to service a hydroelectric scheme) and is perfectly safe. With reasonable energy you can walk it in well under a day – or you could, like many Spanish day-trippers, get a taste of it by walking just a section from Caín. Such is the popularity of this route that in August it can seem to be a stream of hikers – unless you're an early riser.

The usual **starting point** is from the southern trail heads, **Posada de Valdeón** and **Caín**, which can be reached from Potes via Portilla de la Reina, from Cangas de Onis via Oseja de Sajambre, or from León via Riaño. There is a single daily bus to Posada de Valdeón from León via **Portilla de la Reina**, an odd little hamlet at the bottom of a lichen-covered chasm of limestone; Portilla itself is on the León–Potes bus line. On foot, you can reach Posada de Valdeón from Fuente Dé in about four hours, over a mix of dirt tracks and footpaths; the occasional Land Rover makes the trip in summer.

Access from the north is, if anything, easier with a Land Rover bus connecting **Poncebos**, the northern trail head, with Arenas de Cabrales – which has a regular bus service to Cangas de Onis, Llanes and Panes. Poncebos can also be reached on foot from Bulnes – see below.

Santa Marina and Posada de Valdeón, Cordiñanes and Caín

The bus from Portilla de la Reina gives out at **SANTA MARINA DE VALDEÓN**, transferring its passengers to a Land Rover for the final 3km ride on the narrow lane leading down to Posada. Santa Marina is a lovely village – still quite unspoilt – with a bar, *La Ardilla,* which rents out **rooms** (☎987 742677; ①), and a **campsite**, *El Cares* (☎987 742676), which offers pony trekking.

POSADA DE VALDEÓN is very much on the tourist trail, though nothing can detract from the views of the huge mountains that hem in the valley to the south and shorten the days. There's a helpful **Turismo** just outside the village (daily 9am–1pm & 4–7pm; ☎987 740549) which can provide information on much of the surrounding area. The most characterful **accommodation** is at the old *Pensión Begoña* (☎987 740516; ③); budget rooms are available at the *hostal* above the *Café-Bar Campo* (☎987 740502; ②), or you can get a dormitory bed at the *Albergue Cuesta-Valdeón* (☎987 740560; ①) on the northern edge of the village. For more comfort, head for *Cumbrés Valdeón* (☎987 742701; ⑤), which also has a smart restaurant. There is also a *casa rural* nearby, *El Friero* (☎987 742658; ③) and a **campsite**, *El Valdeón* (☎987 742605), 3km east of the village, at the hamlet of Soto de Valdeón. For **meals**, *Pensión Begoña* does a good set menu, or try the *Cafetería Campo* for more choice.

The **Río Cares** runs through Posada, and its gorge begins just north of the village. Over this first section – to Caín – it is relatively wide and is trailed by a road. However, it's still pretty delightful, with odd pockets of brilliant green meadows at the base of the cliffs. If you're pushed for time (or energy) there is a **Land Rover** service from Posada to the trail head – 4000ptas per carload – and hitching is easy enough. Most people will prefer to walk the distance, though, and some of the tarmac can be bypassed by taking a dirt track from the lower end of Posada to the **Mirador del Tombo**, just past the village of Cordiñanes. From there to Caín it's around 6km, along a downhill road.

CORDIÑANES makes for a pleasant night's stop – a quieter base than Posada or Caín – and has a couple of small **pensiones**: *El Tombo* (☎987 740526; ④) and *El Rojo* (☎987 740523; ④). In summer, **CAÍN** itself is quite a honeypot, full of cars, groups, day-trippers and trekkers. It has a handful of bars and a supermarket, plying the trade. There is a single **hostal**, *La Ruta* (☎987 742702; ③; March–Oct), right at the opening of the gorge path, although the *Casa Cuevas* (☎987 742720; ②) also offers beds, and the nearby hotel, *La Posada del Montañero* (☎987 742711; ④), is reasonable value, with a large restaurant and terrace. Alternatively, you can **camp** in the meadow nearby for the princely sum of 200ptas (no amenities whatsoever). For food supplies, *Casa Chevas* and *Bar La Senda* are reliable and convenient.

Into the gorge

Just beyond Caín the motorable road ends, the valley briefly opens out, then, following the river downstream, suddenly seems to disappear as a solid mountain wall blocks all but a thin vertical cleft. This is where the **gorge** really begins, the path along its course dramatically tunnelled within the rock in the early stages before emerging on to a broad, well-constructed and well-maintained footpath.

The path owes its existence to a long-established hydroelectric scheme, for which a canal was constructed (often buried inside the mountain) all the way from Caín to Poncebos, and into which the river can be diverted in varying quantities. The path is still used for maintenance and each morning a power-plant worker walks the entire length, checking water volume in the canal and waking up those who have elected to spend a night out in the mountains. If you feel like camping, but with more privacy, there is a side valley leading off to the east about 1km into the gorge.

The first stretch of the path is more of an engineering spectacle than anything else and in midsummer or at weekends is thronged with day-trippers strolling through the dripping tunnels and walkways. Once you get 4km or so from Caín, you're down to more committed walkers, and the mountains, freed of most waterworks paraphernalia, command your total attention. They rise pale and jagged on either side, with griffon vultures and other birds of prey circling the crags. The river drops steeply, some 150m below you at the first bridge but closer to 300m down by the end.

A little over halfway along, the canyon bends to the right and gradually widens along the **descent to Poncebos**. At about 7km and 9km into the gorge some enterprising individuals have cornered the summer market with makeshift refreshments stands, handy as there are no springs. Just before Poncebos another side path leads up to the cliffside village of **CAMARMEÑA**, where *La Fuentina* (☎98 584 66 25; ①) has a bar, *camas* and tremendous perspectives on the Naranjo de Bulnes peak. However, most people stick to the main route and finish at Poncebos.

Poncebos – and a trail to Bulnes

At **PONCEBOS** you'll find **places to stay**, including the *Pensión El Garganta del Cares* (☎98 584 64 63; ③) and, a bit farther down past the bridge (coming from Caín), next to the power plant, the modern *Hostal Poncebos* (☎98 584 64 47; ③), and the large *Mirador de Cabrales* (☎98 584 66 73, fax 98 584 66 85; ⑥), which has a rather ugly self-service restaurant. Any of these might be welcome facilities at the end of a long day, but they're a bit institutional and somewhat gloomy due to blocked sunlight. They are, incidentally, the only buildings at Poncebos – in no sense is the place a village. If daylight permits, you might prefer to make the superb, but steep, hour-and-a-half trek up the gorge of the Tejo stream to **Bulnes** (see p.462) and stay overnight there. The path begins over the photogenic medieval bridge of Jaya, located just to the right (south) at the end of the marked Cares path – there's no need to descend to the hotels. From summer 1999, you should be able to take the **funicular railway** as well (see p.462).

Arenas de Cabrales

The foothill area to the north of the Picos is known as **Cabrales**, as is the delicious and exceptionally strong fermented sheep's cheese made in a dozen-odd villages here. The C6312 runs through the valley; there are buses four times a day (Mon–Sat) between Cangas de Onis and Arenas de Cabrales, two of which run through to Panes and on to

La Mancha windmills

Guggenheim Museum, Bilbao   Arcos de la Frontera, Andalucía

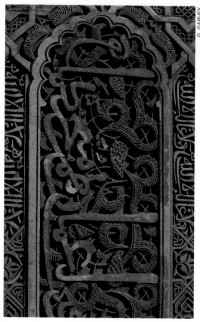

Detail from the Alhambra, Granada

Patio de los Leones, Alhambra, Granada

Detail from the Mesquita, Córdoba

Galician countryside

Flamenco postcards, Andalucía

"Bigheads", Semana Grande fiesta, Bilbao

Rioja vineyard

Sevilla house front

Asturian fishing village

Picos de Europa

the coast. If you're driving, the minor roads to the coast are pleasant, allowing you to bypass traffic on the Cangas road.

ARENAS DE CABRALES (Las Arenas on some maps) is the main village of this region: a friendly place, and an excellent first or last stop in the Picos. There are three good **hotels**, the *Naranjo de Bulnes* (☎98 584 65 19; ⑥), the luxurious *Los Picos de Europa*, (☎98 584 64 91, fax 98 584 65 45; ⑦), and the elegant *Villa de Cabrales* (☎98 584 67 19, fax 98 584 67 33; ⑤). You'll also find a pair of *pensiones* just around the corner, *El Castañeu* (☎98 584 65 73) and *Covadonga* (③), and there's a **campsite**, *Camping Naranjo de Bulnes* (☎98 584 65 78), 1km to the east. If all of the accommodation is full, there are three further *hostales* 3km down the road in Carreña de Cabrales, the best of which is *Hostal Cabrales* (☎98 584 50 06; ④). Back in Arenas, the *Mesón Castañeu* has outstanding à la carte **food** at *menú* prices, while *Bar Palma*, past the BBV bank, is a lively spot for an evening's drinking – they serve *queimadas* (hot Galician punch) if you're in a large enough group.

Arenas also has a helpful **Turismo** booth (Tues–Sun 10am–2pm & 4–8pm; ☎98 584 52 84), to fill you in on mountain or transport details, two **banks** and various stores. On the last Sunday in August the village plays host to the **Asturian Cheese Festival**, an excuse for plenty of dancing and music but, oddly enough, not all that much cheese.

Over to the west: the Sella valley and Riaño

The road running along the western end of the Picos, the N625 between Cangas de Onis and Riaño, is arguably quite as spectacular as the Cares gorge. Mountains rear to all sides and for much of the way the road traces the gorge of the **Río Sella**. The central section of this, the **Desfiladero de los Beyos**, is said to be the narrowest motorable gorge in Europe – a feat of engineering rivalling anything in the Alps and remarkable for the 1930s.

In summer there are daily EASA **buses** in each direction between Cangas and Posada de Valdeón via Oseja de Sajambre.

The Sajambre villages

Coming from Posada de Valdeón, you turn on to the N625 right by the 1290m **Puerto del Pontón**, a pass almost continually fogged in since the reservoir was built at Riaño to the south (see below). Heading north, the road passes through **OSEJA DE SAJAMBRE**, a very pretty village, high on the steep slope of a broad and twisting valley. Comfortable **rooms** and good **meals** are available at *Hostal de Pontón* (☎987 740348; ④).

Six kilometres above Oseja, to the east of the road, is **SOTO DE SAJAMBRE**, an excellent base for walkers, with a lovely **hostal**, the *Peña Santa* (☎987 740395; ③) which also has dormitory beds and a restaurant. This is a possible starting point for a south-to-north traverse of the western Picos massif to the Lakes of Covadonga, as well as for treks in the valley of the Río Dobra. There is a refuge, *Vegabaño*, one hour above the village.

Riaño and south towards León

South from the **Puerto del Pontón**, you descend to the spectacular **Pantano de Riaño** (see box p.466). The creation of this reservoir flooded half a dozen villages and a swathe of farmland – leaving just the odd tree top above water.

The main village of the valley, **RIAÑO**, was relocated just above the reservoir, and has a hotel and a few bars. There are plans to turn it into a winter- and water-sports resort, though little has come of this so far.

RIAÑO: THE MAKING OF A RESERVOIR

Travelling in Asturias, you often see posters with the slogan "Don't let them destroy our Picos". The threat to the mountains is real: the Picos is a small range, and every year the despoliation of previously pristine areas seems to increase. The Asturians are doing what they can, but if you enter the Picos from the south, from León through Riaño, you'll see the worst that can (and has) happened – the loss of a whole valley.

In 1966 the Franco regime claimed right of eminent domain over the entire valley of **Riaño**, prior to turning it into a reservoir. Compensation of sorts was paid at that time, and then plans stalled until the 1980s, when the project was revived by the PSOE government. The inhabitants of Riaño, most of them children of those who had accepted the "settlement" in the 1960s, were forcibly evicted, with no further compensation offered. The newer generation erected a tent village overlooking their destroyed homes, but that too was bulldozed, after demonstrations broken up by riot police. On December 31, 1987, the dam was suddenly sealed, and flooding commenced. The authorities claimed that conditions were optimal – there was a storm in progress – but the reality was that the government had imposed a deadline and wanted no more protests.

The dam, clearly, has a value for the Spanish agricultural economy, irrigating the plains of León and Palencia to the south. But the investment came from outside corporations, and that's where the profits will go. The water from the reservoir will benefit no one locally.

Cangas de Onis, Covadonga and the lakes

The main routes between the Picos and central Asturias meet at **Cangas de Onis**, a busy market town, and a bit of a traffic bottleneck, especially so in summer and at weekends. If you're not intent on a visit to **Covadonga**, with its pilgrim shrine and **mountain lakes** beyond, or on making a canoe trip down the Río Sella, you may prefer to make a detour.

Cangas de Onis

The distant peaks around **CANGAS DE ONIS** provide a magnificent backdrop to its big sight – the so-called **Roman bridge**, festooned with ivy, which you'll see splashed across the front of many Asturian tourist brochures, although it has in fact been re-built many times, including this century. The town's other attraction, less photogenic but perhaps more curious, is the **Capilla de Santa Cruz**, a fifteenth-century rebuilding of an eighth-century chapel founded over a Celtic dolmen stone. This, like the Liébana monastery at Potes, is among the earliest Christian sites in Spain, and Cangas, as an early residence of the fugitive Asturian-Visigothic kings, lays claim to the title of "First Capital of Christian Spain". Today, however, it belies such history: a functional town, muscled-in upon by new developments, though good for a comfortable night and a solid meal after a spell in the mountains, and a better base than Arriondas itself for the popular **canoe descents** of the Río Sella. These morning trips tend to last three hours or so, cost around 3000ptas including transport, and are bookable through various tour operators in town.

Practicalities

Most facilities lie within a few hundred metres of the **bus station** (in front of the *Ayuntamiento*). A **Turismo** kiosk (July–Sept Mon–Fri 10am–10pm, Sat 10am–9pm, Sun 10am–3pm) is on Avenida Covadonga, next to the park. More comprehensive information for trekkers and mountaineers is available from Casa Dago (☎98 584 91 54), a headquarters of the National Park, just up the road from the Turismo.

There's a wide range of **accommodation**, although budget places tend to get booked out in summer. Good choices include the friendly *Pensón Principado*, Avda. Covadonga 6 (☎98 584 83 50; ③), or *Hostal El Sella* (☎98 584 80 11; ③), by the old bridge at Avda. de Castilla 2. More upmarket are the *Hotel Covadonga* in the same street (☎98 584 81 35, fax 98 594 70 54; ⑤), and the *Hotel Puente Romano*, at Puente Romano 8 (☎98 584 93 39, fax 98 594 72 84; ⑥). If you want to camp, there is a **campsite** in Soto de Cangas; *Covadonga* (☎98 594 00 97). Two kilometres down the road to Arriondas there's the new *Parador de Cangas de Onis* (☎98 584 94 02; ⑧) in the sumptuously restored monastery of La Vega, and a youth hostel, *La Posada del Monasterio* (☎98 584 85 53; ①), a useful fallback when everywhere's full in town.

Freshwater fish and *sidra* are the specialities in the **bars and restaurants** here. The *Sidrería/Mesón Puente Romano* by the bridge has a grand outdoor setting under the plane trees, with good-value *menúo*, while *Restaurante Los Arcos*, on Avenida Covadonga, has a less romantic setting but excellent, if slightly pricey, cooking.

Covadonga and the lakes

The **reconquista** is said to have begun at **COVADONGA**, 11km southeast of Cangas in a northerly sierra of the Picos. Here in 718 the Visigothic King Pelayo and a small group of followers repulsed the Moorish armies – at odds, according to Christian chronicles, of 31 to 400,000. In reality the Moors can hardly have been more than an isolated expeditionary force and their sights were already turned to the more lucrative lands beyond the Pyrenees, where in 732 they were defeated at Poitiers by Charles Martel. But the symbolism of the event is at the heart of Asturian, and Spanish, national history, and the defeat probably did allow the Visigoths to regroup, slowly expanding Christian influence over the northern mountains of Spain and Portugal.

Certainly, Covadonga is a serious religious shrine, with signs proclaiming it as a place of prayer, and daily masses in the **cave** (8am–10pm; free), which is the focus of the pilgrimage. This shrine, said to have been used by Pelayo and containing his sarcophagus, is now a chapel, sited impressively on the side of a mountain above a waterfall and plunge pool. Across the road is a grandiose nineteenth-century pink basilica, and, opposite this, a **Museo del Tesoro** (daily 10.30am–2pm & 4–7.30pm; 50ptas) displaying various religious artefacts.

There is one inexpensive **fonda** on the road into town, the *Hospedería del Peregrino* (☎98 584 60 47, fax 98 584 60 51; ④), which has an excellent restaurant, specializing in *fabada asturiana*. There is also a *casa rural*, *Casa Priera* (☎98 584 60 70; ④), with bath, TV and telephone. For more upmarket accommodation, you'll find the *Hotel Pelayo*, right next to the caves (☎98 584 60 61, fax 98 584 60 54; ⑦).

Lakes Enol and Ercina

Beyond Covadonga the road begins to climb sharply, and after 12km you reach the **mountain lakes** of **Enol** and **Ercina**. These are connected by a bus service from June 15 to September 15 (leaving Covadonga at 11am, 12pm, 3.30pm and 5.30pm; the last bus back from the lakes leaves at 6.30pm), but it's not difficult to hitch if you miss out. The **Mirador de la Reina**, a short way before the lakes, gives an inspiring view of the assembled peaks.

The **lakes** themselves are placid, but subject to quirky weather. Even if it's misty at Cangas or Covadonga, you may find that the cloud cover disperses abruptly just before the lakes. There is a basic **refugio** (☎98 584 80 43), with no eating or washing facilities, a **campsite** at the southwest corner of Lake Enol, and a bar-restaurant beside Ercina.

The Cornión Massif

From the higher Lake Ercina a good path leads east-southeast within three hours to the **Vega de Ario**, where there's a newly refurbished **refugio** (☎989 524553), lots of campers on the meadow, and unsurpassed **views** across the Cares Gorge to the highest peaks in the central Picos. Unless you have serious hiking experience for the steep descent to the Cares, this is something of a dead end, since to cross the bulk of the western peaks you'll need to backtrack at least to Lake Ercina to resume progress south.

Most walkers, however, trek south from the lakes to the **Vega Redonda refugio** (☎98 584 85 16). This popular route initially follows a dirt track but later becomes an actual path through a curious landscape of stunted oaks and turf. Vega Redonda, about three hours' walk, overlooks the very last patches of green on the Asturias side of the Cornión massif. From here the path continues west for another hour up to the viewing point, the **Mirador de Ordiales**.

Beyond the Vega Redonda refugio, walks are in a different category of difficulty altogether. Nerve and skill are required to cross the barren land to **Llago Huerta**, the next feasible overnight spot – and like Redonda popular with potholers who disappear down various chasms in the area. From Llago Huerta it's possible to descend to Cordiñanes, Santa Marina de Valdeón or Oseja de Sajambre.

Oviedo

OVIEDO likes to set itself apart from the other cities of the region, and some would say sets itself above them too, its bourgeois culture in stark contrast with the working-class ethos of its neighbours. As the Asturian capital, it has long been fairly wealthy, a history which can be traced through its plethora of grand administrative and religious buildings, right down to the recent restoration and pedestrianization works which have transformed it into one of the most attractive cities in the north. The old quarter is a knot of squares and narrow streets built in warm yellow stone, while the newer part is redeemed by a huge public park right in the centre. Throughout the city are excellent bars and restaurants, many aimed at the lively student population. There are good transport links, too, with buses to just about everywhere in the province, and trains on both the FEVE and RENFE lines.

The principal reason for visiting the city, however, is to see three small **churches**. They are among the most remarkable in Spain, built in a style unique to Asturias which emerged in the wake of the Visigoths and before the Romanesque style had spread south from France. All of them date from the first half of the ninth century, a period of almost total isolation for the Asturian kingdom, which was then just 65km by 50km in area and the only part of Spain under Christian rule. Oviedo became the centre of this outpost in 810 with the residence of King Alfonso II, son of the victorious Pelayo (see "Covadonga", above).

Arrival, information and orientation

Coming in by public transport, points of arrival can be a little confusing. There are two separate **FEVE train stations** in addition to the regular **RENFE** one on c/Uría (which serves León). The FEVE Asturias, between the RENFE and the bus station, is for the line towards Santander; the FEVE Vasco, on c/Victor Chavarri, serves stations west to El Ferrol – they're a good fifteen minutes' apart, so don't try to make too tight a connection.

Most long-distance **buses**, and those to the airport, run from an underground station (☎98 528 12 00) in the Plaza Primo de Rivera, with the important exception of Alsa-Turytrans services, to inland Asturias and the smaller coastal towns, which run from opposite the FEVE Asturias, just above the plaza; the ticket office is here too, on c/Jerónimo Ibrán.

Central Oviedo is bounded by a loop of roads. At its heart is the extensive **Campo de San Francisco**; the **cathedral** is a couple of blocks to the east of this, with the **Plaza de la Constitución** and **Ayuntamiento** to its south. The city has a **Turismo**

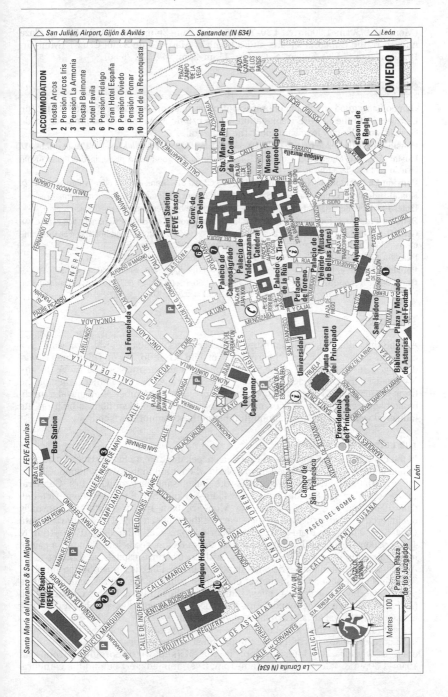

OVIEDO

△ San Julián, Airport, Gijón & Avilés   △ Santander (N 634)   △ León

ACCOMMODATION
1 Hostal Arcos
2 Pensión Arcos Iris
3 Pensión La Armonia
4 Hostal Belmonte
5 Hotel Favila
6 Pensión Fidalgo
7 Gran Hotel España
8 Pensión Oviedo
9 Pensión Pomar
10 Hotel de la Reconquista

(Mon–Fri 9.30am–1.30pm & 4.30–7.30pm, Sat 9am–2pm; ☎98 521 33 85) in Plaza Alfonso II, the cathedral square, and a booth at Marqués de Santa Cruz 1 (Mon–Fri 10.30am–2pm & 4.30–7.30pm, Sat & Sun 11am–2pm; ☎98 522 75 86).

Accommodation

Oviedo has a good supply of **accommodation**, with a concentration of *hostales* on c/de Uría, opposite the RENFE train station, along c/9 de Mayo and its continuation c/de Caveda, and along c/Jovellanos near the cathedral.

Pensión Arco Iris, c/de Uría 39 (☎98 524 59 08). Clean, friendly *pensión*, offering large rooms. ③.

Hostal Arcos, c/Magdalena 3 (☎98 521 47 73). Friendly, good-value place, in the heart of old Oviedo, just off Plaza Mayor. ④.

Pensión La Armonia, c/Nueve de Mayo 14 (☎98 522 03 01). Small and excellent-value *pensión*. ②.

Hostal Belmonte, c/de Uría 31 (☎98 524 10 20). Pleasant and newly refurbished rooms. ④.

Hotel Favila, c/de Uría 37 (☎98 525 38 77). Comfortable business hotel. ⑤.

Pensión Fidalgo, c/Jovellanos 5 (☎98 521 32 87). Cosy rooms with television, near the centre. ④.

Gran Hotel España, c/Jovellanos 2 (☎98 522 05 96, fax 98 522 21 40). Grand hotel, just as the name claims, close by the cathedral. Expensive, but reduced weekend rates. ⑦.

Pensión Oviedo, c/Uría 43 (☎98 524 10 00). Good, mid-priced *pensión*. ④.

Pensión Pomar, c/Jovellanos 7 (☎98 522 27 91). A little dingy, but central and very cheap. ②.

Hotel de la Reconquista, Gil de Jaz 16 (☎98 524 11 00, fax 98 524 11 66). Luxury accommodation in a seventeenth-century palace near Parque da San Francisco. ⑧.

The Town

Around the cathedral, enclosed by scattered sections of the medieval town walls, is a compact, attractive quarter, the remains of **Old Oviedo**. As at Gijón, much was destroyed in the Civil War when Republican Asturian miners laid siege to the Nationalist garrison; the defenders were relieved by a *gallego* detachment when on the brink of surrender. The centre nevertheless preserves a number of medieval churches and squares, and some fine government buildings and town houses built on the industrial wealth of the area, although most of these cannot be visited.

The cathedral and around

In the ninth century, King Alfonso II built a chapel, the Cámara Santa (Holy Chamber), to house the holy relics rescued from Toledo when it fell to the Moors. Remodelled in the twelfth century, this now forms the inner sanctuary of Oviedo's **Catedral** (May–Sept Mon–Fri 8.45am–8pm, Sat 8.45am–6.30pm, Sun 8.45am–9.30pm; Oct–Feb daily 10am–1pm & 4–6pm; March–May Mon–Fri 10am–1pm & 4–7pm), an unusually uncluttered Gothic structure at the heart of the modern city. The **Cámara Santa** (July–Sept Mon–Fri 10am–8pm, Sat 10am–6.30pm; Oct–June daily 10am–1pm & 4–6pm; 200ptas, 400ptas including cloisters and museum, see below) is in fact a pair of interconnecting chapels. The innermost, with its primitive capitals, is thought to be Alfonso's original building. The antechapel, rebuilt in 1109, is a quiet little triumph of Spanish Romanesque; each of the six columns supporting the vault is sculpted with a pair of superbly humanized apostles. Built around the attractive Gothic **cloister**, itself built on pre-Romanesque foundations, the diocesan museum has a higher quality collection of devotional art and artefacts than is typical.

Around the cathedral, some of the city's ancient **palaces** – not least the archbishop's, opposite – are worth a look, though most are in government use and none is open to visitors. Of interest, too, is the **Museo Arqueológico** (Mon–Sat 10am–1.30pm & 4.30–6pm, Sun 11am–1pm; free), immediately behind the cathedral in the former convent of San Vicente. This displays various pieces of sculpture from the "Asturian-Visigoth" churches.

The nearest of these churches, **San Julian de los Prados**, or **Santullano** (Tues–Sun: July–Sept 9.30am–1pm & 4.30–6pm; May, June & Oct 11am–1pm & 4.30–6pm; Nov–April noon–1pm & 4–5pm), is ten minutes' walk to the northeast along the c/de Gijón and by some unfortunate quirk of local city planning stands right next to a highway. However, it's well worth seeing. Built around 830, it is considerably larger and more spacious than the other Asturian churches, with an unusual "secret chamber" built into the outer wall. It is kept locked but the keys are available at the priest's house to the left; there are original frescoes inside, executed in similar style to those of Roman villas.

Santa María del Naranco

The greatest of the Asturian churches, indeed the architectural gem of the principality, is **Palacio de Santa María del Naranco** (daily: May–Oct 9.30am–1pm & 3–7pm; Nov–April 10am–1pm & 3–5pm; closed Sun pm; 200ptas, free on Mon), majestically located on a wooded slope 3km above the city. It's a 45-minute walk from the centre, or half an hour from the station; the local tourist office has marked out a walking route, starting on one of the pedestrian streets in the town centre and leading on to a beautiful trail.

Perhaps it's the walk, providing glimpses of the warm stone and simple bold outline of the church through the trees, that makes Santa María so special, almost mystical, a building. But when you've arrived and gazed upon it from all sides it still seems quite perfect in its harmony of form, decoration, and natural surroundings – "formidable beyond its scale", to use Jan Morris's phrase. Curiously, it was designed not as a church but as a palace or hunting lodge for Ramiro I (842–52), Alfonso's successor. The present structure was just the main hall of a complex that once included baths and stairways, features which the caretaker may point out. Architecturally, the open porticos at both ends are most interesting – an innovation developed much later in Byzantine churches – as well as the thirty or so decorative medallions which give the appearance of being suspended from the roof. The crypt bears a notable resemblance to the Cámara Santa back in town.

A couple of hundred metres beyond Santa María is King Ramiro's palace chapel, **San Miguel de Lillo** (same hours as Santa María), built with soft golden sandstone and red tiles. This is generally assumed to be by the same architect as Santa María, Tiodo (whom some scholars credit also with the Cámara Santa and San Julian de los Prados), though its design, the Byzantine cross-in-square, is quite different. Much of its interior sculpture has been removed to the archeological museum.

Further up from the two little churches is a Rio-style **figure of Christ** that looks out over the city and is spectacularly illuminated at night. It was built by Republican prisoners of war and although ugly close up (it's constructed from concrete blocks), there are wonderful views from the site.

Eating, drinking and nightlife

Head to the area around the cathedral for the best **eating and drinking**. You can't help but notice the *sidrerías*, spit-and-sawdust places with a lot of people pouring a lot of drink from a great height. These will baffle the newcomer, but just order a bottle (about 275ptas), and you'll soon pick up the right drinking method. Most of the best are along c/Gascona, down from the cathedral. There are plenty of cafés and bars too, most with remarkable-value *menús* – anything over 800ptas is expensive – as well as more pricey traditional *mesones* serving *fabada* and other Asturian fare. A pleasant place to while away some time is the café in the Corrada del Obispo, one of the most beautiful of Oviedo's squares. Internet junkies can get online in the funky *Café Bhet@* (daily 4pm to midnight); look for the restored railway carriage next to the RENFE station.

Restaurants and tapas bars

Bocamar, Plaza Trascorrales 14. Terrific *sidrería-marisquería*: try the *fabas con almejas* (beans with clams) and the delicious rice dishes.

Canela, c/Campoamor 20 (☎98 522 00 45). Great little restaurant with quality cooking at a remarkable price; the *menú* is 2000ptas. Closed Sun, Feb 15–28 & Aug 1–15.

Casa Fermín, c/San Francisco 8 (☎98 521 64 97). A classic, much-written-about restaurant, serving imaginatively recreated Asturian dishes. The *menú* is a hefty 3000ptas and you could easily spend a lot more. Closed Sun.

Casa Manolo, c/Altamirano 9 (☎98 521 25 61). Superior and pricey *sidrería* known for its game and *tapas*.

El Fontan, c/Fierro. Café-restaurant overlooking the market with good-value *menú*.

Los Italianos, Avda. de Galicia 15. Reliable pasta and pizza.

Los Lagos, Plaza del Carbayón 3. Excellent *sidrería* filled with the heady smell of strong Asturian foods, cider and sawdust. Another branch on c/Cervantes 7.

El Mirador, midway up the road to Naranco. Very decent restaurant with a terrace that looks out over the whole city and mountains beyond.

El Raitán, Plaza Trascorrales 6 (☎98 521 42 18). Superb restaurant in a delightful square off Plaza Mayor. The huge 4000ptas *menú* offers a taste of several Asturian dishes, but you can eat for as little as half that.

Nightlife and entertainment

Oviedo can be quiet in summer when the local youth tends to flock to nearby resorts and the student population is away, but during the rest of the year there's a huge scene. The **pubs** and **bars** have a strong Celtic tradition, and you'll find Guinness on tap and loud Irish music playing at the extremely popular *Ca Beleño*, c/Martínez Vigil 4. Calle Mon is the place to go for the thriving **disco-pub** scene, with music to cater for most tastes. The trendy *Diario Roma* is loud and crowded with a great atmosphere, while *Montañes* is a quieter refuge with cheaper drinks. *Monster* on the nearby Plaza de Sol plays indy/alternative rock and on the tiny c/Carta Puebla off c/Postigo Alto, *El Planeta Tierra* and *La Misión* host a more dance-oriented scene. *Salsipuedes*, c/Salsipuedes 3, is a relaxed place with a trio of bars and a great summer terraza.

Places on c/Altamirano stay open a bit later – *La Botica* has a good selection of dance music and *La Tamara* wonderful decor and a trendy mixed crowd – but if you want to keep going into the small hours, a younger crowd moves out to the bars and **clubs** on c/Rosal and c/Gonzalez Besada ten minutes west of the old town; *Movie* on the latter is hugely popular. Two big popular clubs are *El Antiguo* on c/del Peso, off Plaza Mayor and *Stavaganza* on c/Santa Clara off Plaza del Carbayón. *La Real* on c/Cervantes is good for house and has a mixed gay/straight crowd.

For **classical music**, watch out for Oviedo's Orquestra de Asturias, who are based here and perform mainly in the Teatro Campoamor. There are usually a couple of concerts each week, and summer performances in the university and cathedral cloisters. For many years there has been an opera festival in September, but financing problems are leaving its immediate future in doubt.

Listings

Airport Aeropuerto de Asturias (☎98 554 77 33 or 98 556 17 09) is 13km away in Ranon, just off the N632.

American Express c/o Viajes Cafranga, c/Uría 26 (☎98 522 52 17).

Books Librería Cervantes, c/Dr Casal 3/9 has a good stock, including walking and wildlife guides to Asturias, and English-language novels.

Car rental Avis, c/Ventura Rodríguez 12 (☎98 524 13 83); Europcar, c/Uría, in RENFE station (☎98 524 57 12); National Atesa, c/Asturias 41 (☎98 524 35 76).

Post office The *Correos Principal* is at c/Alonso Quintanilla 1 (Mon–Fri 8.30am–8.30pm, Sat 9.30am–2pm).

Telephones The *Telefónica* is at c/Foncalada 6 (Mon–Sat 10am–2pm & 4–10.30pm).

Trekking The Federacíon Asturiana de Montaña, Avda. Julian Clavería (☎98 525 23 62), provides information and organizes treks in the Picos. The student agency, TIVE, c/Calvo Sotelo 5 (☎98 523 11 12), also offers good-value trekking trips.

Avilés and Oviedo to Galicia

The **coast west of Avilés**, as far as the Río Navia, is pretty rugged, with scarcely more than a handful of resorts carved out from the cliffs. The most attractive by far is the old port and resort of **Luarca**. West again from the Río Navia, the coast becomes marshy and, save for an honorary mention to the unspoilt fishing village of **Tapia de Casariego**, unexceptional. Again, the FEVE line trails the coast, with some spectacular sections, though some of the stations (including Cudillero and Luarca) are inconveniently sited some way out of town.

Inland from Oviedo, the N634 and C630 offer a winding approach over the hills to Lugo in Galicia. The old town of **Salas**, with its castle, is of passing interest, but the main appeal of the route is the mountainous wildness of this area, which sees hardly a tourist from one year to the next.

Cudillero

CUDILLERO is a small, active and picturesque fishing port, with brightly coloured arcaded houses rising one upon each other over a steep horseshoe of cliffs around the port. Despite encroaching tourism, the town retains its charm. As there's no beach as such here – the nearest is **Playa Aguilar**, 3km to the east – the most obvious attractions are the **fish tavernas** in its narrow, cobbled, seaside plaza; at weekends these are packed out, with prices geared to tourist rather than local trade. For good *sidra* and *calamares*, *Méson El Pescador* is excellent.

Practicalities

Cudillero can be reached by **FEVE trains** from Avilés or Oviedo; the station is at the top of town, a fifteen-minute walk from the centre. The **bus station** is midway between here and the town centre, with twelve daily buses to Avilés and a sporadic service to Oviedo and Gijón, although you can walk 3km to **El Pito** on the main road to pick up the full coastal service. In summer, there's a **Turismo** (Mon–Fri 10am–9pm, Sat & Sun 3–8pm; ☎98 559 00 20) on Plaza de San Pedro, just behind the port, and a booth next to the harbour which can help find accommodation.

In the village proper, there is a single **hotel**, the pricey *San Pablo*, c/Suarez Inclán 36–38 (☎98 559 11 55; ⑥), and two *pensiónes* on the main road just above the centre: *El Camarote* (☎98 559 12 02; ④) and *Pensión Alver* (☎98 559 15 28; ④). There is a **campsite**, *L'Amuravela* (☎98 559 09 95; June–Sept), in El Pito 2km back from Playa Aguilar, and you'll find another, *Yolimar* (☎98 559 04 72; April–Sept), 2km back from the stunning deep cove at Artedo, 4km west of the port. On the hill above is a FEVE stop, La Magdalena.

Luarca

Beyond San Pedro the coast is rocky and the road winds through dark hills before dipping down through thick woods to the port of **LUARCA**. This is one of the most attractive towns along the whole northern coastline, a mellow place, built around an

S-shaped cove amid sheer cliffs. Down below, the town is bisected by a small, winding river, and knitted together by numerous narrow bridges.

Luarca is a seaside resort in a very modest sort of way, with a slim beach of slightly murky sand, a scattering of accommodation, and some excellent bars and restaurants. In contrast to Cudillero, Luarca has defiantly retained its traditional character, including a few *chigres* – old-fashioned Asturian taverns – where you can be initiated into the art of *sidra* drinking. The fishing harbour area is the best place for meals, too: cross the bridge from the plaza, follow the river, and pick from a line of good-value restaurants here, among them the huge and popular *Mesón de la Mar*. You can watch the small fishing boats returning at around midnight and see the catch auctioned off at the *lonja* at around 3pm the following afternoon.

Practicalities

The **Turismo** (Tues–Sun 11am–2pm & 4–7pm; ☎98 564 00 83), at c/Olavarrieta 27, provides lists of private rooms and apartments. On the way into town, there are some good budget **places to stay**, including *El Redondel* (☎98 564 07 33; ③), on the main highway, 3km from the centre, in Almuña. In town, *El Cocinero* (☎98 564 01 75; ③) is a fine, ramshackle eighteenth-century *fonda* in the main plaza, and there are modest rooms at *Bar Oviedo* (☎98 564 09 06; ②) on c/del Crucero, a pedestrianized street behind the plaza. The upmarket choices are the *Hotel Gayoso*, Paseo Gómez 4 (☎98 564 00 54, fax 98 547 02 71; ⑤–⑦), a grand old hotel, with a cheaper annexe nearby in Plaza Alfonso, and well-situated *Hotel Baltico* (☎98 547 01 34; ⑤), overlooking the harbour.

The town **beach** is divided in two. The closer strip is narrower but more protected, the broader one beyond the jetty is subject to seaweed litter. On the cliff-top on the other side of town is a hermitage chapel and a lighthouse, and facing these across a rocky cove is a **campsite**, *Los Cantiles* (☎98 564 09 38; open all year), with facilities to match its superb setting.

You'll find an excellent **restaurant**, *Casa Consuelo*, on the main road (Carreterra San Sebastián), which attracts people from miles around; try the *merlunza con angulas* (hake with eels). In town, the gourmet choice is the excellent *Villablanca* on Avda. de Galicia.

Luarca has good **bus** connections to Oviedo, Gijón, Avilés and into Galicia; you'll find the bus station just off c/del Crucero. The FEVE station is 2km out of town.

Luarca to Ribadeo

West from Luarca, you cross the wide Río Navia – a foretaste of Galicia's *rías* or estuaries – at **NAVIA**, a pleasant little port, though lacking the style and life of Luarca. If you have transport, the inland route from here to Lugo is fascinating. At **COAÑA**, 5km south of Navia and connected by local buses, there's a *castro*, or Celtic settlement (Tues–Sun 11–2.30pm & 4–7.30pm; free), and beyond that the road winds above the reservoirs of the Navia River before twisting into Galicia and the remote mountainous region around Fonsagrada.

The best beach along this stretch is the last in Asturias, the **Playa de Los Campos**, which flanks the unspoilt fishing village of **TAPIA DE CASARIEGO**. This is a lively little place, with an entertaining "alternative" Teatro Popular, and a very helpful **Turismo** in a small kiosk in the plaza. There are three reasonably priced **hotels**, including *La Ruta* (☎98 562 81 38; ⑤) which is great value, and *Puente de los Santos* (☎98 562 81 55, fax 98 562 8437; ⑥), just opposite, which is slightly more expensive. Just outside town are two **campsites**, about 1km towards Ribadeo; *Playa de Tapia* (☎98 547 27 21; June–Sept) and *El Carbayín* (☎98 562 37 09; open all year). The port area is again the place to eat and drink; walk down to the beaches and turn left.

CASTROPOL, set back from the coast on the Río Eo – the border with Galicia – is a tiny, pretty place with a pair of *hostales*. However, you're better off staying across the border in Ribadeo. There's a **Turismo** (Tues–Sat 10am–2pm & 5–8pm, Sun 10am–3pm) on the main highway, if you're entering from Galicia and want pamphlets and information on Asturias.

Salas

SALAS, 35km west of Oviedo, was the home of the Marqués de Valdés-Salas, founder of Oviedo University and one of the prime movers of the Inquisition. The town **castle** is actually the Marqués's old palace; you can climb an adjoining tower from the **Turismo** (☎98 589 09 88) for fine views of the town and surrounding countryside. Among the other monuments are a sixteenth-century **Colegiata** and, in the main square, the tenth-century church of **San Martín**.

If you want to **stay**, there are two options: the *Hotel Castillo de Valdés-Salas* (☎98 583 22 22, fax 98 583 22 99; ⑤), in the castle, with an out-of-the-ordinary restaurant; and the *Pensión Soto*, c/Arzobispo Valdés 9 (☎98 583 00 37; ④), which has big, clean rooms. **Buses** to Oviedo leave on the hour from outside the *Café Berlin*.

travel details

BUSES

The majority of buses along the coast, and all those covering longer distances, are run by the Alsa bus company. Some of these buses covering shorter distances are also labelled EASA or Turytrans, but the livery is the same distinctive blue-grey and all buses carry the Alsa logo. A number of smaller companies operate more local services between coastal resorts and inland destinations, but you should note that these buses often have reduced services outside July and August.

Castro Urdiales to: Bilbao (7 daily; 1hr); Santander (11 daily; 1hr); Vitoria (3 daily; 1hr 15min).

Comillas to: San Vicente (3 daily; 30min); Santander (7 daily; 45min); Santillana (4 daily; 35min).

Gijón to: Irún via Oviedo (6 daily; 7hr 30min); Léon via Oviedo (8 daily; 2hr); Madrid via Oviedo (11 daily; 5hr 30min); Oviedo (every 15min; 30min); Ribadeo via Luarca, Navia, Castropol and Vegadeo (7 daily; 4hr); Sevilla (2 daily; 12hr 30min); Salamanca (5 daily; 4hr 30min); Villaviciosa (hourly; 45min).

Llanes to: Arenas (3 daily; 1hr); Madrid via Cangas and Oseja (daily; Monday, Wednesday and Friday only in winter); Oviedo via Ribadesella (12 daily; 1hr 30min); San Vicente (11 daily;

45min); Santander (11 daily; 1hr 30min); Unquera (11 daily; 30min).

Oviedo to: Avilés (every 30min; 30min); Cangas de Onis (10 daily; 1hr–1hr 30min); La Coruña via Betanzos (2 daily; 4hr 30min/5hr); Covadonga (5 daily; 1hr 45min); Cudillero (10 daily – but 3 more by changing at Avilés; 1hr); Gijón (every 15min; 30min); León (8 daily, 1hr 30min); Lugo (5 daily; 5hr 30min); Madrid (12 daily; 5hr 30min); Pontevedra (2 daily; 8hr); Ribadeo via Luarca (7 daily; 3hr 30min); Ribadesella (12 daily; 1hr 20min–2hr); Santander (8 daily; 3hr 30min); Santiago (3 daily; 5hr 30min–7hr); Sevilla (2 daily; 12hr); Valladolid (4 daily; 3hr 30min); Vigo (2 daily; 8hr 30min); Villaviciosa via San Pedro de Ambas (8 daily; 1hr 15min).

Picos buses Arenas de Cabrales–Cangas de Onis (4 daily; 45min), Bustio–Arenas via Panes (2 daily; 50/20min), Cangas de Onis–Covadonga (9 daily; 45min), Cangas de Onis–Posada de Valdeón via Sajambre (1 daily in summer; 2hr 15min); Llanes–Madrid via Cangas, Sajambre and Riaño (1 daily in summer; 3 weekly in winter; 6hr 15min); León–Posada de Valdeón via Riaño and Portilla de la Reina (1 daily; 3hr). Potes–Espinama –Fuente Dé (3 daily; 1hr). Also **Land Rover service** between Valdeón and Caín.

Ribadesella to: Lastres (every 2hr in summer; 45min); Llanes (11 daily; 45min); Oviedo via Arriondas (change at Arriondas for Cangas; 12

daily; 1hr 20min–2hr); San Vincente (3 daily; 2hr); Villaviciosa (3 daily; 1hr).

San Vicente to: Comillas (3 daily; 30min); Llanes (12 daily; 45min); Potes via Unquera (2 daily; 1hr 30min); Ribadesella (3 daily; 2hr); Santander (12 daily; 1hr).

Santander to: Barcelona (2 daily; 9hr); Bilbao (25 daily; 10 of which continue to French border; 1hr 30min); Burgos (6 daily; 4hr); Castro Urdiales (11 daily; 1hr); Comillas (7 daily; 45min; more by changing in Torrelavega); Laredo (21 daily; 40min); Llanes (11 daily; 1hr 30min); Madrid (6 daily; 8hr); Oviedo (8 daily; 3hr 30min); Potes via San Vicente and Unquera (3 daily; 3hr); Puente Viesgo (5 daily; 40min); Santiago, Vigo, and Portuguese border (2 daily; 10–12hr); Santillana (7 daily, 4 daily in winter; 45min); San Vicente la Barquera (12 daily; 1hr); Vitoria via Castro Urdiales, skips Bilbao (7 daily; 2hr).

TRAINS
RENFE

Oviedo to: Alicante (1 daily; 11hr); Barcelona (2 daily; 12hr–13hr 30min); León (7 daily; 2hr 30min); Madrid (5 daily; 6hr); Vigo (2 daily; 9hr).

Santander to: Madrid (3 daily; 5hr 30min), change at Palencia for east–west routes including León.

FEVE

This delightful independent service runs along the north coast between **Bilbao, Santander, Oviedo and Ferrol**. The narrow-gauge railway has recently been modernized, and the line is punctual and scenic, though still slow for longer trips. Timetables can be picked up at any main station but these can be confusing. In practical terms it is best to think of the service divided between **through trains** that cover the longer distances between the big cities, and **local trains**, which run more frequently between the smaller towns. There are also a few *cercanías*, or local **branch lines**, most of which are centred around Gijón. The full journey from Ferrol to Bilbao can't be done in one day, and you should also note that there are two separate stations in Oviedo, Oviedo Asturias for trains east to Bilbao, and Oviedo Vasco for trains west to Ferrol. Connecting in Oviedo between the first train from Ferrol and the last train on to Santander is particularly tight.

Though trains: Bilbao to Santander (3 daily; 2hr 20min); Santander to Oviedo Asturias (2 daily; 2hr 20min); Oviedo Vasco to Ferrol (2 daily; 7hr).

Local trains: Bilbao to Orejo (3 daily; 2hr 20min); Orejo to Santander (18 daily; 24min); Santander to Puente de San Miguel (42 daily; 33–40min); Puente de San Miguel to Cabezon de la Sal (20 daily; 22min); Cabezon to Llanes (2 daily; 1hr 5min); Llanes to Ribadesella-Infiesto (3 daily; 30min–1hr 30min); Ribadesella to Nava (7 daily; 18min); Nava to Oviedo Asturias (21 daily; 39min); Oviedo Vasco to Pravia (21 daily; 1hr 5min); Pravia to Cudillero (18 daily; 20min); Cudillero to Navia (3 daily; 1hr 30min); Navia to Ribadeo (2 daily; 1hr); Ribadeo to Ferrol (3 daily; 3hr 5min).

Branch lines: Gijón to Avilés (30 daily; 40min); Gijón to Pravia (for main line to Ferrol; 15 daily; 30min).

FERRIES

Car/passenger ferry from **Santander** to **Plymouth** (Tues & Thurs, 24hr; runs weekly to Poole only in February and early March, 28 hr).

CHAPTER EIGHT

GALICIA

Remote, rural, and battered by the Atlantic, Galicia is a far cry from the popular image of Spain. It not only looks like Ireland; there are further parallels in the climate, culture, and music, as well as the ever-visible traces of its Celtic past. Above all, despite its green and fertile appearance, Galicia has a similar history of famine and poverty, with a decline in population owing to forced emigration which is only now being reversed with government subsidies for returning emigrants of *gallego* ancestry.

Galicia is lush and heavily wooded in native oaks and pines, although subsidized plantations of imported eucalyptus are becoming dominant. The coastline is shaped

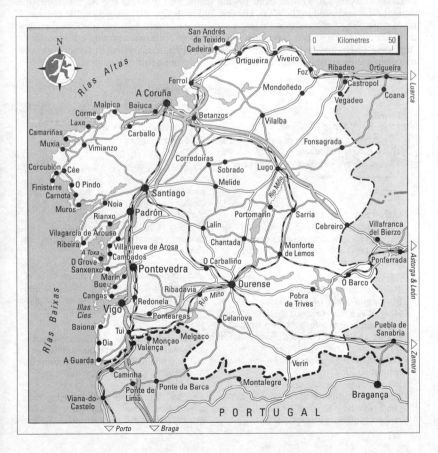

by fjord-like inlets, source of some of the best seafood in Europe. In the north these *rías* shelter unspoiled old villages and fine beaches, while the sunnier southern coast is becoming increasingly built up with new resorts and roads. As you enter Galicia from the east, the rolling meadows of Asturias are replaced by a patchwork of tiny fields, with terraces of vines supported on granite props and allotments full of turnip-tops and cabbages growing on stalks. Archaic inheritance laws have meant a constant division and redivision of the land into little plots too small for machinery and worked with primitive agricultural methods; ox carts with solid wooden wheels are still seen on the backroads. Everywhere you see *hórreos*, granaries made here of granite rather than wood, with saints and sculpted air-vents, standing on pillars away from rodents and the damp.

While it is a poor, "backward" part of the country, unlike the south it never seems oppressively so, and the wave of road improvements, motorways and new building in the 1990s is rapidly changing the character of the region. Food is plentiful, most people being involved in its production, and there's a strength and solidity in the culture, run, uniquely for Spain, by the women. In the countryside, women and children frequently work the land while the men work at sea, whether as merchant seamen or fishermen, catching octopus and lobster from rowing boats, and minding the *mejilloneiras* (the mussel rafts anchored in the *rías*). Others, undoubtedly, are engaged in the old stand-by of smuggling – which, these days, means drugs as well as more traditional contraband. For centuries men have also sought their fortunes abroad, traditionally in Argentina (there are said to be more *gallegos* in Buenos Aires than in Galicia), though more often these days as migrant labourers in northern Europe.

FIESTAS

January

1 Livestock fair at Betanzos.

6 Horseback procession of *Los Reyes* (the Three Kings) in Baiona.

15 *San Mauro* – fireworks at Vilanova de Arousa.

March

1 Celanova's big festival, of *San Rosendo*, at the monastery above town.

Pre-Lenten *carnavales* throughout the region, along with the *Lazaro* festival, a gathering of both *gallego* and Portuguese folk groups, at Verín.

April

Palm Sunday Stations of the Cross at Monte San Tecla, near A Guarda.

Holy Week Celebrations include a symbolic *descendimiento* (descent from the Cross) at Viveiro on Good Friday and a resurrection procession at Finisterre.

Second Monday after Easter *San Telmo* festival at Tui.

25 *San Marcos* observance at Noia.

Late April (dates vary from year to year) Festival at Ribadavia celebrating and promoting Ribeiro wines.

May

1 *Romería* at Pontevedra.

22 *Santa Rita* at Vilagarcía de Arousa.

June

Sundays Country fairs and roundups of wild horses, known as *curros*, are held on successive Sundays in the hills above Baiona and Oia; villages include La Valga, Torroña, Mougas and Pinzas.

Corpus Christi Flower festival, with flower "carpets" in the streets, in Ponteareas.

24–25 Two days of celebration for *San Juan* in many places, with processions of bigheads and *gigantones* on the 24th and spectacular parades with fireworks and bands through the following evening.

July

First weekend *Rapa das Bestas* – capture and breaking in of wild mountain horses – at Viveiro and San Lorenz (Pontevedra). At the latter the horses are raced before being let loose.

11 *San Benito* fiesta at Pontevedra, with river processions and competitions, and folk groups, and a smaller *romería* at Cambados.

With so many men absent, and little heavy industry beyond the failing shipbuilding yards in Ferrol and Vigo, there is little of the radicalism of Asturias. Galicia has always been deeply conservative and since 1875 has provided Spain with a gallery of prominent right-wing leaders; it was the birthplace of General Franco, and is today dominated by the right wing Partido Popular, whose founder, Manuel Fraga, is another local boy. Nonetheless, there is a strong and proud *gallego* nationalist movement, which may not approach the scale – or political intensity – of the Catalans and the Basques, but has formed links with Brittany and Ireland, and championed the revival of the long-banned local language.

Gallego today sounds like a fusion of Castilian and Portuguese, but has existed every bit as long as either, and is still spoken by an estimated 85 percent of the population. In the smaller communities few people speak anything else. It is definitely a living language, taught in schools and with its own literary heroes such as the poet Rosalia de Castro and the essayist and caricaturist Castelao. Road signs and maps these days tend to be in **Gallego**. We have therefore used the *gallego* name for towns, supplying the Castilian version in parentheses where it varies significantly, or is helpful. The most obvious characteristic of *gallego* is the large number of *X*s, which in Castilian might be *G*s, *J*s or *S*s; these are pronounced as a soft *sh*. You will also find that the Castilian *plaza* becomes *praza* and *playa* becomes *praia,* while *la* is *a* (as in A Coruña), *el* is *o* (as in O Grove), *de la* is *da* and *del* is *do.*

The obvious highlight of the region is **Santiago de Compostela**, the greatest goal for pilgrims in medieval Europe and once again a flourishing centre for tourists. The cathedral, and the unified architecture of the whole city, with its granite colonnades

---

16 *Virgen del Carmen.* Sea processions at Muros and Corcubión.

25 Galicia's major fiesta, in honour of Saint James, at Santiago de Compostela. It's worth attending Mass to see the National Offering to the Shrine (of the country and government) as well as the swinging of the *botafumeiro.* The evening before, there's a fireworks display and symbolic burning of a cardboard effigy of the mosque at Córdoba. The festival – also designated Galicia Day – has become a nationalist event with traditional separatist demonstrations and an extensive programme of political and cultural events for about a week on either side.

29 Octopus festival at Vilanova de Arousa.

August

First Sunday Wine festival at Cambados; bagpipe festival at Ribadeo; *Virgen de la Roca* observances outside Baiona.

9 *Percebe* (barnacle) festival in Finisterre.

16 *San Roque* festivals at all churches that bear his name: at Betanzos there's a Battle of the Flowers on the river; at Sada (10km

east of A Coruña) there are boat races and feasts.

24 Fiesta (and bullfights) at Noia.

25 *San Ginés* at Sanxenxo.

28 *Romería del Naseiro* outside Viveiro.

Last Sunday *Romería* sets out from Sanxenxo to the Praia de La Lanzada.

September

6–10 *Fiestas del Portal* at Ribadavia.

8 *San Andreu* at Cervo (20km east of Viveiro).

First Sunday after 8th *Romería* at Muxia.

14 Seafood festival at O Grove; *romería* with bigheads at Viveiro.

October

13 *Fiesta de la Exaltación del Marisco* at O Grove – literally "a celebration in praise of shellfish".

November

11 *Fiesta de San Martín* at Bueu.

Last Sunday Oyster festival at Arcade (10km south of Pontevedra).

December

Last week Crafts fair, *O Feitoman,* at Vigo.

GALLEGO FOOD AND DRINK

One of the most compelling attractions of Galicia is the local **food**. Gourmets claim the quality of the **seafood** here is to be equalled only in Newfoundland, and with a few exceptions it is not expensive, at least when eaten as *tapas* in bars. Local wonders to look out for include *vieiras* (the scallops whose shells became the symbol of St James), *mejillones* (the rich orange mussels from the *rías*), *cigallas* (a kind of crayfish usually and inadequately translated as shrimp), *anguilas* (little eels from the River Minho), *navajas* (razor-shells), *percebes* (barnacles) and *choquitos* and *chipirones* (different kinds of small squid best served in their own ink). *Pulpo* (octopus) is so much a part of *gallego* eating that there are special *pulperías* cooking it in the traditional copper pots, and it is a mainstay of local country fiestas. In the province of Pontevedra alone, Vilanova de Arousa has its own octopus festival, Arcade has one devoted to oysters, and O Grove goes all the way with a generalized seafood fiesta. One word of warning, however; although a wide variety of crab and lobster is always on display in the restaurants, make sure to have a price quoted in advance – the cost of these specialities is often exorbitant, and the demand so great that certain items such as *necoras* (spider crab) even have to be imported from England to keep up the supply.

Throughout Galicia there are superb **markets**; the coastal towns have their rows of seafront stalls with supremely fresh fish, while cities such as Santiago and Pontevedra have grand old arcaded market halls, piled high with farm produce from the surrounding countryside. Most enjoyable of all are the ports (such as Cambados and Marín), with *lonjas* open to the public, where you can wait for the fishing boats to come home (usually around midnight, but more like 6am in A Coruña) and watch the auctioning of their catch – much of which will have left Galicia well before dawn for the restaurants of Madrid, on the nightly special train.

Another speciality, imported from the second *gallego* homeland of Argentina, is the **churrasquería** (grill house). Often unmarked and needing local assistance to find, these serve up immense *churrascos* – what we inadequately call "spare ribs" (it's more like a steak with bones in it). The *gallegos* don't normally like their food highly spiced, but *churrascos* are traditionally served with a devastating garlic-based *salsa picante*. Other common dishes are *caldo gallego*, a thick stew of cabbage and potatoes in a meat-based broth, *caldeirada*, a filling fish soup, *lacon con grelos*, ham boiled with turnip greens, and the ubiquitous *empanada*, a light-crusted pasty, often filled with tuna and tomato.

The local **wines** can be great – both the whites (especially Albariño) and the thick portlike reds (some bars even serve a "black" wine) – and are still usually drunk from *tazas*, handleless ceramic cups; the best regions are Ribeiro and the Rias Baixas. The local **beer** is Estrella Galicia, good and strong. **Liqueurs** tend to be fiery, based on the clear *aguardiente* (which is elsewhere known as *eau de vie* or *aquavit*) nowadays often flavoured with herbs or coffee liquor; one much-loved *gallego* custom is the *queimada*, when a large bowl of *aguardiente* with fruit, sugar and coffee-grains is set alight and then drunk hot.

and mossy facades, together make Santiago quite unforgettable. But there are smaller and equally charming old stone towns throughout Galicia, and those that have retained a vibrant sense of life and atmosphere, such as **Pontevedra** and **Betanzos**, are enjoyable bases for a touring holiday. The coastal countryside is always spectacular, but the best and safest swimming beaches are along the booming **Rías Baixas** towards Portugal, with **O Grove** and **Baiona** two of the most popular resorts. Far fewer visitors come here than to the Mediterranean, and while the sea is never as warm, the pine-fringed coves are delightful. Outside July and August accommodation prices drop considerably and you'll have the beaches virtually to yourself. Further north, the tiny, picturesque ports of the harsh **Costa da Morte** – the stretch of coast between **A Coruña** and **Noia** – still preserve the traditional *gallego* lifestyle of smallholdings and small-scale fishing.

Inland, Galicia can be bleak and empty; the most rewarding route is to follow the Minho river upstream from the Portuguese border to towns such as **Ribadavia** and **Celanova**, and then up to the Roman walls of **Lugo**.

THE RÍAS ALTAS AND SANTIAGO

It's not nearly as difficult as it once was to move around the north coast of Galicia, where the **Rías Altas** (High Estuaries) include both the northernmost and westernmost points of Spain. Roads, which until recently were poorly surfaced and barely frequented, are now reliable and safe, and the facilities for visitors have improved with the increasing importance of the revenues from tourism. The savagery of the ocean has created a wild and dramatic coastline that slows down travel, and even if you have a car it's advisable to choose just a couple of targets. **Viveiro**, to the east, and the **Costa da Morte**, the section of coastline to the west of A Coruña, are particularly good to explore. No words of praise could be too extravagant for **Santiago de Compostela**, and if you really want to appreciate this pilgrimage centre to the fullest it makes sense to approach it by the ancient Pilgrim Route from León. Its one drawback, often exaggerated, is the weather; Santiago must be one of the few cities in the world which actually boasts about its excessive rainfall. With the exception of Santiago and **A Coruña**, which preserves a beautiful medieval quarter amid the sprawl of the modern port, the cities of this area are best avoided; **Ferrol** in particular is deep in the throes of industrial decay.

The north coast

The closing stretch of the FEVE **railway** (see p.437) from Luarca to Ferrol, is perhaps the best, as long as you're in no hurry to arrive. It clings to every nuance of the coastline, looping around a succession of *rías* and rambling through the eucalyptus forests and wild-looking hills which buffer the villages from the harsh Atlantic. Settlements are concentrated at the sides of the estuaries, with the occasional beach tacked beside or below them. By **road**, too, it's a slow route. Most buses to A Coruña and Ferrol detour inland as far as Lugo rather than tackle the endless bends of the C642 (at their most severe around Ortigueira), even though this stretch has recently been improved.

Along the FEVE

RIBADEO, the first *gallego* town and *ría*, makes a poor introduction to the region. It does have a certain crumbling charm, as well as a few places to stay – such as the *Galicia*, c/Virgen del Camino 1 (☎982 128777; ④), and a *parador* on c/Amador Fernández (☎982 128825, fax 928 100346; ⑥) – but overall it's drab. The nearest **beach**, the Praia do Castro, is a few kilometres further west, with **campsites** at Benquerencia (☎982 124450; June–Sept) and Reinante (☎982 134005), but by now you're getting a bit

---

ACCOMMODATION PRICE CODES

The codes used in our hotel listings denote the following price ranges:

① Under 2000ptas	④ 4500–6000ptas	⑦ 12,000–17,500ptas
② 2000–3000ptas	⑤ 6000–8000ptas	⑧ Over 17,500ptas
③ 3000–4500ptas	⑥ 8000–12,000ptas	

See p.34 for more details.

too close to the industrial port of Foz. Beyond that, Cervo has little more to boast of than a huge, rust-red aluminium factory, although Mondoñedo, 20km up the valley of the Río Masma, is an attractive old riverside town.

Viveiro

Once a remote, elegant port, the area around **VIVEIRO** has seen an influx of summer visitors over the last five years or so, changing the character of the large *ría* with a rash of holiday homes spreading up the hillsides. The old town however, is protected by a circuit of Renaissance walls, and its narrow streets are largely closed to traffic and lined with glass-fronted houses in delicate white wooden frames.

The sloping main drag down to the harbour is crammed with lively bars full of the local youth, and the bay shelters several peaceful **beaches**, particularly the Praia de Faro up towards the open sea. The large town beach, the Praia de Covas, is a good ten minutes walk from town across a causeway, with a **campsite**, the *Viveiro* (☎982 560004; June–Oct) behind.

PRACTICALITIES

Buses stop on Travesía de la Marina, the waterfront road below the old town; right opposite the station you'll find the **Turismo** (mid-June to mid-Sept 11am–2pm & 5–9pm). Inside the walls there are a couple of good, inexpensive **places to stay**: *Hospedaje García*, Praza Mayor (☎982 560675; ③), has a few simple but immaculate balconied rooms overlooking the square – look for the blue "CH" sign as there's no other marker; nearby, *Nuevo Mundo*, c/Teodoro de Quirós 14 (☎982 560025; ③), also has attractive balconied rooms (although those at the front are within ear-splitting distance of the bells of Santa María church, opposite). More upmarket, but somewhat character-less is the *Hostal Villa*, c/Nicolás Montenegro 57 (☎982 561331; ④), just outside the wall at the Porta del Vallado at the top end of town. For real luxury, try the well-cared for *Hotel Orfeo*, c/García Navia Castrillón 2 (☎982 562101, fax 982 560453; ⑤), with private parking and rooms overlooking the bay.

The *Nuevo Mundo* has a good **restaurant** upstairs – 1000ptas for a four-course feast. As you might expect, seafood is a local speciality: the excellent *Laurel*, c/Melitón Cortiñas 26, three streets east of the main square, is a busy *bodega* with wooden barrels and tables, and the cooks on view, battling away to fill the orders; expect to pay around 3000ptas for two, including the fine local wine. Just above San Francisco church at c/Antonio Bas 2, *Restaurante Serra* serves decent seafood and *menús* for around 1500ptas.

Porto do Barqueiro, Ortigueira and Porto de Vares

The next two *ría* villages (and FEVE stops) are **PORTO DO BARQUEIRO**, a tiny and very picturesque fishing port of slate-roofed houses near Spain's northernmost point, and the larger **ORTIGUEIRA**, set amid a dark mass of pines. The former has three places to stay dotted around its tiny harbour: *Estrellas del Mar* (☎981 414105; ③), with great sea views; *La Marina* (☎981 414098; ③), a little smarter and pricier but with only two sea-facing rooms; and the stylish and very comfortable *Bodegón O Forno* (☎981 414124; ④), also looking on to the sea. Ortigueira, too, has a couple of decent *hostales*, including the *Monterrey*, at Avda. Franco 105 (☎981 400135; ②). Ortigueira was for a few years the home of a particularly raucous Celtic festival, but that seems now to have been discontinued in view of its tendency to degenerate into violence (dark mutterings hold *agents provocateurs* responsible).

Drivers and cyclists, though, should take the opportunity to head the 7km north of Barqueiro up to the headland, through pine and eucalyptus forest, to straggly Vila de Vares. Two kilometres beyond, **PORTO DE VARES** is a highly attractive clump of fishermen's houses overlooking the bay, flanked to the south by a superb, wide, sandy beach, where you can camp. In the hamlet, there's a single *hostal*, the brand-new *Hostal Porto Mar* (☎981 562803; ③), with smart rooms and beautiful sea views. There's also a terrific seafood restaurant, *Marina*, with outdoor tables and window seats overlooking bay and beach. Fresh seafood meals – including great octopus and an *especial paella* – start from 1500ptas a head (though the *paella* will set you back considerably more).

San Andrés de Teixido and around

The FEVE heads inland after Ortigueira, but drivers or the very determined could make a side-trip to the hermitage at **SAN ANDRES DE TEIXIDO**, which, like so many of Galicia's sanctuaries, is based on a pre-Christian religious site. The hermitage occupies an important place in the mythology of Galicia, where the saying goes: *a San Andrés de Teixido vai de morto o que non foi de vivo* ("those who don't go to San Andrés alive, will go once they're dead"). Those failing to make the pilgrimage in their lifetime become one of the dreaded Santa Compaña, their souls trapped in the skins of lizards and weasels living in the rocks around the hermitage. Even in recent times, some older Galicians have been known to buy bus tickets for recently deceased relatives in an attempt to avoid this fate. It is a dramatic spot, with the nearby cliffs at **Vixia de Herbeira** claiming the title of highest in Europe at over 600 metres. There are a couple of places to stay in **CEDEIRA**, a port with a long sweep of beach set in an attractive *ría* 12km away: try the comfortable *Avenida*, c/Cuatro Caminos 6 (☎981 480998; ⑤), or the basic *Hostal Chelsea*, Plaza Sagrado Corazón 15 (☎981 481111; ③).

Ferrol

The city of **FERROL**, historically one of Spain's principal naval bases and dockyards, is now struggling to survive the collapse of the shipbuilding industry. Unfortunately the navy and dockyards have usurped the best of the coastline, leaving a provincial centre dominated by a status-conscious, navy-orientated community and a large statue of El Caudillo (the Chief), Francisco Franco, who was born here in 1892. Although frequently considered a bastion of conservatism, Ferrol was also the birthplace of Pablo Iglesias, founder of the Spanish Socialist Party, which until March 1996 ruled Spain for over a decade.

Getting out shouldn't be too difficult; the **FEVE** and **RENFE** stations are housed in the same building, and the **bus station** is just outside – exit and make two quick lefts, and you'll see it some 50m ahead of you. If you need **accommodation**, one of the more reasonable places is the spartan *Noray* on c/Venezuela 117 (☎981 310079; ②), and there are plenty of other choices along c/Pardo Bajo – the *Aloya* is at number 28 (☎981 351231; ③) – or c/del Sol and c/María, all within a few minutes' walk of the station and the central Praza de España. If you're driving, beware of outrageous traffic jams out of Ferrol on Friday and in again on Sunday nights, when the entire community heads out of the city for the weekend, blocking local roads solid.

The Ría de Betanzos

Ferrol stands more or less opposite A Coruña, only 20km away across the mouth of the **Ría de Betanzos**, but a seventy-kilometre trip by road or rail. The coast between the two cities is surprisingly rural, with the contours of the *ría* speckled with forests and secluded beaches.

Pontedeume, Perbes and Sada

Heading south from Ferrol, you cross the Río Eume either by the vast medieval bridge at **PONTEDEUME** (Puentedeume), or the vaster-still new motorway flyover nearby.

The stones on either side of the old bridge as you enter town are, in fact, boars from the arms of the once-powerful overlords, the counts of Andrade. Their tower overlooks the river at Pontedeume, and the Castelo de Andrade is perched on a hill over the town.

Just beyond, *Camping Perbes* (☎981 783104; June–Sept) is sandwiched between woods and water on the popular **Praia Perbes** near Minho. At **SADA**, opposite, you'll find the *Marina Española* **youth hostel** (☎981 620118; ①), and there are also several **campsites** in the area.

Betanzos

The town of **BETANZOS** is an enjoyable place to stay, although as most visitors are day-trippers from A Coruña, accommodation is fairly limited. The site it's built on is so old, dating back from before the Romans, that what was once a steep seaside hill is now set well back from the coast, at the spot where the rivers Mendo and Mandeo meet. The base of the hill is surrounded by still-discernible medieval walls composed largely of houses, above which rises a mass of twisting and tunnelling narrow streets. Follow these, and you'll come to the twelfth-century church of **Santa María de Azogue**, reconstructed by the Andrade lords in the fourteenth century; Andrade influence probably explains the unlikely stone pig with a cross on its back over the adjacent and contemporary church of San Francisco.

The focus of Betanzos is the large, attractive main square, **Praza de García Hermanos**, to the right of the town walls as you approach from the RENFE station. Nearby, in Rúa Emilio Romay, is the excellent **Museo das Mariñas** (10am–1pm & 4–8pm; 100ptas), which provides a fascinating insight into Betanzos and neighbouring *mariñas* (sea-facing villages) throughout their long history. Among the exhibits are an impressive collection of medieval sculpture, a roomful of eighteenth- and nineteenth-century *gallego* regional costumes and some photographs of the intriguing O Pasatempo, Parque Enciclopédico – a sort of fantasy park founded by the García brothers at the turn of the century (and now in ruins).

PRACTICALITIES

Right behind the main *praza*, in Rúa de Emilio Romay, you'll find the **Turismo** (10am–1pm & 4–8pm) in the same building as the Museo das Mariñas. If you need a **place to stay**, there are a few options just off the main square: at Rua do Rollo 6, directly behind the statue of the Garciá brothers, *Hostal Barreiros* (☎981 772259; ②) fills up quickly in summer, but has pleasant, if basic rooms; just around the corner, the very basic *Fonda Universal*, Avda. Linares Rivas 18 (☎981 770055; ②), is a cheap fallback; and on the far side of the square, *Hotel Los Ángeles*, c/de los Ángeles 11 (☎981 771511, fax 981 771213; ⑤), is professionally run, if a bit anonymous.

Eating and drinking centre around the row of bars on the main square – with outdoor seating – and the two tiny alleys leading off it to the right of *Café La Galeta*. The popular *O Pote* on the second alley, the Travesía do Progreso, has a great range of *tapas*, though you may have to stand. The owner of the *Hostal Barreiros* also runs the rather classy, wood-panelled *Mesón dos Arcos* below the *hostal*, whose dining room serves an excellent-value *menú del día* and great grills.

It's a ten-minute walk into town from the Betanzos Ciudad RENFE **station** (across the park and over the bridge to the town walls), but it's used only for the three daily trains to and from Ferrol. Other trains use the Betanzos Infesta station, 2.5km away at the top of a steep climb – or wait for a Ferrol-bound connection. ALSA **buses** arrive in the main square every half hour or so from A Coruña, a twenty-minute journey; buses also run from Lugo, Ferrol (hourly) and Santiago.

A Coruña

Despite its long history, the port of **A CORUÑA** is surprisingly modern, focused more on the office blocks and apartments of its rising middle class than on its past. However, its situation is impressive, crammed onto a peninsular with one side looking across the *rías* to Ferrol, the other exposed to the Atlantic, and its medieval quarter remains fairly extensive. It's also a major transport nexus, with a cosmopolitan range of shops and services, a surprisingly good beach right in the centre, an excellent array of seafood restaurants and a vibrant nightlife that ends with 5am *chocolate con churros*, watching the fishing boats come in.

Arrival, information and accommodation

The newly constructed **Paseo Marítimo** walkway edges the city's extensive coastline, bending around the port and marina, where it's overlooked by an elegant lacework of glassed-in balconies – a practical innovation against A Coruña's wind and showers. The **Turismo** is here at the Darsena de la Marina (Mon–Fri 9am–2pm & 4.30–6.30pm, Sat 9am–2pm & 5–7pm, Sun 10am–2pm & 5–7pm; mornings only in winter), a good thirty-minute walk across the city from the **bus** and **train** stations, which are 200m apart across a pedestrian flyover opposite El Corte Inglés department store; take bus #1 or #1a to the Praza de María Pita.

Finding a **place to stay** is easy – the Turismo has extensive and up-to-date listings. Try *Fonda Alba*, c/San Andrés 145 (☎981 220242; ②–③), which offers spotless rooms and the use of a kitchen, or the *Centro Gallego*, c/Estrella 2 (☎981 222236; ③), which is pleasant and well-located, as is the nearby *Hostal Merche*, c/Estrella 12 (☎981 223447; ④). There are plenty more options down c/Riego de Agua, the best of which is the homely *Fonda María Pita* at number 38 (☎981 221187; ③). For a step up in comfort, *Hostal El Sol* has stylish rooms on c/Sol 10 (☎981 210019, fax 981 210362; ④–⑤), while at the very top of the scale is the *Hotel Finisterre* (☎981 205400, fax 981 208462; ⑦–⑧) on the Paseo del Parrote alongside the old town.

The City

Departure point of the doomed 1588 Armada, and veteran of the Peninsular Wars, A Coruña has a lengthy history of naval combat. The restored Castelo San Antón, an easy walk along the Paseo Marítimo from the marina, was once a garrison and, until the 1960s, a military and political prison. It now houses the **Museo Arqueológico e Histórico** (Tues–Sat 11am–9pm (closes 7pm in winter), Sun 11am–2.30pm; 300ptas), worth the entrance fee if only for the view across the bay from the top and the medieval stone carvings at the back. Inland from here are the walled **Jardines de San Carlos** and, inside, the **tomb of Sir John Moore**, killed in 1809 during the British retreat from the French in the Peninsular Wars, and immortalized in the jingoistic rhythms of Reverend Charles Wolfe ("Not a drum was heard, not a funeral note . . .") which you will find here inscribed. Across the road, a new military museum contains relics from the city's various miltary adventures. Keep going and you'll find yourself in the narrow streets of the medieval town, which wind around the Romanesque churches of **Santiago** and **Santa María del Campo**, and are shielded from the sea by a high wall, much of which still remains, notably some fine sixteenth- and seventeenth-century gates. To the west of the old town, directly behind the café-terraces of the Darsena de la Marina, the huge, colonnaded **Praza de María Pita** is the city's grandest square, with some of the finest glass frontages you'll see, and a thriving café scene that continues into the early hours.

From the gardens just behind the Turismo, bus #3 or #3a runs out to the rocky outcrop where the much-trumpeted lighthouse, the **Torre de Hercules**, the city's symbol,

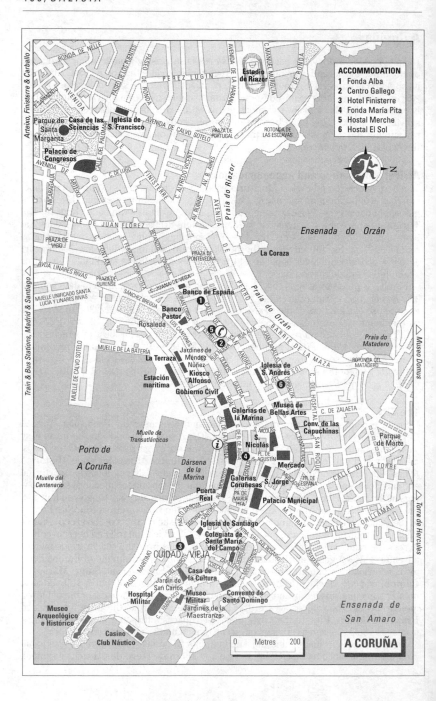

ACCOMMODATION
1 Fonda Alba
2 Centro Gallego
3 Hotel Finisterre
4 Fonda María Pita
5 Hostal Merche
6 Hostal El Sol

A CORUÑA

has been warning ships off the treacherous Costa da Morte since Roman times. It was entirely recased in the eighteenth century and there's not a trace of ancient stone to be seen. The latest victim of the coast was an oil tanker that went down in 1993; only a typically vicious storm saved the region from absolute ecological disaster, by breaking up the slick.

At the north end of the huge Praia del Orzán is the superbly designed **Museo Domus** (Mon–Sat summer 11am–9pm, winter 10am–7pm, Sun 11am–2.30pm; 400ptas), the museum of mankind. It's mostly aimed at children, but adult visitors may also find the playful interactive displays on how the human mind and body works seductive. The joint entry ticket also get you in to the less-interesting **Casa de las Sciencias** (same hours), an interactive science museum in Parque de Santa Margarita, out towards the bus station.

Eating, drinking and nightlife

The chain of small streets leading west from Praza de María Pita, from c/Franja, through to c/La Galera, c/Los Olmos and c/Estrella, are crowded with **bars** that, at their best, offer some of Spain's finest seafood, and excellent *tapas*. The **late-night** scene moves to the other side of the isthmus around the two beaches of Praia de Ríazor and Praia do Orzán; try the bars *Grietas*, *Cotobelos* or *Latino*, all on the Pasadizo Orzán (just off the Praia do Orzán, towards the Rotonda do Matadero). At the other end of the bay you can dance the night away in the *discoteca*, *Praia Club*, on the seafront Avenida de Pedro Barrić da Maza. Inland, the more yuppified c/de Juan Florez has jazz, salsa and the perennial *Pirámide* nightclub. Five kilometres out of town, the bars and clubs at **Praia Santa Cristina**, a lovely wooded spit of sand further up the *ría*, are lively throughout the summer. You can pick up a bus from the main station until 10pm, or a boat from the Darsena de la Marina until 8pm, but once there you'll either have to stay the course until the following morning or get a taxi back to town.

Inland to Santiago

The **Camino de Santiago**, the pilgrims' route, is the longest-established "tourist" route in Europe, and its final section through Galicia provides a fair representation of the medieval pilgrimage to the thousands who walk it every year, armed with the traditional staff and the shell emblem of St James. Hundreds more cycle the route, and it's possible to drive, too, although this is the least satisfying way of making the journey, offering tantalizing glimpses of ancient footpaths winding through woods as the road and footpath intertwine and then separate. Both routes are well-signposted with yellow scallop shell symbols, and local buses cover much of the road route, a boon to the footsore. Basic hostels for pilgrims are set up along the way, with priority given to walkers. Walking or cycling, the *camino* is a tough but unforgettable experience. Local Turismo offices have lists of the hostels and special pilgrim facilities (there are phone lines for medical emergencies); you'll also need a hat to guard against the hot sun, rainwear against *gallego* deluges, and a big stick to keep the dogs at bay.

The Pilgrim Route branches off the main Ponferrada–Lugo road at the **Pedrafita do Cebreiro** pass which marks the *gallego* frontier. This is a desolate spot, where hundreds of English soldiers froze or starved to death during Sir John Moore's retreat towards A Coruña in 1809. In such a forbidding landscape, you can only be impressed by the sheer scale of work that medieval builders put into providing spiritual and material amenities for the pilgrims. Crumbling castles, convents and humble inns line the road, and it's not hard to imagine what a welcome sight each must have been.

Cebreiro

The village of **CEBREIRO** itself is quite appallingly situated to catch the worst of the *gallego* wind and snow – not that you would realize that on one of the rare fine days of summer. It's highly picturesque, an undulating settlement of thatched stone huts (*pallozas*) surrounding a stark ninth-century church. No one actually lives in the *pallozas* any more, which are maintained as a national monument, with a guide on site to answer visitors' questions. In high season up to 1000 people per day pass this way; at other times it feels as remote as it ever did, and it's even possible to take refuge for the night in the former monastery next to the church. There are similar villages in the vicinity, where a few farmers still choose to live in the ancient dwellings; their children, however, seem to be unanimous in the desire to move away in pursuit of creature comforts, and the old way of life must surely be coming to an end.

Following the Pilgrim Route through Galicia

Many of the places along the Pilgrim Route that medieval travellers stopped at are now little more than ruins, but some survive. For example, the **Monasterio de Samos** (daily 10.30am–1pm & 4.30–7pm), 40km west of Cebreiro, famous for its library in the Middle Ages, and badly damaged by fire in 1951, has been restored, and its *hospedería* re-opened for pilgrims. Its moss-covered exterior, pierced only by two small barred windows, leads to two sunny and peaceful cloisters.

The once-great monastery of **Sobrado dos Monxes** (daily 10.15am–1.30pm & 4.15–6.45pm), midway between Lugo, Santiago and Betanzos, was also allowed to decay for a long time, but the provincial government is beginning to repair and restore it, and with your own transport this remains a highly worthwhile detour. After the empty approach road, the huge cathedral church with its strong west towers comes as a dramatic shock. The range of the abbey buildings proclaims past royal patronage, their scale emphasized by the tiny village below. The church itself sprouts flowers and foliage from every niche and crevice, its honey-coloured stone blossoming with lichens and mosses. Within, all is immensely grand – long, uncluttered vistas, mannerist Baroque, and romantic gloom; there are superb, worm-endangered choir stalls (once in Santiago cathedral), and, through a small arch in the north transept, a small, ruined Romanesque chapel. These are the highlights, but take time to explore the outbuildings, too, including a magnificent thirteenth-century kitchen, in good condition and imaginatively lit, with a massive chimney flue. A small community of monks maintain the monastery and operate a small shop.

Equipped with a handful of *hostales* and cafés, **SARRÍA** makes a logical stopover on this part of the *camino*; try the *Londres*, Calvo Sotelo 153 (☎982 532456, fax 982 533006; ④). The lower part of town is unimpressive, but old Sarría straggles gloriously uphill, topped by a (privately owned) castle. Further along the route, the whole town of **PORTOMARÍN** was flooded by the damming of the Minho, but its Templar castle and church were carried stone by stone to a new site further up the hillside.

Lugo

The Camino de Santiago bypassed **LUGO**, although it was already an ancient city even a thousand years ago. Built on a Celtic site above the Minho (and named after the Celtic sun god Lug), it is the only Spanish town to remain completely enclosed within superb **Roman walls**. These are ten to fifteen metres high, with 85 circular towers along a circuit of almost three kilometres, and are broad enough to provide a pleasant thoroughfare for walks around the city. Sadly, insensitive building has blocked out

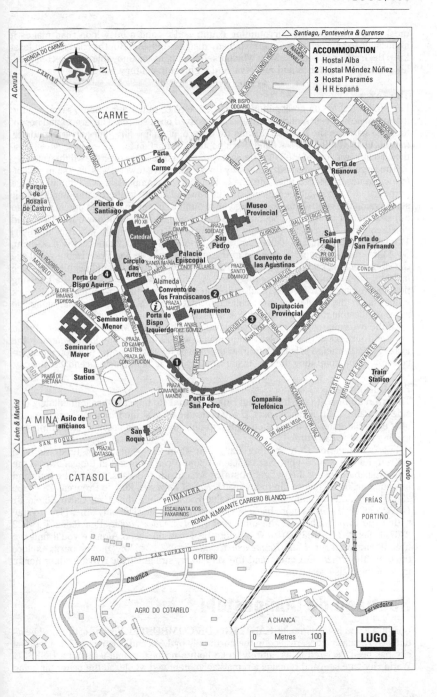

△ Santiago, Pontevedra & Ourense

ACCOMMODATION
1 Hostal Alba
2 Hostal Méndez Núñez
3 Hostal Paramés
4 H H España

LUGO

most of the views of the surrounding countryside – and a busy loop road makes it impossible to appreciate the walls from any distance outside. But the road does at least keep the traffic out of the centre, which itself maintains an enjoyable if neglected medley of cultivated patches and medieval and eighteenth-century buildings.

The Town

Lugo may be short on great sights, but it's a fine place to wander around, savouring the many granite staircases, narrow arcades and relaxed open spaces. The largest and best of the city's gardens, the **Parque Rosalia de Castro**, has a fine little café and weekend performances by the local brass band. It's a popular destination for the evening *paseo*, positioned a little way out of the Porta de Santiago, with good views over the Minho valley.

The large mossy **Catedral**, flanked by three distinctive towers, was, like so many *gallego* churches, modelled after the one at Santiago de Compostela, with imitation here perpetuated by the eighteenth-century Baroque additions to the facade. Inside, choir stalls cramp the central space, forcing you around a ring of chapels, in one of which an imperial soldier in cherubic posture tramples a dying Moor. Walk down Rúa Nova and you'll come to Lugo's exceptionally good **Museo Provincial** (July & Aug Mon–Fri 11am–2pm & 5–8pm, Sat 10am–2pm; Sept–June Mon–Fri 10.30am–2pm & 4.30–8pm, Sat 11am–2pm; free), partly housed in the old Convento de San Francisco – you'll see the stone kitchen, complete with a fireplace big enough to sit in (and people did). Well laid out, the museum features *gallego* art, including a wonderful statue of a kneeling peasant woman, staff in one hand, priest in the other; Spanish contemporary work swiped from the Prado; an early collection of Galicia's Sargadelos china; alongside more predictable displays of Roman remains and ecclesiastical clutter.

Of the two squares, the graceful colonnades of the **Praza Maior** shelter some good cafés and a couple of reasonable restaurants (as well as the Turismo in the *galerías*); the Praza Santo Domingo is less inviting, watched over by a black statue of a Roman imperial eagle, commemorating the 2000th anniversary of Caesar Augustus's entry to the city.

Practicalities

The **train station** (to the north) and **bus terminal** (to the east) are immediately outside the walls, a fair distance apart. If you enter the town at the **Porta de Santiago**, the best of its old gates, you can then climb up onto the most impressive stretch of wall, leading past the cathedral.

Lugo's **Turismo** (July & Aug daily 9am–2pm & 4–8pm; Sept–June Mon–Fri 9.30am–1.30pm & 4.30–6pm, Sat 10.30am–1.30pm) can be found in the *galerías* of the Praza España. Most of the budget **hostales** are outside the walls, around the train and bus stations, but it's more fun to be inside. *Hostal Paramés*, Rúa do Progreso 28 (☎982 226251; ③), offers comfortable, good-value rooms, while the *Alba*, Calvo Sotelo 31 (☎982 226056; ②–③), is more basic but perfectly adequate. The only other place to stay within the town walls is at the upmarket *Hotel Méndez Núñez*, Rúa Raiña 1 (☎982 230711, fax 982 229738; ⑥). Just outside the Porta do Bispo Aguirre you'll find the friendly and well-run *Hotel Residencia España* (☎982 231540; ④). For **bars**, explore those on the Praza do Campo and the very long, straight **Rúa Nova** leading north; most of them also serve *tapas*.

Santiago de Compostela

Built in a warm golden granite, **SANTIAGO DE COMPOSTELA** is one of the most beautiful of all Spanish cities, rivalled in the north only by León and Salamanca. The medieval city has been declared in its entirety to be both a national monument and a UNESCO World Heritage site, and remains a remarkably integrated whole, all the better for being almost completely pedestrianized. The buildings and the squares, the long stone arcades and the statues, are hewn from the same granite blocks and blend imperceptibly one into the other, often making it impossible to distinguish ground level from raised terrace.

The **pilgrimage** to Santiago captured the imagination of Christian Europe on an unprecedented scale. At the height of its popularity, in the eleventh and twelfth centuries, the city was receiving over half a million pilgrims each year. People of all classes came to visit the supposed shrine of Saint James the Apostle (Santiago to the Spanish, Saint Jacques to the French), making this the third holiest site in Christendom, after Jerusalem and Rome.

The atmosphere of the place is much as it must have been in the days of the pilgrims, with tourists now as likely to be attracted by Santiago's art and history as by religion. Not that the function of pilgrimage here is dead. It fell into decline with the Reformation – or as the local chronicler Molina reported, "the damned doctrines of the accursed Luther diminished the number of Germans and *wealthy* English" – but fortunes have revived of late. Each year at the **Festival of St James** (see p.479) on July 25, there is a ceremony dedicating the country and government to the saint at his shrine, and recent pilgrims have included Generals de Gaulle and Franco, and, to put his seal on the myth, Pope John Paul II (in 1982). Years in which the saint's day falls on a Sunday are designated "Holy Years", and the activity becomes even more intense; the next Holy Years are 1999 and 2004.

With its large population of students, most of whom live in the less appealing modern city slightly downhill, Santiago is always a lively place to visit, far more than a mere historical curiosity. Uniquely, it's also a city that's at its best in the rain; in fact it's situated in the wettest fold of the *gallego* hills, and suffers brief but constant showers. Water glistens on the facades, gushes from the innumerable gargoyles, and flows down the streets. As a result vegetation sprouts everywhere, with the cathedral coated in orange and yellow mosses, and grass poking up from the tiles and cobbles. It's also a manageable size – you can wander fifteen minutes out of town and reach wide open countryside. You may well find yourself staying longer than you'd planned, particularly if you arrive when the great July 25 Festival is in full swing.

Arrival, orientation and information

Arriving at the **bus station** you are 1km or so northeast of the town centre; bus #10, on to which everyone climbs, will take you in to Praza de Galicia. If you're walking, the easiest way into town is to turn right as you exit the bus station and walk down the Rúa de Rodriguez Vigun as far as the second roundabout; here, take the second right up Rúa dos Concheiros, which becomes Rúa de San Pedro, leading to the Porta do Camiño. Santiago is a major nexus for buses; as well as comprehensive local services, buses run to Portugal, France, Switzerland and England. The **train station** is a shorter distance from the centre; if you arrive here, simply walk (or take a bus) up Rúa do Horreo directly to the Praza de Galicia. Labacolla **airport** (☎981 547500) is some 13km out east on the road to Lugo. Eleven buses a day run into the centre via the train and bus stations; you can also pick the bus up on Rúa Xeneral Pardiñas opposite the the Iberia office at number 24. The **Turismo**, at Rúa do Vilar 43 (Mon–Fri 10am–2pm & 4–7pm, Sat 11am–2pm & 5–7pm, Sun 11am–2pm; ☎981 584081), can provide complete lists of accommodation and facilities. There is also a less useful municipal office on the Praza de Galicia.

Accommodation

You should have no difficulty finding an inexpensive **room** in Santiago, though note that *pensiones* here are often called *hospedajes*, as elsewhere in Galicia. The biggest concentration of places is on the three parallel streets leading down from the cathedral: Rúa Nova, Rúa do Vilar, and Rúa do Franco (this last named after the French pilgrims,

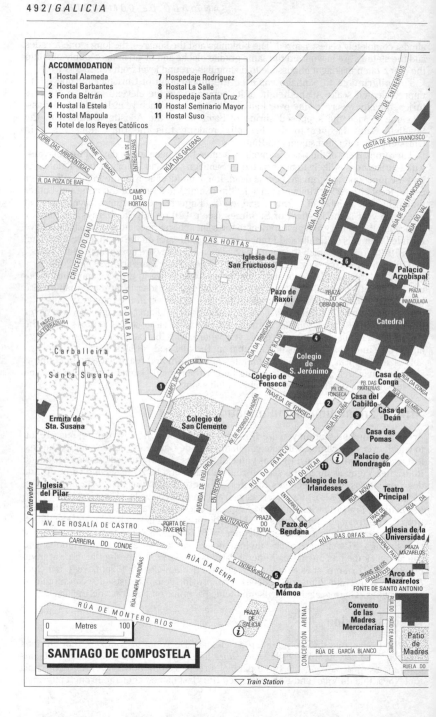

ACCOMMODATION

1 Hostal Alameda
2 Hostal Barbantes
3 Fonda Beltrán
4 Hostal la Estela
5 Hostal Mapoula
6 Hotel de los Reyes Católicos
7 Hospedaje Rodríguez
8 Hostal La Salle
9 Hospedaje Santa Cruz
10 Hostal Seminario Mayor
11 Hostal Suso

SANTIAGO DE COMPOSTELA

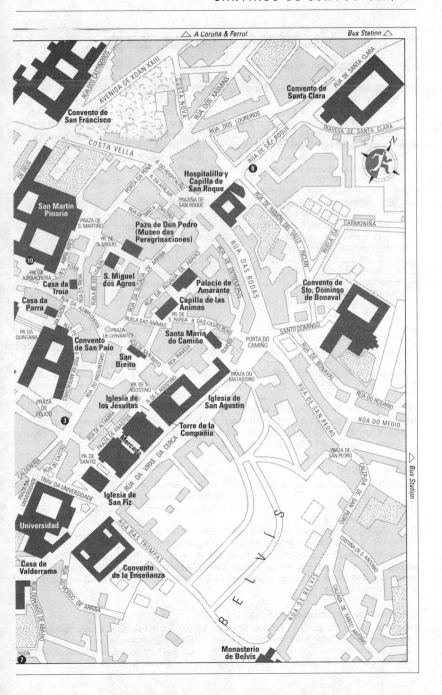

△ A Coruña & Ferrol   Bus Station △

Convento de Santa Clara

RÚA DE SANTA CLARA

TRAVESA DE SANTA CLARA

CARMONIÑA

RÚA DOS CASTIÑEIROS

AVENIDA DE XOÁN XXIII

COSTA NOVA

RÚA DOS XASMINS

RÚA DOS LOUREIROS

RÚA DE SAN ROQUE

Convento de San Francisco

COSTA VELLA

DE DEUS

PORTA DA PENA

R. DO HOSPITALIÑO

R. DA ATALAIA

RÚA DE SANTA CRISTINA

Hospitalillo y Capilla de San Roque

PRAZIÑA DE SAN ROQUE

RÚA DE RAMÓN DEL VALLE - INCLÁN

RUELA DA

San Martín Pinario

PRAZA DE S. MARTIÑO

PR DE S. MIGUEL

Pazo de Don Pedro (Museo das Peregrinaciones)

RÚA DE ENTREMURAS

RÚA DAS RODAS

Convento de Sto. Domingo de Bonaval

DAS ÁGRILARES

RÚA DE SAN XOÁN

RÚA DA TROIA

RÚA DE XERUSALÉN

RÚA DA ALGALIA DE ARRIBA

RÚA DA ALGALIA DE ABAIXO

PR. DA AZABACHERÍA

Casa da Troia

S. Miguel dos Agros

Palacio de Amarante

Capilla de las Ánimas

Casa da Parra

VÍA SACRA

RÚA DA AZABACHERÍA

RUELA DAS ÁNIMAS

PR. DE S. PARGA

R. DAS CASAS REAIS

SANTO DOMINGO

RÚA DE BONAVAL

PR. DA QUINTANA

Convento de San Paio

PRAZA DE CERVANTES

RÚA DE SAN BIEITO

Santa María do Camiño

OLARRIBA

PORTA DO CAMIÑO

RÚA DO ROSARIO

RÚA DE SAN PAIO DE ANTEALTARES

RÚA DO PREGUNTOIRO

San Bieito

RÚA TRAVESA

PRAZA DO MATADOIRO

RÚA DO MEDIO

PRAZA DE FEIXOO

PR DE S. AGOSTIÑO

R. DE S. AGOSTIÑO

Iglesia de los Jesuitas

Iglesia de San Agustín

RÚA DE ALTAMIRA

PRAZA DE ABASTOS

Mercado

Torre de la Compañía

RÚA DE SAN PEDRO

PRAZA DE SAN PEDRO

△ Bus Station

CALDERERÍA

RÚA D'O CASTRO

PR. DE SAN FIZ

RÚA DA VIRXE DA CERCA

CALZADA DE SAN PEDRO

PRAZA DA UNIVERSIDADE

TRAV. DA UNIVERSIDADE

Iglesia de San Fiz

COSTIÑA DE S. ANTONIO

Universidad

RÚA DAS TROMPAS

RÚA DE BELVÍS

CALZADA DE SANTO ANTONIO

Casa de Valderrama

RÚA DO PEXIGO DE ARRIBA

RÚA DO PEXIGO DE ABAIXO

Convento de la Enseñanza

BELVÍS

PISÓN

Monasterio de Belvís

❼   ❿   ❽   ❸

THE PILGRIMAGE TO SANTIAGO

The great **pilgrimage to Santiago** was the first exercise in mass tourism. Although the shrine was visited by the great – Fernando and Isabella, Carlos V, Francis of Assisi – you didn't have to be rich to come. The various roads through France and Northern Spain which led here, collectively known as El Camino de Santiago (The Way of Saint James, or the Pilgrim Route), were lined with monasteries and charitable hospices for the benefit of the pilgrims. Villages sprang up along the route, and an order of knights was founded for the pilgrims' protection. There was even a guidebook – the world's first – written by a French monk called Aymery Picaud, which recorded, along with water sources and places to stay, such facts as the bizarre sexual habits of the Navarrese Basques (who exposed themselves when excited, and protected their mules from their neighbours with chastity belts). All in all it was an extraordinary phenomenon in an age when most people never ventured beyond their own town or village.

Why did they come? Some, like Chaucer's Wife of Bath, who had "been in Galicia at Seynt Jame", had their own private reasons: social fashion, adventure, the opportunities for marriage or even for crime. But for most pilgrims, it was simply a question of faith. They believed in the miraculous power of Saint James, and were told that the journey would guarantee them a remission of half their time in purgatory. Not for a moment did they doubt that the tomb beneath the high altar at Compostela Cathedral held the mortal remains of James, son of Zebedee and Salome and first cousin of Jesus Christ. It seems scarcely credible that the whole business was an immense ecclesiastical fraud.

Yet **the legend**, at each point of its development, bears this out. It begins with the claim, unsubstantiated by the Bible, that Saint James came to Spain, at some point after the Crucifixion, to spread the gospel. He is said, for example, to have had a vision of the Virgin in Zaragoza. He then returned to Jerusalem, where he was undoubtedly beheaded by Herod Agrippa. His body should, by all rights and reason, be buried somewhere in the Nile Delta. But the legend records that two of James's disciples removed his corpse to Jaffa, where a boat appeared, without sails or crew, and carried them to Padrón, twenty kilometres downstream from Santiago. The voyage took just seven days,

rather than the late dictator). Even during the July festival, there's rarely a problem, with half the bars in the city renting out beds, and landladies dragging you off on arrival; if anything, things can be more difficult out of season, when much of the cheaper accommodation is let long-term to students.

Budget options

Fonda Beltrán, Rúa do Preguntoiro 36 (☎981 582225). Attractive rooms in a beautiful, ancient house with friendly owners. The large living room has wonderful views of the cathedral. ①–②.

Hostal La Estela, Avda. Rajoy 1 (☎981 582796). Quiet, good-value *hostal* on a pretty street just off the Praza do Obradoiro. ③.

Hospedaje Rodríguez, Ruela do Pison 4 (☎981 588408). Simple budget rooms in a peaceful street off Patio de Madres, with a well-equipped kitchen for guests' use. ③.

Hospedaje Santa Cruz, Rúa do Villar 42 (☎981 582815). Large, basic rooms near the cathedral. ①–②.

Hostal La Salle, Rúa do San Roque 6 (☎981 584611, fax 981 584221). A modern students' residence, annexed to the Colexio la Salle, containing sixty or so small, functional rooms, all with private shower or bath. ③.

Moderate and expensive options

Hostal Alameda, Rúa do San Clemente 32 (☎981 588100, fax 981 588689). Smart, stylish rooms with polished floors, large windows, bathroom and TV. Pleasantly located by a park. ⑤.

Hostal Barbantes, Rúa do Franco 1 (☎981 581077). Clean and light en-suite rooms, some with balconies overlooking a little square. There's a good bar and restaurant below. ④.

at once proving the miracle "since", as Ford wrote in 1845, "the Oriental Steam Company can do nothing like it".

At this stage the body was buried, lost and forgotten for the next 750 years. It was redis-covered at Compostela in 813, at a time of great significance for the Spanish church. Over the preceding century, the Moors had swept across the Iberian peninsula, gaining control over all but the northern mountain kingdom of Asturias, and in their campaigns they had introduced a concept entirely new to the West: *jihad*, or holy war. They also drew great strength from the inspiration of their champion, the Prophet Muhammad, whose death (in 632) was still within popular memory and a bone from whose body was preserved in the Great Mosque of Córdoba. Thus the discovery of the bones of Saint James, under a buried altar on a site traditionally linked with his name, was singularly opportune. It occurred after a hermit was attracted to a particular spot on a hillside by visions of stars, and the hill was known thereafter as Compostela, from the Latin *campus stellae*, meaning "field of stars". Alfonso II, king of Asturias, came to pay his respects, built a chapel, and the saint was adopted as the champion of Christian Spain against the Infidel.

Within decades the saint had appeared on the battlefield. Ramiro I, Alfonso's succes-sor, swore that he had fought alongside him at the Battle of Clavijo (844), and that the saint had personally slaughtered 60,000 Moors. Over the next six centuries *Santiago Matamoros* (Moor-killer) manifested himself at some forty battles, even assisting in the massacre of American Indians in the New World. It may seem an odd role for the fish-erman-evangelist, but presented no problems to the Christian propagandists who por-trayed him most frequently as a knight on horseback in the act of dispatching whole clutches of swarthy, bearded Arabs with a single thrust of his long sword. (With con-summate irony, when Franco brought his expert Moroccan troops to Compostela to ded-icate themselves to the overthrow of the Spanish Republic, all such statues were dis-creetly hidden under sheets.)

The cult of Santiago was strongest during the age of the First Crusade (1085) and the Reconquest; people wanted to believe, and so it gained a kind of truth. In any case, as Ford acidly observed, "If people can once believe that Santiago ever came to Spain at all, all the rest is plain sailing."

Hostal Mapoula, Rúa do Entremurallas 10 (☎981 580124, fax 981 584089). Good, friendly *hostal* with spacious, en-suite rooms (with TV and phone). ③–④.

Hostal de los Reyes Católicos, Praza do Obradoiro 1 (☎981 582 200, fax 981 563094). Spain's most famous *parador*, and reputed to be the oldest hotel in the world –see also p.497. ⑧.

Hostal Seminario Mayor, Praza da Inmaculada 5 (☎981 583008 or 981 572880). Students' resi-dence open as a hotel in summer. Rooms are basic for the price, but the setting, in a stunning for-mer Benedictine monastery, is superb. ④.

Hostal Suso, Rúa do Vilar 65 (☎981 586611). Neat, comfortable *hostal*, with a good bar-restaurant downstairs, located in a lively street, a few doors along from the Turismo. ④.

Camping

Camping As Cancelas (☎981 580266). Open all year and within reasonable walking distance of the town (2.5km northeast of the cathedral). Reached via the road to A Coruña, branching off at the Avda. del Camino Francés; the route is also served by regular buses to the airport and the city bus #9.

Camping Las Sirenas (☎981 898722). Reasonable second choice 6km out on the Santa Comba road, with less frequent connecting buses.

The cathedral

All roads to Santiago lead to the **Catedral**. And this, as Jan Morris asserts, "is still, as it was for those ancient pilgrims, one of the great moments of travel". Traditionally the first member of a party of pilgrims to catch sight of their goal would cry "Mon Joie!"

and become "king" of the group; the hill on the eastern side of Santiago thus became known as "Mountjoy". But you first appreciate the sheer grandeur of the cathedral upon venturing into the vast expanse of the Praza do Obradoiro. Directly ahead stands a fantastic Baroque pyramid of granite, flanked by immense bell towers and everywhere adorned with statues of Saint James in his familiar pilgrim guise with staff, broad hat, and scallop-shell badge. This is the famous **Obradoiro facade**, built in the mid-eighteenth century by an obscure Santiago-born architect, Fernando Casas y Novoa. No other work of Spanish Baroque can compare with it, nor with what Edwin Mullins (in *The Road to Compostela*) sublimely calls its "hat-in-the-air exuberance".

The main body of the cathedral is Romanesque, rebuilt in the eleventh and twelfth centuries after a devastating raid by the Muslim vizier of Córdoba, al-Mansur, in 977. He failed to find the body of the saint (perhaps not surprisingly), but forced the citizens to carry the bells of the tower to the mosque at Córdoba – a coup which was later dramatically reversed (see p.280). The building's highlight – indeed one of the great triumphs of medieval art – is the **Pórtico de Gloria**, the original west front, which now stands inside the cathedral behind the Obradoiro. Completed in 1188 under the supervision of one Maestro Mateo, this was both the culmination of all Romanesque sculpture and a precursor of the new Gothic realism, each of its host of figures being strikingly relaxed and quietly humanized. They were originally painted, and still bear traces of a seventeenth-century renovation.

The real mastery, however, is in the assured marshalling of the ensemble. Above the side doors are representations of Purgatory and the Last Judgement, while over the main door Christ presides in glory, flanked by his Apostles (Matthew writing on his knees, Luke writing on a bull, John on an eagle and Mark on a lion), and surrounded by the 24 Elders of the Apocalypse playing celestial music. Saint James sits on the central column, beneath Christ and just above eye level in the classic symbolic position of intercessor, since it was through him that pilgrims could gain assurance of their destiny. To either side are the Prophets of the Old Testament, most famously Daniel, apparently smiling seraphically across at Esther on the other side of the portico. The pilgrims would give thanks at journey's end by praying with the fingers of one hand pressed into the roots of the Tree of Jesse below the saint. So many millions have performed this act of supplication that five deep and shiny holes have been worn into the solid marble. Finally, for wisdom, they would lower their heads to touch the brow of Maestro Mateo, the humble squatting figure on the other side.

The spiritual climax of the pilgrimage, however, was the approach to the **High Altar**. This remains a peculiar experience. You climb steps behind the altar, embrace the Most Sacred Image of Santiago, kiss his bejewelled cape, and are handed, by way of certification, a document in Latin called a *Compostela*. The altar is a riotous creation of eighteenth-century Churrigueresque, but the statue has stood there for seven centuries and the procedure is quite unchanged. (You also get a God's-eye view from up there, during services, of the priest and congregation.) The pilgrims would then make confession and attend a High Mass. You should try to do the latter at least, as a means of understanding Santiago's mystique.

You'll notice an elaborate pulley system in front of the altar. This is for moving the immense incense-burner, "**Botafumeiro**", which, operated by eight priests, is swung in a vast 25–30-metre ceiling-to-ceiling arc across the transept. It's stunning to watch, but takes place only at certain services and is unusual outside Holy Years. The saint's bones are kept in a **crypt** beneath the altar. They were lost for a second time in 1700, having been hidden before an English invasion, but were rediscovered during building work in 1879. In fact they found three skeletons, which were naturally held to be those of Saint James and his two disciples. The only problem was identifying which one was the Apostle. This was fortuitously resolved as a church in Tuscany possessed a piece of Santiago's skull which exactly fitted a gap in one of those here. Its identity was confirmed in 1884 by Pope Leo XIII, and John Paul II's visit presumably reaffirmed official sanction.

The cathedral is full of collecting boxes; there are two on either side if you wish to kneel before the bones. But to visit the **Treasury**, **Cloister**, **Buchería** (Archeological Museum), and Mateo's beautiful **Crypt of the Portico**, you need to buy a collective ticket for 500ptas. The late Gothic cloisters in particular are well worth seeing; from the plain, mosque-like courtyard you get a wonderful view of the riotous mixture of the exterior, crawling with pagodas, pawns, domes, obelisks, battlements, scallop shells and cornucopias. Underneath the cloister in the Buchería, is Mateo's original stone choir and the remains of the thirteenth-century cloister. The crypt lies directly under the Portico de Gloria, accessed from beneath the main entry staircase, the museum and cloister entrance is just to the right on the cathedral square. These parts of the building – unlike the cathedral itself, which stays open throughout the day – are limited to set opening hours of 10.30am–1.30pm and 4–6.30pm (Sun 10.30am–1.30pm).

The rest of the city

The whole city, with its flagstone streets and arcades, is quietly enchanting, but if you want to add direction to your wanderings, perhaps the best plan is first to examine the buildings around the cathedral – the Archbishop's palace and Hostal de los Reyes Católicos – and then head for some of the other monasteries and convents. Finally, to get an overall impression of the whole architectural ensemble of Santiago, take a walk along the promenade of the **Paseo da Ferradura** (Paseo de la Herradura), in the spacious public gardens just southwest of the old part, at the end of Rúa do Franco.

Around the cathedral

The **Pazo de Xelmírez** (Palacio Arzobispal Gelmírez; 10am–1.30pm & 4.30–7.30pm; 200ptas) occupies the north side of the cathedral, balancing the cloister, with its entrance just to the left of the main stairs. Gelmírez was one of the seminal figures in Santiago's development. He rebuilt the cathedral in the twelfth century, raised the see to an archbishopric, and "discovered" a ninth-century deed which gave annual dues to St James's shrine of one bushel of corn from each acre of Spain reconquered from the Moors. It was enforced for four centuries, and repealed only in 1834. In his palace, suitably luxuriant, are a vaulted twelfth-century kitchen and some fine Romanesque chambers.

As late as the thirteenth century the cathedral was used to accommodate pilgrims (the *Botafumeiro* was used at least in part as a fumigator), but slowly its place was taken by convents founded around the city. Fernando and Isabella, in gratitude for their conquest of Granada, added to these facilities by building a hostel for the poor and sick. This, the elegant Renaissance **Hostal de los Reyes Católicos**, fills the northern side of the Praza do Obradoiro in front of the cathedral. It is now a *parador*, which means that unless you're staying here, it's not all that easy to get in to see the four superb patios, the chapel with magnificent Gothic stone carving, and the vaulted crypt-bar (where the bodies of the dead were once stored). However, although do-it-yourself tours are frowned on, you can always stop in for a drink in the bar (which isn't that expensive, unlike the restaurant).

You could easily spend half an afternoon just getting to know the squares around the cathedral. Each of these is distinct. The largest is the **Praza da Quintana**, where a flight of broad steps joins the back of the cathedral to the high walls of a convent. The "Porta Santa" doorway in this square is only opened during those Holy Years in which the Feast of Santiago falls on a Sunday. To the south is the **Praza das Platerías**, the silversmiths' square, dominated by an extravagantly ornate fountain, and to the north is the **Praza da Azabachería**, which at one time was the financial centre of Spain.

Central churches and museums

The enormous Benedictine **San Martín** stands close to the cathedral, the vast altarpiece in its church ("a fricassee of gilt gingerbread", according to Ford) depicting its patron riding alongside Saint James. Nearby is **San Francisco**, reputedly founded by the saint himself during his pilgrimage to Santiago.

East of San Martín, the fascinating museum of pilgrimage, the **Museo das Peregrinaciόns** (Tues–Fri 10am–8pm, Sat 10.30am–1.30pm & 5–8pm, Sun 10.30am–1.30pm; 400ptas), lies just off Praza de San Miguel in a sixteenth-century mansion, the Pazo de Don Pedro, also known as the Gothic House. It traces the history of the *camino*, the city and cathedral using excellent models and displays, and there is a comprehensive (and free) guide in English. The real jewel of the museum is the original copy of the twelfth-century *Codex Calixtinus*, a travel guide for pilgrims, which recommended routes and lodgings and pointed out the various dangers of the *camino*, such as the "malicious, swarthy, ugly, depraved, perverse, despicable, disloyal and corrupt" Navarrese.

Farther out of the city you'll find two more churches: to the north, Baroque **Santa Clara**, with a unique curving facade, and, to the east, **Santo Domingo**. This last is perhaps the most interesting of the buildings, featuring a magnificent seventeenth-century triple stairway, each spiral leading to different storeys of a single tower, and the fascinating **Museo do Pobo Gallego** (Mon–Sat 10am–1pm & 4–7pm; free), featuring *gallego* crafts and traditions. Many aspects of the way of life displayed haven't yet entirely disappeared, though you're today unlikely to see *corozas*, straw overcoats worn until recent decades by mountain shepherds. The exhibits are labelled in *gallego*, but guides are available in major European languages.

Santa María do Sar

Outside the main circuit of the city, the one really worthwhile visit is the curious Romanesque church of **Santa María do Sar**. This lies about a kilometre down the c/de Sar, which begins at the Patio das Madres. Due to the subsidence of its foundations Santa María has developed an extraordinary slant of about fifteen degrees, though it remains utterly symmetrical. It also has a wonderfully sculpted cloister, reputedly the work of Maestro Mateo. The church is supposed to stay open all day, but you may have to ask around in the buildings at the back.

Eating, drinking and nightlife

The presence of so many students in Santiago guarantees that the city has a healthy animation to go with its past. In term-time the main **bar** scene is down in the new town, particularly on Rúa Nova de Abaixo. The slightly more expensive old town is lively throughout the year, particularly if you're lucky enough to witness (or foolhardy enough to attempt) the legendary **Paris–Dakar race**: participants must start at *Bar Paris* at the top of end of Rúa do Franco and have one drink at each of the 48 bars on the way down to *Bar Dakar* on Rúa da Raiña, finishing by midnight. It's on this street that you'll find the best **tapas bars**, although after midnight people tend to move on to the pubs scattered around the city.

Gallego food is also plentiful and excellent in Santiago, with a plethora of good, solid **places to eat**, particularly on Rúa do Franco which is lined with seafood restaurants, most with your dinner displayed (live) in the window. If you're shopping for your own food, don't miss the large covered **market** held daily until 3pm in the old halls of the Praza de Abastos. Thursday is the main market day, when it is bustling. There are also a number of tiny delicatessens throughout the town which sell the traditional breast-shaped **cheese**, the rich *queso de tetilla*.

Santiago is also the best place in Galicia to hear the local Celtic **music**, played on *gaitas* (bagpipes), often by student groups known as *tunas* – they'll probably try and sell you a tape in Praza do Obradoiro.

Restaurants

Abellá, Rúa do Franco 30. Generous portions and good service – their *caldo gallego* is particularly good.

Bodegón de Xulio, Rúa do Franco 24. Good seafood place on this long restaurant-lined street.

Cabaliño do Demo, Porta do Camino 7. Imaginative vegetarian food and excellent 850ptas *menú*.

Casa Manolo, Rúa Travesa 27. A superb and justly popular student haunt, with a vast 750ptas *menú* and wide choice. No smoking. Closed Sun pm.

Cuatro Vientas, c/Santa Cristina 19. The cheapest restaurant in town and very friendly – try the *tortas*. Just behind the pilgrimage museum.

Don Gaiferos, Rúa Nova. Superb – but expensive – seafood in highly attractive cellar-like surroundings.

Toñi Vicente, c/Rosalía de Castro 24. Very expensive nouvelle cuisine with *gallego* elements; winner of the 1998 prize for Spanish cuisine.

Bars and tapas

Bar-Restaurante Entrerúas, Ruela de Entrerúas 2. Hidden up a tiny alley between Rúas Nova and Vilar, this bar offers excellent seafood *raciones*.

O Beiro, Rua da Raiña 3. An excellent place to try practically any Spanish wine.

Café-Pub Metata, c/Preguntoiro. Potent liquor-laced hot chocolate served up on the site of an old chocolate-making cellar.

Casa das Crechas, Via Sacra 3. Well-known folk bar, often with live *gallego*, Celtic or international folk music.

Fuco Lois, Rúa Xelmirez 25. Popular bar with eclectic live music, particularly mid-week.

Galo d'Ouro, Rúa (Cuesta) Conga 14. Cellar bar with a famous old-style jukebox.

O Gato Negro, Rua da Raiña. Unmissable old *tasca* that's been the place to go for the last eighty years.

Klausura, Rúa de San Paio de Antealtares 20 (San Pelayo). One of a cluster of popular summer-night pubs on the tiny square.

Ventosela, Rua da Raiña 28. Basic, but characterful bar where many of the *tunas* come to refresh their singing voices.

Listings

Airlines Labacolla airport is served by a number of airlines, including: Iberia (☎981 333111); Air Europa (☎981 594950); and Spanair (☎902 131415).

Airport information ☎981 547500.

American Express c/o Ultratur, Avda. de Figueroa 6 (Mon–Fri 9.30am–2pm & 4.30–7.30pm, Sat 10am–12.30pm; ☎981 587000).

Bookshops Variable second-hand selection, including foreign-language titles and book-exchange, from Librería Vetusta, Rúa Nova 31. Huge choice of new titles at Librería Follas Novas, Rúa Montero Ríos 37, in the new town.

Bus information ☎981 589090.

Car rental Operators include: Autos Brea, Rúa Xeneral Pardiñas 21 (☎981 565056); Avis, Rúa República Salvador 10 (☎981 573908); Autotur-Budget, Rúa Xeneral Pardiñas 3 (☎981 586496); and Atesa, Parador de los Reyes Católicos (☎981 581904).

Internet cafés *Ciber...¿Qué?*, Praza Cruceiro de San Pedro, halfway towards the bus station; *Ciber Dreams*, Rúa Diego do Muros 5, just south of Praza Roxa in the new town.

Laundry Lavandería la Económica is a self-service launderette at Rúa Ramón Cabanillas 1 (off Praza Roxa, a few blocks west of Praza de Galicia).

Post office The main office is on the corner of Travesía de Fonseca and Rúa do Franco.
Trains RENFE information ☎981 520202; information and booking also available from many of the travel agents in town.

The Costa da Morte

The wild, indented coastline to the west of A Coruña and Santiago is known as the **Costa da Morte** or Coast of Death; hundreds of shipwrecks litter the cliffs and rocks, and Celtic legends, here as at the Breton Finisterre, tell of doomed cities drowned beneath the sea. The climate and landscape are harsher than that of the Rías Baixas farther south, but beautiful nonetheless, with forests covering the mountain slopes and occasional fishing villages huddled up against the bleak headlands, battered by mighty Atlantic waves. For the medieval pilgrims this was the **end of the world**, and it remains relatively inaccessible and somewhat forbidding. Regular Transportes Finisterre buses connect all the places mentioned below, but can be as infrequent as one a day, and often leave very early in the morning. Although some stretches have been improved, roads tend to be slow and winding, and there are no trains. If you have your own car, or you're prepared to hitch (it's one of the best places in Spain to try), it's well worth following the length of the coastal road from A Coruña down to **Finisterre** and around to **Muros** and **Noia**. Celtic dolmens and *castros* (forts) abound, but you'll need a good map and plenty of patience to find most of them.

You should also be warned that even where the isolated coves do shelter fine beaches, you will rarely find resort facilities. While the beaches may look splendid, braving the water is recommended only to the hardiest of swimmers, and the weather is significantly wetter and windier here than it is a mere 100km further south.

Malpica to Traba

There are few potential stopping points immediately west of A Coruña (see p.485); your best bet is to get on a Transportes Finisterre bus and stay on it until you're well past Carballo (a busy inland road junction) after which the bus takes you to a succession of tiny seaside harbours. The first of these is **MALPICA**, crammed onto the neck of a narrow peninsula, with a harbour on one side and a marvellous – though exposed – beach hardly 100m away on the other. Out to sea are three desolate islands which make up a seabird sanctuary; access is possible only if you come to some informal arrangement with a fisherman. If you want a **place to stay**, *Hospedaje Choucina* (☎981 720223; ②) is fairly basic, but four of the rooms offer splendid sea views; the rooms at *Hostal Panchito*, Praza Villar Amigo 6 (☎981 720307; ④), are smarter and have private bath, but the views aren't as good; *Hostal JB* (☎981 721906; ④) is right on the beach. The best seafood **restaurants** here are *San Francisco*, Rúa Eduardo Pondal, where you can choose your dinner from a tankful of live sea creatures, and *O Burato*, overlooking the port off the square.

Unlike its neighbours, **CORME** lacks a developed seafront and so is hardly visited by tourists, which can be a relief in the high season. Across the headland from Malpica, it is set back above a deep, round bay, with three beaches just to the east: two in small rocky inlets and a larger one backed by sand dunes a walkable distance around the bay. The town itself has few bars or restaurants, only a few cramped streets leading to a minute *praza*. Even by the standards of local villages whose social structures are still clan-based, Corme is fiercely insular. In the 1940s and 1950s, it was the stamping-ground of *gallego* guerrillas, who swooped down from the hills to beat up the Civil Guard. In August 1993, 650 kilos of hashish appeared in the nets of a local fishing boat – to the amazement of no one. **CORME ALDEA**, an agricultural settlement on the hill above the port, has perhaps more charm than its sea-based sister, but back in Corme the view across the harbour from the back of *O Biscoiteiro* bar-restaurant, on Avenida Remedios, is lovely, and the food's good, too. There are **beds** available at *O'Cabazo*, c/Arnela 23 (☎981 738077; ③), if you want to stay.

Midway between Malpica and Corme, Spanish people set up tents around small fires on the sheltered **Praia de Niñóns**. Follow the signposts from Corme and turn left at the granite cross – then follow the road between fields of maize to the sea. There's a *fuente* (fountain) beneath the granite church that overlooks the beach, and a solitary bar that closes at night; otherwise, you'll need to bring your own supplies. Another great, though illegal, campsite is at **Praia de Balarés**, below Corme and approaching Ponteceso; a lovely sheltered inlet with a couple of high-season bars, and relatively safe swimming.

An ancient bridge crosses the River Anllóns at **PONTECESO**, just beyond the stone mansion that was the home of the *gallego* poet, Eduardo Pondal (1835–1917) – you'll see roads named after him all over Galicia. A long sweep of fine, clean sand is backed by café-lined streets at **LAXE** (pronounced *lashay*), which offers the area's safest swimming, thanks to a formidable sea wall which also protects a small harbour. *Bar Mirador*, off the square, is owned by the descendant of a family of photographers who began work here in the 1870s – there's a pictorial history of the area up on the bar walls. The only **places to stay** here are the pleasant *Hostal Beira Mar*, c/Rosalía de Castro 30 (☎981 728109; ③), and the *Hospedaje Pescador*, c/del Río (☎981 728195; ③), just off the plaza. Basic rooms are available at the *Restaurante Sardiñeira*, c/Rosalía de Castro 51 (☎981 728029; ②). Close by are two beaches, the deserted **Praia de Soesto**, which, though exposed, more than rivals the town beach, and a perfect cove, the **Praia de Arnado**. Nearby **TRABA** has its own massively long beach, the **Praia de Traba**, remote as anything, and backed by sand dunes and the jigsaw mini-fields of what is still basically strip-farming, although newly collectivized.

Camariñas to Finisterre

The stretch of coast from Camariñas to Finisterre is the most exposed and westerly of all, and has long been known as the end of the world, or *finis terrae*, since a Roman expedition under Lucius Florus Brutus was brought short by what seemed to them an endless sea. The savagery of the currents and weather are notorious, and even scavenging for shellfish along the rocks can be lethal. This is prime territory for hunting *percebes* (barnacles), which have to be scooped up from the very waterline, and collectors have been known to be swept away by the dreaded "seventh wave", which can appear out of nowhere from a calm sea. *Percebes*, shrivelled little things which look for all the world like mummified toes, are one of Galicia's most popular delicacies – you'll see them on sale in the markets at vastly inflated prices.

Camariñas

Picturesque **CAMARIÑAS** is back on the bus route: if you're planning a night's stay it has a definite edge over Finisterre. Curled around an attractive harbour containing a fishing fleet and the yachts of well-heeled visitors, Camariñas's buildings have white-painted, glassed-in balconies while the town sports a tradition in lace-making – you'll see old women, with lace-making pillows and extensive experience in markets, strategically placed to corner tourists.

For **accommodation**, *La Marina* (☎981 736030; ③), c/Miguel Freijo 3, at the beginning of the harbour wall, has clean rooms, great views and a good restaurant. There's also *Hostal Plaza* in the old market square (☎981 736103; ③) and, about 1km out of town on Area de Vilá (by the sandy beach), *Triñanes II* (☎981 736108; ③).

You can trek out from Camariñas to **Cabo Vilán**, five kilometres away, where a lighthouse rising out of a huge mansion guards a rocky shore; climb the adjacent rocks for a stunning sea view. Winds whip viciously around the cape, which is why it was chosen for the site of the towering experimental windfarm park next door to the lighthouse. Huge, sci-fi propellers spin in the wind – dramatic and, in the evening when lit by the searchlight beam of the lighthouse, rather eerie.

Muxía

On the tip of a rocky promontory across the *ría* from Camariñas, the small port of **MUXÍA** is nothing special, but from the Romanesque church on the hill above, there's a fabulous view to either side of the headland and a footpath down to the eighteenth-century **Santuario de la Virgen de la Barca**, once the second most important site of Galicia's pre-Christian animist cult after San Andrés de Teixido (see p.483). The cult was centred around the strangely shaped granite rocks at the furthest point of the headland, some of which are precariously balanced and said to make wonderful sounds when struck correctly; others are supposed to have healing power. In later times, the rocks were re-interpreted as being the remains of the stone ship which brought the Virgin to the aid of Santiago, an obvious echo of the saint's own landing at Padrón.

The best **place to stay** is the delightful *Casa Isolina* (☎981 742367; ①), a beautiful old house one block back from the seafront, with a vine-terraced garden behind. For great **seafood**, visit the tiny tumbledown *Casa Marujita*, up left from the far end of the seafront road.

On to Finisterre

The inland road (C552) from Carballo to Finisterre is surprisingly good, a result of the unprecedented burst of 1990s' road-building that is changing Galicia forever. **VIMIANZO** has spent years restoring its picture-postcard thirteenth-century castle (Mon–Sat: summer 10.30am–2pm & 4–8.30pm; winter 9am–1pm & 3–6pm), which now makes a wonderful setting for a new cultural centre with paintings, photographs and costumes.

Heading west, 2km past the industrialized port of Cée, **CORCUBIÓN**, 14km northeast of Finisterre, retains some elegance, though ribbon-strip development has now joined it with its uglier neighbour. For a cheap room, try the small *La Sirena*, c/Antonio Porrua 15 (☎981 745036; ②), above the bar of the same name just off the square, or, if you're after luxury, *El Hórreo* on the seafront (☎981 745550, fax 981 745563; ⑥). Halfway between Corcubión and Finisterre, a fine white-sand beach nestles in a small cove at **ESTORDE**, 1km short of the larger village of **SARDIÑEIRO**. Overlooking the beach is a pleasant **hostal**, the *Praia de Estorde* (☎981 745585; ⑤), and just across the road, a small wooded **campsite**, *Ruta de Finisterre* (☎981 746302; June–Sept).

Finisterre

The town of **FINISTERRE** (Fisterra) still feels as if it's ready to drop off the end of the world, but other than for its symbolic significance, there's no great reason to stay. It's no more than a grey clump of houses wedged into the rocks on the side of a headland away from the open ocean, but it does have a number of inexpensive **hostales**, the cheapest of which is the *Casa Velay* (☎981 740127; ②), overlooking the tiny bay just beyond the long harbour wall. *Hospedaje Lopez* (☎981 740449; ②–③) on the north side of the harbour has some rooms with balconies and views, and the *Rivas*, Carreterra de Faro (☎981 740027; ③), is excellent value. For more luxury, the *Cabo Finisterre* (☎981 740000, fax 981 740054; ④) has both a *hostal* and a hotel on c/Santa Catalina. For **food**, bypass the fancier restaurants with giant lobster tanks and head for the south side of the harbour where you'll find a cluster of places with *sardiñadas* (open-air sardine grills) and fresh *mariscos*.

The actual tip of the **headland** is a four-kilometre walk beyond, along a heathered mountainside, then through a newly planted pine forest. On the way out of town, stop at **Santa María das Areas**, a small, but atmospheric church with Romanesque and Gothic elements and a beautiful carved altar, which like the strange weathered tombs to the left of the main door, is considerably older than the rest of the building. At the cape, a lighthouse perches high above the waves and when, as so often, the whole place is shrouded in thick mist and the mournful foghorn wails across the sea, it's an eerie spot. When the sun shines, you're better steering clear of the ice-cream kiosks and shell-necklace sellers, and turning right up the zigzag road that climbs to the **Vista Monte do Facho**, high above the lighthouse, for stupendous views.

Ezaro, O Pindo and Carnota

Around **EZARO**, where the Río Xallas meets the sea, the scenery is marvellous. The rocks of the sheer escarpments above the road are so rich in minerals that they are multicoloured, and glisten beneath innumerable tiny waterfalls. Upstream there are warm natural lagoons and more cascades. In Ezaro itself, the *hostal* above the *Bar Stop* (☎981 7125777; ③), has inexpensive en-suite **rooms**, or you could continue another couple of kilometres to the little port of **O PINDO**. Beneath a stony but thickly wooded hill dotted with old houses, there's a small beach here and two **places to stay**, the *Hospedaje La Morada* (☎981 764870; ④) and *La Revolta* (☎981 764927; ④), with a recommended *marisquería*.

Towards **CARNOTA** the series of short beaches finally join together into a long unbroken line of dunes, swept by the Atlantic winds. The village of Carnota is 1km from the shore, but its palm trees and old church are still thoroughly caked in salt. Set in fields just outside town, *Casa Fandiño*, c/Calvo Sotelo 23 (☎981 857020; ②), is an excellent choice, with spotless, quiet rooms, while *Hostal Miramar*, Praza de Galicia (☎981 857016; ④), is nice but expensive.

Muros and Noia

Some of the best traditional *gallego* architecture outside Pontevedra can be found in the old town of **MUROS**. It rises in tiers of narrow streets from the curve of the seafront to a Romanesque church; almost everywhere you look are squat granite columns and arches, flights of wide steps, and benches and stone porches built into the housefronts. The old market building in particular is delightful.

Any of the **hostales** along the seafront Rúa Castelao would make for a pleasant stay, although you'll have to book ahead to get a sea-facing room; *Hostal Ría de Muros* (☎981 826056; ④) at no. 53, has spacious double rooms with views and balconies, while *La Muradana* (☎981 826885; ④), at no. 107 (where **buses** stop), is also recommended. There's also a **campsite**, *A Bouga* (☎981 826025), beside the beach 3km out at Louro. For **dinner**, *Pulpería Pachanga*, also on Rúa Castelao, has a stone-vaulted interior, fresh seafood and grilled meats, while the Plaza de la Pescadería one block back from the seafront has a couple of good café-restaurants under the arches.

The larger town of **NOIA** (Noya), near the head of the first of the Rías Baixas, is, according to a legend fanciful even by *gallego* standards, named after Noah, whose Ark is supposed to have struck land nearby. Scarcely less absurd is Noia's claim to be a "Little Florence", principally on the strength of a couple of nice churches and an arcaded street. Nevertheless, with its white sandy beach (about 1km from the town centre) and picturesque setting, Noia makes a pleasant enough stopover, and has a welcoming atmosphere. **Places to stay** include *Hostal Sol y Mar*, down by the small bridge, on Avenida de San Lázaro (☎981 820900; ③), a bit grim from the outside but with lovely views over the river. Smarter and pricier is *Ceboleiro*, Rúa Galicia 15 (☎981 820531, fax 981 824497; ④–⑤), opposite the grand *Ayuntamiento*.

The southern side of the Ría da Noia, which is sometimes called the "Cockle Coast", is dauntingly exposed, although in good weather the dunes serve as excellent beaches. At **BAROÑA** (Basonas), a rocky outcrop juts from the sand into the sea, and built on top of it you can still see the ruins of an impregnable pre-Roman settlement, with round stone huts enclosed behind a fortified wall. From here you can follow the increasingly bleak coastal road around into the Ría de Arousa, or take a short cut through the deep lush gorges along the AC301 to Padrón.

THE RÍAS BAIXAS AND THE MINHO

In the three lowest of the **Rías Baixas** (Rías Bajas) – the *rías* of **Arousa**, **Pontevedra** and **Vigo** –Galicia is expanding its tourist industry at an enormous rate. The summer sun is fairly dependable and the climate mild, avoiding the worst of the Atlantic storms, which tend just to brush the northwest corner. Each of these inlets is sheltered by islands and sandbanks offshore. They are deep and calm beneath mountains of dark pines, busy with bright fishing boats and mussel rafts, and fringed with little towns of whitewashed houses and safe bathing beaches. Most visitors are Spanish or Portuguese and although there is none of the overexploitation of the Mediterranean resorts, the coastline is becoming increasingly built up along the new roads, particularly around Vigo and Vilagarcía.

To the south, the slow, wide, mist-filled Río Minho marks the border with Portugal, and can be followed inland in search of unspoiled towns and hill-top monasteries. The chief pleasures of the region however, are to be found by the sea, and the two most obvious places to base yourself are **Pontevedra** and **Vigo**, each dominating its own magnificent and spacious *ría*.

The region is also famous for its wines, although they are less well-known outside Spain than the ubiquitous Rioja. The areas along the Minho and between Vilagarcía and Sanxenxo are particularly heavily cultivated, most famously with the pale Albariño grape which produces wonderful, flowery wine.

Ría de Arousa

Following the road and rail route south from Santiago, it will take you a while to realize that things are changing. **Padrón** and Catoira are not especially appealing, and in fact the train swings inland again at Vilagarcía without reaching the main resorts of this first *ría*, **Cambados** and **O Grove**. The northern shore is pretty inaccessible, and is still not sufficiently far south for travellers in search of beaches to feel confident of favourable weather.

Padrón and the north shore

According to legend, the corpse of Saint James arrived in Galicia by sailing up the Ría de Arousa as far as **PADRÓN**, where his miraculous voyage ended. The modern town along the highway has surprisingly little to show for the years of pilgrimage, except an imposing seventeenth-century church of Santiago in which, if you can find the boy in charge of the key, you can see the *padrón* (mooring post) to which the vessel was tied. Padrón is no longer on the sea – the silt of the Río Ulla has stranded it a dozen kilometres inland – and it is not an exciting place to stay, despite having several **hostales** and a top-quality octopus restaurant, the *Pulpería Rial* on Plazuela de Traviesas. The best-value accommodation is probably at *Hostal Jardín*, c/Salgado Araújo 3 (☎981 810950; ③), a beautiful eighteenth-century house overlooking a park.

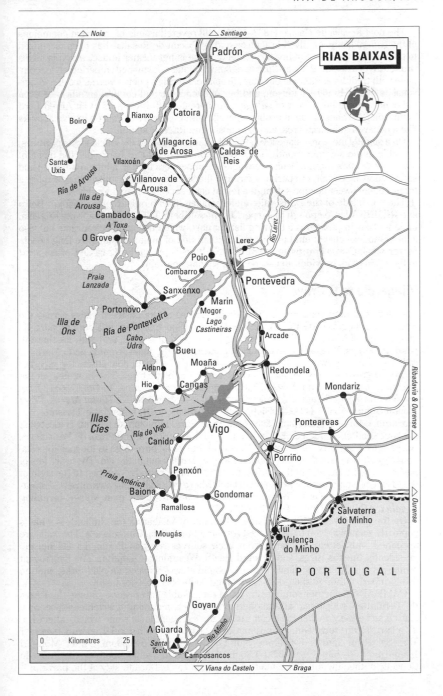

The poet Rosalia de Castro (1837–1885), still revered as one of the great champions of the *gallego* language, lived in Padrón and a "Circuit de Rosalia" has been organized to take in the main sites of her life. Chief of these is her former house, which is now a **museum** (Tues–Sun 9.30am–2pm & 4–8pm; 200ptas), furnished in period style, complete with traditional kitchen and huge fireplace. Rosalia's poetry was as fresh and personal as that of Emily Dickinson, and her public image and cultural significance even today have made her a sort of *gallego* poet laureate with the status of an Alfred Lord Tennyson. The house is an unpromising walk from the centre of Padrón into what looks like a decayed industrial area, and is opposite the RENFE station.

On a slightly more mundane level, Padrón is also renowned in Galicia for its **peppers**, available in the summer months only. What you get in a *tapas* bar under the name of *pimientos de Padrón* might look like whole green peppers fried in a bit too much oil and sprinkled with sea salt, but perhaps through the intercession of Santiago they acquire a transcendent sweet flavour – though a few in each serving are memorably hot.

The north side of the *ría* is quite underpopulated, with only Rianxo (Rianjo), Boiro and **RIBEIRA** large enough to support *hostales*. Ribeira (also known as Santa Eugenia, or Santa Uxia in *gallego*) is a thriving fishing port, which has good restaurants but also a lot of modern apartment buildings. On either side of the town there are long beaches; the small *Coroso* **campsite** (☎981 838002; June–Sept) on the Praia de Coroso, next to the C550 road, provides an escape from staying centrally.

Vilagarcía to O Grove

The slow, cluttered road around the Ría de Arousa offers postcard views across the water. Sprawling **VILAGARCÍA**, on the Coruña–Vigo train line, is a serious port, its quays lined with trucks. The drug-smuggling capital of Galicia, and with its share of passing tourists, Vilagarcía isn't short of a buck, and the main Avenida de la Marina – rather ugly and set well back from the sea – is sprinkled with chic **cafés**; the pleasant *Mesón da Marina* at no. 58, has a terrace under the plane trees. The **hostales** on the Avenida – *León XIII* at no. 7 (☎986 506500; ③) and *San Luís* at no. 16 (☎986 507120, fax 986 504735; ④) – are nice but pricey; better value is the attractive *Hostal Martis*, Praza Martín Gómez Abal 2 (☎986 505410, fax 986 504310; ③–④), behind the Turismo. The **Turismo** (Mon–Fri 10am–2pm & 5–9pm, Sat & Sun 11am–2pm & 5–8pm) is located at the south end of Avenida de la Marina, next to the market on the Praza de Pescadería. Buses leave from here for Vilaxoán (Villajuán), but you'll have to go to the main bus station to get further south to the wooded **Isla de Arousa** out in the *ría*. There are lots of pleasant beaches here, but the easiest to get to is the **Praia de Vao**, just to the right of the bridge as you cross over onto the island, where you'll also find a **campsite**, *Salinas* (☎986 527444; June–Oct). There are a couple of *hostales* in the main village, including *Benalua*, c/Méndez Núñez (☎986 551335; ④).

On the road towards Villajuán, about 1km out of Vilagarcía (on the left), is what is popularly acknowledged to be the best restaurant in Galicia, **Chocolate's**. The walls are festooned with letters of praise from such sources as Juan Perón, La Oficina del Presidente, Buenos Aires, and Edward Heath, Westminster, London. The flamboyant owner personally serves clients with two-pound steaks impaled on pitchforks, and the fish is superb – though the prices are around 3000–5000ptas per head.

CAMBADOS, further south again, has a remarkable paved stone square, the **Praza de Fefiñanes**, with beautiful buildings on all sides, including a seventeenth-century church and a *bodega* where you can sample the excellent local white wines; otherwise, it's a fairly sleepy town with an unremarkable seafront. The helpful **Turismo** (summer Mon–Sat 10am–2pm & 5–9.30pm, Sun 11am–1.30pm & 5–9.30pm; winter Mon–Fri 10am–1pm 4.30–7pm & Sat 10.30–1.30pm) is housed in a small booth on the Praza do Concello at the junction of the main roads. If you can't afford to stay at the **parador** –

the *Albariño* (☎986 542250, fax 986 542068; ⑦) – try *El Duende*, c/Orense 10 (☎986 543075; ④), just off the seafront and Praza do Concello, or the nearby *Pazos Feijoo*, c/Curros Enríquez 1 (☎986 542810; ④).

O Grove and A Toxa

The coast road curves back on itself to the resort of **O GROVE**, one of the few towns in Galicia whose principal raison d'être is the tourist trade. O Grove is specifically a "family" resort, full of inexpensive, small-scale bars, restaurants and places to stay, and not altogether without charm. There are dozens of **hostales**, most of them concentrated along Avenida González Besada, c/Teniente Domínguez, and Rúa Castelao, including the *Casa Otero*, Rúa Castelao 133 (☎986 730110; ③), and the *Casa Campaña*, in the same street at no. 60 (☎986 730919; ③). As for **eating**, there are plenty of *tapas* bars around.

There are a number of **campsites** on the road west across the peninsula between Reboredo and San Vicente, served by a regular bus from O Grove. Try *Miami Playa* (☎986 738012), *Sol y Mar* (☎986 738136) or the larger *Siglo XXI* on the Praia de Barrosa a little further along; these are packed throughout the summer, but there's room for everybody on the local beaches, the largest of which is La Lanzada (see p.511).

It's also possible to walk across a bridge to the pine-covered islet of **A TOXA** (La Toja), much-loved by Galicia's nouveaux riches, who stay in the couple of upmarket hotels and play the casino. Heavily coated with expensive holiday homes, A Toxa is fast becoming horrible, its little shell-covered church shedding cockles among a throng of pushy souvenir sellers. A Toxa actually owes much of its nationwide fame to the soap that's made from the salts of the spa here; Magno, the original brand, is pitch black and available from the shops on the island (and most Spanish supermarkets).

The inland route: Caldas de Reis

The motorway between Santiago and Pontevedra is expensive, though it does circumvent traffic jams around Padrón. If you take the inland road (the N550) you come, halfway between Padrón and Pontevedra, to the thermal spa town of **CALDAS DE REIS**, where there's a Roman fountain, the waters of which guarantee you will be married within a year should you be so foolhardy as to drink them. At the exact point where the road crosses the Río Umia, there's a gorgeous bar-restaurant, *O Muiño*, down under the bridge next to a broad, clear weir. The barbecues and the octopus are unbeatable; the one hazard is that a local fly-fisherman may land a trout on your plate.

SMUGGLERS

Smuggling is a long-established tradition in Galicia. Not all the boats you see sailing into the picturesque fishing harbours are carrying fish; not all the lobster pots sunk offshore are used for holding crustaceans; not all those huts on the mussel-rafts are occupied by shellfish-growers. All along the coast you'll find beaches known locally as the "Praia de Winston", notorious for the late-night arrivals of shipments of foreign cigarettes.

Recently, however, it has become more difficult to laugh off the smugglers as latter-day Robin Hoods. Taking advantage of the infrastructure developed over the years by small-time tobacco smugglers, and of the endlessly corrugated coastline frequented by innumerable small boats, the big boys have moved in. At first, there were stories of large consignments of hashish brought in at night; now heroin abuse has become a major concern. At some point, the Medellín cartel of Colombia began to use Galicia as the European entrance point for large consignments of cocaine. Several major police crackdowns, particularly on the Isla de Arousa where certain segments of the population seemed all of a sudden to have become inexplicably rich, have yet to reverse the trend that has locals worrying that Galicia is heading towards becoming "another Sicily".

Ría de Pontevedra

Of all the Rías Baixas, the long narrow **Ría de Pontevedra** is the archetype, closely resembling a Scandinavian fjord with its steep and forested sides. **Pontevedra** itself is a lovely old city, now set slightly back from the sea at the point where the Río Lérez begins to widen out into the bay. It's a good base for expeditions along either shore of its *ría* – such expeditions made necessary by the fact that the town itself doesn't have a beach. The **north coast** of the *ría* is the more popular with tourists, Sanxenxo (Sangenjo), the best-known resort with well over fifty hotels, often full of British and German visitors. If you want to avoid the crowds, head for the **south coast**, which stretches out past lovely beaches towards the rugged headland, ideal for camping in privacy.

Pontevedra

PONTEVEDRA is the definitive old *gallego* town, a maze of cobbled alleyways and colonnaded squares, with granite crosses and squat stone houses with floral balconies. There are some "sights" to see – the museum is good, and there are several interesting churches – but the real joy of visiting Pontevedra is to spend time in an ancient town so lively and lived-in. It's perfect for a night out, with the traditional local food and drink both at their best. The town is very compact, despite being the administrative capital of a district which includes the much larger city of Vigo. Pontevedra's growth was curtailed by the silting up of its medieval port (from which one of Columbus's ships supposedly sailed; there is even a long-standing claim that Columbus was born a *gallego* in Pontevedra). There are some slightly dismal industrial suburbs, but the old quarter, the *zona monumental*, remains distinct and unchanged, hard against the Río Lérez within the sweeping crescent of the main boulevards.

Arrival and orientation

Both the **bus** and **train** stations are about 1km southeast of the centre, side by side, and served by intermittent buses which will drop you at the **Praza da Peregrina**. If you're coming in on foot, walk north from the bus or train station up the Avenida Alfereces Provisionales, keep going straight at the first roundabout, up the Avenida de Vigo, and you'll end up in the Praza da Peregrina. The **Turismo** is nearby at c/General Mola 3 (summer daily 9.30am–2pm & 4.30–8pm; winter Mon–Fri 9.30am–2pm & 4.30–8pm, Sat 9.30am–2pm; ☎986 850814).

Accommodation

Finding a **place to stay** in Pontevedra should be straightforward, but if you get stuck the Turismo can help. The best-value places are in the winding streets of the *zona monumental*; the widest choice is among budget places, but there are also a couple of good upmarket options here. The new town offers a number of hotels on and around Avenida de Vigo, but these are mostly characterless and overpriced.

Casa Alicia, Avda. de Santa María 5 (☎986 857079). Good-value, spotless rooms in a pleasant house in the old quarter. ③.

Fonda Chiquito, c/Charino 23 (☎986 862192). The cheapest in town, but perfectly adequate. ②.

Bar O Fidel Pulpeiro, c/San Nicolás 7 (☎986 851234). Pleasant, well-kept rooms above a friendly bar with great *pulpo*. ②.

Casa Maruja, Rúa Alta (☎986 854901). Neat and comfortable *pensión* opposite Casa Alicia. ③.

Parador Casa del Barón, c/del Barón 19 (☎986 855800, fax 986 852195). The best – and most expensive – place to stay in Pontevedra. ⑦.

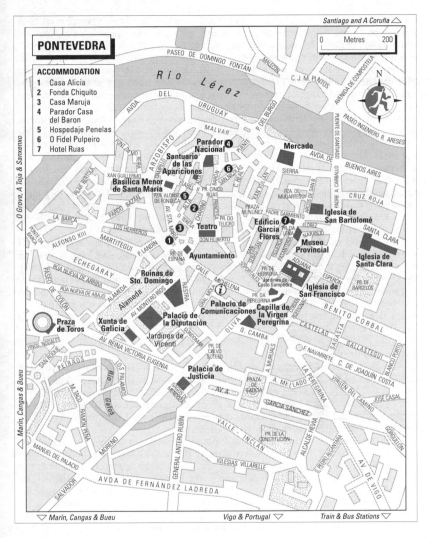

PONTEVEDRA

ACCOMMODATION

1 Casa Alicia
2 Fonda Chiquito
3 Casa Maruja
4 Parador Casa del Baron
5 Hospedaje Penelas
6 O Fidel Pulpeiro
7 Hotel Ruas

Hospedaje Penelas, Rúa Alta 17 (☎986 855705). Wafer-thin walls here, but the simple rooms are spotlessly clean. ③.

Hotel Rúas, c/Padre Sarmiento 37 (☎986 846416, fax 986 846411). A handsome old hotel in an excellent location, next to the museum. ⑤.

The Town

The boundary between Pontevedra's old and new quarters is marked by the **Praza da Peregrina** (site of a small pilgrim chapel built in the shape of a scallop shell) and the **Praza da Herrería** (known simply as the "Herrería"), a paved square lined by arcades on one side and rose trees on the other. To the east is the town's main church, **San Francisco**. Amid the surrounding fountains, gardens, and open-air cafés, are old women playing cards, teenagers courting and all the daily rituals of life in a town small enough for everyone to know everyone else.

A selection of narrow lanes leads north from the Herrería into the **Zona Monumental**. Following c/Figueroa, you come to the small and shaded **Praza de Leña**, the postcard image of Pontevedra, a typical *gallego* square complete with granite columns and a calvary. Two of its mansions have been joined to form an elegant and well-conceived **Museo Provincial** (June–Sept Tues–Sat 10am–2.15pm & 5–8.45pm, Sun 11am–1pm; Oct–May Tues–Sat 10am–1.30pm & 4.30–8pm, Sun 11am–1pm). Star exhibits include jet jewellery from Santiago de Compostela, which held a monopoly on the stone throughout the Middle Ages, pre-Roman gold, and a fair – though badly lit – selection of Spanish masters; Ribera, Zubarán and Murillo. The museum's real draw is a top-floor room in the second building devoted to the twentieth-century artist, caricaturist and writer Alfonso Castelao, author of *Sempre en Galizia*, the Bible of *gallego* nationalists and now a set text for the region's schools. His drawings, at their most moving when depicting pre-war poverty and the horror of the Civil War, celebrate the strength and resilience of the *gallego* people and their culture.

The covered **market** beside the river is an attractive old two-tier building, well worth taking a look at even if you don't intend to buy anything – as long as you can cope with the sight of disembowelled cows hanging from meathooks, and still-hairy muzzles poking out from buckets of blood. The fish stalls are full of glistening goodies, while the walls on all sides are stacked high with muddy piles of nameless edible greenery. Finally, the **Alameda** leading down from Praza de España is a grand promenade down to the sea, with a monument to Columbus where the river empties into the Atlantic.

Eating and drinking

The twisting streets of the *zona* are packed with tiny **bars** and **restaurants** and jammed late into the night with revellers. You'd probably do best to eat in the bars, although vegetarians will be glad to find a good restaurant, *Sabor Sabor*, on c/Santa Clara 33, just east of the *zona*. Platters of fish and jugs of rich white wine are available everywhere, particularly on c/Figueroa, which runs between the Herrería and Praza de Leña; *Bar Puerta a Puerto* and *La Chiruca* are recommended.

Try to end up at *Os Maristas*, in Praza I. Armesto, next to Praza de Leña, one of two unmarked bars on the right as you face the police station. This bar is sought after for the astonishing liqueur **Tumba Dios** (translated as "God falls down"), an esoteric blends of *aguardiente* (firewater) and *licor de café*, laced with sundry secret herbs and spices. The alcohol is devastating, the coffee invigorating, and the herbs verge on the hallucinogenic.

For late night drinking, the area around Praza das Cinco Rúas and down Rúa do Baron has drawn a young crowd with the disco-pub craze. If you're determined to see the dawn, *Carabás* is the best-known *discoteca*, on c/Cobián Roffignac.

The north shore of the Ría

To the north, 5km from Pontevedra, is the seventeenth-century Benedictine **Monasterio de Poyo**, with a *hospedería* (☎986 770000) and farther along the coast the village of **COMBARRO**, justly famed for its large collection of waterfront *hórreos*, resembling miniature chapels with their granite crosses. Beyond is the resort of **SANXENXO** (Sangenjo), the area's main venue for a serious summer night out. From 10pm onwards, the seafront bars and cafés are packed with revellers, the clubs playing Eurodance music to a lively crowd. You can judge the scale of things from the fact that there are over sixty hotels between here and the similar resort of **PORTONOVO**, but prices are high; you'd be lucky to find a room under 4000ptas.

A few kilometres beyond begins the vast **beach** of **La Lanzada**, a favourite with strong swimmers and windsurfers. In the summer there are temporary enclaves of cafés and restaurants, and **campsites** such as the recommended *Muiñeira* (☎986 738404), or *O Espiño* (☎986 738048); during the rest of the year it's left to the wild ocean waves.

The south shore and the Península do Morrazo

The southern side of the Ría de Pontevedra is less developed and has fewer visitors, although once past Marín (see below) it's quite superb. The first stretch, however, is off-putting in the extreme. Just outside (and upwind from) Pontevedra sits a monstrous paper factory, **La Cellulosa**, where a titanic yellow metal spider spouts mountains of sawdust and emits a staggering stench; on a bad day you can smell it fifty kilometres away. Plenty of orange buses run from Pontevedra's bus station, right around the headland to Marín.

Marín

Nearby **MARÍN** is not on first impression all that appealing. It's a very busy port, with the seafront cut off from the town by forbidding walls for most of its length, and is populated largely by bored cadets from the local naval academy. Even the wooded island in the middle of the *ría* belongs to the navy, and is inaccessible.

However, Marín does boast the best **churrasquería** in Spain, the *Cantaclara*, which is very cheap and almost impossible to find, housed in what looks like a deserted blue shed very near the harbour, about a mile back towards Pontevedra from the middle of town. The window display has been known to feature two completely skinned dead lambs, one wearing a pair of green plastic sunglasses and with its teeth firmly clamped into the throat of the other. Inside, there's a huge roaring flame from the wooden fire of the barbecue, and the restaurant itself is screened from the bar by stacked boxes of the Rioja house wine. The charcoal-grilled meat of all kinds is delicious.

Mogor, Bueu and beyond

Once past Marín, the scenery rapidly improves, the bay broadening into a whole series of breathtaking sandy coves. A narrow side road drops away from the main coast road immediately beyond the naval academy outside Marín, leading to three beaches. The second of these, the **Praia de Mogor** (on the bus route from Pontevedra), is perfect, with fields of green corn as the backdrop to a crescent of fine, clean sand. There are a couple of bars overgrown with vines, and the villagers' rowboats are pulled up in the shade of the trees next to some weird, bald rocks. One side is shielded by a thick headland of dark green pines; at the other end you'll find the rocks are deeply carved with religious and fascist symbols and slogans.

Interestingly, rocks all over the surrounding hills were carved by the same man, a shoemaker who spent the afternoons of his declining years glorifying God and Franco with a hammer and chisel on every available surface. In the late 1970s, when the carver was in his nineties, a professor found some carvings in Mogor and announced that they were prehistoric. The villagers said no, that's just the old shoemaker. So the professor and the shoemaker spent days combing the area, the shoemaker having to separate his carvings from those which had already been there. Some of the cruder stone spirals were duly authenticated as megalithic remains, and the professor wrote a book and made a TV documentary. The shoemaker died discredited.

BUEU (pronounced *bwayo*) is a quiet market town and port about 12km beyond Marín, and offers pleasant strips of **beach** stretching away from its rambling waterfront;

the quieter spots are round the headland to the west. **Accommodation** here is mostly expensive; you'll get little for less than 5000ptas in the summer, although the unmarked *Hostal Fazanes*, c/Eduardo Vincenti 29 (☎986 320046; ③) has cheap, basic rooms in the town centre. Other options include the *Incamar*, c/Montero Ríos 147 (☎986 320067, fax 986 320784; ⑤), or to the east, *A Centoleira*, Praia de Beluso (☎986 320896; ④).

A smaller road turns away from the sea at Bueu, towards Cangas, and is served by half-hourly buses in summer, but if you make your way along the coast, towards the village of **ALDÁN** and the cape of **Hio**, you'll find an unspoiled expanse of pine trees and empty beaches – an ideal place to go **camping** if you stock up in advance. Particularly worth following is the unpaved road to the huge boulders at **Cabo Udra**, where wild horses roam the hillsides and the waves come crashing down in deserted coves. For those without transport, it may be easier to access the more southerly areas via Cangas. Hio itself has Galicia's best-known granite *cruceiro* (not a "passenger liner" as the official brochure translates it, but a crucifix), looking down on the spectacular *ría* of Vigo.

Ría de Vigo

Following the main road south from Bueu, you cross the steep ridge of the Morrazo peninsula to astonishing views on the far side over the **Ría de Vigo**, one of the most sublime natural harbours in the world. This region was once a hotbed of witchcraft, although *gallegos* are careful to distinguish between *brujas* (malevolent witches) and *meigas* (wise women herbalists with healing powers). Tradition tells of a local woman who was accused of trafficking with the Devil by the Inquisition in the seventeenth century; she proved her claim to be a *meiga*, and was sentenced to stand outside Cangas church in her oldest clothes every Sunday for six months. Presumably she fell foul of the Holy Inquisition in one of its more lenient moods. Even today, you'll find charms against witches (in the shape of a clasped hand) on sale everywhere in Galicia, often next to crucifixes.

The *ría*'s narrowest point is spanned by a vast suspension bridge which carries the Vigo–Pontevedra highway; you'll see its twin towers from all around the bay. On the inland side is what amounts to a saltwater lake, the inlet of **San Martín**. The road and railway from Pontevedra run beside it to **Redondela**, separated from the sea by just a thin strip of green fields, and pass close to the tiny San Martín islands, once a leper colony and used during the Civil War as an internment centre for Republicans. The calm waters here are deceptive; somewhere under them lies a fleet of galleons lost in 1702. Seeking shelter from a storm, the ships foundered on hidden sandbanks and went down with the largest single shipment of silver ever sent from the New World.

The city of **Vigo** looks very appealing, spread along the waterfront, but apart from its possibilities for sleeping and eating, it's not a particularly interesting place to stay. If Vigo is your point of arrival in this region, one obvious alternative is to head down to the waterfront and get a **ferry** across to the little resort of **Cangas**; another would be to take a bus (the train doesn't follow the coast any farther) out to **Baiona**, at the edge of the ocean. Wherever you end up staying, be sure not to miss the boat trip out to the wonderful **Illas Cíes**.

Cangas and Moaña

CANGAS, where the road south from Bueu descends, is today a burgeoning resort, at its most lively during the Friday **market**, when the seafront gardens are filled with stalls. The town spreads perhaps 1km along the coast, though not up the hillside, to reach the **Praia de Rodeira**. The cheapest **rooms** in town are at *Hostal Belén*, c/Antonio Nores (☎986 300015; ③–④), and the *Playa*, Avda. de Orense 78 (☎986

303674; ④), but both of these fill quickly in summer. A **Turismo** booth is located at the port, behind the bus station (July & Aug daily 10am–2pm & 5–8pm, closed Sun pm).

The main cluster of **bars and restaurants** is around the port. *O Porrón* at Paseo de Castelao 15 (behind the fish market), and *Taberna O Arco*, on Plaza Arco, are two very good bars specializing in seafood, while the *Bar Celta* at c/A. Saralegui, up some steps slightly to the left of the jetty as you face the town, and looking out over the bay, is an excellent old-fashioned *tapas* bar whose *comedor* serves bargain, budget meals. You can monitor the ferries from here, and hurry down when the hooter announces a departure. A few doors along from *Bar Celta* is *O Balcón do Porto*, a wonderful little restuarant with excellent home cooking and great views out to sea. There's a pleasant, twenty-minute **ferry** trip (foot passengers only) to Vigo, half-hourly between 6am and 9pm (225ptas), with a reduced service on weekends. There are also ferry services (subject to irregularities) to the Illas Cíes (see below).

Hourly boats to Vigo (6am–9pm; 200ptas) also leave from **MOAÑA**, 5km along the coast. Similar in feel to Cangas, Moaña boasts a fine, long beach, but fewer facilities for travellers. **Places to stay** include *Hostal Prado Viejo*, c/Ramón Cabanillas 16 (☎986 311634; ④), with en-suite rooms and private parking, and *Hostal Antonio*, c/Méndez Núñez 2 (☎986 313684; ④), which has rooms with and without baths. The appeal of the Moaña trip is that you sail right alongside the *mejilloneiras* of the *ría*. These ramshackle rafts, perched on the sea like water-spiders and sometimes topped by little wooden huts, are used for cultivating mussels.

West of Cangas, the beaches and hills are stunning and all but deserted. In summer, hourly buses take you from Cangas to **Nerga**, from where it's a short walk to the huge sandy strip extending from the Praia de Nerga to the nudist Praia de Barra. There is also a 2pm bus (returning at 7.30pm) to **Donon** from where it's a two-kilometre walk to the Praia de Melide on the tip of the peninsula, an isolated cove backed by woods and a lighthouse, with superb walks along the cape.

Vigo

VIGO is a large and superbly situated city, dominating the broad expanse of its *ría*. Seen from a ship entering the harbour, it is magnificent, though once ashore you may find the views back out to sea to be its most attractive feature. It is so well sheltered from the Atlantic that the wharves and quays which make up Spain's chief fishing port stretch along the shore for nearly 5km.

Arrival and information

Vigo's **Turismo** is located at the port (Mon–Fri 9.30am–2pm & 4.30–8pm, Sat & Sun 10am–12.30pm, winter closed Sun; ☎986 810144), and offers a free map with accommodation marked on it. The **RENFE station** at the opposite end of town has direct services to Santiago, Barcelona and Madrid, and down into Portugal. **Buses** to all major destinations, including Baiona, use the terminal, a fair way out from the centre, at the junction of Avda. de Madrid and Avda. Gregorio Espiño. From the stop just outside the station entrance, buses #7 and #12 run infrequently to the central Porta do Sol, and #23 to c/Areal, just east of the port.

Accommodation

Places to stay tend to be reasonably priced and are concentrated in two main areas: up by the train station, and down by the port. The latter is more atmospheric and is also where you'll find the best restaurants and bars.

Hotel El Águila, Rúa Victoria 6 (☎986 431398). Friendly, old-fashioned hotel in the old area, with lots of charm. Some of the rooms (all en-suite) are small. ④.

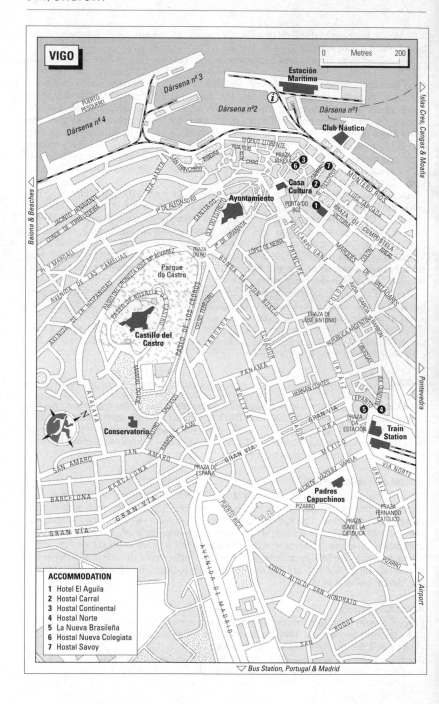

VIGO

0 Metres 200

Puerto Pesquero

Dársena nº 4

Dársena nº 3

Dársena nº2

Estación Marítima

Dársena nº1

Club Náutico

Islas Cres, Cangas & Moaña

Baiona & Beaches

MONTERO RÍOS

TEÓFILO LLORENTE

RIBEIRA

RÚA REAL

PRAZA IGREXA

6 3

7

SAN FRANCISCO

STA MARÍA

CHAO

Casa Cultura

2

LUIS TABOADA

PORTA DO SOL

1

PRAZA DE VICTORIA

PRAZA DE COMPOSTELA

Ayuntamiento

Pº DE ALFONSO XII

SANTIAGO

C/X DESTRUCTO

Pº DE GRANADA

PRAZA DO REI

POLICARPO SANZ

PRÍNCIPE

MÁRQUES DE VALLADARES

COLÓN

AREAL

Parque do Castro

PASEO DEL CRONISTA XOSÉ Mª ALVAREZ

PASEO DE ROSALÍA DE CASTRO

BEIRA DE DON BOSCO

PRAZA DE JOSÉ ANTONIO

AVDA GARCÍA BARBÓN

URUGUAY

REPÚBLICA ARGENTINA

JACINTO BENAVENTE

CONDE DE TORRECEDEIRA

PI Y MARGALL

AVENIDA DE LAS CAMELIAS

AVENIDA DE LA HISPANIDAD

Castillo del Castro

MARQUÉS DE VALLADARES

PASEO DE LOS PEROS

CELSO TERCEIRO

TARGADA

ECUADOR

PANAMÁ

BOLIVIA

HERNÁN CORTÉS

LEPANTO

5 4

PRAZA DA ESTACIÓN

Train Station

ATALAYA

SALCODS

RAMÓN Y CAJAL

Conservatorio

SAN AMARO

SAN AMARO

BARCELONA

GRAN VÍA

PRAZA DE ESPAÑA

ECUADOR

GRAN VÍA

CUBA

MÉXICO

ALCALDE VÁZQUEZ VARELA

VÍA NORTE

URZÁIZ

Pontevedra

BARCELONA

GRAN VÍA

PUERTO RICO

Padres Capuchinos

PIZARRO

PRAZA ISABEL LA CATÓLICA

PRAZA FERNANDO CATÓLICO

PIZARRO

Airport

GRAN VÍA

AVENIDA DE MADRID

COUTO ALTO DE SAN HONORATO

SAN

ROQUE

ACCOMMODATION

1 Hotel El Aguila
2 Hostal Carral
3 Hostal Continental
4 Hostal Norte
5 La Nueva Brasileña
6 Hostal Nueva Colegiata
7 Hostal Savoy

Bus Station, Portugal & Madrid

Hostal Carral, Rúa Carral 18 (☎986 224927). Reasonable budget rooms (if the owner isn't in, ask in the amusement arcade a couple of doors down, which he also runs). ②–③.
Hostal Continental, Bajada a la Fuente 3 (☎983 220764). Good en-suite rooms in a lovely location. ⑤.
Hostal Norte, Rúa Alfonso XIII 29 (☎986 223805). Conveniently located next to the train station; most rooms have bath, TV and phone, and there are some cheaper ones without. ④.
La Nueva Brasileña, Rúa Lepanto 26 (☎986 439311). Comfortable, recently refurbished rooms close to the train station. ③–④.
Hostal Nueva Colegiata, Plaza de la Iglesia 3 (☎986 220952). Well-kept *hostal* on a lovely central square. ③.
Hostal Savoy, Rúa Carral 20 (☎986 432541). A large and characterful *hostal*; probably Vigo's best budget option. ③.

The City

Today Vigo's passenger port may be declining, but it has kept the prime spot in the middle of this stretch of shore. This was where Laurie Lee disembarked "with the whole of Spain to walk through", a journey marvellously recorded in *As I Walked Out One Midsummer Morning*. Here, too, generations of *gallego* emigrants have embarked for and returned from South America, and Caribbean immigrants have had their first glimpse of Europe. Although, these days, the only tourists who arrive at the **Estación Marítima de Ría** are those who have come on the ferry from Cangas and Moaña, the steep, winding streets of the old city remain crammed with tiny shops and bars catering for the still-plentiful sailors.

The cobbled streets around the **Rúa Real** (once the main street, and what Todman calls "the best drinking street in Christendom") remain a focal point for visitors. Along the seafront early in the morning, kiosks revive fishermen with strong coffee, while there and in the nearby **market** their catch is sold: from early morning to mid-afternoon women stand at granite tables rooted in **Rúa Teófilo Llorente**, with plates of fresh oysters set out for passers-by. On **Rúa Carral** shops sell pocket knives and exotic marine souvenirs, and in the evening the myriad bars on all the tiny streets come alive. A surprising, old-fashioned red-light district still operates on the **Rúa Abeleira Menández**, tucked away behind the town hall.

For the most part, the **beaches** adjacent to Vigo are crowded and not nearly as appealing as those further along, or across the *ría* – and certainly not a patch on the Illas Cíes (see below). Heading south, however, the beaches of **Samil** and **Vao** are better, and very popular for late Saturday night revels; take bus #L15 or #L27 from Rúa Colón and return on the #LN. A little further on, the beach at **Canido**, 10km from Vigo, is also quite reasonable, and equipped with campsites (try *Canido*, ☎986 491920) and *hostales*, though it's spoilt by seaweed wrack.

Eating and drinking

Among the budget **restaurants**, *O'Meu Lar* on Rúa Fermín Penzal, off Rúa Carral, offers a decent set menu for around 800ptas. If you're prepared to pay 3500ptas and up, *El Mosquito* on the Praza A Pedra is a classy option. Virtually all of the **bars** in the old streets serve great *tapas*, but *Chavolas* (for cuttlefish) and *Taberna Ramón*, on Rúa Cesteiros, off the Praza Almeida, and *La Parra* on Rúa Alta (try the octopus) stand out. More expensive tastes will lead you to seek out the local delicacy, *anguilas*, the baby eels which come swimming up the Río Minho fresh from the Sargasso Sea, all ready to be eaten.

The Illas Cíes

The most irresistible sands of the Ría de Vigo must be those of the **Illas Cíes**. These three islands protect the entrance to the *ría*, and can be reached by boat from Vigo, Baiona and Cangas. The islands were once a refuge used by Sir Francis Drake when conducting pirate raids on Spanish shipping, and are now a nature reserve. One is an off-limits bird sanctuary; the other two are joined by a narrow causeway of sand, which forms a beach open on one side to the Atlantic and on the other to a placid lagoon. Most visitors stay on the beach, with its sprinkling of bars and a campsite in the trees, so it's easy to escape the crowds and find a deserted spot all your own – which can feel particularly remote on the Atlantic side of the islands. A long climb up a winding rocky path across desolate country leads to a lighthouse with a commanding ocean view.

The **campsite** (☎986 438358; June–Oct) is the only legal accommodation on the islands, so if you want to stay in midseason, phone ahead to make sure there's room. You have to buy a camping token before you get on the boat – this acts as a deposit (1000ptas per person), deducted from your camping bill; the difference is either made up or refunded when you leave the site. There is a small shop, as well as a couple of restaurants which aren't at all bad, but these are free to charge more or less what they choose, so you might prefer to take your own food and drink. In the summer there are ten **boats** per day **from Vigo** (Estación Marítima; hourly 9am–1pm & 3–7pm), the last one back leaving the islands at 8pm, with the return trip costing 2000ptas. In addition, there are four daily boats **from Baiona** (at 10.45am, 12.45pm, 3.45pm and 6.30pm) and there is a summer service from Cangas (you can call Vigo's Estación Marítima on ☎986 225272 to confirm all timetables). Only a certain number of visitors are allowed to go to the Cíes on any one day; aim for an early boat to make sure. The season lasts from mid-June to mid-September, and during the rest of the year you can't get out there at all.

Baiona and around

BAIONA (Bayona) is situated just before the open sea at the head of a miniature *ría*, the last and the smallest in Galicia. It is arguably the region's best resort, not yet over-exploited for all its popularity with the Spanish. This small and colourful port was the first place in Europe to hear of the discovery of the New World, when Columbus's *Pinta* appeared on March 1, 1493. Nowadays the harbour contains at least as many pleasure yachts as fishing boats.

The **medieval walls** surrounding the wooded promontory which is Baiona's most prominent feature, enclose the idyllic *Parador Conde de Gondomar* (☎986 355000, fax 986 355076; ⑨), which boasts a reputation as Spain's best hotel. It has a couple of bars, including a nice one standing alone in the grounds.

It's definitely worth paying the 100-ptas fee to walk around the parapet, with an unobstructed view in every direction, across the *ría* and along the chain of rocky islets which leads to the Illas Cíes. There's a footpath beneath the walls at sea level, barely used, which gives access to several diminutive beaches. These are not visible from the town proper, which has only a small patch of sand despite its fine esplanade.

Practicalities

Baiona's **Turismo** (June 15–Sept 15 daily 10am–8pm; ☎986 687067) is by the entrance to the *parador*; out of season, the *Ayuntamiento* on Praza de Castro will supply you with a free map and various leaflets. The only budget **place to stay** in the centre is at the cramped but well-located *Hospedaje Kin*, c/Ventura Misa 27 (☎986 357215; ②–③); for a step up in comfort, take a short walk out to the *Mesón del Burgo* (☎986 355309; ④) by the Praia Santa María (next to the Campsa petrol station), which has sunny, spacious rooms looking out to sea. The hotel *Tres Carabelas* (☎986 355441, fax 986 355921; ④–⑤), in the cobbled alleyway just behind the seafront, is very atmospheric. The **bars** along the alleyway are excellent, too; look for *tapas* at *Jalisco*, on the square behind the alley. All around Praza de Castro and along c/Ventura Misa, **restaurants** such as *El Túnel* have enticing window displays of live lobsters and assorted shellfish.

Praia de América, Ramallosa and Sabaris

There are two good **beaches** next to the road in from Vigo a couple of kilometres before Baiona. The first is the **Praia de América** – take the Vigo–Baiona bus via Panjón (Panxon), not Nigrán – a superb, long curve of clean sand backed by rows of vacation villas. This has its own **campsite**, *Praia América* (☎986 365404; March–Oct); the *Baiona Praia* (☎986 350035; June–Sept), however, is nearer the town (and accessible on both bus routes) on the shorter and scruffier Praia Ladeira at **SABARIS**. The inlet here is popular with **windsurfers**.

Look out for the wonderful Roman stone footbridge at **RAMALLOSA**, next to the road between the two beaches, and in Sabaris climb up the hill opposite the Ladeira beach road for good food at the very welcoming and gregarious *Churrasquería Franky*. If you keep going up this road, you'll reach the bleak plateau at the very top. It's a great place for long walks in the woods, and there's a scattering of old villages up there where life seems to go on as it always did, oblivious to the developments below.

Buses from Baiona run from c/Carabela la Pinta, just off the seafront, near the market building, except for the A Guarda buses which carry straight on around the headland; catch them opposite the *O Moscón* restaurant by the port.

The coastal route towards Portugal

The road between Baiona and A Guarda, which once threaded through a deserted, windswept wilderness, has recently been improved and is now scattered with *hostales* and hotels. There are no beaches (although the sight of the ocean foaming through the rocks is mightily impressive), or even shops, and only three buses per day.

Just outside Baiona on this road is the **Virgen de la Roca**, a massive granite image overlooking the sea; it's possible to climb up inside it and on to the boat she holds in her right hand on appropriately solemn religious occasions. Halfway between Baiona and A Guarda is the town of **OIA**, no more than a very tight bend in the coast road, beneath which nestles a remarkable Baroque **monastery**, with its sheer stone facade surviving the constant battering of the Atlantic.

A Guarda and around

At the mouth of the great Río Minho stands the dishevelled and slightly disappointing port of **A GUARDA** (La Guardia), which is largely the modern creation of emigrants

---

HORSES AND CURROS

The scrubby exposed hills around here are home to hundreds of **wild horses**, who sometimes venture down to graze by the sea. In May and June a series of day-long fiestas known as **curros** are held on successive Sundays on the hilltops farther inland. At these absolutely unmissable events the horses are rounded up, counted and branded, and set free again. Wooden corrals are built at clearings in the pine woods, and surrounded by makeshift stalls and bars set up among the trees. The misty dawns see riders swathed in crude, poncho-like blankets scouring the countryside, standing in stirrups like solid wooden wedges as they chase and lasso the fleeing horses. Penned together the animals are magnificent, all sleek brown bodies and flashing eyes, tossing their unkempt manes and whinnying their disgust at being handled for the first time. It's very much a country festival, hugely enjoyed by the *gallegos* you never see in the towns below, feasting on *pulpo* and picnicking in the woods, splashing dark wine from great barrels into chipped white bowls. Those villages currently holding *curros* include La Valga, Torroña, Mougas and Pinzas. Ask at local tourist offices or in the bars for details; they're not organized for tourists, and so may not be advertised.

returned from Puerto Rico. In consolation you can **eat seafood** well and inexpensively, and search out **rooms**, possibly with a harbour view. The *Hostal Martirrey* at José Antonio 8 (☎986 610349; ③) is recommended, as is the *Hostal Fidel Mar* (☎986 610208; ④), a fifteen-minute walk from the centre out on the Praia Arena Grande, with wonderful sea views (follow the main Baiona road until you see signs for the *praia*). If it's real comfort you're after, head for the beautiful *Hotel Convento de San Benito* down by the port (☎986 611116, fax 986 611517; ⑤), which until ten years ago was a convent occupied by Benedictine nuns. There's **camping** out towards the river at *Camping Santa Tecla* (☎986 613011), signposted from town. ATSA **buses** leave every 30 minutes to Tui, and there are three services a day to Baiona.

Just above the town are the thick woods of **Monte Santa Tecla**, with extensive remains of a *celta* (pre-Roman fortified hill settlement), common in this part of Galicia, and even more so in northern Portugal. The ruins are about two-thirds of the way up the mountain, about half an hour's climb up a footpath-stairway cut through the forest; the way starts at the edge of A Guarda nearest Tui. There's also a tarmac road up to the summit, but drivers should note that each person in the car will be charged 100ptas at a ticket box by the road.

The **celta** was probably occupied between around 600 and 200 BC, and abandoned when the Romans established control over the north. It consists of the foundations of well over a hundred circular dwellings, crammed tightly inside an encircling wall. A couple of them have been restored as full-size thatched huts; most are excavated to a few feet, though some are still buried. Set in a thick pine grove on the bleak, seaward hillside, the ancient village with its winding stone paths, wells or cisterns, and grand entranceways forms a striking contrast to the humdrum roofscape of A Guarda below. On the north slope of the mountain there is also a large **cromlech**, or stone circle, while continuing upwards you pass along an avenue of much more recent construction, lined with the Stations of the Cross, and best seen looming out of a mountain mist.

At the top are a church, a small **museum** (Tues–Sun 11am–2pm & 4–7.30pm; free) of Celtic finds, and a relatively inexpensive one-star **hotel**, the *Pazo Santa Tecla* (☎986 610002, fax 986 611072; ③), whose café-restaurant has an outdoor balcony with breathtaking views up and down the Portuguese and Spanish coasts, and along the Minho.

A Guarda itself has only a couple of small **beaches**, but you can walk around the Monte Santa Tecla and down to the village of **Camposancos** (about 3km) where, facing Portugal and a small islet capped by the ruins of a fortified Franciscan monastery, you'll find an adequate stretch of sand along the riverbank and a café. The council in A Guarda, along with promises to improve the look of the place, has pledged to revive a long-defunct ferry service linking Camposancos with Caminha in Portugal.

Along the Minho

The **RÍO MINHO** (Río Miño), the border between Spain and Portugal, so wide and beautiful upstream, is surprisingly narrow at its mouth. Only about one hundred metres, mostly of sandbank, separate the two countries, and it's barely navigable. No large ships can make their way inland to **Tui** or **Valença**; Viana is the first port of any size down the Portuguese coast. The miles of dunes that stretch down to Viana make for better beaches than those few around A Guarda on the Spanish side. At present, the first place you can cross the river is a few miles upstream at **GOIAN** (Goyan), where a car ferry makes hourly journeys to the delightful walled village of Vila Nova da Cerveira.

Tui

TUI (Tuy, pronounced *twee*), 30km from A Guarda, is the main *gallego* frontier town, staring across to the neat ramparts of Portuguese Valença and worth a visit even if you don't plan to continue across the border. There is, of course, the usual border-crossing otrect of tacky wares, but old Tui stands back, tiered amid trees and stretches of ancient walls above the fertile riverbank. Sloping lanes, paved with huge slabs of granite, climb to the imposing fortress-like **Catedral** dedicated to San Telmo, patron saint of fishermen; its military aspect is a distinctive mark of Tui, scene of sporadic skirmishes with the Portuguese throughout the Middle Ages. There are other churches of interest, too, such as the Romanesque San Bartolomeo, or Gothic Santo Domingo with its ivy-shrouded cloisters. More memorable, though, is the lovely rambling quality of the place, coupled with a pair of enticing little river beaches. There's a large **market** on Wednesdays along the main road through town.

Practicalities

If you're looking to **stay**, there's the inexpensive *Habitaciones Otilia*, c/Generalísimo 8 (☎986 601062; ②), on the edge of the old town, just up the steps from the main road – rickety and down-at-heel, but friendly enough. Other slightly more expensive places include the *Hostal San Telmo*, Avda. de la Concordia 91 (☎986 603011; ③–④), opposite the train station, or *Hostal La Generosa*, c/Calvo Sotelo 37 (☎986 600055; ②). Tui's *parador* (☎986 600309, fax 986 602163; ⑦) is a splendid, high-class alternative, on the road to Portugal. There's a fine **pizzeria** just around the corner from *Habitaciones Otilia*, which is surprisingly good and not at all expensive.

Tui is well-connected with Vigo by **bus**; there's at least one departure every half hour. If you're heading inland by rail towards Ribadavia and Ourense, it's much quicker to catch your **train** from Guillarei station, 3km east of town, than to wait for a connection in Tui itself.

Crossing the border

It's a twenty-minute walk to the Portuguese border, across an iron bridge designed by Eiffel; the little town of **VALENÇA**, dwarfed behind its mighty ramparts, lies a similar distance beyond. There's no border control at the bridge any more: just stroll (or drive) across and head up the hill to Valença, past a **Turismo** which can provide details about onwards Portuguese transport. A **ferry**, from Salvaterra do Minho farther upstream, crosses to the similarly attractive old Portuguese town of Monção.

North of Tui

There is a road from Tui to Gondomar, and from there to Baiona, which avoids Vigo and makes a spectacular drive through thick virgin forests, but no buses run this way. From Porriño, halfway between Tui and Vigo, the new motorway is the most direct route to Ourense, up very steep bleak mountains with not a habitation in sight. On the way, **PONTEAREAS** has a **Corpus Christi** festival (in June) when the streets are spread out with gorgeous patterned "carpets" of bright flowers. Nearby, **MONDARIZ** is a pretty spa town with bathing beaches by a secluded river.

Upstream to Ribadavia and Celanova

Whether you follow the N120 highway or the train line parallel to the Minho, there are numerous rewarding stops along the way. If you want to get away from it all, head for the tiny hamlet of **ALBEOS** where you'll find *La Levada* (☎986 666413, fax 986 666413; ③), an English-run guesthouse situated on an organic farm spilling down the terraces of the valley (if you're arriving by train the owners will pick you up from Albeos station). The views across the Minho are breathtaking from here, and the food (vegetarian) is good.

One of the best larger towns to end up in is **RIBADAVIA**. The trip there by train from Tui is a lovely riverside journey, although the valley of the Minho does tend to fill up with freezing mist until midday or so. The town stands among woods and vineyards above the river, looking grander than its size would promise, with several fine churches, including the Visigothic **San Ginés** and a sprawling **Dominican monastery** which was once the residence of the kings of Galicia. There's also an interesting *Judería* (Jewish quarter), dating from the eleventh century when Ribadavia received its first Jewish immigrants; by the fourteenth century these had become half the town's population, and formed one of the most important and prosperous Jewish communities in Spain. Head for the fountain behind the *Iglesia de la Magdalena* for a wonderful view of the hillside terraces.

Several pleasant **bars** serve the region's excellent, port-like wine, and there is a handful of **hostales**: the *Hostal Plaza* on the Plaza Mayor (☎988 470576; ③) has good, en-suite rooms and is the only *hostal* in the old town; *Hostal Evencio*, Avda. Rodriguex Valcarcel 30 (☎988 471045; ④), is rather soulless but has spacious, well-equipped rooms with great views.

The first hydroelectric dam blocks the Minho about 30km below Ribadavia, and it's from then on up that the flooding of the valley makes the river so broad and smooth-flowing, with forests right to the water's edge. The high and winding road along the south bank through Cortegada to the border at São Gregorio makes a good excursion, and can also be used as part of the route to **CELANOVA**. This is hardly more than a village, dominated by a vast and palatial **Benedictine monastery**. It was here that Felipe V retired into monastic life, having spent much of his reign securing the throne in the War of the Spanish Succession (1701–13). The monastery is now a school, but you can borrow the key to explore its two superb cloisters – one Renaissance, the other Baroque – and the cathedral-sized church. Most beautiful of all is the tiny Mozarabic chapel of **San Miguel** in the garden of the monastery. This dates from the tenth century, and is the work of "Arabicized" Christian refugees from *al-Andalus*. **Buses** also come in from Ourense, and the **hotel** *Betanzos* on Castor Elices 12 (☎988 451036; ③) is excellent.

Ourense

OURENSE (Orense) is worse than disappointing, having lost most of its atmosphere (along with its old buildings) in a sprawl of anonymous modern suburbs. There are a few attractive small squares, and the approach is deceptively magnificent, across a seven-arched, thirteenth-century bridge. The Praza Maior is an attractive old arcaded square below the dark **Catedral**, an imitation of Compostela's, with a painted (but greatly inferior) copy of the Pórtico de Gloria, and a museum in the cloisters. From here, the old town disappears rapidly into the dilapidated areas around Rúa Dois de Mayo, while Rúa Calvo Sotelo takes you into Rúa do Paseo and the new town, a pleasant café-lined stroll. You'll find a **Turismo** kiosk in the new town at the corner of Rúa do Paseo at Parque San Lázaro.

Several **fondas** are scattered around the long main street which leads from the centre to the train station, but Ourense has a rather drab, soulless feel – astonishing when you consider that it was the birthplace of Julio Iglesias. (Fidel Castro's family was also from Ourense.) It's a half-hour walk out to the **RENFE station** on the opposite side of the river, so you can't expect to be able to drop in and see anything between trains. You'd do better to stay the night in Ribadavia and just pass through.

Gorges of the Río Sil

The Minho is more spectacular the farther you go upstream; it arrives at Ourense having flowed south from Lugo through the harsh landscape traversed by the Camino de Santiago. Twenty kilometres northeast of Ourense it meets the Río Sil at Los Peares, a crumbling old village on the main train line. You can walk from there along the **Gorges of the Sil**, with precarious farm terraces tumbling down to a chaos of rocks and foam. High above San Esteban is another monastery, the three-cloistered **Monasterio de Ribas do Sil**. On the plain to the north, **MONFORTE DE LEMOS** is a major rail junction. Again, the station is a long way from the town centre, but Monforte is a satisfyingly unspoilt and ancient place. Its **Torre de Lemos** looks out across a featureless expanse from the top of a hill full of tumbledown old houses, and there's a strikingly elegant Renaissance **Colegio** lower down.

To the south of the Sil, **MANZANEDA** is the only *gallego* ski resort, offering most of the necessary facilities but not always the snow, and on the other side of the mountains is **VERÍN**, where a fine castle above the fortified town, on a site occupied since prehistoric times, is now a *parador* (☎988 410075, fax 988 412017; ⑦). The town itself is quite modern, though a few traditional balconied houses remain around the main square, near which c/Mayor is a promising area for cheaper accommodation. There's a swimming area, with a few bars and a grassy bank for sunbathing, down beside the Tamega river. Here you're once more within a dozen kilometres of Portugal; buses run alongside the river to the rugged Portuguese frontier town of **Chaves**.

travel details

BUSES

A Coruña to: Betanzos (every 30min; 45min); Camariñas (3 daily; 1hr 45min); Carnota (2 daily; 2hr 40min); Cee (5 daily; 2hr 15min); Corme (3 daily; 1hr 30min); Ferrol (15 daily; 1hr); Finisterre (6 daily; 2hr 30min); Laxe (1 daily; 1hr); Lugo (11 daily; 2hr); Madrid (6 daily; 8hr); Malpica (2 daily; 1hr 15min); Ourense (5 daily; 3hr 30min); Oviedo (4 daily; 5hr); Pontevedra (10 daily; 2hr); Ribadavia (4 daily; 3hr); Santiago de Compostela (hourly; 1hr 30min); Ribadeo (6 daily; 4hr); Vigo (10 daily; 3hr); Viveiro (5 daily; 3hr 30min).

Costa da Morte buses: Camariñas–Muxia–Cee (3 daily; 30min/1hr30 min); Finisterre–Corcubión– Muxia–Camariñas (3 daily; 15min/1hr 15min/2hr); Finisterre–Muros (3 daily; 1hr); Laxe–Muxia (1 daily; 1hr 30min); Muros–Cee (9 daily; 1hr); Muxia–Camariñas (3 daily; 30min).

Lugo to: A Coruña (11 daily; 2hr); Foz (5 daily; 2hr); Ourense (5 daily; 2hr); Pontevedra (6 daily; 2hr); Santiago de Compostela (7 daily; 2hr); Vigo (7 daily; 3hr); Viveiro (7 daily; 2–3hr).

Ourense to: Celanova (1 daily; 1hr 30min); A Coruña (5 daily; 3hr 30min); Lugo (5 daily; 2hr);

Oporto (1 daily; 8hr); Santiago de Compostela (9 daily; 2hr 30min); Vigo (13 daily; 2hr).

Pontevedra to: Bueu (16 daily; 30min); Cambados (11 daily; 1hr); Cangas (21 daily; 1hr); O Grove (every 30min; 1hr); A Coruña (10 daily; 2hr); Isla de Arousa (7 daily; 1hr 30min); Lugo (6 daily; 3hr); Moaña (5 daily; 45min); Noia (1 daily; 1hr 30min); Ourense (8 daily; 2hr); Padrón (hourly; 1 hr); Santiago de Compostela (every 30min; 1hr); Tui (2 daily; 1hr); Vigo (every 30min; 30min–1hr); Vilagarcía (16 daily; 45min).

Santiago de Compostela to: Betanzos (4 daily; 1hr 30min); Camariñas (3 daily; 3hr); Cambados (5 daily; 2hr); Cee (3 daily; 2hr); A Coruña (hourly; 1hr 30min); Ferrol (4 daily; 2hr 30min); Finisterre (3 daily; 2hr 30min); Lugo (6 daily; 2hr); Madrid (3 daily; 9hr 30min); Malpica (2 daily; 2hr); Muros (13 daily; 2hr 30min); Noia (16 daily; 1hr 30min); Ourense (9 daily; 2hr 30min); Padrón (every 30min; 45min); Pontevedra (every 30min; 1hr); Vigo (15 daily; 1hr 30min–2hr); Vilagarcía (5 daily; 1hr).

Vigo to: Baiona (every 30min; 1hr); Barcelona (1 or 2 daily; 14hr); Cangas (2 daily; 1hr); A Coruña (10 daily; 3hr); O Grove (3 daily; 1hr 15min); Lugo (7 daily; 3hr); Madrid (6 daily; 8hr); Noia (1 daily;

3hr); Ourense (13 daily; 2hr); Oviedo (2 daily; 8hr); Padrón (13 daily; 2hr); Pontevedra (every 30min; 30min–1hr); Ribadavia (13 daily; 1hr 30min); Oporto and Lisbon (4 weekly; 3hr 30min/6hr); Santiago de Compostela (every 30min; 2hr 30min); Tui (every 30min; 45min); Vilagarcía (2 daily; 2hr).

TRAINS

As well as the FEVE line (see p.437) which journeys along the north coast from Asturias to Ferrol, there are two main lines into and out of Galicia: one from Madrid via Avila, Medina del Campo and Zamora to Ourense; the other from León to Monforte, the junction between Lugo and Ourense. Many of these trains continue to Santiago and A Coruña, but you can usually get about more easily using the *regionales*. Galicia has two regional lines: the first runs from A Coruña to Vigo via Santiago; the second from Vigo to Ourense and on to Monforte. Two further minor lines connect Ferrol with A Coruña, and A Coruña with Lugo and Monforte.

A Coruña to: Ávila (2 daily; 7hr); Barcelona (3 daily; 14–17hr); Betanzos (4 daily; 30min); Bilbao (1 daily; 12hr); Burgos (3 daily; 8–9hr); Ferrol (2 daily; 1hr 30min); Irún (1 daily; 12hr 30min); León (4 daily; 6–7hr); Lugo (7 daily; 1hr 40min–2hr 15min); Madrid (2 daily; 8hr 30min–11hr 30min); Ourense (3 daily; 2hr 15min–3hr); Palencia (3 daily; 7hr 30min–8hr 30min); Santiago de Compostela (18–24 daily; 1hr–1hr 30min); Vigo (19 daily; 2hr–3hr 30min); Zamora (2 daily; 5hr 20min); Zaragoza (2–3 daily; 12hr 30min).

Ourense to: Burgos (4 daily; 6–8hr); A Coruña (3 daily; 2hr 30min–3hr 30min); León (3–4 daily; 4hr);

Madrid (2–4 daily; 6–8hr); Medina del Campo (3 daily; 3hr 30min–4hr 30min); Monforte (3–4 daily; 45 min); Ponferrada (8 daily; 2hr 30min); Pontevedra (2 daily; 2hr 45min); Ribadavia (6 daily; 25min); Santiago de Compostela (6–8 daily; 1hr 20min–2hr); Vigo (8–12 daily; 2hr); Zamora (3–4 daily; 2hr 50min).

Santiago de Compostela to: Ávila (2 daily; 6hr); A Coruña (18–24 daily; 1hr); Bilbao (1 daily; 10hr 45min); Burgos (1 daily; 8hr); Irún (1 daily; 11hr 30min); León (1 daily; 6hr); Madrid (2 daily; 8–10hr); Medina del Campo (2 daily; 5hr 20min); Ourense (6–8 daily; 1hr 20min–2hr); Palencia (1 daily; 7hr); Vigo (20 daily; 1hr 15min–1hr 45min); Zamora (2 daily; 4hr 30min–6hr 30min).

Vigo to: Ávila (3 daily; 6hr 30min–8hr 30min); Barcelona (3 daily; 15hr–16hr 30min); Burgos (2–4 daily; 8hr); A Coruña (19 daily; 2hr–3hr 30min); Irún (1–2 daily; 11hr 30min); León (4 daily; 6hr); Madrid (2–3 daily; 8–10hr); Medina del Campo (2–3 daily; 3hr); Ourense (8–12 daily; 2hr); Ponferrada (6 daily; 4–5hr); Pontevedra (21 daily; 30min); Oporto (3 daily; 2hr 15min); Ribadavia (4 daily; 1hr 30min); Santiago de Compostela (20 daily; 1hr 15min–1hr 45min); Tui (3 daily; 45min); Zamora (2–3 daily; 5–6hr); Zaragoza (5 daily; 11–12hr).

FERRIES

Goyan to: Vilanova do Cerveira, Portugal (hourly; 5min).

Salvaterra do Minho to: Monção, Portugal (hourly; 5min).

Vigo to: Cangas (every 30min; 20min); Moaña (hourly; 20min); Illas Cíes (10 daily in summer only; 1hr); Isla de Ons (daily in summer; 2hr).

CHAPTER NINE

ARAGÓN

Politically and historically **Aragón** has close links with Catalunya, with which it formed a powerful alliance in medieval times, exerting influence over the Mediterranean as far away as Athens. It is a Castilian rather than Catalan-speaking area, though, and, locked in on all sides by mountains, has always had its own identity, with traditional *fueros* like the Basques. The modern *autonomía* – containing the provinces of Zaragoza, Teruel and Huesca – is well out of the Spanish political mainstream, especially in the rural south, where Teruel is the least populated region in Spain. Coming from Catalunya or the Basque country, you'll find the Aragonese pace, in general, noticeably slower.

It is the **Pyrenees** that draw most visitors to Aragón, with their stunning valleys, old farming villages, and trekking. The mountains are remarkably unspoilt – and much less commercialized than across the border in France – and they have a stunning focus in the **Parque Nacional de Ordesa**, with its panoply of canyons, waterfalls and peaks. Aragón's Pyrenean villages are also renowned for their Romanesque architecture; **Jaca** has the country's oldest Romanesque cathedral.

The most interesting monuments of central and southern Aragón are, by contrast, **Mudéjar**: a series of churches, towers and mansions built by Muslim workers in the early decades of Christian rules. **Zaragoza**, the Aragonese capital, and the only place of any real size, sets the tone with its remarkable **Aljafería Palace**, the most spectacular Moorish monument outside Andalucía. Other examples are to be found in a string of smaller towns, in particular **Tarazona**, **Calatayud** and – above all – the southern provincial capital of **Teruel**.

In southern Aragón, two mountainous regions are also of interest. West of Teruel, the Montes Universales, a frontier with Cuenca province, offer some gorgeous routes and walking, especially around the massively walled village of **Albarracín**. To the east is the isolated region of **El Maestrazgo**, a wild countryside stamped with dark peaks and gorges, whose villages feel extraordinarily remote.

This chapter is arranged in two sections: **Zaragoza, Teruel and southern Aragón** (covering Zaragoza and Teruel provinces); and **The Aragonese Pyrenees** (covering Huesca province).

ZARAGOZA, TERUEL AND SOUTHERN ARAGÓN

Zaragoza houses over half of Aragón's one million population, and most of its industry. It's a big but enjoyable city, with a lively zone of bars and restaurants tucked in among remarkable monuments, and is a handy transport nexus, both for Aragón and beyond. Its province includes the Mudéjar towns of **Tarazona, Calatayud** and **Daroca**, and, along the border with Navarra, the old **Cinco Villas**, really just ennobled villages, of which the most interesting is **Sos del Rey Católico**. Wine enthusiasts may also want to follow the **ruta de los vinos**, south from Zaragoza through Cariñena to Daroca.

Teruel province is a lot more remote, and even the capital doesn't see too many passing visitors. It is unjustly neglected, considering its superb Mudéjar monuments,

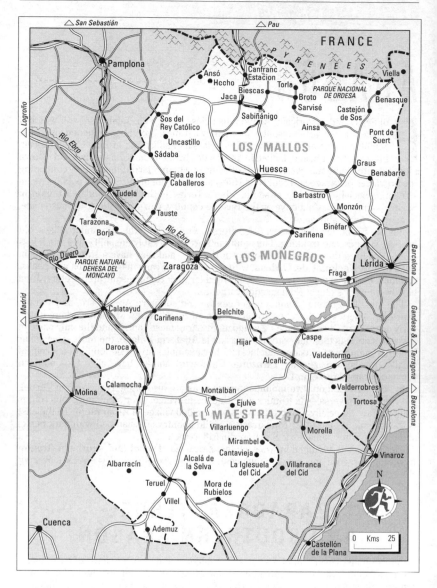

and if you have transport of your own there are some superb rural routes to explore: especially east, through **Albarracín** to Cuenca, or south through to Valencia. The valleys and villages of the **Maestrazgo**, which border Valencia province, are the most remote of the lot: a region completely untouched by tourism, foreign or Spanish, and where transport of your own is a big help.

FIESTAS

April

8–9 Pilgrimage to the Santuario de Nuestra Señora de la Alegría in Monzón, the journey made in decorated carriages.

Holy Week Small-scale but emotional celebrations at Calatayud and elsewhere. On Maundy Thursday/Good Friday there's the festival of *La Tamborrada* in Calanda, near Alcañiz.

May

First Friday Jaca commemorates the Battle of Vitoria against the Moors with processions and folkloric events.

25 More of the same at Jaca for the *Fiesta de Santa Orosia*.

Monday of Pentecost *Romería Nuestra Señora de Calentuñana* at Sos del Rey Catolico.

June

Nearest Sunday to the 19th Cantavieja celebrates the *Fiesta de los Mozos*: a serious religious event but with dancing and the usual fairground activities.

30 *Ball de Benas*: small festival at Benasque.

July

First Sunday *Romería del Quililay*, pilgrimage and picnic up the mountain above Tarazona.

First–second week Teruel bursts into ten days of festivities for the *Vaquilla del Ángel*, one of Aragón's major festivals.

Late July/early Aug International Folklore Festival of the Pyrenees alternates between France and Spain: it's at

Jaca in odd-numbered years, accompanied by a very full programme of traditional music and dance.

August

Early August Fiesta at Huesca in honour of San Lorenzo.

14–15 *Fiestas del Barrio* in Jaca – street markets and mass parties.

16 Patron saint's festival at Biescas – "bigheads" and eats.

27–28 *Encierros* – crazy local bull running – at Cantavieja.

September

Early September Teruel fair.

4–8 Fiesta at Barbastro includes *jota* dancing, bullfights and sports competitions (like pigeon-shooting contests).

8 Virgin's birthday signals fairs at Alcañiz, Hecho, Catalayud, Alcalá de la Selva and Villel.

12–15 Three days of patron saint festivities at Graus including stylized traditional dances and "dawn songs". *Romería* at L'Iglesuela del Cid, with the "Mojiganga", a socially satiric procession, held on the Sunday closest to the14th.

8–14 Bull running and general celebrations at Albarracín.

October

Second week Aragón's most important festival in honour of the Virgen del Pilar. Much of the province closes down around the 12th and at Zaragoza there are floats, bullfights and *jota* dancing.

Zaragoza

ZARAGOZA is an interesting and inviting place, having managed to absorb its suburbs and rapid growth with a rare grace. Its centre, at least, reflects an air of prosperity in its wide, modern boulevards, stylish shops and bars. In addition, the city preserves the spectacular Moorish **Aljafería**, and an awesome basilica, devoted to one of Spain's most famous icons, **Nuestra Señora del Pilar**.

The city's **fiestas** in honour of Nuestra Señora del Pilar – which take place throughout the second week of October – are well worth planning a trip around, so long as you can find accommodation. In addition to the religious processions (which focus on the 12th), the local council lays on a brilliant programme of cultural events, featuring top rock, jazz and folk bands, floats, bullfights and traditional *jota* dancing. It's a pretty lively town for

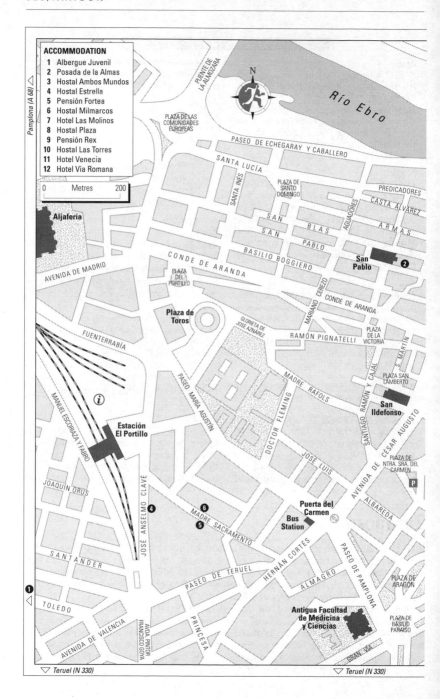

ACCOMMODATION
1 Albergue Juvenil
2 Posada de la Almas
3 Hostal Ambos Mundos
4 Hostal Estrella
5 Pensión Fortea
6 Hostal Milmarcos
7 Hotel Las Molinos
8 Hostal Plaza
9 Pensión Rex
10 Hostal Las Torres
11 Hotel Venecia
12 Hotel Vía Romana

0   Metres   200

Pamplona (A 68)

Aljafería

PUENTE DE LA ALMOZARA

Río Ebro

N

PLAZA DE LAS COMUNIDADES EUROPEAS

PASEO DE ECHEGARAY Y CABALLERO

SANTA LUCÍA

SANTA INÉS

PLAZA DE SANTO DOMINGO

PREDICADORES

CASTA ÁLVAREZ

SAN BLAS

AGUADORES

ARMAS

SAN

PABLO

BASILIO BOGGIERO

San Pablo ❷

CONDE DE ARANDA

AVENIDA DE MADRID

PLAZA DEL PORTILLO

MARIANO CEREZO

CONDE DE ARANDA

Plaza de Toros

GLORIETA DE JOSÉ AZNÁREZ

RAMÓN PIGNATELLI

PLAZA DE LA VICTORIA

FUENTERRABÍA

S. MARTÍN

PLAZA SAN LAMBERTO

PASEO MARÍA AGUSTÍN

MADRE RÁFOLS

SANTIAGO RAMÓN Y CAJAL

San Ildefonso

ⓘ

MANUEL ESCORIAZA Y FABRO

DOCTOR FLEMING

PLAZA DE CÉSAR AUGUSTO

Estación El Portillo

JOSÉ LUIS

PLAZA DE NTRA. SRA. DEL CARMEN

AVENIDA DE CÉSAR AUGUSTO

Ⓟ

JOAQUÍN ORÚS

JOSÉ ANSELMO CLAVÉ

❹

❻

MADRE SACRAMENTO

❺

Puerta del Carmen

Bus Station

ALBAREDA

SANTANDER

PASEO DE TERUEL

HERNÁN CORTÉS

ALMAGRO

PASEO DE PAMPLONA

PLAZA DE ARAGÓN

❶

TOLEDO

AVDA PINTOR FRANCISCO GOYA

PRINCESA

Antigua Facultad de Medicina y Ciencias

PLAZA DE BASILIO PARAÍSO

AVENIDA DE VALENCIA

GRAN VÍA

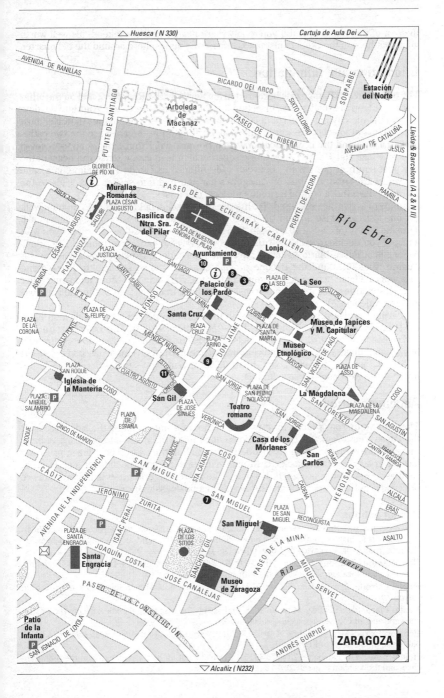

△ Huesca (N 330)

Cartuja de Aula Dei △

AVENIDA DE RANILLAS

RICARDO DEL ARCO

SOBRARBE

Estación
del Norte

Arboleda
de
Macanaz

PUENTE DE SANTIAGO

PASEO DE LA RIBERA

SIXTO CELORRIO

AVENIDA DE CATALUÑA

△ Lleida & Barcelona (A 2 & N II)

JESÚS

GLORIETA
DE PÍO XII

PASEO DE

Río Ebro

RAMBLA

Murallas
Romanas

PLAZA CÉSAR
AUGUSTO

ECHEGARAY Y CABALLERO

ABENAIRE

SALDUBI

Basílica de
Ntra. Sra.
del Pilar

PLAZA DE NUESTRA
SEÑORA DEL PILAR

PUENTE DE PIEDRA

AUGUSTO

CÉSAR

PLAZA
LANIZA

C/ PRUDENCIO

SANTIAGO

Lonja

AVENIDA

Ayuntamiento

PLAZA
JUSTICIA

SANTA ISABEL

10

La Seo

TOBRE

ALFONSO I

ESPOZ Y MINA

8

3

PLAZA DE
LA SEO

12

SEPULCRO

PLAZA DE
S. FELIPE

Palacio de
los Pardo

C/ LIBRES

PLAZA
DE LA
CORONA

GALO PONTE

Santa Cruz

MÉNDEZ NÚÑEZ

PLAZA
CRUZ

DON JAIME I

PLAZA DE
SANTA
MARTA

Museo de Tapices
y M. Capitular

PLAZA
ARIÑO

Museo
Etnológico

PLAZA DE
SAN ROQUE

C/ CUATRO AGOSTO

ESTÉBANES

9

SAN JORGE

MAYOR

SAN VICENTE DE PAÚL

PLAZA DE
ASSO

PLAZA
MIGUEL
SALAMERO

Iglesia de
la Mantería

COSO

11

C/ PREGON

San Gil

PLAZA
DE JOSÉ
SINUÉS

PLAZA DE
SAN PEDRO
NOLASCO

La Magdalena

SAN LORENZO

PLAZA DE LA
MAGDALENA

COSO

SAN AGUSTÍN

AZOQUE

CINCO DE MARZO

PLAZA
DE
ESPAÑA

VERÓNICA

Teatro
romano

SAN JORGE

CADENA

FRANCISCO
CANTÍN Y GAMBOA

ALCALÁ

CÁDIZ

AVENIDA DE LA INDEPENDENCIA

C/ BLANCAS

STA. CATALINA

COSO

Casa de los
Morlanes

San
Carlos

ROMEA

HEROÍSMO

ERAS

JERÓNIMO
ZURITA

SAN MIGUEL

PLAZA DE
SAN MIGUEL

RECONQUISTA

ASALTO

Río

Huerva

PLAZA DE
SANTA
ENGRACIA

ISAAC PERAL

7

SAN MIGUEL

San Miguel

PASEO DE LA MINA

MIGUEL SERVET

Santa
Engracia

JOAQUÍN COSTA

PLAZA
DE LOS
SITIOS

SANCHO Y GIL

Museo
de Zaragoza

JOSÉ CANALEJAS

Patio
de la
Infanta

PASEO DE LA CONSTITUCIÓN

SAN IGNACIO DE LOYOLA

ZARAGOZA

ANDRÉS GURPIDE

▽ Alcañiz (N232)

the rest of the year too, and if you're anywhere nearby at the weekend, it's well worth going out here in the evening just to experience the atmosphere around the old quarter.

Orientation and information

The **old centre** of Zaragoza is bordered to the north by the **Río Ebro**, and on the other sides by a loop of broad *paseos*; bisecting it is the **Avenida de César Augusto**, leading in from the old city gate, Puerta del Carmen. With the exception of the **Aljafería**, most other points of interest are within this loop. Backing on to the river are the two cathedrals, **La Seo** and the **Basilica de Nuestra Señora del Pilar**, flanked on their south side by **Plaza del Pilar**, a huge stone square which is in every sense the heart of the city. Just south of the square, between c/de Alfonso and c/de Don Jaime, is a zone known as **El Tubo**, the hub of Zaragoza's bar and nightlife scene. This leads to the **Plaza de España**, a central terminus for local city buses.

Points of arrival are scattered. **Trains** use the Estación del Portillo, a 25-minute walk (or bus #21 clockwise around the Paseo María Agustín) to Plaza de España; a small Turismo booth (Mon–Sat 10am–9pm, Sun 9am–3pm) at the station can supply you with a map if you decide to walk. By **bus**, you could arrive at various terminals. The principal one is at Paseo María Agustín 7, near the Puerta del Carmen; Agreda services for Madrid, Catalunya and the Basque provinces, and Oscense services to Huesca and Jaca, operate from here. Services south to Daroca, Cariñena and Muel, and some other local destinations, use a terminal across the railway tracks (south of the train station) at Avda. Valencia 20.

Leaving for elsewhere, best check with the **Turismo** opposite the basilica on Plaza del Pilar (Mon–Sat 10am–8pm, Sun 10am–2pm; ☎976 201200). This caters for the city and province of Zaragoza. For pamphlets and maps on destinations and routes throughout Aragón, make your way to the **regional office** in the Torreón de la Zuda (Mon–Fri 8.15am–2.45pm & 3.15–8pm, Sat 10am–1.30pm, Sun 9am–2pm; ☎976 393537), the tower at the west end of Plaza del Pilar.

Accommodation

There are numerous **places to stay** close to the train station, along the side streets off the Paseo María Agustín. However, if you don't mind the noise and company of bars, there's more atmosphere in **El Tubo**, where you'll find upwards of a dozen *pensiones* located in airy mansion blocks; c/Méndez Núñez here, and the smaller streets off it, such as c/Estabañes, are good locations. The more upmarket hotels in Zaragoza are pricey and not very special, catering mainly to a business market.

Budget options

Albergue Juvenil Baltázar Gracián, c/Franco y López 4, off Avda. de Valencia (☎976 551504). Zaragoza's refurbished youth hostel is on the fifth street on the right as you walk down Avda. de Valencia from Avda. Francisco de Goya. Open Jan–July & Oct–Dec. ①.

Hostal Ambos Mundos, Plaza del Pilar 16 (☎976 299704, fax 976 299702). Large *hostal* (50 rooms) in an excellent location; spacious rooms with small ensuite baths. ③.

Hostal Estrella, Avda. de Clave 27 (☎976 283061). Decent rooms with en-suite baths, near the train station. ③.

Hostal Plaza, Plaza del Pilar 14 (☎976 294830). Possibly the best budget choice: decent rooms with showers, and, of course, an excellent location. ③.

Pensión Rex, c/Méndez Núñez 31 (☎976 392633). Large, quiet rooms (some en-suite) in a lovely old house in the heart of El Tubo. ③.

Hostal Venecia, c/Estabañes 7 (☎976 393661). Don't be put off by the tatty exterior; the rooms are clean and the location is great. ②.

ACCOMMODATION PRICE CODES

The codes used in our hotel listings denote the following price ranges:

① Under 2000ptas ④ 4500–6000ptas ⑦ 12,000–17,500ptas
② 2000–3000ptas ⑤ 6000–8000ptas ⑧ Over 17,500ptas
③ 3000–4500ptas ⑥ 8000–12,000ptas

See p.34 for more details.

Moderate and expensive options

Posada de las Almas, c/San Pablo 22 (☎976 439700, fax 976 439143). Soak up the faded grandeur in this well-located old hotel, with its own restaurant and garage. ⑤.

Pensión Fortea, c/Madre Sacramento 45 (☎976 282229). Clean rooms, some with private bath, and handy for the train and bus stations. It's worth trying to bargain the rates down. ⑤.

Hostal Milmarcos, c/Madre Sacramento 40 (☎976 284618). Modern, comfortable rooms with TV and bath. Tends not to get too busy so worth trying to negotiate a cheap deal. ⑤.

Hotel Los Molinos, c/San Miguel 28 (☎976 224980, fax 976 211032). Good-value hotel with its own café; central location. ⑤.

Hotel Las Torres, Plaza del Pilar 11 (☎976 394250, fax 976 394254). Comfortable en-suite rooms in an unbeatable position, looking directly onto the basilica. ⑤.

Hotel Vía Romana, c/Don Jaime I 54 (☎976 398215, fax 976 290511). Smart hotel just off the Plaza del Pilar; cheaper at weekends. ⑥.

Camping

Camping Casablanca, Valdefierro – 2km from the centre along the Avda. de Madrid (☎976 753870). A rather barren-looking site, but large and well equipped, with a swimming pool. Bus #36 from Plaza del Pilar or Plaza de España runs past. Open April 1–Oct 15.

The City

The **Plaza del Pilar** is the obvious point to start exploring Zaragoza. The square, paved in a brilliant, pale stone, was remodelled in 1991, creating a vast, airy expanse from the old cathedral, **La Seo**, past the great **Basilica del Pilar**, and over to the Avenida César Augusto. A look around the square spans the whole extent of the city's history: at one end a patch of Roman wall remains; between the churches is a Renaissance exchange house, **La Lonja**; while at the centre is some modern statuary and a waterfall shaped like a map of South America.

Even if you plan only to change trains or buses in Zaragoza, it is worth coming into the centre to see the square and basilica, and making your way over to **La Aljafería**, either on foot (around 20min) or by taxi.

The Basilica de Nuestra Señora del Pilar

Majestically fronting the Río Ebro, the **Basilica de Nuestra Señora del Pilar** (daily 6am–8pm) is one of Spain's greatest and most revered religious buildings. It takes its name from a pillar – the centrepiece of the church – on which the Virgin is said to have descended from heaven in an apparition before Saint James the Apostle. The structure around this shrine is truly monumental, with great corner towers and a central dome surrounded by ten brightly-tiled cupolas; it was designed in the late seventeenth-century by Francisco Herrera el Mozo and built by Ventura Rodríguez in the 1750s and 1760s.

The **pillar**, topped by a diminutive cult image of the Virgin, is constantly surrounded by pilgrims, who line up to touch an exposed (and thoroughly worn) section, encased in a marble surround. The main artistic treasure of the cathedral is a magnificent alabaster reredos on the high altar, a masterpiece sculpted by Damien Forment in the first decades of the sixteenth century.

Off the north aisle is the **Museo Pilarista** (daily 9am–2pm & 4–6pm; 150ptas), where you can inspect at close quarters the original sketches for the decoration of the domes by Francisco de Goya, González Velázquez, and Francisco and Ramón Bayeu. Your ticket also admits you to the **Sacristía Mayor**, off the opposite aisle, with a collection of religious paintings and tapestries.

Around the square

The old cathedral, **La Seo**, stands at the far end of the Plaza del Pilar, shrouded in scaffolding for an extensive restoration programme. It is at present (and, it seems, for some time to come) closed to visitors, though you can still admire the exterior, which is essentially Gothic-Mudéjar, with minor Baroque and Plateresque additions. To the left of the main entrance is a Mudéjar wall with elaborate geometric patterns. Inside, the superb *retablo mayor* contains some recognizably Teutonic figures executed by the German Renaissance sculptor, Hans of Swabia.

Midway between the two cathedrals stands the sixteenth-century **Lonja**, the old exchange building, a Florentine-influenced structure, with an interior of elegant Ionic columns, open periodically for art exhibitions. Over to the other side of the basilica, and now housing one of the city's tourist offices, is the **Torreón de la Zuda**, part of Zaragoza's medieval fortifications, and the remains of **Roman walls**, insignificant ruins but a reminder of the city's Roman past. Zaragoza's name derives from that of Caesar Augustus (César Augusto in the Spanish form).

South of the Plaza del Pilar

A block south of the square, in the impeccably restored Palacio de los Pardo at c/Espoz y Mina 23, the **Museo Camón Aznar** (Tues–Fri 9am–2.15pm & 6–9pm, Sat 10am–2pm, Sun 11am–2pm; 100ptas) houses the private collections of José Camón Aznar, one of the most distinguished scholars of Spanish art. Highlights include a permanent display of most of Goya's prints (the artist was born at nearby Fuendetodos, see p.533). At the far end of the street, which becomes c/Mayor, the church of **La Magdalena** has the finest of Zaragoza's several Mudéjar towers.

You can see more works by Goya at the **Museo de Zaragoza** (Tues–Sat 9am–2pm, Sun 10am–2pm; free), in the Plaza de los Sitios. Other exhibits span the city's Iberian, Roman and Moorish past.

Close by the museum are a pair of interesting churches: **San Miguel**, with a minor *retablo* by Forment and a Mudéjar tower, and **Santa Engracia**, with a splendid Plateresque portal and palaeo-Christian sarcophagi in its crypt. Two further Mudéjar towers are to be seen at **San Pablo** (daily 9–10am & 8–8.30pm, fiestas 8am–1pm), over to the west of Plaza del Pilar, with another *retablo* by Damien Forment, and **San Gil**, near the Plaza de España.

The Aljafería

Moorish Spain was never very unified, and from the tenth to the eleventh century Zaragoza was the centre of an independent dynasty, the Beni Kasim. Their palace, the **Aljafería** (June–Sept Mon–Sat 10am–2pm & 4–8pm, Sun 10am–2pm; Oct–May Mon–Sat 10am–2pm & 4–6.30pm, Sun 10am–2pm; free), was built in the heyday of their rule in the mid-eleventh century, and as such predates the Alhambra in Granada and Sevilla's Alcázar. Much, however, was added later, under twelfth- to fifteenth-century Christian rule, when the palace was adapted and used by the *Reconquista* kings of Aragón. Since 1987, the Aragonese parliament has met here; a move which adds prestige to both the building and the institution.

From the original design the foremost relic is a tiny and beautiful **mosque**, adjacent to the entrance. Farther on is an original and intricately decorated court, the **Patio de Santa Isabella**. Crossing from here, the **Grand Staircase** (added in 1492) leads to a succession of mainly fourteenth-century rooms, remarkable for their carved *artesonado* ceilings; the most beautiful is in the Throne Room, currently under restoration.

Eating, drinking and nightlife

Zaragoza's **bars** – for both *tapas* and *copas* – are neatly concentrated in the old quarter, along with many of the best-value **restaurants** – no-nonsense *comedores*, often incorporated into the *fondas* and *pensiones*. As you'd expect in a place of this size, there are some very good, more upmarket restaurants, too, scattered all over the city. The old quarter also has a *zona* of **music bars** and **nightclubs** around c/Cantamina and c/Temple, which get pretty lively at the weekends, and another, more alternative, *zona* right behind El Corte Inglés at the bottom of Avenida de la Independencia.

Tapas bars and restaurants

Posada de las Almas, c/San Pablo 22. An attractive old inn with a cheap *menú*.

Casa Amadico, c/Jordán de Urriés 3. A popular *cervecería* with a large range of *tapas*, especially seafood. Closed Mon & Aug.

Bar Arranque, c/Jordan de Urriés 5. A must for Spanish music-lovers, this *tapas* bar only plays flamenco and Spanish records, the sleeves of which have been used to decorate the walls. There are 27 varieties of *tapas* and an excellent selection of Aragonese wines too.

Los Borrachos, Paseo Sagasta 64 (☎976 275036). A classic Zaragoza restaurant, just south of the Plaza de Aragón, whose specialities are mostly game dishes. It is fairly expensive: reckon on 3000ptas and up for a meal with wine.

Circo, c/Blancas 4. Serious *tapas*, including some terrific casserole dishes (*cazuelas*), line the bar at this *cervecería*.

Dominó, Plaza Santa María. *Tapas* include a fine selection of local cheeses, hams and *chorizo*, and there's a good range of Aragón wines to accompany them.

Mundo Mundial, c/San Lorenzo 5. Counterculture eatery serving world food, from Caribbean to Oriental. Tasty *menús* are 975 and 1200ptas and there's a vegetarian *menú* for only 850ptas.

Fonda La Peña, c/de Cinegio 3. The *comedor* here, open to all, dishes up particularly vast quantities of simple home cooking with its 900ptas *menú*.

Restaurant Savoy, Coso 42, facing c/Alfonso. The best place to treat yourself without splashing out. High-class international cuisine and a decent house wine make the 1300ptas *menú* a bargain.

Music bars and nightlife

Ángel Azul, c/Blancas 7. Good café to sit and unwind in an artistic atmosphere.

Bar Azul, c/Pizaro 10. Ideal place to get your finger on the pulse of Zaragoza, with arty photography and up-to-date DJs: Thurs for big beats and trip-hop, Fri funk, Sat hip-hop and Sun for an ambient and trip-hop chill-out.

bassLAB, c/la Paz 29. One of many bars along this street which specialize in *macina* (techno).

La Campana de los Perdidos, c/Prudencio 7. Great atmosphere and regular comedy acts at this bar; you can pick up a programme at the Turismo. Closed mid-June to mid-August.

Chastón, c/Plaza Ariño 4. Pleasant city centre bar with jazz and blues sounds and a summer *terraza*. Starts getting busy after 11pm.

Oasis, c/Boggiero 28. Grand old concert hall transformed into a traditional cabaret – a kind of Aragonese equivalent of the Parisian *Moulin Rouge*, though locals complain it's losing its magic. Open Sat only; closed June–Sept.

Sala Morrisey, Gran Vía 33. Irish pub with bogus olde worlde interior but great alternative DJs Thurs–Sun and occasional live music.

La Taberna de Harry McNamara, c/Méndez Núñez 36. So you didn't expect to end the evening in a Scottish pub? Think again . . . Open daily 5pm–3am.

Listings

Ambulance ☎976 358500.

American Express c/o Viajes Turopa, Paseo Sagasta 47 (☎976 383911).

Bike rental You can rent mountain bikes from the Parque Primo de Ribera, at the south end of Gran Vía (bus #30 or #40 from Plaza de España). From the park, paths lead out into forest land on the edge of the city.

Bus enquiries Main station on Paseo María Agustín (☎976 229343); terminal at Avda. de Valencia (☎976 554588). Eurolines Julia, at c/Marceliano Isabel 2 (☎976 238373), have the most extensive international services and depart from c/Hernan Cortes 6.

Car rental Hertz (☎976 284460) is at the train station; Avis is at Paseo Fernando el Católico 9 (☎976 357863); Atesa is at Avda. Valencia 3 (☎976 352805).

Cinemas The Filmoteca, on Paseo Sagasta, opposite El Corte Inglés, is a beautiful old cinema, with an arts programme, including original-language movies.

Hospital Miguel Servet, Plaza Isabel la Católica 1 (☎976 355700).

Flea market *El Rastro* takes place near the football stadium, La Romadera, every Sun and Wed morning for clothes, accessories and household objects. The more eclectic *Mercadillo* is held on Sun mornings outside the bullring.

Laundry If you're staying in or around El Tubo there's a self-service launderette at c/San Vicente Paul 25; by the train station, Lavomatique is the nearest, on c/San Antonio María Claret 5, just off Avda. Pintor Francisco Goya.

Post office The *Correos Central* is at Paseo de la Independencia 33 (Mon–Fri 9am–8pm, Sat 9am–2pm). Poste restante (*Lista de Correos*) is downstairs at window 4.

Shops The big shopping street is Paseo de la Independencia, south of Plaza de España; it is full of fashion shops, and at the end is a large branch of El Corte Inglés – good for English-language books and everything department store-ish. The news-stands outside carry foreign newspapers and magazines.

Skiing If you plan to go skiing in the Pyrenees you are probably better off buying a package deal from a travel agent in Zaragoza than turning up and going your own way. For the **Astún** resort, for instance, you could buy a weekend or week-long package that includes bed and breakfast in Jaca, bus transport daily to the slopes and ski equipment. One of the best agents to try is Marsans, Avda. de la Independencia 18 (☎976 236965, fax 976 236974); there are others on Paseo María Agustín.

Swimming pools There's a pleasant open-air pool in the Parque Primo de Ribera, at the south end of Gran Vía (bus #30 or #40 from Plaza de España). It is open 10.30am–10pm, from mid-June to mid-Sept.

Taxis Radio-Taxi Aragón (☎976 383838); Radio-Taxi Cooperativi (☎976 373737); Radio-Taxi Zaragoza (☎976 424242).

Train information ☎976 280202.

Around Zaragoza

Few tourists spend much time exploring the sights and towns around Zaragoza, and with the Pyrenees just a step to the north, it is perhaps no wonder. However, wine buffs heading south might want to follow the **ruta del vino** south through **Cariñena**, and for Goya enthusiasts there are murals at the monastery of **Aula Dei** (though entry is restricted to men only) and at **Muel**.

Farther afield, northwest of the capital, the **Cinco Villas** stretch for some 90km along the border with Navarra. These are really little more than villages, set in delightful, scarcely visited countryside; their title is owed to Felipe V, who awarded it for their services in the War of the Succession (1701–13). The most interesting of the five is the northernmost "town", **Sos del Rey Católico**, on the C127 to Pamplona.

The Cartuja de Aula Dei

At the **Cartuja de Aula Dei**, 12km north of Zaragoza, Goya painted a series of eleven murals depicting the lives of Christ and the Virgin in 1774. They suffered badly after the Napoleonic suppression, when the buildings were more or less abandoned, but subsequent repainting and restoration have revealed enough to show the cycle to be one of the artist's early masterpieces. The monastery is today a strict Carthusian community – and thus open only to male visitors (Wed & Sat 10am–1pm & 3–7pm).

To reach Aula Dei, take the Montañana road out of the city, along the east bank of the Río Gallego. The Agreda bus to San Mateo de Gallego runs past the monastery. For times (and advice on how much you can see amid the ongoing restoration work) check at the Turismo in Zaragoza.

Tho wino routc and Coya

There are vineyards all over Aragón, but the best wines – strong, throaty reds and good whites – come from the region to the south of Zaragoza, whose towns and villages are accessible from both the road and rail line down to Teruel. The tourist authorities have marked out a **ruta del vino** through the area; an alternative route could take you on a brief **Goya trail**, to see further frescoes and his birthplace.

Muel
MUEL marks the northernmost point of the region and was once a renowned pottery centre. It has seen much better days, however, and few trains stop here any more. The town's interest lies in a Roman fountain and a hermitage, **La Ermida de Nuestra Señora del Fuente**, which has some early (1771) frescoes of saints by Goya. The artist, who became court painter to Carlos IV, was in fact born at the village of **FUEN-DETODOS**, 24km southeast, where a little **Casa Museo** has been done up with period furnishings (Tues–Sun 11am–2pm & 4–7pm; 300ptas).

Cariñena
Continuing south from Muel, **CARIÑENA** is a larger, rather ramshackle old town, with a clutch of **wine bodegas**. Out on the main road behind the church (cross the bridge on to the *carretera* and turn left), the *Bodega Morte* (daily 8am–8pm; free) welcomes visitors to sample its wines, and buy bottles, or fill their own for next to nothing from the huge barrels. If you want **to stay** – and Cariñena, with its open-air swimming pool, is a quiet alternative to Zaragoza – you'll find good rooms at the *Hostal Iliturgis* on the Plaza Ramón, near the church (☎976 620492; ②), and the newly refurbished *Hotel Cariñena*, on the main Zaragoza road, near the wine *bodegas* (☎976 620250, fax 976 622000; ③). The town also has a **Saturday market**.

Sos del Rey Católico and the Cinco Villas

Moving north from Zaragoza, the **Cinco Villas** comprise: **Tauste**, **Ejea de los Caballeros**, **Sádaba**, **Uncastillo** and **Sos del Rey Católico**. They make a pleasant rambling approach to the Pyrenees (the road past Sos continues to Roncal in Navarra) or to Pamplona, though you really need transport to explore more than one of them. Only one bus a day makes it up from Zaragoza to Sos.

Zaragoza to Sos
TAUSTE, closest of the "towns" to Zaragoza, has an interesting parish church built in the Mudéjar style – and **accommodation** at *Hostal Casa Pepe* (☎976 855832; ③) and *Hospedaje Nuestra Señora de Sancho Abarca*, c/Sierra de la Virgen (☎976 863011; ③ or dorm bed ①).

Nearby **EJEA DE LOS CABALLEROS** retains elements of Romanesque architecture in its churches, and has a handful of **places to stay**, including *Fonda Goya*, Plaza

Goya 2 (☎976 661006; ②), and *Hostal Aragón*, c/Media Villa 21 (☎976 660630; ③), for simple rooms without bath. For more comfort, try *Hostal Cuatro Esquinas*, c/Salvador 4 (☎976 661003; ④).

SÁDABA boasts an impressive medieval castle, thirteenth-century in origin, as well as the remains of an early synagogue. The only **place to stay** is at the basic *Hospedaje Cinco Villas*, c/Urriti Castelón 32 (☎976 863011; ③). UNCASTILLO, on a minor road to Sos, through the Sierra de Santo Domingo, also has a castle, as its name suggests, this time dating from the twelfth century, and the remains of an aqueduct. Again, **accommodation** is limited to one option, the attractive but expensive *Equestre*, c/Mediavilla 71 (☎976 679481; ⑤), which also has a very good – though fairly pricey – **restaurant**.

Sos del Rey Católico

SOS DEL REY CATÓLICO is the most interesting town of the five and an excellent place to relax, especially if you're on your way to or from Navarra. The town derives its name from Fernando II, El Rey Católico, born here in 1452 and as powerful a local-boy-made-good as any Aragonese town could hope for. The narrow cobbled streets, like so many in Aragón, are packed with marvellously grand mansions, including the **Palacio de Sada** where Fernando is reputed to have been born, and there's an unusually early parish **church**, with a curious crypt dedicated to the Virgen del Pilar. These are the real attractions of the place, but you could wander up, too, towards the **Castillo de la Peña Fernando** for lovely views over the village's terracotta rooftops and surrounding countryside, and into the **Ayuntamiento**, which displays – as ever – interesting tidbits of information about local government in a town whose population scarcely tops a thousand.

There are three **places to stay**: the *Fonda Fernandina*, c/Emilio Alfaro (☎948 888120; ②), which is great value; the modern *Hostal Las Coronas*, opposite the *Ayuntamiento* (☎948 888408; ④); and the superb *parador* (☎948 888011, fax 948 888100; ⑦), whose rooms give sweeping panoramic views across the hills.

Tarazona and around

The Aragonese plains are dotted with reminders of the Moorish occupation, and nowhere more so than TARAZONA, which the local tourist authorities promote as "La Ciudad Mudéjar" and even "the Aragonese Toledo". The latter is a bit of an overstatement but Tarazona is a fine-looking place, and if you're en route to Soria or Burgos, makes a good place to break the journey. Don't miss out, either, on the superb Cistercian monastery of **Veruela**, 15km southeast, off the N122 to Zaragoza.

The Town

It is the **Barrios Altos**, the old "upper quarters" of Tarazona, that are the main attraction here. They stand on a hilly site, overlooking the river, with medieval houses and mansions lining the *callejas* and *pasadizos* – the lanes and alleyways.

At the heart of the quarter, as ever, is a Plaza de España, which is flanked by a truly magnificent **Ayuntamiento**, a sixteenth-century town hall, with a facade of coats of arms, sculpted heads and figures in high relief. A one-foot-high frieze, representing the capture of Granada, runs the length of the building. From here, a *ruta turística* directs you up to the church of **Santa Magdalena**, whose Mudéjar tower dominates the town. The *mirador* (viewpoint) here gives a good view of the town, and especially the eighteenth-century **Plaza de Toros** – a circular terrace of houses, with balconies (now filled in) from which spectators could view the *corrida*. Farther uphill lies another church, **La Concepción**, again with a slender brick tower.

In the lower town, the main sight is the **Catedral**, built mainly in the fourteenth and fifteenth centuries. It is a typical example of the decorative use of brick in the Gothic-Mudéjar style, with a dome built to the same design as that of the old cathedral in Zaragoza. The interior has been closed for restoration for the past fifteen years, but the Mudéjar inner **cloisters** (July & Aug only: Sat & Sun 10am–1pm; free) have recently been opened up to the public again, and are well worth a look.

Practicalities

The **Turismo**, next door to the cathedral on c/de la Iglesia (Mon–Fri 9am–1.30pm & 4.30–7pm, Sat & Sun 10am–2pm & 4–7pm; ☎976 640074), will arrange a guided tour of the town if you give them some notice. Going your own way, take a look at the **town plan**, showing the principal sights, outside the nearby church of San Francisco.

There are three **accommodation** choices: *Hostal María Cristina*, Ctra de Castilla 3 (☎976 640084; ②), on the Soria road, across from the municipal swimming pool; *Hotel Brujas de Becquer*, Ctra de Zaragoza (☎976 640404, fax 976 640198; ④–⑤), just out of town on the Zaragoza road; and the upmarket *Hotel Ituri-Asso* (☎976 643196, fax 976 640466; ⑥), down by the river, near the stone bridge. The *Marisquería Galeón*, in the lower town at Avda. La Paz 1, is a reasonably priced **restaurant**, with good seafood and a *menú* for 1200ptas.

Veruela

El Monasterio de Veruela (Tues–Sun: summer 10am–2pm & 4–7pm; winter 10am–1pm & 3–6pm; 200ptas) is one of Spain's greatest religious houses. Isolated in a fold of the hills, it stands within a massively fortified perimeter. It makes an easy excursion from Tarazona, or a break in the journey to Zaragoza: if you are travelling by bus, you need to get off at **Vera de Moncayo** and then walk uphill for 3km. The monastery is uninhabited now but the great church, built in the severe twelfth-century transitional style of the Carthusians, is kept open. The monastery admission ticket also gives access to the fourteenth-century cloisters and convent buildings, as well as a small and not terribly interesting **Museo del Vino** that sits rather uneasily in the monastic grounds.

Calatayud, Piedra and Daroca

Like Tarazona, **Calatayud** is a town of Moorish foundation, with some stunning Mudéjar towers, and again it offers access to a Cistercian monastery, **Piedra**, set in lush parkland. The town itself, however, is an uninviting, impoverished place, where you wouldn't choose to be stranded, especially with the delightful old town of **Daroca** so close, on the train line and main road southeast to Teruel.

Calatayud

If you are passing, it's worth climbing up to the old upper town of **CALATAYUD**, where amid a maze of alleys are the churches of **San Andrés** and **Santa María**, both of which have ornate Mudéjar towers, reminiscent of Moroccan minarets. Santa María, the collegiate church, also has a beautifully decorative Plateresque doorway, while **San Juan**, towards the river, has frescoes attributed to the young Goya.

Ruins of the Moorish **castle** survive, too, on high ground at the opposite end of town from the train station. The views from here are outstanding, though for a closer view of the towers you'd do best to climb the hill to the hermitage in the centre of the old town.

If you have to **stay** in Calatayud, there are a couple of *fondas* immediately across the square from the train station, the most salubrious being *Fonda Los Ángeles* (☎976 881133; ② –③). In the centre you've got a choice between the rather basic *Fonda El Comercio* on c/Dato 33 (☎976 881115; ②), and the considerably more comfortable *Hotel Fornos*, Paseo Cortes de Aragón (☎976 881300, fax 976 883147; ⑤).

El Monasterio de Piedra

El Monasterio de Piedra – "The Stone Monastery" – lies 20km south of Calatayud, 4km from the village of **NUÉVALOS**. The monastic buildings, once part of a grand Cistercian complex, are a ruin, but they stand amid park-like gardens (daily 9am–8pm; 1000ptas for joint park/monastery ticket), which seem all the more gorgeous in this otherwise harsh, dry landscape.

There are two **routes** through the park. The blue arrows lead around the cloister and shell of the church to the twelfth-century **Torre del Homenaje**, whose *mirador* gives a panoramic view over the park. The red ones take you past a series of romantically labelled waterfalls, grottoes and lakes. If there are crowds, it will be easy enough to escape them, though be warned that you're not allowed to take food into the park; if you've brought a picnic you'll have to eat it before you enter the grounds.

There are two **places to stay** up here; the luxurious *Hotel Monasterio de Piedra*, near the park entrance (☎976 849011, fax 976 849054; ⑥) and, a little farther down the road, the well-equipped and reasonably priced *Hotel Las Truchas* (☎976 849040, fax 976 849137; ④), with its own pool, tennis courts and gym. Down in the village, the *Hostal Río Piedra*, at the foot of the road up to the monastery (☎976 849007; ④), has a range of rooms, some with bath. Alternatively, there is a very well-equipped **campsite**, *Lago Park Camping* (☎976 849038; April–Sept), 3km from Nuévalos (in the other direction from the monastery) on a promontory by a reservoir. There are good fishing opportunities here, if you're an enthusiast.

Just one **bus** daily runs from Zaragoza to Nuévalos, leaving at 1.45pm and returning at 5pm. If you have your own transport, the **roads south** to Cuenca or Albarracín (see p.540) are enjoyable routes.

Daroca

DAROCA, southeast of Calatayud, is a lovely old place, set within an impressive run of **walls** that comprise no fewer than 114 towers and enclose an area far greater than that needed by the present population of 2300. The last major restoration of the walls was in the fifteenth century, but today, though largely in ruins, they are still magnificent.

You enter the town through its original gates, the **Puerta Alta** or stout **Puerta Baja**, the latter endowed with a gallery of arches and decorated with the coat of arms of Carlos I. Within, the Calle Mayor runs between the two gates, past ancient streets dotted with Romanesque, Gothic and Mudéjar churches. The principal church, the **Colegiata de Santa María**, is sixteenth-century Renaissance and has a small museum. But the interest of Daroca lies more in the whole ensemble rather than any specific monuments.

There are two choices of **accommodation**, the nicer being *Bar-Pensión El Ruejo*, c/Mayor 88 (☎976 800962; ③), which has a range of rooms and a pleasant patio restaurant that serves a substantial 1000ptas *menú*. The *Hostal Legido* (☎976 800190; ⑤) is a characterless modern fallback on the main road outside town. Daroca is on the Calatayud–Teruel **train line**, though the station is 2km outside town and **buses** are easier. There are a couple of daily services each to and from Calatayud, Teruel and Cariñena/Zaragoza.

Teruel

The little provincial capital of **TERUEL** is basically a market town, catering for its remote and sparsely populated rural hinterlands. It is hard to overestimate how much of a backwater this corner of Aragón is: a recent survey found that it was the only part of Spain where deaths outnumbered births. The land is very harsh, and very high, with the coldest winters in the country. If you like back-of-beyond villages, with medieval sights that haven't been prettified, it is a region that merits a fair bit of exploring.

Arrival, information and accommodation

Teruel doesn't feel quite like a city, despite its capital status, and the separation of the old town from the new reinforces this. Nonetheless, it has most facilities you might need, **trains** from Zaragoza and Valencia, and **buses** from most destinations in the province. The train and bus stations are both close to the city centre: from the former, cross the ring road and walk north up c/Nueva, and from the latter walk north a short way up the ring road, taking the first left to Plaza Judería. There are no fewer than thirteen bus companies in Teruel, many serving the same destinations, so check the timetables in the windows before buying a ticket on departure, as some buses are considerably slower than others.

You're unlikely to want to stray out of the old quarter, and finding your way around it isn't too difficult, thanks to its size. The city's focal point is Plaza del Torico (shown as Plaza Carlos Castel on some maps); just south of here, at c/Tomás Nogués 1, is the **Turismo** (July–Sept Mon–Sat 9am–2pm & 4.30–9pm, Sun 9.30am–2pm; Oct–June Mon–Fri 8am–3pm & 5–7.30pm, Sat 9am–2pm & 5–8pm).

Accommodation

Accommodation is rarely a problem, though be warned that if you're here for the raucous **Fiesta Vaquilla del Ángel** (at the beginning of July) every place in town will be booked solid, and you may have to join other exhausted revellers sleeping in the park down by the train station.

Hostal Alcazaba, c/El Tozal 34 (☎978 610761). Immaculate rooms, with a restaurant below. ④.

Hostal Aragón, c/Santa María 4 (☎978 601387). Small but comfortable rooms, with some triples and quadruples. ③.

Hostal Continental, c/Juan Pérez 9 (☎978 602317). If *Hostal Aragón* is full, this is just around the corner, with similar rooms, though marginally more expensive. ③.

Parador de Teruel, 2km out on the Zaragoza road (☎978 601800, fax 978 608612). This is a modern building but its position is inspired, on a wooded hillside overlooking the town and towers. ⑦.

Hotel Reina Cristina, Paseo del Óvalo 1 (☎978 606860, fax 978 605363). Attractive hotel with an excellent restaurant, located by the Torre del Salvador. ⑦.

Fonda El Tozal, c/Rincón 5 (☎978 601022). A spotless if rather chilly old *fonda*. ②–③.

The Town

Teruel is a likeable and impressively monumental place, with some of the finest Mudéjar work to be found. Like Zaragoza, it was an important Moorish city and retained significant Muslim and Jewish communities after its Reconquest by Alfonso II in 1171. Approaching the town, the Mudéjar towers, built by Moorish craftsmen over the next three centuries, are immediately apparent. These – and the fabulous Mudéjar ceiling in the cathedral – should not be missed. The old town, **El Casco Histórico**, stands on a hill above the Río Turia: a confusing lay-out, enclosed by the odd patch of wall, and with a viaduct linking it to the modern quarter to the south. Leading off to the north is a sixteenth-century aqueduct, **Los Arcos**, a slender and elegant piece of monumental engineering.

If you arrive by train, you will see straight ahead of you **La Escalinata**, a flight of steps decorated with bricks, tiles and turrets that is pure civic Mudéjar in style. From the top of the steps c/El Salvador leads to the **Torre de San Salvador** (summer daily 11am–2pm & 5–7pm; winter Sat & Sun only 11am–2pm; 200ptas), the finest of the town's four Mudéjar towers, and the only one you can go up; you must however be with a group of at least ten so ask at the Turismo to see if there are any groups in town you can tag along with. It's covered with intricately patterned and proportioned coloured tiles, to stunning effect, echoed closely in its more modest sister tower, **San Martín**, best reached via c/de los Amantes (third left off c/El Salvador just at the corner of

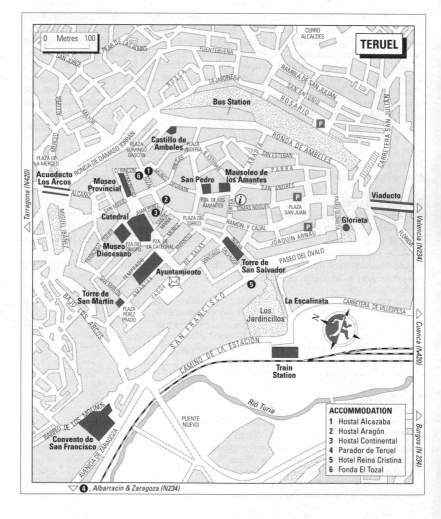

Plaza del Torico). A common feature of all the towers is that they stand separate from the main body of the church, a technique surely influenced by the freestanding minarets of the Muslim world.

The **Catedral**, built in the twelfth century, but gracefully adapted over subsequent years, boasts another fine Mudéjar tower, incorporating Romanesque windows, and a lantern that combines Renaissance and Mudéjar features. The interior follows a more standard Gothic-Mudéjar pattern and at first sight seems unremarkable, save for its brilliant Renaissance *retablo*. Climb the stairs by the door, however, and put money in the illuminations box, and the fabulous **artesonado ceiling** is revealed. This was completed between 1260 and 1314 by Moorish craftsmen, in a gorgeous and fascinating mix of geometric Islamic motifs and medieval painting of courtly life.

Standing next to the cathedral, the sixteenth-century Palacio Episcopal houses the **Museo Diocesano** (Mon–Sat 10am–2pm; 150ptas). Inside, look out for *Calvario*, a beautiful wood carving of Jesus (whose arms are missing), Saint John and the Virgin Mary, carved in the fifteenth century but for many years hidden behind a wall in a church in Sarrón, where it was discovered in 1946. Another highlight is the *Arbol de la Vida*, a striking seventeenth-century ivory carving of Christ.

A couple of blocks from the museum is Plaza del Torico (aka Plaza Carlos Castell), the centre of the old quarter, and flanked by a trio of *modernista* houses. Just beyond here, in another attractive square, is the church of **San Pedro**, once again endowed with a Mudéjar tower. Its fame, however, relates to the adjacent **Mausoleo de los Amantes** (Mon–Sat 10am–2pm & 5–7.30pm, Sun 10am–2pm; 50ptas), a chapel containing the alabaster tomb of the *Lovers of Teruel*, Isabel de Segura and Juan Diego Martínez de Marcilla. This pair's thirteenth-century tale of thwarted love is a legend throughout Spain. The story goes that Diego, ordered by his lover's family to go away and prove himself worthy, left Teruel for five years, returning only to find that Isabel was to be married that same day. He asked for a last kiss, was refused, and expired, heartbroken; Isabel, not to be outdone, arranged his funeral at San Pedro, kissed the corpse, and died in its arms. The lovers' (reputed) bodies were exhumed in 1955 and now lie illuminated for all to see; it is a macabre and popular pilgrimage for newly-weds.

Lastly, if you intend heading out to the Teruel countryside, the **Museo Provincial** (Tues–Fri 10am–2pm & 4–7pm, Sat & Sun 10am–2pm; free), close by the cathedral, could be worthwhile. Its range of exhibits include objects of local folklore and traditional rural life.

Eating and drinking

The main *zona* for **food and drink** in Teruel is at the eastern side of the old quarter, principally Plaza Judería, c/Bartolomé Esteban, c/Abadía and c/San Esteban (the first street into the old town, from the bus station).

Bar Gregori, Paseo Ovalo, 6. This friendly *tapas* bar is the locals' choice, as can be seen from the sheep's head on the menu. Outside tables and inexpensive drinks – 550ptas for a litre of sangria – make it a pleasant place to pass the evening.

La Menta, c/Bartolomé Esteban – behind the Mausoleo de los Amantes. The city's top restaurant – pricey, with dishes 1200ptas and up, but a good choice for a splurge in southern Aragón. Closed Sun, last week of July & Aug 1–14.

Mesón Óvalo, Paseo del Óvalo 2. Very popular *mesón* with quality cooking (the trout dishes are excellent) and a pretty good-value 1400ptas *menú*. Closed Mon & Jan 8–28.

La Parrilla, c/San Esteban 2. Good-value grill restaurant, with traditional interior, where the meat is flame-grilled on a wood fire.

Bar El Plata, c/Amantes 7. *Tapas* bar with lots of local treats. Located on the street leading from the Plaza del Torico to the *Ayuntamiento*.

EL RINCÓN DE ADEMUZ

El Rincón de Ademuz, due south of Teruel, is a strange little region: a Valencian province enclosed within Aragonese territory. It is a very remote corner of Spain, with a bleak kind of grandeur, and scarcely a tourist from one year to the next.

The place to head for – and if you are bussing it, the only realistic place to get to from Teruel – is **ADEMUZ** itself, without a doubt Spain's tiniest and least significant provincial capital. Strung along a craggy hill at the confluence of two long rivers, this could make a beautiful base for walking, and there's a fascination just in wandering the streets with their dark stone cottages and occasional Baroque towers. If you want to stay, there's a single **hostal**, *Casa Domingo* (☎978 782030, fax 978 782056; ④ with bath), which also serves a 1425ptas *menú*.

For energetic trekking, **Torre Baja** lies to the north along the Río Turia, and beyond it the beautiful village of **Castielfabib**. The most interesting of these little Ademuz hamlets, **Puebla de San Miguel**, lies to the east, in the Sierra Tortajada, most easily accessible by road from Valencia, but also from a small route just out of Ademuz in the Teruel direction, east over the Río Turia bridge and signposted to Sabina, Sesga and Mas del Olmo.

Albarracín

ALBARRACÍN, 37km west of Teruel, is one of the more accessible targets in rural southern Aragón – and one of the most picturesque towns in the province, poised above the Río Guadalaviar and retaining, virtually intact, its medieval streets and tall, balconied houses. There's a historical curiosity here, too, in that from 1165 to 1333 the town formed the centre of a small independent state, the kingdom of the Azagras.

Over the last few years a small trickle of tourism has begun, and some of the houses have been prettified a bit too much. But Albarracín's dark, enclosed lanes and those buildings that remain unrestored, with their splendid coats of arms, still make for an intriguing wander – reminders of lost and now inexplicably prosperous eras. Approaching from Teruel, you may imagine that you're about to come upon a large town, for the **medieval walls** swoop back over the hillside – protecting, with the loop of the river, a far greater area than the current or past extent of the town.

The town follows the line of a ridge, above the river, and breaks into two main parts. On the Teruel side, you enter through a gate known as El Túnel, and shortly reach the **Plaza Mayor** and **Ayuntamiento**. Follow the c/de Santiago, up towards the walls, and you reach Santiago church and a gateway, the Portal del Molina. If you take instead the c/de la Catedral, a quiet rural lane, you reach a small square (cars can access this from the other side) with the **Catedral** – a medieval building remodelled in the sixteenth and eighteenth centuries – and Palacio Episcopal.

Practicalities

If you want to stay – and you'll have to if you arrive on the daily bus from Teruel – there is a cluster of **hostales** at the foot of the hill, where the buses stop. These are all pleasant, housed in converted mansions, but tend to be quite pricey. Choices include the *Hostal El Gallo* (☎978 710032; ④), the *Olimpia* (☎978 710083; ④) and the *Arabia* (☎978 710212; ⑤). There's also a **youth hostel**, the *Albergue Juventud Rosa Brios* (☎978 710005; closed Sept ; ①), just past the cathedral at c/Santa María 1. The local **fiesta** takes place from September 8 to 17.

Moving on from Albarracín, if you have transport, there's a fabulous route west to Cuenca through beautiful country, by way of **Frías de Albarracín** and the **source of the Río Tajo** (see p.167).

El Maestrazgo

The mountains of **El Maestrazgo**, northeast of Teruel, are an area of great variety and striking, often wild, beauty, with their severe peaks, deep gorges and lush meadows. Tourism isn't a presence here, though you will find at least one simple *fonda* in most of the tiny, scattered villages. The places below are just a small selection and are geared to the more accessible; armed with a decent map, your own transport, or the will to do some walking, the choice is very much your own.

Inevitably **buses** are infrequent (often their main purpose is to deliver the mail) but most villages are connected once a day, with each other and/or Teruel; an alarm clock is useful since they have a nasty habit of leaving before dawn. The main approaches to the region are from Teruel (daily bus to Cantavieja and Villafranca del Cid), or from Morella in the province of Castellón (see "Valencia" chapter on p.753).

Southern Maestrazgo

Approaching the Maestrazgo from Teruel, you take a minor road off the N420, just a kilometre or so out of town. This passes **Cedrillas**, with its conspicuous, ridge-top castle ruin, and then starts climbing into the hills, over a sequence of *puertos* – gates, or passes. At the **Puerto de Villaroya** (1655m) you cross the highest point of the Maestrazgo, a hair-raising trip on the bus which twists its way down across the valleys, following dried-up rivers, and thundering over narrow, crumbling stone bridges. The first village of any size beyond here is **Cantavieja**.

Cantavieja and El Cid country

CANTAVIEJA, dramatically situated by the edge of an escarpment, at an altitude of 1300m, is a little livelier and larger than most Maestrazgo villages, though its population is still about a thousand. The whitewashed and porticoed **Plaza Mayor** here is typical of the region, and the escutcheoned *Ayuntamiento* bears a Latin inscription with suitably lofty sentiments: "This House hates wrongdoing, loves peace, punishes crimes, upholds the laws and honours the upright". It is a useful base for exploring – or walking in – the region, with a **Turismo** (June–Sept daily 11am–2pm & 5–8pm; ☎ 978 185001), an exceptionally good-value **hotel**, the *Balfagón Alto Maestozgo* (☎964 185076, fax 964 185076; ④) near the municipal swimming pool, and a reasonable *fonda*, the *Julián* (☎964 185005; ②). There's also an unexpectedly stylish **restaurant**, *Buj* (closed Feb), run by a woman and her two daughters. The food at the *Balfagón* is also good, and it has a 1425ptas *menú*.

MIRAMBEL, 15km northeast of Cantavieja and walkable in about four hours, has a population of a mere 160 and preserves a very ancient atmosphere, with its walls, gateways and stone houses. The village was temporarily thrown into a whirl of excitement when Ken Loach and his team filmed *Land and Freedom* here some years ago, but these days it's back to its usual, sleepy self. The main **bar** offers **accommodation** (though it has no sign to indicate it) and a good atmosphere; there is also an excellent little *fonda*, the *Guimera* (☎964 178269; ②), with good en-suite rooms at bargain rates.

A similar distance to the southeast of Cantavieja, and another fine walk along a rough country road, is **LA IGLESUELA DEL CID**. The village's name bears witness to the exploits of El Cid Campeador, who came charging through the Maestrazgo in his fight against the Infidel. Its ochre-red, dry stone walls, ubiquitous coats of arms and stream flowing right through the centre are striking enough in this remote countryside, though these features aside, it's a shabby sort of place. There is, however, a characterful **fonda**, *Casa Amada* (☎964 443373; ③ with bath), which offers good and substantial country cooking.

Continuing east for 10km brings you to **VILLAFRANCA DEL CID**, across the border in Castellón Province – and at the end of the bus route from either Teruel or Morella. Straddling the hillside, this is a lively, attractive village, and with a population of 3000 it's larger than most places around here. The only **place to stay** in the centre is the *Hostal Prismark*, c/Sagrado Corazón de Jesús (☎964 441110; ③), which has good-value en-suite rooms; *L'Om de Llosar* (☎964 441325; ④), 2km out of town by a little *ermita*, is also good. If you decide to turn around from here, the **bus** to Teruel departs at 5.45am (Mon–Fri only), passing through La Inglesuela del Cid at 6am.

Northwest from Cantavieja

Another dramatic, almost Alpine route is in store if you head northwest from Cantavieja, past Cañada de Benatanduz, to **VILLARLUENGO**, a beautiful village of ancient houses stacked on a terraced hillside. Just beyond here, you cross a pass, and the Río Pitarque, with a side valley leading to a hamlet of the same name. Here, by the riverside, in isolated and magnificent countryside, is the stylish *Hostal de la Trucha* (☎978 773008, fax 978 773100; ⑥), with a **restaurant** which serves trout caught a few yards away. Back in Villarluengo, *Fonda Villaluengo*, on Plaza Carlos Castell (☎978 773014; ②) is rather more affordable.

Over another higher pass, the Puerto de Majalinos (1450m), the road drops down to **EJULVE**, a small village with just one **place to stay**, *Pensión Navarra*, c/Tomás Ariño (☎978 753074; ③), and a bar decorated with the fearsome head of a boar – wild country indeed. Just a few more kilometres north, you reach the N420 between Montalbán and Alcañiz.

The **bus** runs this way once a day from Cantavieja, taking nearly four hours to cover the ninety-kilometre journey to **Alcorisa** on the N420.

Northern Maestrazgo: Alcañiz and Valderrobres

The northern limits of the Maestrazgo edge into Tarragona Province in Catalunya, and can be approached from Tarragona/Gandesa, or from Zaragoza through Alcañiz. This town also lies at the end of the N420, east of Alcorisa.

Alcañiz

The castle-topped town of **ALCAÑIZ** is quite a sight as you approach, though close up it's a bit of a disappointment. The **Castillo** has been unsympathetically modernized as a **parador**, *Parador de Alcañiz* (☎978 830400, fax 978 4830366; ⑦), and the best thing about the place is the panorama from its heights. These allow a grand bird's-eye view of the huge Baroque church of **Santa María** which dominates the town below.

The town (and this is a big place in comparison to the Maestrazgo villages, with a population of some 12,000) gives access by bus to Valderrobres (see below), and, by bus or rail, east to Zaragoza and west to the coast at Tortosa or Viñaros via Morella. You probably won't need or want to stay but – in addition to the *parador* – there are several cheapish **places to stay**; try the comfortable *Guadalupe* (☎978 830750; ⑤), near the *castillo* or, for those on a tight budget, the basic *Villar* at c/Calderos 28 (☎978 830256; ①).

Valderrobres

VALDERROBRES is one of the Maestrazgo's most accessible and most attractive towns. It stands 36km from Alcañiz, near the border with Catalunya and astride the Río Matarrana, whose crystal waters teem with trout. The old quarter is crowned by a **castle-palace** (Tues–Sun 11am–1pm & 5–8pm), once occupied by the kings of Aragón, and a Gothic parish church – **Santa María** – which has a fine rose window. In the Plaza

Mayor, the unassuming seventeenth-century **Ayuntamiento** was considered so characteristic of the region that it was reproduced in Barcelona's *Pueblo Español* in 1929.

Places to stay include the *Fonda La Plaza* (☎978 850106; ③), opposite the *Ayuntamiento*, which has an excellent *comedor*, and the newly refurbished *Hostal Querol* (☎978 850192; ③–⑤), across the river in a fourteenth-century inn, which also offers great cooking, with basic, cheap rooms on the first floor and smart, more expensive, en-suite ones on the second. There's also a *casa rural* at c/Pilar 35, up by the castle (☎978 854056; ③).

THE ARAGONESE PYRENEES

Aragón has the best stretch of the **Pyrenees** on the Spanish side: a fabulous region, where you can enjoy anything from casual day-walks in the high valleys to long-distance treks across the mountains. There are numerous trails, marked out by the Aragón mountain club as **GR** (*grande recorrido* – long-haul) or **PR** (*pequeño recorrido* – short-haul) trails.

The most popular jumping-off point for the mountains is **Jaca**, an attractive town in its own right and with an important cathedral. From here, most walkers head to the **Parque Nacional de Ordesa** – the most spectacular mountainscape, with its canyons and waterfall valleys. Over to the east, the highest Pyrenean peaks, Aneto (3404m) and Posets (3371m) are accessible from **Benasque**, while to the west the valleys of **Ansó and Hecho** offer less serious rambles amid wonderful scenery. If you're here in winter, there is also **skiing** at the resorts of (from west to east) Astún-Candanchú, Sallen de Gallego and Cerler; they are reasonably inexpensive.

There are a number of possible **routes into the region**. For Jaca and Ordesa, the most obvious way is via **Huesca**, the provincial capital; this is no great shakes in itself but is poised for the great castle of **Loarre** and the sugarloaf **Los Mallos** mountains that are among the country's most amazing landscapes. Alternatives might include a slow approach to Anso/Hecho or Jaca via the Cinco Villas (see p.533), or, if you're coming from Catalunya (or aiming for Benasque), the scenic route via **Fraga** and **Barbastro**.

You can **travel by rail** through Huesca, Jaca and up to the Spanish border at Canfranc – though there, sadly, the trains stop. Buses, however, continue **into France** over the **Puerto de Somport**, while drivers can also cross over the pass to the east, the **Puerto del Portalé**, or, over towards Benasque, take the **Biesca tunnel**. All of these are open year-round, except for during periods of exceptionally heavy snow.

From the east: Fraga, Monzón and Barbastro

If you're coming to the Pyrenees from Catalunya, it's possible to approach either Huesca or Benasque via **Monzón** and **Barbastro**; both have regular bus connections with Lleida (Lérida), and interesting sights. If you have time and transport, you could approach more slowly from Lleida, following a little-used minor route along the Río Cinca valley from **Fraga**, a pleasant medieval town.

Fraga

It's worth taking a morning to visit **FRAGA**, 25km from Lleida, and just off the *autopista* to Zaragoza. An array of fine brick buildings helps maintain the medieval air of the old town, which is perched high over the Río Cinca. If you're arriving by bus, cross back over the river from the bus station and strike uphill through the steep and convoluted streets of the old town. The tower of the twelfth-century (restored and restyled) church of San Pedro keeps disappearing and reappearing until you reach a tiny square, dominated entirely by the church. If you want to stay, the cheapest **rooms** are at *Hostal Flavia*, Paseo Barón 13 (☎974 471540; ②); for more comfort (and rooms with a bath), head for the *Trébol*, Avda. de Aragón 9 (☎974 471533; ④).

North of Fraga, a tiny road follows the east bank of the Río Cinca to Monzón; it starts out immediately below Fraga's old town. If you have transport, it is a highly recommended route: great steppes fall away to the west beyond the river while coarse vegetation and red clay cliffs flank the road.

If you don't have transport, Fraga is still a good stop. It has **bus** connections with Lleida (4 daily) and Huesca (leaving Mon–Sat at 6.45am).

Monzón

MONZÓN, 50km from Fraga, stands in a triangle between the rivers Cinca and Sosa (the latter now dry), a strategic position that explains its **Templar castle**, forgotten on the crumbling rock above. Originally a ninth-century Moorish fort, it was later endowed for the Templars by Ramón Berenguer IV and was the residence of Jaime I (king of Aragon 1213–76) in his youth. The ruins (summer Tues–Sun 11am–1pm & 5–8pm) include a tenth-century Moorish tower and a group of Romanesque buildings, with a small chapel.

The town below is reasonably substantial – 15,000 population – and has old and new quarters, the former with many fine Aragonese mansions and a Romanesque *colegiata*. Most of the budget **accommodation** is by the train station, including the basic but clean *Habitaciones Rech* (☎974 402241; ②) at c/Cervantes 8. The most comfortable place to stay is *Hotel Vianetto*, Avda. Lérida 25 (☎974 401900; ⑤), which has an excellent restaurant and a secure garage. Two other very good **restaurants** are *Jairo*, c/Santa Barbara 10 (closed Mon), and *Piscis*, Plaza de Aragón 1; both specialize in fish and are reasonably priced, with *menús* at 1200ptas.

Barbastro

BARBASTRO, 20km farther along the Río Cinca, is a historic town of no small importance. It was here that the union of Aragón and Catalunya was declared in 1137, sealed by the marriage of the daughter of Ramiro of Aragón to Ramón Berenguer IV, Lord of Barcelona. Although it's now little more than a provincial market town, Barbastro retains an air of importance in its *casco viejo*, or old quarter. Up on the hill, the Gothic **Catedral**, on a site once occupied by a mosque, has a high altar whose construction was under the authority of Damián Forment: when he died in 1540 only part of the alabaster relief had been completed, and the remainder was finished by his pupils. The **Ayuntamiento**, a restored fifteenth-century edifice designed by the Moorish chief architect to Fernando el Católico, is also worth seeing. Elsewhere, there are some lovely fading **mansions** in the narrow, pedestrianized shopping streets which tumble down towards the river, while a central, tree-lined *paseo* at the top of the town is home to most of the town's bars and cafés.

Practicalities

The **bus** station is at the top of the *paseo*, and offers six departures daily for Huesca and Lleida and two to Benasque. There's an English-speaking **Turismo** (July & Aug daily 10am–2pm & 4.30–8pm; Sept–June Tues–Sat 10am–2pm & 4.30–8pm; ☎974 308350) right next door, which can give you a map and help out with accommodation.

There are several inexpensive **hostales** in town. *La Sombra* (☎974 315332; ①), on c/Argensola, one block back from the river, has the cheapest rooms, though the

---

JOSÉ-MARÍA ESCRIVA AND OPUS DEI

Barbastro was the birthplace of **José-María Escriva** (1902–75), the founder of **Opus Dei**. This fundamentalist and ultra-conservative Catholic movement today has a worldwide following of around 80,000, including sympathetic ears at the Vatican, where, in 1992, Pope John Paul II "beatified" Escriva, putting him on the first rung to sainthood. Its power, however, has been far greater. In the latter years of Franco's regime, three of the Generalísmo's cabinet were Opus Dei members, and the organization looked, for a while, set to control the government in the years to come.

Escriva launched the movement in 1928, while a young priest in Madrid. His followers were to be encouraged to dedicate their lives to God, following an ascetic spiritual programme, but to work within the world rather than withdrawing into monastic orders. The **members** were (and are) designated in one of three categories. At the top are the *numenaries*, who have pledged celibacy and live in Opus Dei houses; some of them become priests but the majority have professional jobs. Next are the *oblates*, lay people who choose celibacy but live with their family. Then there are the *supernumenaries*, who live regular lives, though, like the rest, follow the "norms" laid down by Escriva in his book, *El Camino*. These are the best-known and most controversial aspects of Opus Dei, for, as well as daily Mass and a day's spiritual retreat each week, they include "mortifications": wearing a spiked bracelet for two hours a day and self-flagellation once a week.

The spiritual home of Opus Dei is at **Torreciudad**, 20km north of Barbastro. At the old hermitage here, the two-year-old Escriva was brought to be cured. On the slopes above, his followers have built the largest modern monastery in Spain, and they have elevated the Virgin of Torreciudad to the highest rank, on a par with those of Zaragoza and Lourdes.

---

cheerful and family-run *Hostal Goya* at number 13 (☎974 311747; ②) is the better option. The *Roxi* (☎974 311064; ③) offers a bit more comfort and your own bathroom, while rooms at *Fonda San Ramón*, just off the *paseo* at Academia Cerbuna 2 (☎974 310250; ③), are old-fashioned, clean and spacious, with private bathroom. This is also the best **place to eat** in town; the superbly decorated first-floor dining room features a chandelier, old tiling, glass cabinets and potted plants – an expertly cooked four-course *cubierto* costs 1600 or 2200ptas. Another good place to eat is the *Bar Stop Meriendas*, next door to *La Sombra*, which has a terrific range of dishes to choose from. Alternatively, try *Restaurante Flor* at c/Goya 3, for food at mid-range prices.

Huesca and around

HUESCA is one of the least memorable Aragonese towns and if you're heading for the mountains, you could bypass it altogether, or stay on the train to Jaca or beyond. However, northwest of the town, the beautiful **Los Mallos** mountains and the castle at **Loarre** represent a very good reason for breaking a journey towards Jaca.

To say Huesca is unmemorable is perhaps a bit of a slight, for it has a reasonably well-preserved **Casco Viejo**, tucked into a loop of *paseos* and the Río Isuela. At the core of this is a late Gothic **Catedral**, whose unusual facade combines the thirteenth-century portal of an earlier church with a brick Mudéjar gallery, and a pinnacled uppermost section that's Isabelline in style. The great treasure inside is the *retablo* by Damián Forment, which is considered this Renaissance sculptor's masterpiece.

Next door, the **Museo Diocesano** (daily 11am–1pm & 4–6pm; 200ptas) contains a rather mixed collection, gathered from churches in the countryside. Across the way is a Renaissance **Ayuntamiento**. These apart, there's little to detain you. The liveliest time to visit is during Huesca's big **fiesta** in honour of San Lorenzo, held over the week that includes August 10.

Arrival and information

Finding your way around Huesca shouldn't be a problem. The **train** station is at the south end of c/Zaragoza, a main thoroughfare, and the **bus station** is up the street at Plaza Navarra. There is a municipal **Turismo** (July–Sept Mon–Fri 10.30am–1pm & 4–6.30pm, Sat & Sun 10.30am–1pm; Oct–June variable opening times; ☎974 292100) opposite the Cathedral in the *Ayuntamiento*, and a regional Turismo (Mon–Fri 9am–2pm & 4.30–8pm, Sat 10am–2pm & 5–8pm, Sun 10am–2pm; ☎974 225778) on c/General Lasheras opposite Plaza de Cervantes, which stocks lots of pamphlets on the Aragonese mountains. The **Correos** is at Coso Alto 14–16.

Accommodation

Places to stay can be hard to find, and in summer, when trekkers from all over are passing through, it is well worth booking ahead. The campsite, *San Jorge* (☎974 227416), is at the end of c/Ricardo del Arco.

Pensión Augusto, c/Ainsa 16 (☎974 220079). Tidy rooms in this good-value *pensión*. ②–③.

Pensión Bandrés, c/Fatás 5 (☎974 224782). Large, clean *pensión*, close to the bus station. ③.

Hostal El Centro, c/Sancho Ramírez 3 (☎974 226823). Large, well-renovated rooms. ③.

Hostal Lizana (☎974 221470) and **Hostal Lizana II** (☎974 220776, fax 974 220776), both on Plaza de Lizana. Nicely located on a quiet square, just downhill from the cathedral. Both ④.

Hotel Pedro I de Aragón, Avda. de Parque 34 (☎974 220300, fax 974 220094). Huesca's top hotel, offering air-conditioned luxury and a swimming pool. ⑦.

Hostal Sancho Abarca, Plaza de Lizana 13 (☎974 220650, fax 974 225169). Another luxury hotel on this well-located square. ⑥.

Eating, drinking and nightlife

Restaurants are plentiful enough, with many places offering solid mountain fare, including lamb and freshwater fish specialities. For excellent **tapas bars** and the centre of the town's **nightlife** head for the *zona* around c/San Lorenzo, between the Coso Bajo and the Plaza de Santa Clara.

Casa Lis, c/Padre Huesca 37. The unique mixture of Spanish and Danish food at this restaurant reflects the parentage of its owner; not only is Marilis *cordon bleu* trained, she serves a 800ptas *menú* – the cheapest in town – and will always accommodate vegetarians.

Restaurante Navas, c/Vicente Campo. The city's top restaurant has delicious fish dishes, exquisite desserts, and a choice of *menús* from a modest 2000ptas up to 4000ptas for the chef's full works. Closed Mon, June 21–30 & Oct 18–27.

Restaurante Las Torres, c/María Auxiliadora 3. A relaxed restaurant with French-influenced cooking; the *menú* is 1800ptas. Closed Sun & Aug 20–Sept 3.

Castillo de Loarre

The **Castillo de Loarre** (April–Sept 10am–1.30pm & 4–7pm; Oct–March 11am–2.30pm; closed Mon & Tues except in August; free, but donation expected) is Aragón's most spectacular fortress – indeed, there are few that can rival it anywhere in Spain. As you approach, the castle at first seems to blend into the hillside but gradually assumes a breathtaking grandeur: superbly compact, it rises dizzily on a rocky outcrop, commanding the landscape for miles around.

Its builder was Sancho Ramírez, king of Navarra (1000–35), who used it as a base for his resistance to the Moorish occupation. Within the curtain walls is a delicately proportioned Romanesque church, with 84 individually carved capitals. There is access, also, to a pair of towers, the Torre de la Reina and the taller Torre del Homenaje, which can be climbed by iron rungs cemented into the wall. Be careful, though, as the rungs, especially those at the top, are not in the best state of repair.

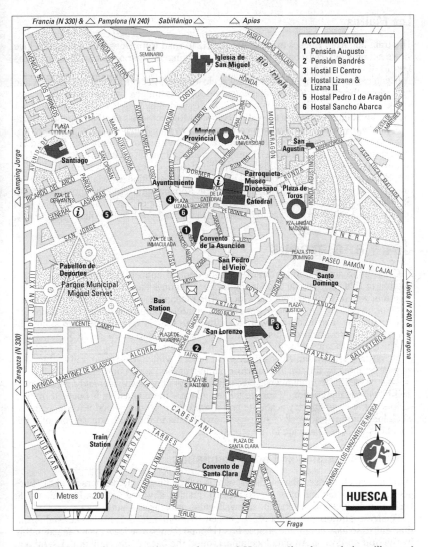

Francia (N 330) & △ Pamplona (N 240)   Sabiñánigo △   △ Apies

ACCOMMODATION
1 Pensión Augusto
2 Pensión Bandrés
3 Hostal El Centro
4 Hostal Lizana &
    Lizana II
5 Hostal Pedro I de Aragón
6 Hostal Sancho Abarca

HUESCA

0 Metres 200

The castle stands some 40km northwest of Huesca, 6km beyond the village of Loarre. By **public transport**, it's an awkward trip and you may decide that the views from the road or rail line are sufficient, as bus and train timetables do their best to conspire against a day trip, and there is nowhere to stay in either Ayerbe (the nearest train station) or Loarre. Loarre village has three buses daily from Huesca, all in the afternoon. If you can get a big enough group together, you could consider hiring a Microbus for the day: try GuarAbus, c/Ballesteros 9 (☎974 227000) in Huesca, and haggle for all you are worth.

Los Mallos

The train line from Huesca to Jaca, and the N240 road from Huesca to Pamplona, give views not only of Loarre but of the fantastic, pink-tinged sugarloaf mountains known as **Los Mallos** – the ninepins.

If you're travelling by train and want a closer look, get off at **Riglos-Concilio** and walk along the road to **Riglos** village, tucked high up underneath the most impressive stretch of the peaks. Along the way, you'll be rewarded by a series of superb views not only of the Mallos, but also of the valley below. At Riglos there's another (unstaffed) station, below the village, from where you can resume your journey.

There's another group of Mallos mountains near **Agüero**, a completely isolated village, 5km off the main Huesca–Pamplona road and easily visible from Riglos. This would make a 7km walk from Riglos-Concilio station, or a 5km walk from Murillo (on the Huesca–Pamplona bus route). The reward, in addition to Mallos views, is an unspoilt village, and a gorgeous, unfinished Romanesque church, the **Iglesia de Santiago** (c. 1200), with portal carvings by the Master of San Juan de la Peña (see p.552); it is reached up a dirt road above the main road – ask in the village for the key.

Jaca and around

JACA is approached through scruffy, traffic-choked suburbs: an unpromising introduction to this early capital and stronghold of Aragón – and the base from which the kingdom was recaptured from the Moors. The old centre, however, is a lot more characterful, overlooked by a huge star-shaped citadel, retaining patches of Roman and medieval walls, and endowed with a **cathedral** that is one of the high points of Romanesque architecture. This, and the monastery of **San Juan de la Peña**, 20km southeast, are the major local sights, though in winter there is a bonus in the proximity of **Astún-Candanchu**, Aragón's best ski resort, while, year-round, rail enthusiasts may be tempted by the trip to **Canfranc**, almost at the French border.

After a spell in the mountains, Jaca's (relatively) "big town" feel and facilities may well be an equal attraction. It can be a lively place – the population is boosted by conscripts at the large military academy and a summer university – and it hosts a terrific week-long **fiesta** (last week of June) with live bands in the main square, lots of traditional costume, and partying in the streets.

Arrival, information and accommodation

Jaca has two characters: the northeast side is a little dingy, and shelters all of the budget accommodation and bars; the southwest quarter, abutting Avenida Regimiento de Galicia, is flashier with a series of sidewalk cafés, restaurants and banks.

The **train station** (the ticket office is open 10am–noon & 5–7pm) is a fair walk from the centre, so look out for the shuttle bus (75ptas). When you leave, you can catch this by the **bus station** on Avenida Jacetania, around the back of the cathedral. Useful bus services include: Pamplona (3 daily), and Biescas via Sabiñánigo (2 daily); there are also more frequent services to Zaragoza and Huesca (4–5 daily). Note that although the timetables don't say so, hardly any buses run on Sundays.

If you're heading for the mountains, look in at the **Turismo**, Avenida Regimiento de Galicia (summer Mon–Fri 9am–2pm & 4.30–8pm, Sat 10am–1.30pm & 5–8pm, Sun 10am–1.30pm; winter Mon–Fri 9am–1pm & 4.30–7pm, Sat 10am–1pm & 5–7pm; ☎974 360098), which has a range of leaflets on trekking, skiing, mountain-biking, horse-riding, and other activities from yoga to weaving.

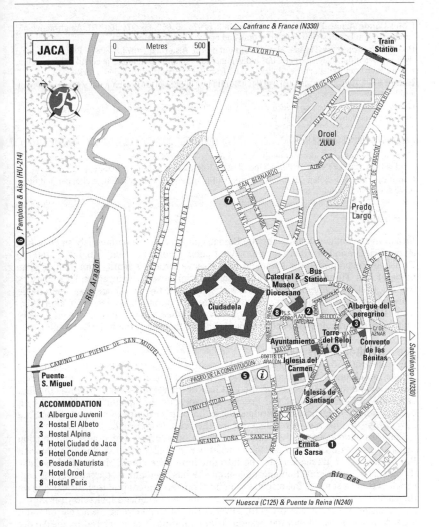

Accommodation

Jaca is a gateway to the peaks, and its **accommodation** facilities are almost always stretched. It's a good idea to book in advance.

Albergue Juvenil, Avda. Perimetral (☎974 360536). The local youth hostel has doubles, triples and five-bed rooms. It is located at the south end of the town by the skating rink. ①.

Hostal Residencia El Abeto, c/Bellido 15 (☎974 361642). A comfortable *hostal*, with en-suite facilities, although it's a bit noisy, with a lot of bars nearby. ③.

Hostal Alpina, c/Mayor 57 (☎974 364026). Modern, attractive rooms in the old town. ⑥.

Hotel Ciudad de Jaca, c/Siete de Febrero 8 (☎974 364311, fax 974 364395). Centrally located with good en-suite rooms. ④.

Hotel Conde Aznar, Paseo de la Constitución 3 (☎974 361050, fax 974 360797). An attractive old family-run hotel, with well-renovated rooms and an excellent restaurant. ⑤.

Posada Naturista las Tienas Altas, 15km out on the Aísa road (☎974 348087). Perched above a river in a beautiful valley, this rural inn and vegetarian restaurant is about as peaceful as you can get. If you haven't got transport they'll pick you up from Jaca. Breakfast included in price. ④.

Hotel Oroel, Avda. de Francia 37 (☎974 362411, fax 974 363804). Modern hotel with its own pool, and large rooms with kitchens. ⑥–⑦.

Hostal París, Plaza de San Pedro 5 (☎974 361020). Best-value *hostal* in town – clean, spacious rooms across from the cathedral. ③.

CAMPING

Camping Peña Oroel, 4km out on the Sabiñánigo road (☎974 360215). An attractive campsite, set amid woods, with excellent facilities. Open Easter week and mid-June to mid-Sept.

Camping Victoria, 1500m out of town on the Pamplona road (☎974 360323). A cheaper and more basic site, near the Río Aragón.

The Town

Jaca is an ancient city, founded by the Romans and occupied continuously since. It had a very brief period of Moorish rule, having been captured around 716, but in 760 the Christians reconquered the town and held it, save for a few years, from then on. The battle of **Las Tiendas** in 795, when Moorish armies were repulsed, in large part by women, is still commemorated on the last Friday in May, in a mock all-women battle between Christians and Moors. The town's greatest period, however, came after 1035, when **Ramiro I**, son of Sancho of Navarre, established a court here. It was in this era that the first parliament on record took place, and that the cathedral was rebuilt.

The cathedral and its museum

The **Catedral** is the main legacy of Jaca's years as an early capital of the kingdom of Aragón, and is one of Spain's most appealing and architecturally important monuments. Rebuilt on old foundations during the first half of the eleventh century, it was the first cathedral in Spain to adopt the French Romanesque architecture, and, as such, it became a huge influence on churches along the pilgrim routes of northern Spain; the new designs themselves were carried along the route from France.

Ramiro's endowment of the cathedral was undoubtedly designed as a confirmation of Jaca's role as a Christian capital, in what was still almost an exclusively Moorish Iberian peninsula. Its design saw the introduction of the classic three-aisled basilica, though sadly the original Romanesque simplicity has been much adapted over the centuries. It retains some of the original sculpture, however, including realistic carving on the capitals and doorway; a sixteenth-century statue of Santiago looks down from the porch. Inside, the main treasure is the silver shrine of Santa Orosía, Jaca's patron saint; a Czech noble, married into the Aragón royal family, she was martyred by the Moors for refusing to renounce her faith.

Installed in the dark cathedral cloisters is an unusually good **Museo Diocesano** (daily except Mon: summer 10am–2pm & 4–8pm; winter 11am–1.30pm & 4–6.30pm; 200ptas). This features a beautiful collection of twelfth- to fifteenth-century Aragonese frescoes, gathered from village churches in the area and from higher up in the Pyrenees. If your interest is sparked, there is a comparable, though far more extensive, display of their Catalunyan equivalents in Barcelona.

The Ciudadela and Puente San Miguel

The **Ciudadela**, a redoubtable sixteenth-century fort, built in the French-style star design, is still part-occupied by the military. You can visit a part of the interior (daily:

summer 11am–12.30pm & 5–6.30pm; winter 11am–12pm & 4–5pm; 200ptas), however, on a guided tour. Its walls offer good views of the surrounding peaks, and of the wooded countryside around.

Below the citadel, reached along a rough track from the end of the Paseo de la Constitución, Jaca preserves a remarkable medieval bridge, the **Puente San Miguel**. It was across this bridge, over the Río Aragón, that pilgrims on the **Camino de Santiago** (see p.494) entered Jaca – a welcome sight, marking the end of the arduous Pyrenean stage for pilgrims following the Camino Aragonés. This branch of the route, from Provence, crossed into Spain over the Puerto de Somport and, from Jaca, headed wootwardo, through Puento la Roina do Jaoa, towardo Navarra, whoro it mot with tho more popular route from Roncesvalles.

This Aragón section of the Camino de Santiago – like other branches of the route – has experienced quite a revival in recent years. In town, there is a **pilgrims' hostel** in the medieval hospital on c/de Aznar, and route maps and pilgrimage-related souvenirs are widely available.

Eating and drinking

Jaca has a lively and inviting selection of **restaurants** and **bars** catering to the needs of hungry walkers. Prices are generally reasonable – though being served on the terrace of any restaurant attracts a ten percent surcharge – and there's a good night-time atmosphere in town, especially during the summer months.

El Arco, c/San Nicolás 4. That rare Spanish breed: a vegetarian, no-smoking restaurant. Fresh, filling, international dishes and a 1200ptas *menú*. Closed Sun in winter.

La Cabaña, c/del Pez 10. Inexpensive *menú* and cheerful surroundings.

La Cocina Aragonesa, Paseo de la Constitución 3. This is the restaurant of the hotel *Conde Aznar* and it is reckoned the best in town. The cooking is elaborate and Basque-influenced. Expect to pay 3000ptas. Closed Wed.

Crepería El Breton, c/Ramiro I 10. An authentic French-run *crêperie*. Closed Mon in winter and last two weeks of June.

Croissanterie Demilune, Avda. Regimiento de Galicia 2. A wide variety of filled croissants and *batidos* (fruit shakes) make this a great place for snacks or breakfast.

Equiza, c/Primer de Rivera. This rather ritzy-looking bar has a big reputation for its *tapas* – especially its *gambas* and other *fritos*.

La Fragua, c/Gil Berges 4. Excellent, reasonably priced grills. Closed Wed.

Mesón El Rancho Grande, c/Arco 2. Fairly expensive but very impressive Aragonese cooking – a good place for a blow-out.

Pizzeria La Fontana, corner of c/Ramiro I and Plaza del Marqués de la Cadena. Dependable and substantial pizzas at above average prices.

Tomás, c/Ferrenal 8. No-nonsense bar with a vast range of *tapas* and *raciones*.

Listings

Bike rental You can rent a mountain bike at short notice for around 2500ptas a day from Jaca Adventura, Avda. Francia 1 (☎974 363521).

Car rental Don Auto, Correos 2 (☎908 833227). In high season all cars must be booked at least a day in advance.

Laundry There's a self-service *lavandería* next to the supermarket, Superpirineos, on c/Astún.

Post office The *Correos* – including poste restante (*lista de correos*) – is at c/Correos 13 (Mon–Fri 9am–2pm, Sat 9am–1pm).

Tours Trekking, rafting, climbing, skiing and other activity expeditions are organized by Jaca Adventura (see "Bike rental" above) or Alcorce-Pireneos Adventura, opposite the Turismo at Avda. Regimiento Galicia 1 (☎974 356437). Both these companies have English-speaking staff.

Trekking maps are available from two bookstores on c/Mayor and at a mountaineering shop, Charli, Avda. Regimiento de Galicia 3.

On to San Juan de la Peña

San Juan de la Peña, up in the hills to the southwest of Jaca, is the best-known monastery in Aragón. In the Middle Ages, it was an important detour on the pilgrim route from Jaca to Pamplona, as it was reputed to hold the Holy Grail – a Roman-era chalice which later found its way to Valencia cathedral. These days, most tourists (and there are a lot – including school parties) visit for the views and Romanesque cloister.

The most direct **route to the monastery** is from the Jaca–Pamplona (N240) road. A turning 10km from Jaca, leads 3km to the village of **Santa Cruz de los Serós**, and from here it's a further 4km up to San Juan. There is no public transport, although you could take a Puente la Reina/Pamplona bus from Jaca and walk from the turn-off to Santa Cruz. **Renting a bike** would be easier: reckon on one hour for Jaca to Santa Cruz, then a further hour up the steep road to San Juan. Descending, you could take the C125 via Bernues – a gradual descent to Bernues, a slight climb to Puerto de Oroel, then a fierce drop to Jaca – this is very scenic, and car-free, but not a leg to do uphill.

Santa Cruz de los Serós

SANTA CRUZ DE LOS SERÓS is a picturesque hamlet, dominated by a fine Romanesque **church** (11am–1pm & 4–6pm; 100ptas), that was once part of a large Benedictine monastery. The nearest place to stay is the *Hostal Aragón* (☎974 377112, fax 974 362189; ④), back on the Jaca–Pamplona road (N240).

From Santa Cruz, walkers can take the **old path** up to San Juan in about an hour. The path is waymarked as a variant of GR65.3 and is signposted from near the church (where there is also a sign with a map). The road takes a more circuitous route around the mountainside, giving wonderful views over a vast panorama, with the peaks of the Pyrenees clearly visible to the north and the oddly shaped Peña de Oroel to the east.

San Juan de la Peña

SAN JUAN DE LA PEÑA actually comprises two monasteries, 2km apart. Coming from Santa Cruz, you reach first the lower (and older) one.

Built into a hollow under the rocks, the **Lower Monastery** (mid-March to mid-Oct Tues–Sun 10am–1.30pm & 4–6pm; mid-Oct to mid-March Wed–Sun 11am–2.30pm; 300ptas) is an unusual and evocative complex, even in its partial state of survival. It was here that the Latin Mass was introduced to the Iberian peninsula and here, too, that the Aragonese maintained a stronghold in the early years of the Reconquest. Entering, you pass first into a ninth-century Mozarabic chapel, which was adapted as the crypt of the main Romanesque **church**; it retains fragments of Romanesque frescoes. Upstairs, alongside the main church, is a **pantheon** for Aragonese nobles, while to the side is a pantheon for the kings of Aragón, remodelled in a cold, Neoclassical style in the eighteenth century and sacked by Napoleon's troops. Reliefs on the Gothic nobles' tombs depict events from the early history of Aragón.

The artistic highlight, however, is the twelfth-century Romanesque **cloisters**. Only two of the bays are complete – another is in a fragmentary state – but the surviving capitals are among the greatest examples of Romanesque carving. They were the work of an idiosyncratic master who made his mark on a number of churches in the region. He is now known as the Master of San Juan de la Peña and his work is easily recognizable by the unnaturally large eyes he gave his figures.

The **Upper Monastery**, a sizeable complex with a Baroque facade, can be seen from the outside only, but it is worth the climb, if only for the views of the Pyrenees from a nearby *mirador*. Facing the monastery, the huge meadow, enclosed by woods, is a very popular picnic ground.

Canfranc-Estación

Ever since the French railways discontinued their part of the trans-Pyrenean line, **CANFRANC-ESTACIÓN**, 30km north of Jaca, has been a white elephant: a train station equipped with a hotel, post office and police station — but no onward traffic. The re-opening of the rail line is periodically mooted, and the planned opening of the Somport car tunnel in around 2000, may bring things to a head. Spanish undercutting of French prices prompted the closure of the line in the first place in the 1970s, amid French mutterings about ostensible safety concerns over the Spanish track.

The village, such as it is, exists solely to catch the passing tourist trade (mostly French), and sports a few gift shops and hotels. It's just about worth the day's trip from Jaca, even if you don't continue into France, for the train ride up the valley. **Places to stay** include the *Albergue Pepito Grillo*, c/Fernando el Católico 2 (☎974 373123; ①), the *Hotel Ara*, c/Fernando el Católico 1 (☎974 373028; ③), and the friendly *Hotel Villa Anayet*, Plaza de Aragón (☎974 373146; ④). There is also a **campsite** (☎908 731604; April to mid-Sept), 5km north on the road towards Candanchú. For meals, *Casa Flores* has the cheapest *menú*, at 1070ptas, or consider the *comedor* at the *Hotel Villa Anayet*, where a set, four-course *menú* is 1200ptas.

Though there's no train, you can travel on into France by public transport. There are four daily **bus** departures, co-run by La Oscense and SNCF. Coming from France, buses arrive in Canfranc from Oloron at 9.53am, 11.30am, 11.47am and 4.05pm, with train connections on to Jaca at 11.35am and 5.55pm. More information, if you need it,

---

SKIING IN ARAGON

There are half a dozen **ski resorts** in Aragón's stretch of the Pyrenees and most of them – following the province's hosting of the 1982 University Winter Olympics – are well equipped. You may find that package deals, bought from any travel agent in northern Spain, work out cheaper than going your own way but there's nothing to prevent you from just turning up. The Spanish National Tourist Organization publishes a special pamphlet on skiing and there are piles of more detailed information at the tourist offices in Zaragoza, Huesca and Jaca. It's easy enough to search through these, decide where you feel like going, and phone ahead to check conditions and reserve a room (the latter vital around Christmas or the New Year).

Perhaps the best, and certainly the most varied, option is the twin resort of **ASTÚN-CANDANCHÚ**, north of Canfranc (buses from Jaca). The resorts – Astún is fairly new, Candanchú established – are just 8km apart, and you can alternate between them. Astún is particularly well organized, rarely crowded and has plentiful (generally new) equipment for hire at reasonably modest rates. The only budget accommodation in Candanchú is the *Hostal Somport*, Ctra de Francia 198 (☎974 373009; ③ for rooms without bath) while the *Tobazo*, Ctra de Francia (☎974 37312, fax 974 373125; ⑥), and the *Candanchú*, Ctra de Francia (☎974 373025, fax 974 373050; ⑥), reflect the more usual prices for this resort. Over in Astún there are a couple of *albergues*, the highly rated *El Águila* (☎974 373291; half-board ③), and the *Valle del Aragón* (☎974 373222; half-board ③), both open all year, in addition to the usual, expensive hotels.

Other good winter resorts in Aragón include **Sallent de Gallego**, to the east of Jaca (buses from Sabiñánigo via Biescas) and **Cerler**, close to Benasque.

can be had from the Canfranc **Turismo** (July–Sept Mon–Sat 9am–1pm & 4–8pm, Sun 9am–1pm; Oct–June Wed–Sat 9am–1.30pm & 3.30–6.30pm, Sun 9am–1.30pm; ☎974 373141), opposite the station.

Arriving from France, the village of **VILLANÚA**, 6km down the valley, offers a much more tranquil and pleasant introduction to Spain. Buses stop on the main road and if you walk over the bridge and down into the old village, you'll find the welcoming *Albergue-Refugio Triton* (☎974 378281; ①) just off the main square at c/Mediodía.

Hecho and Ansó

Hecho and **Ansó** are two of the most attractive valleys in the Pyrenees. Their rivers water the Río Aragón, to the west of Jaca, and, until very recently, both valleys felt extremely remote, with villagers wearing traditional dress and speaking a dialect, *Cheso*, descended from medieval Aragonese. These days, they're on the tourist map for Spanish weekenders and summer walkers, though the rural life goes on pretty much unaffected.

If you don't have transport of your own, renting a **mountain bike** in Jaca would be a good investment for exploring the valleys, as there is only a single **daily bus** (calling first at Hecho and continuing to Ansó; it leaves Jaca at 6.30pm and begins the journey back from Ansó at 6am, passing Hecho 45min later). By bike, reckon on around two-and-a-half-hours from Jaca to Hecho village, turning off the N240 at Puente la Reina de Jaca, or much the same to Ansó village, turning off at Berdún.

For **trekking in the region**, the Editorial Alpina booklet, *Guía Cartográfica de las Valles de Ansó y Hecho* (500ptas) is extremely useful.

Valle de Hecho

HECHO (the first H is silent – you'll also see it spelt Echo) is a splendid old village, with stone and whitewash houses, and a claim to fame in Aragonese history as the seat of the embryonic Aragonese kingdom under Aznar Galíndez in the ninth century, and the birthplace of the "warrior king", Alfonso I. Today it is very much a farming community, although the influx of tourists in July and August has led to high prices at the hotels and, especially, restaurants where a *menú* will cost around 1600ptas. There is a **Turismo** in the *Ayuntamiento* (daily June–Sept 10am–2pm & 6–8pm; ☎974 375329), which also has information about much of the surrounding area; if it's shut ask upstairs and they may open it for you.

There used to be an annual arts festival which has left a permanent legacy in an open-air **gallery of sculpture**, on the hillside west of the village. Created by a group of artists led by Pedro Tramullas, these pieces are not too stunning individually but the location makes up for them; unfortunately, the venture does not enjoy whole-hearted backing from the locals, who have resisted its expansion. Near the village church, there is also a more conventional museum, the **Museo Etnológico** (daily 11am–2pm & 6–9pm; 150ptas), with interesting collections on Pyrenean rural life and folklore.

In summer or at the weekend you would be well advised to book ahead at one of Hecho's three **hostales**. The clear first choice is *Casa Blasquico*, unmarked at Plaza de la Fuente 1, next door to the bar (☎974 375007; closed Sept; ③–④); this is a wonderful six-bedroomed place, based on trust and disregarding locks and keys. Fallbacks are the modern *Hostal Lo Foratón* (☎974 375247; ④–⑤) and *Hostal de la Val* (☎974 375028; ④), both at the north end of the village. There is also a **campsite**, *Valle de Hecho* (☎974 375361), just south of the village.

For **meals**, don't miss the chance to eat at *Casa Blasquico* (closed Sept) – definitely worth a splurge à la carte, but, if money's tight, there's usually also a great-value 1500ptas *menú de la casa*, including good house wine. The owner-chef here, Gaby Coarasa, is brilliant and her tiny *comedor* is often singled out in Spanish magazines as the most creative restaurant in the Pyrenees; the walls inside are lined with awards to prove it. She starts serving at 2pm and 9pm; you can drink beforehand at the village bar next door. It's extremely popular so making a reservation is a good idea, especially in the summer.

Sirooa and boyond

Two kilometres north of Hecho – a fine walk down the valley – is the beautiful, quiet village of **SIRESA**. Standing watch over the river – which boasts a lovely spot for swimming – is a remarkable ninth-century church, **San Pedro** (daily 10am–2pm & 4–8pm), once the core of a monastery. There is a pleasant **hotel** here, the *Castillo d'Acher* (☎974 375011; ④, depending on season); this also operates the *fonda* (②), over the village bar, and a **restaurant** which serves *menús* from 900ptas.

Walkers may be tempted to continue 10km up the valley from Siresa, to **SELVA DE OZA**, where there's a **campsite**, *Selva de Oza* (☎974 375168; mid-June to mid-Sept), with hot water and a restaurant, and a refuge, *Refugio Oza* (140 places; staffed all year). These are both excellent bases for following trails up the surrounding limestone peaks of **Bisaurin** (2669m), **Agüerri** (2449m) and **Castillo de Acher** (2390m). The finest of these is Agüerri, whose summit is a fairly strenous 6–7hr walk from the *refugio*.

North of Selva de Oza, the frontier peaks of **Lariste** (2168m) and **Laraille** (2147m) are classic trekking targets, again around 6–7hrs walking from the *refugio*. Walkers also have tempting routes in the long-distance **GR11 footpath**, which cuts across the valleys 2km north of Oza: west to Zuriza in the Ansó valley (see below) and east to Candanchú; either route will take you a full 7–9hr day's trekking.

On to Ansó

The daily **bus** from Jaca to Hecho continues to Ansó: a good route, along 12km of narrow, twisting road, up over the ridge and then, through two tunnels and a gorge, dropping into the **Valle de Ansó**, which is guarded by two strangely shaped rocks known locally as "the Monk and the Nun".

There's also a very enjoyable two-and-a-half-hour **trail** from **Siresa to Ansó**, shakily signposted by the stream below Siresa.

Valle de Ansó

Once a prosperous, large village, **ANSÓ** fell upon hard times during the depopulation of rural Aragón in the 1950s and 1960s. These days, though, there are signs of revival, with Jaca and Pamplona professionals keeping weekend residences here, as well as a growing stream of tourists. It's certainly an attractive weekend base, with a little river beach for splashing around in the Río Veral. Sights are a bit thin on the ground, though, as at Hecho, there's a **Museo Etnológico** (daily 10.30am–1.30pm & 4–8pm; 200ptas), housed in an ancient church building.

Ansó's growing popularity is reflected in five places to **stay**, all of which fill quickly in summer. Best are the *Posada Magoria* (☎974 370049; ③), which serves communal vegetarian meals (preference is given to guests); *Hostal Estanés* (☎974 370146; ④), which has good-value rooms with and without baths; and the Peruvian-run *La Posada Veral*, Cocorro 6 (☎974 370119; ③). *Hostal Kimboa* (☎974 370184; ④) has less character, but the rooms are new and comfortable. There's no campsite but tents are tolerated on the grass down by the riverside municipal swimming pool, at the south end of the village.

All of the *hostales* have their own **restaurants**, and there's also one at the swimming pool, plus a number of **bars**, the liveliest of which are *Zuriza* on the main street and the one in *La Posada Veral*.

Zuriza and beyond

Other than the path in from Siresa, the lower Ansó valley has little trekking potential; to start **walking** you really must go to **ZURIZA**, 14km north. There's no bus service, and the paved road up the valley is tedious, so try to arrange a lift if you don't have transport. At Zuriza, there is a combined **refugio/campsite**, *Zuriza* (☎974 370196; ① beds and a few ④ rooms), a general store and a bar-restaurant. Equipped with the Editorial Alpina booklet, you're well poised here to tackle the popular day-trek up **Pico Sorbacal**, one of the highest in the area, or **Pico Chipeta**.

Other popular, longer outings from Zuriza include the traverses east to **Selva de Oza**, or west to **Isaba** in Navarra, along the GR11. Serious walkers might also continue north from Zuriza, along a track by the Petrachema stream, to the camping area at **Plano de la Casa** (5km). From here, you could make a day walk to Tres Reyes, at the heart of the karst region around the French border, or reach the high-level HRP, near the *Refugio Belagos* (☎976 236355).

Parque Nacional de Ordesa

The **PARQUE NACIONAL DE ORDESA Y MONTE PERDIDO** was one of Spain's first protected national parks, and it is perhaps the most dramatic: a place – as the tourist leaflet poetically puts it – "where all the different elements of nature seem to have agreed that here was the perfect spot to offer an uninterrupted spectacle of enjoyable surprises". The reality almost lives up to this brief, with beech and poplar forests, mountain streams, dozens of spring and early summer waterfalls, and of course a startling backdrop of peaks. The **wildlife**, too, is impressive, including golden eagles, lammergeiers, griffon vultures and Egyptian vultures, and Pyrenean chamois – mountain goat – so common that at certain times hunters are allowed to cull the surplus.

The park is an increasingly popular destination for walkers, and its foothill villages are becoming more and more commercialized each year. In midsummer, you will need to book accommodation well in advance, unless you plan to camp. Nevertheless, this is the Pyrenees at its very best, and well worth a few days of anyone's time.

Getting to Ordesa

Heading for Ordesa from the south, the place to make for is the gateway village of **Torla**, from where the GR15 leads into the park.

There's a daily **bus** service from Sabiñánigo to Ainsa, which stops at Torla and all the other villages on the way, including Biescas, Linas de Broto, Broto and Sarvisé. If you're coming **from the south**, it leaves Sabiñánigo at 11am, reaches Biescas fifteen minutes later, and gets to Torla at noon. In July and August there's an additional service between Sabiñánigo and Sarvisé, leaving the former at 6.30pm. Sabiñánigo and Biescas can be reached by bus from Jaca: there are two buses a day, leaving at 10.15am and 6.15pm (taking thirty minutes to get to Sabiñánigo and about an hour to Biescas).

Coming **from the east**, the same bus leaves Ainsa at 2.30pm, arriving in Torla at 3.30pm, and the summer service leaves Sarvisé at 8pm, calling at Torla about fifteen minutes later.

Sabiñánigo, Biescas and Linas de Broto

There's not much to industrial **SABIÑÁNIGO** and you'll probably want to push straight on. The **train station** is 300m northwest of the **bus terminal**, on the same street. Should you need to stop over, there are a half-dozen mostly overpriced places **to stay** along this road, the nicest and cheapest being the *Hostal Laguarta* (☎974 480004; ③), above the *Bar Lara*, just southeast of the bus station. During the evening this street is surprisingly lively, the bar clientele – a mix of locals and walkers – spilling out on to the pavement.

If you miss the morning through-service to Torla, there is a year-round evening service to **BIESCAS**, 17km north, from where you could try your luck hitching the remaining 25km to Torla (or pick up the Torla bus the following morning). If you get stuck (likely), Biescas is very pleasant, with a picturesque setting and several places to stay: *Habitaciones Las Herras* (☎974 485027; ③) offers spotless rooms in an old stone house, across the river from the *Ayuntamiento*, while *Hotel Ruba*, just off the Plaza del Ayuntamiento (☎974 485001; ④), has been in the same family since 1884 and is one of the oldest hotels in Aragón. There's also a central **campsite**, *Edelweiss* (☎974 485084; mid-June to mid-Sept), and a **Turismo** (June–Sept 10am–2pm & 4–6pm) next to the bridge. The tiny stone hamlet of **LINAS DE BROTO**, 17km east on the way to Torla, with three *hostales* and a fine position, would also be a reasonable spot to stop over: the best **place to stay** here is at *Hostal Jal* (☎974 486106; ③–④), right next to the bus stop.

Torla

The old stone village of **TORLA**, just 8km short of Ordesa, is fast being hidden away behind concrete blocks of rooms and apartments. It exists very much as a walkers' base and almost everything is geared to the trade. The **bus** from/to Sabiñánigo/Ainsa stops at the north end of town, by the pharmacy. Backtracking 100m or so to the main Ainsa/Biescas road, you'll find the **Turismo** (late June to mid-Sept, 9am–2pm & 4–6pm, closed Thurs & Sun pm; ☎974 229804), which offers free maps showing the main paths in the park. Inside the village there's a bank (with an ATM) next to the main supermarket.

In July and August, you'll need to book **accommodation** in Torla at least a week ahead; at other times, it is rarely a problem. In addition to the places listed below, there are two **campsites** along the road out to Ordesa: the *Río Ara* (☎974 486248), on the riverside, 2km from Torla, and the pricier *Ordesa* (☎974 486146), just under a kilometre from the village, with a pool, shop and a decent restaurant.

Albergue L'Atalaya (☎974 486022; ①). A French-run walkers' hostel, with 21 bunks and – getting its priorities right – a classy restaurant, probably the best in town. A kitchen is currently being added to the hostel. ①.

Albergue Lucien Briet (☎974 486221). A friendly thirty–bed hostel (but no kitchen), run by the nearby *Bar Brecha*, which serves good and inexpensive meals. ①.

Hostal Alto Aragón (☎974 486172). Friendly *hostal*, with smart en-suite rooms. ④.

Casa Carpintero (☎974 486256). Pleasant rooms in a private house, behind the *Bar Brecha* (through the small arch next to the bar); they may have space left when everyone else is full. ③.

Hotel Ordesa (☎974 486125, fax 974 486381). Peacefully located about 1km towards the park, with a pool, a restaurant and excellent views. ⑤.

Hotel Villa de Torla (☎974 486156, fax 974 486365). Located on the village square, this is the best of the more upmarket hotels, again with its own pool. ⑤.

Broto, Oto, Sarvisé, Fiscal and Ainsa

If you find Torla full, you may need or prefer to stop in one of the villages just to the east, along the road to Ainsa.

BROTO, 4km south of Torla, is a noisy, teeming place, its old quarter hemmed by traffic and new construction, a plight symbolized by the collapsed Roman bridge just upriver. Just beside this bridge is the quietest place to stay, and one of the last to fill:

Tabierna Bar O Puente (☎974 486072; ③ including breakfast). The **Turismo** (June–Sept Tues–Sun 10am–2pm & 4.30–8.30pm; ☎974 486002) can advise on vacancies in high season. If you are walking, you can follow a well-trodden *camino* to Torla in 45 minutes; it begins near the ruined bridge.

OTO, 2km south, is a more attractive village, with traditional architecture and a pair of medieval towers. It has two **casas rurales**: *Herrero* (☎974 486093; ③) and *Pueyo* (☎974 486075; ③), and a large **campsite** (☎974 486075; April to mid-Oct).

The lowest village of the Valle de Broto, a further 4km from Broto, is **SARVISÉ**. This again has a fair bit of accommodation, including the mid-range *Casa Frauca* (☎974 486182; ③) and *Casa Puyuelo* (☎974 486140; ③).

East of Sarvisé, the landscape widens into a broad valley with evidence of large-scale depopulation; medieval villages just off the road are largely deserted, their fields gone to seed. Indeed, Aragón has the highest proportion of abandoned settlements in Spain. One village that's found a new lease of life through a growing number of visitors is **FISCAL**: it has two **campsites**, *El Jabalí Blanco* (☎974 503074) and *Ribera del Ara* (☎974 503035), an outdoor pool and a gorgeous, eighteenth-century *casa rural*, *El Arco* (☎974 503042; ③), run by a Dutchman. There's also a *hostal* on the main road by the bus stop, and a **Turismo** (June–Sept 10am–2pm & 4.30–8.30pm) close by.

The next place of any size is **AINSA**, which has of late been prettified with walkways and boutiques in an attempt to cash in on some of the cross-border trade pouring over from the Bielsa tunnel to the north. Its **old quarter** up on the hill remains attractive, centred on an exceptional Romanesque church with a dark, primitive interior, and a vast, arcaded Plaza Mayor. The only place offering **rooms** up here is *Casa El Hospital* (☎974 500750; ③), an old stone house right next to the church. The rest of the accommodation is down in the new town and includes *Hostal Ordesa* (☎974 500009; ③) and *Hotel Sánchez* (☎974 500014; ③). The *Bodegas del Sobrarbe* (closed Nov to Easter), at Plaza Mayor 2, is an attractive, if somewhat pricey, **restaurant**, housed in a medieval cellar.

The Ordesa Canyon and central park treks

A tarmac road from Torla leads to the new **information office** (Centro de Visitantes; July–Oct 10am–1pm & 4–8.30pm), and from here continues about 1km to the car park at the entrance to the **Ordesa Canyon**. At the Centro de Visitantes you can buy a range of **maps** of the park; the clearest is the 1:50,000 IGN sheet (which also covers Gavarnie, across the French border), though cheaper ones are perfectly adequate if you're going to stick to the popular, signed paths. All the maps mark the park's network of very basic stone **refugios**, where you will need to stay on longer treks, as camping is prohibited in the park (except when the *refugios* are full, which happens in July and August, when you're allowed to camp alongside them).

If you're coming to the Centro on foot (there's no bus), you can cover the first half of the two-hour walk on the GR11 footpath: starting from the *Hotel Bella Vista* in Torla, walk down to the river and cross the bridge, then take the first (sharp) left to join the **Camino de Turieto**; at the next fork, take the left-hand path to join the road to the information office, or the right-hand path to bypass this and go directly to the car park, which is where most of the marked-out treks begin. There's no shop here or inside the park, so be sure to bring your own supplies.

Treks in the park

Most day-trippers to Ordesa aim no farther than a loop to the *mirador* (viewing point) at the **Cascada del Abanico**, six easy and well-waymarked kilometres from the car park, with a return path on the opposite bank of the Río Arazas. However, there are dozens of trails, encompassing most levels of enthusiasm and expertise. The following is just a selection.

Be aware that some of the "paths" marked on the maps are actually climbing routes and don't underestimate their time and difficulty.

CIRCO DE SOASO
This is one of the most popular and rewarding short-distance treks. It's not especially difficult: a steep, 7.5km-walk, along a signposted path, which brings you out at the **Cola de Caballo** (Horsetail Waterfall) in three to four hours (reckon on 6–7hr, there and back). The path sets out through beech forest and then climbs past a *mirador*, to emerge into the upper reaches of a startling valley gorge.

The path is not usually crowded, except in July and August, but for more solitude an alternative approach from the car park would be to climb the steep **Senda de los Cazadores** (the Hunters' Path) which brings you to the *mirador de Calcilarruego*; from here the path levels out along the Faja de Pelay, which joins up with the Circo de Soaso.

COTATUERO FALLS AND BEYOND
A shorter and easier walk is to the impressive **Cotatuero Falls**. Starting from the top of the car park, the Cotatuero route takes you steeply but easily through the woods to a vantage point below the waterfall.

An exciting onward route takes over here, if you have a head for heights. With the help of iron pegs, you can climb above the falls on to the Brecha de Rolando and trek onwards to Gavarnie (see below).

CARRIATA FALLS AND BEYOND
Another waterfall route is signposted from the old information office, near the car park, to the **Carriata Falls**. You head into the trees, fork left, and begin a steep zigzag up to the falls, which are most impressive in late spring when melted snow keeps them flowing.

If you want to continue, the left-hand route (at a fork on the open mountainside) ascends to the top of the gorge walls via a series of thirteen iron pegs, not nearly as intimidating as those on the Cotatuero route and feasible for any reasonably fit, active walker. The right-hand fork contours spectacularly along the canyon's north wall to meet up with the path up to Cotatuero.

REFUGIO GÓRIZ AND MONTE PERDIDO
A path climbs up from the top of Circo de Soaso, in around an hour, to the **Refugio Góriz** (2169m; ☎974 341201; open year round), which is more elaborate than the other refuges, equipped with beds and sheets, and an overpriced restaurant. It can also be reached on a path from the car park, in around four hours' walk. In July and August, it is usually packed to the gills, but you can camp alongside.

For most walkers, the refuge is a starting point for the ascent of **Monte Perdido**. This is a scramble rather than a climb but a serious expedition nonetheless, for which you should be properly equipped and prepared; the Góriz guardian can advise. The summit takes around 5hr and is reached via a mountain lake, Lago Helado.

TORLA TO GAVARNIE
The Ordesa park adjoins the French **Parc National des Pyrénées** and it is possible to trek across to the French border town of **Gavarnie**. This is a fair haul and most easily done from Torla; the routes from the Ordesa park office are longer and harder.

Leaving Torla, you follow the path to Ordesa, out beyond the campsites and as far as the signposted left fork for the Puente de los Navarros (around 45min), then climb down to the river and follow the GR11 markers up the valley. There's a **campsite**, *Camping Valle Bujaruelo* (☎974 486348; mid-April to mid-Oct), after another 4km, and, farther beyond, the hamlet of San Nicolás, from where the path, now mostly track, heads over the mountains and down to Gavarnie in six to eight hours.

The Southern canyons: Escuaín and Añisclo

In the southeast corner of the Ordesa park yawn a pair of **canyons** – the *gargantas* of **Escuaín** and **Añisclo** – which are every bit the equal of the Ordesa gorge but with far fewer visitors. The lack of transport to the trail heads, and limited accommodation, contribute to this, but the extra effort is amply rewarded.

The Añisclo canyon

The **Garganta de Añisclo** is the most spectacular of the two canyons, and more frequently visited. If you have transport, you can reach this on a minor but paved road from Sarvisé to Escalona (10km north of Ainsa). This road runs through a narrow gorge, the Desfiladero de las Cambras, at the west end of which knots of parked cars announce the mouth of Añisclo.

From here, two broad paths – each as good as the other – lead north into this marvellous, wild gorge; it's five hours' round-trip through the most spectacular section to La Ripareta. Long-haul trekkers also use the canyon as an alternate approach to the Góriz hut, exiting the main gorge via the Fon Blanca ravine.

If you're doing a day-walk, the best place to stay locally is **NERÍN**, 45 minutes' walk west of the canyon, via the deserted hamlet of Sercué, along a trail marked as part of the GR15. Nerín has a fine Romanesque church – typical of these settlements – and an *albergue* (☎974 486138; ①); this serves meals but requires reservations, or else you may end up camping. **FANLO**, 6km west, is the biggest place hereabouts; *Casa Nerein Sese*, La Plaza 1 (☎974 489009; ①–②), has rooms and dorms, though you'll definitely need to call first to reserve.

The Escuaín canyon

The **Garganta de Escuaín**, more properly the valley of the Río Yaga, is easiest reached from **Lafortunada**, 17km northwest of Ainsa and a convenient overnight base, with congenial rooms and filling *menús* at the *Casa Sebastián* (☎974 505120; ②) or the adjacent *Hotel Badain* (☎974 505134; ③).

From here, if you don't have transport, the quickest way into the canyon country is along the newly marked **GR15** trail; this climbs within two hours to the picturesque village of **Tella**, with a clutch of Romanesque churches and a park **information office** (daily July–Oct 8.30am–9pm), but no other facilities. Beyond, the trail drops to the river at Estaroniello hamlet before climbing through thick woods to **Escuaín**, an abandoned settlement taken over in summer by enthusiasts exploring **the gorge**, which lies just upstream. If you arrive early enough, you can lunch at the *albergue* (☎974 500939; ①) here, before continuing along paths into the water-sculpted ravine.

These routes through the gorge emerge at or near Revilla, a similarly desolate hamlet on the opposite bank. From there you can backtrack to Tella or follow a lovely and little-trodden *pequeño recorrido* path through Estaroniello to Hospital de Tella, 3km west of Lafortunada. You can complete this figure-of-eight itinerary in a single, long summer's day, taking in the best this limestone Shangri-la has to offer.

The Benasque area

Serious climbers and trekkers gravitate to **Benasque**, in the Valle del Ésera, for, above the town, just out of sight, loom the two highest peaks in the Pyrenees – **Aneto** (3404m) and **Posets** (3371m). The town can be reached most easily from Huesca (see p.545) or Barbastro (see p.544) on the daily **bus** that leaves Huesca at 10am, calling at Barbastro at 10.50am and arriving at Benasque at 1pm.

Over to the west of Benasque, and reachable from it on an HRP trail, or more easily on a road from Castejón de Sos, is the **Valle de Gistau**, a remote area which should appeal to walkers wanting to get away from the more established trekking areas.

Castejon de Sos, should you get stuck en route, has a trio of *hostales* along c/El Real, an **albergue**, the *Pajaro Loco* (☎974 553016; ①), and a **campsite** (☎974 553456) near the bridge to the Benasque road.

Benasque and its peaks

Surrounded by hay fields in a wide stretch of the Valle del Ésera, **BENASQUE** might seem spoiled if you knew it a decade ago. But otherwise it's an agreeable place, combining modern amenities with old stone houses, some of them built as summer homes for the Aragonese nobility in the seventeenth century. It is a good place to rest up before or after the rigours of the nearby peaks.

The cheapest **places to stay** are *Casa Bardanca*, c/Las Plazas 6 (☎974 551360; ②), which offers pleasant rooms above a bar, and *Fonda Barrabés*, c/Mayor 5 (☎974 551654; ②), a little shabby but with great mountain views. *Casa Gabás*, c/El Castillo (☎974 551275; ③), is on a quiet street and has self-catering studios as well as rooms with and without baths. For more comfort, try *Hotel Aneto*, Ctra de Anciles (☎974 551061, fax 974 551509; ⑤), which has a pool, tennis courts, gym, sauna and parking facilities; the *Hostal Valero* (③) shares the same building and facilities but has less luxurious rooms. There is also *Hotel Avenida*, Avda. de los Tilos (☎974 551126, fax 974 551515; ⑤), one of the most characterful – if pricey – hotels in the village.

Competition for walkers' custom means that 900—1400ptas *menús* abound at the **bars and restaurants**. Try the *comedores* of the *Salvaguardia*, c/San Marcial 3, or the *Bardanca*, c/Las Plazas 6. Another good place to head for is *Les Arkades* behind the church; it's an old stone building with an interior patio – on one side is a pub-*crepería*, and on the other a more expensive *comedor*, serving good-quality Aragonese dishes.

Climbs and treks around Benasque

Benasque attracts committed climbers and trekkers, and if you already count yourself among their number you'll probably be intent on bagging the **peaks of Aneto and Posets**. These are ascents for the experienced only, requiring crampons, ice-axe and a rope, and a helmet to guard against falling rocks.

For casual walkers, however, there are plenty of possibilities. The Aragón mountain club has marked out a number of blue-and-white- and yellow-and-white-painted **pequeño recorrido** (PR) paths, and they are documented in a locally available guide prepared by the club. The trails, to surrounding villages and also to all three local refuges, are routed so that you avoid roads as much as possible.

Farther afield: Viados and the Valle de Gistau

With a full pack and the stamina for day-long traverses, Benasque is a jump-off point for some of the best parts of the Spanish Pyrenees. Moderate itineraries include following the GR11 east to **Aigües Tortes** in Catalunya (a day and a half, tent necessary until the refuge at Llausets is completed); or heading west on the same numbered trail, around the Posets massif, for a two-day trek. No tents are necessary there, since the **refugios** of **Estós** (4hr from Benasque) and **Viadós** (9hr from Benasque) are well placed. From Viadós you could walk in another day to **Bielsa**, an eastern gateway to Ordesa National Park, with the Parador de Bielsa (☎974 501011, fax 974 501188; ⑦) and a few *hostales*, or descend by track to the villages of the **Valle de Gistau**.

Valle de Gistau

A mesh of trails links the villages of the Valle de Gistau. **PLAN** is the biggest place, with shops, a **Turismo** and three **casas rurales** (the norm for accommodation in this area), *Casa Mur* (☎974 506123; ②), *Casa Ruche* (☎974 506072; ②) and *Casa Buisan* (☎974 506051; ②) on the Plaza Mayor. Heading west out of the valley, a new GR19 trail leads through **SIN**, with an *albergue* (☎974 506212; ①), and on to Salinas and Lafortunada (see "The Southern Canyons", p.560).

Alternatively, you can descend from Sin on another PR trail to **SARAVILLO**, near the mouth of the valley. This has a large **campsite**, *Los Vives* (☎974 506171; mid-April to mid-Sept), and a **casa rural**, *Casa Cazcarreta* (☎974 506273; ②). It is also the starting point for excursions into the evocatively shaped mountains to the south and the **lakes and refugios** of the Circo de Armeña.

travel details

TRAINS

Huesca to: Calatayud (1 daily; 2hr 30min); Jaca (3 daily; 2hr 15min); Madrid (1 daily except Sat; 5hr); Sabiñánigo (3 daily; 2hr 15min); Zaragoza (5 daily except Sat; 1hr).

Zaragoza to: Barcelona (14 daily; 3hr 30min–4hr 30min); Bilbao (4–5 daily; 4hr 30min); Burgos (4–5 daily; 4hr); Cáceres (2 daily; 8hr 30min); Cádiz (1 daily; 9hr); Córdoba (3 daily; 8hr); Gijón (2 daily; 9hr); Girona (3 daily; 5hr); Huesca (1 daily except Sat; 1 hr); Irún (2–3 daily; 4hr 30min); Jaca (1 daily except Sat; 3hr 20min); León (3 daily; 6hr); Lleida (10–12 daily; 1hr 40min); Logroño (5–6 daily; 1hr 45min); Lugo (2–3 daily; 10hr 45min); Madrid (12–14 daily; 3hr); Málaga (2 daily; 9hr–10hr 30min); Medina del Campo (1–3 daily; 5hr 30min); Orense (1–2 daily; 10hr 30min); Oviedo (2 daily; 8hr 30min); Palencia (3 daily; 4hr); Pamplona (5–6 daily; 2hr); Sabiñánigo (1 daily; 3hr); Salamanca (3–4 daily; 6hr 30min); San Sebastián (2–3 daily; 4hr 30min); Sevilla (2 daily; 7hr 20min); Tarragona (8–12 daily; 3hr); Teruel (3 daily; 3hr 30min); Valladolid (1–2 daily; 5hr); Vigo (1–2 daily; 12hr 30min); Vitoria (1 daily; 3hr).

BUSES

Huesca to: Barbastro (6 daily; 50min); Barcelona (2–4 daily; 4hr 15min); Fraga (1 daily; 2hr 15min); Jaca (4–5 daily; 1hr); Lleida (6 daily; 2hr); Loarre (3 daily; 45min); Monzón (4 daily; 1hr 10min);

Pamplona (3 daily; 2hr 50min); Sabiñánigo (6 daily; 55min); Zaragoza (18 daily; 1hr 15min).

Jaca to: Anso via Hecho (1 daily; 1hr 15min); Astún/Candanchú (5 daily; 45min); Biescas (2 daily; 1hr); Estación Canfranc (5 daily; 30min); Huesca (3 daily; 1hr); Pamplona (3 daily; 2hr 30min); Sabiñánigo (2 daily; 30min); Zaragoza (3 daily; 2hr 30min).

Teruel to: Albarracín (1 daily; 2hr); Barcelona (3 daily; 6hr or 4hr 45min); Cantavieja/L'Iglesuela del Cid/Villafranca del Cid (1 daily; 2hr 30min/3hr/3hr 30min); Cuenca (2 daily; 2hr 30min); Valencia (5 daily; 2hr). All services reduce dramatically on Sundays.

Zaragoza to: Astorga (2 daily; 8hr); Barcelona (13 daily; 3hr 30min); Bilbao (5 daily; 4hr 30min); Burgos (2 daily; 3hr 45min); Cariñena (2 daily; 1hr 15min); A Coruña (1 daily; 11hr 30min); Huesca (10 daily; 1hr 15min); Jaca (3 daily; 2hr 30min); León (2 daily; 8hr); Lleida (4 daily; 2–3hr); Logroño (6 daily; 2–3hr); Lourdes via Huesca, Jaca, Canfranc, Pau, Oloron (June–Sept Sat 7.30am, Sun 2.30pm; 7hrs; passes through Jaca at 9.45am & 5.45pm); Lugo (2 daily; 7hr); Madrid (15 daily; 3hr 45min); Palencia (2 daily; 5hr); Ponferrada (2 daily; 9hr); Salamanca (2 daily; 6hr); Santiago de Compostela (1 daily; 12h 30min); Soria (5 daily; 2hr 15min); Sos del Rey Católico (1 daily; 2hr 15min); Tarragona (6 daily; 3hr); Valladolid (3 daily; 7hr 30min); Zamora (3 daily; 3hr 30min).

CHAPTER TEN

BARCELONA

B arcelona, the self-confident and progressive capital of Catalunya, is a tremendous place to be. A thriving port and the most prosperous commercial centre in Spain, it has a sophistication and cultural dynamism way ahead of the rest of the country. There's an awful lot to do here: the city boasts outstanding Gothic and *modernista* (Art Nouveau) buildings, and some superb **museums** – most notably the individual art museums dedicated to Picasso, Joan Miró and Antoni Tàpies, the striking new Museu d'Art Contemporani, and the excellent Museu d'Art de Catalunya. Barcelona has also evolved an individual and eclectic cultural identity, most perfectly and eccentrically expressed in the architecture of **Antoni Gaudí**, reason in itself for visiting the city. But there's also a multitude of very agreeable ways of doing very little. In part this reflects Barcelona's position, near France, whose influence is apparent in the parks, the elegant boulevards – most notably the famous **Ramblas** – and in the city's imaginative cooking. The energy of Barcelona will impress you, too. It is channelled into its industry and business, art and music, political protest and merrymaking. Even on a brief visit you'll probably be aware of this – certainly if you stay during the city's main **fiestas**. There's a list on p.620, but the main ones of which to be aware are April 23 (*Día de Sant Jordi*, or St George's Day), June 24 (*Día de Sant Joan*) and September 24 (*Festa de la Mercè*).

Barcelona has long had the reputation of being the most cosmopolitan city in Spain, especially in design and architecture, though in the 1980s much of the real intellectual impetus passed to Madrid. Gaining the 1992 **Olympics** was an important boost: the enormous popular support for sports in Barcelona (especially for football, the chief focus of the incessant rivalry with Madrid) helped win the nomination in the first place, and the legacy of the games was an outstanding set of new facilities and a spruced-up city centre. The Olympic Village and **Parc de Mar** development arose from the ruins of the old industrial area of Poble Nou, while the Olympic stadium on Montjuïc, built in 1929 and used for the alternative (anti-Nazi) games to the Berlin Olympics in 1936, was entirely refitted. Latterly, the harbour area at the foot of the Ramblas has been completely overhauled as part of the **Port Vell** development, while even parts of the Barri Chino/Raval neighbourhood have been rescued from neglect in the wake of the addition of the contemporary art museum. And the reforms do not stop there: as Barcelona enters its "second phase" of renovation, plans are ever more ambitious and include new theatres, concert halls and a World Trade Centre, as well as a UNESCO-funded project to promote diversity and world peace, the *Forum Universal de Cultures*, set to take place in 2004.

But there are darker sides to this prosperity and confidence. As more money is poured into the sleek image, residents of previously poor neighbourhoods are edged out as house prices rocket. Indeed, despite the constant drive for improvement and the high-tech edge to much of the city infrastructure, there is a great deal of poverty here and hard drugs are much in evidence. This means that **petty crime** is rife and it's not unusual for tourists to feel threatened in their peregrinations around the seedier areas flanking the Ramblas. If you're *very* unlucky you'll be mugged, so take a few precautions; leave passports and tickets locked up in your hotel, don't be too conspicuous with expensive cameras and, if you are attacked, *never* offer any resistance. If you've brought your car, don't leave anything in view, and always remove the radio and tape deck.

Orientation

Despite a population of over three million, Barcelona is a surprisingly easy place to find your way around. Most things of historic interest are in the **old town** – or La Ciutat Vella – which is small enough to master quickly on foot. This spreads northwest from the harbour for about 1.5km up to the southern borders of the city's nineteenth-century grid system. At its heart is the **Barri Gòtic** (*Barrio Gótico* in Castilian), the medieval nucleus of the city – around 500 square metres of gloomy, twisted streets and historic buildings. Bisecting the old town, at the western edge of the Barri Gòtic, are the famous **Ramblas**, Barcelona's main thoroughfare, its northern end marked by **Plaça de Catalunya**. At the southern end of the Ramblas lies the **harbour** and the **Port Vell** (old port) development, where walkways and a swing bridge skip across the harbour to a popular shopping, restaurant and cinema complex. West of the Ramblas, between the harbour and c/de l'Hospital, lies the warren of streets known locally as the **Barrio Chino** (or China Town), though officially the neighbourhood is called **El Raval**.

The medieval streets continue on either side of the Ramblas: reaching northeast through the Barri Gòtic – and past the celebrated **Museu Picasso** in the area known as **La Ribera** – to the **Parc de la Ciutadella** (*Parque de la Ciudadela*); and southwest to the fortress-topped hill of **Montjuïc** (*Montjuich*), where some of the city's best museums and the main Olympic stadium are sited. A cable car connects Montjuïc with **Barceloneta**, the waterfront district east of the harbour, below the Parc de la Ciutadella. Further northeast, the old industrial suburb of Poble Nou has been thoroughly transformed over the last few years into the **Parc de Mar** site, which incorporates the Port Olímpic and the Vila Olímpica (Olympic Village).

Beyond Plaça de Catalunya stretches the modern city and commercial centre. Known as the **Eixample** (*Ensanche*), it was conceived in the last century as a breathing space for the congested old town, its simple grid plan split by two huge avenues that lead out of the city; the **Gran Vía de les Corts Catalanes** and the **Avinguda Diagonal**. It's in the Eixample that some of Europe's most extraordinary architecture – including Gaudí's **Sagrada Familia** – is located.

Beyond the Eixample lie suburbs which were until relatively recently separate villages. The nearest, and the one you're most likely to visit, is trendy **Gràcia**, with its small squares and lively bars. Gaudí left his mark in these areas, too, particularly in the splendid **Parc Güell**, but also in a series of embellished buildings and private suburban houses which the enthusiastic will find simple to track down. **Out of the city**, the mountain-top monastery of **Montserrat** is the most obvious day trip to make, though the **beaches** on either side of the city also beckon in the summer.

Arrival and information

Most **points of arrival** are fairly central, with the obvious exception of the airport. If you're aiming to stay on the Ramblas or in the Barri Gòtic – much the best idea – there are fast city transport connections right there from most termini.

By air

Barcelona's **airport** is 12km southwest of the city at El Prat de Llobregat. There's an information office in each terminal (see below), as well as exchange facilities and car rental offices; for details of these and flight information numbers, see "Listings", p.622.

The airport is linked to the city by regular and direct train or bus services. The **train** (6am–10.40pm; journey time 30min; 305ptas weekmdays, 350ptas weekends and public holidays; info on ☎93 490 02 02) runs every 30 minutes to Estació-Sants and – more usefully if you're staying in the Barri Gòtic – continues to the station at Plaça de Catalunya, with the exception of the very last train which terminates in Sants. There's also a very useful **Aerobus** service (Mon–Fri 6am–midnight, Sat & Sun 6.30am–midnight; 475ptas) which leaves every 15 minutes from outside both terminals, stopping in the city at Plaça d'Espanya, Gran Via (at c/Comte d'Urgell), Plaça Universitat, Plaça de Catalunya and Passeig de Gràcia (at c/de la Diputació) – this takes around thirty minutes to reach Plaça de Catalunya, though allow longer in the rush hour. A **taxi** from the airport costs roughly 2400ptas to Estació-Sants, and 2500–2700ptas to somewhere more central in the old town.

When leaving town, always allow yourself plenty of time to get to the airport Aerobus departures (Mon–Fri 6am–midnight, Sat, Sun and bank holidays 6.30am–midnight) are from Plaça de Catalunya (in front of El Corte Inglés), Avda. de Roma (at c/Comte d'Urgell) or Estació-Sants. The advantage of the **train** is that it doesn't get stuck in traffic – services back to the airport leave every half an hour (6am–10.40pm), either from Plaça de Catalunya, or from Estació-Sants (platform 3).

By train

The main station for national and some international arrivals is **Estació-Sants**, west of the centre. Again, there are exchange, information and car rental offices here, as well as a hotel booking service (see "Accommodation" below). From Sants, metro line 3 runs direct to Liceu for the Ramblas.

Estació de França, next to the Parc de la Ciutadella, east of the centre, handles many of the long-distance arrivals and departures: essentially, this means Talgo services from Madrid, Sevilla and Málaga, Intercity services from other major Spanish cities, and international trains from Paris, Zürich, Milan and Geneva. Some trains stop at both Sants and França – check the timetable first. From França either take metro line 4 from nearby Barceloneta, or simply walk into the Barri Gòtic, up Vía Laietana and into c/Jaume I.

Other possible arrival points by train are the stations at **Plaça de Catalunya**, at the top of the Ramblas (for trains from coastal towns north of the city, the airport, Lleida, and towns on the Puigcerdà-Vic line); **Plaça d'Espanya** (FF.CC trains from Montserrat and Manresa); and **Passeig de Gràcia** (trains from Port Bou/Girona).

By bus

The main bus terminal, used by most international, long-distance and provincial buses, is the **Estació del Nord** on Avda. Vilanova (main entrance on c/Ali-Bei), three blocks north of the Parc de la Ciutadella (nearest metro, Arc de Triomf, a five-minute walk away). There's a bus information desk on the ground floor, with the ticket offices above at street level. When **leaving**, it's a good idea to reserve a seat in advance on the popular long-distance routes; the day before is usually fine. There's a round-up of bus companies and their destinations in "Listings", p.622.

By ferry

Ferries from the Balearics dock at the **Estació Marítima** at the bottom of the Ramblas. There are daily services from Palma (Mallorca) and several times weekly from Ibiza and Menorca. From the ferry terminal you're only a short walk from Plaça Portal de la Pau at the bottom of the Ramblas; nearest metro, Drassanes. Schedules and tickets for departures are available from Transmediterránea, at the Estació Marítima; see "Listings", p.622.

Information

It's a good idea to visit a **Turismo** as soon as possible after arrival, where you can pick up a free large-scale map of the city and a public transport map – as well as more

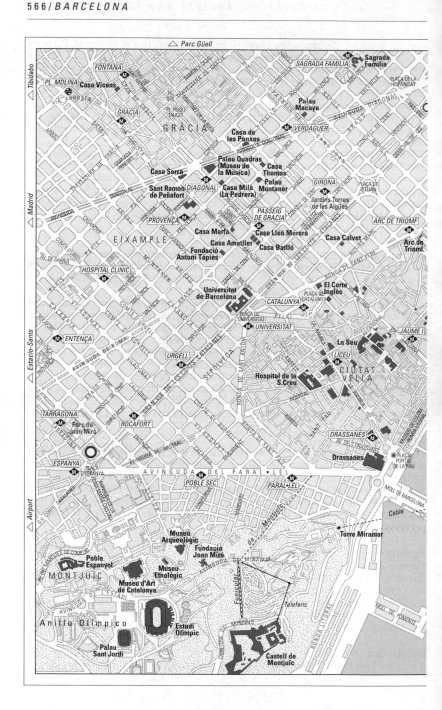

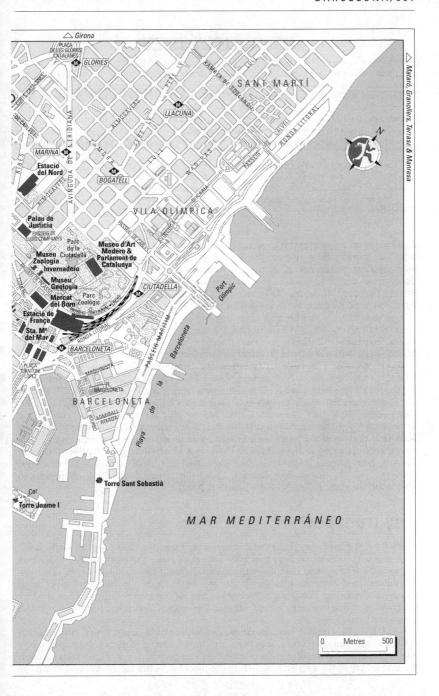

FINDING AN ADDRESS

Addresses in Barcelona are all written in Catalan, though a lot of maps – including official ones – haven't yet caught up and still use Castilian spellings. In this book, the text and maps use Catalan names and addresses.

Addresses are written as: c/Picasso 2, 4° – which means Picasso street (*carrer*) no. 2, fourth floor. You may also see left- (*esquerra*) hand apartment or office; *dreta* is right; *centro* centre. C/Picasso s/n means the building has no number (*sin número*). In the gridded streets of the Eixample, **building numbers** run from south to north (lower numbers at the Plaça de Catalunya end) and from west to east (lower numbers at Plaça d'Espanya).

The other main address **abbreviations** used in Barcelona are: Avda. (for *Avinguda*, avenue); Pg. (for *Passeig*, more a boulevard than a street); Bxda. (for *Baixada*, alley); Ptge. (for *Passatge*, passage); and Pl. (for *Plaça*, square).

For a full rundown of the Catalan language – and a list of useful words – see the feature on p.628.

---

detailed pamphlets and brochures on aspects of the city's architecture, history and culture. The tourist offices also sell the **Barcelona Card**, which gives free travel on public transport, reductions of up to fifty percent on entry into many museums and between ten and thirty percent in some shops and restaurants. The card is valid for 24 hours (2500ptas), 48 hours (3000ptas) or 72 hours (3500ptas), and is worth considering if you are only going to be in town for a short time.

The main office is at **Plaça de Catalunya** (daily 9am–9pm; ☎906 30 12 82 if calling from within Spain, ☎93 304 34 21 if calling from abroad and ☎93 304 32 32 for accommodation enquiries). There are also offices at the **airport** (Terminal A, Mon–Sat 9.30am–3pm; ☎93 478 47 04: Terminal B, Mon–Sat 9.30am–8.30pm, Sun and holidays 9.30am–3pm; ☎93 478 05 65), **Estació-Sants** (June–Sept daily 8am–8pm; Oct–May Mon–Fri 8am–8pm, Sat & Sun 8am–2pm; ☎93 491 44 31), and inside the **Ajuntament** building on Plaça Sant Jaume (Mon–Sat 10am–7pm, Sun 10am–2pm ☎93 270 24 29). For information about Catalunya go to **Palau Robert**, Passeig de Gràcia 107 (Mon–Fri 10am–7pm, Sat & Sun 10am–2pm; ☎93 238 40 00), the tourist office run by the Generalitat (the Catalan government). There is also a summer information **kiosk** (open May–Oct) in front of the Sagrada Familia and wandering tourist information officers in red jackets operating in the old town. There is a **Municipal Information Office** in Plaça de Sant Miquel (Mon–Fri 8.30am–6pm; ☎93 270 24 29), which is not really for tourists, but is invariably helpful. For the English-speaking **Informació Metropolitana** line (Mon–Sat 8am–10pm), call ☎010.

City transport

Apart from the medieval Barri Gòtic where you'll want to (and have to) walk, you'll need to use the city's excellent transport system to make the most of what Barcelona has to offer. The system comprises the metro, buses, trains and a network of funicular railways and cable cars: to sort it all out, pick up a free **public transport map** (*Guía del Transport Públic de Barcelona*) at any of the tourist offices, or at the city information office in Plaça de Sant Miquel; the map is also posted at bus stops and metro stations.

On all the city's **public transport** you can buy a single **ticket** every time you ride (140ptas, night buses 150ptas), but even over only a couple of days it's cheaper to buy one of the available *targetes* – discounted ticket strips which you either pass through the box on top of the barrier or punch in the machine at the metro entrance or on the

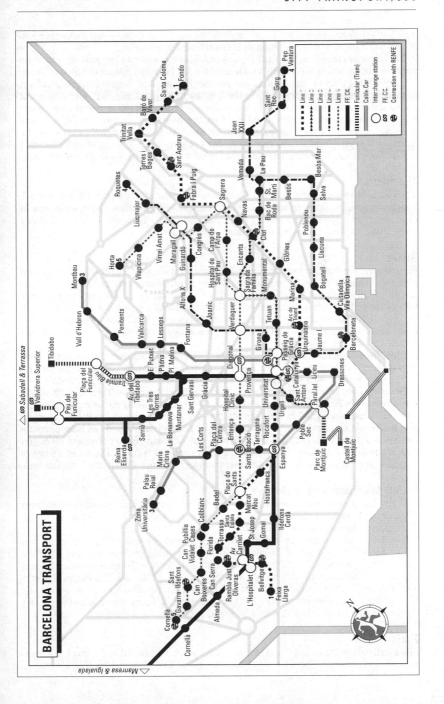

BARCELONA TRANSPORT

bus. These tickets can be used by more than one person at a time – just make sure you punch it the same number of times as there are people travelling.

There are two **targetes**: the T1 (775ptas), valid for ten separate journeys on either the metro or the buses; or the T2 (760ptas), used for ten journeys just on the metro. These *targetes* are not valid on night buses, but you can buy a *nitbus targeta* for 990ptas which is valid for ten rides and available on the bus itself. You can buy the other *targetes* at metro station ticket offices and at FF.CC stations (see below). Other **travel passes** are available at station ticket offices and valid on the buses and metro: the T-Dia (1 day 575ptas; 3 days 1350ptas; 5 days 2000ptas) or the T-Mes (1 month; 5250ptas) – for the latter you'll need a transport ID card, available from the TMB office at Plaça Universitat metro. Anyone caught without a valid ticket is liable to an **on-the-spot fine** of 5000ptas.

The metro

The quickest way of getting around Barcelona is by the modern and efficient **metro**, which runs on five lines; entrances are marked with a red diamond sign. Its **hours of operation** are Mon–Thurs 5am–11pm; Fri, Sat and the night before a holiday 5am–2am; Sun 6am–midnight; and holidays 6am–11pm.

Buses

Bus routes are easy to master if you get hold of a copy of the transport map and remember that the routes are colour-coded: **city centre buses** are red and always stop at one of three central squares (Catalunya, Universitat or Urquinaona); **cross-city buses** are yellow; green buses run on all the **peripheral routes** outside the city centre; and **night buses** are blue (and always stop near or in Plaça de Catalunya). In addition, the route is marked at each bus stop, along with a timetable – where relevant, bus routes are detailed in the text.

Most buses **operate daily**, roughly from 4–5am until 10.30pm, though some lines stop earlier and some run on until after midnight. The **night buses** fill in the gaps on all the main routes, with services every thirty minutes from around 10pm to 4am.

Between April and November, there's also a **tourist bus**, Bus Turistic (#100) (daily 9am–7pm; every 20min), starting at Plaça de Catalunya and linking all the main sights and tourist destinations, including the Sagrada Familia, Parc Güell and the Poble Espanyol. The bus is colour-coded according to its direction: red for northbound and blue for southbound. Tickets cost 1700ptas and are valid for a day, allowing you to get on and off as you please; a two-day ticket costs 2300ptas and a child's ticket is 900ptas. The ticket also gives discounts at various attractions and on other transport systems, such as the Tibidabo tram.

Trains, funiculars and cable cars

The city has a commuter **train line**, the Ferrocarrils de la Generalitat de Catalunya (FF.CC), with its main stations at Plaça de Catalunya and Plaça d'Espanya. You'll use this going to Montserrat and Tibidabo.

You may also use the **funicular railway** (215ptas one-way, 375ptas return) and **cable car** (375ptas one-way, 575ptas return) when going to Montjuïc, and there's a tram (200ptas one-way, 325ptas return) and funicular service (300ptas one-way, 400ptas return) to Tibidabo, too – full details in those sections of the text. On these services, your *targeta* (the T1) is valid only for the Tibidabo tram. You also have to pay separately for the **cross-harbour cable car** (1000ptas one-way, 1200ptas return, plus 600ptas for the Jaume I lift), which is well worth taking at least once for the views.

Taxis

Black-and-yellow **taxis** (with a green roof-light on when available for hire) are inexpensive and plentiful. There's a minimum charge of 295ptas and after that it's around

100ptas per kilometre. But taxis won't take more than four people and charge extra for baggage and on public holidays, or for picking up from Sants, or for a multitude of other things. Asking for a *recibo* should ensure that the price is fair. **Cabs** can be called on the following numbers: ☎93 490 22 22; ☎93 433 10 20; ☎93 330 08 04; ☎93 357 77 55; ☎93 392 22 22; and ☎93 391 22 22.

Accommodation

You can pick up a list of hotels and *hostales* at any Turismo, though these don't usually include the less expensive categories of accommodation. If you don't want to wander the streets when you first arrive, **hotel reservations offices** at the airport and at Sants station (daily 8am–10pm) or in the tourist office in Plaça de Catalunya (daily 9am–9pm) will book you a place to stay on arrival but they don't handle the very cheapest places and, of course, you won't get to see the room beforehand.

Hotels and hostales

Most of the **budget accommodation** in Barcelona is to be found in the **Barri Gòtic**, a convenient and atmospheric place in which to base yourself. However, what may be atmospheric by day can seem plain threatening after dark, and the farther down towards the harbour you get, the less salubrious, and noisier, the surroundings. As a rule, anything above c/Escudellers tends to be acceptable (though not necessarily fancy or modern); anything right on the Ramblas or on the streets above c/Portaferrissa should be reliable and safe. The best hunting-ground is between the Ramblas and Plaça de Sant Jaume, in the area bordered by c/Escudellers and c/de la Boqueria, where there are loads of options, from *fondas* to three-star hotels. Beyond, in the wider streets of the **Eixample**, are found most of the city's more expensive places to stay, though you'll be able to find reasonably priced rooms here. There are more possibilities in the **Gràcia** district, which – though farther out – is easily reached by metro.

On (and just off) the Ramblas

The further up the Ramblas you go, towards Plaça de Catalunya, the quieter, more pleasant and more expensive the places become. Alternatively, there are several places on Plaça Reial, halfway down the Ramblas, a fine square dotted with palm trees and arcaded walks.

Pensión Colom 3, c/Colom 3 (☎93 318 06 31, fax 93 302 40 02). The least expensive choice on the square. Adequate singles, doubles and triples, some with bath – book in advance if possible. Dorm beds available, too (see "Youth Hostels", below). ④

Hostería Grau, c/Ramalleres 27 (☎ & fax 93 301 8135). Only five minutes from Plaça de Catalunya, this excellent-value *hostal* offers rooms with or without bath, in a charming building above a café. There is also a small open-plan breakfast area and reading room. ④.

ACCOMMODATION PRICE CODES		
The codes used in our hotel listings denote the following price ranges:		
① Under 2000ptas	④ 4500–6000ptas	⑦ 12,000–17,500ptas
② 2000–3000ptas	⑤ 6000–8000ptas	⑧ Over 17,500ptas
③ 3000–4500ptas	⑥ 8000–12,000ptas	
See p.34 for more details.		

Hotel Lloret, Ramblas 125 (☎93 317 33 66, fax 93 301 92 83). A grand Ramblas building whose large rooms are better value than most in this category – most have TV and air conditioning and lots have Ramblas views. Rooms with just washbasins are cheaper. ⑤.

Hotel Mare Nostrum, Ramblas 67 (☎93 318 53 40, fax 93 412 30 69). Pleasant new hotel with smart double or triple rooms with TV and air conditioning, and some with street views. The price drops considerably for rooms without bath. ④.

Hostal Marítima, Ramblas 4 (☎93 302 31 52). Popular backpackers' choice next to the Wax Museum, offering basic doubles and triples with and without showers; there's a washing machine and luggage storage service too. ③.

Pensión Noya, Ramblas 133 (☎93 301 48 31). The best choice in this block and a popular stop for young travellers. Nice rooms, separate showers; you might find prices in high season fall into the next category up. ③.

Hotel Oriente, Ramblas 45 (☎93 302 25 58, fax 93 412 38 19). Appealing, turn-of-the-century decor and smart, modern rooms, some with Ramblas views. ⑦.

Hotel Roma Reial, Plaça Reial 11 (☎93 302 03 66, fax 93 301 18 39). Lots of airy rooms overlooking the square; others give on to an indoor patio. Book ahead since it's good value for its location and fills quickly. ⑤.

Between Carrer de Ferran and Carrer de la Boqueria

These two streets, and the alleys that run between them, are a good place to start for budget possibilities back from the Ramblas.

Hotel California, c/Rauric 14 (☎93 317 77 66, fax 93 317 54 74). Tucked down a side street that crosses c/de Ferran, this friendly hotel is popular with gay travellers. Rooms have TV and air conditioning, and breakfast is included in the price. ⑥.

Pensión Dalí, c/de la Boqueria 12 (☎ & fax 93 318 55 80). Not terribly inspiring, but often has space; expect a few hundred pesetas discount on all rooms from Sept–June. ③–④.

Pensión Europa, c/de la Boqueria 18 (☎93 318 76 20). A bit on the dingy side but cheap but popular with groups of young travellers. Some rooms with a balcony, with or without bath. ③.

Pensión Fernando, c/Ferran 31 (☎93 301 79 93). Newly renovated with an entrance on the main street, this *pensión* is welcoming and friendly and pretty good value for money. Rooms available for up to six people, some with bath. ②.

Hostal Palermo, c/de la Boqueria 21 (☎93 302 40 02, fax 93 238 03 55). Friendly place with clean, high-ceilinged rooms with or without bath. Probably the most attractive of the budget places on this street. ③.

Plaça de Sant Miquel, Plaça de Sant Jaume and c/Princesa

The streets between and around the Barri Gòtic's two central squares are rather more attractive than most in the area and contain several decent budget hotels.

Hostal Canadiense, Baixada de Sant Miquel (☎93 301 74 61). Down a quiet side street off Plaça de Sant Miquel, this is a slightly dark and labyrinthine *hostal*. However, it's in a good, fairly quiet, central location and worth trying if the *Levante* over the road is full. ④.

Hostal Levante, Baixada Sant Miquel 2 (☎93 317 95 65, fax 93 268 20 42). This welcoming wood-panelled *hostal* is a good first choice. Nice, plain rooms (with and without shower) on two floors in a well-kept building. Recommended. ④.

Hostal Lourdes, c/Princesa 14 (☎93 319 33 72). Absolutely basic but cheap and well-located for the Barri Gòtic and Passeig Born with clean bathrooms, and a TV room. ②.

Hotel Rey Don Jaime I, c/Jaume I 11 (☎ & fax 93 310 62 08). Fine location, and better value than most in this area, this small hotel is being slowly renovated, and has comfortable rooms with bath, almost all with balconies overlooking the busy main street below. ⑤.

Near the cathedral: Plaça Sant Josep Oriol and Carrer Portaferrissa

Around and beyond the cathedral, from Plaça Sant Josep Oriol northwards, the price and quality of accommodation take a general step up. Carrer Portaferrissa in particular has several decent choices.

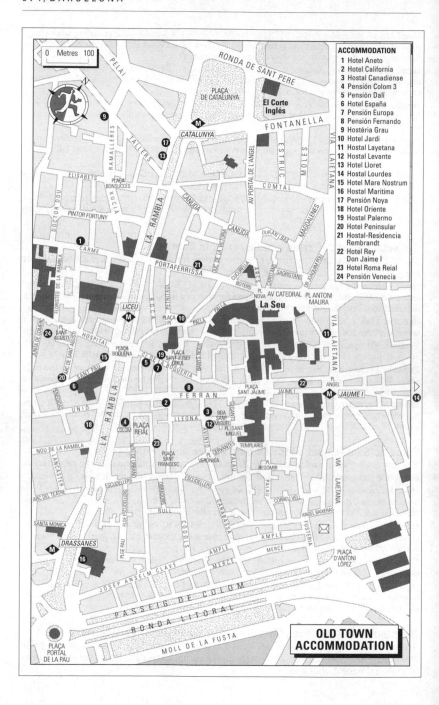

ACCOMMODATION

1 Hotel Aneto
2 Hotel California
3 Hostal Canadiense
4 Pensión Colom 3
5 Pensión Dalí
6 Hotel España
7 Pensión Europa
8 Pensión Fernando
9 Hostéria Grau
10 Hotel Jardi
11 Hostal Layetana
12 Hostal Levante
13 Hotel Lloret
14 Hostal Lourdes
15 Hotel Mare Nostrum
16 Hostal Maritima
17 Pensión Noya
18 Hotel Oriente
19 Hostal Palermo
20 Hotel Peninsular
21 Hostal-Residencia Rembrandt
22 Hotel Rey Don Jaime I
23 Hotel Roma Reial
24 Pensión Venecia

OLD TOWN ACCOMMODATION

Hotel Jardi, Plaça Sant Josep Oriol 1 (☎93 301 59 00, fax 93 318 36 64). Very popular by virtue of its extremely attractive position and pleasant rooms. Overlooking the square, and above a trendy café – rooms without balcony are cheaper. Try and book ahead. ⑤.

Hostal Layetana, Plaça Ramón Berenguer el Gran 2 (☎ & fax 93 319 20 12). Close to the cathedral, and with airy rooms, some without showers, for which you'll pay around 1500ptas less. ③.

Hostal-Residencia Rembrandt, c/Portaferrissa 23 (☎ & fax 93 318 10 11). An excellent place, run by accommodating people. Spotless rooms with shower and balcony; less expensive rooms without, too. ③.

West of the Ramblas

There are lots of places to stay on the west side of the Ramblas, though the proximity of the Barrio Chino red-light district doesn't make it the most enticing part of Barcelona. Look especially on c/de Sant Pau and c/Hospital, and c/Junta del Comerç, which runs between these two streets.

Hotel Aneto, c/Carmen 38 (☎93 301 99 89, fax 301 98 62). Small, reasonably priced hotel in a good location, on one of the safer streets in this area. All rooms with bath and air conditioning; ask for one with a view of the lovely square below. ⑤.

Hotel España, c/de Sant Pau 9–11 (☎93 318 17 58, fax 93 317 11 34). Designed by Domènech i Montaner; the highlight of this elegant hotel is the splendid *modernista* dining room. The rooms are spacious and comfortable, many giving onto delightful interior patios. ⑥.

Hotel Peninsular, c/de Sant Pau 34 (☎ & fax 93 302 31 38). An interesting old building originally belonging to Carmelite nuns, which explains the slightly cell-like quality of the rooms. The main attractions are the attractive covered inner courtyard hung with dozens of plants and the well-restored dining room area. ④.

Pensión Venecia, c/Junta del Comerç 13 (☎93 302 61 34). A clean, spacious place that's a cut above most of the budget choices on this street. Rooms without shower available too. Some rooms have access to a terrace where you can sit or hang clothes. ③.

Around Plaça de Catalunya and the Eixample

The top end of the Ramblas, around Plaça de Catalunya, is a safe and central place to stay – with the added advantage of being reached directly from the airport by train or bus. On the whole, the extra money it costs to stay in this part of town is well spent if you're concerned about looks and safety, less so if you're after character and a central position.

Residencia Australia, Ronda Universitat 11, 4° (☎93 317 41 77, fax 93 302 52 82; Metro Universitat). Good rooms (some with bath), well cared for by a pleasant English-speaking management, although the owner is due to retire in 1999. You'll need to reserve ahead as this place is always busy – try at least a fortnight in advance in summer. ③.

Hotel Claris, c/de Pau Claris 150 (☎93 487 62 62, fax 93 215 79 70; Metro Passeig de Gràcia). Renovated Eixample house featuring stylish, modern accommodation and up-to-the-minute facilities, including roof terrace, restaurant and pool. ⑧.

Hostal Ciudad Condal, c/Mallorca 255 (☎93 215 10 40; Metro Passeig de Gràcia). Plain but comfortable and one of the few budget options in this expensive area. All rooms come with bath and TV, some look onto the busy street and those at the back give onto an indoor patio. ④.

Hotel Ginebra, Rambla de Catalunya 1 (☎93 317 10 63, fax 93 317 55 65; Metro Catalunya). Small hotel on the third floor of a well-kept building. All rooms come with TV and air conditioning, and some have impressive views of Plaça de Catalunya. ④.

Hostal-Residencia Neutral, Rambla de Catalunya 42 (☎93 482 63 90; Metro Passeig de Gràcia). Excellent location and great views of the avenue, alongside decent rooms with shower or bath for two, three or four people. ④.

Hostal-Residencia Oliva, Passeig de Gràcia 32 (☎93 488 17 89 or ☎93 488 01 62; Metro Passeig de Gràcia). Nice old building, fine rooms on the fourth floor (reached by elevator), and a bit of a bargain if you can do without an en-suite shower. Ask for a room with a balcony. ④–⑤.

Hostal-Residencia Palacios, Gran Vía de les Corts Catalanes 629 (☎93 301 37 92; Metro Catalunya). A full range of decent rooms, some with street-facing balconies; singles and doubles, with and without shower or bath. ④.

Hotel Paseo de Gràcia, Passeig de Gràcia 102, (☎93 215 5828, fax 93 215 3724; Metro Diagonal). In a good location at the top of Passeig de Gràcia – handy for both the Eixample and Gràcia – this is a comfortable quiet hotel with some stunning views. ⑤.

Hostal Windsor, Rambla de Catalunya 84 (☎93 215 11 98; Metro Passeig de Gràcia). Small *hostal* in a lovely building on the Eixample's nicest avenue. There are only fifteen rooms (some without shower) so book ahead. ⑤.

Gràcia

Staying in Gràcia, you're farther away from the old town sights but the trade-off is the pleasant local neighbourhood atmosphere and the proximity to some excellent bars, restaurants and clubs.

Pensión Abete, c/Gran de Gràcia 67 (☎93 218 55 24; Metro Fontana). Friendly, family-run hotel, whose pleasant, if somewhat basic, fourteen rooms all have showers. Triples are available at a good rate, too. ④.

Pensión San Medín, c/Gran de Gràcia 125 (☎93 217 30 68, fax 93 415 44 10; Metro Fontana). Better looking inside than out, this friendly and well-located *pensión* has twelve rooms, some with shower. Situated on the first floor of a nice building but on an extremely busy street, so ask for an interior room. ④.

Pensión Norma, c/Gran de Gràcia 87 (☎93 237 44 78; Metro Fontana). Unpromising from the outside and up quite a lot of stairs, this is actually a pleasant place with keenly-priced, spotless rooms, with or without shower. ③.

Youth hostels

There are several official (IYHF) and not-so-official **youth hostels** in Barcelona, where accommodation is in multi-bedded dorm rooms; you'll need a membership card only for the IYHF hostels. Prices are around 1000–1500ptas per person, more in an IYHF hostel if you're over 26 or a non-member. Always ring ahead in summer.

Albergue Pere Tarrés, c/Numància 149 (☎93 410 23 09, fax 93 419 62 68; Metro Les Corts). Near Sants station, but otherwise inconvenient for most things. There's a maximum five-night stay, and an 11pm curfew, though entry is possible at hourly intervals throughout the night. Breakfast included and there's also a laundry and parking. Closed Jan & Feb. Open 4–10pm.

Albergue Verge de Montserrat, Passeig de la Mare de Déu del Coll 41–51 (☎93 210 51 51, fax 93 483 83 42; Metro Vallcarca and follow the signs, or bus #28 from Plaça de Catalunya). An IYHF hostel (membership essential) a long way out of the city – near Parc de la Creueta del Coll – but worth the trip for its facilities and setting. Open 7.30am–midnight with breaks in mid-morning and afternoon. Maximum five-night stay; breakfast is included, and there's an optional dinner. It is possible to arrive later than midnight if arranged with the management.

Pensión Colom 3, c/Colom 3 (☎93 318 06 31, fax 93 238 03 55; Metro Liceu). With an entrance inside Plaça Reial, this is the better hostel choice in the square; open 24-hr. Small balconied rooms stuffed with bunk beds; laundry facilities available.

Hostal de Joves, Passeig de Pujades 29 (☎ & fax 93 300 31 04; Metro Arc de Triomf). An IYHF hostel right by the Parc de la Ciutadella that usually has space. You can stay one night without a card, five nights with. Open 7.30–10am & 3pm–midnight, but opens at regular intervals throughout the night.

Campsites

Although there are hundreds of **campsites** on the coast in either direction, none of them is less than 7km from the city. The prices – around 500–600ptas per person, often the same again per tent – do you no favours either, and you'd be better saving your camping for later. The two sites closest to the city are:

Albatros, Gavá (☎93 662 20 31, fax 93 633 06 95). Bus #L90 or #L93 from Plaça d'Espanya or Plaça de Universitat. Open April–Sept.

Cala-Gogo-El Prat, Prat de Llobregat (☎93 379 46 00, fax 93 379 47 11). Bus #65 from Plaça d'Espanya. Open all year.

The Ramblas and the Old Town

It is a telling comment on Barcelona's character that one can recommend a single street – **the Ramblas** – as a highlight. No day in the city seems complete without a stroll down at least part of what, for Lorca, was "the only street in the world which I wish would never end". Littered with cafés, shops, restaurants and newspaper stalls, it's at the heart of Barcelona's life and self-image – a focal point for locals every bit as much as for tourists, and one to which you'll return again and again.

The Ramblas bisect Barcelona's **old town** (La Ciutat Vella), which spreads north from the harbour in an uneven wedge, and is bordered by the Parc de la Ciutadella to the east, Plaça de Catalunya to the north and the slopes of Montjuïc to the west. Contained within this jumble of streets is a series of neighbourhoods – originally separate medieval parishes and settlements – that retain certain distinct characteristics today. Some of these old town neighbourhoods are accessible by diving off the Ramblas into the side streets as you go – such as the **Raval/Barrio Chino**, and the area back from the **harbour** around c/de la Mercè. But by far the greatest concentration of interest is in the cramped **Barri Gòtic**, where you'll find the city's finest medieval buildings and churches tucked into unkempt streets and alleys. East of here, across the broad **Vía Laietana**, the old town streets continue in the area known as **La Ribera** encompassing two of Barcelona's most favoured sights: the graceful church of **Santa María del Mar** and the showpiece **Museu Picasso**.

You could see most of the places and buildings described in this section in a long day's outing. To start your tour, the nearest **metro** stops are Catalunya, Liceu or Drassanes (top, middle and bottom of the Ramblas respectively), or Jaume I for the Barri Gòtic.

Along the Ramblas

Everyone starts with the **RAMBLAS**, no bad thing since they're the city's most famous feature – and deservedly so. The name, derived from the Arabic *ramla* (or "torrent"), is a reminder that in earlier times the Ramblas marked the course of a seasonal river. In the dry season, the channel created by the water was used as a road, and by the fourteenth century this had been paved over in recognition of its use as a link between the harbour and the old town. In the nineteenth century, benches and decorative trees were added, overlooked by stately, balconied buildings, and today – in a city choked with traffic – this wide swathe is still given over to pedestrians, with cars forced up the narrow strip of road on either side.

For the visitor, the first eccentricity is that the tree-lined Ramblas is (or rather are) **five separate streets** strung head to tail – from north to south, Rambla Canaletes, Estudis, Sant Josep, Caputxins and Santa Monica – though this plurality of names doesn't amount to much more than a subtle change in what's being sold from the kiosks as you head down the street. Here, under the plane trees, you'll find pet canaries, rabbits, tropical fish, flowers, plants, postcards and books. You can buy jewellery from a

---

OPENING AND CLOSING TIMES

Note that although a few of Barcelona's most important **monuments** and **museums** open throughout the day in summer, most things **close** for an extended lunchtime, so be prepared to sit out two or three of your midday hours in a bar or restaurant; many also close all day on **Monday**.

blanket stretched out on the ground, cigarettes from itinerant salespeople, have your palm read and your portrait painted, or just listen to the buskers and watch the pavement and performance artists. If you're around when Barça (FC Barcelona) wins an important match you'll catch the Ramblas at its best: the street erupts with instant and infectious excitement, fans driving up and down with their hands on the horn, cars bedecked with Catalan flags, pedestrians waving champagne bottles.

The following account of the Ramblas runs from **north to south**, from Plaça de Catalunya at the top down to the Columbus monument.

From Plaça de Catalunya to Palau de la Virreina

The huge **Plaça de Catalunya** is many people's first real view of Barcelona. If you've emerged blinking from the metro and train station here, the first few minutes can be a bit bewildering as you try to figure out which way to go for the Ramblas. The square, with its central gardens, seats and fountains, is right at the heart of the city, with the old town and port below it, the planned Eixample above and beyond. The massive **El Corte Inglés** department store, in the northern corner, has some stupendous views of the city from its ninth-floor cafeteria. The latest additions to the square are branches of Marks and Spencers and the Hard Rock Café, their presence illustrating the increasing investment of multinationals in the city; the **Ramblas** begin at this southern corner. It's a good idea to fix the *plaça* in your mind early on, since you'll probably pass through on several subsequent occasions as you go about the city.

Heading down the Ramblas, the first two stretches are **Rambla Canaletes**, with its iron fountain (a drink from which supposedly means you'll never leave Barcelona), and **Rambla Estudis**, named for the university (L'Estudi General) that was situated here until the beginning of the eighteenth century. This part is also known locally as Rambla dels Ocells as it contains a bird market, the little captives squawking away from a line of cages on either side of the street. Over on the right, the **Església de Betlem** was begun in 1681, built in Baroque style for the Jesuits, but destroyed inside during the Civil War. Opposite, the arcaded **Palau Moja** dates from the late eighteenth century and still retains a fine exterior staircase and elegant great hall. The ground floor of the building, restored by the Generalitat, is now a cultural bookshop.

Another restored palace on the opposite side of the Ramblas – the graceful eighteenth-century Baroque **Palau de la Virreina** (Tues–Sat 11am–9pm, Sun 11am–3pm; free), at no. 99, on the corner of c/del Carme, contains a fine display of period decorative art, a select collection of European masters, and a collection of coins, the **Gabinet Numismàtic de Catalunya** (Mon–Fri 9am–2pm; free, organized visits only; ☎93 301 77 75 for details), as well as hosting various miscellaneous temporary exhibitions. The ground floor of the palace is a walk-in **information centre** and ticket office for cultural events run by the *Ajuntament*; drop in and pick up a programme.

Rambla Sant Josep

Beyond the Palau de la Virreina starts **Rambla Sant Josep**, the switch in names marked by the sudden profusion of flower stalls at this point of the Ramblas. The city's main food market – the glorious **Mercat Sant Josep** (Mon–Sat 8am–8pm) – is over to the right, a cavernous hall stretching back from the high wrought-iron entrance arch facing the Ramblas. Built between 1836 and 1840 – though the arch was added 30 years later – and known locally as the *Boqueria*, it's a riot of noise and colour with great piles of fruit, vegetables, herbs and spices, mounds of cheese and sausage, fish so fresh it's alive, and bloody meat counters.

Past the market, c/Hospital leads off to the right to the interesting Hospital de la Santa Creu (see "Barrio Chino/El Raval", below). This part of the Ramblas is known as

Plaça de la Boqueria, and is marked (in the middle of the pavement) by a large round **mosaic** by Joan Miró, just one of a number of the artist's city works.

By now you've reached the Liceu metro station, a little way beyond which is what remains of the **Gran Teatre del Liceu**, Barcelona's celebrated opera house, which burned down for the third time in January 1994, when a worker's blowtorch set fire to the scenery during last-minute alterations to an opera set. The building has had an unfortunate history, to say the least. Founded in 1847, it was first rebuilt after a fire in 1861 to become Spain's grandest opera house. Regarded as a bastion of the city's late nineteenth-century commercial and intellectual classes, the Liceu was devastated again in 1893 when an anarchist threw two bombs into the stalls during a production of *William Tell*. He was acting in revenge for the recent execution of a fellow anarchist assassin – twenty people died in the bombing. The latest devastation came as a severe blow to the city: Spain's king and queen offered their sympathy, while opera stars like Montserrat Caballé immediately pledged support to raise funds to rebuild it. It is now set to reopen in October 1999, in time for the 1999–2000 season.

Across the way, at Rambla 74, is the famous **Café de l'Opera**, which remains a very fashionable meeting place, as it has been for a century or so.

Plaça Reial

A hundred metres or so farther down the Ramblas, now the **Rambla de Caputxins**, the elegant nineteenth-century **Plaça Reial** is another good place to call a halt – it's hidden behind an archway on the left and is easy to miss. Laid out in around 1850, the Italianate square is studded with tall palm trees and decorated iron lamps (by the young Gaudí), bordered by arcaded buildings, and centred on a fountain depicting the Three Graces. Stop for a drink at one of the terrace cafés, or call in on Sunday (10am–2pm) when there's a **coin and stamp market**, attended by serious dealers but with enough lightweight exhibits and frenetic bargaining to be entertaining.

Rambla de Santa Mònica

Continuing down the Ramblas, Gaudí's magnificent Palau Güell stands on c/Nou de la Rambla (see "Barrio Chino/El Raval" below), just over the way from Plaça Reial, beyond which you're on the final stretch, the **Rambla de Santa Mònica**. There's little to see until you reach the bottom of the Ramblas, though you can derive some diversion from the pavement artists and palm readers who occasionally set up stall here, augmented in the afternoons at the weekend by a small street market selling jewellery, ornaments and clothes. There's a wax museum here, too, the **Museu de Cera**, on the left-hand side at no. 4–6 (July–Sept daily 10am–8pm; Oct–June Mon–Fri 10am–1.30pm & 4–7.30pm, Sat & Sun 10am–1.30pm & 4.30–8pm; 900ptas), though it's of little relevance to Barcelona, or even Spain; the usual trawl through the international famous and infamous.

The Ramblas end at **Plaça Portal de la Pau**, coming up hard against the teeming traffic that runs along the harbourside road. In the centre stands Columbus, pointing out to sea at the top of a tall, grandiose, iron column built for the Universal Exhibition in 1888: the **Monument a Colom**. You can get inside (June–Sept daily 9am–8.30pm; Oct–May Mon–Sat 10am–1.30pm & 3.30–6.30pm, Sun 10am–6.30pm; 250ptas) and take the lift to his head 52m up for aerial views of the city.

The harbour and Port Vell

Columbus is the most obvious landmark down at Barcelona's **harbour**, an area spruced up considerably over recent years. A harbourside *passeig*, the **Moll de la Fusta** – the city's old timber wharf – is landscaped with benches and trees from the

Colombus monument as far as the Post Office building. Cross the little bridges which span the ring road (built to link Montjuïc with the Olympic Village to the east), and you'll find seats from which you can look out over the marina. There are a few trendy clubs in summer along the promenade, and some bar-restaurants providing meals with pricey views.

PORT VELL (or old port), across the harbour from Moll de la Fusta and linked to it by a series of undulating wooden walkways and a swing bridge (called La Rambla del Mar), is the city's latest dockside development. The old wharves now accommodate **Maremàgnum**, a modernistic leisure complex jammed with shops, fast-food outlets, restaurants and bars. Other attractions here include a multi-screen cinema and the Imax Port Vell, showing giant format movies, as well as **L'Aquàrium** (daily 10am–9.30pm, closes 11pm July & Aug; 1400ptas), an impressive series of 21 different aquariums showing off Mediterranean marine life.

To the south of the Columbus monument is a stretch of the port leading to the central cable car station and the Estació Marítima at the Moll de Barcelona, where the ferries leave for the Balearics. This area has been earmarked for another big development in the form of a World Trade Centre (due to open by 1999), which will be yet another zone of offices, congress centres, hotels and restaurants, and which will also incorporate the ferry port itself.

The Drassanes: Museu Marítim

Opposite Columbus, set back from the road on the western side of the Ramblas, are the **Drassanes**, unique medieval shipyards dating from the thirteenth century. Originally used to fit and arm Catalunya's war fleet, in the days when the Catalan kingdom was vying with Venice for control of the Mediterranean, the shipyards were in continous use (and frequently refurbished) until well into the eighteenth century. The basic structure – long parallel halls facing the sea – has changed little; its size and position couldn't be bettered, whether the shipbuilders were fitting out medieval warships or eighteenth-century trading vessels destined for South America.

Nowadays the huge, stone-vaulted buildings make a fitting home for an excellent **Museu Marítim** (Tues–Sat 10am–7pm; 400ptas), whose centrepiece is a copy of the sixteenth-century Royal Galley (Galeria Reial), a red-and-gold barge rowed by enormous oars. It's surrounded by smaller models, fishing skiffs, sailing boats, old maps and charts, and other nautical bits and pieces – none of which, worthy though they are, can really compete with the soaring building itself. Recently added is a permanent exhibition about the dangers of the sea, in which you can take a virtual reality trip in a submarine.

Harbour rides and views

From a couple of points along the Moll de la Fusta, regular sightseeing boats, **Las Golondrinas** (daily 11.30am–8pm; departs every 45min Mon–Fri, every 25min Sat & Sun; less frequent in winter; 465ptas), make the half-hour ride across the harbour through the modern docks to the breakwater. There's also a ninety-minute ride east to the Port Olímpic (daily 11.30am, 1.15pm, 4.30pm & 6pm with an extra trip at 8.15pm on Sat & Sun; 1250ptas), including a twenty-minute stop at the port.

A more dramatic view of the city is offered by the **cable car** (daily noon–7pm; 1000ptas one way, 1200ptas return, plus 600ptas for the Jaume I lift), which sweeps right across the water from the base of Montjuïc to the middle of the new docks and on to Barceloneta – film buffs may remember Jack Nicholson riding it in Antonioni's film, *The Passenger*. The central **cable-car tower**, Jaume I, is just a few minutes' walk up the Moll de Barcelona from the Columbus monument, and even if you're saving the ride for a full trip from either Barceloneta or Montjuïc, you might consider taking the lift to the top of the tower, as at this point the views over the city are supreme.

The Barrio Chino/El Raval

West of the Ramblas, from the harbour roughly as far north as c/de Hospital, the triangular **BARRIO CHINO** is not the most obvious area of Barcelona in which to sightsee, but – during the day at least – you'll find it's an interesting place to wander around. Officially, this entire neighbourhood is known as **EL RAVAL** and historically it has been the city's red-light area (the name is misleading; there are no Chinese here). You may see the area referred to on maps as the "Barri Xines" which is the correct translation of its name in Catalan; Catalans however tend to refer to it as the "Barri Xino" or simply "el Xino". Like any port, Barcelona has a long history of prostitution: Orwell relates how after the 1936 Workers' Uprising "in the streets were coloured posters appealing to prostitutes to stop being prostitutes". Franco, for rather different reasons, was equally keen to clear the streets. Neither succeeded, though measured by its former reputation, the Barrio Chino is pretty tame these days – indeed, it's undergoing a gradual process of gentrification, with house prices going through the roof as the district becomes fashionable. The area's bygone golden age of sleaze is commemorated in a series of photographs in the new **Museu de l'Erotica** near Plaça de Catalunya, c/Bergara 3 (Tues–Sun 9am–2pm; 200ptas).

It may be rather hard to credit, given the often shabby surroundings, but the quarter also contains several sights firmly on the tourist map. During the day, don't be unduly concerned as you make your way to the destinations below – which include one of Gaudí's early works. At night, sensible precautions (such as not carrying large wallets down unlit side streets) should see you right: certainly, it would be a shame not to patronize some of the excellent **restaurants** that thrive in the area.

Architecturally, most of the *barri* is fairly undistinguished, though in among the down-at-heel surroundings is a splash of **modernista** colour worth keeping an eye out for: the **Hotel España** at c/de Sant Pau 9–11 is perhaps the best-known of the buildings, with a hugely attractive tiled dining room designed by Domènech i Montaner.

The Palau Güell

Much of Antoni Gaudí's early career was spent constructing elaborate follies for wealthy patrons. The most important was Don Eusebio Güell, a shipowner and industrialist, who in 1885 commissioned the **Palau Güell**, at c/Nou de la Rambla 3, just off the Ramblas (Mon–Sat 10am–2pm & 4–8pm; 300ptas). The first modern building to be declared a world heritage building by UNESCO, it is open to the public so, unusually, you can see the interior: most of the Gaudí houses are still privately owned. Here, Gaudí's feel for different materials is remarkable. At a time when architects sought to conceal the iron supports within buildings, Gaudí turned them to his advantage, displaying them as attractive decorative features. The roof terrace, too, makes a virtue of its functionalism, since the chimneys and other outlets are decorated with glazed tiles, while inside, columns, arches and ceilings are all shaped and twisted in an elaborate style that was to become the hallmark of Gaudí's later works – most of which are in the Eixample. The Palau is also one of the places where you can buy your ticket for the **Ruta del Modernisme**, which allows entry to all the *modernista* buildings (see p.596).

Sant Pau del Camp

Behind the Gran Teatre del Liceu on the Ramblas, c/de Sant Pau leads down through the heart of the Barrio Chino to the church of **Sant Pau del Camp** (St Paul of the Plain), its name a reminder that it once stood in open fields beyond the city walls. The oldest and one of the most interesting churches in Barcelona, Sant Pau was a Benedictine foundation of the tenth century, built on a Greek Cross plan. Above the main entrance are curious, primitive (and faded) thirteenth-century carvings of fish, birds and faces, while other animal forms adorn the capitals of the twelfth-century cloister; at the back of the church the delicately curved apses are worth a detour, too.

Hospital de la Santa Creu

On the northern fringes of the Barrio Chino the **Hospital de la Santa Creu** is the district's most substantial relic. The attractive complex of Gothic buildings here, reached down c/de Hospital (from where you get the best views of the building's facade), was built in the fifteenth century on the site of a tenth-century refuge, later transformed into a hospital for pilgrims. The hospital itself shifted site earlier this century and most of the remaining buildings have been converted to educational use, leaving you free to wander among the spacious cloisters and courtyards. Just inside the entrance are some superb seventeenth-century *azulejos* of various religious scenes; note the figure with the word *Iesus* written in mirror image – a formula signifying death. You may also be allowed into the eighteenth-century Academia de Medicina whose lecture theatre is decked out in red velvet and chandeliers, complete with revolving marble dissection table.

The Museu d'Art Contemporani de Barcelona

Carrer de Hospital acts as a sort of frontier for the Barrio Chino, but the Raval itself stretches as far north as c/Pelai and the Ronda Sant Antoni. The whole of this part of the Ravel has also been undergoing renovation; entire blocks are being pulled down, open spaces created and old buildings cleaned up, while the most ambitious plan is already under construction – a boulevard stretching from Avda. Drassanes across the *barri* to Ronda Sant Antoni. However, the most dramatic manifestation of the changes being wrought to the neighbourhood is the building of the **Museu d'Art Contemporani de Barcelona** – or MACBA (Mon & Wed–Fri noon–8pm, Sat 10am–8pm, Sun 10am–3pm; 500ptas, Wed 350ptas), which you can approach from c/dels Àngels or from the Ramblas (take c/Bon Succés). The contrast between the huge, white, almost luminous structure of the museum and the old buildings around it couldn't be more stark and it has inevitably been the subject of controversy since it opened in 1995.

The collection represents the main movements in contemporary art since 1945, mainly in Catalunya and Spain, but with a smattering of foreign artists too. The works are shown in rotating exhibitions and, depending when you visit, you may catch works by Miró, Tàpies or Chillida, or by the more contemporary Joan Brossa, leading light of the Catalan Dau al Set group.

Adjoining MACBA is the **Centre de Cultura Contemporània de Barcelona** (Tues, Thurs & Fri 11am–2pm & 4–8pm, Wed & Sat 11am–8pm, Sun 11am–7pm; 600ptas, Wed 400ptas), which hosts temporary art exhibitions as well as movies and concerts. This, too, is another fine example of the juxtaposition of old and new: built as the Casa de la Caritat in 1714, it was for centuries an infamous workhouse and lunatic asylum and at the entrance you can see the old *azulejos* and facade in a patio presided over by a small statue of Sant Jordi.

The Barri Gòtic

A remarkable concentration of beautiful medieval Gothic buildings just a couple of blocks northeast of the Ramblas, the **BARRI GÒTIC** forms the very heart of the old town. Once it was entirely enclosed by fourth-century Roman walls, but what you see now dates principally from the fourteenth and fifteenth centuries, when Barcelona reached the height of her commercial prosperity before being absorbed into the burgeoning kingdom of Castile. Parts of the ancient walls can still be seen incorporated into later structures, especially around the cathedral.

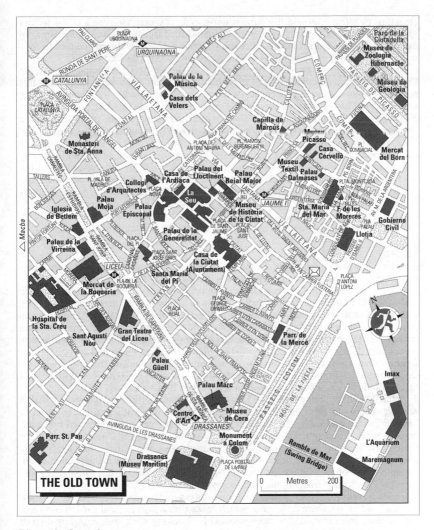

THE OLD TOWN

0 Metres 200

Plaça de Sant Jaume

The quarter is centred on the **Plaça de Sant Jaume**, a spacious square at the end of the main c/de Ferran. Once the site of Barcelona's Roman forum and marketplace, it's now one venue for the weekly dancing by local people of the Catalan folk dance, the *sardana*, and is also the traditional site of demonstrations and gatherings.

The square contains two of the city's most significant buildings. On the south side stands the restored town hall, the **Ajuntament**, from where the Spanish Republic was proclaimed in April 1931. The most interesting part, the restored fourteenth-century council chamber, the Saló de Cent, is on the first floor and is open to visitors at the weekend (10am–2pm). Otherwise, you get a much better idea of the grandeur of the original structure by nipping around the corner, down c/de la Ciutat, for a view of the former main entrance. It's a typically exuberant Catalan-Gothic facade, but was badly damaged during renovations in the nineteenth century – a move which led the city council to commission the much less pleasing Neoclassical facade on Plaça de Sant Jaume.

Right across the square rises the **Palau de la Generalitat**, traditional home of the Catalan government, which since 1977 has once again been operating from this address. Begun in 1418, this presents its best – or at least its oldest – aspect around the side, on c/del Bisbe, where the early fifteenth-century facade by Marc Safont contains a spirited medallion portraying Saint George and the Dragon. As you go in through the Renaissance main entrance facing the square, there's a beautiful cloister on the first floor with superb coffered ceilings, while opening off this gallery are the chapel and salon of **Sant Jordi** (St George, patron saint of Catalunya as well as England), also by Safont, and other chambers of the former law courts. The only time you can visit the interior is each year on Sant Jordi's Day, April 23 (expect a two-hour wait), when the whole square is festooned with bookstalls and flower sellers. Celebrated as a nationalist holiday in Catalunya, Sant Jordi's Day is also a kind of local Valentine's Day – tradition has it that you give a man a book and a woman a rose, and the stalls set up on Plaça de Sant Jaume and the Ramblas to sell them are mobbed all day with customers.

La Seu

La Seu (daily 8am–1.30pm & 4–7.30pm, at weekends it opens an hour later in the afternoon; free), Barcelona's cathedral, is one of the great Gothic buildings of Spain. Located just behind the Generalitat, on a site previously occupied by a Roman temple and Moorish mosque (a familiar pattern), it was begun in 1298 and finished in 1448, with one notable exception commented on by Richard Ford in 1845: "The principal facade is unfinished, with a bold front poorly painted in stucco, although the rich chapter have for three centuries received a fee on every marriage for this very purpose of completing it." Perhaps goaded into action, the authorities set to and completed the facade within a ten-year period in the 1880s. Some critics complain that this delay cost the cathedral its architectural harmony, though the facade is Gothic enough for most tastes – and is seen to startling effect at night when it's lit up.

Artificial lighting has transformed the **interior**, replacing the dank mystery with a soaring airiness to echo the grandeur of the exterior. The cathedral is dedicated to Santa Eulàlia, martyred by the Romans for daring to prefer Christianity, and her tomb rests in a crypt beneath the high altar; if you put money in the slot the whole thing lights up to show off its exemplary Catholic kitschiness. See, too, the rich altarpieces, and carved tombs of the 29 side chapels. Among the finest of these is the painted wooden tomb of Ramón Berenguer I, Count of Barcelona from 1018 to 1025, who was responsible for establishing many of the *usatges*, ancient Catalan rights.

The most renowned part of the cathedral is its magnificent fourteenth-century **cloister** (daily 8.45am–1.15pm & 4–7pm), which looks over a lush tropical garden complete with soaring palm trees and – more unusually – honking white geese. If they disturb the tranquillity of the scene, they do so for a purpose: geese have been kept here for over five hundred years, either (depending on which story you believe) to reflect the virginity of Santa Eulàlia or as a reminder of the erstwhile Roman splendour of Barcelona.

Plaça de la Seu and Plaça Nova

Outside La Seu is the **Museu Diocesà de Barcelona** (Tues–Sat 10am–2pm & 5pm–8pm, Sun 11am–2pm; 200ptas), a small collection of religious art and artefacts from around Catalunya, while flanking the cathedral, to the west of the **Plaça de la Seu**, are two fifteenth-century buildings closely associated with it. The **Casa de l'Ardiaca** (once the archdeacon's residence, now the city archives) boasts a tiny cloistered and tiled courtyard with a small fountain, while the **Palau Episcopal**, just beyond on c/del Bisbe, was the bishop's palace. This is on a grander scale altogether. Though you're not allowed inside either building, you can go as far as both courtyards to see their fine outdoor stairways, a frequent local feature; there's a patio at the top of the Palau Episcopal's stairway with Romanesque wall paintings.

The large **Plaça Nova**, facing the cathedral, marks one of the medieval entrances to the old town – beyond it, you're fast entering the wider streets and more regular contours of the modern city. Even if you're sticking with the Barri Gòtic for now, walk over to study the frieze surmounting the modern **Collegi d'Arquitectes** (College of Architects) building on the other side of the square. Designed in 1960 by Picasso, it has a crude, almost graffiti-like quality at odds with the more stately buildings to the side.

Plaça del Rei and around

The cathedral and its associated buildings aside, the most concentrated batch of historic monuments in the Barri Gòtic is the grouping around the neat **Plaça del Rei**, behind the cathedral apse. The square was once the courtyard of the rambling palace of the Counts of Barcelona, and across it stairs climb to the great fourteenth-century **Saló del Tinell** (Tues–Sat 10am–2pm & 4–8pm, Sun 10am–2pm; joint ticket with Museu d'Historia de la Ciutat 500ptas), the palace's main hall and a fine, spacious example of secular Gothic architecture; the interior arches span seventeen metres. At one time the Spanish Inquisition met here, taking full advantage of the popular belief that the walls would move if a lie was spoken; nowadays it hosts various exhibitions, while concerts are occasionally held in the hall, or outside in the square. It was on the steps leading from the Saló del Tinell into the Plaça del Rei that Fernando and Isabella stood to receive Columbus on his triumphant return from America.

The palace buildings also include the late-medieval, five-storeyed **watchtower** which rises above one corner of the square, as well as the beautiful fourteenth-century **Capella de Santa Agata**, with its tall single nave and unusual stained glass. This is entered through the building that closes off the rest of the square, the Casa Clariana-Padellás, a fifteenth-century mansion moved here brick by brick from nearby c/de Mercaders earlier this century to house the splendid **Museu d'Historia de la Ciutat** (June–Sept daily 10am–8pm; Oct–May Tues–Sat 10am–2pm & 4–8pm, Sun 10am–2pm; joint ticket with Saló del Tinell 500ptas, free Wed afternoons and first Wed of month); the entrance is on c/del Veguer. Underground, extensive Roman and Visigothic remains (including whole streets and a fourth-century Christian basilica) have been preserved where they were discovered during works in the 1930s.

The surrounding streets, between Plaça del Rei and the cathedral, reveal a similar kind of historical cross-section. The mid-sixteenth-century **Palau del Lloctinent**, the viceroy's palace, has a facade facing the Plaça del Rei and a fine courtyard with staircase and coffered ceiling (enter on c/dels Comtes).

Perhaps the most engaging sight in the area, however, is the **Museu Marès** (Tues–Sat 10am–5pm, Sun 10am–2pm; 300ptas, 150ptas Wed, free first Sun of month), which occupies another wing of the old royal palace, behind Plaça del Rei (entrance on c/dels Comtes), and whose large, arcaded courtyard is the most impressive so far. The bulk of this museum consists of an important body of religious sculpture, including a vast number of wooden crucifixes showing the stylistic development of this form from the twelfth to the fifteenth century. This is infinitely more interesting than it might sound, but in case boredom should set in, the upper floors house the **Museu Sentimental** of local sculptor Frederico Marès (not always open), an incredible retrospective jumble gathered during fifty years of travel, with everything from tarot cards to walking sticks by way of cigarette papers.

Plaça Sant Felip Neri to Plaça Sant Josep Oriol

Heading east back towards the Ramblas from the cathedral, you snake through a series of interconnecting squares and dark streets. Behind the Palau Episcopal, **Plaça Sant Felip Neri** is wholly enclosed by buildings and used as a playground by the kids at the square's school. Beyond are three more delightful little squares, with the fourteenth-century **Església de Santa María del Pi** at their heart. Burned down in 1936, and restored in the 1960s, the church boasts a Romanesque door but is mainly Catalan Gothic in style, with just a single nave with chapels between the buttresses. The rather plain interior only serves to set off some marvellous stained glass, the most impressive of which is contained within a huge rose window, often claimed (rather boldly) as the largest in the world.

The church stands on the middle square, **Plaça Sant Josep Oriol**, the prettiest of the three, overhung with balconies and scattered with seats from the excellent *Bar del Pi*, a fine place for a drink in the evening. This whole area becomes an artists' market at the weekend, while buskers and street performers often appear here, too. The squares on either side – Plaça del Pi and Placeta del Pi – are named, like the church, for the pine tree that once stood here.

North towards Plaça de Catalunya

Beyond Plaça Sant Josep Oriol, two or three diversions on the way north to Plaça de Catalunya make it worthwhile to stick to the backstreets, avoiding the Ramblas. Much of the area is devoted to antique shops and art galleries: one of the most famous is at c/Petritxol 5, where the **Sala Pares** was already well-established when Picasso and Miró were young; it still deals exclusively in nineteenth- and twentieth-century Catalan art.

The large **Plaça Vila de Madrid** features some well-preserved Roman tombs in its sunken garden, and here you're close to c/Montsió and **Els Quatre Gats** (The Four Cats; see p.614), the bar opened by Pere Romeu and other *modernista* artists in 1897 as a gathering place for their contemporaries. Also known as the Casa Martí, the building itself is gloriously decorated inside – it was the architect Puig i Cadafalch's first commission – and *Els Quatre Gats* soon thrived as the birthplace of *modernista* magazines, the scene of poetry readings and shadow-puppet theatre and, in 1901, the setting for Picasso's first public exhibition.

A small diversion across the nearby Via Laietana takes you to another *modernista* classic, Domonech i Montaner's **Palau de la Música Catalana**, which doesn't seem to have enough breathing space in the tiny c/Sant Pere Mes Alt. If you can get a ticket

---

JEWISH BARCELONA

Barcelona's medieval **Jewish quarter**, El Call, was just to the south of Plaça Sant Josep Oriol, centred on today's c/Sant Domingo del Call (*Call* is the Catalan word for a narrow passage). In the narrow, dark alleys on either side of the street, a closed ghetto survived and even prospered for some 300 years before the Jews were expelled from Spain in the fifteenth century. Excavations have proved that the main synagogue was on the site of the building that now stands at c/Sant Domingo del Call 7, but today little except the street name survives as a reminder of the Jewish presence – after their expulsion, the buildings used by the Jews were torn down and used for construction elsewhere in the city, a pattern repeated throughout Catalunya. There are still some echoes of the Jewish presence in Barcelona, however: on the eastern side of Montjuïc (Mountain of the Jews) was the Jewish cemetery, already a long-established burial place by the eleventh century, and many records of medieval Jewish life are preserved in the archives of the Aragón crown housed at c/Almogovares 77. You won't get inside to see these but the castle at Montjuïc does display around thirty tombstones recovered from the cemetery earlier this century.

for one of the many fine concerts here, do so, since the building is as fantastic acousti-cally as it is visually. Alternatively, there are hour-long **guided tours** of the interior (July & Sept Mon–Fri 2pm, 3pm, 4pm; Aug daily 10am–2pm hourly; Nov–June pre-arranged visits only; call ☎93 268 10 00 to reserve a place; 500ptas).

Vía Laietana to Parc de la Ciutadella

In 1859, as the plans for the Eixample took shape, a wide, new avenue was also con-structed to the south, cutting through the old town. This was the **Vía Laietana**, running roughly parallel to the Ramblas. Nowadays it delineates the eastern extent of the Barri Gòtic, but not to push on over the road into the equally dense network of medieval streets beyond would be a mistake. True, there isn't the same concentration of pre-served buildings here as in the Barri Gòtic, but there is the major attraction of the **Museu Picasso**, while the street on which it lies (c/de Montcada) and the church at the end of it (Santa María del Mar) encapsulate some of Barcelona's most perfect Catalan-Gothic features.

Carrer de Montcada and the Passeig del Born

Everyone makes the trip to **c/de Montcada** sooner or later, a narrow street lined with leaning, late-medieval mansions. The draw is the Museu Picasso, housed in one of the grander buildings, but the street itself is one of the best-looking in the city. Laid out in the fourteenth century, until the Eixample was planned almost 500 years later it was home to most of the city's leading citizens who occupied spacious mansions built around central courtyards, from which external staircases climbed to the living rooms on the first floor. The Picasso Museum aside, several of the other mansions are also used as exhibition space today.

Almost opposite the Picasso Museum, at no. 12, the fourteenth-century Palau de Lliò and its next-door neighbour contain the extensive collections of the **Museu Textil i d'Indumentaria** (Tues–Sat 10am–5pm, Sun 10am–2pm; 400ptas, joint ticket with Museu Barbier-Mueller 700ptas, free first Sun of month) – 4000 items altogether, including textiles from the fourth century onwards and costumes from the sixteenth, dolls, shoes, fans and other accessories. Next door at no. 14 there's the **Museu Barbier-Mueller** (Tues–Sat 10am–8pm, Sun and holidays 10am–3pm; 500ptas, joint ticket with Museu Textil i d'Indumentaria 700ptas, free first Sat of month) – a collec-tion of Pre-Columbian art housed in the specially renovated sixteenth-century Palau Nadal. Close by there's a private gallery at no. 25, the Galeria Maeght, spread across two floors of the former Palau dels Cervelló, and at no. 20, the Palau Dalmases has been opened as a bar, allowing you to see the interior. C/de Montcada ends at the church of Santa María del Mar (see below), fronting which is the fashionable **Passeig del Born**, once the site of medieval fairs and tournaments and now lined with trendy bars.

The Museu Picasso

The **Museu Picasso** (Tues–Sat 10am–8pm, Sun 10am–3pm; 600ptas, free first Sun of month), at c/de Montcada 15–19, is Barcelona's biggest tourist attraction, housed in a strikingly beautiful medieval palace converted specifically for the museum. It's one of the most important collections of Picasso's work in the world and certainly the only one of any significance in his native country. Even so, some visitors are disappointed: the museum isn't thoroughly representative, it contains none of his best-known works, and few in the Cubist style. But what *is* here provides a unique opportunity to trace Picasso's development from his early paintings as a young boy to the major works of later years.

The museum opened in 1963 with a collection based largely on the donations of Jaime Sabartes, friend and former secretary to the artist. The **early drawings** in which Picasso – still signing with his full name, Pablo Ruíz Picasso – attempted to copy the nature paintings in which his father specialized, and the many studies from his art school days, are fascinating. Indeed, it's the early periods that are the best represented: some works in the style of Toulouse-Lautrec, such as the menu Picasso did for *Els Quatre Gats* restaurant in 1900, reflect his interest in Parisian art at the turn of the century; other selected works show graphically Picasso's development of his own style – there are paintings here from the famous **Blue Period** (1901–04), the Pink Period (1904–06), and from his Cubist (1907–20) and Neoclassical (1920–25) stages.

The large gaps in the main collection (for example, nothing from 1905 until the celebrated *Harlequin* of 1917) only underline Picasso's extraordinary changes of style and mood. This is best illustrated by the large jump after 1917 – to 1957, a year represented by two rooms on the first floor which contain the fascinating works Picasso himself donated to the museum, his fifty-odd interpretations of Velázquez's masterpiece *Las Meninas*.

Santa María del Mar

At the bottom of c/de Montcada sits the graceful church of **Santa María del Mar** (daily 9am–12.30pm & 5–8.15pm; Sun choral Mass at 1pm), built on what was the seashore in the fourteenth century. The church was at the heart of the medieval city's maritime and trading district (c/Argentería, named after the silversmiths who worked there, still runs from the church square to the city walls of the Barri Gòtic), and its soaring lines were the symbol of Catalan supremacy in Mediterranean commerce, much of it sponsored by the church. Built quickly, and therefore largely pure in style, it's an exquisite example of Catalan-Gothic architecture, with a wide nave and high, narrow aisles, and for all its restrained exterior decoration is still much dearer to the heart of the average local than the cathedral, the only other church in the city with which it compares.

Ciutadella to Montjuïc

Recreational space has always been high up the list with every redesign of the city. Recently, peripheral bits of industrial wasteland have benefited from the drive to provide some greenery and relative peace, but the late-nineteenth-century expansion of

Barcelona relied instead on transforming previously fortified, and very central, sections of the city. The quickest respite from the centre is still in the **Parc de la Ciutadella**, east of the old town and within easy walking distance of the Barri Gòtic. Once the site of a Bourbon fortress, this is a formal park, with several museums and other attractions spread about its attractive paths and gardens. To the south lies the fishing (and seafood-eating) district of **Barceloneta**, jutting out into Barcelona's central harbour, while a short walk from here, the newly built **Parc de Mar** has totally transformed a previously redundant section of the city's coastline.

You'll probably want to reserve most of a day for the more substantial attraction of **Montjuïc**, the hill that rises over on the other side of the harbour, to the west of the Barrio Chino. This still retains its castle, while the museums, monuments and gardens are connected by an extensive series of paths and viewpoints; some of the attractions are also linked by cable car – a method of transport that also connects Montjuïc with Barceloneta, enabling you to jump fairly swiftly between all the areas described in this chapter. For **transport details**, see the information boxes.

Parc de la Ciutadella

The **PARC DE LA CIUTADELLA** seems to have a peculiar ability to take in far more than would seem possible from its outward dimensions. As well as a lake, Gaudí's monumental fountain and the city zoo, you'll find here the meeting place of the Catalan parliament and a modern art museum. The last two occupy parts of a fortress-like structure right at the centre of the park, the surviving portion of the star-shaped **citadel** from which the park takes its name. It was erected by Felipe V in 1715, to subdue Barcelona after its spirited resistance to the Bourbons in the War of the Spanish Succession, and a whole city neighbourhood had to be destroyed to make room for the citadel. The Bourbon symbol of authority survived uneasily, until it too was destroyed in 1869 and the surrounding area made into a park. It seems a fitting irony that the main palace structure is once again home to the autonomous Catalan parliament, which first sat here between 1932 and 1939.

Perhaps the most notable of the park's sights is the **Cascada**, the monumental Baroque fountain in the northeast corner. Designed by Josep Fontseré, the architect chosen to oversee the conversion of the former citadel grounds into a park, this was the first of the major projects undertaken here. Fontseré's assistant in the work was the young Antoni Gaudí, then a student, who was also thought to have had a hand in the design of the Ciutadella's iron park gates, at the entrance on Avda. Marqués de l'Argentera.

The Park and the 1888 Exhibition

In 1888, barely twenty years after it was first created, the park was chosen as the site of the **Universal Exhibition**, which helped start the cultural regeneration of Barcelona. Many of the *modernista* giants called upon to help left their mark here, beginning with Josep Vilaseca i Casanoves's giant brick **Arc de Triomf**, outside the main gates at the top of Passeig Lluís Companys.

Just inside the main entrance, Domènech i Montaner designed a castle-like building intended for use as the exhibition's café-restaurant. Dubbed the Castell dels Tres Dragons, it became a centre for *modernista* arts and crafts, and is now the **Museu de Zoologia** (Tues–Sun 10am–2pm; 300ptas, free first Sun of month), whose decorated red-brick exterior knocks spots off the rather more mundane interior. Just beyond is the the attractive late-nineteenth-century conservatory – the *hivernacle* – which now houses a pleasant outdoor **bar**.

The Museu d'Art Modern de Catalunya

In the centre of the park, the surviving parts of Felipe's citadel – the governor's palace and old arsenal – stand on the Plaça d'Armes. They are now shared by the Catalan parliament and the **Museu d'Art Modern de Catalunya** (Tues–Sat 10am–7pm, Sun 10am–2.30pm; 500ptas). The museum has often been seen as a sort of collection of also-rans – Barcelona has separate galleries for Picasso, Miró and Tàpies, and Dalí gets his own place in Figueres – but there's enough fine work here to dispel the charge effectively.

The museum is devoted to Catalan art dating from the mid-nineteenth century until around 1930 and, as you might expect, it's particularly good on *modernista* and *noucentista* painting and sculpture, the two dominant schools of the period. There are fine examples of the work of Ramón Casas (whose work once hung on the walls of *Els Quatre Gats*) and Santiago Rusiñol, while later *modernista* works include the landscapes of Joaquim Mir and the astonishingly varied output of Isidre Nonell. The museum's latter rooms cover *noucentista* works, a style at once more classical and less consciously flamboyant than *modernisme* – Joaquim Sunyer, perhaps the best-known *noucentista* artist, is among those displayed here, though there are works by a host of others, too, including Xavier Nogués and the sculptor Pau Gargallo.

The Parc Zoològic

For all Ciutadella's cultural appeal, the most popular attraction – apart from the green spaces of the park itself – is the city's zoo, the **Parc Zoològic** (daily summer 10am–7.00pm, winter 10am–5pm; 1400ptas), taking up most of the southeast of the park. There's an entrance on c/de Wellington if you've arrived at Metro Ciutadella, as well as one inside the park. Here the star exhibit is Snowflake, a unique (in captivity at least) and much-gawped-at, pure white albino gorilla.

Barceloneta and Parc de Mar

South of the park, and across the tracks of the Estació de França, the port district of **BARCELONETA** is the closest to the centre of the self-contained village suburbs that used to ring the city and are now part of greater Barcelona. The triangular wedge of development was laid out in 1755 – a classic eighteenth-century grid of streets where previously there had been mud-flats – to replace the neighbourhood destroyed to make way for the Ciutadella fortress. The long, narrow streets are still very much as they were planned, broken at intervals by small squares and lined with low-built, multi-windowed houses.

The main reason most people – city inhabitants included – come to Barceloneta is to eat in one of the district's many **fish and seafood restaurants**. It used to be possible to eat right on the beach but the redevelopment of the whole of this waterfront area means that the best restaurants are now found elsewhere – on the main **Passeig de Bourbó** (still Passeig Nacional on some maps), in the narrow streets of Barceloneta itself, or in the **Palau del Mar**, a renovated warehouse at the northern end of Passeig

BARCELONETA TRANSPORT

• **Metro**: line 4 to Barceloneta, from where it's a short stroll down to the Passeig de Bourbó.
• **Buses**: #17 and #45 from Vía Laietana, #39 from Arc de Triomf, #59 from the Ramblas, and #57 and #64 from Avda. Paral·lel and Passeig de Colom, all dropping on Passeig de Bourbó. Stay on any bus (except the #45 and #59) until the end of the line in Barceloneta, at the top of Passeig de Bourbó, and you're very close to the cable car station.
• **Cable car**: connects Montjuïc (Torre de Miramar) and the Moll de Barcelona (Torre de Jaume I), in the centre of the docks, to Barceloneta (Torre de Sant Sebastià) – daily noon–7pm; 1000ptas one way, 1200ptas return, plus 600ptas for the Jaume I lift.

de Bourbó. The Palau del Mar is also home to the **Museu d'Historia de Catalunya** (Tues–Thurs 10am–7pm, Fri & Sat 10am–8pm, Sun 10am–2.30pm; 500ptas), which traces the history of the region from the Stone Age to the present time. Don't miss the bar on the fourth floor which has a glorious view of the harbour and city skyline.

It's only a short walk through the Barceloneta streets to the **beach**, much cleaned up recently, furnished with outdoor showers, and backed by the long promenade of the Passeig Maritim.

Parc de Mar: the Vila Olímpica and the Port Olímpic

On the beach at Barceloneta you're within walking distance of perhaps the most adventurous urban development project undertaken by the city since the nineteenth-century extension to the north. The old industrial suburb of Poble Nou and its waterfront were torn apart to make way for the **Parc de Mar**, a huge seafront development that incorporates the **Port Olímpic** and **Vila Olímpica** (Olympic Village), home to the athletes and administrators during the 1992 Games. The project was the brainchild of a specialist firm of urban architects led by Josep Martorell, Oriol Bohigas and an Englishman, David Mackay, which planned to turn the 5km of shoreline from Barceloneta to the Río Besòs to the east into a high-tech but user-friendly corridor of apartment blocks, conference and shopping centres, hotels, offices, parks and transport links. The Olympic Village itself was built to house 15,000 competitors and support staff, the idea being to convert it into permanent housing for around 7000 people after the Games.

Not everyone, of course, supported the redevelopment, and the promise of new housing, particularly, had a hollow ring in Barceloneta and Poble Nou, two of the poorer areas of the city, since it was soon clear that the apartment blocks and residential complexes were not exactly being built on low-cost lines. Little by little, however, the Port Olímpic has filled with restaurants, bars and fast-food joints, making it a major target for visitors and city dwellers at weekends and on summer nights. And from just about any point the country's two tallest buildings – the office-filled Torre Mapfre and the steel-framed Hotel Arts – are visible, casting their shadows over the frolics below.

Montjuïc

Easily visible from Barcelona's harbourside, the steep hill of **MONTJUÏC** is much the largest green area in the city and contains the most of interest. It took its name from the Jewish community that once settled on its slopes, and there's been a castle on the heights since the mid-seventeenth century, which says much about the hill's obvious historical defensive role. But since the erection of buildings for the International Exhibition of 1929, Montjuïc has been the city's greatest cultural draw – it takes a full day at least to sample its varied attractions, which include five museums, an amusement park, various gardens and the famous "Spanish Village". The architecture on Montjuïc is disappointing if you've been inspired by the remnants from 1888 in the Ciutadella park; *modernisme* was a spent force by 1929 and the bland, monumental designs here seem purely functional. However, spurred on by the Olympics, a new spate of building and improvement work produced some rather more unorthodox designs. With these set alongside the few unusual relics from 1929, Montjuïc has never looked so spruce as it does now.

From Plaça d'Espanya to the Palau Nacional

From the **Plaça d'Espanya**, past the square's 47-metre-high twin towers and up the imposing Avda. de la Reina Maria Cristina, you can either make the stiff climb on foot, or take the long outdoor escalators which were part of the improvements sponsored by the 1992 Olympic Games: either is worth doing at least once for the rewarding views

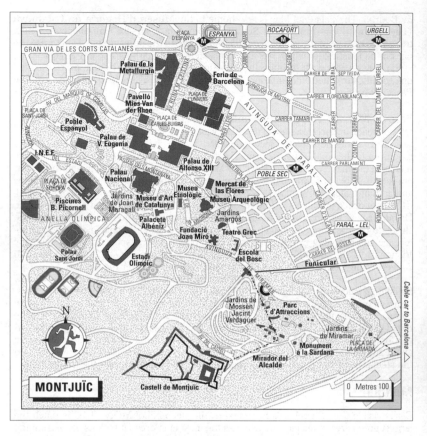

MONTJUÏC

0 Metres 100

Cable car to Barcelona

as you go. On either side of the avenue and terraces (laid out by Puig i Cadafalch) are various exhibition buildings from 1929, still in use as venues for the city's trade fairs, while central position is given over to the illuminated fountains, the **Font Mágica**, in front of the Palau Nacional; these have recently been renovated, and now form part of a spectacular sound and light show (Thurs–Sun 8pm–midnight, sound and light show Thurs–Sun10.30pm; free).

The Museu d'Art de Catalunya

The towering **Palau Nacional**, set back at the top of the flight of steps, was the centre-piece of Barcelona's 1929 International Exhibition; it was due to be demolished once the exhibition was over but gained a reprieve and later became home to one of Spain's great museums, the **Museu d'Art de Catalunya** (Tues, Wed, Fri & Sat 10am–7pm, Thurs 10am–9pm, Sun 10am–2.30pm; 800ptas). This is by far the best art museum in Barcelona, though it is currently undergoing a massive long-term refit and reorganization which will not be completed until the year 2001, when the huge collection will finally be shown together under one roof. The renovation is being carried out chronologically, so you will have to wait several years to see the Renaissance and Baroque art, which includes works by El Greco, Zurbarán and Velázquez, or the drawings, engravings and posters from the eighteenth to the twentieth century. In time, it's also proposed to show the modern art collection currently in the Parc de la Ciutadella here, as well as Catalan coins and medallions and an extensive photographic collection – eventually making this one of Europe's largest museums. In the meantime, you'll have to be content with the museum's enormous medieval collection.

This collection has two main sections, one dedicated to Romanesque art and the other to Gothic – periods in which Catalunya's artists were pre-eminent in Spain. Medieval Catalan studios concentrated on decorating churches with murals, but they also produced painted altar frontals, often based on a figure of a saint surrounded by scenes from his life. In time, these grew in scale into the large *retablos* over the high altar – a key feature of Spanish churches for centuries.

The **Romanesque** collection is remarkable, perhaps the best of its kind in the world. It is laid out chronologically, starting with stone sculptures from the sixth to the tenth century and ending with late thirteenth-century paintings. A series of rooms is filled with eleventh- and twelfth-century frescoes, meticulously removed from a series of small Catalan Pyrenean churches to prevent them being stripped and sold off. Great numbers of Romanesque churches were built in the Catalan Pyrenees as the Reconquest spread, far more than further south, where Christianity arrived later. For the most part, these churches and their decorative frescoes were either ruined by later renovations or lay abandoned, prone to theft and damage, until a concerted effort from 1919 onwards to remove the murals to the museum for preservation.

The frescoes are beautifully displayed – all with explanatory notes in English, some in a reconstruction of their original setting – and while you're unlikely to be familiar with such art, since surviving examples are rare and invariably remote, you're equally unlikely not to be converted to its charms. For the most part the pieces have a vibrant, raw quality, best exemplified by those taken from churches in the Boí valley in the Catalan Pyrenees – like the work of the so-called Master of Taüll, whose decoration of the apse of the church of Sant Climent in Taüll (see p.705) combines a Byzantine hierarchical composition with the imposing colours and strong outlines of the contemporary manuscript illuminators.

The **Gothic** collection is also fascinating, and extensive, ranging over the whole of Spain – particularly good on Catalunya, Valencia and Aragón – and again, laid out chronologically, from the thirteenth to the fifteenth century. The evolution from the

---

MONTJUÏC TRANSPORT

• From **Plaça d'Espanya Metro**, you can **walk** (or take the escalators) up to the Palau Nacional, or take one of three **buses** – #61, which runs past most of the sights, stopping at the amusement park (last bus 8.30pm); the #13, which links the Plaça to the Poble Espanyol (last bus 10.30pm); or the summer tourist route, the #100, which runs past the Poble Espanyol (see p.570 for full details of this service). In the summer there is also a toy train, the **Tren Turístic de Montjuïc**, which leaves Plaça d'Espanya every half hour (April–Oct Sat & Sun 11am–10pm; summer and Easter daily 11am–10pm; 300ptas for one ride or 500ptas for a one-day unlimited use ticket).

• Starting at the eastern end of the hill, there's a dramatic **cable-car** ride from Barceloneta or from the Moll de Barcelona, near the Columbus statue, to Jardins de Miramar (daily noon–8pm; 1000ptas one way, 1200ptas return, plus 600ptas for the Jaume I lift). Just beyond, you can then pick up a second cable car to the amusement park and the castle; or simply walk to the nearby museums.

• There's also a **funicular** which runs every 15min from Paral·lel Metro station to the cable-car station for the castle (summer daily every 15min 11am–10pm; winter Sat, Sun & holidays only 10.45am–8pm; 215ptas one way, 375ptas return). From here, you're only a few minutes' walk from the Fundació Miró.

Romanesque to the Gothic period was marked by a move from mural painting to painting on wood, and by the depiction of more naturalistic figures showing the lives of the saints and later portraits of kings and patrons of the arts. In the early part of the period, Catalan and Valencian schools were particularly influenced by contemporary Italian styles and you'll see some outstanding altarpieces, tombs and church decoration as well as colourful, if less refined, paintings. Later began the so-called "International Gothic" or "1400" style in which the influences became more widespread; the important figures of this time were the fifteenth-century artists Jaume Huguet and Lluís Dalmau. Works from the end of this period show the strong influence of contemporary Flemish painting, seen in the use of denser colours and the depiction of crowd scenes and perspective.

The Museu Etnològic and Museu Arqueològic

Downhill from the Palau Nacional, just to the east, are a couple more collections to find time for; the city's excellent ethnological and archeological museums. The **Museu Etnològic** (Tues & Thurs 10am–7pm, Wed & Fri–Sun 10am–2pm; 300ptas, free first Sun of month) boasts extensive cultural collections from Central and South America, Asia, Africa, Australia and the Middle East, housed in a series of glass hexagons.

More compelling, or at least more relevant to Catalunya, is the important **Museu Arqueològic** (Tues–Sat 9.30am–7pm, Sun 10am–2.30pm; 400ptas, free Sun), lower down the hill. Mostly devoted to the Roman period, the museum also has Carthaginian relics (especially from the Balearics), Etruscan bits and pieces and lots of prehistoric objects: it's of particular interest if you're planning to visit Empúries on the Costa Brava (see p.642), since most of the important finds from that impressive coastal site, and some good maps and photographs, are housed here. Among the more unusual exhibits in the museum is a reconstructed Roman funeral chamber whose walls are divided into small niches for funeral urns; a type of burial known as *columbaria* (literally pigeon-holes), which may be seen in situ in the south of Spain, at Carmona in Andalucía.

Over the way, cut into the hillside, is a reproduction of a Greek theatre, the **Teatre Grec**, again built for the 1929 Exhibition and now used during Barcelona's summer cultural festival, the *Grec* season. The Teatre Grec is part of another ambitious project, La Ciutat del Teatre, a huge arts complex which will also incorporate the nearby Mercat de les Flors, plus two new buildings, the Institut del Teatre and the Teatre Lliure, both currently situated in Gràcia: the complex is planned to be up and running by 1999.

From the Poble Espanyol to the Olympic area

A short walk over to the western side of the Palau Nacional brings you to the **Poble Espanyol** or "Spanish Village" (Mon 9am–8pm, Tues–Thurs 9am–2am, Fri & Sat 9am–4am, Sun 9am–midnight; 950ptas). This was designed for the International Exhibition and its streets and squares consist of famous or characteristic buildings from all over Spain. At the time, it was an inspired concept and as a crash-course in Spanish architecture it's still not at all bad – everything is well labelled and reasonably accurate and there are a couple of museums on site (both open daily 9am–2pm), displaying ethnographical and folk items.

Amid the pre-Olympic frenzy, the city authorities brought in Barcelona's hippest designers, Alfredo Arribas and Xavier Mariscal, who installed a club, the *Torres de Ávila*, in the Ávila gate. Other trendy venues followed and, of course, this being Barcelona, the whole complex now stays open until the small hours, a vibrant and exciting centre of Barcelona nightlife.

Just down the road from the village, the 1986 reconstruction by Catalan architects of the **Pavelló Mies van der Rohe** (April–Oct daily 10am–8pm; Nov–March daily 10am–6.30pm; 300ptas) recalls part of the German contribution to the 1929 Exhibition. Originally designed by Mies van der Rohe, the pavilion has a startlingly beautiful conjunction of hard straight lines with watery surfaces, its dark green polished onyx alternating with shining glass.

The Olympics on Montjuïc

From the Poble Espanyol, the main road through Montjuïc climbs around the hill and up to the city's principal **Olympic area**. It's a superb spot, sporting some amazing views of the city and its suburbs, and the road leads you right past some of Barcelona's most celebrated new buildings – such as Ricardo Bofill's **Sports University** (the Institut Nacional d'Educacio Fisica de Catalunya), the **Complex Esportiu Bernat Picornell** (swimming pools and sports complex), and the low-slung, Japanese designed, steel-and-glass **Palau Sant Jordi**, a sports and concert hall seating 17,000 people which opened in 1990 with Pavarotti in attendance.

Even this, however, is overshadowed by the **Estadi Olímpic** (visits daily 10am–6pm; free), which comfortably holds 65,000. Built originally for the 1929 Exhibition, and completely refitted by Catalan architects to accommodate the 1992 opening and closing ceremonies, it's a marvellously spacious arena. Remarkably, the only part not touched in the rebuilding was the original Neoclassical facade – everything else is new. The **Galeria Olímpica** (Tues–Fri 10am–1pm & 4–6pm, Sat and Sun 10am–2pm; 390ptas) exhibits items from the opening and closing ceremonies, and displays videos of the Games themselves.

The 1992 Olympics were the second planned for Montjuïc's stadium. The first, in 1936 – the so-called "People's Olympics" – were organized as an alternative to the Nazis' infamous Berlin games of that year, but the day before the official opening Franco's army revolt triggered the Civil War and scuppered the Barcelona games. Some of the 25,000 athletes and spectators who had turned up stayed on to join the Republican forces.

Fundació Joan Miró

Continuing down the main Avda. l'Estadi, heading towards the cable-car station, you pass Barcelona's possibly most adventurous museum, the **Fundació Joan Miró** (Tues–Sat 11am–7pm, Thurs closes 9.30pm, Sun 10.30am–2.30pm; 700ptas) – an impressive white structure, opened in 1975, and set in gardens overlooking the city. Joan Miró (1893–1983) was one of the greatest of Catalan artists, establishing an international reputation whilst never severing his links with his homeland. He had his first exhibition in 1918 and after that spent his summers in Catalunya (and the rest of the time in France) before moving to Mallorca in 1956, where he died. His friend, the architect Josep-Luís Sert, designed the beautiful building that now houses the museum, a permanent collection of paintings, graphics, tapestries and sculptures donated by Miró himself and covering the period from 1914 to 1978.

The **paintings and drawings**, regarded as one of the chief links between surrealism and abstract art, are instantly recognizable. Miró showed a childlike delight in colours and shapes and developed a free, highly decorative style – one of his favourite early techniques was to spill paint on the canvas and move his brush around in it. But for all that, perhaps the most affecting pieces in the museum are those of the *Barcelona Series* (1939–44), a set of fifty black-and-white lithographs executed in the immediate post-Civil War period. Other exhibits include his enormous bright **tapestries** (he donated nine to the museum), pencil drawings (particularly of misshapen women and gawky ballerinas) and **sculpture** outside in the gardens.

As well as the permanent exhibits, excellent temporary exhibitions, which may or may not be related to aspects of Miró's own work, are a regular feature. There is work by other artists, too, on permanent display, including pieces conceived in **homage to Miró** by the likes of Henri Matisse, Henry Moore, Robert Motherwell and the Basque sculptor Eduardo Chillida. The single most compelling exhibit, however, has to be Alexander Calder's **Mercury Fountain**, which he built for the Republican pavilion at the Paris Universal Exhibition of 1936 – the same exhibition for which Picasso painted *Guernica*. It is housed in a corridor on the ground floor.

The Parc d'Atraccions and the Castell de Montjuïc

Over in the eastern corner of Montjuïc, in a huddle above the port, are the hill's final set of attractions. From a point on the main road by the **Jardins de Mossen Jacint Verdaguer**, a cable-car system climbs to Montjuïc's amusement park, the **Parc d'Atraccions** (Sat, Sun and public holidays 11.30am–8pm, closes earlier in winter; 600ptas; ticket including unlimited rides 1800ptas), which has forty or so rides.

From the amusement park, the cable car tacks up the hillside, offering magnificent views across the city, before coming to rest close to the eighteenth-century **Castell de Montjuïc**. Built on seventeenth-century ruins, the castle has been the scene of much bloodshed – the first president of the Generalitat, Lluís Companys, was executed here by the Franco regime on October 15, 1940 – and perhaps appropriately now houses a remarkably good **Museu Militar** (Tues–Sun 9.30am–7.30pm; 200ptas). Inside are models of the most famous Catalan castles and an excellent collection of swords and guns, medals, uniforms, maps and photographs, capped by a collection of suits of armour down in the dungeons.

The Eixample

As Barcelona grew more prosperous throughout the nineteenth century, the Barri Gòtic was filled to bursting with an energetic, commercial population. By the 1850s it was clear that the city had to expand beyond the Plaça de Catalunya. The plan that was accepted was that of an engineer, Ildefons Cerdà, who drew up a grid-shaped new town marching off to the north, intersected by long, straight streets and cut by broad, angled avenues. Work started in 1859 on what became known as the *Ensanche* in Spanish – in Catalan, the **EIXAMPLE**, or "Extension".

It was a fashionable area in which to live, and the moneyed classes soon started moving from their cramped quarters by the port in the old town to spacious new apartments and business addresses. As the money in the city moved north, so did a new class of *modernista* architects who began to pepper the Eixample with ever more striking examples of their work, which were eagerly snapped up by status-conscious merchants and businessmen. These buildings – most notably the work of **Antoni Gaudí, Lluís Domènech i Montaner** and **Josep Puig i Cadafalch**, but others too (see "Modernisme" p.598) – are still often in private hands, restricting your viewing to the outside, but turning the Eixample into a huge urban museum around which it's a pleasure to wander. If you are thinking about doing a serious exploration of *modernista* architecture, something definitely worth considering is the **Ruta del Modernisme** ticket. The price of the ticket (available from Palau Güell, see p.581, or Casa Lleó Morera, see p.597; 1500ptas) includes entry into all buildings usually open to the public and a map and written guide (in English) marking a route with the most emblematic as well as minor examples of buildings from this movement; the ticket is also valid for a month, meaning you can spread your visits out.

The Eixample is still the city's main shopping and business district, spreading out on either side of the two principal (and parallel) thoroughfares, **Passeig de Gràcia** and **Rambla de Catalunya**, both of which cut northwest from the Plaça de Catalunya. The former features several of the best-known examples of Barcelona's *modernista* architecture, including the famous **Manzana de la Discòrdia** and Gaudí's **La Pedrera**.

The latter is the district's most attractive avenue, largely pedestrianized and sporting benches and open-air cafés. Almost all the things you're likely to want to see are on the eastern side of the Rambla de Catalunya – an area known as Dreta de l'Eixample – and south of the wide **Avinguda Diagonal**, which slices across the entire Eixample. There's less to get excited about on the west side of Rambla de Catalunya – the so-called Esquerra de l'Eixample – which housed many of the public buildings contained within Cerdà's nineteenth-century plan.

If you're not interested in shopping or architecture, it's not immediately clear why you might spend time in the Eixample, though one bonus is that many of the buildings also contain noteworthy exhibitions and museums; the **Fundació Antoni Tàpies** is Barcelona's latest gallery dedicated to the work of just a single artist. Moreover, the Eixample contains the one building in the city to which a visit is virtually obligatory: Gaudí's extraordinary **Sagrada Familia** church, beyond the Diagonal, in the northeast of the district.

Along Passeig de Gràcia

If you want to walk in the Eixample, the stretch you'll get most out of is the wide **Passeig de Gràcia** which runs northwest from the El Corte Inglés store on the corner of Plaça de Catalaunya. Laid out in its present form in 1827, it's a splendid, showy avenue, bisected by the other two main city boulevards, the Gran Vía and Avda. Diagonal, and continues as far as Gràcia itself – but you're probably not going to walk that far. Stick with it, though, as far as Metro Diagonal for a view of some of the best of the city's *modernista* architecture, flaunted in a series of remarkable buildings on and just off the avenue.

Manzana de la Discòrdia

The most famous grouping of buildings, the so-called **Manzana de la Discòrdia** or "Block of Discord", is just four blocks up from Plaça de Catalunya (nearest metro: Passeig de Gràcia). It gets its name because the adjacent buildings – built by three different architects – are completely different in style and feeling.

On the corner with c/de Consell de Cent, at Passeig de Gràcia 35, the six-storey **Casa Lleó Morera** (daily 10am–7pm; entry with Ruta del Modernisme ticket only) is by Domènech i Montaner, completed in 1906. It's the least appealing of the buildings in the block (in that it has the least extravagant exterior), and has suffered more than the others from "improvements" wrought by subsequent owners, which included removing the ground-floor arches and sculptures. However, it's still got a rich Art Nouveau interior (of which you can see the first floor only) – flush with ceramics and wood – and its semicircular jutting balconies are quite distinctive.

A few doors up at no. 41, Puig i Cadafalch's **Casa Amatller** is more striking, an apartment block from 1900 created largely from the bones of an existing building and paid for by Antoni Amatller, a Catalan chocolate manufacturer. The facade rises in steps to a point, studded with coloured ceramic decoration and with heraldic sculptures over the doors and windows. Step inside the hallway for a peek: the ceramic tiles continue along the walls and there are twisted stone columns, fine stained-glass domes and an interior glass roof. The block contains an Hispanic art institute, the Institute Amatller d'Art Hispanic (library open Sept–June Mon–Fri 10am–1.30pm, also Tues & Thurs 3.30–7pm), located inside the old Amatller family apartments; if you want to ensure a look inside, there are guided tours on Thursdays (11am & noon; free).

Perhaps the most extraordinary creation on the Block of Discord is next door, at no. 43, where Gaudí's **Casa Batlló** (finished in 1907) – designed for the industrialist Josep Batlló – was similarly wrought from an apartment building already in place but

MODERNISME

Modernisme, the Catalan offshoot of Art Nouveau, was the expression of a renewed upsurge in Catalan nationalism in the 1870s. The early nineteenth-century economic recovery in Catalunya had provided the initial impetus, and the ensuing cultural renaissance in the region – the *Renaixença* – led to the fresh stirrings of a new Catalan awareness and identity after the dark years of Bourbon rule.

Lluís Domènech i Montaner (1850–1923) – perhaps the greatest *modernista* architect – was responsible for giving Catalan aspirations a definite direction with his appeal, in 1878, for a national style of architecture, drawing particularly on the rich Catalan Romanesque and Gothic traditions. The timing was perfect, since Barcelona was undergoing a huge expansion: the medieval walls had been pulled down and the gridded Eixample was giving the city a new shape, with a rather French feel to it, and plenty of new space to work in. By 1874 **Antoni Gaudí** (1852–1926) had begun his architectural career. He was born in Reus to a family of artisans, and his work was never strictly modernist in style (it was never strictly anything in style), but the imaginative impetus he gave the movement was incalculable. Fourteen years later the young **Josep Puig i Cadafalch** (1867–1957) would be inspired to become an architect (and later a reforming politician) as he watched the spectacularly rapid round-the-clock construction of Domènech's *Grand Hotel* on the Passeig de Colom. It was in another building by Domènech (the café-restaurant of the Parc de la Ciutadella) that a craft workshop was set up after the Exhibition of 1888, giving Barcelona's *modernista* architects the opportunity to experiment with traditional crafts like ceramic tiles, ironwork, stained glass and decorative stone carving. This combination of traditional crafts with modern technology was to become the hallmark of *modernisme* – a combination which produced some of the most fantastic and exciting modern architecture to be found anywhere in the world.

Most attention is usually focused on the three protagonists mentioned above; certainly they provide the bulk of the most extraordinary buildings that Barcelona has to offer. But keep an eye out for lesser-known architects who also worked in the Eixample; **Josep María Jujol**, renowned as Gaudí's collaborator on several of his most famous projects, can also boast a few complete constructions of his own, or there's the hard-working **Jeroni Granell** (1867–1931), and **Josep Vilaseca i Casanoves** (1848–1910), who was responsible for the brick Arc de Triomf outside the Ciutadella park.

It's Antoni Gaudí, though, that most have heard of – by training a metalworker, by inclination a fervent Catalan nationalist. His buildings are the most daring creations of all Art Nouveau, apparently lunatic flights of fantasy which at the same time are perfectly functional. His architectural influences were Moorish and Gothic, while he embellished his work with elements from the natural world. Yet Gaudí rarely wrote a word about the theory of his art, preferring its products to speak for themselves. Like all the *modernista* buildings in the city, they demand reaction.

considered dull by contemporaries. Gaudí was hired to give it a face-lift and contrived to create a facade which Dalí later compared to "the tranquil waters of a lake". There's an animal aspect at work here, too: the stone facade hangs in folds, like skin, and from below, the twisted balcony railings resemble malevolent eyes.

Casa Montaner i Simon: the Fundació Antoni Tàpies

Turn the corner on to c/d'Aragó and at no. 255 (just past Rambla de Catalunya) you'll find Domènech i Montaner's first important building, the **Casa Montaner i Simon**, finished in 1880. The building originally served the publishing firm of Montaner i Simon, but, as the enormous aluminium tubular structure on the roof now announces, it's been converted to house the **Fundació Antoni Tàpies** (Tues–Sun 11am–8pm; 500ptas).

The third of Barcelona's showpiece single-artist collections is devoted to the life and work of Antoni Tàpies, born in the city in 1923. His first major paintings date from 1945, at which time Tàpies was interested in collage (using newspaper, cardboard, silver wrapping, string and wire) and engraving techniques. Later, coming into contact with Miró among others, he underwent a brief surreal period (the fruits of which are displayed in the basement). After a stay in Paris he found his feet with an abstract style that matured during the 1950s, during which time he held his first major exhibitions, including a show in New York. His large works – splashed across the main gallery – are deceptively simple, though underlying messages and themes are signalled by the inclusion of everyday objects and symbols on the canvas, while he has also experimented with unusual materials, such as oil paint mixed with crushed marble. His work became increasingly political, too, during the 1960s and 1970s: the harsh colours of *In Memory of Salvador Puig Antich* commemorate a Catalan Anarchist executed by Franco's regime.

La Pedrera and Vinçon

Gaudí's weird apartment block, the Casa Milà, at Passeig de Gràcia 92 (Metro Diagonal) is another building not to be missed, worked on between 1905 and 1911. Its rippled facade, curving around the street corner in one smooth sweep, is said to have been inspired by the mountain of Montserrat, and the apartments themselves, whose balconies of tangled metal drip over the facade, resemble eroded cave dwellings. The building – still split into private apartments – is more popularly known as **La Pedrera**, the "rock pile" or "stone quarry". This was one of Gaudí's last secular commissions – and one of his best – but even here he was injecting religious motifs and sculptures into the building until told to remove them by the building's owners. You can visit **the roof**, to see at close quarters the enigmatic chimneys, as well as an exhibition about Gaudí's work in the top rooms of the building (Tues–Sat 10am–8pm, Sun 10am–3pm; 500ptas).

Right next to La Pedrera, in the same block, the **Casa Casas** dates from 1899, a huge building designed for the artist Ramón Casas who maintained a home here. In 1941, the **Vinçon** store was established in the building, which emerged in the 1960s as the country's pre-eminent purveyor of furniture and design, a position today's department store (Mon–Sat 10am–2pm & 4.30–8.30pm) still maintains; there are entrances at Passeig de Gràcia 96, c/de Provença 273 and c/Pau Claris 175.

East: between Passeig de Gràcia and Avinguda. Diagonal

The buildings along Passeig de Gràcia are perhaps the best-known in the Eixample, but the blocks contained within the triangle to the east, formed by the Passeig and **Avinguda. Diagonal**, sport their own important, often extraordinary structures. Several are by the two hardest working architects in the Eixample, Domènech i Montaner and Puig i Cadafalch, while Gaudí's first apartment building, the Casa Calvet, is also here. Apart from the Casa Calvet, all the buildings are within a few blocks of each other between the Passeig de Gràcia and Diagonal metro stops.

Just a few blocks from the Plaça de Catalunya, Gaudí's **Casa Calvet** (c/de Casp 48) dates from 1899. This was his first apartment block and, though fairly conventional in style, the Baroque inspiration on display in the main facade was to surface again in his later, more elaborate buildings on the main Passeig de Gràcia. If you need another target, aim for the church and market of **La Concepció**, in between c/de Valencia and c/d'Aragó. The early fifteenth-century Gothic church and cloister once stood in the old town, part of a convent abandoned in the early nineteenth century and then transferred here brick by brick in the 1870s by Jeroni Granell. The market was added in 1888, its iron-and-glass tram-shed structure reminiscent of others in the city. One block north, the neo-Gothic **Casa Thomas** at c/de Mallorca 291, with its understated pale ceramic tiles, has a ground floor that welcomes visitors into its furniture design showroom. A little way along, set back from the crossroads in a little garden, the **Palau Montaner** (c/de Mallorca 278) was finished a few years later, in 1893. By comparison, it's rather a plain, low structure, though enlivened by rich mosaic pictures on the facade and a fine interior staircase (open Sat only, 9am–1pm).

From here you can head up to Avinguda. Diagonal, and the soaring Casa Terrades at no. 416–420. More usually known as the **Casa de les Punxes** (House of Spikes) because of its red-tiled turrets and steep gables, it is Puig i Cadafalch's largest work. Farther along Avinguda. Diagonal, on the other side of the road at no. 373, Puig's almost Gothic **Palau Quadras** from 1904 now houses the **Museu de la Música** (Tues & Thurs–Sun 10am–2pm, Wed 5–8pm; 300ptas, free Wed afternooon & first Sun of month). The collection of instruments from all over the world, dating from the sixteenth to the twentieth century, gives an excuse to see inside.

La Sagrada Familia

While diverting, and occasionally provocative, the pockets of architectural interest throughout the Eixample hardly command mass appeal. The same is not true, however, of the new town's most famous monument, Antoni Gaudí's great **Templo Expiatiorio de la Sagrada Familia** (daily: March, Sept & Oct 9am–7pm; April–Aug 9pm-8pm; Nov–Feb 9pm–6pm; 800ptas; metro line 2 or 5 to Sagrada Familia), a good way northeast of the Plaça de Catalunya and just north of the Diagonal. It's an essential stop on any visit to Barcelona, for more than any building in the Barri Gòtic it speaks volumes about the Catalan urge to glorify uniqueness and endeavour.

Begun in 1882 by public subscription, the Sagrada Familia was conceived originally by its progenitor, the Catalan publisher Josep Bocabella, as an expiatory building which would atone for the city's increasingly revolutionary ideas. Bocabella appointed the architect Francesc de Paula Villar to the work, and his plan was for a modest church in an orthodox neo-Gothic style. After arguments between the two men, **Gaudí** took charge two years later and changed the direction and scale of the project almost immediately, seeing in the Sagrada Familia an opportunity to reflect his own deepening spiritual and nationalist feelings. Indeed, after he finished the Parc Güell in 1911, Gaudí vowed never to work again on secular art, but to devote himself solely to the Sagrada Familia (where, by now, he lived in a workshop on site), and he was adapting the plans ceaselessly right up to his death. (He was run over by a tram on the Gran Vía in June 1926 and died in hospital two days later – initially unrecognized, for he had become a virtual recluse, rarely leaving his small studio. His death was treated as a Catalan national disaster, and all of Barcelona turned out for his funeral procession.)

Today the church remains unfinished, though amid great controversy **work restarted** in the late 1950s and still continues. Although the church building survived the Civil War, Gaudí's plans and models were destroyed in 1936 by the Anarchists, who regarded Gaudí and his church as conservative religious relics that the new Barcelona could do without: George Orwell – whose sympathies were very much with the Anarchists during the Civil War – remarked that the Sagrada Familia had been spared because of its supposed artistic value, but added that it was "one of the most hideous buildings in the world" and that "the Anarchists showed bad taste in not blowing it up when they had the chance". However, since they didn't, and as no one now knows what Gaudí intended, the political arguments continue. Some maintain that the Sagrada Familia should be left incomplete as a memorial to Gaudí's untimely death, others that he intended it to be the work of several generations, each continuing in their own style.

The building

The size alone is startling. Eight **spires** rise to over one hundred metres. They have been likened to everything from perforated cigars to celestial billiard cues, both of which are good descriptions. For Gaudí they were symbolic of the twelve Apostles; he planned to build four more above the main facade and to add a 180-metre tower topped with a lamb (representing Jesus) over the transept, itself to be surrounded by four smaller towers symbolizing the Evangelists.

A precise **symbolism** also pervades the facades, each of which is divided into three porches devoted to Faith, Hope and Charity. The east facade further represents the Nativity and the Mysteries of Joy; the west (currently the main entrance and nearing completion) depicts the Passion and the Mysteries of Affliction. Gaudí meant the south facade, the Gloria, to be the culmination of the Sagrada Familia – designed, he said, to show "the religious realities of present and future life . . . man's origin, his end and the ways he has to follow to achieve it", Everything from the Creation to Heaven and Hell, in short, was to be included in one magnificent ensemble.

Use the **elevator** which runs up one of the towers around the rose window, or face the long, steep climb to the top (a twisting 400 steps). Either route will reward you with partial views of the city through an extraordinary jumble of latticed stonework, ceramic decoration, carved buttresses and sculpture. You're free to climb still farther around the walls and into the other towers, a dizzy experience to say the least.

On site, there's the small **Museu de la Sagrada Familia**, which traces the career of the architect and the history of the Sagrada Familia. Models, sketches and photographs help to make some sense of the work going on around you.

Esquerra de l'Eixample: Plaça de Catalunya to Estació-Sants

The long streets **west of the Passeig de Gràcia** – making up the Esquerra de l'Eixample – are no competition when it comes to planning a route around the Eixample, and most visitors only ever travel this part of the city underground, on their way into the centre by metro. This was the part of the Eixample meant by Cerdà for public buildings, and many of these still stand: the grand **Universitat** building, at Plaça de la Universitat; the local **Hospital Clinic** (1904); the prison – the **Preso Model** – with its star-shaped cell blocks; and **Les Arenes** bullring, the last a beautiful structure from 1900 with fine Moorish decoration. However, probably your only venture into this part of the Eixample will be a window-shopping stroll along the **Gran Vía de les Corts Catalanes** (usually shortened to just the Gran Vía), which links Plaça d'Espanya with Plaça de les Glòries Catalanes to the east.

However, there is one part of the Esquerra de l'Eixample that it is possible to justify a short walk around, starting at the Plaça d'Espanya. Between here and **Sants** station, several public spaces have been created over the last decade or so in a style known as **nou urbanisme** – typified by a wish to transform former industrial sites into urban parks accessible to local people.

Parc Joan Miró and around Sants station

Built on the site of the nineteenth-century municipal slaughterhouse, the **Parc Joan Miró** (Metro Tarragona) features a raised piazza whose main feature is Miró's gigantic mosaic sculpture *Dona i Ocell* (Woman and Bird), towering above a small lake. It's a familiar symbol if you've studied Miró's other works, and was originally entitled "The Cock", until the city authorities suggested otherwise.

Even more controversial are the open park areas created around Sants station, just up the road. Directly in front of the station, the **Plaça dels Països Catalans** features a series of walls, raised meshed roofs and coverings designed by Helio Piñon – a rather comfortless "park" in most people's eyes, more intimidating than welcoming. It's easier to see the attraction of Basque architect Luís Peña Ganchegui's **Parc de l'Espanya Industrial**, two minutes' walk away around the side of the station. Built on an old textile factory site, it has a line of red-and-yellow striped lighthouses at the top of glaring white steps with an incongruously classical Neptune in the water below, seen to best effect at night.

The suburbs

Until the Eixample stretched out across the plain to meet them, a string of small towns ringed the city to the north. Today, they're firmly entrenched as **suburbs** of Barcelona, but most still retain an individual identity worth investigating even on a short visit to the city. **Gràcia**, particularly – the closest to the centre – is still very much the liberal, almost bohemian stronghold it was in the nineteenth century, with an active cultural life and night scene of its own. Apart from mere curiosity, each of the other suburbs also has a specific sight or two that makes it a worthwhile target. Some, like Gaudí's **Parc Güell**, between Gràcia and Horta, and the Gothic monastery at **Pedralbes**, are included in most people's tours of the city, and for good reason. Other sights are more specialized – such as the football museum at FC Barcelona's superb **Camp Nou** stadium or the ceramics collection in the **Palau Reial** – but taken together they do help to counter the notion that Barcelona begins and ends in the Barri Gòtic. Finally, if you're saving yourself for just one aerial view of Barcelona, wait for a clear day and head for **Tibidabo**, way to the northwest; a mountain with an amusement park and a couple of bars with the best views in the city.

Gràcia

GRÀCIA is the most satisfying of Barcelona's peripheral districts, and, given its concentration of bars, clubs and restaurants, the one you're most likely to visit. Beginning at the top of the Passeig de Gràcia, and bordered roughly by c/de Balmes to the west and the streets above the Sagrada Familia to the east, it has been a fully fledged suburb of the city since late last century – traditionally home to arty and political types, students and the intelligentsia, but also still supporting a very real local population which lends Gràcia an attractive, no-frills, small-town atmosphere. **Getting there** by public transport means taking the FF.CC railway from Plaça de Catalunya to Gràcia station; bus #22 or #24 from Plaça de Catalunya up c/Gran de Gràcia; or taking the metro to either Diagonal, to the south, or Fontana, to the north.

Plaça del Sol is an enjoyable place to sit out during the day at one of the cafés, admiring the solid nineteenth-century buildings that surround the square and the more recent architectural additions by Gabriel Mora and Jaume Bach. At night, especially at the weekend, the square becomes an outdoor meeting-place, a base from which to launch yourself at the bars, clubs and restaurants in the vicinity. A couple of blocks down is another pleasant stop, **Plaça Rius i Taulet**, whose most obvious feature is a thirty-metre-high bell tower.

Gaudí's first major private commission, the **Casa Vicens** (which he finished in 1885), is at c/de les Carolines 24 (closest metro: Fontana). Here he took inspiration from the Mudéjar style, covering the facade in linear green-and-white tiles with a flower motif.

Parc Güell

From 1900 to 1914 Gaudí worked for Don Eusebio Güell (patron of his Palau Güell, off the Ramblas) on the **Parc Güell** (daily: July–Sept 10am–9pm; Oct–June 10am–6pm; free), on the outskirts of Gràcia. This was Gaudí's most ambitious project after the Sagrada Familia – which he was engaged on at the same time – commissioned as a private housing estate of sixty dwellings and furnished with paths, recreational areas and decorative monuments. In the end, only two houses were actually built, and the park was opened to the public instead in 1922.

Laid out on a hill which provides fabulous views back across the city, the park is an almost hallucinatory expression of the imagination. Pavilions of contorted stone, giant decorative lizards, a vast Hall of Columns (intended to be the estate's market), the meanderings of a huge ceramic bench – all combine in one manic swirl of ideas and excesses. The immediate and obvious comparison is with an amusement park, something not lost on a variety of literary visitors. The Hall of Columns was described by Sacheverell Sitwell (in *Spain*) as "at once a funfair, a petrified forest, and the great temple of Amun at Karnak, itself drunk, and reeling in an eccentric earthquake".

The ceramic mosaics and decorations found throughout the park were mostly executed by J.M. Jujol, who assisted on several of Gaudí's projects, while one of Gaudí's other collaborators, Francesc Berenguer, designed and built a house in the park in 1904, in which Gaudí was persuaded to live until he left to camp out at the Sagrada Família for good. The house is now the **Casa Museu Gaudí** (Mon–Fri & Sun 10am–2pm & 4–6pm, closes 7pm in summer; 250ptas), a diverting collection of some of the furniture he designed for other projects – a typical mixture of wild originality and brilliant engineering – as well as plans and objects related to the park and to Gaudí's life.

To get to the park, take **bus** #24 from Plaça de Catalunya right to the side gate by the car park, or the **metro** to Vallcarca, from where you walk down Avinguda. de l'Hospital until you see the mechanical escalators on your left, then follow the path right to the park entrance. Be warned, however, that the escalators are often not working and the climb up on foot is a particularly stiff one. **Walking from Gràcia**, head straight up the main c/Gran de Gràcia and you'll pass Metro Lesseps, where you should turn right on to the Travessera de Dalt.

Pedralbes and around

Northwest of the city, **PEDRALBES** is a well-to-do, residential neighbourhood of wide avenues and fancy apartment blocks. Allow yourself the best part of a day and you can include the Gothic monastery here in a longer route that takes in the Camp Nou stadium, an early Gaudí creation, and the ceramics museum in the Palau Reial.

Camp Nou: the Museu del Futbol Club Barcelona

Within the city's Diagonal area, the magnificent **Camp Nou** football stadium of FC Barcelona (Metro Collblanc or María Cristina) will be high on the visiting list of any sports fan. Built in 1957, and enlarged to accommodate the 1982 World Cup semi-final, the comfortable stadium seats a staggering 120,000 people in steep tiers that provide one of the best football-watching experiences in the world – on a par with the famous Maracaña stadium in Brazil. The club is Spain's most successful in recent years, domestic league and cup winners on a regular basis, and European Cup winners in 1992. But it's more than just a football club to most people in Barcelona. During the Franco era, it stood as a Catalan symbol, around which people could rally, and perhaps as a consequence FC Barcelona has the world's largest football club membership – currently 106,000 – including the planet's most celebrated clerical goalkeeper, the Pope, who was persuaded to join on his visit to Spain in 1982.

If you can't get to a game, a visit to the club's **Museu del Futbol** (Mon–Sat 10am–6.30pm, Sun 10am–2pm; 450ptas), is a good second-best: a splendid celebration of Spain's national sport. There are team and match photos dating back to 1901, and a gallery of foreign players who have graced Barça's books.

Palau Reial de Pedralbes and the Finca Güell

On the other side of Avinguda. Diagonal, the **Palau Reial de Pedralbes** (Metro Palau Reial) is an Italianate palace set in pleasant, formal **grounds** (daily: winter 10am–6pm; summer 10am–8pm). The interior is open to the public as the **Museu de Ceràmica** (Tues–Sun 10am–3pm; 500ptas, free first Sun of month), where the many exhibits range from the thirteenth to the nineteenth century, and include fine Mudéjar-influenced tiles and plates from the Aragonese town of Teruel, as well as whole rooms of Catalan water stoups (some from the seventeenth century), jars, dishes and bowls. In the modern section, Picasso, Miró and the *modernista* Antoni Serra i Fiter are all represented. Adjoining the Museu de Ceràmica and included in the ticket price is a new museum, the **Museu de les Arts Decoratives** (times as for the Museu de Ceràmica), a collection of household objects and industrial design from the Middle Ages to the modern day.

From the palace, it's a walk of fifteen minutes or so up Avinguda. Pedralbes to the monastery. Just a couple of minutes along the way, you'll pass Gaudí's **Finca Güell** on your left. Built as a stables and riding school for the family of Gaudí's old patron, Don Eusebio Güell, and now a private residence, you can see no farther than its extraordinary metal dragon gateway, with razor teeth snarling at the passers-by.

Monestir de Pedralbes

At the end of Avinguda. Pedralbes, the Gothic **Monestir de Pedralbes** (Tues–Sun 10am–2pm; 300ptas, free first Sun of month, joint ticket with Collecció Thyssen-Bornemisza 500ptas) is reached up a cobbled street that passes through a small archway set back from the road. If you're coming from the city centre, the monastery is about a thirty-minute journey by **bus** (#22 from the Passeig de Gràcia, just north of Plaça de Catalunya, to the end of the line), or take the metro to Palau Reial (see above).

Founded in 1326 for the nuns of the Order of St Clare, this is in effect an entire monastic village, preserved on the outskirts of the city. The harmonious **cloisters** are built on three levels and adorned by the slenderest of columns, and rooms opening off here give the clearest impression of monastic life you're likely to see in Catalunya: there's a large refectory, a fully equipped kitchen, infirmary (complete with beds and water jugs), separate infirmary kitchen, and windows overlooking a well-tended kitchen garden. The adjacent **church**, a simple, single-naved structure which retains some of its original stained glass, is also well worth looking in on. In the chancel, to the right of the altar, the foundation's sponsor, Elisenda de Montcada, wife of Jaume II, lies in a superb, carved marble tomb.

After years of negotiations, a selection of religious paintings from the Thyssen-Bornemisza art collection is now on permanent view in one of the monastery's old dormitories. The immense private art collection of Baron Heinrich Thyssen-Bornemisza came to Spain in 1989, and the bulk of it is displayed in Madrid's Villahermosa palace, but the promptings of the baron's Catalan wife ensured a cache of paintings found its way to Barcelona. This now forms the **Collecció Thyssen-Bornemisza** (Tues–Sun 10am–2pm; 300ptas, joint ticket with Monestir de Pedralbes 500ptas), a superb body of work which includes priceless pieces from all the major movements in European art from the fourteenth to the eighteenth century.

Tibidabo

If the views from the Castell de Montjuïc are good, those from the 550-metre heights of **Mount Tibidabo** – which forms the northwestern boundary of the city – are legendary. On one of those mythical clear days you can see across to Montserrat and the Pyrenees, and out to sea even as far as Mallorca. The very name is based on this view, taken from the Temptations of Christ in the wilderness, when Satan led him to a high place and offered him everything which could be seen: *Haec omnia tibi dabo si cadens adoraberis me* ("All these things will I give thee, if thou wilt fall down and worship me").

At the summit there's a modern **church** topped with a huge statue of Christ, and – immediately adjacent – a wonderful **Parc d'Atraccions** (July & Aug Mon–Thurs noon–10pm, Fri & Sat noon–1am; Sept Mon–Fri noon–8pm, Sat & Sun noon–10pm; Oct–April Sat, Sun & holidays only, noon–8pm; May–June Wed–Fri 10am–6pm, Sat &

Sun noon–9pm), where the amusements are scattered around several levels of the mountain-top, connected by landscaped paths and gardens. It's a good mix of tradition-al rides and high-tech attractions, at all of which large queues form at peak times. There are various **admission** charges depending on what you want to do: entry only is 700ptas, and with this you pay separately for each ride and attraction (up to 500ptas); if you want to go on everything, or even just three or four rides, it'll be cheaper to buy an ticket for 2400ptas.

Take the FF.CC **train** (Sarrià line) or **bus** #17 (both from Plaça de Catalunya) to Avinguda. Tibidabo. From there a regular **tram** service (the Tramvia Blau; every 30min or every 15min at weekends, 7am–9.30pm; 225ptas one way, 350ptas return) runs you up to Plaça Doctor Andreu (there's a bus service instead if the tram's not run-ning). Here, there are a couple of café-bars, and a **funicular station** with regular con-nections to the top (Mon–Thurs & Sun noon– 10.30pm; Fri & Sat noon–1.30am; 300ptas one way, 400ptas return).

Out of the city

Day trips out of the city are easy and popular, particularly up or down **the coast** to one of the beach-resorts that city-dwellers have appropriated for themselves. The best coastal destination is Sitges, forty minutes away along the Costa Daurada, dealt with in the "Catalunya" chapter. However, there are plenty of other beaches closer to the city that are worth considering, such as **Castelldefels** to the south, and those of the **Costa Maresme** to the north – all of them are connected to Barcelona by very frequent train services that run throughout the summer. Otherwise, the one essential excursion is to **Montserrat**, the extraordinary mountain and monastery 40km northwest of the city: few visitors are disappointed.

The coast: Castelldefels and the Costa Maresme

All **trains** to the beaches below depart from Estació-Sants, which is where you should go for current timetables. Those heading south to Castelldefels also stop at the station at Passeig de Gràcia; north to the Costa Maresme, you can pick the train up at Plaça de Catalunya.

South, the first coastal stop is at **CASTELLDEFELS**, 20km from Barcelona. Don't get off at the earlier town stop; you want Castelldefels-Platja, where vast numbers alight in summer to descend upon this extremely long beach, which starts just a couple of blocks from the station. **GARRAF**, another five minutes or so south on the train, has a much smaller beach, and more of a family atmosphere, but the town itself is far pretti-er, with a small port to take up some of your time as well.

Immediately **north** of Barcelona, before you reach the Costa Brava, is a stretch of coast known as the **Costa Maresme**. On the whole it's far more industrial and less attractive than the Costa Brava, but its proximity to the city means clogged-up roads and packed trains in the summer, as people head out of in search of a change of scenery. The first 40km of coastline is dominated by the grim industrial towns of Badalona and Mataró, and if you're after a town with a bit more to it than interesting chemical smells, you should continue at least as far as **ARENYS DE MAR**, an hour from Barcelona. It's the largest fishing port hereabouts and consequently has a har-bour that bears investigation and a beach that's serviceable. **CALDETES**, a couple of kilometres south from here, is visited for its thermal baths, first exploited by the Romans; while **CANET DE MAR**, just to the north, also has a decent beach.

SANT POL DE MAR, 45km from Barcelona, is probably your best bet if you're heading for just one spot on the coast. Small, and as unspoiled as these coastal villages get, it offers rocky coves and crowd-free swimming around fifteen minutes' walk from the station, and has several restaurants along the main street. From the train station, cross the tracks and walk to the left, around the corner.

The mountain and monastery of Montserrat

The **mountain of MONTSERRAT**, with its strangely shaped crags of rock, its monastery and ruined hermitage caves, stands just 40km northwest of Barcelona, off the road to Lleida. It is one of the most spectacular of all Spain's natural sights, a saw-toothed outcrop left exposed to erosion when the inland sea that covered this area around 25 million years ago was drained by progressive uplifts of the earth's crust. Legends hang easily upon it. Fifty years after the birth of Christ, Saint Peter is said to have deposited an image of the Virgin carved by Saint Luke in one of the mountain caves, and another tale makes this the spot in which the knight Parsifal discovered the Holy Grail. Inevitably the monastery and mountain are no longer remote; in fact they're ruthlessly exploited as a tourist trip from the Costa Brava. But don't be put off – the place itself is still magical and you can avoid the crowds by striking out on to the mountainside, along well-signposted paths, to potent and deserted hermitages. The main **pilgrimages** to Montserrat take place on April 27 and September 8.

Practicalities

The most thrilling approach is by train and cable car from Barcelona. FF.CC **trains** leave from beneath Plaça d'Espanya daily 9.07am, 10.10am, 11.07am then at two-hourly intervals until 7.07pm; get off at Montserrat Aeri, just over an hour away. From here, a cable car (the Teleferic de Montserrat Aeri; every 15min, daily 10am–1.45pm & 3–6.35pm) completes the journey, a five-minute swoop up the sheer mountainside to a spot just below the monastery – probably the most exhilarating ride in Catalunya. A return ticket, including train and cable car, costs 1770ptas, and there is also a combined ticket including the train, cable car and the two funiculars on the mountain for 2530ptas return; both tickets are available from the FF.CC station.**Returning to Barcelona**, the trains back from Montserrat Aeri station are again two-hourly, this time from 10.35am to 6.35pm.

Otherwise, daily **buses** run from Barcelona (Julia Tours, Plaça Universitat 12; ☎93 490 40 00), usually leaving at 9am and returning at around 6pm. These cost around 1200ptas per person, and tickets are available from Julia Tours or any travel agent. **Drivers** should take the A2 motorway as far as Martorell, and then follow the N11 and C1411 before zig-zagging up to the monastery.

Food at the couple of self-service restaurants is pricey and uninspiring – and the restaurants themselves are crammed at peak times. There's a lot to be said for taking your own picnic and striking off up the mountainside. **Staying over** at Montserrat can be an attractive option: it's a very different place once the tour groups have departed. The three-star *Hotel Abat Cisneros* (☎93 835 02 01, fax 93 828 40 06; ④) has double rooms with or without shower or bath, while the *Hotel-Residencia Monestir* (same telephone and fax number) is slightly cheaper. The **campsite** (☎93 835 02 51), signposted *Camping*, is up beyond the Sant Joan funicular, with a clean shower and toilet block and excellent views overlooking the monastery and mountains.

The monastery

It is the "Black Virgin" (*La Moreneta*), the icon supposedly hidden by Saint Peter (and curiously reflecting the style of sixth-century Byzantine carving), which is responsible for the existence of the **monastery of Monserrat**. The legend is loosely wrought, but it appears the icon was lost in the early eighth century after being hidden during the Moorish invasion. It reappeared in 880, accompanied by the customary visions and celestial music and, in the first of its miracles, would not budge when the Bishop of Vic attempted to remove it. A chapel was built to house it, and in 976 this was superseded by a Benedictine monastery, set about three-quarters of the way up the mountain at an altitude of nearly 1000m.

Miracles abounded and the Virgin of Montserrat soon became the chief cult-image of Catalunya and a pilgrimage centre second in Spain only to Santiago de Compostela. Over 150 churches were dedicated to her in Italy alone, as were the first chapels of Mexico, Chile and Peru; even a Caribbean island bears her name. For centuries, the monastery enjoyed outrageous prosperity, having its own flag and a form of extraterritorial independence along the lines of the Vatican City. Its fortunes declined only in the nineteenth century; in 1835 the monastery was suppressed for its Carlist sympathies – monks were allowed to return nine years later but by 1882 their numbers had fallen to nineteen. In recent decades Montserrat's popularity has again become established; today there are over 300 brothers and, in addition to the tourists, tens of thousands of newly married couples come here to seek *La Moreneta*'s blessing on their union.

The monastery itself is of no particular architectural interest, save perhaps in its monstrous bulk. Only the Renaissance **Basilica** (dating largely from 1560–92) is open to the public. **La Moreneta**, blackened by the smoke of countless candles, stands above the high altar – reached from behind, by way of an entrance to the right of the basilica's main entrance. The best time to be here is at the chanting of Ave Maria, around 1pm, when Montserrat's world-famous **boys' choir** sings.

Near the entrance to the basilica, the **Museu de Montserrat** (500ptas) is split into two parts: the section adjoining the cloister (10.30am–2pm) contains paintings by Caravaggio and El Greco and a few archeological finds; while under the *plaça* in front of the basilica (3–6pm) are Catalan paintings from the nineteenth century.

Walks on the mountain

After you've poked around the monastery grounds, it's the **walks** around the woods and mountainside of Montserrat which are the real attraction. Following the tracks to various caves and the thirteen different hermitages, you can contemplate what Goethe wrote in 1816: "Nowhere but in his own Montserrat will a man find happiness and peace."

Two separate **funiculars** run from points close to the cable car station. One drops to the **Santa Cova** (Holy Grotto), a seventeenth-century chapel built where the icon is said to have originally been found (every 15–20min 10am–1pm & 3.20–7.30pm; 875ptas return, joint ticket with Sant Joan funicular 1000ptas). The other rises to the hermitage of **Sant Joan** (every 15–20min 10am–7.30pm; 350ptas return, joint ticket with Santa Cova funicular 1000ptas), from where it's another hour or so's walk to the **Sant Jeroni** hermitage, near the summit of the mountain at 1300m.

Eating

There is a great variety of **food** available in Barcelona and even low-budget travellers can do well for themselves, either by using the excellent markets and filling up on sandwiches and snacks, or eating cheap meals in bars and cafés. Good **restaurants** are easily found all over the city, though you'll probably do most of your eating where you do most of your sightseeing, in the old town, particularly around the **Ramblas** and in the **Barri Gòtic**. Venture into the **Barrio Chino** too, and you'll find some excellent restaurants, some surprisingly expensive, others little more than hole-in-the-wall cafés. In the **Eixample** prices tend to be higher, though you'll find plenty of lunchtime bargains around; **Gràcia**, farther out, is a nice place to spend the evening, with plenty of good mid-range restaurants. For the food which Barcelona is really proud of – elaborate *sarsuelas* (fish stews), and all kinds of fish and seafood – you're best off in the **Barceloneta** district, down by the harbour, or in the **Port Olímpic**. Sitting down here for a huge plateful of prawns or mussels and a beer, you'll get away for around 1200ptas. A full seafood dinner will be considerably more expensive, even the paellas starting at around 1300–1500ptas a head.

If you can find a place serving a *menú del día* – usually three or four courses and wine – it's nearly always great value. There's one available at most restaurants and cafés, and at some bars, too, though it's generally a lunchtime affair; indeed, some of the smaller places open only at lunchtime. Otherwise you can put together a full meal by eating *tapas* in bars and restaurants, and these small dishes are available right through the day and night.

Breakfast, snacks and sandwiches

You can get coffee and bread or croissants almost anywhere, but a few **café-bars** and specialist places – *granjas* and *orxaterias* especially – are worth looking out for. Snacks and sandwiches abound, too, and you'll be tempted by *ensaimadas* (pastry spirals), pizza slices and cakes at any bakery or pastry shop.

Antiga Casa Figueres, Ramblas 83 (Metro Liceu). Wonderful *modernista*-designed pastry shop with a few tables outside. Open Mon–Sat 9am–3pm & 5–8.30pm.

The Bagel Shop, c/Canuda 25 (Metro Catalunya). Run by a friendly Canadian who is trying to introduce the bagel to Barcelona. Open Mon–Sat 9am–8.30pm.

Forn de Sant Jaume, Rambla de Catalunya 50 (Metro Passeig de Gràcia). A croissant and sweet specialist, either to take away or eat at the adjacent café. Open Mon–Sat 9am–9pm.

Granja La Pallaresa, c/Petritxol 11 (Metro Liceu). Bow-tied waiters glide around this specialist snack and breakfast stop, dispensing superb *xurros*, pastries, *crema catalana*, croissants, milk shakes and whipped-cream hot chocolates. Open Mon–Sat 9am–1.30pm & 4–9pm, Sun 5–9pm.

Granja M. Viader, c/Xuclà 4–6, off c/del Carmen (Metro Liceu). Homemade *flan*, cakes and hot chocolate with cream in a traditional *granja* bar. Open Mon 5–8.45pm and Tues–Sat 9am–1.45pm & 5–8.45pm.

Horchateria Sirvent, c/Parlament 56 (Metro Paral-lel). *Orxata* lovers regard this as the best in town. Standing room only or takeaway. Open May–Sept daily 9am–12.30pm.

Mesón del Café, c/Llibreteria 16 (Metro Jaume I). Tiny, off-beat bar where you'll probably have to stand to sample the pastries and the excellent coffee, including a "cappuccino" laden with fresh cream. Open Mon–Sat 7am–11pm.

Santa Clara, Plaça de Sant Jaume (corner of c/de la Llibreteria; Metro Jaume I). Marvellous coffee and cakes, right on the square; especially busy on Sunday mornings. Open daily 8am–9.30pm.

La Xicra, Plaça Sant Josep Oriol (Metro Liceu). A decorative *xocolateria* with a touch of "ye olde worlde" about it, but lovely cakes and coffee. Open Mon–Sat 9am–9pm, Sun 9am–2pm & 5–9.30pm; closed two weeks in Aug.

Tapas bars

For a more substantial snack, you can't beat Barcelona's **tapas bars**. The best (and most famous) concentration in the Barri Gòtic is down by the port, between the Columbus monument and the post office – along c/Ample, c/de la Mercè, c/del Regomir and their offshoots. Jumping from bar to bar, with a bite to eat in each, is as good a way as any to fill up on some of the best food that the city has to offer. Done this way, your evening needn't cost more than a meal in a medium-priced restaurant – say 2000–2500ptas a head for enormous amounts to eat and drink.

Ramblas and the Old Town

Bar Celta, c/de la Mercè 16. Galician *tapas* specialities, including octopus and excellent fried *calamares*, and heady Galician wine. Very popular. Open Mon–Sat 10am–1am, Sun 10am–midnight.

La Bodega, c/del Regomir 11. A great barn of a place with long wooden benches, delicious food and jugs of wine as rough as a rat-catcher's glove. Open Tues–Sun 1pm–2am; closed first two weeks of Aug.

Cal Pep, Plaça de les Olles 8 (☎93 310 79 61). Pricey but excellent *tapas* bar. Eat at the crowded bar or in the dining room at the back. Open Mon–Sat 1pm–4.30pm & 8pm–midnight.

Casa del Molinero, c/de la Mercè 13. Huge doors open into a wood-panelled bar with small tables and benches. The speciality is cooked and cured meats, including spicy *chorizo* which hangs from the ceiling. Open daily 1.30–3pm & 6pm–3am.

Euskal Etxea, Placeta Montcada 1–3 (☎93 310 21 85). A Basque restaurant specializing in *pintxos*, which are served around 12.30pm and 7.30pm. Fight for a place at the bar or join the crowds spilling onto the street. Open Tues–Sat 9am–midnight, Sun 12.30pm–4.30pm.

La Socarrena, c/de la Mercè 21. Asturian bar serving strong goat's cheese, cured meats and fine Asturian cider (*sidra*). Open daily 1.30–3pm & 6pm–3am.

El Xampanyet, c/de Montcada 22. Terrific, bustling, blue-tiled champagne bar with fine seafood *tapas*, *cava* by the glass or bottle, and local *sidra*. Open Tues–Sat noon–4pm & 6.30–11pm, Sun noon–4pm; closed Aug.

Eixample and Gràcia

Els Barrils, c/de Aribau 89 (Metro Hospital Clinic). Lavish, expensive *tapas* bar specializing in seafood and cured meat. Open daily except Tues 9am–2am; closed first two weeks of July.

Bodega Sepúlveda, c/Sepúlveda 173 (Metro Universitat). An anchovy specialist, which boasts more than a hundred different types of *tapas* and *torradas*. Open Mon–Sat 9.30am–1am.

La Bodegueta, Rambla Catalunya 98 (Metro Passeig de Gràcia). Long-established basement *bodega* with *cava* and a serious range of other wines by the glass or bottle, and cheese and cured meat to soak it all up. It gets very crowded – you may have to stand to snack. Open daily 7am–2am; closed mornings in Aug.

Cervecería Catalana, c/Mallorca 236 (☎93 216 03 68; Metro Passeig de Gràcia). Excellent *tapas* lined up along two bars, a good choice of beers and a small terraza. Open daily 7.30am–1am.

O'Nabo de Lugo, c/Pau Claris 169 (Metro Passeig de Gràcia). Pricey Galician restaurant with a separate, excellent *tapas* bar. Open Mon–Sat 1–4pm & 8.30pm–midnight.

Tapa Tapa, Passeig de Gràcia 44 (Metro Passeig de Gràcia). Modern bar with an impressive range of *tapas* and beers from around the world. Open daily 7.30am–1.30am.

Restaurants

The most common **restaurants** in Barcelona are those serving local **Catalan** food, though more mainstream Spanish dishes are generally available too. There are several speciality **regional Spanish and colonial Spanish** restaurants as well, which are nearly always worth investigating, while the fancier places tend towards a refined Catalan-French style of cooking that's as elegant as it's expensive. The range of **international cuisine** is not as wide as in other European capitals, but if you've been in Catalunya (or other parts of Spain) for any length of time, you may be grateful that there's a choice at all – pizzas, Chinese and Indian/Pakistani food provide the main choices, though the cuisines of Mexico, North Africa, the Middle East and Japan are represented, too.

Restaurants are generally **open** approximately 1 to 4pm and 8 to 11pm. A lot of restaurants **close on Sundays, on public holidays and throughout August** – check the listings for specific details but expect changes since many places imaginatively interpret their own posted opening days and times. At the more expensive restaurants, it's recommended that you **reserve a table** in advance; either ring the number provided, or call in earlier in the day.

Ramblas and the Barri Gòtic

All the restaurants in this section are easily walked to from Metro Liceu or Metro Jaume I, unless stated otherwise.

Amaya, Rambla Santa Mónica 20–24 (☎93 302 10 37). Famous Basque restaurant that gets packed out, especially on Sunday. Expect to pay around 3000ptas a head; more if you have the excellent fish, less if you have the *menú del día* (2000ptas) or *tapas* in the adjacent bar. Open daily 1pm–midnight. Moderate.

Los Caracoles, c/Escudellers 14 (☎93 302 31 85). Reasonably priced, cavernous Barcelona landmark whose name means "snails", so it would be churlish not to have them, or the fine spit-roast chicken on display in the street outside. Around 3500ptas a head if you include both as part of a big meal. Reserve ahead. Open daily 1pm–midnight. Moderate.

La Fonda, c/Escudellers 10. Modern, spacious, rattan-decorated restaurant on two floors that serves good-value Catalan dishes, including paella. Be prepared to queue, as this place is incredibly popular. Open Tues–Sun 1–3.30pm & 8.30–11.30pm. Inexpensive.

Gallo Kirico, c/d'Avinyó 19. Pakistani-run joint with bargain rice and couscous combinations (around 500ptas a plate) served at the long bar or at tables in a dining room hacked out of the old Roman wall. Open noon–1.30am. Inexpensive.

Juicy Jones, c/Cardenal Casañas 7. Bright restaurant/juice bar with a good value *menú del día* and other dishes served all day. Open Tues–Sun noon–midnight. Inexpensive.

Margarita Blue, c/Josep Anselm Clavé 6. Trendy bar-restaurant serving Mexican style food. A good place to come for supper or for a cocktail in the evenings; the *menú del día* is good value at 1000ptas too. Open 10.30am–2am, 3am at weekends. Moderate.

Mesón Jesús, c/dels Cecs de la Boqueria 4 (off c/de la Boqueria). Come here for the extremely good 1000ptas *menú del día;* otherwise you'll eat for around 2000ptas. Open Mon–Fri 1–4pm & 8–11pm, Sat 1–4pm; closed Aug. Inexpensive.

Peimong, c/Templarios 6–10. Friendly Peruvian restaurant with cheap filling platefuls at around 600ptas each. Open Tues–Sun 1–5pm & 8pm–midnight. Inexpensive.

Les Quinze Nits, Plaça Reial 6. Big restaurant owned by the people who run *La Fonda* (see above); budget-price meals in elegant surroundings and fine views of Plaça Reial. Get there early and join the queue. Open daily 1–4pm & 8pm–midnight. Moderate.

Restaurant Pitarra, c/d'Avinyó 58 (☎93 301 16 47). A renowned Catalan cookery in operation since 1890, lined with paintings and serving good, reasonably priced local food from around 2500ptas a head and a very good value *menú del día*. Open Mon–Sat 1.15–4pm & 8.30pm–11pm. Moderate.

La Rioja, c/Duran i Bas 5 (off Avda. Portal de l'Ángel). Bright, welcoming, white-tiled restaurant with a fine selection of Riojan dishes and wines. Open Mon–Fri 1–4pm & 8–11pm, Sat 1–4pm; closed Aug. Moderate.

Set Portes (*Las Siete Puertas*), Passeig d'Isabel II 14 (☎93 319 30 46 or 93 319 30 33; Metro Barceloneta). The wood-panelled decor in the "Seven Doors" has barely changed in 150 years, and while very elegant, it's not exclusive – though you will need to book ahead. The seafood is excellent, particularly the paella. Around 4500ptas a head and up. Open daily 1pm–1am. Expensive.

La Verònica, c/d'Avinyó 30. Crunchy pizzas and delicious cakes in a loud, buzzing, orange restaurant with a great terraza on the newly named Plaça George Orwell. Open Mon–Sat 1pm–2am. Inexpensive.

C/de Montcada and the Born

The nearest metro stations for the restaurants in this section are Jaume I or Barceloneta.

Bunga Raya, c/Assaonadors 7 (☎93 319 31 69). Good-value Malaysian and Indonesian restaurant. The menu is short, but the food is highly spiced and filling – the house set-meal at 1785ptas is a bumper spread. Open daily 8pm–midnight. Inexpensive.

Bar-Restaurant Can-Busto, c/de Rera Palau (off Plaça de les Olles). Basic dining room with a limited menu, quick service and budget-priced food. Open daily except Tues 12.30–4pm & 8–11.30pm. Inexpensive.

Al Passatore, Plaça del Palau 8 (☎93 319 78 51). Book ahead if you want a pavement seat at this very popular restaurant serving fresh pasta and pizzas cooked in a wood stove, with a good *menú del día* for 975ptas. Open daily 1–4.30pm & 8pm–12.30am. Moderate.

Restaurante Carpanta, c/Sombrerers 13 (☎93 319 99 99). Intimate restaurant housed in a candlelit Gothic house around the back of Santa María del Mar; a great place to sample *arroz negre* (1000ptas) or paella (1300ptas), though other meals will set you back 3500–4000ptas. Reserve a table in advance. Open Tues–Sat 1–5pm & 8.30pm–midnight, Sun 1–5pm. Expensive.

El Salón, c/L'Hostal d'en Sol 6–8. Renovated old building serving imaginative dishes and British-style desserts in a relaxed laid-back atmosphere. You can stay late and drink at the bar, too. Open Mon–Sat 1pm–midnight, Sun 7pm–midnight. Inexpensive.

Barrio Chino/El Raval

All the restaurants in this section are close to Metro Liceu, unless otherwise stated.

La Bella Napoli, c/Margarit 14 (☎93 442 50 56; Metro Poble Sec). Lively pizzeria run by Neopolitans so the pizzas are pretty authentic. Good desserts too. Open daily 8pm–midnight. Inexpensive.

Can Margarit, c/Concòrdia 21 (☎93 441 67 23; Metro Poble Sec). Extremely popular with people wanting to celebrate, this is a huge place where you help yourself to wine from the barrels at the entrance and eat from the simple Catalan menu. Booking essential. Open Mon–Sat evenings only, two sittings at 9pm and 11.30pm. Moderate.

Pollo Rico, c/de Sant Pau 31. Great spit-roast chicken, French fries and glass of *cava* for under 650ptas make this one of the area's most popular budget joints. A Barcelona institution, and always busy. Open daily except Wed 10am–1am. Inexpensive.

Restaurant España, c/de Sant Pau 9–11 (☎93 318 17 58). Eat in *modernista* splendour in a building designed by Domènech i Montaner, though the decor is more memorable than the food. However, the *menú del día* is good value at 1200ptas (1500ptas at night). Open daily 1–4pm & 8.30pm–midnight. Moderate.

Restaurant Garduña, c/Morera 17–19. Tucked away at the back of La Boqueria market, off the Ramblas, this recommended restaurant (busiest at lunch, when there's a 1000ptas *menú del día*) offers excellent paellas and good, fresh market produce. Around 2500ptas. Closed Sun. Moderate.

Restaurant Tallers, c/dels Tallers 6–8 (Metro Catalunya). A good-value *menú del día* (you pay a bit more if you opt for the fine baked chicken). Open Tues–Sun 1–3pm and 8–10pm; closed Aug. Inexpensive.

Silenus, c/dels Àngels 8. A pleasant airy place near the MACBA where the *menú del día* costs 1200 ptas. Open 1–4pm & 9–11.30pm, closed Sun and Mon evening. Moderate.

Els Tres Bots, c/de Sant Pau 42. An extensive list of Catalan favourites served quickly and efficiently at tables at the back of the bar. The *menú del día* is great value at 875ptas, otherwise put together a nourishing meal for well under 1500ptas. Open daily 7am–1am. Inexpensive.

The harbour, Port Vell, Barceloneta and Port Olímpic

The nearest Metro station for the restaurants in this section is Metro Barceloneta, unless otherwise stated.

Agua, Passeig Marítim 30 (☎93 225 12 72; Metro Vila Olímpica). Nice restaurant right on the sea front, with reasonably priced food including pasta, salads and hamburgers. Immensely popular, so book ahead in summer. Open 1.30–4pm & 8.30pm–midnight, 1am at weekends; closed Sun pm. Moderate.

Can Ganassa, Plaça de Barceloneta 4–6. An extensive range of *tapas*, snacks and *torradas* on Barceloneta's central square, a cheap and filling 925ptas *menú del día* at lunchtime, and more expensive seafood if you want it. Open daily except Wed 12.30–11pm; closed Nov. Moderate.

Can Ramonet, c/Maquinista, 17 (☎93 319 30 64). Reputedly the oldest restaurant in the port area, this restaurant now has the added attraction of a terraza on a newly opened square in the heart of Barceloneta. Good seafood and *jamón* and charming service. Open daily noon–midnight. Moderate.

Can Ros, c/Almirall Aixada 7, off Pg. de Bourbó (☎93 221 45 79). Intimate, wood-panelled seafood restaurant with superb appetizers and a rich paella or *arroz negre*, both of which cost just 1200ptas. Open daily except Wed 1–5pm & 8pm–midnight. Moderate.

El Rey de la Gamba, Passeig de Bourbó 46–48, 49 & 53 (☎93 221 75 98). Much promoted restaurant, whose various extensions now occupy half the street and whose outdoor tables are always busy. It's popular for its prawns and dried meats, but the food is overpriced. Open daily noon–midnight. Expensive.

Eixample

Aire, c/Enric Granados 48 (☎93 451 84 62; Metro Passeig de Gràcia). Gay-run restaurant serving imaginative French-Catalan dishes in roomy civilized surroundings. Open daily 1–4pm and 9.30pm–midnight. Moderate.

Comme-Bio II, Gran Vía de les Corts Catalanes 603 (corner Rambla de Catalunya; Metro Catalunya). Vegetarian restaurant that doubles as a health food store. There's another branch in Via Layetana. Open Mon–Sat 9am–midnight, Sun noon–midnight. Moderate.

La Diva, c/de la Diputació 172 (☎93 454 63 98; Metro Urgell). New gay-managed restaurant serving classy food in mock Baroque surroundings for around 5000ptas a head. Booking recommended. Open daily 8pm–12.30am. Expensive.

La Flauta, c/Aribau 23 (Metro Universitat). Standard Catalan food though with a decent *menú del día* for around 1000ptas. More interesting for the great selection of sandwiches which you eat at the bar. Open daily 7am–1.30am; restaurant open daily 1–4pm & 8pm–1am. Moderate.

L'Hostal de Rita, c/Aragó 279 (Metro Passeig de Gràcia). Good Catalan cooking at reasonable prices. Always packed and you can't book in advance so be prepared to wait in line. Open daily 1–3.30pm & 8.30–11.30pm. Inexpensive.

Mordisco, c/Rosselló 265 (Metro Diagonal). Trendy café-restaurant specializing in tasty salads and out-of-the-ordinary sandwiches. Open daily 8am–1.30am. Moderate.

Xix Kebab, c/Còrsega 193 (☎93 321 82 10; Metro Hospital Clinic). Highly recommended Syrian restaurant serving couscous and less typical dishes in a pleasant but not overdone Middle Eastern setting. Open daily except Tues 1.30–4pm & 9pm–midnight. Moderate.

Gràcia

Bar-Restaurante Candanchu, Plaça Rius i Taulet 9 (Metro Fontana). Sit beneath the clock tower in summer and enjoy a sandwich, or choose from the wide selection of local dishes. The *menú del día* is around 1000ptas and usually splendid. Open daily 1–5pm & 8pm–1am, Fri & Sat until 3am; closed two weeks in Nov. Inexpensive.

Ca l'Augusti, c/Verdi 28 (Metro Fontana). Popular local choice, with reasonably priced *torradas*, grilled meats, omelettes and paella on Sunday. There's a very reasonably priced lunchtime *menú del día*, while other meals run to 2000ptas and upwards. Open daily except Wed noon–4pm & 8.30pm–midnight. Inexpensive.

Equinox, c/Torrent de l'Olla 143 (Metro Fontana) and **Equinox Sol**, Plaça del Sol 14 and c/Verdi 21–23. By far the best falafels and shawarma in town, plus other delicious Lebanese dishes, and wicked baklava. Eat your fill for under 1000ptas. Open Mon–Thurs 6pm–2.30am, Fri–Sun 6pm–3.30am. Inexpensive.

Flash, Flash, c/de la Granada del Penedés 25 (Metro Diagonal). Very 1970s, with white leatherette booths in which to eat one of around fifty different types of *tortilla*, priced from 500–900ptas. Open daily 1.30pm–1.30am. Moderate.

El Galliner, c/Martínez de la Rosa 71 (Metro Diagonal). Intimate restaurant in an old house offering cod cooked in over forty different ways. Between 2000ptas and 3000ptas a head. Open 1.30–4pm & 8pm–midnight; closed Tues lunch. Moderate.

El Glop, c/Sant Lluís 24 (Metro Joanic). Authentic Catalan taverna, with enough *torradas* and salads to satisfy vegetarians, as well as grilled meats. Lively and popular; around 2000ptas a head, less if you're careful. There are also branches at Rambla de Catalunya 65 and c/Casp 21. Open Tues–Sun 1–4pm & 7pm–1am. Moderate.

Illa de Gràcia, c/Sant Domenec 19 (Metro Fontana). Bright vegetarian restaurant serving decent salads, pasta, rice dishes, omelettes and crêpes – all around 600ptas. Open Tues–Fri 1–4pm & 9pm–midnight, Sat & Sun 2pm–midnight; closed mid-Aug to mid-Sept. Inexpensive.

El Tastavins, c/Ramón y Cajal 12 (Metro Fontana). Good local cooking in attractive, down-to-earth surroundings (try the chicken stuffed with prunes or the steak in anchovy sauce), and with a 850ptas lunch *menú*; otherwise around 1500–2500ptas a head. Highly recommended. Open Mon 10am–1.30am, Tues–Sat 9am–5pm & 8.30pm–1.30am. Moderate.

Buying your own food: markets, supermarkets, delis

If you want to buy fresh food, or make up your own snacks and meals, use the city's **markets**. There's less choice in the **supermarkets**, though they're worth trying for tinned products, as are the **delicatessens** and small central shops which specialize in tinned fish and meat, cheeses and cooked meats. The best-value food and provisions shops are those in the Barrio Chino, particularly down c/de Sant Pau.

Centre Comercial Simago, Rambla 113. Department store with food department in the basement. Open Mon–Thurs 9am–8pm, Fri & Sat 9am–9pm.

Día, c/del Carme; and at c/Comtessa de Sobradiel. Fairly basic supermarket, with the first branch just around the corner from the much pricier Simago (see above).

La Fuente, c/de Ferran 20 (Metro Liceu). A *xarcuteria*, but better visited for its wide selection of tinned and preserved food, wines and cheeses. Open Mon–Fri 9am–1pm & 4–8pm, Sat 9am–1pm; closed Aug.

Mauri, Rambla de Catalunya 100 (Metro Passeig de Gràcia). Superb deli specializing in cakes and pastries, with an attached café. Open Mon–Sat 9am–9pm, Sun 9am–3pm.

Mercat Sant Antoni, Ronda de Sant Pau (junction with c/del Comte). Food stalls in the middle of this large market – though most are shut in Aug. Open Mon–Sat 8am–3pm & 5–8pm.

Mercat Sant Josep/La Boqueria, Rambla Sant Josep 89 (Metro Liceu). The best place in the city for fresh fruit, vegetables, meat, fish and dried foods. Open Mon–Sat 8am–8pm.

Drinking and nightlife

There are lively **bars and cafés** throughout the centre – in the Barri Gòtic as well as the Eixample and Gràcia – catering for all types and styles. One of the city's great pleasures is to pull up a pavement seat outside a bar, sip a coffee or a beer, and watch the world go by. There's little difference between a bar and café (indeed, many places incorporate both words in their name), but some of the other names you'll see do actually mean something – a *bodega* specializes in wine; a *cervesería* in beer; and a *xampanyería* in champagne and *cava*. Alongside the regular bars and cafés, Barcelona also has a range of **designer bars** geared towards late-night drinking, and there's a disco and club **nightlife** that, at present, is one of Europe's most enjoyable.

For **listings** of bars and clubs, get the weekly *Guía del Ocio* from newsstands, or SexTienda's map of **gay** Barcelona with a list of bars, clubs, and contacts (see p.623 for SexTienda's address). It's worth noting, that – unlike restaurants – most bars and cafés stay open throughout August.

Bars and cafés

Generally, the bars in the **old town** are a mixture of traditional tourist haunts, local drinking places or trendy downbeat bars. The area around the Museu Picasso is currently one of the places to be at night – **Passeig del Born**, the square at the end of c/de Montcada behind Santa María del Mar, is the main focus, while the streets around c/d'Avinyó and c/Escudellers also have their share of the action. The **Port Olímpic** and the Maremàgnum complex have become more mainstream summer night-time playgrounds for locals and tourists alike. Barcelona is also known for its *bars modernos* or *bars musicals*: hi-tech, music-filled places concentrated mainly (though not exclusively) in the **Eixample** and the streets in the western part of **Gràcia** around c/Santaló and c/Marià Cubí. The "in" places change rapidly, with new ones opening up all the time; the decor is often astounding, the drinks always expensive. For more low-key, lateish drinking (though still pricey), the centre of Gràcia itself is the place, full of little squares bordered by busy café-terraces.

Ramblas and the Barri Gòtic

L'Antiquari, c/Veguer 13. A former antique shop, this late-opening bar attracts a decent mix of locals. There's terrace seating in Plaça del Rei and live music at weekends, but you can end up waiting ages for your drinks. Open daily 10am–2am.

Café del Born Nou, Plaça Comercial 10. Relaxed gay-friendly bar with pavement tables in summer; a popular meeting place. Come for breakfast and relax with the papers, or later when it livens up a bit. Open daily 8.30am–3.30am.

Café de l'Opera, Rambla Caputxins 74. Morning coffee, afternoon tea or late-night brandies in this fashionable, turn-of-the-century bar. Always busy. Open daily 9am–3am.

Dot, c/Nou de Sant Francesc 7. Down a dark side street off the hectic c/Escudellers, this is an extremely trendy bar with different music every night, guest DJs and a very cool crowd. Open daily 9pm–3am.

La Gloria, c/d'Avinyó 42. Smart new bar with fairly minimalist decor but friendly all the same. Look out for the unusual lampshades. Bar snacks available. Open daily 5pm–2am, 3am at weekends.

Mudanzas, c/Vidrieria 15. Very popular relaxed café-bar in black, cream and wood surroundings. Open daily 6pm–2.30am.

La Palma, c/Palma de Sant Just 7. Comfortable, traditional *bodega*, with large wooden tables and antiques on display. Open Mon–Sat 8am–4pm & 7–10pm.

Els Quatre Gats, c/Montsío 3. *Modernista*-designed haunt of Picasso and his contemporaries (see p.588), and still an interesting, arty place for a drink or meal. Open 10am–midnight; closed Sun lunch.

Salero, c/del Rec 60. The name in English means salt cellar, which may explain the all-white decor of this stylish new bar which attracts a chic clientele. Food available too. Open 2pm–2.30am; closed Sun night and Mon morning.

Schilling, c/Ferran 23. Fashionable café-bar packed all day with a mixture of locals and tourists; shout for your drink over the music and be prepared to wait for it. Open daily 10am–2.30pm.

Barrio Chino/El Raval

Bar Pastis, c/Santa Monica 4 (just behind Centre d'Art Santa Monica). Tiny, dark French bar, right in the red-light district, awash with artistic and theatrical memorabilia, and soothed by wheezy French music. Open 7.30pm–2.30am, Fri & Sat until 3.30am; closed Tues.

La Bata de Boatiné, c/Robador 23. Friendly gay bar in the middle of the Barrio Chino. Open Tues–Sun 11pm–3am.

Bar Fortuny, c/Pintor Fortuny 31. A good place for a quiet drink, attracting a mixture of people from the *barrio*, and popular with local lesbians. Food available at lunchtime. Open Tues–Sun 10am–12.30pm.

Bar Kasparo, Plaça Vicenç Matorell 4. Tucked away in the corner of a quiet square off c/Bon Succés, this tiny bar has a nice *terraza* popular with locals. Sandwiches, *tapas* and some hot dishes available too. Open daily 9am–10pm (until midnight in summer).

Bar London, c/Nou de la Rambla 34. Opened in 1910, this well-known *modernista* bar today attracts a mostly tourist clientele, puts on live jazz and hosts fortune-telling sessions. Open Wed–Sun 5pm–3.30am.

El Café Que Pone "Muebles Navarro", c/Riera Alta 4–6. Big, airy café-bar in a converted furniture store (hence the name) which is a friendly comfortable place to have a drink or a snack. Open Mon–Sat 11am–midnight, Sun 5pm–midnight.

Marsella, c/de Sant Pau 65. Turn-of-the-century bar now frequented by a spirited mix of local characters and young trendies. Occasional live music and performances. Open Mon–Thur & Sun 9am–2.30am, Fri & Sat 6pm–3.30am.

The harbour, Port Vell and Port Olímpic

Café Café, Moll de Mestral 30, Port Olímpic. One of the neighbourhood's more relaxed and better decorated bars, serving lots more besides coffee. Open daily noon–3am, 5am at weekends.

Distrito Marítimo, Moll de la Fusta 1. Large *terraza* overlooking the harbour, playing techno and house to a trendy pre-club gay crowd. Open Fri & Sat 11pm–3am.

Insólit, Local 111, Maremagnum/Port Vell. A multi-space venue which doubles as restaurant and Internet café during the week, only to turn into a big dance floor after 1am at weekends, where a mixed crowd dance to 60s' and 70s' sounds or enter cyberspace on the computers upstairs. Open daily 1pm–midnight (until 5am at weekends).

Jugolandia, Moll de Mestral 6, Port Olímpic. Huge range of tropical fruit juices, some laced with alcohol, served on a terrace overlooking the marina. Open daily 3pm–3am.

Octopussy, Moll de la Fusta 4. Hip, happening club with a big *terraza* overlooking the port with guest DJs playing soul, dub, drum and bass, with live music as well. Packed at weekends in the summer. Open Thurs, Fri and Sat midnight–3am.

Eixample

L'Arquer, Gran Vía de les Corts Catalanes 454. Bar with good *tapas* and – believe it or not – an archery range where you can have a go under the careful supervision of someone more sober than you. Open daily 6pm–3am.

Café Internet, Gran Vía de les Corts Catalanes 656. Barcelona's first cybercafé; half an hour's connection costs 600ptas. Open Mon–Thurs 7am–midnight, Fri & Sat 7am–2am, Sun 4–10pm.

Dietrich Gay Teatro Bar, c/Consell de Cent 255 (between c/Muntaner and c/Aribau). This extremely popular gay hangout serves food until midnight and becomes a disco after that. Open daily 6pm–3am.

La Fira, c/de Provença 171 (between c/Muntaner and o/Aribau; Metro Provença). One of the city's most bizarre – and fun – bars, complete with turn-of-the-century fairground rides, and decorated with circus paraphernalia. Open Tues–Thurs 10pm–3am, Fri & Sat 7pm–4.30am, Sun 6pm–1am.

Jazz Matazz, Ptge Domingo 3 (Metro Passeig de Gràcia). Situated on a little side street between Rambla de Catalunya and Passeig de Gràcia, this is a new venue run by owners from Senegal, Ireland and Catalunya whose intention is to provide an eclectic mix of live music every night. Open Wed–Sat 10pm–4pm.

Nick Havanna, c/del Rosselló 208 (Metro Diagonal). One of the most futuristic bars in town, the 1986 brainchild of Eduardo Samso. The cool crowd have deserted it of late, but it's still worth taking a look at what's been dubbed the "ultimate bar". Open daily 11pm–4am, Fri & Sat until 5am.

Punto BCN, c/Muntaner 63–65 (Metro Diagonal). Stylish gay bar, with good music – a popular meeting place. Open daily 6pm–3am.

El Velòdrom, c/Muntaner 213 (Metro Diagonal). Old-style bar and pool hall, resembling an airy student beer cellar – and none the worse for that. Open Mon–Sat 6pm–1.30am; closed Aug.

Velvet, c/Balmes 161 (Metro Diagonal). The creation of designer Alfredo Arribas, this was inspired by the velveteen excesses of film-maker David Lynch. Slightly cosier and smoother than others, with an older clientele which appreciates the mainly 60s' and 70s' sounds. Open daily until 5am.

Zsa Zsa, c/del Rosselló 156 (between c/Muntaner and c/Aribau). A designer bar showing off its fashionable wall hangings, and serving up loud music and pricey cocktails to the trendy set. Open daily 7pm–3am, Fri & Sat until 4am.

Gràcia

Bahia, c/Séneca 12. Relaxed and attractive bar with gay, lesbian and straight punters. Open daily 7pm–2.30am.

La Bolsa, c/Tuset 17 (Metro Diagonal). Music-bar where the drinks prices go up and down according to the demand – *bolsa* being the Spanish for "stock exchange". Open 8.30pm–2.30am.

Café del Sol, Plaça del Sol 9. Popular, split-level neighbourhood bar attracting the local cool types. Seats outside in the square make this pleasant at any time of the day or night. Open daily except Mon 1pm–3am.

Gimlet, c/Santaló 46 (FF.CC Plaça Molina). Cocktails, snacks and outdoor tables packed with the local beautiful people. Open daily 7.30pm–2.30am.

Roma, c/Alfons XII 4 (FF.CC Plaça Molina). Spacious relaxed gay bar with friendly staff, which gets full around midnight with a pre-club crowd. Open daily 8pm–3am.

Triptic, c/Mozart 4 (Metro Diagonal). Lively, hippyish locals' bar, with marble-topped tables, mirrors and loud music. Open daily 8pm–3am.

Universal, c/Marià Cubi 184 (FF.CC Plaça Molina). A classic designer bar that's been at the cutting edge of Barcelona style since 1985 and there are still queues to get in. Be warned, they operate a strict door policy here and if your face doesn't fit you won't get in. Open 11pm–3am.

Virreina, Plaça de la Virreina 1. Popular bar with seats outside in one of Gràcia's loveliest squares. Open daily except Wed noon–2am.

Zig Zag, c/de Plató 13 (FF.CC Muntaner). This long-established place (open since 1980) was designed by Alicia Nuñez and Guillem Bonet (creators of *Otto Zutz*; see "Discos and Clubs" below). It has all the minimalist designer accoutrements – chrome and video – but better, quieter music than usual, and a young, rich clientele. Open daily 10pm–3am.

Elsewhere

Carpe Diem, Avda. Dr Gregorio Marañón 17 (Metro Palau Reial). Near the university campus and Camp Nou stadium, *Carpe Diem* is a huge tent containing various bars, restaurants and dance floors. Open all year, but best and most packed in summer. Open daily 6pm–5am.

Firestiu, Plaça Univers y Palau 4 de la Fira (Metro Espanya). Multi-space entertainment in a series of tents and awnings in the exhibition centre zone. Inside are dozens of bars set up by well-known city venues, as well as dance floors, fairground rides, mini-golf and even bungee-jumping. Open June–Aug Thurs–Sat 10pm–5am.

Mirablau, Plaça del Dr Andrea, Avda. Tibidabo (at the top of the Tibidabo tram line, opposite the funicular station). Unbelievable city views from a chic, expensive bar, that fills to bursting at times. Open daily 11pm–5am.

Torres de Ávila, Avda. Marqués de Comillas, Poble Espanyol, Montjuïc. The creation of Mariscal and Arribas, located inside the mock twelfth-century gateway in the "Spanish Village" built for the 1929 fair. It's a stunning fantasy, with a fabulous panoramic terrace. Beware that the dress code is strict (no sports shoes) and drinks are very expensive. Open Thurs–Sat 10pm–4am.

Discos and clubs

Quite why Barcelona is one of Europe's hippest nightspots is something of a mystery to everyone except the Catalans, who knew all along. There aren't, in fact, too many places which are *that* good – but gripped by Friday and Saturday night fever it's eminently possible to suspend disbelief.

Be warned that clubbing in Barcelona is extremely expensive and that in the most exclusive places a beer is going to cost you roughly ten times what it costs in the bar next door. If there is free entry, don't be surprised to find that there's a minimum drinks charge of anything between 500–1000ptas – if you're given a card as you go in and it's punched at the bar, be prepared to pay a minimum charge. Also note that the distinction between a music-bar and a disco is between a closing time of 2 or 3am and 5am – with a corresponding price rise. Barcelona stays open **very late** at the weekends, if you can take it; some of the places listed below feature a second session of action some time between 5am and 9am.

Antilla Cosmopolita, c/Muntaner 244, on the north side of Avda. Diagonal. Popular disco dedicated to salsa, offering live bands and free classes to get you into practice for the serious dancing. There's a cover charge to get in. Open daily 10.30pm–5am.

Arena, c/Balmes 32. Popular club catering to a mainly gay male crowd with a back room. Entry 500ptas. Open daily midnight–5am.

Bikini, c/Deu i Mata 105, off Avda. Diagonal, behind the shopping centre L'Illa (Metro Maria Cristina). This traditional landmark of Barcelona nightlife offers regular live music and a popular disco, specializing in salsa and tangos on Sundays. Open Tues–Sun 11pm–5am.

Jamboree, Plaça Reial 17 (Metro Liceu). Live music every night followed by a disco with great jazz, funk and dance, attracting a very mixed crowd. Open daily 9pm–5am.

The Mad Monkie, Marià Cubí 183. Roomy disco with two floors, pool tables and chill-out spaces catering to a good mix of lesbian, gay and gay-friendly punters. Funk and soul and surprisingly little techno. Open weekends 11pm–4am.

Moog, Arc del Teatre 3. Lively disco playing techno and house to a young trendy crowd. Open daily 11pm–5am.

Nitsa Club, at Sala Apolo, c/Nou de la Rambla 113. Late disco playing house and techno with guest DJs. Open weekends 12.30am–very late.

Otto Zutz, c/de Lincoln 15. Still one of the most fashionable places in the city, a three-storey warehouse converted by architects Núñez and Bonet into a nocturnal shop window for everything that's for sale or hire in Barcelona. With the right clothes and face you're in (you may or may not have to pay – around 2000ptas – depending on how impressive you are, the day of the week, etc); the serious dancing is 2–5.30am. Open Tues–Sat midnight–5.30am.

Paradís, c/Paradís 4. Underground club playing reggae, African and Latin sounds in the heart of the Barri Gòtic. Open daily till late.

Satanassa, c/Aribau 27, Eixample. A mural-covered interior and a friendly, funky gay and straight crowd. There's no admission charge, but it gets very busy at the weekends. Open daily 11pm–5am.

La Terrazza, Avda. Marquès de Comillas s/n (behind Poble Espanyol). Non-stop techno, and the place to be in summer, though don't get there until at least 4am. Open midnight–7am weekends.

Music, the arts and festivals

Quite apart from the city's countless bars, restaurants and clubs, there's a full **cultural life** worth sampling. Barcelona hosts a wide range of **live music** events throughout the year and **film** and **theatre** are also well represented, as you'd expect in a city this size. Even if you don't speak Catalan or Spanish there's no need to miss out, since several cinemas show films in their original language, while Barcelona also boasts a series of old-time music hall/**cabaret** venues putting on largely visual shows, appealing in any language. Catalan performers have always steered away from the classics and gone for the innovative, and so the city also boasts a long tradition of **street and performance art.** Finally, if you're lucky (or you've planned ahead), you'll coincide with one of the city's excellent **festivals** and open-air events, in which case you'll be able to immerse yourself in what Barcelona does best: enjoying itself.

The most important ticket office is the **Centre d'Informació** in the Palau de la Virreina, Rambla Sant Josep 99 (Metro Liceu; Mon–Sat 10am–7pm; ☎93 318 85 99), which dispenses programmes, advance information and tickets for all the *Ajuntament*-sponsored productions, performances and exhibitions, including the *Grec* season events. The booth on the corner of c/Aribau and the Gran Vía, close to Plaça Universitat (Mon–Sat 10.30am–1.30pm & 4–7.30pm) sells **tickets** for major rock and pop concerts and for most theatre productions; record shops also carry concert tickets; or go straight to the relevant box office at the venue. With a credit card you can use the ServiCaixa automatic dispensing machines in many branches of La Caixa to obtain tickets for many events. Theatre and some concert tickets can be bought over the phone through Tel-Entrades on ☎902 10 12 12.

For **listings** of almost anything you could want in the way of culture and entertainment, buy a copy of the weekly *Guía del Ocio* from any newspaper stand. This has full details of film, theatre and musical events (free and otherwise), as well as extensive sections on bars, restaurants and nightlife. It's in Spanish but easy enough to decipher. There are similar listings in *El País*, and there's also a free monthly guide published by the *Ajuntament*, available from tourist offices. For listings in English look for *Barcelona Metropolitan*, available free in hotels and bars.

Live music

Many major bands now include Barcelona on their tours at a variety of big venues (including the Camp Nou stadium, Olympic stadium, and Palau d'Esports), and tickets for these are every bit as pricey as they are elsewhere in the world. However, lots of the city's clubs and discos regularly feature bands, too – the more reliable places are listed below, and entrance to these is a lot less expensive than to a stadium gig. June sees the **Festival de Jazz Ciutat Vella**, and a **European jazz festival**; and there's also the annual **jazz festival** in October/November, which highlights visiting bands in the clubs and hosts street concerts and events. Most of Barcelona's **classical music** concerts take place in Domènech i Montaner's Palau de la Música Catalana, a splendid turn-of-the-century *modernista* creation (for more on which see p.586). **Opera** (and to a lesser extent, **ballet**) used to be confined to the Gran Teatre del Liceu on the Ramblas, though since this burned down at the beginning of 1994 (see p.579 for more details) performances have been held at the Teatre Victòria, Avda. del Paral-lel 67 (☎93 443 29 29) or at the Palau de la Música Catalana.

Rock, pop, folk and jazz

Antilla Cosmopolita, c/Muntaner 244, Eixample (☎93 200 77 14; Metro Diagonal). Salsa and other Latin American sounds as well as dance classes. Bands come on after midnight at weekends and the place stays open very late.

Barcelona Pipa Club, Plaça Reial 3 (☎93 302 47 32; Metro Liceu). Small club with jazz most nights; admission around 500–600ptas.

Centre Artesà Tradicionàrius, Trav. de Sant Antoni 6–8, Gràcia (☎93 218 44 85; Metro Fontana). Folk recitals by local performers on Thurs and Fri around 10pm. Watch out for the festival organized here in the spring.

La Cova del Drac, c/Vallmajor 33, Gràcia (☎93 200 70 32; FF.CC Muntaner). One of Barcelona's best jazz clubs serves up live music Tues–Sat 11pm–5am. Cover charge 1500–3000ptas depending on the act. Closed Aug.

Garatge Club, c/Pallars 195, Poble Nou (☎93 309 14 38; Metro Poble Nou). Local rock and pop bands, never on much before midnight. Thurs–Sun only.

Harlem Jazz Club, c/Comtessa de Sobradiel 8 (☎93 310 07 55; Metro Jaume I). Small, central venue for mixed jazz styles; live music most nights from around 9–10pm. Usually no cover charge, and reasonably priced drinks. Closed Aug.

Luz de Gas, c/Muntaner 246, Eixample (☎93 209 77 11; Metro Diagonal). Smart venue popular with a slightly older suit and tie crowd; live music every night around midnight.

La Tierra, c/Aribau 230, Eixample (☎93 302 47 32; Metro Diagonal). Popular club with live bands most nights. Admission around 1000ptas. After the gigs the venue turns into *Costa Breve*, a popular funk and soul disco.

Zeleste, c/Almogavers 122 (☎93 309 12 04; Metro Llacuna). Foreign rock and pop bands play regularly at the warehouse-style club.

Classical music and opera

Auditori Winterthur, L'Illa, Avda. Diagonal 547 (☎93 218 48 00). New privately owned concert hall in the Illa shopping centre.

Centre Cultural de la Fundació La Caixa, Passeig Sant Joan 108 (☎93 458 89 05; Metro Verdaguer). Regular concerts and recitals.

L'Espai, Trav. de Gràcia 63, Gracia (☎93 414 31 33; Metro Diagonal). Performances by a variety of soloists and groups especially good for dance.

Fundació Joan Miró, Parc de Montjuïc s/n (☎93 329 1908; see also p.595). Regular contemporary music concerts especially during the summer when the venue puts on its *Nits de Música* sessions, usually on Thursdays.

Palau de la Música Catalana, c/Sant Francesc de Paula 2, off c/Sant Pere Més Alt (☎93 268 10 00; Metro Urquinaona). Home of the Orfeó Català choral group, and venue for concerts by the Orquestra Ciutat de Barcelona among others. Concert season runs Oct–June. Box office open Mon–Fri 10am–9pm, Sat 3–9pm.

Sala Cultural Caja de Madrid, Plaça de Catalunya 9 (☎93 301 44 94). Regular, free concerts and recitals.

Saló del Tinell, Plaça del Rei (☎93 315 11 11; Metro Jaume I). Choral music in the Gothic hall of the Palau Reial; usually free entry.

Teatre Grec, Passeig de la Exposició s/n, Montjuïc (☎93 301 77 75; Metro Espanya). Impressive open-air summer venue for concerts and recitals. The amphitheatre is used extensively during the summer *Grec* season.

Theatre and cabaret

Barcelona has nothing like the **theatrical life** of Madrid, but it does have some worthy venues and happenings. Ninety-nine percent of the regular theatre productions, however, are in Catalan and you'll rarely see a Spanish classic. The centre for commercial theatre is on Avinguda. Paral-lel and the streets immediately around. Some theatres draw on the city's strong **cabaret** tradition – more music-hall entertainment than stand-up comedy, and thus a little more accessible to non-Catalan/Spanish speakers.

CATALAN THEATRE COMPANIES

In Barcelona, check for forthcoming appearances of the following theatre companies:

Els Comediants use Catalan popular theatre tradition in a modern context; they've just set up their own theatre at Canet de Mar, north of Barcelona on the coast.

La Cubana is a highly original and popular company that started life as a street theatre group. It still hits the streets occasionally, taking on the role of market traders in the Boqueria or cleaning cars in the street in full evening dress.

Els Fura del Baus (Vermin of the Sewer) are performance artists who aim to shock and lend a new meaning to audience participation.

Els Joglars is a political theatre company, particularly critical of the church.

El Tricicle is a three-man mime group.

Tickets for most theatres are available from the kiosk on the corner of c/Aribau and the Gran Vía, and from the Centro de Localidades at Rambla Catalunya 2. For advance tickets for the Mercat de les Flors productions, you have to go to the Palau de la Virreina (Ramblas 99). Theatre tickets can also be bought over the phone through Tel-Entrades on ☎902 10 12 12.

Bodega Bohemia, c/Lancaster 2 (☎93 302 50 61; Metro Drassanes). Old performers doing old turns in a decrepit cabaret venue. Somehow the faded decor and jaded routines gel into an entertaining night out. Nightly performances from 11pm until late. Sunday afternoons too; closed Wed.

Café Concert Llantiol, c/Riereta 7 (☎93 329 90 09; Metro Paral·lel). Daily cabaret featuring curious bits of mime, song, clowns and magic. Shows begin at 9pm.

Mercat de les Flors, c/de Lleida 59 (☎93 426 21 02 or ☎93 425 18 75; Metro Poble Sec). A nineteenth-century building worth visiting for the architecture alone. Hosts visiting fringe theatre and dance companies.

Teatre Lliure, c/Montseny 47, Gràcia (☎93 218 92 51; Metro Fontana). The "Free Theatre" is the home of a progressive Catalan company, due to move to a new home in the Ciutat del Teatre on Montjuïc in 1999. Also hosts visiting dance companies, concerts and recitals.

Teatre Malic, c/Fussina 3 (☎93 310 70 35; Metro Jaume I). Tiny theatre with off-beat productions and the occasional concert or performance artist.

Teatre Nacional de Catalunya, Plaça de les Arts 1 (☎93 306 57 00, tickets by credit card ☎900 12 11 33). Designed by Ricardo Bofill, and intended to foster Catalan works, this brand new theatre has so far disappointed.

Teatre Romea, c/Hospital 51 (☎93 301 55 04). Built in 1863, the theatre was forced to use Castilian under Franco, but has now come back as the Centre Dramàtic de la Generalitat de Catalunya with exclusively Catalan productions.

Film

All the latest international films reach Barcelona fairly quickly (though they're usually shown dubbed into Spanish) – central **main screens** include those at Rambla de Canaletes 138, Rambla Catalunya 90, Plaça de Catalunya 3, Passeig de Gràcia 13 and Maremagnum at Port Vell. More accessibly, the **cinemas** listed below show mostly original-language ("V.O.") foreign films. **Tickets** cost 650–750ptas, and most cinemas have one night (usually Mon or Wed) – a *día del espectador* – when entry is discounted, usually to around 500ptas.

Casablanca, Passeig de Gràcia 115, Eixample (☎93 218 43 45; Metro Diagonal). Late-night film on Fri and Sat; discount night Mon.

Cines Icaria-Yelmo, c/de Salvador Espriu 61, Vila Olímpica (☎93 221 75 85; Metro Ciutadella). No fewer than fifteen screens showing "V.O." movies; late-night screenings on Fri and Sat; discount night Mon.

Filmoteca, Avda. de Sarrià 33, Eixample (☎93 410 75 90; Metro Hospital Clinic). Run by the Generalitat, the Filmoteca has an excellent programme, showing three or four different films (often foreign, dubbed or subtitled) every night; 400ptas per film, or buy a pass for 2500ptas allowing entry to ten films.

Renoir-Les Corts, c/Eugeni d'Ors 12 (☎93 490 55 10; Metro Les Corts). Six screens showing good "V.O." films. Late-night sessions on Fri & Sat; discount night Mon.

Verdi, c/Verdi 32, Gràcia (☎93 237 05 16; Metro Fontana). Five screens showing quality "V.O." movies. Late-night films on Fri & Sat; discount night Mon.

Arts festivals, open-air events, and the sardana

Best of the annual arts events is the Generalitat's summer *Grec* season, when theatre, music and dance can be seen at various venues around the city, including the Teatre Grec at Montjuïc. But there are plenty of other times when Barcelona lets its hair down: the main arts-orientated events are listed below. Catalunya's national **folk dance**, the *sardana*, can be seen for free at several places in the city: in front of the cathedral (Sat 6.30pm and Sun noon) and Plaça Sant Jaume (Sun 6pm). Mocked in the rest of Spain, the Catalans claim theirs is a very democratic dance. Participants (there's no limit on numbers) all hold hands in a circle, each puts something in the middle as a sign of community and sharing, and since it is not overly energetic (hence the jibes) old and young can join in equally.

April/May *Tamborinada* is a day of children's entertainment in Ciutadella – theatre, dancing giants and music.

May The *Marató de l'Espectacle* (Entertainment Marathon) takes place at the Mercat de les Flors theatre, a non-stop, two days' worth of local theatre, dance, cabaret, music and children's shows.

June The *Grec* season starts in the last week (and runs throughout July and into August), a summer festival incorporating a wide variety of events, some of which are free. Information and booking is at the Palau de la Virreina. Also, the *Día de Sant Joan* celebrations on the 23rd involve fireworks, dancing and music throughout the city. The *Caixa Flamenco Festival* takes place in the same month; while the *Barcelona Film Festival* starts at the end of the month and continues throughout July.

August The *Festa Major* in mid-August is in Gràcia; bands and events in the streets and squares.

September *Festa de la Mercè* at the end of the month: parades, free concerts, fireworks and general mayhem.

Shopping and markets

While not on a par with Paris or the world's other style capitals, Barcelona is head and shoulders above the rest of Spain when it comes to **shopping**. It's the country's fashion and publishing capital, and there's a long tradition of innovative design which is perhaps expressed best in the city's fabulous architecture but which is also revealed in a series of shops and malls selling the very latest in designer clothes and household accoutrements.

Shops

Shop **opening hours** are typically Monday–Friday 10am–1.30/2pm and 4.30–7.30/8pm, Saturday 10am–1.30/2pm, although various markets, department stores and shopping centres open right through lunch.

As well as the places picked out below, visit one of the city's **department stores and shopping arcades**: Bulevard Rosa, at Passeig de Gràcia 55, and Avda. Diagonal 609–615, Barcelona's first shopping mall, both arcades featuring around 100 shops; El Corte Inglés, Plaça de Catalunya 14, and Avda. Diagonal 617, the city's biggest department store; and Centre Comercial Barcelona Glòries, Plaça de les Glòries 1 (Metro Glòries), a shopping, restaurant and cinema complex. El Mercadillo, c/Portaferrissa 17

(Metro Liceu), is a small complex of clothes and shoe shops, together with a restaurant and nice patio garden.

Antiques, arts and crafts

Art Escudellers, c/Escudellers 23–25 (Metro Liceu). An enormous shop selling ceramics from different regions of Spain. Not cheap but a good selection. Open daily 11am–11pm.

La Bola, c/Sepúlveda 184 (Metro Universitat). Old things, bric-a-brac and antique clothing.

La Caixa de Fang, c/Freneria 1 (Metro Jaume I). Off Baixada de la Llibretaria, behind the cathedral, this has very good-value ceramics and recycled glass.

La Cubana, c/de la Boqueria 26 (Metro Liceu). Old shop selling fans and mantillas.

La Manual Alpargatera, c/Avinyó 7 (Metro Liceu). Workshop making and selling *alpargatas* (espadrilles) to order, as well as other straw and rope work.

Populart, c/de Montcada 22 (Metro Jaume I). Delightful shop filled with antiques and crafts.

1748, Plaça de Montcada 2 (Metro Jaume I). Good ceramic shop with one of the widest selections.

Books

You'll find English-language books, newspapers and magazines at the stalls along the Ramblas, and a good selection of English-language books (novels and general unless otherwise stated) at the following shops:

BCN, c/Aragó 277, Eixample (Metro Passaig de Gràcia). Good selection of novels and TEFL books.

The Book Store, c/la Granja 13, Gràcia (Metro Fontana). Second-hand English-language books. Closed Aug.

Crisol, Rambla de Catalunya 81, Eixample (Metro Passaig de Gràcia). Magazines, books and music – open until 1am.

Llibreria Mallorca, Rambla de Catalunya 86, Eixample (Metro Passaig de Gràcia). Big selection of British and American newspapers and magazines.

Llibreria Pròleg, c/Dagueria 13. A women's/feminist bookshop, though with most works in Spanish/Catalan. Closed Aug.

Llibreria Quera, c/Petritxol 2 (Metro Liceu). Maps and trekking guides in a cramped little Barri Gòtic store.

Clothes, shoes and accessories

Adolfo Domínguez, Passeig de Gràcia 89 (Metro Passaig de Gràcia). Men and women's designs from the well-known *gallego* designer.

Camper, c/Muntaner 248; c/València 249; Avda. Pau Casals 5; Bd. Rosa Pedralbes. These are the four branches of Spain's most stylish value-for-money shoe-shop chain.

Groc, Rambla Catalunya 100 bis; c/Muntaner 385 (Metro Passaig de Gràcia). The shops of Barcelona's most innovative designer, Antoni Miró; the first is for men, the second for women.

Joaquín Berao, c/Roselló 277, Eixample (Metro Diagonal). Avant-garde jewellery in a stunningly designed shop.

Jean Pierre Bua, Avda. Diagonal 469 (Metro Diagonal). The city's temple for fashion victims: a postmodern shrine for Yamamoto, Gaultier, Miyake, Westwood, Miró and other international stars.

Lailo, c/Riera Baixa 20 (Metro Liceu). Off the west side of the Ramblas, this second-hand clothes shop is usually worth a look.

Obach Sombrería, c/del Call 2 (Metro Liceu). An excellent selection of hats of all types.

Pedro Morago, Avda. Diagonal 520 (Metro Diagonal). Morago is a classic Barcelona designer, producing everything from suits to sports shirts for men and women.

Sara Navarro, Avda. Diagonal 598 (Metro Hospital Clinic). Original leather clothes, shoes and accessories.

Design and decorative art

BD Ediciones de Diseño, c/Mallorca 291, Eixample (Metro Diagonal). The building is by Domènech i Montaner, the interior filled with the very latest in furniture and household design.

D. Barcelona, Avda. Diagonal 367, Eixample (Metro Diagonal). Up the road from Dos i Una, and with a similar but much bigger selection.

Dom, Passeig de Gràcia 76, Eixample (Metro Passeig de Gràcia). Original, amusing household and personal items at accessible prices.

Dos i Una, c/Rosselló 275, Eixample (Metro Diagonal). Contemporary, imaginative household and personal items.

Vinçon, Passeig de Gràcia 96, Eixample (Metro Passeig de Gràcia). This palace of design houses stylish and original items, pioneered since the 1960s by Fernando Amat, and with logo and carrier bags by the ubiquitous Mariscal. Temporary art and design exhibitions are held here, too.

Markets

Barcelona's **daily food markets**, all in covered halls, are open Monday–Saturday 8am–3pm and 5–8pm, though the most famous, La Boqueria on the Ramblas, opens right through the day. Other **specialist markets** are open only on certain days.

Good ones to try include:

Antiques: every Thurs in Plaça del Pi (Metro Liceu) from 9am; not Aug.

Coins, books and postcards: every Sun outside Mercat Sant Antoni 10am–2pm.

Crafts: first Sun of the month at Avda. Pau Casals, Eixample (Metro Hospital Clinic), from 10am – ceramics, textiles, glassware, wrought iron.

Flea market: Els Encants, every Mon, Wed, Fri and Sat in Plaça de les Glòries (Metro Glòries) from 8am – clothes, jewellery, junk and furniture.

Food: Mercat Abaceria Central, c/de Puigmartí, Gràcia (Metro Diagonal); Mercat Sant Antoni, Ronda de Sant Pau (Metro Sant Antoni); Mercat Sant Josep/La Boqueria, Ramblas (Metro Liceu); Mercat Santa Catarina, Avda. Francesc Cambó 16 (Metro Jaume I).

Listings

Airlines Almost all are located on Passeig de Gràcia or around the corner on the Gran Via. The main ones include: Air France, Passeig de Gràcia 56 (☎93 214 7900); British Airways, Passeig de Gràcia 85 (☎93 215 69 00); Iberia, Passeig de Gràcia 30 (☎902 400 500).

Airport El Prat de Llobregat (all enquiries on ☎93 298 38 38).

American Express The office is at Passeig de Gràcia 101 (Mon–Fri 9.30am–6pm, Sat 10am–noon; Metro Diagonal; ☎93 217 00 70). There's also an Amex cash machine at the airport.

Banks and exchange Main bank branches are in Plaça de Catalunya and Passeig de Gràcia. El Corte Inglés department store in Plaça de Catalunya, and American Express (see above) also have efficient exchange facilities which offer competitive rates. Banco de Santander on c/de Ferran (corner Plaça de Sant Jaume) and Caja de Madrid on Plaça de Catalunya both have automatic money exchanges, which accept British, French and German paper currency. Exchange offices include: Plaça de Catalunya tourist office (daily 9am–9pm); airport (daily 7.30am–10.45pm); Estació-Sants (daily 8am–10pm); and El Corte Inglés, Plaça de Catalunya (Mon–Sat 10am–9.30pm).

Buses For buses to all destinations, go to the Estació del Nord (☎93 265 65 08) on Avda. Vilanova (Metro Arc de Triomf). Companies represented include: Alsina Graells (☎93 265 68 66; to Andorra, Lleida, La Pobla de Segur and Vall d'Aran); Autocares Julia (☎93 490 40 00; London and Europe, Montserrat, Zaragoza); Bacoma (☎93 231 38 01; Córdoba, Granada, Sevilla); Barcelona Bus (☎93 232 04 59; Girona); Empresa Sarfa (☎93 265 10 77; Costa Brava); Enatcar (☎93 245 25 28; Madrid, Palencia, Valencia); Iberbus (☎93 265 07 00; London, Rome, Paris and Amsterdam); Viacarsa (☎93 490 40 00; Bilbao, Vitoria); Vibassa (☎93 491 101 10; Vigo, Galicia); Zatrans (☎93 231 04 01; Burgos, Logroño, Valladolid, Zamora).

Car rental Atesa, c/Muntaner 45 (☎93 298 34 33) and airport (☎93 302 45 78); Avis, c/Casanova 209 (☎93 209 95 33), c/Aragó 235 (☎93 487 87 54) and airport (☎93 298 36 00); Europcar, c/Viladomat 214 (☎93 439 84 01); Hertz, c/Tuset 10 (☎93 217 32 48), airport (☎93 298 36 36) and Estació-Sants (☎93 490 86 62); Ital, Trav. de Gràcia 71 (☎93 201 21 99); Vanguard, c/Londres 31 (☎93 439 38 80).

Consulates Australia, Gran Vía Carlos III 98 (☎93 330 94 96); Britain, Avda. Diagonal 477 (☎93 419 90 44); Canada, Gran Via Carlos III 989 (☎93 330 9496); Ireland, Gran Vía Carles III 94 (☎93 491 50 21); New Zealand, Trav. de Gràcia 64 (☎93 209 03 99); USA, Passeig de la Reina Elisenda 23 (☎93 280 22 27).

Cultural institutes The British Council at c/Amigó 83 (☎93 209 60 90 or 93 414 68 88) has an English-language library, lists of language schools and a good noticeboard advertising lessons and accommodation. The American Institute, Vía Augusta 123 (☎93 240 51 10), has newspapers, magazines and a reference library.

Emergencies For an ambulance or emergency doctor, dial ☎061. Or go to the accident and emergency departments of the Hospital Clinic or Hospital Sant Pau (see below).

Ferries Departures to the Balearics are from the Estació Marítima (☎93 301 2598; Metro Drassanes) at the bottom of the Ramblas. Buy tickets here at the Transmediterránea office (☎93 245 46 45). The ferries get very crowded in July and August – book ahead.

Gay and lesbian Barcelona There's a lesbian and gay city telephone hotline on ☎900 601 601 (6–10pm only). Cómplices, c/Cervantes 2, and Antinous, c/Josep Anselm Clavé 6, are gay bookshops with useful contacts and information. For a map of gay Barcelona, detailing bars, clubs, hotels and restaurants, contact either SexTienda, c/Rauric 11 (Mon–Sat 10am–9pm), or Zeus, c/Riera Alta 11 (Mon–Sat 10am–9pm; ☎93 442 97 95). Look out also for a free magazine called *Nois* which carries an up-to-date list of the scene. Most of the city's lesbian groups meet at Ca la Dona (see "Women's Barcelona", below): these include the Grup de Lesbianes Feministes de Barcelona, which meets on Thurs at 8pm, and L'Eix Violeta, a young lesbian group; another lesbian group meets on Tues at 8pm at the Coordinadora Gai-lesbiana, c/Bonaventura Muñoz 4 (☎93 309 79 97 or 902 120 140). Other contacts include Casal Lambda, c/Ample 5 (☎93 412 72 72; Mon–Thurs 5–9pm, Fri 5–11pm, Sat & Sun noon–9pm), a gay and lesbian group with a wide range of social, cultural and educational events; the Front d'Alliberament Gai de Catalunya, c/Verdi 88 (☎93 217 26 69), an association for gay men, with a library, meetings and video shows, and a gay youth group at the same address; and the Col.lectiu Gai de Barcelona, c/Paloma 12 (☎93 318 16 65), a gay men's organization with groups for young men and older men, and a magazine, *Infogai*. Finally, the city's annual lesbian and gay pride march is on June 28, starting in the evening at Plaça Universitat.

Hospitals Hospital de la Creu Roja, c/Dos de Maig 301 (☎93 433 15 51); Hospital Clinic, c/Casanovas 143 (☎93 227 54 00); Hospital de Sant Pau, c/Sant Antoni Mari Claret (☎93 291 91 91); Centro Diagnostic Malalties Sexuales (Sexually Transmitted Disease Clinic), Avda. Drassanes 17–19 (☎93 329 44 95).

Language schools The cheapest Spanish/Catalan classes in Barcelona are at the Escola Oficial d'Idiomes, Avda. Drassanes (☎93 329 24 58), where a lottery system is in force – queue up for a ticket, then see if you've won a place to sit the exam that day. Expect big queues at the start of term. Or try International House, c/Trafalgar 14 (☎93 268 45 11).

Laundries Self-service launderettes (*lavanderías automáticas*) are rare – you normally have to leave your clothes for the full works. Try Lava Super, c/Carme 63 (off the Ramblas). Note that you're not allowed by law to leave laundry hanging out of windows over a street, and some *hostales* can get shirty if you're found doing excessive washing in your bedroom sink.

Left luggage At Estació-Sants the *consigna* is open daily from 4am–midnight and costs 400–600ptas a day; at the Estació Maritima the hours are daily 8am–midnight and it costs 300–500ptas.

Library Biblioteca Nacional de Catalunya at c/de Hospital 56, next to the Hospital de la Santa Creu (Mon–Fri 9am–8pm, Sat 9am–2pm). The university public library is at Gran Vía 585 (Mon–Fri 8am–8.30pm, also Oct–June Sat 9am–2pm).

Lost property If you lose anything, try the *Ajuntament* (*objetos perdidos*) in c/de la Ciutat 9 (Mon–Fri 9.30am–1.30pm; ☎93 402 31 61), or the transport office in the Metro in Plaça Universitat, but you'll be lucky to get it back.

Newspapers You can buy foreign newspapers, magazines and trade papers at the stalls down the Ramblas, around Plaça de Catalunya and at Estació-Sants.

Noticeboards For apartment-sharing, lifts, lessons and other services check the noticeboards at the cultural institutes (see above); at International House (c/Trafalgar 14); at the university (in the main building; take door on far left and, inside, bear left and then right); at Escola Oficial d'Idiomes (see "Language schools"), and at Llibreria Prolèg (see "Books", p.621).

Police The main police station is at Via Laietana 49 (☎93 290 30 00) where there is also a department for women who've suffered violent crime. The tourist police – the Centro Atencíon Policial – are at

Rambla 43 (open 24hr in summer; ☎93 301 90 60). The various police bodies in the city can be contacted on the following numbers: Guàrdia Civil ☎062; Policia Nacional ☎091; Guàrdia Urbana ☎092.

Post office The main post office (*Correus*) in Barcelona is at Plaça d'Antoni López, facing the water at the end of Passeig de Colom (Mon–Sat 8am–8pm). Poste restante is at window 17 (Mon–Fri 9am–8pm, Sat 9am–2pm). Another post office is at c/Aragó 282 (Mon–Fri 8am–9pm, Sat 9am–2am).

Residence permits In Barcelona, residence permits are issued by the Servicio de Extranjeros at Avda. Marqués de l'Argentera 4 (Mon–Fri 9am–1pm; ☎93 482 05 44 or 93 482 05 30). It's advisable to apply a few weeks before your time runs out, keeping bank exchange forms every time you change money.

Swimming pools To swim at one of Barcelona's pools, take your passport along; you may need to show it at some of the pools before being allowed in. Central pools include Club Natació at Passeig Marítim (daily 6.30am–10pm; 1000ptas) and, best of all, the Olympic Piscines Bernat Picornell, Avda. de l'Estadi 30–40, Montjuïc (Mon–Fri 7am–midnight, Sat 7am–9pm, Sun 7.30am–2.30pm; summer 1200ptas, winter 650ptas).

Telephone offices There are *Telefónica* offices at c/Fontanella 4, off Plaça de Catalunya (Mon–Sat 8.30am–9pm), and at Estació-Sants (daily 8am–10pm).

Trains For train information, call RENFE (☎93 490 02 02; international routes on ☎93 490 11 22, 10am–2pm). You can buy train tickets at the RENFE office in the underground foyer at Passeig de Gràcia (corner of c/Aragó). Otherwise, at Estació-Sants there's both a RENFE information office (daily 6.30am–10.30pm; English-speaking) and an International Train Information Office (daily 7am–10pm), where you can reserve seats and couchettes on international trains. This is recommended in high season, compulsory on some trains, and should be done in advance – at least a couple of hours before departure, the day before if possible.

Travel agencies General travel agencies are found on the Gran Vía, Passeig de Gràcia, Vía Laietana and the Ramblas. For specific deals try: Julia Tours, Plaça Universitat 12 (☎93 317 64 54 or 93 317 62 09) for city tours, Catalunya holidays and trips; Oficina de Turisme Juvenil, c/Rocafort 116 (☎93 483 83 78) for discounted youth and student bus, train and flight deals; Viajes Marsans, Rambla 134 (☎93 318 72 16), for discounted train tickets, flights and holidays; and Wasteels, inside Estació-Sants, for youth train tickets.

Women's Barcelona The most useful contact address in the city is Ca la Dona, c/Caspe 38 (☎93 412 71 61; Mon–Fri 10am–2pm), a women's centre used for meetings of over twenty feminist and lesbian organizations; information available to callers. There's also La Illa, c/Reig i Bonet 3, Gràcia (☎93 210 00 62; 7.30pm–1am, later at weekends), a women's bar and cultural centre.

Youth information There's a youth information office at c/Ferran (☎93 402 78 00 or 93 402 78 01; Mon–Fri 10am–2pm and 4–8pm), with city information and advice, a library and English-speakers.

travel details

BUSES

Barcelona to: Alicante (5 daily; 9hr); Andorra (2 daily; 4hr 30min); Banyoles (2–3 daily; 1hr 30min); Besalú (2–3 daily; 1hr 45min); Cadaqués (2–4 daily; 2hr 20min); Girona (Mon–Sat 6–9 daily, Sun 3 daily; 1hr 30min); Lleida (9 daily, Sun 3 daily; 2hr 15minr); Lloret de Mar (July–mid-Sept 10 daily; 1hr 15min); Madrid (4 daily; 10hr); Olot (2–3 daily; 2hr 10min); Palafrugell (8 daily; 2hr); Perpignan, France (2 daily; 4hr); La Pobla de Segur (1 daily; 3hr 30min); La Seu d'Urgell (2 daily; 4hr); Tarragona (18 daily; 1hr 30min); Torroella (3 daily; 4hr 30min); Tossa de Mar (July–mid-Sept 12 daily; 1hr 35min); Valencia (7 daily; 6hr); Vall d'Aran (1 daily; 7hr); Viella (June–Nov 1 daily; 7hr); Zaragoza (4 daily; 5hr).

TRAINS

Barcelona to: Cerbère, France (18 daily; 2hr 55min); Girona (21 daily; 1hr 20min); Figueres (21 daily; 1hr 30min); Lleida via Manresa (3 daily; 4hr); Lleida via Valls or Tarragona/Reus (14 daily; 2–3hr); Madrid (4 daily; 12hr); Paris (7 daily; 11–15hr); Port Bou (18 daily; 2hr 50min); Puigcerdà (6 daily; 3hr 30min); Ripoll (12 daily; 2hr); Sitges (every 30min; 25–40min); Tarragona (every 30min; 1hr 30min); Valencia (7 daily; 4–5 hr); Vic (6 daily; 1hr); Zaragoza (13 daily; 4hr 30min–6hr 30min).

FERRIES

Barcelona to: Palma, Mallorca (1–2 daily; 8hr); Ibiza (2– 4 weekly; 9hr); Maó, Menorca (2–3 weekly; 9hr).

CHAPTER ELEVEN

CATALUNYA

Y ou can't think of visiting Barcelona without seeing something of its surroundings. Although the city is fast becoming international, the wider area of Catalunya (Cataluña in Castilian Spanish, traditionally Catalonia in English) retains a distinct regional identity that borrows little from the rest of Spain, let alone from the world at large. Out of the city – and especially in rural areas – you'll hear Catalan spoken more often and be confronted with better Catalan food, which is often highly specialized, varying even from village to village. Towns and villages are surprisingly prosperous, a relic of the early industrial era, when Catalunya developed far more rapidly than most of Spain; and the people are enterprising and open, celebrating a unique range of festivals (see the list on p.632) in almost obsessive fashion. There's a confidence in being Catalan that traces right back to the fourteenth-century Golden Age, when what was then a kingdom ruled the Balearics, Valencia, the French border regions, Sardinia and Corsica, too. Today, Catalunya is officially a semi-autonomous province, but it can still feel like a separate country – cross the borders into Valencia or Aragón and you soon pick up the differences.

Catalunya is also a very satisfying region to tour, since two or three hours in any direction puts you in the midst of varying landscapes of great beauty; from rocky coastlines to long, flat beaches, from the mountains to the plain, and from marshlands to forest. There are some considerable distances to cover, especially in the interior, but on the whole everything is easily reached from Barcelona, which is linked to most main centres by excellent bus and train services. The easiest targets are the **coasts** north and south of the city, and the various **provincial capitals** – Girona, Tarragona and Lleida – all destinations that make a series of day trips or can be linked together in a loop through the region.

The best of the beach towns lie on the famous **Costa Brava**, which runs up to the French border. This was one of the first stretches of Spanish coast to be developed for mass tourism, and though that's no great recommendation, the large, brash resorts to the south are tempered by some more isolated beaches and lower-key holiday and fishing villages further north. Just inland from the coast, the small town of **Figueres** contains another reason to visit the area: the Museu Dalí, Catalunya's biggest tourist attraction. South of Barcelona, the **Costa Daurada** is less enticing, though it has at least one fine beach at **Sitges** and the attractive coastal town of **Tarragona** to recommend it; inland, the romantic monastery of Poblet figures as one approach to the enjoyable provincial capital of **Lleida**.

Travels in inland Catalunya depend on the time available, but even on a short trip you can take in the medieval city of **Girona** and the surrounding area, which includes the isolated Montseny hills and the extraordinary volcanic **Garrotxa** region. With more time you can head for the **Catalan Pyrenees**, with their magnificent and relatively isolated hiking territory, particularly in and around the **Parc Nacional de Aigües Tortes**. East of here is **Andorra**, a combination of tax-free hellhole and mountain retreat set amidst quieter, generally neglected border towns, all offering great hiking and, in winter, good skiing.

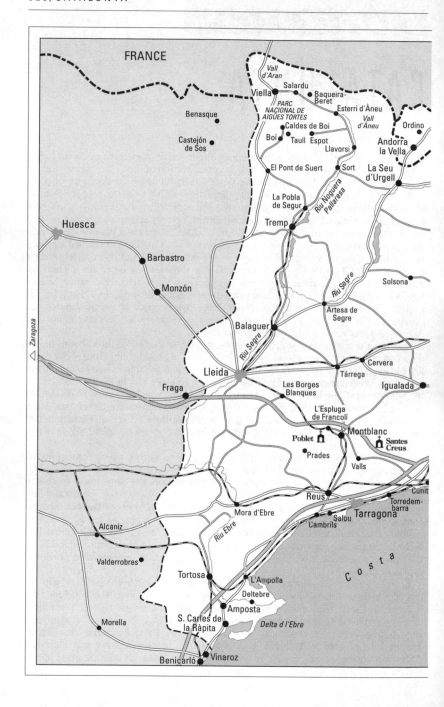

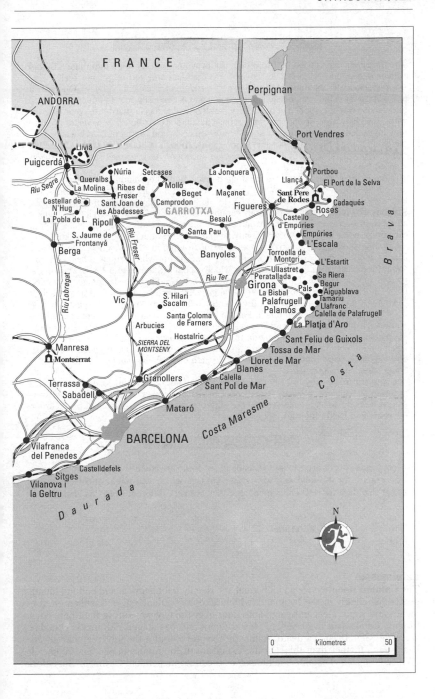

FRANCE

ANDORRA

Perpignan

Port Vendres

Llivià

Puigcerdá

Núria   Setcases   La Jonquera   Portbou
Queralbs   Llançá   El Port de la Selva
La Molina   Ribes de   Molló   Maçanet
Castellar de   Freser   Beget   Sant Pere   Cadaqués
N'Hug   Sant Joan de Camprodon   Figueres   de Rodes   Roses
La Pobla de L. les Abadesses   GARROTXA
Ripoll   Besalú   Castello
S. Jaume de   Olot   Santa Pau   d'Empúries
Frontanyá   Empúries
Berga   Banyoles   L'Escala
                                    Torroella de
                                    Montgrí   L'Estartit
                   Riu Ter   Ullastret
                             Peratallada   Sa Riera
               S. Hilari   Girona   Pals   Begur
Vic   Sacalm   La Bisbal   Aiguablava
                         Santa Coloma Palafrugell   Tamariu
            Arbucies   de Farners   Palamós   Llafranc
                   Hostalric   Calella de Palafrugell
            SIERRA DEL   La Platja d'Aro
            MONTSENY   Sant Feliu de Guixols
Manresa   Tossa de Mar
Montserrat   Lloret de Mar
Terrassa   Granollers   Blanes
Sabadell   Calella
            Mataró   Sant Pol de Mar

Riu Segre

Riu Freser

Riu Lobregat

BARCELONA   Costa Maresme

Vilafranca
del Penedes
      Castelldefels
Sitges
Vilanova i
la Geltru

Daurada

Brava

Costa

N

0   Kilometres   50

CATALÀ

The traveller's main problem throughout the province is likely to be **language** – *Català* (Catalan) has more or less taken over from Castilian and you might not realize that *Dilluns Tancat*, for example, is the same as *Cerrado Lunes* (closed Monday). On paper it looks like a cross between French and Spanish and is generally easy to understand if you know those two but, spoken, it has a very harsh sound and is far harder to come to grips with, especially away from Barcelona where accents are stronger. Few visitors realize how ingrained and widespread *Català* is, and this can lead to resentment because people won't "speak Spanish" for you. Increasingly, though, *Català* is replacing Castilian rather than cohabiting with it, a phenomenon known as the *venganza* (revenge). Never commit the error of calling it a dialect!

When Franco came to power, publishing houses, bookshops and libraries were raided and *Català* books destroyed. While this was followed by a let-up in the mid-1940s, the language was still banned from the radio, TV, daily press and, most importantly, schools, which is why many older people today cannot read or write *Català* (even if they speak it all the time). Conversely, in the capital virtually everyone *can* speak Castilian, even if they don't, while in country areas, many people can only understand, not speak it.

Català is spoken in Catalunya proper, part of Aragón, most of Valencia, the Balearic islands, the Principality of Andorra, and in parts of the French Pyrenees, albeit with variations of dialect (it is thus much more widely spoken than several better-known languages such as Danish, Finnish and Norwegian). It is a Romance language, stemming from Latin and more directly from medieval Provençal and *lemosi*, the literary French of Occitania. Spaniards in the rest of the country belittle it by saying that to get a *Català* word you just cut a Castilian one in half. In fact, the grammar is much more complicated than Castilian and it has eight vowel sounds (three diphthongs). There is a deliberate tendency at present in the media to dig up old words not used for centuries, even when a more common, Castilian-sounding one exists. In Barcelona, because of the mixture of people, there is much bad *Català* and much bad Castilian spoken, mongrel words being invented unconsciously.

In the text we've tried to keep to *Català* names (with Castilian in parentheses where necessary) – not least because street signs and Turismo maps are in *Català*. Either way, you're unlikely to get confused as the difference is usually only slight; ie Girona (Gerona) and Lleida (Lérida)

CATALÀ GLOSSARY

Most **Català** words are similar to Castilian, but some are completely unrecognizable. The criteria for the following words and phrases which you might encounter are either that they are very common or that they are very different from Castilian.

One	*Un(a)*	Four	*Quatre*
Two	*Dos (dues)*	Five	*Cinc*
Three	*Tres*	Six	*Sis*

Catalanisme

The **Catalan people** have an individual and deeply felt historical and cultural identity, seen most clearly in the language, which takes precedence over Castilian on street names and signs. Despite being banned for over thirty years during the Franco dictatorship, Catalan survived behind closed doors and has staged a dramatic comeback since the Generalísimo's death. As in the Basque country, though, regionalism goes back much further than this. On the expulsion of the Moors in 874, Guifré el Pelós (Wilfred the Hairy) established himself as the first independent **Count of Barcelona**;

Seven	*Set*	None, some, any,	*Cap*
Eight	*Vuit*	towards	
Nine	*Nou*	In	*Dins*
Ten	*Deu*	With	*Amb*
Eleven	*Onze*	Still/yet/even	*Encara*
Twelve	*Dotze*	A lot, very	*Força*
		A little	*Una mica*
Monday	*Dilluns*	Near	*(a) Prop*
Tuesday	*Dimarts*	Far	*Lluny*
Wednesday	*Dimecres*	(Six) years ago	*Fa (sis) anys*
Thursday	*Dijous*	Self/same	*Mateix*
Friday	*Divendres*	Half/middle	*Mig/mitja*
Saturday	*Dissabte*	Stop, enough!	*Prou!*
Sunday	*Diumenge*	Too much/too	*Massa*
		many	
Day before	*Abans d'ahir*		
yesterday		To work	*Treballar*
Yesterday	*Ahir*	To go	*Anar*
Today	*Avui*	To call, phone	*Trucar*
Tomorrow	*Demà*	To have dinner	*Sopar*
Day after	*Demà passat*	(evening)	
tomorrow		To eat	*Menjar*
Left, Right	*Esquerre (a),*		
	Dret(a)	Girl	*Una noia*
Ladies, Gents	*Dones, Homes*	Boy	*Un noi*
(WC)	*(Toaleta)*	Child/term of	*Nen(a)*
		affection	
Open, Closed	*Obert(a), Tancat*	Dog	*Gos*
Good morning/	*Bon dia*		
Hello		Place	*Lloc*
Good evening/	*Bona nit/Adéu*	Light	*Llum*
Goodbye		Chief, head	*Cap*
Very well	*Molt bé*	Time, occasion	*Vegada*
Bad	*Malament*		
Got a light?	*Tens foc?*	Drinking glass	*Got*
I like	*M'agrada*	Table	*Taula*
Well, then	*Sisplau*	Milk	*Llet*
What do you	*Que vols?*	Egg	*Ou*
want?		Strawberry	*Maduixa*
Where is?	*On és?*	Orange	*Taronge*
Sometimes	*A vegades*	Carrot	*Pastanaga*
Never, ever	*Mai*	Lettuce	*Enciam*
More	*Més*	Salad	*Amanida*
Nothing	*Res*	Apple	*Poma*

his kingdom flourished and the region became famous for its seafaring, mercantile and commercial skills, characteristics which to some extent still set the region apart. In the twelfth century came union with Aragón, though the Catalans kept many of their traditional, hard-won rights (*usatges*), and from then until the fourteenth century marked Catalunya's **golden age**. By the end of that time the kingdom ruled the Balearic islands, the city and region of Valencia, Sardinia, Corsica and much of present-day Greece. In 1359 the Catalan Generalitat formed Europe's first parliamentary government.

In 1469, through the marriage of Fernando V (of Aragón) to Isabella I (of Castile), the region was added on to the rest of the emergent Spanish state. Throughout the following centuries the Catalans made various attempts to secede and to escape from the stifling grasp of the central bureaucracy, which saw Catalan enterprise as merely another means of filling the state coffers. Early industrialization, which was centred here and in the Basque country, only intensified political disaffection. In the 1920s and 1930s, anarchist, communist and socialist parties all established major power bases in Catalunya. In 1931, after the fall of the dictator General Primo de Rivera, a **Catalan Republic** was proclaimed and its autonomous powers guaranteed by the new Republican government. Any incipient separatism collapsed, however, with the outbreak of the Civil War, during which Catalunya was a bastion of the Republican cause, Barcelona holding out until January 1939.

In return, Franco pursued a policy of harsh suppression, attempting to wipe out all evidence of the Catalan cultural and economic set-up and finally to establish the dominance of Madrid. Among his more subtle methods – employed also in Euskadi – was the encouragement of immigration from other parts of Spain in order to dilute regional identity. Even so, Catalunya remained obstinate, the scene of protests and demonstrations throughout the dictatorship. After Franco's death there was massive and immediate pressure – not long in paying dividends – for the reinstatement of a **Catalan government**. This, the semi-autonomous Generalitat, enjoys a very high profile, whatever the complaints about its lack of real power. It controls education, health and social security, with a budget based on taxes collected by central government and then returned proportionally. The province's official title is the Comunitat Autonoma de Catalunya and it is also known internally as the Principalitat. Since autonomy was granted, the region has consistently elected right-wing governments, which may be difficult to understand in view of the recent past, but which might be explained by the fact that such regimes are seen to be better able to protect Catalan business interests.

THE COSTA BRAVA

The **Costa Brava** (Rugged Coast), stretching from Blanes, 60km north of Barcelona, to Portbou and the French border, was once the most beautiful part of the Spanish coast with its wooded coves, high cliffs, pretty beaches and deep blue water. In parts it's still like this: the very northern section of the coast retains its handsome natural attractions and boasts a string of small towns and villages, which – while hardly undiscovered – are at least frequented only by locals and passing French motorists. The rest of the coast, however, to the south, is an almost total scenic disaster: thirty years of package-holiday saturation have taken their inevitable toll, and the concrete development has been ruthless. In places, there's a density of hotel and apartment blocks worse even than on the Costa del Sol.

Although the development appears all-encompassing at first glance, the Costa Brava splits into two distinct parts. The southern string of resorts, beginning at **Blanes**, *is* fairly horrible, though it's redeemed in a couple of places: the old town and medieval walls of **Tossa de Mar** are as attractive as anything you'll see in Catalunya, and **Sant Feliu de Guixols** farther north has more going for it than most towns along the coast. Even the area's most notorious resort, **Lloret de Mar**, is a matter of taste: a brash, tacky concrete pile it may be, but if you like your nightlife loud, late and libidinous, you'll have few complaints.

Beyond **Palamós** the main road runs inland and the coastal development here is relatively low-key; the beaches and villages close to the small inland town of **Palafrugell**, in particular, are still wonderfully scenic. An added attraction is the ancient Greek site of **Empúries**, within walking distance of **L'Escala**, itself a resort on an eminently reasonable scale. Beyond here, the hinterland of the large bay, the **Golfo**

GETTING AROUND THE COSTA BRAVA

Driving is the easiest way to get around, though you can expect the smaller coastal roads to be very busy in summer and parking to be tricky in the major resorts. **Buses** in the region are almost all operated by the SARFA company, but although they are reasonably efficient, it can be a frustrating business trying to get to some of the smaller coastal villages. Consider using Figueres, or even Girona, as a base for lateral trips to the coast; both are big bus termini and within an hour of the beach. The **train** from Barcelona to Portbou and the French border runs inland most of the time, serving Blanes, Girona and Figueres, but emerging on the coast itself only at Llançà.

There's also a daily **boat service** (Cruceros) in the summer – June to September – from Calella (south of Blanes and not to be confused with the one near Palafrugell) to Palamós, calling chiefly at Blanes, Lloret, Tossa, Sant Feliu and Platja d'Aro. The Lloret–Tossa trip, for example, costs around 900ptas return, and it's worth taking at least once as the rugged coastline makes for an extremely beautiful ride.

---

de Roses, is rural and fairly isolated, crossed by only a few minor roads and encompassing a nature reserve, the Parc Natural dels Aiguamolls de l'Empordá. Around the bay, **Roses** is the last of the Costa Brava's massive tourist developments; nearby **Cadaqués** is becoming more popular by the year, though you can find quieter coastal fishing villages right the way up to the French border, including the likeable small resort of **Portbou**, last stop before France. Inland, the region's largest town, **Figueres**, is the birthplace of Salvador Dalí and home to his superb, surreal museum.

There's more accommodation along the Costa Brava than anywhere else in Catalunya, but that doesn't necessarily make **rooms** any easier to find. In the large resorts block-booking by tour operators reduces the supply considerably and if you're heading independently to Lloret or Tossa, for example, in the summer, you'd be wise to book well in advance. You *will* generally find something if you arrive on spec, but you'll almost certainly pay over the odds for it. There are few problems with **camping,** provided you can put up with enormous, crowded sites often some way out of the towns and villages.

Blanes

Just over an hour from Barcelona, **BLANES** is the first town of the Costa Brava, though this apart there's little to distinguish it from the other resort towns back down the coast towards the city. With its industrial base and heavy-duty fishing port, it's an uninspiring stop. If you rose to the challenge you could doubtless derive some satisfaction from the town's botanical garden, which covers five hectares, the remains of a tenth-century castle keep and the surviving fourteenth-century church, but the main interest – inevitably – is provided by the pine-sheltered, sandy **beach**, one of the coast's longest. With Lloret de Mar only 8km away, and Tossa another 13km beyond, there's little incentive to do much more than dip a toe in the sea and then press on.

Practicalities

Blanes at least has the advantage over many similar places of being a real town rather than just a tourist settlement. There are dozens of largely indistinguishable **hotels and hostales** here, and no fewer than thirteen local **campsites** as well. The **Turismo** in Plaça de Catalunya (June–Sept Mon–Sat 9am–8pm, July & Aug also Sun 9am–2pm; May & Oct Mon–Fri 9am–2pm & 4–7pm; Nov–April Mon–Fri 9am–3pm; ☎972 330348) can help you find a room should you decide to stay.

If endless *platos combinados* and fast food don't appeal, there's an excellent Catalan **restaurant**, *Les Brases*, about ten minutes' walk from Plaça de Catalunya at c/Antiga 40

FIESTAS

In some cases, dates may vary slightly from year to year.

January
20–22 Traditional pilgrimage in Tossa de Mar, the *Pelegri de Tossa*, followed by a lively fiesta. Annual festival at Llança.

February/March
Carnaval Sitges has Catalunya's best celebrations (see p.706). Celebrations also at Solsona, Sort, Rialp and La Molina.

Easter
The *Patum* festival in Berga (see p.679) is the biggest and best festival in Catalunya; Holy Week celebrations at Besalú and La Pobla de Segur.

April
23 *Semana Medieval de Sant Jordi* in Montblanc – a week of exhibitions, games, dances and medieval music to celebrate the legend of St George.

May
11–12 Annual *Festival* in Lleida; and the annual wool fair, *Festa de la Lana*, in Ripoll. *Festa de Corpus Christi* in Sitges – big processions and streets decorated with flowers.
Third week *Fires i Festes de la Santa Creu* in Figueres; processions and music.

June
21–23 *Festival* in Camprodon.
24 *Día de Sant Joan* celebrated everywhere; watch out for things shutting down for a day on either side.
29 Annual *Festival* at Tossa de Mar.
Last week The *Raiers* (rafters) *Festival* and river racing in Sort.

July
First Sunday Annual *Festival* at Puigcerdà.

10 *Sant Cristobal* festival in Olot, with traditional dances and processions.
Third week *Festa de Santa Cristina* at Lloret de Mar. Also, annual *Festival* at Palafrugell.
25 *Festival* at Portbou in honour of St James.
26 Annual *Festival* at Blanes.

August
First week *Festa Major* at Andorra la Vella; annual festival at Sant Feliu de Guixols.
10–12 Annual festival at Castelló d'Empúries.
15 *Festival* at La Bisbal and Palafrugell.
19 *Festa de Sant Magi* in Tarragona.
Last week *Festa Major* in Sitges, to honour the town's patron saint, Sant Bartolomeu.

September
First week *Festival* at Cadaqués and at L'Escala.
8 Religious celebrations in Cadaqués, Núria and Queralbs. Processions of *gigantes* at Solsona. *Festivals* at Sort and Esterri d'Aneu.
22 Annual *Festival* at Espot.
23 *Festa de Sant Tecla* in Tarragona, with processions of *gigantes* and human castles.
24 Annual *Festival* at Besalú.

October
8 Annual fair at Viella.
Last week *Ferias de Sant Narcis* in Girona, and *Festa de Sant Martiriano* in Banyoles.

November
1 *Sant Ermengol* celebrations in La Seu d'Urgell.

December
18 *Festival* at Cadaqués.

– left off Rambla Joaquim. This has a delicious 975ptas *menú* and is situated on a quiet residential street, so you can enjoy your meal in peace.

The **train** station is inland, a little way out of town – there's a half-hourly service to Barcelona and several trains daily to Girona and Figueres. Regular buses run from the station to the beach, and **buses** also connect Blanes with Lloret every twenty minutes until 9.35pm.

Lloret de Mar

Despite the increasingly developed character of the coast as you head north, nothing will prepare you for **LLORET DE MAR**, one of the most extreme resorts in Spain. It's the one place on the Costa Brava that most people have heard of, with a sky-high tourist profile that puts many off and attracts countless others for roughly the same reasons – the bars, the discos, bastardized European cuisine, English pubs, German beer, and visitors who, on the whole, do their best to ignore the fact that they're in Spain at all.

On the surface, Lloret is a mess: highrise concrete tower blocks, a tawdry mile or so of sand and alongside it the most prosaic, unimaginative display of cafés, restaurants and bars you'll ever see. Looking for cultural distraction is a waste of effort, and only a tiny portion of the town – around Plaça de l'Església and the sixteenth-century parish church – hints at what Lloret once was. But to see the town in this way is misguided, since Lloret makes no pretence that it's anything other than an out-and-out holiday resort. And as out-and-out holiday resorts go, Lloret de Mar is as accommodating as they come, excelling in giving its guests what they want. During the day, the central **beach** is packed with oily bodies, but it's flanked by attractive little coves and lookout points which you can either reach by footpath or view from the coastal boat service that calls at Lloret. Budget meals abound – in Dutch and German bars, overly convivial cafés, pizzerias and Chinese restaurants – while there are plenty of more expensive, and more impressive, Catalan and Spanish **restaurants** too. Beer and *sangría* flow ceaselessly, mopped up in the loud bars, pubs and discos along c/de la Riera and the surrounding streets.

Practicalities

Cruceros and other coastal **boats** dock at the beach, which is where the ticket office is, too (info on ☎972 314969); there are services eleven times daily to Tossa de Mar, 45min away. The **bus station** is north of the town centre, on Carretera de Blanes, in front of the football ground. As well as regular services from nearby Blanes and Tossa, there are ten daily buses from Barcelona. There's a **Turismo** (May–Oct Mon–Sat 9.30am–1pm & 4–8pm; Nov–April closes 7pm; ☎972 365788) at the bus station if you want to pick up a map and hotel listings, and another one in the centre close to the seafront at Plaça de la Vila 1 (June–Sept Mon–Sat 9am–9pm, Sun 9.30am–2pm; March–May & Oct Mon–Sat 9.30am–1pm & 4–8pm; ☎972 364735).

If you're intending **to stay**, arm yourself with a list of hotels and *hostales* and start looking early in the day. Among the more reasonable places close to the sea are *Pensión Reina Isabel*, c/Vall de Venecia 12 (☎972 364121, fax 972 369978; ③–④), the friendly *Pensión Proa Astor*, c/Venecia 51 (☎972 364216; ④) and *Pensión Tropicana*, Avda. Joan Llaverias 19 (☎972 364130; ④), which is clean and has sea views. Farther back from the sea in the quieter part of town, *Hotel Montserrat*, c/Del Carme 54–56 (☎972 364493; June–Sept; ④), and *Pensión Valls*, c/Santa Teresa 11 (☎972 364389; June–Aug; ③), are good bets.

ACCOMMODATION PRICE CODES

The codes used in our hotel listings denote the following price ranges:

① Under 2000ptas	④ 4500–6000ptas	⑦ 12,000–17,500ptas
② 2000–3000ptas	⑤ 6000–8000ptas	⑧ Over 17,500ptas
③ 3000–4500ptas	⑥ 8000–12,000ptas	

See p.34 for more details.

If you're determined to eat Spanish **food** – a heretical choice in Lloret – then the heavily Catalan *Ca l'Avi*, at Avda. Vidreres 30, should satisfy you, though look to pay around 3000ptas a head.

Tossa de Mar

Arriving by boat at **TOSSA DE MAR**, 13km north of Lloret, is one of the Costa Brava's highlights, the medieval walls and turrets pale and shimmering on the hill above the modern town. Although an unashamed resort, Tossa is still very attractive and – if you have the choice – infinitely preferable to Lloret as a base.

Arrival and information

There are plenty of day-trippers in Tossa, which is linked to Lloret by half-hourly **buses**. If you're going to stay, pick up a free map and accommodation lists from the **Turismo** (May & Oct Mon–Sat 10am–1pm & 4–8pm; early June & late Sept Mon–Sat 9.30am–8.30pm, Sun 10am–1pm; late June to early Sept Mon–Wed, Fri & Sat 9am–9pm, Thur & Sun 10am–1pm; Nov–April Mon–Fri 10am–1pm & 4–7pm, Sat 10am–1pm; ☎972 340108), in the same building as the **bus station**. To reach the centre, and the beaches, head straight down the road in front of you and turn right at the roundabout. The Cruceros **boats** dock at the main beach, where there's a ticket office (info on ☎972 716081).

Accommodation

There is plenty of **accommodation** to be had in the warren of tiny streets around the church and below the old city walls; in summer, the more obscure streets away from the front are the ones to check. There are five local **campsites**, all within a two- to four-kilometre walk of the centre. *Cala Llevado* (☎972 340314, fax 972 341187; May–Sept) is 3km out, off the road to Lloret; and costs around 850ptas per person and per tent. The bus to Lloret should drop you close by if you ask.

Pensión Can Lluna, c/Roqueta 20 (☎972 340365 or 972 340757). Comfortable, reasonably priced *pensión*, open March–Nov. ③.

Pensión Can Tort, c/Pescadores 1 (☎972 341185). Clean and friendly option; price includes breakfast. ⑤.

Hotel Diana, Plaça d'Espanya 6 (☎972 341886, fax 972 341103). Nicely located in an attractive square; open April to mid-Nov. Prices drop dramatically outside summer. ⑥.

Hotel Mar Blau, Avda. de la Costa Brava 16 (☎972 340282). Pleasant, slightly more expensive than *Pensión Can Lluna* but with a commensurate increase in comfort. ④.

Pensión Moré, c/Sant Telm 9 (☎972 340399). Basic but perfectly adequate and very friendly. ②.

The Town

Founded originally by the Romans, Tossa has twelfth-century walls surrounding an old quarter, the **Vila Vela**, which is all cobbled streets, whitewashed houses and flower boxes, offering terrific views over beach and bay. Within the quarter you'll eventually happen upon the **Museu de la Vila Vela** at Plaça Roig I Soler 1 (June–Sept Tues–Sun 10am–7pm; Oct–May Tues–Sun 10am–1pm & 3–6pm; 200ptas), which features some Chagall paintings, a Roman mosaic and remnants from a nearby excavated Roman villa.

Tossa's best **beach** (there are four) is the Mar Menuda, around the headland away from the old town. The main central beach, though pleasant and clean enough, gets crowded even on the gloomiest of days. Booths here sell tickets for **boat trips** around the surrounding coastline, a reasonable way to blow 1000ptas or so if you're not going to take the Cruceros coastline service beyond Tossa. Fonda Crystal, with a booth right next to that of Cruceros, run glass-bottomed boat trips (☎972 342229; April–Oct; 1000ptas),

Out of season Tossa's attraction is even greater, simply because there are fewer people to disturb the tranquil old town streets. It's in winter, too, that you'll see something of the Costa Brava's previous, more traditional, life. This is best represented by the annual *Pelegri de Tossa*, on January 20 and 21, a **pilgrimage** from Tossa to the inland town of Santa Coloma in honour of Saint Sebastian, followed by a winter fair.

Eating
Most of Tossa's **restaurants** feature *menús del día* of varying quality, while there are endless "Full English Breakfast" bargains offered in places on the way out to the bus station. More atmospherically, there is a whole host of excellent restaurants up in the old quarter and just outside the walls, where you'll require big money or a credit card. For local specialities, two well-known places are *Bahía*, Passeig del Mar (☎972 340322), whose swish interior is the setting for reasonably priced seafood meals, and *Es Molí*, c/Trull 3 (open Oct–April, closed Tues), expensive but with a garden patio and fine local cooking. A less exclusive place, with reliable Catalan food and a 1600ptas *menú del día* is *Tito's*, at c/Sant Telmo 6. The *Roqueta Mar*, c/de la Roqueta 2, is similarly priced and has a lovely setting, with a creeper-shaded terrace in a rambling corner of the old town.

Sant Feliu to Palamós

Tossa is something of an aberration and the coast immediately to the north is again heavily developed and often thoroughly spoiled. Fairly regular buses ply the route, though, and the ride isn't bad in parts, particularly the winding section between Tossa and Sant Feliu. Even nicer is to use the **boat service**, which continues up the coast via Sant Feliu to Palamós – another lovely ride, and really the only reason to be stopping in most of the towns below. Incidentally, many of the buses on this coastal route originate in Girona or Palafrugell, so it's easy enough to see the various towns on day trips from either of those places, too.

Sant Feliu de Guixols

SANT FELIU DE GUIXOLS is probably the best stop between Tossa and the beaches of Palafrugell. It's another full-blown resort, but at least a reasonably pleasant one with only low-rise hotels, a decent sweep of coarse sand, a yacht harbour, and an attractive seafront, Passeig del Mar, decked out with pavement cafés and plane trees. Back from the beach, the narrow streets of the old town – thick with café-bars – are commercial but undeniably appealing, while a weekly market in the central Plaça de Mercat adds a bit of local colour. Sant Feliu owes its handsome buildings and air of prosperity to the nineteenth-century cork industry which was based here, but the origins of the town go back as far as the tenth century, when a town grew up around the Benedictine **monastery**, whose ruins still stand in Plaça Monestir. The squat round tower and tenth-century arched gateway, the Porta Ferrada, sit back from the square, and if you want to look inside, the complex is usually open from 8am Mass until noon, and again at 8pm Mass. A **museum** around the back houses a permanent display of work by local artist Josep Albertí, who died in April 1993.

Practicalities
Cruceros **boats** dock on the main beach, where there's a ticket office (☎972 372692). There are two **bus terminals**: Teisa services to and from Girona stop opposite the monastery, next to which you'll also find the **Turismo**, at Plaça Monestir (June–Sept Mon–Sat 10am–2pm & 4–8pm, Sun 10am–2pm; Oct–May Mon–Sat 10am–1pm &

4–7pm, Sun 10am–2pm; ☎972 820051); the SARFA bus station (for buses to and from Palafrugell, Girona and Barcelona) is five minutes' walk north of the centre on the main Carretera de Girona, at the junction with c/Llibertat.

A score of family-run **pensiones and hotels** can be found in the old town streets, all within a five-minute walk of each other and the sea; pick up a list and current prices from the Turismo. The most obvious is the *Hostal Zürich*, Avda. Juli Garreta 43–45 (☎972 321054; ④), just off Plaça Monestir, opposite the Turismo; while a favourite budget choice is the *Gas Vell*, c/Santa Magdalena 29 (☎972 321024, fax 972 321024; ③), though it's a long way from the sea. Of the two **campsites**, *Camping Sant Pol*, c/Doctor Fleming (☎972 321029; April–Sept), is more expensive – but less sprawling – and only 1km from the seafront.

There are **restaurants** everywhere, although those on the Passeig del Mar are overpriced, certainly if you're eating fish. Probably the best-value *menú del día*, at 1200ptas, is at *Optimus II*, c/Major 23. Otherwise, try the *Club Nautic*, at the far end of the harbour in among the yachts, less for the food than for the unimpeded sea views, and *Segura*, c/Sant Pere 11–13, or *Amura*, Placeta Sant Pere 7, for fish. For *tapas*, *El Gallo*, down the backstreets at c/Especiers 13, is very popular with locals.

The *modernista*-influenced *Nou Casino de la Constancia*, which faces the water on Passeig dels Guixols, is also worth a visit at some point. It's open daily from 9am to 1am (10pm in winter), and you can get a beer here and watch the old-timers fleecing each other at cards.

La Platja d'Aro, Calonge and around

There's another immense concrete concentration a few kilometres to the north, in the area around **LA PLATJA D'ARO** (Playa de Aro), whose only recommendation is its three-kilometre beach – though as it recommends itself to thousands of others, too, you may as well give it a miss.

Beyond Platja d'Aro, buildings are still going up, and around **Sant Antoni de Calonge** the main road traffic kicks up swirls of concrete dust. Four times daily the Palafrugell bus detours to **CALONGE** itself, just 2km inland but hardly visited by the beach hordes. It has a closely packed medieval centre with a church and castle, and there's a **restaurant**, *Can Muni*, at c/Major 5, whose speciality mussel recipes and 1650ptas *menú del día* are alone worth the trip. The village also has several upmarket *hostales*, though you'd be better off moving back to the coast for the night.

Eleven kilometres west of Calonge, along a minor road (no public transport), the ancient, megalithic stone of **Cova d'en Dayna** at **ROMANYÁ DE LA SELVA** is one of the very few surviving examples in Catalunya. If you're driving, the diversion is warranted, though under your own steam getting there involves taking the bus between Sant Feliu and Girona and asking to be put off at the turning outside Llagostera, from where it's a tiring seven-kilometre walk.

Palamós

Heading for Palafrugell, the only other realistic stop is at **PALAMÓS**, a modern-looking resort set around a harbour full of yachts, and last stop on the Cruceros boat run (information on ☎972 314969). The town was originally founded in 1277, and the old part is set apart from the new, on a promontory at the eastern end of the bay. Palamós still retains its fishing industry, the day's catch being auctioned off on the busy quayside in the late afternoon. You can kill time until then on the town's good beach. Don't bother with the small Museu de la Pesca, signposted from various points in the town; you'll spend more time finding it than you will inside.

The **bus station** (for services to and from Sant Feliu, Palafrugell and Girona) is one block back from the **Turismo** (daily: June–Sept 8am–9pm; Oct–May 8am–3pm; ☎972 600550) at Passeig de Mar 22.

Palafrugell and around

The small town of **PALAFRUGELL**, 4km inland from a delightful coastline, has managed somehow to remain almost oblivious to its tourist-dominated surroundings. An old town at its liveliest during the morning market, Palafrugell maintains a cluster of old streets and shops around its sixteenth-century church that aren't entirely devoted to the whims and wants of foreigners. The central square, it's true, is ringed with pavement cafés, but you're as likely to fetch up next to a local as a tourist, and elsewhere in town there are only five or six hotels, and a similar number of restaurants. All of which means that Palafrugell is still a very pleasant place to visit, while it's also a convenient place to base yourself if you're aiming for the nearby coastline – and considerably less expensive than staying at the beach.

The coast, too, makes a marked change from what's gone before. With no true coastal road, this stretch boasts quiet, pine-covered slopes backing the little coves of Calella, Llafranc and Tamariu, all with scintillatingly turquoise waters. The beach development here has been generally mild – low-rise, whitewashed apartments and hotels – and although a fair number of foreign visitors come in season, it's also where many of the better-off Barcelonans have a villa for weekend and August escapes. All this makes for one of the nicest (though hardly undiscovered) stretches of the Costa Brava.

Arrival and information

Buses arrive at Palafrugell's SARFA **bus terminal** at c/Torres Jonama 67: the town centre is a ten-minute walk away to the right; while you turn left from the terminal and left again at the roundabout to find the **Turismo**, c/Carrilet 2 (April–June & Sept Mon–Sat 10am–1pm & 5–8pm, Sun 10am–1pm; July & Aug Mon–Sat 10am–9pm, Sun 10am–1pm; Oct–March Mon–Sat 10am–1pm & 4–7pm; ☎972 300228), which supplies a map (including a useful plan of the local coastline) and accommodation lists. **Drivers** should be warned that finding a metered parking space in the narrow central streets can take hours.

Accommodation

Places to stay can be found at any of the nearby beaches (see "Around Palafrugell" below), though rooms here are expensive and zealously sought after. It's easier and cheaper to stay in Palafrugell itself and get the bus to the beach with everyone else: in summer it's wise to try and book ahead.

Pensión Andalucia, c/Sant Ramon 1 (☎972 301505). Small *hostal*, low on facilities but a good fallback if the other budget places are full. ④.

Fonda L'Estrella, c/de les Quatre Cases 13 (☎972 300005). The best budget choice on a little street near the main Plaça Nova. The rooms are simple and cool, arranged around a cloistered courtyard with tables and potted plants. ③.

Pensión Familiar, c/Sant Sebastià 29 (☎972 300043). On the other side of the square from *L'Estrella*, but not nearly as charming, with separate baths and showers. ③.

Hostal Plaja, c/Sant Sebastià 34 (☎972 300526, fax 972 300526). On the same street as the *Pensión Familiar*, but slightly pricier and more comfortable. Also has a secure garage. ④.

Eating, drinking and entertainment

If you stay in Palafrugell, you'll have to **eat** there as well since the last bus back from the beaches is at around 8.30pm. There's not a great deal of choice, but what there is is generally good value. *El Rebost del Pernil*, c/Major 3, has a decent 1000ptas *menú del día*, and substantial *platos del día* for much less. Up a few steps from Plaça Nova, *Restaurant l'Arc* is recommended for pizzas and other main dishes for well under 1000ptas. Pricier are *La Xicra*, c/de Sant Antoni 17, a very pleasant Catalan restaurant where a meal will run to 2500–3000ptas a head, and the similarly priced and highly praised *Mas Olivier*, on the ring-road at Avda. d'Espanya 70. The town **market** runs daily (not Mon) from 7am onwards; it's on c/Pi i Margall, leading north from Plaça Nova.

Drinking and entertainment revolve entirely around Plaça Nova, where the café-bars are reasonably priced and well-placed for idling the time away. In July and August, on Tuesday and Thursday nights from around 10pm, there's dancing to a piano-and-drum-machine combo, while Friday nights at the same time see a more traditional *sardana* in the square.

Around Palafrugell

Such is the popularity of the **nearby beaches** that a new highway has been built from Palafrugell and, in the summer, an almost non-stop shuttle service runs from the bus terminal to Calella and then on to Llafranc. You might as well get off at Calella, the first stop, since Llafranc is only a twenty-minute coastal walk away and you can get a return bus from there. Other less frequent services run to the more distant beach at Tamariu, and **inland** to Begur.

All **bus services** are drastically reduced before June and after September. Basically, buses from Palafrugell run to Calella and Llafranc (8am–9pm, July and Aug every 30min, June & Sept roughly hourly), to Tamariu (June–Sept 3–4 daily), and to Begur (June–Sept 3–4 daily). However, it's also reasonably inexpensive to make the trip to the coast from Palafrugell by **taxi** – around 900ptas to Calella.

Calella and Llafranc

CALELLA is still (just) a fishing port. Its gloriously rocky coastline is punctuated by several tiny sand beaches which are always packed, but the water is inviting and the village's whitewashed villas and narrow streets are very attractive. If you want to do more than lounge about, a 45-minute walk south leads to the **Castell i Jardins de Cap Roig** (daily: June–Sept 8am–8pm; Oct–May 9am–6pm; 200ptas), a cliff-top botanical garden which took fifty years to lay out. **Bars and restaurants** line the coastline at Calella; one to look out for is the *Continental Bar*, where you can admire the art on the walls of the cool, airy interior as you tuck into a 1000ptas *menú*.

A gentle, hilly, twenty-minute walk high above the rocks brings you to **LLAFRANC**, tucked into the next bay, with one goodish stretch of beach and a glittering marina. Llafranc seems a little more upmarket, its hillside villas glinting in the sun, its beachside restaurants expensive, but essentially the development in both places remains on a human scale. While you're here, try *cremat*, a typical drink of the fishing villages in this region, reputedly brought over by sailors from the Antilles. The concoction contains rum, sugar, lemon peel, coffee grounds and sometimes a cinnamon stick; it will be brought out in an earthenware bowl and you have to set fire to it, occasionally stirring until (after a few minutes) it's ready to drink.

The **bus back to Palafrugell** leaves from the roundabout on the main road outside Llafranc. If you want to stay in either village, pick up a **hotel** list in Palafrugell and ring from there: a good place in Calella is the *Hostería Plancton* at c/Codina 16 (☎972 615081; ③), open in the summer only. In Llafranc, the *Hotel Casamar*, c/d'el Nero 3 (☎972 300104, fax 972 610651; ⑥), is up 113 steps from the seafront, a climb well worth making for the view of the bay from the hotel's balconies. There's probably more chance of a space at one of the villages' **campsites**, which are open only from April to

September: *Moby Dick* (☎972 614307) and the less good *La Siesta* (☎972 615116) in Calella, or *Kim's Camping* (☎972 301156) in Llafranc.

Tamariu

TAMARIU, 4km north of Llafranc, is even lovelier, and although it has a smaller beach than either of the other two villages, there are fewer buses and consequently fewer people. You could just about walk through the woods from Llafranc (around ninety minutes), although the last part of the winding road, with its speeding traffic, is rather dangerous. In any case, walk at least as far as the **lighthouse** above Llafranc, with grand views over the beach villages and Palafrugell set in the plain behind. There's a **campsite** in Tamariu, 200m from the beach (☎972 620422; May–Sept), and several *hostales* and **hotels**, though only the relatively basic *Hotel del Sol*, Reieri 1 (☎972 300424; ④), costs less than 6000ptas a night in July and August. The *Hotel Tamariu* (☎972 620031; mid-May to mid-Sept; ⑤) is small and friendly, and has a mid-priced restaurant that faces the sea.

Begur, Aiguablava and other nearby beaches

For something other than just beaches, and for fewer people, head instead for **BEGUR**, about 8km from Palafrugell and slightly inland. It's a crumbling hill town, and the remnants of its seventeenth-century castle command extensive views of the central Costa Brava. The peeling medieval streets harbour a squat church and a couple of empty restaurants – and nothing but peace and quiet in the heat of the day. *Hotel Plaja* (☎972 622197; ⑤), opposite the church, has decent rooms, and serves a remarkably good-value *menú del día*.

With a little energetic walking from Begur, you can reach the beaches at **AIGUAFREDA** and **FORNELLS** or, if you have transport, the tranquil hamlets of **SA RIERA** and **SA TUNA** to the north. There are *hostales* at several of these beaches, open only in summer, and Sa Riera also has a selection of bars and restaurants for lunch. Drivers can also detour to **AIGUABLAVA** where the views are even more scenic than from Begur. The magnificent *Parador Nacional de la Costa Brava* (☎972 622162, fax 972 622166; ⑧) is the best place to soak up the scenery; non-guests can fork out for a couple of drinks at the bar just for the sheer luxury of enjoying the pool and getting a look at the marble and mosaic opulence within. If you're thinking of staying, book in advance and expect to pay over 20,000ptas a night in high season.

Inland: La Bisbal, Pals and Torroella

Inland from Palafrugell there are several towns and villages that can provide an afternoon's escape from the beaches. A couple would even serve as overnight stops if you prefer tranquil medieval streets to the teeming coastal promenades.

La Bisbal and around

LA BISBAL, 12km northwest of Palafrugell and on the bus route to Girona, is a medieval market town in an attractive river setting. Since the seventeenth century, La Bisbal has specialized in the production of **ceramics**, and pottery shops line the main road through town, where – with a bit of browsing – you can pick up some terrific local pieces. Ceramics apart, La Bisbal makes a pleasant stop anyway, as its handsome old centre retains many impressive mansions, the architectural remnants of a once thriving Jewish quarter and parts of a medieval castle built for the bishops of Girona.

From La Bisbal, a couple of tiny medieval villages to the northeast – now undergoing restoration work – are worth visiting, though you'll need to have your own transport. At **ULLASTRET** there was an Iberian settlement, whose ruins can be seen a little way outside the village. Nearby **PERATALLADA** is especially beautiful, with a ruined castle whose origins have been dated back to pre-Roman times, a fortified church and a number of houses embellished with coats of arms and arches. There's good local food and wine at *Can Nau*, c/d'en Bas 12 (closed Wednesday).

Pals

The bus journey north to L'Escala can be broken 8km north of Palafrugell at **PALS**. This fortified medieval village was long-neglected, but has just received rather an alarming new sheen at the hands of enthusiastic restorers. It's inevitably attracting an increasing number of day-trippers, and ceramic and pottery shops are proliferating in the old quarter, whose buildings date largely from the fourteenth century. However, the commercialization can't detract from the beauty of Pals's quiet hill-top setting: golden-brown buildings cluster around a stark tower, all that remains of the town's Romanesque castle. Below is the beautifully vaulted Gothic parish church, while you could also look into the town **museum** (June–Sept Mon–Sat 10am–2pm & 4–8pm, Sun 10am–2pm; Oct–May opening hours vary; 200ptas), an eclectic collection housed in a restored mansion. Exhibits here include odds and ends retrieved from an English warship sunk in the siege of Roses in the 1808 War of Independence, and there's a steady turnover of art exhibitions, too.

Pals has a regular programme of dances and concerts throughout the summer, including a **wine festival** in mid-August, for which you might be tempted to stay. There are a couple of newish hotels, but the best **budget accommodation** is at the *Hostal Barris* at c/Enginyer Algarra 51 (☎972 636702; ④), in the nondescript new quarter of town, which also does meals. **Buses** stop right in front of the post office, while the **Turismo** (June & Sept Mon–Sat 10am–2pm & 5–8pm; July & Aug daily 9am–2pm & 3–8pm; ☎972 667857) is on the road out to Torroella de Montgrí.

Torroella de Montgrí and L'Estartit

TORROELLA DE MONTGRÍ, 9km beyond Pals on the Ter River, was once an important medieval port which has been left high and dry by a receding Mediterranean. It now stands 5km inland, beneath the shell of a huge, battlemented thirteenth-century castle (a stiff thirty-minute walk away), and remains distinctly medieval in appearance with its narrow streets, fine mansions and fourteenth-century parish church. Oddly, only a couple of coachloads of tourists a day come to look round, and hardly anyone stays. If you do decide to **stay**, the *Fonda Mitja*, at Plaça d'Església 14 (☎972 758003; ③), just off the arcaded Plaça de la Vila, is excellent, and there are several other *hostales* scattered about town; for a list, there is tourist information in the police station at Avda. Lluís Companys 51 (Mon–Fri 8.30am–1.30pm & 4–7pm; ☎972 758300).

The town is probably best known for its annual **classical music festival**, held over July and August in the main square and church. Advance bookings can be made from early June at the Festival Internacional de Música, Apt 70, Codina 28 (☎972 761098, fax 972 760648).

The nearest beach is 6km to the east at **L'ESTARTIT**, a typical Costa Brava resort, though one with a quieter, more family-oriented atmosphere than many. There's a wide, though not particularly stunning, beach, and boat services to the nearby **Illes Medes**, Catalunya's only offshore islands. These form a protected nature reserve, hosting the most important colony of herring gulls in the Mediterranean, numbering some 8000 pairs. There are hourly **buses** from Torroella to L'Estartit.

L'Escala and Empúries

From either Palafrugell or Figueres you're only 45 minutes by bus from **L'ESCALA**, a small holiday resort at the southern end of the Golfo de Roses. On nothing like the

Nuestra Señora del Pilar, Zaragoza   La Virgen statue, Las Fallas, Valencia

Pyrenean foothills near Hecho, Aragon

Roof terrace of Gaudí's La Pedrera, Barcelona

Mosaic lizard, Parc Guell, Barcelona

La Manzana de la Discòrdia, Barcelona

Parade of *gigantones*, Valencia

Casa Figueres shop front, Barcelona

Cadaqués, Costa Brava

Beach scene, Mallorca

Renaissance courtyard, Palma, Mallorca

same scale as the resorts to the south, it caters mainly for local tourists, which means that the steeply sloping streets and rocky coastline are genuinely appealing. L'Escala's proximity to the archeological site of **Empúries** (Ampurias), which lies just a couple of kilometres out of town, is a considerable further attraction. One of Spain's most interesting sites, Empúries's fascination derives from the fact that it was occupied continuously for nearly 1500 years. You can see the ruins in a leisurely afternoon, spending the rest of your time either on the crowded little sandy **beach** in L'Escala or on the more pleasant duned stretch in front of the ruins. The wooded shores around here hide a series of lovely cove-beaches with terrific, shallow water and soft sand. At weekends the woods are full of picnicking families, setting up tables, fridges and gas stoves from the backs of their cars. L'Escala is also widely known for its canning factories where Catalunya's best **anchovies** are packaged. You can sample them in any bar or restaurant, or buy small jars to take home from shops around town.

L'Escala practicalities

Buses all stop on Avinguda. Girona, just down the road from the **Turismo** at Plaça de las Escueles (July & Aug Mon–Sat 9am–1pm & 4–9pm, Sun 10am–1pm; Sept–June Mon–Sat 9am–1pm & 4–7pm, Sun 10am–1pm; ☎972 770603). Here, you can pick up a map, local bus timetables – for Figueres, Palafrugell, Girona and Barcelona – and an up-to-date list of hotels. Drivers can find **free parking** at the football stadium on Cami Ample, around the corner from the bus stop, near the campsite.

Accommodation

L'Escala usually has plenty of **rooms** available, mostly in the streets sloping back from the sea, around the central Plaça Victor Català. Of these streets, Carrer de Gràcia has the most choice. There are **campsites** at each of the little bays that surround L'Escala, or – in the centre of town – at *Cami Ample* (☎972 770084; April–Sept), which is down the hill and right from the bus stop.

Alberg Les Coves, Les Coves 41 (☎972 771200, fax 972 771572). Popular youth hostel with campsite attached, right on the beach by the ruins. Price includes breakfast; other meals are available. Advance booking is advised. Closed mid-Dec to mid-Jan. ①.

Hotel Ampurias, La Platja Portitxol (☎972 770207). Located practically on the beach near the archeological sites. ③.

Hotel Mediterrà, c/Riera 22–24 (☎972 770028). Relaxed and comfortable hotel; prices drop outside July and Aug. ③.

Hostal Poch, c/de Gràcia 10 (☎972 770092). Friendly *hostal* just off the seafront. ③.

Hostal Torrent, c/Riera 28 (☎972 770278). Friendly, clean and good value. ③.

Eating, drinking and entertainment

The best deals for food are in the **restaurants** attached to the small hotels and *hostales*. Both the *Poch* and *Mediterrà* have decent menus, while the shabby *Hostal Riera* at the top of c/de Gracia (no. 20) is a bit hit-and-miss but at best serves very tasty meals for around 1300ptas. The restaurant at the *Hostal Garbi*, just back from the beach at c/Sant Maxima 7, is more formal, but still affordable, while if you're missing *tapas*, you can get a wide choice at the *Taberna Gallego*, c/Gràcia 77.

Otherwise, there are sea views with the food at any of the bars and restaurants overlooking the town beach, but bear in mind that you'll often pay through the nose for the privilege, particularly if you occupy one of the appealing cliff-top seats. As for **entertainments** other than beach-going, a *sardana* (Catalan folk dance) is held on the seafront every Wednesday night in July and August.

Empúries: the site

Empúries was the ancient Greek *Emporion* (literally "Trading Station"), founded in 550 BC by merchants who, for three centuries, conducted a vigorous trade throughout the Mediterranean. In the early third century BC, their settlement was taken by Scipio, and a Roman city – more splendid than the Greek, with an amphitheatre, fine villas and a broad marketplace – grew up above the old Greek town. The Romans were replaced in turn by the Visigoths, who built several basilicas, and *Emporion* disappears from the records only in the ninth century when, it is assumed, it was wrecked by either Saracen or Norman pirates.

The **site** (June–Sept Tues–Sun 10am–7.15pm; Oct–May Tues–Sun 10am–6pm; 400ptas) lies behind a sandy bay about 2km north of L'Escala. The remains of the original **Greek colony**, destroyed by a Frankish raid in the third century AD – at which stage all moved to the Roman city – occupy the lower part of the site. Among the ruins of several temples, to the left on raised ground, is one dedicated to *Asklepios*, the Greek healing god whose cult was centred on Epidavros and the island of Kos. The temple is marked by a replica of a fine third-century BC statue of the god, the original of which (along with many finds from the site) is in the Museu Arqueològic in Barcelona. Nearby are several large cisterns: *Emporion* had no aqueduct so water was stored here, to be filtered and purified and then supplied to the town by means of long pipes, one of which has been reconstructed. Remains of the town gate, the **agora** (or marketplace, in the centre) and several streets can easily be made out, along with a mass of house foundations, some with mosaics, and the ruins of Visigoth basilicas. A small **museum** (300ptas) stands above, with helpful models and diagrams of the excavations as well as some of the lesser finds. Beyond this stretches the vast but only partially excavated

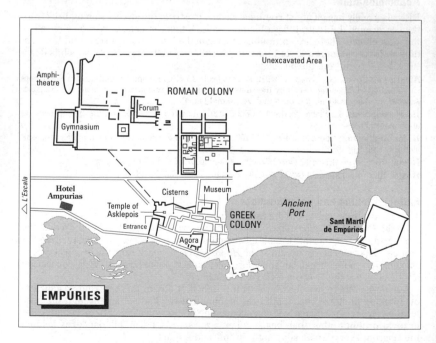

Roman town. Here, two luxurious villas have been uncovered, and you can see their entrance halls, porticoed gardens and magnificent mosaic floors. Further on are the remains of the **forum, amphitheatre** and outer walls.

Sant Marti d'Empúries

A short walk along the shore from the site brings you to the tiny walled hamlet of **SANT MARTI D'EMPÚRIES**. What was once a lovely, decaying place has been entirely taken over by visiting tourists who descend upon the shaded bar-restaurants in the square for lengthy lunches. Though it's still undeniably pretty, there are usually too many people around for comfort – generally, it's less oppressive in the evenings, when Sant Marti can still be perfect for a drink amid the light-strung trees. From the walls outside the village you can see the whole of the Golfo de Roses, with kilometre after kilometre of beach stretching right the way round to Roses itself, glinting in the distance. The only place to stay is *Hotel Riomar* (☎972 770362; May–Sept; ⑦), next to the beach, which requires you to take half-board.

Figueres and around

The northernmost resorts of the Costa Brava are reached via **FIGUERES**, a provincial town with a population of some 30,000. Although it's the capital of Alt Empordà – the upper part of the massive alluvial plain formed by the Muga and Fluvià rivers – it would pass almost unnoticed were it not for the **Museu Dalí**, installed by Salvador Dalí in a building as surreal as the exhibits within. As it is, Figueres itself tends to be overshadowed by the museum, which is the only reason most people come here. Stay longer and you'll find a pleasing town with a lively central *rambla* and plenty of cheap food and accommodation. It's also a decent starting point for excursions into the little-visited **Albères mountains** to the north, which form part of the border with France.

Arrival, information and accommodation

Arriving at the **train station**, you reach the centre of town by simply following the "Museu Dalí" signs. The **bus station** is just a couple of minutes' walk up on the left, at the top of Plaça Estació above the train station. There's a small **tourist information booth** just outside the bus station (June–Sept Mon–Sat 9.30am–1pm & 4–7pm), and a full-blown **Turismo** at the other end of town, on Plaça del Sol, in front of the Post Office building (July & Aug daily 9am–9pm; rest of the year varies; ☎972 503155). Both dish out a town map, handy hotel lists, and timetables for all onward transport.

Accommodation

There's a good choice of **places to stay**, ranging from the most basic to the more upmarket; though many of the better hotels and *hostales* lie on the main roads out of town. Best-value budget accommodation is *Pensión Bartis*, c/Méndez Núñez 2 (☎972 501473; ②), not far from the train and bus stations; if you want to be more central, *Pensión Isabel II*, c/Isabel II 16 (☎972 504735; ③) and the very cheap – if slightly shabby – *Bar La Vinya*, c/Tins 18 (☎972 500049; ②), are both handy for the museums. Near the top right-hand corner of the Rambla is the friendly *Pensión La Venta del Toro*, c/Pep Ventura 5 (☎972 510510; ②). For more comfort, try *Hostal España*, c/Jonquera 26 (☎972 500869; ④), which offers good discounts out of the summer season. On the other side of town, *Hostal Fenix*, Via Emporitana 3 (☎972 503185; ③), is friendly and relaxed. There's a good youth hostel off the Plaça del Sol, *Alberg Tramuntana*, c/Anicet Pagès

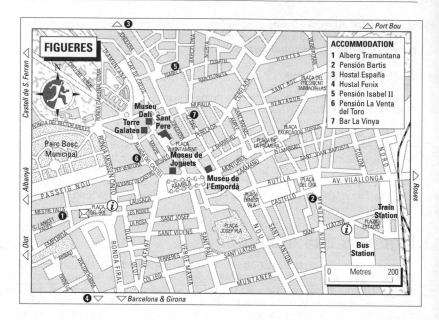

2 (☎972 501213; ①; closed Sept) and a clean, good-value campsite, *Pous* (☎972 675496; closed Nov & Dec), 2km out on the road to France.

The Museu Dalí

The **Museu Dalí** (July–Sept daily 9am–7.15pm, plus 10.30pm–12.30am in Aug, 1200ptas; Oct–June Tues–Sun 10.30am–6pm, 1000ptas) is the most visited museum in Spain after the Prado, a real treat, appealing to everyone's innate love of fantasy, absurdity and participation. Dalí was born in Figueres in 1904 and gave his first exhibition here when he was just fourteen. In 1974, in a reconstruction of the town's old municipal theatre, the artist inaugurated his Museu Dalí, which he then set about fashioning into an inspired repository for some of his most bizarre works. Having moved back to Figueres at the end of his life, Dalí died here on January 23, 1989; his body now lies behind a simple granite slab inside the museum.

Although it does contain paintings (some by other artists) and sculpture, the thematically arranged display is not a collection of Dalí's "greatest hits" – those are scattered far and wide. Nonetheless, what you do get beggars description and is not to be missed.

The very building (signposted from just about everywhere, on Plaça Gala i Salvador Dalí, a couple of minutes' walk off the Rambla) is an exhibit in itself, as it was designed to be. Topped by a huge metallic dome and decorated with luminous egg shapes, it gets even crazier inside. Here, the walls of the circular central well are adorned with stylized figures preparing to dive from the heights, while you can water the snail-infested occupants of a steamy Cadillac by feeding it with coins. There's also a soaring totem pole of car tyres topped with a boat and an umbrella. Climb inside to the main building and one of the rooms contains an unnerving portrait of Mae West, viewed by peering through a mirror at giant nostrils, red lips and hanging tresses. Other galleries on various levels contain a complete life-sized orchestra, skeletal figures, adapted furniture (a bed with fish tails), sculpture and ranks of surreal paintings.

DALÍ: WHOSE LIFE IS IT ANYWAY?

Controversy surrounds **Salvador Dalí**'s final years, with some observers believing that he didn't so much choose to live as a recluse as find himself imprisoned by his three guardians. Dalí suffered severe burns in a fire in 1984, after which he moved into the Torre Galatea, the tower adjacent to the museum. Fitted with a pacemaker and suffering psychological problems, Dalí became increasingly depressed, and several Spanish government officals and friends fear that, in his senile condition, he was being manipulated. In particular, it's alleged that he was made to sign blank canvases – and this has inevitably led to the questioning of the authenticity of some of his later works. Since the mid-1980s, there has been a series of trials in the US based on charges that various individuals have exploited bogus prints and lithographs. In 1990, two Americans, William Mett and Marvin Wiseman, were found guilty of art fraud – in particular of promoting spurious Dalí reproductions – and were fined nearly $2 million and sentenced to three years in prison.

The divison of his legacy of (genuine or otherwise) paintings is made yet more complicated by the fact that Dalí, by the terms of his last will made in 1982, left his entire estate, valued at $130 million, to the Spanish state, with the works of art to be divided between Madrid and Figueres. The Catalan art world was outraged, and promised a battle to keep the canvases from being carted off to Madrid – plans are underway to exhibit over a hundred of the paintings in an as yet undecided location in Catalunya.

Around the rest of town

After the museum, the main sight in town is the huge seventeenth-century **Castell de Sant Ferran**, 1km northwest of the centre – follow Pujada del Castell from just beyond the Dalí museum, going straight on at the roundabout along c/Al Castell de Sant Ferran. This was the last bastion of the Republicans in the Civil War, when the town became their capital after the fall of Barcelona. Earlier in the war, it had been used as a barracks for newly arrived members of the International Brigades before they moved on to Barcelona and the front: the sculptor Jason Gurney, in his *Crusade in Spain*, recorded how he slept in the dungeons but was still excited enough to describe it as the "most beautiful barracks in Spain . . . the building, and its setting in the Pyrenean foothills . . . exquisite". The castle is still in use by the military, but the five-kilometre circuit around the outside of the star-shaped walls makes a good walk.

Back in the centre, pavement cafés line the Rambla, and you can browse around the art galleries and gift shops in the streets and squares surrounding the church of Sant Pere. There are two more museums, too. The **Museu de l'Empordà** at Rambla 2 (July–Sept Mon–Sat 11am–1pm & 4–9pm, Sun 5–9pm; Oct–June Mon–Sat 11am–1pm & 3.30–7pm, Sun 11am–2pm; free), has some local Roman finds and work by local artists, and the **Museu de Joguets** (same hours as Museu de l'Empordà; free) further up the Rambla on the same side, is a toy museum with over 3000 exhibits from all over Catalunya. The statue at the bottom of the Rambla is a monument to Narcis Monturiol, a local who distinguished himself by inventing the submarine.

Eating and drinking

A gaggle of tourist **restaurants** is crowded into the narrow streets around the Dalí museum, particularly along c/Jonquera. Here you'll be able to find a decent *menú del día*, while the cafés on the Rambla are good for snacks and sandwiches. For a food treat, head for the *Hotel Duran,* at c/Lausaca 5, at the top of the Rambla, where they serve generous regional dishes with a modern touch; it's expensive but has an excellent reputation. Eating aside, Figueres is generally fairly comatose **at night**: on weekend evenings there are traffic jams on the road to Roses as everyone heads out to the coast.

North of Figueres: the Albères mountains

The region north of Figueres, which encompasses the **Albères mountains**, is virtually unknown to foreigners; a slow-moving mix of semi-ruined villages hidden among resin-scented hills, dotted with occasional vineyards, olive groves and shady cork plantations. During World War II the area was so deserted that there were no Guardia Civil stationed in the area, which made the eastern Albères a favoured escape route from France. These days, local bus services from Figueres can take you to a few of the more accessible villages, though as departures are only once or twice a day you may have to stay overnight.

The Maçanet region

One of the best routes is to **SANT LLORENÇ DE LA MUGA**, 15km northwest of Figueres, near the shore of a reservoir that looks huge on the map but turns out to be less impressive in the flesh. Across the other side of the reservoir, **MAÇANET DE CABRENYS** (linked to Sant Llorenç by a long hiking trail) looks down on wetlands that are a haven for herons. There are two or three *hostales* here, including the *Cal Ratero* – also known as *Hostal Oliveros* – c/de les Dòmines 6 (☎972 544068; ⑤ including full board), just off the main square. The village is also linked directly with Figueres by bus – the service passing through **DARNIUS**, where there's another place to stay, the *Darnius*, Cra. de Maçanet 19 (☎972 535117; ③). Maçanet is much the livelier of the two places.

The Espolla region

Northeast of Figueres, a daily bus heads for **ESPOLLA**, which boasts at least ten prehistoric sites in the immediate area. Easiest to find is the **Dolmen de la Cabana Arqueta**, dating from around 2500 BC; from Espolla take the **Sant Climent** road, and at the rising bend 1km beyond the village turn down the farm track to the right – the dolmen is ten minutes' walk on. The most important, however, is the **Dolmen del Barranc**, the only carved tomb yet found in the area; it lies 3km from the village off the track leading north to the Col de Banyuls.

Espolla itself is an authentic Alt Empordà village, its shuttered houses crammed into a labyrinth of streets that buzz each year with the flurry of the grape harvest. The only accommodation here is the friendly, family-run *La Manela*, at Plaça del Carmé 7 (☎972 563065; ②), which also cooks good, inexpensive meals with a substantial *menú* at 1000ptas.

The Golfo de Roses

The **Golfo de Roses** stretches between L'Escala and Roses, a wide bay backed for the most part by flat, rural land, well-watered by the Muga and Fluvia rivers. Left to its own quiet devices for centuries, it's quite distinct from the otherwise rocky and touristy Costa Brava, and has really only suffered the attention of the developers in towns at either end of the bay, most notably in the few kilometres between the marina-cum-resort of Ampuriabrava and Roses. Probably the most you'll do is cross the attractive farmlands on your way to or from Figueres, but there are a couple of specific targets if you want to avoid the beach for a while, as well as the excellent beach itself at the resort of Roses.

Parc Natural dels Aiguamolls de l'Empordà

Halfway around the bay is one of Spain's newest and most accessible nature reserves, the **PARC NATURAL DELS AIGUAMOLLS DE L'EMPORDÀ**. Made up of two blocks of land, one on either side of Ampuriabrava, it encompasses what's left of the Empordà marshland, which once covered the entire plain of the Golfo de Roses, but has gradually disappeared over the centuries as a result of agricultural developments and cattle-raising. Relying heavily on the botany students of Barcelona University and volunteers, the park looks a little raw in places, but attracts a wonderful selection of birds to both its coastal terrain and the paddy fields typical of the area. There are several easy paths around lagoons and marshes, and hides have been created along the way: morning and early evening are the best times for bird-watching in the marshes and you'll see the largest number of species during the migration periods (March–May & Aug–Oct).

Entrance to the park is free, and routes to follow around it are all marked on a brochure that you can pick up at the **information centre** at El Cortalet (daily: March–Sept 9.30am–2pm & 4.30–7.30pm; Oct–Feb 9.30am–2pm & 3.30–6pm; ☎972 454222), on the road between Castelló d'Empúries and Sant Pere Pescador (see below). To get the most out of the park, take a pair of binoculars – and in summer and autumn you'll need mosquito repellent. The only **camping** allowed within the park is at the massive "first-class" *Nàutic Almatà* (☎972 454477, fax 972 454686; May–Sept).

Sant Pere Pescador and Torroella de Fluvià

The nearest village to the park is **SANT PERE PESCADOR**, 3km south of the information centre. The village is easily reached by SARFA bus from Figueres and there are also services from Palafrugell, L'Escala and (once-daily) Girona. Despite being a drab place in the middle of nowhere, the village is relatively developed, and this does at least mean that there's plenty of choice if you need to spend the night here: there are half a dozen *hostales* and hotels (most open only from June–Sept), and several bars and restaurants. There's also a bike rental shop.

The Figueres–Palafrugell bus also makes a stop in the little village of **TORROELLA DE FLUVIÀ**, 4km southwest of Sant Pere, where there's a lovely country house, *El Sugué*, at c/de Sant Pere Pescador 1 (☎972 550067; ③), which takes guests. You can cook for yourself here if you wish, though the owners will provide good Catalan and vegetarian meals for anyone who wants them.

Castelló d'Empúries

The delightful small town of **CASTELLÓ D'EMPÚRIES**, halfway between Roses and Figueres and connected to both by very frequent buses, makes a much more attractive base for the park – and indeed is worth a stop in passing anyway. A five-minute walk from the main road where the bus drops you, transports you into a little medieval conglomeration, astride the Riu Muga, that's lost little of its genteel charm despite being so close to the beach-bound hordes. Formerly the capital of the Counts of Empúries, the town's narrow alleys and streets conceal some fine preserved buildings, a medieval bridge, and a thirteenth-century battlemented church, **Santa María**, whose ornate doorway alone is reward enough for the trip.

The nature reserve lies around 5km south, reached on the minor road to Sant Pere Pescador, and the beach at Roses is also close by – only fifteen minutes away by bus. There are several **places to stay** and while prices are a little higher here than usual, it's a price worth paying for the peace and quiet when the day-trippers have all gone home. On the way into the village, *Fonda Ca l'Avi*, Rambla 52 (☎972 250507; ④), is one of the least expensive options, while *Hostal Canet* (☎972 250340, fax 250607; ④) enjoys a fine position on Plaça Joc de la Pilota. Both these places serve food – a meal on the terrace of the *Canet* is particularly good value. There are also two places next to each other on the main road, near where the bus stops, which are much nicer than their position suggests. The *Hostal Ca L'Anton* (☎972 250509; ④) has parking facilities, and an attached restaurant with a fine *menú del día* and plenty of local cuisine. The slightly cheaper, very smart *Fonda Serratosa* (☎972 250508; ④) also has a dining room.

Roses

ROSES itself enjoys a brilliant situation, beneath ruined medieval fortress walls at the head of the grand, sweeping bay. It's a site that's been inhabited for over three thousand years – the Greeks called the place *Rhoda*, when they set up a trading colony around the excellent natural harbour in the ninth century BC – but apart from the castle, the extensive ruined citadel and the surviving sections of the city wall, there's little in present-day Roses to hint at its long history. Instead, the town trades exclusively on its four kilometres of sandy beach, which have fostered a large and popular water-sports industry. Roses is a full-blown resort, with the usual supermarkets, discos and English breakfasts; if you're staying, apart from the beach action, one of the better entertainments is to take the bus ride to more attractive Cadaqués (see below), which runs across the plain and up over the bare hills giving superb views back over the resort and bay. Another option is a **boat trip**: there are regular excursions to Cadaqués or the Illes Medes throughout the summer.

Buses stop outside the post office, with the town centre and restaurants to the left, hotel blocks to the right. There's a **Turismo** (daily: June–Sept 9am–9pm; Oct–May 9am–1pm & 4–8pm; ☎972 257331) on the seafront promenade, and any number of **hotels** and *hostales* in the town; all are marked on the map given away by the Turismo, but, as ever, many are likely to be booked solid throughout the summer. Out of town, there are several enormous **campsites** on the road between Roses and Figueres.

Cadaqués and around

CADAQUÉS is a far more pleasant place to stay, accessible only by the steep winding road over the hills behind Roses and consequently retaining an air of isolation. With box-like, whitewashed houses lining the narrow, hilly streets, a tree-lined promenade and craggy bays on either side of a harbour that is still a working fishing port, it's genuinely picturesque. Sitting on the seafront, you can watch the fishermen take their live catches straight to the restaurant kitchens. In the 1960s Salvador Dalí built a house on the outskirts of the town (see below) and for some years Cadaqués became a distinctly hip place to be, hosting an interesting floating community. Over the last few years, though, it has been "discovered" and is now too trendy for its own good. Nonetheless, Cadaqués remains accessible. There are beautiful people around and more than a few Mercedes, but it all falls far short of, say, a South-of-France snobbery. Out of season Cadaqués could be great and even in midsummer – if you can bear the company and the high prices – you'll probably have fun.

The **beaches** are all tiny and pebbly, but there are some fine local walks around the harbour and nearby coves, while the town itself makes for an interesting tour, clambering around the streets below the church. The number of private art galleries here has mushroomed since the moneyed set began stopping by, and a couple of good museums soak up browsers, too: the **Museu Perrot-Moore**, in the middle of town at c/Vigilant 1 (daily 10.30am–1.30pm & 4.30–8.30pm; 700ptas), has paintings, drawings and graphics by Dalí and Picasso, while the **Museu Municipal d'Art** on c/Monturiol (daily 11am–1.30pm & 3–8pm; 700ptas), features work by local artists whose efforts are mostly inspired by the spectacular local coastline.

Arrival and information

Buses stop at the little SARFA bus office on c/Sant Vicens, on the edge of town. It's less than ten minutes from here, following c/Unió and c/Vigilant, to the central beach and square. Just off the square, the **Turismo** is at c/des Cotxe 2 (July–Sept Mon–Sat 9.30am–2pm & 4–9pm, Sun 10am–1pm; Oct–June Mon–Sat 5–7pm; ☎972 258315).

Accommodation

Finding **rooms** is likely to be a big problem unless you're here outside peak season: a town plan posted at the bus stop marks all the possibilities. The cheapest rooms are at one of three *fondas* scattered about the town: *Fonda Vehí*, c/de l'Església 5 (☎972 258470; ③), has the best position, just below the church, but is open only from June to September. Just back from the main square, very close to the seafront, the *Hostal Marina* (☎972 258199; ④) and *Hostal Cristina* (☎972 258138; ④), the latter with parking facilities, are the next step up – similarly priced, with more expensive rooms with bath, too, and discounts out of season. The *Cristina* won't accept reservations, so there's usually a good chance of a room in high season if you arrive early enough. *Hostal Ubaldo*, on the way into town from the bus stop at c/Unió 13 (☎972 258125; ⑤), is quite good value with all rooms en suite. There's a noisy **campsite** (☎972 258126; mid-April to late-Sept) on the road to Port Lligat, a steep 1km out of town; it also rents out cabins for around 4400ptas a double, with shower.

Eating

The harbourside promenade is lined with pizzerias and **restaurants**, all offering the same kind of deals. If you're not sick of it yet, then Cadaqués is a nice place to sit outside and dive into a paella, which most places offer as part of a *menú del día*. One very attractive possibility is *El Pescador* on c/Nemesi Llorens, which is around the harbourside, to the right as you face the water. There's an elegant two-floored dining room, or seats outside, an authentic Catalan paella (with seafood, sausage and spare ribs) and a 1800ptas *menú del día*. On Avda. Caritat Serinyana, which is the main road running away from the water, the *Don Quijote* (no. 6), has pleasant courtyard seating and a *menú del día* for 2100ptas.

Around Cadaqués: the Casa-Museu Salvador Dalí

A well-signposted twenty-minute walk north of Cadaqués lies the tiny harbour of **PORT LLIGAT**, former home of Salvador Dalí. The artist lived here with his wife and muse, Gala, having converted a series of waterside fishermen's cottages into a sumptuous home that has all the quirks you would expect of the couple, such as speckled rooftop eggs and a giant fish painted on the ground outside. The house is now open to the public as the **Casa-Museu Salvador Dalí** (June–Sept Mon–Sat 9.30am–2pm & 4–9pm, Sun 10am–1pm; Oct–May Mon–Sat 10am–1pm & 4–8pm; 1200ptas), and although there's not much in the way of artworks, and visitor numbers are strictly controlled (you're given an entry time on your ticket), it's worth the wait to see first-hand how the bizarre couple lived until Gala's death in 1982, after which Dalí moved to Figueres.

Tours take in most of the house, and include Dalí's studio, the exotically draped model's room, the couple's master bedroom and bathroom, and, perhaps best of all, the oval-shaped sitting-room that Dalí designed for Gala, which, apparently by accident, boasts stunning acoustics. Upstairs you can see the garden and swimming pool where the couple entertained guests – they didn't like too many strangers trooping through their living quarters. The phallic swimming pool and its various decorative features, including a giant snake and a stuffed lion, are a treat.

El Port de la Selva and Sant Pere de Rodes

Inexplicably, there is no bus service north of Cadaqués and you are forced to backtrack to Figueres for onward transport. Alternatively, you can venture to make the relatively easy 13-kilometre walk/hitch across the cape, **Cap de Creus**, from Cadaqués to **EL PORT DE LA SELVA**, at which point you're back on a bus route. An intensive fishing port set on the eastern side of a large bay, El Port de la Selva isn't terribly enticing, its beaches and campsites mainly used by families who retire early for the night. The town does, however, allow access to Sant Pere de Rodes (see below), the most important monastery in the region. From Selva de la Mar, 2km above the port, a good dirt road takes you right there (a further 4km), or you can approach from Vilajüiga on the Figueres–Portbou rail line, an eight-kilometre walk from the monastery.

If you need to **stay** there are a few choices: the *Fonda Sol y Sombra*, c/Nou 8 (☎972 387060; ④), requires you to take half-board, while the more expensive *Hotel Porto Cristo*, at c/Major 59 (☎972 387062; ⑦), is about twice the price, though good value out of season. Perhaps the most attractive place is the *Hostal L'Arola* (☎972 387005; ④), right on the beach opposite the turning to Selva de la Mar. The views from the *hostal* are unbeatable, and it's not too expensive for a room without a bath as the price includes half board. There are also three **campsites** all within 2km of the beach.

Sant Pere de Rodes

The Benedictine monastery of **Sant Pere de Rodes** (July & Aug Tues–Sun 10am–7pm; Sept–June Tues–Sun 9am–1.30pm & 3–6pm; 200ptas) was one of the many religious institutions founded in this area after the departure of the Moors. Legend has it that, with Rome threatened by barbarians, Pope Boniface IV ordered the Church's most powerful relics – including the head of St Peter – to be hidden. They were brought to this remote cape for safe-keeping and hidden in a cave, though when the danger had passed the relics couldn't be found. A monastery was duly built on the site and dedicated to St Peter. More certainly, the first written record of the monastery dates back to 879, and in 934 it became independent, answerable only to Rome: in these early years, and thanks especially to the Roman connection, the monks became tremendously rich and powerful, administrating huge territories. At the same time they aroused local jealousy, so that from the beginning there were disputes between the monastery and the feudal lords of the surrounding country. As the monastery was enlarged it was also fortified against attack, starting a period of splendour that lasted four hundred years before decadence set in. Many fine treasures were looted when it was finally abandoned in 1789, and it was also pillaged by the French during the Peninsular War; some of the rescued silver can be seen in Girona's Museu d'Art.

The monastery may originally have been built over a pagan temple dedicated to the Pyrenean Venus, *Afrodita Pyrene* – a theory based on a second- or first-century BC Egyptian map, written narratives of the third and fourth centuries AD, and the discovery of fragments of pagan sculptures and Corinthian capitals in the area. Whatever its origins, the daunting ruins are a splendid sight, with the monastery-church universally recognized to be the precursor of the Catalan Romanesque style. The eleventh-century columns in the barrel-vaulted nave are decorated with wolves' and dogs' heads, and there's an irregular cloister adjacent to the church.

Nearby is the pre-Romanesque church of **Santa Elena**, all that stands of the small rural community which grew up around the monastery. Above the monastery (and contemporary with it) stands the very ruined **Castell de Sant Salvador**, of which only the walls remain. This provided the perfect lookout site for the frequent invasions (French or Moorish), which normally came from the sea. In the event of attack, fires were lit on the hill to warn the whole surrounding area.

Llançà

The train line from Barcelona finally joins the coast at **LLANÇÀ**, 8km north of El Port de la Selva and a handier base for touring. Once a small fishing town, Llançà has been opened up to the passing tourist trade by the road and rail route to France – and is shameless in its attempts to cash in. Unlike many such towns, however, it does have compensatory attractions. The beach is a good 2km from the train station (the buses stop outside), but the **old town** is much closer, just off to the right – set back so far from the water to escape the attentions of pirates. A tiny Plaça Major houses an outsize Romanesque church (currently under restoration) and the renovated remains of a later defensive tower, which houses an exhibition (summer daily 10am–1pm & 6–9pm; winter Sat & Sun 4–6pm) of photographs of bygone Llança.

The road down to the **port**, where there's a market each Wednesday, is lined with dozens of restaurants, souvenir shops and miniature golf courses. At the end, though, you'll still find a proper working port and a coarse sandy beach, all reassuringly undeveloped and concrete-free.

Practicalities

There are nine **buses** a day to Llançà from El Port de la Selva in the summer (only two in winter); the **Turismo** (June & Sept Mon–Sat 10am–1pm & 4.30–8pm, Sun 10am–1pm; July & Aug Mon–Sat 9.30am–9pm, Sun 10am–1pm; Oct–May Mon–Fri 10am–1pm & 5–8pm, Sat 10am–1pm & 5–7pm, Sun 10am–1pm; ☎972 380855) is on the road into town. For **accommodation**, there are some cheap *habitaciones* and *hostales* in the old town, or you can stay down at the harbour. Try the pleasant *Habitaciones Can Pau*, c/Puig d'Esquer 4 (☎972 380271; ③), as an example of the former; or the harbourside *Pensión Miramar*, Passeig Marítim 7 (☎972 380132; ④). There are two **campsites** signposted on the way in from the train station: *L'Ombra* (☎972 380335; open all year) and the smaller *Camping Llansa* (☎972 380485; mid-June to Aug).

A couple of recommended **restaurants** are the pricey *La Brasa*, Plaça de Catalunya 6 (open March–Nov), which specializes – as its name suggests – in grilled meat and fish, and a seafood restaurant, *Can Manel*, Paseo Marítimo 9 (closed Thurs in winter), which is a bit cheaper.

Colera

At Llançà you can pick up trains heading for Portbou. At several, usually inconvenient, times throughout the day these will also stop at **COLERA**, only a few kilometres to the north. One of the smallest villages left on this coast, it seems little frequented by passing drivers – partly, one suspects, because it's easy to miss; you need to turn off at the sign to Sant Miquel, Colera's official name. There's only fitful development here, and it's mostly locals using the very pebbly beaches. The water is clean and clear (despite the town's name), and quite safe for children to splash about in. For all these reasons it makes a pleasant stop, at least for lunch: there are a couple of pricey **restaurants** overlooking the beach and harbour, or some more reasonable, equally congenial, alternatives in the village square, Plaça Pi i Margall.

If you want to **stay**, *Hostal Bon Repos*, just off the square at c/Francesc Ribera 12 (☎972 389012; ④), is an adequate place to sleep and eat, while you've also the choice of a couple of more upmarket *hostales* down by the two small beaches. The well-kept *Hostal La Gambina* (☎972 389172; ⑥) is right on the seafront, and discounts its rooms out of season. There's also a good **campsite**, *Sant Miquel* (☎972 389018; April–Sept), set well back from the beach, just off the main road.

Portbou

PORTBOU, 7km farther north, and only 3km from the French border, is a fine place to approach by road, over the hill and around the bay. It's even worth walking from

Colera (it takes around two-and-a-half hours) and suffering the initial steep climb to enjoy the view down over the green hills, deep blue water and small, pebbled beach. Close up, it's still a very pretty place, with a natural harbour and stone beach used by the local fishermen to mend their nets. There are some excellent outdoor **restaurants**, both in the backstreets of the old town and lining the quay, none of them outrageously expensive; you can get an excellent meal here for around 1200ptas. And you can spend the rest of your day pottering around the little coves nearby, reached on footpaths scratched out of the rocks and all clean and relatively uncrowded.

If you arrive on the **train** the massive station with its souvenir stalls creates entirely the wrong impression, although it is true that the railway has transformed the place. Before the Barcelona–Cerbère line came into operation, Portbou was a small fishing village; now it's a stop on the dash in and out of Spain, getting much of its trade from French tourists who come to stock up on booze and souvenirs before crossing straight back into France. Other visitors include those killing the afternoon hours before the night train from Cerbère to Paris, certainly a better way to pass the time than sitting in the Cerbère station bar.

Practicalities

There's a **Turismo** (May–Sept daily 9am–8pm; ☎972 125161) right at the harbour, which has a map and list of **hotels** to give away; staff here are friendly and more than willing to help with recommendations. The rock-bottom choice in town is the *Hostal Comercio*, Rambla de Catalunya 16 (☎972 390001; ③), on the pleasant *rambla* close to the beach – friendly, welcoming and utterly run-down, with no hot water. Around the harbour, and just back from the sea, *Hostal Juventus*, Avda. de Barcelona 2 (☎972 390241; ③), has small, basic quarters for a similar price, or there are much better rooms with bath at the pleasant *Hotel Comodoro* (☎972 390187; ④), one block from the beach at c/Méndez Núñez 1. If you want to overlook the sea, you're going to have to pay a little more: try *Hostal Costa Brava,* c/Cervera 20 (☎972 390386; June–Oct; ⑤), whose rooms with bath are at the top of this price category, those without at the bottom.

There's a similarly wide choice when it comes to **eating**. Of the restaurants along the seafront promenade, Passeig de la Sardana, *L'Ancora* serves a fabulous seafood paella; it also serves beer in virtual buckets if you're set for an afternoon's chat with the barman. Other great seafood establishments are at the *Hostal de Francia*, c/del Mar 1, and the *Tauro*, on Avinguda. de Barcelona (the Figueres road). A particularly attractive setting for breakfast or an afternoon drink is the garden-courtyard of the *Hotel Comodoro*. For sandwiches, or just a drink, *Casa David* in the main Plaça del Mercat has popular outdoor seating, and over the road is the little **market** hall itself, open in the mornings for picnic fixings.

The road **border crossing** into France is open 24 hours from mid-June to September, but closes from midnight until 7am for the rest of the year.

GIRONA AND AROUND

Just an hour inland from the coast, the city of **Girona** with its medieval core provides a startling and likeable contrast to the wilder excesses of the Costa Brava. It's easy to make the day trip here from the coast, or from Barcelona (to which it's connected by regular trains and buses), but it really warrants more time than that – two or three nights in Girona would show you the best of the city and let you enjoy some of the striking surrounding countryside. The quickest trip is to the lakeside town of **Banyoles**, only half an hour from Girona, and it's not much farther on to beautiful **Besalú**, one of the oldest and most attractive of Catalan towns.

To see more of the province of which Girona is capital you have to head for **Olot**, an hour and a half west of the city, at the heart of the **Garrotxa** region. Much of this is an ancient volcanic area, now established as the **Parc Natural de la Zona Volcànica**, whose rolling, fertile countryside is pitted with spent craters. Some of these are within the town boundaries of Olot itself, but the best of the scenery is around the village of **Santa Pau**, just to the east. North of here, and also close to Olot, **Castellfollit de la Roca** is the starting point for several good treks which take you into the foothills of the nearby Pyrenees.

In the other direction, south towards Barcelona, those with a little more time can veer off into the mountainous **Serra del Montseny**, whose spa towns and precipitous roads are a restful diversion – though one you'll find easiest to see if you have your own transport, since buses are infrequent.

Girona

The ancient, walled city of **GIRONA** stands on a fortress-like hill, high above the Riu Onyar. It's been fought over in almost every century since it was the Roman fortress of *Gerunda* on the Via Augusta, and, perhaps more than any other place in Catalunya, it retains the distinct flavour of its erstwhile inhabitants. Following the Moorish conquest of Spain, Girona was an Arab town for over two hundred years, a fact apparent in the maze of narrow streets in the centre, and there was also a continuous Jewish presence here for six hundred years. The intricate former Jewish quarter of houses, shops and community buildings is now visible again after centuries of neglect. By the eighteenth century, Girona had been besieged on twenty-one occasions, and in the nineteenth it earned itself the nickname "Immortal" by surviving five attacks, of which the longest was a seven-month assault by the French in 1809. Not surprisingly, all this attention has bequeathed the city a hotch-potch of architectural styles, from Roman classicism to *modernisme*, yet the overall impression for the visitor is of an overwhelmingly beautiful medieval city, whose attraction is heightened by its river setting.

Considering Girona's airport serves most of the Costa Brava's resorts, the city can seem oddly devoid of tourists, which makes browsing around the streets and cool churches doubly enticing. It's a fine place, full of historical and cultural interest, and one where you can easily end up spending longer than you'd planned. There are two or three excellent museums and a cathedral that's the equal of anything in the region. Even if these leave you unmoved it's hard to resist the lure of simply wandering the superbly preserved medieval streets, fetching up now and again at the river, above which high blocks of pastel-coloured houses lean precipitously on the banks.

Arrival and information

Girona's **airport**, 13km south of the city centre, is used mainly for Costa Brava charter flights; there's no bus into town, so you'll have little choice but to take a taxi which will cost around 2000–2500ptas. Most arriving passengers are bussed direct to their resorts, an hour away to the east. The **train station** is at Plaça d'Espanya, across the river in the new part of the city – from here, it's a twenty-minute walk into the old centre, where you're most likely to want to stay. The **bus station** is around the back of the train station, with frequent services to the Costa Brava and inland to towns in Girona Province and beyond. This is also where international buses from London and other parts of western Europe stop (for route information, phone the numbers given in "Listings", p.659). Girona's old town area is compact and easily explored on foot. Buses cover the greater city; but you're more likely to use a **taxi** for short hops – there are ranks at the train station, Plaça Catalunya and Plaça Independencia.

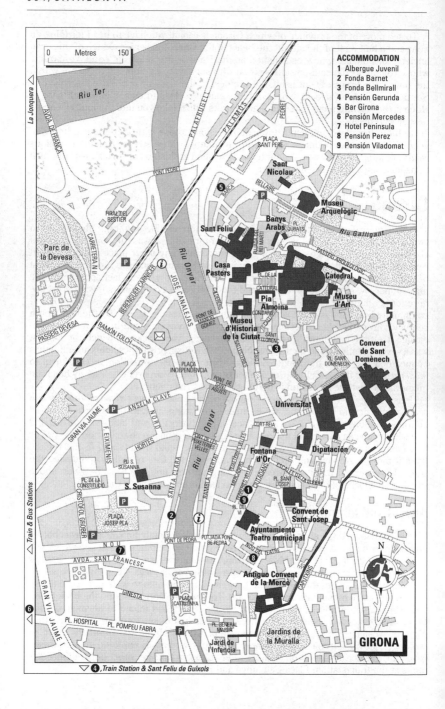

ACCOMMODATION
1 Albergue Juvenil
2 Fonda Barnet
3 Fonda Bellmirall
4 Pensión Gerunda
5 Bar Girona
6 Pensión Mercedes
7 Hotel Peninsula
8 Pensión Perez
9 Pensión Viladomat

GIRONA

There's a **Turismo** inside the train station (July & August Mon–Sat 9am–2pm), while the main office is at Rambla de la Llibertat 1 (Mon–Fri 8am–8pm, Sat 8am–2pm & 4–8pm, Sun 9am–2pm; ☎972 226575), right on the river at the southern end of the old town. Both offices have useful maps and accommodation lists, English-speaking staff, and bus and train timetables for all onward services.

Accommodation

There are plenty of **places to stay** in Girona, including one or two *hostales* near the train station, though if you arrive at any reasonable time during the day it's much better to look for a place in or near the old town, which is also where you'll find the youth hostel. The nearest **campsite** is at Fornells de la Selva, 8km south of town and open all year (☎972 476117), with excellent amenities and an English-speaking proprietor, though you might prefer to camp at livelier Banyoles, half an hour by bus to the west (see p.659).

Albergue Juvenil, c/dels Ciutadans 9, off Plaça del Vi (☎972 218121 or 972 218003). Girona's youth hostel has a good old town location and smart new facilities, including laundry, TV and video; reception open 8–11am and 6–10pm; breakfast included in the price, dinner available. But note that it's hardly any better value than the very cheapest of the *hostales*, and if you're over 25 it's actually more expensive. ①–②.

Fonda Barnet, c/Santa Clara 16 (☎972 200033). In a shambolic old block facing the river from the west side, near the Pont de Pedra. Basic rooms above the *comedor*, separate showers. ③.

Pensión Bellmirall, c/Bellmirall 3 (☎972 204009). Attractive *pensión*, close to the cathedral and nicely turned out, with stone walls, artefacts and paintings. There are only seven rooms (with and without bath), so book ahead. The price includes breakfast. ④.

Pensión Gerunda, c/de Barcelona 34 (☎972 202285). Just to the right of the train station, on the main road, this reasonably priced standby is handy for late arrivals, though the rooms are somewhat claustrophobic. ③.

Bar Girona, c/Barca 31 (☎972 210998). Cheap, cheerful and situated in the less salubrious end of the old town, this bar has six rooms, all with bathrooms. Also has a pretty cheap *menú del día* at only 900ptas. ③.

Pensión Mercedes, c/de Barcelona 99 (☎972 203028). Family-run *pensión*, close to the station, right in front of El Corte Ingles. ②.

Hotel Peninsular, c/Nou 3 (☎972 203800, fax 972 210492). Well-located (if rather bland) hotel on a busy shopping street, near the bridge and river. One advantage is a roof that affords excellent views of the old town. Cheaper rooms without bath also available. ③–⑤.

Pensión Pérez, Plaça Bell-lloc 4 (☎972 224008). The most basic rooms (mainly singles) in Girona, in a very gloomy building in an even gloomier part of town. It's off c/Nou del Teatre, just over Pont de Pedra. ②.

Pensión Viladomat, c/Ciutadans 5 (☎972 203176). Popular place whose airy rooms (with bath) fill quickly in July and Aug due to its very central location. At the bottom end of its price category. Breakfast available for 350ptas. ③.

The City

Although the bulk of modern Girona lies on the west side of the Riu Onyar, bordered to the north by the large riverside Parc de la Devesa, most visitors spend nearly all their time in the **old city**, over the river. This thin wedge of land, tucked under the hillside, contains all the sights and monuments, and as it takes only half an hour or so to walk from end to end it's easy to explore thoroughly. A zone of high walls, stepped streets, closed gates and hidden courtyards, the old city has been zealously preserved. Recent restorations mean that many of the oldest buildings and arcades now house trendy galleries, exclusive shops, restaurants and bars. But here and there – around a corner or up a side alley – real life goes on much as it's always done, in local bars and shops.

The cathedral

The centrepiece of the old city is Girona's **Catedral** (summer Tues–Sat 10am–2pm & 4–6pm, Sun 10am–2pm; winter opening hours vary), a mighty Gothic structure built on to the hillside and approached by a magnificent flight of seventeenth-century Baroque steps. This area has been a place of worship since Roman times, and a Moorish mosque stood on the site before the foundation of the cathedral in 1038. Much of the present building dates from the fourteenth and fifteenth centuries, but a few earlier parts can still be seen – including the eleventh-century north tower, the Torre de Carlomagno ("Carlemany" in Catalan), and the Romanesque cloisters with their exquisite sculpted capitals.

The main facade, remodelled in the eighteenth century, bursts with exuberant decoration: faces, bodies, coats-of-arms, and with Saints Peter and Paul flanking the door. Inside, the cathedral is awesome – there are no aisles, just one tremendous single-naved Gothic vault with a span of 22m, the largest in the world. This emphasis on width and height is a feature of Catalan Gothic with its "hall churches", of which, unsurprisingly, Girona's is the ultimate example. Contemporary sceptics declared the vault to be unsafe, and building went ahead only after an appeal by its designer, Guillermo Bofill, to a panel of architects. The huge sweep of stone rises to bright stained glass, the only thing obstructing the grand sense of space being the enormous organ, placed there a century ago.

You can visit the cloisters by buying a ticket to the **Museu Capitular** (summer Tues–Sat 10am–2pm & 4–6pm, Sun 10am–2pm; winter opening hours vary; 400ptas), inside the cathedral, which in this case is certainly a good idea. The museum is rich in religious art, including a perfect *Beatus* illuminated by Mozarabic miniaturists in 975, and the famous eleventh- to twelfth-century *Creation Tapestry* in the end room – the best piece of Romanesque textile in existence, depicting in strong colours the months and seasons, and elements of the earth. The irregularly shaped **cloisters** themselves (1180–1210) boast minutely carved figures and scenes on double columns, while steps lead up to a chamber above full of ecclesiastical garb and adornments.

The Museu d'Art

If you find the collection in the cathedral's museum remotely interesting, the large **Museu d'Art** (Tues–Sat 10am–7pm, winter closes 6pm, Sun 10am–2pm; 200ptas) is well worth a visit; it's housed on the eastern side of the cathedral in the restored Episcopal Palace. The early rooms deal with Romanesque art, including some impressive *Majestats* (wooden images of Christ wrapped in a tunic) taken from the province's churches, and there are relics here from the monastery of Sant Pere de Rodes, too. Among the manuscripts on display are an eleventh-century copy of Bede and an amazing martyrology from the Monastery of Poblet. The collection then progresses chronologically as you climb the floors, passing a room of bright fifteenth-century *retables* (their intricate scenes almost 3D in effect), some splendid *Renaixement* works – such as a lovely set of sixteenth-century liturgical items – and nineteenth- and twentieth-century Catalan art on the top two floors. Here you'll find some fine nineteenth-century Realist works, as well as pieces by the so-called Olot School of artists (better represented in the museum at Olot itself; p.666), and even examples of local *modernista* and *noucentista* art.

Around Sant Feliu

Climb back down the cathedral steps for a view of one of Girona's best-known landmarks, the blunt tower of the large church of **Sant Feliu**, whose huge bulk backs on to the narrow main street. Shortened by a lightning strike in 1581 and never rebuilt, the belfry tops a hemmed-in church that happily combines Romanesque, Gothic and Baroque styles; you can usually get in for a look around in the morning and late afternoon.

The streets behind the church, by the river, are a bit more down-at-heel than most in the neighbourhood; c/de la Barça is typical, with its bare bars and grocery stores. There's even a red-light area of sorts, though that's rather overstating the importance of the couple of hidden stairways and the odd loitering person. In any case, it's not at all threatening and provides a contrast with the streets just on the other side of Sant Feliu church, which have undergone a genteel transformation. Walk along arcaded c/Ballesteries and you'll immediately see the difference – the ancient houses along here have been converted into swish gallery space and antique shops.

Tho Banys Arabs

Close to Sant Feliu, through the twin-towered Portal de Sobreportas below the cathedral, are Girona's so-called **Banys Arabs** (April–Oct Tues–Sat 10am–7pm, Sun 10am–2pm; Nov–March Tues–Sun 10am–2pm; 200ptas), a civil building probably designed by Moorish craftsmen in the thirteenth century, a couple of hundred years after the Moors' occupation of Girona had ended. They are the best preserved baths in Spain after those at Granada and show a curious mixture of Arab and Romanesque styles. The layout, a series of three principal rooms for different temperatures, with an under-floor heating system, is influenced ultimately by the Romans. The cooling room (the *frigidarium*) is the most interesting; niches (for your clothes) and a stone bench provide seats for relaxation after the steam bath, while the room is lit, most unusually, by a central skylight-vault supported by octagonally arranged columns.

The Museu Arqueològic and the city walls

From the cathedral square, the main street, Pujada Rei Marti, leads downhill to the Riu Galligans, a small tributary of the Onyar. The **Museu Arqueològic** (Tues–Sat 10am–1pm & 4.30–6pm, Sun 10am–2pm; 200ptas) stands on the far bank in the former church of Sant Pere de Galligans, a harmonious setting for the varied exhibits. The church itself holds Roman statuary, sarcophagi and mosaics, while the beautiful Romanesque cloisters contain the heavier medieval relics, such as inscribed tablets and stones, including some bearing Jewish inscriptions. These are the best parts of the museum, since the graceful form of the church adds much to the visit; perhaps in recognition of this, there's a full-size copy of the church's ornate twelfth-century rose window planted amidst the Roman finds. The extensive rooms above the cloisters go on to outline rather methodically the region's history from Paleolithic times to the Romanization of the area: unless you read Spanish or Catalan you'll get little out of the lines of exhibit-filled cases and explanatory maps.

From the museum you can gain access to the **Passeig Arqueològic**, where steps and landscaped grounds lead up to the walls of the old city. There are fine views out over the rooftops and the cathedral, and endless little diversions into old watch towers, down blind dead-ends and around crumpled sections of masonry. The walls and the little paths lead right around the perimeter of the city, with several other points of access or egress along the way: by the Banys Arabs, behind the Sant Domènec convent, and down by Plaça Catalunya at the southern end of the old city.

Carrer de la Força and the Call

Quite apart from its Roman remains and Arab influences, Girona also contains the best preserved **Jewish quarter** in western Europe. There is evidence that Jews settled in Girona before the Moorish invasion, although the first mention of a real settlement – based in the streets around the cathedral – dates from the end of the ninth century. Gradually, the settlement spread, having as its main street the c/de la Força, which in turn followed the course of the old Roman road, Via Augusta. The area was known as the **Call** and at its height was home to around three hundred people who formed a sort of independent town within Girona, protected by the king in return for payment. From the eleventh century onwards, however, the Jewish community suffered systematic and escalating persecution, with attacks on them and their homes by local people: in 1391 a mob killed forty of the Call's residents, while the rest were locked up in a Roman fortress until the fury had subsided. For the next hundred years, until the expulsion of the Jews from Spain in 1492, the Call was effectively a ghetto, its residents restricted to its limits, forced to wear distinguishing clothing if they did leave, and prevented from having doors or windows opening on to c/de la Força.

For an idea of the layout of this sector of tall, narrow houses and maze-like interconnecting passages, visit the **Centre Bonastruc Ça Porta**, formerly the Centre Isaac el Cec (July & Aug Tues–Sat 10am–8pm, Sun 10am–2pm; Sept–June Tues–Sat 10am–6pm, Sun 10am–2pm; free), which is signposted (to *Call Jeue*) up the skinniest of stepped streets off c/de la Força. Opened to the public in 1975, the complex of rooms, staircases, a courtyard and adjoining buildings off c/de Sant Llorenç is an attempt to give an impression of the cultural and social life of Girona's medieval Jewish community – this was the site of the synagogue (though the exact spot hasn't yet been identified), the butcher's shop and the community baths. Work is still going on here, with other nearby alleys currently sealed off but awaiting re-opening, and there's an information office on the site, a café and a quiet place just to sit and contemplate the difficulties of a life confined to these dark nooks and crannies.

The Museu d'Historia de la Ciutat

A little way back up c/de la Força, at no. 27, the **Museu d'Historia de la Ciutat** (Tues–Sat 10am–2pm & 5–7pm, Sun 10am–2pm; 100ptas, free Sun) completes Girona's set of museums. For casual, non-specialist browsing it's the most rewarding of the lot, housed in an eighteenth-century convent. Remains of the convent's cemetery are visible as you enter, with niches reserved for the preserved bodies of the inhabitants. The rest of the collection is fascinating, less for the insights into how Girona developed as a city – though this is explained efficiently through text, exhibits and photos – than for the strange, miscellaneous bits and pieces displayed. A circuit of the rooms shows you old radios from the 1930s, a 1925 Olivetti typewriter, a printing press, cameras, machine tools, engines and a dozen other mechanical and electrical delights.

Eating and drinking

Girona's chic **bars** and **restaurants** are grouped on c/de la Força, on and around the riverside Rambla Llibertat and on the parallel Plaça del Vi – the last two places are also where you'll find the best daytime cafés with outdoor seating. Another little enclave of restaurants with good *menús del día* is over the river in Plaça de la Independencia. For something less touristy – and much less expensive – explore the streets near Sant Feliu church, where there's a run of old-men's bars and some inexpensive *comedors*. Carrer Ballesteries, nearby, is more upmarket: the trendy *La Terra*, at no. 23, with window seats looking out over the river, is typical of the places Girona's youth frequent. During the summer there are also some pricey open-air bars along Terrejes de Noche, next to the Parc de la Devesa, which have live music or dancing from Wednesday to Saturday.

Restaurants

Boira, Plaça de la Independencia 17. The best food on the square and very popular with locals and visitors alike – 1100ptas or so buys a very Catalan *menú*.

Bar-Restaurant Força Vella, c/de la Força 4. The best value on this central street, with a big budget *menú del día* served in the stone-walled *comedor* behind the bar. The waiter rattles off plenty of choices to hungry local workers from 1 to 4pm and also in the evening.

La Crêperie Bretonne, Cort Reial 14. A piece of France in Girona. Delicious crêpes for 450–800ptas and while you wait for your food you can use the crayons provided to draw on the tablecloths.

Fonda Barnet, c/Santa Clara 16. The *comedor* of this *fonda* is the best value in Girona, and the food, though hardly gourmet, is much better than the fairly basic surroundings suggest.

La Penyora, c/Nou del Teatre 3. Staunchly Catalan restaurant hidden away and worth seeking out. There's a 1500ptas *menú del día* and a reasonable if limited à la carte choice. Closed Tues.

La Polenta, Cort Reia l6 (☎972 209374). This tiny vegetarian restaurant serves delicious organic grub and is always busy. Look at paying around 550–1000ptas per plate. Closed Sun and Aug.

Bars and cafés

Antiga, Plaça del Vi 8. Marble-tabled *xocolateria*, with a good line in cakes, *orxata* and other delights.

L'Arcada, Rambla Llibertat 38. Bar-restaurant situated underneath the arcade serves good breakfast pastries. Outdoor tables are a nice place to relax in summer though you'll pay for the privilege.

Café Bistrot, Pujada de Sant Domènec. Snacks, crêpes and drinks either outside on the steps below the church, or inside in cool, jazzy surroundings.

Cafetería Sol, Plaça del Vi. Stylish and friendly hang-out for *tapas* and snacks, with seats inside or in the arcade.

Excalibur, Plaça de l'Oli 1. Friendly bar, frequented by both ex-pats and locals, and decorated in the Spanish idea of traditional English style. Guinness and bitter on tap, and a fine international selection of bottled beers.

Listings

Airport Call ☎972 186600 for flight information.

Banks and exchange There's an exchange office at the train station, and you'll find banks along the Rambla Llibertat.

Buses From the bus station (☎972 212319), there are Rafael Mas services (☎972 213227) to Lloret de Mar; SARFA (☎972 201796) to Tossa, Palafrugell and Sant Feliu; Teisa (☎972 200275) to Olot; and Barcelona Bus (☎972 202432) express services to Barcelona and Figueres. International bus services are run by Eurolines, Via and Julia (all on ☎972 211654).

Car rental Most agencies are close to the train station on c/Barcelona: Avis (☎972 206933) and Hertz (☎972 210108). Local companies such as Cabeza (☎972 218208) are much cheaper, though all cars have to be returned to Girona.

Emergencies Dial ☎092 or contact the Cruz Roja (☎972 222222).

Hospital Hospital Doctor Trueta, Avda. França 60 (☎972 202700).

Newspapers British and American newspapers available at the train station and at shops along Rambla Llibertat.

Police Policia Municipal at c/Bacià 4 (☎972 204526 or 092); Guardia Civil (☎972 201100).

Post office At Avda. Ramón Folch 2; Mon–Sat 8am–9pm.

Train information RENFE information on ☎972 207093.

Banyoles

For an escape into the countryside around Girona, take a bus to **BANYOLES**, half an hour (17km) north of the city. Here, the Pyrenees are on the horizon and the town basks around its greatest attraction – the **lake**, famed for its enormous carp. The lake has been under state protection since 1951, something that kept Banyoles little developed until it was announced that the 1992 Olympic rowing events would be held here. Most of the lakeside closest to town was consequently redeveloped, with tourist boats, new hotels and fancy restaurants much in evidence. Even so, it remains an attractive place to visit, with an old town which has escaped much of the recent building and plenty of opportunities for walking around the lake on shaded footpaths, beyond the new development.

Arrival, information and accommodation

Buses all stop on Passeig de la Industria, with the bus office (where you buy onward tickets) nearby at the corner of the main road, c/Álvarez de Castro. Cross this road and signs point you down to Plaça Major, two minutes' away. The **Turismo** is in the other direction, along Passeig de la Industria at no. 25 (Mon–Fri 10am–2pm & 4.30–7.30pm, Sat 10am–2pm; June–Aug also open Sat afternoon & Sun 10am–2pm; if shut you can get leaflets from the *Ajuntament* next door; ☎972 575573) – and the lake ten minutes further away. For local **trekking information**, the Centre Excursionista de Banyoles, c/del Puig 6, near Sant Esteve, seems to be open most evenings and has a wide range of maps available and tips on local routes.

With Girona so close, there is no advantage in staying in Banyoles, whose **hotels** are expensive anyway. If you do want to stay – and the prospect of a lakeside hotel in summer might persuade you – the Turismo can give you an accommodation list. The most pleasant old town hotel is *Fonda Comas*, c/del Canal 19 (☎972 570127; ④), off Plaça dels Estudis, near the Darder museum: this immaculate building, with stone staircases and its own courtyard and restaurant, has nice rooms with and without bath (closed Sat in winter). **Camping** is perhaps a more attractive proposition here than in most places. There's a large site, *El Llac* (☎972 570305), which you'll pass on the walk to Porqueres, just before the church, and a few more in the vicinity – ask at the tourist office.

The Town

Banyoles grew up around a monastery originally founded by Benedictines in 812. This, the **Monestir de Sant Esteve** at the eastern end of town, is still easily the biggest structure in old Banyoles, and though it's usually locked, you might try asking around for the key holder who lives nearby. If you do get in, don't miss the magnificent fifteenth-century *retablo* by Joan Antigo. The medieval streets which lead back into town from here are full of other ancient buildings, including an almshouse and a dye market. In the end, all streets lead to the central **Plaça Major**, a lovely tree-lined, arcaded space with several café-bars and a Wednesday market that has been held here since the eleventh century.

From the square, signs point the way to the **Museu Arqueològic Comarcal** (July & Aug daily 10.30am–1pm & 4.30–8pm; Sept–June Tues–Sun 10.30am–1.30pm & 4–6.30pm; combined ticket with Museu Municipal Darder d'Historia Natural 250ptas), installed in a fourteenth-century poorhouse in Plaça de la Font. The museum used to contain the famous jawbone of a pre-Neanderthal man found in the nearby Serinya caves, but nowadays you have to make do with a replica: authentic specimens include Palaeolithic tools, and bison, elephant and lion bones, all found locally. The **Museu Municipal Darder d'Historia Natural** (same hours as Museu Arqueològic; combined ticket 250ptas), in nearby Plaça dels Estudis, has a useful display of local flora and fauna.

The lake itself – the **Estany de Banyoles** – is a fifteen-minute walk from Plaça Major. It's long been used for water sports, so the Olympic choice wasn't surprising, and although there's little that's distinctive or attractive about the area nearest the centre, a thirty-minute walk through the woods around the southern edge takes you to the tiny hamlet of **PORQUERES**, where the water is at its deepest (63m). Here the elegant Romanesque church of **Santa María** was consecrated in 1182 and has a barrel-vaulted interior, and unusual capitals with plant and animal designs. The lake itself boasts a whole series of **boating** options – cruises, rowing boats and pedaloes – all of which run to a few hundred pesetas for an hour's fooling about on the water.

Eating and drinking

There are plenty of places to **eat and drink** in the old town. The *menú del día* at the *Fonda Comas* is 1500ptas, and usually very good, while cheaper meals are served at *Les Olles*, Plaça dels Estudis 6, whose main attraction is an English-language menu offering such rare treats as "Coptel Toad Fish" and "Pork Cheeks". Eating in the hotel-restaurants overlooking the lake is more expensive, though the *Mirallac*, Passeig Darder 50, won't break the bank as long as you eat meat rather than fish. The best place for an evening drink or just a sandwich is Plaça Major, whose café-bars spill under the medieval arcades.

Besalú

From the road, the imposing eleventh-century bridge by the confluence of the Fluvià and Capellada rivers is the only sign that there is anything remarkable about **BESALÚ**, 14km north of Banyoles (and connected by regular daily buses). But walk a couple of minutes into the town and you enter a medieval settlement virtually untainted by tourism – probably the most attractive and interesting small town in Catalunya, perfect for a half-day's outing.

Although the restorers' cement is barely dry in places, the steep narrow streets, dusty squares and dark archways exude a sense of history. Besalú was an important town from early times, and, when the Moors were expelled from this corner of Spain, it was one of several independent kingdoms that arose to fill the vacuum. Despite a total population of just eight hundred it prospered, as it had done in a small way since Roman times, and remained a place of importance well into the fourteenth century. In appearance the town is almost completely medieval, boasting some striking monuments quite out of proportion to its current humble status. Unfortunately, most of the churches and sights in Besalú are firmly locked due to renovation work – not a great disappointment in a place where just strolling around is a real pleasure – but if you ask at the Turismo, they might be able to arrange a visit if you are especially keen or you are in a group.

Arrival, information and accommodation

The **bus** stop is on the main Olot–Banyoles road, from where the quickest way into the centre is to walk down the main road towards the *Hotel Siqués* (see below) and then turn right down the little street that leads past the back of Sant Vicenç straight into Plaça Llibertat. The **Turismo** is on Plaça de la Llibertat 1 (daily 10am–2pm & 4–7pm; ☎972 591240), where you can pick up a map and plan your tour.

The town has three very comfortable and quite reasonable **places to stay**, a very attractive proposition, as in the daytime Besalú is prey to whirlwind coach parties, while by early evening it has settled down to its own infinitely preferable pace of life. The *Hotel Siqués* (☎972 590110; ③) is at Avda. Lluís Companys 6, on the main road just down from the bus stop; the *Residencia María* (☎972 590106; ③ including breakfast) is better positioned, right on Plaça Llibertat; while the best budget choice is perhaps the *Fonda Venència*, c/Major 8 (☎972 591257; ③), which is very spick and span and at the lower end of the price scale.

The Town

The most striking reminder of Besalú's grandeur is the splendid eleventh-century **Pont Fortificat** – fortified bridge – over the river Fluvià. In the middle stands a fortified gate-house complete with portcullis. Down to the left beyond the bridge the **Miqwé**, or Jewish bath-house, was originally attached to a synagogue positioned in the old Jewish quarter in the heart of the lower town, along the riverbank.

Plaça **Llibertat**, in the centre of Besalú, is entirely enclosed by medieval buildings, including the elegant thirteenth-century Casa de la Vila, which now houses the *Ajuntament*. There's a weekly **market** in the square each Tuesday. The majestically porticoed c/Tallaferro leads up from here to the ruined shell of **Santa María** (you can't get inside), which for just two years (1018–20) was designated Cathedral of the Bishopric of Besalú; union with Barcelona meant the end of its short-lived episcopal independence.

In the other direction, the twelfth-century monastery church of **Sant Pere** is the sole remnant of the town's Benedictine community, which was founded in 977. It stands in its own square, El Prat de Sant Pere, from where the most eye-catching feature is the window in the otherwise severe main facade, flanked by a pair of grotesque stone lions. Across the square – almost all of which has been heavily restored over the last few years – is the **Casa Cornellà**, a rare example of a Romanesque domestic building, which houses a museum of assorted antique domestic and agricultural implements. Elsewhere in the web of cobbled streets radiating from Plaça Llibertat, you'll come across other attractive buildings – many sporting stone flourishes, ornate windows and columns. Finally, you can work your way around to the delightful little church of **Sant Vicenç**, close to the main Olot–Banyoles road in a plant-decked square with a café-restaurant and outdoor seating. The church (its entrance arches decorated with mythical monsters) is a lovely example of Catalan Romanesque.

Eating and drinking

For **meals**, the *Hotel Siqués* has an enormous *menú del día* for around 1100ptas (closed Mon Nov–Easter), while at the *Curia Reial* (closed Tues and Feb), you can sit on the out-door terrace next to the square, or on the beautiful patio at the rear overlooking the bridge. Eating at both places can lead to rather large bills if you don't have the *menú del día*. Cheaper meals can be found at the *Can Quei*, Plaça Sant Vicenç 4, outside the church of the same name, where there's a 900ptas *menú del día*, as well as sandwiches and *platos combinados*. *Pont Vell*, c/Pont Vell 28, is much more expensive (around 3000ptas a head), but beautifully situated, with outdoor tables more or less under the bridge.

The Garrotxa region

Besalú is on the eastern edge of the lush and beautiful **GARROTXA REGION**, bisected by the Fluvià River and the main C150 road. The northern part – the **Alta Garrotxa** – is an area of deserted farms set amid low mountains, bursting with attractive trekking possibilities. The bus runs through Alta Garrotxa on its way from Besalú to Olot – the main town of the Garrotxa region, described on p.666 – and in parts the route is spectacular, as at **Castellfollit de la Roca**, where the houses peer over a sheer basalt cliff. South of the Fluvià lies volcanic **Baixa Garrotxa**, where over ten thousand years of erosion have moulded the dormant cones into rounded and fertile hills. The tiny C524, from Banyoles to Olot via **Santa Pau** (an infrequent bus route), takes in the terrific walking in the **Parc Natural de la Zona Volcanica** and the remnants of the great beech wood known as **La Fageda d'en Jorda**.

Alta Garrotxa: around Castellfollit de la Roca

Fourteen kilometres west of Besalú, along the C150, **CASTELLFOLLIT DE LA ROCA** presents its best aspect as you climb up the main road to the village. It's built on the edge of a precipice that falls sixty metres sheer to the Fluvià river, with the church crowded by houses onto the very rim of the cliff. It's an impressive sight from a distance (even more so at night, when spotlights play on the natural basalt columns), but as you pass through the village itself on the busy main road you could be forgiven for wondering what happened: it's a dirty, dangerous bottleneck, with tightly packed rows of grubby brown buildings which give no hint of anything out of the ordinary.

If you're in no hurry to reach Olot, however, you can get off the bus to take in the view from the top of the village over the edge of the cliff. Walk down past the clock tower, by the *fonda* on the main road, and you'll come out by the church at the head of the cliff, which juts out above the valley for a kilometre or more. Having gasped at the drop, and poked around the huddled houses, you can simply hang around for the next bus to Olot, or you could walk on to nearby Sant Joan les Fonts. Thrill-seekers will also want to stay long enough to view Castellfollit's unlikely **Museum of Sausages** (Mon–Sat 9.30am–1.30pm & 4–8pm, Sun 9.30am–2pm & 4.30–8pm; free), which celebrates the local Sala family's 150 years in the skin-stuffing business. The family is almost certainly right in claiming the museum as unique.

Castellfollit is the starting point for some of the region's best **treks** (see below), heading north and northeast through the Alta Garrotxa. You could easily enough **stay** in Olot, but if you want an early start then the *Casa Paula*, Plaça de Sant Roc 3 (☎972 294032; ③), on the main road through Castellfollit, is very reasonable and has a restaurant and decent bar attached.

Alta Garrotxa treks

The **Alta Garrotxa** stretches north from the main C150 road as far as the peaks along the French border. For speleologists, the region is amost inexhaustible, with more than a hundred catalogued caves, and for walkers it's a fabulous area as well. Whichever of the three routes given below you follow (all begin just outside Castellfollit), the Editorial Alpina *Garrotxa* map is an invaluable aid.

It's around 7km from Castellfollit up the **Llierca valley** past **MONTAGUT DE FLUVIÀ** and another 6km on to **SADERNES** (minor road all the way), from where you can continue on the trail to the *Refugi de Santa Aniol*, right on the northern edge of the Garrotxa. From here, the Col de Massanes (1126m) border-crossing can be reached by continuing north on the footpath from the refuge, spending the next night at Coustouges or Saint-Laurent-de-Cerdans, both French villages in the Tech valley.

Staying in Spain, two more routes head northeast into the **Ripoll region**. If you take the paved road to **OIX** (9km), you've a choice of tracks towards Camprodon, either passing just north of the summits of El Tallo (1288m) and Puig Ou (1306m), or going on through the hamlet of Beget. The route continues through Rocabruna to Camprodon (see p.674), a day's hike all told. Alternatively, there's the shorter **Carreras valley** track to **SANT PAU DE SEGURIES** via the Col de Collcarrera; the only **place to stay** en route is the *Can Planes* (☎972 294478; ⑤ half-board), well before the pass, where you might be able to get a snack at short notice. At Sant Pau, you're on the Ripoll–Camprodon bus route.

Sant Joan les Fonts

For less energetic souls, **SANT JOAN LES FONTS** is no more than a three-kilometre walk from Castellfollit, along the less direct road to Olot. You'll soon see its enormous monastery-church in the distance, high above the river, and, although on a main road, the walk is scenic and enjoyable. Once in the village follow the signs to the *Columnes*

Basaltiques – basalt cliffs – and you'll cross the restored medieval bridge, which stands beneath the massive twelfth-century walls of the Romanesque Sant Esteve (usually locked). From the bridge, a path leads up along the right-hand side of the church and then snakes down to the impressive basalt cliffs, part of the *fonts*, or waterfalls, which give the village its name. It all makes for a very pleasant diversion, splashing around the rocks and river, having a drink in one of the small village bars – and afterwards you can either walk or hitch the 4km on to Olot, or wait for the bus, which passes through Sant Joan on its way from Besalú.

Baixa Garrotxa: along the C524

Most of the **Baixa Garrotxa** region – accessible on the minor C524 which runs between Banyoles and Olot – is volcanic in origin, and has been within the **Parc Natural de la Zona Volcanica de la Garrotxa**, which covers almost 12,000 hectares, since 1985. It's one of the most interesting such areas in Europe, the road passing through a beautiful wooded landscape, climbing and dipping around the craters, offering some lovely valley views. It's not, however, a zone of belching steam and boiling mud. It's been 11,500 years since the last eruption, during which time the ash and lava have weathered into a fertile soil whose luxuriant vegetation masks the contours of the dormant volcanoes. There are thirty cones in all in the area, the largest of them some 160m high and 1500m across the base.

If you don't have your own transport, you'll find **access** a little problematic, since the only **bus** is the twice-weekly Olot–Santa Pau–Banyoles service (currently Wed & Sat at 12.45pm from Banyoles, 6.15am from Olot) to Santa Pau, the central village of the volcanic zone. As it's certainly worth making the effort to see the region, you might consider instead **staying in Olot** (see p.666) and walking to Santa Pau from there – it's three hours by track and trail, with the added bonus of passing through the beautiful Fageda d'en Jordà beech forest.

THE GARROTXA REGION'S FLORA AND FAUNA

The lower slopes of the Garrotxa region's distinctive hills are clothed with evergreen oak **forests**, grading into deciduous oak and beech woods, with sub-alpine meadows and pastures at higher altitudes. More than 1500 species of vascular plant have been recorded within the park, ranging from typical **forest herbs** like snowdrops, yellow wood anemones and rue-leaved isopyrum to high-altitude specialities like ramonda and Pyrenean saxifrage. In addition, the Garrotxa contains a number of Iberian rarities, several of which are found nowhere else in the world: the white-flowered *allium pyrenaicum*, typical of rocky limestone cliffs, Pyrenean milkwort (*polygala vayredae*), a woody species with large pinkish-purple flowers, and shrubby gromwell (*lithodora oleifolia*), a scrambling plant with pale pink flowers that turn blue with age.

A phenomenal 143 species of **bird** have been observed in the region. Since three-quarters of the park is covered with forest, goshawks, tawny owls, short-toed treecreepers, great spotted woodpeckers and nuthatches are common. Flocks of bramblings and hawfinches take refuge in the beech woods during winter, while the more barren volcanic summits support alpine choughs and alpine accentors. Summer visitors include short-toed eagles, hobbies, wrynecks, red-backed shrikes and Bonelli's warblers, along with Mediterranean species such as sub-alpine warblers, golden orioles and bee-eaters.

Forest-dwelling **mammals** include beech martens, wildcats, genets, badgers and wild boar, as well as a number of small insectivores – common, pygmy and Etruscan shrews – and the noctural oak dormouse, characterized by its "Lone Ranger" mask and long, black-tufted tail. Otters are also sighted along the rivers from time to time.

Santa Pau

Medieval **SANTA PAU** presents to the outside world a defensive perimeter of continuous and almost windowless house walls. Inside the village, balconies drip with flowers, steps and walls are tufted with grass and huge potted plants line the pavement arcades – it's a village positively reeking with atmosphere, that would make a smashing base for some gentle local walking. Santa Pau is usually quiet, busy only on Sunday with trippers, who crowd into the local restaurants. The rest of the time you're likely to be on your own as you negotiate the cobbled alleys, which converge on the thirteenth-century arcaded Plaça Major, with its dark Romanesque church of Santa María and an information centre that's open only sporadically, but which is good for trekking information and for a free map of the volcanic zone.

In the square adjacent to Plaça Major, Plaçeta dels Balls, you'll find the *Cal Sastre* (☎972 680049; ⑤–⑦ half-board), which has seven **rooms** available, a decent restaurant, and tables outside in the medieval arcade which are just right for a beer. There are a couple of other places to eat in the village, but nowhere so nice to stay. If the *Cal Sastre* is full, you'll have to fall back on the less desirable alternative out of the village on the main road, or **camp**: *Lava* (☎972 680357; open all year) is 3km up the road towards Olot, a large, well-positioned site in the shadow of two volcanic cones.

A loop walk

An excellent way to get acquainted with the Baixa Garrotxa is to take a **loop walk** out of Olot which almost totally avoids paved roads and can easily be completed by any reasonably fit person in a single day. If you're not up for the full distance, you could arrange to be fetched at Santa Pau, roughly halfway.

Begin in Olot by following the multiple signposts directing you across the Riu Fluvià, from where it's an hour south along surfaced country lanes, equally suited to horse-riding or mountain-biking (as is most of this circuit), to the **Fageda d'en Jordà**. Although much reduced, this beech forest is still a treat in the autumn when the leaves are turning; it takes about half an hour more to emerge on the far side of the spooky, maze-like groves, deserted except for the tourist *carruatges* (horsecarts) visiting from Santa Pau.

Turn left when you meet the helpfully marked **GR2** long-distance trail, then right twice in succession when you encounter the track to Sa Cot. Follow the signposts to stay on the GR2, soon becoming a proper path as it heads east for thirty minutes to the medieval chapel of **Sant Miquel de Sa Cot**, a popular weekend picnic spot.

The **Volcà Santa Margarida** is visible just behind and, within forty minutes more, you should be up on its rim and then down into its grassy caldera, where another tiny chapel sits at the bottom. From the turn-off to the cone – just fifteen minutes from Sant Miquel – you descend to the **Font de Can Roure**, source of the only water en route, before skirting Roca Negra with its disused quarry, then entering Santa Pau 45 minutes from the shoulder of Santa Margarida, and some three hours from Olot (not counting the detour to the caldera).

From Santa Pau the GR2 continues north towards the scenic **Serra de Sant Julià del Mont**, just east of which are two **places to stay**: the English-run *Can Jou* (☎972 190263; ③ including breakfast, ④ half-board), over two hours from Santa Pau, and *Rectoria de la Miana* (☎972 590397; ③ including breakfast, ④ half-board), further east and housed in a twelfth-century monastery.

However, for day-trekkers, this would inconveniently lengthen the circuit, so you're best advised to bear west at **Can Mascou** and approach **Volcà Croscat** via the *Lava* campsite (see "Santa Pau"). You skirt the northeast flank of Croscat, badly scarred by quarrying, and from the campsite it's another hour, along a progressively narrowing track unsigned except for "BATET" painted on hunting-zone signs, to the high (720m) plateau of **Batet de la Serra**, scattered with handsome farms.

Here you meet a marked path-and-track coming west from the Serra de Sant Julià, turning west yourself to follow the road briefly before adopting the well-marked *camí* – beautiful and partly cobbled in basalt – which passes the hamlet of Santa María de Batet on its way down to Olot. It takes just under another hour of downhill progress, or a total of something less than seven hours, to emerge at the top of c/Sant Cristòfor, which runs right down to the main boulevard through Olot.

Olot

OLOT, the main town of the Garrotxa region, is a far nicer place than first impressions suggest. As you penetrate towards the centre, the industrial outskirts and snarling through-roads give way to a series of narrow, old town streets and a pleasant *rambla* where the inhabitants go about their prosperous business. The centre is largely made up of attractive eighteenth- and nineteenth-century buildings, evidence of the destructive geological forces that surround the town: successive fifteenth-century earthquakes levelled the medieval town, and – thankfully dormant but easily accessible – three small volcanoes can be seen just to the north, reminders of the volcanic zone beyond.

Olot makes a good base for the Garrotxa: Santa Pau, Sant Joan les Fonts and Castellfollit are all easily reached, and there's a good choice of food and accommodation. It's a position not lost on the local authorities who have done their best to counter Olot's previously rather dour tourist image – *Olot és natural* proclaim the noticeboards and, off the main roads, so it is.

Arrival and information

The **bus station** is on the main road through town and there's a **Turismo** right opposite on c/Bispe Lorenzana (Mon–Fri 9am–3pm & 5–7pm, Sat 10am–1pm & 5–7pm, Sun 11am–4pm; ☎972 260141), and another privately funded one farther down at c/Mulleras 33 (Mon–Fri 9am–1pm & 4–7pm; ☎972 270242) – take your pick. Both have English-speaking staff, contain a good stock of local brochures, maps and timetables, and hand out accommodation lists and information on the volcanic zone. More local **trekking information** can be had from the Centro Excursionista de Olot, irregularly open, next to the theatre on the Passeig d'en Blay; maps and guides are sold at the DRAC bookshop, at the bottom of the *passeig*.

Accommodation

Olot has a reasonable range of **places to stay**, with many central budget options. The closest **campsites** are the slightly noisy *Les Tries* (☎972 262405; May–Oct), 1km east of town on the way to Girona, and *La Fagueda* (☎972 271239; open all year), 4km out on the minor road to Santa Pau.

Alberg Torre Malagrida, Passeig de Barcelona 15 (☎972 264200). Youth hostel southwest of the centre overlooking the river, about halfway to the Casal dels Volcans. It's open 8–10am and 1pm–midnight and is closed Sept and Sun & Mon Oct–May. ①.

Pensión Narmar, c/Sant Roc 1 (☎972 269807). Very pleasant and well-located (off Plaça Major) *pensión*, with clean, modern rooms with sinks, and its own restaurant-patisserie downstairs. ③.

Hostal Sant Bernat, Ctra. de les Feixes 31 (☎972 261919). Although it's a bit out of the way towards the northeast end of town, this *hostal* is quiet and friendly and its garage makes it the best choice if you've got a car or a bike. Some rooms have bath. ③.

Hostal Stop, c/Sant Pere Màrtir 29 (☎972 261048). Large rooms with separate shower in this shabby-looking but good-value *hostal*. ③.

The Town

If you arrived by bus on the busy main through-road, the older streets nearby, between Plaça Major and Sant Esteve church, are a revelation. Filled with fashionable shops, art galleries and smart patisseries, they tell of a continuing wealth, historically based on textiles and the production of religious statuary. **Sant Esteve** lies right at the heart of town, built high above the streets on a platform, its tower a useful landmark. Beyond the church, the central **rambla**, Passeig d'en Blay, is lined with pavement cafés and benches, and adorned by the delightful nineteenth-century Teatre Principal. Between 6 and 8pm, this whole area teems with life as the well-dressed *passeig* swings into action.

Museu Comarcal de la Garrotxa

The substantial cotton industry that flourished here in the eighteenth century led indirectly to the emergence of Olot as an artistic centre: the finished cotton fabrics were printed with coloured drawings, a process that provided the impetus for the foundation of a Public School of Drawing in 1783. Joaquim Vayreda i Vila (1843–94), one of the founders of the so-called **Olot School** of painters, was a pupil of the school, but it was his trip to Paris in 1871 that was the true formative experience. There he came under the spell of Millet's paintings of rural life and scenery, and must have been aware of the work of the Impressionists. From these twin influences, and the strange Garrotxa scenery, evolved the distinctive and eclectic style of the Olot artists.

Some of the best pieces produced by the Olot School can be seen in the town's excellent museum, the **Museu Comarcal de la Garrotxa** (11am–2pm & 4–7pm, closed Sun afternoon & Tues; 300ptas), which occupies the third floor of a converted eighteenth-century hospital at c/Hospici 8, a side street off c/Mulleras. The first part of the museum traces the development of Olot through photos and models of its industries. The bulk of the collection, though, is work by local artists and sculptors, and it's an interesting and diverse set of paintings and figures. There's characteristic work by Ramón Amadeu, whose sculpted rural figures are particularly touching; Miquel Blay's work is more monumental, powerfully influenced by Rodin, while Joaquim Vayreda's *Les Falgueres* is typical of the paintings in its recreation of the Garrotxa light. By way of contrast – and indicative of a continuing artistic tradition in the town – there's also a room of modern ironwork sculpture and a few striking postwar paintings.

Jardí Botànic and the Casal dels Volcans

A twenty-minute walk from the centre are the town's landscaped botanical gardens, the **Jardí Botànic** (daily: July–Sept 10am–2pm & 5–7pm; Oct–June 10am–2pm & 4–6pm; free); follow the signs for Casal dels Volcans. They're worth walking out to, not least because they contain the fascinating **Casal dels Volcans** itself (July–Sept 10am–2pm & 5–7pm; Oct–June 10am–2pm & 4–6pm; closed Tues; 200ptas or free with Museu Comarcal ticket), a small museum devoted to the local volcanic region and housed in a Palladian building. Even if you don't speak Catalan or Castilian, you'll get a pretty good idea of the displays: there are photos and maps of the local craters, rock chunks and a seismograph, and even a "what to do in an earthquake" series of explanatory drawings (the answer appears to be run like hell). The building also houses an information centre on activities in the Garrotxa volcanic zone.

Eating, drinking and nightlife

Olot's attractive historical centre boasts numerous lively **bars** and **restaurants**, where you'll find the grilled meat specialities of the region, as well as a surprisingly wide range of non-regional dishes.

Can Guix, c/Mulleras 3. Cheerful bar-restaurant where queues form for large servings. Eat heartily for 1200ptas – the local wine is served in a *porrón*, but you get a glass to decant it into if you chicken out. Closed Sun.

Font de l'Àngel, Plaça Móra. Snack-bar/café with garden seating and inexpensive *menús*. Closes Sundays after characteristically lively Saturday nights.

Pensión Narmar, c/Sant Roc 1. The restaurant attached to the *pensión* has reasonably priced, well-cooked food and a *menú* for 1100ptas. Especially good is the free-range – *de montaña* – chicken.

Ramón, Plaça Clara 10. Middle- to high-priced Catalan dishes; the bar under the arches is a good vantage point if you just want a drink.

Set al Gust, Passeig d'en Blay 49. Smart and trendy pizzeria, though it includes things you hoped you'd never see on a pizza (like *bacalao*). Pizza and local wine runs to around 1500ptas a head.

La Vegetal, c/dels Sastres 43. Attached to a health-food store, this vegetarian restaurant is a rare sight in a Catalan town. Tasty, but on the expensive side. Open noon–7pm; closed Tues & Sun.

Nightlife

More than a dozen **bars and cafés** are scattered between the bullring and Plaça Carme at the eastern end of the Barri Antic. Aside from some obvious ones on the Passeig d'en Blay (itself the best place for an outdoor drink), try the genteel *Cocodrilo* on c/Sant Roc, the *Crêperie* on Plaça del Mig, *Bar 6T7* at c/dels Sastres 35, or the Senegalese-run *Bar-Restaurant Central*, c/Pare Antoni Soler 6, a spacious converted clothing factory decorated with original art-works, that serves 800ptas Catalan *menús* and has live rock, blues or funk at the weekend. There are even two **cinemas**: Colom, on the *passeig*, being classier than Núria, near Plaça Carmé. Most events of the **summer festival** take place in the Plaça del Mig, behind the museum.

The Montseny region

South of Girona, the train line and main road to Barcelona both give a wide berth to the province's other great natural attraction, the **Serra del Montseny**, a chain of mountains that rises in parts to 1700m. It's a well-forested region, and from it comes the bulk of Catalunya's mineral water, which is bottled in small spa villages. You can approach either from Girona or Barcelona, though if you're using public transport you'll have to be prepared to stay the night in whichever village you aim for, since the infrequent services rarely allow for day trips. The company which operates most of the routes below is La Hispano Hilariense, whose buses leave from the bus station in Girona or from the *Bar La Bolsa*, c/Consolat 45, in Barcelona's Plaça de Palau.

Breda and Riells

The bus route from Girona into the region passes through **HOSTALRIC**, an old walled village in the heart of a cork-oak growing district, but **BREDA**, about 6km farther on, is a better place to call a halt – known for its ceramic shops, and adorned by a Gothic church with an eleventh-century tower.

There's a fork at Breda, with a minor road (and occasional local bus) running the 7km up to **RIELLS**, which provides your first real glimpse of the hills. There's not much to Riells, and little to do except stroll around the pretty surroundings, but there is a good **place to stay** just before the village: *Hostal Marlet* (☎972 870943; ③), with a garden and restaurant. It's open July and August, and weekends throughout the year, and you have to take full board.

Sant Hilari Sacalm

The main bus route continues up the other road, past Arbúcies, with the views getting ever more impressive as you approach **SANT HILARI SACALM** (1hr 20min from

Girona, 2hr from Barcelona). Perched at around 800m above sea level, Sant Hilari is a pleasant spa town that could make an enjoyable base for a couple of days. It's big enough to support a whole range of hotels and **hostales** – many catering for people taking the curative local waters, and consequently open only during the summer (July–Sept). The central *Hostal Torras*, Plaça del Dr Gravalosa 13 (☎972 868096; ⑤), seems to stay open most of the year, and serves good food, as does the excellent *Hostal Brugués*, c/Valls 4 (☎972 868018; ③), which conjures up delicious Catalan cooking. A **Turismo** (July to mid-Sept Mon–Sat 10am–2pm & 4–8pm, Sun 11am–2pm; ☎972 868826), at the junction of the main roads through town, has details of all bus connections in the area.

Viladrau

If you're driving, it's a splendid, winding twelve-kilometre ride southwest to **VILADRAU**, another spa town set slightly higher in the mountains though not as large as Sant Hilari. By public transport, you have to approach from the other side of the range, by taking the train from Barcelona to Balenyá (on the line to Vic) and connecting with the local bus from there for the twenty-kilometre ride to Viladrau. Even this is not easy, as there are currently only two services a week from Balenyá; check first in Barcelona.

Being more difficult to reach, Viladrau manages to preserve a very tranquil feel within its old streets and attractive surrounding countryside. There are plenty of local wooded walks, and half a dozen places to stay should the area appeal to you. *Fonda del Raco*, c/Pare Claret 1 (☎972 8849061; ③), is about the least expensive.

THE CATALAN PYRENEES

Away from the coast and city you don't have to travel very far before you reach the foothills of the **Catalan Pyrenees**, the easternmost stretch of the mountain chain that divides Spain and France. From Barcelona, you can reach **Ripoll** by train in just a couple of hours. The area north of here has been extensively developed as a skiing centre: out of season (in summer) it's much quieter, which is all to the good if you just want some gentle rambling in and around places like **Camprodon**. A longer trip can take in the private train line up to **Núria** (itself a major ski centre), one of the most stunning rides in Catalunya. Further north, by the French border, **Puigcerdà** boasts the only surviving train link with France over the Pyrenees, while wholly enclosed within France lies the odd Spanish enclave of **Llívia**.

For serious Pyrenean walking – and a wider range of scenery, flora and fauna – you need to head further west, beyond **La Seu d'Urgell** and the adjacent duty-free principality of **Andorra**, which mark roughly the middle of the Catalan Pyrenees. Although more developed (with hydroelectric projects in particular) than, say, the Aragonese stretch to the west, the trekking is some of the best in the whole Pyrenees. The **Noguera Pallaresa** valley, the **Vall d'Aran** and the superbly scenic **Parc Nacional d'Aigües Tortes** are all reasonably accessible, containing routes and treks that novices will be able to follow as well as more specialist terrain. A further lure is the **Boí** valley, on the western edge of the national park, which has a magnificent concentration of **Romanesque churches**.

One complication that faces anyone intent upon seeing more than a small part of the Catalan Pyrenees in one go is the geographical layout of the region. The central Aran valley (Vall d'Aran), in the northwestern corner of Catalunya, lies east–west in orientation, but most of the others run north–south, which means that connecting between them is not always easy. Determined hikers and climbers can follow various passes between the valleys, but most visitors will have to content themselves with **approaching** from the towns and villages to the south of the range, and heading out of the mountains each time before they venture up a new valley.

This section is arranged accordingly, starting in the east, closest to Barcelona, and moving west; it details the easiest approaches and emphasizes the routes that can be followed by **public transport**. Obviously if you have your own transport you've more freedom, and you're helped in your travels by an increasing number of road tunnels, which are being built to connect the valleys.

Vic

The quickest approach to the mountains from Barcelona is to take the train north to Ripoll. About an hour out of the city, the route passes through **VIC**, a handsomely sited small town with a long history, whose few well-preserved relics are worth stopping to see. Capital of an ancient Iberian tribe, Vic was later a Roman settlement (part of a second-century temple survives in town) and then a wealthy medieval market centre. The **market** continues to thrive here, taking place twice weekly (Tuesday and Saturday) in the enormous arcaded main square. Vic is also renowned for its excellent sausages, especially those known as *fuet* and *butifarra*, which you'll see on sale in the market and throughout the town.

Beyond and to the right of the square lies the old quarter of town, dominated by a reworked late-eighteenth-century **Catedral**. A rather dull, Neoclassical edifice, this doesn't make much of a claim on your attention, though it does retain its original Romanesque bell tower and, inside, impressive wall paintings by Josep María Sert. Sert completed two original sets, both of which were lost during the Civil War when the church was burned down, and these date from his third attempt, just before he died in 1945.

Perhaps most interesting in Vic, though, is the **Museu Episcopal** (daily: mid-May to mid-Oct 10am–1pm & 4–6pm, closed Sun afternoon; mid-Oct to mid-May 10am–1pm; 350ptas), next door in Plaça del Bisbe Oliba. As well as the usual local archeological finds, some early Catalan paintings, and a few Gothic pieces, the museum houses the second most important collection of Romanesque art outside Barcelona's Museu d'Art de Catalunya, featuring a wealth of eleventh- and twelfth-century frescoes and wooden sculptures rescued from local Pyrenean churches. As with the Barcelona collection, you don't need to be a specialist to appreciate the craft that went into these objects, and the work here is likely to set you off on the trail of other similar pieces scattered throughout the region.

SKIING IN THE PYRENEES

If you want to go **skiing** in the Catalan Pyrenees – still relatively undeveloped compared to the French side – it will almost certainly prove cheaper to buy an inclusive package from a travel agency than turn up at the resort and do it yourself. The main destination is Andorra (p.687), though some agents do offer Spain, too; you'll get most choice if you go through a travel agency in Barcelona.

The best resorts are those around the La Molina-Super Molina complex (p.681), including Masella, which have a more extensive terrain and more challenging pistes than most. And even in summer, it's possible to see how good Núria (p.678) is for skiing, with a whole range of graded terrain. For **cross-country skiing**, the whole of the Cerdanya (p.681) and much of the Cadí (p.679) are covered with trails, which are drenched with sunshine in spring.

The system for **grading pistes** used in local ski literature is based on a colour code: green for beginner, blue for easy, red for intermediate and black for difficult. It's not a completely dependable system – black in one resort might be red in another – but it does give a fair idea of what to expect.

Practicalities

From the **train station**, walk straight up the road opposite to reach the main market square, Plaça Major. The **Turismo** (Mon–Fri 9am–8pm, Sat 9am–2pm, Sun 10am–1pm; ☎93 8862091) is based here, along with a handful of small **hotels** should you want to stay – though you're close enough to either Barcelona or Ripoll to make it unnecessary. A good place for **lunch** or dinner is the renowned *La Taula*, Plaça Don Miquel de Clariana 4 (☎93 886 32 29; closed Sun night, Mon & Feb), a restaurant in an old mansion, with fine local food at around 3500ptas a head, and exceedingly slow service.

If you have transport (and plenty of cash), you might be tempted to drive the 14km north to the Embalse de Sau reservoir, overlooking which is the grand **Parador Nacional de Vic** (☎93 812 23 23, fax 93 812 23 68; ⑦). The converted country house has all the upmarket facilities you'd expect, including a good Catalan restaurant.

Ripoll

At **RIPOLL**, an hour or so up the train line, you're between the foothills and the peaks, perfectly poised for walking in the surrounding green countryside. Most of the town itself, at the confluence of the Ter and Freser rivers, is modern and industrial, but at its heart it boasts an old quarter containing one of the most famous and beautiful monuments of Romanesque art, the monastery of Santa María. Ripoll is refreshingly free of other tourists, save for the odd coachload that descends upon the monastery and then departs, and it's also small enough to get to grips with quickly, all of which makes it an attractive base.

Arrival, information and accommodation

The **train station** and **bus station** are close together, from where it's a ten-minute walk into town, over the Pont d'Olot and up to Plaça Ajuntament; the adjacent Plaça Abat Oliba is where you'll find the monastery as well as the **Turismo** (Mon–Sat 10am–1pm & 5–7pm; ☎972 702351), just to the left of the Museu dels Pirineos, underneath the sundial. Only a little English is spoken here, but the office has maps, lots of pamphlets and local transport timetables posted on the wall.

Leaving Ripoll, **trains** continue to Puigcerdà and the French border, which is also the way you have to go if you're heading for Andorra. Transport elsewhere is by **bus**: heading northeast to Sant Joan (6–7 daily) and Camprodon (3 daily); or east to Olot (3–4 daily); all departures from the bus station. There's an unofficial – and rather pleasant – waiting room for both stations in the small park nearby.

Accommodation

The handiest **places to stay** are in the old streets close to Santa María, but none is particularly inspiring. Least expensive is the *Hotel Payet*, Plaça Nova 2 (☎972 700250; ③), 300m south of the Turismo off Plaça Sant Eudald, halfway down c/Sant Pere: it's a rambling old place with some dreadful singles, largish double rooms with and without bath, and an all-pervading mustiness. You could also try the *Fonda Ca la Paula*, c/Pirineos 6 (☎972 700011; ④), which, if you face the Turismo, is above a bar-restaurant just thirty seconds' walk beyond, to the left. Some of the rooms are fairly small and windowless, however, so be sure to ask to see yours first. There's a better alternative farther down on the arcaded Plaça Gran, where the more upmarket *Hotel Monasterio* (☎972 700150; ④–⑤) has comfortable rooms with bath. *La Trobada*, Passeig Honorat Vilamanya 4 (☎972 702353, fax 972 700841; ⑤), across the Pont d'Olot, is perhaps the best of all: quiet rooms with bath, with a view of the town over the river and a bar-restaurant on the ground floor. The local **campsite**, *Solana del Ter* (☎972 701062; closed Nov & Dec), is 2km south of town on the Contrada Barcelona.

The Town

An obvious landmark in the centre of town, the Benedictine **Monestir de Santa María** was founded in 888 by Guifré el Pelós (Wilfred the Hairy), Count of Barcelona, as a means of resettling the surrounding valleys after the expulsion of the Moors. Guided by one Olivia, a cousin of the Counts of Besalú, the monastery rose to prominence as a centre of learning in the eleventh and twelfth centuries. Under Olivia and succeeding abbots it was completely rebuilt, using some of the finest craftsmen of the age.

Sadly, much was destroyed by a fire in 1835, though some of the original work can still be seen intact in the **west portal** (presently the main entrance to the church), which is protected from the elements by a sort of glass-fronted conservatory. The delicate columns and arches of the portal contain ornamental designs, zodiac signs and an agricultural-year calendar. These are enclosed by a tremendous sculpted facade of biblical scenes, historical and allegorical tales, and symbols of the Evangelists. The portal and the lower gallery of the adjacent two-storey **cloister** (June–Aug daily 10am–1pm & 3–7pm; Sept–May Tues–Sun varying opening hours; 200ptas), with its rhythmic arches and marvellous capitals, both date from the twelfth century, probably the greatest period of Spanish Romanesque. With their monks and nuns, beasts mundane and mythical, plus secular figures of the time, the capitals completely overshadow the works on display in the cloisters' own museum, the **Museu Lapidari**, which displays assorted stonework, masonry, sarcophagi and funerary art laid out along the walls. The monastery **church** itself (open all day for prayer) is less compelling, heavily restored over the years though still with an impressive barrel-vaulted nave.

Sant Pere

Adjacent to the monastery in Plaça Abat Oliba is the rather severe facade of the fourteenth-century church of **Sant Pere**. Inside, on the top floor, is the rambling and eclectic **Museu dels Pirineos** (Tues–Sun 9.30am–1.30pm & 3.30–7pm; 300ptas), detailing – among other things – Ripoll's history as an important seventeenth-century arms-producing and metalworking centre. There's a whole room of pistols and rifles, along with exhibits ranging from old coins through to ancient clothing, church art, archeology and folkloric items. Incidentally, the church is also the venue for Ripoll's music festival, staged on scattered weekends during July and August – providing the only opportunity to see the interior of the church itself.

The rest of town

Once you've seen the monastery and church you've exhausted the real sights of Ripoll, though it's worth taking the time to climb up around the back of Sant Pere church to the **terrace** from where you can overlook the monastery. There's a bar here, too, which is much the nicest place in town to sit.

Beyond these few old town streets there's little temptation to wander; the river, certainly, is resolutely dirty. A **street market** on Saturday mornings fills up the town centre, while the only other gleam of interest is to track down the several *modernista* buildings found in Ripoll, perhaps the last place you'd expect to come across them. The most notable is the tiny church of **Sant Miquel de la Roqueta**, built in 1912 by Gaudí's contemporary, Joan Rubió – it looks like a pixie's house with a witch's hat on top. You'll pass this on the way to or from the train station, as you will the more easily found **Can Bonada**, c/del Progrés 14, with its sprouting stone flourishes and battlements.

Eating and drinking

The **restaurant** attached to the *Fonda Ca la Paula* is pretty popular, serving Catalan dishes with wonderful *canelones* and trout the specialities. Note that it's never open before 9pm. The *Restaurant Perla*, Plaça Gran 4, has a filling, if limited, 1400ptas *menú del día* (wine extra) and other Catalan dishes which are more adventurous – and pricy – than usual. The adjacent *Hotel Monasterio* has an altogether more expensive menu, but also sports an affordable snack bar.

Two other places to try are the *comedor* at *Hostal del Ripolls*, Plaça Nova 11, which serves a 1000ptas *menú*, and the *Cafetería, c/Berenguer el Vell*, opposite the monastery, a bright, modern bar with outdoor seating, sandwiches and the best array of **tapas** in town. There's more of the same (and traffic-free outdoor tables) at the *Bar Stop*, on Plaça Tomàs Raguer, just to the south.

Northeast: the Romanesque Trail

From Ripoll an important **Romanesque Trail** of beautiful churches and monasteries leads northeast into the mountains. To follow the whole route by public transport you'll have to be prepared to wait (sometimes overnight) for buses, which get more scarce the farther north you go. The first two towns, Sant Joan de les Abadesses and Camprodon, are easy to reach on day trips from Ripoll or from Olot (see p.666). The other, more distant villages take more time and effort but are correspondingly less developed; **trekking** between them is a real pleasure.

Sant Joan de les Abadesses

SANT JOAN DE LES ABADESSES lies just 11km from Ripoll and is connected to it by a regular twenty-minute bus ride. The small town owes its existence to the foundation of another convent by Count Guifré el Pelós, whose daughter became the first abbess here. Later, the convent was turned into a canonical monastery, and the surviving building is still the main reason to make a stop in town; even today the austerity of its single-nave twelfth-century church makes a powerful impression.

Arrival, information and accommodation

The **bus terminal** (a grand name for a couple of bus shelters in a car park) is opposite the monastery and just around the corner from the town's main *rambla*, Passeig Comte Guifré, with the **Turismo** at no. 5 (daily 9am–2pm & 4–8pm; ☎972 720599).

Accommodation is easy to find, not least because it's signposted throughout town. *Hostal Ter*, overlooking both the new and old town bridges from c/Vista Alegra 2 (☎972 720005; ③), is a good first choice, genuinely family-run and with decent meals. Otherwise, *Pensión Nati*, on the road leading down from the bus terminal (c/Pere Rovira 3; ☎972 720114; ③), has large, bright rooms (separate showers): ask in the bar on the ground floor. Nearby, one block below the bus terminal, the *Pensión Janpere*, c/del Mestre Andreu 3 (☎972 720077; ⑤), has rooms at slightly higher prices, though some come with shower or bath, too. *Apartaments Mateu* is almost next door on the corner, at c/Mossèn Masdèu 10 (☎972 720186; ④), but it's fairly unprepossessing.

The Town

This **Monestir** (mid-June to mid-Sept daily 10am–7pm; rest of the year opening times vary; 200ptas), which replaced the original ninth-century foundation, was built in a Latin Cross shape and has five apses, seen to their best effect from outside. Inside, the central apse houses a famous wooden sculpture group, the *Santíssim Misteri* of 1251, depicting Christ's deposition from the Cross. It's a fine work of simple proportions and, if the literature you're given on the way in is to be believed, "On Christ's forehead a piece of Holy Bread has been preserved untouched for 700 years."

Your admission ticket also covers entry to the fifteenth-century Gothic cloisters and the **Museu del Monestir**, whose oldest item is a page from an eleventh-century sacramental book. If that doesn't sound like much, you'll probably be more impressed by the other well-presented exhibits, which include a fine series of Renaissance and Baroque altarpieces, plenty of medieval statuary, ornate chalices, and curiosities such as a crucifix in rock crystal.

The monastery apart, there's not much to Sant Joan, but it's quiet and relaxing – a more attractive (and only slightly less convenient) base than Ripoll for touring the area. The slender twelfth-century **bridge** sets the tone, with the wide valley below terraced and farmed as far as the eye can see. The bridge was destroyed in fierce fighting in February 1939 during the final Republican retreat in the Civil War, and was fully restored only in 1976. Set back from the river there's a fair-sized cluster of ancient houses, where the street names are longer than the streets themselves, centred on a lovely, arcaded **Plaça Major**, west of the *rambla*. Having strolled around and scared the pigeons out of the abandoned shell of the Sant Pol church in the centre, you've pretty much exhausted the excitements in town.

Eating and drinking

Possibilities for **eating and drinking** are a little limited, though there are a couple of pleasant cafés along the *rambla* where you can sit outside – at the *Restaurant La Rambla* you can enjoy the 1200ptas *menú del día* or a *plato combinado* at a pavement table. The restaurant at the back of *Pensión Nati* is the most economical choice, with a full 1000ptas *menú del día* on offer at lunch and dinner; you can also pick a dish from the pictures on the wall. The food isn't spectacular by any means, but it's a friendly enough place. *Pensión Janpere*'s attached diner promises better gastronomic treats, with a *menú del día* at around 1300ptas.

Camprodon

It's another twenty minutes by bus from Sant Joan to **CAMPRODON**, 14km further to the northeast, and the drive is promising – a gradual climb into the low hills alongside the lively Ter River. Coming this way, Camprodon – at 950m – is the first place with the character of a real mountain town, something that was exploited in the nineteenth century by the Catalan gentry who arrived by the (now defunct) railway to relax in the hills. The town still retains the prosperous air of those times, with ornate villas set amongst rows of towering trees, and high town houses embellished now and again with striking *modernista* flourishes.

Like Ripoll, Camprodon is at the confluence of two rivers, this time the Ter and the Ritort, and is knit together by little bridges. The principal one, the sixteenth-century **Pont Nou**, still has a defensive tower. From here you can follow the narrow main street, c/València, to the restored Romanesque monastic church of **Sant Pere** (first consecrated in 904), at the top of town, and complete your sightseeing. There is a small castle above the confluence of the two rivers, but no apparent way up.

More important is Camprodon's character as a mountain town: the shops are full of leather goods, ski gear, and mounds of local sausage and cheese. In winter it's packed with skiers, and in summer the countryside is ideal for walking (see below); in autumn, when the woods are ablaze with the different hues of turning trees, it is more scenic still.

Arrival and information

Buses stop some way south of the centre at the Teisa terminal: there are two daily services to Olot and two daily to and from Setcases. Walk up to the central Plaça d'Espanya, where the *Ajuntament* building houses the **Turismo** (July–Nov daily 10am–2pm & 4–8pm; Oct–June opening times vary; ☎972 740010). You can pick up a map here, though you'll hardly need it, and some information about the surrounding area (in English if you're lucky).

Accommodation

Places to stay in Camprodon are pricier than back down the valley, and you should consider booking in advance if you want to stay (particularly in the winter ski season). Best budget option is *Can Ganasi* at c/Josep Morera 11 (☎972 740134; ④), a street that leads off Plaça d'Espanya, though rooms here are much in demand. *Hostal Sayola*, on the same street at no. 4 (☎972 740142; ④), is reasonable and has some cheaper rooms without bath. A couple of other choices can be found in Plaça del Carme, the first square as you come into town, which lies east of c/Josep Morera: *Hostal Sant Roc* (☎972 740119; ⑥) and *Hotel La Placeta* (☎972 740807; ⑤). Alternatively, head for the best-placed of the town's hotels, the *Hotel Güell* (☎972 740011; ⑤), right on Plaça d'Espanya, where the well-appointed rooms, and parking facilities, justify the expense. There's also a local **campsite**, *Els Solans* (☎972 130099), on the Molló road.

Eating

There are several places in and around Plaça d'Espanya where you'll get good **food**, including the excellent *Bar-Restaurant Núria* at no. 11, which has a dining room that backs onto the river and a hearty 1000ptas *menú del día*, though at night you have to choose from the more expensive à la carte menu. *Hotel La Placeta* has a good attached restaurant (dinner only), or try the restaurant at the *Can Ganansi*, which features lots of differently priced *menús del día* and local dishes. The latter include *pinyes*, extremely rich and dense pine-nut balls, which you can find on sale at bakeries throughout town.

Trekking and skiing: the Ter and Ritort valleys

Beyond Camprodon you have to rely more and more on your own transport and, ultimately, on your own legs. It's not all hard-core trekking by any means, though, and there are a couple of nearby targets which you could reach quite easily in a day trip from Camprodon – or even from Sant Joan or Ripoll if you timed the transport right. The basic choice is between heading northwest up the **Ter valley**, which is the route most skiers follow since it ends at the resort of Vallter 2000, or northeast up the **Ritort valley**, better if you just want some medium-grade hiking.

Llanars, Vilallonga and Tregurà

A couple of kilometres northwest of Camprodon, the first potential stop on the Ter valley route is **LLANARS**, where there's a fine twelfth-century church. From here it's only three or four kilometres more to **VILALLONGA DE TER**, set in lovely green surroundings and with a couple of mid-range *hostales* and a year-round campsite to tempt you to stay. Two or three times a day a bus from Camprodon passes through both places on its way to Setcases.

A couple of kilometres past Vilallonga, there's a turn-off for **TREGURÀ DE DALT**, standing on a sunny shelf at 1400m. The upper part of the village has a church dating from about 980 and there are a few small hotels here, too. From Tregurà, serious hikers have the option of making the all-day **walk to Queralbs**, across to the west on the Núria rack-railway line. From the village, a path climbs to Puig Castell (2125m) and then through the Col dels Tres Pics (2hr) to the *Refugi Coma de Vaca* (4hr) at the top of the Gorges del Freser. From just before the *refugi*, on the south side of the Freser River, a path drops westwards through a stunning gorge to Queralbs (7hr), from where you can pick up the train down to Ribes de Freser or up to Núria.

Setcases

Back in the Ter valley, beautifully situated **SETCASES**, 11km from Camprodon, is a strange mixture of the moderately chic and the decrepit. It was once an important agricultural village but was almost totally abandoned in the years before the ski station brought in a new wave of hoteliers and second-home owners. The bus from Camprodon takes just thirty minutes to get here, so it's one of the few mountain villages that sees much casual trade. If you want to **stay** there's plenty of choice, though again it makes sense to book ahead. Try the *Can Japet* (☎972 136104; ④), *Ter* (☎972 740594; ④) or *Nueva Tiranda* (☎972 136037; ③), all right in the centre; the first two options have parking facilities.

Vallter 2000

Situated at the head of the Ter valley right on the French border, **VALLTER 2000** (no public transport) is the most easterly ski resort in the Pyrenees. Despite the altitude its snow record isn't particularly reliable, but if the snow is good it's worthwhile for the range of pistes laid out in its glacial bowl – three green runs, three blue, five red and four black. There are also plenty of options for ski mountaineers, with possible routes west to Núria or east via the 2507-metre-high Roc Colom to the French *Refuge de Mariailles* (1718m). Less ambitious off-piste skiers can traverse from Vallter's top lift to the **Portella de Mantet** (2415m), dropping down to the French village of Mantet: it takes about three hours to get there and twice that to return the next day.

The Ritort valley

Heading northeast from Camprodon, one daily bus (not Sunday) makes the short ride up the Ritort valley to **MOLLÓ**, 8km away, whose slight attraction is the Romanesque church of Santa Cecilia with its skinny, four-storey bell tower. If you're heading for France by road, over the Col d'Ares, Molló has virtually the only food or accommodation en route to the pass in its two **hotel-restaurants**, the *Calitxó* (☎972 740386; ⑤) and the *François* (☎972 740388; ④); rooms in both are discounted outside July and August.

Rocabruna and Beget

There's more attraction, for hikers at least, in turning off the road about halfway to Molló and following the minor road to **ROCABRUNA**. Here you'll find another small twelfth-century church, plus a couple of good restaurants with simple Catalan food.

From Rocabruna, a tortuous road winds down and down again through terraced slopes to the tiny rustic village of **BEGET**, 12km from Camprodon. Like so many villages in this area it has suffered crippling depopulation, coming to life only in summer when it's a popular Spanish holiday destination. There are two impressive medieval bridges, but the jewels are the late-twelfth-century church of **Sant Cristofor** (two distinct construction periods can be distinguished in the bell tower) and the *Majestat* it houses. Many of the best of these Romanesque wooden images, portraying Christ fully clothed, were produced in this region, though most were destroyed in 1936. This is a particularly solemn and serene example, dating from the late twelfth or early thirteenth century, and is one of the very few that can still be admired in its original setting. If the church is locked, ask in the souvenir shop opposite.

Beyond Beget, it's possible to continue walking on tracks which lead southeast to Oix, from where a road runs the 9km down to Castellfollit de la Roca – a trek that takes a whole day and puts you within striking distance of Olot and the Garrotxa region.

The Upper Freser valley and Núria

From Ripoll, the striking **Freser valley** rises to the town of Ribes de Freser and then climbs steeply to Queralbs, where it swings eastwards through a gorge of awesome beauty. Just above Queralbs, to the north, the Riu Núria has scoured out a second gorge, beyond which lies the sanctuary and ski station of Núria.

You can take the **train** all the way from Barcelona on this route, one of Catalunya's most extraordinary rides. The first stretch is by RENFE train to Ribes de Freser, about a two-and-a-half-hour ride (or just twenty minutes from Ripoll). From there, the *Cremallera* (Zipper) rack-railway takes over: the small trains of this private line, built in 1931, take another 45 minutes to reach Núria.

Ribes de Freser

The simple riverside town of **RIBES DE FRESER** is invariably bypassed in the rush to Núria, no great shame since it has little to offer beyond a few uninspiring hotels and a quiet country-town atmosphere. Its shops sell sacks of grain, seeds, oils and other agricultural and domestic paraphernalia, and there's an important weekly market, too (on Saturday).

You probably won't see any of this: the train from Barcelona/Ripoll stops at the station of Ribes de Freser-Renfe, ten minutes' walk from the centre, and if you're heading for Núria you simply cross the platform to Ribes-Enllaç, where you catch the *Cremallera*, which makes a stop in the middle of town (Ribes-Vila) before heading up into the mountains.

Taking the Cremallera: Queralbs

The *Cremallera* is a fabulous introduction to the mountains. After a leisurely start through the lower valley, the tiny train lurches up into the Pyrenees, following the river between great crags before starting to climb high above both river and fir forests. Occasionally it stops, the track only inches from a drop of hundreds of metres into the valley, a sheer rock face soaring way above you.

One such halt, about twenty-five minutes into the journey, is at **QUERALBS**, an attractive stone-built village, sympathetically renovated and suffering from the attentions of too many tourists only in peak season. Reasonable **accommodation** and **eating** here is provided by the recommended *Fonda Can Constans*, 200m above the village on the Fontalba road (☎972 727370; ⑤ for an apartment for 4–5 people), and *Hostal* Sierco, c/Major 5 (972 727377; ④).

THE FERROCARRIL CREMALLERA

Services on the train line to Núria, the **Ferrocarril Cremallera**, run every day – except Christmas Day and during November when the line is closed – though there are two timetables. During the summer (July to mid-Sept), at weekends and on festival days, trains depart hourly from 9.22am through to 8.55pm, with returning services from Núria running every hour from 8.26am until 9.46pm. During the winter (from mid-Sept to June), the service is reduced during the week to seven trains, which operate between the same hours. The journey takes about 45 minutes and return **tickets** to Núria cost around 2200ptas – rail passes are *not* valid. For latest information see *www.valldenuria.com/valldenuria/crem.htm* or phone ☎972 732020.

Núria

Beyond Queralbs, the train hauls itself up the precipitous valley to **NÚRIA**, twenty minutes further on. The views are dramatic and the drop sometimes terrifying, the impact being enhanced by a sequence of tunnels. Through a final tunnel the train emerges into a south-facing bowl containing a small lake and, at the far end, the one giant building that constitutes Núria, the **Santuario de Nuestra Senyora de Núria**. This "Sanctuary of Our Lady of Núria" was originally established in the eleventh century on the spot where an image of the Virgin was said to have been found. Believed to bestow fertility, the Virgin of Núria is the patroness of shepherds of the Pyrenees, and local baby girls are often named after her. The main **religious celebrations** in Núria are on September 8 every year.

A severe stone structure, the sanctuary combines church, **Turismo**, café, hotel and ski centre all in one. The **hotel**, the *Hotel Vall de Núria* (☎972 732000, fax 972 730326; ⑦), is expensive (though at the bottom of its price category, and less than half price in winter) but the sanctuary maintains a few simple former cells as a kind of budget hostel. In addition, there's an official **youth hostel** at the top of the cable car above Núria: the *Alberg Pic de l'Aliga* (☎972 730048; ①–②) – make reservations in advance to stay here. There are also several bunk-bedded refuges around, although these are often full of Spanish school groups, or you might want to **camp**: a site has been prepared behind the sanctuary complex.

A shop in the hotel sells **food**; fresh bread arrives by train every day. You can also buy hot snacks or breakfast at the *Bar Finestrelles* and there's a self-service place for midday or evening meals. The hotel dining room provides a not-too-expensive set meal.

Trekking and skiing

Despite the day-trippers and hordes of kids, solitude is easily found amid the bleak, treeless scenery. Serious **walkers** and **climbers** can move on from Núria to the summit of **Puigmal** (2909m), a four-to-five-hour hike: the 1:25,000 *Puigmal-Núria* Editorial Alpina contoured map/guide is recommended. The **skiing** here is usually more reliable than at Vallter 2000, but the lift system is very limited (passes cost around 1200ptas) and the top station is at only 2262m, so it's best for beginners and intermediates. There are two green runs, two blue, four red and one black. Off-piste, the summits of Pic de Finistrelles (2829m) and Puigmal are both fairly easy, each ascent taking three to four hours depending on conditions.

Most people, in fact, aren't this committed, but a good **trekking** option if you're reasonably energetic is to look around for a while and then walk back down, at least as far as Queralbs. This is the best part of the route and more than half the total distance: you trek along a beautiful, mostly marked four-hour mountain path down in the river valley below the train line.

Bergueda

An alternative approach to this eastern section of the Catalan Pyrenees is to aim initially for the *comarca* (district) of **Bergueda**, west of Ripoll. It's easiest with your own transport: from Barcelona, the road (the C1411) runs through Manresa and then heads due north to Puigcerdà, via the **Túnel del Cadí**, Spain's longest tunnel. You can come this way by bus, too – heading first for **Berga**, the region's main town, from Barcelona – though this approach is much slower than the train journey to Puigcerdà, via Ripoll.

In this region there's nothing as immediately spectacular as the Núria train journey, though northeast of Berga there's plenty of straightforward trekking at hand, in and around villages like La Pobla de Lillet and Castellar de N'Hug. To the west, the vast

Serra del Cadí contains more serious walks, including treks around (and a possible ascent of) the twin peaks of that most recognizable of Catalan mountains, **Pedraforca**.

Berga

The centre of the *comarca* is **BERGA**, where the Pyrenees seem to arrive with an amazing abruptness. You can get here by bus from Barcelona, a two-hour ride, and though it's a fairly dull place it does have a ruined castle, a well-preserved medieval centre and – more importantly – connections on to more interesting villages.

There's one other reason to come to Berga, and that's at Corpus Christi in May, when the town hosts the **Festa de la Patum**, one of the grandest and most famous of Catalunya's festivals. For three days, it features huge figures of giants and dwarves processing to hornpipe music along streets packed with red-hatted locals. A dragon attacks onlookers in the course of a symbolic battle between good and evil, firecrackers blazing from its mouth, while the climax comes on the Saturday night, when a dance is performed by masked men covered in grass.

Not surprisingly, **accommodation** is impossible during the festival unless you've booked weeks in advance. At other times you should have few problems. There are at least eight places to stay, all reasonably priced: try *Residencia Passeig*, Passeig de la Pau 12 (☎93 812 04 15; ③), which has some less expensive rooms without bath, too; and *Hostal del Guiu*, Cra de Queralt (☎93 821 03 15; ③). The local **campsite** (☎93 821 12 50; open all year) is out on the C1411. If you need help, try the **Turismo** behind the campsite (June–Sept daily 9am–1pm & 4–8pm; Oct–May reduced hours; ☎93 822 15 00), which deals with enquiries for the whole region.

Northwest of Berga: the Serra del Cadí

If you're a fully equipped and experienced trekker, the **Serra del Cadí** range to the northwest of Berga potentially offers three or four days' trekking through lonely areas not served by public transport. There are a number of paths and tracks crossing the range, though the favourite excursion remains the ascent of Pedraforca. As with other limestone massifs, finding fresh water is a problem, and that – combined with intense summer heat at the relatively low altitude – means the peak visitors' season is during May–June and September. In recognition of its unique landscape, the Cadí was declared a national reserve some years ago, and it maintains two fairly well-placed refuges, accessible from a number of foothill villages – themselves served poorly, or not at all, by bus, so you'll have to walk or hitch to them from the larger towns down-valley. For extended explorations of this region, you'll need the Editorial Alpina 1:25,000 *Serra del Cadí/Pedraforca* and *Moixeró* maps and guide.

Guardiola de Berguedà, Bagà, Saldes and Gòsol

The best approaches to the Cadí are from **GUARDIOLA DE BERGUEDÀ**, 21km north of Berga (one daily bus in summer) or the equally small town of Bagà (see below), another 5km further north. If you get stuck in Guardiola – likely if you've just arrived on the afternoon bus from Ripoll – **places to stay** include the *Fonda La Llobregat* (☎93 822 73 35; ③), within sight of the bus terminal, or *Fonda Guardiola* (☎93 822 70 48; ③), on the way south out of town. There are no proper buses from here west towards the mountains, though the mailman stops at the *Bar L'Avellaner* at 11am on weekdays; if you don't have too much equipment you can hitch a ride with him as far as Gòsol (see below). Otherwise, you'll have to hitch from the crossroads 1500m south of town, along the secondary paved road up the Saldes river valley.

The first significant habitation along this, after 18km, is the small village of **SALDES**, set dramatically at the foot of Pedraforca. Here, you'll find two stores with staple provisions suitable for trekking, and two *fondas* at which **rooms** must be reserved in advance: the *Carinyena* near the church (☎93 825 80 25; ②), and the pricier *Can Manuel* (☎93 825 80 41; ⑤) half-board), serving meals.

GÒSOL, 10km further, is an ancient stone village whose peaceful surroundings attracted Picasso back from Paris in 1906: he stayed for several weeks, in fairly primitive conditions, inspired to paint by the glorious local countryside. There is a handful of *hostales* here (more expensive than in Saldes), the bars on the square serve food, and you'll have passed a couple of campsites along the way from Saldes.

From **BAGÀ** (*hostal* and campsite – the *Bastareny*, ☎93 824 44 20; ③), you have a slightly shorter but steeper tramp or hitch 12km west to **GISCLARENY**, not really a village, but rather a pair of campsites and a primitive refuge amidst scattered farms. From here it ultimately takes longer to get to grips with the mountains, which require a further five-hour contour walk to the base of Pedraforca, or a sharp drop into the Gresolet valley followed by an equally hard climb up to Saldes, all of this on jeep tracks.

Up Pedraforca – and beyond

Most people tackle **Pedraforca** (the "stone pitchfork") from Saldes: a good ninety-minute path short-cuts the road up, which passes fifteen minutes below the **Refugi Lluís Estasen** (staffed most of the year; ☎93 822 00 79 or 908 315312; advance booking recommended). From here the ascent of the 2491-metre peak is a popular outing, steep but not technically demanding if you approach clockwise via the scree-clogged *couloir* heading up the "fork"; at the divide between the two summits you'll meet a proper path coming up from Gòsol. The anti-clockwise climb from the refuge via the Canal de Verdet is harder; descent that way is almost impossible, and however you do it count on a round trip of five to six hours.

From the *Estasen* refuge, a day's walk separates you from the Segre valley to the north. The easiest traverse route, on a mixture of jeep tracks and paths, goes through the Pas dels Gosolans, a notch in the imposing, steeply dropping north face of the Cadí watershed. An hour below, the *Refugí Prat d'Aguilo* (primitive facilities, always open) is well placed near one of the few springs in these mountains; from here it's best to hitch a ride along the 18km of dirt track down to Martinet on the main valley road linking La Seu d'Urgell with Puigcerdà.

Around La Pobla de Lillet

From Berga a daily bus heads northeast to **LA POBLA DE LILLET**, an hour away, picturesquely situated with two ancient bridges arching a shallow river and the snowy peaks of the Pyrenees framing the whole. You can also get here by afternoon bus from Ripoll, 28km to the east.

The village is handily placed for some gentle local trekking; otherwise, apart from taking a turn around a couple of minor Romanesque churches – ruined, monastic Santa María and circular Sant Miquel, both 1500m east of town – you're really here only to find overnight **accommodation**. Neither of the two *hostales* – *Pericas*, c/Furrioles Altes 2 (☎93 823 61 62; ④), and *Cerdanya*, c/Pontarró 3 (☎93 823 61 07; ③) – is particularly good value, but both speak excellent English. There is **camping** 4km away at *L'Espelt* (☎93 8236502; open all year).

The route to Castellar de N'Hug

From La Pobla it's a steady twelve-kilometre ascent to Castellar de N'Hug, and since you can't really leave the road, except for short sections at the beginning and at the end, you miss little by hitching if you get the chance. A little way out of La Pobla de Lillet, on the left, is a disused **cement factory**, a flamboyant *modernista* building designed by Rafael Guastavino in 1901; it looks like a stack of cave dwellings, now eerily empty.

Approaching Castellar, you'll come to the **Fonts del Llobregat**, source of the river which divides Catalunya in two, entering the sea at Barcelona. The *fonts* receive many Catalan visitors, who come here almost as a pilgrimage. Summer droughts frequently beset Catalunya, temporarily drying up many of the rivers, so there's great pride in any durable source of water, even if it's only a trickle by outsiders' standards.

To reach the village from here you can stay with the road or take a steep climb up the back way. **CASTELLAR DE N'HUG** is magnificently situated, an old place heaped up the sides of a hill at the base of the Pyrenees. It makes a good base for some splendid local treks, while a farm beyond the village, on the path going into the mountains, has a couple of horses which are available for treks. There's good local **accommodation** too. First choices are *Fonda Fanxicó*, Plaça Major (☎93 825 70 15; ③), and *Fonda Armengou*, Plaça Església (☎93 825 70 94; ④). Alternatively, there's the slightly more expensive *Hostal Alt Llobregat* in c/Portell (☎93 825 70 74; ⑤ including breakfast).

Sant Jaume de Frontanyà

The beautiful eleventh-century church at **SANT JAUME DE FRONTANYÀ** is a ten-kilometre trek southeast from La Pobla. Again, it's wonderfully sited at the foot of a naturally terraced cliff, and is the finest Romanesque church in the region, built in the shape of a Latin cross, with three apses.

Around it are just a few scattered stone houses, a couple of restaurants and a *hostal*, and a road that leads 10km south to **BORREDÀ**, where it joins the main road (C149) back to Berga, 21km away. There's no public transport on any part of this route.

To the French border: the Cerdanya

The train from Barcelona, via Ripoll and Ribes de Freser, ends its run on the Spanish side of the border at Puigcerdà, having cut through the historical region of the **Cerdanya**. A wide agricultural plain, ringed by mountains to the north and south, the region shares a past and a culture with French Cerdagne over the border. The division of the area followed the 1659 Treaty of the Pyrenees, which also gave France control of neighbouring Roussillon, but left Llívia as a Spanish enclave just inside France. Today, the **train** continues over the border into France (the only surviving trans-Pyrenean rail route), providing a good alternative method of leaving or entering Spain. Note that if you're heading to France by train, via Puigcerdà, it's wise to reserve a seat in advance in Barcelona.

From Ripoll to Puigcerdà by train

The railway (and road) **from Ripoll** follows the Freser river north to Ribes de Freser (p.677), and cuts west, climbing gradually up the Rigart river valley. **PLANOLES**, 7km from Ribes de Freser in the valley bottom, has a **youth hostel** (☎972 736177; closed Sept & Oct; ①). Road and rail then enter Cerdanya at the **Collada de Toses** (1800m) – the railway by tunnel – and the views to the west begin a breathtaking sequence, over bare rolling mountains and swathes of deep green forest.

Beyond, the broad meadows of Tossa d'Alp form the pistes of **LA MOLINA/SUPER MOLINA** and **MASELLA**, adjacent ski resorts strung out along the north-facing slopes. By Spanish Pyrenean standards, the skiing here is impressive, both resorts having lifts almost to the top of the 2537-metre-high peak, while in summer all the resorts become upmarket holiday camps for organized activities such as riding, archery and trail-biking. There are lots of **places to stay**, both in La Molina and nearby **ALP**, but prices are high. If all you want to do is come out to La Molina for a walk among the trees and hills, you're better off staying in Puigcerdà and making a day trip of it.

Puigcerdà

Although it was founded as long ago as 1177 as a new capital for the Cerdanya, **PUIGCERDÀ** (pronounced "Poo-eeg-chair-dah") retains no very compelling attractions, partly due to the heavy bombing it suffered in the Civil War. One of the few things in the centre that survived the bombs was the forty-metre-high **bell tower** in Plaça de Santa María. The other end of town, down the pleasant, tree-lined Passeig de 10 Abril, escaped more lightly. Here, the church of **Sant Domènec**, the largest in the Cerdanya, is enveloped in an interior gloom that has helped preserve what little is left of some medieval murals. The only other interesting building, the thirteenth-century convent next door, has been recently renovated and is now used as a local cultural and youth centre. Work is still going on to restore what's left of the medieval cloisters to the rear.

The best thing about Puigcerdà, though, is the atmosphere of the place itself. Certainly if you've just arrived from France, or are just leaving, the attractive streets and squares with their pavement cafés and well-to-do shops are worth allowing at least enough time for lunch, if not an overnight stop. Lots of French trippers think the same, so in summer there's a decidedly lively ambience in the bars and restaurants. The most enjoyable of the outdoor **cafés** are in the Plaça de Santa María and adjacent Plaça dels Herois – both fine places to rest up over a beer. Between drinks, you can stroll the narrow old town streets between Plaça Ajuntament and Passeig de 10 Abril, or amble up to the small recreational **lake**, five minutes from the centre.

Arrival and accommodation

From the **train station** (buses stop outside and continue up to the centre), it's a seriously steep climb up to the centre: take the steps in front of you, go right at the top and up more steps, and then left and up even more steps, to arrive at Plaça Ajuntament, which has superb views over the hills to revive you. The **Turismo** (mid-June to mid-Sept Mon–Sat 9am–2pm & 3–8pm, Sun 10am–2pm; mid-Sept to mid-June 10am–1pm & 4–7pm, Sun 10am–2pm; ☎972 880542) is on the right, behind the Casa de la Vila at c/Querol 1, and has plenty of printed information to give away.

There's lots of **accommodation**, including two hotels right outside the station, but unless you're at death's door and can't face the climb into town there's absolutely no advantage in staying down here. Instead, try one of a dozen *hostales* and *pensiones* in town. *Hostal La Muntanya*, c/Coronel Morera 1, just off Plaça Barcelona (☎972 880202; ④), is one of the best value, comfortable enough and close to all the bars, as is the very central and friendly *Hotel Alfonso*, c/Espanya 3 (☎972 880246; ④). Clean and friendly, *Hostal Residència Rita-Belvedere*, c/Carmelites 6–8 (☎972 880356; ④–⑤), offers excellent views and a choice between old rooms and new ones (2000ptas more expensive). Or splash out on the *Hostal del Lago*, Avda. Dr Puiguillém (☎972 881000; ⑥), off Plaça Barcelona, just a short walk from the lake – this is the most pleasant large hotel in Puigcerdà and superbly appointed.

The **campsite**, *Stel* (☎972 882361; open all year), is 1km out of Puigcerdà on the road to Llívia, just before you cross into France; there's another, *Pirineus* (May–Sept), 3km out of town in the opposite direction, beyond the RENFE station.

Eating and drinking

Passing French tourists are responsible for the bilingual menus and relatively high prices in Puigcerdà, but there are still plenty of reasonable places to eat. At the budget end, *Sant Remo* at c/Ramón Cosp 9 is a straightforward bar that serves large, freshly cooked meals for 1100ptas and 1400ptas. *La Cantonada*, c/Major 48, beyond the bell tower, has more attractive surroundings and a four-course 1300ptas *menú*, while *El Mesón* in the corner of Plaça Cabrinety does a down-to-earth *menú* for only 900ptas.

The bar-restaurants in Plaça dels Herois all serve 1400–1500ptas *menús* and expensive à la carte – they're strictly for the tourists. If the locals want to splash out they head for *Casa Clemente* at Avda. Dr Puiguillém 6, just up past the cinema, where prices are similar but the food is far superior. Another more expensive place is *Tapa Nyam* at Plaça l'Aguer 2, which is worth a visit if only for the spectacular views from the terrace.

The three **bars** with outdoor seats in Plaça dels Herois – the *Miami, Kennedy* and *Sol i Sombra* – are usually busy; the *Sol i Sombra* does a fine sideline in cured meat and serves up that most decadent of Catalan breakfasts, *pa amb tomàquet* with slices of meat, washed down with local wine. If you find these a little crowded then just round the corner you will find *Bar Arenas* on Rambla J.M. Marti which is quieter, considerably cheaper and also has outdoor seating. The atmospheric *Bodega* at c/Miguel Bernades 4, has a clientele of locals and French tourists and the wine is served and sold from the barrels that line the walls: enjoy a glass or two in its intimate interior or take in your own bottle and you can buy a litre of pretty good wine for as little as 135ptas.

Moving on: west to Andorra and north to France

If you're heading **west towards Andorra**, you may have to spend the night in Puigcerdà as there are only three buses a day to La Seu d'Urgell, via Bellver de Cerdanya (see below): currently at 7.30am, 3.10pm and 5.45pm. Heading into **France**, three trains daily cross the border to **LA TOUR DE CAROL**, five minutes away, where you change for Toulouse (4hr) and Paris (12hr). If you're **driving**, you enter France at the adjacent town of **BOURG-MADAME**; the **border** is open 24 hours, all year round, and formal checks here are almost non-existent – the French don't bother much and the Spanish just want to see that you have a valid passport. It's also a simple matter to walk across to Bourg-Madame, 2km from the centre of Puigcerdà.

Llívia

The Spanish enclave of **LLÍVIA**, 6km from Puigcerdà but completely surrounded by French territory, is a curious place indeed. There are only a couple of buses a day (from in front of the train station), but the walk isn't too strenuous: bear left at the junction 1km outside Puigcerdà and keep to the main road.

French **history** books claim that Llívia's anomalous position is the result of an oversight. According to the traditional version of events, in the exchanges that followed the Treaty of the Pyrenees the French delegates insisted on possession of the thirty-three Cerdanya villages between the Ariège and newly acquired Roussillon. The Spanish agreed, and then pointed out that Llívia was officially a town rather than a village and was thus excluded from the terms of the handover. Llívia had, in fact, been the capital of the Cerdanya until the foundation of Puigcerdà, and Spain had every intention of retaining it at the negotiations, which were held in Llívia itself.

Once in Llívia, and off the built-up main road, things become positively medieval. Although there's lots of new building throughout the nucleus of the town itself, it's mostly sympathetic, done in local stone and wood. The narrow streets wind up to a solid fifteenth-century fortified **church** (daily 10am–1pm & 3–7pm; winter closed Mon), with an older defensive tower. On the hill behind are the remains of an even earlier castle, destroyed on the orders of Louis XI in 1479.

It's claimed that the **Museu Municipal** (Tues–Sun 10am–1pm & 3.30–6.30pm; 150ptas), opposite the church, occupies the site of the oldest pharmacy in Europe. The display features pots, powders and jars of herbs, plus a reconstruction of the dispensary, while the rest of the museum is given over to various local finds – Bronze Age relics, maps, and even the eighteenth-century bell mechanism from the church. The ticket also includes entry to the fifteenth-century tower adjoining the church, the Tour

Bernat. The **Turismo** (☎972 896313) is sited in the tower as well: if it's not open (quite probable), the museum may have a little pamphlet about the town to give you.

Practicalities

Most people just stay long enough for **lunch**, not a bad idea. In the main square, Plaça Major, there's the upscale *Can Ventura* restaurant (the building dating from 1791), as well as an excellent *xarcuteria* if you're making your own picnic. The *Fonda-Restaurant Can Marcelli*, visible just up the street, has a pleasant dining room above the bar with a 1300ptas *menú del día*. In the *Bar Esportiv*, below the church, the most athletic item in evidence is a rickety pool table, though the one-armed bandit may help generate a bit of excitement. Just behind here, *Can Francesc* at c/Forns 7 has probably the least expensive food in town – not bad for all that – with courtyard dining during the summer.

There are a few **places to stay** if you're so inclined but the only budget option is *Can Marcelli* (☎972 146096; ④) which has eight reasonable rooms all with bathrooms; ask at the bar. A couple of much more expensive hotels are on the main road below town, but there's little attraction in staying down here.

Bellver de Cerdanya

Three daily buses run between Puigcerdà and La Seu d'Urgell, and although there's no real reason to get off in this part of the Cerdanya, you might be sufficiently taken by the sight of **BELLVER DE CERDANYA**, 18km west of Puigcerdà, to do so. A trout-fishing centre, standing on a low hill on the left bank of the Segre river, Bellver is a fine example of a mountain village, with a ruined castle and a sprinkling of old, balconied houses. The Romanesque church of **Santa María de Talló** is a short stroll south of the town. Known locally as the "Cathedral of the Cerdanya", this is a rather plain building, but has a few nice decorative touches in the nave and apse, and contains a wooden statue of the Virgin that's as old as the building itself.

The **Turismo** at Plaça Sant Roc 9 (July–Sept Mon–Fri 10am–1pm & 4–7pm, Sat & Sun 10am–1pm; ☎973 510229) can fill you in on **accommodation** details, but if it's closed, the *Bianya*, c/Sant Roc 11 (☎973 510475; ②), and the *Hostal Pendis*, Avda. Cerdanya 4 (☎973 510479; ③), are the budget choices; *Casa Martí*, c/Martí de Bares (☎973 510022; ④), and *Mesón Matías*, Contrada Puigcerdà (☎973 510039; ④), have slightly more expensive rooms, available with or without bath.

Towards Andorra and the west

The semi-autonomous principality of Andorra (p.687) is not much of an end in itself, and you'll get immeasurably better trekking (if that's what you're after) in the Pyrenees to either side. However, if you're curious – or travelling back through France – the route there is a reasonably interesting one, covered regularly by buses **from Barcelona**. These end their run in La Seu d'Urgell, the last Spanish town before Andorra. You can also approach Andorra **from Puigcerdà**, by taking the bus west along the C1313 to La Seu d'Urgell; see p.683 for details.

Ponts, Cardona and Solsona

The bus service from Barcelona to La Seu d'Urgell is run by the Alsina Graells company (Ronda Universitat 4), and takes three-and-a-half to four hours. There are two different routes: travelling either via **PONTS**, an undistinguished, flyblown town where there's a drinks stop and a chance to stretch your legs, or the more interesting journey via Cardona and Solsona on the C1410 (see below). The two eventually converge when the buses join the C1313 for the final run up the Segre valley to La Seu. These same routes are the quickest if you're driving towards Andorra or the western Pyrenees, though less attractive than the roads farther east.

Cardona

CARDONA lies about halfway between Barcelona and Andorra, and is dominated by a medieval hillside castle, whose eleventh-century chapel contains the tombs of the Dukes of Cardona. The castle has been converted into a *parador* (☎93 869 12 75, fax 869 16 36; ⑦), which as a luxurious overnight stop would be hard to beat, particularly since it also contains an excellent Catalan restaurant, where dinner runs to around 3500ptas a head. Perhaps the most remarkable thing about Cardona, however, is its salt "mountain", the *Salina*, close to the river – a massive saline deposit which has been in existence since ancient times.

Solsona

Twenty kilometres further on, **SOLSONA** is a smallish, ramshackle town of considerable charm, with medieval walls and gates, and a ruined castle. The **Catedral** here is gloomy and mysterious, in the best traditions of Catalan Gothic, and has fine stained glass and a diminutive twelfth-century Virgin, reminiscent of the Montserrat icon. Inside the adjacent seventeenth-century Bishop's Palace is the **Museu Diocesano** (June–Sept Tues–Sat 10am–1pm & 4.30–7pm, Sun 10am–2pm; Oct–May Tues–Sat 10am–1pm & 4–6pm, Sun 10am–2pm; 100ptas), a collection of Romanesque frescoes, altar panels and sculpture taken from local churches.

If you want to break the journey to Andorra without splashing out on Cardona's *parador*, Solsona is probably the best place. There's a good *fonda* (the *Vilanova*; ②) just off the cathedral square, and the even more reasonable *Pensió Pilar* nearby (☎973 480156; ②–③), with a *comedor* attached. Or try the *Sant Roc*, Plaça de Sant Roc 2 (☎973 480827; ③), just off the road to La Seu opposite the *Bar San Fermín* (where most of the buses stop).

The Segre valley: Organyà

Once you've left Solsona, and the bus has edged its way on to the main highway from Lleida (the C1313), the drama begins. Amid tremendous mountain vistas the road plunges through a great gorge, lined with terraces of rock jutting to over 600m above. This journey through the **Segre valley** alone makes the trip worthwhile, and Andorra starts to seem an exciting prospect by the time you reach La Seu d'Urgell.

There's only one reason to stop on the way, and that's at **ORGANYÀ** – some 20km short of La Seu – for the small, round building on the main road which contains what is possibly the oldest document in the Catalan language. Written in the twelfth century, the **Homilies d'Organyà** are annotations to some Latin sermons, discovered in a local presbytery at the beginning of this century. Opening times for the *Homilies* and the adjacent **Turismo** are the same (Mon–Sat 11am–2pm & 5–7pm, Sun 11am–2pm). There's a reasonable **hostal** (②) on the bend of the road almost opposite, or if you want something smarter go to *La Cabana*, c/Dr Montanyà 2 (☎973 383000; ③), which also has more expensive rooms with bath.

La Seu d'Urgell

The historic town of **LA SEU D'URGELL**, capital of the Alt Urgell region, provides the best base for the area if you don't want to stay in Andorra itself. For years a run-down sort of place, with a neglected medieval quarter, La Seu has undergone a mild transformation since the 1992 Olympic canoeing competitions were held nearby. There are two or three new hotels, as well as the purpose-built canoeing facilities by the River Segre, but as the greater part of the new development is outside the old centre, you should still be able to enjoy a fairly relaxed stay before heading off for the wild excesses of Andorra.

Arrival, information and accommodation

The **bus station** is on c/Joan Garriga Masso, just north of the old town: Alsina Graells buses connect La Seu with Puigcerdà (at 11.45am & 6.30pm), Lleida and Barcelona; more frequent La Hispano-Andorrana services run to Andorra. The **Turismo** (Tues–Sat 10am–2pm & 5–8pm; ☎973 351511) is on the main road coming into town, Avinguda. del Valira, not far from the campsite, but if all you want is a brochure and map try the *Ajuntament* behind the cathedral first.

Accommodation

There's not much decent budget **accommodation** available in La Seu, the standard set by the *Habitaciones Palomares*, c/dels Canonges 34 (☎973 352178; ②–③), in the old town, a warren of chipboard, windowless closets rented out as rooms, tolerable only if you can obtain one of the multi-bedded front rooms with balcony. Only the *Pensio Jové*, c/Santa Maria 38 (☎973 350260; ②), near the Parc del Segre, is cheaper. If you're counting every peseta, you're probably best off in the *La Valira* **youth hostel** (☎973 353897; closed Sept; ①), at the western end of c/Joaquim Fuerza, close to the Parc del Valira, though this is often full with groups.

There are a few more expensive hotels on the main road through town; best placed is the one-star *Hotel Andría*, Passeig Joan Brudieu 24 (☎973 350300; ③–⑤), full of faded elegance, which means things don't always run as smoothly as they should. Top-of-the-range places include the modern *parador* (☎973 352000, fax 973 352309; ⑦), very near the cathedral at c/Sant Domènec 6, and the better-sited *El Castell* (☎973 350704; ⑦), which is on the main Lleida road and incorporated within the Castell de Castellciutat. Or you might consider staying in the village of **Castellciutat** itself, though without your own transport there's no alternative but to walk there with your luggage or take a taxi: the *Pensió Fransol* in the main Plaça de l'Arbre 2 (☎973 350219; ③) is nicely positioned.

The nearest **campsite** is *En Valira* (☎973 351035; open all year), just out of town on the Lleida road at Avda. del Valira 10.

The Town and around

Named after the imposing twelfth-century cathedral at the end of c/Major, La Seu has always had a dual function – as an episcopal seat and commercial centre. A bishopric was etablished here as early as 820, and it was squabbling between the Bishops of La Seu d'Urgell and the Counts of Foix over local land rights that led directly to the independence of Andorra in the thirteenth century. Although consecrated at the time of the foundation of the episcopal see, the **Catedral** (Mon–Sat 9.30am–1pm & 4–6pm, Sun 10am–1pm; May & Oct Sun noon–1pm only) itself was completely rebuilt in 1175, and has been restored several times since. Nevertheless, it retains some graceful interior decoration and fine cloisters with droll capitals, which you can see by buying an inclusive ticket around the back of the church – 350ptas gets you into the cloisters, the adjacent eleventh-century church of Sant Miquel and the **Museu Diocesano** (same hours as cathedral), containing a brightly coloured tenth-century Mozarabic manuscript with miniatures, the *Beatus*. To see only the cloister and church costs 125ptas.

Other than these few sights, time is most agreeably spent strolling the dark, cobbled and arcaded **old town streets** below the cathedral, which is where you'll find many of the town's best bars and restaurants. There's a strong medieval feel here, accentuated by the fine buildings lining c/dels Canonges (parallel to c/Major), and it seems appropriate that the town's fourteenth-century stone corn measures should still stand under the arcade on c/Major.

Castellciutat

Fine views of the whole valley can be enjoyed from the village of **CASTELLCIUTAT**, just 1km out of town, and its nearby ruined castle. Follow c/Sant Ermengol, cross the river and climb up to the village, which glories in the views that La Seu never gets. There's still some farming going on here, on the slopes below the tiny stone church, and a *pensión* in the square (see "Accommodation" above) which makes a nice retreat from La Seu. To continue your walk from Castellciutat, follow the path around the base of the castle and cross the main road for the nearby **Torre Solsona**. A sign here says "danger" and the scanty remains of the old fortifications are indeed crumbling away, assisted by the quarry below – take care at the edges. You can vary your route there or back by following the walkways through the post-Olympic Valira riverside park: from La Seu, head west from Avinguda. de Pau Claris (north of c/Sant Ot) to intercept it.

Eating and drinking

Lively **tapas bars** are plentiful in La Seu's old town: try *Bar Lalin*, c/Major 24, one of the best, or *Bodega Fabrega*, c/Major 81 (closed Sun). For **restaurant meals**, the mid-priced *Restaurant Cal Pacho*, c/la Font 11 (at the southern end of c/Major, to the east), has a very Catalan menu, an outdoor terrace, and is worth trying for lunch or dinner.

Out of the old town there are plenty of choices too. *Palace*, out by the bus station, at the corner of c/Joan Garriga Masso and the highway, has an all-you-can-eat buffet for 1300ptas. More centrally, *Bambola Pizzeria-Creperia*, c/Andreu Capella 4 (east of the main Passeig) serves – no surprises here – tasty and reasonable pizzas and crêpes. The *Nazario*, next door, is a good *orxateria/gelateria* with outdoor seating, though it's rather pricey. For budget Catalan food, the bustling *Restaurant Canigó*, c/Sant Ot 3 (at the north end of the Passeig), has a 975ptas *menú del día* and a fistful of *platos combinados*. Much more expensive is the restaurant of the *Hotel Andría*, on the Passeig; the food is no great bargain – though they do have a 1475ptas *menú* – but it's an attractive venue for a drink, with a terrace-garden.

Andorra

After 700 years of feudalism, the twentieth century has finally forced itself upon the **PRINCIPALITY OF ANDORRA**, 450 square kilometres of mountainous land between France and Spain. A referendum held in March 1993 produced an overwhelming vote to accept a democratic constitution, replacing the semi-autonomous system in place since 1278, when the Spanish Bishops of La Seu d'Urgell and the French Counts of Foix settled a long-standing quarrel by granting Andorra independence under joint sovereignty. Despite a certain devolution of powers – the counts' sovereignty passed successively to the French King and then the French President – the principality largely managed to maintain its independence over the centuries. The bishops and counts, and later the French King and President, appointed regents who took little interest in the nitty-gritty of day-to-day life in the principality. The country was run instead by the Consell General de les Vals (General Council of the Valleys), made up of appointed representatives from Andorra's seven valley communes, who ensured that the principality remained well out of the European mainstream – it even managed to maintain its neutrality during the Spanish Civil War and World War II.

It was during these conflicts that Andorra began its meteoric economic rise, as locals first smuggled in goods from France during the Civil War and, later, goods from Spain during the occupation of France. After the war, this trade was largely replaced by the legitimate duty-free business in alcohol, tobacco and electronics, and by the money generated by the huge demand for winter skiing. Much of the principality became little more than a drive-in supermarket, with the main road through the country and into France clogged with French and Spanish visitors after cut-price hi-fi and electrical gear, mountain bikes, ski equipment, car parts and a tankful of discount petrol. Seasoned Spain-watcher John Hooper has called Andorra "a kind of cross between Shangri-la and Heathrow Duty Free". Ironically, though, this **tax-free status** held the seeds of Andorra's belated conversion to democracy. Although the inhabitants enjoyed one of Europe's highest standards of living, the twelve million visitors a year began to cause serious logistical problems: the country's infrastructure was sorely stretched, the valleys increasingly laid open to speculative blight, while the budget deficit grew alarmingly. Spanish entry into the EC in 1986 only exacerbated the situation, affecting the difference in price of imported goods in Spain and Andorra.

The 1993 referendum was an attempt to come to terms with the economic realities of twentieth-century Europe. Or rather, some of the economic realities, since none of the parties involved in the negotiations and arguments seriously suggested that the solution would be to introduce direct taxation: there is still no income tax in Andorra, and barely any indirect taxes either. Instead, the idea is to transform Andorra into a kind of "offshore" banking centre, to rival the likes of Gibraltar, Lichtenstein and

---

ANDORRA PRACTICALITIES

GETTING THERE
From Spain, there are four daily direct buses from Barcelona (6am, 7am, 2.30pm & 7pm; 4hr), and regular buses from La Seu d'Urgell, at 8am, 9.30am, 12.15pm, 2pm, 3.20pm, 6pm and 7.15pm (Sun at 8am, 9.30am, 12.15pm, 2pm, 4.15pm and 7.15pm), which take forty minutes to reach the capital, Andorra La Vella.

From France, the bus leaves L'Hospitalet at 7.35am, 10.30am 1.15pm, 5pm (summer only; 4.20pm from Ax-les-Thermes) and 7.45pm, arriving at Pas de la Casa twenty to thirty minutes later; services leave La Tour de Carol at 10.30am and 1.15pm, taking 45min to Pas de la Casa.

If you're **driving** you might as well leave the car behind and take the bus – in high season (summer or winter) the traffic is so bad that the bus isn't much slower, and parking in Andorra La Vella is an ordeal.

CURRENCY AND POST
Andorra has no money of its own, so both pesetas and French francs are accepted; prices in shops and restaurants are quoted in both currencies. There's also a dual-operation postal system, with both a French and Spanish post office in Andorra La Vella.

LANGUAGE
Catalan is the official language, but Spanish and, to a slightly lesser extent, French are widely understood.

LEAVING ANDORRA
Buses back to La Seu d'Urgell leave from Plaça Guillemó in Andorra La Vella, parallel to the main road. Departures are Monday–Saturday 8.05am, 9.05am, 11.30am, 1.30pm, 4.05pm, 6pm and 8.05pm (Sun 9.05am, 11.30am, 1.30pm, 4.05pm and 8.05pm).

Luxembourg. Following the referendum, the state's first **constitutional election** was held in December 1993. Only the 10,000 native Andorrans were entitled to vote (out of a total population of 60,000) and an eighty percent turnout gave the outgoing head of the Consell General, Oscar Ribas Reig, the biggest share of the vote. His Agrupament Nacional Democratic took eight seats in the new 28-seat parliament and formed a coalition with other right-wing parties to usher in the new democratic era. For the first time, Andorrans (ie, those born there, or who have lived there for over twenty years) can vote freely, and join trades unions and political parties, while their government now has the right to run its own foreign policy and establish its own judicial system: the principality has already been accepted as a full member of the United Nations.

For many visitors, though, the attractive quaintness stops at the border. As little as thirty years ago Andorra was virtually cut off from the rest of the world – an archaic region which, romantically, happened also to be a separate country. There are still no planes and no trains, but the rest of the development has been all-encompassing: it can take an hour in packed traffic to drive the few kilometres from La Seu d'Urgell to Andorra La Vella, the main town, while the large-scale ski resorts have already taken up much of the most attractive corners of the state – another is currently planned in the beautiful Prat-Primer upland. If you're curious, it can be worth a day or so for the cheap shopping and eating, and it's worth getting at least a little way out of the capital to see some of the scenery that brought the early visitors here. Don't expect to find an unspoiled spot anywhere, though, unless you're prepared to strike off up the mountains on foot – and if you are, there are much more rewarding places on either side of Andorra where you could spend time.

Andorra La Vella

At just over 1000m, **ANDORRA LA VELLA**, with its stone church, river and enclosing hills, must once have been an attractive little town. Now it's ghastly; a seething mass of electrical hardware stores, tourist restaurants (six-language menus a speciality), tacky discos and parked cars. It's consumerism gone mad, which is a shame in light of the spectacular setting, with crags and green *sierra* to either side. There's a partial respite in the old quarter, the **Barri Antic**, which lies on the heights above the river, to the south of the main through-road, Avinguda. Princep Benlloch. But even here, the sole monument is the sixteenth-century stone **Casa de la Vall** in c/de la Vall (free guided tours Mon–Fri 10am–1pm & 3–6pm, Sat 10am–1pm), once a family house, but now housing the Sala de Sessions of Andorra's parliament and a small museum on the top floor.

Practicalities

The **Turismo** is east of the Barri Antic, closer to the river, on c/Dr Vilanova (Mon–Sat 9am–1pm & 3–7pm, Sun 10am–1pm; ☎376 820214), and has complete lists of local accommodation, restaurants, bus timetables and sells a good topographical map of the principality.

Most of the two dozen or so modest **hotels** here are reasonably priced, but there's absolutely no reason to stay. If you're at all taken with the old quarter, the only place within it is *Racó d'en Joan*, c/de la Vall 20 (☎376 820811; ④), which is quiet enough.

A better plan is to stick around just long enough for something to eat, since there's no shortage of **restaurants** and competition fosters low prices, and then head out into the more attractive rural surroundings. *Pizzeria Primavera*, c/Dr Nequi 4, near the Barri Antic, and *Restaurant Macary*, c/Mossèn Tremosa 6, are both fine. For filling combo specials, *Les Arcades*, Plaça Guillemó 5, is the place – it's a hotel, too (☎376 821355; ③). South of the centre, on the far side of the river, *Pizzeria Taverneta*, in an alley off Avinguda. Tarragona, is good but has shoved up its prices a lot recently. For something a little more exotic, *El Canton,* c/Joan Maragall 22, provides the only Chinese food for miles around.

Up the Valira d'Ordino

It's hard to convince yourself that not all of Andorra is like this (sadly, much of it is) but with a bit of effort you can effect a partial escape into the magnificent mountain scenery by heading up the **Valira d'Ordino**. At **LA MASSANA**, 7km out of Andorra La Vella, the road splits, the left-hand fork climbing the 4km up to the ski resorts of **ARINSAL** and **PAL**. The former is the most developed (with a bus from Andorra La Vella in season), while the latter is a pretty, stone-built village with limited skiing.

The right fork at La Massana is for **ORDINO** itself (regular half-hourly buses from Andorra La Vella; catch them from where the La Seu bus sets you down, near the church), an intriguing and steep eight-kilometre climb from Andorra La Vella. Construction work is rapidly making its small-village existence a thing of the past, but Ordino still retains a handful of old stone buildings and some infinitely quieter surroundings.

El Serrat and Ordino-Arcalis

From Ordino it's an easy eight-kilometre (two-hour) walk up the gently undulating valley towards El Serrat; there are also two buses daily from Andorra La Vella, run by Interurbana. The views get better and better as you go and there are several tiny hamlets on the way, mere clusters of houses built over the river. Given its proximity to the main road it's all remarkably pleasant, but even here the excursion trade is beginning to make itself felt: a suspiciously good restaurant here, a tourist bar there, and everywhere the foundations and works that tell of another nascent hotel or apartment block.

At **EL SERRAT** there are some tumbling waterfalls and a couple of hotels offering tea and views from their restaurant terraces. If you wanted to **stay** (and these parts are certainly attractive enough), then there's the odd *hostal* on the Ordino–El Serrat road, as well as hotels in both Ordino (*Hotel Casamanya*, on the main road, ☎376 837166, fax 376 836704; ④) and El Serrat (*Hotel Tristaina*, ☎376 850081, fax 376 850730; ③), and two **campsites**; the first and nicest 2km beyond Ordino, the second just before El Serrat.

From El Serrat, the road climbs steeply to the new ski resort of **ORDINO-ARCALIS**, probably the best place to ski in Andorra, set in remote high-mountain scenery, above the Tristaina lakes. In season, three ski buses a day run there from Sant Julia through Andorra La Vella.

The road to France: the Valira del Orient

It's around 35km from Andorra La Vella to the French border at Pas de la Casa, a route you can follow by bus, in which case you're unlikely to be tempted to get off anywhere en route. If you're driving, it's easier to stop off at the couple of places of minor interest.

Just a few kilometres northeast of Andorra La Vella, **ESCALDES** is little more than a continuation of the capital – all cars, coaches, hotels and restaurants. On a shelf of land just to the north is **Sant Miquel d'Engolasters**, one of Andorra's most attractive Romanesque churches. Its frescoes, like those of many Andorran churches, have been taken to the Museu d'Art de Catalunya in Barcelona, but this eleventh-century chapel is still an evocative sight. To get there, take the road that climbs to the dammed lake of Engolasters, passing the church after 4km.

Beyond Encamp, **CANILLO** is one of the best compromise bases in Andorra – fairly close to the shops of Andorra La Vella, but far enough away to retain some dignity and character. On the eastern fringe of town, the bell tower of the Romanesque church of **Sant Joan de Caselles** is original, but the porch is a fifteenth-century addition. Just short of Canillo, a small road climbs to **Notre-Dame-de-Meritxell**, the ugly new sanctuary designed by architect Ricardo Bofill to replace a Romanesque building that burned down in 1972. Five kilometres on, **RANSOL** is set just above the main road, at the start of the Ransol valley – one of the few pleasant villages left in Andorra, with apartments available for rent if you fancied overnighting here.

SOLDEU, 3km further on, is one of Andorra's biggest ski resorts and has plenty of hotel accommodation, but here you're fast entering the built-up area close to the French border. You can escape the development by heading off up the lovely **Vall d'Incles**, at the head of which is a campsite (about an hour's walk from the main road). Once over the **Port d'Envalira**, the road tumbles down to the border town of **PAS DE LA CASA**, a combination of duty-free bazaar and ski-station and, again, of no more than passing interest.

The Noguera Pallaresa valley

The **Noguera Pallaresa**, the most powerful river in the Pyrenees, was once used to float logs down from the mountains to the sawmills at La Pobla de Segur, a job now done by truck. These days, the river is known for its river-rafting opportunities, while for those with less specialized enthusiasms, its primary interest is as a way of getting into the high Pyrenees, particularly to the celebrated Vall d'Aran.

Getting there: Artesa de Segre and Tremp

Access to the valley is easiest through La Pobla de Segur (see below), which can be reached direct from Barcelona or Lleida. Approaching from the east, there's a road from La Seu d'Urgell to Sort, at the northern end of the valley (see below), through 53km of gorgeous scenery; no buses run this way, though, and hitching can be very slow – you do so from the turn-off at Adrall, 7km southwest of La Seu.

One **bus** a day (run by Alsina Graells) leaves Barcelona (from Plaça de la Universitat) for La Pobla de Segur, a three-and-a-half-hour ride. It passes through **ARTESA DE SEGRE** (on the C1313), a town which also lies on the bus route between La Seu d'Urgell and Lleida, and therefore can provide a roundabout connection if you're coming from La Seu or Andorra. Unless you have to change here, don't even think of stopping in dismal Artesa de Segre – you can hear jaws drop at the very thought as you make your way to the front of the bus.

After Artesa, the first major halt in the Noguera Pallaresa valley itself is at **TREMP**, which can also be reached on a spectacular **train** ride direct from Lleida. Tremp is at the centre of the huge hydroelectric project that supplies much of Catalunya's power, and although it's a distinct improvement on Artesa de Segre – people here walk around with their mouths closed – there's still no real reason to delay, since the best of the scenery is yet to come. If you do get stuck, there are a few places to stay, a pleasant central square, and even a tourist office. With your own transport, though, and a big **meal** in mind, you can do immeasurably better by heading north a few kilometres to the small town of **TALARN**, where the *Casa Lola*, c/Soldevilla 2 (☎973 650814) is widely recognized as providing abundant portions of superb local food – from around 3000ptas a head.

La Pobla de Segur

Thirteen kilometres further north, **LA POBLA DE SEGUR** sits on the Noguera Pallaresa river, at the head of the Embalse de Talarn. You only come to La Pobla really because all the region's transport connects here, but it's lively enough if you want to break your journey. **Trains** from Lleida terminate here, while **buses** run from La Pobla

WATER SPORTS ON THE NOGUERA PALLARESA

Rafting season on the Noguera Pallaresa is between April and the end of August. The original rafts were logs lashed together ten-wide, controlled by a long, stern-mounted oar, for the journey downstream to the sawmills of La Pobla de Segur. (These perilous vessels are commemorated by raft races at Pobla on the first Sunday in July, as well as at the valley festival.) Today's water-sport versions are reinforced inflatables, up to 6.5m long. If you sign on for a trip you'll share the raft with as many as a dozen others, all togged out with crash helmets, buoyancy jackets, lightweight paddles and – if it's early in the season – wet suits. The man who actually knows what he's doing sits at the rear, wielding a pair of long oars. The passengers spread around the sides, feet wedged into stirrups. At the very least you're in for a soaking and about as much excitement as any well-balanced person would want. But it can be more dangerous – people do fall out and rafts do sometimes capsize. If you get pitched in, the advice is to "go with the flow", feet first, and wait until you drift past an easy place to get ashore.

The 12km or so below Llavorsí is the most challenging section of the river, and apart from rafting you can also try out **canoeing** and the relatively new sport of **hydrospeed**. Best described as tobogganing on water, hydrospeed requires an outfit of Day-Glo helmet, flotation jacket, knee pads and wet suit; once encased in this kit, you launch yourself into waterfalls and whirlpools clutching a streamlined plastic float. It's great fun, but can be dangerous, despite the armour.

to El Pont de Suert, Boí and Capdella for the western side of Aigües Tortes (see p.698), and direct to Viella via the Túnel de Viella for the Vall d'Aran (p.694). Most excitingly, though, the bus from Barcelona continues from La Pobla **up the Noguera Pallaresa valley**, travelling through Sort and Llavorsí (see below) and passing within 7km of Espot, the major entry point to the Aigües Tortes national park. From June to October, the bus continues to Viella in the Vall d'Aran; during the winter it stops short of the pass at Esterri d'Aneu. Arriving from Lleida, morning train and bus services should connect with the onward bus up the Noguera Pallaresa (it leaves at around 11.40am; there's another at 6.30pm).

Trains arrive in the new town, from where you must walk up the road, cross the bridge and head along the main street to the Alsina Graells **bus terminal**, at c/Sant Miquel de Puy 3, next to the *Hostal Montañyà*. Should you miss your connection, there are a few reasonably cheap **places to stay**; try the *Torrentet*, Plaça Pedrera 5 (☎973 680352; ②), or *Faceria*, Major 4 (☎973 680227; ③).

Gerri de la Sal and around

From La Pobla de Segur, the road threads through the spectacular **Desfiladero de Collegats**, a mighty gorge forged by the Noguera Pallaresa through 300-metre-high cliffs. Stalactites hang heavy here in huge caves gouged out of the rock. Unfortunately, since a new tunnel has been blasted through part of the defile, drivers see little of the spectacular valley, though the abandoned old road is still a marvellous route for walkers.

As the gorge widens you come suddenly upon the rickety village and enchanting twelfth-century Benedictine monastery of **GERRI DE LA SAL** – "de la Sal" because of the local salt-making industry. You'll see the surviving salt pans at the side of the river as you pass by. Village and monastery are linked by an ancient stone bridge, and though the monastery, Santa María, is normally closed, it's worth a look even from outside, where an arched hay-loft runs the entire length of the building. If you have your own car this is a fine place for a short break, but it's inconvenient without transport: there are only a handful of bars, and the nearest accommodation is 4km north, at the tiny village of **BARO**, where there are two or three places to stay strung along the main road, a riverside campsite, the *Pallars Sobirà* (☎973 662033; open all year) and a supermarket.

West to Pobleta de Bellveí
The minor road from Gerri to **POBLETA DE BELLVEÍ**, 17km west, is a pristine and tranquil run, passing the idyllic little Estany de Montcortès, and providing wonderful views of the Collegats gorge from the village of **BRETUI** (10km). The chances of a lift are remote, but at Pobleta de Bellveí you can pick up the Capdella bus (see p.699).

Sort, Rialp and Llavorsí

SORT, 30km from La Pobla de Segur, has an attractive old centre of tall, narrow houses, now hemmed in by modern apartment blocks. The main reason for this rapid development is that Sort and its neighbouring villages have suddenly found themselves among the premier **river-running** spots in Europe. After spring snow-melt the area swarms with canoeists and rafters, mostly foreign and encumbered with high-tech gear. And every year in late June/early July, the communities in the valley stage their own festival of the *Raiers* (Rafters), re-enacting the exploits of the old-time timber pilots who still put the slick new daredevils to shame.

Because of the upmarket sports types it attracts, Sort has priced itself out of any casual trade, and in any case it's not a place to linger unless you're here for the action (which can be exhilarating; see box, p.692): its main street is almost exclusively devoted to rafting/adventure shops and information centres, and there's nowhere cheap to stay or eat, unless you get a sandwich in one of the bars. The bus stops outside the *Bar Cayote* on the main road.

RIALP, 3km north, is a similarly uninviting mix of new buildings and boutiques; the bus stop/office is next to the *Hotel Victor*. **LLAVORSÍ**, 10km further, would be the most attractive place to stay on this stretch if you were determined to do so. Despite extensive renovation, and a scattering of new bar-restaurants and rafting paraphernalia, this tight huddle of stone-built houses at the meeting of the Noguera Pallaresa and Cardós rivers still retains much of its character. There's a riverside **campsite** (☎973 622153; open March–Aug) 1km out of town, and any number of **hostales** catering for the new trade. In rafting season (April to end–August), reserve in advance: try the *Hostal Lamoga*, Avda. Pallaresa 1 (☎973 622006; mid-March to Oct; ⑤), or the *Hostal del Rey*, right on the riverfront at c/Santa Ana 7 (☎973 622011; ④).

The Vall d'Àneu

From Llavorsí the bus from Barcelona/La Pobla de Segur continues along the Noguera Pallaresa, past the turning for Espot and the artificially placid lake of Panta de la Torrassa, to **LA GUINGUETA D'ÀNEU**. This is the first of three villages that incorporate the name of the local valley, the **Vall d'Àneu**, and it has a small cluster of roadside **accommodation** (a couple of *fondas* and one hotel) and a decent **campsite** across from the lake.

Esterri d'Àneu
ESTERRI D'ÀNEU, 4km on at the head of the lake, has changed so quickly that the former farming community doesn't know what's hit it. Taken in isolation, the few huddled houses between the road and the river, the arched bridge and slender-towered Sant Vicenç church are as graceful an ensemble as you'll see, but the new apartment blocks on the north side of the village, the sports shops, fancy hotels and "pub" have altered its once somnolent character irretrievably. Which is not to deny that it's a pleasant place to

fetch up in the evening if you're looking for an overnight stop. There are several **places to stay**, the pick of which (and easily the best value) is the delightful *Fonda Agustí* (☎973 626034; ③) in Plaça de l'Església, just behind the church. This serves meals, too, and has an inexpensive bar. You can also get a drink and a good *bocadillo* at *Els Cremalls*, on the main street. The **campsite**, *La Presalla* (☎973 626221; open all year), is 1km south of the village.

Esterri has a couple of banks, three or four supermarkets for provisions, and a building at the end of the village that houses a post office, **Ajuntament** and **Turismo** (Mon–Sat 9.30am–2pm & 4.30–8pm, Sun 10am–2pm). From November to May, the village is also the end of the line for the bus from Barcelona: the pass itself is closed throughout the winter.

València d'Àneu and the Port de la Bonaigua
Further up the hill, **VALÈNCIA D'ÀNEU** is a village of traditional stone and rendered houses that has been far less disrupted by development. There are two places to stay here, *La Morera* (☎973 626124; ⑤) and the more reasonable *Cortina* (☎973 626124; ③), both of which have parking facilities. If you're staying in Esterri, it's a pleasant three-kilometre walk: there's a restaurant, a bar for drinks and the small Romanesque church of Sant Andreu to explore.

Soon after València, the road starts to climb away from the river and the quilt of green and brown fields that mark the valley. The views get ever more impressive as it heads above the treeline, passing an isolated *bar-restaurant* and *refugi* before reaching the bleak pass of **Port de la Bonaigua** (road closed in winter). Near the top (2072m) snow patches persist year-round, and you get a brief glimpse of half-wild horses grazing and simultaneous panoramas of the valley you've just left and the Vall d'Aran to come.

The Vall d'Aran

The **Vall d'Aran**, with its majestic alpine feel, is completely encircled by the Pyrenean mountains. Although it has belonged to Spain since 1192, the valley, with the Garonne river cleaving down the middle, opens to the north, and is actually much more accessible from France. Like Andorra, it was virtually independent for much of its history, and for centuries it was sealed off from the rest of Spain by snow for eight months of the year, but in 1948 the Viella tunnel was cut to provide a year-round link with the provincial capital of Lleida along the N230 highway.

In recent years, life in the valley has changed beyond recognition. The old scythe-wielding hay-reapers of summer have been replaced by Massey Ferguson balers, overlooked by holiday chalets for city folk, which have sprouted at the edge of each and every village. Although the development is undeniably sympathetic – the new Aranese-style stone buildings fit closely with the originals – the increasing number of restaurants and sports shops sits uneasily with the dark little villages they surround. By getting off the main road through the valley and trekking it's still possible to get some idea of the region as it was fifty years ago, but on the whole the Vall d'Aran has lost its claim to be one of the most remote, unspoiled valleys in the Pyrenees. If all you're doing is making the bus ride to Viella you shouldn't expect great undiscovered rural expanses – generally speaking, someone's been there first and has built an apartment.

The valley's legendary greenness derives from the streams that drain into it, mostly from lakes on the south side, and this means that hikers have a better than even chance of enjoying the region's **wildlife** at first hand. When the weather is wet, black and yellow fire salamanders move with unconcerned slowness on the damp footpaths; before and after the rain, there are the equally brilliant butterflies, for which the Vall d'Aran and Aigües Tortes are both famous; and on the heights you should see izards (chamois).

Among themselves the inhabitants speak Aranés, a **language** (not a dialect, as a glance at the bizarre road signs will tell you) apparently consisting of elements of Catalan and Gascon with a generous sprinkling of Basque. *Aran*, in this language, means "valley": *Nautaran*, (High Valley) is the most scenic eastern portion. The Aranese spelling of local place names is given in parentheses below.

Baqueira-Beret

The ride down from Port de la Bonaigua is adventurous, to say the least – and often plain scary as you contemplate the choice between the terrifying drop on one side and the sheer rock wall on the other. The first place you encounter coming down from the pass is **BAQUEIRA-BERET**, a mammoth skiing development, much frequented by the French. This is the biggest engine of change in the region, and the surrounding land is virtually all divided into lots waiting to be sold off. No doubt in winter the skiing fraternity have a ball (the resort is a favourite of the Spanish royal family), but in summer – as W.C. Fields said of Philadelphia – Baqueira-Beret is closed. Stay on the bus.

Salardú

SALARDÚ, a few kilometres farther west, is the biggest of the villages of the *Nautaran* and the obvious base for visiting the others, being large enough to offer a reasonable choice of accommodation and food, but small enough to feel pleasantly isolated (except in August, or in peak ski season). With its steeply pitched roofs clustered around the church, it still retains some of its traditional feel, though the main attraction in staying is to explore the surrounding villages, all – like Salardú – centred on beautiful Romanesque churches. Salardú's is the roomy, thirteenth-century church of **Sant Andreu**, at the top of the village. The doors here are usually open, and you'll be able to see the *Sant Crist de Salardú*, a detailed wooden crucifix contemporary with the church. The church grounds are a pleasant place for a picnic.

Information and accommodation

There's a wooden **Turismo** hut (Tues–Sun 10.30am–1.30pm & 4.30–8pm) just off the main road at the turning for Bagergue. The one **bank** in the village has normal opening hours throughout the year, plus 4.30–7.45pm in the ski season. There is also a **swimming pool** (mid-June to Aug daily 11am–7pm; 500ptas) if you fancy a dip.

Even at the height of the summer you should be able to find a **bed** (if not a room) easily enough in Salardú. The cheapest place is the **youth hostel**, *Alberg Era Garona* (☎973 645271, fax 973 644136; ①), where you'll need an IYHF card and a reservation; it's above the village on the main road to Baqueira. The hostel serves evening meals (bed and breakfast only in September). This is followed by the lovely little wood-furnished rooms above the *Pensión Bar Muntanya*, at c/Major 8 (☎973 644108; ③), which fills quickly in summer.

Accommodation aimed at **trekkers** includes the *Refugi Rosti*, Plaça Major 4 (☎973 64 53 08; July to mid-Sept; rooms ③, dorms ①), in a 300-year-old building on the main square, and *Refugi Juli Soler Santaló* (☎973 645016; ①) in c/del Port, close to the youth hostel on the main Baqueira road. In addition to these, eight more expensive **hostales** and **hotels** advertise themselves around the village. In any of these you can expect to pay at least 5000–6000ptas for a double.

Eating and drinking

Most of the places to stay in the village serve good-value **meals**: non-guests can eat at the highly recommended *Refugi Juli Soler Santaló*. Alternatives are scarce, especially as the couple of village restaurants are overpriced for what you get: the *Bar Montaña* does a basic eggs-and-bacon meal or sandwiches (and has a pool table); there's a smart pizzeria on the main road; and the *Granja Era Lera*, on c/Major, is a fine crepêrie and sweet shop. While the restaurant at the *Refugi Rosti* is decent enough, too, its main draw is the nicest **bar** in town: *Delicatesen*.

Villages around Salardú

The Barcelona bus gets into Salardú at around 2pm, leaving plenty of time to find accommodation and then strike off into the surrounding villages. Houses here are traditionally built sturdily of stone, with slate roofs, and there's surprisingly little to distinguish a 400-year-old home from a four-year-old one. Fortunately, many display dates on the lintels – not of the same vintage as the churches but respectable enough, with some going back as far as the sixteenth century.

UNYA (Unha), 700m up the hill, boasts a shrine of the same age as the church in Salardú, as does **BAGERGUE**, 2km higher up the road. Bagergue is the most countrified of the *Nautaran* settlements, sheltered from the view of Baqueira by the rounded contours of Roc de Macia. In the other direction, the church at **GESSA** (1km downhill, towards Arties) has a square, keep-like belfry. A signposted two-kilometre walk from Salardú runs along a delightful country lane into the heart of **TREDÒS**, a small village overlooked by a neglected church impressive mostly for its massive bulk and separate bell tower. A river runs through the middle of the old village, and once you've fooled around in this, and stopped for a drink in the village bar-restaurant, there's nothing to stop you from walking back to Salardú.

In terms of **trekking**, there are no really hard-core walks in the valley except for the eight-hour (round-trip) excursion up to the Liat lakes (2130m) by the French border, starting from Bagergue. This doesn't have many fans – the way up is along a steep, rutted track through shadeless, bleak scenery, more suited for jeeps or mountain bikes than walkers. The local paths joining Unya with Gessa, and Salardú with Tredòs, are only short, but everywhere – even from the asphalt road up to Bagergue – the scenery and views are spectacular. On a clear day, **Aneto**, highest peak in the Pyrenees at 3404m, looms snowcapped to the west.

Arties

ARTIES, the next valley community of any size, features the usual complement of new holiday homes. Nevertheless, if you're driving and can afford the time, it has some attraction, particularly in its Romanesque church which has fine furnishings, including a delightful painted screen. The village is otherwise known for its hot springs, but these are currently shut down. However, the *camí* leading past them cuts out 3km of the busy main highway, rejoining it at the river bridge below Garòs, a boon if you're cycling.

There's **accommodation** in Arties, too, which takes up the overflow from Salardú. Besides the very comfortable *Parador Don Gaspar de Portolà* (☎973 640801, fax 973 641001; ⑧), there are two or three hotels and a few places with rooms, like the *Bar Consul* (☎973 640803; ④) on the main road; *Portolà*, c/Major 17, in the village (☎973 640828; ④); or *Pension Barrie* (☎973 640828; ③–④), a few doors down at no. 21. The *Montarto*, also on the main road (☎973 640803; ④), has a decent bar-restaurant, and there's a **campsite**, *Era Yerla d'Arties* (☎973 641602; open all year), just below the village on the main road to Viella.

Viella

From *Nautaran*, the highest of the three divisions of the Vall d'Aran, you move into *Mijaran* (Mid-Aran), whose major town is **VIELLA** (Vielha), the end of the line for the bus from Barcelona/La Pobla de Segur in summer. This arrives at 2.30pm, with the daily service in the opposite direction leaving at about 11.45am. You may also arrive in Viella on the more direct run from Lleida, via El Pont de Suert, a spectacular route in its final stages that culminates in the awesome **Túnel de Viella**, nearly 6km long. This brings you right out at the southwest corner of the valley, the road swirling down to the town below.

In truth, the ride to Viella from either direction is more attractive than the town itself, and there's no great reason to stay, particularly if you can make a bus connection onwards. Viella has become intensely developed and smartened up of late, a trend aggravated by French day-trippers who patronize the numerous supermarkets, gift shops and restaurants. Yet some old smallholdings still lurk by the side of the Garona River as it runs through town, and the parish **church** in the central square is as decrepit as ever. There's a pleasant little café with outdoor seats just outside the church, and if you've got more time to kill, the **Museu Etnològico** (Tues–Sat 10am–1pm & 5–8pm, Sun 10am–1pm; 200ptas), on c/Major, west of the river, is worth a look for its coverage of Aranese history and folklore.

Practicalities

Buses stop on the roundabout at the west end of town; information and tickets from inside the booth. The **Turismo** (June–Sept Mon–Sat 9am–1pm & 4–8pm, Sun 10am–1pm & 4.30–7.30pm; Oct–May opening times vary; ☎976 640110) is near the post office at c/Sarriulera 10, just off the church square; it has maps and accommodation lists.

As you might expect there's no shortage of **accommodation** in Viella, though little of it is particularly good value. Starting at the church, you'll find the best of the budget places by turning left along the main street and then right down the lane just across the bridge. Just off to the left, at Plaça Sant Orenç 3, is the *Hostal El Ciervo* (☎973 640165; ④); *Pensió Puig*, c/Camín Reiau 4 (☎973 640031; ②), has rock-bottom prices and consequently is often full; or there's also the tiny *Pensión Casa Vicenta* at c/Camín Reiau 3 (☎973 640819; ③–④). You'll find other inexpensive *habitaciones* at *Busquets* (☎973 640238; ③) at c/Major 11, above the *Restaurant Ali Oli*. Otherwise, the *Verneda* **campsite** (☎973 641024; June–Sept) is 5km away on the road towards France.

Meals aren't particularly memorable in Viella either. About the best you can do without excessive spending is to eat at the *Restaurant Basteret* at c/Major 6b, a smartish Catalan place that has a relatively cheap 1200ptas *menú*. You can also get an authentic snack in the *Era Puma* on the main Avinguda. Pas d'Orro, or a good sandwich at the nearby *Frankfurt Aran*.

Les Bordes, Arròs and Bossost

You can continue from Viella by bus, through **LES BORDES** (6km) and **ARRÒS** (9km), two places that play a key role in Aranese domestic architecture. Les Bordes supplies the granite for the walls and Arròs the slates for the slightly concave roofs that the planners generally demand in *Nautaran* and *Mijaran*. Arròs itself, though, is almost in the lower *Baixaran* region, and the balconied houses here, around the octagonal bell tower, have rendered white walls and red-tiled roofs. There are two **campsites** at Arròs – the *Artigane* (☎973 640189; June–Sept) and the *Verneda* (see "Viella", above) – and another just past Les Bordes.

The focus of *Baixaran* is the large village of **BOSSOST**, 18km from Viella, where the houses are strung out along the main road and on both sides of the curving river. This being the direct road between France and the Viella tunnel, accommodation is highly priced, but there's no real reason to stop: it's only around 10km to the **French border**, and 20km to the first significant French town, Saint-Béat.

Parc Nacional d'Aigües Tortes i Sant Maurici

The most popular target for trekkers in the Catalan Pyrenees is the **PARC NACIONAL D'AIGÜES TORTES I SANT MAURICI**, a vast and beautiful mountainous area constituting Catalunya's only national park. Established in 1955, and covering some 130 square kilometres, it is a rock- and forest-strewn landscape of harsh beauty, including spectacular snow-spotted peaks of up to 3000m, cirques and dramatic V-shaped valleys. For the less adventurous, there are any number of mid-altitude rambles to be made through some lovely scenery. The Sant Nicolau valley (in the west) has many glacially-formed lakes and cirques, as well as the Aigües Tortes (Twisted Waters) themselves; in the east, the Escrita valley, slightly craggier, contains the Sant Maurici lake.

AIGÜES TORTES: PRACTICALITIES

• **Entry** to the park is free, but private cars are prohibited between 10am and 6pm, and only 175 vehicles are allowed in before 10am. A total access ban for vehicles except for the jeep-taxis into the park from Espot and Boí is under consideration. You can get **information** at one of the summer park information offices in Espot or Boí (see text for details).

• **Accommodation in the park** is limited to four mountain refuges (with a warden during the summer – you'll need sleeping bags at all of them), but there are several more in nearly as impressive alpine areas just outside the park boundaries. Each refuge has a kitchen, emergency transmitter and bunk beds. **Camping** in the park (and in a peripheral "zone of influence") is officially forbidden, but there are campsites close to Caldes de Boí and at Taüll in the west, and at Espot in the east. All the approach villages have *hostales* and hotels.

• The region is covered by three Editorial Alpina **map/booklets**: the two you'll need for walking any of the routes described below are *Sant Maurici* for the east, and *Montardo* for the west, both 1:25,000 and available in Boí, Espot and good bookshops throughout the Pyrenees and in Barcelona. An English-language leaflet/map about the park is also available from park information offices. Beware some of the "paths" marked on maps: even where a bona fide trail exists, you may eventually find yourself at the base of steep, snowed-in passes which require special equipment to negotiate – check routes with information offices and refuge wardens.

• Be aware of **weather conditions**. In winter the park is covered in snow. In mid-summer many rivers are passable which are otherwise not so, but temperature contrasts between day and night are still very marked and you should always be prepared for foul weather higher up. Local summer patterns in recent years have alternated between daily rain showers throughout July and August, or prolonged drought – the general trend is towards drier summers. The best time to see the wonderful colour contrasts here are in autumn or early summer.

• In winter, the park is excellent for cross-country and high-mountain **skiing**, though there are no marked trails. There are two ski resorts on the fringes of the park: Boí-Taüll in the west and Super Espot in the east.

The most common **trees** are fir and Scotch pine, along with silver birch and beech, especially on north-facing slopes. There's also an abundance of flowers in spring and early summer (don't forget that when spring is in the air lower down, winter still has a grip on the higher slopes). As for the **fauna**, wild boar apparently roam here and at the very least you should see izards (chamois); **birds** you might spot include the golden eagle, ptarmigan and black woodpecker.

Which **approach** to the park you use rather depends upon which zone you intend to explore, and how strenuous you want your walking to be. Access to the Sant Maurici zone is via the village of **Espot**, just beyond the eastern fringes of the park and within 7km of the La Pobla de Segur–Viella bus route. Quickest access to the high and remote peaks is via **Capdella**, south of the park at the head of the Flamicell river – this is the next valley west from Noguera Pallaresa, served by bus from La Pobla de Segur. Finally, for the western Aigües Tortes zone, the entrance is from **Boí**, approached via **El Pont de Suert**, which has a bus service from La Pobla de Segur and Viella.

If you can afford only a day or two, then Boí is probably the best place for which to aim. It's easy to reach, and though the village itself is some 7km from the park entrance, there's enough mountain grandeur in the immediate surroundings to compensate if you're not going all the way into the park. All the approaches – and details of how to move on into the park – are dealt with fully below, while for **practical details** about the park itself check the boxed feature opposite.

Capdella

There's one daily bus (La Ocense; not Sunday) from La Pobla de Segur to **CAPDEL-LA**, 30km upstream. The village, the highest of half a dozen in the unsung Vall Fosca, is in two quite distinct parts: the upper part has no facilities, while the lower, 2km below – where the bus stops – is based around the Central (de Energia), one of the oldest hydroelectric power plants in these parts. For **accommodation** here, *Hostal Leo* (☎973 663157; half board ⑥), originally built to host the power company workers, is very elegant; *Hostal Monseny* (☎973 663079; half board ⑥), 800m below, is newer but equally good value. Since there's no shop or restaurant (apart from the *hostales*), meals are included: both charge around 4800ptas per person for a bed and evening meal.

Into the park

From Capdella it's a half-day trek, past the Sallente dam, to the wonderful **Refugi Colomina** (2395m; open year-round, but staffed only early Feb, mid-March to mid-April & mid-June to Sept; call ☎973 681042 for reservations), an old wooden chalet ceded to mountaineers by the power company and set among superb high mountain lakes on the southern perimeter of the park. You can cut out much of the trek by taking the *teleféric* (cable car) from the back of the Sallente reservoir to within 45 minutes' walk of the refuge: departures in summer only at 9am and 3pm, 500ptas one-way.

The immediate surroundings of the refuge have several short outings suitable for any remaining daylight. The more adventurous will set out the following day to Boí via the Estany Tort and Dellui Pass. Alternatively, there's the classic (if difficult) traverse due north into the national park via the Peguera Pass (2726m). You end up near the base of the Sant Maurici dam, having covered the length of the beautiful Monastero valley, at the *Refugi Ernest Mallafré*, poised for further walks (see p.702). If you enter the park this way, there's a summer information post (July–Sept daily 9.30am–2pm & 4–6.30pm) at Sant Maurici.

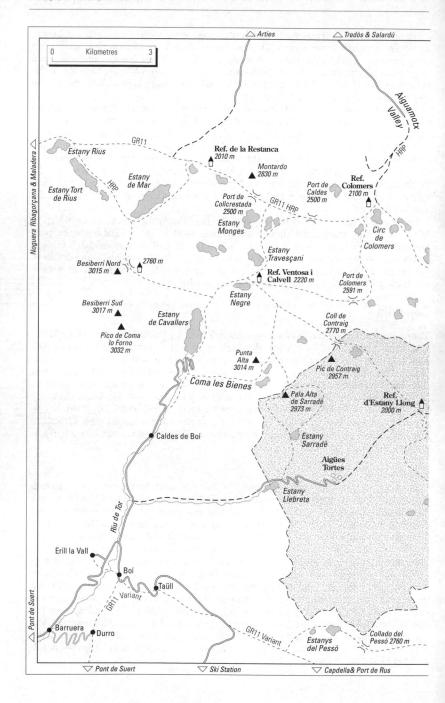

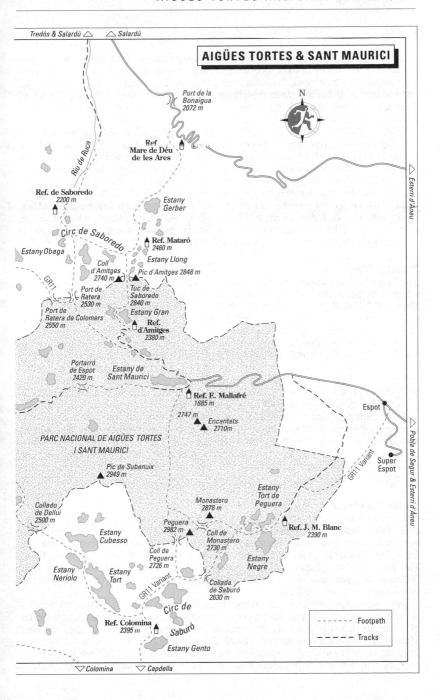

AIGÜES TORTES & SANT MAURICI

Espot

The approach from Espot is less strenuous, though purists (and people with heavy backpacks) will object to the probable necessity of road-walking both the very steep 7km up from the turning on the main road where the Barcelona–Viella bus drops you, and the similar distance beyond the village to the park entrance. If there's a jeep-taxi waiting at the turn-off, take it and save your legs for later – it should cost around 300ptas each for the short run up to Espot.

ESPOT (1430m) itself is still fairly unspoiled, though hovering on the edge of exploitation as a tourist centre. There are four or five places to stay in the predominantly rural village, where hay spills out of neighbouring lofts and the cobbled streets and riverside pastures are still reassuringly splattered with goat shit. Most of the old farm buildings downstream from the La Capdella bridge and around the church are original, and the only discordant note is struck by the rank of jeep-taxis waiting at the head of the village, all for hire on into the park. There's a **park information office** (daily 9am–1pm & 3.30–6.45pm; ☎973 624036) at the edge of Espot, where you can pick up **maps** of the park and wonderful wildlife books (unfortunately only in Spanish or Catalan), as well as check on conditions if you intend to stay and trek for some time.

Practicalities

The best-value **accommodation** in the village is at *Residencia Felip* (☎973 624093; ④), which is simple but very clean with all rooms ensuite. Other possibilities are the *Hotel Roya* (☎973 624040, fax 973 624041; ⑤), *Hostal Parimar* (☎973 624072; ④) and, if you've more money, the large, rambling *Hotel Saurat* (☎973 624162, fax 973 624037; ⑤), which dominates the centre. Espot also participates in the *casa de pagès* (old house lodging) programme; details from the information office. There are three **campsites** close by: the *Sol i Neu* (☎973 624001; June–Sept;) is excellent and just a few hundred metres from the village; *La Mola* (☎973 624024; June–Sept), 2km farther down the hill, has a swimming pool. At the far (upstream) edge of Espot, beyond the old bridge, the *Solau* (☎973 624068), in the *barrio* of that name, isn't a brilliant campsite, but it also rents out rooms (④), a good fallback if the village itself is full.

As for **eating**, you pay for the fact that you're in a tourist mill, miles from anywhere; there are no *menús del día* for less than 1000ptas. Most of the bars serve sandwiches and *platos combinados*, though the surly *Cabana d'Espot* is worth avoiding. In contrast, the adjacent *L'Isard* is welcoming and as fair value as you'll find in the village. There are also two well-stocked **supermarkets** and another shop selling maps, camping gas cartridges, and the like.

Walks from Espot

Coming from Espot, you see clearly how development is starting to encroach on the park. Two kilometres above the village, **SUPER ESPOT** is already established as a substantial ski-resort, and a recent road also leads to the park boundary (3km) and from there to the end of the tarmac at the **Estany de Sant Maurici** (a further 4km). The jeep-taxis from Espot run this far: they carry eight people and cost around 5000ptas, so if you can share a full one it's not a terribly expensive way to cut out the initial, fairly dull, road-walking.

One of the classic walks – demanding but realistic for anyone in reasonable shape – is right across the park from east to west, starting at Espot, or further in at the Sant Maurici lake: Espot to Boí is about 30km, or around twelve hours' walking. The Sant Maurici lake itself, beneath the twin peaks of Els Encantats (2749m), is one of the most beautiful spots in the Catalan Pyrenees and the **Refugi Ernest Mallafré** (open early-June to mid-Oct) offers the chance to stay here. There's another refuge, **Refugi**

d'Estany Llong (mid-June to mid-Oct; ☎973 696107 for reservations) at **Estany Llong**, three or four hours along the wide track, with Caldes de Boí then within easy reach.

Heading north from Sant Maurici, you can reach the **Refugi-Xalet Amitges** (mid-June to Sept; ☎973 250109 for reservations) with a couple of hours' walking up the Ratera valley. The fourth of the park's refuges, **Refugi Josep Mariá Blanc** (mid-June to Sept), in the Peguera valley, is reached by a direct trail from Espot in around three-and-a-half hours. You can continue to the Colomina refuge in another three-and-a-half to four hours from here: this is a well-travelled route, marked as a variant of the GR11 trail. Unless you're very committed to trekking, and proficient and well-equipped, the east–west traverse described above is the best option. Really serious walkers regard it as altogether too easy, but if you spread it over two or three days there are some excellent day treks to be enjoyed from the refuges at which you'll stay.

El Pont de Suert: the route to Boí

The route into the western area of Aigües Tortes begins at **EL PONT DE SUERT**, a small town 41km northwest of La Pobla de Segur: currently, there's a La Ocense **bus** at 2pm from La Pobla, as well as services from Viella (two daily) and from Lleida. The buses all stop close to the church on the main road through town, with timetables posted in the window of the adjacent *Las Cumbres* bar-restaurant.

El Pont de Suert is pleasant enough if you have to spend the night before catching the bus north to Boí the next day (which operates June–Sept only). There are several **cafés** with outdoor tables, and places doing sandwiches and *platos combinados*, while you can stock up in the supermarkets and bakeries for the days ahead. **Rooms** are available at *Habitaciones Gallego* (☎973 690273; ③), opposite where the bus stops. There are also a few places in the next price category, including the *Can Mestre* at Plaça Major 8 (☎973 690306; ④), which has a good dining room.

Coll, Barruera, Durro and Erill la Vall

From El Pont de Suert, a bus (June to Sept once daily, currently at 11.15am) runs north up the Noguera de Tort valley towards Caldes de Boí, passing Boí on the way. It's an area crammed with **Romanesque churches** and is far from an impossible route to walk or hitch: Boí is 21km away, and there's some local traffic to the villages on the way.

After about 8km the twelfth-century church of Santa María appears on the hillside to the left at **COLL** (the village is 2km off the main road); the ironwork on the door is particularly fine, but you're in for a long walk afterwards if you get off the bus to see it. However, Coll is also where you'll find the family-run *Hostal Casa Peyro* (☎973 297002; ⑤) which has one of the best restaurants in the area. It isn't cheap but the food is fantastic – especially the *entrantes*. **BARRUERA**, 4km further on and much larger, has several places to stay, the least expensive being the *Noray* (☎973 694021; ③), right on the main road. For a bit more of an outlay, the *Farre d'Avall* (☎973 694029; ⑤), in the village centre, is much more pleasant and quiet. There is also camping at the cramped *Camping Boneta* (☎973 694086; April–Sept). Barruera boasts the main **Turismo** for the entire valley (June–Sept Mon–Sat 10am–2pm & 4.30–7.30pm, Sun 11am–1pm; Oct–May Mon–Sat 8am–3pm; ☎973 694000), right opposite the petrol station. There's also a **riding stable** – the Hipica Casa Coll (☎973 694072) – if you fancy saddling up.

There are two Romanesque churches hereabouts: the eleventh-century Sant Feliu, down by the river and campsite, and La Nativitat de la Mare de Déu at the small village of **DURRO**, 3km away by road, on the hillside to the east, with a massive bell tower. Here, you can stay and eat at *Casa Xuqúin* (☎973 694059), where an apartment for up to four people costs around 6000–7000ptas. Finally, just before the turn-off for Boí, you pass **ERILL LA VALL**, whose twelfth-century church of Santa Eulalia has an attractive arcaded porch and a six-storey tower.

Boí

BOÍ lies 1km off the main road, which continues up to Caldes de Boí (see below): if you're dropped at the turn-off instead of being taken into the centre, it's a twenty-minute walk. With a few stone houses clinging to steep, mud-spattered alleys, the core of Boí remains attractive despite the inevitable surrounding development. This amounts to extensive parking facilities, several overpriced hotels and a choice of restaurants, though if you've just walked across the park and want to rest up for a couple of days this kind of development is most welcome. If you're on your way in, there's plenty of chance to get used to the stunning scenery first with some lovely local walks, on relatively gentle, green slopes beneath the peaks.

Practicalities

The **park information office** is in Boí's square (daily 9am–1pm & 3.30–7pm; ☎973 696189), and you can buy an Editorial Alpina map in the **supermarket** (open Sunday morning too) behind the *Hostal Beneria*. The **bank**, around the back of the supermarket, is open in the summer, on Monday, Wednesday and Thursday only, from 5–7pm.

Prime **accommodation** is at the splendid *Hostal Pascual* (☎973 696014; ③), at the turn-off from the main road, 1km below the village by the bridge. This is open out of season, and has helpful owners and a decent menu in its dining room. In the village, more expensive and similarly endowed choices include the *Pensió Pey* (☎973 696036, fax 973 696191; ⑤), in the square; *Hostal Beneria* (☎973 696030; ④), just off the square; and *Pensió Fondevila* (☎973 696011; ⑤), 200m down towards the main road. There are also some clean, modern rooms (②) just through the stone archway from the village square – look for the *habitaciones* sign.

For **eating**, you'll not do better than the *Casa Higinio*, 200m up the road to Taüll, above the village. Its wood-fired range produces excellent grilled meat dishes, or try the fine local trout – a big meal accompanied by the local *vi negre* comes to around 1800ptas, but there's no *carta* advising you of this, so don't order separate items unnecessarily. Other restaurants in the village also have ranges, and the *Hostal Pascual* serves hearty *menús del día* for around 1500ptas.

Into the park

It's 6km from Boí to the **park entrance**, and another 4km to the scenic springs of **Aigües Tortes**, where there's an unstaffed park information point. Jeep-taxis from Boí's village square run as far as this, past the artificial Llebreta reservoir, and, as at Espot, this will cost around 500ptas per person each-way. You can either wander around for an hour or so, or if you miss the last taxi back (taxis run July–Sept 8am–7pm; Oct–June 9am–6pm) walk back down later (no great hardship). If you walk on further into the park, it's relatively level as far as **Estany Llong**, but beyond that point the ascent to the pass overlooking Sant Maurici begins.

Around Boí: Taüll and Caldes de Boí

The added advantage of approaching (or leaving) the park via Boí is that you get the chance to visit the area's numerous **Romanesque churches**. Only one original apse and the bell tower remain of the renovated twelfth-century church of Sant Joan in Boí village, but within reasonable walking distance are the churches at Erill la Vall, Barruera and Durro (see above). The path to Erill la Vall from Boí, across the valley, takes half an hour; the best route to Durro is the well-signposted path which you can pick up behind Boí village – it starts just over the little bridge at the back of the village and takes around an hour to follow.

Taüll
The most popular local excursion, however, is the walk to **TAÜLL**, three or four kilometres by road above Boí (or there's a steep forty-minute path from the village that cuts across the road). Either way, you arrive at the six-storeyed tower of Romanesque **Sant Climent** (10am–2pm & 4–8pm; if shut try ☎973 696179; 100ptas), whose interior is like a dusty junk shop. The ticket lets you climb the rickety wooden steps to the top of the bell tower for scintillating village and valley views. There's an appealing bar with a garden, the *Mallador*, just outside the church, run by nice folks with a good taste in music; it's the only place in the village that serves any sort of to-order breakfast (pricey, like their lunches and dinners). Up in the village, the church of **Santa María** was consecrated, like Sant Climent, in 1123, though its belfry has only four storeys. After a millennium of subsidence, there's not a right angle remaining in the building. Admission is free and it's normally open, as it's also the parish church.

Accommodation options, mostly under the *casa de pagès* scheme, include *Casa Barò* (☎973 696027; ③) at the village entrance, with *Sant Climent* (③) across the way. Other budget options are *Casa Llovet*, Plaça Franc 5 (☎973 696032; ②–③), and *Casa Xep* (☎973 696054; ③), just below Plaça Santa María – information from the adjacent supermarket. A **campsite** (☎973 696174) perches on the hill below Sant Climent. For restaurants, *El Caliu*, at the top of Taüll in a new apartment block, is good, though pricey.

Boí-Taüll and Caldes de Boí
The character of both Taüll and Boí has been changed by the ski resort – known as **BOÍ-TAÜLL** – established on the mountains above them. Even in summer, Taüll is prey to tour coaches and drivers seeking out panoramic picnic spots, and there's a new and enormous holiday complex 1500m beyond the village, en route to the ski station. Even before the ski resort was built, one other local place that had already seen radical transformation is the spa resort of **CALDES DE BOÍ**, 5km above the park entrance, built below the highest peaks in the immediate area and within sight of one of the highest dams, at the southern end of Estany de Cavallers. This is where the bus that passes Boí ends its run, and there's an (unstaffed) park information point here, though no budget accommodation.

THE SOUTH

The great triangle of land **south** of Barcelona is not the first place you think of going when you visit Catalunya. It's made up of the province of Tarragona and part of the province of Lleida (the rest of which takes in the western Pyrenees) and, with the exception of the obvious attractions of the coast and one medieval monastery, almost all the interest lies in the provincial capitals themselves.

The main target is the **Costa Daurada** – the coastline that stretches from Barcelona to Tarragona and beyond – which is far less exploited than the Costa Brava. Although this might be reason in itself to visit, it is easy enough to see why it has been so neglected. All too often the shoreline is drab, with beaches that are narrow and characterless, backed by sparse villages overwhelmed by pockets of villas. There are exceptions, though, notably vibrant **Sitges**, which is just forty minutes from Barcelona. This is one of the great Spanish resorts, bolstered by its reputation as a major gay summer destination. If all you want to do is relax by a beach for a while, there are several other less trendy and perfectly functional possibilities, ranging from tiny **Cunit** to the region's biggest holiday resorts at **Salou** and **Cambrils**.

The Costa Daurada really begins to pay dividends, however, if you can forget about the beaches temporarily and plan to spend a couple of days in **Tarragona**, the provincial capital. It's a city with a solid Roman past – reflected in an array of impressive ruins and monuments – and it makes a handy springboard for trips inland into Lleida province. South of Tarragona, Catalunya peters out in the lagoons and marshes of the **Delta de l'Ebre**, a riverine wetland that's rich in bird life – perfect for slow boat trips, fishing and sampling the local seafood.

Inland attractions are fewer, and many travelling this way are inclined to head on out of Catalunya altogether, not stopping until they reach Zaragoza. It's true that much of the region is flat, rural and dull, but nonetheless it would be a mistake to miss the outstanding monastery at **Poblet**, only an hour or so inland from Tarragona. A couple of other nearby towns and monasteries – notably medieval **Montblanc** and **Santa Creus** – add a bit more interest to the region, while by the time you've rattled across the huge plain that encircles the provincial capital of **Lleida** you've earned a night's rest. Pretty much off the tourist trail, Lleida makes a very pleasant overnight stop: from here, it's only two and a half hours to Zaragoza, or you're at the start of dramatic road and train routes into the western foothills of the Catalan Pyrenees.

Sitges

SITGES, 40km from Barcelona, is definitely the highlight of the Costa Daurada. Established in the 1960s as a holiday town whose loose attitudes openly challenged the rigidity of Franco's Spain, it has now become the great weekend escape for young Barcelonans, who have created a resort very much in their own image. It's also a noted **gay** holiday destination, with a nightlife to match: indeed, if you don't like vigorous action of all kinds, you'd be wise to avoid Sitges in the summer – staid it isn't. As well as a certain style, the Barcelona trippers have brought with them the high prices from the Catalan capital – the bars, particularly, can empty the deepest wallets – while finding anywhere to stay (at any price) can be a problem unless you arrive early in the day or book well in advance. None of this deters the varied and generally well-heeled visitors, however, and nor should it, since Sitges as a sort of Barcelona-on-Sea is definitely worth experiencing for at least one night.

The town itself is reasonably attractive – a former fishing village whose pleasing houses and narrow streets have attracted artists and opted-out intellectuals for a century or so. The beaches, though crowded, are far from oppressive, and Sitges even has a smattering of cultural interest – though no one is seriously suggesting you come here just for that.

Arrival and information

Trains to Sitges leave Barcelona-Sants every thirty minutes throughout the day; the station is about ten minutes' walk from the town centre and seafront. **Buses** stop in front of the train station. If you're driving, it's probably best to pay for a **car park** rather than leave your vehicle on the street: there are car parks at Plaça Espanya (open-air), c/Sant Francesc (covered) and at the Mercat Nou, c/Artur Carbonell (covered).

On arrival you may as well drop in at the **Turismo** (July to mid-Sept daily 9am–9pm; mid-Sept to June Mon–Fri 9.30am–2pm & 4–6.30pm, Sat 10am–1pm; ☎93 894 5004 or 93 894 4251; *www.sitgestur.com*), at the Oasis shopping mall, which is a right-turn out of the train station and then right again up Passeig Vilafranca. It has a useful free map with local listings on the back, and all sorts of English-language information about the town. From July to September, there's also tourist information available from a building on Plaça Ajuntament (Wed–Sun 10am–1pm & 5–9pm).

SITGES

Train Station

Museu Romantic

Platja de la Ribera

Museu Cau Ferrat

Museu Maricel de Mar

ACCOMMODATION

1 Hotel Bahia	6 Hostal-Residencia Lido
2 Hostal Casa Bella	7 Hotel Mariangel
3 Hotel Celimar	8 Residencia Parellades
4 Hostal-Residencia Internacional	9 Hotel Romantic
5 Hostal Casa Julián	10 Hotel Terramar
	11 Hotel El Xalet

0   Metres   200

Accommodation

If you're offered a **room** by someone as you get off the train, take it: if it's sub-standard, you can always look for a better one later. Otherwise, try one of the places listed below, though note that in July and August they are all liable to be full; it's always best to book ahead. If you arrive without a reservation, a short walk through the central streets and along the front (particularly Passeig de la Ribera) reveals most of the possibilities – places near the station are not exactly glamorous, but are more likely to have space. Come **out of season** (after October and before May) and the high prices tend to soften a little, though in mid-winter you may have real difficulty finding anywhere that's open, especially at the budget end of the scale.

The nearest local **campsite** is *El Rocà* (☎93 894 00 43), well-signposted north of the Turismo under the railway bridge.

Hotel Bahia, c/de les Parellades 27 (☎93 894 00 12). Not far from the beach, though on a fairly noisy street, this comfortable hotel-restaurant drops its prices out of season. Open mid-April to mid-Oct. Price includes breakfast. ⑤.

Hostal Casa Bella, Avda. Artur Carbonell 12 (☎93 894 4322, fax 93 894 7331). On the main road down from the station. Large, spartan rooms: some have balconies but these are noisy. Open May–Oct. ⑤.

Hotel Celimar, Passeig de la Ribera 18 (☎93 811 0170, fax 93 811 0403). Seafront hotel at the bottom end of this range, worth trying early on for a balconied room with a view. Prices fall a category outside high season. ⑦–⑧.

Hostal-Residencia Internacional, c/Sant Francesc 52 (☎93 894 26 90). Clean and simple place where the family owners have made a bit of effort with the decor; the rooms are light and crisp. Nearer the station than the beach, but not massively inconvenient. Open all year. ③–④.

Hostal Casa Julián, Avda. Artur Carbonell 2 (☎93 894 03 06). Just down the hill from the station, this is clean and more likely than most to have room – probably because one look at the wallpaper puts many off. Open June–Sept. ④.

Hostal-Residencia Lido, c/Bonaire 26 (☎93 894 48 48). Just back from the sea, this popular *hostal* has its own lounge-bar. Rooms with bath are in the next category. Open April to mid-Oct. ⑤.

Hostal Mariangel, c/de les Parellades 78 (☎93 894 13 57). One of the town's most popular budget places, so it fills quickly. There's a small lounge. Closed mid-Sept to mid-Nov. ④.

Residencia Parellades, c/de les Parellades 11 (☎93 894 08 01). The large airy rooms and decent location make this a good first choice. Open April–Sept. ⑤.

Hotel Romàntic, c/Sant Isidre 33 (☎93 894 83 75, fax 93 894 81 67). Attractive, old converted nineteenth-century villa in the quiet streets away from the front, not far from the train station. It's a favourite with gay visitors. Many rooms have a terrace overlooking the gardens; those with showers are in the next category. Open April to mid-Oct. The similar *La Renaixença,* owned by the same management (same telephone number and prices), is open all year. ⑥.

Hotel Terramar, Passeig Marítim 80 (☎93 894 00 50, fax 93 894 56 04). Superb position at the end of the long promenade, and splendid views from its large, balconied rooms, but a bit dated in style and decor. Open April–Dec. ⑦.

Hotel El Xalet, c/Illa de Cuba 35 (☎93 811 00 70, fax 93 894 55 79). Charming, discreet hotel in a beautiful *modernista* house near the train station. There are only ten rooms – booking ahead is a necessity in summer. Price includes breakfast. ⑦.

The Town

It's the **beach** that brings most people to Sitges, and it's not hard to find, with two strands right in town, to the west of the church. From here, a succession of beaches of varying quality and crowdedness stretches west as far as the *Hotel Terramar*, a couple of kilometres down the coast. A long seafront promenade, the **Passeig Marítim**, runs all the way there, and all along there are beach bars, restaurants, showers and watersports facilities. Beyond the hotel, following the train line, you eventually reach the more notorious nudist beaches, a couple of which are exclusively gay. It's worth noting that as the town's popularity has increased, petty crime seems' to have been exported from Barcelona to Sitges. Watch your possessions on the beaches and exercise care at night.

Back in town, make the effort at some stage to climb up the knoll overlooking the beaches, topped by the Baroque parish church – known as *La Punta* – and a street of old whitewashed mansions. One contains the **Museu Cau Ferrat**, an art gallery for want of a better description. Home and workshop to the artist and writer Santiago Rusiñol (1861–1931), its two floors contain a massive jumble of his own paintings, as well as sculpture, painted tiles, drawings and various collected odds and ends – such as the decorative ironwork Rusiñol brought back in bulk from the Pyrenees. Two of his better buys were the minor El Grecos at the top of the stairs on either side of a crucifix. The museum also contains works by the artist's friends (including Picasso) who used to meet in the *Els Quatre Gats* bar in Barcelona.

All **museums** in Sitges have the same opening hours and prices: Mon–Sat 9.30am–2pm & 4–9pm, Sun 9.30am–2pm; 500ptas each (free first Wed of month) or 800ptas for a **combined ticket** for all the museums, valid for a month.

Two other museums are worth giving a whirl on a rainy day. The **Museu Maricel de Mar**, next door to the Museu Cau Ferrat, has more minor art works, medieval to modern, and maintains an impressive collection of Catalan ceramics and sculpture. More entertaining is the **Museu Romàntic** (guided tour every hour), which aims to show the lifestyle of a rich Sitges family in the eighteenth and nineteenth centuries by displaying some of their furniture and possessions. It's full of nineteenth-century knick-knacks, including a set of working music boxes and a collection of antique dolls. The museum is right in the centre of town, at c/Sant Gaudenci 1, off c/Bonaire.

Eating

International tourism has left its mark on Sitges: multilingual menus and "English breakfasts" are everywhere. Fortunately there are reasonable **restaurants** among them, and though you're unlikely to be sampling Catalan cuisine at its finest you'll find plenty of good *menús del día*. Some suggestions appear below, but good general areas to explore are the side streets around the church, or the beachfront for more expensive seafood restaurants. For picnic supplies, the town's **market** – the Mercat Nou – is very close to the train station, on Avinguda. Artur Carbonell. **Ice cream** fiends should check out *Ribera*, Passeig de la Ribera 5, *Italiana*, c/Jesús, or *Heladería* and *Il Gelatieri*, both on c/Parellades.

El Argentino, Passeig Aiguadolç 22. If you're sick of seafood this is the place for serious charcoal-grilled meat – especially beef – though a meal here will set you back 3000ptas upwards.

Calitja, c/Marqués de Mont Roig 5. Catalan place open in the evenings that's well thought of and reasonably priced by Sitges standards. There's not a wide choice of dishes, though.

El Cisne, c/Sant Pere 4 (junction with c/de les Parellades). Nothing adventurous here, but you'll get well-cooked food in a dining room at the back of the bar – around 1600ptas for a four-course *menú del día*.

Dubliner, c/Illa de Cuba 9. It's bold and it's tacky, but this pub-restaurant knows its clientele – it offers two aspirins with its full English breakfast.

Flamboyant. c/Pau Barrabeig, off c/Carreta. Rather expensive, but with a beautiful garden setting. Around 2500ptas a head.

Mare Nostrum, Passeig de Ribeira 60. Long-established fish restaurant situated on the seafront, with a menu that changes according to the catch and season. Around 3000ptas a head, though you may find a *menú del día* for half that.

Nieuw Amsterdam, c/de les Parellades 70. The "English Chef" can recommend what he likes, but the only real reason to come is for the medium-priced Indonesian and Dutch specialities – not spectacular, but then you're not in Indonesia.

Olivers, c/Illa de Cuba 39. A mid-priced Spanish, rather than Catalan, restaurant, but the menu has some interesting flourishes that make the food memorable. Meals from around 2000ptas a head.

El Trull, c/Mossèn Félix Clarà 3, off c/Major. Fairly pricey French-style restaurant in the old town, though with a 1500ptas *menú del día* of mainly Spanish food (drinks excluded).

Los Vikingos, c/Marqués de Mont Roig 18. Good, cheap restaurant right on the main tourist drag serving anything and everything (including fresh fish) accompanied by loud music.

Bars and nightlife

The main part of the action in Sitges is concentrated in a block of streets just back from the sea in the centre of town. Late-opening bars started to spring up here in the late-1950s: today, **c/1er (Primer) de Maig** (marked as c/Dos de Mayo on some old maps) and its continuation, **c/Marqués de Montroig**, are fully pedestrianized, while c/de les Parellades and c/Bonaire complete the block – not somewhere to come if you're looking for a quiet drink. This is basically one long run of disco bars, pumping music out into the late evening, interspersed with the odd restaurant or fancier cocktail bar, all with outdoor tables vying for your custom. The bars are all loud and their clientele pre-dominantly young, and you can choose from just about any style you care to imagine: pool-hall chic, colonial cane, Costa Brava excess or sleek dance-party. The best policy is to browse and sluice your way around until you find a favourite, though a few are picked out below. More **genteel bars** are not so easy to come by, though the places right on the seafront are generally quieter.

Afrika, c/1er de Maig. One of the best of the music bars.

Atlántida, Sector Terramar, 3km out of town. The town's favourite club, the clifftop *Atlántida* can be reached by regular buses which run there and back all night from the bottom of c/1er de Maig.

Bar Bodega Talino, c/de les Parellades 72. That rare thing in Sitges – a real *tapas* bar.

Café-Bar Roy, c/de les Parellades 9. An old-fashioned café with dressed-up waiters and marble tables. It's good for breakfast, or for a glass of *cava* and a fancy snack.

Parrots Pub, Plaça de la Industria. Stylish bar at the top of c/1er de Maig that's a required stop at some point of the day; it's just one place you can pick up the free gay map of Sitges (see below).

The gay scene and Carnaval

The **gay scene** in Sitges is frenetic and ever-changing, but chronicled on a gay map of town available from *Parrots Pub*, in Plaça de la Industria, as well as from several other bars and clubs.

During the day, a current favourite hang-out is the *Picnic Bar* on Passeig de la Ribera (opposite *Les Anfores* restaurant in the *Calipolis* hotel), popular for its sand-wiches. By early **evening**, everyone's moved on to *Parrots Pub* for cocktails. The best concentration of bars and discos is in c/Bonaire and c/Sant Buenaventura: at *Bourbons*, c/Sant Buenaventura 9, gay women are especially welcome, as they are in the *Bar Azul* (at no. 10), where happy hour is 9–10.30pm. The best gay disco is at *Trailer* at c/Àngel Vidal 14, in the old town. *Bar el 7*, at c/Nou 7, is a bar serving late breakfasts before an afternoon on the beach.

Carnaval

Carnaval in Sitges (Feb/March) is outrageous, thanks largely to the gay populace. The official programme of parades and masked balls is complemented by an unwritten but widely recognized schedule of events. The climax is the Tuesday late-night parade (not in the official programme), in which exquisitely dressed drag queens swan about the streets in high heels, twirling lacy parasols and coyly fanning themselves. Bar doors stand wide open, bands play, and processions and celebrations go on until four in the morning; *Bar el 7* has photos of parades from days gone by if you miss the action.

Listings

Banks Banco Español de Credito, Plaça Cap de Vila 9; Banco de Sabadell, Plaça Cap de Vila 7; La Caixa, c/de les Parellades 16.

Cinema Casino Prado, c/Francesc Gumà 4, and El Retiro, c/Àngel Vidal 13.

Hospital Hospital Krankenhaus Sant Camil, Plaça del Hospital (☎93 896 00 25); in emergencies, call Ambulancis Urgències (☎904 100904).

Pharmacist Two central *farmacias* are Ferret de Querol, c/de les Parellades 1, and Planas, c/Artur Carbonell 30.

Police Plaça de l'Ajuntament (☎93 811 76 25).

Post office Plaça Espanya, open Mon–Fri 8.30am–2.30pm, Sat 9.30am–1pm.

Sports Other than in the sea, there's swimming in the Piscina Municipal, on Passeig Maritím; there's a windsurfing school at Platja Riera Xica, a beach about 500m west of the church; and ten-pin bowling at the Oasis commercial centre.

Taxis There's a rank outside the train station (☎93 894 13 29), and you should find someone prepared to take you to/from Barcelona airport, which is 30km away.

Train information Call ☎93 490 02 02.

Travel agencies Viajes Sitges, c/Marquès de Montroig 21 and Plaça Cap de Vila 19; Viajes Playa de Oro, c/de les Parellades 22. For train tickets and local tours.

Vilanova i la Geltrú

Eight kilometres south down the coast is the large fishing port of **VILANOVA I LA GELTRÚ**. Sitges gets most of its fish from here, but Vilanova borrows little in return – this is a real working port, whose quayside is lined with great refrigerated trucks waiting to load the catches from the hundreds of boats moored alongside. Although the town itself is nothing special, it's fascinating to wander along the docks through the scattered fishing nets, and when you tire of this there's a tourist side to Vilanova which is a pleasant contrast to the excesses of Sitges. There are two **beaches**: one beyond the port, the second – better – at the end of the seafront promenade. This road changes its name: near the port it's Passeig Marítim, while beyond, up by the Turismo, it becomes the Passeig de Ribes Roges, a palm-lined stretch with some nice café-bars open to the pavement.

You might be tempted by Vilanova's fair smattering of **museums**, two of which are found straight out of the train station door: one of Spain's few railway museums to the right (July & Aug Tues–Fri 5–9pm, Sat & Sun 10am–2pm; Sept–June Tues–Fri 10am–2pm & 5–7pm, Sat & Sun 10am–2pm; 300ptas), probably best left to the specialists, and the **Biblioteca Museu Balaguer** (Tues–Sat 10am–2pm & 4–8pm, Sun 10am–2pm; free) to the left, founded by a local nineteenth-century politician. This is actually a quite rewarding stop, featuring pieces loaned from the Prado alongside a hoard of Catalan nineteenth- and twentieth-century paintings. Best of all, though, is the town's **Museu Romàntic Can Papiol**, on c/Major 32, behind the church at the very top of the Rambla Principal (Tues–Sat 10am–1pm & 4–6pm, Sun 10am–2pm; 300ptas). It's the sister museum to the one in Sitges, and the entrance fee includes a guided tour around the lavishly furnished eighteenth-century town house in which the collection is housed.

Practicalities

Trains and **buses** run about every twenty to thirty minutes from Sitges, and there are daily bus connections between Vilanova and Vilafranca del Penedés if you want to take an inland loop back to Barcelona. The bus might drop you off on the seafront; otherwise the main stop is in front of the train station – from here, cross the tracks by turning left out of the station, left again and heading under the tunnel. The port is on the left, while to the right is the Passeig Marítim where you'll find the **Turismo** (June–Sept Mon–Sat 10am–8pm, Sun 10am–2pm; Oct–May Tues–Sat 10am–2pm & 5–8pm, Sun 10am–2pm; ☎93 815 45 17).

There are a few **hotels** opposite the tourist office – and the town's best beach just beyond – though a less expensive *hostal*, the *Costa d'Or*, is at Passeig Marítim 49 (☎93 815 55 42; ⑥ full board). If you don't mind being away from the beach, there are a couple of budget choices near the station on Rambla Ventosa: *Bar Restaurant Central* (☎93 815 54 69; ③), at no. 13, is the better of the two, but if it's full, try no. 25. If you want to pitch a tent, Vilanova might be a better bet than Sitges as it has three **campsites**, including the friendly beach-based *Platja Vilanova* (☎93 895 07 67; April–Sept). There are a dozen or so **restaurants** along the seafront *passeig*, which on the whole are better value than the equivalents in Sitges. All have outdoor seating and while the views may not be quite so special as further up the coast, the atmosphere is a lot more down to earth. A good choice is the *Daviana,* at no. 104, which has a hearty *menú del día* for around 1500ptas or a terrific paella for the same price. If you fancy a snack there is also the *L'Orient Express*, opposite the port at Passeig de Carme 48, which serves Eastern Mediterranean *tapas* from 300ptas.

Cunit, Puerta Romana and Torredembarra

If the Costa Daurada beaches so far seem too crowded and frenetic – a distinct possibility in high season – there are a couple of other possible stops before Tarragona. Travelling by train, make sure you catch a local and not an express which will run straight through.

Cunit

CUNIT, about 15km south of Sitges, is the first stop inside Tarragona province. Rather soulless – more a collection of villas than a village – nonetheless it has a good, long beach. There's a **campsite**, *Mar de Cunit* (☎977 674058; March–Sept), behind the beach and a few good places to **stay**: *Los Almendros* (☎977 675437; ②–③), at the top of the village, but cut off from it by the highway, or the more pricey *Hostal La Diligencia* at Plaça Major 4 (☎977 674081; ⑤ half-board), opposite the church in the centre. The former has an outdoor grill and a decent 900ptas *menú del día*, while *La Diligencia* has a particularly good restaurant, with a 1200ptas *menú*.

Puerta Romana and Torredembarra

Again little more than a few streets of villas, the hamlet of **PUERTA ROMANA**, 15km before Tarragona, has perhaps the best swimming and sunbathing on this stretch of coast, with clean sand and clear water. It's not on the map or signposted from the main road, and the nearest train station is at the small resort of **TORREDEMBARRA** (a few hotels here), from where you could walk the 4km north. Coming by bus, ask to be put down at *Camping Sirena Dorada* (☎977 801103 or 977 801303) by the main road; this is open all year, changes money and has huts to rent. From there walk straight towards the sea, across the railway line, and you'll reach Puerta Romana, where there's another campsite – *Gavina* (☎977 801503; April–Oct) – slap-bang on the beach. Puerta Romana is also easily reached from the nearest village, **CREIXELL**, where signposts point the way to the *platja* (over the new railway bridge). The closest place to eat is at the *Puerta Romana*, a bar serving basic meals, on the street just back from the beach.

Tarragona

Majestically sited on a rocky hill, sheer above the sea, **TARRAGONA** is an ancient place. Settled originally by Iberians and then Carthaginians, it was later used as the base for the Roman conquest of the peninsula, which began in 218 BC with Scipio's march south against Hannibal. The fortified city became an imperial resort and, under Augustus, *Tarraco* became capital of Rome's eastern Iberian province – the most elegant and cultured city of Roman Spain, boasting at its peak a quarter of a million inhabitants. Temples and monuments were built in and around the city and, despite a history of seemingly constant sacking and looting since Roman times, it's this distinguished past which still asserts itself throughout modern Tarragona.

Time spent in the handsome upper town quickly shows what attracted the emperors to the city: strategically – and beautifully – placed, it's a fine setting for some splendid Roman remains and a few excellent museums. There's an attractive medieval part, too, while the rocky coastline below conceals a couple of reasonable beaches. If there's a

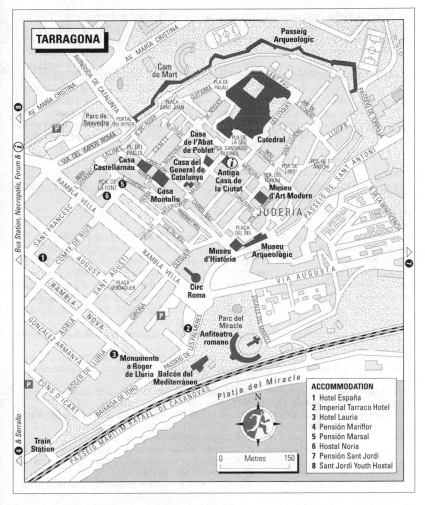

downside, it's that Tarragona is today the second largest port in Catalunya, so the views aren't always unencumbered – though the fish in the Serrallo fishing quarter is always good and fresh. Also, the city's ugly outskirts to the south have been steadily degraded by new industries which do little for Tarragona's character as a resort: chemical and oil refineries, and a nuclear power station.

Arrival and information

The city divides clearly into two parts, on two levels: a predominantly medieval, walled upper town (where you'll spend most time), and a prosperous modern extension below. Heart of the upper town is the sweeping **Rambla Nova**, a sturdy provincial rival to Barcelona's, lined with fashionable cafés and restaurants. Parallel, and to the east, lies the **Rambla Vella,** marking – as its name suggests – the start of the old town. To either side of the *ramblas* are scattered a profusion of relics from Tarragona's Roman past, including various temples, and parts of the forum, theatre and amphitheatre.

The **train station** is in the lower town: when you arrive, turn right and climb the steps ahead of you and you'll emerge at the top of the Rambla Nova, from where everything is a short walk away. The **bus terminal** is at the other end of the Rambla Nova, at Plaça Imperial Tarraco. The **Turismo** is at c/Major 39 (July–Sept Mon–Fri 9.30am–8.30pm, Sat 9.30am–2pm & 4–8.30pm, Sun 10am–2pm; Oct–June Mon–Fri 10am–2pm & 4.30–7pm, Sat 10am–2pm, Sun 10am–2pm; ☎977 245064); and there are also seasonal information booths (July–Sept) at Plaça Imperial Tarraco and at the beginning of Vía Augusta. If you're travelling further afield the regional tourist office is near Rambla Nova at c/Fortuny 4 (Mon–Fri 9am–2pm & 4–6.30pm, Sat 9am–2pm; ☎977 233415).

You're unlikely to use the city's **local bus** network, other than for trips out to the campsite or to the aqueduct (the relevant details are given below), but the Turismo can let you know the routes if you're interested.

Accommodation

Tarragona makes a great stopover, and is certainly less exhausting than Sitges. The nicest **rooms** in town, or at least the ones in the best location, are in the newly pedestrianized Plaça de la Font, just in the old town off Rambla Vella. If these are full, there are a couple of less desirable places near the train station. Cheapest lodgings are at the *Sant Jordi* youth hostel (see list below for details), while down towards the beach, Platja Arrabassada, a few kilometres out of town, are some more small hotels and **campsites:** to get to *Camping Tarraco* (☎977 239989; April–Sept) take bus #1, #3 or #9 (every twenty minutes) from Plaça de Corsini, near the market and local forum.

Hotel España, Rambla Nova 49 (☎977 232712). Affordable mid-range hotel on the *rambla*, with bath in every room. ④–⑤.

Imperial Tarraco Hotel, Passeig de Palmeres (☎977 233040, fax 977 216566). The city's best and most expensive hotel, modern but beautifully positioned, sitting on top of the cliff and facing out to sea. ⑧.

Hotel Lauria, Rambla Nova 20 (☎977 236712, fax 977 236700). Posh three-star hotel on the main *rambla*. Outside July and Aug, room prices become eminently reasonable. ⑥.

Pensión Mariflor, c/General Contreras 29 (☎977 238231). Only two blocks from the train station, and much less shifty than its location suggests. Housed in a modern apartment block, this has fairly large rooms and is clean and friendly; hot showers cost 100ptas extra. ③.

Pensión Marsal, Plaça de la Font 26 (☎977 224069). Above the *Bar/Restaurante Turia*, this is the square's best-value choice, with modern, well-kept rooms at the bottom of this price range; ask for one with a view of the square. Bathrooms are separate and spotless. ④.

Hostal Noria, Plaça de la Font 53 (☎977 238717). Smarter and more upmarket than most around the *plaça*, but good value out of season. Ask inside the bar/cafetería. ③.

Pensión Sant Jordi, Vía Augusta s/n (☎977 207515). Long-standing favourite that recently moved from its previous berth in Plaça de la Font into these more roomy premises. Well-run and friendly; all rooms have bath. ⑤.

Sant Jordi Youth Hostel, Avda. President Companys 5 (☎977 240195). An IYHF hostel with four-or six-bedded rooms (over-26s pay fifty percent more) and sports facilities; breakfast included in the price. Reception open 7–10am & 2–8pm; reservations advised in July & Aug; closed Sept. ①–②.

The City

Much of the attraction of Tarragona lies in the **Roman remains** dotted around the city. Some of the most impressive monuments are a fair way out (see "Out of the centre" below), but there's enough within walking distance to occupy a good day's sightseeing and to provide a vivid impression of life in Tarragona in imperial Roman times. It's worth noting in advance, though, that almost all Tarragona's sights and museums are **closed on Mondays**; while the admission price to the Passeig Arqueològic buys a **combined ticket** (475ptas) which also allows entry to the Circ Roma, the Amfiteatre, the Casa Museu de Castellarnau and Museu d'Historia, all of which are free to ISIC card holders.

Passeig Arqueològic

For an overview of the city and its history, start at the **Passeig Arqueològic** (Tues–Sun: April & May 10am–1.30pm & 3.30–4.30pm; June–Sept 9am–midnight; Oct–March 10am–1.30pm & 3.30–5.30pm; 475ptas combined ticket), a promenade which encircles the northernmost half of the old town. From the entrance at the Portal del Roser, a path runs between **Roman walls** of the third century BC and the sloping, **outer fortifications** erected by the British in 1707 to secure the city during the War of the Spanish Succession. Megalithic walls built by the Iberians are excellently preserved in places, too, particularly two awesome gateways; the huge blocks used in their construction are quite distinct from the more refined Roman additions. Vantage points (and occasional telescopes) give views across the plain behind the city and around to the sea, while various objects are displayed within the Passeig – several Roman columns, a fine bronze statue of Augustus, and eighteenth-century cannons still defending the city's heights.

Roman Tarragona: the Necropolis, Forum and Amphitheatre

The most interesting remains in town are those of the ancient Necropolis, a twenty-minute walk out of the centre down Avinguda. Ramón i Cajal, which runs west off Rambla Nova. Here, both pagan and Christian tombs have been uncovered, spanning a period from the third to the sixth century AD. They're now contained within the fascinating **Museu i Necropolis Paleocristians** (Tues–Sun: June–Sept 10am–8pm; Oct–May 10am–1pm & 4–7pm; combined ticket with Museu Nacional Arqueològic 300ptas, free on Tues), whose entrance is on Passeig de la Independencia. The museum is lined with sarcophagi and displays a few fragmented mosaics and photographs of the site, but it's outside in the covered trenches and stone foundations that you get most sense of Tarragona's erstwhile importance. Scattered about are amphorae, inscribed tablets and plinths, rare examples of later Visigothic sculpture, and even the sketchy remains of a mausoleum. Most of the relics attest to Tarragona's enthusiastically Christian status: Saint Paul preached here, and the city became an important Visigothic bishopric after the break-up of Roman power. Back in the centre, the Roman forum has survived too. Or rather forums, since – as provincial capital – Tarragona sustained both a ceremonial **provincial forum** (the scant remnants of which are close to the cathedral) and a **local forum**, whose more substantial remains are on the western side of Rambla Nova, near the market hall and square. Located on the flat land near the port, this was the commercial centre of imperial *Tarraco* and the main meeting place for locals for three centuries. The site (Tues–Sun: April & May 10am–1.30pm & 3.30–6.30pm; June–Sept 9am–8pm; Oct–March 10am–1.30pm & 3.30–5.30pm; free), which contained temples and small shops ranged around a porticoed square, has been split by a main road: a footbridge now connects the two halves where you can see a water cistern, house foundations, fragments of stone inscriptions and four elegant columns.

Tarragona's other tangible Roman remains lie close to each other at the seaward end of the Rambla Vella. Most rewarding is the **Amfiteatre** (open as forum site; 475ptas combined ticket), built into the green slopes of the hill beneath the *Imperial Tarraco* hotel. The tiered seats backing on to the sea are original, and from the top you can look north, up the coast, to the headland; the rest of the seating was reconstructed in 1969–70, along with the surviving tunnels and structural buildings.

Above here, on the Rambla Vella itself, are the visible remains of the Roman Circus, the **Circ Roma**, also known as Las Voltas del Circ, whose vaults disappear back from the street into the gloom and under many of the surrounding buildings. If you want a closer look, the Circ now forms part of the **Museu de la Romanitat** (June–Sept Tues–Sat 10am–8pm, Sun 10am–3pm; Oct–May Tues–Sat 10am–5.30pm, Sun 10am–3pm; 475ptas combined ticket). Built at the end of the first century AD to hold chariot races, the Circ has been restored and presented to spectacular effect. The rest of the museum contains computer-generated pictures of Roman Tarragona's buildings, and an elevator cuts right through the building and onto the roof for the best views in Tarragona.

The old town

For all its individual Roman monuments, the heart of Tarragona is still the steep and intricate streets of the medieval **old town** which spreads east of the Rambla Vella. Here and there the towering mansions in the side streets incorporate Roman fragments, while the central c/Major climbs to the quarter's focal point, the **Catedral** (mid-March to June Mon–Sat 10am–1pm 4–7pm; July to mid-Oct Mon–Sat 10am–7pm; mid-Oct to mid-Nov Mon–Sat 10am–12.30pm & 3–6pm; mid-Nov to mid-March Mon–Sat 10am–2pm; 300ptas, free on Tues), which sits at the top of a broad flight of steps. This, quite apart from its own grand beauty, is a perfect example of the transition from Romanesque to Gothic forms. You'll see the change highlighted in the main facade, where a soaring Gothic portal is framed by Romanesque doors, surmounted by a cross and an elaborate rose window. Except for services, entrance to the cathedral is through the **cloisters** (*claustre*; signposted up a street to the left of the facade), themselves superbly executed with pointed Gothic arches softened by smaller round divisions. The cloister also has several oddly sculpted capitals, one of which represents a cat's funeral being directed by rats. The ticket lets you proceed into the cathedral, and into its chapter house and sacristy, which together make up the **Museu Diocesa**, piled high with ecclesiastical treasures – pick up the English-language leaflet for a rundown of what's in every nook and cranny.

Strolling the old town's streets will also enable you to track down Tarragona's excellent clutch of museums. The least obvious – but worth seeing for the setting inside one of the city's finest medieval mansions – is the **Casa Museu de Castellarnau** on c/Cavallers 14 (June–Sept Tues–Sun 10am–8pm; Oct–May Tues–Sat 10am–1.30pm & 4–7pm; 475ptas combined ticket). The interior courtyard alone rewards a visit, with its arches and stone coats-of-arms built over Roman vaults. Otherwise, the small-scale collections are largely archeological and historical (coins and jars), rescued from banality by some rich eighteenth-century Catalan furniture and furnishings.

Museums of archeology and history

The most stimulating exhibitions in town are in adjacent buildings off Plaça del Rei at the edge of the old town. The splendid **Museu Nacional Arqueològic** (June–Sept Tues–Sun 10am–8pm; Oct–May Tues–Sat 10am–1.30pm & 4–7pm; combined ticket with Museu i Necropolis Paleocristians 300ptas, free Tues) has a mutual admission ticket with the Necropolis and shouldn't be missed. The huge collection is a marvellous reflection of the richness of imperial *Tarraco*, and admirably laid-out, starting in the basement with a section of the old Roman wall preserved in situ. On other floors are thematic displays on the various remains and buildings around the city, accompanied by pictures, text and relics, as well as whole rooms devoted to inscriptions, sculpture, ceramics, jewellery – even a series of anchors retrieved from the sea. More importantly, there's an unusually complete collection of mosaics, exemplifying the stages of development from the plain black-and-white patterns of the first century AD to the elaborate polychrome pictures of the second and third centuries.

Out of the centre: ruins, port and beaches

Tarragona is compact enough not only to be able to walk everywhere in the city, but to reach most of the outlying districts on foot, too. It's less than half an hour to either the port area of **Serrallo** or, across town, to the best local beach at **Arrabassada**. The Roman **Aqueduct**, 4km inland, is best reached by bus, but for most of the other Roman remains dotted around the surrounding countryside you'll need transport of your own.

Other Roman remains

Perhaps the most remarkable (and least visited) of Tarragona's monuments stands outside the original city walls. This is the **Roman Aqueduct**, which brought water from the Riu Gayo, some 32km distant. The most impressive extant section, nearly 220 metres long and 26 metres high, lies in an overgrown valley, off the main road in the middle of nowhere: take bus #5, marked *Sant Salvador* (every twenty minutes from the stop outside Avda. Prat de la Riba 11, off Avda. Ramón i Cajal; last bus back at around 10.45pm) – a ten-minute ride. The trip is undoubtedly worthwhile; the utilitarian beauty of the aqueduct is surpassed only by those at Segovia and the Pont du Gard, in the south of France. Popularly, it is known as El Pont del Diable (Devil's Bridge) due, remarked Richard Ford, to the Spanish habit of "giving all praise to 'the Devil', as Pontifex Maximus".

Other local Roman monuments of similar grandeur are more difficult to reach: in fact, without your own transport, almost impossible. If you're determined, keep a wary eye out for signs, and expect to have to ask directions locally from time to time. The square, three-storeyed **Torre dels Escipions**, a funerary monument built in the second century AD and nearly ten metres high, stands just off the main Barcelona road, the N340, 6km northeast up the coast. A couple of kilometres farther north, the **Pedrera del Medol** is the excavated quarry that provided much of the stone used in Tarragona's constructions, while 20km from the city, after the turn-off for Altafulla, is the triumphal **Arc de Bera**, built over the great Via Maxima in the second century AD.

Serrallo

A fifteen-minute walk west along the industrial harbourfront from the train station (or the same distance south from the Necropolis) takes you right into the working port of **SERRALLO**, Tarragona's so-called "fisherman's quarter". Built a century ago, the harbour here is authentic enough – fishing smacks tied up, nets laid out on the ground for mending – but the real interest for visitors is the line of **fish and seafood restaurants** which fronts the main Muelle Pescadores. You'll get something to eat, somewhere, on most days, though the weekend is when the locals descend and then you'll need to arrive early to grab a table. None of the restaurants is designed for budget eaters, but there are a couple of more basic joints hidden in the parallel backstreet, and it's also worth checking the *menús del día*. Where these are available you should be able to eat for around 1500ptas a head; otherwise, commit yourself to the higher à la carte prices in the knowledge that the fish is as fresh as can be. *La Puda* (no. 25), at the far end, has tables overlooking the harbour inside and out, a short selection of seafood *tapas*, and a main menu that's overpriced but very good – the full three-course seafood works for two, plus wine, will cost around 8000ptas.

After your meal, you can walk back to Tarragona through the tangle of boats and nets, following the rail lines – or wait on the main road for city bus #2 back up to the old town.

Tarragona's beaches

The closest beach to town is the long **Platja del Miracle**, over the rail lines below the amphitheatre. The nicest, though, is a couple of kilometres further up the coast, reached by taking Vía Augusta (off the end of Rambla Vella) and turning right at the *Hotel Astari*. Don't despair upon the way: the main road and railway bridge eventually give way to a road which winds around the headland and down to **Platja Arrabassada**, an ultimately pleasant walk with gradually unfolding views of the beach. There are regular buses in summer (#1, #3, or #9) from various points throughout town.

Arrabassada isn't anything very special, though it's roomy enough and has a few other diversions that make it worthwhile. Top of the list is the *Brasilmos* beach **bar-restaurant**, at the far end by the headland, which features seafood *tapas*, Latin American sounds, a pool table and occasional live music on summer evenings. There are a couple of other beach bars, too, and under the railway line, by *Brasilmos*, tiny **ARRABASSADA** village itself, which boasts two or three restaurants, a couple of hotels and *hostales*, a supermarket and two **campsites**, including *Camping Tarraco* (see "Accommodation", p.714). A bit further along the coast at **Platja Llarga**, a cluster of restaurants offer good food at low prices and stay open late. There's also a very lively Cuban **disco**, the *Corason*, where you'll find local familes – including grandparents – dancing the night away, fuelled by potent cocktails. Entrance is free, but you'll be expected to buy at least one drink.

Eating and drinking

There are plenty of good **restaurants** in the centre of Tarragona, as well as the fish and seafood places down in Serrallo. Many – particularly in and around Plaça de la Font – have outdoor seating in the summer. *Pescado romesco* (fish with *romesco* sauce) is the regional **speciality** and you'll find it on several *menús del día* around town: *romesco* sauce has a base of dry pepper, almonds and/or hazelnuts, olive oil, garlic and a glass of Priorato wine. Beyond this, there are many variations, as cooks tend to add their own secret ingredients. Good **bars** are less in evidence in Tarragona, though there are a few recommended ones listed below. Instead, you can join the locals in their nocturnal search for **cakes and ice cream**: Rambla Nova particularly is groaning with pavement cafés, all doing a roaring trade. For the location of Tarragona's **markets**, see "Listings", below.

Restaurants

Bar-Restaurant Turia, Plaça de la Font 26. Basic *comedor* with home-cooked food. No great choice, just the daily 900ptas *menú del día*, but as cheap as it comes, and not at all bad.

Can Llesques, c/Natzaret 6, on Plaça del Rei. Cramped, atmospheric restaurant with low stone arches serving endless variations of *Pa amb tomaquet*, accompanied by drinks dished up in ceramic pitchers. It's amazingly popular; go early or prepare to hang around for a table. Sitting outside attracts a ten percent surcharge.

El Caseron, c/de Cos del Bou 9. Small restaurant just off Plaça de la Font, with a decent menu of staples – rabbit, paella, grills and fries – and a very good-value *menú del día*. Closed Mon after 5pm & Sat & Sun.

Les Coques, c/Nou del Patriarca. Fine dining in an upmarket Catalan restaurant, just off Plaça de la Seu near the cathedral. Around 3000ptas a head. Closed Sun.

Mistral, Plaça de la Font 17. Pizzas around the 500ptas mark, plus the usual (Spanish) menu, including pricey *pescado romesco*. Tables on the square in summer are its main attraction, though. Closed Sun in winter.

La Pizzeria, c/Cos del Bou 6. There are cheaper pizzerias, but this family-run place has a relaxed and friendly atmosphere. Closed Mon lunch & Sun.

El Plata, c/August 20. Summer outdoor dining in the pedestrian zone between the two *ramblas*. A decent *menú del día* at 1125ptas and a wide *tapas* selection.

Bars and cafés

Bar Frankfurt el Balcon, Rambla Nova 3. Outdoor tables in the best spot on the *rambla*, on the balcony of land next to the statue of Roger de Lluria. Sandwiches and *tapas*.

Bar Musical El Cau, c/Trinquet Vell 2. Situated in an underground Roman vault in the old town, this dark venue has live indie-pop or rock every Saturday night. Open daily 10pm–4am with reasonable bar prices.

Café L'Antiquari, c/Santa Anna 3. Laid-back café-bar with funk and rock sounds and a liberal use of borrowed religious artefacts and statues, including a confessional box converted into a telephone cabin. A noticeboard at the entrance has details of events around town.

Café Cantonada, c/Fortuny 23. Civilized café-bar whose roomy interior and pool table encourage extended visits. Breakfast served from 8.30am to midday; closed Mon.

El Candil, Plaça de la Font 13. Fashionable, friendly bar with a wide selection of herbal teas and coffees as well as alcohol.

Frankfurt, c/Canyelles (off Rambla Nova, on the left before the fountain). A bar with good hot and cold sandwiches prepared in front of you – a wide selection for 200–400ptas a go.

La Geladeria, Plaça del Rei 6. Popular ice-cream parlour outside the archeological museum.

Moto Club Tarragona, Rambla Nova 53. Busy *rambla* bar with televised soccer if it's on. Open daily from 7am to midnight for drinks and snacks.

Patisseria Granta, c/Major 32. Cakes and pastries in a swish, modern *patisseria*. Counter or table service; popular on Sundays.

La Penya, Plaça de la Font 35. Friendly, hippyish bar offering hearty Catalan cuisine, with generous shots of *vermouth de la casa* (at 125ptas a go), and, if you ask a couple of days beforehand, excellent Mexican food too.

Tupac'Amaru, c/Via de l'Imperi Romà 11. Weird and wonderful bar with acid decor, table-football and a fine collection of techno sounds.

Listings

Airlines Iberia, Rambla Nova 116 (☎977 240696 or 977 240751).

Banks and exchange Many banks have offices along Rambla Nova. Outside banking hours you can exchange money and travellers' cheques at Viajes Eurojet, Rambla Nova 42 (Mon–Fri 9am–1.30pm & 4.30–8.30pm, Sat 9am–1pm). This agency also handles American Express matters, and will exchange cheques and hold mail.

Bus information Local bus information is available from the tourist offices or the cabin on c/Cristòfor Colom (☎977 549480). Bus station information on ☎977 229126.

Car rental Atesa, at Viatgens Marsans, c/Lleida 11 (☎977 219867); Racc, Rambla Nova 114 (☎977 211962); Avis, at c/Pinsoler 10 (☎977 219156); Hertz, Vía Augusta 91 (☎977 384137).

Cinemas Movies are shown at Oscars, c/Ramón i Cajal 15; Lauren Multicines, c/Vidal I Barraquer 15-17; and Catalunya, Rambla Vella 9. Listings from the tourist offices or in the local newspaper.

Consulates UK, c/Reial 33 (☎977 220812).

Emergencies Call ☎092 or ☎977 222222 for an ambulance.

Hospitals Hospital de Sant Pau i Santa Tecla, Rambla Vella 14 (☎977 259900).

Markets Daily food market (not Sun) on and around Plaça Cosini, near the provincial forum; indoor food market at Plaça de Corsini (Mon–Fri 9am–1pm & 4–8pm, Sat 7am–1pm). On Sundays, there's an antiques market at the top of the cathedral steps, with jewellery, bric-a-brac, ornaments and antiques spilling over into the arcades along c/Mercería.

Newspapers Foreign newspapers are on sale at the kiosks on Rambla Nova.

Post office At Plaça de Corsini (Mon–Fri 8am–8.30pm, Sat 8am–2pm).

Taxis There are ranks on Rambla Nova (in Plaça del Font, and at the Moto Club), in Plaça del Font, and at the bus and train stations. Or call ☎977 221414, 977 236064 or 977 215656.

Train information Information on ☎977 240202. RENFE has an office at Rambla Nova 40 for tickets and enquiries (Mon–Fri 9am–1pm & 4–7pm; ☎977 232534).

Travel agencies For local tours, train and bus information, and tickets, contact Viajes Eurojet,

Rambla Nova 40; Viatgens Marsans, c/Comte de Rius; Vibus, Rambla Nova 125; or Wagon Lits, c/Cristòfor Colom 8.

Salou-Cambrils

The coast south of Tarragona is an uninspiring prospect. The occasional beaches are not easily reached by public transport, and few of them have anything to encourage a stop: long, thin strips of sand, they are almost universally backed by gargantuan caravan-camping grounds, packed full and miles from anywhere. This part of the Costa Daurada also boasts one of Catalunya's biggest tourist developments, the extended coastal stretch that is the resort of **Salou-Cambrils**. It's actually two separate towns, but the few kilometres between them have long been filled and stacked with holiday apartments, bars and restaurants. You may wish to give them a miss altogether – understandable in high summer when every inch is block-booked and smothered in sunscreen – though Cambrils does have its good points, especially out of season.

Salou

The ten-minute train ride from Tarragona to **SALOU** makes an unpromising start, passing through a mesh of petro-chemical pipes and tanks before rounding on the resort itself – an almost entirely unrelieved gash of apartment blocks and hotels spilling down towards the sea. There are three or four separate beaches here, ringed around a sweeping bay and backed by a promenade studded with palms. From the seafront it's quite an attractive prospect, but the town is resolutely downmarket and stuffed to the gills in summer, the streets back from the sea teeming with "English pubs" and poor restaurants serving overpriced food and beer. Just outside town lies **Port Aventura** (daily: mid-June to mid-Sept 10am–midnight; mid-Sept to mid-June 10am–8pm; information ☎902 202220; 4100ptas). This massive theme park, with its own RENFE station, boasts five themed "lands" including China and the Wild West, each offering death-defying rides, garish restaurants and live entertainment. If it's your bag, you might want to buy a two-day pass (6250ptas) and stay in Salou, which is packed with hotels and *pensiones*. Otherwise, you're much better off heading for Cambrils, 7km south. Buses regularly ply the coastal road between the two, or it's one more stop on the train.

Cambrils

Smaller **CAMBRILS** is nicer in every way, the town set back from a large harbour which still has working boats and fishing nets interspersed among the restaurants and hotels. In summer it's as full as anywhere along the Catalan coast, and Cambrils is probably better seen as a day trip from Tarragona, only fifteen minutes to the north. Out of season, though, it's more relaxed and while inexpensive accommodation isn't easy to come by, it might be worth persevering for a night to eat in the good fish restaurants and amble around the harbour and nearby beaches. There's a **market** in town every Wednesday (the one in Salou is on Monday).

Arrival and information
Arriving by bus from Tarragona, you'll pass through Salou and can ask to be dropped in Cambrils on the harbour front. By **train**, you're faced with a fifteen-minute walk from the inland part of town down to Cambrils-Port and the harbour: from the station, turn right and then right again at the main road, heading for the sea. Across the bridge on

your left is the main **Turismo** (daily 10am–1pm & 5–8pm; ☎977 361159), which has free maps, local bus and train timetables posted on the door, and may be able to help find a room. From here, Cambrils-Port is straight ahead, down any of the roads in front of you.

Accommodation

Finding **rooms** can be a problem, since accommodation in town is mainly in apartments. The hotels that exist are pricey, and not inclined to reduce their rates out of season. On the square outside the train station, and on the way to the harbour, a few places advertise *habitaciones*: you'd probably do best to take whatever's going in summer, even though here you're fifteen minutes or so from all the action.

Down at the harbour, hotels mingle with places just offering rooms. Try the *Hostal Moncusi*, c/Roger de Llúria 8 (☎977 360029; marked CH; ③), whose clean, bright rooms (without bath) are about the best value in town; ask at the *Restaurant Playa* for directions. The *Hotel-Restaurant Miramar*, Passeig Miramar 30 (☎977 361394; ⑥), is a deal more expensive, but nicely positioned overlooking the sea; the price here includes breakfast.

There are no fewer than eight **campsites** in and around Cambrils, and the Turismo has a free map showing where they all are. Closest to the centre is *Camping Horta* (☎977 361243; April–Oct), north of the harbour at the top of Rambla Regueral; the others are spread up and down the coast in both directions.

Eating

Food prices in Cambrils are on the steep side, but there's plenty of choice and some splendid fish **restaurants** along the harbour if you're prepared to dust off your wallet. The *Restaurant Playa* (see above) makes a good start, with three variously priced *menús del día*, the most expensive of which – at around 1500ptas a head – guarantees you a fine feast. Elsewhere, you're looking at a *menú del día* for around 1200ptas in most of the restaurants, though à la carte seafood at one of the harbour front restaurants comes in at considerably more than that.

Less expensive meals are found at several places along c/Pau Casals – including *Restaurant-Pizzeria El Capi* at no. 16 – or go for the modestly priced *platos combinados* at *Cafetería La Sirena*, c/Sant Pere 2 (entrance on c/Roger de Llúria; closed Thursday). The bar opposite the train station has seafood *tapas* and the usual *comedor* standbys.

South of Cambrils

Beyond Cambrils the train shoots past a scrappy coastline that resolutely fails to impress. The sporadic concrete development is punctuated by campsites and beaches that might tempt drivers but shouldn't persuade you off the infrequent trains. If disaster strikes, or the fancy takes, the only place even to consider delaying your progress is at **L'AMETLLA DE MAR**, a tourist town of rooms and restaurants but of no other intrinsic interest. Once you're past here, the landscape of the Delta de l'Ebre (see below) soon begins to make itself felt, before the train suddenly cuts inland to Tortosa, framed by the mountains behind.

Tortosa

The only town of any size in Catalunya's deep south is **TORTOSA**, slightly inland astride the Riu Ebre. In the Civil War the front was outside Tortosa for several months until the Nationalists eventually took the town in April 1938. The battle cost 35,000 lives – a traumatic event that is commemorated by a gaunt metal monument standing on a huge stone plinth in the middle of the river in town. The fighting took its toll in other ways, too: there's little left of the medieval quarter in the few old streets around the **cathedral**, though the building itself is worth a look. Founded originally in the twelfth century on the site of an earlier mosque, it was rebuilt in the fourteenth century, and its Gothic interior and quiet cloister – although much worn – are very fine. Several *modernista* houses around town (marked on the Turismo map) also add a bit of interest.

Tortosa's brightest point is also its highest. **La Suda**, the old castle, sits perched above the cathedral, glowering from behind its battlements at the Ebre valley below and the mountains beyond. Like so many in Spain, the castle has been converted into a luxury *parador*, but there's nothing to stop you climbing up for a magnificent view from the walls, or even from marching into the plush bar and having a drink. From the cathedral, c/de la Suda takes you straight there.

On the other side of La Suda, a garden beneath the castle houses a collection of **sculptures** (April to mid-Sept Tues–Sat 10am–1pm & 4.30–7.30pm, Sun 10am–2pm; mid-Sept to March Tues–Sat 10am–1pm & 3.30–5.30pm, Sun 10am–2pm; 300ptas) by Santiago de Santiago. The human figures are based loosely on themes such as "Ambition" and "Love", and the central feature is a ten-metre-high tower of seething bodies apparently depicting the struggle of humanity.

Practicalities

Tortosa is the main transport terminus for the region: in particular, regular buses run from here out to the principal towns and villages of the Delta de l'Ebre (see below). This, really, is the main reason to come, since the town is otherwise hardly an inspirational stopover, unless you stay at the *parador*. Moving on **out of Catalunya**, regular **buses** run from Tortosa to Vinaròs (in Castellón province to the south), from where you can reach the wonderful inland mountain town of Morella; and less regularly west to Alcañiz (in Aragón). **Trains** head south, passing through Vinaròs, on their way to Valencia.

The main **Turismo** (Mon–Fri 10am–1pm & 4–7pm, Sat 10am–1pm; ☎977 510822) is in the Plaça Bimil Lenari, to the south of the town, and there's a more central summer Turismo (April–Sept Tues–Sat 10am–1pm & 4–8pm, Sun 10am–1pm; ☎977 442567) on the main road into town, Avinguda. de la Generalitat, in the park on the left-hand side. To get there from the bus or train stations, follow the train tracks towards the river and turn left – away from the centre – under the bridge. Further out of town along here is the *Pensión Virginia*, at no. 133 (☎977 444186; ②), a good place to stay if your budget doesn't run to the **parador** (☎977 444450; fax 977 444458; ⑦) at La Suda. If you do stay at the *parador* you should eat there as well, since it has the best **restaurant** in town, open to non-guests. The *Virginia* also has a decent restaurant, but other good places to eat are thin on the ground in Tortosa.

The Delta de l'Ebre

In the bottom corner of Catalunya is the **Delta de l'Ebre** (Ebro Delta), 320 square kilometres of sandy delta constituting the biggest wetland in Catalunya and one of the most important aquatic habitats in the western Mediterranean. Designated a natural park, its brackish lagoons, marshes, dunes and reed beds are home to thousands of wintering birds and provide excellent fishing; around fifteen percent of the total Catalan catch comes from this area. The delta has been inhabited since the time of the Moorish conquest – some of the local names are Arab-influenced – but endemic malaria and heavy flooding kept the population in check for centuries, and only comparatively recently has there been any stability in the various settlements within the delta.

Much of the area of the **Parc Natural de Delta de l'Ebre** is a protected zone and hence access is limited. It's also difficult to visit without your own transport, though the effort of doing so is rewarded by tranquillity and space. If you're relying on buses, aim for one of the three main towns – Amposta, Sant Carles de la Ràpita or Deltebre – where you'll find accommodation and boat services on into the delta. Outside the towns, camping is allowed in certain areas.

Amposta

AMPOSTA, at the far western edge of the delta, is the largest and least attractive of the towns in the region, and not really somewhere you need to stay long. There are a couple of places to stay on the edge of town and a **Turismo** at Sant Gaime 1 (April to mid-Sept Mon–Sat 10am–1pm & 4–7pm, Sun 10am–2pm; Oct to mid-Sept March Mon–Fri 11am–1pm; ☎977 703453), which can advise you about the possibility of renting a boat to take you down to the river mouth: with costs shared between a group of people, this is not too expensive.

Sant Carles de la Ràpita

SANT CARLES DE LA RÀPITA, to the south, is a more inviting place, with regular daily buses from Tortosa – though few at the weekend – and a **Turismo** (June–Sept Mon–Fri 9am–2pm & 4–6pm, Sat & Sun 11am–1pm & 5–7pm; Oct–May Mon–Sat morning only, closed Sun; ☎977 740100) in the *Ajuntament*. It's quite a busy town in summer, drawing families to the several campsites stretching away down the coast – prepare to fend off swarms of mosquitoes if you stay at them – and to the dozens of restaurants which are said to serve the best prawns in the Med. Unless you've access to a car, though, you'll be able to explore only the immediate surroundings.

For **rooms** in town, try the large *Pensión Roca Mar*, Avda. Constitució 8 (☎977 740458; ③), whose rooms without bath are fine, or *Pensión Agusti*, c/Pilar 2 (☎977 740427; ④), whose rooms with bath are only a shade dearer. The latter also has some rooms with air conditioning, a rare treat in these parts. The *Agusti*'s excellent **restaurant** is much frequented by locals, as is the *Can Victor*, signposted from all over town, whose position right beneath the market guarantees the freshest of produce. Throughout July, local restaurants take turns to lay on special promotional menus, at the end of which you'll either have turned into a prawn or be off seafood for life.

Deltebre, Sant Jaume d'Enveja and around

From Amposta, road and river run to **DELTEBRE** (buses from Tortosa), at the centre of the delta. The **park information office** here, on the edge of town at c/Ulldecona 22 and well-signposted (Mon–Fri 10am–2pm & 3–6pm, Sat 10am–1pm & 3.30–6pm, Sun 10am–1pm; ☎977 489679), can provide you with a map of the delta, and has information about tours and local walks. At the same place there's an interesting **Ecomuseum** (same opening hours; 100ptas), which has an aquarium displaying (non-edible) species from the delta, and also maintains hides for bird-watchers which overlook a pond. There are three or four places to stay in Deltebre, all reasonably priced, as well as a **youth hostel** (☎977 480136; ①) at Avda. de les Goles del Ebre, and a ferry across to **SANT JAUME D'ENVEJA** on the opposite shore. The local restaurants serve wonderful fish dishes, the speciality being *arròz a banda*, similar to paella except that the rice is brought before the seafood itself.

Three islands lie between Amposta and the open sea, the biggest being the **Illa de Buda** just by the river mouth. It's covered with rice fields (the main local crop) and you can reach it on excursion boats from Deltebre or by scheduled ferry from Sant Jaume. The road which runs along the south bank of the river leads to the so-called Eucaliptus **beach**, where there's a campsite, *Mediterrani Blau* (☎977 479046). Sunbathers should be careful not to burn in these flat, windy zones.

Inland: the route to Lleida

The train line from Barcelona forks at Tarragona, and the choice is either south towards Tortosa or **inland** for the fairly monotonous three-hour ride northwest across the flat lands to Lleida. The Tarragona–Lleida bus is a slightly more attractive proposition than the train, if only because it climbs the odd bluff and ridge on the way for good views over the plain. The bus also takes you directly to the region's only major attraction, the monastery of Poblet, which you could see in half a day and then move on to Lleida. Access to the monastery by train is possible, but means walking some of the way – not an unpleasant task by any means if the weather's fine since the surroundings are lovely.

Montblanc

The walled medieval town of **MONTBLANC**, 8km before the turning to the monastery at Poblet, is also on the train line to Lleida, so it's easy enough to see both on the same trip. It's a surprisingly beautiful place to discover in the middle of nowhere, and astonishingly lively during the evening *passeig* around the picturesque Plaça Major. There are many fine little Romanesque and Gothic monuments contained within a tight circle of old streets; all are marked on a map attached to the town's medieval gateway, the **Portal de Boue**, which is just a hundred metres or so up from the train station.

The grand Gothic parish church of **Santa María**, just above the central square, is perhaps the first thing to look out for: its elaborate facade has lions' faces on either side of the main doorway and cherubs swarming up the pillars. There's a fine view from the once-fortified mound that rises behind the church – over the rooftops, defensive towers and walls, and away across the plain. A couple of other churches to track down are Romanesque Sant Miquel (usually locked) and Sant Marcel, on the other side of the mound, which contains the **Museu Marès** (June–Sept Tues–Sat 10am–2pm & 4–8pm, Sun 10am–2pm; Oct–May Sat & Sun only; free). Like the one in Barcelona (p.585), it's an eclectic collection of religious sculpture and art. Montblanc also has a fine local history museum, the **Museu Comarcal de la Conca de Barberà** (June–Sept Tues–Sat 10am–2pm & 5–8pm, Sun 10am–2pm; Oct–May Tues–Sat 10am–1pm & 4–7pm, Sun 10am–2pm; 400ptas), just off Plaça Major below the church, which is bright and informative, although all annotated in Catalan.

Practicalities

There's a very friendly and helpful **Turismo** inside the Casa de la Vila building in the arcaded Plaça Major. When it's closed, the policeman on the door should hand over a map if he's asked nicely. If you're driving, Montblanc would make a fine base for visiting Poblet – even on foot, it's only 8km to the monastery. The friendliest place to stay is the *Fonda dels Àngels*, Plaça Àngels 1 (☎977 860173; ④), in the first square you reach after passing through the town gate; it also serves meals.

The Monestir de Poblet

There are few ruins more stirring than the **MONESTIR DE POBLET**. It lies in glorious open country, vast and sprawling within massive battlemented walls and towered gateways. Once *the* great monastery of Catalunya, it was in effect a complete manorial village and enjoyed scarcely credible rights, powers and wealth. Founded in 1151 by Ramón Berenguer IV, who united the kingdoms of Catalunya and Aragón, it was planned from the beginning on an immensely grand scale. The kings of Aragón-Catalunya chose to be buried in its chapel and for three centuries diverted huge sums for its endowment, a munificence that was inevitably corrupting. By the late Middle Ages Poblet had become a byword for decadence – there are lewder stories about this than any other Cistercian monastery – and so it continued, hated by the local peasantry, until the Carlist revolution of 1835. Then, in a passionate frenzy of destruction, a mob burned and tore it apart, so remorselessly that Augustus Hare, an English traveller who visited it 36 years later, recorded that "violence and vengeance are written on every stone".

The monastery was repopulated by Italian Cistercians in 1940 and over the past decades a superb job of restoration has been undertaken. Much remains delightfully ruined but, inside the main gates, you are now proudly escorted around the principal complex of buildings. As so often, the **cloisters**, focus of monastic life, are the most evocative and beautiful part. Late Romanesque, and sporting a pavilion and fountain, they open onto a series of rooms: a splendid Gothic **chapter house** (with the former abbots' tombs set in the floor), wine cellars, a parlour, a **kitchen** equipped with ranges and copper pots, and a sombre, wood-panelled **refectory**.

Beyond, you enter the **chapel** in which the twelfth- and thirteenth-century tombs of the kings of Aragón have been meticulously restored by Frederico Marès, the manic collector of Barcelona. They lie in marble sarcophagi on either side of the nave, focusing attention on the central sixteenth-century altarpiece. You'll also be shown the vast old **dormitory**, to which there's direct access from the chapel choir, a poignant reminder of Cistercian discipline. From the dormitory (half of which is sealed off since it's still in use), a door leads out onto the cloister roof for views down into the cloister itself and up the chapel towers.

Entry to the monastery costs 500ptas, and it's open daily from 10am to 12.30pm and from 3 to 6pm (closing half an hour earlier in the winter). Officially, it can be toured only by members of a **guided group**. The tours take an hour and depart roughly every half-hour (every fifteen minutes Sunday and holidays). However, the porter may let you in to walk around alone if there aren't enough people within a reasonable period of time. There's a **Turismo**, on the left as you enter (daily 10am–1.30pm & 3–6pm; ☎977 871247).

Getting there by bus

Three **buses** a day run to Poblet from Tarragona or Lleida, passing right by the monastery. It's an easy day trip from either city, or can be seen on the way between the two – the gap between buses is roughly three hours, which is enough time to get around the complex. You could also **stay overnight** at Poblet, an even more attractive proposition if you have your own transport, since there are several pleasant excursion targets in the surrounding countryside (see below). The solitary *Hostal Fonoll* outside the main gate of the monastery (☎977 870333; ②; closed mid-Dec to mid-Jan) has a decent restaurant and bar, functional standard rooms and more expensive rooms with bath; while 1km up the road, around the walls, the hamlet of **LES MASIES** has a couple more hotels and restaurants, including the *Villa Engràcia* (☎977 870308, fax 977 870326; ③), which has a pool, tennis courts and parking facilities.

Getting there by train: L'Espluga de Francolí

The approach by **train** is much more atmospheric. You get off at the ruined station of **L'ESPLUGA DE FRANCOLÍ**, from where it's a beautiful three-kilometre walk to the monastery. Unfortunately there's no baggage *consigna* at the station, and L'Espluga itself is such a one-horse town that there's not much to do when it's not your turn with the horse. However, there are a couple of places to stay, including the *Hotel del Senglar* (☎977 870121, fax 977 871012; ⑤), a very comfortable set-up – with a decent restaurant, pool, tennis courts and parking – on the main road through town that leads to Poblet.

You can of course vary your approach to the monastery, taking the bus one way and choosing to walk to or from L'Espluga (3km), Montblanc (8km) or even Vimbodi (5km), at all of which the Tarragona–Lleida train stops.

Around Poblet: excursions

If you have time and transport, a couple of excursions into the countryside surrounding Poblet are well worth making. The red-stone walled village of **PRADES**, in the Serra de Prades, 20km from the monastery, is a beautifully sited and tranquil place that needs no other excuse for a visit. The *Pensión Espasa*, c/Sant Roc 1 (☎977 868023; ④), offers simple accommodation if you decide you like it enough to stay on. Prades is also the place to be during the second weekend of July, when they replace the water in the fountain with *cava*, and for a mere 1200ptas you can join in and help yourself.

The other option is to take in two more twelfth-century Cistercian monasteries. **Santes Creus** (summer daily 10am–1.30pm & 3–7pm; winter Tues–Sun 10am–1.30pm & 3–6pm; 300ptas) is the easier to reach, northeast of **VALLS** on the other side of the Tarragona–Lleida highway. It's built in Transitional style, with a grand Gothic cloister and some Romanesque traces, and you can explore the dormitory, chapter house and royal palace. There's a once-daily bus from Tarragona to Valls, which connects with a local service to Santa Creus, but check on return times because you don't want to get stranded in these parts. Trickier to find, though worth the drive, is the monastery of **Vallbona de les Monges** (Mon–Sat 10am–1.30pm & 4.30–6.45pm, Sun noon–1.30pm & 4.30–6.45pm; free), north of Poblet, reached up the C240 from Montblanc. This has been occupied continuously for 800 years, and the church is particularly fine.

Lleida

LLEIDA (Lérida), at the heart of a fertile plain near the Aragonese border, has a rich history. First a *municipium* under the Roman empire and later the centre of a small Arab kingdom, it was reconquered by the Catalans and became the seat of a bishopric in 1149. Little of those periods survives in today's pleasant city but there is one building of outstanding interest, the old cathedral, which is sufficient justification in itself to find the time for a visit. If you have to spend the night in Lleida – and you will if you're heading north to the Pyrenees by train or bus – there are a couple of museums and a steep set of old town streets to occupy any remaining time. Little known it may be, but Lleida certainly isn't dull, and the lack of visitors makes an overnight stop doubly attractive: rooms are easy to come by, and the students at the local university fill the streets and bars on weekend evenings in good-natured throngs.

Arrival and information

Plaça de Sant Joan is a fifteen- to twenty-minute walk east of the **train station**, with the **bus station** a similar distance in the other direction, down Avinguda. de Blondel. The **Turismo** (June–Sept Mon–Fri 9am–8pm, Sat 9am–2pm; Oct–May Mon–Fri 9am–7pm, Sat 9am–2pm; ☎973 270997) is at Avda. Madrid 36, overlooking the river. Pick up a map and a brochure, but don't expect too much English to be spoken.

Accommodation

There are a couple of **places to stay** right outside the train station, and more along the road straight ahead – Rambla Ferrán – which leads into the centre. Otherwise, press on to the central Plaça Sant Joan, around which there are several possibilities. There's a **campsite**, *Les Basses* (☎973 235954; mid-May to Sept), a couple of kilometres out of town on the Huesca road. Take the bus labelled *BS* or *Les Basses* (every 45min from Rambla Ferrán).

Alberg Sant Anastasi, Rambla d'Aragó 11 (☎973 266099, fax 973 266099). Lleida's youth hostel, centrally located but only open in July and Aug. ①.

Pensión Alex, c/Tallada 33 (☎973 260193). Good *pensión* on a quiet street near the market. ④.

Habitaciones Brianso, c/Pi i Maragall 22 (☎973 236339). A short walk from Plaça Sant Joan, along the continuation of c/Magdalena, these rooms are in a modern apartment block close to La Seu Vella. Phone first. ②.

Hostal-Residencia Caribe, c/Anselm Clavé (973 243584). No great shakes, but the cheapest accommodation near the train station. ②.

Hostal España, Rambla Ferrán 20 (☎973 236440). More upmarket than either of the neighbouring *habitaciones*, this *hostal* offers some rooms with a shower, but remember it's a busy road – so ask to see the room first. ③.

Residencia Mundial, Plaça de Sant Joan 4 (973 242700). Central and friendly *residencia*, with a break-fast bar and parking facilities. Some of the rooms (with and without bath) overlook the square. ④.

Hotel Principal, Plaça de la Paeria 8 (☎973 230800). Just off the Plaça de Sant Joan, a more luxurious and, inevitably, more expensive option. ⑤.

The City

The **Seu Vella** (Tues–Sat 10am–1.30pm & 4–7.30pm, closes 5.30pm in winter, Sun 9.30am–1.30pm; 400ptas), or old cathedral, is entirely enclosed within the walls of the ruined castle (La Suda), high above the Riu Segre, a twenty-minute climb from the centre of town. It's a peculiar fortified building, which in 1707 was deconsecrated and taken over by the military. It remained in military hands until 1940 since, wrote Richard Ford, "in the piping times of peace the steep walk proved too much for the pursy canons, who, abandoning their lofty church, built a new cathedral below in the convenient and Corinthian style!" Enormous damage was inflicted over the years (documented by photos in a side chapel) but the church remains a notable example of the Transitional style, similar in many respects to the cathedral of Tarragona. Once again the Gothic cloisters are masterful, each walk comprising arches different in size and shape but sharing delicate stone tracery. They served the military as a canteen and kitchen. Outside, the views from the walls, away over the plain, are stupendous.

You can climb back down towards the river by way of the aforementioned new cathedral, the **Seu Nova**, a grimy eighteenth-century building only enlivened inside by a series of minuscule, highly stained-glass windows. Nearby, halfway up the steep c/Cavallers at no. 15, is the **Museu Morera** (on the second floor; June–Sept Tues–Sat 11am–1pm & 6–9pm, Sun 10am–1pm; Oct–May Tues–Sat 11am–2pm & 5–8pm, Sun 10am–1pm; free), a permanent display of contemporary art by local artists, housed in an old monastery building. On the other side of the cathedral, on Avinguda. de Blondel, the **Museu Arqueològic** (Tues–Sat noon–2pm & 6–9pm; free) is a fairly negligible collection, but again is housed in an interesting building, this time the fifteenth-century Santa María hospital.

Once you've seen the cathedral and museums, you've just about seen the lot that Lleida has to offer, though its central pedestrianized shopping streets are good for a browse, and you can wind up in the **Plaça de Sant Joan** for a drink in one of the outdoor cafés. This square has been in the throes of regeneration for years, the last addition being a lift from the *plaça* to the Seu Vella. Much of the new stone and concrete infrastructure is already in place, and according to your point of view it's either making bold use of new materials to link the lower town with La Suda, or making a pig's ear of the square and its surroundings – so far the town seems unable to decide whether to love it or hate it.

Eating and drinking

Finding anything to **eat** or **drink** can be surprisingly difficult in the evening in Lleida, particularly on Sunday when many places are closed (including most of those detailed below).

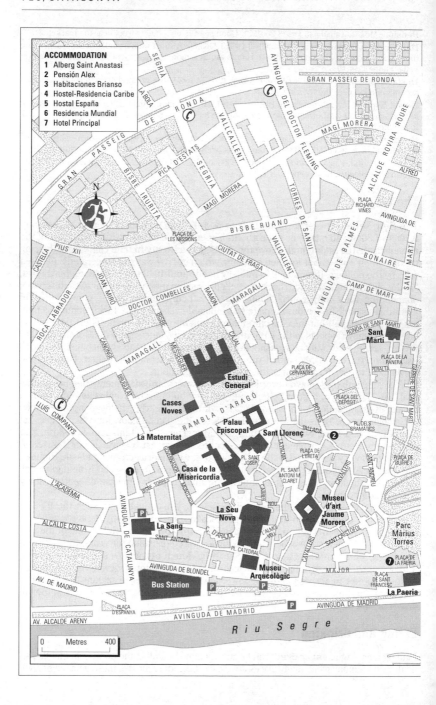

ACCOMMODATION
1 Alberg Saint Anastasi
2 Pensión Alex
3 Habitaciones Brianso
4 Hostel-Residencia Caribe
5 Hostal España
6 Residencia Mundial
7 Hotel Principal

N

GRAN PASSEIG DE RONDA

AVINGUDA DEL DOCTOR FLEMING

MAGÍ MORERA

ALCALDE ROVIRA ROURE

ALFRED

PLAÇA RICHARD VINES

AVINGUDA DE

SEGRIA

A BOLA

RONDA

DE

PASSEIG

GRAN

BISBE IRURITA

PICA D'ESTATS

SEGRIA

MAGÍ MORERA

BISBE RUANO

VALLCALLENT

TORRES DE SANUI

AVINGUDA DE BALMES

SANT MARTI

BONAIRE

CAMP DE MART

CASTELLA

PIUS XII

JOAN MIRO

PLAÇA DE LES MISSIONS

CIUTAT DE FRAGA

VALLCALLENT

ROCA LABRADOR

DOCTOR COMBELLES

BISBE

CANONGE

BRUGULAT

MARAGALL

MESSEGUER

RAMON

MARAGALL

Y CAJAL

PLAÇA DE CERVANTES

RONDA DE SANT MARTI

Sant Marti

PLAÇA DE LA PANERA

PERALTA

TORRENT DE SANT MARTI

LLUÍS COMPANYS

Estudi General

RAMBLA D'ARAGÓ

Cases Noves

Palau Episcopal

La Maternitat

Sant Llorenç

BOTERS

PLAÇA DEL DEPÒSIT

PL. DELS DRAMÀTICS

2

TALLADA

PLAÇA DE 'BUIRE I'

SANT ANDREU

L'ACADEMIA

1

Casa de la Misericordia

PL. SANT JOSEP

PL. SANT ANTONI M. CLARET

CATALUVERS

AVINGUDA DE CATALUNYA

BISBE TORRES

CONSERVAT

MONTCADA

La Seu Nova

C. D'ARAJOL

TORRE

NOU

PL. CATEDRAL

VALMU

Museu d'art Jaume Morera

SANT CRISTOFOL

Parc Màrius Torres

ALCALDE COSTA

P

La Sang

SANT ANTONI

CAVALLERS

7

PLAÇA DE LA PAERIA

AV. DE MADRID

AVINGUDA DE BLONDEL

Museu Arqueològic

MAJOR

PLAÇA DE SANT FRANCESC

La Paeria

Bus Station

P

P

AVINGUDA DE MADRID

P

AVINGUDA DE MADRID

AV. ALCALDE ARENY

PLAÇA D'ESPANYA

Riu Segre

0   Metres   400

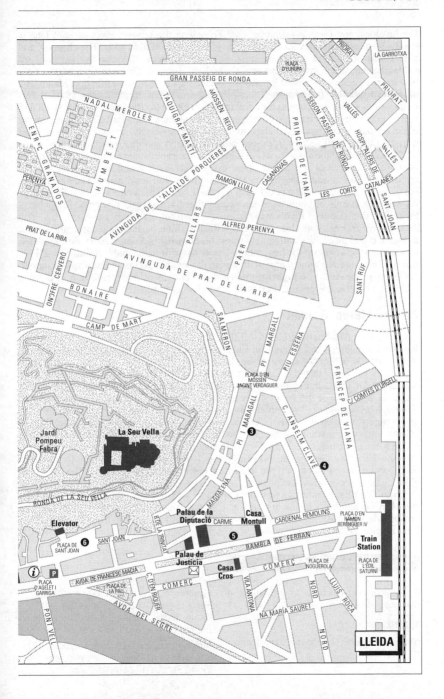

LLEIDA

For breakfast and *platos combinados*, *Café Triunfo* on the edge of Plaça de Sant Joan is good – step inside anyway for a look at the photographs of old Lleida. The cheapest and best meals are at the unpretentious *Casa José*, c/Botera 17 (near the Auditori, off c/Magdalena), which is very popular with the locals – especially for the *mariscos* – so it's best to arrive before 9pm when it really starts filling up. Nearby *Casa Marti*, c/Magdalena 37, is much smarter: the restaurant above the bar serves fine, locally inspired food at mid-range prices – 1500 to 2000ptas for a full meal or 975ptas for the *menú del dia*. You'll find more budget dining along c/de Cavallers, on the way up to the Seu Vella, where a string of rickety bars serve *tapas* (including snails, the local speciality) and meals. The **market** is just at the top of this street (Mon–Sat 9am–2pm), in Plaça dels Gramàtics.

If you're looking for more variety and better restaurants, head for the block of streets north of the church of Sant Marti. The university is close by, and this is where the students come to eat and hang out, in the restaurants and loud **music-bars** along the block formed by c/Sant Marti, c/Camp de Marti, c/Balmes and Avda. Prat de la Riba. As well as a couple of budget Catalan places, there are several pricier pizzerias here, including the popular *Restaurant-Pizzeria Travestere*, c/Camp de Marti 27. The *Marisquería Bar Lugano*, close by at Plaça Ricard Viñes 10, has a strong seafood *tapas* menu, and one place that is definitely **open on Sunday** is *Snoopy*, Avda. de Blondel 9, on the main road close to the bus station. Ignore the naff name and the pink-bowed interior: inside, there are good *platos combinados*, reasonable pizzas and a friendly English-speaking proprietor. For **nightlife**, there are a couple of good clubs on c/Comtes d'Urgell, near the station, but they don't start kicking until after 3am.

Around Lleida: Raimat

Twelve kilometres north of Lleida, off the road to Monzon, the little-known village of **RAIMAT** (meaning "grape-hand" in Catalan), with a population of just three hundred, is the location of Europe's biggest single **vineyard**. They've been making wine here since 1627 but only started commercial production in 1978 and have quickly built up a reputation for producing some of Spain's best, though least-known wines. There are tours (in Spanish) of the factory at weekends (10.30am, 11.30am & 12.30pm; ☎973 724000; free), although, if you phone first, it may be possible to visit during the week or to arrange a tour with Carlos Negrillo, who speaks excellent English. The tour, of course, ends with a small tasting (200ptas) and a visit to the shop, where you can purchase some of Raimat's finest for very reasonable prices. Particularly good is the Cava and the Cabernet Sauvignon, especially the 1994 vintage. Other than the factory, there's not a lot else to occupy you in Raimat, unless you fancy a drink at the bar of the village's summer-only swimming pool.

If you don't have your own transport, the only way to get to the vineyard is to take the Monzon bus from Lleida bus station (3–4 daily) and ask the driver to stop at the crossroads, which they usually will if you don't have any luggage in the hold; from here, it's a twenty- to thirty-minute walk.

travel details

For services from Barcelona to destinations in Catalunya, see p.624.

TRAINS

Blanes to: Figueres (2 daily; 1hr 30min); Girona (10 daily; 45min).

Figueres to: Barcelona (21 daily; 1hr 30min); Blanes (2 daily; 1hr 30min); Colera (8 daily; 25min); Girona (21 daily; 35min); Llançà (12 daily; 20min); Portbou (12 daily; 30min).

Girona to: Barcelona (21 daily; 1hr 20min); Blanes (10 daily; 45min); Figueres (21 daily; 35min); Portbou (12 daily; 1hr 10min).

Lleida to: Barcelona via Valls or Reus/Tarragona (14 daily; 2–3hr); Barcelona via Manresa (3 daily; 4hr); La Pobla de Segur (4 daily; 2hr); Tarragona (3 daily; 2hr); Zaragoza (15 daily; 1hr 40min).

Puigcerdà to: La Tour de Carol (3 daily; 6min).

Ribes de Freser to: Núria (9–10 daily; 45min); Queralbs (9–10 daily; 25min).

Ripoll to: Barcelona (12 daily; 2hr); Puigcerdà (6 daily; 1hr 30min).

Sitges to: Barcelona (every 30min; 25–40min); Cunit (12 daily; 20min); Tarragona (15 daily; 1hr); Vilanova (12 daily; 10min).

Tarragona to Barcelona (every 30min; 1hr 30min); Cambrils (11 daily; 20min); Cunit (10 daily; 40min); Lleida (3 daily; 2hr); Salou (11 daily; 10min); Sitges (direct every 30min; 1hr); Tortosa (10 daily; 1hr 15min); Valencia (8 daily; 4hr); Vilanova i la Geltrú (17 daily; 50min); Zaragoza (6 daily; 3hr 30min).

BUSES

Banyoles to: Besalú (Mon–Sat 8 daily, Sun 4; 15min); Girona (Mon–Sat 15 daily, Sun 2; 30min); Olot (Mon–Sat 8 daily, Sun 4; 50min); Santa Pau/Olot (8 daily; 45min/1hr).

Cadaqués to: Barcelona (2–4 daily; 2hr 20min); Castelló d'Empúries (5 daily; 1hr); Figueres (5 daily; 1hr 15min); Roses (5 daily; 35min).

Camprodon to: Molló (Mon–Sat 1 daily; 15min); Olot (1–2 daily; 1hr); Setcases (1–2 daily; 30min).

L'Escala to: Barcelona (July–Sept 3 daily; 2hr 40min); Figueres (5 daily; 45min); Girona (3 daily; 1hr); Palafrugell (4 daily; 45min); Pals (3 daily; 35min); Sant Pere Pescador (5 daily; 20min); Torroella de Montgrí (4 daily; 20min).

Figueres to: Barcelona (3–8 daily; 1hr 30min); Cadaqués (5 daily; 1hr 15min); Castelló d'Empúries (every 30min; 15min); El Port de la Selva (4 daily; 40min); L'Escala (5 daily; 45min); Espolla (1 daily; 35min); Girona (Mon–Sat 4–8 daily, Sun 3; 1hr); Llançà (Mon–Fri 5 daily; 20min); Olot (2–3 daily; 1hr 30min); Palafrugell (3 daily; 1hr 30min); Pals (3 daily; 1hr 20min); Roses (every 30min; 40min); Sant Pere Pescador (5 daily; 25min); Torroella de Montgrí (3 daily; 1hr).

Girona to: Banyoles (Mon–Sat 15 daily, Sun 2; 30min); Barcelona (Mon–Sat 6–9 daily, Sun 3; 1hr 30min); Besalú (Mon–Sat 8 daily, Sun 4; 45min); L'Escala (3 daily; 1hr); Figueres (Mon–Sat 4–8 daily, Sun 3; 1hr); Olot (Mon–Sat 8 daily, Sun 4; 1hr 15min); Palafrugell (hourly; 1hr 15min); Palamós (14 daily; 1hr); Platja d'Oro (14 daily; 45min); Sant Feliu (11 daily; 2hr); Sant Hilari Sacalm (Mon–Fri 2 daily, Sat 1; 1hr 20min); Tossa de Mar (July–Sept 2 daily; 1hr).

Lleida to: Artesa de Segre (3 daily; 1hr); Barcelona (Mon–Sat 9 daily, Sun 3; 2hr 15min); Huesca (5 daily; 2hr 30min); La Seu d'Urgell (2 daily; 3hr 30min); Montblanc (6 daily; 1hr 30min); Pobla de Segur (1 daily; 2hr); Poblet (3 daily; 1hr 15min); Tarragona (3 daily; 2hr); Viella, via Túnel de Viella (Mon–Sat 2 daily; 3hr); Zaragoza (Mon–Sat 4 daily, Sun 1; 2hr 30min).

Lloret de Mar to: Barcelona (July to mid-Sept 10 daily; 1hr 15min); Blanes (every 15min; 15min); Girona (5 daily; 1hr 20min); Palafrugell (2 daily; 1hr 30min); Palamós (2–4 daily; 1hr); Platja d'Oro (2–4 daily; 50min); Sant Feliu (2–4 daily; 40min); Tossa de Mar (every 30min; 15min).

Olot to: Banyoles (Mon–Sat 8 daily, Sun 4; 50min); Barcelona (2–3 daily; 2hr 10min); Besalú (Mon–Sat 8 daily, Sun 3; 30min); Camprodon (1–2 daily; 1hr); Figueres (2–3 daily; 1hr 30min); Girona (Mon–Sat 8 daily, Sun 4; 1hr 20min); Ripoll (3–4 daily; 1hr 10min); Sant Joan les Abadesses (1 daily; 50min); Santa Pau/Banyoles (1–2 weekly; 15min/1hr).

Palafrugell to: Barcelona (8 daily; 2hr); L'Escala (4 daily; 45min); Figueres (3 daily; 1hr 30min); Girona (15 daily; 1hr 15min); Lloret de Mar (2 daily; 1hr 30min); Palamos (12 daily; 15min); Pals (4 daily; 10min); Sant Feliu (hourly; 45min); Sant Pere Pescador (4 daily; 1hr); Torroella de Montgrí (4 daily; 25min).

La Pobla de Segur to: Barcelona (1 daily; 3hr 30min); Caldes de Boí (July to mid-Sept 1 daily; 2hr); Capdella (Mon–Sat 1 daily; 1hr); Lleida (1 daily; 2hr); El Pont de Suert (Mon–Sat 1 daily; 1hr); Viella (Mon–Sat 1 daily; 2hr).

El Port de la Selva to Figueres (4 daily; 40min); Llançà (July to mid-Sept 9 daily, rest of the year 2–4 daily; 25min).

Ripoll to: Camprodon (3 daily; 40min); Olot (3–4 daily; 1hr 10min); Sant Joan de les Abadesses (6–7 daily; 20min).

Sant Feliu to: Barcelona (8 daily; 1hr 30min); Girona (July–Sept 11 daily; 2hr), Lloret de Mar (July & Aug 2 daily; 40min); Palafrugell (hourly; 45min); Palamós (hourly; 30min); Platja d'Oro (hourly; 15min).

La Seu d'Urgell to: Andorra La Vella (6–7 daily; 1hr); Artesa de Segre (2 daily; 2hr); Lleida (2 daily; 3hr 30min); Puigcerdà (3 daily; 1hr).

Tarragona to: Andorra (1–2 daily; 4hr 30min); Barcelona (18 daily; 1hr 30min); Berga (July & Aug 1 daily, rest of the year Sat & Sun only; 3hr 10min); L'Espluga (3 daily; 1hr); La Pobla de Lillet (July & Aug 1 daily, rest of the year Sat & Sun only; 4hr 15min); La Seu d'Urgell (daily at 8am; 3hr 45min); Lleida (3 daily; 2hr); Montblanc (3 daily; 50min); Poblet (3 daily; 1hr 5min); Salou-Cambrils (every 30min; 20min); Tortosa (Mon–Fri 1 daily; 1 hr 30min); Valencia (7 daily; 3hr 30min); Zaragoza (4 daily; 4hr).

Tortosa to: Deltebre (Mon–Fri 5 daily, Sat 2; 1hr); Sant Carles de la Ràpita (Mon–Sat 5 daily, Sun 1; 40min); Tarragona (Mon–Fri 1 daily; 1hr 30min).

Tossa de Mar to: Barcelona (July–Sept 12 daily; 1hr 35min); Girona (July–Sept 2 daily; 1hr); Lloret de Mar (every 30min; 15min).

Viella to: Lleida (Mon–Sat 2 daily; 3hr); La Pobla de Segur (Mon–Sat 1 daily; 2hr); Salardú (Mon–Sat 1 daily; 20min).

CRUCEROS BOATS

Calella to: Palamós and vice versa, stopping at all intermediate ports (June–Sept 3 daily; 4hr).

Blanes to: Lloret de Mar/Tossa de Mar (June–Sept 5 daily; 20min/45min).

Tossa de Mar to: Sant Feliu (June–Sept 5 daily; 45mins); Platja d'Oro/Sant Antoni de Calonge/Palamós (June–Sept 4 daily; 1hr 15min/1hr 25min/1hr 45min).

CHAPTER TWELVE

VALENCIA AND MURCIA

The area known as the Levante (the East), combining the provinces of Valencia and Murcia, is a bizarre mixture of ancient and modern, of beauty and beastliness. The rich *huerta* of **Valencia** is said to be the most fertile slab of land in Europe, crowded with orange, lemon and peach groves, and with rice fields still irrigated by systems devised by the Moors. Unsurprisingly, a farmhouse is the most characteristic building of the Valencian *huerta*: called a *barraca*, its most striking feature is its steeply pitched thatched roof. *Valenciano*, a dialect of Catalan, is spoken in some parts of the region and, as it's been recently revived in schools, it now receives a higher profile in the capital. There's even an extreme nationalist group who deny the dialect's Catalan origins, but they haven't managed to convince anyone else. Evidence of the lengthy Moorish occupation can be seen throughout the province, in the castles, irrigation systems, crops and place names – Benidorm, Alicante, Alcoy, all come from Arabic.

Murcia is quite distinct, a *comunidad autónoma* in its own right, and there could hardly be a more severe contrast with the richness of the Valencian *huerta*. This southeastern corner of Spain is virtually a desert and is some of the driest territory in Europe. It was fought over for centuries by Phoenicians, Greeks, Carthaginians and Romans, but there survives almost no physical evidence of their presence – or of five hundred years of Moorish rule, beyond an Arabic feel to some of the small towns and the odd date palm here and there. As if the sterility of the land weren't enough, the unfortunate Murcians rank lowest in the popularity stakes in Spain, according to a survey taken in the 1970s of where people would prefer their son- or daughter-in-law to come from. The prejudice probably originated in the 1920s, when Murcians flooded into Catalunya in search of work and later spread to the entire country.

Much of the region's **coast**, despite some fine beaches, is marred by the highway to the south, the industrial development which has sprouted all around it (with consequent pollution), and of course the heavy overdevelopment of villas and vacation homes. The coves around **Denia** and **Xábia** (Jávea) in Valencia are the prettiest beach areas, but access and accommodation are difficult. The resorts of the **Mar Menor** in Murcia are similarly attractive, but again don't even think of turning up in season if you don't have a reservation. For the "wild" beaches of **southern Murcia**, transport is the major hurdle, but crowds won't be a problem. **Valencia** and **Alicante** are the major urban centres, and there are several historic small towns and villages a short way inland, such as **Xátiva**, **Orihuela** and **Lorca**. Throughout the region, trains are usually less expensive and faster than buses on shorter journeys.

There's no shortage of **culinary pleasures** in the region. Gourmets tend to agree that the best paellas are to be found around (but not *in*) Valencia, the city where the dish originated. It should be prepared fresh, and cooked over wood (*leña*), not scooped from some vast, sticky vat; most places will make it for a minimum of two people, with advance notice. Of the region's other rice-based dishes, the most famous is *arròz a banda*, which is served in two stages: first the rice, then the fish. Another speciality is eels served with piquant *all i pebre* (garlic and pepper) sauce. The sweet-toothed should try *turrón*; made of nuts and honey, it traditionally comes in a soft, flaky variety or very hard like a nougat (the *turrón* from Jijona is the finest). You could follow it with an *horchata*, a milky drink made from tiger nuts (*chufas*) or almonds (*almendras*).

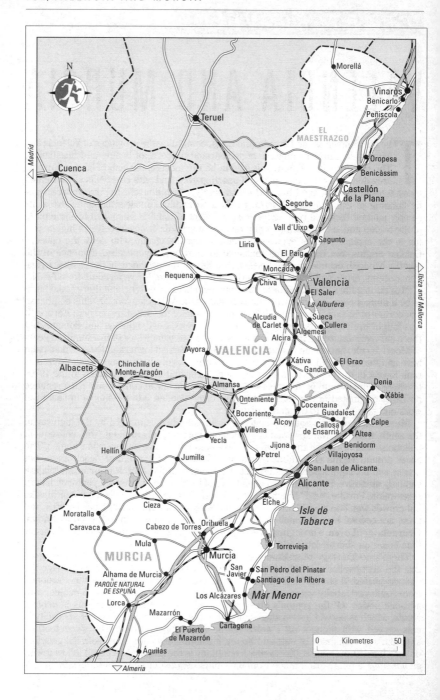

The Valencia area has a powerful tradition of **fiestas** and there are a couple of elements unique to this part of the country. Above all, throughout the year and more or less wherever you go, there are mock battles between Moors and Christians (*Moros y Cristianos*). Recalling the Christian Reconquest of the country – whether through symbolic processions or recreations of specific battles – they're some of the most elaborate and colourful festivities to be seen anywhere. The other recurring feature is the *fallas* (bonfires) in which giant carnival floats and figures are paraded through the streets before being ceremoniously burned.

Valencia

Valencia, the third largest city in Spain, may not approach the cosmopolitan vitality of Barcelona or the cultural variety of Madrid, but it does boast some of the best nightlife to be found in mainland Spain. *Vivir Sin Dormir* (live without sleep) is the name of one of its bars, and could be taken as the Valencian motto. The city is alive with noise and colour throughout the year, with unexpected explosions of gunpowder, fireworks and festivities. Although in summer the air becomes heavy with pollution, the clear Levante light, special to the area, flatters the city, and while the traffic is still a problem, four new metro lines are reducing the congestion in the centre.

Always an important city, Valencia was fought over for the agricultural wealth of its surrounding *huerta*. After Romans and Visigoths, it was occupied by the Moors for over four centuries with only a brief interruption (1094–1101) when El Cid recaptured it. He died here in 1099 but his body, propped on a horse and led out through the gates, was still enough to cause the Moorish armies – previously encouraged by news of his death – to flee in terror. It wasn't until 1238 that Jaime I of Aragón permanently wrested Valencia back. It has remained one of Spain's largest, richest and most stylish cities ever since. Despite its size, however, Valencia retains a strong feeling of *pueblo*. You won't hear much English spoken here and there are as yet few tourists outside *Fallas* time.

Valencia's **fiestas** are some of the most riotous in Spain. The best is *Las Fallas*, March 12–19 (see box p.740), which culminates in a massive bonfire when all the processional floats are burned. In July the city celebrates the *Feria de Julio* with bullfights, concerts, the "battle of the flowers" and fireworks. In September, there's a spectacular fireworks competition held in the river-park.

Arrival and information

Arriving by train at Valencia's beautifully tiled **Estación del Nord**, you're very close to the town centre; walk down Avenida. Marqués de Sotelo to the Plaza del Ayuntamiento, the central square. The **bus station** is some way out on the north side of the river, take local bus #28, or allow fifteen minutes if you decide to walk. The **Balearic ferry terminal** connects with the central plaza via bus #4 and with the train station via the #19 bus.

ACCOMMODATION PRICE CODES

The codes used in our hotel listings denote the following price ranges:

① Under 2000ptas	④ 4500–6000ptas	⑦ 12,000–17,500ptas
② 2000–3000ptas	⑤ 6000–8000ptas	⑧ Over 17,500ptas
③ 3000–4500ptas	⑥ 8000–12,000ptas	

See p.34 for more details.

FIESTAS

February

2–5 Moors and Christians battle for the castle in Bocariente, with wild firework displays at night.

Carnaval (forty days before Easter Week) in Águilas is one of the wildest in the country after Tenerife and Cádiz. Good carnival celebrations also in Cabezo de Torres and Vinaròs.

March

12–19 *Las Fallas de San José* in Valencia is by far the biggest of the bonfire festivals, and indeed one of the most important fiestas in all Spain. The whole thing costs as much as 200 million ptas, most of which goes up in smoke (literally) on the final *Nit de Foc* when the grotesque cardboard and wooden caricatures are burned. These *fallas* may be politicians, film stars or professional athletes, and anyone else who may be a popular target for satirical treatment. Throughout, there are bullfights, music and stupendous fireworks.

The middle of the month, especially around the **19th** (*San José*) also sees smaller *fallas* festivals in Xátiva, Benidorm and Denia.

Third Sun of Lent *Fiesta de la Magdalena* in Castellón de la Plana is marked by major processions and pilgrimages.

April

Holy Week is celebrated everywhere. In Elche there are, naturally, big Palm Sunday celebrations making use of the local palms, while throughout the week there are also religious processions in Cartagena, Lorca, Orihuela, Moncada and Valencia. The **Easter processions** in Murcia are particularly famous and they continue into the following week with, on the Tuesday, the *Bando de la Huerta*, a huge parade of floats celebrating local agriculture and, on the Saturday evening, the riotous "Burial of the Sardine" which marks the end of these spring festivals.

22–24 Famous *Moros y Cristianos* in Alcoy. After a colourful procession, battle commences between the two sides.

25 Morellá holds the traditional fiesta of *Las Primes*.

May

1–5 *Fiestas de los Mayos* in Alhama de Murcia, and *Moros y Cristianos* in Caravaca de la Cruz.

Second Sun *La Virgen de los Desamparados* in Valencia. The climax of this celebration is when the statue of the Virgin is transferred from her basilica to the cathedral.

Third Sun Moors and Christians battle in Altea.

On the **Plaza del Ayuntamiento**, you'll find the **Correos** crowned with trumpeting angels, and the **Turismo** (Mon–Fri 8.30am–2.15pm & 4.15–6.15pm, Sat 9.15am–12.45pm; ☎96 351 04 17), which gives out an excellent map. There's another Turismo in c/de la Paz 48 (Mon–Fri 10am–6pm, Sat 10am–2pm) and an information point with a hotel reservation service at the **train station**.

Accommodation

Valencia's budget **accommodation** is centred around the train station, in c/Bailén and c/Pelayo, parallel to the tracks off c/Játiva. C/Pelayo is the quieter of the two streets, but the area is not the most salubrious; for nicer – and not necessarily much pricier – places, head for the centre of town, around the market and out near the beach. There are **campsites** all along the coast, but none less than 10km from the city.

Albergue Juvenil Colegio Mayor "La Paz", Avda. del Puerto 69 (☎96 361 74 59). This youth hostel is out of town halfway to the port. Inexpensive but not too attractive, with a midnight curfew. Open July–Sept only. Bus #19 from Plaza Ayuntamiento. ①.

Albergue Juvenil Camino de Santiago, Plaza Hombres del Mar 28 (☎96 356 42 88). Situated in the fishermen's quarter a stone's throw from the beach, this friendly air-conditioned 22-bed hostel, with

June

23–24 *Día de San Juan* Magnificent *hogueras* festival around this date on the beaches of San Juan de Alicante. Similar to the March *fallas* of Valencia, with processions and fireworks, and celebrated on a smaller scale on the beaches of Valencia (Malvarossa, Cabanyal and Aloboraya), with bonfire-jumping.

July

Early July *Fiestas de la Santísima Sangre* in Denia with dancing in the steets, music and mock battles.

15–20 *Moros y Cristianos* in Orihuela.

16 In San Pedro del Pinatar a maritime *Romería* in which an image of the Virgin is carried in procession around the Mar Menor.

Second week *Feria de Julio* in Valencia with much music and above all fireworks, ending with the Battle of the Flowers in the Alameda. Festival of music in Valencia throughout the month, featuring open-air concerts in Viveros park.

25–31 *Moros y Cristianos* battle in Villajoyosa by both land and sea.

August

15 Local festivities in Denia, Jumilla, and Requena.

21–23 Local festivities in Jijona.

Last Wed Local fiesta in Sagunto and at the same time the great Moors and Christians and a mystery play in Elche. *La Tomatina* in Buñol, a tomato-throwing free for all, with some of Europe's finest orchestras playing in an open-air auditorium.

September

4–9 *Moros y Cristianos* in Villena.

8 *Mare de Deu de la Salut* – colourful folkloric processions in Algemesi.

10–13 International Mediterranean Folk Festival in Murcia.

13 Rice festival in Sueca includes a national paella contest.

22 Fiesta of *Santo Tomás* in Benicàssim with bands and a "blazing bull".

October

Second Sunday Benidorm celebrates its patron saint's day.

18–22 Moors and Christians in Calpe.

November

1 *Fiesta de Todos los Santos*; All Saints' festival in Cocentaina.

December

6–8 *La Fiesta de la Virgen* in Yecla when the effigy of Mary is carried down from the sanctuary on top of the hill amid much partying.

14 The weekend after this date sees four days of Moors and Christians in Petrel.

a women-only dorm, is ideally situated for the throbbing nightlife along Las Arenas. Facilities include TV, kitchen and washing machine. Silence after 11pm as the fishermen rise at 6am or earlier. Take bus #19 from the train station or bus #1 or #2 from the bus station. Pilgrims on their way to Compostela can stay free of charge. ③.

Hotel Alkázar, c/Mosén Femades 11 (☎96 351 55 51, fax 96 351 25 68). Dependable and well-cared-for town centre hotel, near the post office. All rooms with shower. ⑤.

Hotel Astoria Palace, Plaza Rodrigo Botet 5 (☎96 352 67 37, fax 96 352 80 78). Luxurious accommodation in this traditional and upmarket hotel, located in a quiet square. ⑧.

Hotel Inglés, Marqués de Dos Aguas 6 (☎96 351 64 26, fax 96 394 02 51). Old-fashioned, stylish hotel next to the Palacio Dos Aguas. ⑦.

Hotel La Marcelina, Paseo de Neptuno 72, near the sea (☎96 372 51 35). Pleasant, comfortable rooms with bath. ④.

Hotel Melia Plaza, Plaza Ayuntamiento 4 (☎96 352 06 12, fax 96 352 63 63). Recently opened upmarket hotel in a central location. All rooms are en suite with satellite TV. ⑧.

Hostal Moratín, c/Moratín 15 (☎96 352 12 20). Good value, central *hostal* with clean and comfortable rooms. ④.

Hotel La Pepica, Avda. Neptuno 2, near the beach (☎96 371 41 11). Comfortable hotel offering good-value rooms with bath. ④.

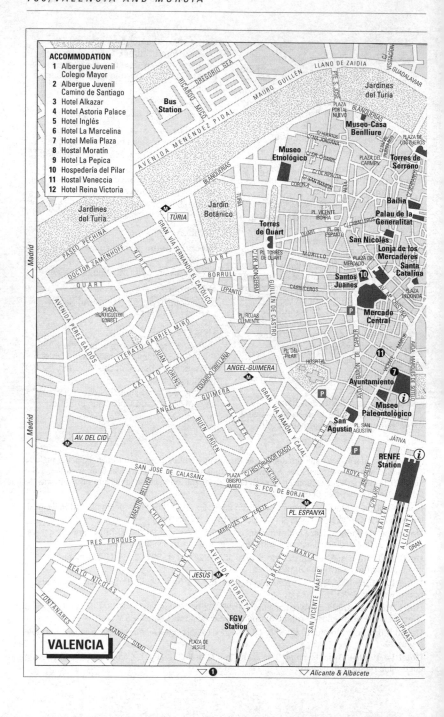

ACCOMMODATION

1 Albergue Juvenil
  Colegio Mayor
2 Albergue Juvenil
  Camino de Santiago
3 Hotel Alkazar
4 Hotel Astoria Palace
5 Hotel Inglés
6 Hotel La Marcelina
7 Hotel Melia Plaza
8 Hostal Moratín
9 Hotel La Pepica
10 Hospedería del Pilar
11 Hostal Veneccia
12 Hotel Reina Victoria

VALENCIA

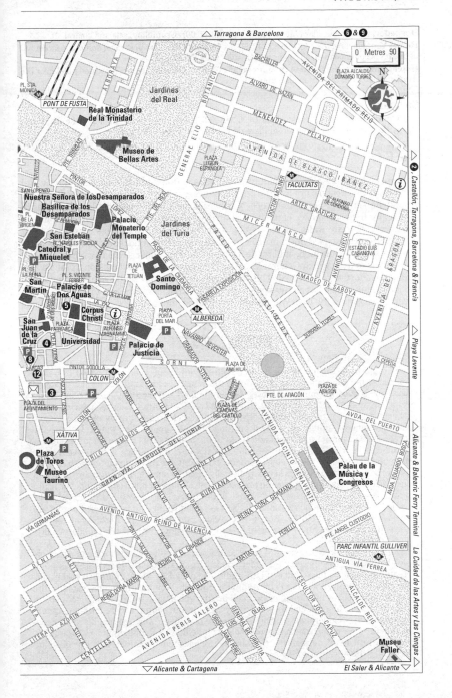

0 Metres 90

N

PL. STA.
MONICA
PONT DE FUSTA

Real Monasterio
de la Trinidad

Jardines
del Real

BACHILLER

AVENIDA DEL PRIMADO REIG

PLAZA ALCALDE
DOMINGO TORRES

ALVARO DE BAZAN

BOTANICO

Museo de
Bellas Artes

GENERAL ELIO

PTE. TRINIDAD

PINTOR

MENENDEZ

PELAYO

PLAZA
LEGION
ESPAÑOLA

AVENIDA DE BLASCO IBAÑEZ

Ⓜ
FACULTATS

PL.
SAN LORENZO

Nuestra Señora de losDesamparados

Basílica de los
Desamparados

San Esteban

Catedral y
Miguelet

PL. DE LA
VIRGEN

Palacio
Monaterio
del Temple

Jardines
del Turia

DOCTOR MOLINER

ARTES GRAFICAS

EL ALFONSO
DE CORDOBA

MICER MASCO

ESTADIO LUIS
CASANOVA

PL. NAPOLES Y SICILIA

PASEO DE LA CIUDADELA

PLAZA
DE
TETUAN

Santo
Domingo

AMADEO DE SABOYA

AVENIDA SUECIA

SERRANO MORRES

AVENIDA DE ARAGON

R. CEPEDA

PL. DE
LA REINA

San
Martin

PL. S. VICENTE
FERRER

Palacio de
Dos Aguas

❺
Corpus
Christi

ⓘ

Ⓜ
ALBEREDA

PLAZA
PORTA
DEL MAR

P

PASADELA EXPOSICION

ALAMEDA

San
Juan
de la
Cruz

❹
Universidad

PLAZA
ALFONSO
MAGNANIMO

P

Palacio de
Justicia

NAVARRO REVERTER

PLAZA DE
AMERICA

PLAZA DEL
AYUNTAMIENTO

❽

⑫

COLON

Ⓜ

❸

COLON

PTE. DE ARAGON

PLAZA DE
ARAGON

XÁTIVA

Ⓜ

P

Plaza
de Toros

Museo
Taurino

P

GRAN VIA MARQUES DEL TURIA

PLAZA DE
CANOVAS
DEL CASTILLO

AVENIDA JACINTO BENAVENTE

AVDA. DEL PUERTO

Palau de la
Música y
Congresos

VIA GERMANIAS

AVENIDA ANTIGUO REINO DE VALENCIA

REINA DOÑA GERMANA

PTE. ANGEL CUSTODIO

PARC INFANTIL GULLIVER

ANTIGUA VIA FERREA

Ⓜ

Museu
Faller

△ ❷, *Castellón, Tarragona, Barcelona & Francia*

△ *Playa Levente*

△ *Alicante & Balearic Ferry Terminal*

La Ciudad de las Artes y Las Ciengas

Hospedería del Pilar, Plaza Mercado 19 (☎96 391 66 00). Crumbling, safe and central. ②.

Hostel Venecia, c/en Llop 5 (☎96 352 42 67, fax 96 352 44 21). The best value *hostal* in a street full of budget accommodation; all rooms are en suite with TV. ⑤.

Hotel Reina Victoria, Barcas 4 (☎ & fax 96 352 04 87). Upmarket, centrally located hotel near the *Ayuntamiento*, with off-season discounts. ⑧.

Camping

El Palmar, Carretera Valencia–Cullera (☎96 162 03 53). 16km out, by La Albufera; take the hourly bus marked Valencia–El Perello from Plaza de los Torros. Open July–Aug.

The City

The most interesting area for wandering around is undoubtedly the mazelike **Barrio del Carmen** (the oldest part of town), roughly between c/de Caballeros and the Río Turia around the Torres de Serranos. In c/de Caballeros, look for the old door knockers placed high up for the convenience of the horse-borne gentlemen residents (hence the name of the street). The **city walls**, which judging from the two surviving gates must have been magnificent, were pulled down in 1871 to make way for a roundabout, and the beautiful church of **Santo Domingo**, in Plaza de Tétuan, has been converted into a barracks – the very barracks from which General Milans del Bosch ordered his tanks on to the streets during the abortive coup of 1981. This fact, however, isn't representative of the city's political inclination, which has always been to the left – Valencia was the seat of the Republican government during the Civil War after it fled Madrid, and the last city to fall to Franco.

LAS FALLAS

From March 12 to 19, around the saint's day of San José, Valencia erupts in a blaze of colour and noise for the **Fiesta de las Fallas**. During the year, each *barrio* or neighbourhood builds a satirical caricature or *falla*. These begin to appear in the plazas of each *barrio* at the beginning of March and are judged and awarded prizes before being set alight at midnight on March 19, the *Nit de Foc*. The festival takes its name from the Valencian word for torch. Traditionally, carpenters celebrated the day of San José and the beginning of spring with a ritual burning of spare wood. They would decorate the torches used over the winter and add them to the bonfire. This simple rite of spring has become an international tourist attraction, and it's an extraordinary sight to watch these painstakingly constructed models, some as tall as buildings, some big enough to walk inside, be strung with firecrackers and literally go up in smoke. The *fallas* are ignited in succession; the last to go up are the prize-winners. Each *falla* has a small model or **ninot** beside it, usually created by the children of the *barrio*. The *ninots* are exhibited in La Lonja before the fiesta begins, and the best is added to the Museu Faller; the rest are burnt with the *fallas*. Finally, around one o'clock, the *falla* of the Plaza Ayuntamiento goes up in flames, set off by a string of firecrackers, followed by the last thunderous firework display of the fiesta.

During the fiesta, processions of *falleros*, dressed in traditional costume and accompanied by bands, carry flowers to the Plaza de la Virgen, where the flowers are massed to create the skirt of a huge statue of La Virgen. The daily **Las Mascaletas** firecracker display takes place at 2pm in the Plaza Ayuntamiento – for a reputedly unpunctual race, the Valencians observe the timing of this celebration religiously. Traffic comes to a standstill, streets are blocked and the whole city races to the central square for a ten-minute series of body-shuddering explosions. There are nightly fireworks, bullfights, paella contests in the streets and *chocolate y buñuelos* stalls selling fresh doughnuts. On March 20, Valencia returns to normality – the streets are cleaned overnight, and the planning begins for the next year's *Fallas*.

The oldest part of the city is almost entirely encircled by the **Río Turia**, which is now a **river-bed park**. The river was diverted in 1956 after serious flooding which damaged much of the old town. The ancient stone bridges remain, and the river bed houses cycle paths and footpaths, football pitches, a stadium, a giant Gulliver for children to climb on and also the **Palau de la Música**, a striking, greenhouse-style glass concert hall, built in 1987, which offers daily classical and jazz concerts.

Around the Plaza del Ayuntamiento

Within the **Plaza del Ayuntamiento** is a central square lined with flower stalls, and an impressive floodlit fountain. The *Ayuntamiento* houses the **Museo Histórico Municipal** (Mon–Fri 9am–2pm; free) whose library has an impressive eighteenth-century map of Valencia showing the city walls intact.

The distinctive feature of Valencian architecture is its wealth of elaborate Baroque facades – you'll see them on almost every old building in town, but none so extraordinary or rich as the **Palacio del Marqués de Dos Aguas**. Hipólito Rovira, who designed its amazing alabaster doorway, died insane in 1740, which should come as no surprise to anyone who's seen it. Inside is the **Museo Nacional de Cerámica** (Tues–Sun 11am–8pm) with a vast collection of ceramics from all over Spain. Valencia itself was a major ceramics centre, largely owing to the size of its *morisco* population. Apart from an impressive display of *azulejos*, the collection contains some stunning plates with gold and copper varnishes (*reflejos*), a trio of evocatively ornate eighteenth-century carriages and, on the top floor, a reconstruction of a traditional Valencian kitchen. In the same decorative vein as the *palacio* is the church of **San Juan de la Cruz** (or San Andrés) next door.

Nearby, in the Plaza Patriarca, is the Neoclassical former **university** with lovely cloisters where free classical concerts are held throughout July, and the beautiful Renaissance **Colegio del Patriarca**, whose small **art museum** (daily 11am–1.30pm; 100ptas) includes excellent works by El Greco, Morales and Ribalta. Another Ribalta, *The Last Supper*, hangs above the altar in the college's chapel; in the middle of the *Miserere* service at 10am on Friday mornings it's whisked aside to reveal a series of curtains. The last of these, drawn at the climactic moment, conceals a giant illuminated crucifix. The whole performance is amazingly dramatic, and typical of the aura of miracle and mystery which the Spanish church still cultivates. The university library contains the first book printed in Spain, *Les Trobes*, 1474.

The cathedral

North from the university, along c/de la Paz, is the **Plaza de la Reina** and Valencia's **Catedral** (daily 7.30am–1pm & 4.30–8.30pm). The plaza is dominated by two octagonal towers, the florid spire of the church of **Santa Catalina** and the fourteenth- to fifteenth-century **Miguelete**, the unfinished tower of the cathedral itself. You can make the long climb up to the roof for a fantastic view over the city with its many blue-domed churches. Entrance to the tower from inside the cathedral costs 200ptas; hours are not fixed but it's usually open in the morning until about 1pm and again from about 5 to 8pm, closing earlier in the winter. The church's most attractive and unusual feature is the lantern above the crossing, its windows glazed with sheets of alabaster, a popular material in the region as it lets in the Valencian light. The lengthy process of removing the later Baroque additions from the original Gothic structure of the main body of the building was completed in 1996.

In the **Museu de la Seu**, the cathedral museum (daily 10am–1pm & 4pm until dusk; 200ptas) is a gold and agate cup (the *Santo Cáliz*) said to be the one used by Christ at the Last Supper – the Holy Grail itself. It's certainly old and, hidden away throughout the Dark Ages in a monastery in northern Aragón, it really did inspire many of the legends associated with the Grail. Other treasures include two Goyas, one of which depicts an exorcism (the corpse was originally naked, but after Goya's death a sheet was painted over it), and a 2300-kilo tabernacle made from gold, silver and jewels donated by the Valencian people. Made in 1939, it is paraded through the streets at Corpus Christi. The bells actually ring, and the silver figures of saints have removeable clothes.

Leaving the cathedral through the **Puerta de los Apóstoles**, you enter the **Plaza de la Virgen**. Here the Tribunal de las Aguas, the black-clad regulatory body of Valencia's water users, meets at noon every Thursday to judge grievances about the water irrigation system of the *huertas*. Blasco Ibáñez (1867–1928) describes their workings in detail in his novel *La Barraca*, which is about peasant life in the Valencian *huerta* and remains the best guide to the life of that region.

Two footbridges allow the clergy (only) to go straight from the cathedral into the Archbishop's Palace and the tiny chapel of **Nuestra Señora de los Desamparados**, also on the Plaza de la Virgen, where thousands of candles constantly burn in front of the image of the Virgin, patron of Valencia.

From the plaza, c/Caballeros leads to the **Palau de la Generalitat**, built in 1510, and today the seat of the Valencian autonomous government. The courtyard can be visited on weekdays (9am–8pm; free), but to see inside you need to make an appointment (Mon–Fri 9am–2pm; ☎96 386 61 00; English-speaking guide available). It's worth the phone call to see the beautifully painted ceilings and frescoes depicting a meeting of the assembly (1592) in the Salón Dorado and Salón de Cortes.

Silk exchange and markets

If you tire of Baroque excesses, visit the beautifully elegant Gothic **Lonja de los Mercaderes** (also known as Lonja de la Seda, or the Silk Exchange; Tues–Sat 9.30am–2pm & 5–9pm, Sun 9.30am–2pm; free) in the Plaza del Mercado. On weekdays it still operates as a commercial exchange. Opposite is the enormous **Mercado Central**, a modernist iron, girder and glass structure built at the beginning of the century and crowned with swordfish and parrot weathervanes. It's one of the biggest markets in Europe, fitting for *huerta* country, with amazing local fruit and vegetables, as well as hard-to-find herbs, health foods and dried goods. It closes around 2pm every day. Valencia's other spectacular market is the Mercado Colón on c/Cirilo Amoros.

Museums

The **Museu de Belles Artes** (Mon–Sat 9am–2.30pm, Sun 10am–2pm; free) on the far side of the river has one of the best general collections in Spain with works by Bosch, El Greco, Goya, Velázquez, Ribera and Ribalta as well as quantities of modern Valencian art. Outside is the largest of Valencia's parks – the **Jardines del Turia** (also called the Viveros Gardens) – in the centre of which is a small **zoo** (daily 10am–dusk; 500ptas). The gardens are the site of various events during the summer: a book fair in May and a music fair in July with open-air concerts.

As you head back into town don't miss the fourteenth-century **Torres Serranos**, an impressive gateway defending the entrance to the town across the Río Turia. The other remaining gateway is the **Torres de Quart**, a simpler structure but equally awesome in scale. Along with the **Museo de Etnología y Prehistoria** (Tues–Sat 10am–2.30pm & 4–7pm, Sun 10am–8pm; free) in the Centro Cultural La Beneficencia, at c/Corona 36, another minor museum that calls for a visit is the **Museo Paleontológico** (Tues–Sat 10am–2pm & 5–8pm; free) in c/Arzobispo Mayoral 3. It's in a building called the *Almudí*, a former grain storehouse built in the thirteenth century and rebuilt in the sixteenth century, now housing an awesome collection of bones and a magnificent collection of shells. If you're interested in bullfighting, the **Museu Taurino** is behind the bull ring on Pasaje Doctor Serra (Mon–Fri 10.30am–1.30pm; free).

If you want to gain insight into Valencia's Fiesta de las Fallas (see box, p.740), head for the **Museu Faller**, Plaza de Monteolivete 4 (Tues–Fri 10am–2pm & 4–7pm, Sat & Sun 10am–2pm; free), near the river-bed park (#13 bus from Plaza del Ayuntamiento). Here you'll find a fascinating array of *ninots* which have been voted the best and consequently saved from the flames. For a more hands-on experience, the **Museo del Artista Fallero** (Mon–Fri 10am–2pm & 4–7pm, Sat 10am–2pm; 300ptas), at c/ del Ninot 24 (#27 bus from behind the Ayuntamiento), which reveals exactly how the *fallas* are made.

La Ciudad de las Artes y las Ciencias

In its bid to attract tourists to the city outside of *Fallas* time, the city's Generalitat has undertaken an ambitious new project – **La Ciudad de las Artes y las Ciencias** (City of Arts and Sciences) – a giant complex set by the Turia between Autopista del Saler and Calle Moreras, consisting of four gigantic futuristic edifices designed by Valencian architect Santiago Calatrava.

The bulk of the project won't be ready until late 1999, but already open is **L'Hemisfèric** (Tues–Sun 10am–11.30pm; all shows 1000ptas; bookings essential on ☎902 115577), a striking eye-shaped building with a huge concave screen used for films, laser shows and a planetarium. Although at first all its nuts and bolts were not quite in place (the fire brigade declared it a safety hazard), it is now a resounding success and already ranks as the fourth most-visited building in Spain.

The other edifices will be the **Palacio de la Artes**, a multi-functional centre with a 2500-seater open-air auditorium, which will host plays, operas and concerts; the **Museo de las Ciencias**; and the **Parque Oceanográfico**, an underwater city with an aquarium housing dolphins, killer whales and an underwater restaurant. The Park will also duplicate the geological coastal formations of each climatic region of the planet.

Eating

Although it's the home of **paella**, the city of Valencia doesn't offer the best opportunities for sampling this most Spanish of dishes. The finest places to eat are, in fact, out of town in Perellonet or El Palmar (see p.748), or along the city beach, **Playa Levante**; Paseo Neptuno is lined with small hotels all with their own paella and *marisco* restaurants. For *tapas* and budget eating, you're best off heading for the Barrio del Carmen.

VALENCIAN CUISINE

Gastronomy is of great cultural importance to the Valencians. Rice is the dominant ingredient in dishes of the region, grown locally in paddy fields still irrigated by the Arabic canal system (*acequias*). The genuine **Paella Valenciana** doesn't mix fish and meat. It typically contains chicken, rabbit, green beans, *garrofón* (large butter beans), snails, artichokes and saffron. Shellfish are eaten as a starter.

Rice dishes vary around the region: *arroz negro* is rice cooked with squid complete with ink which gives the dish its colour, and served with *all i oli*, a powerful garlic mayonnaise. *Arroz al horno* is drier, baked with chickpeas. *Fideuá* is seafood and noodles cooked paella-style.You'll find *arroz a banda* further south on the coast around Denia – it's rice cooked with seafood, served as two separate dishes: soup, then rice. Around Alicante you can try *arroz con costra*, which is a meat-based paella topped with a baked egg crust. Apart from rice, vegetables (best *a la plancha*, brushed with olive oil and garlic) are always fresh and plentiful.

Restaurants and tapas bars

Alcabar, c/Sorní 35 (☎96 395 10 05). Stylish restaurant near Plaza de America serving modern Mediterranean cuisine. Closed Sat lunchtime Sat, Sun & Aug 7–Sept 7.

Bar Amorós, c/en Llop 3, just off Plaza de la Ayuntamiento (☎96 395 10 05). Inexpensive *tapas* bar which has specialized in seafood *tapas* for nearly seventy years.

El Asador de Aranda, c/Félix Pizcheta 9 (☎96 352 97 91). Fine Spanish delicacies, including *lechazo asado*. Closed Sun.

Bar Almudín, c/Almudín. Situated just behind the cathedral and renowned for its good seafood *raciones*.

Bar Ancoa, Plaza San Lorenzo at c/Novellos. Mid-range bar on the pedestrianized streets between the *Ayuntamiento* and the Turia. Also serves inexpensive *platos*.

Bar Cánovas, Plaza Cánovas Castillo. One of the city's best *tapas* bars.

Bar Glorieta, Plaza Alfonso Magnánimo. Large old bar serving *tapas* and excellent coffee (closes about 9pm).

Bar Manolin, c/Luís Oliaz 6. Basic and inexpensive *tapas* and *bocadillos*.

Bar Pilar, on the corner of c/Moro Zeit, just off Plaza del Esparto. Traditional place for *mejillones* (mussels), where they serve them in a piquant sauce and you throw the shells into buckets under the bar.

Bar Todo a Cien, c/Bailen 42. Great budget eat beside the train station; as the name suggests, all *tapas* cost just 100ptas.

Barbacoa, Plaza del Carmen 6 (☎96 392 24 48). Serves a wonderful *menú del día* including barbecued meat for 1500ptas. Be prepared to wait as it's small and very popular.

Civera, c/Lérida 11 & 13 (☎96 347 59 17). Valencia's best seafood restaurant, situated across the river from the Torres de Serranos.

Gargantua, c/Navarro Reverter 18 (☎96 334 68 49). Good Valencian restaurant serving regional specialities. Closed Sun evening & Mon.

La Hacienda, c/Navarro Reverter 12 (☎96 373 18 59). Best and most expensive restaurant in town where the speciality is bull's tail Cordoban-style. Closed Sat lunchtime, Sun & Easter.

La Lluna, c/San Ramón (☎96 392 21 46). Good vegetarian restaurant right in the heart of the Barrio del Carmen.

Mey Mey, c/Historiador Diago (☎96 384 07 47). Popular Chinese restaurant where you'll need to book at weekends. Closed Easter & last 3 weeks of Aug.

Restaurante Patos, c/de la Mar 28 (☎96 392 15 22). Handy if you're staying in c/Conde Montornes, this small, quiet restaurant has reasonably priced, interesting dishes.

La Riua, c/ de la Mar 27. Good restaurant serving up home-made paella and *fideuá*.

Rotunda, Plaza Redonda. Moderately priced restaurant, superbly situated on Valencia's distinctive round plaza.

HORCHATA

Valencia is also known for its **horchata** – a drink made from *chufas* (tiger nuts) served either liquid or *granizada* (slightly frozen). It is accompanied by *fartóns* (long, thin cakes). Legend has it that the name *"horchata"* was coined by Jaume I, shortly after he conquered Valencia. He was admiring the *huerta* one hot afternoon, and an Arab girl offered him a drink so refreshing that he exclaimed, *"Aixó es or, xata"* (this is gold, girl).

You can get *horchata* all over the city but the best traditionally comes from Alboraya, formerly a village in the Valencian suburbs, now absorbed into the city. The oldest *horchatería* in town is the *Santa Catalina* on the bottom corner of Plaza de la Reina. The various *horchaterías* and *heladerías* on Plaza San Lorenzo, just in from the Torres de Serranos, are excellent and very good value. To get to **Alboraya**, take the #70 bus, or metro line 3 to Metro Alboraya from Estación Pont de Fusta (across the river from Torres de Serranos). The most renowned *horchatería* is *Daniel*, Avda. de la Horchata 41, where you can sit on the terrace and escape from the summer heat of the city.

Bars and nightlife

Valencia takes its **nightlife** very seriously and has one of the liveliest bar scenes in mainland Spain. However, the action is widely dispersed, with many locations across the Turia, and if you don't know where to go, the city can seem dead at night. To get across the Turia, or go from one zone to another as the Spanish do, you'll either have to do a lot of walking or take taxis. Surprisingly, the area where you would expect at least some action, around the cathedral, is quite dead after dark.

There are two weekly **listings guides**, *Qué y Dónde*, and the slightly less comprehensive *Cartelera Turia*.

Barrio del Carmen

In town, the youngest crowd and loudest music are to be found on c/Bailén and c/Pelayo. The **Barrio del Carmen** has dozens of small café-bars and is one of the liveliest areas at night, especially around Plaza San Jaume. The popular *La Marxa* is worth searching out, located in an imaginatively decorated town house, with a small, sweaty dance floor and varied music. You'll find plenty of other lively options along c/Serranos, c/de Quart (running into c/de Caballeros), c/Alta and c/Baja, c/Beneficiencia, and the four parallel streets of Na Jordana, San Ramón, de Ripalda and Dr Chiarri. Current favourites include *Ghecko*, in Plaza del Negrito, *Coyote*, in c/Padre Huérfanos, and the wildly imaginative *Johnny Maracas*, in c/de Caballeros. For good salsa, head for *Rincón Latino*, c/Gobernador Viejo 10.

Across the Río Turia

You'll also find plenty of bars on the **other side of the river** beyond the Barrio (around c/Ruaya, c/Visitación and c/Orihuela), and behind the Gran Vía de Fernando el Católico (along c/Juan Llorens and c/Calixto). In the latter area, the *Café Carioca* and *Café La Habana*, at c/Juan Llorens 52 and 41, are currently in favour, as are *La Torna* at c/Carmen 12 and *Bésame Mucho* in Ciudad Jardín at c/Explorador Andrés 6, which has live music every Wednesday and Thursday.

Most of the "in" places are across the Turia in the new **university** region. The trendiest bars are on Avda. Blasco Ibáñez – *Picasso* at no. 109, *Hipódromo* at no. 146 and *El Asesino*. The bars of Plaza Xuquer, just off the Blasco Ibáñez, are popular meeting places – *Cuba Litro*, in the corner, serves litre plastic cups of *combinados* (see box on p.746), while the *Pan de Azúcar* serves snack food until late. Wherever you look around here there's a bar worth calling in at – they're particularly thick on the ground in c/Artes Gráficas, c/Rodrigo Poros, c/Alfonso de Córdoba (the town side of Blasco Ibáñez, towards the Jardín del Real) and c/Menéndez Pelayo (on the opposite side).

Malvarrosa beach

In summer, the bars lining the **Malvarrosa beach** are the places to be, especially the *Genaro*, *Tropical*, *ACTV* and *Casablanca*, large bar-discos on c/Eugenio Vines (the beach road). To get there, take bus #1 or #2 from the bus station, or #19 from Plaza del Ayuntamiento. All three buses go along the Avda. del Puerto and turn into c/Dr Lluch; get off about halfway along and go down to the beach along c/Virgen del Sufragio – *Genaro* is on your right, *Tropical* is along on the left. The stop for the return bus is one road back from where you got off. You'll probably need a taxi late at night. There are also several bars between Paseo Neptuno and the new Paseo Marítimo next to the port which are less rowdy. The best is *Vivir Sin Dormir*, where you can play pool or sit at candlelit tables. Also very popular is the open-air *La Floridita* which serves up Latin sounds to an older crowd.

COMBINADOS VALENCIANOS

The *valencianos* really seem to like *combinados*, or **cocktails**, which don't necessarily have the upmarket connotation they have elsewhere. The *Rincón Latino*, c/Gobernador Viejo 10, off c/Conde Montornes, near Plaza San Vicente Ferrer, is a smoky cellar where the speciality is inexpensive Nicaraguan drinks – order a rum and pineapple cocktail and you'll get a tiny glass of each, the idea being to toss back all the rum in one go, quickly followed by the juice. A classic cocktail goes under the name of *Agua de Valencia* and is served by the jug in a series of old bars. The *Cervecería de Madrid*, c/de la Abadía de San Martín, just below Plaza de la Reina, is a popular old-fashioned bar with walls crammed full of paintings, where they serve the orthodox *Agua de Valencia* made with orange juice, champagne and vodka. The *Café Malvarrosa*, c/Ruíz de Lihoro, off c/de la Paz, has its own *Agua de Malvarrosa*, made with lemon instead of orange. The nearby cafés, *Paris* and *Madrid*, also have their own versions of the same.

Plaza Cánovas Castillo

At the end of Gran Vía Marqués del Turia, lies the fashionable area in and around **Plaza Cánovas Castillo**, which is full of *pubs* (music bars) where people go to see and be seen. The bars along c/Serrano Morales (especially *Champán*) and c/Grabador Esteve are yuppie haunts (the cars outside are a good indicator), but those off the opposite side, down c/Salamanca, c/Conde de Altea and c/Burriana are more mixed. In both cases, each bar has its own particular age group and style – there's something for everyone from salsa to flamenco to *bacalao* (see below). In many of the bars around Plaza Cánovas you can ask the waiters for discount/free entrance cards for discos, but these will be available only early in the evening. One of the more unusual places in this area is *Johan Sebastian Bach* in c/del Mar (1500ptas entry charge). They used to keep a lion in a cage in the bar, but even without the lion, it's impressive.

Discos

Most discos play exclusively rave techno music. Known as **bacalao** or *makina* (machine) music, this scene has ruled in Valencia since the late 1980s. One of the best *bacalao* spots is *Calcatta*, in a converted old house in c/Reloj Viejo off c/Caballeros. There's plenty of **alternative music** around, however; try *La Marxa* off c/Caballeros, *Un Sur* in c/Maestro Gozalbo, *Época* in c/Cuba, *Raza* in c/Pedro III El Grande (often with live music) and *Jerusalem*, c/Jerusalem off Plaza de España, all in or near the city centre.

There are also lots of good discos in the **university area**: the slick *Jardines del Real*, off c/General Elio in Plaza Legión Española 13, just over the Puente del Real, *Acción* in Blasco Ibáñez, the teenage *Woody*, c/Menéndez Pelayo and *Arena*, c/Emilio Baró, which as well as a disco is a venue for visiting bands.

The rest of the discos are **out of town** on the main road heading south along the coast. *Spook Factory* on Carretera El Salér and *The Face* are near each other, on the Playa de Pinedo, Camino Montañares. Farther out on the Nazaret–Oliva road in El Perelló, you'll find *Heaven* and *Puzzle*. In Les Palmeretes, *La Barraca* is a pop disco and *Chocolate Cream* is pop-rock.

For **jazz**, the current favourite is the *Black Note Club* at c/Polo y Peyrolon 15, off Avda. Blasco Ibáñez near the football stadium, which offers quality jazz, blues, soul and flamenco on a nightly basis.

Gay scene

Valencia has a thriving **gay scene**, and there are scores of bars and discos, varying from "mixed" to a heavier, gay male-only scene. Most of the gay bars/discos are found around Central Market and c/Quart. *Venial*, c/Quart, is young and trendy, and you pay to get in only at weekends (1300ptas). Or try the very popular *Dakota*, c/San Mártir, near Plaza de la Reina, a bar with a Wild West theme. Also worth trying is *Victor's* at c/Dr Monserrat 23, near the Torres de Quart.

Listings

Airlines Iberia and Aviaco, c/de la Paz 14 (☎96 352 05 00); British Airways, Plaza Rodrigo Botet 6 (☎96 351 22 84).

Airport Manises, 15km away (☎96 370 95 00); bus #15 from bus station (hourly).

Banks Main branches of most banks are around the Plaza del Ayuntamiento or along c/Játiva. There's a Barclays at c/Correos 10, and a Londres y América Sur at Plaza Rodrigo Botet 6. Outside banking hours, two branches of the Caja de Ahorros are open Mon–Sat 9am–8pm: one at c/Játiva 14, to the left as you come out of the train station, and the other in the Nuevo Centro, near the bus station. As savings banks, they can only do certain transactions. Banco de Valencia, División Internacional, c/Colón 20, charges one of the lowest commission rates for changing money.

Beaches The city beach, Malvarrosa, is polluted, but is being cleaned up and does have an elegant promendade. It's best go to El Salér, a long, wide stretch with pine trees and a campsite behind it. A bus goes from the Puerta del Mar at the end of Glorieta Park, leaving from just next to the newspaper kiosk (May–Sept on the hour and half-hour, Oct–June on the hour). The ride takes 20min and it stops in the village before heading down to the beach and then turning back.

Bookstores English books are available from the International Bookshop on c/Ruzafa, the English Book Centre on c/Pascual y Genis and Crisol, Antic Regne de Valencia.

Bus information Main station is at Avda. Menéndez Pidal 3, across the Turia (☎96 349 72 22). Regular services to northern Europe and to London leave from here – offices in the station.

Car rental Best value is probably Cuñat Car Hire, c/Burriana 51 (☎96 374 85 61). Otherwise, there's Avis at the airport and at c/Isabel la Católica 17 (☎96 351 07 34), Hertz at the airport and c/Segorbe 7 (☎96 341 50 36), Atesa at the airport and Avda. del Cid 64 (☎96 379 91 08), and many more.

Cinema Original-language films are shown regularly at the subsidized municipal Filmoteca, Plaza del Ayuntamiento, and are sometimes also shown at Albatros Mini-Cines, Plaza Fray Luís Colomer, Xerea, c/En Blanch 6, and Babel, c/Vincente Sancho Tello 10.

Consulates USA, c/Ribera 3 (☎96 351 69 73). No British consulate, but there is a British Institute at c/Gen Sanmartín 7 (☎96 351 88 18).

Cycling There are various cycle paths (marked in green) running through the city; watch out for straying pedestrians. For info on the excursions and longer routes organized by the Consellería de Cultura, Educación y Ciencia de la Generalitat de Valencia, ask at ITVA (Institut Turistic Valencia), Avda. Aragón 30 (☎96 398 60 00).

Ferries Leave at least twice weekly for Mallorca (9hr) and once a week for Ibiza (7hr); information and tickets from any of the half-dozen travel agents on the *Ayuntamiento* plaza.

Hospital Avda. Cid, at the Tres Cruces junction (☎96 379 16 00). First-aid station at Plaza América 6 (☎96 352 67 50).

Laundry El Mercat, Plaza Mercado 12.

Left luggage Self-store lockers at RENFE; 24hr access, 100–300ptas a day.

Markets Check out the crowded flea market around the Plaza Redonda (off Plaza de la Reina) and also Plaza San Esteban behind the cathedral. There are also a few stalls alongside the cathedral – best for crunchy sugar cane. Every day except Sun and Tues there are stalls selling jewellery, clothes and knick-knacks off c/de la Paz in Plaza Alfonso Magnánimo. On Sun it's held in Plaza de la Virgen, and on Tues in Plaza España.

Police Headquarters are on Gran Vía Ramón y Cajal 40 (☎96 351 08 62).

Post office Main *Correos* is at Plaza del Ayuntamiento 1 (Mon–Fri 8.30am–8.30pm, Sat 9.30am–2pm). There is a *poste restante* on the first floor.

Telephones Pasaje Rex 7, just off Avda. Marques de Sotelo, close to Plaza del Ayuntamiento (Mon–Fri 9am–3pm & 4–9pm, Sat 9am–2pm).

Train information RENFE is on c/Játiva 24 (☎96 352 02 02). Several trains depart daily for Barcelona, Madrid and Málaga. For destinations around Valencia, there's the FGV (metro) from Plaza España (lines 1 & 2) and Puente de Madera (line 3).

Trekking Treks through various mountain areas in the region are organized year-round. You can either join a guided group or, if you want to go it alone, they'll provide route maps and info. Details from Centro Excursionista de Valencia, Plaza Tabernes de Valldigna 4 (☎96 391 16 43), or ITVA (see "Cycling" above).

Around Valencia

There are a number of good **day trips** to be made from Valencia, including visits to the region's very best paella restaurants at El Palmar, El Perelló and Perellonet. The city can get extremely hot in the summer and the cool mountains of the Alto Turia are an enticing option.

La Albufera and the paella villages

La Albufera is a vast lagoon separated from the sea by a sandbank and surrounded by rice fields. Being one of the largest bodies of freshwater in Spain it constitutes an important wetland, and attracts tens of thousands of migratory birds – a throng composed of 250 species, of which ninety breed here regularly. In the Middle Ages it was ten times its present size but the surrounding paddies have gradually reduced it. After growing contamination by industrial waste, domestic sewage and insecticide, the area was turned into a natural park.

Whether you're into bird-watching or not, the lagoon area makes a relaxing change from the city and you can eat paella and local speciality, *all i pebre* (piquant eels), in the nearby villages of El Palmar and El Perelló. **EL PALMAR**, the prettier of the two, was once a settlement of fishing huts; today it's packed with **restaurants**, as struggling fishing families turn to the catering business. One of the better restaurants is *Mateu* (☎96 162 02 70). On August 4 El Palmar celebrates its **fiesta**; the image of Christ on the cross is taken out on to the lake in a procession of boats to the *illuent*, or centre, of the lake, where hymns are sung.

Further along the road to El Perelló is the small – and rather unexceptional – village of **PERELLONET**, where you can eat some of the best paella around. Try *Vert i Blau*, Avda. Gariotas 72, for *patatas Amparín* – a potato *tapa* with a kick – and *Blayet*, also a **hostal** (☎96 177 71 84, fax 177 73 66; ⑤), or *Gaviotas*, next door (☎96 177 75 75), where you need to book, for paella, *mariscos* and *all i pebre*. The nearest campsite is *Devesa Gardens* (☎ & fax 96 161 11 36; open all year) on the Carretera El Saler, near the golf course of the same name. Regular hourly **buses** run from the city via El Salér and on to the lagoon, El Palmar and El Perelló.

Manises

Fifteen kilometres southwest of the city at **MANISES**, where Valencia's airport is located, is the centre of the region's ceramics business. The **Museo de Cerámica**, c/Sagrario 22 (Tues–Sat 10am–2pm & 4–7pm, Sun & festivals 11am–2pm; free), has displays of ceramics from medieval blue and metallic varnishes to award-winning modern examples, and a demonstration of the traditional process of ceramic-making.

North of Valencia – the Costa del Alzahar

The best **beaches** along the Costa del Alzahar are around **Benicàssim**, north of the provincial capital, **Castellón de la Plana**. Farther north, **Peñíscola**, a historic town with good beaches and seafood restaurants, is worth a visit, and **Benicarló** is pleasant too. Perhaps the best place to stop en route to Catalunya or Morellá is **Vinaròs** at the mouth of the tiny Río Servol – a real town, not developed exclusively for tourists.

Real Monasterio de El Puig de Santa Maria

Eighteen kilometres north of Valencia on the road to Sagunto is the small town of **EL PUIG**, where it's well worth spending a couple of hours visiting the impressive **Real Monasterio de El Puig de Santa Maria** (10am–1pm & 4pm–7pm, closed Mon afternoon; 300ptas), a huge building, flanked by four towers, which dominates the town and surrounding countryside. The Orden de la Merced – the order who act as guardians of the sanctuary – was founded by Pedro Nalaso in 1237 after he'd seen a vision of the Virgin Mary on the nearby hill. It is a favourite pilgrimage of Valencians and royalty alike, from Jaime I to the present monarchs Juan Carlos I and Dona Sofia, although in Franco's time, it was put to a rather different use – as a prison.

In the lower cloister, the **museum of print and graphics** (one of the most important in Europe) contains a wealth of artefacts, including the smallest book in the world – the size of your thumbnail – which reveals the Padre Nuestro (Lord's Prayer) in half a dozen languages which you can read through a magnifying glass. Other star exhibits include a copy of the Gothenburg Bible and a wonderful pictorial atlas of natural history, both from the sixteenth century. In the upper cloister, the ceramics room houses various Roman pieces, but its real treasures are the fourteenth-century plates, bowls and jars recovered from the sea bed close to El Puig. Keep an eye out too throughout the monastery for the neck manacles which the monks use as candle holders.

El Puig is served by **train** (14 daily; 20min) and **bus** (30 daily; 25min) from Valencia.

Sagunto and around

Twenty-four kilometres north of Valencia are the fine Roman remains of **SAGUNTO** (Sagunt). This town passed into Spanish legend when, in 219 BC, it was attacked by Hannibal in one of the first acts of the war waged by Carthage on the Roman Empire. Its citizens withstood a nine-month siege before burning the city and themselves rather than surrendering. When belated help from Rome arrived, the city was recaptured and rebuilding eventually got under way. Chief among the ruins is the second-century Roman amphitheatre, the **Teatro Romano** (May–Sept Tues–Sat 10am–8pm, Sun 10am–2pm; Oct–April Tues–Sat 10am–6pm, Sun 10am–2pm; free), the basic shape of which survives intact. Debate continues about its restoration: it's now functional, but for many people has lost its authenticity. Plays are performed here during the summer. The wonderful views from its seats take in a vast span of history – Roman stones all around, a ramshackle Moorish castle on the hill behind, medieval churches in the town below, and, across the plain towards the sea, the black smoke of modern industry. Further Roman remains are being excavated within the walls of the huge **acropolis-castle** (Tues–Sat 10am–2pm & 4–7pm, Sun & festivals 10am–2pm; free). Sagunto's Jewish quarter has been preserved, and here you'll find medieval houses among the cobbled alleyways. Twenty-eight kilometres north, at **Vall d'Uixo**, is the underground river of San José, featuring wonderful stalactites – you can tour the river by boat (☎964 690576; 950ptas).

Practicalities

The main road passes below the town – with frequent **buses** from Valencia – as do the main Valencia–Barcelona (7 daily) and Valencia–Zaragoza (4 daily) **rail** lines. If you want to **stay** near Sagunto, try the inexpensive *La Pinada* (☎96 266 08 50, fax 265 05 43; ③), which has a swimming pool and sauna; it's 3km out of town on the CN234, the road to Teruel. Alternatively, *Hostal Carlos*, near the station on the busy Avda. País Valencia 43 (☎96 266 09 02; ②), is cheap and conveniently located.

Segorbe and Montanejos

About 30km inland from Sagunto is **SEGORBE**, the Roman Segóbriga, which is worth a visit more for its tranquillity and surrounding scenery than its sights. It lies in the valley of the Río Palancia, among medlar and lemon orchards. Segorbe's cathedral was begun in the thirteenth century, but suffered in the Neoclassic reforms and only the cloister is original. The museum (daily 11am–1pm, closed beginning of Sept; 200ptas) contains a few pieces of Gothic Valencian art, with a *retablo* by Vicente Maçip. Only part of the old city wall remains, but the views are more rewarding. One kilometre outside Segorbe on the road to Jérica, you'll find the "fountain of the provinces" which has fifty spouts, one for each province of Spain, each labelled with the coat of arms. If you want **to stay**, the only option is the *Fonda Aparicio*, c/Colón 74 (☎964 710172; ①), opposite the museum. Segorbe lies on the main **train** line from Valencia to Teruel and Zaragoza and there are five trains a day. Segorbe has its **fiestas** at the beginning of September, when *La Entrada* takes place, and bulls are run through the town by horses.

From Segorbe, it's an easy trip to **MONTANEJOS** (not to be mistaken for Montan, the village just before). Turn off at Jérica for the road to Montanejos, or catch the bus in Segorbe. This tiny village has two hotels and four *hostales*, and is popular with visitors to the hot springs, **Fuente de Baños**, where the water emerges at 25°C and has medicinal properties. Walks around the village join up with the *Gran Recorrido* route. If you want to **stay** here, there's *Hotel Rosaleda del Mijares*, Carretera de Tales 28 (☎964 131079, fax 964 131466; ④), *Hostal Valenciana*, c/Elviro Peiró 40 in the centre (☎964 131062; ④ full board), or *Hostal Gil*, Avda. Fuente de Baños (☎964 131063; ②).

Castellón de la Plana

Continuing north along the coast, **CASTELLÓN DE LA PLANA** is a pleasant enough place to stop off; it's also one of the least expensive places to stay along this stretch of coast and there are some surprisingly good **beaches** within easy reach.

In the old part of town, there's a fine seventeenth-century **Ayuntamiento** (Mon–Fri 7.45am–1.15pm) with a collection of works by local artists and a painting of San Roque attributed to Francisco Ribalta. Nearby is the sixteenth-century bell tower **El Fadrí** and the striking, neo-Gothic **Concatedral de Santa Mariá** (the original eleventh-century building was destroyed in the Civil War). Crossing the square, the **Convento de Capuchinas** (daily 2–8pm; free) has some valuable works by Francisco Zurbarán. Also worth a visit is the **Museo de Bellas Artes** on c/Caballeros 25, between Plaza Mayor and Plaza de Aulas (Mon–Fri 10am–2pm & 4–6pm, Sat 10am–12.30pm; free), with displays of ceramics, pictures and sculptures by local artists.

The beaches are at the Grao (port) and continue along the coast to Benicàssim. **Buses** for both leave regularly from Plaza Hernán Cortés.

Practicalities

There is a helpful **Turismo** off the Plaza María Agustina 5 (July & Aug Mon–Fri 9am–7pm, Sat 10am–2pm; Sept–June Mon–Fri 9am–2pm & 4–7pm, Sat 10am–2pm; ☎964 358688) which produces a useful list of accommodation and restaurants. If you do decide to **stay the night** you have several options. The basic but clean *Hostal Residencia Marti*, c/Herrero 19 (☎964 224566; ②), is good value and central, while the *Hostal La Esperanza*, c/Trinidad 37 (☎964 222031; ③), has immaculate rooms and a good restaurant, with a *menú* for 900ptas. For a beach base, *Pensión Los Herreros*, Avda. del Puerto 28 (☎964 284264; ④), is a good bet; more upmarket is *Hotel del Golf* at Playa del Pinar (☎964 280180, fax 964 281123; ⑥), with a pool and tennis courts.

There are plenty of **places to eat**, especially around the Grao: *Club Nautico*, Escollera de Poniente, serves good *arroz* and *pescado al horno*, while *Casa Juanito*, Paseo Buenavista 11, offers an excellent selection of seafood. For the best *arroz negro* (rice cooked with squid), head for *Tasca del Puerto*, at Avda. del Puerto 13.

At night, **bars** spring to life along c/Puerta del Sol, and you'll find plenty of *tascas* and pubs on c/Poeta Guimerà y Alloza. *Bacalao* aficionados should head for *Aqui Me Quedo* and *Volumen*.

Villafamés

VILLAFAMÉS, 24km inland from Castellón, is an attractive hill town which successfully mixes the medieval, Renaissance and modern. In the highest part of the town there's an ancient ruined castle, conquered by Jaime I in 1233. The fifteenth-century Palau del Batle houses the **Museo Popular del Arte Contemporáneo** (daily 11am–1pm & 5–8pm; free), a collection of over five hundred sculptures and paintings including works by Miró, Lozano and Mompó. There are good **rooms** at *El Rullo*, c/de la Fuente (☎964 329384; ③), which also has a restaurant.

Benicàssim

BENICÀSSIM, a few kilometres north of Castellón, is heavily developed and budget accommodation is scarce – the **Turismo**, Médico Segura 4 (Mon–Fri 8.30am–3pm; ☎964 300962), has a list of **hostales** and will provide a free map of the town. Among the better-value *fondas* in the old village near the train station, *Fonda Garamar*, c/Queipo de Llano 3 (☎964 300011; ②), and *Hostal Residencia Almadraba*, Santo Roméas 137 (☎964 301000; ②), are good bets. The *Buenavista*, c/San Antonio 13 (☎964 300905; closed Oct–March; ③), is large and inexpensive for rooms with bath. More upmarket is the *Hostal Montreal*, in the town at c/Barracas 5 (☎964 300681; ⑤), which has lots of facilities and even a swimming pool. There's also a year-round **youth hostel**, *Argentina*, on Avda. de Ferrandis Salvador (☎964 300949), and at least seven **campsites** in the area; *Camping Florida*, Sigalero 34 (☎964 392385; April–Sept), is close to the beach, with a pool and tennis courts.

Six kilometres inland from Benicàssim is the **Desierto de las Palmas**, a Carmelite monastery in an idyllic setting which dates from 1694. The Carmelites run meditation courses here (☎964 300950) and there is also a museum of religious history (daily 10.30am–1pm & 4.30–7pm; free). Climb the nearby Monte Bartolo for a great view across the plains. Parts of the mountain were unfortunately stripped of trees by a forest fire in 1992 – a serious problem throughout the whole of Valencia and often caused by arsonists. Back in town, wine-tasting visits are on offer at *Bodegas Carmelito*, Avda. Castellón (daily 9am–1.30pm & 3–7.30pm; ☎964 300849; free); Benicàssim is famed for its Moscatel wine, and was once well known as a wine-producing area, although today very few vineyards remain.

In summer there is a regular **bus** service to Castellón (buses leave from Sant Tomàs every 15min in summer, every 30min in winter).

Peñíscola

There's not much else along this stretch until you reach Peñíscola, although the resort of **OROPESA** just beyond Benicàssim does have reasonable beaches, good campsites and a lively atmosphere in the summer.

PEÑÍSCOLA occupies a heavily fortified promontory jutting out into the Mediterranean. There was a Phoenician settlement here, and later it saw Greek,

Carthaginian, Roman and Moorish rulers, but the present castle was built by the Knights Templar with alterations by Pedro de la Luna. Pope Benedict XIII, (Papa Luna) lived here for six years after he had been deposed from the papacy during the fifteenth-century church schisms. The castle today (daily: summer 10am–2.30pm & 5–9.30pm; winter 10am–1.30pm & 3.15–5.30pm; 200ptas), where part of *El Cid* was filmed, is heavily restored and largely a museum to Papa Luna, but it's impressive from a distance and the old town that clusters around its base is extremely picturesque, if heavily commercialized. There are small **beaches** on either side of the castle but the best one is on the town side, even though it's accordingly more crowded.

Practicalities

You'll find a **Turismo** on Paseo Marítimo (summer Mon–Sat 9am–8pm, Sun 10am–1pm; winter Mon–Fri 9.30am–1.30pm & 4–7pm; ☎964 480208), which will provide a free map of the town. Peñíscola is best visited off-season to avoid the crowds and to make sure of finding **accommodation** in the old town. For sea views, try *Chiqui Bar*, c/Mayor 3 (☎964 480284; ③), run by a friendly couple. The *Hostería del Mar*, Avda. Papa Luna 18 (☎964 480600, fax 964 480759; ⑤), offers more luxury and also specializes in medieval banquets every Saturday, with music and dancing. There are several reasonably priced *hostales* near the base of the castle and along the beach road; *Simo*, Porteta 5 (☎ & fax 964 480620; ④), is right on the beach, while the no-frills *Hostal-Residencia El Torcio*, c/Jose Antonio 18 (☎964 480202; ③), is just 100m from the sea. Around here you'll find the town's many **restaurants**, serving local dishes, such as *susquet de peix* (fish stew), and *all i pebre de polpet* (small octopus with garlic and pepper). **Buses** run down the coast from Vinaròs (every half-hour) and Benicarló (every 15min) from 8am to 11pm.

Benicarló

BENICARLÓ, seven kilometres farther along the coast, boasts a church with a fine octagonal tower and blue-tiled dome and a small but tranquil beach. There are several inexpensive places to **stay** right in the centre – *Pensión Las Palomas*, Hernán Cortés 14 (☎964 474771; ②), is decent, while *Hostal Residencia Mateu*, Ferreras Breto 8 (☎964 471085; ④), has good views of the church. For more luxury, head for the modern *Parador de Benicarló*, Avda. Papa Luna 3 (☎964 470100, fax 964 470934; ⑦), with pool, garden and a good restaurant. There's a **youth hostel** at Avda. de Yecla 29 (☎964 470500; ①) and **campsites** on the coast nearby, including *Camping Alegria del Mar* (☎964 470871; open all year), 1.5km north on the Carretera Valencia–Barcelona. The docks are important for shipbuilding and worth a look.

Vinaròs

The **beaches** of **VINARÒS**, next along the coast, are small but rarely packed and in town there's an elaborate Baroque church, with an excellent local produce market nearby. The **Turismo** (10am–2pm & 5–9pm; ☎964 455904), close to the church, can help you to find **accommodation**. The *Salom*, Plaza de San Antonio 13 (☎964 455849; ③), is good value if you're not looking for private facilities; the small *El Pino*, c/San Pascual 47 (☎964 450553; ③) is the least expensive *hostal* with bathrooms; while *Pensión Casablanca*, c/San Pascual 8 (☎964 450425; ②) is run by a friendly couple and offers clean rooms with shared bathroom. For more comfort, head for *Hotel Roca*, on Avenida San Roque (☎964 401312; ④).

The **fish** is locally caught and excellent; the *langostinos* are reputedly the best in Spain. Go down to the dockside market in the early evenings to watch the day's catch being auctioned and packed off to restaurants all over the region. *Bar Neus* (which makes excellent iced coffee), opposite the bus terminal, is the main source of informa-tion for all timetables or routes from the town; the bus to Morella currently leaves at 7.30am and 4pm. The town's **train station** is a good 2km from the centre.

Morellá

MORELLÁ, 62km inland on the road from the coast to Zaragoza, is the most attractive town in the province of Castellón and one of the most remarkable in the entire area. A medieval fortress town, it rises from the plain around a small hill crowned by a tall, rocky spur and a virtually impregnable **castle** which dominates the countryside for miles around. A perfectly preserved ring of ancient walls defends its lower reaches. The city was recovered from the Moors in the thirteenth century by the steward of Jaime I. He was reluctant to hand it over to the crown, and it is said that the king came to blows with him over the possession of the city.

Chief among the monuments, apart from the castle, is the church of **Santa María la Mayor** (*Iglesia Arciprestal*, May–Sept daily 11am–2pm & 4–7pm; Oct–April Mon–Fri noon–2pm & 4–6pm, Sat & Sun 11am–2pm & 4–6pm), a fourteenth-century Gothic construction with beautifully carved doorways (*dels Apòstols*) and an unusual raised *coro* reached by a marble spiral stairway. A few minutes' walk to the left, at the foot of the castle, is the restored **Monasterio de San Francisco** (daily 10.30am–7.30pm). Its elegant Gothic cloister and chapter house are worth visiting, along with the **fortress**, itself in ruins but still impressive. It's a tiring climb but there are tremendous views in every direction from the crumbling courtyard at the top – down over the monastery, bullring and town walls to the plains. In the distance are the remains of the weird Gothic **aqueduct** which once supplied the town's water.

Not far from the monastery is the curious **Museo Tiempo de los Dinosaurios** (Tues–Sun: May–Sept 11am–2pm & 4–7pm; Oct–April closes 6pm; free), containing fos-sils of dinosaurs found in the area. In the c/de la Virgen de Villavana is a house where San Vicente Ferrer performed the prodigious miracle of resurrecting a child who had been chopped up and stewed by its mother – she could find nothing else fit for a saint to eat. There's an annual **festival of classical music** in Morellá in the last week of August.

Practicalities

Be prepared for lower temperatures in Morellá than elsewhere in the province, and for snow in winter. The **Turismo** (daily 10am–2pm & 4–7pm; ☎964 173032) is a five-minute walk from the bus station, in Plaza de San Miguel, and has useful maps and leaflets on town sights.

Budget **accommodation** can be found at *La Muralla*, Muralla 12 (☎964 160243; ③), and at *Hostal El Cid*, Puerta San Mateo 2 (☎964 160125; ②), right by the bus stop and town gate, with views of the hills from its balconied rooms (but it can be noisy). There's also a basic *fonda,* the *Moreno* (☎964 160105; ①), at c/San Nicolás 12. During fiestas and national holidays, you should book rooms in advance, as Morellá is very popular with Spanish holidaymakers. If you are stuck without accommodation, the neighbour-ing village of **FORCALL** has a good *albergue*, as well as a comfortable hotel, *Palau dels Osset*, Playa Major 16 (☎964 177524, fax 964 177556; ⑤).

The main porticoed street, **Els Porxos**, bisected by steep steps leading down to the lower walls, is the place to focus on for food, a good source of **bars, bakeries and cafés**. *Vinatea* and *Rourera* are both excellent for *tapas*. Below the monastery are a couple of small plazas where you can sit at outdoor cafés – especially pleasant in the evening.

Morellá is one possible approach to the Maestrazgo region of southern Aragón. In summer, daily **buses** leave for Alcañiz, (at 10am) and Cantavieja/Villafranca del Cid (6.30pm), as well as to Vinaròs (Mon–Fri 4pm & 7.30pm) and Castellón (Mon–Fri 4pm & 7.30pm).

The Costa Blanca

South of Valencia stretches a long strip of country with some of the **best beaches** on this coast, especially between Gandía and Benidorm. Much of it, though, suffers from the worst excesses of **package tourism** and in the summer it's hard to get a room anywhere – in August it's virtually impossible. Campers have it somewhat easier – there are hundreds of campsites – but driving can be a nightmare unless you stick to the toll roads.

Leaving Valencia, both road and rail pass the vast **Ford factory**, one of the Spanish government's earliest successes in persuading multinational companies to invest in the country's cheap labour and favourable tax measures. If you're taking the inland route as far as Gandía, you'll get the opportunity to see the historic town of **Xátiva** (Játiva).

Xátiva and around

The ancient town of **XÁTIVA** (Játiva), 50km south of Valencia, was probably founded by the Phoenicians and certainly inhabited by the Romans. Today it's a scenic, tranquil place to kill a few hours in the relative coolness of the hills, and makes a good day trip from the capital. Medieval Xátiva was the birthplace of Alfonso de Borja, who became Pope Calixtus III, and his nephew Rodrigo, father of the infamous Lucrezia and Cesare Borgia. When Rodrigo became Pope Alexander VI, the family moved to Italy. **Fiestas** are held during Holy Week and in the second half of August when the *Feria de Agosto* is celebrated with bullfights and livestock fairs, but beware, it can get unbearably hot at this time of year.

Xátiva has a fine collection of mansions scattered around town, but most are private and cannot be entered. Many of the churches have been recently renovated, and the **old town** is a pleasant place to wander. If you arrive by train, follow c/Baixada Estación up towards the central tree-lined Alameda, and then keep heading up towards the castle.

It's a long and tiring walk up the steep hill to the **castle** (Tues–Fri 10am–7pm, Sat & Sun 11am–7pm; 300ptas) – follow signposts from the Plaza del Españoleto, or take a taxi or train from outside the Turismo. On the way, you'll pass the thirteenth-century **Ermita de San Feliu** (May–Sept Mon–Sat 10am–1pm & 4–7pm, Sun 10am–1pm; Oct–April Mon–Sat 10am–1pm & 3–6pm, Sun 10am–1pm), a hermitage built in transitional Romanesque-Gothic style; ancient pillars, fine capitals and a magnificent Gothic *retablo* are the chief attractions of the interior.

The **Museo Municipal** (Tues–Fri 9.30am–2.30pm, Sat & Sun 10am–2pm; free) consists of two separate sections, one an archeological collection, the other an art museum. The latter includes several pictures by José Ribera (who was born here in 1591) and engravings by Goya – *Caprichos* and *Los Proverbios*. A portrait of Felipe V is hung upside down in retribution for his having set fire to the city in the War of Succession and for changing its name.

Xátiva practicalities

You'll find the town **Turismo** opposite the *Ayuntamiento*, at c/Alameda 50 (daily 10am–2.30pm; ☎96 227 33 46). If you're enjoying Xátiva's peace and quiet and want to **stay**, the best place is the *Hostal Margallonero*, Plaza Mercat 42 (☎96 227 66 77; ②) – they also serve food. If you can afford to splash out, head for the wonderful *Hostería de Mont Sant* (☎96 227 50 81, fax 96 228 19 05; ⑦), on the way up to the castle. Another excellent place is *Calixto III* (☎ 96 228 34 91) at Plaza Calixte III 8, though rooms are rented on a weekly basis only. Flanked by the impressive Basillica La Seu on one side and the fifteenth-century hospital on the other, this *hostal* has spotlessly clean en-suite rooms with TV and kitchenette, and with a day's notice they will knock you up a meal of paella and pumpkin pie. Prices for a three- or four-bed room are 50,000ptas a week.

Keep an eye open for *arnadí* in the **bakeries** – it's a local speciality of Moorish origin, a rich (and expensive) sweet made with pumpkin, cinnamon, almonds, eggs, sugar and pine nuts. For a good **restaurant** head for the *Casa La Abuela*, c/Reina 17 (☎ 96 228 10 85; closed Sun); many Valencians drive out here to savour its traditional fare.

Xátiva is served by **buses** and **trains** from Valencia; the train (1hr) is half the price of the bus and leaves every half-hour. There are also connections to Gandía by bus and to Alicante by train.

Llosa de Ranes

Five kilometres from Xátiva lies the small town of **LLOSA DE RANES**, of little note other than for its fourteenth-century hermitage, **Santa Maria**, which sits astride the mountain where James I first set eyes on Xátiva. The Turismo in Xátiva will lend you the ancient and only keys. Aside from a decorative arched ceiling and an amazing echo, the hermitage's real highlight is the spectacular view, which during the summer is a favourite local pilgrimage at sunset. Llosa de Ranes is served erratically by bus from Xátiva.

Gandía

There's not much along the coast until you get to **GANDÍA**, the first of the big resorts. A few kilometres inland from the modern seafront development, the old town is quiet and provincial, with one sight that's well worth seeing, and some good, inexpensive accommodation.

Gandía was once important enough to have its own university but the only real testimony to its heyday is the **Palacio Ducal de los Borja**, built in the fourteenth century but with Renaissance and Baroque additions and modifications. There are regular guided tours (daily 11am–noon & 6–7pm; 250ptas) throughout the year. Tours are in Spanish, but photocopied translations are available at the reception; it is essential to book (☎96 287 12 04). The lifetime of Duke Francisco de Borja coincided with the golden age of the town (late fifteenth to early sixteenth century) in terms of urban and cultural development, a process in which he played an important part; learned and pious, the duke opened colleges all over Spain and Europe, and was eventually canonized. The palace contains his paintings, tapestries and books, but parts of the building itself are of equal interest, such as the *artesonado* ceilings and the pine window shutters, so perfectly preserved by prolonged burial in soil and manure that resin still oozes from them when the hot sun beats down. There are also several beautiful sets of *azulejos*, but these are outshone by the fourteenth-century Arab wall tiles, whose brilliant lustre is now unattainable, derived from pigments of plants that became extinct soon after the Moors left.

Practicalities

Both **buses** and **trains** arrive on Marqués de Campo. The **Turismo** (Mon–Fri 10am–2pm & 4.30–7.30pm, Sat & Sun 10am–1pm; ☎96 287 77 88) occupies a brown hut, cleverly camouflaged behind some trees opposite the train station. There is a handful of **hostales** in town; good bets include *Hostal Residencia Los Naranjos*, c/Pío XI 57 (☎96 287 31 43, fax 96 287 31 44; ④), and the nearby *Hostal La Safor*, Avda. de Valencia 40 (☎96 286 40 11, fax 286 41 79; ④), with phone and TV in all rooms. More luxurious is *Hotel Borgia*, Avda. República Argentina 5 (☎96 287 81 09, fax 96 287 80 31; ⑥). For a base on the beach, there's *Hotel Clibomar* (☎96 284 02 37; ⑤), in c/Alcoy by the Playa de Gandía, or the cheaper *Hostal Mengual* at Plaza de Mediterráneo 4 (☎96 284 21 02; ④). The exceptionally nice **youth hostel** (☎96 283 17 48; ①) is on the beachfront at **Playa de Piles**, 5km down the coast and there are buses every hour from outside the train station

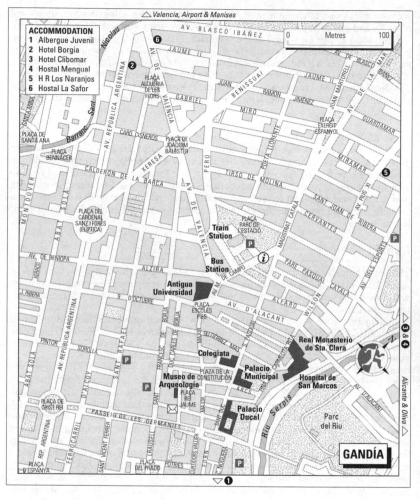

ACCOMMODATION
1 Albergue Juvenil
2 Hotel Borgia
3 Hotel Clibomar
4 Hostal Mengual
5 H R Los Naranjos
6 Hostal La Safor

GANDÍA

(8am–8pm). Gandía's best **restaurants** and **bars** are ten minutes from town at the beach. *Flash* and *Fakata* discos are also out of town on the Carretera de Valencia.

Gandía beach

Buses run regularly from the Turismo down to the enormous **beach**, Gandía Playa. The beach is packed in summer (especially with Spanish families) and lined with high-rise apartments which out of season can be remarkably good value. You'll find the town's second **Turismo** on Paseo Neptuno (July & Aug Mon–Fri 10am–2pm & 5–8pm, Sat 10am–1pm & 5–8pm, Sun 10am–1pm). The beach zone is a good place for **seafood** and paellas; don't miss *fideuà*, a local speciality with a strong seafood flavour, cooked with vermicelli instead of rice, and freshly made *cocques* (similar to pizzas) from *Taro* bakery on Passeig de los Germaines. *La Gamba* (☎96 284 13 10), Carretera Nazaret-Oliva, a few blocks back from the beach, is one of the best places to eat here.

Gandía to Altea – around the cape

A string of lovely little towns and beaches stretches from Gandía to Altea before you reach the developments of Benidorm and Alicante, but your own transport is essential to enjoy the best of them and accommodation can be pricey. The most inexpensive option along this coast is to camp. There are scores of decent **campsites** and a useful booklet listing them is available from local Turismos. Try *La Merced* in Calpe, Urb La Merced 1a (☎96 583 00 97; open all year), and *El Naranjal* in Xàtiva, Pda Morer 15 (☎96 646 02 56; open mid-March to Sept).

Oliva

OLIVA, 8km south beyond Gandía, is a much lower-key development. Again the village is set back from the coast and, although the main road charges through its centre, it's relatively unspoiled and there's a number of **hostales and fondas**. *La Tropical* is a rather upmarket *hostal* on Avda. del Mar 9 (☎96 285 06 02; ③), with seasonal reductions and a variety of rooms. There's a **Turismo** on Passeig Luís Vives (May–Sept Mon 10am–1.30pm & 5–8pm, Tues–Fri 9.30am–1.30pm & 5–8pm, Sat 10am–1pm; Oct–April Mon 10am–1.30pm & 4–7pm, Tues–Fri 9.30am–1.30pm & 4–7pm, Sat 10am–1pm; ☎96 285 55 28), who can provide you with a map of the town. Oliva's beach is served by frequent buses, and stretches a long way to the south, almost as far as Denia, so if you're prepared to walk, or better still if you've got transport, you can escape the crowds altogether. **Playa de Oliva** itself has hundreds of villas and apartments (booked up throughout July and Aug) but is refreshingly free of concrete and tackiness. A good place to eat is *Restaurante El Rebollet*, near the filling station at the entrance of the village.

Denia

DENIA, at the foot of the Montgó Natural Park, is a far bigger place, a sizable town even without its summer visitors. There is a combined train and bus service to Alicante airport throughout the day, and a rattling narrow-gauge railway (FEVE) runs down the coast from Denia to Alicante, with seven trains a day from 6.25am to 7.25pm. There is currently also an unreliable boat service to Palma, Mallorca and Ibiza which, when in operation, runs daily; try Balearia Lines (☎96 578 40 11) for information. Beneath the wooded capes beyond, bypassed by the main road, stretch probably the most beautiful beaches on this coastline – but you'll need a car to get to most of them, and there's little inexpensive accommodation. If you want to stay, try the *Hostal Residencial Llacer*, Avda. del Mar 37 (☎96 578 51 04; ③), or *Hostal Residencial Cristina*, Avda. del Cid 5 (☎96 578 61 00; ③). Slightly more upmarket is *Hotel Costablanca*, Pinto Llorens 3 (☎96 578 03 36, fax 96 578 30 27; ④) – handy for the centre and train station. If you want to stay on the beach, *Hostal Noguera*, Ptda Estanyo, Las Marinas (☎96 647 41 07; ③), is a good option.

Xàbia

At the heart of this area, very near the easternmost Cabo de la Nau, is **XÀBIA** (Jávea), an attractive village surrounded by hillside villas, and with two smallish beaches hemmed in by hotels, and a very pleasant old town. In summer both Denia and Xàbia are lively in the evenings, especially at weekends, as they're popular with young people from Valencia. One of Xàbia's best-value *hostales* is the *Hostal Residencia Portichol*, Partida Portichol 157 (☎96 646 10 50; ③–④); alternatively, there's *Hostal Jávea*, Pío X 5 (☎96 579 54 61; ⑤). There is also a *parador*, the modern *Parador de Jávea* (☎96 579 02 00, fax 96 579 03 08; ⑧) at Avenida del Mediteraneo, which has good low-season rates at around 15,000ptas for two nights' half board. **Nightlife** is centred around the beach; good bars include *Mongo di Bongo* and *Terra*. Later in the evening, the crowds move to *La Hacienda* on the Xábia–Denia road, *Trance* on the road to Calpe and *Moli Blanc* in Xábia itself.

Calpe

If you have a car, you could make a detour to the busy family resort of **CALPE** (Calp) and the dramatic rocky outcrop known as the **Peñón de Ifach**. The Peñón has been declared a national park to prevent encroaching tourist development; you can reach the top via a pathway through the rock, and, on a clear day, the island of Ibiza is visible. The harbour at its foot is used by a small fleet of fishing vessels. There is a helpful **Turismo** on Avda. de los Ejércitos Españoles (summer Mon–Sat 9am–9pm, Sun 10am–2pm; winter Mon–Sat 9am–2pm & 4–6pm; ☎96 583 74 13), who can provide you with a free map of the town.

Calpe has plenty of **accommodation** on offer; good bets include *Hostal Centrica*, Plaza Ifach 5 (☎96 583 55 28; ②), the basic but clean *Hostal le Vieux Bruxelles*, Avda. Isla Formentera 18 (☎96 583 43 57; ②), and *Hostal El Hidalco* near the beach in Plaza Calalga, Edif. Santa Marta 1–2 (☎96 583 67 14; ④). If you feel like splashing out, *Hotel Galetamar*, c/Urb la Caleta 28 (☎96 583 23 11, fax 96 583 23 28; ⑥), has en-suite rooms with TV and a swimming pool. For a good set **menú** for 1500–2500ptas, try out *Restaurante Club Nautico*, on Puerto Pesquero.

There is a daily **bus** service (run by Ubesa) between Alicante and Valencia (nearly every hour in summer), which leaves from Capitán Pérez Jorda in front of the Centro de Salud.

Altea

Back on the main road again is **ALTEA**, set on a small hill overlooking this whole stretch of coastline. Restrained tourist development is centred on the seafront, and the town has retained its character and charm. The old village up the hill is picturesquely attractive with its white houses, blue-domed church and profuse blossoms. You can eat and drink well here: the main square has a host of bars; pizzerias are lined up along the front, and the *L'Obrador*, c/Concepción 8, serves some of the best pasta in the whole area. For accommodation, try *Hostal Fornet*, c/Beniards 1 (☎96 584 01 14; ③), high up on the northern edge of the old town with shared bathroom, or *Hostal Paco* on Avenida Alt Rei en Jaime I (☎96 584 05 41; ⑤).

Benidorm

Vaguely Vegas and hugely highrise, **BENIDORM** is the king when it comes to package tourism. Just over thirty years ago Rose Macaulay could describe Benidorm as a small village "crowded very beautifully round its domed and tiled church on a rocky peninsula". The old part's still here, but it's so overshadowed by the miles of towering concrete that you'll be hard-pressed to find it. If you want hordes of British and Scandinavian sunseekers, scores of "English" pubs, almost two hundred discos and disco-bars, and bacon and eggs for breakfast, then this is the place to come. The **Playa de la Levante**, Benidorm's biggest highlight, with its 2km of golden sand, is undeniably pleasant when you can see it through the hordes of roasting corpses. A little further from the centre is the slightly more relaxed and less exposed **Playa de Ponienete**.

Arrival and information

Buses and trains arrive at the top of town, off Avenida de Beniarda. You'll find Benidorm's helpful **Turismo** in the old town, on Avda. Martínez Alejos 16 (Mon–Sat 10am–2pm & 4–8pm; July–Sept closes at 9pm; ☎96 586 81 89), which provides a useful

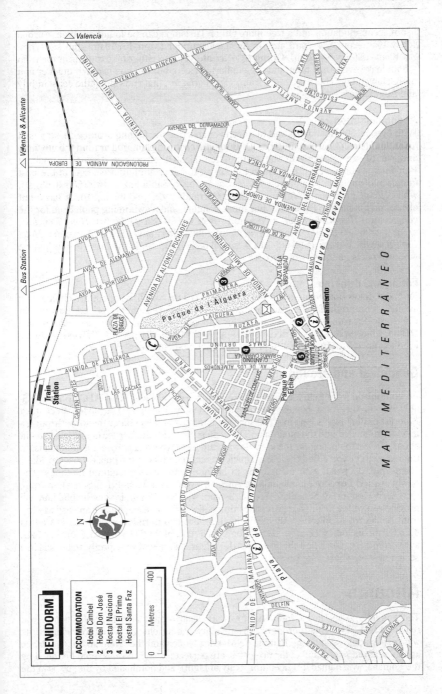

list of accommodation and a free map. Other Turismos can be found on Avda. Europa (daily 10am–2pm & 4–7pm) and on Avda. Derramoor (Mon–Fri 10am–2pm & 4–7pm, Sat 10am–1.30pm & 4–7pm). **Going to Alicante** you can either take the bus or the train – both leave every half-hour and are similarly priced, but the bus is much quicker and more convenient. There is a night train, *Trensnochador*, that runs along the coast in July and August.

Accommodation

With over 35,000 hotel beds and hundreds of apartments, finding a **place to stay** isn't a problem (except perhaps in August). Budget places are clustered around the old town and out of season many of the giant hotels slash their prices drastically, making Benidorm a cheap base from which to explore the surrounding area. One of the best *hostals* in town is the comfortable *Hostal Santa Faz*, c/Santa Faz 18 (☎96 585 40 63; ④), while *Hostal El Primo*, c/Antonio Ramos Carratalá (☎96 586 69 43; ③), is basic but clean, and not far fom the beach. For more comfort, and a swimming pool, head for the very central *Hostal Nacional*, c/Verano 9 (☎ & fax 96 585 04 32; ④); *Hotel Don José*, c/Alt 2 (☎96 585 50 50; ⑤) nearby, is an attractive alternative. For real comfort, *Hotel Cimbel*, Avda. Europa (☎96 585 21 00, fax 96 586 06 61; ⑧), is the last word in luxury, with two pools and plenty of comfort.

Eating and drinking

Fish and chips dominate, and if you're after a fry-up, you'll be spoilt for choice. For authentic **Spanish food**, head for the pleasant and reasonably priced *Enrique*, in Carrer de Ricardo, with its set *menú* for 1400ptas, or *La Palmera*, in Avda. Severo Ochoa, which specializes in rice dishes – allow 3000ptas per person. *Tiffany's*, at Avda. Mediterráneo 51, offers great, if pricey, international cuisine.

Guadalest and around

An hour inland from Benidorm, accessible by three daily buses, is **GUADALEST**, justifiably one of the most popular tourist attractions in Valencia. The sixteenth-century Moorish castle town is built into the surrounding rock and you enter the town through a gateway tunnelled into the mountain. If you can put up with the hordes of tourists and gift shops, it's worth visiting for the view down to the reservoir and across the mountains. In the main street you'll find the Casa Típica, an eighteenth-century house-museum (daily 10am–7pm; 300ptas), with exhibitions of antique tools and agricultural methods. The newly opened **Turismo**, c/Avenida de Alicante (May–Sept Mon–Fri & Sun 11am–7pm; Oct–April Mon–Fri & Sun 10am–2pm & 3–6pm; ☎96 588 52 98), is very helpful and will provide you with a map. There's no accommodation in Guadalest, but it's an easy day trip from Benidorm or Alicante. Alternatively, there are two **pensiones** close by in Callosa d'En Sarrià, including *Pensión Avenida* on Ctra d'Alacant 9 (☎96 588 00 53; ③). Just 3km away from here, you'll find the **Fuentes del Algar**, a series of very pretty waterfalls in a secluded spot, where you can swim.

Alicante

There is little to see in the industrial town of Villajoyosa, or anywhere else before you reach **ALICANTE**. This thoroughly Spanish city has an elegant Mediterranean air; its wide esplanades, such as the Rambla de Méndez Núñez and the Avenida. Alfonso Sabio, and its seafront *paseos*, full of terrace cafés, are perfect for stylish relaxation. Founded by the Romans, who named it "Lucentum" (City of Light), and dominated by the Arabs in the second half of the eighth century, the city was finally reconquered by Alfonso X in 1246, for the Castillian crown. In 1308 Jaime III incorporated Alicante in the kingdom of Valencia.

Today Alicante is Valencia's second largest city, and receives millions of visitors through its airport each year. With its long sandy beaches, mild and pleasant climate, recently renovated old town and lively nocturnal offerings, this is definitely a city to spend at least one night in.The main fiesta, *las hogueras*, is at the end of June, and ignites a series of cracking celebrations second only to the *fallas* in Valencia.

Arrival and information

The main **train station**, Estación de Madrid, on Avenida. Salamanca, has direct connections to Madrid, Albacete, Murcia and Valencia, but trains on the FEVE line to Benidorm and Denia leave from the small station at the far end of the Playa del Postiguet. The **bus station** for local and international services is in c/Portugal. Arriving by air, the **airport** is 12km west from the centre of Alicante, in El Altet. Airport buses into town operate between 6.30am and 11.35pm and stop outside the bus station.

Alicante's main **Turismo** is in the Explanada de España 2 (summer Mon–Fri 10am–7pm, Sat 10am–2pm & 3–7pm; winter Mon–Fri 10am–2pm; ☎96 520 00 00). Another office with town and regional information is in the *Ayuntamiento* (Mon–Fri 8am–3pm; ☎96 514 92 90). For those arriving by bus, there's a useful municipal office on c/Portugal (summer Mon–Fri 9am–2pm & 3–8pm, Sat 10am–2pm; winter Mon–Sat 9am–2pm).

Accommodation

Except in August you should have little problem finding a **room**, with the bulk of the possibilities concentrated at the lower end of the old town, above the Explanada de España (a weirdly tiled seafront walk seen on all local postcards), in c/San Fernando and c/San Francisco. Among several **campsites** along the coast, *Internacional La Marina* (☎96 541 90 51), 29km out on the Ctra Alicante–Cartagena, is pleasantly located in some woods, near a good beach and is open all year.

Hostal Garcia, c/Castaños 3 (☎96 520 58 66). Small, modern rooms, some with bath. The balconies overlook a busy street full of bars, so it can be noisy in summer. ③.

Hotel Gran Sol, Rambla Mendez Núñez 3 (☎96 520 30 00, fax 96 521 14 39). Old 1970s-style residence; the rooms have TV, and some have sea views. Well-placed for the old town. ⑧.

Habitaciones La Orensa, c/San Fernando 10 (☎96 520 78 20). Five simple rooms with shared bath beside *Café Bolero*. Useful for old town and nightlife. ② .

Pensión Milán, c/San Fernando 6 (☎96 520 45 15). Large, clean rooms with balconies and shared facilities. ①.

Pensión les Monges, c/Monges 2 (☎96 521 50 46). Friendly *pensión* with comfortable rooms, some en suite. ④.

Hotel Palas, c/Cervantes 5 (☎96 520 93 10, fax 96 514 01 20). Old-fashioned set-up with charm and character very near to the *Ayuntamiento*. The restaurant is famous for its cannelloni. ⑥.

Hostal Residencia Portugal, c/Portugal 26 (☎96 592 92 44). Light, airy rooms near the bus station in this clean and convenient *hostal*. ③.

Hotel La Reforma, c/Reyes Católicos 7 (☎96 592 81 47, fax 96 592 39 50). Clean, modern and functional rooms with air conditioning, TV and phone. ⑥.

Hostal Ventura, c/San Fernando 10 (☎ & fax 96 520 83 37). Simple, clean double rooms with bath, in this *hostal* on the fifth floor of the building. ③.

The Town

The rambling **Castillo de Santa Bárbara**, an imposing fortress on the bare rock behind the town beach, is Alicante's only real "sight" – with a tremendous view from

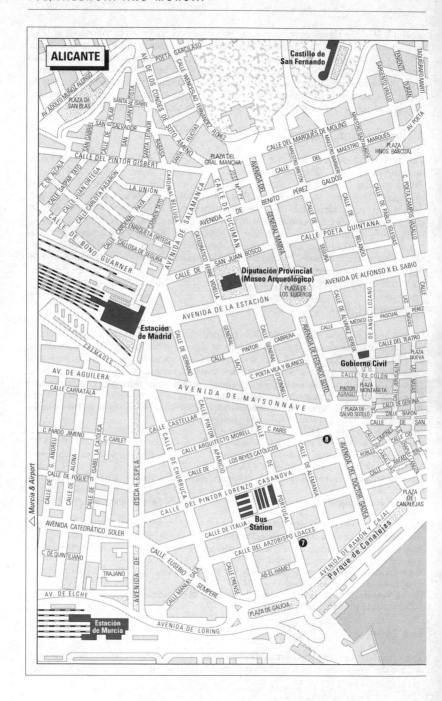

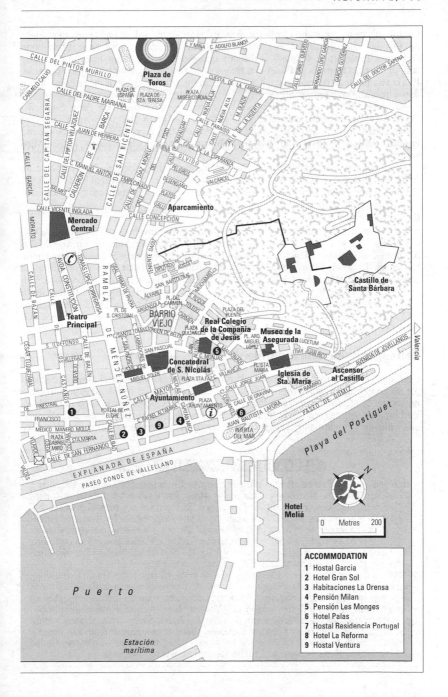

ACCOMMODATION

1 Hostal Garcia
2 Hotel Gran Sol
3 Habitaciones La Orensa
4 Pensión Milan
5 Pensión Les Monges
6 Hotel Palas
7 Hostal Residencia Portugal
8 Hotel La Reforma
9 Hostal Ventura

the top. It's best approached from the seaward side where a shaft has been cut straight up through the hill to get you to the top. The lift (daily: April–Sept 10am–8pm; Oct–March 9am–7pm; 400ptas) is directly opposite Meeting Point Five on the other side of the road from Playa Postiguet. Drivers can reach the castle from the other side. Iberian and Roman remains have been found on the site, but most of the present layout dates from the sixteenth century.

Alicante's other main attraction is a remarkably good **Museo de Arte Siglo 20** (May–Sept Tues–Sat 10.30am–1.30pm & 6–9pm, Sun 10am–1pm; Oct–April Tues–Sat 10am–1pm & 5–8pm, Sun 10am–1pm; free), close to the impressive *Ayuntamiento* and opposite Alicante's oldest church of Santa María, with works by Picasso, Tápies, Miró and Dalí.

The town also has a small **Museo Arqueológico** in the Palacio de la Diputación on Avda. de l'Estación, which is well laid out, though you have to be a real buff to enjoy it (Mon–Fri 9am–1.30pm, bring your passport, sign the book and get security clearance!).

Beaches

For the best local **beaches** head for **San Juan de Alicante**, about 6km out, reached either by bus #21 (every 15–20min) from the Plaza del Mar or on the FEVE Alicante–Denia railway. The town beach – **Playa del Postiguet** – is crowded and none too clean. Between Playa Agua Amarga and Playa del Saladar/Urbanova, there's a *playa libre* (nudist beach); take the Line A bus for El Palmeral or the airport bus. You can also take a day trip to the **island of Tabarca** (a marine reserve), to the south –boats leave, weather permitting, from the Explanada de España (April–Nov daily at 10.45am, returning at 6pm; 2200ptas) – but the rock tends to get very cramped and crowded during the summer.

Eating, drinking and nightlife

Inexpensive **restaurants** are clustered around the *Ayuntamiento*, including a couple of places on c/Miquel Saler where you can eat couscous, and a couple of excellent *churrerías*; try *La Madrileña* in c/San José. Over on the other side of town, c/San Francisco, leading off a square near the bottom end of the *rambla*, has a group of restaurant/*tabernas* with seats outside. For *tapas* try the *Taberna Castellana* on c/Loaces, on the other

---

FIESTA DE MOROS Y CRISTIANOS

One of the most important fiestas in the region and the most important of its kind is the three-day **Fiesta de Moros y Cristianos** in **Alcoy**, about 60km from Alicante. It happens around Saint George's Day (*San Jorge*, April 23), but the date varies slightly according to when Easter falls. Magnificent processions and mock battles for the castle culminate in the decisive intervention of Saint George himself — a legend that originated in the Battle of Alcoy (1276) when the town was attacked by a Muslim army. New costumes are made each year and prizes are awarded for the best which then go into the local museum, Museu de la Festa Casal de San Jordi, at c/San Miguel 60.

On day one the Christians make their entrance in the morning, the Moors in the afternoon; day two is dedicated to Saint George, with several religious processions; day three sees a gunpowder battle, leading to the saint's appearance on the battlements. Access from Alicante is easy, with five buses a day. You may have to commute since reasonably priced accommodation in Alcoy is not plentiful; try *Hostal Savoy*, c/Casablanca 5 (✆96 554 72 72; ③ with bath), or the more expensive *Hotel Reconquista*, Puente San Jorge 1 (✆96 533 09 00, fax 96 533 09 55; ⑥). After Alcoy's fiesta, the *Moros y Cristianos* fiestas in **Villena** (beginning of Sept) and **Elche** (August) are two of the best.

side of Avenida Dr Gadea – sample their *montaditos* (tiny bread rolls), *croquetas* and *patatas bravas* (spicy potatoes). Further along the road at no. 15 is the smarter *Museo del Jamón* – the restaurant is expensive, but they also serve *tapas*. On the waterside *paseo*, near the Turismo, the *Boutique de Jamón* specializes in *jamón serrano*. On c/San Fernando the *Venta del Lobos* does very low-priced *carnes a la brasa* (barbecued meats), and in Plaza Santa María, opposite the Gothic portico of the church, you'll find a good vegetarian restaurant, *Mixto Vegetariano*.

If you want to buy your own food, visit the enormous **Mercado Central**, housed in a wonderful old Art Deco-meets-Modernism building on Avenida Alfonso X el Sabio. Another **market** (a major outdoor event) is held by the **Plaza de Toros**, 9am–?pm Thursdays and Saturdays. There's also an excellent **supermarket** at the junction of Avenida Álvarez Serena and Avenida Médico Pasqual. It's a good place to buy Alicante's famous nougat-like *turrón* – Turrón 1880 is the best.

Bars and nightlife

For **drinking** and the best **nightlife**, head into the Barrio Santa Cruz, whose narrow streets lie roughly between the cathedral, Plaza Carmen and Plaza San Cristóbal. At night El Barrio, as it's called, covers the old town area, and there are so many bars here that you can easily steer clear of the questionable places. If you enter via the Plaza San Cristóbal or c/Santo Tomás below it, you'll quickly hit the main area. Both the *Armstrong* bar and *Desafinado*, Santo Tomás 6, have great jazz, and *El Paseito*, on c/San Fernando, is a *sevillanos* bar with dancing. The best *discotecas* currently are *Discoteca Pacha* on Avda. de Aguileras, *Zoo* in c/Colón and *Bugatti* on c/San Fernando.

Another good area to check out for nightlife is on the other side of town, in particular along c/Italia and c/Loaces. *El Lobo Marinero* is a pub-style bar on c/Alemania; *Hollywood* is a more modern music bar on c/Italia; and on c/San Fernando, the *Plátano* bar is extremely popular. For trendy cafés and upmarket restaurants, head for Explanada de España, which also has lively *mesones* and noisy bars. In summer the bars along Playa San Juan are always packed, especially along Avenida. de Niza, beside the sea.

Listings

Airlines Iberia offices are at Paseo de Soto 9 (☎96 520 99 66) and British Airways is at Explanada de España 3 (☎96 520 05 94).
Airport Located in El Altet, 12km from Alicante city centre; ☎96 691 90 00.
Banks Most banks are around the Plaza de los Luceros and along the Avda. de la Estación/Alfonso el Sabio. Caja Alicante, on c/Mayor, is open in the afternoons.
Bus information ☎96 520 07 00.
Cinema The Cine Astoria, in the middle of El Barrio, often has original-language films (all shows 450ptas on Wed nights).
Consulates British Consulate, Plaza Calvo Sotelo 1 (☎96 521 60 22).
Hospital Hospital General, c/Alicante Sant Joan (☎96 590 83 00).
Police The *Comisaría* is at c/Médico Pascual Pérez (☎96 514 22 22).
Post office The *Correos* is in Plaza Gabriel Miró (Mon–Fri 8am–9pm, Sat 9am–2pm).
Telephones Avda. Constitució 10 (9am–10pm).
Train information Estación de Madrid ☎96 592 02 02. For FEVE trains call ☎96 526 26 78.

Inland – Elche and Orihuela

ELCHE, 20km inland and south from Alicante, is famed throughout Spain for its exotic **palm forest** and for the ancient stone bust known as La Dama de Elche discovered here in 1897 (and now in the Museo Archeológico in Madrid). The palm trees, originally planted by the Moors, are still the town's chief industry – not only do they attract tourists, but the female trees produce dates, and the fronds from the males are in demand all over the country for use in Palm Sunday processions and as charms against lightning. You can see the forest, unique in Europe, almost anywhere around the outskirts of the city; the finest trees are those in the specially cultivated **Huerto del Cura** on c/Federico García Sánchez.

Elche is also the home of a remarkable **fiesta** in the first two weeks of August which culminates in a centuries-old mystery play – *Misteri*, held in the eighteenth-century **Basilica Menor de Santa María** over August 14–15. Additional celebrations include one of the best examples of the mock battles between Christians and Moors. Over several days the elaborately costumed warriors fight it out before the Moors are eventually driven from the city and the Christian king enters in triumph.

There are **buses** more or less hourly from Alicante to Elche. Outside fiesta time you should have no problem finding somewhere to **stay**, though there are few budget options: try *Pensión Juan*, c/Pont dels Ortissos 15 (☎96 545 86 09; ②), for basic but clean rooms with shared bathroom. Elche also has a smart *parador*, *Hotel Huerto del Cura*, Porta de la Morera 14 (☎96 545 8040, fax 96 542 19 10; ⑦). The *Bar Águila* on c/Dr Coro 31 is highly recommended for convivial drinking and good **tapas**, while the restaurant in the park, *Parque Municipal*, serves *arroz con costra*, the delicious local rice dish.

Elche is also regularly connected with **SANTA POLA** on the coast – previously a village but now quite developed, with good rooms to let, clean beaches, and ferries to **Tabarca** on the Islote de la Cantera, a strange little islet offshore. Inland, the road continues to Orihuela.

Orihuela

Just over 50km southwest of Alicante lies the capital of the Vega Baja district, **ORIHUELA**, where in 1488 los Reyes Católicos held court. The town's aristocratic past is reflected in the restored old quarter, and the impressive renovation of the **Teatro Circo**. Despite its proximity to the coast, Orihuela retains its provincial charm and is worth wandering around. Though it doesn't take long to see the monuments, it's worth spending a whole day (and maybe even a night) to enjoy its pace – you're unlikely to run into other tourists here. Orihuela also has a natural attraction in **El Palmeral**, the second largest palm forest in Spain – walk out beyond Colegio de Santo Domingo or take the Alicante bus (from the centre) and ask to be dropped off. Many of the town's seventeenth- and eighteenth-century mansions are closed to the public; however, you can roam around the one occupied by the Turismo (see "Practicalities", below) and the *Ayuntamiento* operates from the Palacio Marqués de Arneva.

Opposite the Turismo is one of the town's three medieval churches, all of which are Catalan Gothic (subsequently altered), a style you won't find any farther south. The oldest part of the **Iglesia de Santiago** (Mon–Fri 10.30am–1.30pm & 5–7.30pm, Sat 10.30am–1.30pm) is the front portal, the Puerta de Santiago, a spectacular example of late fifteenth-century Isabelline style. Inside, the furniture is Baroque, and there is a *retablo* by Francisco Salzillo. Heading back down towards the town centre, just past the *Ayuntamiento*, you'll see the **Iglesia de Santas Justa y Rufina** – its tower is the oldest construction in the parish and has excellent gargoyle sculptures.

Right in the centre of the old town is the **Catedral** (Mon–Fri 10.30am–1.30pm & 5–7.30pm, Sat 10.30am–1.30pm), no bigger than the average parish church, built with spiralling, twisted pillars and vaulting. A painting by Velázquez, *The Temptation of St Thomas,* hangs in a small museum in the nave – and don't overlook the Mudéjar-influenced, fourteenth-century Puerta de las Cadenas. The **Museo Diocesano de Arte Sacro** (Mon–Fri & Sun 10.30am–1.30pm & 4.30–6.30pm, Sat 10.30am–1.30pm;

100ptas) above the cloister, contains an unexpectedly rich collection of art and religious treasures (including a painting by Ribera), many of which are brought out during *Semana Santa*, the town's most important fiesta. There's also a **Museo Semana Santa** (Mon–Fri 10.30am–1.30pm & 5–7.30pm, Sat 10.30am–1.30pm; 100ptas) not far from the cathedral, containing religious artefacts, photos and costumes particular to the Easter celebrations.

Orihuela's other main sight is the Baroque **Colegio de Santo Domingo** (call the Turismo to make an appointment; free), out towards the palm forest. Originally a Dominican monastery, it was converted into a university in 1569 by Pope Pío V, then closed down by Fernando VII in 1824. The two cloisters are well worth seeing, along with the fine eighteenth-century Valencian tiles in the refectory. For a view of the town and surrounding plains, walk up to the seminary on top of the hill. From Plaza Caturla in the centre of town, take the road leading up on the right; not far from the top, there are a couple of steeper short cuts to the right.

Practicalities

The **Turismo** is located in the impressive Palacio Rubalcara, c/Francisco Die 25 (Mon–Fri 8am–2.30pm; ☎96 530 27 47). The best **hostal** in town, *Hostal Rey Teodomiro* (☎96 674 33 48; ⑤), is at the top of the long avenue from the train station – it's clean, and there are plenty of rooms, all with bath. Alternatively, there are some good budget places a bit farther into town: *Pensión Joaquina*, c/del Río 23 (①), is a good bet. Out by El Palmeral, *Casa Corro* (☎96 530 29 63; ③) and *Hostal El Palmeral* (☎96 674 35 00; ③) are two more options, but neither is very convenient.

Cross over the road from the *Hostal Rey Teodomiro* and take the first right, and you'll come to the best **place to eat** – *Mesón Don Pepe* at c/Valencia 3. It has great *tapas* and a good lunch menu during the week – try the *consomé al Jerez* (soup with sherry) or the region's speciality, *arroz con costra* (literally "rice and crust", made with rice, eggs, *embutidos*, chicken and rabbit). Orihuela's **nightlife** is surprisingly good. In the early evening, head for the bars along c/Duque de Tamames, and later on try c/Castellón, c/Valencia and the surrounding area. There are also a lot of big *bacalao* discos just outside town, but you'll need a car to get to them – they include *Thumesis* (one of the biggest discos in Europe) in Redován, *Metro* in Bigastro and *Blue Sky* in Benijófar.

Frequent **trains** and **buses** go on to Murcia and Alicante. Buses for Torrevieja on the coast are run by Costa Azul (☎96 530 15 67) – they leave six times a day from the Plaza de Toros (a provisional arrangement while a bus station is being built).

Murcia

MURCIA, according to the nineteenth-century writer Augustus Hare, would "from the stagnation of its long existence, be the only place Adam would recognize if he returned to Earth". Things have changed slightly – there is industrial development on the outskirts and a gathering movement to spruce up the centre – but it remains basically a slow-moving city. Founded in the ninth century on the banks of the Río Segura (no more than a trickle now), by the Moors, Murcia soon became an important trading centre and, four centuries later, the regional capital. It was extensively rebuilt in the eighteenth century, and the buildings in the old quarter are still mostly of this era.

Today it's the commercial centre of the region and most of the industry is connected with the surrounding agriculture. There are very few tourists and a refreshing lack of tawdry souvenir and postcard stands. Surrounded by mountains, Murcia has a tranquillity and unspoilt air impossible to find in most modern cities.

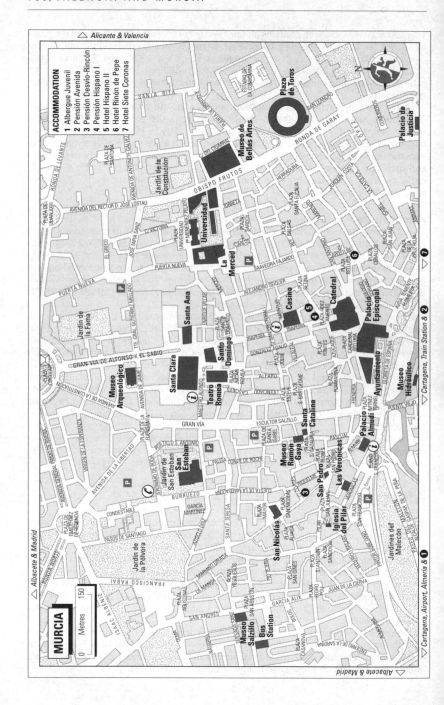

MURCIA

Metres
0   150

ACCOMMODATION
1 Albergue Juvenil
2 Pensión Avenida
3 Pensión Desvío-Rincón
4 Pensión Hispano I
5 Hotel Hispano II
6 Hotel Rinon de Pepe
7 Hotel Siete Coronas

Arrival and accommodation

Both bus and train stations are on the edge of town. If you're arriving by **bus**, either walk down to the Plano de San Francisco, then follow the river until you see the cathedral or take bus #3 to the town centre. The **train station** is across the river at the southern edge of town – take bus #9 or #11 to the centre. Murcia's **Turismo** is on c/San Cristóbal (Mon–Fri 9.30am–2.30pm & 5–7pm, Sat 11am–1.30pm; ☎968 366100). Murcians seem to know it's hard to find and will tell you the way; it's an unusually helpful office, full of ideas and generous with their posters and postcards. If you're planning on travelling around the region, their publication *A Day Around Murcia* is excellent. Two other information offices can be found at Plana de San Franscisco 8 (Mon–Fri 9am–2pm) and on c/Maestro Alonso Vega (Mon–Sat 10am–1.30pm & 5–7.30pm, Sun 10am–1.30pm).

Accommodation

There are plenty of **hostales** dotted around the city, mainly in the old town.

Albergue Juvenil, Albergue del Valle (☎968 607185). Beautiful youth hostel in a *parque natural* in La Alberca, 5km outside Murcia. Catch #29 bus from the Jardín de Floridablanca over the bridge on the south side of town. The YH is signposted about 1km beyond the last stop.

Pensión Avenida, c/Canalejas, 10 (☎968 215294). Basic budget *pensión* on the other side of the river across Puente Viejo, offering rooms without bath. ③.

Pensión Desvío-Rincón, c/Cortés 27 (☎968 218436). Basic rooms near bus station. ②.

Pensión Hispano I, c/Trapería 8 (☎968 216152, fax 968 216859). Comfortable and convenient spot in the pedestrianized zone with easy access to surrounding sights. ④.

Hotel Hispano II, c/Radio Murcia 3 (☎968 216152, fax 968 216859). Upmarket hotel with good restaurant. ⑥.

Hotel Rincón de Pepe, c/Apósteles 34 (☎968 212239, fax 968 221744). One of the best hotels in Murcia with a famous restaurant downstairs. ⑧.

Hotel Siete Coronas, Ronda de Garay 5 (☎ 968 217771, fax 968 221294). Expensive hotel overlooking the river, especially popular for Spanish weddings, but not as central as *Rincón de Pepe*. ⑧.

The City

The **Catedral** (daily 10am–1pm & 5–7pm) towers over the mansions and plazas of the centre. Begun in the fourteenth century and finally completed in the eighteenth, it's a strange mix of styles, known as "Mediterranean Gothic" because of the relations between the crown of Aragón and the kingdom of Murcia. The outside is more interesting architecturally, particularly the south side, with its Gothic facade and tower which you can climb for great views of the city. Inside, the most remarkable aspect is the florid Plateresque decoration of the chapels – particularly the Capilla de los Vélez (1491–1505). It's one of the finest examples of medieval art in Murcia and one of the most interesting pieces of Hispanic Gothic, originally designed as a funeral area but never completed. It does, however, house the heart of Alfonso the Wise in an urn in the niche of the main altar. The museum (10am–1pm & 5–7pm; 200ptas) has some fine primitive sculptures and, above all, a giant processional monstrance – 600 kilos of gold and silver twirling like a musical box on its revolving stand.

The **Museo Salzillo**, in Plaza San Agustín, near the bus station (Tues–Sat 9.30am–1pm & 3–6pm, Sun 11am–1pm; 450ptas), has an extraordinary collection of the figures carried in Murcia's renowned Holy Week procession (which is when they are seen at their best). They were carved in the eighteenth century by Francisco Salzillo and they display all the cloying sentimentality and delight in the "rustic" of that age. Other museums include the **Museo de Bellas Artes** at c/Obispo Frutos 12 (Mon–Fri 9am–2pm & 5–8pm, Sat 10am–2pm; 300ptas, free to EU citizens), with a representative collection of local art from medieval to contemporary, some of it good; and the **Museo Arqueológico**, Paseo Alfonso X 5 (Mon–Fri 9am–2pm & 5–8pm, Sat 11am–2pm; free), for which you should be keenly interested in potsherds (broken fragments of pottery), but there's a great deal to see and staff are very friendly.

The **Casino** (daily 9.30am–9pm; free), at c/Trapería 22, dates from 1847, and eclectically combines an Arabic patio and vestibule, an English-style library-reading room, a Pompeian patio with Ionic columns, a billiard room and French ballroom. Most extraordinary of all, perhaps, is the neo-Baroque ladies' powder room (open to all) whose ceiling depicts angelic ladies among the clouds, powdering their noses and tidying their hair.

Eating, drinking and nightlife

Murcia is known as *la huerta de Europa* (the orchard of Europe), and although this might be a slight exaggeration, you'll find local produce in all the city's restaurants. Murcia is an important rice-growing region, and the local variety, *Calasparra*, is renowned in Spain. It's the vegetables, though, that the area is really known for, and you'll find that vegetable soups, grills and paellas are a speciality.

Restaurants and tapas bars

Just before **lunchtime** the whole of the Gran Vía Alfonso X and the Plaza de las Flores (towards the river end of Gran Vía Salzillo) is packed with people drinking aperitifs and picking at *tapas*. If you're on a budget, any one of the *mesones* in the Plaza de Julián Romea (beside the theatre) and Plaza San Juan is a safe bet. For an excellent *menú del día* for 1700ptas, head for *Mesón del Corral de José Luís*, Plaza de Santo Domingo 23. You'll find the best **tapas** at *Barra del Rincón* (which shares the same chef as *Hotel Rincón de Pepe*), which also has a superb *menú* for 1500ptas and is easily one of the liveliest places to eat in town. For dinner, *La Cocina del Cardenal* in Plaza Belluga is very good, but for the ultimate gastronomic experience, visit the famous *Hotel Rincón de Pepe*, at c/Apósteles 34, and try their *leche frita* for dessert.

Bars and nightlife

As a university town, Murcia has a good **nightlife** during semesters. The liveliest area is around the university, near the Museo de Bellas Artes, in particular the c/de Saavedra Fajardo and the side streets off it. There is also a big gay scene in Murcia, unusual for a provincial Spanish town.

A good place to start the evening is in Plaza de la Universidad in the bar *Ideales*, then head towards c/de Saavedra Fajardo for a next drink at *Icaro*, or the popular *A Los Toros* a bit further down. There are plenty more bars in nearby c/Vara de Rey, and *Latino* in c/Victorio is good. Later on, the crowds stumble off to the disco-bars of c/Doctor José Tapia; *Pasadena* is currently all the rage. For late-night venues head for *Salsa* and *Cha Cha Cha*, off Gran Vía Alfonso X. Nearby, in Gran Vía Escultor Salzillo, you will find the disco *Capitulo*, while *Centro*, in Plaza Julián Romea, is also very lively. *Metropol*, on c/San Andrés, near the bus station, is almost exclusively **gay** and plays rave and techno until the early hours.

Listings

Airlines For reservations on Iberia, call ☎968 240050. Most of the others are represented by travel agencies. The airport (☎968 570550) is at San Javier on the Mar Menor. There are limited internal flights to Almería, Barcelona and Madrid.

Banks All the big ones, with foreign exchange desks, are on the Gran Vías.

Bookshops Antaño, on c/Puerta Nueva, sells a good selection of English books.

Bus information The bus station is on c/Sierra Nevada (☎968 292211).

Car rental Hertz is next to the train station on Plaza de la Industria (☎968 268938), Eurocar, c/Primo de Rivera 10 (☎968 249215), Sol Mar, c/Doctor Fleming 10 (☎968 823 93 87), and Avis, Florida Blanca 26 (☎968 264366).

Dentist Jesús Pérez de Vega, Marcos Redondo 4 (☎968 283424), is an English-speaking practice.

Hospitals The General Hospital is near the river on Avda. del Intendente Jorge Palacios (☎968 256900). Red Cross (☎968 222222).

Market The Mercado Municipal, c/Verónicas, has stacks of wonderful local produce including kiwi fruit, dates, bananas and, of course, citrus fruit.

Police, Avda. San Juan de la Cruz (☎968 266600).

Post office The *Correos* is at Plaza Circular (Mon–Fri 9am–2pm & 5–8pm, Sat 9am–2pm).

Shopping El Corte Inglés is on Gran Vía Salzillo. The main shopping area is around the Gran Vías.

Train information RENFE, Plaza de la Industria (☎968 252154).

Telephones The *Telefónica* is on c/Jerónimo de Roda, off Gran Vía Salzillo.

The coast south of Torrevieja

The stretch of coast around the south of **Torrevieja** has been developed at an alarming rate, and is now home to a mix of Europeans, Russians and Spaniards. Just to the south is a series of pleasant beaches, known collectively as **Las Playas de Orihuela** (as they come within Orihuela's provincial boundary). Both Playa La Zenía and Playa Cabo Roig are good, clean options with car parks and cafés (the restaurant at Cabo Roig is also exceptionally good and enjoys good views over the harbour).

The Murcian Costa Cálida starts at the **Mar Menor** (Lesser Sea), a broad lagoon whose shallow waters (ideal for kids) warm up early in the year, making this a good out-of-season destination. With its highrise hotels, the "sleeve" (*la manga*) looks like a diminutive Miami Beach; the upmarket resorts on the land side of the lagoon are more appealing, and they do have a few *hostales*. The main problem is getting a room in season – the area is immensely popular with Spaniards and by April all the cheaper places are often booked up for the summer.

San Pedro del Pinatar

SAN PEDRO DEL PINATAR, the first resort, is probably your best bet in season as it's not as polished-looking as the others, and is actually more pleasant as a result. The **bus station** is up in the old town, but it's not worth spending much time here. Head down Avenida. de Generalísimo or take a bus straight to the seafront. On Monday there's a big market (on the inland side of the main road) with a large selection of food, clothes and shoes.

Much of the town **beach** area, called Lo Pagán, was reconstructed after terrible floods in 1986. Year after year people return to La Puntica beach to coat themselves in its **therapeutic mud**, a product of the salt pools behind, which reputedly relieves rheumatism and is good for the skin. The best beach near here is Playa de las Llanas, the other side of the salt pool area; it's a long way to walk though – from town, go down Emilio Castelar and turn off into Avenida Salinera Española (*puerto* direction).

Practicalities

If you do get stuck in the old town and need a **bed** for the night, try *Pensión Mariana*, Avda. Dr Artero Guirao 136 (☎968 181013; March–Oct; ④). There are plenty of *hostales* down at the resort, including *Pensión Alas Playa*, Bartolomé Gil 3 (☎968 181017; ④), very good value and virtually on the beach but only open April to October, and the clean and friendly *Hostal Lucrecia*, c/Nacional 22 (☎96 818 92 81; ④), half a kilometre out of town towards Cartagena, with a good and inexpensive restaurant.

Places to **eat** are in good supply – the *Hogar del Pescador* is an inexpensive seafood restaurant at c/Lorenzo Morales 2, near the main square; *Restaurante La Pradera*, c/Emilio Castelar is ranch-style, good for barbecues; *Mesón La Panocha*, c/Muñoz Delgado, near the seafront, has excellent *tapas*; and *El Venezuela* is a high-quality if rather expensive seafood place virtually on the beach. Most of San Pedro's bars and discos are along Avenida de Generalísimo.

There are at least ten daily **buses** from San Pedro to Cartagena and Murcia.

Santiago de la Ribera

The next town on the Mar Menor, and within walking distance, is **SANTIAGO DE LA RIBERA**, a fancy resort that's popular with *murcianos*. There's an important sailing club here, as the calm sea is perfect for novices.

One of the best budget **pensiones** is *Manida*, near the sea at c/Muñoz 11 (☎968 570011; ③), with a range of rooms and good full-board deals. Alternatively, *Pensión K Hito*, c/López Peña 9 (☎968 570002; ③ with bath, open July–Sept only), and *Hotel Trabuco*, Avda. Mar Menor 1 (☎968 570051, fax 968 570638; ④), are close together at the back of the town. More expensive is *Hotel Don Juan*, Avda. Nuestra Señora de Loreto 2 (☎968 571043, fax 968 572976; ④). Also worth trying on c/Zarandona are *Pensión La Obrera*, at no. 7 (☎968 570042; ④ with bath), and *Hotel Madrid* at no. 18. (☎968 570504; ③). If you're looking for seafood, you'll get the best in town at *Mesón El Pescador* on Explanada Barnuevo. There are three **campsites** in the area, all open all year: *Alcázares* (☎968 575100) in Los Alcázares, with a pool, *Andrómeda* (☎968 571876) on the Balsicas road, and *Mar Menor* (☎968 570133) on the Alicante–Cartagena road.

From the military airport at San Javier you can get **flights** to Madrid, Barcelona and London. The nearest **train station** for this area is Balsicas (connected with San Pedro and Santiago by bus). A train called the *Costa Cálida* runs direct to here from Barcelona and Madrid in summer.

Cartagena

Whether you're approaching **CARTAGENA** from one of the numerous resorts along Mar Menor, inland from Murcia, or from Almería to the south, it's not a pretty sight. Scrub and semi-desert give way to a ring of hills littered with disused factories and mines, eventually merging into the newer suburbs. It's only when you reach the old part of town down by the port, with its narrow medieval streets, packed with bars and restaurants, that the city's real character emerges.

Cartagena was Hannibal's capital city on the Iberian peninsula, named after his Carthage in North Africa, and a strategic port and administrative centre for the Romans. International Nautical Week is celebrated here in June, and in November the city hosts an International Festival of Nautical Cinema. The **fiestas** of *Semana Santa* are some of the most elaborate in Spain with processions leaving from the church of Santa María de Gracia in the early hours of Good Friday morning.

Arrival, information and accommodation

Cartagena has a new **bus station** in c/Plaza Mexico. The **train** stations, both RENFE and FEVE, are also here. You'll find the city's **Turismo** at the corner of the *Ayuntamiento* (Mon–Fri 10am–2pm & 5–8pm, Sat 10am–2pm; ☎968 506483); they can provide a free map of the town.

Places to stay are somewhat thin on the ground, and not particularly low in price. For good value and a central location, head for *Hotel Peninsular*, c/Cuatro Santos 3 (☎968 500033, fax 968 500033; ③), just off c/Mayor. *Pensión Isabelita*, Plaza María José Artes (☎968 507735; ③), adjacent to Plaza del Ayuntamiento, is clean and fairly decent, while two places on c/Jara, *Pensión Garrido* at no. 27 (☎968 503736; ③), and *Hostal Cartagenera* at no. 32 (☎968 502500; ④), are also good bets, although the *Garrido* can be noisy. For a more upmarket choice, try the nearby *Hotel Los Habaneros*, c/San Diego 60 (☎& fax 968 505250; ⑤).

The City

Cartagena does not have an excess of sights and much of what it does have is in ruins or not open to the public. The vast military **Arsenal** that dominates the old part of the town dates from the mid-eighteenth century and, like the Captaincy General building, is still in use, heavily guarded and not open to the public. However, you can visit the **Naval Museum** (Tues–Sun 10am–1pm; free), c/Menéndez Pelayo 6, set in the walls of the Arsenal, and the **National Museum for Underwater Archeology** (Tues–Sun 10am–3pm; free), which is a long walk round the outer walls of the Arsenal on the way to the lighthouse, and has a reconstructed Roman galley and a lot of interesting exhibits salvaged from shipwrecks. The **Museo Archeológico**, c/Ramón y Cajal 45 (Tues–Fri 10am–1pm & 4–6pm, Sat & Sun 10am–1pm; free), in the new part of town, is built on a Roman burial ground and has an excellent collection of Roman artefacts and a good introduction to the ancient history of the city.

The best of Cartagena's churches is **Santa María de Gracia**, on c/San Miguel, which contains various works by Salzillo, including the figures on the high altar. There are more works by Salzillo and a fine art collection in the Neoclassical church **La Caridad** on c/la Caridad. You'll see a large number of Art Nouveau buildings around the city. Most of these are the work of former Cartagenian and disciple of Gaudí, Victor Beltri (1865–1935). In particular, have a look at Casa Maestre in Plaza San Francisco, Casa Cervantes, c/Mayor 15 and the *Hotel Zapata*, Plaza de España.

To get a feel of the city's distinguished past, wander along the sea wall towards the old military hospital. It's a huge, empty, but evocative building, now falling into disrepair and no-one will mind you looking around. From the lighthouse there are great views of the harbour and city, but perhaps the best **city views** are from Torres Park, reached along c/Gisbert. Past the ruins of the old cathedral, the road winds down back into Plaza del Ayuntamiento.

Eating, drinking and nightlife

There are plenty of unexploited **bars** and **restaurants** in the old town with Spanish-only menus and uninflated prices. The best places to look for food are Plaza del Ayuntamiento and Plaza María José Artes – best value is *Casa Pedrero* on the corner of Plaza María José Artes with very low-priced *platos combinados* and a 900ptas *menú del día*. *Mesón Artes*, opposite, has a vast range of *tapas*, and the popular *El Mejillonería*, c/Mayor 4, just off Plaza del Ayuntamiento, is definitely worth trying to squeeze your way into. The side streets around the squares also contain plenty of good places: on c/Escorial, *El Bahia* is a tiny seafood restaurant with meals cooked straight from its tanks of live fish, and the more expensive *Mare Nostrum*, down by the port, also offers excellent seafood dishes as well as *tapas*.

In the evening, try *El Macho*, corner of c/Aire and c/del Cañon, which specializes in *pulpo* and *patatas bravas*; *Mi Bodega* has excellent *tortilla;* and *La Uva Jumillana*, on c/Jara, serves extremely strong wines from the barrel. You'll find Cartagena's **discos** and late-night bars on c/del Cañon, on the streets of Plaza de San Agustín, and along c/Jiménez de la Espada.

The Golfo de Mazarrón

South of Cartagena, on the coast of the **Golfo de Mazarrón**, only Mazarrón and Águila are easily accessible. Very little building has been allowed around the beaches between these two towns, because the area is a breeding ground for **tortoises** and a species of **eagle** – for the last decade there have been plans to make it a nature reserve. The few roads that lead down to the better beaches usually end up as tracks.

Mazarrón and around

The inland village of **MAZARRÓN** is small and peaceful with an attractive plaza, and a few **places to stay**; both *Pensión Calventus*, Avda. de la Constitución 60 (☎968 590094; ③), and *Guillermo II*, c/Carmen 7 (☎968 590436; ③), are worth trying. Puerto de Mazarrón resort is 6km away, served by three daily buses from Cartagena.

Despite a fair amount of development, **PUERTO DE MAZARRÓN** is pretty quiet even in season, but most of the **accommodation** is in expensive resort hotels. If you're looking for something a little less pricey, *Pensión Delfín*, c/Mayor 13 (☎968 594639; ③), and *La Linea*, c/Cartagena 2 (☎968 594549; ③), are both clean and reasonable. For more comfort, head for *Hotel Durán*, Playa de la Isla (☎968 594050; ④) or *Hotel Playa Grande*, Ctra Bolnuevo (☎968 594684, fax 968 153430; ⑤). The massive **campsite**, *Garoa Playa de Mazarrón* (☎968 150660) on Crta Bolnuevo, is open year round. You'll find a useful **Turismo** at Doctor Meca 47 (summer Mon–Sat 9am–2pm & 6–10pm, Sun 10am–1pm; winter Mon–Sat 9am–2pm; ☎968 590119). The better **beaches**, Cabo Tiñoso to the north and Punta Calnegre to the south, are not served by public transport, but the best one, Bolnuevo, is just about walkable from Puerto de Mazarrón. Nearby is the "Enchanted City of Bolnuevo", a small area of weird, eroded rocks. If you get tired of sunbathing, the nature reserve at **La Rambla de Moreras** has a lagoon which attracts a variety of migratory birds.

For **food** the best place to head for is *Virgin del Mar* on Paseo de la Sal, which serves excellent *arroz con bogavante* (rice with lobster). Slightly cheaper is the seafood restaurant *Beldemar*, Avda. Costa Cálida, where you buy fresh fish and have it cooked for you on the spot. In summer, the **nightlife** is centred along Vía Axial; *Casona-Mundo Noche* and *Legarto Verde* are currently popular haunts.

Totana and Aledo

Inland from Mazarrón is the town of **TOTANA**, at the foot of the Sierra Espuña, home to wild boars and royal eagles. The strange stone domes dotted around in the mountains are "snow wells", used to store snow before the thaw. The sanctuary La Santa, 7km outside the town, has a beautifully carved wooden ceiling, and houses a collection of sixteenth- and seventeenth-century paintings. Totana is served by hourly buses and trains from Murcia, and buses continue on to **ALEDO**, another ancient mountain town with Arabic walls and a tower. Medieval traditions are still strong here and on January 6 it hosts the **Auto Sacramental** (mystery play). Just outside the town is the *Hotel El Pinito de Oro* (☎ & fax 968 484436; ②–④) with magnificent views.

Águilas

ÁGUILAS lies at the southern end of the Golfo de Mazarrón, bordered inland by fields of tomatoes, one of the few things that can grow in this hot, arid region. Fishing, along with the cultivation of tomatoes, is the mainstay of the economy here, and a fish auction is held at around 5pm every day in the port's large warehouse. **Carnaval** is especially wild in Águilas, and for three days and nights in February the entire population lets its hair down with processions, floats and general fancy-dress mayhem.

Arrival and information

You'll find the **Turismo** (summer Mon–Fri 9am–2pm & 6–9pm, Sat 9am–1pm; winter Mon–Fri 9am–2pm & 5–7pm; ☎968 413303) on Plaza de Antonio Cortijos, near the port; they can provide free maps of the town. **Buses** stop at the *Bar Peña Aguileña*, with services to Almería, Cartagena, Murcia (6 daily) and Lorca (9 daily). There are also three **trains daily** to both Murcia and Lorca. If you plan on exploring the surrounding beaches, hiring a car or bike is a good idea; **car rental** is available from Auriga, c/Iberia 65 (☎968 447046), and **mountain bikes** can be found at c/Julián Hernández Zaragoza.

Accommodation

Pensiones tend to be full from mid-July to mid-August. *Pensión Cruz del Sur,* Avda. de la Constitución 37 (☎968 410171; ④), is very good value, with its seafront position on Levante beach. In the centre of town, *Hostal La Aguileña*, at c/Isabel la Católica 8 (☎968 410303; ③ without bath), is another good bet, as is *Pensión Rodríguez*, Ramón y Cajal 3 (☎968 410615; ③). For more comfort, head for *Hotel Carlos III*, near the pretty Plaza de España, on c/Rey Carlos III 22 (☎968 411650, fax 968 411658; ⑥). The **youth hostel**, *Albergue Juvenil* (☎968 413029; ①), is 4km out of town at Calarreona along the Carretera Almería, and there is no bus out this way. There are two **campsites** in the area, both open all year; *Águilas* (☎968 419205) is 2km from the beach, and *Bellavista* (☎968 449151) is on the Vera–Almería road in a quiet green spot.

The town and its beaches

Águilas is a popular spot as the beaches (see below) are plentiful, reasonably served by public transport and the area has a superb year-round climate. The town itself has managed to escape the excesses of tourism, and retains much of its rural charm and character.

You'll find two fine **beaches**, and over thirty small *calas* (coves) in the vicinity. Those to the north are rockier and more often backed by low cliffs; to the south they are grittier and more open. The main attraction, however, is the lack of surrounding development – some are totally wild, others have a smattering of villas, others have just one bar. The beaches are cleaned daily from May onwards, as a lot of seaweed is washed up.

Heading north from Águilas, Playa Hornillo (on the summer-only Calabardina bus route) is a nice beach with a couple of bars nearby. From here, it's possible to walk round to Playa Amarillo, probably the most secluded and beautiful of the beaches. A string of beaches are served by the Calabardina bus in summer; Playa Arroz, La Cola and Calabardina itself (7km from town). If you feel energetic you could walk across Cabo Cope to yet another chain of beaches beginning at Ruinas Torre Cope, but there's really no need to go so far.

South of Águilas, the Las Lomas bus serves the rocky Playa Las Lomas from where you can walk to Playa Matalentisco with shallow stretches, ideal for kids. The Las Palomas beach (known locally as La Cabaña) has the added attraction of a restaurant; beside it is Calarreona beach, then comes La Higuérica, 5km from town. Further south, Playa Cuatro Calas has a drinks stall, but no other unnatural presence, and by the time you get to La Carolina, on the border of Andalucía, the shore is completely wild.

Eating and drinking

You won't go hungry in this part of the world as **fresh fish** is always in supply. For a fine selection of fish and *arroz a la piedra* (a tasty rice dish), head for *Las Brisas* on Explanada del Puerto (closed Mon), or the excellent *El Puerto*, Plaza Robles 18 (closed

Wed), which specializes in *pulpo* (octopus). Good choices at the lower end of the price scale include *El Pequeño Mesón*, Jiménez Crouseilles 5, which specializes in *cocina catalana* (Catalan cooking), and *Mesón Maribel* at c/ Rambla 22 (closed Wed), which is good for meat dishes.

Inland to Lorca

Many of the historic villages of inland Murcia are accessible only with your own transport, but one place you can reach easily is **Lorca**, a beautiful former frontier town. The villages around all have their share of Renaissance and Baroque architecture and are surrounded by stunning countryside.

Lorca

Despite being slowly shaken to pieces by the traffic that hammers straight through its centre, **LORCA** still has a distinct aura of the past. For a time it was part of the caliphate, but it was retaken by the Christians in 1243, after which Muslim raids were a feature of life until the fall of Granada, the last Muslim stronghold. Most of the town's notable buildings – churches and ancestral homes – date from the sixteenth century onwards.

Arrival, information and accommodation
Arriving by **train**, get off at Lorca Sutullera; buses will also drop you at the station, but the bus stop before is closer to town. The **Turismo**, on c/López Gisbert (daily: summer 9am–2pm & 5.30–7pm; winter 10am–2pm & 5.30–7pm; ☎968 466157), can provide a good map and an excellent guided architectural walk of about an hour around the town. Both **trains** and **buses** connect Lorca with Murcia; the train is cheaper and quicker. Heading south to Granada there are two buses daily, at 10.40am and 4pm.

Even though it really only takes an hour or two to look around Lorca, it's still a good place to stop overnight, with inexpensive **rooms** all along the highway. *Pensión del Carmen*, c/Rincón de los Valientes 3 (☎968 466459; ④) and *Casa Juan*, c/Guerra 10 (☎968 468006; ③), are decent and reasonably priced, while *Hotel Félix*, Avda. Fuerzas Armadas 141 (☎968 467654, fax 968 467 650; ④), is an old-fashioned place and very good value. If you have trouble finding a room, the enormous *La Alberca*, Plaza Juan Moreno 1 (☎968 468850; ③ without bath), is clean and friendly and is likely to have space. If you're coming for Holy Week you'll have to book at least a month in advance, or stay in Murcia or Águilas.

The Town
Next door to the Turismo, is the **Centro de Artesanía**, displaying and selling work combining traditional crafts with avant-garde design (Mon–Fri 10am–2pm & 5–8pm; free).

The old part of town lies up the hill from c/López Gisbert. The **Casa de los Guevara**, above the Turismo, is an excellent example of civic Baroque architecture from the end of the seventeenth century and the best mansion in town. On the corner of Plaza San Vicente and c/Corredera, the main shopping artery, is the **Columna Milenaria**, a Roman column dating from around 10 BC: it marked the distance between Lorca and Cartagena on the *Vía Heraclea*, the Roman road from the Pyrenees to Cádiz. The Gothic **Porche de San Antonio**, the only gate remaining from the old city walls, lies at the far end of the Corredera. On Plaza de España, the focal point of the town, and seemingly out of proportion with the rest, you'll find the imposing **Colegio de San Patricio** (Mon–Fri 11am–1pm & 4.30–6.30pm, Sat & Sun 11am–1pm; free), with its enormous proto-Baroque facade, built between the sixteenth and eighteenth centuries – there's a marked contrast between the outside and the sober, refined interior, which is largely Renaissance. Nearby is the **Ayuntamiento**, with its seventeenth- to eighteenth-century facade. An equally impressive front is presented by the sixteenth-century **Posito**, down a nearby side street – originally an old grain storehouse, it's now the municipal archive.

The thirteenth- to fourteenth-century **Castillo** overlooking the town seems an obvious destination but it's a very hot walk and not really worth it, as the two towers of interest are open only on November 23, the day the fortress was recovered from the Moors. The impoverished *barrio antiguo*, huddled below the castle, can be a little dangerous at night, but it's worth wandering around it in daylight.

Lorca is famed for its **Semana Santa** celebrations which out-do those of Murcia and Cartagena, the next best in the region. There's a distinctly operatic splendour about the dramatization of the triumph of Christianity, with characters such as Cleopatra, Julius Caesar and the royalty of Persia and Babylon attired in embroidered costumes of velvet and silk. The high point is the afternoon and evening of Good Friday.

Eating and drinking

A good place to **eat** is the *Restaurante El Teatro*, Plaza Colón 12 (closed Sun & Aug) – the square is on the same road as the Turismo. Also try the *Restaurante Barcas Casa Cándido*, c/Santo Domingo 13, for their very good *menús*. Up the road from here in c/Tintes, on the corner of Est. Cava, is a great, seedy **bodega**, where they serve powerful shots of port-like *vino tinto* for next to nothing.

Caravaca de la Cruz and Moratalla

CARAVACA DE LA CRUZ, an important border town, can be reached from Lorca by daily bus, although there are more direct buses from Murcia (hourly; 1hr 30min). The town is dominated by the *castillo* which contains a beautiful marble and sandstone church, **El Santuario de Vera Cruz**. The church houses the cross used in the Easter celebrations, and on May 3 the cross is "bathed" in the temple at the bottom of town to commemorate the apparition of a cross to the Moorish king, Ceyt Abuceit, in 1231. Just outside the church, cloisters lead to the **museum** (Mon–Sat 8am–2pm & 4.30–8.30pm, Sun 10am–2pm & 4.30–8pm; 250ptas) which concentrates on religious art and history. The churches that tower over the rest of the town, **La Iglesia del Salvador** and **La Iglesia de la Concepción**, are also worth a visit; the latter contains some excellent examples of carved Mudéjar wood. **Accommodation** is limited; good bets include *Pensión Victoria*, c/María Girón 1 (☎968 708624; ③), and *Hotel Central*, Gran Vía 18 (☎968 707055, fax 968 707369; ⑤).

Moratalla

Fourteen kilometres on is **MORATALLA**, a pretty village spread around the foot of a fortress. The steep, winding streets of the old town lead up to the castle from where there are stunning views of the surrounding countryside and its vast forests.

Moratalla is a lovely place to **stay** if you want to relax: *Pensión Levante*, Carretera del Canal 21 (☎968 730454; ③), although slightly out of town has comfortable rooms and modern bathrooms, while *Pensión Reyes*, c/Tomas el Cura 10 (☎968 730377; ①) is simple but clean. There is a **campsite** 8km out of town in La Puerta (☎968 730008; open all year). If you're driving, you might head out to *Hotel Cenajo* (☎968 721011, fax 968 720645; ⑤), hidden away in the hills (but signposted), overlooking a beautiful reservoir. Moratalla is full of little **bars**; the *Alhameda* is one of the best for food; for *tapas*, head for *Bar Luquillas*, c/Ctra San Juan 34, which serves delicious ham-filled *croquetas*.

travel details

TRAINS

Alicante to: Albacete (8 daily; 1hr 30min); Denia (7 daily; 2hr 15min); Benidorm (15 daily; 1hr 10min); Madrid (6 daily; 6–10hr); Murcia (12 daily; 1hr 30min); Valencia (8 daily; 1hr 30min–2hr 30min); Xativa (5 daily; 1hr 30min).

Murcia to: Águilas (4 daily, 1 on Sunday; 2hr); Barcelona (2 daily; 7hr); Cartagena (9 daily; 1hr); Granada (2 daily; 8hr); Lorca (14 daily; 1hr); Madrid (3 daily; 6–8hr).

Valencia to: Alicante (7 daily; 2–3hr); Barcelona (10 daily; 5hr); Benicassim (7 daily; 45min); Castellón (11 daily; 1hr 30min); Gandía (12 daily; 1hr); Madrid (3 daily via Cuenca; 6–7hr: 5 daily via Albacete; 7hr); Malaga (2 daily; 10hr); Murcia (2 daily; 3hr 45min); Orihuela (2 daily; 3hr 15min); Peniscola (8 daily; 1hr 20min); El Puig (30 daily; 25min); Sagunto (34 daily; 20min); Segorbe (5 daily; 1hr); Zaragoza (4 daily; 6hr); Xátiva (16 daily; 1hr).

BUSES

Alicante to: Albacete (2 daily; 2hr 30min); Almería (2 daily; 7hr); Barcelona (7 daily; 10hr); Cartagena (10 daily; 2hr); Granada (4 daily; 12hr); Orihuela (8 daily; 1hr 20min); Madrid (3 daily; 6hr); Málaga (4 daily; 9hr); Murcia (9 daily; 2hr); San Pedro del Pinatar (11 daily; 1hr 15min); Torrevieja (10 daily; 1hr).

Murcia to: Águilas (daily Mon–Fri, 2 daily Sat & Sun; 2hr); Albacete (2 daily; 2hr 30min); Alicante (10 daily; 2hr); Almería (5 daily; 4hr); Barcelona (5 daily; 8 hr); Cartagena (14 daily; 1hr); Granada (5 daily; 6hr); Lorca (11 daily; 1hr 15min); Orihuela (6 daily; 1hr); Madrid (8 daily; 8 hours); Málaga (4 daily; 8hr); Mazarrón (8 daily; 1hr 30min); Valencia (6 daily; 4hr 30min).

Valencia to: Alicante (6 daily, 10 in summer; 4hr); Barcelona (7 daily; 6hr); Benidorm (6 daily, 10 in summer; 3hr 15min); Castellón (11 daily; 1hr 30min); Cuenca (3 daily; 4hr); Gandía (6 daily, 10 in summer; 1hr); Madrid (6 daily; 6hr); Murcia (3 daily; 4hr 30min); Oliva (6 daily, 10 in summer; 1hr 30min); Orihuela (2 daily; 3hr); El Puig (14 daily; 20min); Sagunto (30 daily; 30min); Segorbe (7 daily; 1hr); Sevilla (1 daily; 12hr).

BALEARIC CONNECTIONS

From Valencia Transmediterránea **sailings** to: Palma, Mallorca (9hr) 2–3 weekly; Ibiza (9hr) 1 weekly. At least 4 **flights** daily to Palma (40min), at least 2 daily to Ibiza (30min).

From Alicante Air Nostrum regular summer **flights** to Palma and Ibiza.

CHAPTER THIRTEEN

THE BALEARIC ISLANDS

Comprising an archipelago to the east of the Spanish mainland, the four chief Balearic islands – Ibiza, Formentera, Mallorca and Menorca – maintain a character distinct from the rest of Spain and from each other. Ibiza, firmly established among Europe's trendiest resorts, is wholly unique with an intense, outrageous street life and a floating summer population that seems to include every club-going Spaniard from Sevilla to Barcelona. It can be fun, if this sounds like your idea of island activity, and above all if you're gay – Ibiza is a very tolerant place. Formentera, small and a little desolate, is something of a beach-annexe to Ibiza, though it struggles to present its own alternative image of reclusive artists and "in the know" tourists. Mallorca, the largest and best-known Balearic, also battles with its image, popularly reckoned as little more than sun, booze and highrise hotels. In reality you'll find all the clichés, most of them crammed into the mega-resorts of the Bay of Palma and the east coast, but there's lots more besides: mountains, lovely old towns, some beautiful coves and the Balearics' one real city, Palma. Mallorca is in fact the one island in the group you might come to other than for beaches and nightlife, with scope to explore, walk and travel about. And last, to the east, there's Menorca – more subdued in its clientele, and here, at least, the grim modern resorts are kept at a safe distance from the two main towns, the capital Maó, and the scenic, pocket-sized port of Ciutadella.

Access to the islands is easy from Britain or northern Europe, with charter **flights** and complete package deals dropping to absurd prices out of season or with last-minute bookings. From mainland Spain, too, there are charters, though believe it or not these can often cost as much or even more. **Ferries** – from Barcelona and Valencia – are less expensive but still overpriced for the distances involved: the single passenger fare from Barcelona to Palma will, for example, set you back some 6660ptas in high season (mid-June to September), 4350ptas in low season (October to early June), with vehicle rates starting at around 18,560ptas one way. More expensive still are the **hydrofoils** which run from the same mainland ports in the period mid-June to mid-September – Valencia to Palma, for instance, costs 8150ptas. Likewise, rates for **inter-island** ferries are also high, and for journeys such as Ibiza–Mallorca or even Mallorca–Menorca it can actually be better value to fly. The catch here is availability: in the high season tickets are snapped up fast, so it's a good idea to book ahead of time — a few days beforehand is usually sufficient. For fuller details on **routes** see "Travel details" at the end of this chapter.

Expense and **over-demand** can be crippling in other areas, too. As "holiday islands", each with a buoyant international tourist trade, the Balearics charge considerably above mainland prices for **rooms** – which from mid-June to mid-September are in very short supply. If you go at these times, it's sensible to try to fix up some kind of reservation in advance or at least get a bag of small change and phone round before tramping the streets (though many places accept only agency bookings). If you plan

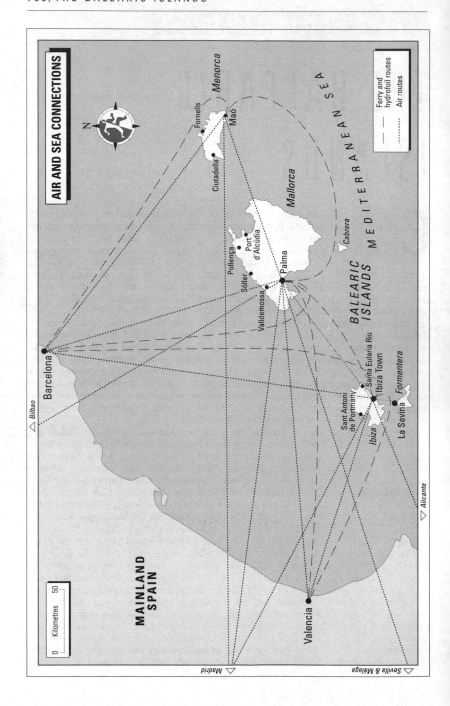

to rent a **car**, these are also in short supply in season. **Mopeds, scooters and bicycles** are a good option on the islands but be sure to check your insurance policy: it should definitely include theft as well as accident. To avoid the latter, store most of your baggage somewhere before setting out – riding with a pack is both exhausting and dangerous. Without your own transport, the **bus** network is reasonably comprehensive – and services are detailed in "Travel Details" as well as the text for the specific islands.

As elsewhere in Spain, the Balearics have revived their own **dialects** since the death of Franco. Throughout the islands a dialect of **Catalan** is spoken, a result of their capture from the Moors by the thirteenth-century king of Catalunya and Aragón, Jaume I. Each of the three main islands has a different sub-dialect, and indeed many inhabitants object to their language being called Catalan at all, though generally the islanders speak their native language and Castilian (Spanish) with equal fluency. For the visitor, confusion arises from the difference between the islands' road signs and street names – which are almost exclusively in Catalan – and many of the maps on sale, which are in Castilian. In particular, note that Menorca now calls its capital Maó rather than Mahón, while both the island and town of Ibiza are usually referred to as Eivissa. The influx of tourists also means that you'll find no shortage of people with fluent English, German or sometimes French. In this chapter we give the Catalan name for towns, beaches and streets with the Castilian name in brackets where helpful, except for Ibiza and Ibiza Town which are not widely known by their Catalan names outside Spain.

IBIZA

IBIZA (*Eivissa* in Catalan) is an island of excess. Beautiful, indented with scores of cove beaches, it's nevertheless the islanders (*ibizencos*) and their visitors who make it special. However outrageous you may want to be (and outrageousness is the norm here) the locals have seen it all before – and remain determinedly blasé about the thousands of lotion-smeared tourists preening themselves on the beaches during the day, in preparation for the nightly flounce through the bars and clubs.

For years Ibiza was *the* European hippie escape, but nowadays the island is as popular with modern youth and sociable gays as it is with its 1960s denizens. Germans, squeezed into their lederhosen, rub bottoms with the trimmest of international designer labels in a remarkably relaxed meeting of the camp and the hip, and you'll find the latest London, Paris, Madrid and Milan fashions in the shops here, often before they've been seen at home. Ibiza Town, in particular, lives glamorously, especially at night – an endless fashion parade that excites and amuses in equal measure.

Ibiza Town, the capital, is the obvious place to base yourself: only a short bus ride from two great beaches – **Ses Salines** and **Es Cavellet** – and crammed with shops, restaurants, bars and clubs to occupy the nights. Nowhere else can compare, certainly not the second city, **Sant Antoni de Portmany**, which is a highly avoidable package resort nightmare, nor **Santa Eulària des Riu**, the only other real town, a mundane little place with a pretty hill-top church. Indeed, the island is small enough to put scores of cove **beaches** – *calas* – within reach of the capital if you have your own transport and, although all the more accessible are developed to some degree, few are actually crowded. **Inland** there's little of anything – a few villages and holiday homes that are exceedingly pretty to drive through but offer little if you stop.

The island has a harsh landscape of tinder-dry scrubland interrupted by the occasional stretch of productive land, and is peppered with small lakes used for salt production. Salt attracted the Greeks, and after them the Phoenicians and **Carthaginians**, who made the island a regular stop on their Mediterranean cruises –

FIESTAS

January

16 *Revetla de Sant Antoni Abat* (Eve of St Antony's Day) is celebrated by the lighting of bonfires (*foguerons*) in Palma and several of Mallorca's villages – especially Sa Pobla, where the inhabitants move from fire to fire, dancing round in fancy dress. Also observed in Sant Antoni de Portmany (Ibiza) and Maó (Menorca).

17 *Beneides de Sant Antoni* (Blessing of St Antony). St Antony's feast day is marked by processions in many of the Balearics' country towns, notably Sa Pobla and Artà on Mallorca.

17 *Processó d'els Tres Tocs* (Procession of the Three Knocks). Held in Ciutadella, Menorca, this procession commemorates the victory of Alfonso III over the Muslims here on January 17, 1287.

19 *Revetla de Sant Sebastià.* Palma, Mallorca, has bonfires, singing and dancing for St Sebastian.

20 *Festa de Sant Sebastià.* Celebrated in Pollença, Mallorca, with a religious procession accompanied by *Cavallets* (literally "merry-go-rounds"), two young dancers each wearing a cardboard horse and imitating the animal's walk. Of medieval origin, you'll see *Cavallets* at many of the islands' festivals.

February

Carnaval Towns and villages throughout the islands live it up during the week before Lent with marches and fancy-dress parades.

March/April

Semana Santa (Holy Week) is as widely observed as everywhere. On Maundy Thursday in Palma, Mallorca, there's a religious procession through the streets. There are also Good Friday (*Divendres Sant*) processions in many towns and villages, especially in Palma, Sineu (Mallorca) and Maó. Most holy of all, however, is the Good Friday *Davallament* (the Lowering), the culmination of Holy Week in Pollença, Mallorca.

May

Mid-May *Festa de Nostra Senyora de la Victòria* in Port de Sóller, Mallorca, features mock battles between Christians and infidels in commemoration of the thrashing of Turkish pirates here in 1561. Lots of booze and firing of antique rifles (in the air).

30 *Festa de Sant Ferran* in Sant Ferran, Formentera.

June

23–25 In Ciutadella, Menorca, the midsummer *Festa de Sant Joan* features jousting competitions, folk music, dancing, and processions. Also wildly celebrated in Ibiza Town.

July

15–16 *Día de Virgen de Carmen.* The patron saint of seafarers and fishermen is honoured with parades and the blessing of boats, especially in Ibiza Town.

Third Week Reconquest of Menorca is celebrated in a festival in Mercadal.

August

2 *Mare de Déu dels Àngels.* Moors and Christians battle it out in Pollença, Mallorca.

Second weekend *Festa de Sant Llorenç*, in Alaior, Menorca; high jinks on horseback through the streets of the town.

20 *Cavallet* Week-long festival in Felanitx, Mallorca.

Throughout August International Festival at Pollença, Mallorca, including art and sculpture exhibitions and chamber music.

September

Second week *Nativitat de Nostra Senyora* (Nativity of the Virgin) in Alaró, Mallorca, with a pilgrimage to a hilltop shrine near the Castell d'Alaró.

December

3 *Día de Sant Francesc* celebrated in Sant Francesc Xavier, Formentera.

Christmas (*Nadal*) is especially picturesque in Palma, Mallorca, where there are Nativity plays in the days leading up to the 25th.

to such an extent that Ibiza has hundreds of (unexcavated) Punic burial sites. Under Roman rule the island continued to prosper until dropping into the familiar pattern of Spanish history, occupied successively by Goths and Moors before being liberated by the Catalans early in the thirteenth century. Thereafter decline set in and, despite occasional imperialist incursions, Ibiza was effectively an abandoned and impoverished backwater until the middle of this century, when it began to acquire status as the most chic of the Balearics.

Ibiza practicalities

Getting around the island is relatively easy. There is a good **bus service** between Ibiza Town, Sant Antoni de Portmany, Santa Eulària des Riu, Portinatx, the airport and a few of the larger beaches, and local **boats** from Ibiza Town serve various destinations along the coast; however, renting some form of **vehicle** will widen your options no end (see p.789). The main problem – and expense – on the island is **accommodation**, which is difficult, sometimes impossible, to find in high season; Ibiza Town is generally your best bet. For information on the island's airport, see p.784.

Ibiza Town

In physical terms as well as in its atmosphere and adventure, **IBIZA TOWN** (*Ciutat d'Eivissa*) is easily the most attractive place on the island. Most people stay in rented apartments or small *hostals* which means there are fewer hotels to ruin the skyline and not so many package tours. Approach by sea and you'll get the full frontal effect of the old medieval walls rising like a natural extension of the rocky cliffs which protect the harbour. Within the walls, the ancient quarter is topped by a sturdy cathedral, whose illuminated clock shines out across the harbour throughout the night.

Daylight hours are usually spent on the **beaches** at Ses Salines and Es Cavellet or the nearer (but not so nice) Figueretes. At night, before the clubs open their doors, the **shops** stay open until 11pm, and behind the harbour you'll find stalls selling everything from jewellery, arts and crafts, though to naive paintings and tawdry souvenirs. **Bars** stay open until 4am, and afterwards the action moves to the **clubs**, which stay open till 6am or later. As a break from the stress of sunbathing and the simple pleasures of wandering the streets, there are a couple of modest museums and fancy modern art galleries with prices that will amaze you even if the displays don't.

Arrival, information and orientation

Ibiza's international **airport** is situated 6km southwest of Ibiza Town. In the airport, the efficient **Turismo** (May–Sept daily 10am–midnight) can provide maps and lists of the island's accommodation as well as details of vehicle rental. Several car rental firms have desks in the Arrivals lounge too (see "Listings", p.789). From the airport you can take a bus (hourly 7.30am–10.30pm; 115ptas), or a taxi (around 1400ptas), into Ibiza Town.

Ibiza Town has two **ferry terminals**: one near the foot of Avgda. Sta Eulària for local boats along the Ibiza coast and to Formentera, and the other on Passeig des Moll for the Spanish mainland, Mallorca and Menorca (via Mallorca). The waterfront is just a stone's throw from the old **lower town**, which divides into two quarters, Sa Marina and Sa Penya. From here, it's a brief walk straight ahead to the walls of the **Dalt Vila**, literally "High Town". The unattractive **new town** is round to the west, beyond the Passeig Vara de Rey. The **bus station** is in the new town on Avgda. Isidor Macabich, but most services – including those from the airport – pass close to the harbourfront.

Ibiza's main **Turismo** is on the harbourfront on Passeig des Moll (June–Sept Mon–Fri 9.30am–1.30pm & 5–7pm, Sat 10.30am–1pm; Oct–May Mon–Fri 9.30am–1.30pm; ☎971 301900).

Accommodation

Most of the **budget accommodation** is in the lower town within easy striking distance of the waterfront, and half a dozen establishments are clustered in the mundane side-streets around the Passeig de Vara de Rey. If you're confident with Spanish telephones, it's obviously easier to phone around, but fortunately the town is small and compact enough to make finding a place on foot perfectly feasible. Even if you stay to the west of the centre in Figueretes, you're not that far removed from the action. The Turismo has a comprehensive list of Ibiza Town accommodation – indeed they have lists that cover the whole island – with details of **hotels** and **hostals** as well as **apartments** for stays of a week or more, but remember that in the height of the season last-minute vacancies are very hard to come by. If you haven't booked ahead, you may well be reduced to one of the island's six **campsites**, three of which are in the vicinity of Santa Eulària des Riu, two at Sant Antoni de Portmany, and one at Portinatx.

ACCOMMODATION PRICE CODES

The codes used in our hotel listings denote the following price ranges:

① Under 2000ptas   ④ 4500–6000ptas   ⑦ 12,000–17,500ptas
② 2000–3000ptas   ⑤ 6000–8000ptas   ⑧ Over 17,500ptas
③ 3000–4500ptas   ⑥ 8000–12,000ptas

See p.34 for more details.

Hostal Residencia El Corsario, c/Ponent 5 (☎971 393212, fax 971 391953). High in Dalt Vila, with excellent views over the old town and the marina, and with its own bar. Fourteen en-suite bedrooms, each decorated to a high standard in a traditional style befitting an old mansion. Lit up at night, the place is something of a landmark. ⑦.

Hostal Residencia Juanito & Hostal Residencia Las Nieves, c/Joan d'Austria 18 (☎971 315822). These two *hostals* have clean rooms, some en suite. Same management and prices for both. Two blocks north of the Passeig de Vara de Rey. ②.

Hotel Residencia Montesol, Passeig de Vara de Rey 2 (☎971 310161). Set on the corner of Vara de Rey, looking across to the marina, this established hotel offers excellent central accommodation. All rooms are air conditioned and have bath, TV and telephone. ⑥.

Hotel Nautico Ebeso, c/Ramón Muntaner 44 (☎971 302300, fax 971 304860). Pretty, modern two-star hotel with a garden terrace, bar, air conditioning and pool. Near the seashore out by Platja Figueretes. ⑥.

Hostal Residencia Parque, Caieta Soler s/n (☎971 301358). Modern *hostal* overlooking a pleasant square, and with its own café/bar. ⑤.

Hostal El Puerto, c/Carles III 22 (☎971 313827, fax 971 317452). Modernized accommodation with pool, bar and TV lounge. Attractively furnished and close to the port area. ⑥.

Hostal Residencia Sol y Brisa, Bartomeu Vicente Ramón 15. (☎971 310818). Very clean and comfortable rooms close to the port area, though it can be noisy at night. ③.

Casa de Huéspedes Vara de Rey, Passeig de Vara de Rey 7 (☎971 301376). Set on the third floor of an old building, this clean and friendly guesthouse offers reasonably priced rooms with fan, some decorated with original driftwood sculptures. Good, central location. ②.

Hostal Residencia La Ventana, Sa Carrossa 13 (☎971 390857, fax 971 390145). High-quality accommodation inside the walls of Dalt Vila. Beautifully furnished, with superb views of the old city from the terraces. Has a stylish, outdoor restaurant and all mod cons. ⑧.

The Town

The stone walls of the Dalt Vila reach a dramatic climax at the imposing main entrance, the **Portal de ses Taules**, a triple gateway designed to withstand the heaviest artillery barrage. Just beyond the main gate is the Plaça Vila, packed with restaurants and bars. The **Museu d'Art Contemporani** (summer Mon–Fri 10am–1.30pm & 5–8pm, Sat 10am–1.30pm; winter Mon–Fri 10am–1pm, Sat 10am–1.30pm; 200ptas) is here as well, above the arch of the Portal de ses Taules, and inside are held contemporary art exhibitions.

Heading east uphill along Sa Carrossa, you'll pass some of the better restaurants and have easy access to the top of the walls, which provide great views down over the town. You'll soon reach c/General Balanzat, where the sixteenth-century church of **Sant Domingo** stands next to its former monastery, converted in 1838 into the *Ajuntament*, which overlooks the Plaça Espanya. Across the square a long, dark tunnel leads through the walls; a ten-minute walk around their exterior will take you back into the old town at the Baluard de Santa Tecla near Plaça Catedral.

Some 90m above sea level, the **Catedral** (Tues–Sun: June–Sept 9am–4pm; Oct–May 10am–2pm; free) was built on the site of a mosque in the fourteenth century, its sturdy

Gothic lines supported by crude, ill-formed buttresses. Inside, the nave is similarly unexciting, its whitewashed walls picked out in vertical stripes of simple design. A plaque commemorates the massacre of churchmen, soldiers and ordinary islanders at the hands of "Marxists" during the Civil War. The cathedral also has a **museum**, a mildly diverting affair stuffed with bishops' regalia: mitres, sandals, gloves, cloaks and some nifty red-and-white velvet slippers which were obviously of great comfort to ecclesiastical feet on the stone floors.

Across the square is the **Museu d'Arqueología** (Tues–Sat 10am–2pm & 5pm–7pm, Sun 10am–2pm; 300ptas) with a collection of local archeological finds. The majority of the objects on display are from Phoenician and Carthaginian (Punic) sites, but there are also some bones from Formentera that date back to 1600 BC, and various Arab and Roman curiosities. If this whets your appetite, check with the Turismo to see if the museum on Via Romana, on the slopes of Puig des Molins – a hill just west of Dalt Vila – has re-opened, as this contains many finds from a huge Punic necropolis that was excavated here. Among the objects unearthed were some splendidly decorated terracotta pieces, clay figurines, amphoras and amulets depicting Egyptian gods. Indeed, so many funerary sites have been found on Ibiza that it was long assumed to be some kind of burial island, and, although this theory is no longer accepted, the finds are still impressive.

Outside the walls

Not quite as grand, nor as ancient as the Dalt Vila, the Sa Penya quarter of the lower town snuggles between the harbour and the ramparts, a maze of raked passages and narrow streets crimped by balconied, whitewashed houses. Here, especially along the waterside promenade and c/d'Enmig, the evening *passeig* reaches its exuberant peak and everyone – local and visitor alike – gravitates towards the bars and restaurants. This is where many of the shops are, too, occupying almost every doorway that isn't a bar.

Finally, and farther to the west, the **new town** is generally of less interest, but there's activity here as well, centred on the Passeig de Vara de Rey. At dusk, birds swoop in and out of the trees that line the square, and both the *Café Montesol* and the *Café Mar y Sol*, on the opposite corner, become popular meeting places.

Eating

Ibiza Town has scores of **cafés** and **restaurants** to cater for the crowds. The pricier places are generally up in Dalt Vila – mostly on or near Plaça de Vila and Sa Carrossa – or down by the waterfront, while the less expensive establishments are dotted round the lower town in between. Opening hours are fairly elastic, with many places staying open from the morning until very late at night. For an **early breakfast**, head for the *Café Montesol*, on Passeig de Vara de Rey, or the *Croissant Show* on Plaça Constitució.

If you plan to prepare your own meal, or want to gather ingredients for a picnic, the covered **market** at the bottom of the ramp into the Portal de ses Taules is not bad, if not quite a match for the main market in the new town between Avingudas Espanya and Isidor Macabich. Be warned, though, that prices are double what they would be in a mainland market and that the selection is not all that great – whereas the Supermercado Spar, on Abel Matutes just off the Passeig de Vara de Rey, does bear comparison with its mainland equivalents.

Restaurants

C'an Alfredo, Passeig de Vara de Rey. Classy restaurant catering for any wallet, with main courses from 700–2000ptas. International dishes set the tone, but there are Balearic specialities too, and the seafood is outstanding.

C'an Costa, c/Crue 19. Smoky, reasonably priced restaurant in the lower town serving good, fresh Spanish dishes. Closed Sun.

Dalt Vila, Plaça de Vila. Quality Spanish food at moderately expensive prices in the heart of atmospheric Dalt Vila.

La Marina, Passeig des Moll 4. Top-notch, pricey seafood restaurant down by the harbour.

El Olivo, Plaça de Vila. First-class international cuisine with prices to match; open until 1.30am.

Los Pasajeros, c/Vicent Soler s/n. On a narrow lane connecting c/d'Enmig with the waterfront, this first-floor restaurant is one of the hippest places to dine, with its unpretentious plain decor and tasty but limited Spanish menu. A good place to find out what's happening, and open until 2am.

Pizzeria Pinocchio, c/d'Enmig 18. Among many pizza and pasta places, this is one of the most popular and inexpensive – and the food is OK, if uninspired.

Restaurante S'Acarda, c/Obrador s/n, off Plaça Anton Riquer. Situated amongst a cluster of similar restaurants, this is a popular spot, with main courses starting at a very reasonable 900ptas. The specialities here are paella and other Spanish dishes.

Rocky's, c/Verge 6. Down near the harbour, one street from c/d'Enmig, this restaurant is famous for serving one of the tastiest paellas in town – and there's a vegetarian version on offer as well.

La Victoria, c/Riambau 1. Popular and well-established restaurant in the lower town, offering generous portions of basic but tasty Spanish cuisine – excellent value.

Drinking and nightlife

However good the restaurant scene in Ibiza Town, it's something of a sideshow compared with the bars and clubs which have made the island internationally famous – you come to Ibiza to party. Together they keep the place going pretty much twenty-four hours a day, and with money, mobility and stamina the night is yours, never mind the morning.

The town's **bars** throng the streets of the lower town and there's a fair assortment up in Dalt Vila too. Meanwhile, **clubs** – amongst which are numbered some of Europe's very best – are dotted across the southern half of the island, but primarily in Sant Antoni de Portmany, Platja d'en Bossa, Sant Rafel and, of course, Ibiza Town itself. It's actually quite easy to hop from one club to the other courtesy of the Voramar bus company, which runs the *Disco Bus* (nightly 6.30pm–6.30am; 225ptas per journey; details from the tourist office). Neither is there much difficulty in finding out what's happening: each club employs PR people, who descend on Ibiza Town to drum up custom by distributing flyers and sticking up posters in bars and shops. Many of the bars also hand out free club entry tickets in return for your custom, which represent a significant saving. None of the clubs opens until midnight, but there again they do carry on until at least 6am. Most have a policy of a free drink with the admission price and the majority accept credit cards.

In the **early evening** in Ibiza Town, things kick off in the Sa Penya district and down along the harbourfront. Here, at the *Zoo* bar (8pm–4am) and its neighbours – such as the innovative *Bar Zuka*, c/Verge (8pm–4am) – you can listen to the latest sounds and admire the harbour view. Another excellent option close by, though it doesn't open until 10pm – and out of season only on the weekend – is the *Blues Music Bar*, above the Estació Marítim, which has a huge, glass-fronted bar with great views over the marina and up to the old town. Close by, along c/d'Enmig and c/Verge, are lots of other places, including several lively **gay bars**, like the small and well-established *JJ's* and *Teatro*, at the end of c/d'Enmig. There are also a couple of transvestite cabaret shows nearby on c/Verge, the best being *Samsara*, but note that although the admission here is free, the first drink costs 2000ptas (subsequently 1000ptas). The busiest gay bars are, however, to be found up by the city walls: *Incognitos* and *Angelos* are the places to head for, beside the Portal de ses Taules. This is a good area to hang out in any case, with loads of lively drinking places – such as *Bar Cueva* (9pm–4am), inside Dalt Vila on c/Conquista, which has low tables with candles, hammocks in the bar and an open-minded music scene.

For **live music**, the prime spot is *Teatro Pereira*, c/Comte de Rosselló 3, housed in the old municipal theatre near the Passeig de Vara de Rey. This splendid old building, easily spotted by its outdoor terrace bar ablaze with fairy lights, has a great atmosphere and showcases live quality acts each night – blues, R&B, reggae, rock and jazz. Open 8pm–5am, it has no admission fee and prices are reasonable considering the quality of entertainment. They also serve homemade burgers. Alternatively, the *Arteca*, across the street at c/Azara 4 (7pm–4am), is a pocket-sized corner bar playing jazz and South American salsa. They also have an extensive jazz library, serve snacks and have newspapers to browse.

Clubs

Amnesia, on the Eivissa/Sant Antoni road before Sant Rafel (☎971 198041). Large, well-established club with the best European house and garage DJs, a domed glass roof, spacious dancing floors and many bars. There's also an outdoor garden bar with carobs and palms and bamboo chairs for chilling out, a boutique and food. This is a young club and they have special nights when the dance floor is filled with foam. Daily mid-June to mid-September, midnight–7am. Admission: 4000ptas; drinks from 800ptas.

Anfora, c/Sant Carles 7, Dalt Vila (☎971 302893). Set in the heart of Dalt Vila, this men-only gay club has a cave-like decor. Daily May to late-September, midnight–6am. Admission: 1000ptas.

El Divino, Passeig Joan Carles I s/n (☎971 190176). Across the bay from the town centre, on the waterfront next to the casino. Superb views of the marina and Ibiza Town from its bean bag and bamboo-cluttered outdoor terrace. Comparatively small – with a capacity of 1400 – El Divino has Indonesian decor, a large dance floor, several bars and comfortable seating areas. There's a smart dress code and mixed age-range with mainstream dance sounds, and guest DJs some nights. Daily mid-June to late-September, midnight–6am (restaurant 8.30pm—2am). Admission: 4000ptas; drinks from 600ptas.

Pacha, Avgda. 8 d'Agost (☎971 313600). On the edge of Ibiza Town, around the marina on the St Eulària des Riu road. In a smart white building surrounded by palms, with an atmospheric salsa/Latino bar, a dance floor, an excellent restaurant, and plush sofa seating areas (outdoors, too, in summer). Music range is broadly garage, funk and techno. The age range is varied and the dress code fairly smart. Daily May–Sept; Oct–April weekends only. Midnight–6am. Admission: 4500ptas; drinks from 1000ptas.

Privelege, off the Ibiza Town/Sant Antoni de Portmany road at Sant Rafel (☎971 198160). Formerly known as Ku, this club was the forerunner of the Ibiza sound and is the sole reason why some people come to the island. High up in the hills, this huge, glass-sided and -roofed building has splendid views over the interior. Inside, the club resembles a movie set, with a huge swimming pool in the centre of the dance floor, fountains, fourteen bars, a capacity of around 8000, an outdoor terrace garden, a restaurant and a main theme of futuristic scaffolding in silver, black and gold. Top-name DJs and special events are regular. Daily mid-June to late-September, midnight–7am, and later on special party nights. Admission: 4000ptas; drinks from 800ptas.

Listings

Airport information (☎971 302200). The Iberia office is at Passeig de Vara de Rey 15 (☎971 302580).

Car rental Avis (☎971 809176); Atesa-Eurodollar (☎971 395393); Hertz (☎971 809178) – all at the airport.

Consulates Britain, Avgda. Isidor Macabich 45 (☎971 301818).

Ferries Mainland, Mallorca and Menorca sailings with Transmediterranea (☎971 315050); local boats along the Ibiza coast and to Formentera operated by several companies, including Transmapi (☎971 310711) and Umafisa (☎971 314513).

Hospital Hospital Can Mises, on the way to the airport at Avgda. d'Espanya 49 (☎971 397000).

Laundry Masterclean, close to *Hostal El Puerto* on c/Felip II.

Moped rental Motos Valentin, Bartomeu Vicent Ramón 19 (☎971 310822); and Motosud, Avgda. d'Espanya s/n (☎971 302442), a 1km walk west of the centre.

Post office The main *Correu* (Mon–Fri 8.30am–2pm) is at c/Madrid 21.

Around Ibiza Town: the beaches

There's sea and sand close to Ibiza Town at **Figueretes**, **Platja d'en Bossa** and **Talamanca**, but the first two of these are built-up continuations of the capital with over-exploited beaches, and only at the third is there any peace and quiet. All are accessible by short and inexpensive ferry rides from the terminal near the foot of Avinguda. Santa Eulària. Everything considered though, it's worth going a little further afield to escape the highrise hotels – unless it's just water you want, in which case the outside pools and water slides of the Aguamar complex at Platja d'en Bossa should satisfy.

Ses Salines and Es Cavallet

To the **south of Ibiza Town**, stretching from the airport to the sea, are thousands of acres of **salt flats**. Ibiza's history, and its powerful presence on ancient trade routes, was based on these salt fields (*salinas*), a trade that was vital, above all, to the ancient Carthaginians. Indeed, salt remained an important economic resource until comparatively recently; the island's only rail line ran from the middle of the marshes to **La Canal**, a dock where an enormous container ship would arrive weekly to be loaded with the bright white sea salt. Even now, though tourism brings in far more money and the rail line has been torn up, salt production continues.

There are two beaches around here and buses from Ibiza Town leave regularly for the more westerly, **SES SALINES**, whose fine white sand arcs around a bay, the crystal clear waters fringed by pines and dunes. The beach also has a handful of beach bars, and sun loungers are for rent at 600ptas per day. From Ses Salines, it's a brief walk around the rocks or along the paths that maze the sand dunes to **ES CAVALLET**, a quieter if broadly similar beach that's long been a favourite of gay visitors – the dunes behind the beach are a well-known cruising area.

Santa Eulària des Riu and around

Heading northeast from Ibiza Town, it's just 15km to **SANTA EULÀRIA DES RIU**, one of the island's more agreeable little towns. Pushed tight against the seashore, it's situated beside the only river in the Balearics and boasts an attractive hill-top **church**, a modest whitewashed affair approached up a slope lined with the Stations of the Cross. The modern seafront is, however, uninspiring and the flat, sandy beach it borders undistinguished, faults that are partly redeemed by the presence of several first-rate **restaurants**, including *El Naranjo*, c/Sant Josep 31, which serves up quality Spanish food amidst a patio of orange trees. There's no real reason to **stay**, but if you do the town has several reasonably priced *hostals*, two of the better ones being *Hostal Residencia Rey*, Sant Josep 17 (☎971 330210; April–Oct; ④), where all rooms have bath and balcony, and the family-run *Hostal Residencia Mayol*, Algemesi 2 (☎971 330282; ③), with spacious, en-suite rooms also with balcony.

The rugged coastline **north of Santa Eulària des Riu** is notched with small sandy coves and beaches. However, almost all of them are developed to some degree – nowhere more so than in and around the resort of Es Canar – and you're better off heading **inland** to **SANT CARLES**, a one-horse town where *Anita's*, a bar on the corner next to the supermarket, attracts islanders and resident hippies in roughly equal proportions. If you decide to press on north, be warned that the resort of Cala Sant Vicent, at the end of the road, has little to recommend it.

The north coast

Cutting straight across the island north from Ibiza Town, it's about 6km to a fork in the road where you veer right for **Portinatx** or left for **Port de Sant Miquel**. Both roads pass through some of the island's finest countryside – burnt-red fields of olive, almond and carob trees, and occasionally a plantation of melons or vines – before they reach their north-coast destinations.

Portinatx

Some 25km from Ibiza Town, the road skirts the hill-top village of Sant Joan before wriggling down to Portinatx along a beautiful, fertile valley flanked by olive-terraced hills and orderly groves of almond and pine. After rain, in particular, there's a distinctive brightness to the air here and a delightful burgundy glow to the soil. At **CALA XARRACA** you emerge above the sea with a path leading down to a tiny beach, with sparklingly clear water, rocks to dive off and a lone bar. **CALA XUCLAR**, next along, is in much the same mould, reached by an even steeper track and great for snorkelling.

After the trip down the valley, the cramped resort of **PORTINATX** comes as a disappointment – once you've walked the length of its three beaches, tried the harbour sports and purchased your quota from the souvenir shops, there's little left to do. The beaches – **Big Beach**, **Little Beach** and **Es Port** – have to serve several medium-sized hotels and there's barely room to squeeze a towel in between the sunbeds, all rotated hourly to follow the path of the sun. About the only thing worth doing is the climb up beyond the *Holiday Club* chalets to the old watch tower (one of very few which survive intact and accessible), from where there's a great view down across the town, its bay and back into the hills.

If you're looking for a **room** and the hotels are all agency-booked to capacity (as they probably will be), try the two-star *Hostal Cas Mallorqui* (☎971 333082, fax 971 333159; ⑦), whose comfortable and commodious rooms overlook the bay from above Es Port beach.

Port de Sant Miquel

The attractive little bay flanking **PORT DE SANT MIQUEL**, about 20km from the capital, has been badly mauled by the developers, and has oodles of beach bars and restaurants – unenticing surroundings for the **Cova de Can Marça** (June–Sept daily 10.30am–7.30pm, guided tours every half hour; 750ptas), a cave complex which is well signposted on the twisting road above the bay. The cave features some spectacular lighting effects and an artificial waterfall cascading over fossil-rich rocks, and there's an excellent **view** of the coastline from outside.

The west coast: Sant Antoni de Portmany

SANT ANTONI DE PORTMANY is seriously out of place on Ibiza; this is package tour territory of the least endearing kind – all sun, sex and booze ad nauseam. Nevertheless, if for some reason you're marooned here, the **Turismo** (Mon–Fri 9.30am–8.30pm, Sat & Sun 9.30am–1pm; ☎971 343363), in the park at the beginning of the waterfront Passeig de ses Fonts, provides information on **places to stay** and is very helpful. Reasonably priced, downtown options include *Hostal Residencia Roig*, c/Progres 44 (☎971 340483; ③), where all the rooms have good-sized bathrooms and pleasant pine furniture, and *Hotel Residencia Vedra*, c/De La Mar 7 (☎971 340150, fax 971 342656; April–Oct; ④), a family-run affair with balconied bedrooms, some of which (on the upper floors) have sea views. Alternatively, there's a pricier-than-average **campsite**, *Camping San Antonio* (☎971 340536; April–Sept), just outside town beside the main road to Ibiza Town. It occupies a surprisingly quiet and palm-shaded area, and comes equipped with a swimming pool, bar and laundry. Pitches cost 600ptas, plus 600ptas per person, and there are also bungalows (②).

There are plenty of **cafés** and restaurants to choose from – though the food is generally either dull or over-priced – and you'll find dozens of bars and a clutch of nightclubs. Amongst them, the better-than-average *Café del Mar* (April–Oct daily 5.30pm–4am), by the coast at the west end of c/Vara de Rey, offers great views of the sunset from an outdoor terrace. To escape the town, **car rental** is available from Avis, down by the harbour on Passeig de la Mar (☎971 342715), and from Ibiza-Betacar, just behind the waterfront on c/General Balanzat (☎971 345068). **Bicycle rental** outlets include Autos Reco, c/Ramón i Cajal (☎971 340388), a few minutes' walk from the harbourfront on the east side of the town centre.

Sant Antoni de Portmany offers a wide range of **boat trips**, from glass-bottomed tours of the harbour and a shuttle service west across the bay to the highrise resort of Cala Bassa, through to a twice weekly circuit of the island of Ibiza, calling in at Wednesday's "hippie market" at Es Canar. **Buses** leave for Ibiza Town every half-hour, four times daily to Santa Eulària des Riu and frequently to local *calas*. **Timetables** are available at the Turismo. All buses leave from the Passeig de la Mar.

Around Sant Antoni de Portmany

Heading out of Sant Antoni de Portmany, you'll find more attractive beaches, and fewer people, within easy striking distance. To the **north**, at the end of a turning off the road to Santa Agnés de Corona (see below), it's just 4km from town to the small cove of **CALA SALADA**, where the beach is of fine sand and the sea excellent for swimming. There's a small and cheerful restaurant here, a beach bar and pedalo rental too. Farther north, and inland, the sleepy hamlet of **SANTA AGNÉS DE CORONA** drapes over a hillside surrounded by picturesque countryside. The village has two small restaurants and a **chapel**, which has a subterranean gallery in which local Christians worshipped secretly during the Moorish occupation. Discovered in 1907, the catacomb is currently under renovation, so check with the Turismo in Sant Antoni before making a special trip. From the village, a rough country road continues east across the scrawny interior of the island to Sant Miquel and ultimately Portinatx (see p.790).

South of Sant Antoni de Portmany are the busy resorts of Port des Torrent and Cala Bassa. If you're after a bit more tranquillity, however, press on to the **southwest** corner of the island via Sant Josep to **CALA D'HORT**, which has a lovely quiet beach and a quaint fishing harbour. There are two excellent seafood restaurants here, *Es Boldado* and *Can Jaime*, and delightful views over **Illa Vedrà**, a canine tooth of rock stabbing through the bay just offshore. Ibiza's highest peak, it allegedly starred in the film *South Pacific* as the mysterious island of Bali Hai.

Sant Antoni de Portmany to Ibiza Town

It's just 15km from Sant Antoni de Portmany to Ibiza Town east along the main road, but you can detour south via Sant Josep, a more scenic route with turnings off to the south coast. Of these, the turning to the **Cova Santa** (Holy Cave) is the one you want, with some impressive drippy stalactites 17m underground, just off the main road. The caves are signposted, but there are no set opening hours – you just have to turn up and hope you're in luck. From the caves, the side road continues south until fields of melons and grapes herald **CALA JONDAL**, a popular spot with the islanders, where you can get delicious seafood at the bar *Tropicana*. The drawback is the beach, an uncomfortable, pebbly affair, though recent dollops of imported sand have changed matters somewhat, while the shallow waters make it safe for swimmers.

FORMENTERA

Just eleven nautical miles south of Ibiza Town, **FORMENTERA** (population 4000) is the smallest of the inhabited Balearics. It's actually two small islets joined together by a narrow sandy isthmus and is just 20km long from east to west. The crossing from Ibiza is short, but strong currents ensure that it's slow – over an hour – and can be rough. Return fares are about 2200ptas (3800ptas on the hydrofoil, which is quicker but less enjoyable) and there are usually rival sailings to choose from: check the return times before deciding.

Formentera's history more or less parallels that of Ibiza, though for nearly three hundred years – from the early fifteenth century to the end of the seventeenth – it was left uninhabited for lack of water and fear of Turkish pirate raids. Under the Romans it had been a major agricultural centre (its name derives from *frumentaria*, "granary"), and when repopulated in 1697 the island was again divided up for cultivation. It never regained its original level of productivity, however, and nowadays is largely barren, the few crops having to be protected, as on Menorca, against the lashing of winter winds. Indeed, most of the island is now covered in rosemary, growing wild everywhere, and crawling with thousands of brilliant green lizards – the **Ibiza wall lizard** (*Podarcis pityusensis*) which flourishes in arid scrubland.

Modern income is derived from tourism (especially German, Italian and British), taking advantage of some of Spain's longest, whitest and least-crowded beaches. The shortage of fresh water continues to keep development within acceptable limits – there are only around thirty *hostals* and hotels on the whole island – and for the most part visitors here are seeking escape with little in the way of sophistication. Nevertheless, Formentera has become increasingly popular with day-trippers from neighbouring Ibiza, and is certainly not the "unspoilt paradise" it once was. Nude sunbathing is tolerated – indeed the norm – just about everywhere.

Arrival, information and accommodation

There is a basic **bus** service from the **port of arrival**, La Savina, but timetables are not always adhered to and buses connect only the settlements that string out along the main island road plus a few of the larger resorts, leaving you long, hot walks to any of the more isolated beaches. **Taxis** are cheap and are the most popular form of island transport. You'll find ranks at La Savina, Sant Francesc and Es Pujols (see box, p.795). Fares are about 1000ptas for 5km but as the distances involved are small, the cost is never extortionate. It's best to book a taxi the day before you need it. For **car rental**, reckon on 5000ptas per day (see box, p.795). **Renting a bicycle** is a popular option too; apart from some of its coastal extremities, the island is extremely flat. You'll find bike rental places at La Savina and Es Pujols and a day's hire will set you back around 500ptas.

The island's main **Turismo** (☎971 322057), is at the ferry port in La Savina, and can provide information on all aspects of the island, including accommodation. If you're staying on the island, buy the IGN 1:25,000 **map** which shows the dirt tracks as well as the tarmac roads.

Accommodation

Most visitors treat Formentera as a **day trip** from Ibiza, and if you want to be one of the few who **stay** you'd be well-advised to make an advance reservation – the bulk of the island's limited supply of beds is snapped up early by the tour operators. Bear in mind also that almost all the hotels and *hostals* close down for the winter – from November to March. Neither does Formentera have a campsite and although people do doss down behind the beaches, it's not encouraged and has, in the past, damaged the delicate ecology of the dunes.

Hostal Bellavista, Passeig de la Marina s/n, La Savina (☎ & fax 971 322255). Next to the harbour, with forty rooms all with sea view. There's a waterside restaurant and terrace bar here as well. Open all year. ⑤.

Hostal Centro, Sant Francesc Xavier (☎971 322063). Basic *hostal* in an old building in the island capital, across the square from the church. The large restaurant, *Plate*, serves reasonable and inexpensive snacks and meals. Open all year. ③.

Hostal Residencia Mayans, Es Pujols (☎ & fax 971 328724). Pleasant, one-star *hostal*, 100m from the beach, in a quiet spot away from the main resort area. Open April–Oct. ⑤.

Pepe, c/Major, Sant Ferran (☎971 328033). Basic but functional rooms with bath and balcony at this bar-restaurant. There is a patio garden and swimming pool too. Open all year. ③.

Hostal La Savina, La Savina (☎ & fax 971 322279). Large blue and white *hostal* about 50m from the harbourfront on the road out of town. Open mid-April to Oct. ⑤.

Around the island

Sailing out of Ibiza Town harbour, there's a stupendous view of the citadel astride its cliff and soon the sand-fringed islets which herald Formentera hove into view – one of the tiniest being the Illa d'es Penjats ("Hanged Men's Island"), once the last stop for Ibiza's criminals. Ferries and hydrofoils then proceed to Formentera's one and only ferry dock at **LA SAVINA**. There's nothing much to the place, apart from a taxi rank and rows of car, bicycle and moped rental agencies, and a couple of places to stay. The island capital, **SANT FRANCESC XAVIER** is a few kilometres inland from the port and is easily reached on foot or by bike, bus or taxi if you're not planning to rent a vehicle. The town is something of a crossroads and serves as the island's commercial and shopping centre with restaurants, cafés, bars, banks, supermarkets, a health-food shop, a pharmacist and open-air markets – but it's an insignificant place all the same, its only real sight being the fortified **church**, now stripped of its defensive cannons, sitting in a large square at the top of the town.

FORMENTERA: USEFUL NUMBERS

Car rental Autos Betacar ☎971 322031;
Avis ☎971 322123;
Hertz ☎971 322242.

Medical emergencies ☎971 322369.

Ferries Umafisa ☎971 323007;
Transmapi ☎971 322703;
Transmediterranea ☎971 315050.

Police ☎092.

Post office Plaça Constitució 1,
Sant Francesc ☎825.

Taxis Taxis La Savina ☎971 328016,
Taxis Sant Francesc ☎971 322243;
Taxis Es Pujols ☎971 322016.

Heading east from the capital, it's just 3km along the main island road to tiny **SANT FERRAN**, the island's second town and home to *Pepe*, c/Major, a long-established and laid-back bar-cum-restaurant, that's something of an island institution. You can also stay here (see "Accommodation").

From Sant Ferran, a side road leads to the north coast at **ES PUJOLS**, Formentera's largest resort development – though it's still tiny by mainland (and Mallorcan) standards. Originally a fishing village, the resort centres on two smallish sandy beaches which nestle in amongst craggy rocks, backed by pines. The islet-studded bay is very pretty, the sand is bright white and the sea is clear and shallow, but behind the shore lurk tasteless tourist hotels, which will probably prompt an early departure. If you do hang around, there's windsurfing and other water sports, late-night bars, and two clubs.

Northwest of Es Pujols, the **Es Trucadors peninsula** pokes a flat and sandy finger out towards Ibiza. There are more long and slender beaches here – notably **Platja de ses Illetes** on the west shore – and at the peninsula's end, across a narrow channel, lies the uninhabited island of **S'Espalmador**.

Back in Sant Ferran, the main island road travels east, passing the rough, dirt turnings which twist south through arable farmland and acres of sand dunes to the middle portion of the **Platja de Migjorn**, whose fine white sands and turquoise waters extend for some 5km. There's some development at either end of the beach – in the west at **Es Ca Mari** and to the east around the equally unenticing **Maryland** – but the centre remains largely untouched and it's here in the dunes you'll find the *Yoga Mari* bar, which provides tasty snacks.

Beyond the Maryland turning, the main road leaves the flatlands to snake up through pine forests, passing a first-rate restaurant, *El Mirador* – where the views of Formentera are exceptional – as it skirts the northern flanks of **La Mola**, at 192m the island's highest point. Soon you reach the drowsy little town of El Pilar, where the road straightens for the final 2km-dash to the **Far de La Mola** (lighthouse), which stands on the cliffs high above the blueness of the ocean. It was here that Jules Verne was inspired to write his *Journey Round the Solar System* as he gazed into the clear night sky – hence the large stone block with the bronze plaque. Before you head back, you can pop into the souvenir shop and the café.

Eating and drinking

Es Pujols, the principal resort, has a plethora of seafront **bars and restaurants**, with menus to suit most wallets, and excellent seafood on offer. Good options include the busy little *Bar Pupit*, and *Can Vent*, which serves great seafood. For breakfast, try *Cafetería Espardell*. There's an especially good Basque restaurant, *Café L'Opera*, at c/Espalmador 32. Here also is where you'll find the island's **nightlife**, with a couple of late bars and discos. Most of Formentera's *hostals* serve meals, or you can get your own supplies from the market and supermarket in Sant Francesc.

MALLORCA

Few Mediterranean holiday spots are as often and as unfairly maligned as **MALLORCA**. The island is commonly perceived as little more than sun, sex, booze and highrise hotels – so much so that there's a long-standing Spanish joke about a mythical fifth Balearic island called *Majorca* (the English spelling), inhabited by an estimated four million tourists a year. However, this image, spawned by the helter-skelter development of the 1960s, takes no account of Mallorca's beguiling diversity. It's true that there are sections of coast where highrise hotels and shopping centres are continuous, wedged beside and upon one another and broken only by a dual carriageway down to more of the same. But the spread of development, even after 25 years, is surprisingly limited, essentially confined to the Badia de Palma (Bay of Palma), a thirty-kilometre strip flanking the island capital, and a handful of mega-resorts notching the east coast. Elsewhere, things are very different. **Palma** itself, the Balearics' one real city, is a bustling, historic place whose grand mansions and magnificent Gothic cathedral defy the expectations of many visitors. And so does the northwest coast, for here is the **Serra de Tramuntana**, a rugged mountain range amongst whose rearing peaks are beautiful cove beaches, a pair of intriguing monasteries at Valldemossa and Lluc, and a string of delightful old towns – Deià, Sóller and Pollença – as well as the picturesque villages of Biniaraix and Fornalutx. There's a startling variety and physical beauty to the land, too, which, along with the mildness of the climate, has drawn tourists to visit and well-heeled expatriates to settle here since the nineteenth century, including artists and writers of many descriptions, from Robert Graves to Roger McGough.

Mallorca practicalities

Palma, the site of the only airport and the principal ferry port of the island is, for all the disasters of its bay, an excellent initial base, especially as it's the hub of an extensive public transport system, with bus services linking the capital to all of Mallorca's principal settlements. There are even a couple of train lines running out of Palma – one, a beautiful ride up through the mountains to Sóller, is an attraction in itself – while by car Palma is within three hours' drive of the island's farthest corner. When you feel you've exhausted Palma's possibilities, your best bet is to move across to the **Serra de Tramuntana** for a few days in the mountains, preferably working your way up the coast to the handsome town of **Pollença** – and perhaps squeezing in a visit to the bird-rich marshlands of the **Parc Natural de S'Albufera** as well.

The main constraint for travellers is **accommodation**. From mid-June to mid-September rooms are in short supply and, if you do go at this time, you're well-advised to make a reservation several months in advance or to book a package. Out of season, things ease up and you can idle round, staying pretty much where you want. Bear in mind also that five of Mallorca's **monasteries** rent out renovated cells at exceptionally inexpensive rates – reckon on 1500ptas per double room per night. The Monastir de Nostra Senyora at Lluc (see p.810) and the Ermita de Nostra Senyora del Puig outside Pollença (see p.810) are both reachable via public transport, while those with their own transport could also try the Ermita de Sant Salvador at Felanitx (☎971 827282), the Ermita de Nostra Sra. de Bonany at Petra (☎971 561101), and the slightly more comfortable Ermita de Nostra Sra. de Cura in Algaida Randa (☎971 660994).

Palma

In 1983 **PALMA** became the capital of one of Spain's newly established autonomous regions, the Balearic Islands, and since then it's shed the dusty provincialism of

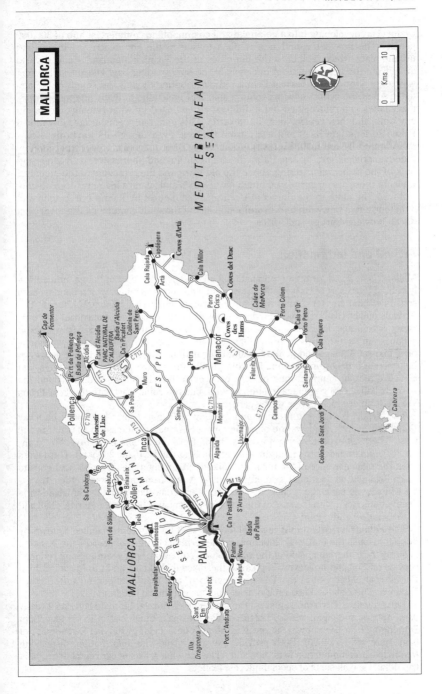

yesteryear, developing into a go-ahead and cosmopolitan commercial hub of 300,000 people. The new self-confidence is plain to see in the city centre, a vibrant and urbane place which is akin to the big cities of the Spanish mainland – and a world away from the heaving tourist enclaves of the surrounding bay. There's still a long way to go – much of suburban Palma remains obdurately dull and somewhat dilapidated – but the centre now presents a splendid ensemble of lively shopping areas, mazy lanes and refurbished old buildings, all enclosed by what remains of the old city walls and their replacement boulevards. This geography encourages downtown Palma to look into itself and away from the sea, even though its **harbour** – now quarantined by the main highway – has always been the city's economic lifeline. Indeed, arriving here by sea, Palma is still beautiful and impressive, with the grand bulk of the cathedral towering above the old town and the remnants of the medieval walls. In these are encapsulated much of the city's and island's history: Moorish control from the ninth to the thirteenth century, reconquest by Jaume I of Aragón and a meteoric rise to wealth and prominence in the fifteenth century as the main port of call between Europe and Africa.

Arrival and information

Mallorca's new and gleaming international **airport** is 11km east of Palma, immediately behind the resort of Ca'n Pastilla. It has one enormous terminal, which handles both scheduled and charter flights with separate floors for Arrivals and Departures. The Arrivals hall has 24-hour **cash card and credit card machines, car rental** and **currency exchange** facilities as well as a provincial **Turismo** (Mon–Sat 9am–2pm & 3–8pm, Sun 9am–2pm), which has lists of hotels and *hostals*, public transport timetables, taxi rates, maps and general island information. The Turismo will not, however, help arrange **accommodation**; for this you'll either have to telephone hotels and *hostals* direct, or approach one of the dozen or so travel agents scattered round the Arrivals hall – it's a good idea to shop around, but you could start with Iberia or Prima Travel, both of which have a wide selection.

The airport is linked to the city and the Bay of Palma resorts by a busy highway (*autopista*), which shadows the shoreline from S'Arenal in the east to Magaluf in the west. The least expensive way to reach Palma from the airport is by **bus** #17 (daily, every 20min from 6am to midnight, plus 1am, 1.35am and 2.10am; 290ptas). This leaves from the main entrance of the terminal building just behind the taxi rank, and goes to Plaça Espanya, on the north side of the centre. A **taxi** from the airport to the city centre will set you back about 2000ptas; taxi rates are controlled and a list of island-wide destinations along with the cost of the taxi fare is displayed both in the Arrivals hall and in the window of the tourist office.

The Palma **ferry terminal** is about 4km west of the city centre, linked to town by bus #1; to catch the bus, walk 200m out of the terminal to the main road – the bus stop is on the near (harbour) side of the road. Buses run every hour (8am to 9pm; reduced service on Sun and holidays; 175ptas) to the Plaça de la Reina and the Plaça Rei Joan Carles I, at either end of the Passeig d'es Born, and then continue on to the Plaça Espanya. There's also a taxi rank outside the ferry terminal building.

The provincial **Turismo** is just off the Passeig d'es Born at Plaça de la Reina 2 (daily 9am–2.30pm & 3–8pm; ☎971 712216), while the main municipal office is at c/Sant Domingo 11, in the subway at the end of c/Conquistador (Mon–Fri 9am–8pm, Sat 9am–1pm; ☎971 724090). Both provide city and island-wide information, dispensing free maps, accommodation lists, bus and ferry schedules, lists of car rental firms, boat trip details and all sorts of special interest leaflets.

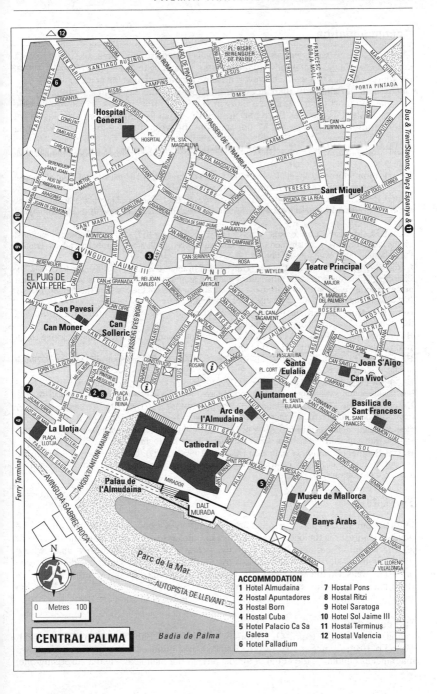

CENTRAL PALMA

Badia de Palma

0 Metres 100

ACCOMMODATION
1 Hotel Almudaina
2 Hostal Apuntadores
3 Hostal Born
4 Hostal Cuba
5 Hotel Palacio Ca Sa Galesa
6 Hotel Palladium
7 Hostal Pons
8 Hostal Ritzi
9 Hotel Saratoga
10 Hotel Sol Jaime III
11 Hostal Terminus
12 Hostal Valencia

Accommodation

There are around twenty *hostals* and thirty hotels dotted around Palma, and if you haven't got a reservation, your first move in the summer should be to pick up the official list from the tourist office. They won't, however, arrange accommodation for you.

The bulk of Palma's **budget accommodation** is in the city centre; fortunately this is by far the most diverting area to stay in. The best areas to look are along the side streets off the Passeig d'es Born and around the Plaça Espanya. There are clusters of **fancier hotels** on the Passeig Mallorca and to the west of the centre along Avinguda Gabriel Roca, overlooking the waterfront.

Hotel Almudaina, Avgda. Jaume III 9 (☎971 727340, fax 971 722599). Smart, modern rooms above a noisy street right in the centre. ⑥.

Hostal Apuntadores, c/Apuntadors 8 (☎971 713491). Appealingly laid-back *hostal* in an old house off the Passeig d'es Born. Rooms are simple but adequate. ③.

Hostal Born, c/Sant Jaume 3 (☎971 712942, fax 971 718618). Comfortable and justifiably popular *hostal* in excellent downtown location. Set in an old, refurbished mansion with its own courtyard café. ⑥.

Hostal Residencia Cuba, c/Sant Magí 1 (☎971 738159, fax 971 403131). Pleasant, functional rooms in an attractively refurbished stone house with a pretty little tower and balustrade; overlooks the bottom of busy Avgda. Argentina. ④.

Hotel Residencia Palacio Ca Sa Galesa, c/Miramar 8 (☎971 715400, fax 971 721579). Charmingly renovated seventeenth-century mansion amongst the narrow alleys of the oldest part of town a couple of minutes' walk from the cathedral. Fine views of the city from the rooftop terrace. Just a dozen luxurious rooms and suites. Very expensive. ⑧.

Hotel Residencia Palladium, Passeig Mallorca 40 (☎971 713945, fax 971 714665). Clean, trim and tidy rooms in a modern high-rise. No dining room. ⑥.

Hostal Residencia Pons, c/Vi 8 (☎971 722658). Simple rooms in a lovely old house with a courtyard and house plants. In the old part of town, near the Passeig d'es Born. ③.

Hostal Ritzi, c/Apuntadors 6 (☎971 714610). Basic, one-star rooms in an ancient, five-storey house off the Passeig d'es Born. ③.

Hotel Saratoga, Passeig Mallorca 6 (☎971 727240, fax 971 727312). Excellent, newly refurbished hotel with rooftop swimming pool. Most rooms have balconies overlooking the boulevard. ⑦.

Hotel Sol Jaime III, Passeig Mallorca 14 (☎971 725943, fax 971 725946). Agreeable three-star hotel with tidy, modern rooms, most with balconies. Very reasonable prices. ⑥.

Hostal Residencia Terminus, c/Eusebi Estada 2 (☎971 750014). Decent hotel next to the train station, with a quirkily old-fashioned foyer and fairly large bedrooms. ④.

Hostal Residencia Valencia, c/Ramón i Cajal 21 (☎971 733147). Modern, thirty-room *hostal* on the northern edge of the city centre. Spruce, almost antiseptic rooms, some with balconies overlooking the boulevard. ④.

The City

Finding your way around Palma is fairly straightforward once you're in the centre. The obvious landmark is the **cathedral** – *La Seu* in Catalan – which dominates the waterfront and backs onto the oldest part of the city, a cluster of alleys and narrow lanes whose northern and eastern limits are marked by the zigzag of avenues built beside or in place of the city walls. On the west side of the cathedral, Avinguda d'Antoni Maura/Passeig d'es Born cuts up from the seafront to intersect with Avinguda Jaume III/Unio at Plaça Rei Joan Carles. These busy thoroughfares form the centre of the modern town.

The cathedral

Palma's **cathedral** (April–Oct Mon–Fri 10am–6pm, Sat 10am–2pm; Nov–March Mon–Fri 10am–3pm, Sat 10am–2pm; 400ptas), five hundred years in the making, is a magnificent building – the equal of almost any on the mainland – and a surprising one, too, with *modernista* interior features designed by Antoni Gaudí. The original foundation came with the Christian Reconquest of the city, and the site taken, in fulfilment of a vow by Jaume I, was that of the Moorish Great Mosque. Essentially Gothic, with massive exterior buttresses to take the weight off the pillars within, the church derives its effect through its sheer height, impressive from any angle but startling when glimpsed from the waterside esplanade. The *reconquista*-era builders had a point to make, and they didn't hold back.

In the central nave, fourteen beautifully aligned, pencil-thin pillars rise to 21 metres before their ribs branch out – rather like fronded palm trees – to support the single-span, vaulted roof. The nave, at 44 metres high, is one of the tallest Gothic structures in Europe and its length – 121 metres – is of matching grandeur. This open, hangar-like construction, typical of Catalan Gothic architecture, was designed to make the high altar visible to the entire congregation, and to express the mystery of the Christian faith, with kaleidoscopic floods of light that filtered in through the **stained-glass windows**. Most of the original glass was lost long ago, but recent refurbishment has returned many windows to their former glory. For once the light isn't trapped by the central *coro* (choir) that normally blocks the centre of Spanish cathedrals. The innovative sidelining of the *coro*, and the fantastic forms of the lighting system above the altar, were Gaudí's work, completed from 1904 to 1914. At the time, these measures were deeply controversial; no *coro* had ever before been removed in Spain. The artistic success of the project, however, was undeniable, and it was immediately popular. Compared to Gaudí's designs in Barcelona, everything here is simple and restrained but there are touches of his characteristic fantasy. The wrought-iron contraption above the altar symbolizes the Crown of Thorns and the railings in front of the altar are twisted into forms inspired by Mallorcan window-grilles.

On the way into the church, you pass through the three rooms of assorted ecclesiastical bric-a-brac that comprise the **Museu de la Catedral**. The first room's most valuable exhibit, in the glass case in the middle, is a gilded silver monstrance of extraordinary delicacy, its fairy-tale decoration dating from the late sixteenth century. On display around the walls are assorted chalices and reliquaries and a real curiosity, the portable altar of Jaume I, a wood and silver chessboard with each square containing a bag of relics. The second room is mainly devoted to the Gothic works of the **Mallorcan Primitives**, a school of painters who flourished on the island in the fourteenth and fifteenth centuries, producing strikingly naive devotional works of bold colours and cartoon-like detail.

The Palau de l'Almudaina and La Llotja

Opposite the cathedral entrance stands the **Palau de l'Almudaina** (April–Sept Mon–Fri 10am–6pm, Sat 10am–2pm; Oct–March Mon–Fri 10am–2pm & 4–6pm; 450ptas), originally the palace of the Moorish *walis* (governors) and later of the Mallorcan kings. Visits here are guided, with energetic commentaries repeated in three languages, though there's nothing much to see – one of the few saving graces being a handful of admirable Flemish tapestries, each devoted to classical themes.

A steep flight of steps leads down from the Palau de l'Almudaina through some pleasant gardens and a restored section of the old city walls to the fifteenth-century **Llotja** (Tues–Sat 11am–2pm & 5–9pm, Sun 11am–2pm), the city's former stock exchange. This carefully composed building, with its octagonal turrets and tall windows, now hosts frequent and occasionally excellent exhibitions.

The rest of the city

Even more engaging is the medina-like maze of streets at the back of the cathedral, and here, at c/Can Serra 7, you'll come upon the **Banys Àrabs** (daily 10am–6pm; 150ptas).

One of the few genuine reminders of the Moorish presence, this *hammam* is an elegant, horseshoe-arched and domed chamber, but if you've been to the ones in Girona or Granada, these are anticlimactic; the garden outside, with tables where you can picnic, is perhaps nicer. Nearby, on c/Portella, the **Museu de Mallorca** (Tues–Sat 10am–2pm & 4–7pm, Sun 10am–2pm; 300ptas), occupying one of the many fifteenth- and sixteenth-century patrician mansions that dot this part of town, has extensive local archeology exhibits and some exceptionally fine medieval religious paintings – further examples of the work of the Mallorcan Primitives.

A five-minute walk away along Pont i Vich and Pare Nadal, and occupying, oddly enough, the site of the old Moorish soap factory, the **Basílica de Sant Francesc** (Mon–Sat 9.30am–12.30pm & 3.30–6pm, Sun 3.30–6pm; 100ptas) is the finest among a host of worthy medieval churches. A vast building founded towards the end of the thirteenth century, the church's main facade displays a stunning severity of style, with a great sheet of dressed sandstone stretching up to an arcaded balcony and pierced by a gigantic rose window. Entered via a trim Gothic cloister, the cavernous interior is disappointing, but you can't miss the monumental **high altar**, a gaudy affair illustrative of the High Baroque. Incidentally, the strange statue outside the church – of a Franciscan monk and an American Indian – celebrates the missionary work of **Junipero Serra**, a Mallorcan priest dispatched to California in 1768, who subsequently founded San Diego, Los Angeles and San Francisco.

From the basilica, it's a couple of minutes' walk west to **Santa Eulalia** (Mon–Fri 7am–1pm & 5.30–8pm, Sat & Sun 8am–1pm & 6–8pm; free), the first church to be built after Jaume's arrival, a typically Gothic construction with a yawning nave originally designed – as in the cathedral – to give the entire congregation a view of the high altar. Close by, the **Ajuntament** is a debonair example of the late Renaissance style with a grand and self-assured foyer.

Eating

Eating in Palma is less pricey – or can be – than anywhere else in the Balearics. Inexpensive **cafés** and **tapas bars** are liberally distributed around the city centre, with a particular concentration in the side streets off the Passeig d'es Born and Avinguda. Antoni Maura. The distinction between *tapas* bars and **restaurants** is blurred as many of the latter serve light snacks as well as full meals – but as a general rule the former are less formal. Some of the city's restaurants are geared up for the tourist trade, especially those along the seafront and Avinguda. d'Antoni Maura; it is, however, unfair to be snooty about them, as many serve delicious food and are also popular with Spaniards. If you venture a little further into the city centre, you'll discover more exclusively local haunts, some offering the finest of Catalan and Spanish cuisine. At all but the most expensive of places, 2500ptas will cover the cost of a starter and main course, as well as a bottle of wine – though you can expect prices to be jacked up in summer.

Cafés and tapas bars

Bar Bosch, Plaça Rei Joan Carles I. One of the most popular and inexpensive *tapas* bars in town, the traditional haunt of intellectuals and usually humming with conversation. At peak times you'll need to be assertive to get served.

Bon Lloc, c/Sant Feliu 7. One of the few vegetarian café-restaurants on the island, centrally situated off the Passeig d'es Born. Informal atmosphere and good food at low prices. Open Mon–Sat 1–4pm and the odd evening, usually Fri, till 9pm.

Ca'n Joan de S'Aigo, c/Can Sanç 10. Long-established coffee house with wonderful, freshly baked *ensaimadas* (cinnamon-flavoured spiral pastry buns) for just 85ptas and fruit-flavoured mousses to die for. Charming decor too. C/Can Sanç is a tiny alley near Plaça Santa Eulalia. Closed Tues.

Mesón Salamanca, c/Sant Jaume 3. Mostly Castilian cuisine in a tastefully refurbished, warren-like mansion off Avgda. Jaume III. Delicious *tapas* on the ground floor (avoid the overpriced, stuffy restaurant upstairs).

El Pilon, c/Can Cifre 4, off the north end of Passeig d'es Born. Vibrant, cramped and crowded *tapas* bar serving all manner of Spanish and Mallorcan dishes at very reasonable prices.

Restaurants
Caballito del Mar, opposite La Llotja at Passeig Sagrera 5. Superb selection of seafood in trim, no-nonsense surroundings, with excellent, friendly service. Main courses around 2500ptas.

Ca'n Carlos, c/Aigua 5, off Avgda. Jaume III. Charming, family-run restaurant featuring exquisite Mallorcan cuisine – cuttle fish, snails etc. The menu isn't extensive, but everything is beautifully prepared and there's a daily special. Main courses average around 1800ptas. Opens for lunch and at 8pm in the evening.

Celler Pagès, off c/Apuntadors at c/Felip Bauza 2. Traditional Mallorcan food in a tiny, inexpensive restaurant near Passeig d'es Born. Easy-going atmosphere, but can be stifling in the summer. Closed Sun.

Celler Sa Premsa, Plaça Bisbe Berenguer de Palou 8. Justly popular restaurant with delicious seafood, a five-minute walk west of the Plaça Espanya. Old bullfighting photos and posters adorn the walls amidst a pot-pourri of dusty bygones; you'll probably share a table with other diners. Prices are surprisingly low – as little as 1600ptas per person for a three-course meal.

Forn de Sant Joan, c/Sant Joan 4. Highly popular Catalan restaurant near La Llotja, one of several busy spots on this narrow alley. Fine fish dishes for around 1900ptas, *tapas* from 850ptas.

Es Parlament, c/Conquistador 11. All gilt-wood mirrors and chandeliers, this old and polished restaurant specializes in paella. The tasty and reasonably priced *menú del día* is recommended too. A favourite hangout of local politicians and lawyers.

Drinking and nightlife

Most of the cafés and all the *tapas* bars detailed above are quite happy just to ply you with drink, making the distinction between these establishments and the bars we've listed separately below somewhat artificial. Nonetheless, there's a cluster of lively **late-night bars** – mostly with music as the backdrop rather than the main event – amongst the narrow and ancient side streets backing onto Plaça Llotja. A second concentration of slightly more upmarket bars embellishes the bayside modernity of Avinguda. Gabriel Roca, about 3km west of the city centre. The grimy suburb of El Terreno, also west of the centre, once accommodated Palma's best late-night bars. The district has gone downhill, and now features topless "entertainment" and porn shops, but it's here you'll find the occasional offbeat bar, as well as several gay bars.

  Nightclubs (*discotecas*) are not Palma's forte, but there are one or two of some merit in El Terreno and on Avinguda Gabriel Roca. They're rarely worth investigating until around midnight and entry charges will cost you anything between 1000ptas and 2000ptas, depending on the night and what's happening.

Late-night bars
Abaco, just off c/Apuntadors at c/Sant Joan 1. Inhabiting a charming Renaissance mansion, this is easily Palma's most unusual bar, with an interior straight out of a Busby Berkeley musical: fruits cascading down its stairway, caged birds hidden amid patio foliage, elegant music and a daily flower bill you could live on for a month. Drinks, as you might imagine, are extremely expensive, but you're never hurried into buying one. It is, however, too sedate to be much fun if you're on the razzle.

La Bóveda, c/Boteria 3, off Plaça Llotja. Classy, bustling bar, one of several on this short alley, with long, wide windows and wine stacked high along the back wall. Be prepared to queue to get in – or come early.

El Globo, at the junction of c/Apuntadors and c/Felip Bauza. Lively bar with a background of modern jazz. One of several bars at the bottom end of c/Felip Bauza – *La Red*, at no. 5, is a cybercafé.

Gotic, Plaça Llotja 4. Cramped bar redeemed by its candle-lit patio and pavement tables which nudge out across the piazza, adding a touch of romance.

Latitude 39, c/Felip Bauza off c/Apuntadors. Tiny, upbeat bar, playing jazz, blues and sometimes classical music.

La Lonja, opposite La Llotja. A popular, well-established haunt, with revolving doors and pleasantly old-fashioned decor; the background music caters for (almost) all tastes.

Twins, c/Sant Joan 7, off Plaça Llotja. Fashionable place with an upbeat tempo and boisterous crowd.

XL, Avgda. Gabriel Roca, next door to Parc Cuarentena. Classy hangout with strikingly conspicuous, abstract decor. Quality cocktails and an upmarket clientèle.

Nightclubs

Discoteca Pacha, Avgda. Gabriel Roca 42. Loud, popular and raucous disco with a dance floor and a couple of bars inside, and another bar outside in the garden. A five-minute walk west of Parc Cuarentena.

Discoteca Tito's, Avgda. Gabriel Roca s/n. With its stainless steel and glass exterior, this long-established nightspot looks a bit like something from a sci-fi film set. Outdoor lifts carry you up to the dance floor, which pulls in huge crowds from many countries. The music lacks conviction, but it's certainly loud. Just on the city centre side of Parc Cuarentena.

Made in Brasil, Avgda. Gabriel Roca 27. Alarming tropical decor in this pocket-sized club-cum-bar on the city centre side of Parc Cuarentena. Great Latin sounds and cocktails.

Listings

American Express Avgda. Antoni Maura 10 (March–Oct 9am–1.30pm & 2–8pm, Sat 10am–2pm & 3–7pm, Sun 9am–2pm; Nov–Feb Mon–Sat only, reduced hours; ☎971 722344).

Banks Many banks are on and around the Passeig d'es Born and Avgda. Jaume III. There are 24-hour cash card and credit card machines dotted round the city too.

Bicycles Rent them at Ciclos Bimont, Plaça Progrés 19 (☎971 731866), for around 3000ptas a day, 12,000ptas a week. They also run a repair service.

Car rental Mallorca's four biggest car rental companies have offices at the airport: Atesa-Eurodollar (☎971 789896); Avis (☎971 789187); Betacar (☎971 789135); and Hertz (☎971 789670). In the city, there's a concentration – including many small concerns – along Avgda. Gabriel Roca: Hertz are at no. 13 (☎971 732374); Avis at no. 16 (☎971 730720); and Betacar at no. 20 (☎971 455111). The tourist office will supply a complete list of rental companies.

Consulates Ireland, c/Sant Miquel 68A (☎971 719244); United Kingdom, Plaça Major 3 (☎971 718501); USA, Avgda. Jaume III, 26 (☎971 725051).

Emergencies General emergency number ☎971 112. For **ambulances** call ☎971 061; **firefighters** ☎971 080; **police** (Policia Local) ☎971 092.

Ferries The tourist offices have ferry schedules and tariffs. Tickets can be purchased at travel agents or direct from the ferry line, Transmediterranea (☎971 405014), at the ferry port. For details of routes see "Travel details" at the end of this chapter.

Hospital Hospital General, Plaça Hospital 3 (☎971 728484).

Laundry The most convenient self-service laundry is Self-Press at c/Annibal 14, off Avgda. Argentina.

Maps Libreria Fondevila, Costa de Sa Pols 18 (Mon–Fri 9.45am–1.30pm & 4.30–8pm, Sat 9.45am–1.30pm; ☎971 725616), has a wide selection of general maps of Mallorca, as well as a fairly comprehensive selection of walking maps.

Mopeds and scooters RTR Rental, Avgda. Joan Miró 338 (☎971 402585).

Post office The central *Correu* is at c/Constitució 5 (Mon–Fri 8.30am–8.30pm, Sat 9.30am–2pm).

Trains The tourist office has timetable details or you can phone direct: Palma to Inca ☎971 752245; Palma to Sóller ☎971 752051.

Around Palma

For a **day out** from Palma, anywhere in the west or centre of the island is accessible, but if you're after a quick **swim** the most convenient option is to stick to the resorts strung along the neighbouring **Badia de Palma** (Bay of Palma). Locals tend to go east on the #15 bus (every 10min; 30min) from Plaça Espanya to the individual *balneario* (beach bar) sections of **S'ARENAL**, where there's an enormously long, if crowded, sandy beach.

Alternatively, you might conceivably be tempted by the **Castell de Bellver** (April–Sept Mon–Sat 8am–8pm, Sun 10am–2pm & 4–7pm; Oct–March Mon–Sat 8am–7pm, Sun 10am–5pm; 260ptas, free Sun), a strikingly well-preserved fortress of canny circular design built for Jaume II at the beginning of the fourteenth century, which boasts superb views of Palma and its harbour from a wooded hill-top some 3km west of the city centre.

Andratx, Sant Elm and Illa Dragonera

Inland from Palma bay, you could certainly find worse ways to spend an afternoon than hopping on a bus to **ANDRATX**, a small, undeveloped town huddled among the hills to the west. From here, there's a strenuous but enjoyable 7km **hike** along a narrow country road out into the pretty, orchard-covered landscape and on to the dishevelled, low-key resort of **SANT ELM** (in Castilian, San Telmo). There are plans to expand the resort, but at present it's a relatively quiet spot where there's a reasonable chance of a **room** in high season, either at the conspicuous *Hotel Aquamarín* (☎971 239105, fax 971 239125; May–Oct; ④) or, preferably, at the *Hostal Dragonera* (☎971 239086, fax 971 239013; ③), a simple, modern building with clean and neat rooms, most of which offer sea views. For such a small place, there's also a surprisingly wide choice of **cafés and restaurants**, the best being *Na Caragola*, which specializes in seafood and has a charming terrace and ocean views – reckon on 6000ptas for a complete meal, including house wine.

If you've walked here, there's no need to trudge back. From May to October, **buses** ply between Sant Elm and Andratx seven times a day Monday to Saturday, and once on Sundays (in winter, once daily). With more time to spare, boats shuttle across from Sant Elm's minuscule harbour to the austere offshore islet of **Illa Dragonera**, an uninhabited chunk of rock, some 4km long and 700m wide, with an imposing ridge of seacliffs dominating its northwestern shore.

Northwest Mallorca

Mallorca is at its scenic best in the gnarled ridge of the **Serra de Tramuntana**, the imposing mountain range which stretches the length of the island's northwest shore, its rearing peaks and plunging seacliffs intermittently intercepted by valleys of olive and citrus groves and dotted with the most beguiling of the island's towns and villages. There are several possible routes which take in the best of the region, but perhaps the most straightforward if you're reliant on public transport is to travel up from Palma to **Sóller**, in the middle of the coast, and use this town as a base, making selected forays along the coastal road, the C710; not far away to the **southwest** lie the mountain village of **Deià** and the monastery of **Valldemossa**, while within easy striking distance to the northeast are the monastery of **Lluc**, the quaint town of **Pollença** and the relaxing resort of **Port de Pollença**.

The Serra de Tramuntana also provides the best walking on Mallorca, with scores of **hiking trails** latticing the mountains. Generally speaking, paths are well marked, though apt to be clogged with thornbushes. There are trails to suit all aptitudes and all levels of enthusiasm, from the easiest of strolls to the most gruelling of long-distance treks, but in all cases you should come properly equipped – certainly with an appropriate hiking map (these are available in Sóller and Palma) and, for the more difficult routes, with a compass. Also available locally are a variety of **hiking books**, the best of which are those by Herbert Heinrich (*12 Classic Hikes through Majorca*), while the *Rough Guide to Mallorca and Menorca* details several of the island's most famous hiking routes, too. Spring and autumn are the best times to embark on the longer trails; in midsummer the heat can be enervating and water is scarce. Bear in mind also that the mountains are prone to mists, though they usually lift at some point in the day. For obvious safety reasons, lone mountain walking is not recommended.

As far as **beaches** are concerned, most of the region's coastal villages have a tiny, shingly strip, and only around the bays of Pollença and Alcúdia are there more substantial offerings. The resorts edging these bays have the greatest number of hotel and *hostal* rooms, but from June to early September, and sometimes beyond, vacancies are extremely thin on the ground. Indeed, **accommodation** – especially if you have a tight itinerary and are travelling in the summertime – requires some forethought, though there's a reasonable chance of getting a room on spec in Sóller, and in the monasteries at Lluc and just outside Pollença. To compensate, distances are small, the roads are good and the **bus** network is perfectly adequate for most destinations. One of the most useful buses is the twice every weekday service (May–Oct) along the C710 from Port de Sóller to Port de Pollença, and on to Port d'Alcúdia. **Taxis** can work out a reasonable deal too, if you're travelling in a group: for instance, the fare for the thirty-kilometre trip from Palma to Sóller is about 4500ptas.

Easily the best way to get to the Serra de Tramuntana is to take the **train from Palma to Sóller**, a 28-kilometre journey that takes about one hour and twenty minutes on antique rolling stock that seems straight out of an Agatha Christie novel. The rail line, constructed on the profits of the nineteenth-century orange and lemon trade, dips and twists through the mountains and across fertile valleys, offering magnificent, almost awe-inspiringly beautiful views. There are five departures daily from Palma station throughout the year (sometimes six from Sóller); a return costs 760ptas (380ptas one-way), though the mid-morning Turist train – whose only distinction is a brief photostop in the mountains – will set you back 1115ptas return (735ptas one-way).

Sóller

Arriving by train at **SÓLLER**, the obvious option is to continue by tram (every 30min; 15min) down to the seashore, a rumbling, 5km-journey ending at **Port de Sóller**. If you pass straight through, however, you'll miss one of the most laid-back and enjoyable towns on Mallorca, an ideal and fairly inexpensive base for exploring the surrounding mountains. Rather than any specific sight, it's the general flavour that appeals, the town's narrow, sloping lanes cramped by eighteenth- and nineteenth-century stone houses, whose fancy grilles and big wooden doors once hid the region's fruit-rich merchants. All streets lead to the main square, Plaça Constitució, an informal, pint-sized affair of crowded cafés and grouchy mopeds just down the hill from the train station. The square is dominated by the hulking mass of the church of **Sant Bartomeu**, a crude neo-Gothic remodelling of the medieval original, its only saving grace the enormous rose window cut high in the main facade. Inside, the cavernous nave is suitably dark and gloomy, the penitential home of a string of gaudy Baroque altarpieces.

Port de Sóller

PORT DE SÓLLER is one of the most popular resorts on the west coast, and its horseshoe-shaped bay must be the most photographed spot on the island after the package resorts around Palma. The high jinks of the Badia de Palma are about the last thing imaginable down here, though – the place is almost stiflingly staid. There's no point in staying just for the swimming either, since, although the water is warm and calm, it's often surprisingly murky (courtesy of the yachts at anchor), and the sandy beach is overlooked on all sides – by the road, hotels and restaurants. Probably the best option is to make the fifty-minute stroll out west to the lighthouse, which guards the cliffs above the entrance to Port de Sóller's inlet. From here, the views out over the wild and rocky coast are spectacular, especially at sunset. Directions couldn't be easier as there's a tarmac road all the way: from the centre of the resort, walk round the southern side of the bay past the beach and keep going along the seashore.

Trams from Sóller clank to a full stop beside the waterfront, bang in the centre of town. En route, you'll pass the **Turismo**, Passeig es Través (May–Sept Mon–Fri 11.30am–3pm, Sat 9.30am–1.30pm; ☎971 633042), with lists of local hotels and *hostals*. Outside peak season there's a chance of a reasonably priced room at the mundane Hotel Miramar, c/de la Marina 12 (☎971 631350, fax 971 632671; April–Oct; ④), a standard-issue skyrise down by the waterfront in the centre, and at the equally unexciting, 100-room Hotel Generoso, nearby at c/de la Marina 4 (☎971 631450, fax 971 632200; ⑤). The string of one- and two-star hotels and *hostals* behind the Platja den Repic on the south side of the bay are worth considering too: the pleasant Los Geranios, Passeig sa Platja 15 (☎971 631440, fax 971 631651; ⑤), is probably the best option.

Port de Sóller has several fine seafood **restaurants** overlooking the bay. The pick of the bunch is the spick-and-span Sa Llotja des Peix beside Moll Pesquer, the old fishing jetty, where a delicious *menú del día* will set you back a very reasonable 2300ptas. Other good alternatives are El Pirata and Es Racó, both on c/Santa Caterina Alejandria, a narrow side street cutting up from the waterfront close to Moll Pesquer.

Southwest from Sóller: Deià

It's a dramatic 13km journey **southwest from Sóller** along the C710 to the beautiful village of **DEIÀ**. The mighty Puig des Teix meets the coast here, and, although its lower slopes are now gentrified by the villas of the well-to-do, the mountain retains a formidable, almost mysterious presence. Doubling as the coastal highway, Deià's main street skirts the base of the Teix, showing off most of the village's hotels and restaurants. At times, this main street is too congested to be much fun, but the tiny heart of the village, tumbling over a high and narrow ridge on the seaward side of the road, still manages a surprising tranquillity. Labyrinthine alleys of old peasant houses curl up to a pretty country church, in the precincts of which stands the **grave of Robert Graves**, the village's most famous resident – marked simply "Robert Graves: Poeta, E.P.D." (*En Paz Descanse*: "Rest In Peace"). From the graveyard, the views out over the coast are truly memorable.

Graves put Deià on the international map, and nowadays the village is the haunt of long-term expatriates. These inhabitants congregate at the **Cala de Deià**, the nearest thing the village has to a beach – some 200m of shingle at the back of a handsome rocky cove of jagged cliffs, boulders and white-crested surf. It's a great place for a swim, the water clean, deep and cool, and there's a ramshackle beach bar, but in summer the cove often gets crowded, especially when the day-trippers arrive by boat from Port de Sóller (usually on Fridays). It takes about twenty minutes to walk from the village to the *cala*, a delightful stroll down a wooded ravine; from the bus stop, walk in the Palma direction to a sharp right bend in the main road, then turn right down the shallow steps and continue downhill, taking a right fork after a few minutes. When the lane ends a signposted footpath continues in the same direction; after about five minutes turn right by a white painted sign and follow the path until it joins a surfaced road about 500m from the cove. Alternatively, driving there takes about ten minutes: head north along the main road out of Deià and watch for the sign.

ROBERT GRAVES IN DEIÀ

Robert Graves lived in Deià from after the end of World War II until his death in 1985. This was his second stay; during the first – in the 1930s – he shared his house at the edge of the village with Laura Riding, an American poet and dabbler in the mystical. Riding came to England in 1926 and, after she became Graves's secretary and collaborator, the two of them had an affair. The tumultuous course of their relationship created sufficient furore for them to decide to leave England and they supposedly chose Mallorca on the advice of Gertrude Stein. Graves and Riding were forced to leave Mallorca in 1936 at the onset of the Spanish Civil War, and back in England Laura ditched Graves, who subsequently took up with a mutual friend, Beryl Hodge. Graves returned to Mallorca in 1946, Beryl joined him and they were married in Palma in 1950. But they didn't live happily ever after; Graves had a predilection for young women, claiming the need for female muses to inspire his poetic vision; outwardly Beryl accepted this waywardness, but without much enthusiasm. Also, while his novels – *Goodbye to All That*; *I, Claudius*; *Claudius the God* – became increasingly well-known and profitable, his romantic poetry – of which he was particularly proud – fell out of fashion, and his last anthology, *Poems 1965–1968*, was widely snubbed.

Practicalities

The Palma–Port de Sóller **bus** scoots through Deià five times daily in each direction. There's no tourist office, but the village's hotels and *hostals* will gladly provide local advice on walks and weather, and can fix you up with a **taxi** – or do it yourself on ☎971 633588. Of the two places where there's a good chance of a reasonably-priced **room** in high season, the *Fonda Villa Verde* (☎971 639037; usually April–Oct; ⑤) has lovely premises near the village church, while the *Hotel d'es Puig* (☎971 639409, fax 971 639210; March to mid-Nov; ⑦) occupies a tastefully converted old stone house close by. Deià also possesses two of the finest hotels on Mallorca, both overlooking the main road – *Es Molí* (☎971 639000, fax 971 639333; April–Oct; ⑧) and *La Residencia* (☎971 639011, fax 971 639370; ⑧), each of which occupies a gracious and beautifully-maintained mansion.

As for **eating** in Deià, you're spoiled for choice. There's a concentration of cafés and restaurants along the main street towards the west end of the village. These include *Café La Fabrica*, which offers reasonably priced *tapas*, *bocadillos* and the traditional *pa amb oli* (bread rubbed with olive oil); and the *Deià Bar-Restaurante*, where you'll pay a little more for a light meal, but with the compensation of a terrace overlooking the valley. Moving up the price range, the *Restaurant Jaime*, which is also at the west end of the village, offers mouth-watering Mallorcan cuisine.

Valldemossa

Some 10km **southwest of Deià** along the C710, the ancient and intriguing hill town of **VALLDEMOSSA** is actually best approached from the south, where, after squeezing through a narrow, wooded defile, the road from Palma enters a lovely valley, whose tiered and terraced fields ascend to the town, a sloping jumble of rusticated houses and monastic buildings backclothed by the mountains. The origins of Valldemossa date to the early fourteenth century, when the asthmatic King Sancho built a royal palace here in the hills where the air was easier to breathe. Later, in 1399, the palace was given to Carthusian monks from Tarragona, who converted and extended the original buildings into a **monastery**, which is now the island's most visited building after Palma cathedral.

Remodelled on several occasions, most of the present complex of the **Real Cartuja de Jesús de Nazaret** (March–Oct Mon–Sat 9.30am–1pm & 3–6pm, Sun 10am–1pm; Nov–Feb Mon–Sat 9.30am–1pm & 3–5.30pm, Sun 10am–1pm; 1100ptas) is of seventeenth- and eighteenth-century construction, its square and heavy church leading to the shadowy corridors of the cloisters beyond. The monastery owes its present notoriety almost entirely to the novelist and republican polemicist **George Sand**, who, with her companion, the composer **Frédéric Chopin**, lived here for four months in 1838–39. Just three years earlier the last monks had been evicted during the Liberal-inspired suppression of the monasteries, so the pair were able to rent a commodious set of vacant cells. Their stay is commemorated in Sand's *A Winter in Majorca*, a stodgy, self-important book that is considerably overplayed hereabouts, being available in just about every European language.

A visit begins in the gloomy, aisleless **church**, which is distinguished by its fanciful bishop's throne, though the lines of the nave are spoiled by the clumsy wooden stalls of the choir. In the adjoining cloisters, the first port of call is the **pharmacy**, which survived the expulsion of the monks to serve the town's medicinal needs well into the twentieth century. Its shelves are crammed with a host of beautifully decorated majolica jars, antique glass receptacles and painted wood boxes, each carefully inscribed with the name of the potion or drug. The nearby **prior's cell** is, despite its name, a comfortable suite of bright, sizeable rooms with splendid views down the valley. It's also, together with the adjoining library and audience room, the proud possessor of a wide assortment of religious *objets d'art*. Further along the corridor, **cell no. 2** exhibits miscellaneous curios relating to Chopin and Sand, from portraits and a lock of hair to musical scores and letters (it was in this cell that the composer wrote the *Raindrop Prelude*). There's more of the same next door in **cell no. 4**, plus Chopin's piano, which arrived only after three months of unbelievable complications – and just three weeks before the couple left for Paris. Considering the hype, these incidental mementoes are something of an anti-climax, but persevere: upstairs, there's a small but outstanding collection of **modern art**, including work by Miró and Picasso, not to mention Francis Bacon and Henry Moore. And be sure too to take the doorway beside the prior's cell, which leads outside the cloisters to the enjoyable **Palace of King Sancho**. It's not the original palace at all – that disappeared long ago – but it is the oldest part of the complex and its fortified walls, mostly dating from the sixteenth century, accommodate a string of handsome period rooms.

Practicalities

Easily reached from Deià, Palma and Andratx, **buses** to Valldemossa stop at the west end of town in the biggest of several car parks that edge the bypass. Services from Palma, 18km away, pause here before continuing to Deià and Sóller; six times weekly a bus also comes from Andratx and points west along the coast. From the bus stop, it's just a couple of minutes' walk to the monastery – cross the bypass and keep going straight on.

Downtown **accommodation** is limited to the *Ca'n Mario*, c/Uetam 8 (☎971 612122; ④), an attractive *hostal* where an elegant, curio-cluttered foyer leads to comfortably old-fashioned rooms; it's situated just a couple of minutes' walk from the monastery – from the pedestrianized area between the church and the palace, go downhill and take the first turning on the right.

The centre of Valldemossa heaves with **restaurants and cafés**, mostly geared up for day-trippers – and many offer dire fast food at inflated prices. Nonetheless, amongst the dross there are one or two quality places, in particular *Ca'n Pedro*, a large café-restaurant beside the main car park.

Northeast from Sóller to Lluc

Beyond a doubt, the most interesting approach to the northernmost tip of the island is the continuation of the C710 northeast from Sóller, slipping through the highest and harshest section of the Serra de Tramuntana. For the most part, the mountains drop straight into the sea, precipitous and largely unapproachable cliffs with barely a cove in sight. The accessible exceptions are the comely beach at Cala Tuent and the horribly commercial hamlet of Sa Calobra next door. But easily the best place to break your journey is at **LLUC**, tucked away in a remote mountain valley about 35km from Sóller. Mallorca's most important place of pilgrimage since the middle of the thirteenth century, supposedly after a shepherd boy named Lluc (Luke) stumbled across a tiny, brightly painted statue here in the woods, Lluc is dominated by the austere, high-sided dormitories of the **Monestir de Nostra Senyora** (daily 10am–5.30pm; free). At the centre of the monastery is the main shrine and architectural highlight, the **Basilica de la Mare de Deu de Lluc**, a dark and gaudily decorated church dominated by heavy jasper columns, whose stolidness is relieved by a dome over the crossing. On either side of the nave, stone steps extend the aisles round the back of the Baroque high altar to a modest chapel. This is the holy of holies, built to display the much-venerated statue of the Virgin, which has been commonly known as **La Moreneta** ("the Dark-Skinned One") ever since the original paintwork peeled off in the fifteenth century to reveal brown stone underneath.

Just before the entrance to the basilica, a stairway climbs up one floor to the enjoyable **Museu de Lluc** (300ptas). After a modest section devoted to archeological finds from the Talayotic and Roman periods, come cabinets of intricate old vestments, medieval religious paintings, and an intriguing assortment of votive offerings – folkloric bits and bobs brought here to honour La Moreneta. The museum also boasts an extensive collection of **majolica**, tin-glazed earthenware whose characteristic shapes are two-handled drug jars and show dishes or plates, of which some two or three hundred are on display. Allow time, too, for a stroll along the **Camí dels Misteris del Rosari** (Way of the Mysteries of the Rosary), a broad pilgrims' footpath that winds its way up the rocky hillside behind the monastery.

Practicalities

Buses to Lluc, which is situated 2km off the C710, stop right outside the monastery. In addition to the Port de Sóller–Port de Pollença–Port d'Alcúdia service, buses run to Lluc at least once a day from Palma via Inca. **Accommodation** at the monastery is highly organized, with simple, self-contained apartment-cells. In summer phone ahead if you want to be sure of space, but at other times simply book at the monastery's information office on arrival (☎971 517025, fax 971 517096; ②). For **food**, there's a café-bar and a restaurant beside the car park, but far preferable, even though it has become a little pricey, is the monks' former dining room, where the food is traditional Spanish – and the meat dishes are much better than the fish.

Pollença

Northeast of Lluc, the C710 twists through the mountains to travel the 27km to **POL-LENÇA**, a tranquil and ancient little town which nestles among a trio of hillocks where the Serra de Tramuntana fades into coastal flatland. Following standard Mallorcan practice, the town was established a few kilometres from the seashore to militate against sudden pirate attack, with its harbour, Port de Pollença (see below), left an unprotected outpost. For once the stratagem worked. Unlike most of Mallorca's old towns, Pollença avoided destruction, but nevertheless little of the medieval town survives today, and the austere stone houses that cramp the twisting lanes of the centre mostly date from the eighteenth century. In the middle, **Plaça Major**, the lazy main square, accommodates a cluster of laid-back cafés and the dour facade of the church of **Nostra Senyora dels Àngels**, a sheer cliff-face of sun-bleached stone pierced by a rose window. Pollença's pride and joy is, however, its **Via Crucis** (Way of the Cross), a long, steep and beautiful stone stairway, graced by ancient cypress trees, which ascends **El Calvari** (Calvary hill) directly north of the town centre. At the top, a much-revered statue of **Mare de Deu del Peu de la Creu** (Mother of God at the Foot of the Cross) is lodged in a simple, courtyarded **Oratori** (chapel), whose whitewashed walls sport some of the worst religious paintings imaginable. However, the views out over coast and town are sumptuous. On Good Friday, a figure of Jesus is slowly carried by torchlight down from the Oratori to the church of Nostra Senyora dels Àngels, in the **Davallament** (Lowering), one of the most moving religious celebrations on the island.

There are further magnificent views from the **Ermita de Nostra Senyora del Puig**, a rambling, mostly eighteenth-century monastery which occupies an extraordinarily serene and beautiful spot on top of the Puig de Maria, a 320-metre-high hump facing the south end of town. The monastic complex, with its fortified walls, courtyard, chapel, refectory and cells, has had a chequered history, alternately abandoned and restored by both monks and nuns. It's now a working monastery again, with a handful of resident Benedictines supplementing their collective income by renting out cells to tourists (see below). To get to the monastery, take the signposted turning left off the main Pollença–Inca/Palma road just south of town; head up this steep, 1500-metre-long lane until it fizzles out, to be replaced by a cobbled footpath which winds up to the monastery entrance. It's possible to drive to the top of the lane, but unless you've got nerves of steel, you're better off leaving your vehicle by the turning near the foot of the hill. Allow just over an hour each way if you're walking from the centre of town.

Practicalities

Regular **buses** from Palma, Inca and Port de Pollença halt immediately to the south of Pollença's Plaça Major. The town doesn't have a tourist office, but there is one central place to **stay**, the excellent *Hotel Juma*, Plaça Major 9 (☎971 535002, fax 971 534155; ⑥), a medium-sized hotel with comfortable, air-conditioned, modern bedrooms. There are cheaper lodgings at the Ermita de Nostra Senyora del Puig (☎971 530235; ①) – see above for directions – where the original monks' cells have been renovated to provide simple accommodation. Be warned, though, that it can get cold and windy at night, and the refectory food is mediocre.

Pollença does well for **cafés** and **restaurants**. On Plaça Major, the *Café Espanyol* offers filling snacks and a good strong cup of coffee, the *Juma* serves up first-rate *tapas* and the *Restaurante Il Giardino* provides superb French-style cuisine. On c/Montisión, in between the main square and El Calvari, you'll also find the upbeat and fashionable *Restaurante Cantonet*, where the seafood is delicious.

Port de Pollença

Over at **PORT DE POLLENÇA** things are a little more touristy, though still pleasantly low-key. With the mountains as a backcloth, the resort arches through the flatlands behind the Badia de Pollença, a deeply indented bay whose sheltered waters are ideal for swimming. The **beach** is the focus of attention, a narrow, elongated sliver of sand that's easily long enough to accommodate the crowds, though as a general rule you'll have more space the farther southeast (towards Alcúdia) you walk. A rash of apartment buildings and hotels blights the edge of town, and the noisy main road to Alcúdia runs close to most of the seashore, but all in all the place is very appealing, especially in the centre behind the marina, where old narrow streets hint at the resort's origins as a small port and fishing harbour.

For a change of scene, **boat-taxis** shuttle between the marina and the Platja de Formentor, one of Mallorca's most attractive beaches (5 daily; 30min; 800ptas each way), whilst **boat trips** cruise the bay (Mon–Fri 1 daily; 2hr; 1500ptas), or work their way along to Cap de Formentor (Mon & Fri 1 daily; 2hr 30min; 1600ptas). There's also the option of making a delightful three-kilometre (each way) **hike** across the neck of the Península de Formentor to **Cala Boquer**. On the seafront northeast of the marina, take a left up Avinguda Bocchoris, then continue along the wide footpath fringed with pine trees on the left. At a sign saying "Predio Bóquer Privada Camin Particular", take the wide path north, with the ridge straight ahead and you'll soon reach an iron gate, beyond which is Bóquer farmhouse. The trail leads on through the mountain-sheltered **Vall de Boquer** (Boquer Valley), a favourite of ornithologists, especially for its migrant birds, and of botanists for its wild flowers and shrubs. After about 45 minutes' walking you reach a small, shingly **beach** offering good swimming in clean water (though the shore is sometimes rubbish-strewn).

Practicalities

Buses to Port de Pollença from Palma, Alcúdia, Port d'Alcúdia and Port de Sóller stop by the marina right in the town centre. A couple of minutes' walk away is the **Turismo**, one block behind the seafront at Carretera Formentor 31 (May–Oct Mon–Fri 9am–1pm & 4–7pm, Sat 9am–1pm; ☎971 865467). The flatlands edging the Badia de Pollença and stretching as far as Alcúdia and Pollença make for easy, scenic cycling. **Mountain bikes** can be rented for 1600ptas a day from a shop called March on c/Joan XXIII 89 (☎971 864784), as can **mopeds** and **motorcycles**. On the same street at no. 9, Viajes Iberia (☎971 866262) is the **American Express** agent for this part of Mallorca. The walking holiday specialist Globespan has an office at Passeig Saralegui 114 (☎971 864711), where you can pay to join one of its day-long guided walks (around 2000ptas per person). The office will provide all the details; you should book a minimum of 24 hours beforehand.

There are several reasonably priced and convenient **accommodation** options, though getting a room in season may be difficult. Overlooking the tiny main square stands the pleasant *Hostal Residencia Borras*, Plaça Miquel Capllonch 16 (☎971 531474; ④), a real bargain, where most of the rooms are comfortably spacious and you can eat breakfast in the pretty little courtyard. On the seafront, the *Hotel Miramar*, Passeig Anglada Camarasa 39 (☎971 867211, fax 971 864075; April–Oct; ⑥), is an attractive three-star hotel, with balconied rooms set behind a grand facade; also by the water is the friendly, unpretentious *Hostal Residencia Eolo*, a hikers' favourite at c/Torres 2 (☎971 866550, fax 971 866301; ⑤).

Among a plethora of **restaurants**, excellent choices include the *Restaurant Stay*, on the marina's Moll Nou jetty, a chic little place which features the freshest of seafood and charges about 5500ptas for a full à la carte meal; and the *El Pozo*, c/Joan XXIII 25, where you can choose from a superb selection of seafood. For something less expensive, head for the seafront around the marina.

The Península de Formentor

Heading northeast out of Port de Pollença, the road clears the military zone at the far end of the resort, before weaving up into the craggy hills of the 20km-long **Península de Formentor**, the final spur of the Serra de Tramuntana. At first, the road (which suffers a surfeit of tourists from mid-morning to mid-afternoon) travels inland, out of sight of the true grandeur of the scenery, but after about 4km the **Mirador de Mal Pas** rectifies matters with a string of lookout points perched on the edge of plunging, north-facing seacliffs. From here, it's another couple of kilometres to the woods backing onto the **Platja de Formentor**, a pine-clad beach of golden sand in a pretty cove. It's a beautiful spot, with views over to the mountains on the far side of the bay, though it can get a little crowded. In summer, you can get here from Palma and Port de Pollença on a twice-daily **bus** service. At the end of the cove, opposite a tiny islet, stands the *Hotel Formentor* (☎971 899100, fax 971 865155; ⑧). Opened in 1930, this wonderful hotel – arguably the island's best – lies low against the forested hillside, its hacienda-style architecture enhanced by Neoclassical and Art Deco features and exquisite terraced gardens. Stay here if you can afford it – there's a surprisingly good chance of a vacant room, even in high summer. Beyond the turn-off for the beach, the main peninsula road runs along a wooded ridge, before tunnelling through Mont Fumat to emerge on the rocky mass of **Cap de Formentor**, a tapered promontory of bleak seacliffs and scrub-covered hills which offers spectacular views.

Alcúdia

Moving **south** from **Port de Pollença**, it's just 10km round the bay to pint-sized **ALCÚDIA**, whose main claim to fame is its imitation medieval wall. Indeed, the whole place is overly spick and span, a poor reflection of the town's true historical importance. Situated on a neck of land separating two large, sheltered bays, the site's strategic value was first recognized by the Phoenicians, and later by the Romans, who built their island capital, Pollentia, here in the first century AD, on top of the earlier settlement. In 426, the place was destroyed by the Vandals and lay neglected until the Moors built a fortress in about 800, naming it *Al Kudia* (On the Hill). After the Reconquest, Alcúdia prospered as a major trading centre, a role it performed well into the nineteenth century, when the town slipped into a long and gentle decline – until tourism refloated its economy.

It only takes an hour or so to walk around the antique lanes of Alcúdia's compact centre, and to explore the town walls and their fortified gates. This pleasant stroll can be extended by a visit to the meagre remains of Roman **Pollentia** (open access; free), whose broken pillars and mashed-up walls lie just outside the walls.

Buses to Alcúdia halt beside the town walls on Plaça Carles V; there's no tourist office. For **food**, there are several good cafés on Plaça Constitució, but it's hard to beat the cosy café-bar of *Ca's Capella*, just east of the church of Sant Jaume along c/Rectoria.

Port d'Alcúdia

PORT D'ALCÚDIA, 2km south of Alcúdia, is the biggest and busiest of the resorts on the Badia d'Alcúdia, its clutch of restaurants and café bars attracting crowds from a seemingly interminable string of high-rise hotels and apartment buildings. This is not, however, to equate this resort with some of its seamier rivals, for the tower blocks are relatively well distributed, and the streets are neat and tidy. Predictably, the daytime focus is the **beach**, a superb arc of pine-studded golden sand, which stretches south for 10km from the combined marina and fishing harbour.

Port d'Alcúdia acts as northern Mallorca's summertime transport hub, with frequent **bus** services to and from Palma, Port de Sóller, Port de Pollença, Pollença and Artà, as well as other neighbouring towns and resorts. All these buses stop in the town centre near the **Turismo** (Mon–Sat 9am–7pm; ☎971 892615), which is situated on Carretera d'Artà, the main drag. The office can supply all sorts of information, most usefully free maps marked with all the resort's hotels — but bear in mind that in season vacant rooms are few and far between, and in winter almost eveywhere is closed. More usefully, perhaps, Port d'Alcúdia has a superabundance of **car, moped and bicycle rental** companies strung out behind the beach: Avis, for example, have an office at Avgda. Casino 1 (☎971 891701); mountain bikes will cost you around 1500ptas per day, 6500ptas for the week.

Parc Natural de S'Albufera

Heading southeast around the bay from Port d'Alcúdia on the C712, it's about 6km to the 2000-acre **Parc Natural de S'Albufera** (daily: April–Sept 9am–7pm; Oct–March 9am–6pm; free), a segment of pristine wetland that is all that remains of the marshes that once extended round most of the bay – the rest has been developed to take advantage of the enormous pine-studded sandy beach. About 1km from the signposted entrance on the main road, footpaths leave the park's **reception area** to explore the reedy, watery tract beyond. It's a superb habitat, where ten well-appointed hides allow excellent **bird-watching**. Over two hundred species have been spotted: resident wetland-loving birds, autumn and/or springtime migrants, and wintering species and birds of prey in their scores. There's no problem getting here by public transport – **buses** from Port d'Alcúdia to Ca'n Picafort stop beside the entrance.

Eastern Mallorca

Mallorca's **east coast**, stretching for about 60km north from Cala Figuera to Cala Rajada, is fretted by narrow **coves**, the remnants of prehistoric river valleys created when the level of the Mediterranean was much lower. Of great natural beauty, all but the least accessible of these coves has, however, been engulfed by a tide of development and, frankly, you're better off staying away, especially if you haven't got your own transport. That said, if you do decide to pass this way, there are one or two incidental attractions, not least the attractive minor road which links the resorts, running, for the most part, a few kilometres inland along the edge of the **Serres de Llevant**, a slim and benign band of grassy hills which rises to over 500m at its two extremities – south outside Felanitx and north around Artà.

Porto Cristo

Halfway up the east coast, **PORTO CRISTO** is the largest town hereabouts, a busy and slightly old-fashioned place near the region's two big excursions. These, announced by multicoloured, multilingual billboards, are the **Coves des Hams** (regular guided tours daily 10.30am–5.30pm; 1300ptas) and the **Coves del Drac** (regular guided tours April–Oct daily 10am–5pm; Nov–March daily 10.30am–4pm; 900ptas), each of which includes underground classical concerts in the price and endurance of a visit. You'd hardly want to see them both; opt for the Drac (Dragon) caverns about fifteen minutes' walk from the centre of Porto Cristo. The lighting here is really very impressive, focused as it is on what the leaflet asserts is "Europe's largest underwater lake", and musicians drift about in boats playing harmoniums.

Artà and around

Heading north from Porto Cristo, it's about 20km to **ARTÀ**, an ancient hill town of sun-bleached roofs clustered beneath a castellated chapel-shrine, with the bunching peaks of the Serres de Llevant providing a dramatic backdrop. It's a delightful scene, though at close quarters the town is something of an anticlimax – the cobweb of cramped and twisted alleys doesn't quite match the setting. Nonetheless, the ten-minute trek to the **Santuari de Sant Salvador**, the shrine at the top of Artà, is a must for the views out over eastern Mallorca. Also make time to visit the substantial remains of the prehistoric settlement of **Ses Paisses** (April–Sept Mon–Fri 9am–1pm & 3–7pm, Sat 9am–1pm; Oct–March Mon–Sat 9am–1pm & 2–5.30pm; 200ptas), tucked away in a grove of olive, carob and holm-oak trees about 1km to the south of the town.

Buses to Artà stop on the edge of the town centre, beside the C715. From the bus stop, it's a couple of hundred metres east to the short main street, c/Ciutat, where there are several **cafés**. The best is *Café Parisien,* at no. 18, a trendy little place with an outside terrace, that offers tasty *tapas* and salads at reasonable prices. The *Ca'n Balague,* at no. 19, is a more traditional café-bar also serving light meals. Artà has no hotels or *hostals*.

Artà is a major crossroads: to the **east**, the main road cuts through the village of **CAPDEPERA** – a dusty, elongated village, crouched below a fine crenellated castle – before descending to the coast at the massive resort of **CALA RAJADA**, whose excellent beach is a favourite haunt of German package tourists. To the **west**, the C712 weaves through the hills to Ca'n Picafort and the Badia d'Alcúdia (see p.813).

MENORCA

Second largest of the Balearics, **MENORCA** has the greatest number of reminders of its prehistoric past: crude stone remains that litter much of the landscape. The island also has its share of modern crudity in its tourist villages and resorts that lie dotted along the coast. Fortunately, there's still the occasional undeveloped cove or beach and, more distinctive still, are the two main towns, **Maó** in the east and **Ciutadella** in the west, which have preserved much of their seventeenth- and eighteenth-century appearance.

Little is known of the island's prehistory, despite the omnipresent physical evidence, but the monuments are thought to be linked to those of Sardinia and representative of the second-millennium BC **Talayot culture**. *Talayots* are the rock mounds found all over the island – popular belief has it that they functioned as watchtowers, but it's a theory few experts accept. They have no interior stairway, and only a few are found on the coast. Even so, no one has come up with a much more convincing explanation. The megalithic *taulas* – huge stones topped with another to form a T, around 4m high and unique to Menorca – are even more puzzling. They have no obvious function, and they are almost always found alongside a *talayot*. One of the best preserved *talayot* and *taula* remains are on the edge of Maó at the **Trepucó** site. Then there are *navetas* (dating from 1400 to 800 BC), stone-slab constructions shaped like an inverted loaf tin. Many have false ceilings, and although you can stand up inside they were clearly not living spaces – communal pantries, perhaps, or more probably tombs.

In more recent history, the long and slender, deep-water channel of the port of Maó promoted Menorca to an important position in European affairs. The British saw its potential as a naval base during the War of the Spanish Succession and achieved their aim in having the island handed over to British rule under the Treaty of Utrecht (1713). Spain regained possession in 1783, but with the threat of Napoleon in the Mediterranean, a new British base was temporarily established under admirals Nelson and Collingwood. The British influence is still considerable, especially in architecture: the sash windows so popular in Georgian design are still sometimes referred to as *winderes*, locals often part with a fond *bye-bye*, and there's a substantial expatriate community. The British also moved the capital from Ciutadella to Maó and constructed the main island road. More importantly they introduced the art of distilling juniper berries: Menorcan **gin** (Xoriguer, Beltran or Nelson) is renowned.

Before much of it was killed off by tourism, Menorcan **agriculture** had become highly advanced. Every field was protected by a dry stone wall to prevent the *tramóntana* (the vicious north wind) from tearing away the topsoil; even olive trees have their roots individually protected in a little stone well. Nowadays, apart from a few acres of rape and corn, many of the fields are barren, but the walls survive. Any vegetation that dares to emerge above their safety is instantly swept away by the gusts.

Menorca practicalities

Menorca is boomerang-shaped, stretching from the enormous natural harbour of Maó in the east to the smaller port of Ciutadella in the west. **Bus** routes are distinctly limited, adhering mostly to the main central road between these two, occasionally branching off to the larger coastal resorts. Consequently, you'll need your own **vehicle**

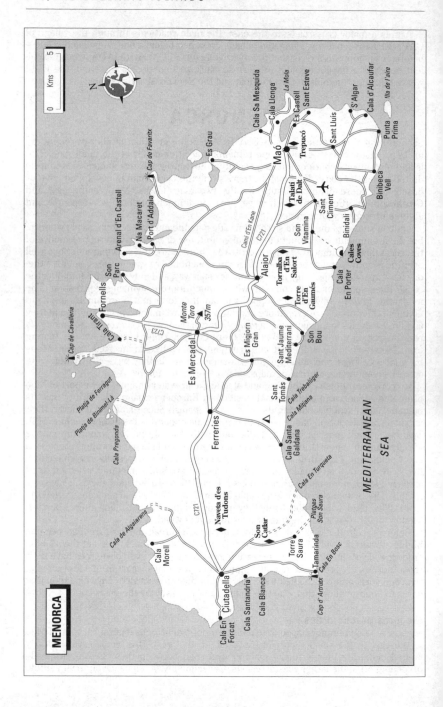

MENORCA

0 Kms 5

N

Cap de Favaritx

Cala Sa Mesquida
Cala Llenga
La Mola
Es Castell
Sant Esteve
S'Algar
Cala d'Alcaufar
Illa de l'aire

Es Grau

Maó

Trepucó

Sant Lluís

Punta
Prima

Talatí
de Dalt

Binibeca
Vell

Arenal d'En Castell

N'a Macaret
Port d'Addaia

Sant
Climent

Son
Vitamina

Binidalí

Son
Parc

Camí d'En Kane

C721

Cales
Coves

Fornells

Alaior

Torralba
d'En
Salort

Cala
En Porter

Cap de Cavalleria

Cala Tirant

C723

*Monte
Toro*
357m

Torre
d'En
Gaumés

Son
Bou

Es Migjorn
Gran

Sant Jaume
Mediterrani

Es Mercadal

Son
Tomàs

Sant Tomàs

Cala Trebalúger
Cala Mitjana

Platja de Ferragut

Platja de Binimel·Là

Ferreries

Cala Santa
Galdana

MEDITERRANEAN

SEA

Cala Pregonda

Cala En Turqueta

Naveta d'es
Tudons

*Platges
Son Saura*

C721

Cala de Algaiarens

Son
Catlar

*Cala
Morell*

Torre
Saura

Tamarinda

Cala En Bosc

Cala En
Forcat

Ciutadella

Cala Santandria

Cala Blanca

Cap d' Artrutx

to reach any of the emptier **beaches** – which are often down a track fit only for four-wheel-drive – and the wind, which can be very helpful when it's blowing behind you, is distinctly uncomfortable if you're trying to ride into it on a **moped.**

Accommodation is at an exploited premium, with little of anything outside Maó and Ciutadella – and you can count on all the beds in all the resorts being block-booked by the tour operators from the beginning to the end of the season (May to October). Advance booking is essential in August.

Maó

MAÓ (*Mahón* in Castilian), the island capital, is likely to be your first port of call. It's a respectable, almost dull little town, the people restrained and polite. So is the architecture – an unusual hybrid of classical Georgian sash-windowed town houses and tall, gloomy Spanish apartment blocks shading the narrow streets. Port it may be, but there's no seamy side to Maó, and the harbour is home to a string of restaurants and cafés that attract tourists in their droves.

Arrival and information

Menorca's **airport** (☎971 369015), just 5km west of Maó, is short on amenities, with just a handful of car rental outlets and a **tourist information desk**, which has a good selection of free literature (May–Oct daily 8.30am–11pm; ☎971 157115). There are no buses into the town, but the taxi fare will set you back only about 1000ptas. **Ferries** from Barcelona and Palma sail right up the inlet to Maó harbour, mooring next to the Transmediterránea offices (☎971 366050) directly beneath the town centre. From behind the ferry dock, it's a two-minute walk up the wide stone stairway to the old part of town.

Maó's **Turismo,** on the landward side of the centre in Plaça S'Esplanada (Mon–Fri 8am–3pm & 5–7pm, Sat 9am–2pm; ☎971 363790), will provide maps of the island and free leaflets giving the lowdown on almost everything you can think of, from archeological sites and beaches to bus timetables, car rental, accommodation and banks. **Island-wide buses** arrive at the stands along Avinguda Quadrado, round the corner from the tourist office; **local buses**, which shuttle up and down the southeast coast, stop on the square just across from the tourist office.

Accommodation

Maó has a limited supply of **accommodation** and excessive demand tends to inflate prices at the height of the season. However, along with Ciutadella, it remains the best Menorcan bet for bargain lodgings, with a small concentration of **hostals** among the workaday streets near Plaça Princep, a few minutes' walk east of the town centre. None of these places is inspiring, but they're reasonable enough and convenient.

Budget options

Hostal La Isla, c/Santa Caterina 4, at the corner of c/Concepció (☎971 366492). Recently refurbished, comfortable one-star with 25 rooms and its own bar and restaurant. ③.

Hostal Residencia Orsi, c/Infanta 19 (☎971 364751). Nicest *hostal* in town, English-owned and a couple of minutes' walk from Plaça Reial; pleasant, spick-and-span old rooms with large windows and green shutters. ③.

Hostal Reynes, c/Comerç 26, just off c/Infanta (☎971 364059). Undistinguished modern block with basic rooms. ③.

Hostal Residencia Roca, c/Carme 37, at the corner of c/Santa Caterina (☎971 351539). No-frills rooms in a plain but quite cheerful modern block with a ground-floor café. ③.

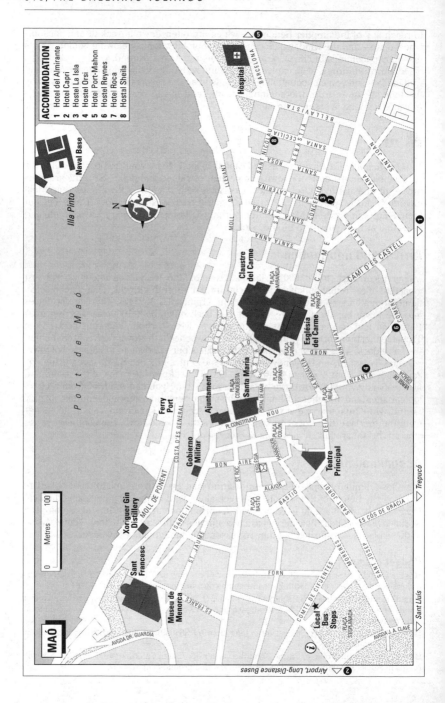

MAÓ

ACCOMMODATION
1 Hotel del Almirante
2 Hotel Capri
3 Hostel La Isla
4 Hostel Orsi
5 Hotel Port-Mahon
6 Hostel Reynes
7 Hotel Roca
8 Hostal Sheila

Illa Pinto
Naval Base

Port de Maó

Ferry Port

Xoriguer Gin Distillery

Sant Francesc

Museu de Menorca

Gobierno Militar

Ajuntament

Santa Maria

Claustre del Carme

Església del Carme

Teatre Principal

Hospital

Local Bus Stops

Metres
0   100

Airport, Long-Distance Buses

Moderate and expensive options

Hotel del Almirante, Carretera de Maó, nearly 2km from Maó by the coastal road to Es Castell (☎971 362700). Once the residence of British admiral Lord Collingwood, this maroon and cream Georgian house has a delightful, antique-crammed interior, though some of the bedrooms are modern affairs overlooking the swimming pool round the back. The package-tour operators Thomson use the place, but there are often vacancies. ⑦.

Hotel Capri, c/Sant Esteve 8 (☎971 361400). Characterless, modern hotel in the centre of Maó, a brief walk west of the tourist office along Avgda. Quadrado. ⑦.

Hotel Port-Mahón, Avgda. Fort de l'Eau 13 (☎971 362600). Elegant colonial-style hotel of columns, pediments and circular windows, in a superb location overlooking the Maó inlet. There's a swimming pool and all mod cons. Room prices vary enormously, with the top whack a hefty 30,000ptas. The hotel is a twenty-minute walk east of the town centre along either c/Carme or the harbourfront. ⑨.

Hostal Sheila, c/Santa Cecília 41, at the corner of c/Sant Nicolau (☎971 364855). This old terraced house has been tastefully refurbished in ultra-modern style, with neat and tidy rooms. ⑥.

The Town

While you'll need transport to get around the island, Maó itself is best seen on foot – its compact centre, with its deep streets rising high above the water's edge, is no more than ten minutes' walk from top to bottom. Maó's fine setting and its crowded old mansions are its charm – rather than any specific sight – and you can explore the place thoroughly in a day. From near the ferry terminal, set beneath the cliff that supports the remains of the city wall, a generous stone stairway leads up to four small squares that are practically adjacent to each other. The first, the **Plaça Espanya**, offers views right across the port and bay. Immediately to the left is the **Plaça Carme**, with a simple Carmelite church whose cloisters have been adapted to house the town's fresh fish, fruit and vegetable market. In the other direction from Plaça d'Espanya lie the **Plaça Conquesta** and the **Plaça Constitució**.

Plaça Constitució boasts the town's main church, **Santa María**. Founded in 1287 by Alfonso III to celebrate the island's Reconquest, its Gothic structure has been much modified – in particular with an unremarkable Baroque high altar. More interesting is the **organ**, a monumental piece of woodwork built in Austria in 1810 and lugged across half of Europe at the height of the Napoleonic wars under the concerned charge of Admiral Collingwood. Its four keyboards and 3000 pipes are quite out of proportion here, and it's a pity the admiral couldn't have found somewhere rather more suitable. Almost next door is the eighteenth-century **Ajuntament**, whose attractive arcaded facade features handsome wrought-iron balconies, a clock presented by the island's first British governor and an inscribed stone proclaiming Roman occupation in the first century AD.

Round the corner, the Baroque facade of **Sant Francesc** at the end of c/Isabel II appears as a cliff-face of pale golden stone set above the rounded, Romanesque-style arches of its doorway. The church was a long time in the making, its construction spread over the seventeenth and eighteenth centuries, following the razing of the town by Barbarossa in 1535. The nave is poorly lit, but it's still possible to pick out the pinkish tint in much of the stone and the unusual spiral decoration of the pillars. In contrast, the **Chapel of the Immaculate Conception**, tucked away off the north side of the nave, is flooded with light; this octagonal wonderland of garlanded vines and roses is an exquisite example of the Churrigueresque style. The chapel is attributed to Francesc Herrara, who trained in Rome and worked in Menorca before moving on to Palma's church of Sant Miquel.

The adjacent monastic buildings now house the **Museu de Menorca** (Tues–Sat 10am–2pm & 5–8pm, Sun 10am–2pm; free) easily the island's biggest and best museum. Entry to the collection is through the **cloister** of Sant Francesc, whose sturdy pillars and vaulted aisles represent the high point of Menorcan Baroque. Beyond, up the stairs, the museum's **first floor** holds a wide sample of prehistoric artefacts, beginning with bits and pieces left by the neolithic pastoralists who settled here about 4000 BC; there's also an extensive range of material from the Talayotic period. Most of the exhibits carry multilingual labels.

From the museum, it's a brisk five-minute walk up through the town to the flowerbeds and fountains of the undistinguished main square, the **Plaça S'Esplanada**. South from Plaça S'Esplanada a twenty-minute walk will take you to the prehistoric remains of **Trepucó** (open access; free) – follow Es Cós de Gràcia to the ring road, cross the traffic island and follow the twisting lane that leads past the cemetery. Surrounded by olive trees and dry-stone walls, the tiny site holds a 4.2-metre-high and 2.75-metre-wide *taula* (T-shaped monolith), the largest monument of its kind on Menorca. There are two cone-shaped *talayots* close by, though the lines of the larger one were mucked up by the French – during the invasion of 1781, they increased the width of the walls and mounted their guns on them.

Back near the ferry terminal, the **Xoriguer gin distillery** (Mon–Fri 8am–7pm, Sat 9am–1pm; free) is where you should go to help yourself to free samples of gin, various liqueurs and other spirits. From here, you can stroll the entire length of the quayside to the southeast edge of town, a half-hour trip that will take you past a long string of restaurants, bars and cafés as well as the town's bulging marinas. By day, this makes a relaxing stroll; at night it's slightly more animated, but not much.

Eating, drinking and nightlife

Maó has a place in culinary history as the eighteenth-century birthplace of **mayonnaise** (*mahonesa*). Various legends, all of them involving the French, claim to identify its inventor: take your pick from the chef of the French commander besieging Maó; a peasant woman dressing a salad for another French general; or a housekeeper disguising rancid meat from the taste buds of a French officer. The French also changed the way the Menorcans bake their bread, while the British started the dairy industry and encouraged the roasting of meat. Unfortunately, traditional Balearic food is not very much in evidence these days, as most of Maó's **restaurants** specialize in Spanish, Catalan or Italian dishes. These tourist-oriented establishments are mainly spread out along the harbourside – the Moll de Ponent west of the main stairway, the Moll de Llevant to the east. There's also a smattering of cheaper restaurants and **coffee bars** in the centre of town, though surprisingly few **tapas bars**.

Nightlife is not Maó's forte, but some fairly lively **bars** dot the harbourfront, staying open till around 2am on summer weekends.

Cafés and tapas bars

American Bar, Plaça Reial 8. Big-windowed, expansive café-bar that was once the most fashionable place in town, and is still a good spot to nurse a coffee or tuck into unexceptional but filling snacks.

Cafeteria Consey, Plaça S'Esplanada 72. Among the string of mundane cafés on the main square, this place stands out for its above-average *tapas* and snacks at reasonable prices.

La Farinera, Moll de Llevant 84. Spruce, modern café-bar offering excellent snacks near the ferry port. Open from 6am.

La Morada, Plaça Bastió 12. A good range of traditional *tapas*, averaging about 400ptas per person.

Restaurants

L'Arpó, Moll de Llevant 124. Cosy and intimate restaurant featuring a superb selection of fish dishes from 1800ptas.

Gregal, Moll de Llevant 43. Chic little establishment at the east end of the harbourfront serving the best of Greek cuisine as well as excellent seafood. Main courses from around 2000ptas.

Pilar, c/Forn 61. Family-run place featuring traditional Menorcan cuisine (main course starting around 1600ptas), near Plaça S'Esplanada; leave the square along c/Moreres, take the first left and then the first right. Closed Nov–April.

Il Porto, Moll de Llevant 225. Enjoyable place to eat with a fountain and an arcaded terrace. The cooks perform in full view, turning out tasty fish and meat dishes from a wide-ranging and moderately priced menu.

Roma, Moll de Llevant 295. Popular, fast-service eatery specializing in well-prepared Italian food at bargain prices. The decor is a tad old-fashioned, but that seems to suit the *Daily Express*-reading clientele.

Bars and nightclubs

Bar Akelarre, Moll de Ponent 41. Relaxed, fashionable bar set in an imaginatively refurbished old stone vault, close to the ferry terminal.

Café Baixamar, Moll de Ponent 17. Modernist decor, great atmosphere and music to suit most tastes.

Nou Bar, c/Nou 1, at the corner of c/Hannover. Old-fashioned café-bar with gloomy lighting, much favoured by locals who come to sip coffee and brandy in the ancient armchairs.

Si, c/Verge de Gràcia 16, at c/Santiago Ramón y Cajal. Low-key nightspot south of Plaça Reial. From 11.30pm to around 3am.

Listings

American Express At Viajes Iberia, c/Nou 35 (☎971 362848).

Banks Banco de Credito Balear, Plaça S'Esplanada 2; Banca March, c/Sa Ravaleta 7.

Bicycle rental Just Bicicletas, c/Infanta 19 (☎971 364751), has mountain bikes for around 1000ptas per day, 5000ptas per week.

Car rental Avis (☎971 361838) and Atesa (☎971 366213) have branches at the airport, while downtown there's another Avis outlet, at Plaça S'Esplanada 53 (☎971 364778), plus many smaller concerns – the tourist office has an exhaustive list.

Emergencies Creu Roja (Red Cross) for an ambulance ☎361180; firefighters ☎092; police (Policia Municipal) ☎092.

Ferries Schedules, tariffs and tickets direct from the ferry line, Transmediterranea (☎971 366050), next to the ferry port.

Hospital Virgen de Monte Toro, on c/Barcelona.

Maps and books Librería Católica, adjoining Plaça Colón at c/Hannover 14, has a reasonable selection of guidebooks and general maps of Menorca, as well as an assortment of island-walking maps.

Mopeds Motos Gelabert, Avgda. J. A. Clavé 12 (☎971 360614).

Post office c/Bon Aire 15, near Plaça Bastió (Mon–Fri 9am–5pm, Sat 9am–1pm).

Taxis There is a taxi rank on Plaça S'Esplanada. Alternatively, telephone Radio Taxis (☎971 367111).

North to Fornells

North of Maó, the road to Fornells runs through some of Menorca's finest scenery – the fields are cultivated and protected by great stands of trees, and the land rises as the road approaches Monte Toro and skirts round it to the north. At the end of the road, just 25km from the capital, **FORNELLS** is a low-rise, classically pretty fishing village at the mouth of a long and chubby bay. Despite the lack of a decent beach, it has been popular with tourists for years, above all for its **seafood restaurants**, whose speciality, *caldereta de llagosta* (*langosta* in Castilian), is a fabulously tasty – and wincingly expensive – lobster stew. Nevertheless, there's been little development, just a slim trail of holiday homes extending north from the village in a suitably unobtrusive style.

The wild and rocky coastline west of Fornells boasts several **cove beaches** of outstanding beauty. Getting to them, however, can be a problem: this portion of the island has barely been touched by the developers so the coast is often poorly signposted and the access roads are of very variable quality – some are just dirt tracks. These byroads usually branch off from the narrow but metalled country lanes which cross the lovely pastoral hinterland. Two excellent beaches to head for are **Binimel-Là** and **Cala Pregonda** – but before you set out you'll need a detailed IGN (1:25,000) map. Public transport around here is, as you might expect, non-existent, though you can rent a **bike or car** in Fornells at Roca-Rosello, c/Major 57 (☎971 376540).

The resort's expensive **restaurants** edge the waterfront on either side of the minuscule main square, Plaça S'Algaret. Such is their reputation that King Juan Carlos regularly drops by on his yacht, and many people phone up days in advance with their orders. The royal favourite is the harbourside *Es Pla* (☎971 376655), which offers a superb paella for two for 7000ptas as well as the traditional lobster stew. More relaxed alternatives include *Sibaris*, Plaça S'Algaret 1, and *El Pescador*, next door, which concentrates on a magnificent *caldereta de llagosta* – as does the *Es Port*, nearby at c/Rosario 17. As a general rule, reckon on about 2000–2500ptas for a seafood main course, twice that for paella or lobster stew.

Fornells has three reasonably priced, comfortable **hostals**. The two-star *S'Algaret* is a neat little place, with slightly old-fashioned furnishings and plain but cheerful rooms, at Plaça S'Algaret 7 (☎971 376674; ⑤), and the nearby *Hostal La Palma* is very similar (☎971 376634; ⑤). The *Hostal Fornells*, c/Major 17 (☎971 376676; ⑥), is slightly smarter, a sprucely modern three-star with a swimming pool.

Across the island

The road from Maó to Ciutadella forms the backbone of Menorca, and what little industry the island enjoys – a few shoe factories and producers of the island's famous cheeses – is concentrated along it.

Alaior

Just 4km out of Maó, you pass the short and clearly signposted country lane leading to **Talatí de Dalt**, another illuminating Talayotic remnant. Much larger than Trepucó, the site is enclosed by a Cyclopean wall and features an imposing *taula*, which is adjacent to the heaped stones of the main *talayot*. All around are the scant remains of prehistoric dwellings. The exact functions of these are not known, but there's no doubt that the *taula* was the village centrepiece, and probably the focus of religious ceremonies. The rustic setting is charming – olive and carob trees abound and a tribe of hogs roots around the undergrowth.

Cheese is a good reason to stop at **ALAIOR**, 12km from Maó, an old market town which has long been the nucleus of the island's dairy industry. There are two major companies, both of which have factory shops near to – and clearly signposted from – the old main road, as it cuts across the southern periphery of the town centre: come off the new bypass at the most easterly of the three Alaior exits and follow the signs. Approaching from Maó, the first shop is owned by La Payesa (Mon–Fri 9am–1pm & 4–7pm), while the second is the bigger and better outlet of Coinga (Mon–Fri 9am–1pm & 5–8pm, Sat 9am–1pm). Both companies sell a similar product, known generically as *queso Mahon*, after the port from which it was traditionally exported. It's a richly textured, white, semi-fat cheese made from pasteurized cow's milk with a touch of ewe's milk added for extra flavour. The cheese is sold at four different stages of maturity, either *tierno* (young), *semi-curado* (semi-mature), *curado* (mature) or *añejo* (very mature). Both shops have the full range and, although quite expensive, their prices are the best you'll see.

The centre of Alaior is a tangle of narrow streets and bright white houses tumbling down the hillside beneath the imposing church of **Santa Eulalia**. Apart, however, from a quick gambol up and down the hill, there's not much reason to hang around – unless you happen to be here in the second weekend of August when Alaior lets loose during the **Festa de Sant Llorenç**.

Es Mercadal and Monte Toro

Nine kilometres northwest of Alaior you arrive at **ES MERCADAL**, squatting amongst the hills at the very centre of the island. Another old market town, it's an amiable little place of whitewashed houses and trim allotments whose antique centre straddles a quaint watercourse. The town also boasts a top-notch **restaurant**, the *Ca N'Aguedet*, at c/Lepanto 30, which serves up traditional Menorcan cuisine, and a simple, one-star **hostal-residencia**, the spick-and-span *Jeni*, in a modern building at Miranda del Toro 81 (☎971 375059; ⑤). To get there, walk south from the main square – Sa Plaça – along c/Nou and take the first left and then the first right. **Buses** from Maó and Ciutadella stop just off the C721 on Avinguda Metge Camps, which leads on to c/Nou.

From Es Mercadal you can set off on the ascent of **Monte Toro**, a steep 3.4-kilometre climb along a serpentine road. At 357m, the summit is the island's highest point and offers wonderful vistas: on a good day you can see almost the whole island, on a bad one to Fornells, at least. From this lofty vantage point, Menorca's geological division becomes apparent: to the north, Devonian rock (mostly reddish sandstone) supports a rolling, sparsely populated landscape edged by a ragged coastline; to the south, limestone predominates in a bumpy plain that boasts both the island's best farmland and, as it approaches the south coast, its deepest valleys.

Monte Toro has been a place of pilgrimage since medieval times, and the Augustinians plonked a monastery on the summit in the seventeenth century. Bits of the original construction survive in the **convent**, which shares the site today with an army outpost and a monumentally ugly statue of Christ. Much of the convent is out of bounds, but the public part, approached across a handsome courtyard, encompasses a couple of gift shops, a delightful terrace café and a cosy, Neoclassical church.

Ferreries

FERRERIES is the next town along the route, though there's little to detain you here unless you're interested in visiting the Jaime Mascaró shoe factory. Ferreries is an appealing little place, no more than a village really, which seems even more insignificant because it's hidden at the bottom of a dip in the road – no sooner do you leave than it has disappeared. One definite plus is the *Vimpi* bar on the plaza at the entrance to town, which serves some of the tastiest *tapas* on the island.

Heading on from Ferreries, you'll find one of the best examples of a *naveta* – the **Naveta d'es Tudons** – beside the main road some 6km from Ciutadella. Seven metres high and fourteen long, the structure is made of massive stone blocks slotted together in a sophisticated dry-stone technique. The narrow entrance on the west side leads into a small antechamber, which was once sealed off by a stone slab; beyond lies the main chamber where the bones of the dead were stashed away after the flesh had been removed. Folkloric memories of the *navetas*' original purpose survived into modern times, for the Menorcans were loathe to go near these odd-looking and solitary monuments well into the eighteenth century.

Ciutadella and around

Like Maó, **CIUTADELLA** sits high above its harbour. Here, though, navigation is far more difficult, up a narrow channel too slender for all but the smallest of cargo ships. Despite this nautical inconvenience, Ciutadella has been at the centre of affairs as the island's capital for most of its history. The Romans chose it, the Moors adopted it as *Medina Minurka*, and the Catalans of *la reconquista* flattened the place and began all over again. In 1558, the Catalan-built town was, in its turn, razed by Turkish corsairs. Several thousand captives were carted off to the slave markets of Istanbul, but the survivors determinedly rebuilt Ciutadella in grand style, its compact, fortified centre brimming with the mansions of the rich. To the colonial powers of the eighteenth century, however, Ciutadella's feeble port had no appeal when compared with Maó's

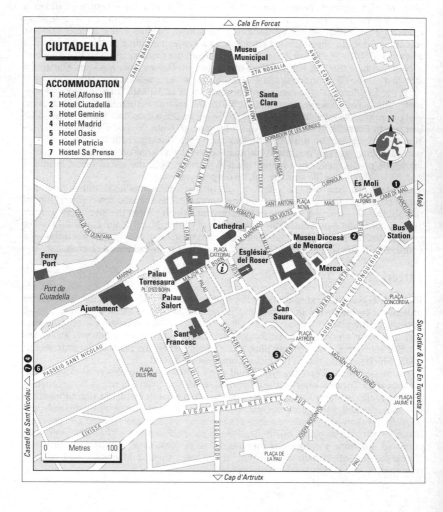

magnificent inlet. In 1722 the British moved the capital to Maó, which has flourished as a trading centre ever since, whilst Ciutadella has stagnated – a long-lasting economic reverie that has, by coincidence, preserved its old and beautiful centre as if in aspic. The bulk of the Menorcan aristocracy remained in Ciutadella, where the colonial powers pretty much left them to stew – an increasingly redundant, landowning class far from the wheels of mercantile power. Consequently, there's very little British or French influence in Ciutadella's **architecture**; instead, the narrow, cobbled streets boast fine old palaces, hidden away behind high walls, and a set of Baroque and Gothic churches very much in the Spanish tradition.

Essentially, it's the whole architectural ensemble that gives Ciutadella its appeal rather than any specific sight, and that, together with some excellent restaurants and an adequate supply of *hostals* and hotels, makes this a lovely place to stay. Allow at least a couple of days, more if you seek out one of the beguiling cove beaches within easy striking distance of town: **Cala En Turqueta** is the pick of the bunch.

Arrival and information

Ciutadella's compact centre could hardly be more convenient. **Buses** from Maó and points east arrive at the station on c/Barcelona, just south off the end of the Camí de Maó, an extension of the main island highway, the C721. **Local buses** shuttle up and down the west coast from Plaça dels Pins, on the west side of the town centre next to the main square, Plaça d'es Born. **Hydrofoils** from Cala Rajada and (less dependably) Port d'Alcúdia, on Mallorca, dock in the harbour below the Plaça d'es Born. The **Turismo** (May–Oct Mon–Fri 9am–1.30pm & 6–pm, Sat 9am–1pm; ☎971 382693) has buckets of information on Menorca as a whole and Ciutadella in particular. It's opposite the cathedral on Plaça Catedral, bang in the middle of the old town, which can only be explored on foot.

Accommodation

There's hardly a plethora of **accommodation** in Ciutadella, but the town does have two quality hotels that aren't booked up by package-tour operators and a handful of fairly comfortable and reasonably priced *hostals* dotted in and around the centre, with a concentration in the vicinity of Plaça Alfons III and Plaça Artrutx.

Budget options

Hostal Oasis, c/Sant Isidre 33, footsteps away from Plaça Artrutx (☎971 382197). Attractive one-star with nine simple rooms set around a courtyard-restaurant. ③.
Hostal Sa Prensa, Plaça Madrid s/n (☎971 382698). Recently refurbished, villa-like, one-star *hostal* with six spartan rooms above a café-bar. It's a fifteen-minute walk west of the centre, close to the rocky seashore at the end of c/Madrid: follow Passeig Sant Nicolau from the Plaça S'Esplanada, take the fifth turning on the left (c/J. Ramis i Ramis) and you'll hit c/Madrid at the first major intersection. ③.

Moderate and expensive options

Hotel Alfonso III, Camí de Maó 53 (☎971 380150, fax 971 481529). Brashly modern but well-maintained hotel with fifty simple one-star rooms. Located beside the main road from Maó, a couple of minutes' walk from the ring road; try to get a room at the back away from the noisy road. ④.
Hostal Residencia Ciutadella, c/Sant Eloi 10 (☎971 383462). Unassuming yet comfortable two-star, in an old terraced house down a narrow side street off Plaça Alfons III. ⑤.
Hotel Residencia Geminis, c/Josepa Rossinyol 4 (☎971 385896). Painted bright pink and white, with blue awnings to add to the effect, this well-tended, central and comfortable one-star certainly hits the eye. Closed Jan. ⑤.

Hotel Madrid, c/Madrid 6 (☎971 380328). Fourteen quite comfortable rooms in a well-maintained, villa-style building with its own ground-floor café-bar. Located near the ocean a fifteen-minute walk west of the town centre, halfway along c/Madrid (directions as for *Hotel Sa Prensa* above). May–Oct. ⑤.

Hotel Residencia Patricia, Camí de Sant Nicolau 90 (☎971 385511). The best hotel in town, popular with business folk and handy for the centre. Extremely comfortable, ultra-modern rooms with all facilities, the only downer being the lack of a sea view – though the best rooms have rooftop balconies with panoramic vistas. ⑦.

The Town

Ciutadella's compact centre crowds around the fortified cliff face shadowing the south side of the harbour. The main plazas and points of interest are within a few strides of each other, on and around the main square, **Plaça d'es Born**, in the middle of which is a soaring **obelisk** commemorating the futile defence against the Turks in 1558. On the western side of the square stands the **Ajuntament**, whose nineteenth-century arches and crenellations mimic Moorish style, purposely recalling the time when the site was occupied by the Wali's Alcázar (palace). In the square's northeast corner, the massive **Palau Torresaura**, built in the nineteenth century but looking far older, is the grandest of several aristocratic mansions edging the plaza. Embellished by self-important loggias, its frontage proclaims the family coat of arms above a large wooden door giving onto an expansive courtyard. The antique interior, however, is off-limits, because the house is still owner-occupied, like most of its neighbours.

From Palau Torresaura, c/Major d'es Born leads to the **cathedral** (Mon–Sat 9am–1pm & 6–8pm; free), built by Alfonso III at the end of the thirteenth century on the site of the chief mosque. So soon after the Reconquest, its construction is fortress-like, with windows set high above the ground – though the effect is somewhat disturbed by the flashy columns of the Neoclassical west doorway, the principal entrance. Inside, light from the narrow, lofty windows bathes the high altar in an ethereal glow, the hallmark of the Gothic style. There's also a wonderfully kitschy, pointed altar arch, and a sequence of glitzily Baroque side chapels.

Cutting down c/Roser from the cathedral, you'll pass the tiny **Esglèsia del Roser**, whose striking Churrigueresque facade, dating from the seventeenth century, boasts a quartet of pillars engulfed by intricate tracery. The church was the subject of bitter controversy when the British commandeered it for Church of England services – not at all to the liking of the Dominican friars who owned the place. At the end of c/Roser, turn left past the palatial, seventeenth-century mansion of **Can Saura**, now an antique shop, and then left again for c/Seminari and the **Museu Diocesà de Menorca** (Tues–Sun 10am–1.30pm; 300ptas), housed in an old and dignified convent. Inside, the convent buildings surround an immaculately preserved Baroque cloister, whose vaulted aisles sport coats of arms and religious motifs. The museum's collection is distributed chronologically, and the first three rooms hold the most interesting pieces – a hotchpotch of Talayotic and early Classical archeological finds, notably a superbly crafted, miniature bull and a similarly exquisite little mermaid, both Greek bronzes dating from the fifth century BC. Moving further on, Rooms 6, 7 and 8 inhabit parts of the old refectory and display all sorts of ecclesiastical tackle: it's the general glitter that impresses, rather than any individual piece. Throughout the collection, the labelling – where it exists – is in Spanish.

Behind the museum lies the **mercat** (market), on Plaça Llibertat, another delightful corner of the old town, where fresh fruit, vegetable and fish stalls mingle with lively and inexpensive cafés selling the freshest of *ensaimadas*. In the opposite direction, c/Seminari intersects with the narrow, pedestrianized main street through the old town, **c/J. M. Quadrado** (though it goes under various names along its route). To the east of this intersection, it boasts a block of whitewashed, vaulted arches, **Ses Voltes**, distinctly Moorish in inspiration and a suitable setting for several attractive period shops and busy cafés. Carrer J. M. Quadrado then leads into **Plaça Nova**, a minuscule square edged by some of the most popular pavement-cafés in town. Nearby, off c/Sant Antoni, a narrow archway cuts through what was once the city wall, which explains the name of the alley beyond – *Qui no Passa*. Continuing east along c/Maó, you leave the cramped alleys of the old town at Plaça Alfons III.

Retracing your steps along c/J. M. Quadrado, turn north down c/Santa Clara for the five-minute walk to the **Museu Municipal** (summer Tues–Sat 10am–4pm; winter Tues–Fri 11am–1pm & Sat 10am–1pm; 200ptas), inhabiting part of the old city fortifications at the end of c/Portal de Sa Font. Inside the museum, a long vaulted chamber is given over to a wide range of archeological finds, amongst which there's a substantial collection of Talayotic remains, featuring artefacts garnered from all over the island and covering the several phases of Talayotic civilization. A leaflet detailing the exhibits in English is available free at reception.

Eating and drinking

For an early **breakfast** make your way to the *mercat* on Plaça Llibertat, where a couple of simple cafés serve coffee and fresh pastries. Later in the day, aim for c/J. M. Quadrado, which is jam-packed with tiny **café-bars** offering reasonably priced snacks and light meals. More ambitious and expensive food is available at a string of excellent **restaurants** down by the harbourside, or at several good places tucked away near Plaça d'es Born.

Cafés and bars

Bar Aladdino, c/Marina s/n. Busy and polished bar at the foot of the steps linking the harbour with the old town. Open till 2am.

Bar Sa Llesca, Plaça Nova 4. One of several pleasant, and largely indistinguishable, café-bars on this tiny square.

Bar Ulises, part of the *mercat*, Plaça Llibertat. No-frills café-bar on the market. Their *ensaimadas* (cinnamon-flavoured pastries), a snip at 200ptas each, are probably the best in town.

Café Central, Plaça Catedral. Busy little place next to the cathedral's main entrance, serving traditional Menorcan *tapas*, including various sausages and cheeses.

Pastisseria Mol, c/Roser 2. Delicious takeaway pizza slices and mouthwatering cakes from this little pastry shop off Plaça Catedral.

Restaurants

El Bribón, c/Marina 115. Excellent harbourside restaurant specializing in seafood, often prepared in traditional Menorcan style. Reckon on 1900ptas for the *menú del día*. Next door to *Casa Manolo*.

Casa Manolo, c/Marina 117. Fabulous seafood, with main courses averaging around 2500ptas, at the end of the long line of restaurants flanking the south side of the harbour.

El Horno, c/Forn 10. French-style basement restaurant, where the food is good and reasonably priced. Near the northeast corner of Plaça d'es Born.

La Payesa, c/Marina 65. Popular tourist restaurant where the menu is wide-ranging and the seafood is usually very good.

Racó d'es Palau, c/Palau 35. Comfortable spot with low-beamed ceilings off c/Major d'es Born. A filling *menú del día* of Spanish food costs just 1100ptas, pizzas from around 700ptas.

Listings

Banks Banca March, Plaça d'es Born 10; Sa Nostra, c/Maó 2, on Plaça Nova,
Bicycle and moped rental Bicicletas Tolo, c/Sant Isidre 28, off Plaça Artrutx (☎971 381576).

Car rental Ciutadella has a handful of car rental firms; amongst them is Avis which has an outlet on the ring road at Avgda. Jaume el Conqueridor 81 (☎971 381174) and Betacar just along the road at no. 59 (☎971 382988).

Emergencies Creu Roja (Red Cross) for an **ambulance** ☎361180; **firefighters** ☎092; **police** (Policia Municipal) ☎092.

Hydrofoils and ferries The main operator of ferry and hydrofoils between Mallorca and Ciutadella has suspended these services until further notice. In the meantime, Cape Balear de Cruceros (☎971 818668) has stepped into the breach running passenger-only hydrofoils to Ciutadella from Cala Rajada. They don't have offices in Ciutadella, but the tourist office should have details of sailings – if not ask down at the harbour. There is generally at least one sailing per day, the journey time is 1hr 15min and the return fare is about 7500ptas, dropping to 6000ptas in winter.

Maps and books Both Punt i Apart, c/Roser 14, and Librería Pau, c/Nou Juliol 23, have a reasonably good selection of travel books, general maps and IGN Menorcan walking maps.

Post office The central *Correu* is just off the ring road at c/Pius 4–6 (Mon–Fri 8.30am–2.30pm, Sat 9.30am–1pm).

Taxis There is a taxi rank on Plaça dels Pins. Alternatively, telephone Auto Taxi (☎971 384179).

Southeast of Ciutadella: Cala En Turqueta

The cross-country route running **southeast from Ciutadella** to **Cala En Turqueta**, the most beautiful of the pristine cove beaches of the south coast, begins in town at Plaça Jaume II, just off the ring road. From here, head southeast along Camí Sant Joan de Missa; after about 3km you reach the clearly marked farmhouse of Son Vivó, where the road branches into two seven-kilometre-long byroads which proceed down to the coast. The more easterly route is the one you want. Following this, you'll pass the hermitage of Sant Joan de Missa, and, with the road now becoming a bumpy track, you should keep going until you round the farmhouse of Sant Francesc. If the gate here is locked, park and follow the track for the last 1km down to the beach; if it's open you can drive down – but only just. Cala En Turqueta itself is a lovely cove backed by wooded limestone cliffs. There are no facilities, and it's most unusual to find a crowd, though boat trips do occasionally drop by in the afternoon.

travel details

MALLORCA

Buses

Ca'n Picafort to: Cala Rajada (May–Oct Mon–Sat 5 daily; 35min); Palma (2–3 daily; 1hr); Port d'Alcúdia (May–Oct every 15min; Nov–April 3 daily; 10min); Porto Cristo (May–Oct Mon–Sat 3 daily; 55min).

Palma to: Alcúdia (May–Oct Mon–Sat 10 daily, 5 on Sun; Nov–April 3 daily; 1hr); Andratx (Mon–Sat every 30min; 11 on Sun; 35min); Artà (Mon–Sat 4 daily, 1 on Sun; 1hr 25min); Ca'n Picafort (2–3 daily; 1hr); Coves del Drac (Mon–Sat 2–4 daily, 1 on Sun; 1hr); Deià (5 daily, except Oct–March Sun 3 on Sun; 45min); Inca (Mon–Sat 8 daily, 4 on Sun; 30min); Lluc (Mon–Sat 2 daily, 1 on Sun; 1hr); Platja de Formentor (May–Oct Mon–Sat 1 daily; 1hr 15min); Pollença (3–5 daily; 1hr); Port d'Alcúdia (May–Oct Mon–Sat 10 daily, 5 on Sun; Nov–April 3 daily; 1hr 10min); Port de Pollença (3–5 daily; 1hr 10min); Port de Sóller (5 daily, except Oct–March 3 on Sun; 1hr 15min); Sóller (5 daily, except Oct–March 3 on Sun; 1hr 10min); Valldemossa (5 daily, except Oct–March 3 on Sun; 30min).

Port d'Alcúdia to: Alcúdia (May–Oct every 15min; Nov–April 3 daily; 5min); Artà (May–Oct Mon–Sat 5 daily; 30min); Cala Rajada (May–Oct Mon–Sat 2 daily; 40min); Ca'n Picafort (May–Oct every 15min; Nov–April 3 daily; 10min); Palma (May–Oct Mon–Sat 10 daily, 5 on Sun; Nov–April 3 daily; 1hr 10min); Platja de Formentor (May–Oct 2 daily; 25min); Pollença (3–5 daily; 20min); Port de Pollença (May–Oct every 15min; Nov–April 3 daily; 15min); Port de Sóller (May–Oct Mon–Sat 2 daily; 1hr 10min).

Port de Pollença to: Alcúdia (May–Oct every 15min; Nov–April 3 daily; 10min); Ca'n Picafort (3 daily; 25min); Palma (3–5 daily; 1hr 10min); Platja de Formentor (May–Oct 2 daily; 20min); Pollença (3–5 daily; 10min); Port d'Alcúdia (May–Oct every 15min; Nov–April 3 daily; 15min); Port de Sóller (May–Oct Mon–Sat 2 daily; 55min); Sóller (May–Oct Mon–Sat 2 daily; 50min).

Port de Sóller to: Deià (5 daily; 20min); Palma (5 daily, except Oct–March 3 on Sun; 1hr 15min); Pollença (May–Oct Mon–Sat 2 daily; 50min); Port d'Alcúdia (May–Oct Mon–Sat 2 daily; 1hr 10min); Port de Pollença (May–Oct Mon–Sat 2 daily; 55min); Sóller (5 daily; 5min); Valldemossa (5 daily; 30min).

Porto Cristo to: Ca'n Picafort (May–Oct Mon–Sat 3 daily; 1hr); Port d'Alcúdia (May–Oct Mon–Sat 3 daily; 1hr).

Valldemossa to: Andratx (Mon–Sat 1 daily; 1hr); Deia (5 daily, except Oct–March 3 on Sun; 15min); Palma (5 daily, except Oct–March 3 on Sun; 30min); Peguera (Mon–Sat 1 daily; 1hr 10min).

Trains
Palma to: Binissalem (hourly; 30min); Inca (hourly; 40min); Sóller (5 daily; 1hr 20min).

MENORCA

Buses
Ciutadella to: Alaior (Mon–Sat 6 daily, 4 on Sun; 40min); Es Mercadal (Mon–Sat 6 daily, 4 on Sun; 30min); Ferreries (Mon–Sat 8 daily, 5 on Sun; 20min); Maó (Mon–Sat 6 daily, 4 on Sun; 1hr)).

Ferreries to: Alaior (Mon–Sat 6 daily, 4 on Sun; 20min); Cala Santa Galdana (6 daily; 35min); Ciutadella (Mon–Sat 8 daily, 5 on Sun; 20min); Es Mercadal (Mon–Sat 6 daily, 4 on Sun; 10min); Maó (Mon–Sat 6 daily, 4 on Sun; 40min).

Fornells to: Es Mercadal (Mon–Fri 1 daily; 15min); Maó (1–2 daily; 35min).

Maó to: Alaior (Mon–Sat 11 daily, 9 on Sun; 20min); Ciutadella (Mon–Sat 6 daily, 4 on Sun; 1hr); Es Mercadal (Mon–Sat 6 daily, 4 on Sun; 30min); Ferreries (Mon–Sat 6 daily, 4 on Sun; 40min); Fornells (1–2 daily; 35min); Cala Santa Galdana (1–2 daily; 1hr).

IBIZA

Buses
Ibiza Town to: Cala Sant Vicenç (hourly; 45min); Figueretes (every 30min; 5min); Platja d'en Bossa (every 30min; 10min); Portinatx (2–6 daily; 45min); Sant Antoni de Portmany (every 30min; 30min); Ses Salines (hourly; 15min); Santa Eulària des Riu (hourly; 20min); Sant Joan (2–6 daily; 35min); Sant Miquel (1 daily; 25min).

Boats
Ibiza Town to: Es Canar (7 daily; 1hr 10min); Platja d'en Bossa (6 daily; 20min); Santa Eulària des Riu (7 daily; 50min).

INTER-ISLAND FLIGHTS, FERRIES AND HYDROFOILS

All inter-island flights are operated by Iberia. All inter-island ferries and hydrofoils are operated by Transmediterranea except for those between Ibiza and Formentera.

Formentera to: Ibiza (4 ferries daily, 1hr; June to Sept 10 passenger-only hydrofoils daily, 20min).

Ibiza to: Palma (4 flights daily, 40min; 1–2 ferries weekly, 4hr; mid-June to mid-Sept 3 hydrofoils weekly, 2hr 15min).

Palma to: Maó (4 flights daily, 40min; 1 ferry weekly, 6hr).

Cala Rajada to: Ciutadella (1 hydrofoil daily; 1hr 15min).

MAINLAND FERRY CONNECTIONS

Barcelona to: Ibiza (2–4 weekly; 9hr); Maó (2–3 weekly; 9hr); Palma (1–2 daily; 8hr).

Valencia to: Ibiza (1 weekly; 9hr); Maó via Palma (1 weekly; 15hr); Palma (2–3 weekly; 9hr).

MAINLAND HYDROFOIL CONNECTIONS

Barcelona to: Palma (mid-June to mid-Sept 3 weekly; 4hr 15min).

Valencia to: Ibiza (mid-June to mid-Sept 3 weekly; 2hr 15min); Palma (mid-June to mid-Sept 3 weekly; 5hr 15min).

PART THREE

THE

CONTEXTS

THE
HISTORICAL
FRAMEWORK

EARLY CIVILIZATIONS

The first identifiably Iberian peoples arrived on the peninsula from southern France towards the close of the Palaeolithic age. They were cave dwellers and hunter-gatherers and seem to have been heavily concentrated in the north of the country, around the modern province of Santander. Here survive the most remarkable traces of their culture (which peaked around 15,000 BC), the deftly stylized cave murals of the animals that they hunted. The finest examples are at Altamira – now closed for general visits, though you can see similar paintings at Puente Viesgo, also near Santander.

Subsequent prehistory is more complex and confused. There does not appear to have been any great development in the cave cultures of the north. Instead the focus shifts south to Almería, which was settled around 5000–4000 BC by the "Iberians", **Neolithic** colonists from North Africa. They had already assimilated into their culture many of the changes that had developed in Egypt and the Near East. Settling in villages, they introduced pastoral and agricultural ways of life and exploited the plentiful supply of copper. Around 1500 BC, with the onset of the **Bronze Age**, they began to spread outwards into fortified villages on the central meseta, the high plateau of modern Castile. At the turn of the millennium they were joined by numerous waves of **Celtic** and **Germanic** peoples. Here, Spain's divisive physical make-up – with its network of mountain ranges – determined its social nature. The incoming tribes formed distinct and isolated groups, conquering and sometimes absorbing each other but only on a very limited and local scale. Hence the Celtic "urnfield people" established themselves in Catalunya, the **Vascones** in the Basque country, and near them along the Atlantic coast, the **Astures**. Pockets of earlier cultures survived, too, particularly in Galicia with its *citanias* of beehive huts.

FIRST COLONIES

The Spanish coast meanwhile attracted colonists from different regions of the Mediterranean. The **Phoenicians** founded the port of Gadir (Cádiz) in 1100 BC and traded intensively in the metals of the Guadalquivir valley. Their wealth and success gave rise to a Spanish "Atlantis" myth, based on the lost kingdom of Tartessus, mentioned in the Bible and probably sited near Huelva; the sophisticated jewellery it produced is on display in Sevilla's archeological museum. Market rivalry later brought the **Greeks**, who established their trading colonies along the eastern coast – the modern Costa Brava. There's a fine surviving site at Empúries, near Barcelona.

More significant, however, was the arrival of the **Carthaginians** in the third century BC. Expelled from Sicily by the Romans, they saw in Spain a new base for their empire, from which to regain strength and strike back at their rivals. Although making little impact inland, they occupied most of Andalucía and expanded along the Mediterranean seaboard to establish a new capital at Cartagena. Under Hannibal they prepared to invade Italy and in 214 BC attacked Saguntum, a strategic outpost of the Roman Empire. It was a disastrous move, precipitating the **Second Punic War**; by 210 BC only Cádiz remained in their control and they were forced to accept terms. A new and very different age had begun.

ROMANS AND VISIGOTHS

The **Roman colonization** of the peninsula was far more intense than anything previously experienced and met with great resistance from the

Celtiberian tribes of the north and centre. It was almost two centuries before the conquest was complete and indeed the Basques, although defeated, were never fully Romanized.

Nonetheless, Spain became the most important centre of the Roman Empire after Italy itself, producing no less than four emperors, along with the writers Seneca and Lucan. Again, geography dictated an uneven spread of influence, at its strongest in Andalucía, southern Portugal and on the Catalan coast around Tarragona. In the first two centuries AD the Spanish mines and the granaries of Andalucía brought unprecedented wealth and Roman Spain enjoyed a brief **"Golden Age"**. The finest monuments were built in the great provincial capitals – Córdoba, Mérida (which boasts the finest remains) and Tarragona – but all across the country more practical structures were undertaken: roads, bridges and aqueducts. Many were still used well into recent centuries – perhaps the most remarkable being the aqueducts of Segovia and Tarragona – and a few bridges remain in use even today.

Towards the third century, however, the Roman political framework began to show signs of decadence and corruption. Although the actual structure didn't totally collapse until the Muslim invasions of the early eighth century, it became increasingly vulnerable to **barbarian invasions** from northern Europe. The Franks and the Suevi (Swabians) swept across the Pyrenees between 264 and 276, leaving much devastation in their wake. They were followed two centuries later by further waves of Suevi, Alans and Vandals. Internal strife was heightened by the arrival of the **Visigoths** from Gaul, allies of Rome and already Romanized to a large degree. The triumph of Visigothic strength in the fifth century resulted in a period of spurious unity, based upon an exclusive military rule from their capital at Toledo, but their numbers were never great and their order was often fragmentary and nominal, with the bulk of the subject people kept in a state of disconsolate servility, and the military elite divided by constant plots and factions – exacerbated by the Visigothic system of elected monarchy and by their adherence to the heretical Arian philosophy. In 589 **King Recared** converted to Catholicism but religious strife was only multiplied: forced conversions, especially within the Jewish enclaves, maintained a constant simmering of discontent.

MOORISH SPAIN

In contrast to the long-drawn-out Roman campaigns, **Moorish conquest** of the peninsula was effected with extraordinary speed. This was a characteristic phenomenon of the spread of Islam – Muhammad left Mecca in 622 and by 705 his followers had established control over all of North Africa. Spain, with its political instability, its wealth and its fertile climate, was an inevitable extension of their aims. In 711 Tariq, governor of Tangier, led a force of 7000 Berbers across the straits and routed the Visigoth army of King Roderic: two years later the Visigoths made a last desperate stand at Mérida and within a decade the Moors had conquered all but the wild mountains of Asturias. The land under their authority was dubbed **"al-Andalus"**, a fluid term which expanded and shrunk with the intermittent gains and losses of the Reconquest. According to region, the Moors were to remain in control for the next three to eight centuries.

It was not simply a military conquest. The Moors (a collective term for the numerous waves of Arab and Berber settlers from North Africa) were often content to grant a limited autonomy in exchange for payment of tribute; their administrative system was tolerant and easily absorbed both Jews and Christians, those who retained their religion being known as "Mozarabs". And al-Andalus was a distinctly Spanish state of Islam. Though at first politically subject to the Eastern Caliphate (or empire) of Baghdad, it was soon virtually independent. In the tenth century, at the peak of its power and expansion, Abd ar-Rahman III asserted total independence, proclaiming himself Caliph of a new **Western Islamic Empire**. Its capital was Córdoba – the largest, most prosperous and most civilized city in Europe. This was the great age of Muslim Spain: its scholarship, philosophy, architecture and craftsmanship were without rival and there was an unparalleled growth in urban life, in trade, and in agriculture aided by magnificent irrigation projects. These and other engineering feats were not, on the whole, instigated by the Moors who instead took basic Roman models and adapted them to a new level of sophistication. In **architecture** and the **decorative arts**, however, their contribution was original and unique – as may be seen in the incredible monuments of Sevilla, Córdoba and Granada.

The Córdoban Caliphate for a while created a remarkable degree of unity. But its rulers were to become decadent and out of touch, prompting the brilliant but dictatorial **al-Mansur** to usurp control. Under this extraordinary ruler Moorish power actually reached new heights, pushing the Christian kingdom of Asturias-León back into the Cantabrian mountains and sacking its most holy shrine, Santiago de Compostela. However, after his death the Caliphate quickly lost its authority and in 1031 disintegrated into a series of small independent kingdoms or *taifas*, the strongest of which was Sevilla.

Internal divisions amongst the *taifas* offered less resistance to the Christian kingdoms which were rallying in the north, and twice North Africa had to be turned to for reinforcement. This resulted in two distinct new waves of Moorish invasion – first by the fanatically Islamic **Almoravids** (1086) and later by the **Almohads** (1147), who restored effective Muslim authority until their defeat at the battle of Las Navas de Tolosa in 1212.

THE CHRISTIAN RECONQUEST

The **reconquest** of land and influence from the Moors was a slow and intermittent process. It began with a symbolic victory by a small force of Christians at Covadonga in the Asturias (727) and was not completed until 1492 with the conquest of Granada by Fernando and Isabella.

Covadonga resulted in the formation of the tiny Christian **Kingdom of the Asturias**. Initially just 65 by 50km in area, it had by 914 reclaimed León and most of Galicia and northern Portugal. At this point, progress was temporarily halted by the devastating campaigns of al-Mansur. However, with the fall of the Córdoban Caliphate and the divine aid of Spain's Moor-slaying patron, Saint James the Apostle (see "Santiago de Compostela"), the Reconquest moved into a new and powerful phase.

The frontier castles built against Arab attack gave name to **Castile**, founded in the tenth century as a county of León-Asturias. Under Fernando I (1037–65) it achieved the status of a kingdom and became the main thrust and focus of the Reconquest. Other kingdoms were being defined in the north at the same time: the Basques founded Navarra (Navarre), while dynastic marriage merged Catalunya with Aragón. In 1085 this period of confident

Christian expansion reached its zenith with the capture of the great Moorish city of Toledo. The following year, however, the Almoravids arrived on invitation from Sevilla, and military activity was effectively frozen – except, that is, for the exploits of the legendary **El Cid**, a Castilian nobleman who won considerable lands around Valencia in 1095.

The next concerted phase of the Reconquest really began as a response to the threat imposed by the Almohads. The kings of León, Castile, Aragón and Navarra united in a general crusade which resulted in the great victory at **Las Navas de Tolosa** (1212). Thereafter Muslim power was effectively paralyzed and the Christian armies moved on to take most of al-Andalus. Fernando III ("El Santo", the saint) led Castilian soldiers into Córdoba in 1236 and twelve years later into Sevilla. Meanwhile, the kingdom of Portugal had expanded to more or less its present size, while Jaime I of Aragón was to conquer Valencia, Alicante, Murcia and the Balearic Islands. By the end of the thirteenth century only the kingdom of Granada remained under Muslim authority and for much of the following two centuries it was forced to pay tribute to the monarchs of Castile.

Two factors should be stressed regarding the Reconquest. First, its unifying religious nature – the **spirit of crusade**, intensified by the religious zeal of the Almoravids and Almohads, and by the wider European climate (which in 1085 gave rise to the First Crusade). This powerful religious motivation is well illustrated by the subsequent canonization of Fernando III, and found solid expression in the part played by the military orders of Christian knights, the most important of which were the **Knights Templar** and the Order of Santiago. At the same time the Reconquest was a movement of **recolonization**. The fact that the country had been in arms for so long meant that the nobility had a major and clearly visible social role, a trend perpetuated by the redistribution of captured land in huge packages, or *latifundia*. Heirs to this tradition still remain as landlords of the great estates, most conspicuously in Andalucía. Men from the ranks were also awarded land, forming a lower, larger stratum of nobility, the *hidalgos*. It was their particular social code that provided the material for Cervantes in *Don Quixote*.

Any spirit of mutual co-operation that had temporarily united the Christian kingdoms disintegrated during the fourteenth century, and independent lines of development were once again pursued. Attempts to merge **Portugal** with Castile foundered at the battle of Aljubarrota (1385), and Portuguese attention turned away from Spain towards the Atlantic. Aragón experienced a similar pull towards the markets of the Mediterranean, although pre-eminence in this area was soon passed to the Genoese. It was **Castile** that emerged as the strongest over this period: self-sufficiency in agriculture and a flourishing wool trade with the Netherlands enabled the state to build upon the prominent military role played under Fernando III. Politically, Castilian history was a tale of dynastic conflict until the accession of the Catholic monarchs.

LOS REYES CATÓLICOS

Los Reyes Católicos – the **Catholic Monarchs** – was the joint title given to **Fernando V of Aragón and Isabella I of Castile**, whose marriage in 1479 united the two largest kingdoms in Spain. Unity was in practice more symbolic than real: Castile had underlined its rights in the marriage vows and Aragón retained its old administrative structure. So, in the beginning at least, the growth of any national unity or Spanish – as opposed to local – sentiment was very much dependent on the head of state. Nevertheless, from this time on it begins to be realistic to consider Spain as a single political entity.

At the heart of Fernando and Isabella's popular appeal lay a **religious bigotry** that they shared with most of their Christian subjects. The **Inquisition** was instituted in Castile in 1480 and in Aragón seven years later. Aiming to establish the purity of the Catholic faith by rooting out heresy, it was directed mainly at Jews – resented for their enterprise in commerce and influence in high places, as well as for their faith. Expression had already been given to these feelings in a pogrom in 1391; it was reinforced by an edict issued in 1492 which forced up to 400,000 Jews to flee the country. A similar spirit was embodied in the reconquest of the **Kingdom of Granada**, also in 1492. As the last stronghold of Muslim authority, the religious rights of its citizens were guaranteed under the treaty of surrender. Within a decade, though, those Muslims under Christian rule had been given the choice between conversion or expulsion.

The year 1492 was symbolic of a fresh start in another way: it was in this year that Columbus discovered America, and the Papal Bull that followed, entrusting Spain with the conversion of the American Indians, further entrenched Spain's sense of a mission to bring the world to the "True Faith". The next ten years saw the systematic conquest, colonization and exploitation of the **New World** as it was discovered, with new territory stretching from Labrador to Brazil, and new-found wealth pouring into the royal coffers. Important as this was for Fernando and Isabella, and especially for their prestige, priorities remained in Europe and strategic marriage alliances were made with Portugal, England and the Holy Roman Empire. It was not until the accession of the Habsburg dynasty that Spain could look to the activities of Cortés, Magellan and Pizarro and claim to be the world's leading power.

HABSBURG SPAIN

Carlos I, a Habsburg, came to the throne in 1516 as a beneficiary of the marriage alliances of the Catholic monarchs. Five years later, he was elected Emperor of the Holy Roman Empire as Carlos V (**Charles V**), inheriting not only Castile and Aragón, but Flanders, the Netherlands, Artois, the Franche-Comté and all the American colonies to boot. With such responsibilities it was inevitable that attention would be diverted from Spain, whose chief function became to sustain the Holy Roman Empire with gold and silver from the Americas. It was only with the accession of **Felipe II** in 1556 that Spanish politics became more centralized. The notion of an absentee king was reversed. Felipe lived in the centre of Castile near Madrid, creating a monument to the values of medieval Spain in his palace, El Escorial.

Two main themes run through his reign: the preservation of his own inheritance, and the revival of the crusade in the name of the Catholic Church. In pursuit of the former, Felipe successfully claimed the Portuguese throne (through the marriage of his mother), gaining access to the additional wealth of its empire. Plots were also woven in support of Mary Queen of Scots's claim to the throne of England, and to that end the ill-fated Armada sailed in 1588, its sinking a triumph for English naval strength and for Protestantism.

This was a period of unusual religious intensity: the **Inquisition** was enforced with renewed vigour, and a rising of *Moriscos* (subject Moors) in the Alpujarras was fiercely suppressed. Felipe III later ordered the expulsion of half the total number of *Moriscos* in Spain – allowing only two families to remain in each village in order to maintain irrigation techniques. The **exodus** of both Muslim and Jew created a large gulf in the labour force and in the higher echelons of commercial life – and in trying to uphold the Catholic cause, an enormous strain was put upon resources without any clear-cut victory.

By the middle of the seventeenth century, Spain was losing international credibility. Domestically, the disparity between the wealth surrounding Crown and Court and the poverty and suffering of the mass of the population was a source of perpetual tension. Discontent fuelled regional revolts in Catalunya and Portugal in 1640, and the latter had finally to be acknowledged as an independent state in 1668.

BOURBONS AND THE PENINSULAR WAR

The **Bourbon dynasty** succeeded to the Spanish throne in the person of Felipe V (1700); with him began the War of Spanish Succession against the rival claim of Archduke Charles of Austria, assisted by British forces. As a result of the Treaty of Utrecht which ended the war (1713), Spain was stripped of all territory in Belgium, Luxembourg, Italy and Sardinia, but Felipe V was recognized as king. Gibraltar was seized by the British in the course of the war. For the rest of the century Spain fell very much under the French sphere of influence, an influence that was given political definition by an alliance with the French Bourbons in 1762.

Contact with France made involvement in the **Napoleonic Wars** inevitable and led eventually to the defeat of the Spanish fleet at Trafalgar in 1805. Popular outrage was such that the powerful prime minister, Godoy, was overthrown and King Carlos IV forced to abdicate (1808). Napoleon seized the opportunity to install his brother, Joseph, on the throne.

Fierce local resistance was eventually backed by the muscle of a British army, first under Sir John Moore, later under the Duke of Wellington, and the French were at last driven out in the course of the Peninsular War. Meanwhile, however, the **American colonies** had been successfully asserting their independence from a preoccupied centre and with them went Spain's last real claim of significance on the world stage. The entire nineteenth century was dominated by the struggle between an often reactionary monarchy and the aspirations of liberal constitutional reformers.

SEEDS OF CIVIL WAR

Between 1810 and 1813 an ad hoc Cortes (parliament) had set up a **liberal constitution** with ministers responsible to a democratically elected chamber. The first act of Fernando VII on being returned to the throne was to abolish this, and until his death in 1833 he continued to stamp out the least hint of liberalism. On his death, the right of succession was contested between his brother, Don Carlos, backed by the Church, conservatives and Basques, and his infant daughter, Isabella, who looked to the Liberals and the army for support. So began the **First Carlist War**, a civil war that lasted six years. Isabella II was eventually declared of age in 1843, her reign a long record of scandal, political crisis and constitutional compromise. Liberal army generals under the leadership of General Prim effected a coup in 1868 and the queen was forced to abdicate, but attempts to maintain a Republican government foundered. The Cortes was again dissolved and the throne returned to Isabella's son, Alfonso XII. A new constitution was declared in 1876, limiting the power of the Crown through the institution of bicameral government, but again the progress was halted by the lack of any tradition on which to base the constitutional theory.

The years preceding World War I merely heightened the discontent, which found expression in the growing **political movements** of the working class. The Socialist Workers' Party was founded in Madrid after the restoration of Alfonso XII, and spawned its own trade union, the UGT (1888), successful predominantly in areas of high industrial concentration such as the Basque region and Asturias. Its anarchist counterpart, the CNT, was founded in 1911, gaining substantial support among the peasantry of Andalucía.

The loss of **Cuba** in 1898 emphasized the growing isolation of Spain in international affairs and added to economic problems with the return of soldiers seeking employment where there was none. A call-up for army reserves to fight in **Morocco** in 1909 provoked a general strike and the "Tragic Week" of rioting in Barcelona. Between 1914 and 1918, Spain was outwardly neutral but inwardly turbulent; inflated prices made the postwar recession harder to bear.

The general disillusionment with parliamentary government, together with the fears of employers and businessmen for their own security, gave **General Primo de Rivera** sufficient support for a military coup in 1923. Dictatorship did result in an increase in material prosperity, but the death of the dictator in 1930 revealed the apparent stability as a facade. New political factions were taking shape: the Liberal Republican Right was founded by Alcalá Zamora, while the Socialist Party was given definition under the leadership of Largo Caballero. The victory of anti-monarchist parties in the 1931 municipal elections forced the abdication of the king and the **Second Republic** was declared.

THE SECOND REPUBLIC

Catalunya declared itself a republic independent of the central government and was conceded control of internal affairs by a statute of 1932. **Separatist movements** were powerful too in the Basque provinces and Galicia, each with their own demands for autonomy. Meanwhile, the government, set up on a tidal wave of hope, was hopelessly divided internally and too scared of right-wing reaction to carry out the massive tax and agrarian reforms that the left demanded, and that might have provided the resources for thoroughgoing regeneration of the economy.

The result was the increasing polarization of Spanish politics. **Anarchism**, in particular, was gaining strength among the frustrated middle classes as well as among workers and peasantry. The **Communist Party** and left-wing **Socialists**, driven into alliance by their mutual distrust of the "moderate" socialists in government, were also forming a growing bloc. On the right the **Falangists**, basically a youth party founded in 1923 by **José Antonio Primo de Rivera** (son of the dictator), made uneasy bedfellows with conservative traditionalists and dissident elements in the army upset by modernizing reforms.

In an atmosphere of growing confusion, the left-wing Popular Front alliance won the general election of **February 1936** by a narrow margin. Normal life, though, became increasingly impossible: the economy was crippled by strikes, peasants took agrarian reform into their own hands and the government failed to exert its authority over anyone. Finally, on July 17, 1936, the military garrison in Morocco rebelled under **General Franco**'s leadership, to be followed by risings at military garrisons throughout the country. It was the culmination of years of scheming in the army, but in the event far from the overnight success its leaders almost certainly expected. The south and west quickly fell into Nationalist hands, but Madrid and the industrialized north and east remained loyal to the Republican government.

CIVIL WAR

The ensuing **Civil War** was undoubtedly one of the most bitter and bloody the world has seen. Violent reprisals were taken on their enemies by both sides – the Republicans shooting priests and local landowners wholesale, the Nationalists carrying out mass slaughter on the population of almost every town they took. Contradictions were legion in the way the Spanish populations found themselves divided from each other. Perhaps the greatest irony was that Franco's troops, on their "holy" mission to ensure a Catholic Spain, comprised a core of Moroccan troops from Spain's North African colony.

It was, too, the first modern war – Franco's German allies demonstrated their ability to wipe out entire civilian populations with their bombing raids on Gernika and Durango, and radio proved an important weapon, as Nationalist propagandists offered the starving Republicans "the white bread of Franco".

Despite sporadic help from Russia and thousands of volunteers in the International Brigades, the Republic could never compete with the professional armies and the massive assistance from Fascist Italy and Nazi Germany enjoyed by the Nationalists. In addition, the left was torn by internal divisions which at times led almost to civil war within its own ranks. Nevertheless, the Republicans held out in slowly dwindling territories for nearly three years, with **Catalunya** falling in January 1939 and armed resistance in **Madrid** – which never formally surrendered – petering out over the next few months. As hundreds of thousands of refugees flooded into France, General Francisco Franco, who had long before proclaimed himself Head of State, took up the reins of power.

FRANCO'S SPAIN

The early reprisals taken by the victors were on a massive and terrifying scale. Executions were commonplace and upwards of two million people were put in concentration camps until "order" had been established by authoritarian means. Only one party, the Falange, was permitted and censorship was rigidly enforced. By the end of World War II, during which Spain was too weak to be anything but neutral, **Franco** was the only fascist head of state left in Europe, one responsible for sanctioning more deaths than any other in Spanish history. Spain was economically and politically isolated and, bereft of markets, suffered – almost half the population were still tilling the soil for little or no return. When General Eisenhower visited Madrid in 1953 with the offer of huge loans, it came as water to the desert, and the price, the establishment of American nuclear bases, was one Franco was more than willing to pay. However belated, economic development was incredibly rapid, with Spain enjoying a growth rate second only to that of Japan for much of the 1960s, a boom fuelled by the tourist industry and the remittances of Spanish workers abroad.

Increased **prosperity**, however, only underlined the bankruptcy of Franco's regime and its inability to cope with popular demands. Higher incomes, the need for better education and a creeping invasion of Western culture made the anachronism of Franco ever clearer. His only reaction was to attempt to withdraw what few signs of increased liberalism had crept through, and his last years mirrored the repression of the postwar period. Trade unions remained outlawed, and the rampant inflation of the early 1970s saw striking workers across Spain hauled out of occupied mines and factories and imprisoned, or even shot in the streets. Attempts to report these events by the liberal press resulted in suspensions, fines and censorship. Basque Nationalists, whose assassination of Admiral Carrero Blanco had effectively destroyed Franco's last hope of a like-minded successor, were singled out for particularly harsh treat-

ment. Hundreds of so-called terrorists were tortured, and the Burgos trials of 1970, together with the executions of August 1975, provoked worldwide protest.

Franco finally died in November 1975, nominating **King Juan Carlos** as his successor. Groomed for the job and very much in with the army – of which he remains official Commander in Chief – the king's initial moves were cautious in the extreme, appointing a government dominated by loyal Francoists who had little sympathy for the growing opposition demands for "democracy without adjectives". In the summer of 1976 demonstrations in Madrid ended in violence, with the police upholding the old authoritarian ways.

THE RETURN OF DEMOCRACY

The violent events leading up to and following his mentor's death seem to have persuaded Juan Carlos that some real break with the past and a move towards **democratization** was now urgent and inevitable. Using the almost dictatorial powers he had inherited, he ousted Franco's reactionary prime minister, Carlos Arias Navarro, and replaced him with Adolfo Suárez, an ambitious lawyer and former head of Spanish TV. In 1976 Suárez pushed a **Law of Political Reform** through the Cortes, reforming the legislature into two chambers elected by universal suffrage – a move massively endorsed by the Spanish people in a referendum. Suarez also passed legislation allowing the setting up of free trade unions, as well as legitimizing the Socialist Party (PSOE) and, controversially, the Communists. Several cabinet ministers resigned in protest and an outraged military began planning their *coup d'état*.

When elections were held in June 1977, Suárez's own hastily formed centre-right party, the Unión del Centro Democrático (UCD), was rewarded with a 34 percent share of the vote, the Socialists coming in second with 28 percent, and the Communists and Francoist **Alianza Popular** both marginalized at 9 percent and 8 percent. Despite the overwhelming victories in Catalunya and the Basque Country of parties appealing to regional sentiment, this was almost certainly a vote for democratic stability rather than for ideology, something reflected in the course of the parliament, with Suárez governing through "consensus politics", negotiating settlements on all important issues with the major parties.

The first parliament of the "New Spain" now embarked on the formidable task of drawing up a **constitution**, whilst the Suárez government applied for membership of the then EEC. On December 6, 1978 the new constitution was overwhelmingly endorsed in a national referendum, and remarkably, only three years after the death of Franco, Spain had become a full democracy.

Elections in March 1979 almost exactly duplicated the 1977 result but when the UCD, a fractious coalition of moderates and extremists, started to crack at the seams, Suárez resigned in January 1981. This provided the trigger for a **military coup**, launched by a contingent of Civil Guards loyal to Franco's memory and commanded by the tragi-comic, moustachioed colonel Antonio Tejero. They stormed into the Cortes with Tejero brandishing a revolver, and sub-machine-gunned the ceiling as MPs dived for cover. The crisis, for a while, was real; tanks were brought out on to the streets of Valencia, and only three of the army's ten regional commanders remained unreservedly loyal to the government. But as it became clear that the king would not support the plotters, most of the rest then affirmed their support. Juan Carlos had taken the decision of his life and emerged with immensely enhanced prestige in the eyes of most Spaniards.

THE GONZÁLEZ ERA

On October 28, 1982, the Socialist PSOE, led by charismatic **Felipe González**, was elected with the biggest landslide victory in Spanish electoral history to rule a country that had been firmly in the hands of the right for 43 years. The Socialists captured the imagination and the votes of nearly ten million Spaniards with the simplest of appeals: "for change".

Once in power, however, the Socialist Party chose the path of pragmatism, and a relentless drift to the right followed. Four successive election victories kept the party in power for fourteen years and by the mid-1990s the PSOE government's policies had become indistinguishable from the conservative administrations of Britain or Germany. The party's abandonment of many of its core principles in favour of a more blatant opportunism was neatly encapsulated in a popular witticism, which redefined the "changes" (*cambios*) promised by González as the "three c's": *coche*

(a new car), *compañera* (a new girlfriend) and *casa* (a new house).

González himself, meanwhile, had been equally transformed, from a radical young labour lawyer, into a careworn elder statesman. Control of inflation had become a more urgent target than reducing unemployment, whilst loss-making heavy industries (steel and shipbuilding especially) were ruthlessly overhauled and other industries privatized. European Community (now **European Union**) membership came in 1986, and the pride which most Spanish people felt at this tangible proof of their acceptance by the rest of Europe bought the Socialists more valuable time.

The issue of **NATO** (or OTAN as the Spaniards know it), perhaps more than any other, demonstrated how much González had sacrificed to pragmatism. During the 1982 election campaign he had made an impassioned speech at a rally against Spain remaining a member of NATO, which the dying UCD administration had rushed into joining at the behest of the military. When the promised referendum was finally held four years later – which surprisingly turned out marginally in favour of staying in – his was one of the main voices in favour of continued membership. González finally buried the question of NATO as a political issue for the mainstream left when in 1995 he agreed to and supported the elevation of his foreign secretary and close colleague, Javier Solana, to the post of Secretary General of the organization he had spent most of his political life reviling.

After long years of being hopelessly divided, in the late Eighties the **Spanish right** realigned itself when former prime minister Adolfo Suárez's UCD Christian Democrats merged with the Alianza Popular to to form the new right-of-centre **Partido Popular** (PP) which came a respectable second in the 1989 elections; a new far-left coalition, **Izquierda Unida** (United Left), comprised of the Communists and smaller leftist parties, came third, albeit with the same number of seats (eighteen) in the Congress of Deputies as the Catalan Nationalists, barely a tenth of the PSOE's representation.

The nation's progressive disillusionment with Felipe González's government in the early 1990s saw the rise to prominence of **José María Aznar** as leader of the PP. A former tax inspector and devoid of charisma, Aznar was dogged in his criticism of government incompetence in

AUTONOMY AND SEPARATISM

Autonomy – the granting of substantial self-rule in the 1978 Constitution to the seventeen *autonomías* into which Spain is now divided – has created as many problems as it has solved. In Franco's time even speaking the regional languages such as Catalan or Basque was banned, and the backlash against this has turned all Spaniards into potential separatists. Although each of the autonomous regions now has its own president, parliament and civil service – all at enormous and spiralling cost – the main beneficiaries of the new arrangement have been the Basques and Catalans in the north who since 1993 have held the balance of power in the Madrid parliament. Spain's chronic economic problems in the late 1980s enabled these two to drive hard bargains with the ailing PSOE administration. Jordi Pujol, a veteran of Franco's jails and the supremely canny regional president of the Catalans, once said that whilst Catalunya had long been the economic locomotive pulling the rest of Spain, it had never been the driver, and that this would change. As good as his word, he managed to secure a concession from the central government which allows the Catalan Regional Government to collect and spend thirty per cent of its income tax. The other autonomies demanded equal treatment and the law has now been retrospectively applied to them, too, with unforeseeable long-term repercussions for the national economy.

Predictably, having won one victory over Madrid and with Catalan regional elections on the horizon, late in 1998 Pujol attempted to use his support for the Aznar government as a bargaining chip to up the fiscal figure to one hundred per cent. The prime minister retorted that he would sooner call a general election than be blackmailed, but it was an ominous sign for the future. When the *autonomías* do get hold of the cash they tend to spend it not on fostering an entrepreneurial spirit or investment for the long term, but

subsidizing benefit payouts to the poor in order to buy votes. Similarly, and to justify their existence, the regional leaders (many of whom earn salaries higher than the Spanish prime minister) have ploughed vast resources into grandiose schemes such as the Sevilla Expo '92, which often leave behind staggering debt mountains. At the same time the *autonomías* have become fiefdoms used by the victorious party to reward its members with jobs in the regional government pyramid, ranging from senior civil service posts, all the way down the social scale to school inspectors and refuse collectors, often with a blind eye turned to lack of qualifications.

But the genie of nationalism is now out of the bottle and it seems unlikely that the powers granted to the *autonomías* will ever return to the centre; in fact, with the Basques and Catalans spearheading demands for ever more powers – Pujol has recently called for Catalunya to control its own justice system – the opposite is more likely.

The violence by the Basque terrorist group **ETA** remains a threat and although it has claimed over eight hundred lives since 1968 there are strong signs that support both for its methods and its political wing, Herri Batasuna, is waning, as more Basques openly condemn the violence and voice their protests at frequent demonstrations. Influenced by the emerging peace settlement in Northern Ireland (ETA and the IRA have long had close links), in the summer of 1998 ETA announced an **indefinite ceasefire**, somewhat catching the hardline Aznar administration on the hop. As both sides move warily towards negotiations, there are hopes that a politically negotiated settlement may now emerge.

Meanwhile, the **sovereignty of Gibraltar** (see box, p.226) continues to be an important issue in Spanish politics, though it's viewed less urgently in London. However, the British – at Spain's bidding – have begun to pressurize the Gibraltar authorities into clamping down on the scourges of drug and tobacco smuggling and money laundering which have exploded in the colony over the last decade.

dealing with its own sleaze and the growing economic crisis. This debilitated the PSOE's position still further in the build up to the **1993 elections**. However, the PSOE confounded the pundits and the opinion polls to hang on to power by the skin of its teeth, albeit with the help of a coalition with Pujol's Catalan

Nationalists. But González's victory was a poisoned chalice, for he had no new ideas to deal with urgent economic problems, whilst his past now began to catch up with him. As illegal financing of the PSOE and corruption and commission-taking on government projects by party officials and ministers were being exposed, the director of the Guardia Civil (appointed by González), jumped the country with millions of dollars of secret service funds, and the governor of the Bank of Spain was caught out making a private (and illegal) fortune. But the most serious of all the scandals to beset González was the **GAL affair** (Grupo Antiterrorista de Liberación), when it was discovered that a semi-autonomous anti-terrorist unit had been carrying out a dirty war against the ETA terrorists in the 1980s, which included kidnapping and wholesale assassinations of suspected ETA members. The press – and a later judicial investigation – exposed police participation in these crimes and a clear chain of command reaching up to the highest echelons of the PSOE government. González's attempts to muzzle journalists' investigations only poisoned further relations between the government and the media and feeling grew that the truth would never come out. However, in the summer of 1998, the legal system confounded the cynics by convicting two senior ex-ministers of sponsoring kidnapping and misappropriating public funds whilst coordinating GAL activities. They were each sentenced to ten years imprisonment.

CONTEMPORARY POLITICS

The PSOE administration limped on towards what looked likely to be a crushing defeat in the **1996 elections**. The surprise result, however, was another **hung parliament** which made everyone a loser. Aznar, the narrow victor, was denied the "absolute majority" he had believed to be his throughout the campaign, which meant that he would have to do a deal with the nationalist parties (whom he had described as "greedy parasites" on the hustings) if he wanted to form a Partido Popular government. The broadest smile of all on election night was on the face of Felipe González, who had avoided the predicted annihilation to win a respectable 141 seats in the new parliament – only fifteen fewer than Aznar's PP.

However, early in 1998, with his party still in turmoil, **Felipe González** finally **resigned** from the leadership of the PSOE, which he had led for 24 years, to be replaced by the former transport minister, **José Borrell**, a Catalan, and not Gonzáles' preferred choice of successor. Whilst Borrell has set about trying to restore the Socialist Party's credibility following the scandals of recent years, González hovers in the background, and many believe that his appetite for power is not yet exhausted.

The reasons for Aznar's failure to win an outright majority are also significant for modern Spain. When Felipe Gonzalez told the king after the PSOE's first election victory in 1982 that his party's success had completed the transition from dictatorship to democracy, the monarch sagely advised him that the end of the transition would be when the Socialists lost an election to the right. The long and repressive Franco period still casts a heavy shadow across the Spanish political scene, and many voters seem to have become nervous in the days before the poll at the prospect of a right-wing party with a big majority curtailing their new-found liberties and dismantling the social security system – a vital lifeline in poorer regions such as Extremadura and Andalucía. Thus it was that Andalucía, one of the largest *autonomías*, performed its traditional role as the *sartenilla* or frying pan of Spanish politics – traditionally frying the votes of the right-leaning north – by confounding the opinion polls and turning out to vote for the discredited government, effectively denying Aznar a majority.

Elected on a centre-right platform, during his period in office Aznar has begun to move his party to the centre, shifting aside the remaining hardliners in the hope of gaining the electorate's confidence and a working majority not dependent on alliances with the northern nationalists. In tandem with this realignment he has declared his admiration for the ideas of British Prime Minister Tony Blair. Despite his shortcomings as a "likeable personality", even his enemies are forced to admit that the Aznar government has proved wrong those who said he would never be able to reach an understanding with the unions, the nationalist leaders or his international colleagues (former German Chancellor Helmut Kohl once said of him "if he ever gets into power he won't last a siesta").

But it is in the domestic economic sphere that Aznar's political future will be decided. And whilst **unemployment** at around twenty per cent remains the highest in the EU, the PP government has engineered a delicate balancing act that has managed to keep the economy on track, while at the same time introducing measures – such as subsidies for seasonally unemployed agricultural workers –to win over the "have-nots" in staunchly socialist areas such as Andalucía.

At the same time the government have accelerated the previous administration's **privatization policy**, culminating in the sale of Iberia, the national airline, and the power group Endesa. The receipts from privatizations, added to a booming tourist industry (now the third largest in the world), have enabled Aznar to promote the expansion of the economy, backed up by massive investment in new nationwide road and rail links. This, added to low inflation, high growth, and income tax cuts scheduled to kick in on the run-up to the next election, are the golden eggs that the PP leader believes will give him his longed-for majority. Although vast discrepancies remain between Spain's richest and poorest regions

(the Balearic islands enjoy a standard of living four times higher than that of Extremadura), a recent survey indicating that Spaniards feel more positive about the economy than at any time since democracy was restored in the 1970s, suggests that he may be right.

The consensus across Spanish politics on Spain's role in **Europe** has continued, with its inclusion in the first wave of EU nations to adopt a **single currency** in 1999. Building on the successful hosting of the Olympic Games in 1992, an event which symbolized the progress made in shaking off the consequences of the Franco era and international isolation, Spain is set to move forward into the next century as a major player on the European stage.

CHRONOLOGY OF MONUMENTS

25,000 BC	Prehistoric settlements, mainly around Santander.	Cave paintings at Altamira and Puente Viesgo; also Las Piletas (near Ronda).
1100 BC	**Phoenicians** found Cádiz.	
C9th–4th BC	**Celts** settle in the north.	Celtic dolmens and "*citania*": both can be seen at La Guardia (Galicia).
	Greeks establish trading posts along east coast.	Empúries, near Barcelona (Greek site).
C3rd BC	**Carthaginians** occupy Andalucian and Mediterranean coast.	**Celto-Iberian** culture develops, with Greek influence: busts of "La Dama de Elche", etc, in Museo Nacional Arqueológico, Madrid.
214 BC	Second Punic War with Rome.	
210 BC	**Roman colonization** begins.	Important **Roman sites** at Mérida, Tarragona, Itálica, Carmona, Sagunto, Segovia, etc.
414 AD	**Visigoths** arrive.	Sculpture and jewellery (in museums at Madrid and Toledo); also isolated churches.
711	**Moors** from North Africa invade, and conquer peninsula within seven years.	
718	Battle of Covadonga: Christian victory leads to formation of **Asturian kingdom**.	Asturian **pre-Romanesque** churches in and around Oviedo and the Picos de Europa.
756	Abd ar-Rahman I proclaims **Emirate of Córdoba**.	Great Mosque (*Mezquita*) begun at Córdoba, the climax of **early Moorish architecture**.
812	Christians discover body of Santiago (St James) at Compostela.	**Mozarabic** churches built by Arabized Christians in Andalucía – and in the north a century later.
C9th	Kingdoms of **Catalunya** and **Navarra** founded.	
939	Abd ar-Rahman III adopts title "Caliph".	Medina Azahara palace and extensions to Mezquita at Córdoba in the **Caliphal style**.
967	**Al-Mansur** usurps caliphal powers, and forces Christians back into Asturias.	
1013	Caliphate disintegrates into *taifas*, petty kingdoms.	Alcazabas built at Málaga, Granada, Almería, Sevilla, Carmona, Ronda, etc.
1037	Fernando I unites kingdoms of Castile and León-Asturias.	**Romanesque architecture** enters Spain along the pilgrim route to Compostela. Superb examples throughout Castile and the north – especially at Salamanca, Segovia, Burgos, Ávila and Santillana.
	Ramón Berenguer I extends and strengthens Catalan kingdom.	
1085	Christians capture Toledo.	
1086	**Almoravids** invade Spain.	
1147	**Almohads** restore Muslim authority in Andalucía.	Sevilla becomes new Moorish capital in Spain: **Almohad minarets** include Giralda and Torre del Oro.
1162	Alfonso II unites kingdoms of Aragón and Catalunya.	**Cluniac monasteries** built along pilgrim route to Santiago; **Cistercian abbeys** at Poblet and elsewhere.
1212	Almohad advance halted at Las Navas de Tolosa.	**Mudéjar** style emerges through Moorish craftsmen working on Christian buildings: good examples in Aragón at Teruel and Tarazona.

1213	Jaime I "El Conquistador" becomes king of Aragón. **Christian Reconquest** of Balearics (1229), Valencia (1238), Alicante (1266).
1217	Fernando III, "El Santo," King of Castile and retakes Córdoba (1236), Murcia (1241) and Sevilla (1248).
1479	Castile and Aragón united under **Isabella and Fernando**.
1492	**Fall of Granada**, the last Moorish kingdom. **Discovery of America** by Columbus.
1516	**Carlos V** succeeds to throne and (1520) becomes the Holy Roman Emperor. "**Golden Age**'.
1519	Cortés lands in Mexico.
1532	Pizarro "discovers" Peru.
1556	**Felipe II** (d. 1598).
1588	Sinking of the Armada.
1609	Expulsion of Moriscos, last remaining Spanish Muslims.
1700	War of Spanish Succession brings Felipe V (1713–46), a Bourbon, to the throne. British seize Gibraltar.
1808	**French occupy Spain**.
1811	Venezuela declares independence: others follow.
1835	**First Carlist War**.
1874	**Second Carlist War**.
1898	Loss of Cuba, Spain's last American colony.
1923	Primo de Rivera dictatorship.
1931	Second Republic.
1936–9	**Spanish Civil War**.
1939	**Franco dictatorship** begins.
1975	Death of Franco; **restoration of democracy**.
1982	Election of Socialist government under Prime Minister Felipe González.
1992	
1996	Election of first minority Partido Popular (Conservative) government led by José María Aznar.
1997	

First **Gothic cathedrals** built at Burgos (1221), Toledo (1227) and León (1258). Catalan Gothic also develops in 1220s, best seen in Barcelona's Barri Gòtic and Girona.

Granada's **Alhambra** palace constructed under Ibn Ahmar (1238–75) and his successors. Craftsmen from Granada also construct Sevilla Alcázar for Pedro the Cruel (1350–69).
Sevilla Cathedral (1402–1506).
Isabelline style of late Gothic age of castle building: Coca and Segovia are outstanding.
Last Gothic cathedrals built at Salamanca (1512) and Segovia (1522).
Renaissance reaches Spain. Elaborate early style is known as Plateresque (best represented at Salamanca). Later, key figures include Diego de Siloé (1495–1563; Burgos, Granada, etc) and Andrés de Valdelvira (d. 1565; Jaén, Úbeda and Baeza).

Juan de Herrera (1530–97) introduces new austerity in the Escorial.
Painters and sculptors include: El Greco (1540–1614; Toledo), Ribalta (1551–1628), Ribera (1591–1652), Zurbarán (1598–1664), Alonso Cano (1601–67), Velázquez (1599–1660), Murillo (1618–1682), Roldán (1624–1700), de Mena (1628–1688), Martínez Montañés (1580–1649). Best collections of all at Madrid's Prado.
Baroque develops in reaction to the severity of High Renaissance and reaches a flamboyant peak in the Churrigueresque style of the C18th. (Salamanca's Plaza Mayor, and altarpieces throughout Spain, and above all the Obradoiro facade at Santiago.) Last great cathedrals built at Valencia, Murcia and Cádiz.
Francisco de Goya (1746–1828). Royal Palaces of Madrid and Aranjuez.

Dissolution of monasteries.

Antoni Gaudí (1852–1926) and **Modernisme**, or *modernista* (Art Nouveau) movement in Barcelona.
Picasso (1883–1973; museum in Barcelona, *Guernica* in Madrid); Joan **Miró** (1893–1982; museum in Barcelona); Salvador **Dalí** (1904–89; museum at Figueres).

Antonio Saura and **abstract artists** (Museum of Abstract Art, Cuenca).

Much new building in Barcelona for the **Olympics** and in Sevilla for **Expo '92**.

Guggenheim museum opened in Bilbao.

ARCHITECTURE

Spain's architectural legacy is a highly distinctive one, made up of a mixture of styles quite unlike anything else in Europe. The country was usually slow to pick up on the main currents of European architecture, and when a new style was adopted it was often in an extreme or stylized form. There are French, Dutch, German and Italian currents, but all were synthesized into something uniquely Spanish. Centuries of Moorish occupation have left an indelible mark, too, manifested both in the handful of wonderful buildings which represent the highpoint of Moorish civilization in Andalucía, and in a powerful influence on Christian and secular architecture, including the layout of entire towns.

There has been less of the wanton destruction of old buildings in Spain than in most other countries, and in general the architecture here is astonishingly well preserved. There's perhaps less purity of form than elsewhere in Europe – additions over the years have left many buildings with a medley of different styles – but no other country can boast quite as many old churches, castles and unspoiled towns and villages.

At the risk of making generalizations, it's possible to identify a number of **trends** in the buildings of Spain. As a rule, there is an emphasis on the longitudinal, and on solidity of construction. A heavy use of surface ornament is often popular, with elaborate doorways and rich decoration. Because of the warm climate there is an interest in outdoor living and a need for cool and open space, which accounts for the prevalence of patios in civic buildings and cloisters in religious edifices, including those which were not monastic. There is also a tendency to break up long vistas by various means, creating a variety of compartments within a large space.

THE ROMAN PERIOD

Although fragments of earlier civilizations do exist, Spain's architectural history (in terms of surviving buildings) begins in the **Roman** period, from which there remain a number of remarkable structures. These have no particular Spanish flavour, nor were they to prove as influential on subsequent developments as in some other countries, but nonetheless the aqueduct at **Segovia**, the bridge at **Alcántara** (the highest in the Roman world and still in use), and the theatre and associated remains at **Mérida** belong among the first rank of Roman survivals anywhere. There's another fine group in and around **Tarragona**, with walls, a necropolis, an arena, a forum and a praetorium in the city itself, and more notably an aqueduct, the Centcelles Mausoleum, the Arco de Bar and the Torre de Scipio all within a radius of a few kilometres.

Other Roman monuments worthy of special note include the walls of Lugo, the amphitheatre and castle at Sagunto, and the three-span triumphal arch at Medinaceli. Excavations of complete towns can be seen at Empúries, Itálica, Numancia and Bilbilis.

VISIGOTHIC AND ASTURIAN PERIODS

The **Visigothic** period, which succeeded the Roman, bequeathed a small number of buildings of uncertain date. Visigothic buildings have simple exteriors, and were the first in Spain to adopt the horseshoe arch (later to be altered and used widely by the Moors). They also developed elements from Roman buildings, the most refined example of which is at **Quintanilla de las Viñas** in Old Castile, a church whose exterior is enlivened by delicately carved stone friezes set in bands; inside there's a triumphal arch over the apse, carved with the earliest surviving representation of Christ in Spain.

Other remnants of the era survive at the modern industrial town of **Tarrasa** in Catalunya, formerly Egara, in the shape of three churches, one of which – the Baptistery of San Miguel – dates from the fifth or sixth century; the other two have apses that are probably of ninth-century construction. Other Visigothic buildings include part of the crypt of Palencia Cathedral, and the nearby basilica of San Juan at Baños de Cerrato, documented as seventh-century.

Hard on the heels of the Visigothic epoch was the **Asturian** period, named after the small kingdom on the northern coast, which developed its own style during the ninth century. This retained Visigothic elements alongside technical developments that anticipated the general European trends still to come. A little group of buildings centred around **Oviedo** – the Cámara Santa, the church of Santulano in the city itself, San Miguel de Lillo and Santa María de Naranco on the slopes of Monte Naranco nearby – are, unusually in Spanish history, clearly superior to and more highly developed than any contemporary work in Europe. The last represents the pinnacle of the style, a perfectly proportioned little building with barrel vaulting and arches supported on pilasters, as well as delicate decoration using Roman and Byzantine elements. The isolated surrounding countryside holds a few similar buildings from the succeeding century, but the Asturian style was soon to be swallowed up by the new Romanesque movement which swept across the north of Spain from France and Italy.

THE MOORISH PERIOD

By this time most of Spain was under Muslim domination. It remained so, at least in part, until the final defeat of the Moors in 1492. During this period Moorish architecture did not develop in the way we understand the word, and it is best to consider the different epochs of building separately.

The first real style was the **Caliphate**, centred around Córdoba, whose great surviving monument – the **Mezquita** – was built and added to over a period from the eighth to the tenth century. The Caliphate style demonstrates most of the vocabulary used by Moorish builders over the years – horseshoe, cusped and multifoil arches, the contrasting use of courses of stone and brick, the use of interlacing as a particular feature of design, doors surmounted by blind arcades, stucco work, and the ornamental use of calligraphy along with geometric and plant motifs. Various technical innovations, too, were introduced in the construction of the Mezquita, from the original solution of two-tiered arches to give greater height to the ribbed dome vaults in front of the *mihrab* (prayer-niche).

Another example of the Caliphate style, the (now ruined) palace-city of **Medina Azahara**, just outside Córdoba, was no less splendid than the Mezquita. Many of its buildings were produced according to the descriptions of Solomon's temple. In **Toledo**, El Cristo de la Luz is a small-scale Caliphate mosque, and the old Bisagra Gate was part of the fortifications of that time. As the Reconquest progressed, other fortifications went up. Gormaz was begun in around 965. Only part of the original Moorish building has survived, including two gateways. Calatayud, in the north, holds more fortifications of the period, probably of an even earlier date.

With the fall of the Caliphate at the end of the eleventh century, Moorish Spain was divided into independent kingdoms or **taifas**, giving rise to the *alcazabas* or castles at Granada, Málaga, Guadix, Almería, Tarifa and Carmona. The Aljafería palace in Zaragoza also dates from this period, much altered over the years but preserving its mosque and a tower. The strongest *taifa* was at Sevilla, where later the **Almohad** dynasty created an art of refined brickwork and left behind the Patio de Yeso in the Alcázar, the Torre del Oro, which originally formed part of the city's fortifications, and the Giralda – former minaret of the mosque and arguably the finest tower ever built in the Arab world.

The apotheosis of pure Muslim art came, however, with the **Nasrid** dynasty in Granada, the last city to fall to the Christians. The gorgeously opulent palace of the **Alhambra** went up between the thirteenth and fifteenth centuries. Built on a hill against the romantic backdrop of the Sierra Nevada, this structure provided the necessary partner in the union between art and nature sought by the Moorish architects, especially in the lush gardens of the more modest Generalife section. As for the palace itself, the buildings are structurally very poor, with no exterior features of note; yet the interior, around the two great courtyards, is one of the most intoxicating creations in the world, the culminating ideal of Moorish civilization, built when it was already in irreversible decline.

MOZARABIC AND MUDÉJAR

The Moorish occupation had an indelible influence on the architecture of Spain, and led directly to two hybrid architectural styles unique to the country – **Mozarabic** and Mudéjar. The former was the style of Christians subjugated by the Moors who retained their old religion but built in the Arabic style. Their churches are mostly in isolated situations – San Miguel de Escalada east of León, Santa María de Lebena near the Picos de Europa and San Baudelio near Berlanga de Duero in Soria Province are the finest examples.

Mudéjar is far more common, the style of the Arabs who stayed on after their homelands had been conquered, or who had migrated to the Christian kingdoms. Often they proved to be both the most skilful builders and the cheapest workforce, and they left their mark on almost all of the country over a period of several centuries. They continued to build predominantly in brick, mainly working on the construction of parish churches, resulting in an odd – though unmistakably Moorish – Christian-Islamic hybrid that some claim is barely a distinct architectural style at all. There are details of Mudéjar buildings under the relevant European headings, below, although a number deserve inclusion here as being more firmly within the Arab tradition. Among these are the palaces of Tordesillas and the Alcázar in Sevilla; various secular buildings in Toledo; the Chapel of the Assumption of Santiago at Las Huelgas; and the synagogues of Toledo and Córdoba.

THE ROMANESQUE

Back in the mainstream of European architecture, the **Romanesque** style in Spain is most associated with the churches, bridges and hospices built along the **pilgrim road** to Santiago de Compostela. None of the hospices has survived, but the Puente la Reina in Navarra is the most famous of a number of Romanesque-era bridges. The churches come in various shapes and forms, but all include beautiful sculpture. The cathedral of Jaca, the monasteries of Santa Cruz de la Seros, San Juan de la Peña and Leyre, and the churches of Santa María la Real at Sanguesa, San Miguel at Estella, San Martín at Fromista and San Isidoro at León are the most notable examples, but the climax, of the style as of the pilgrimage, came with the great **Cathedral of Santiago** itself. This is now almost entirely encased by Baroque additions, but preserves the original shape of the interior. Begun around 1070, it was built to allow as much space as possible for the pilgrims to circulate – hence the large triforium gallery, and the ambulatory with radiating chapels. Santiago's cathedral also served as a model for many contemporary derivations, particularly the nearby cathedrals of Lugo, Orense and Tuy.

Elsewhere, the influence of the great Burgundian abbey of Cluny, which so influenced the development of the pilgrimage, can be seen most clearly at **San Vicente** in Ávila. Another building closely related to the pilgrimage churches is the monastery of **Santo Domingo de Silos**, where the architecture and superb bas-reliefs of the cloisters, the only surviving part of the original building, are clearly derived from French models. There's an additional ingredient, too: most of the capitals here show an unmistakable Moorish influence – a very early example of the mix of East and West to be found in Spain.

Other Romanesque buildings tend towards regional variants. In **Catalunya**, whose architectural history so often diverges from that of the rest of Spain, the influence was more from Lombardy than France, with tall, square bell towers, prominent apses, blind arcading and little sculptural detail – although this last was later to become important, for example in the cloisters of the cathedral and San Pedro in Girona.

Belfries were a dominant feature in **Segovia**, where the main innovation was the construction of covered arcades in the manner of cloisters built against the sides of the building, making the parish churches of this city amongst the most distinctive in Spain. **Soria**'s churches, particularly San Domingo, recall those of Poitiers, although the fantastic cloister of San Juan de Duero defies classification in its combination of the round-headed Romanesque, early pointed Gothic, and Moorish horseshoe and intersecting arches in one extraordinarily capricious composition. **Zamora** was unusual in having a

Byzantine influence; also its portals tended to lack tympana, but had richly carved archivolts. Finally, there are a number of churches in a crossover **Mudéjar**/Romanesque style in such places as Toledo, Sahagún, Cúellar and Arévalo.

Military architecture of this period is dominated by the complete walls of Ávila, the best preserved in Europe, and by the castle at Loarre, the most spectacular of the early Christian castles built to defend the conquered lands. Survivors of civil buildings are few and far between, but there are precious examples in the form of the palaces of Estella and Huesca.

THE TRANSITIONAL STYLE

With the advent of the Cistercian reforms, the **Transitional** style was introduced to Spain in the middle of the twelfth century, first in a series of monasteries – La Oliva, Veruela, Poblet, Santes Creus, Las Huelgas and Santa María la Huerta – that are notable for massiveness of construction combined with the introduction of such Gothic characteristics as the pointed arch and the ribbed vault.

In some ways, **La Oliva** can claim to be the first Gothic building in Spain, although in both its solidity and ground plan it is still Romanesque in spirit. The severe, unadorned style of the Cistercians was to have a great impact at a time when the rest of Europe was moving towards an appreciation of the structural advantages of Gothic, not quickly realized in Spain. The late twelfth and early thirteenth centuries saw the construction of a number of cathedrals in the Transitional style – Siguenza, Ávila, Santo Domingo de la Calzada, Tarragona and Lleida – all of which had fortress-like features and were indeed at times used for defensive purposes. Similar is the Collegiate church at Tudela, although the sculpture here, in direct contravention of Cistercian rules, is among the richest in Spain.

A few buildings of the same period show clear **Byzantine** influence – the Old Cathedral of Salamanca, Zamora Cathedral and the Colegiata at Toro – each with a distinctive central dome, although their design otherwise shows normal Transitional elements. Closely related are the cathedral of Ciudad Rodrigo and the often octagonally shaped buildings associated with the Knights Templar: La Vera Cruz in Segovia, and two mysterious buildings on the Pilgrim Route whose exact nature is uncertain – Eunate and Torres de Río.

THE GOTHIC STYLE

Examples of the early **Gothic** style in Spain are rare, and those that there are seem to derive from French and English sources. The refectory of Santa María la Huerta is as pure and elegant as the best in France; Cuenca Cathedral, begun about 1200, seems to derive from a Norman or English model. Later, buildings began to develop a more specifically Spanish style, eschewing any notions of purity of form.

Three great cathedrals commenced in the 1220s best exemplify the increasingly Spanish features of the churches of the time. Of these, the overall plans and building of **Burgos** and **Toledo** are obviously indebted to French models, but they are far from the grace and lightness of the great French Gothic cathedrals. The windows are much smaller – partly, perhaps, to cut down on excessive sunlight, partly to preserve a greater sense of mystery than their French equivalents did. Both were also given the rich interior decoration that soon became the norm for Spanish cathedrals, most characteristic of which was the *coro*, an elaborate set of choir stalls often enclosed by a *trascoro* or retrochoir, situated in the nave – a feature that looks odd to those used to the chancel-based choirs of northern Europe. The reasons for this are unclear, but it seems it was associated with the predominance of the choir services of the clergy, which meant that the construction of the *coro* made the best use of the space; it may also have been felt that the chancel should be reserved solely for the Holy Sacrament, and not downgraded for any other purpose.

Equally typical are the giant *retablos*, the most important of which are situated over the high altar, again masking the architecture. Generally these were carved and multicoloured, and contained a series of scenes from the life of Christ and of the Virgin, perhaps along with statues of saints. Basically their function was similar to that of stained-glass windows in the cathedrals of France, providing pictorial representation of the Bible to an illiterate population. Smaller *retablos*, either painted or carved, were placed over smaller altars. In addition, tombs of monarchs, aristocratic families, bishops and saints were often placed in specially built chapels, and sometimes enclosed by iron gates or grilles (*rejas*) which were often of a highly elaborate workmanship and would enclose the entrances to the *coro* and the chancel too. The overall effect of all this decoration can appear oversumptuous to the modern eye, but it gives a better impression of a medieval cathedral than anything that can be found in northern Europe, where reformation, revolution, war and restoration have combined to leave buildings that are architecturally far purer but spiritually far less authentic.

The third great cathedral of the 1200s, **León**, was the only one to adopt the normal French system of triple portal, prominent flying buttresses and large windows filled with brilliantly coloured stained glass. Even here, however, there were Spanish touches, such as the cloister and its dependencies, and the later construction of a *coro*.

All the other cathedrals followed the model of Burgos and Toledo. **El Burgo de Osma** is in a way a miniature version of them, although it's purer Gothic in form. **Palencia**, built in the fourteenth and fifteenth centuries, is unusual in that most of its decoration is roughly contemporary with the architecture, with very few later additions. At **Pamplona** and **Huesca**, the architects built in the knowledge that there would be a *coro* in the nave – though ironically these were removed relatively recently by restorers. Pamplona's cloister, the earliest part of the building, is perhaps the most beautiful Gothic cloister in Spain. It has several fine doorways and a chapel with an exquisite star vault, a feature that was to be Spain's main contribution to the vocabulary of Gothic architecture, as characteristic as fan vaulting in England, although far more common – and with an obvious debt to Moorish models. There are other, equally grand examples of the national Gothic style: **Murcia** and **Oviedo** are two, **Sevilla** a more spectacular one, its vast size determined by the ground plan of the mosque that preceded it.

REGIONAL STYLES

Regional forms of Gothic are found in Catalunya and Aragón. In **Catalunya**, churches were built with huge arcades, omitting the triforium and including only a small clerestory. Long spans were also common; aisles, if there were any, were very nearly the same height as the nave; buttresses were internalized by the construction

of tall, straight-walled chapels built between them, lending a rather sober appearance to the outside. Barcelona's **Cathedral of Santa María del Mar** is a good example of all these features, as is **Palma Cathedral**, although the most spectacular of the Catalan cathedrals is **Girona** – so daring structurally as to be admired more for its engineering than its aesthetic appeal.

In **Aragón** there was strong Mudéjar influence, which extended even to the cathedrals of **Zaragoza**, **Tarazona** and **Teruel**. The towers of these cities, and of **Calatayud**, tend to be either square in shape and decorated with ceramic tiles that glisten in the sun, or else octagonal and of brick only. Both show a virtuoso skill in decoration with what appear to be very basic and unpromising materials. Each of the cathedrals has a central cupola, while Tarazona has an amazing cloister filled with Mudéjar ornament. There's another unusual cloister far away in Guadalupe, while more orthodox Mudéjar Gothic churches are all over, though there's a fine concentration in **Toledo**.

MILITARY ARCHITECTURE

Turning to **military architecture**, a number of fortified towns from the Gothic period still survive. Toledo has several gateways and two bridges of the era, and there are fine examples of walls at Albarracín, Daroca, Morella, Berlanga de Duero, Madrigal de las Altes Torres and Montblanch. Spain's castles of this period are without parallel in Europe. However, those that had a genuine function in the Reconquest are as a rule in the poorest condition, while those that look most impressive today often had little if any defensive purpose. It should be remembered that there is no Spanish equivalent at any time to the English or French country house. Where great houses were built by the nobility in Spain, they often resembled castles, even if they were never used for military purposes.

Perhaps the finest fourteenth-century castle is that of **Bellver** near Palma, a circular structure built as a summer residence by the kings of Mallorca. The great fifteenth-century castle at **Olite** is a palace in the pastiche form on a grand scale. For all the monumentality of its towers, many are wholly ornamental and would have been quite useless in time of war. Unfortunately, what you see today gives little hint of the richness of the former interior decoration.

Along the banks of the Duero are castles which were genuinely in action at the time of the Reconquest. **Gormaz** is particularly interesting, showing how an originally Moorish building was adapted by the Christians after its capture. **Peñafiel**'s fifteenth-century castle is actually the successor to the one that was built as protection against the Moors; apart from its own severe beauty, it clearly shows the importance of a strong strategic location. The many brick castles in the **area of Segovia and Valladolid** should be thought of more as expressions of the wealth and power of the nobility than as genuine military constructions of the time. These often incorporated Mudéjar features, and their construction was often in reality rather delicate: **Coca** is the best example of this.

CIVIL BUILDINGS AND LATE GOTHIC

The legacy of **Gothic civil architecture** is also impressive. Large numbers of towns preserve their medieval character in layout and design, even if many of the houses are not, strictly speaking, original. Important town mansions survive all over the country, often characterized by the carving of a coat of arms on the facade. **Cáceres**, in Extremadura, is probably the richest place for seigneurial houses, although most of the other towns in this province are also notable for vernacular architecture of this, and later dates. Elsewhere, the shipyards of **Barcelona** constitute a unique survival from the Gothic period, as do parts of the Barri Gòtic, which contains a number of original municipal buildings. Barcelona also has the earliest lonja, or exchange – later and more exotic examples of which can be found in Valencia, Palma and Zaragoza.

Spanish **late Gothic** architecture is particularly spectacular, the increasing ornamentation partly the result of the mid-fifteenth-century influx of artists from Germany and the Netherlands to Spain. **Burgos** and **Toledo** were the centre of the developing style. Juan de Colonia built the superb openwork spires of Burgos Cathedral, modelled on those of his native Cologne – which themselves, ironically, existed only on paper until the nineteenth century. His son, Simon, was responsible for other work on the same building, particularly the Capilla del Condestable at the east end, and worked with his father on the Cartuja de

Miraflores. At the same time, Anequin de Egas from Brussels began a series of additions to Toledo Cathedral.

A little later the focus shifted to **Valladolid** and became increasingly florid – the **Isabelline** style – reaching its most extreme in the facades of San Pablo and the Colegio San Gregorio. It's not known who was responsible for these, or for the equally ornate facade of Santa María in Aranda de Duero, though a variety of people have been suggested, not least Juan Guas, who is known to have built San Juan de los Reyes in Toledo, the gallery of the castle at **Manzanares el Real** and perhaps the Palacio del Infantado in **Guadalajara**. The Isabelline style, at its best, combined the Moorish penchant for hanging decoration with standard European motifs, and has been seen by some commentators as the one chance Spain had to create its own special, unified architectural style. However, Isabelline had a very short life. The queen after whom it was named became more enchanted by the Italians before long, and encouraged the adoption of the Renaissance in Spain.

There was also a counter-movement towards a purer Gothic form. The New Cathedral of **Salamanca** and the Cathedral of **Segovia** were both begun in the sixteenth century in what was then a wholly archaic language by Juan Gil de Ontañón, and continued by his son Rodrigo. Juan de Álava also built a number of monuments in this style – San Esteban in Salamanca, part of the cathedral at Plasencia, and the cloisters at Santiago. **Segovia Cathedral**, too – unusually for Spain – displays a remarkable unity of form, using the traditional Gothic elements rejected by earlier builders.

THE RENAISSANCE

Oddly enough, the **Renaissance** was introduced to Spain with the **Collegio Santa Cruz** in Valladolid, just a few hundred metres from the simultaneous construction of two Isabelline facades. The architect, Lorenzo Vázquez, for all his historical importance, remains a rather shadowy figure. (Later, he was to build an Italian Renaissance palace at La Calahorra in Andalucía.) Enrique de Egas, who built the hospitals at Toledo (Santa Cruz), Granada and Santiago, and who also worked in a late Gothic style, as witnessed by his Capilla Real in Granada and his design for the adjoining cathedral, is much better documented.

Much early Spanish Renaissance architecture is termed **Plateresque**, from the profusion of carving which allegedly resembled the work of silversmiths. The term is now applied rather loosely, but it is most associated with **Salamanca**, which is built of an extremely delicate rose-coloured sandstone. The supreme masterpiece of the style is the facade of the **University** here, where instead of the wild and irregular carvings of Valladolid, a generation before, all is order and symmetry while equally ornate. The motifs used in Plateresque carving are wholly Italianate – figures in medallions, *putti*, candelabra, grotesques, garlands of flowers and fruit, scrollwork and coats of arms. No convincing attribution has been made for the university facade, but one Plateresque architect whose work can be traced is **Alonso de Covarrubias**. He built the Capilla de los Reyes Nuevos in Toledo Cathedral, part of the Alcázar and probably the Hospital de Tavera in the same city, and worked on Sigüenza Cathedral, particularly the amazing sacristy. The facade of the University of Alcalá de Henares is a more severe Plateresque masterpiece by Rodrigo Gil de Ontañón; other important works are San Marcos in León by Juan de Badajoz, and the Hospital del Rey near Burgos.

The **High Renaissance**, by contrast, centred around **Andalucía**, the part of the country that was most lacking in Christian architecture following its liberation from the Muslim powers. The real masterpiece of the style is the **Palace of Carlos V** in Granada – incongruously located in the Alhambra, but a superbly pure piece of architecture. It is rare in being based on a round courtyard, and is the only surviving building by Pedro Machuca. As for churches, the leading architect of the Andalucian Renaissance in this field was Diego de Siloé, who began his career as a sculptor in Burgos under his father, Gil, and built the marvellous Plateresque Escalera Dorada in the cathedral there. Following study in Italy, he worked as an architect, devising an ingenious east end for the cathedral at Granada, and designing Guadix Cathedral and El Savador at Úbeda. The last-named was actually built by his pupil, Andrés de Vandelvira, whose own main work is the monumental Cathedral of Jaén. All these buildings show a strongly classical influence.

The severest, purest and greatest Spanish Renaissance architect was **Juan de Herrera**, who succeeded Juan Bautista de Toledo as architect of **El Escorial**, to which he devoted much of his working life. To many, this vast building is excessively sober, particularly in a country where ornamentation has so often reigned supreme. However, it does have a unique grandeur, and illustrates the Spanish penchant for taking any style to its extremes. Herrera's other main building is the **Cathedral of Valladolid**, though sadly only half of this was ever built, and some of that well after Herrera. In this truncated form it can appear rather cold and sombre, although the model for the complete building shows what a well-proportioned, harmonious and majestic edifice it might have become.

THE BAROQUE

For a time, Herrera's style was to spawn a number of imitations, and early **Baroque** architecture was remarkably restrained – Madrid's early seventeenth-century **Plaza Mayor** by Juan Gomez de Mora being a case in point. In the east, Neapolitan influence was paramount, and led to the building of a large number of dignified churches.

Before long, however, this early phase gave way to an exuberant, playful and confident style that is perhaps Spain's most singular contribution to European architecture, the **Churrigueresque** – taken from the name of the family of architects, the Churrigueras, with whom the style was most associated. Ironically, their own work in architecture was far less ornate than that of many of their successors, although they also designed **retablos**, which are as embellished as anything that followed, so large as to seem almost pieces of architecture in themselves. These were typically of carved wood, painted and gilded, with twisted columns populated by saints in visionary or ecstatic mood and swirling processions of angels. *Retablos* of this type were soon to be found in churches all over Spain. Often the work of far cruder imitators, they raised the ire of visiting Protestant travellers, who used the term "Churrigueresque" to signify all that was basest in art. It's still a pejorative term, although the Churrigueras did actually create a number of masterpieces.

José, the eldest brother, created a complete planned town in **Nuevo Baztán**, not far from Madrid. Alberto, the youngest and most talented, laid out the **Plaza Mayor** in Salamanca in collaboration with Andrés García de Quiñones – a superb and harmonious piece of town planning, integrated wonderfully with the town's older buildings, and with the plain sides enlivened by carvings deriving from Plateresque work, and the rhythmic facade of the *Ayuntamiento* providing a central focus on the north side.

The Churrigeras's contemporaries were more profusely ornate, often imitating the form of the *retablos* in their portals, perhaps the finest example of which is the **Hospicio San Fernando** in Madrid by Pedro de Ribera. Another new architectural feature was the transparente, in which a lavish altarpiece is lit from above by a window cut in the vault, giving a highly theatrical effect. The most famous example is that in **Toledo Cathedral** by Narciso Tomé, a brilliant piece of illusionism when the sun shines through, though in an utterly incongruous setting.

The Baroque style was also, of course, used when making additions to existing buildings, something you see all over Spain. Sometimes the merging of Baroque and medieval was triumphantly successful, as in the mid-eighteenth-century Obradoiro facade of **Santiago Cathedral** by Fernando Casas y Novoa, the climax of about a century's work, encasing the old Romanesque building in a lively Baroque exterior. While the loss of the Romanesque exterior is regrettable, particularly as some of the Baroque building is mediocre, the facade ranks as one of the most joyous creations in all architecture, and the ultimate triumph of Spanish Baroque. Other notably successful Baroque additions are the towers of the cathedrals of El Burgo de Osma, Santo Domingo de la Calzada and Murcia, which all harmonize surprisingly well with the existing structures, and give them a dimension they previously lacked. Many other additions, however, were far less fortunate: much of the time Baroque builders paid insufficient attention to the scale, style and materials of the existing work, and even when each is a competent piece of work in its own right, old and new scream at each other in horror.

Because of the trend towards enlivening old buildings, only one complete Baroque cathedral was built in Spain, at **Cádiz**. Nor are there many notable Baroque monasteries, although a number of charterhouses (*cartujas*) were built, not least at **Granada**, which became more and

more extreme as construction progressed, culminating in the outrageous *sagrario* (sacristy) by Francesco Hurtado Izquiero. However, Spanish Baroque never found favour at court, where Italian and French models were preferred, and architects and decorators were imported from these countries, producing the Bourbon palaces of Aranjuez, La Granja de San Ildefonso and Madrid, which stand apart from Spanish buildings of the period. Filippo Juvara, the famous architect of Turin, was summoned to Spain in the penultimate year of his life to design the garden front of La Granja and the overall plan for Madrid, although both were executed by his pupil, Giovanni Battista Sachetti.

NEOCLASSICISM

In time, the court taste changed to **Neoclassical**, enforced by the mid-century establishment of academies, and the presiding architectural style became heavy and monumental in scale. The dominant figure was **Ventura Rodríguez**, a technically competent architect who built a lavish Augustinian church in **Valladolid** and completed the **Basílica del Pilar** in Zaragoza – a colossal building with elements drawn from a variety of styles that is more notable for its grandiose outline than for any other feature. But Rodríguez's talents were not put to their best use: his facade for **Pamplona Cathedral** would look fine on a bank but is wholly incongruous for a church, and a serious distraction in what is otherwise a fine building; and his plain, rather nondescript church at **Santo Domingo de Silos** is a similarly poor partner for the great cloister there. Another leading Neoclassical architect was **Juan de Villanueva**, who built the **Prado** (actually as a natural history museum) and the two **Casitas** at El Escorial.

Spain's subsequent provincial history is mirrored in the paucity of buildings of much consequence. The slow process of industrial and social change meant that there were few of the self-confident expressions of prosperity found all over northern Europe. There were a host of imitative styles, but it is really only on the small scale that they give much pleasure. **Neo-Gothic**, also, was nowhere near as vital or as prevalent as elsewhere: the cathedrals built in this style, at **San Sebastián** and **Vitoria**, are not especially notable, and the most satisfying work was probably the completion of **Barcelona Cathedral**, which was actually accomplished according to a fifteenth-century plan.

MODERNISME

Barcelona provides the one bright spot in Spain's otherwise gloomy architectural history of the past two centuries, showing once again how distinctive Catalunya's heritage is. The last quarter of the nineteenth century was a turbulent time there – a fact mirrored in the **Modernisme** (or *modernista*) movement in architecture, which created a remarkable number of challenging, Art Nouveau-type buildings until well into the present century.

The dominant genius was **Antoni Gaudí**, one of the most distinctive voices of the age – indeed, of any age. He was interested not merely in architecture but also in sculpture and interior design, including lighting. His main architectural influences were Moorish and Gothic, which he considered the greatest European style. From the former he took towers, *trompe l'oeil* effects, repeated elements, ceramics, cornices, dragons and the use of water, all employed, like his Gothic influences, in a free and fantastic way. He was also influenced by the natural world: trees, rocks, embankments, animals, birds, eroded and organic forms. He combined all these elements in an amazing – and distinctive – architectural vocabulary. Some of his projects were almost impossibly ambitious. He worked for over forty years on the **Sagrada Familia**, yet only built a small portion. The **Parc Güell** was another vast project for a complete garden city, a commercial failure that has become a successful public park. Still, many less grandiose plans in a variety of forms were completed in Barcelona, and his work can also be seen in Astorga, León and Comillas.

Gaudí stands out among his **contemporaries**, but there are a number of other architects of the time worthy of note, such as Lluís Domènech i Montaner, who was responsible for the sumptuous Palau de la Musica in Barcelona and who, with Juan Martorell, built at Comillas. These other architects, though, came nowhere near to developing the personal style of Gaudí and were far less utopian in their thinking.

MODERN

Beyond the *Modernisme* movement, much of Spain's **modern architecture** is best passed over. The buildings for the abortive "Fair of the Americas" in Sevilla in 1929 do have a certain period charm, but there's not much that's good about the bloated public buildings that went up in Madrid before and after the Civil War. The last thirty years have seen the wholesale destruction of large sections of the coast, particularly the south and east, as Spain led the way in speculative building projects, wiping out old communities in order to develop the country's tourist facilities; in addition, many of the larger cities have been spoiled by ugly and unchecked modern sprawl – Valladolid and Zaragoza are particularly good examples of irretrievably damaged cities.

The most prestigious (if politically obnoxious) building project of recent years was Franco's **Valley of the Fallen** outside Madrid, which commemorates the dead of the Civil War, and also houses the Generalísimo's own tomb. It's a typical example of the sort of building favoured by dictators – classical in inspiration, overbearing in style.

More exciting is the project to complete Gaudí's **Sagrada Familia**, which is likely to take a century or more. It remains to be seen whether the finishing process will take the form of pastiche of the master or modern innovation. Regrettably, the continuing construction of **Madrid Cathedral** is another opportunity missed. The Neo-Romanesque crypt built at the end of the last century has been succeeded by a dull medley of Neo-Gothic and Neoclassical, unlikely to produce anything very challenging.

Only in Catalunya was modern architecture kept alive at all, through the work of local architects such as Oriol Bohigas, Ricardo Bofill and Federico Correa. The post-Franco period which ushered in the autonomous governments saw architects throwing off the shackles as each region vied to create a unique identity following the long years of severe centralization. Barcelona was at the forefront of this movement and the city streaked ahead with a burst of creativity, culminating with a series of massive projects undertaken for the 1992 Olympics. Recently, Barcelona has been joined by Madrid and Sevilla (with cities such as Bilbao, with its spectacular new Guggenheim museum designed by American Frank O'Gehry, coming up fast), which have produced landmark buildings generally regarded as being at the cutting edge of European design. Among the notable projects of the last decade a handful will serve to indicate the riches which have drawn in architects and designers worldwide to learn from and be inspired by Spain's dramatic architectural revolution: Santiago Calatrava's Bilbao Airport and bridges in Sevilla and Barcelona; Rafael Moneo's Atocha Station and Thyssen–Bornemisza Museum (both Madrid), Sevilla Airport and Roman Museum (Mérida); Mackay, Bohigas and Martorell's Olympic Village (Barcelona); Kruz and Ortíz's Santa Justa Station (Sevilla); Bofill's Barcelona Airport and Teatro Nacional de Catalunya (Barcelona); Miralles and Pinos's cemetery at Igualada (Catalunya); Viaplana and Piñon's Rambla del Mar and Maremagnum (Port Vell, Barcelona); Miralles' sports stadium (Huelva); Junquera and Perez-Pita's Caja de Madrid (Majadahonda, Madrid).

Away from the big cities, and to Spain's further credit, most of the smaller towns have been untouched by modern building programmes, and remain delightfully unspoiled. There has grown up, since the return to democracy, a genuine concern about the country's heritage, which was pretty much taken for granted in the past, and a good deal of restoration work is now under way. Spain's great monuments remain, but there are still equally potent joys to be found in the country's townscapes, whether they be simple agricultural villages, complete small towns such as Santillana del Mar and Covarrubias, or formerly important cities such as Toledo, Segovia, Salamanca and Santiago.

Gordon McLachlan

SPANISH PAINTING

From the Middle Ages to the present day, the history of Spanish painting is a chequered one, more a series of high spots – El Greco, Velázquez, Goya, Picasso – than a continuous process of development. Influence from abroad has often been a factor, with somewhat mixed results. Yet at its best Spanish painting can stand comparison with that of any other country, not least in its intensity: the great masterpieces of Spain have a power that has seldom been equalled elsewhere.

BEGINNERS

Early examples of this strength of expression can be found in the **illuminated manuscripts** and **mural paintings** of the eleventh and twelfth centuries. Dominant among the manuscripts are the many versions of Beatus's *Commentaries on the Apocalypse*, the original text of which, written by an eighth-century Spanish monk, inspired a whole series of versions illuminating the text with brilliantly coloured miniatures. These books have found their way into libraries all over the world, but many still remain in Spain, with those in Girona and El Burgo de Osma particularly worthy of note.

The great decorative plans of village churches are also characteristic of the period, especially in Catalunya, though for the most part these are

no longer in situ; many were saved earlier this century, just in time to prevent them from deteriorating irrevocably, and have been removed to museums, of which Barcelona's have by far the finest collection. The most imposing example of this style is by the so-called **Master of Tahull**, whose decoration of the apse of the church of San Clemente combines a Byzantine hierarchical composition with the vibrant colours and strong outlines of the manuscript illuminators. His overall rawness and monumentality seem strangely anticipatory of much of the best modern art.

Amazingly, two other highly talented painters also worked in the village of Tahull in the 1120s: art historians have christened them the **Master of Maderuelo** and the **Master of the Last Judgement**. Another notable artist of the period is the **Master of Pedret**, who incorporated scenes of everyday and natural life into his paintings.

Catalan studios also produced painted wooden altar frontals, often based on a central figure of a saint, surrounded by scenes from his life. In time, this grew in scale into the large *retablo* over the high altar – a key feature of Spanish churches for centuries. The most remarkable frescoes outside Catalunya are those of the Panteón de los Reyes in San Isidoro in León. These date from the second half of the twelfth century, and show a softer, more courtly style, perhaps influenced by French models.

THE CATALAN SCHOOL

In the Gothic period, Catalunya's predominance continued, rivalled only by Valencia. The leader of the school was **Ferrer Bassa** (c.1285–1348), court painter to Pedro IV of Aragón and a manuscript illuminator. Unfortunately, his only certain surviving work comes from late in his long career – a series of murals in the Convent of Pedralbes in Barcelona. These are charming, notable for their colouring and descriptive qualities, along with a sense of movement and skilled draughtsmanship, and are clearly influenced by the paintings of the Sienese school, though they're freer and less refined. Bassa may also have been influenced by the rounder qualities of Giotto and the Florentine school – Italian currents that are also found in the work of the artist's followers, along with various French trends.

The most notable names of this school were **Jaume Serra** (d. 1395), his brother, **Pere**

Serra (d. 1408), **Ramón Destorrents** (1346–91), **Luís Borrassa** (d. 1424) and **Ramón de Mur** (d. 1435). **Bernat Martorell** (d. 1452) is perhaps the most appealing of the group, a notable draughtsman who worked very carefully and deliberately, striving to give character to faces in his paintings. **Luís Daimau** (d. 1460) came strongly under the influence of contemporary Flemish painting, in particular that of Jan van Eyck, and no other foreign currents are discernible in his work. **Jaume Huguet** (c.1414–92) blended this new realism to the traditional forms of the Catalan school, and can thus be seen as a representative of the International Gothic style of painting.

THE VALENCIAN SCHOOL

The Valencian school tended towards a more purely Italian influence, although one of its main painters, **Andrés Marzal de Sax** (d. 1410), may have been German. Other notable names are **Pedro Nicolau** (d. 1410), **Jaime Baco** ("Jacomart") (d. 1461), **Juan Rexach** (1431–92) and **Rodrigo de Osona** (d. 1510), the last of whom was influenced by the Renaissance. The greatest of all the Spanish Primitives, however, was **Bartolomé Bermejo** (d. 1495/8), originally from Córdoba, who worked in both Valencia and Barcelona. He seems to have had a fairly long career but only a few works, of a consistently high quality, survive. His earlier paintings, of which the Prado's *Santo Domingo de Silos* is a good example, are sumptuous; the later works, particularly the *Pietà* in Barcelona Cathedral, are altogether more complex, with a haunting sense of mystery and a Flemish and French influence that marks the introduction of oil painting to Spain.

THE CASTILIAN SCHOOL

In Castile, artists of foreign origin predominated – **Deillo Delli** ("Nicolas Florentino") (d. 1470) in Salamanca, **Nicolás Frances** (1425–68) in León, **Jorge Inglés** (dates unknown) in Valdololid, and **Juan de Flandes** (d. 1514) in Salamanca and Valencia. The last became court painter to Isabella la Católica and introduced a Renaissance sense of space along with the beautiful modelling and colouring typical of the Flemish school. There was a rustic local school active in Ávila, however, and towards the end of the century native artists came increasingly to

the fore. Particularly notable is **Fernando Gallego** (c.1440–1507), who worked in Zamora and Extremadura. Superficially, his paintings seem strongly reminiscent of Flemish types, but his exaggerated sense of drama – manifested in distorted expressions, strange postures and movements frozen in mid-course – is far removed from these models. Nonetheless, the garments are correctly drawn, and landscape is often a feature of the backgrounds.

Pedro Berruguete (c.1450–1504) was originally trained in the Flemish style, but spent an extended period in Italy at the court of Urbino, where he remained until 1482. His productions from this period are so close to those of the Fleming Justus van Gent that art historians have frequently been unable to distinguish between them. On his return to Spain, Berruguete worked in a hybrid style: although his drawing was precise and he introduced chiaroscuro to Spanish art, he persisted in using the traditional gold backgrounds – an anachronistic mixture that is surprisingly satisfying. Berruguete was never a slavish imitator of Italian models, like too many of his successors, and his most impressive works are those with crowd scenes, where the differentiation of types and attitudes is remarkable. **Alonso Berruguete** (1486–1561), his son, also went to Italy, and his paintings are heavily Mannerist in style, with strong drawing and harsh colours. His work as a sculptor is more significant: uneven in quality but sometimes truly inspired, with many powerful and intensely personal images. Certainly, he was the most distinctive and arguably the greatest native Spanish artist of the Renaissance.

THE LATE RENAISSANCE

Too often the quality of Italian art was diluted in Spain: neither nudes nor mythological subjects – both of crucial importance in Italy – had any attraction here, and there is hardly an example of either. Instead, there was a sweetening and sentimentalization of religious models. In Valencia, **Fernando Yáñez** (d. 1531) and his collaborator **Fernando de los Llanos** (dates unknown) adopted this facet of the art of Leonardo da Vinci, while **Juan Vicente Masip** (c.1475–1550) and his son of the same name, usually referred to as **Juan de Juanes** (1523–79), drew more from Raphael, becoming ever more saccharine as time went on.

Sevilla also had a school of painters, beginning with **Alejo Fernández** (d. 1543), but although less slavishly imitative of Italian models than the Valencian, it also failed to produce an artist of the very first rank. The Extremaduran **Luís Morales** (c. 1509–86) is more notable: he was revered by the common people, who referred to him as "El Divino", but he never found favour with authority, and much of his work is still in village churches. He is at his best with such small-scale subjects as Madonna and Child, which he repeated many times with slight variations. Strongly Mannerist in outlook, his drawing is rather stiff and his colours often cold, but he has a genuine religious feeling.

Ironically enough, it took a foreigner, Domenico Theotocopoulos (1540–1614), universally known as **El Greco**, to forge a truly great and quintessentially Spanish art in the late Renaissance period. He arrived in Toledo in 1575, having come from his native Crete via Italy. Presumably he hoped to find favour at court, particularly in the decoration of El Escorial, but was soon disappointed, and spent the rest of his life painting portraits of the nobility, along with a host of religious works for the many churches and monasteries of Spain's ecclesiastical capital. Having shown himself adept at both the Byzantine and Venetian styles of painting, he drew from both to create a highly idiosyncratic art that was ideally suited to the mood of Spain at the time. Distinguished features of his style include elongated faces and bodies, together with a sense of spiritual ecstasy that gives a strong feeling of the union of the terrestrial and the celestial. El Greco's gift for portraiture, too, is shown not only in his paintings of real-life sitters, but also in those of historical subjects, most notably in the several series of Apostles he was required to produce. His greatest work, *The Burial of the Count of Oryaz*, in Santo Tomás in Toledo, displays all the facets of his genius in a single canvas. Later, El Greco's style became increasingly abstract, with a freeing of his brushwork that anticipates many subsequent developments in the history of art. Sadly, although he maintained a flourishing studio which produced many replicas, none of El Greco's followers picked up much on his master's style. Most talented was **Luís Tristán** (1586–1624), whose own output was very uneven.

At court, a school of portraiture was founded by a Dutchman, **Antonio Moro** (1517–76), who emphasized the dignity of his sitters in their facial expressions and by giving prominence to clothes and jewellery – a style that was followed by two native artists, **Alonso Sánchez Coello** (1531–88) and **Juan Pantoja de la Cruz** (1553–1608). At El Escorial, minor Italian Mannerists were imported in preference to native artists. An exception was the deaf-mute **Juan Navarret** (1526–79).

In Valencia, **Francisco Ribalta** (1565–1628) began working in a similar Mannerist style, but soon came under the influence of Caravaggio and introduced naturalism and the sharp contrasts of light associated with "tenebrism" into Spain. He was followed by a yet more significant painter, **Jusepe (Jose) de Ribera** (1591–1652). Ribera spent nearly all his career in Naples under the protection of the Spanish viceroys, who sent many of his works back to his native land. He had two distinctive periods: early on in his career he used heavy chiaroscuro and small, thick brushstrokes; later he brightened his palette considerably. Above all he was interested in the dignity of human beings, and whether he painted ancient philosophers in contemplation, saints in solace, or martyrs resigned to their fate, his art is a concentrated one, with the spotlight very much on the main subject. His subjects at times can appear gruesome, but they are very much of their period in that respect, and the treatment is never mere sensationalism. For a long time out of critical favour, Ribera now appears as one of the most accomplished artists of European Baroque.

THE SEVENTEENTH CENTURY

In the early seventeenth century, Sevilla and Madrid replaced Valencia and Toledo as the main artistic centres of Spain. **Francisco Pacheco** (1564–1654) was the father figure of the Sevillan school, although nowadays his work as a theorist is more significant than his paintings. He adopted a naturalistic approach as a reaction against Mannerism, and was followed in this by **Francisco Herrera** (c.1590–1656) and his son of the same name (1622–85), who painted in an increasingly bombastic and theatrical manner.

Towering high above these, Pacheco's son-in-law, **Diego Velázquez** (1599–1660), is probably the artist the Spanish people take most pride in. Velázquez was a stunning technician. His genre scenes of Sevillan life, painted while he was still in his teens, have a naturalistic quality that is almost photographic. In contrast to many of his fellow countrymen, Velázquez was a slow and meticulous worker: he probably painted fewer than 200 works in his entire career, some 120 of which survive, almost half of them in the Prado.

In 1623 Velázquez went to Madrid to work for the court, a position he retained for the rest of his life. As well as the many royal portraits, he portrayed the jesters and dwarfs of the palace, giving them a Spanish sense of dignity. In *The Surrender of Breda* he revolutionized history painting, ridding it of supernatural overtones. His greatest masterpieces, *Las Hilanderas* and *Las Meninas*, date from near the end of his life, and are remarkable for the way they immortalize fleeting moments, as well as for their absolute technical mastery, particularly of aerial perspective.

Juan Bautista del Marzo (c.1615–67), son-in-law and assistant to Velázquez, was so adept at imitating his style that it is often difficult to determine which works are the originals and which are copies. His independent work, however, is altogether of inferior quality. **Juan Carreno de Miranda** (1614–85) also followed Velázquez's portrait style very closely, and was very active as a painter of religious subjects, a field largely abandoned by Velázquez in his maturity.

In Sevilla, the greatest painter was **Francisco de Zurbarán** (1598–1664), who is best known as an illustrator of monastic life of the times. He painted mainly for the more austere orders, such as Carthusians and Hieronymites, and many of his portraits of saints are modelled on real-life monks, some of them single figures of an almost sculptural quality. Zurbarán's palette was a bright one, his lighting effects are subtle rather than dramatic, and he ranks as one of the supreme masters of still lifes, which have a frequent presence in his larger paintings as well as in a few independent compositions. A complete example of one of his decorative schemes is still extant at Guadalupe, but sadly his later work sometimes shows a fall-off in quality: to pay off his debts he was forced to produce a large number of works for export to religious foundations in Latin America.

Zurbarán also sentimentalized his style in order to meet the competition of his highly successful younger contemporary, **Bartolomé**

Esteban Murillo (1618–82), who spent his entire career in Sevilla. Murillo's light, airy style was in perfect accord with the mood of the Counter-Reformation, and he was to have an important impact on Catholic imagery. His versions of subjects such as the Immaculate Conception, Madonna and Child, and the Good Shepherd, became the norm in terms of the portrayal of traditional dogma. His genre scenes of street urchins and portraits in the manner of van Dyck made him popular in northern Europe, too, and for a long time he was considered one of the greatest artists of all time. His reputation slumped considerably in the nineteenth century, and it is only in the last few years that critical opinion has turned again in his favour. Certainly his subject matter can seem cloying to modern tastes, but Murillo nearly always painted beautifully, and he was a marvellous storyteller. His later works were particularly successful, employing the *vaporoso* technique of delicate brushwork and diffuse forms, and there's no doubt that he was a substantial influence on much subsequent eighteenth- and nineteenth-century painting in Spain, France and England.

In complete contrast to Murillo, **Juan Valdés Leal** (1622–90) preferred the violent and macabre side of the Baroque. His work was very uneven in quality; the paintings in the Hospital de la Caridad in Sevilla are the most celebrated. **Alonso Cano** (1601–67) was the leading painter of Granada and also active as an architect and sculptor. He led a rather dissolute life, and changed his working style abruptly several times. Perhaps the most successful of his paintings are the mature, pale-coloured religious works, which reveal debts to van Dyck and Velázquez.

A large number of artists can be grouped together under the **Madrid school**. One of the earliest was the Florentine-born **Vicente Carducho** (1576–1638), who painted large-scale works in sombre colours for the Carthusians and other orders. **Fra Juan Rizi** (1600–81) illustrated contemporary monastic life in a different and less mystical way than Zurbarán. His brother, **Francisco Rizi** (1614–85), favoured full-blown canvases of Baroque pomp. **Fra Juan Bautista Maino** (1578–1649) was more influenced by the classical aspects of seventeenth-century art; he painted some notable religious and historical canvases with strong colouring, but with little interest in lighting effects. **Juan de Arellano** (1614–76) and **Bartolomé Pérez** (1634–93) worked mainly with landscape and historical religious works, while **José Antolínez** (1635–75) was particularly renowned for his versions of the Immaculate Conception. **Mateo Cerezo** (1626–66) painted fluid religious canvases under the influence of the works by Titian and van Dyck in the royal collections. The last major figure was probably also the most accomplished: **Claudio Coello** (1642–93), who was a master of the large-scale decorative style, using techniques of spatial illusion and very complicated arrangements of figures. His work at El Escorial shows his style at its best.

THE EIGHTEENTH AND NINETEENTH CENTURIES

The late seventeenth century and the first half of the eighteenth century was a very thin time in the history of Spanish painting: even the French and Italian artists imported by the Bourbon court were seldom of great merit. One native artist worthy of mention, however, is **Luís Meléndez** (1716–80), a master of still-life subjects. **Anton Raphael Mengs** (1728–79) came to Spain from Bohemia in 1761 as court painter, and in this capacity was a virtual dictator of style for a while, spearheading the adoption of an academic, Neoclassical tone, particularly in portraiture. His assistant, **Francisco Bayeu** (1734–95), was a prolific fresco painter for both royal and religious patrons, and was also in charge of the cartoons for the Royal Tapestry Factory. His brother, **Ramón Bayeu** (1746–93), worked on similar projects but was far less accomplished.

It was the Bayeus' brother-in-law, however, **Francisco Goya** (1746–1828), who was the overwhelmingly dominant personality of the period. Goya's output was prolific and his range of subject matter and style so immense that it is hard to believe one man was responsible for so much. Interestingly, he was no prodigy. In his twenties he became a highly competent painter of religious murals, his work at Zaragoza and Aula Dei already surpassing that of his contemporaries. After moving to Madrid, he worked for many years on tapestry cartoons (preparatory drawings), which in their graceful handling and skilful grouping made the most of their rather frivolous subject matter and gave Goya an entry into court circles, after which he became a fashionable portrait painter. It was in this role that

his originality began to show through: his portraits eschew any attempt at flattery, and it's clear that he was less than impressed by his sitters. A serious illness in the early 1790s left him deaf and led to a more bitter and sarcastic art; his increasingly fantastic style may have emerged from his developing interest in witchcraft, which resulted in many paintings and two series of etchings: *Los Caprichos* and, later, *Los Disparates*. The marvellous frescoes in San Antonio de la Florida in Madrid are the exception here, among his most beautiful creations ever and containing a remarkable representation of the various social types of the day. But the Peninsular War further darkened Goya's mood, as shown by *May 2nd* and especially *May 3rd*, and by the engravings *The Disasters of War*. The last paintings are probably his most remarkable, especially those of bullfights, in which he showed an extraordinary visual perception, the exactness of which was proved only with the development of the slow-motion camera. Finally, there were the despairing "black paintings" made on the walls of his own house, the Quinta del Sordo, now detached and hung in the Prado.

Of Goya's contemporaries, the most interesting are **Luís Paret y Alcázar** (1746–99), who painted Rococo scenes under French and Italian influence, and **Vicente López** (1772–1850), an academic portrait painter in the manner of Mengs whose severe portrait of Goya hangs in the Prado. The nearest artist to Goya in style was **Eugenio Lucas** (1824–70), who followed his interest in bullfighting and Inquisition scenes, but did little of stylistic advance. Indeed, most of the nineteenth century was extremely barren in Spanish art history, a period of imitation, largely of French models, at least twenty years late. The most gifted painter was perhaps **Mariano Fortuny** (1838–74), who specialized in small, very highly finished canvases, often of exotic subjects. Other artists worthy of mention are **Dario de Regoyos y Valdés** (1857–1913), the nearest thing to an Impressionist working in Spain at the time; **Joaquín Sorolla** (1863–1923), who was noted for his beach scenes; and **Ignacio Zuloaga** (1870–1945), who painted portraits against landscape backgrounds.

THE TWENTIETH CENTURY

As with architecture, it was Catalunya that took the lead in painting towards the end of the nineteenth century. **Isidoro Nonell** (1873–1911) was best known as a naturalistic painter of the poor. In contrast, **José María Sert** (1874–1945) was at his best in large-scale mural decorations, particularly in the powerful sepia and grey frescoes he produced for Vic Cathedral, replacements for two earlier sets.

Although born in Málaga, **Pablo Picasso** (1881–1973), the overwhelmingly dominant figure in twentieth-century art, spent many of his formative years in Barcelona, achieving great technical facility at a very early age, and creating many accomplished works in a representational style before the age of twenty. In 1900 he first visited Paris, where the influence of Toulouse-Lautrec made itself felt in the "blue period" of 1901–4, during which he depicted many of society's victims in Paris and Barcelona, following the lead of Nonell. The "rose period" of 1904–6 was perhaps Picasso's most "Spanish" phase (although by now he was living in Paris). Actors, clowns and models featured among his subjects, and his interest turned to the work of El Greco and ancient Iberian sculpture. The following "negro period" of 1907–9 marked the break with traditional forms, as manifested in the key work, *Les Demoiselles d'Avignon*. After this Picasso returned to representational painting only for a short time in the 1920s, and from 1910 onward developed Cubism in association with Frenchman Georges Braque.

The movement's first phase, analytical Cubism, was largely concerned with form, with being able to depict objects as if seen from different angles at the same time. This was followed by synthetic Cubism, which showed a revival of interest in colour and handling. For a time in the 1920s and 1930s, Picasso combined Cubism with Surrealism, inventing a new anatomy for the human form, and eventually becoming noted as a painter of protest, most markedly in *Guernica*, a cry of despair about the Civil War in his native land (which he had by then left for good). Until his death, Picasso worked in a variety of styles, active in sculpture and ceramics as well. He was prolific to an almost unimaginable degree – in 1969 alone he produced almost as many canvases as Velázquez did in his lifetime, among the most notable of which were variations on well-known paintings such as *Las Meninas*.

One of the most faithful Cubists was **Juan Gris** (1887–1927), who favoured stronger colours and softer forms than others in the group. In **Surrealism**, two Catalans were among the leading figures: **Joan Miró** (1893–1983) and **Salvador Dalí** (1904–1989). Miró created the most poetic and whimsical works of the movement, showing a childlike delight in colours and shapes, and developing a highly personal language that was freer in form and more highly decorative than that of the other Surrealists. One of his favourite techniques during the Thirties was to spill paint on the canvas and move his brush around in it. He was also active in a variety of artistic media besides paint and canvas: collage, murals, book illustrations, sculpture and ceramics. Aside from an early period as a Futurist and Cubist, Dalí was more concerned with creating his own vision of a dream world. He was particularly interested in infantile obsessions and in paranoia, and his works often showed wholly unrelated objects grouped together, the distortion of solid forms, and unrealistic perspectives. He also worked on book illustrations, some of them his own texts, and on films. In later years he looked for other stimuli and painted a number of religious subjects. Few other artists in history have shown such talent for self-publicity. There are few artists, either, who have been so easily forged: in his later years Dalí reputedly made millions by signing thousands of blank pieces of paper.

Artists of the same generation include **Óscar Domínguez** (1906–57), who used both the Cubist and Surrealist idioms, at times combining the two in a wholly individualistic way. Another isolated figure of note was **José Gutiérrez Solana** (1885–1945), whose impoverished background led him to seek out his subjects amongst the low-life of Madrid he knew so well, adopting a realist approach with strong use of colour.

THE PRESENT DAY

Among the most important living Spanish artists are the members of the "abstract generation", who run a museum at Cuenca devoted solely to their works. By far the most individual figure of the group is **Antonio Saura** (b. 1930), whose violently expressive canvases, the earlier of which are painted in black and white only, are overtly political in tone, showing Man oppressed but unbowed. He uses religious themes in a deliberately humanist or even blasphemous way in his triptychs of crowd scenes, and transformation of the Crucifixion into a parable of secular oppression. The Catalan **Antoni Tàpies** (b. 1923) is an abstractionist in the tradition of the Dada movement; he began by making collages out of newspaper, cardboard, silver wrapping, string and wire. For a period he turned to graffiti-type work with deformed letters, before returning to experiments with unusual materials, particularly oil paint mixed with crushed marble.

For those who despair of the theoretical and iconoclastic side of the modern movement, **Antonio López García** (b. 1936) comes as a refreshing change. Whilst obviously using modern idioms, he is a representational painter of landscapes, cityscapes, still lifes and nudes of an immediately appealing effect which clearly have their roots firmly in artistic tradition. **Eduardo Arroyo** (b. 1937) is a follower of the Pop Art movement, with its emphasis on large-scale depictions of familiar everyday faces and objects.

Gordon McLachlan

WILDLIFE

Despite its reputation as the land of the package holiday, you can't beat Spain for sheer diversity of landscape and wildlife. When the Pyrenees were squeezed from the earth's crust they created an almost impenetrable barrier stretching from the Bay of Biscay to the Mediterranean Sea. Those animals and plants already present in Spain were cut off from the rest of Europe, and have been evolving independently ever since. In the same way, the breach of the land bridge at what are now the Straits of Gibraltar, and the subsequent reflooding of the Mediterranean basin, stranded typical African species on the peninsula. The outcome was an assortment of wildlife originating from two continents, resulting in modern-day Iberia's unique flora and fauna.

Spain is the second most **mountainous** country in Europe after Switzerland. The central plateau – the Meseta – averages 600–700m in elevation, slopes gently westwards and is surrounded and traversed by imposing sierras and *cordilleras*. To the north, the plateau is divided from the coast by the extensive ranges of the Cordillera Cantábrica, and in the south the towering Sierra Nevada and several lesser ranges such as the Serranía de Ronda run along the Mediterranean shores (where these southern sierras continue across the Mediterranean basin, the unsubmerged peaks are today known as the Balearic Islands). The Pyrenean chain marks the border with France, and even along Spain's eastern shores the narrow coastal plain soon rises into the foothills of the Sierras of Montseny, Espuña and los Filabres, among others. The ancient Sierras de Guadarrama and Gredos cross the Meseta just north of Madrid, and the Sierra Morena and the Montes de Toledo rise out of the dusty southern plains. So it is not surprising to find that both flora and fauna of Spain possess a distinctly alpine element, with many species adapted to high levels of ultraviolet light and prolonged winter snow-cover.

The centre of Spain lies many kilometres from the coast, and thus the **climate** is almost continental in character. The summers are scorching, the winters bitter, and what rain there is falls only in spring and autumn. Moving eastwards, the Mediterranean Sea has a moderating effect on this weather pattern, favouring the coastal lands with mild winters and summers which become progressively hotter as you move south towards Africa. What most people tend to forget, however, is that the northern and western parts of the country are endowed with a climate that, if anything, is even worse than that of Britain. Depressions coming in from the Atlantic Ocean are responsible for almost continual cloud cover, high rainfall and persistent mists along the appropriately named Costa Verde; when the sun does show its face the high humidity can make life very uncomfortable.

These climatic variations have produced a corresponding diversity in Spanish wildlife. The wet, humid **north** is populated by species common throughout Atlantic Europe, especially Ireland, whilst the **southern** foothills of the Sierra Nevada, situated only a stone's throw from Africa, have an almost subtropical vegetation. The continental weather pattern of much of the **interior** has given rise to a community of drought-resistant shrubs, together with annual herbs which flower and set seed in the brief spring and autumn rains, or more long-lived plants which possess underground bulbs or tubers to withstand the prolonged summer drought and winter cold.

LANDSCAPE

The Iberian peninsula was once heavily forested, although it is estimated that today only about ten percent of the original **woodland** remains, mostly in the north. Much of the Meseta was covered with evergreen oaks and associated shrubs such as laurustinus and strawberry tree, but the clearance of land for arable and pastoral purposes has taken its toll, as have the ravages of war. Today tracts of Mediterranean woodland persist only in the sierras and some parts of Extremadura. When it was realized that much of the plateau was unsuitable for permanent agricultural use, the land was abandoned, and is now covered with low-growing, aromatic scrub vegetation, known as *matorral* (maquis). The southeastern corner of the Meseta is the only part of Spain which probably never supported woodland; here the arid steppe **grasslands** – *calvero* – remain basically untouched by man. In northern Spain, where vast areas are still forested, the typical tree species are more familiar: oak, beech, ash and lime on the lower slopes, grading into pine and fir at higher levels.

Much of the Meseta is flat, arid and predominantly brown. Indeed, in Almería, Europe's only true **desert** is to be found, such is the lack of rainfall. But the presence of subterranean water supplies gives rise to occasional **oases**: flashes of green and blue, teeming with wildlife. The numerous tree-lined **watercourses** of the peninsula also attract birds and animals from the surrounding dusty plains. The great Ebro and Duero rivers of the north, and the Tajo and Guadiana in the south, have been dammed at intervals, creating **reservoirs** which attract wildfowl in winter.

The Spanish **coastline** has a little of everything: dune systems, shingle banks, rocky cliffs, salt marshes and sweeping sandy beaches. In Galicia, submerged river valleys, or *rías*, are reminiscent of the Norwegian fjords, and the offshore islands are home to noisy sea-bird colonies; the north Atlantic coast is characterized by limestone promontories and tiny, sandy coves; the Mediterranean coast, despite its reputation for wall-to-wall hotels and beach towels, still boasts many undeveloped lagoons and marshes, and west of Gibraltar lies perhaps the greatest of all coastal marshlands: the Coto Doñana.

The Spanish **landscape** has changed little since the early disappearance of the forests. While the rest of Europe strives for agricultural supremacy, in Spain the land is still **farmed** by traditional methods. The olive groves of the south, the extensive livestock-rearing lands of the north and even the cereal-growing and wine-producing regions of the plains are still havens for the indigenous wildlife of the country. It is only since Spain joined the European Community that artificial pesticides and fertilizers and huge machines have made much impact. Even so, Spain is still essentially a wild country compared to much of Europe. Apart from a few industrial areas around Madrid and in the northeast, the landscape reflects the absence of modern technology, and the low population density means that few demands are made of the wilderness areas that remain.

FLOWERS

With such a broad range of habitats, Spain's **flora** is nothing less than superb. Excluding the Canary Islands, about 8000 species occur on Spanish soil, approximately ten percent of which are endemic: that is, they are found nowhere else in the world. Due to the plethora of high **mountains**, an alpine flora persists in Spain well beyond its normal north European distribution, and because of the relative geographical isolation of the mountain ranges, plants have evolved which are specific to each (there are about 180 plants which occur only in the Pyrenees, and over forty species endemic to the Sierra Nevada).

The **buttercup** family makes a good example. In the Pyrenees, endemic species include the pheasant's-eye *Adonis pyrenaica* and the meadow-rue *Thalictrum macrocarpum*; the Sierra Nevada has *Delphinium nevadense* and the monkshood *Aconitum nevadense*, and of the columbines *Aquilegia nevadensis* occurs here alone. *A. discolor* is endemic to the Picos de Europa, *A. cazorlensis* is found only in the Sierra de Cazorla and *A. pyrenaica* is unique to the Pyrenees. Other handsome montane members of this family include alpine pasque flowers, hepatica, hellebores, clematis and a host of more obvious buttercups.

The dry Mediterranean grasslands of Spain are excellent hunting grounds for **orchids**. In spring, in the meadows of the Cordillera Cantábrica, early purple, elder-flowered, woodcock, pink butterfly, green-winged, lizard and tongue orchids are ten a penny, and a little searching will turn up sombre bee, sawfly and Provence orchids. Farther into the Mediterranean zone, exotic species to look for include Bertoloni's bee, bumblebee and mirror orchids. Lax-flowered orchids are common on the Costa Brava and high limestone areas will reveal black vanilla orchids, frog orchids and summer lady's tresses a bit later in the year.

The Mediterranean **maquis** is a delight to the eye and nose in early summer, as the cistus bushes and heaths come into flower, with wild rosemary, thyme, clary and French lavender adding to the profusion of colour. The dehesa grasslands of southwest Spain are carpeted with the flowers of *Dipcadi serotinum* (resembling brown bluebells), pink gladioli and twenty or so different trefoils in May. In the shade of the ancient evergreen oaks grow birthworts, with their pitcher-shaped flowers, bladder senna and a species of lupin known locally as "devil's chickpea".

Even a trip across the **northern Meseta**, although apparently through endless cereal fields, is by no means a dull experience: arable weeds such as cornflowers, poppies, corncockle, chicory and shrubby pimpernel are sometimes more abundant than the crops themselves. Where the coastal **sand dunes** have escaped the ravages of the tourist industry you can find sea daffodils, sea holly, sea bindweed, sea squill and the large violet flowers of *Romulea clusiana*.

MAMMALS

Spain's mammalian fauna has changed little since the Middle Ages: only the beaver has been lost since that time. Unfortunately, that doesn't mean that the remaining creatures are easy to see. Although still quite common in the mountains of the north and west, **wolves** keep out of man's way as much as possible (they're sporadically protected in Spain, but are widely regarded as a threat to livestock; the shepherds complain that wolves seem to know when a man is carrying a rifle and react accordingly). Neither are you likely to come across any of the few remaining brown **bears**. In fact, of Spain's enormous wealth of mammals, only a few species are active during the day and present in sufficient numbers for regular sightings to be made.

In the **northern mountains** – the Pyrenees and the Cordillera Cantábrica – you should get at least a glimpse of chamois, roe and red deer, and possibly wild boar, which can be seen at dusk

during the winter when they conduct nightly raids on village potato patches. Wildcats sometimes cross the road in front of you, and red squirrels are quite common, especially in the pine forests. Ibex, with robust scimitar-shaped horns, are common in the Sierras de Cazorla and Gredos, and marmots can occasionally be seen in the Pyrenees.

The typical mammals of **southern Spain** are seldom seen, but include the pardel lynx (paler than the north European one), the Egyptian mongoose, the Mediterranean or blind mole, and fallow deer in the umbrella pine woods of the Coto Doñana. No fewer than 27 species of **bat** occupy caves and woodlands throughout Spain, including four types of horseshoe. Over a score of **whale** and **dolphin** species frequent Spanish waters and the Mediterranean shores are still home to some of the last remaining Mediterranean **monk seals**.

BIRDS

If you care to spend your vacation with binoculars trained on the sky, trees or marshes, then Spain is one of the best venues in Europe for **bird-watching**. Most people head for the Coto Doñana National Park if it's birds they're after, but other parts of the country are just as rewarding, even if the list of sightings isn't quite so long at the end of the day.

If you have the patience to search out and identify **birds of prey**, Spain is an ideal destination, especially in **summer**, as about 25 species breed here. Some, such as red kites, goshawks, Bonelli's and golden eagles, griffon vultures, peregrine falcons and marsh harriers can be seen at all times of year in almost any part of the country. Others are confined to certain parts of the peninsula, where climate, landscape and vegetation combine to provide the right environment in which to raise their young. You will see the rare black-shouldered kite, for example, only in the southwest, or the majestic lammergeier in the high Pyrenees (and sometimes in the peaks behind the eastern coast), while black vultures (about 240 pairs) and the rare Spanish race of the imperial eagle are restricted to the southern half of the country.

Some of these raptors visit Spain only in the **winter**; these are best seen in late autumn or early spring on migration, and include the kestrel-like red-footed falcon and magnificent spotted eagle. By contrast, when these birds are leaving for their African and Asian nesting sites, others, like Montagu's harriers, short-toed and booted eagles, Eleonora's falcons and Egyptian vultures are coming the other way, having spent the winter in warmer climes, but returning to breed in Spanish territory.

There is no less variety in other types of birds; woodpeckers, for example, are most abundant in the extensive forests of the **northern mountain ranges.** White-backed woodpeckers are confined to the Pyrenees, other such rarities as black and middle-spotted woodpeckers may also be seen in the Cordillera Cantábrica, and the well-camouflaged wryneck breeds in the north and winters in the south of the country. Other typical breeding birds of these northern mountains are the turkey-like capercaillie, tree pipits, wood warblers, pied flycatchers, ring ouzels, alpine accentors, citril and snow finches, ptarmigan in the Pyrenees, and that most sought-after of all montane birds: the wallcreeper.

In the open **grasslands** and cereal fields of the Meseta, larks are particularly common. Look out for the Calandra lark, easily identified by the trailing white edge to the wing, although loads of patience and good binoculars are needed to distinguish between short-toed, lesser short-toed, crested and Thekla larks. Other small brown birds of the plains are rock sparrows and corn buntings, but more rewarding, and a lot easier to identify, are great and little bustards – majestic at any time of year, but especially the males when they fan out their plumage during the springtime courtship display. Look out also for the exotically patterned pin-tailed sandgrouse, the only European member of a family of **desert-dwelling birds**, as well as stone curlews and red-necked nightjars, the latter seen (and heard) mainly at dusk.

If you come across an ancient olive grove, or an area of southern Spain where the evergreen oak **forests** are still standing, then stop! A colourful assemblage of birds is typical of such oases of natural vegetation: hoopoes, azure-winged magpies, golden orioles, great grey and woodchat shrikes, bee-eaters, rollers, greater-spotted cuckoos, redstarts and black-eared wheatears. On a sunny summer's day, these birds are active and easy to spot.

Natural inland bodies of **water** often have wide marshy borders owing to the fluctuating water level. In these rushy margins look out for

water rail and purple gallinule, as well as the diminutive Baillon's crake, and scrutinize reed beds carefully for signs of penduline and bearded tits. The airspace above the water is usually occupied by hundreds of swifts and swallows; you should be able to pick out alpine, pallid and white-rumped swifts and red-rumped swallows if you are in the southern half of the country, as well as collared pratincoles. These lakes are also frequented by wintering waterfowl (although Spain has no breeding swans or geese), European cranes and sometimes by migrating flamingos.

The **coastal wetlands** are certainly a must for any serious bird-watcher, with common summer occupants including black-winged stilts, avocets and most members of the heron family: cattle and little egrets, purple, squacco and night herons, bitterns and little bitterns. On the Mediterranean coast, especially in low-growing scrub, keep an eye out for a small quail-like bird called the Andalucian hemipode: strangely enough it is closely related to the graceful crane. Wintering waders are not outstandingly distinctive, though wherever you go, even on the Atlantic coast, spoonbills are frequently encountered. Grey phalaropes visit the northwest corner, as do whimbrel, godwits, skuas and ruff, taking a break from their northern breeding grounds.

The **Balearic Islands** can provide you with a few more exotic cliff-nesting species, such as Cory's shearwater and storm petrels; and the Islas Cíes, off the Galician coast, provide breeding grounds for shags, the rare Iberian race of guillemot and the southernmost colony of lesser black-backed gulls in the world.

Hundreds more birds could be listed: with a good field guide you should find many of them for yourself.

REPTILES AND AMPHIBIANS

As with other types of wildlife, Spain is especially rich in amphibians and reptiles, with about sixty species in total. Some of the easiest to see are **fire salamanders**, which occur throughout Spain, albeit with coloration varying from yellow stripes on a black background to vice versa, depending on the exact locality. The best time to see them is in cool, misty weather in the mountains, or immediately after rain.

Three other species of **salamander** live in Spain. The golden-striped salamander (a slender, rather nondescript beast, despite its name) is endemic to northwest Iberia; the large sharp-ribbed salamander is found only in the southwest of the peninsula; and the Pyrenean brook salamander is confined to the Pyrenees.

Closely related to the salamanders are the **newts**, of which there are only four species in Spain. If you take a trip into the high mountain pastures of the Cordillera Cantábrica, where water is present in small, peaty ponds all year round, you should see the blackish alpine newt; marbled newts can be seen round the edges of many of Spain's inland lakes, and reservoirs.

Midwife **toads** strike up their chorus at dusk, and can often be heard well away from water, sometimes causing confusion with the call of the Scops owl. If you search through tall waterside vegetation you may be rewarded by the sight of a tiny, lurid-green tree-frog: striped in the north and west, but stripeless along the Mediterranean coast.

Two species of **tortoise** occur in Spain; spur-thighed tortoises can still be found along the southern coast and on the Balearic Islands, which are also the only Spanish locality for Hermann's tortoise. European pond terrapins and stripe-necked terrapins are more widely distributed, but only in freshwater habitats.

Perhaps the most exotic reptilian species to occur in Spain is the **chameleon**, although again this swivel-eyed creature is confined to the extreme southern shores. **Lizards** are numerous, with the most handsome species being the ocellated or eyed lizard – green with blue spots along the flank. Some species are very restricted in their range, such as Ibiza, Italian and Lilford's wall lizards, which live only in the Balearic Islands.

Similarly, **snakes** are common, although few are venomous, and in any case it's sometimes quite difficult to spot them before they spot you and take evasive action themselves. Asps and western whip snakes occur in the Pyrenees, but you are likely to see horseshoe whip snakes and false smooth snakes only in the extreme south.

INSECTS

Almost 100,000 insects have been named and described in Europe and an untold number await discovery. In Spain, with areas where no one knows for sure how many bears there are, insects have barely begun to be explored.

From early spring to late autumn, as long as the sun is shining, you will see **butterflies**: there are few European species which do not occur in Spain, but by contrast there are many Spanish butterflies which are not found north of the Pyrenees. These seem to be named mostly after obscure entomologists: Lorquin's blue, Carswell's little blue, Forster's furry blue, Oberthur's anomalous blue, Lefèbvre's ringlet, Zapater's ringlet, Chapman's ringlet, Zeller's skipper, and many others. You need to be an expert to identify most of these, but the more exciting butterflies are in any case better-known ones: the Camberwell beauty, almost black and bordered with gold and blue; swallowtails, yellow and black or striped like zebras, depending on the species, but always with the distinctive "tails"; the lovely two-tailed pasha, which is often seen feeding on the ripe fruit of the strawberry tree; and the apollo (papery white wings with distinctive red and black eyespots), of which there are almost as many varieties as there are mountains in Spain. Other favourites include the small, bejewelled blues, coppers, fritillaries and hairstreaks that inhabit the hay meadows.

Aside from the butterflies, keep an eye open for the largest **moth** in Europe, the giant peacock, which flies by night but is often attracted to outside lights, or the rare, green-tinted Spanish moon moth, a close relative of tropical silk moths. During the day, take a closer look at that hovering bumble bee, as it may be a hummingbird hawkmoth, or a broad-bordered bee-hawk, flying clumsily from flower to flower. Oleander and elephant hawkmoths (resplendent in their pink and green livery) are often seen around flowering honeysuckle bushes at dusk. Many moths have bizarre caterpillars, for example the lobster moth, which feeds on beech, or the pussmoth, found on willows and poplars, although the adults may be quite nondescript in appearance.

Grasslands and arid scrub areas are usually good hunting grounds for **grasshoppers and crickets**, which you can locate by following their calls. Mole crickets and field crickets live in burrows they have excavated themselves, but look to the trees for the adult great green bush cricket, about 7–8cm long. French lavender bushes in the maquis are a favourite haunt of the green mantis *Empusa pennata*, identified by a large crest on the back of the head (the nymphs are brown, with a distinctive curled-up abdomen). **Stick insects** are harder to spot, as they tend to sit parallel with the stems of grasses, where they are well camouflaged.

ENVIRONMENT AND CONSERVATION

Protecting the environment of a country which encourages well over forty million tourists to leave their footprints in the sand each year could easily be perceived as a lost cause. But since most of these visitors flock to, and stay on, a comparatively narrow coastal strip, the damage is contained.

The environmental impact of "**costa**" tourism, with its pressures on water supply, sewage disposal and landscape, is a specialist subject in its own right, and one in which the battles are by no means over. According to the Barcelona-based environment group DEPANA, there is cause for worry over the second boom in coastal tourism as foreigners start to buy holiday homes. Meanwhile in inland, rural areas encroachment is fostered by domestic second-home buyers.

Concerned people in Spain have a common complaint: while there may be lip service paid to environmental matters, actually goading bureaucracy into action is a different matter. The only language understood by all sides is an economic one, the good news being that the value of the environment to tourism is becoming increasingly evident and important in bargaining terms.

Protection, then, is the name of a game increasingly played in the political arena, in which environmental benefit becomes almost incidental. Spain is still one of the wilder places of Europe, and wilderness can be found surprisingly close to some of the major urban and touristic centres. There are about a dozen **Parques Nacionales** (National Parks) with a total protected area of more than 17,000 square kilometres, or 3.4 percent of Spain's total land area. This, of course, is chicken feed compared to the level of ecological threat, but protection of the environment isn't yet on the worry list of the average Spaniard, and doesn't attract priority spending.

The stirrings of a movement towards environmental education can be seen in the creation of regionally nominated and managed **Parques Naturales**. So far the majority of these are in Catalunya, Galicia and Andalucía, but they now exist in every part of the country, and natural parks, with their fairly comprehensive protection, already cover an area some three times larger than national parks.

Even Spain's highest-profile national park, though, the **Coto Doñana**, was in the headlines in

1998 with one of the worst ecological catastrophes in recent Spanish history. A dam used for storing toxic waste just outside the park burst, unleashing five million cubic litres of heavy metals into the Guadiamar river which carried it towards the park. The deadly tide was stopped just two kilometres from the park's boundary, but catastrophic damage was done to farmland surrounding Doñana, devastating nesting birds and poisoning fish, which provide a vital food source for much of the park's wildlife. At the time of writing the long-term extent of the pollution is still being assessed. The **Parque Nacional de Aigües Tortes**, too, has lost international recognition as a national park because of continuing hydroelectric exploitation of its lakes.

WETLANDS

In 1980 Spain had 10,852 square kilometres of wetlands, six times more than France. It has not been so ready as some other nations to condemn wetland out of hand and rush to get it drained. Spain was an early signatory of the Ramsar Convention, an international agreement (the only one of its kind) to protect wetland. Three Spanish sites of international importance had been nominated by 1985. None of this, however, has prevented the steady decline of wetland areas, either by pollution or indirect draining.

The **Coto Doñana**, perhaps the most important wetland, is facing chronic drought and is suffering both from chemical run-off pollution (which caused the disaster mentioned above) and from detrimental agricultural practices. Just across the Río Guadalquivir from the Doñana, the last remaining unprotected wetland of the region has been drained and converted into farms.

The **Tablas de Daimiel** in La Mancha, too, are well-known in conservationist circles for their deteriorated condition. Once recognized as being one of Europe's most important wetlands, and designated Reserva Nacional in 1966, then Parque Nacional in 1973, the area has nonetheless suffered terribly. Most blame is put on local viniculture upstream, with its irrigation and resultant heavy demand on artesian water. The Río Guadiana dried up in 1982 and the nearby Cigüela is heavily polluted. In the summer months particularly, the region can hardly support wildlife at all and certainly no longer attracts the once fabulous amounts of waterfowl which earned it worldwide fame.

There is some comfort in knowing that the plight of the Tablas has been officially recognized, with the launch of a project aimed at restoring former water levels. Naturalists are certain that if the water returns, so will the birds and ditto the visitors. **La Albufera de Valencia** was once one of the largest bodies of fresh water in Spain, but it too is shrinking rapidly and is now ten times smaller than it was in the Middle Ages. On a more positive note, the most accessible wetland of the lot, **Alguamolls de l'Emporda**, just behind the tourist beaches of the Costa Brava, has very recently been established as a Parque Natural.

HUNTING

The greatest confrontation over environmental issues in Spain involves hunting and farming groups. Many middle-aged and older men in Spain believe a shotgun is an accessory that they shouldn't be seen without in the countryside, and feel personally threatened at the news of the establishment or expansion of protected areas. One of the most emotive subjects is the protection of **wolves**. In areas where they have been protected, in the north especially, numbers have grown rapidly. Over recent years, outraged farmers have taken to increasingly militant demonstrations in an attempt to "protect" their land.

The figures speak for themselves. Although national parks protect more than 1200 square kilometres, **hunting reserves** (*reservas nacionales de caza*) cover a vastly greater area – almost four million acres to date. Largest is Saja in Cantabria, which is larger than all the mainland national parks put together. And although more species than ever before are protected and now forbidden to the hunter (ibex, bears, capercaillie and most of the major birds of prey, for instance) there is no shortage of demand for other hunting trophies such as wild boar, deer and chamois. Supermarkets stock all hunting gear, including shotgun cartridges, and walkers have to take care not to look shootable on weekends in season, when the hills are alive with the sound of double barrels.

As long ago as 1970 there were well over a million hunting licences issued annually, and exceeding quotas or **poaching** is considered virtually normal procedure, especially in areas where shooting and trapping provide an extra source of income for the poor. **Waterfowl** is a popular target, with huge numbers being killed each year.

The shooting and netting of **common birds** is also a major problem, as it is in much of southern Europe and North Africa. The annual slaughter of migrating birds in the Pyrenees, for a start, contributes substantially to the overall global figure of 900 million bird deaths each year. Latest European estimates for Spain are that about 30 million birds, often accused of being agricultural pests, are caught each year.

ACID RAIN

Spain was among the first countries to sign and ratify the UN's Convention on Long Range Transboundary Pollution, which came into effect in 1983, claiming that: "Spain recognises the need to take the prevention of air pollution into account in overall energy policies." However, as the time for accession to the European Community in 1986 drew near, the tone changed. There were strong political hints at this stage that the adoption of environmental policies was going to prove "difficult and costly". Spain's rapid growth as an industrial nation is a further blow to the environment.

In 1983, 235 square kilometres of Spanish forests were showing signs of damage from acid rain. But most of this is home-produced: as far as Europe is concerned, Spain is one of the six countries receiving the least acid rain (18 percent of its total) from foreign sources. On the other hand Spain's domestic sulphur pollution accounts for 63 percent of its total. The country is the sixth largest source of sulphur in western Europe. Worst affected by acid deposition are parts of the north coast downwind from major industrial centres such as **Bilbao** and **Avilés**, and around the power stations of **Serchs** (Barcelona), **Andorra** and **El Serrallo** (Castellón). It is believed that industry in Avilés alone has been generating 24,000 metric tons of SO annually. A technical commission established to study pollution in the forests of **El Maestrazgo** and **El Port de Tortosa-Beseit**, which spread over three provinces, blamed emissions from Andorran industry for the damage, which seems, on the face of it, like an attempt to whitewash Spain's own problem.

Paul Jenner and Christine Smith

Members of the *Arachnidae* (**spiders**) to be found include two species of **scorpion** in the dry lands of southern Spain. Look out also for long-legged *Gyas*, the largest harvest-spider in Europe, which can be about 10cm in diameter, although the body is little larger than a pea. Spanish **centipedes** can grow to quite a size too: *Scutigera coleoptra*, for example, often live indoors – they have fifteen pairs of incredibly long, striped legs, which create a wonderful rippling effect when they move across walls

WHERE AND WHEN TO GO

Virtually anywhere in Spain, outside the cities and most popular tourist resorts, rewards scrutiny in terms of wildlife. Perhaps the best thing about this country is that so much wilderness remains to be discovered on your own, without guidebooks to tell you where to go.

The main drawback, however, is getting anywhere on public transport, which often doesn't stop between departure point and destination. There is rarely any problem getting off a bus when you feel the urge, but you may have problems stopping the next one, which in any case may not arrive until the following day.

The following suggestions, then, are largely limited to those which are easily accessible by public transport. Inevitably this means that other people will be there, too: you'll have to head off into the hills on foot in order to experience the best of Spanish wildlife.

Southern Spain is a good choice for any **time of year**, since even in the depths of winter the climate is mild and many plants will be in full bloom. If you decide on the **northern mountain ranges**, spring and early summer are best. The weather can be temperamental, but for the combination of snowy peaks and flower-filled meadows, it's worth taking the risk. The **interior** of Spain is freezing in winter and almost too hot to bear in midsummer, so spring or autumn – to coincide with the occasional rains and the flowering of the maquis and steppe grasslands – are best. Again, if your real interest is the **coastal bird life** of Spain, visit in spring or autumn, not only to catch the phenomenal migrations of birds between Africa and northern Europe, but also because accommodation in the resorts can be incredibly low-priced outside the tourist season.

THE PYRENEES

The Moors called these mountains El Hadjiz – the barricade – which is effectively what they are, isolating Spain from the rest of Europe. The Spanish flanks of the Pyrenees are somewhat hotter and drier than their northern counterparts, but the high passes are nevertheless snowbound for several months in the winter.

If you avoid the ski resorts there are still many unspoiled valleys to explore, with their colourful alpine meadows studded with Pyrenean hyacinths and horned pansy, and some of the highest forests in Europe, extending up to 2500m in places. The **Vall d'Aran**, close to Pico de Aneto (the highest point of the chain, at 3408m), is a botanical paradise at any time of year. Go in spring and you will find alpine pasque flowers, trumpet gentians and sheets of daffodils, among them pale Lent lilies and pheasant's-eye narcissi. A little later in the year sees the flowering of Turks'-cap lilies, dusky cranesbill and Pyrenean fritillaries, sheltering among the low-growing shrubs on the hillsides; while in autumn, following the annual hay-making, the denuded meadows shimmer with a pink-purple haze of merendera and autumn crocuses.

Farther west, the **Parque Nacional de Ordesa y Monte Perdido** in the Aragonese Pyrenees shelters valleys clothed in primeval pine, fir and beech forests which are home to pine martens, wildcats, genets, red squirrels, polecats and wild boar among the 32 mammal species that live within the park boundaries. Dominating the forests are sheer cliffs with spectacular waterfalls and towering rock formations, the haunt of the sprightly chamois which thrive here in profusion. Although these antelope-like creatures are easily spotted, you will need to have your sights set firmly on the heavens to see the most renowned occupant of Ordesa: the lammergeier. A vulture of splendid proportions, it is now almost completely confined to the Pyrenees and a few eastern ranges in Spain. Its Spanish name – *quebrantahuesos*, or "bone-breaker" – refers to its habit of dropping animal bones from great heights to smash on the rocks below, exposing the tender marrow.

The second national park in the Spanish Pyrenees is that of **Aigües Tortes**, centred on the glacial hanging valleys and impressive cirques of northern Catalunya. The extensive coniferous forests of Scots pine and common silver fir are populated by capercaillie and black woodpeckers. Just above the timberline, early purple orchids and alpine and southern gentians flourish in the superb alpine meadows, and the rocky screes conceal pale, delicate edelweiss and yellow mountain saxifrage. The fast-flowing mountain rivers are home to otters; and the tiny secretive Pyrenean desman, Pyrenean brook salamanders and alpine newts live in the clear waters of the glacial lake of San Mauricio. In the airspace above the peaks look out for honey buzzards and golden eagles soaring on the thermals, and if you scrutinize the cliff faces you might be rewarded with the sight of a wallcreeper.

CORDILLERA CANTÁBRICA

This mountain chain runs more or less parallel to the north coast from the Portuguese border eastwards into the Basque country. It has long formed a barrier between the northern coast and the rest of Spain since there are few crossing points, of which a good proportion are impassable during the winter. The vegetation is clearly affected by the rain-laden clouds which constantly sweep in from the Atlantic, as can be seen by the extensive oak and beech forests that shroud the slopes. Extensive beef and dairy farming is the traditional way of life, and the majority of the flower-filled meadows have never been subjected to artificial fertilizers and pesticides. One of the most fascinating aspects is the abundance of meadow flowers now rarely found in northern Europe: lizard orchids, heath lobelia, greater yellow rattle, moon carrot, Cambridge milk-parsley, galingal and summer lady's-tresses – a delicate, white-flowered orchid.

The high point of the Cordillera Cantábrica is the small limestone mountain range of the **Picos de Europa**, visible from miles offshore in the Bay of Biscay. Over sixty species of mammal have been recorded here, ranging from such typical wilderness creatures as brown bears and wolves to snow voles, tiny denizens of the high peaks. Red squirrels, roe deer and chamois are easy to see, but many of the mammals which haunt these mountains, such as genets, beech martens and wildcats, are secretive nocturnal beasts.

One of the most outstanding landscape features of the Picos de Europa is the **Cares gorge**, where the river bed lies almost 2000m below the peaks on either side. The sheltered depths of the gorge are home to a number of

shrubs more typical of Mediterranean Spain – figs, strawberry trees, wild jasmine and barberry – and the sheer rock-faces are home to the exotic wallcreeper, a small ash-grey bird with splashes of crimson under the wings, the sight of which is highly coveted by bird-watchers.

The **Covadonga National Park** covers much of the western massif of the Picos de Europa, its focal point being the glacial lakes of Enol and Ercina. In spring the verdant pastures which surround the lakes are studded with pale yellow hoop-petticoat daffodils and tiny dog's-tooth violets, but a visit later in the year will be amply rewarded by the discovery of hundreds of purple spikes of monkshood and the steel-blue flowers of Pyrenean eryngo. A few hours scrambling across the limestone crags away from the lake should be sufficient for excellent views of griffon and Egyptian vultures, or you don't even have to leave the small café in the car park to see alpine choughs scavenging among the litter-bins.

For those who prefer a more gentle scenery, **Galicia**, with its green rolling hills and constant mists, is hard to beat. Few people live in the countryside, which as a consequence is teeming with wildlife. The oak and beech woods of Ancares provide shelter for deer and wild boar; although the chamois were hunted to extinction for food during the Civil War. The meadows benefit from the frequent rains and you can find all manner of wet-loving plants, such as large-flowered butterwort, bog pimpernel, globe flowers, marsh helleborines, whorled caraway and early marsh orchids.

THE INTERIOR

If you believed everything you read you'd be tempted to regard inland Spain as a flat, barren plain covered with mile after mile of bleached cornfields. But the wildlife is there – if you know where to look.

A good place to start is the **central sierras**. Just to the north of Madrid, almost bisecting the vast plain of the Meseta, run several contiguous mountain ranges which are well worth a visit. They may not have the rugged grandeur of the Pyrenees but there is plenty of wildlife to be found on the rocky, scrub-covered slopes. Venture into the extensive pine forests of the **Sierra de Guadarrama** to see Spanish bluebells and an unmistakable toadflax, *Linaria triornithophora*, which has large snapdragon-like flowers each with a long tail, sometimes pink, sometimes white. Birds of prey are abundant, and not too difficult to tell apart; both red and black kites can be seen, easily distinguished from other raptors by their distinctly forked tails (the red kite has clear white patches under its wings). Booted eagles are identified by the black trailing edge to their wings, and the Spanish short-toed eagle, here known as *águila culebrera*, the "snake eagle", is almost pure white below, with a broad, dark head.

Farther west the granite bulk of the **Sierra de Gredos** boasts some of the highest peaks in Spain after the Sierra Nevada and the Pyrenees. Scots and maritime pines occur in the higher levels, sweet chestnut and Pyrenean and cork oaks on the southern slopes. The springtime flora is superb, including lily-of-the-valley, conspicuous St Bernard's and martagon lilies, and several species of brightly coloured peonies. On some of the drier slopes, where the trees have been cleared, the aromatic gum cistus forms a dense layer up to 2m high. There is no need to fight your way through their sticky branches to discover the delights of the flora here: even the edges of the shepherds' tracks are ablaze with asphodels, French lavender, a strange-looking plant called the tassel hyacinth and the closely related grape hyacinth. But best of all in the Gredos are the ibex, very common in the pine zones between the cirques of Laguna Grande and Cinco Lagunas. Look out also for Egyptian and griffon vultures, red and black kites and Bonelli's eagles overhead, crossbills and firecrests in the coniferous forests, and rock buntings, identified by their striped heads, almost everywhere.

Moving away from the mountains there are still sights to be seen in the plains. *Dehesa* parkland is the best habitat, especially for birds: **Monfragüe Natural Park**, in Extremadura, contains some excellent areas of *dehesa*. Golden orioles, woodchat and great grey shrikes, hoopoes and bee-eaters are impossible to miss, and you might even see a roller. In winter about 7000 common cranes descend on the Monfragüe grasslands, and the flooded river valleys which are an integral part of this park are good viewing points for red-rumped swallows and collared pratincoles in summer.

Monfragüe is perhaps best known for its breeding population of the endangered Spanish **imperial eagle**, easily identified by the distinct white shoulder markings. The central reserve where this raptor nests is open only to permit holders, but you may see them soaring over the *dehesa*. The same can be said for the rare black vulture: a huge bird which is impossible to miss. Monfragüe has the largest known breeding colony (about sixty pairs). Most people head for the huge rock outcrop known as Peñafalcón, where black storks, now extremely rare as a breeding bird in Spain, can be seen perched up on the cliff face, and the sky is constantly filled with griffon vultures coming and going. And look out for a smallish, light-coloured hovering bird – it might be a rare black-shouldered kite, which you certainly won't see elsewhere in Europe.

Heading in the other direction, towards Zaragoza in the northeastern corner of the plains, you might consider visiting the **Laguna de Gallocanta**. This is Spain's largest natural inland lake, and has a lot to recommend it. Look out for birds more typical of the arid plains – pin-tailed sandgrouse and stone curlews – as well as those usually associated with fresh water. Gallocanta is a national stronghold for red-crested pochard.

MEDITERRANEAN COAST

Spain's Mediterranean coast conjures up visions of sandy beaches packed with oiled bodies and a concrete wall of hotels stretching from the French border to Gibraltar. Even in the heart of the Costa Brava, though, there's rich wildlife to be found. The **Parc Natural dels Aiguamolls de L'Empordá** in Catalunya is a salt marsh and wetland reserve sandwiched between the A7 motorway and the hotel developments in the Gulf of Roses. It is the nearest thing in Spain to a British nature reserve, with signposted nature trails, a well-equipped information centre and several bird hides. This rather detracts from the wilderness aspect of the site, but it is nevertheless a good place to watch out for the 300 species of birds that have been observed here. Apart from the more typical water birds look out for little bittern, black-winged stilt, bearded tit and purple heron, all of which breed here. Spring is perhaps the best time, when flamingos, glossy ibis and spoonbills drop in on migration.

If you can't stand the mosquitos from the marshes, try the drier, Mediterranean scrub areas nearby, which are ideal for spotting red-footed falcons on migration, breeding lesser grey shrikes (the only Spanish locality), stone curlews, great spotted cuckoos and moustached and Marmora's warblers in summer. And of course, marsh and Montagu's harriers are always present.

Other promising wildlife locations include the fan-like **Delta de l'Ebre** (Ebro Delta), with up to 100,000 wintering birds and a large colony of purple herons. Again isolated from the mainland by the A7 motorway, the lagoons and reed beds here attract squacco and night herons, avocets and red-crested pochard, with isolated islands providing nesting areas for the rare Audouin's and slender-billed gulls. Look out, too, for lesser short-toed larks, and a multitude of terns, including gull-billed, whiskered, roseate and Sandwich.

Further south again lies a smaller coastal wetland known as the **Albufera de Valencia**. It is so close to the city of Valencia that to learn it supports a breeding colony of the rare ferruginous duck is quite a surprise. Other water birds to look out for are red-crested pochard and, during the winter, the extremely rare crested coot, as well as cattle and little egrets, breeding night, purple and squacco herons, little bitterns, black-necked grebes and bearded and penduline tits.

SOUTHERN SPANISH SIERRAS

Stretching for miles behind the coastal metropolises of the Costa del Sol, these lofty mountains are a complete contrast from the sun-and-sea image of southern Spain. Perhaps the best-known is the **Sierra Nevada** at the eastern end of the range, which peaks at Mulhacén (3482m), the highest mountain in mainland Spain. Snow persists for much of the year at the highest levels, but the south-facing foothills are only about 150km from Africa. Environmental conditions thus range from alpine to almost tropical. Not surprisingly there is an incredible range of plant and animal life. If you are equipped to visit the high mountains when the snow is starting to melt you should see such attractive endemic plants as glacier eryngo, looking not unlike its Pyrenean counterpart, and Nevada daffodils, saxifrages and crocuses. Later on in the year there is still plenty to see, including the strange, spiny mountain tragacanth, wild tulips, peonies, pinks, alpine gentians, the Nevada monkshood and columbine, and the white-flowered rockrose *Helianthemum apenniunum*.

Owing to the extreme altitude of the Sierra Nevada, birds more commonly found farther north – crossbills, alpine accentors and choughs – have a final European outpost here. You should also see many of the smaller birds which favour dry, rocky hillsides. Perhaps the most distinguished of these is the black wheatear, the males identified by their funereal plumage and white rump. Farther north, in the limestone **Sierras de Cazorla y Segura**, raptor-watching will be amply rewarded. Cazorla is the only Spanish locality outside the Pyrenees where lammergeiers regularly breed, and the smaller Egyptian vultures are common here. Small numbers of golden and Bonelli's eagles nest in the peaks and goshawks frequent the extensive forests (black, maritime and Aleppo pines at high levels and holly, holm and Lusitanian oaks, with narrow-leaved ash and strawberry trees, on the lower slopes).

These mountain ranges, birthplace of the great Río Guadalquivir, are rather unusual in Spain in that they run approximately north–south rather than east–west. They also have a flora of some 1300 unique species including such handsome rock-dwelling plants as the crimson-flowered Cazorla violet (*Viola cazorlensis*), the columbine *Aquilegia cazorlensis*, a relict carnivorous butterwort (*Pinguicula vallisneriifolia*) and several endemic narcissi.

To the west lie some extraordinary Jurassic limestone ranges, eroded over centuries into formations known collectively as *torcales*. One of the more famous of these is at **Grazalema**, renowned for its Spanish fir forest. This tree *(Abies pinsapo)* is now restricted to just a handful of localities in southern Spain, including the **Serranía de Ronda**, and a specialized flora has evolved to cope with the dense shade that the trees cast. You should be able to find the colourful peonies *Paeonia coriacea* and *P. broteri*, as well as paper-white daffodils and the winter-flowering *Iris planifolia*, with a large, solitary flower on a ridiculously short stem. A whole range of typical Mediterranean shrub species grow here, including laurustinus, grey-leaved and poplar-leaved cistus, Spanish barberry, Etruscan honeysuckle, the nettle tree (*Celtis australis*) and *Acer granatense*, a maple species confined to the mountains of southern Spain. Also, in these woods the eagle owl breeds: the largest in Europe, it even preys on roe deer and capercaillie.

As a break from the mountains you might consider a visit to **Fuente de Piedra**, the largest inland lagoon in Andalucía (about 15 square kilometres). Partly because the water is never more than 1.5m deep (the level being further reduced by intense evaporation in summer) and also due to the lack of pollution, large numbers of flamingos construct their conical mud nests here every year. Fuente de Piedra is thus one of only two regular breeding places for greater flamingos in Europe, and has recently been declared a *Reserva Integral*, the most strictly protected type of nature reserve in Spain. Altogether about 120 species of bird, 18 mammals and 21 reptiles and amphibians have been recorded here.

SOUTHERN ATLANTIC COAST

The more or less tideless Mediterranean ends at Gibraltar, so the coast stretching westwards up to the Portuguese border is washed by the Atlantic Ocean. Here, the low-lying basin formed by the Río Guadalquivir contains one of Europe's finest wetlands: the **Coto de Doñana**, Spain's most famous national park.

Perhaps the most renowned spectacles are the breeding colonies of spoonbills and herons in the cork oaks which border the marshes, but equally impressive are the huge flocks of **waterfowl** which descend on the lagoons during the winter. As for breeding ducks, Doñana is the European stronghold for the marbled teal, a smallish, mottled-brown dabbling duck which rarely breeds in Europe outside Spain. Ruddy shelduck – large, gooselike birds, generally confined to the eastern Mediterranean – are also present throughout the year, but breeding has not yet been proved. White-headed ducks definitely nest and rear their young here, although the more renowned nursery for this is at the Lagunas de Córdoba in central Andalucía. One of Europe's rarest birds is the crested coot, distinguished from the common coot only at close range by two small red knobs on its forehead, or in flight by the absence of a white wing-bar. It breeds in Morocco, migrating northwards into southern Spain for the winter; Doñana is the only Spanish locality where this species is resident all year round, although again no one is quite sure whether it breeds here or not.

Water birds aside, keep an eye out for large flocks of pin-tailed sandgrouse, which perform prodigious aerobatics in perfect time, rather like a shoal of fish; and, at ground level, cattle egrets in the grasslands, usually in the company of some of the renowned black bulls of the region. Cattle egrets are most easily distinguished from other egrets by their pinkish legs (black or yellow in all other species). A smaller bird to watch out for is the Spanish sparrow, which commonly makes its home in the nether regions of the large, untidy nests of the white stork. Doñana also boasts an impressive roll call of birds of prey, including imperial eagle and black vulture.

Some large **mammals** are relatively easy to see in Doñana: red and fallow deer and wild boar display an inordinate lack of fear when approached by people, despite the fact that this area was a Royal Hunting Reserve until quite recently. The same, unfortunately, cannot be said for Doñana's pardel lynxes, of which there are some 25 pairs, estimated to represent about half the total Spanish population. Egyptian mongooses also frequent the dry, scrubby areas, and genets are occasionally seen by day in the more remote, forested parts of the national park. If you can drag your eyes from the veritable feast of bird life you might spot a curious creature known as Bedriaga's skink. Endemic to Iberia, this small lizard has only rudimentary legs; you are most likely to see it burrowing rapidly into the sand in an effort to escape detection.

The nearby **Marismas de Odiel**, which lie within the boundaries of the city of Huelva a little to the west, are also very worthwhile. Apart from the flamingos, which are increasingly preferring these saline coastal marshes as breeding grounds to the nearby Doñana, you will also be rewarded by the sight of large numbers of spoonbills, purple herons and other typical southern Spanish waterbirds.

THE BALEARIC ISLANDS

Despite the sun-seeker image of the Balearic Islands, there are many remote spots which have escaped the ravages of the tourist industry. Even on the big ones you can escape easily enough, and in total there are fifteen islands (most uninhabited).

One of the wilder regions is the **Sierra de Tramuntana** which runs along the northern coast of Mallorca, dropping abruptly into the sea for much of its length. It is a good place to see the diminutive Eleonora's falcon and enormous black vulture. Around your feet you can feast your eyes on an array of exotic plants such as *Cyclamen balearicum*, an autumn-flowering crocus (*Crocus cambessedesii*), *Helleborus lividus* (a rare member of the buttercup family), the pink-flowered *Senecio rodriguezii*, and many other endemic species of peony, birthwort and hare's ear. Even in January many plants are in flower, but the best time of year to see the blossoming of the islands is from March to May.

Away from the mountains, other wildlife refuges are the low-lying coastal marshes which have to date defied the hotel trade. On Mallorca that of **S'Albufera** is a bird-watcher's paradise. The maze of tamarisk-lined creeks and lagoons is the summer haunt of water rail, spotted crake and little egrets, and a little careful scrutiny may reveal more secretive denizens: Savi's, Cetti's, Sardinian, moustached, fan-tailed and great reed warblers. Also easy to get to are the saltpans known as **C'an Pastilla**, close to the airport at Palma, where whiskered and white-winged black terns, as well as Mediterranean and Audouins's gulls (this latter bird is the rarest breeding gull in Europe), are frequently seen.

The Balearics are also ideal places for watching the endemic races of lizards; they are usually quite undeterred by your presence, and make excellent subjects for portrait photography! If you are keen on marine life, don't forget your flippers and snorkel, as the underwater scenario is superb.

Teresa Farino

MUSIC

Spain is remarkable for the extraordinary variety and abundance of its popular music, a music which enjoys certain continuity despite dramatic changes from a predominantly rural to urban life this century. Much of this distinctive richness is rooted in the determination of what are now autonomous regions to preserve their regional identities, which has meant that traditions from Euskadi to Galicia, Catalunya to Andalucía, have continued to thrive.

At a local and live level, almost every type of music can be heard, the performers sustained by enthusiastic groups of aficionados. The recent emergence of small, specialist record labels means that much of it finds its way onto CD, if not into the main record stores.

FLAMENCO

Flamenco is one of the great musical forms of Europe, with a feeling few folk cultures can match. Twenty years or so ago, however, it looked like a music on the decline, preserved only in the clubs or *peñas* of its aficionados, or in travestied castanet-clicking form for tourists. But in the 1980s and '90s, flamenco has returned to the Spanish mainstream, with styles infused by jazz, salsa, blues and rock making their way in the charts and clubs, and a new respect for the old "pure flamenco" artists.

Flamenco owed its new-found influence in part, perhaps, to the first southern-dominated socialist governments of post-Franco democratic Spain; the Prime Minister Felipe Gonzalez came from Sevilla, as did many of his associates. Perhaps, too, it was down to Spain's unconscious desire then, just having joined the EU, to establish a national identity which challenged the European stereotype of flamenco as sanitized kitsch, all frills and castanets.

The initial impetus, however, began much earlier, at the end of the 1960s, with the innovations of guitarist Paco de Lucia and, especially, the late, great singer El Camarón de la Isla. These were musicians who had grown up learning flamenco but whose own musical tastes embraced international rock, jazz and blues.

ORIGINS

Flamenco evolved in southern Spain from many sources: Morocco, Egypt, India, Pakistan, Greece, and other parts of the Near and Far East. How exactly they came together as flamenco is a subject of great debate, though most authorities believe the roots of the music were brought to Spain by gypsies arriving in the fifteenth century. In the following century, it was fused with elements of Arab and Jewish music in the Andalucían mountains, where Jews, Muslims and "pagan" gypsies had taken refuge from the forced conversions and clearances effected by the Catholic kings and Church. The main flamenco centres and families are still to be found today in quarters and towns of gypsy and refugee origin, such as Alcalá, Jerez, Cádiz, Utrera and the Triana *barrio* of Sevilla. Although it's linked fundamentally to **Andalucía**, emigration from that province has long meant the flamenco map encompassing Madrid, Extremadura and the Levante – indeed, wherever Andalucían migrants have settled.

Flamenco aficionados enjoy heated debate about the purity of their art and whether it is more validly performed by a **gitano** (gypsy) or a **payo** (non-gypsy). Certainly, flamenco seems to have thrived while preserved by the oral tradition of the closed gypsy clans. Its power too, and the despair which its creation overcomes, seem to have emerged from the precarious and vulnerable life of a people surviving for centuries at the margins of society. Flamenco reflects their need to preserve, and aggressively protect, their self-esteem.

These days, there are as many acclaimed *payo* as *gitano* flamenco artists. The concept of dynasty, however, remains fundamental. The veteran singer **Fernanda de Utrera**, one of the great voices of "pure flamenco", was born in 1923 into a gypsy family in Utrera, one of the *cantaora* (flamenco singer) centres. The granddaughter of the legendary singer "Pinini", she and her younger sister Bernarda, also a notable singer, both inherited their flamenco with their genes. This concept of an active inheritance is crucial, and has not been lost in contemporary developments: even the members of *Ketama*, the Madrid-based flamenco-rock group, come from two gypsy clans – the Sotos and Carmonas.

If flamenco's exact origins are debated, it is generally agreed that its "laws" were established in the nineteenth century. Indeed, from the mid-nineteenth into the early twentieth centuries flamenco enjoyed a Golden Age, the tail-end of which is preserved on some of the earliest 1930s recordings. The musicians found a home in the **café cantantes**, traditional bars which had their own groups of performers (*cuadros*). One of the most famous was the *Café de Chinitas* in Málaga, immortalized by the poet Gabriel Garciá Lorca in his poem *A las cinco de la tarde* (At five in the afternoon), in which he intimates the relationship between flamenco and bullfighting, both sharing root emotions and flashes of erratic genius, and both also being a way to break out of social and economic marginality.

Just such a transformation happened in 1922 when the composer Manuel de Falla, the guitarist Andrés Segovia and the poet Lorca were present for a legendary *Concurso de Cante Jondo* (Deep Song Gathering). A gypsy boy singer, **Manolo Caracol**, reportedly walked all the way from Jerez and won the competition with the voice and the flamboyant personality that was to make his name throughout Spain and South America. The other key figure of this period, who can be heard on a few recently remastered recordings, was Pastora Pavón, known as **La Niña de Los Peines**, and popularly acclaimed as the greatest woman flamenco voice of the twentieth century.

In the 1950s several crucial events in flamenco history took place, establishing for the music a culture beyond its aficionados in the *café cantantes*. In 1954, the Spanish label Hispavox recorded all the flamenco greats on the *Antología del Cante Flamenco*; two years

later the first national contest of *cante jondo* was launched in Córdoba; and in 1958 a Chair of Flamencology was established at Jeréz. Each of these events brought media attention (and deserved respectability), and were accompanied by the appearance of numerous *tablaos* (clubs – heirs of *café cantantes*), which became the training ground for a new and more public generation of singers and musicians.

THE ART OF FLAMENCO

Flamenco is played at *tablaos*, fiestas, in bars, and at *juergas* – informal, more or less private parties. The fact that the Andalucían public are so knowledgeable and demanding about flamenco means that musicians, singers and dancers found at even the most humble local club or festival are usually very good indeed.

Flamenco songs often express pain, with a fierceness that turns that emotion inside out and beats it up against violent frontiers. Generally, the voice closely interacts with improvising guitar, which keeps the *compás* (rhythm), the two inspiring each other, aided by the **jaleo** – the hand-clapping *palmas*, finger-snapping *palillos* and shouts from participants at certain points in the song.

Aficionados will shout encouragement, most commonly *¡olé!* – when an artist is getting deep into a song – but also a variety of other less obvious phrases. A stunning piece of dancing may, for example, be greeted with *¡Viva la maquina escribir!* (long live the typewriter), as the heels of the dancer move so fast they sound like a clicking machine; or the cry may be *¡agua!* (water), for the scarcity of water in Andalucía has given the word a kind of glory.

The encouragement of the audience is essential for an artist, as it lets them know they are reaching deep into the emotional psyche of their listeners. They may achieve the rare quality of **duende** – total communication with their audience, and the mark of great flamenco of any style or generation. *Duende* is an ethereal quality: moving, profound even when expressing happiness or deep sadness, in one sense mysterious but nevertheless felt, a quality that stops listeners in their tracks. Many of those listeners are intensely involved, for flamenco is not just a music; for many it is a way of life, a philosophy that influences daily activities.

It is an essential characteristic of flamenco that a singer or dancer takes certain risks, by putting into their performance feelings which arise direct from their own life experience, exposing their own vulnerabilities. Aficionados tend to acclaim a voice that gains effect from surprise and startling moves more than one governed by recognized musical logic. Vocal prowess or virtuosity can be deepened by sobs, gesticulation and an intensity of expression that can have a shattering effect on an audience. Thus pauses, breaths, body and facial gestures of anger, pain and transcendence transform performances into cathartic events.

SONGS AND SINGERS

There is a classical repertoire of more than sixty flamenco **songs** (*cantes*) and dances (*danzas*) – some solos, some group numbers, some with instrumental accompaniment, others *a cappella*. These different styles (or *palos*) of flamenco singing are grouped in families according to more or less common melodic themes, establishing three basic types of *cante flamenco*: **cante grande** – comprising songs of the *jondo* type – **cante chico**, and **cante intermedio** between the two. Roughly speaking the *jondo* and *chico* represent the most and the least difficult *cantes* respectively in terms of their technical and emotional interpretation. **Cante jondo** (deep song) comprises the oldest and "purest" songs of the flamenco tradition, and is the profound flamenco of the great artists, whose *cantes* are outpourings of the soul, delivered with an intense passion, expressed through elaborate vocal ornamentation. To a large extent however, such catagories are largely arbitrary, and few flamenco musicians talk about flamenco in this way; what matters to them is if the flamenco is good or bad.

The basic *palos* include **soleares**, **siguiriyas**, **tangos** and **fandangos**, but the variations are endless and often referred to by their place of origin: *malagueñas* (from Málaga), for example, *granaínos* (from Granada), or *fandangos de Huelva*. Siguiriyas, which date from the Golden Age, and whose theme is usually death, have been described as cries of despair in the form of a funeral psalm. In contrast there are many songs and dances such as tangos, *sevillanas*, *fandangos* and *alegrías* (literally "happinesses") which capture great joy for fiestas.

The **sevillana** originated in medieval Sevilla as a spring country dance, with verses improvised and sung to the accompaniment of guitar and castanets (rarely used in other forms of flamenco). **El Pali** (Francisco Palacios), who died in 1988, was the most well-known and prolific *sevillana* musician. He combined an unusually gentle voice and accompanying strummed guitar style, with an enviable musical pace and ease for composing the popular poetry of the genre. In the last few years, dancing *sevillanas* has become popular in bars and clubs throughout Spain, but their great natural habitats are Sevilla's April Fería and the annual *romería* or pilgrimage to El Rocio.

Another powerful and more seasonal form are the **saetas**. These are songs in honour of the Virgins carried on great floats in the processions of *Semana Santa* (Easter Week), and traditionally they are quite spontaneous – as the float is passing, a singer will launch into a *saeta*, a sung prayer for which silence is necessary and for which the procession will therefore come to a halt while it is sung.

Camarón – or more fully **El Camarón de la Isla** – was by far the most popular and commercially successful singer of modern flamenco. Collaborating with the guitarists and brothers Paco de Lucía and Ramón de Algeciras, and latterly, Tomatito, Camarón raised *cante jondo* to a new art. He died in 1992, having almost single-handedly revitalized flamenco song, inspiring and opening the way for the current generation of flamenco artists.

Among the best contemporary singers are Enrique Morente, the aforementioned Fernanda and Bernarda de Utrera, El Cabrero, Juan Peña El Lebrijano, the Sorderos, Fosforito, José Menese, Carmen Linares, Carmen Amaya, El Potito. **Enrique Morente** is considered one of the great artists of his generation through his renovation and adaptations of modern and classic poets. **Carmen Linares** has been a major female figure of the 1990s who, like many other great artists of her generation, works by innovating from within the tradition. **El Potito** was hailed as one of the voices to watch when just twenty years old, in the search for a successor to the late, great Camarón.

FLAMENCO GUITAR

A flamenco performance is filled with pauses. The singer is free to insert phrases seemingly on the spur of the moment. The guitar accompaniment, while spontaneous, is precise and serves one major purpose – to mark the *compas* (measures) of a song and organize rhythmical lines. Instrumental interludes which are arranged to meet the needs of the *cantaor* not only catch the mood and intention of the song and mirror it, but allow the guitarist to extemporize what are called *falsetas* (short variations) at will. When singer and guitarist are in true rapport the intensity of a song develops rapidly, the one charging the other, until the effect can be overwhelming.

The guitar used to be simply an accompanying instrument – originally the singers themselves played – but in the early decades of this century it began developing as a solo instrument, absorbing influences from classical and Latin American traditions. The greatest of these early guitarists was **Ramón Montoya**, who revolutionized flamenco guitar with his harmonizations and introduced a whole variety of arpeggios – techniques of right-hand playing adapted from classical guitar playing. Along with Niño Ricardo and Sabicas, he established flamenco guitar as a solo medium, an art extended from the 1960s on by **Manolo Sanlucar**, whom most aficionados reckon the most technically accomplished player of his generation. Sanlucar has kept within a "pure flamenco" orbit, and not strayed into jazz or rock, experimenting instead with orchestral backing and composing for ballet.

The best known of all contemporary flamenco guitarists, however, is undoubtedly **Paco de Lucía**, who made the first moves towards "new" or "fusion" flamenco. A *payo*, or non-gypsy, he won his first flamenco prize at the age of 14, and went on to accompany many of the great singers, including a long partnership with Camarón de la Isla. He started forging new rhythms for flamenco following a trip to Brazil, where he was influenced by *bossa nova*, and in the 1970s established a sextet with electric bass, Latin percussion, flute and saxophone. Over the past twenty years he has worked with jazz-rock guitarists like John McLaughlin and Chick Corea, while his own regular band, featuring his other brother, the singer Pepe de Lucía, remains one of the most original and distinctive sounds on the flamenco scene.

Other modern-day guitarists have equally identifiable sounds and rhythms, and fall broadly into two camps, being known either as accompanists or soloists. The former include **Tomatito** (Camarón's last accompanist),

Manolo Franco and Paco Cortés, while among the leading soloists are the brothers Pepe and Juan Habichuela; Rafael Riqueni, an astonishing player who is breaking new ground with classical influences; Enrique de Melchor; Gerardo Nuñez and Vicente Amigo. Jerónimo Maya was acclaimed by the Spanish press as the "Mozart of Flamenco" when he gave his first solo performance, aged seven, in 1984.

NUEVO FLAMENCO

The reinvention of flamenco in the 1980s was hated by purists, but gave the music a new public. Paco de Lucía set the new parameters of innovation and commercial success, followed by others including Lolé y Manuel, who updated the flamenco sound with original songs and huge success, and Jorge Pardo, Paco de Lucía's sax and flute player, who was in fact originally a jazz musician. Meanwhile, Enrique Morente and Juan Peña El Lebrijano both worked with Andalucían orchestras from Morocco, and *Amalgama* recorded with southern Indian percussionists, revealing perhaps unsurprising stylistic unities.

Another interesting composition came with Paco Peña's 1991 *Missa Flamenca* recording, a setting of the Catholic Mass to flamenco forms with the participation of established singers like Rafael Montilla "El Chaparro" from Peña's native Córdoba, and a classical academy chorus from London.

The encounter with rock and blues was pioneered at the end of the 1980s by Ketama and Pata Negra. **Ketama** (named for a Moroccan village famed for its hashish) were hailed by the Spanish press as creators of the music of the "New Spain", after their first album which fused flamenco with rock and Latin salsa, adding a kind of rock-jazz sensibility, a "flamenco cool" as they put it. They then pushed the frontiers of flamenco still further by recording the two *Songhai* albums in collaboration with Malian kora-player Toumani Diabate and British bassist Danny Thompson. The group **Pata Negra**, a band led by two brothers, Raímundo and Rafael Amador, introduced a more direct rock sound with a bluesy electric guitar lead, giving a radical edge to traditional styles like *bulerías*. Their *Blues de la Frontera* album caused an equal sensation.

Collectively, these young and iconoclastic musicians have become known, in the 1990s, as

nuevo flamenco: a movement associated in particular with the Madrid label Nuevos Medios. They form a challenging, versatile and at times musically incestuous scene in Madrid and Andalucía, with musicians guesting at each others' gigs and on each others' records. Members of *Ketama* crop up, for instance, along with the astonishing guitarist Tomatito on an album by Duquende, one of the powerful singers of flamenco's new wave.

The music is now a regular sound of nightclubs, too, through the appeal of young singers like **Aurora** – whose salsa-rumba song *Besos de Caramelo*, written by Antonio Carmona of Ketama, was the first 1980s number to crack the pop charts – and pop singer **Martirio** (Isabel Quinones Gutierrez), one of the most flamboyant personalities on the scene, who has appeared dressed in lace mantilla and shades like a cameo from a Pedro Almodovar film, and records songs with ironic, contemporary lyrics, full of local slang, about life in the cities.

Martirio's producer, **Kiko Veneno**, who wrote Camarón's most popular song, *Volando Voy*, is another key artist on the scene. His own material is basically rock music but has a strongly defined sense of flamenco. **Rosario**, one of Spain's top woman singers, has also brought a flamenco sensibility to Spanish rock music.

Other more identifiably *nuevo flamenco* bands and singers to look out for on the scene include *La Barbería del Sur* (who add a dash of salsa); Wili Gimenez and Raimundo Amador; and José El Frances. In the mid-1990s *Radio Tarifa* emerged as an exciting group who started out as a trio, expanding to include African musicians, and mixing Arabic and medieval sounds onto a flamenco base.

FOLK AND REGIONAL

Spain has a centuries-long tradition of folk song and dance. At the beginning of the twentieth century certain dances became emblematic of certain regions and their communities – for example, the *muiñeira* in Galicia, the *zortziko* in the Basque country and the *sardana* for Catalunya. In common with many other totalitarian regimes however, the Franco dictatorship exploited folklore as a way of promoting nationalism, with the women's section of the Falange party collecting folk songs. As a result, what became known as "folklorism" was somewhat discredited, particularly among those most opposed to the regime.

The inspiration of the 1970s, '80s and '90s has therefore been to give new value to folk music and rescue it from patriotic cliché and Francoesque kitsch. While the restoration of democracy has been crucial, great impetus has also come from the fact that Spain is now composed of several different autonomies, each with their own financial support and official nurturing from regional government.

THE KEY MUSICIANS

Currently, folk and regional music is at its most developed in the northwest, from Galicia to Euskadi – Celtic Spain. The *Fiesta del Mundo Celta* at Ortigueira has played a leading role in this revival, and there is a regular summer scene of local festivals in the Basque country, Asturias and Galicia.

Galician music is in particularly fine fettle, rooted in pipes, bagpipes and drums. Best known of the groups is **Milladoiro**, regulars on the European festival scene. The music of Galician bagpiper **Carlos Nuñez** exemplifies that of a new generation who have grown up steeped in tradition, with classical training and a passion for many other musics. Nuñez, who served a kind of touring apprenticeship with Irish group *The Chieftains*, constantly searches out collaborations which bring out different aspects of Galician music, such as the inspiring *pandereta* (tambourine) group and singers of *Cantegueiras Xiradella*, from Martezo, near La Coruña, who have learnt traditional spirited work songs and *jotas* from older women in the countryside. Nuñez has also collaborated with North American guitarist Ry Cooder and Cuba's *Vieja Trova Santiaguera*, while his 1999 project, *Os Amores Libres*, explores the rhythmic connections between Celtic and flamenco music. Other Galician musicians who have helped revitalize the scene include *Na Lua* (who combine saxophone with bagpipe); *Doa, Citania, Trisquell, Fía Na Roca* and *Xorima* (all traditional and acoustic); *Palla Mallada* (hyper-traditional); and *Alecrín, Brath* and *Matto Congrio* (electric folk). Emilio Cao switches back and forth between traditional folk and more modern singer-songwriting.

The Basque country, **Euskadi**, is home to a wild accordion music called *trikitrixa* (meaning the devil's bellows). *Trikitrixa* maestro, **Josepa**

Tapia, who plays with *pandereta* player Leturia in the *Tapia et Leturia* band, is one of the stars. **Kepa Junkera** has taken *trikitrixa* further afield playing with Carlos Nuñez, and in 1998 created an exciting disc *Bilbao 00:00 hrs*, playing with musicians from Madagascar, Sweden and beyond.

The fine Basque singer-songwriter **Ruper Ordorika**, whose music has a rock edge to it, has recently worked on an imaginative project with the poetry of Bernardo Atxaga (the first Basque to win Spain's National Prize for Literature), who has written lyrics previously for rock and folk bands. Producing a book with stories, interviews, poems and photographs, with an accompanying CD, and working with veteran songwriter Mikel Laboa and *Tapia et Leturia*, *Nueva Etiopia* (the New Ethiopia) is an exciting collaborative venture.

Oskorri are a fine, politicized electro-acoustic group, who were instrumental in keeping Basque music publicly alive in the latter years of Franco and who have gone from strength to strength. Also impressive are Ganbara and Azala, and singer-songwriter Benito Lertxundi, whose energies generally go into traditional Basque music but who has also recently experimented with the Celtic sounds of the northern coast. Younger artists include Txomin Artola, his former companion Amaia Zubiría, and *Imanol*.

A Celtic movement exists in **Asturias** centring on two festivals in Oviedo (the Oviedo Folk Festival and the *Noche Celta*). Most groups are fairly traditional, particularly *Ubiña* and *Lliberdón*, though *Llan de Cubel* are adventurous and challenging.

Turning to the **Balearics**, Mallorcan **Maria del Mar Bonet** has brought the rich treasury of her own island to huge acclaim at home and abroad. Starting in the 1960s, Bonet was part of the Catalan singer-composer group *Els Setge Jutges*, and the movement of *nova cançó* (new song) which incurred the displeasure of Franco's censors by singing in Catalan. Key Bonet songs include Mallorca's unofficial hymn, *La Balanguera*, ballads like *La Mort de la Margalida* as well as lively dances like *La Jota Marinera* and the apocalyptic medieval *La Sybilla*, sung only on Christmas Eve in certain churches in Mallorca. Some of Bonet's arrangements of Mallorcan work-songs have been choreographed as a ballet, first by the Spanish National Dance Company, then by the Netherlands Ballet.

Bonet has also delved into Mallorca's Mediterranean connections, translating Zülfü Livaneli's songs, including *Merhaba* and *Leylim Ley*, from Turkish into Catalan, and worked closely with Greek composer Mikis Theodorakis on the Catalan translation of his songs for her album, *El Las*. Other Balearic musicians of interest include the groups *Musica Nostra*, *Sis Som*, *Calitja* and *Aliorna*, who play traditional styles; *Coanegra* and *Siurell Electric*, with a more progressive sound, and *Calabruix*, an electro-acoustic duo.

In **Catalunya**, Maria del Mar Bonet's colleague and friend in *Els Setge Jutges*, **Lluís Llach**, has enjoyed a long career, as has fellow Catalan **Joan Manuel Serrat**. Serrat, one of the big record sellers in Spain, sings both in Catalan and Spanish and enjoys a huge reputation in Latin America. Llach comes from the small village of Verges, near the French border, which is home to the oldest medieval Dance of Death of its kind; this still takes place as part of the ritual of Holy Week, with Llach regularly attending the event in his youth.

Earlier Llach songs such as *El bandoler* and *L'estaca*, from the period when Franco censored Catalan song, are still highly esteemed and sung today. For Llach they resulted in four years exile in France, when his seminal recording at the Paris Olympia with its classic version of *País Petit* (My Small Country) circulated clandestinely. Returning as Franco died, to great celebration, Llach is now a Spanish superstar, touring with a superb group of musicians, and mixing jazz and rock in his arrangements. His lyrics retain an acute political awareness, as exemplified by his 1997 suite of songs, *Porrera*, about his mother's village and the problems of life in rural areas.

Another member of *Els Setge Jutges* who celebrated thirty years singing in 1997, is **Raïmon**, composer of many key songs including *Al Vent*, a song about being free in the wind, which conjured up images of liberty during the 1960s and '70s. Other interesting Catalan groups, mostly playing folk music, include *La Murga* and the newer *Tradivarius*.

Catalunya also has a number of **orchestras** playing traditional dance music: some closer to salsa like the *Orquesta Platería* and the *Salseta del Poble Sec*, others more traditional like *Tercet Treset* and the *Orquesta Galana*. The emblematic *sardana* dance remains important

All the recommendations below are CDs, which in Spain, as elsewhere, have virtually taken over from records, with reissues and remasters coming on the market all the time.

CLASSIC FLAMENCO

Various *Arte Flamenco: Excerpts from the collection* (Mandala).

Various *Arte Flamenco: Vol. 7 La Nina de los Peines* (Mandala).

Various *Arte Flamenco: Vol. 9 El cante en sevilla* (Mandala).

Various *Concurso de Cante Jondo* (Sonifolk).

Various *Duende: The Passion and Dazzling Virtuosity of Flamenco* (Ellipsis Arts; 3 CDs).

Various *Magna Antología del Cante Flamenco* (Hispavox; 10 volumes).

Various *Early Cante Flamenco: Classic Recordings from the 1930s* (Arhoolie).

Various *Fiesta: Flamenco Vivo* (Auvidis).

Various *Flamenco: Grande Figures* (Chant du Monde).

Various *Flamenco: The Rough Guide* (World Music Network).

Various *Noches Gitanas* (EPM; 4CDs).

Various *Sevillanas: the soundtrack of Carlos Saura's film* (Polydor).

Escudero & Ramos de Almaden *Flamenco de Triana* (Tradition).

Remedios Amaya *Me voy contigo* (Hemisphere).

Agustín Carbonell Bola *Carmen* (Messidor).

Duquende *Duquende y La Guitarra de Tomatito* (Nuevos Medios).

Federico Garcia Lorca & La Argentina *Colección de Canciones Populares Españolas* (Sonifolk).

El Indio Gitano *Nací gitano por la gracia de Dios* (Nuevos Medios).

Camarón de la Isla *Potro de Rabia y Miel* (Polygram).

Camarón de la Isla *Calle Real* (Polygram).

Camarón de la Isla *Una leyenda flamenca*, *Vivire* and *Autorretrato* (Philips).

Carmen Linares *Cantaora* (Riverboat).

Paco de Lucía *Luzía* (Polygram).

Paco de Lucía *Siroco* (Philips).

Paco de Lucía y Paco Peña *Paco Doble* (Philips).

Enrique de Melchor *Cuchichi* (Fonodisc).

José Menese *El viente solano* (Nuevos Medios).

Moraíto *Morao y oro* (Auvidis).

Enrique Morente *Negra, si tú supieras* (Nuevos Medios).

Paco Peña *Flamenco Guitar Music of Ramon Montoya and Niño Ricardo* (Nimbus Records).

Ramón el Portugués *Gitanos de la Plaza* (Nuevos Medios).

Saetas *Cante de la Semana Santa Andaluza* (Auvidis).

Tomatito *Barrío Negro* (Nuevos Medios).

NUEVO FLAMENCO

Various *Los Jóvenes Flamencos Vol I–5* (Nuevos Medios).

Amalgama y Karnataka College of Percussion (Nuba).

La Barbería del Sur (Nuevos Medios).

Chano Domínguez *Chano* (Nuba).

Ray Heredía *Quien no corre, vuela* (Nuevos Medios).

Jazzpaña (Nuevos Medios).

Ketama *Canciones hondas* (Nuevos Medios) and Ketama (Hannibal).

Lolé . . . y Manuel (Gong Fonomusic).

Paco de Lucía Sextet *Solo Quiero Caminar* and *Live in America* (Philips), *Live . . . One Summer Night* (Phonogram).

Pata Negra *Blues de la Frontera* (Nuevos Medios/Hannibal).

Radio Tarifa *Rumba Argelina* (World Circuit).

Radio Tarifa *Temporal* (World Circuit).

Songhai (Ketama/Toumani Diabate/Danny Thompson) *Songhai* and *Songhai 2* (Nuevos Medios/Hannibal).

Juan Peña Lebrijano y Orquestra Andalusi de Tanger *Encuentros* (Ariola/Globestyle).

FOLK AND REGIONAL

Various *El gusto es nuestro* (Ariola).

Various *Magna Antología del Fulklore Musical de España* (Hispavox; 17 LPs).

Various *La sal de la vida* (NubeNegra).

Various *Voice of Spain: Spanish regional music* (Heritage).

Rafael Alberti y Paco Ibañez *A galopar* (PDI).

Bernardo Atxaga *Nueva Etiopia* (Colleccion Lcd el Europeo).

Luís Eduardo Aute y Silvio Rodríguez *Mano a mano* (Ariola).

Ana Belen *Veneno para el corazón* (Ariola).
María del Mar Bonet *Salmaia* (Ariola).
María del Mar Bonet *El cor del temps* (Picap, Spain, 2CDs).
María Del Mar Bonet *Anells D'Aigua* (Ariola).
María Del Mar Bonet *Cancons de fiesta* (Ariola).
María Del Mar Bonet *Canta M.Theodorakis* (Ariola).
Olaio Centenera *No soy la Piquer* (RNE).
Carlos Cano *Quedate con la Copla* (CBS).
Llan de Cubel *L'otru llaou de la mar* (Fono Astur).
Vainica Doble *1970* (RNE).
Fía na Roca (Arpafolk).
Pablo Guerrero *Todo la vida es ahora* (Polygram).
Habas Verdes *En el jardin de la yerba buena* (Gam).
Imanol *Alfonsina, viaje de mar y luna* (Ediciones Cúbicas).
Kepa Junkera *Bilbao 00.00* (Resistencia).
Kepa Junkera *Trikitixa zoom* (Nuba).
Kepa, Zabaleta & Imanol *Triki Up* (Elkar).
Mikel Laboa *Lau-Bost* (Elkar).
Leilía *Leilía* (Discmedi Blau).
Benito Lertxundi *Hyunkidura kuttunak* (Elkar).
Lluís Llach *Lluis Llach A L'Olympia* (Fonomusic).
Lluís Llach *Ara 25 anys en directe* (Picap).
Lluís Llach *Mon porrera* (Picap).
Manuel Luna *Como hablan las sabinas* (RNE).
La Musgaña *El Diablo Cojuelo* (Sonifolk).
Mestisay *El cantar viene de lejos* (Manzana).
Milladoiro *As Fadas de Estrano Nome* (Green Linnet records).
Milladoiro *Galicia no temp* (Discmedi).
Nuevo Mester De Juglaria *25 Aniversario* (Polygram).
Aurora Moreno *Aynadamar* (Saga).
Carlos Nunez *A Irmandade das Estrelas* (Ariola, Spain).
Ruper Ordorika *Ez da posible* (Gasa) and *Hiru truku* (Nuevos Medios).
Ruper Ordorika *Bilduma Bat* (Elkar).
Oskorri *Badok hamahiru* (Elkar).
La Paloma *One Song For All Worlds* (Indigo).
Albert Pla *No solo de rumba vive el hombre* (Ariola).
Port-Bo *Arrel de tres* (Picap).
Port-Bo *Canela y Ron* (Picap).
Raímon *Cancons* (Auvidis).

Marina Rossell *Marina* (PDI).
Bleizi Ruz, Leilía, La Musgaña *Hent Sant Jakez* (Shamrock Records).
Maria Salgado *Mirandote* (NubeNegra).
Salpicão (RNE).
Joan Manuel Serrat *Utopia* (Ariola).
Joan Manuel Serrat *Nadie es perfecto* (Ariola).
Joan Manuel Serrat *Sombras de la China* (Ariola).
Joan Manuel Serrat *Serrat en directo* (Ariola).
Al Tall y Muluk el Hwa *Xarq al-Andalus* (RNE).
Tapia Eta Leturia *Dultzemeneoa* (Elkar).
Els Trobadors *Et ades sera l'Alba* (Lyricon).
Uxia *Estou vivindo no ceo* (NubeNegra).

ROCK
Arrajatabla *Sevilla blues* (Fonomusic).
Ana Belen, Miguel Rios, Víctor Manuel, Joan Manuel Serrat *El gusto es nuestro* (Ariola).
Celtas Cortos *Cuentame un cuento* (DRO).
Celtas Cortos *Tranquilo majete* (Dro).
Ciudad Jardín *Ojos mas que ojos* (Hispavox).
Corcobado *Tormenta de tormento* (Triquinoise).
Fangoria *Una ola cualquiera en Vulcano* (Gasa).
Héroes del Silencio *El espíritu del vino* (Hispavox).
Illegales *Regreso al sexo químicamente puro* (Hispavox).
Luz *A contraluz* (Hispavox).
Negu Gorriak *Borreroak baditu milaka aurpegi* (Esan Ozanki).
Presuntos Implicados *Alma de blues* (WEA).
Radio Futura *Tierra para bailar* (Ariola).
Los Rebeldes *La rosa y la cruz* (Epic).
Os Resentidos *Están aqui* (Gasa).
Miguel Ríos *Así que pasen 30 años* (Polydor).
Los Rodríguez *Sin documentos* (Gasa).
Rosario *De Ley* (Epic).
Los Secretos *Cambio de planes* (Dro).
Seguridad Social *Furia Latina* (Gasa).
Tam Tam Go! *Vida y color* (Hispavox).
Manolo Tena *Sangre Española* (Epic).
El Ultimo de la Fila *Astronomía razonable* (EMI).
Antonio Vega *El sitio de mi recreo* (Polygram).
Kiko Veneno *La Pequeña Salvaje* (Nuevos Medios) and *Échate un cantecito* (BMG).

too in every local festival, as does a tradition of popular singing linking Catalunya with Cuba, known as *habanera*, which thrives today in summer festivals on the Costa Brava coast. With maritime connections strong in the nineteenth and twentieth centuries, the music of *ida y vuelta*, coming and going, of greeting and farewell, has endured in fishermen's choirs and small groups, and has now been taken up again by young people.

Other Spanish musicians to take note of include *Al Tall*, an interesting band from Valencia, whose last major project was a joint effort with *Muluk El Hwa*; *Alimara*, a group from Marrakesh who are involved with both music and traditional dance; *Salpicao*, who have experimented with flamenco-based fusions; and *La Vella Banda*, an innovative horn band.

Joaquín Díaz, a phenomenally hard-working and prolific artist, has for many years dominated the musical life of Castile, as have the prolific *Nuevo Mester de Juglaría*, a distinguished group who established an alternative roots music to Franco's folkloristic ventures. Manuel Luna and *La Musgaña* have created fine sounds, as has the singer María Salgado, who has made recordings of the *habanera* tradition found outside Catalunya, and who worked on *La sal de la vida* (The Salt of Life), with two other women musicians, Uxía from Galicia and Rasha from the Sudan – together they explore the similarities and differences, rhythms and cadence, of each other's cultures, including largely unheard-of songs from Galicia and Asturias. Other musicians to listen out for include the Segovian group, *Rebolada*, who include eight *dulzainas* (flutes) in their line-up, and *Habas Verdes* from Zamora, who produce spirited, vivid versions of traditional tunes on instruments such as the hurdy-gurdy and the *dulzaina*, as well as the cello, organ and guitar.

Andalucía is home not only to flamenco but also other musics: *Almadraba* from Tarifa explore the highly traditional, while *Lombarda* from Granada are more revivalist. Andalucía is also where you'll find **Sephardic** (Iberian Jewish) music, often a cross between folk and traditional styles. Rosa Zaragoza and Aurora Moreno are two female singers who have produced interesting work in this field; Moreno is also involved in Mozarabic *jarchas* (Arabic verse set to music). *Els Trobadors* and *Cálamus* have both also successfully revived medieval tradi-

tions, while the outstanding Luís Delgado works with sephardic, medieval and Spanish Arabic music.

ROCK AND POP

Even when it comes to rock and pop music, it is hard to talk of Spain as a single entity. In the 1970s Anglo-American rock inspired the first rock groups, including Miguel Ríos and *Los Bravos*, as well as the progressive proto-rock of *Los Canarios*, *Maquina* and *Música Dispersa*, pioneers of the musical underground. Madrid was dominated by **heavy rock**, with a series of groups like *Burning*, *Mermelada* and *Indiana*, whose fans lived in the working-class districts of the capital and in the dormitory towns of the outskirts. Meanwhile, in Barcelona, the scene was split between musicians who were producing a very cool **jazz-rock**, and those into a warmer **Catalan salsa**, or Barcelona's own gypsy music – **Catalan rumba**, popularized by Peret, a Barcelona musician with a liking for Elvis Presley. On the fringes were the singer-songwriters and the Latin American groups who, despite Franco, managed to tour Spain.

At the end of the 1970s, a **punk** reaction began to take hold among teenagers, just as it did in Britain and the US. Some older rockers, like Ramoncín, attempted to take punk on board, but punk challenged and broke up the old order, setting the scene for the future, with an explosion of diverse groups.

Since then, straight **pop** has been the main area of activity, but there have been various phases in which punks, technos, *garajistas*, *siniestros*, Romantics and rockabillies have had success, crossing over between genres.

Today, **Madrid** has an active scene, with bands covering a wide range of styles and stances. A key figure on the scene since the punk days is **Alaska**, a club owner and one-time muse of modernity, whose records are less significant than his brilliant live performances. Female singer **Mecano**, accompanied by two male musicians, has become the most successful Spanish pop group ever, popular in Latin America, France and Italy, as well as Spain. Other established bands include the country-influenced *Los Secretos*; the futuristic *Aviador Dro*; Miguel Ríos and Ramoncín, both of whom stick to classic rock; and the heavy-metal groups, *Rosendo*, *Obús* and *Barón Rojo*. A slightly younger generation includes *Gabinete*

Caligari (macho Hispano-pop), *Los Coyotes* (Latin rockabilly) and *La Frontera* (cowboy), while Luz, and Rosario, an interesting and original singer from a flamenco dynasty (the daughter of Rosa Flores), have become big new stars.

In **Barcelona** one of the most innovative bands has been *El Ultimo de la Fila*, a duo with engaging lyrics and a sophisticated Mediterranean sound. Equally enjoyable are *Los Rebeldes*, former rockabilly heroes, who have been exploring new directions.

Euskadi has witnessed a two-part musical scene: radical rock has been represented by *Negu Gorriak*, *Potato*, *Hertzainak* and *La Polla Records*, who use hot rhythms, reggae and ska as a base for a message with an undeniable political conscience. On a more straightforward rock level, *21 Japonesas* and *La Dama se Esconde* have demanded attention.

From **Galicia** (especially Vigo) a surprising number and diversity of bands have emerged, including *Siniestro Total* and *Os Resentidos* in the 1980s, with *Os Diplomaticos* an interesting new arrival of the 1990s. *Los Ilegales*, powerful rockers with a strong live set, have emerged in **Asturias**, while in **Aragón**, *Heroes del Silencio* have been one of the major chart rock groups of the 1990s.

In **Andalucía**, the *malagueño* combo *Danza Invisible* have had some unforgettable catchy hits, and the long list of artists from Sevilla include the astonishing Martirio (who combines pop and traditional songs with a playful, witty sense of challenging Spanish stereotypes); Arrajatabla and Kiko Veneno. Veneno's sporadic albums are clever, literate, utterly Spanish rock songs and come highly recommended.

JAZZ

Jazz in Spain has always had loyal fans tucked away in small clubs, but since the end of the 1970s it has really taken off. There are many festivals and a good number of established groups. Bop and hard bop predominate, but there are also many experiments with fusion and traditional jazz.

Two great musicians exemplify the best in current Spanish jazz: the Madrid saxophonists **Pedro Iturralde** and **Jorge Pardo**. Both head their own groups and Jorge also works on flamenco projects with Paco de Lucía. Other combos which stand out are the Madrid-based *Canal Street Band* and *Clamores Band*, both trad; the ultramodern *O C Q*; Vlady Bas's group; and the groups led by Tomás San Miguel, José Antonio Galicia and Gerardo Núñez – all of them working in Madrid.

The country's biggest **jazz festival** is held at San Sebastián in July. Vitoria celebrates one in the same month, and there are two in Madrid: one in May (*Fiestas de San Isidro*), the other in November. November is jazz month in Spain, when there's also a festival in Barcelona, and many smaller events which take the opportunity of featuring some of the artists who are playing in the two major cities. Other worthwhile events are the *Fiesta de Jazz* in the streets of Murcia and the *Muestra de Jazz* for young exponents, organized by the Instituto de la Juventud in Ibiza.

Jan Fairley and Manuel Domínguez

CINEMA

It has not always been easy for cinema to take root in Spain. The lack of a proper infrastructure, the devastation of the Civil War, and the restrictions of the Franco regime all meant that Spanish film-makers had to struggle to get films made, and then often to struggle again to get them released.
The vast majority of Spanish films remain unseen outside Spain. From the 1950s onwards, Spanish films would periodically appear on the film festival circuit and, on occasion, be taken up by an art-house cinema. One director in particular, **Carlos Saura**, achieved international prestige even while working under the restrictions of the Franco regime. From an earlier generation, **Luis Buñuel** has long been accepted as one of the major figures in the history of cinema. But Saura was something of an exception, while Buñuel made almost all of his films in either France or Mexico.

The end of the dictatorship, however, has been followed by a remarkable degree of film-making activity, and today the films of Spanish directors, **Pedro Almodóvar** in particular, are capable of filling cinemas within and beyond Spain. The garishly modern Madrid of *Women on the Edge of a Nervous Breakdown*, the dusty Los Monegros plains of *Jamón Jamón*, the magical-realist Basque landscape of *Vacas* – these have all helped to establish Spain on the world cinema map.

THE EARLY DECADES

The history of Spanish film goes back to the last century, and Spain even produced one of the pioneers of early cinema, **Segundo de Chomón**, a man whose use of trick photography rivalled that of the French director, Georges Méliès. Overall, however, Spanish cinema developed slowly. Spain entered the twentieth century lacking the technology, the capital and the urban audiences that produced a thriving film industry in neighbouring France. "In my own village of Calanda," wrote Luis Buñuel in his autobiography, "...the Middle Ages lasted until World War I." Like Buñuel, Segundo de Chomón spent most of his career abroad, and ended up producing special effects for other directors in Italy and France. By the 1920s, a Spanish film industry had been established, but its modest scale and pretensions are indicated in the slogan used to promote one film made in 1925 – "It's so good that it doesn't seem Spanish."

Without a strong production base, cinema in Spain was particularly susceptible to the rapidly developing power of **America**. In the early 1930s "Spanish" films were being produced, but often in Hollywood rather than Madrid, as the major American film companies dealt with the coming of sound (and the threat that an active Spanish film industry might have provided) by producing Spanish-language versions of their English-speaking product. In the process they deprived Spain of a number of its film-makers.

However, in 1934, a major production and distribution company, **CIFAS**, was founded in Madrid. With a degree of support from the Republican government, and with the native product proving more popular than subtitled American movies (though dubbing was gradually adopted as a standard practice), the Spanish film industry began to appear relatively healthy. Luis Buñuel returned to Spain from France – where, with fellow Spaniard Salvador Dalí, he had directed a couple of surrealist classics, *Un Chien Andalou* (1928) and *L'Age d'Or* (1930) – to make *Land Without Bread* (1932). This film, an unremitting documentary about rural poverty, was promptly banned, but Buñuel stayed on, dubbing films for Warner Bros, and working as executive producer (and reputedly occasional director) on four more mainstream projects.

The **Civil War** and the eventual Nationalist victory drove Buñuel into exile. It also ended the brief flowering of popular Spanish cinema that had been exhibited in films such as *Paloma Fair* (1935) and *Clara the Brunette* (1936), the latter featuring the first "star" of Spanish cinema, Imperio Argentina.

During the war, the Communists and the anarcho-syndicalists produced numerous short works extolling their cause; there were also appeals for international support for the Republican cause in films such as Joris Ivens's *The Spanish Earth* (1937). Some **propagandist** films were produced by the victorious Nationalist regime, including *Madrid Front* (1939) and *Race* (1941), the latter an adaptation of Franco's own novel. More significant was the establishment of the **Supreme Board of Film Censorship**, inaugurating four decades in which censorship became the strongest force in Spanish cinema.

THE FRANCO YEARS

Under Franco, both scripts and completed films had to be submitted for approval, and films had to be dubbed into the "official" Castilian dialect. No actual code of censorship was laid down until 1963, but this only gave greater freedom to the censors. Film-makers also needed to placate the Catholic Church, which in 1950 established the **National Board of Classification of Spectacles** which made its own "recommendations".

Some efforts were made to support an indigenous Spanish film industry. In 1947 a **film school** was established in Madrid (where students were able to see foreign films banned from public exhibition), and in 1952 state **subsidy** regulations were changed to allow for the award of fifty percent of the costs of films deemed to be of "national interest". In practice this did little to vary the diet of epics, dramas, musicals and comedies which glorified the Spanish past and presented **idealized images** of the state, the Church and the family.

It was against this background that a group of **left-wing film-makers** met in 1955, declaring contemporary Spanish cinema to be "1. Politically futile. 2. Socially false. 3. Intellectually worthless. 4. Aesthetically valueless. 5. Industrially paralytic." Inspired by the example of Italian neo-realism, such film-makers

were, in fact, already beginning to present a less idealized picture of Spanish society. Films such as Luis Berlanga's *Welcome Mr Marshall* (1952), a satire about the effect of America's Marshall Plan on a Spanish village, and Antonio Bardem's *Death of a Cyclist* (1956), suggested that there was some room for alternative voices in the Spanish film industry.

The restrictions continued (in 1956 Bardem was briefly imprisoned for his political views), but the Spanish government did institute a slightly more flexible policy, if largely to attract international support and investment. While American film companies were being persuaded to use relatively inexpensive **Spanish locations** for films such as *Alexander the Great* (1955), the prestige offered by the international film festival circuit meant that even films offering a critical view of Spanish institutions could be used as a means of "selling" Spain abroad.

The contradictions inherent in this policy were shown up most blatantly when Buñuel was invited back to Spain to make a film for the production company **UNINCI**, which had been formed by a group of film-makers including Bardem, Berlanga and Carlos Saura. The resulting film, *Viridiana* (1961), revealed that the director of *L'Age d'Or* could be as uncompromising as ever. Astonishingly, the film was initially passed by the censor despite scenes including a parody of The Last Supper, acted out by an assortment of drunks and beggars – and was only banned after it had been attacked in the Vatican newspaper. The result was that Buñuel resumed his career in Mexico and France, and the promise and short life of UNINCI was brought to a close.

Buñuel returned to Spain to make *Tristana* in 1970 and *That Obscure Object of Desire* in 1977, though both were French-Spanish co-productions rather than exclusively Spanish. *Viridiana* was not publicly shown in Spain until 1977.

In the slightly liberalized but still restrictive atmosphere of the 1960s and 1970s, some directors managed to develop the problem of getting round the censor into something of a fine art. **Carlos Saura**, in particular, who had quickly left behind the naturalism of his earliest films, used the power of suggestion, allegory and symbol to attack Francoist pretensions in films such as *The Hunt* (1965) and *The Garden of Delights* (1970). Working in association with the actress Geraldine Chaplin and the producer Elías Querejeta, he used his developing international prestige to retain a remarkable degree of control over his own films.

Other directors lacked Saura's prestige, though the loose movement known as the **Barcelona School** attempted to challenge the dominance of Madrid and the lack of adventure in mainstream Spanish cinema. Meanwhile, another side of Spanish cinema was revealed in the developing market for **low-budget horror films**, capitalizing on the fact that violence was less censored than directly sexual or political.

In the last years of the Franco regime, Saura continued to maintain his independence, exploring the scars of the Civil War in *Cousin Angelica* (1973), and the consequences of repression in *Raise Ravens* (1975). The aftermath of the Civil War also provided the theme for Victor Erice's remarkable debut feature, *The Spirit of the Beehive* (1973), a lyrical film set in a bleak Castilian village and featuring, like *Raise Ravens*, the young **Ana Torrént**.

A more violent picture of rural Spain was presented in Ricardo Franco's *Pascale Duarte* (1975) and José Luis Borau's *Poachers* (1975). In its story of **disintegrating authority**, the latter film, released shortly before Franco's death, seemed almost to anticipate the demise of the dictatorship: it was shown despite objections from the censor, and drew large crowds at the box-office.

AFTER FRANCO

In 1977 censorship was formally abolished, and though a none too sympathetic portrayal of the Civil Guard in Pilar Miró's *The Cuenca Crime* (1980) initially led to that film being seized by the police, Miró's film also went on to break box-office records. In 1982 Miró herself – whose *Gary Cooper, Who Art in Heaven* (1980) told of the difficulties of a woman working in a male-dominated industry – was appointed Director General of Cinema by the incoming Socialist government.

With the **death of Franco**, and the **lifting of censorship**, Spanish film-makers were able to engage with politics more directly: *Black Brood* (1977), directed by Manuel Gutiérrez Aragón, dealt with right-wing terrorists; *The Truth About the Salvatore Affair* (1978), directed by Antonio

Drove, returned to history (Barcelona between 1917 and 1923) to examine the economic roots of political change; while Juan Bardem mixed thriller and documentary in his *Seven Days in May* (1978).

Liberalization brought its own problems. Under Franco the Spanish film industry had been restricted but also cushioned; now filmmakers found themselves competing against an influx of American imports for a share of a declining audience. As Director General of cinema, Miró set out to halt this trend by reintroducing **protectionist measures** and government subsidies. Efforts were also made to decentralize the film industry, and to move away from Franco's exclusive emphasis on Spain's Castilian heritage. For the first time, films using the Catalan language became possible following the establishment in 1975 of the **Institute of Catalan Film**, while the Basque government also financed a number of projects. National and regional subsidies have continued, although since the Socialist's fall from power they have been significantly reduced.

For directors who had mastered the art of indirect statement under Franco, the end of the dictatorship necessitated a change of direction. For **Carlos Saura** this change bore fruit in the form of *Blood Wedding* (1981), which showed Antonio Gades and his troupe rehearsing and performing a ballet version of the Federico Garcia Lorca play; his collaboration with Gades continued with *Carmen* (1983) and *Love the Magician* (1986). Saura returned to the Civil War with the tragi-comic *Ay, Carmela* (1990), and has continued to explore subjects from dance to neo-fascism in films such as *Flamenco* (1995) and *Taxi* (1996).

Since *The Spirit of the Beehive*, **Victor Erice** has directed just two films. In *The South* (1983), he gave a further poetic and unsentimental exploration of a father-daughter relationship under the shadow of the Civil War. *The Quince Tree Sun* (1991) – a slow but ultimately rewarding study of an artist at work – recorded the meticulous preparations made by the Spanish artist Antonio López while he waited to capture the exact light needed for his painting. A further film, *The Shanghai Gesture*, is reported to be in preparation.

Julio Medem, one of a number of Basque directors to emerge in recent years, has carved an individual, sometimes mystifying, but also striking path with *Vacas* (1991), which tells four interrelated stories about a feud between two families, *The Red Squirrel* (1993) and *Earth* (1996).

Vicente Aranda, who directed his first film in 1964, achieved his international breakthrough with *The Lovers* (1991), a highly-charged story of fatal attraction in 1950s Madrid starring **Victoria Abril**, who had made her debut in Aranda's *Change of Sex* (1976). More recently Aranda has had commercial if not critical successes with both *Turkish Passion* (1995) and the big-budgeted Civil War drama, *Libertarians* (1996).

The past has continued to figure prominently in Spanish films, though most directors have tended to avoid directly confronting the Civil War. Pedro Olea's *The Fencing Master* (1993) returned to nineteenth-century Madrid for its narrative of love, fate and death; Fernando Trueba's *Belle Epoque* (1993), set in a nostalgic recreation of the Republican 1930s, became the second Spanish film to win the Best Foreign Film Oscar (the first being *Begin the Beguin* (1982), directed by José Luis Garci); while before her death in 1997, Pilar Miró had a box-office success with *The Dog in the Manger* (1996), an adaptation of Lope de Vega's seventeenth-century comedy.

Other directors who came to prominence after the dictatorship seemed intent on turning their back on history. The cinema of **Pedro Almodóvar**, in particular, represents a break with both the idealized films that towed the Franco line, and the social commitment of directors such as Bardem and Berlanga. "I never speak of Franco," he has stated. "I hardly acknowledge his existence. I start after Franco."

Almodóvar made his feature film debut in 1980 with the cheap and transgressive *Pepi, Lucy, Bom and a Whole Load of Other Girls*. His prodigious output during the 1980s included *What Have I Done to Deserve This* (1982), a black comedy about drugs, prostitution and the forging of Hitler's diaries, *Matador* (1986), a dark thriller linking sexual excitement with the violence of the bullfight, *The Law of Desire* (1987), a story involving a gay film director, his transsexual brother/sister, murder and incest, as well as the internationally successful *Women on the Edge of a Nervous Breakdown* (1988). He has remained one of the very few directors able to attract audiences across the globe with films in a language other than English.

Almodóvar's films have benefited from the performances of actors such as Carmen Maura, Victoria Abril, Rosy de Palma and Antonio Banderas, and over time they have gained in narrative coherence and production values while retaining the capacity to offend (notably with *Tie Me Up, Tie Me Down* (1990)). If his work was seen as losing something of its edge in the mid-1990s, his most recent film, *Live Flesh* (1997), has been praised as heralding a more mature film-maker, interested in moving beyond his trademark concern with shock and style.

Bigas Luna is another director capable of simultaneously offending and delighting audiences within and beyond Spain. He achieved notoriety with *Jamón Jamón* (1992), and has continued his relentless preoccupation with sex, food and machismo in films such as *Golden Balls* (1993) and *The Tit and the Moon* (1994). **Alex de la Inglesia**'s *Mutant Action* (1993) imagined (in gruesome detail) a future in which the disabled wage war on the beautiful, while **Juanma Bajo Ulloa**, director of the disturbing psychological thriller, *The Dead Mother* (1993), had a hit at the Spanish box-office with *Airbag* (1995), a gleefully tasteless comedy about three men searching for a missing wedding ring through a succession of brothels.

New directors have continued to emerge. The camp comedy of **Felix Sabroso** and **Dunia Ayaso**'s *I'm Sorry Darling, but Lucas Loved Me* (1997) has been described as reminiscent of early Almodóvar. **Iciar Bollaín**, after acting roles that included the daughter in Erice's *The South* and a fiery freedom fighter in Ken Loach's Civil War drama, *Land and Freedom* (1995), wrote and directed *Hi, Are You Alone?* (1996), a sympathetic portrait of a pair of young women, travelling through Spain with an uncertain destination. **Alejandro Amerábar** made his directorial debut with *Thesis* (1995), an intelligent thriller about a student researching violence in the media, which collected a handful of awards at the Goya ceremony (the Spanish version of the Oscars). Ana Torrént, now a 29 year-old veteran of Spanish cinema, played the student; Amerábar, aged 23 when he made the film, belongs to a generation with barely a memory of Spain under Franco.

Guy Barefoot

BOOKS

Listings below represent a highly selective reading list on Spain and matters Spanish, especially in the sections on history. Most titles are in print, although we've included a few older classics, many of them easy enough to find in second-hand bookshops and libraries. For all books in print, publishing details are in the form (UK publisher; US publisher), where both exist; if books are published in one country only, this follows the publisher's name (eg Serpent's Tail, UK). University Press has been abbreviated as UP.

If you have difficulty finding any title, an excellent source for books about Spain – new, used, and out of print – is Books On Spain, PO Box 207, Twickenham, TW2 5BQ, UK; ☎ & fax 0181/898 7789; email *keith_harris_books @compuserve.com.*

IMPRESSIONS, TRAVEL AND GENERAL ACCOUNTS

THE BEST INTRODUCTIONS

Ian Gibson *Fire in the Blood: the New Spain* (Faber/BBC, UK). Gibson is a Madrid-based writer, resident since 1978, and a Spanish national since 1984. He is a passionate enthusiast and critic of Spain and the Spanish, both of which he gets across brilliantly in this 1993 book – the accompaniment to a gripping TV series – in all their mass of contradictions, attitudes, obsessions, quirks and everything else. It received flak from outraged Spanish reviewers, and it's dating somewhat, but still hugely recommended.

John Hooper *The New Spaniards* (Penguin, UK/US). This excellent, authoritative portrait of post-Franco Spain was written by *The Guardian's* correspondent in 1986 and published in a revised edition in 1995. Along with Ian Gibson's book (above), it is the best possible introduction to contemporary Spain.

Lucy McCauley (ed) *Spain: Travelers' Tales* (O'Reilly, US). It would be hard to better this anthology of writing on Spain, which gathers its stories and journalism predominantly from the last ten years. Featured authors include Gabriel García Márquez, Colm Tóibín and Louis de Bernières, whose "Seeing Red", on the tomato-throwing festival of Buñol, is worth the purchase price on its own.

RECENT TRAVELS/ACCOUNTS

Alastair Boyd *Essence of Catalonia* and *The Sierras of the South: Travels in the Mountains of Andalucia* (Harper Collins, UK). Part travel books, part history, these are good general introductions to their respective regions, with entertaining discourses on food, drink, art, literature and language.

Carrie B. Douglass *Bulls, Bullfighting and Spanish Identities* (Arizona UP, US). Anthropologist Douglass delves into the symbolism of the bull in the Spanish national psyche, and then goes on to examine the bullfight's role in some of the thousands of fiestas countrywide that support it.

Nina Epton *Grapes and Granite* (out of print). One of the few English books on Galicia – full of folklore and rural life in the 1960s – and well worth hunting down in libraries or second-hand bookshops.

David Gilmour *Cities of Spain* (John Murray; Ivan R Dee). A modern cultural portrait of Spain, but very much in the old tradition; it is a little fogeyish at times but excellent, nonetheless, in its evocation of history, especially on the Moorish cities of Andalucía.

Adam Hopkins *Spanish Journeys: a Portrait of Spain* (Penguin, UK). Published in 1993, this is an enjoyable and highly stimulating exploration of Spanish history and culture, weaving its (considerable) scholarship in an accessible and unforced travelogue form, and full of illuminating anecdotes.

Robert Hughes *Barcelona* (Harvill/Vintage). This is the best of the 1992 books on the Olympic city: a text that, in the author's stated ambition, "explains the zeitgeist of the place and the connective tissue between the cultural icons".

Michael Jacobs *Between Hopes and Memories: a Spanish Journey* (Picador, UK). The thorough and entertaining account of a journey through Spain in 1992 with lively digressions on food, art, literature and the characters met along the way. *Andalusia* (Viking UK/US), by the same author, is an outstanding introduction to the region.

Peter B. Meyer *A True Story About Doing Business in Spain* (Avon Books, UK). This quirkily written insider's view of Spanish business life features encounters with corrupt bureaucracy, shifty lawyers, crooked business partners and a parade of police and politicos straight out of central casting. Sometimes skewed, but always fascinating.

Cees Nooteboom *Roads to Santiago: Detours and Riddles in the Land and History of Spain* (Harvill; Harcourt Brace). This is one of the most literary travel books of recent decades: an almost Shandyesque tale (few of the roads travelled lead anywhere near Santiago), garnished from the notebooks of this quirky, architecture-obsessed Dutch writer. Very highly recommended.

Eamonn O'Neill *Matadors: a journey into the heart of modern bullfighting* (Mainstream, UK). Part autobiographical travelogue, part sociological study of the role of bullfighting in modern Spain.

Paul Richardson *Not Part of the Package* (Macmillan, UK). Published in 1993, this is the best account yet of tourism in Spain – in this case a year's hedonism on Ibiza, which emerges in all its disco-dazzled lights.

Paul Richardson *Our Lady of the Sewers* (Little Brown, UK) An articulate and kaleidoscopic series of insights into rural Spain's customs and cultures, fast disappearing.

Chris Stewart *Driving Over Lemons – An Optimist in Andalucía* (Sort Of/Penguin, UK). A funny, insightful and very charming account of life on a remote peasant farm in the Alpujarras. The author, oddly enough, was the original drummer in *Genesis*.

Robert White *A River in Spain* (I.B. Tauris UK/US). Well-written account of an American's love affair with the Duero valley; strong on towns, history, architecture and local folklore.

James Woodall *In Search of the Firedance: Spain through Flamenco* (Sinclair-Stevenson, UK). A terrific history and exploration of flamenco.

EARLIER TWENTIETH-CENTURY WRITERS

Gerald Brenan *South From Granada* (Penguin, UK). An enduring classic. Brenan lived in a small village in the Alpujarras in the 1920s, and records this and the visits of his Bloomsbury contemporaries Virginia Woolf, Lytton Strachey and Bertrand Russell.

Camilo José Cela *Journey to the Alcarria* (Penguin; Wisconsin UP). A Nobel Prize-winner for literature, Cela explored a hidden corner of New Castile in 1946 – a study of a rural world that no longer exists.

Laurie Lee *As I Walked Out One Midsummer Morning* (Penguin, UK), *A Rose For Winter* (Penguin, UK), *A Moment of War* (Penguin; New Press). *One Midsummer Morning* is the irresistibly romantic account of Lee's walk through Spain – from Vigo to Málaga – and his gradual awareness of the forces moving the country towards Civil War. As an autobiographical novel, of living rough and busking his way from the Cotswolds with a violin, it's a delight; as a piece of social observation, painfully sharp. In *A Rose For Winter* he describes his return, twenty years later, to Andalucía, while in *A Moment of War* he looks back again to describe a winter fighting with the International Brigade in the Civil War – by turns moving, comic and tragic.

James A. Michener *Iberia* (Corgi; Crest). A bestselling, idiosyncratic and encyclopedic compendium of interviews and impressions of Spain on the brink – in 1968 – looking forward to the post-Franco years. Fascinating, still.

Jan Morris *Spain* (Penguin; Prentice-Hall). Morris wrote this in six months in 1960, on her (or, at the time, his) first visit to the country. It is an impressionistic account – good in its sweeping control of place and history, though prone to see everything as symbolic. The updated edition is plain bizarre in its ideas on Franco and dictatorship – a condition for which Morris seems to believe Spaniards were naturally inclined.

George Orwell *Homage to Catalonia* (Penguin; Harvest Books). Stirring account of Orwell's participation in the early exhilaration of revolution in Barcelona, and his growing disillusionment with the factional fighting among the Republican forces during the ensuing Civil War.

OLDER CLASSICS

George Borrow *The Bible in Spain* and *The Zincali* (both out of print). On first publication in 1842, Borrow subtitled *The Bible in Spain* "Journeys, Adventures and Imprisonments of an English-man"; it is one of the most famous books on Spain – slow in places but with some very amusing stories. *Zincali* is an account of the Spanish gypsies, whom Borrow got to know pretty well.

Richard Ford *A Handbook for Travellers in Spain and Readers at Home* (Centaur Press; Gordon Press); *Gatherings from Spain* (out of print). *The Handbook* (1845) must be the best guide ever written to any country and stayed in print as a *Murray's Handbook* (one of the earliest series of guides) well into the twentieth century. Massively opinionated, it is an extremely witty book in its British, nineteenth-century manner, and worth flicking through for the proverbs alone. Copies of *Murray's* may be available in second-hand bookshops (Stanfords in London sometimes have the Centaur edition) – the earlier the edition the purer the Ford. *The Gatherings* is a rather timid – but no less entertaining – abridgement of the general pieces, intended for a female audience who wouldn't have the taste for the more cerebral stuff. . . .

Washington Irving *Tales of the Alhambra* (originally published 1832; abridged editions are on sale in Granada). Half of Irving's book consists of oriental stories, set in the Alhambra; the rest of accounts of his own residence there and the local characters of his time. A perfect read in situ.

George Sand *A Winter in Majorca* (Academy Press, US). Sand and Chopin spent their winter at the monastery of Valldemossa. They weren't entirely appreciated by the locals, in which lies much of the book's appeal. Local editions, including a translation by late Mallorcan resident Robert Graves, are on sale around the island.

ANTHOLOGIES

Jimmy Burns (ed) *Spain: A Literary Companion* (John Murray, UK). A good anthology, including nuggets of most authors recommended here, amid a whole host of others.

David Mitchell *Travellers in Spain: An Illustrated Anthology* (Cassell, UK). A well-told story of how four centuries of travellers – and most often travel-writers – saw Spain. It's interesting to see Ford, Brenan, Laurie Lee and the rest set in context. Also published as *Here in Spain* (Lookout, Spain), widely available at bookshops in tourist areas.

HISTORY

GENERAL

Juan Lalaguna *A Traveller's History of Spain* (Windrush; Interlink). A lucid – and pocketable – background history to the country, which spans the Phoenicians to the 1990s and the maturing of democratic Spain.

M. Vincent & R.A. Stradling *Cultural Atlas of Spain and Portugal* (Andromeda, UK). A formidable survey of the Iberian peninsula from ancient times to the present, in coffee-table format, with excellent colour maps and well-chosen photographs.

PREHISTORIC AND ROMAN SPAIN

James M. Anderson *Spain: 1001 Archaeological Sites* (Hale; Calgary UP). A good guide and gazetteer to 95 percent of Spain's archeological sites, with detailed instructions of how to get there.

María Cruz Fernandez Castro *Iberia in Prehistory* (Blackwells, UK). A major study of the Iberian peninsula prior to the arrival of the Romans which surveys recent archeological evidence relating to the remarkable technical, economic and artistic progress of the early Iberians.

Roger Collins *Spain: An Archeological Guide* (Oxford UP, UK). Covering just 130 sites, this book's more detailed coverage makes it a more useful guide to the major sites than Anderson's work (above).

S.J. Keay *Roman Spain* (British Museum Publications; California UP). Definitive survey of a neglected subject, well illustrated and highly readable.

John Richardson *Roman Spain* (Blackwells, UK). This new assessment of the period, which includes recent discoveries and excavations, is part of a fourteen-volume history of Spain, covering prehistoric times to the present.

EARLY, MEDIEVAL AND BEYOND

J.M. Cohen *The Four Voyages of Christopher Columbus* (Cresset Library, UK). The man behind the myth; one of the best books on Columbus in English.

Roger Collins *The Arab Conquest of Spain 710–97* (Blackwells, UK). Controversial study which documents the Moorish invasion and the significant influence that the conquered Visigoths had on early Muslim rule. Collins's earlier *Early Medieval Spain 400–1000* (Macmillan, UK), takes a broader overview of the same subject.

John A. Crow *Spain: The Root and the Flower* (California UP, UK/US). Cultural/social history from Roman Spain to the present.

J.H. Elliott *Imperial Spain 1469–1716* (Penguin, UK/US). The best introduction to "the Golden Age" – academically respected and a gripping tale.

Richard Fletcher *The Quest for El Cid* (OUP, UK) and *Moorish Spain* (Orion–Phoenix/ California UP). Two of the best studies of their kind – fascinating and highly readable narratives.

L. P. Harvey *Islamic Spain 1250–1500* (Chicago UP, UK/US). Comprehensive account of its period – both the Islamic kingdoms and the Muslims living beyond their protection.

David Howarth *The Voyage of the Armada* (Penguin, US). An account from the Spanish perspective of the personalities, from king to sailors, involved in the Armada.

Henry Kamen *The Spanish Inquisition* (Mentor, US). Highly respected examination of the causes and effects of the Inquisition and the long shadow it cast across Spanish history. *The Spanish Inquisition: An Historical Revision* (Weidenfeld & Nicolson, UK), by the same author, returns to the subject in the light of more recent evidence, while his *Philip of Spain* (Yale UP, UK/US) is the first fully researched biography of Felipe II, the ruler most associated with the Inquisition.

Elie Kedourie *Spain and the Jews: the Sephardi Experience, 1492 and After* (Thames & Hudson, UK/US). A collection of essays on the three million Spanish Jews of the Middle Ages and their expulsion by the Catholic kings.

John Lynch *Spain 1598–1700* and *Bourbon Spain: 1700–1808* (Blackwells, UK). Two further volumes in the Blackwells project, written by the General Editor. It's an academic series but one

readable enough for anyone with an interest in the period(s) in question.

Colin Smith, Charles Melville & Ahmad Ubaydli *Christians and Moors in Spain* (Aris & Phillips, UK; 3 vols). A fascinating collection of documents by Spanish and Arabic writers from the Muslim conquest to the Christian supremacy, which are intended for the lay reader as well as the academic.

THE TWENTIETH CENTURY

Gerald Brenan *The Spanish Labyrinth* (CUP, UK/US). First published in 1943, Brenan's account of the background to the Civil War is tinged by personal experience, yet still an impressively rounded account.

Raymond Carr *Modern Spain 1875–1980* (OUP, UK/US) and *The Spanish Tragedy: the Civil War in Perspective* (Weidenfeld, UK). Two of the best books available on modern Spanish history – concise and well-told narratives.

Ronald Fraser *Blood of Spain* (Pantheon, US). Subtitled "The Experience of Civil War, 1936–39", this is an equally impressive piece of research, constructed entirely from oral accounts. *In Hiding* (Penguin, UK), by the same author, is a fascinating individual account of a Republican mayor hidden by his family for thirty years until the Civil War amnesty of 1969.

Ian Gibson *Federico García Lorca* (Faber & Faber; Pantheon), *The Assassination of Federico García Lorca* (Penguin, UK) and *Lorca's Granada* (Faber & Faber, UK/US). The biography is a compelling book and *The Assassination* a brilliant reconstruction of the events at the end of his life, with an examination of fascist corruption and of the shaping influences on Lorca, twentieth-century Spain and the Civil War. *Granada* contains a series of walking tours around parts of the town familiar to the poet.

Gerald Howson *Arms for Spain: the Untold Story of the Spanish Civil War* (John Murray, UK). This important book uses recently opened Russian and Polish archives to reveal how the Republicans were double-crossed by almost every foreign government they attempted to purchase arms from (including the Nazis) during the war – with their avowed ally Moscow one of the major culprits.

Robert Low *La Pasionaria* (Hutchinson, UK). Dolores Ibarruri – La Pasionaria – coined the battle cry *¡No Pasaran!* ("They shall not pass!") during the siege of Madrid and was a crucial figure in the leadership of the Spanish Communist Party during the Civil War, and in her subsequent exile. This is a skilful tale of her sad and extraordinary life.

Paul Preston *Franco* (Harper Collins, UK/US), *Concise History of the Spanish Civil War* (Harper Collins, UK/US). *Franco* is a penetrating – and monumental – biography of Franco and his regime, which provides as clear a picture as any yet published of how he won the Civil War and survived in power so long. *Civil War* is a compelling introduction to the subject and more accessible for the general reader than Thomas's work (below).

Adrian Shubert *A Social History of Spain* (Routledge, UK). Comprehensive and highly readable analysis of social development in Spain from 1800 to the 1980s.

Hugh Thomas *The Spanish Civil War* (Penguin; Touchstone). This exhaustive 1000-page study is regarded (both in Spain and abroad) as the definitive history of the Civil War.

ART, ARCHITECTURE, PHOTO-GRAPHY, FILM AND DESIGN

Marianne Barrucand and Achim Bednoz *Moorish Architecture* (Taschen, Germany). A beautifully illustrated guide to the major Moorish monuments.

Hugh Broughton *Madrid: A Guide to Recent Architecture* (Ellipsis Könemann, UK). Modern Spanish architecture is at the cutting edge of world design and this is a fluent and pocketable guide to a hundred of the best examples in Madrid, each with its own photo and directions on how to get there.

Jerrilyn D. Dodds *Al-Andalus* (Abrams, UK/US). An in-depth study of the arts and monuments of Moorish Andalucía, put together as a catalogue for a major exhibition at the Alhambra.

Godfrey Goodwin *Islamic Spain* (Chronicle Books, US). Portable architectural guide with descriptions of virtually every significant Islamic building in Spain, and a fair amount of background.

Cristina García Rodero *Festivals and Rituals of Spain* (Abrams, US), *España Oculta* (Little, Brown, US). *Festival and Rituals* is a mesmerizing photographic record of the exuberance and

colour of Spain's many fiestas by Spain's most astonishing contemporary photographer. *Oculta* is an equally atmospheric collection of black and white pictures celebrating the country's religion and mysticism.

Meyer Schapiro *Romanesque Art* (Thames & Hudson; Braziller). An excellent, illustrated survey of Romanesque art and architecture – and its Visigothic and Mozarabic precursors.

Suzanne Slesin et al *Spanish Style* (Thames & Hudson; Clarkson N. Potter). A gorgeous photographic compendium of Spanish style, old and new, in everything from its statuary and *azulejo* tilework to modern furniture and interiors.

Fréderic Strauss *Almodóvar on Almodóvar* (Faber & Faber, UK). Frank conversations between Strauss (co-editor of *Cahiers du Cinema*) and the Spanish film director concentrate on the work rather than the hype, punctuated by Almodóvar's contagious humour.

Anatxu Zabalbeascoa *The New Spanish Architecture* (Rizzoli, UK/US). A superb, highly illustrated study of the new Spanish architecture of the 1980s and 1990s in Barcelona, Madrid, Sevilla and elsewhere.

Numerous individual studies of Picasso, Miró, Dalí and Gaudí, as well as the classic Spanish painters, are, of course, also available.

FICTION AND POETRY

SPANISH CLASSICS

Pedro de Alarcón *The Three-Cornered Hat* (Everyman, UK). Ironic nineteenth-century tales of the previous century's corruption, bureaucracy and absolutism.

Leopoldo Alas *La Regenta* (Penguin, UK/US). Alas's nineteenth-century novel, with its sweeping vision of the disintegrating social fabric of the period, is a kind of Spanish Madame Bovary (a book that it was in fact accused of plagiarizing at time of publication).

Ramón Pérez de Ayala *Belarmino and Apolonio* (Quartet; California UP) and *Honeymoon*, *Bittermoon* (Quartet/California UP). A pair of tragi-comic picaresque novels written around the turn of the century.

Emilia Pardo Bazán *The House of Ulloa* (Penguin, UK/US). Bazán was an early feminist intellectual and in this, her best-known book, she charts the decline of the old aristocracy in the time of the Glorious Revolution of 1868.

Miguel de Cervantes *Don Quixote* (Penguin; Signet) and *Exemplary Stories* (Penguin, UK). *Quixote* is of course *the* classic of Spanish literature and still an excellent read. If you want to try Cervantes in a more modest dose, the *Stories* are a good place to start.

Benito Pérez Galdós *Fortunata and Jacinta* (Penguin, UK/US). Galdós wrote in the last decades of the nineteenth century and his novels of life in Madrid combine comic scenes and social realism; he is often characterized as a "Spanish Balzac". Other Galdós novels available in translation include *Misericordia* (Dedalus, UK), *Mazarín* (Oxford, UK), and the epic *"I"* (Columbia, US).

Saint Teresa of Ávila *The Life of Saint Teresa of Ávila* (Penguin, UK/US). Saint Teresa's autobiography is said to be the most widely read Spanish classic after *Don Quixote*. It takes some wading through but it's fascinating in parts. Various translations are available.

MODERN FICTION

Felipe Alfau *Locos: A Comedy of Gestures* (Penguin; Vintage), *Chromos* (Viking; Vintage). Though Alfau emigrated to New York and wrote in English (in the 1930s and 1940s), his recently republished novels are very Spanish; also well ahead of their time in terms of style, so perhaps not the easiest of reads.

Bernardo Atxaga *Obabakoak* (Vintage; Pantheon). This challenging novel by a Basque writer won major prizes on its Spanish publication. It is a sequence of tales of life in a Basque village and the narrator's search to give them meaning.

Francisco Ayala *Usurpers* (Penguin, UK/US). Ayala wrote these stories of corrupt power and ambition after the Civil War, in which his father and brother were killed by fascists. They are set in the middle ages, but with a clearly contemporary resonance.

Arturo Barea *The Forging of a Rebel* (out of print). Superb autobiographical trilogy, taking in the Spanish war in Morocco in the 1920s, and Barea's own part in the Civil War. The books have been published in UK paperback editions under the individual titles *The Forge*, *The Track* and *The Clash*.

Michel del Castillo *The Disinherited* (Serpent's Tail; Consort). Gripping tale of Madrid during the Civil War, written in 1959.

Victor Català (Caterina Albert i Paradís) *Solitude* (Readers International, UK/US). This tragic tale of a woman's life and sexual passions in a Catalan mountain village is regarded as the most important pre-Civil War Catalan novel.

Juan Luís Cebrián *Red Doll* (Grove-Atlantic, US). Easy-to-read thriller set in post-Franco years, involving Basque terrorists, the KGB, right-wing backlash and, of course, romance.

Camilo José Cela *The Family of Pascual Duarte* (Little Brown, UK/US). Cela should be the grand old man of Spanish fiction – a Nobel Prize-winner and integral to the revival of Spanish literature after the Civil War – though his reputation in Spain is compromised by his past involvement with Franco's government. *Pascual Duarte*, his first and best-known novel, portrays the brutal story of a peasant murderer from Extremadura, set against the backdrop of the fratricidal Civil War.

Juan Goytisolo *Marks of Identity* (Serpent's Tail; Consort), *Count Julian* (Serpent's Tail, UK/US), *Juan the Landless* (Serpent's Tail, UK/US), *Landscapes after the Battle* (Serpent's Tail/Seaver Books), *Quarantine* (Quartet Books, UK). Born in Barcelona in 1931, Goytisolo became a bitter enemy of the Franco regime, and has spent most of his life in self-exile, in Paris and in Morocco. He is perhaps the most important modern Spanish novelist, confronting, above all in his great trilogy (comprising the first three titles listed above), the whole ambivalent idea of Spain and Spanishness, as well as being one of the first writers to deal openly with homosexuality. The more recent *Quarantine* documents a journey into a Dante-esque netherworld in which the torments of hell are set against reportage of the Gulf War. Goytisolo has also written an autobiography, *Forbidden Territory* (Serpent's Tail, UK).

Montserrat Lunati (ed) *Rainy Days: Short Stories by Contemporary Spanish Women Writers* (Aris & Phillips, UK). This impressive collection (with Spanish parallel text) has work by celebrated literary lights such as Rosa Montero and Maruja Torres.

Javier Marías *Tomorrow in the Battle Think on Me* (Harvill, UK). There are many who rate

Marias as Spain's finest contemporary novelist – and the evidence is here in this searching, psychological thriller, with its study of the human capacity for concealment and confession. Harvill also publishes two other Marias novels, *A Heart So White* and *All Souls*.

Ana María Matute *School of the Sun* (Quartet; Columbia UP). The loss of childhood innocence on a Balearic island, where old enmities are redefined during the Civil War.

Eduardo Mendoza *City of Marvels* (Harvill, UK). Mendoza's first (and best) novel is set in the expanding Barcelona of 1880–1920, packed with underworld characters and riddled with anarchic and comic turns. It's a milieu repeated in *The Truth About The Savolta Case* and *The Year of the Flood* (also Harvill, UK).

Manuel Vázquez Montalban *Murder in the Central Committee*, *Southern Seas*, *An Olympic Death*, *The Angst Ridden Executive* and *Off Side* (all Serpent's Tail, UK). Montalban is one of Spain's most influential writers, through his weekly political column in *El País* newspaper. A long-time member of the Communist Party, he lives in Barcelona, like his great creation, the gourmand private detective Pepe Carvalho, who stars in all of his wry and racy crime thrillers. The one to begin with – indeed, a bit of a classic – is *Murder in the Central Committee*.

Julián Ríos *Larva* (Quartet; Dalkey Archive). Subtitled *Midsummer Night's Babel*, *Larva* is a large, complex, postmodern novel by a leading Spanish literary figure, originally published to huge acclaim in Spain.

Javier Tomo *The Coded Letter* and *Dear Monster* (Carcanet, UK). A pair of Kafkaesque tales from one of Spain's leading post-Franco era novelists.

Maruja Torres *Desperately Seeking Julio* (Fourth Estate, UK). The Julio is of course Iglesias (the original Spanish title – "It's Him!" – had no need for names) in this enjoyable romp of a novel. Torres is quite a name in Spain, writing for gossip magazines, as well as a regular opinion column in *El País*.

If you can read **Spanish**, the following modern novelists are also of interest: **Luís Martín Santos** (*Tiempo de Silencio*); **Alfonso Grosso** (*Con Flores a María*); **Mariano Antolín** (*Wham!*, *Hombre Arañal* – the Spanish William Burroughs); **Montserrat Roig** (best of

contemporary feminist writers); **Rafael Sánchez Ferlosio** (*El Jarama*, *Alfanhui*); **Pío Baroja** (*El Arbol de la Ciencia*); and **Miguel Delibes** (*El Camino*, or any others).

PLAYS AND POETRY

Pedro Calderón de la Barca *Life is a Dream and other Spanish Classics* (Nick Hern Books; Players Press), *The Mayor of Zalamea* (Absolute Press; Dramatic Publications). Some of the best works of the great dramatist of Spain's "Golden Age".

Federico García Lorca *Five Plays: Comedies and Tragicomedies* (Penguin; New Directions). The great pre-Civil War playwright and poet. Arturo Barea's *Lorca: the Poet and His People* is also of interest.

Lope de Vega. The nation's first important playwright (b. 1562) wrote literally hundreds of plays many of which, including *Lo Cierto por lo Dudoso* (A Certainty for a Doubt) and *Fuenteobvejuna* (The Sheep Well), remain standards of classic Spanish theatre.

J. M. Cohen (ed.) *The Penguin Book of Spanish Verse* (Penguin, UK/US). Spanish poetry from the twelfth century to the modern age, with (parallel text) translations from all the major names.

SPAIN IN FOREIGN FICTION

Harry Chapman *Spanish Drums* (Mainstream, UK). An engaging thriller, telling of an Englishwoman outsider's entry into the life of a family in Teruel – and her discovery of all the terrible baggage of its Civil War past.

Douglas Day *Journey of the Wolf* (Penguin, UK). Outstanding first novel by an American writer, given the seal of approval by Graham Greene ("gripping and poignant"). The subject is a Civil War fighter, "El Lobo", who returns to his village in the Alpujarras as a fugitive, forty years on.

Graham Greene *Monsignor Quixote* (Penguin; Pocket Books). The journey of a small-town priest around modern Spain; Greene at his comic best.

Kathryn Harrison *A Thousand Orange Trees* (Fourth Estate, UK). A complex and intense novel set during the Inquisition in the seventeenth century.

Ernest Hemingway *Fiesta/The Sun Also Rises* and *For Whom the Bell Tolls* (both Arrow;

Scribner). Hemingway remains a big part of the American myth of Spain – *Fiesta* contains some lyrically beautiful writing, while the latter is a good deal more laboured. He also published an enthusiastic and not very good account of bull-fighting, *Death in the Afternoon*.

Arthur Koestler *Dialogue with Death* (out of print). Koestler was reporting the Civil War in 1937 when he was captured and imprisoned by Franco's troops – this is essentially his prison diary.

Matthew Lewis *The Monk* (Oxford UP, UK/US). You'd be hard-pressed to find a more gripping holiday read than this thriller, set in a Capuchin monastery in Madrid, with its tale of lustful monks, evil abbesses, rape, incest and murder. And oddly enough it's a classic novel, the most gothic of the genre, first published in 1796.

Norman Lewis *Voices of the Old Sea* (Picador, UK) and *The Day of the Fox* (Robinson, UK). Lewis lived in Catalunya from 1948 to 1952, just as tourism was starting to arrive. These two books are each ingenious blends of novel and social record, charting the breakdown of the old ways in the face of the "new revolution".

Amin Malouf *Leo the African* (Quartet, UK). A wonderful historical novel, recreating the life of Leo Africanus, the fifteenth-century Moorish geographer, in the last years of the kingdom of Granada, and on his subsequent exile in Morocco and world travels.

Colm Tóibín *The South* (Penguin, UK). First novel by the Irish writer, who spent the early 1990s in Barcelona. The city is the setting for his tale of an Irish woman looking for a new life.

SPECIALIST GUIDEBOOKS

TREKKING AND CYCLING

Robin Collomb *Picos de Europa, Sierra de Gredos* and *Sierra Nevada*, plus others (West Col, UK). Detailed guides aimed primarily at serious trekkers and climbers.

Valerie Crespi-Green *Landscapes of Mallorca* (Sunflower Books, UK). Aimed at fairly casual walkers and picnickers. Sunflower Books also publish reliable and well-researched walking and trekking guides on the Picos de Europa, the Canary Islands, Menorca, Catalunya, the Costa Blanca, Andalucía and the Costa del Sol.

Paul Lucia *Through the Spanish Pyrenees: GR11 Long Distance Footpath* (Cicerone Press, UK). New guide to the GR11, a high-level and recently waymarked trail which crosses the Spanish Pyrenees from coast to coast.

Jacqueline Oglesby *The Mountains of Central Spain* (Cicerone Press, UK). Walking and scrambling guide to the magnificent Sierras de Gredos and Guadarrama by resident author

June Parker *Walking in Mallorca* (Cicerone Press, UK). This popular guide is now in its third edition, with many new treks.

Kev Reynolds *Walks and Climbs in the Pyrenees* (Cicerone Press, UK). User-friendly guide for trekkers and walkers, though half devoted to the French side of the frontier.

Bob Stansfield *Costa Blanca Mountain Walks* (Cicerone Press, UK). Walks within this little-known, but spectacular, area near Alicante.

Robin Walker *Walks and Climbs in the Picos de Europa* (Cicerone Press, UK). New guide by experienced resident mountaineer.

Andy Walmsley *Walking in the Sierra Nevada* (Cicerone Press, UK). Reliable coverage of 45 routes, with details of flora and fauna – from easy short walks in the Alpujarras to ascents of the highest peaks.

In Spanish, look out for the excellent series of guides published by **Sua Edizioak** of Bilbao. These include *Topoguias* and *Rutas y Paseos* covering most of the individual **Spanish sierras and mountain regions**, and a superb range of **regional guides for cyclists**, *En Bici*, functionally ring-bound, with detailed maps and route contours. The reliable **Penthalon** guides, available from major bookshops in Spain, detail walks in various regions throughout the country.

THE PILGRIM ROUTE TO SANTIAGO

Abbé G. Bernes, Georges Veron and L. Laborde Balen *The Pilgrim Route to Compostela* (Robertson-McCarta, UK). This is the most practical of the many guides to the route – thorough on the paths, clear on maps and with basic details of accommodation. It is translated from the French, however, and is not that inspiring a read.

John Higginson *Le Puy to Santiago – A Cyclist's Guide* (Cicerone Press, UK). A cyclist's guide to the pilgrim route which follows as closely as possible (on tarmac) the walker's path, visiting all the major sites en route.

Michael Jacobs *The Road to Santiago de Compostela* (Penguin, UK). An architectural guide, excellent on the buildings but with no practicalities.

Edwin Mullins *The Pilgrimage to Santiago* (out of print). This is a travelogue rather than a guide, but is by far the best book on the Santiago legend and its fascinating medieval pilgrimage industry.

Alison Raju *Le Puy to Santiago – A Walker's Guide* (Cicerone Press, UK). The first guide in English to cover the whole route, this is a British equivalent of the Bernes book (above) by an experienced Iberian hiker.

Pilgrim Guide to Spain (Confraternity of Saint James, UK). A pamphlet, revised annually, with information on the routes and places to stay and eat. The confraternity can also supply many other relevant publications, as well as pilgrim accreditation. Their address is: c/o Marian Marples, Confraternity of St James, 1st floor, 1 Talbot Yard, Borough High St, London SE1 1YP, UK (☎0171/404 4500, fax 407 1468).

WILDLIFE

Frederic Grunfeld and Teresa Farino *Wild Spain* (Sheldrake Press; Prentice Hall). A knowledgable and practical guide to Spain's national parks, ecology and wildlife. Highly recommended.

Heinzel, Fitter and Parslow *Collins Guide to the Birds of Britain and Europe* (Collins, UK). Alternative to the other Collins guide below. Also includes North Africa and the Middle East.

John Measures *The Wildlife Travelling Companion: Spain* (Crowood Press, UK). Clearly laid-out field guide to specific wildlife areas complete with an illustrated index of the most common flora and fauna.

Peterson, Mountfort and Hollom *Collins Field Guide to the Birds of Britain and Europe* (Collins Reference; Houghton Mifflin). Standard reference book – covers most birds in Spain.

Oleg Polunin and Anthony Huxley *Flowers of the Mediterranean* (Chatto, UK). Useful if by no means exhaustive field guide.

K.J. Stoba *Bird Watching in Mallorca* (Cicerone Press, UK). Island guide listing 282 species and where and when to see them.

FOOD AND WINE

Coleman Andrews *Catalan Cuisine* (Headline, UK). Best available English-language book dealing with Spain's most adventurous regional cuisine.

Nicholas Butcher *The Spanish Kitchen* (Macmillan, UK). A practical and knowledgeable guide to creating Spanish food when you get back. Informative detail on olive oil, *jamón serrano* and herbs.

Penelope Casas *The Foods and Wines of Spain* (Penguin; Knopf). Superb Spanish cookbook, covering classic and regional dishes with equal, authoritative aplomb. By the same author is the useful *Tapas: the little dishes of Spain*. (Pavilion, UK).

Mark and Kim Millon *Wine Roads of Spain* (HarperCollins, UK/US). Everything you ever wanted to know about Spanish wine and sherry: when, how and where it's made, with a good array of useful maps.

Jan Read *Guide to the Wines of Spain* (Mitchell Beazley, UK). Encyclopedic (yet pocketable) guide to the classic and emerging wines of Spain by a leading authority. Includes maps, vintages and vineyards.

LANGUAGE

Once you get into it, Spanish is the easiest language there is – and you'll be helped everywhere by people who are eager to try and understand even the most faltering attempt. English is spoken, but only in the main tourist areas to any extent, and wherever you are you'll get a far better reception if you at least try communicating with Spaniards in their own tongue. Being understood, of course, is only half the problem – and getting the gist of the reply, often rattled out at a furious pace, may prove far more difficult. Nevertheless, you'll be getting there.

The rules of **pronunciation** are pretty straightforward and, once you get to know them, strictly observed. Unless there's an accent, words ending in d, l, r, and z are **stressed** on the last syllable, all others on the second last. All **vowels** are pure and short; combinations have predictable results.

A somewhere between the "A" sound of back and that of father.

E as in get.

I as in police.

O as in hot.

U as in rule.

C is lisped before E and I, hard otherwise: *cerca* is pronounced "thairka" (though in Andalucía many natives pronounce the soft "c" as an "s").

G works the same way, a guttural "H" sound (like the ch in loch) before E or I, a hard G elsewhere – *gigante* becomes "higante".

H is always silent.

J the same sound as a guttural G: *jamón* is pronounced "hamon".

LL sounds like an English Y or LY: *tortilla* is pronounced "torteeya/torteelya".

N is as in English unless it has a tilde (accent) over it, when it becomes NY: *mañana* sounds like "manyana".

QU is pronounced like an English K.

R is rolled, RR doubly so.

PHRASEBOOKS, DICTIONARIES AND TEACHING YOURSELF

SPANISH
Numerous **Spanish phrasebooks** are available, not least the *Spanish Rough Guide Phrasebook*, laid out dictionary-style for instant access. For **teaching yourself** the language, the BBC tape series *España Viva* and *Dígame* are excellent, as is their two week crash-course *Get By in Spanish*. *Breakthrough Spanish* (Macmillan) is probably the best of the tape and book home study courses.

Many of the books available in North America are geared to New World, Latin American usage – more old-fashioned publications may be better for Spain itself. Langenscheidt, Cassells, Collins and others all produce useful dictionaries; Berlitz and others publish separate Spanish and Latin American phrasebooks.

CATALÀ
The best book for learning **Català** is a total immersion course called *Digui Digui* (published by the Generalitat de Catalunya), a series of books and tapes that's presented entirely in Catalan; you'll need to speak Spanish to take this on. In Britain, the best place to find it is Grant & Cutler, 55 Great Marlborough St, London W1 (☎0171/734 2012). *Teach Yourself Catalan* (Hodder & Stoughton) is less ambitious (and presented in English); while if you're serious you'll also need *Catalan Grammar* (Dolphin Book Company) and *Parla Català* (Pia), the only available English–Catalan phrasebook.

SPANISH WORDS AND PHRASES

BASICS

Yes, No, OK	*Sí, No, Vale*	With, Without	*Con, Sin*
Please, Thank you	*Por favor, Gracias*	Good, Bad	*Buen(o)/a, Mal(o)/*
Where, When	*Dónde, Cuando*	Big, Small	*Gran(de), Pequeño/a*
What, How much	*Qué, Cuánto*	Cheap, Expensive	*Barato, Caro*
Here, There	*Aquí, Allí*	Hot, Cold	*Caliente, Frío*
This, That	*Esto, Eso*	More, Less	*Más, Menos*
Now, Later	*Ahora, Más tarde*	Today, Tomorrow	*Hoy, Mañana*
Open, Closed	*Abierto/a, Cerrado/a*	Yesterday	*Ayer*

GREETINGS AND RESPONSES

Hello, Goodbye	*Hola, Adiós*	Do you speak English?	*¿Habla (usted) inglés?*
Good morning	*Buenos días*	I don't speak Spanish	*(No) Hablo español*
Good afternoon/night	*Buenas tardes/noches*	My name is . . .	*Me llamo . . .*
See you later	*Hasta luego*	What's your name?	*¿Como se llama*
Sorry	*Lo siento/disculpéme*		*usted?*
Excuse me	*Con permiso/perdón*	I am English/	*Soy inglés(a)/*
How are you?	*¿Como está (usted)?*	Australian/	*australiano(a)/*
I (don't) understand	*(No) Entiendo*	Canadian/	*canadiense(a)/*
Not at all/You're wel-	*De nada*	American/	*americano(a)*
come		Irish/	*irlandés(a)*

NEEDS – HOTELS AND TRANSPORT

I want	*Quiero*	How do I get to . . . ?	*¿Por donde se*
I'd like	*Quisiera*		*vaa . . . ?*
Do you know . . . ?	*¿Sabe . . . ?*	Left, right, straight on	*Izquierda, derecha,*
I don't know	*No sé*		*todo recto*
There is (is there)?	*(¿)Hay(?)*	Where is . . . ?	*¿Dónde está . . . ?*
Give me . . .	*Deme . . .*	. . . the bus station	*. . . la estación de*
(one like that)	*(uno así)*		*autobuses*
Do you have . . . ?	*¿Tiene . . . ?*	. . . the railway	*. . . la estación de*
. . . the time	*. . . la hora*	station	*ferro-carril*
. . . a room	*. . . una habitación*	. . . the nearest bank	*. . . el banco mas*
. . . with two	*. . . con dos*		*cercano*
beds/double bed	*camas/cama matrimonial*	. . . the post office	*. . . el correos/la ofic-*
...with shower/bath	*. . . con ducha/baño*		*ina de correos*
It's for one person	*Es para una persona*	. . . the toilet	*. . . el baño/aseo/ser-*
(two people)	*(dos personas)*		*vicio*
. . . for one night (one	*. . . para una noche*	Where does the bus	*¿De dónde sale el*
week)	*(una semana)*	to . . . leave from?	*autobús para . . . ?*
It's fine, how much is	*¿Está bien, cuánto es?*	Is this the train for	*¿Es este el tren para*
it?		Mérida?	*Mérida?*
It's too expensive	*Es demasiado caro*	I'd like a (return)	*Quisiera un billete (de*
Don't you have any	*No tiene algo más barato?*	ticket to . . .	*ida y vuelta)*
thing cheaper?			*para . . .*
Can one . . . ?	*¿Se puede . . . ?*	What time does it	*¿A qué hora sale*
. . . camp (near) here?	*¿ . . . acampar aquí*	leave (arrive in . . .)?	*(llega a . . .)?*
	(cerca)?	What is there to eat?	*¿Qué hay para comer?*
		What's that?	*¿Qué es eso?*
Is there a hostel near-	*¿Hay un hostal aquí*	What's this called in	*¿Como se llama este*
by?	*cerca?*	Spanish?	*en español?*

NUMBERS AND DAYS

1	*un/uno/una*	13	*trece*	90	*noventa*	first	*primero/a*
2	*dos*	14	*catorce*	100	*cien(to)*	second	*segundo/a*
3	*tres*	15	*quince*	101	*ciento uno*	third	*tercero/a*
4	*cuatro*	16	*diez y seis*	200	*doscientos*	fifth	*quinto/a*
5	*cinco*	20	*veinte*	201	*doscientos*	tenth	*décimo/a*
6	*seis*	21	*veintiuno*		*uno*	Monday	*lunes*
7	*siete*	30	*treinta*	500	*quinientos*	Tuesday	*martes*
8	*ocho*	40	*cuarenta*	1000	*mil*	Wednesday	*miércoles*
9	*nueve*	50	*cincuenta*	2000	*dos mil*	Thursday	*jueves*
10	*diez*	60	*sesenta*	1992	*mil novecien-*	Friday	*viernes*
11	*once*	70	*setenta*		*tos noventa*	Saturday	*sábado*
12	*doce*	80	*ochenta*		*y dos*	Sunday	*domingo*

V sounds more like B, *vino* becoming "beano".

X has an S sound before consonants, normal X before vowels. More common in Basque, Gallego or Catalan words where it's sh or zh.

Z is the same as a soft C, so *cerveza* becomes "thairvaitha" (but again much of the south prefers the "s" sound).

The list of a few essential words and phrases opposite and above should be enough to get you started, though if you're travelling for any length of time a dictionary or phrasebook is obviously a worthwhile investment. If you're using a **dictionary**, bear in mind that in Spanish CH, LL, and Ñ count as separate letters and are listed after the Cs, Ls and Ns respectively.

SPANISH AND ARCHITECTURAL TERMS: A GLOSSARY

ALAMEDA park or grassy promenade.

ALCAZABA Moorish castle.

ALCÁZAR Moorish fortified palace.

APSE semicircular recess at the altar (usually eastern) end of a church.

AYUNTAMIENTO town hall.

AZULEJO glazed ceramic tilework.

BARRIO suburb or quarter.

BODEGA cellar, wine bar or warehouse.

CALLE street.

CAPILLA MAYOR chapel containing the high altar.

CAPILLA REAL Royal Chapel.

CAPITAL top of a column.

CARTUJA Carthusian monastery.

CASTILLO castle.

CHANCEL part of a church containing the altar, usually at the east end.

CHURRIGUERESQUE extreme form of Baroque art named after José Churriguera (1650–1723) and his extended family, its main exponents.

COLEGIATA collegiate (large parish) church.

CONVENTO monastery or convent.

CORO central part of church built for the choir.

CORO ALTO raised choir, often above west door of a church.

CORREOS post office.

CORRIDA DE TOROS bullfight.

CRYPT burial place in a church, usually under the choir.

CUSTODIA large receptacle for Eucharist wafers.

DUEÑO/A proprietor, landlord/lady.

ERMITA hermitage.

IGLESIA church.

ISABELLINE ornamental form of late Gothic developed during the reign of Isabella and Fernando.

LOGGIA covered area on the side of a building, usually arcaded.

LONJA stock exchange building.

MERCADO market.

MIHRAB prayer niche of Moorish mosque.

MIRADOR viewing point (literally balcony).

MODERNISME (MODERNISTA) Catalan/Spanish form of Art Nouveau, whose most famous exponent was Antoni Gaudí.

MONASTERIO monastery or convent.

MORISCO Muslim Spaniard subject to medieval Christian rule – and nominally baptized.

MOZÁRABE Christian subject to medieval Moorish rule; normally allowed freedom of worship, they built churches in an Arab-influenced manner (MOZARABIC).

MUDÉJAR Muslim Spaniard subject to medieval Christian rule, but retaining Islamic worship; most commonly a term applied to architecture which includes buildings built by Moorish craftsmen for the Christian rulers and later designs influenced by the Moors. The 1890s to 1930s saw a Mudéjar revival, blended with Art Nouveau and Art Deco forms.

NARTHEX entrance hall of church.

NAVE central space in a church, usually flanked by aisles.

PALACIO aristocratic mansion.

PARADOR luxury hotel, often converted from minor monument.

PASEO promenade; also the evening stroll thereon.

PATIO inner courtyard.

PLATERESQUE elaborately decorative Renaissance style, the sixteenth-century successor of Isabelline forms. Named for its resemblance to silversmiths' work (*platería*).

PLAZA square.

PLAZA DE TOROS bullring.

PORTICO covered entrance to a building.

POSADA old name for an inn.

PUERTA gateway, also mountain pass.

PUERTO port.

REJA iron screen or grille, often fronting a window.

RELIQUARY receptacle for a saint's relics, usually bones. Often highly decorated.

REREDOS wall or screen behind an altar.

RETABLO altarpiece.

RÍA river estuary in Galicia.

RÍO river.

ROMERÍA religious procession to a rural shrine.

SACRISTÍA, SAGRARIO sacristy or sanctuary of church – room for sacred vessels and vestments.

SARDANA Catalan folk dance.

SEO, SEU, LA SE ancient/regional names for cathedrals.

SIERRA mountain range.

SILLERÍA choir stall.

SOLAR aristocratic town mansion.

TAIFA small Moorish kingdom, many of which emerged after the disintegration of the Córdoba caliphate.

TELEFÓNICA the phone company; also used for its offices in any town.

TRANSCEPTS the wings of a cruciform church, placed at right angles to the nave and chancel.

TYMPANUM area between lintel of a doorway and the arch above it.

TURISMO tourist office.

VAULT arched ceiling.

POLITICAL PARTIES AND ACRONYMS

CNT anarchist trade union.

CONVERGENCIA I UNIO conservative party in power in Catalunya.

ETA Basque terrorist organization. Its political wing is Herri Batasuna.

FALANGE Franco's old fascist party, now officially defunct.

FUERZA NUEVA descendants of the above, also on the way out.

IU Izquierda Unida, broad-left alliance of communists and others.

MC Movimiento Comunista (Communist Movement), small radical offshoot of the PCE.

MOC Movimiento de Objeción de Conciencia, peace group, concerned with NATO and conscription.

OTAN NATO.

PCE Partido Comunista de España (Spanish Communist Party).

PNV Basque Nationalist Party – in control of the right-wing autonomous government.

PP Partido Popular, the centre-right alliance formed by Alianza Popular and the Christian Democrats. The PP is currently Spain's minority government, under José María Aznar.

PSOE Partido Socialista Obrero Español, the Spanish Socialist Workers' Party, led since 1998 by José Borrell.

UGT Unión General de Trabajadores, the Spanish TUC.

INDEX

Stay in touch with us!

ROUGH*NEWS* **is Rough Guides' free newsletter. In three issues a year we give you news, travel issues, music reviews, readers' letters and the latest dispatches from authors on the road.**

I would like to receive ROUGH*NEWS*: please put me on your free mailing list.

NAME . . . .

ADDRESS . . . .

Please clip or photocopy and send to: Rough Guides, 62–70 Shorts Gardens, London WC2H 9AB, England or Rough Guides, 375 Hudson Street, New York, NY 10014, USA.

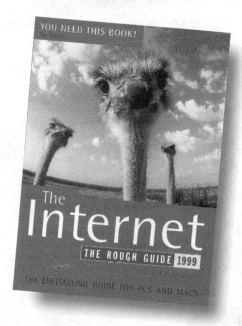

Small

but perfectly informed

Every bit as stylish and irreverent as their full-sized counterparts, Mini Guides are everything you'd expect from a Rough Guide, but smaller – perfect for a pocket, briefcase or overnight bag.

Available 1998
Antigua, Barbados, Boston, Dublin, Edinburgh, Lisbon, Madrid, Seattle

Coming soon
Bangkok, Brussels, Florence, Honolulu, Las Vegas, Maui, Melbourne, New Orleans, Oahu, St Lucia, Sydney, Tokyo, Toronto

 Everything you need to know about everything you want to do

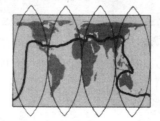